The China Station, Royal Navy

The China Station, Royal Navy:

A History as seen through the careers of the Commanders in Chief, 1864-1941

Jonathan Parkinson

Matador
9 Priory Business Park,
Wistow Road, Kibworth Beauchamp,
Leicestershire. LE8 0RX
Tel: 0116 279 2299
Email: books@troubador.co.uk
Web: www.troubador.co.uk/matador
Twitter: @matadorbooks

ISBN 978 1788035 217

British Library Cataloguing in Publication Data.
A catalogue record for this book is available from the British Library.

Printed and bound in the UK by TJ International, Padstow, Cornwall
Typeset in 11pt Minion Pro by Troubador Publishing Ltd, Leicester, UK

Matador is an imprint of Troubador Publishing Ltd

Foreword

The Royal Navy has a long and very varied history and tradition, much of it glorious, inspiring and exciting, some of it inevitably less creditable and successful but most of it very educative. Some of it is somewhat obscure and took place in distant corners of the world, which have long since changed very much. But all of it provides context, lessons, examples both good and bad and all of it has much to teach us if we will learn.

Of late, it has become less fashionable to study history, our successes and failures of the past and the people who forged them. In recent times, it has led us, naval officers and political leaders alike, to make some very avoidable mistakes ourselves. Jonathan Parkinson is a most honourable exception to this. Recognising the significance of the Far East, both on our own national conscience and on the history and formation of the modern world, he has set out to examine the substantial part played in that by the Royal Navy through the prism of the successive Commanders in Chief of the long-gone China Station.

Most of these Admirals, in those happy days when the speed of modern communications was not even a dream, had a responsibility, authority and independence of action which their modern successors could scarcely even imagine. It is not too much to say that the skills, both professional and diplomatic, judgement and temperament of these men had a huge influence on the early development of a region which may in this century become the world leader. It is, then, well worth the effort to understand the role played by the Commanders in Chief of the China Station, their Navy and their nation in that development.

Jonathan Parkinson has researched his subject in compelling detail and has produced a wealth of information and understanding which illuminates an almost forgotten but hugely important chapter in the Royal Navy's long involvement in global affairs. He has produced a fascinating and most readable account and all those of us who are students of naval history, or even have a passing interest are very much in his debt.

Vice Admiral Sir Jeremy Blackham KCB MA

(The author is most grateful for his generous appraisal. As Naval readers will know for fifteen years to 2017 Sir Jeremy edited that British quarterly, 'The Naval Review').

Introduction

In addition to a precis of the lives and naval careers of each of the Commanders in Chief, China Station, relevant information is given outlining something of the concurrent internal affairs of China and of Japan. Both are very different but sad tales, the former in decline towards the end of the Manchu Ch'ing dynasty then into the chaotic 1920s and 1930s, and the latter increasingly adopting a militaristic attitude which was to result in their disaster of the Pacific War of 1941-1945.

As a reminder of days long gone are interwoven brief references to the British Consular Service, especially relevant in China, and for a shorter period in Japan, during that era of extraterritoriality, and the British Colonial Service with whom necessarily the Navy worked very closely. In addition, being one important reason for it all, frequent references are made to a few British shipping and trading interests together with those of some other nations.

In respect of the career of each Admiral the appropriate references are given at the conclusion of each entry.

The Tokugawa Shogunate era in Japan endured from 1603 to 1868. During the last years of the Shogunate His Imperial Majesty The Emperor Komei reigned in Kyoto between 1846 and 1867. Largely powerless, the aura of mystique surrounding his person was maintained by the Shogunate, and, especially during the early days of this twenty year period just mentioned, then in particular when it so suited them. As will be seen, opposition groups desiring to overthgrow the Shogunate, and centred around various of the fiefdoms or 'han' situated in the west of the country, latterly were to use this Imperial aura as a feature around which to rally others. The Meiji era was to result, a period largely controlled by the interests of two powerful 'han' or fiefdoms, Satsuma and Choshu.

The eventual Pacific War of 1941 – 1945 was to be won by the armed forces of the United States of America, latterly with modest assistance from Great Britain and her Empire. Occasional reference is made to the earlier careers of the senior Naval officers to be involved in that conflict.

Reference also is made to the gradual development of Naval aviation.

The *Navy List* for April 1864 is the first to show China as a separate Station. The East Indies, previously including China, now was combined with The Cape Station (1).

The outbreak of the Pacific War in December 1941 was to signal the end of that era.

As befits the age the Wade-Giles system of romanization is used where appropriate.

I should like to express my gratitude to my wife Geraldine who, over many years, uncomplainingly has tolerated, in fact has encouraged this naval interest of mine. Also to Tom and Monica Mayhew who most kindly and generously always have put up with my frequent visits to England in the practically never ending search for data and information.

Dunkeld, March 2012

NOTES

1.   William Laird Clowes, *The Royal Navy – a History,* Vol. VII (London, 1903), 88. Here it is stated that the East Indies and China Stations separated on 17 January 1865. Later the East Indies Station was to assume an individual identity, the Cape being combined with the West Coast of Africa.

The list of Royal Naval officers who held this post in the Far East follows:-

8 February 1862 to 17 January 1865
Rear Admiral Augustus Leopold **Kuper**

Augustus was born in London on 16 August 1809, son of William Kuper, D.D, chaplain to Her Majesty Queen Adelaide, she being the consort of King William IV (1). He, the 'Sailor King', as Captain H.R.H. Prince William Henry, Duke of Clarence had commanded *Pegasus* in the West Indies in 1786/7. There he had renewed his friendship with Horatio Nelson (2). On 20 June 1837 H.R.H. was to die in Windsor Castle. H.M. Queen Victoria, who at age eighteen ascended to the throne that day, was his niece.

As Sir Augustus he died in South Brent, Devon on 29 October 1885.

'Entered the Navy: 19 April 1823 as a first class volunteer in *Isis*, 50, Flagship of Sir Geo. Eyre in South America, where he continued to serve until the summer of 1827, the greater part of the time as **Midshipman**, in *Spartiate*, 76, Captain Thos. Gordon Falcon, *Mersey*, 26, Captain John Macpherson Ferguson, and *Cambridge*, 80, Captain Thos. Jas. Maling. He was then (--) employed on the Channel and Mediterranean stations in *Royal Sovereign*, yacht, Captain Sir William Hoste, *Isis* again, Captain Sir Thos. Staines, and *Raleigh*, 18 Captain Sir Wm. Dickson (3).'

Lieutenant: 26 February 1830 (4). From 17 October 1831 served in the 90' brig *Savage*, 10 guns, Irish Station, then from 9 April 1832 in sloop *Nimrod*, 20 guns, coasts of Spain and Portugal. Subsequently, and briefly from 30 March 1836, in the Bombay teak built third rate *Minden*, 74, fitting out for service off Lisbon (5).

On 19 June 1837 he married Emma Margaret, eldest daughter of Sir James Gordon Bremer (1786-1850) by his first wife, Harriet (6).

Appointed first Lieutenant in the teak built frigate *Alligator*, 28, Captain Sir James Gordon Bremer: 12 July 1837, Australia Station.

'He assisted his father-in-law, Bremer, in forming the settlement of Port Essington in North Australia and on 27 July 1839 was promoted by him to command of the *Pelorus*, 18. In a violent hurricane at Port Essington the *Pelorus* was driven on shore, high and dry, and was got off with great difficulty and labour after 86 days (7).'

This high wind drove *Pelorus* ashore during the night of 25/26 November 1839, eight members of her company being killed. Another warship in company at the new settlement on that occasion was the brig *Britomart*, 10 guns, 297 tons, then commanded by Lieut. Owen Stanley (8).

With regard to the *Pelorus* incident in due course Their Lordships at the Admiralty were to express themselves as follows. On 6 April 1841 the C. in C. wrote to Kuper:

'Having transmitted to the Lords Commissioners of the Admiralty your letter detailing the damage sustained by Her Majesty's Sloop *Pelorus* in a hurricane at Port Essington in November 1839 (--) I have the satisfaction to acquaint you that I have received their Lordships' commands to convey to yourself, the Officers and Ship's Company of Her Majesty's Sloop late under your command their approval of your conduct on the occasion (9).'

Commander: acting appointment confirmed by the Admiralty with seniority from 27 July 1839. Aged thirty years, as an acting Captain on 17 January 1840 appointed in command of *Alligator*, East Indies. In addition to other waters further to the East, at the time the East Indies Station also included those of the Malay peninsula. As will be seen the ship was to spend much time on the China coast. While proceeding further East naturally *Alligator* called at Singapore.

It was while at Singapore during May 1840 that the assistant surgeon then serving in the troopship *Rattlesnake*, 500 tons bm (builders measurement), Edward Hodges Cree, made some notes in his diary describing the community. Bear in mind that it was then barely twenty one years since Sir Thomas Stamford Raffles first had negotiated the terms of the subsequent British settlement. Clearly most significant progress had been made during this short period of time:-

'Went on shore to have a look at the place, which is quite novel to me and very amusing – a sort of mixture of Indian and Chinese. There are good quays and warehouses on each side of a small river, which does not smell very sweet from the amount of drainage running into it. The houses are mostly of two storeys, with the upper one projecting beyond the lower. (-) Some of the houses are Chinese looking, turning up at the corners and altogether put me in mind of the pictures on an old china plate of the willow pattern. (-) The country round is hilly and pleasant and pretty well cleared and planted for a mile or two. Beyond is all jungle, where tigers and other wild beasts abound. A reward is given by the Government for every tiger's head brought in, as they are so destructive to cattle as well as men. There are many spice plantations, principally nutmegs and cloves. (-) The harbour presents a busy scene, filled with ships of all sorts.

This was a time of considerable unrest in those Far Eastern waters however in giving their attention to various matters not always was local British leadership to be firm and positive. An example follows from which it is clear that some opinion concerning activity during the summer of 1840 did not approve of this apparent vacillation in high places within the British administration, Kuper himself being ordered prematurely to break off one successful operation:-

'At Amoy, also, where Commander Augustus Leopold Kuper of the *Alligator*, 28, maintained a blockade, the threatening attitude of a large fleet of war junks led to the destruction of several of them, and to other reprisals. But Kuper had to abandon an attempt, which he made, to force the passage between Kulangsu and Amoy harbour; and consequently the Chinese were left with the conviction that they had won an important success. Nowhere were they made to feel that they were dealing with foes who were vastly their superiors (10).'

Nevertheless in due course he was to receive an appropriate letter of approval. Writing in *Wellesley*, Captain Thomas Maitland, at Chusan on 5 October 1840 the C. in C., Rear Admiral Rt. Hon. George Elliot, expressed himself:-

'… and that it has given me very great pleasure to see the zeal and gallantry with which the Chinese were met by yourself and those serving under your orders in the *Alligator* and *Braemar* when opposed to so very superior a force. I beg you will acquaint them how highly I approve of their conduct (11).'

In addition to the above, early in 1841 while still in command of *Alligator*, he participated in the attack on the forts at the Bogue which commanded the entrance to the long approach upriver to Canton:

'In February 1841 it was his fortune to elicit the thanks of the Commander in Chief for his conduct in the action with the Bogue forts; as he again did for the gallant and able support he afforded Captain Thos. Herbert in an attack upon the enemy's camp, fort, and ship *Cambridge*, bearing the Chinese Admiral's flag, at their position below Whampoa Reach, when 98 guns were in the whole destroyed. On 13 March Captain Kuper was once more mentioned in terms of praise for the assistance he rendered at the capture of the last fort protecting the approaches to Canton (12).'

Sir Thomas Stamford Raffles, (1781-1826). His grave may be seen, by arrangement, at the Church of St. Mary's in Hendon. The rather naughty tale regarding the positioning of his grave follows. The story goes that at the time of his burial the vicar of the day would not permit the grave actually to be sited within his church building as said vicar did not approve of the late Sir Stamford's work to abolish the slave trade. Apparently the vicar's family earlier had made money in the slave trade. However during the years 1913-1915 the church building was greatly extended in size and fortunately Sir Stamford's grave then found itself as it may be seen today, within the main structure. A memorial statue to Sir Stamford Raffles may be seen within Westminster Abbey.

Sir Henry Pottinger, 3 October 1789 – 18 March 1856. On 26 June 1843 appointed as the first Governor of Hong Kong.

Meanwhile, on Tuesday, 26 January 1841, in the presence of, 'Commodore Sir J.G. Bremer, accompanied by the other officers of the squadron, under a feu de joie from the marines, and a Royal salute from ships of war,' formal possession was taken of the island of Hong Kong (13).

Captain: 8 June 1841.

From 14 June 1841 until 15 March 1843 in command frigate *Calliope*, 26, East Indies Station. In her participated in the British advance up the Yangtse River to Nanking, a very considerable maritime undertaking. The C. in C. was Vice Admiral Sir William Parker with his Flag in the Bombay teak built third rate *Cornwallis*, 72. Much assistance from hydrographic surveyors (see Kellett, C. in C., 1869) was required in making a safe passage upstream. The Treaty of 29 August 1842 resulted. By this Treaty the island of Hong Kong was ceded in perpetutity to the British Crown, and five ports were opened to foreign trade, the 'Treaty Ports' of Canton, Amoy, Fuchow, Ningpo and Shanghai. Shortly thereafter, by order in Council dated 5 April 1843, Hong Kong island was to receive the status of a Colony, the first Governor being H.E. Sir Henry Pottinger (1789-1856), he who had been Plenipotentiary at Nanking in August the previous year.

CB: 21 January 1842.

Another pleasant sequel was the receipt of a letter dated 14 February 1843 from the Speaker of the House of Commons. The extract relevant to his command of *Calliope* follows:-

> '... desiring me to convey to you and the officers of Her Majesty's ship under your command (--)
> the high sense entertained by the House of Commons of the zeal and gallantry of all those who
> shared in the achievements of the British arms... (14).'

Having returned home, his next appointment was to be on the Pacific Station in command of the frigate *Thetis*, 38 guns: 3 July 1850 – 4 February 1854 (15). Her voyage out to the Pacific was to occupy several months.

After commissioning and fitting out *Thetis* sailed from Devonport on Thursday, 10 October 1850. The First Lieutenant in the ship was John James Steven Josling of whom more will be heard below during the year 1862. Following a short stay at Funchal, 20 to 22 October, she continued across the Atlantic and on 20 November 1850 passed Fort Santa Cruz to starboard to anchor in the bay at Rio de Janeiro at 2 p.m. that afternoon (16). On arrival a salute was fired to the British C. in C., Rear Admiral Barrington Reynolds with his flag in the frigate *Southampton*, 1,468 tons bm (17).

From Rio de Janeiro on 14 December 1850 the ship proceeded to Montevideo where, on 22 May 1851, Mr. Noel Salmon, Midshipman, 'passed his examination' (see C. in C., 1887) (18).

This was a particularly unfortunate period in the history of Uruguay as the civil war, Guerra Grande, of 1843-1852 gradually came to an end. Aided by Brazil and the liberation army of Argentina, the Colorado Liberal party were to defeat the Blanco party which was supported by the then Argentine dictator. Not surprisingly the country of Uruguay itself was to be left in a ruined state.

Sailing from Montevideo on 9 July 1851 *Thetis* passed through Drake's Passage south of Diego Ramirez Island during the afternoon of Thursday, 24 July 1851 and shortly afterwards, by then in the Pacific Ocean, altered course in a northerly direction to anchor off Valparaiso at 11.50 a.m. on Monday, 11 August 1851.

In the frigate *Portland*, 52, a sister ship to *Southampton*, on 20 September the C. in C., Rear Admiral Fairfax Moresby arrived and was saluted with thirteen guns (19). At the time his son, John, was serving as the Gunnery Lieutenant in *Thetis*. John Moresby will appear again below, as a Commander in 1864, sloop *Argus*.

From Valparaiso on 27 September Captain Kuper sailed the short distance north to Coquimbo to attend to a local problem involving British interests, thereafter returning to Valparaiso on 30 October. There he remained until 12 December when *Thetis* sailed south to spend Christmas and New Year at Talcahuano, today (year 2008) the premier Chilean naval base. From there she returned to Valparaiso on 6 January 1852.

Following exercises off the port, on 16 January she returned in a southerly direction to cruise via Talcahuano and Valdivia as far south as Carlos Harbour, north Chiloe Island near present day Ancud. There she remained overnight, 8/9 February, thereafter retracing her steps to anchor off Valparaiso again on 20 February 1852.

Next came a longer voyage north, leaving Valparaiso on 10 March 1852.

In those years prior to the War of the Pacific, Guerra Del Pacifico of 1879-1883, the northern border of Chile fell far short of the present point adjacent to Peru just north of Arica. Bolivia, for example, in those days possessed a considerable Pacific sea coast. *Thetis* first visited Caldera, still in Chile, then proceeded further north into what were then Bolivian waters to anchor off Cobija for a night 24/25 March. Lieut. Moresby was not impressed:

> 'We saw Cobija, the only seaport of Bolivia, with its one well of brackish water, and not a blade
> of vegetation within 150 miles, all vegetables and fruits being brought from Valparaiso 700 miles
> away – a place where no rain has fallen within the memory of man, guarded by its scorched hills
> and desolate as the Mountains of the Moon (20)'

Continuing on to the north the ship anchored off Arica from 28 to 30 March. It was only as recently as in 1929 that Peru finally was to formally award that most northern province to Chile. However, following her earlier conquests, the entire region was to have been administered by Chile since the War had ended with the Treaty of Ancon, 20 October 1883.

Thetis next called at the Chincha Islands, well into Peruvian waters opposite Pisco. These were an important source of guano. Again a quote taken from Lieut. Moresby's recollections follows:-

> 'Anchoring off the largest islet in 33 fathoms, we landed by means of an accommodation ladder,
> fastened to the rock as to a ship's side; and as we stepped on it we looked downards to the transluscent
> ocean depths, and upwards to a mountain of guano, from which proceeded volatile ammonia so
> powerful that it choked and blinded us for a time. The irritation gradually wore off and we were able
> to look around at the busy scene. Some six or eight ships were loading with guano from great shoots
> on the cliff tops let into their holds. These were fed by at least a thousand labourers (21).'

Having remained at anchor off these islands for a night, on 5 April *Thetis* weighed to continue to Callao where she arrived the following day. Founded by Francisco Pizarro in 1537 Callao was the leading port for the export of gold and silver taken by Spain from the Inca people. Lieut. Moresby held a somewhat jaundiced view of the place, but there was to be good news too:-

> 'Next day we were at anchor at Callao, with apparently no prospect of escape from the desolate
> shores of Peru. But a sailor's life is happily full of surprises, and one day when the captain came
> onboard the joyful tidings spread that we were ordered to Vancouver (22).'

Indeed, from Callao on 10 April *Thetis* proceeded to sea. In due course she was to pass to the west of the Galapagos, east of Clipperton, quite close to but west of Clarion Island in the Reviliagigedo Archipelago, and at 1.20 p.m. on Sunday, 23 May 1852 sight Cape Flattery bearing 'ENE 6 or 8 miles (23).'

Shortly thereafter she entered the Strait of Juan de Fuca and early the following morning, 05.30 a.m., passed the Race Rocks, some ten miles S.W. of Victoria and at the southernmost point of Vancouver's Island, to anchor off Esquimalt at 10.00 a.m. Monday, 24 May 1852.

There was no road to Victoria therefore a familiar mode of transport was used:

> 'A row of three miles brought us to the fort (of Victoria). Is it possible for any of those who know
> the stately capital of British Columbia to close their eyes and see, as I do, the little wood palisaded
> building which then represented it? There it stood, defended by bastions at opposite angles, and
> mounting the four 9 pounder guns which were its protection against the surrounding tribes of the
> red man (24).'

At the Fort Captain Kuper was re-acquainted with the prime reason for his detachment to Vancouver's Island. In 1851 gold had been discovered in the Queen Charlotte Islands further north and, without further elaboration here, the authorities feared that 'marauders without title' might endeavour to annexe the islands. The British intended to make it clear to those involved, thought to consist of the, 'lawless floating population of California', that no flouting of British authority over the island, and in particular the region of Mitchell Inlet in which the gold had been discovered, would be tolerated (25). The presence of *Thetis* would add weight to this British declaration. Further, in 1852 Britain formally declared that the Queen Charlotte Islands were a dependency of the Colony of Vancouver Island.

To clarify this matter of the possession of various territories, by act of Parliament British Columbia formally was to be declared a British Colony on 2 August 1858. Prior to this however British jurisdiction over Vancouver Island and British Columbia had been recognised since the signing of the Oregon Treaty, 15 June 1846. In 1849 Vancouver Island already had become a Colony. The two territories were to be united in 1866 and in turn on 20 July 1871 were to join the Dominion of Canada, the Confederation of Canadian Provinces. It was by the British North American Act of 1867 that the country first had been named and known as Canada.

H.E. the Governor of Vancouver's Island, James Douglas, who together with Admiral Fairfax Moresby embodied British authority, visited the ship on Wednesday, 26 May (26).

It was on 5 June 1852 that *Thetis* weighed and proceeded from Esquimalt and at 3 p.m. on 16 June anchored off an 'Indian Village' on the west coast of Queen Charlotte Island up the creek, Mitchell Inlet, just to the south of Hibben Island. Lieut. Moresby elaborated:-

> 'Four miles farther up the fiord slanted sharply to the east; the wind followed; and three miles farther the fiord ended, where a rushing torrent plunged from a mountain gorge. Here we found bottom with 36 fathoms, and secured the ship with hawsers to the trees on either side. It was a wild scene in itself, and its strangeness was increased by a flotilla of large Indian canoes. (-). Our business was to report on the gold prospects, and there it was, running in quartz veins through the granite rocks overhanging the deep inlet. The Americans had left, but they and a Hudson's Bay craft had tried to work it by placing nets and rafts on the surface of the water and exploding the gold bearing rock above. Splendid specimens were obtained, but it could not be made to pay, so it was abandoned (27).'

Having satisfied himself as to the state of affairs prevailing at the site of this minute source of gold, at 11 a.m. on Tuesday, 22 June 1852 Captain Kuper weighed and, 'ran out of the Inner Harbour under the jibs.' Then:-

> 'Noon – boarded the American Schooner *Susan Sturgiss* (*Sturgis*) from San Francisco come to take away a party of men left here on a former visit to this place (28).'

The Americans having been reminded of the British ability to maintain their jurisdiction over their possessions, *Thetis* continued on to spend from 26 to 29 June at anchor in Beaver Harbour within Hardy Bay (today: Port Hardy) inside the Golita Channels, North Vancouver Island.

From that place she returned to Esquimalt to anchor at 2 p.m. on Sunday, 4 July 1852.

Thereafter, leaving Esquimalt on 9 July, followed a short visit south to San Francisco where the ship remained an anchor off the settlement from Friday, 16 July to Thursday, 29 July 1852. These were relatively lawless days and there were a number of enticements, real or imagined, for men to remain ashore. In order to discourage any such tendency on Sunday, 18 July Captain Kuper made his feelings clear:-

> 'In consequence of information having been received of arrangements made by some of the ship's company for deserting, the Captain (warned) the Petty Officers that in case of any man attempting to leave the ship the Sentries have orders to shoot him in Boats (29).'

Also there in San Francisco she received onboard 348 lbs. of beef and 174 lbs. of vegetables.

From San Francisco *Thetis* returned to the Queen Charlotte Islands arriving off the seaward entrance to Moore Channel at the Denham Point of Cape Henry on 11 August. This southern island of the group in due course was to be named after the C. in C., Moresby Island. Further, at the western part of Hibben Island is to be found Cape Kuper.

On this occasion the weather was too stormy and misty to enable the ship to proceed in towards Mitchell Inlet so she lay off the coast and instead sent in a boat to establish that all was well within.

Sailing from those unpleasant waters on 14 August *Thetis* once again returned to anchor off Esquimalt at 7.30 p.m. on Friday, 20 August 1852.

Then followed another journey to San Francisco, sailing on 11 September and arriving back in that bay on 17 September 1852. His business complete, at 2 p.m. on 30 September Captain Kuper endeavoured to put to sea but owing to high adverse winds and a heavy sea running at the entrance to the harbour, the present day Golden Gate, he had no option but to bear up and at 5.10 p.m. that afternoon return to anchor in the bay once more. A few days later the gale abated and on Tuesday, 5 October he was able to proceed safely to sea. Unfortunately off Cape Flattery the tides were found to be adverse, there was much fog, and 'showers obscured the land'. In consequence it took him two days to work up the Strait of Juan de Fuca finally to return to anchor at Esquimalt at 3.10 p.m. on Sunday, 17 October 1852.

There *Thetis* remained through Christmas of 1852 into the New Year.

It was at 3 p.m. on Monday, 3 January 1853 that, 'arrived the steamer *Beaver* with H.E. The Governor onboard (30).' Lieut. Moresby tells more:-

> '... news was brought that a Scotsman had been murdered near the fort (of Victoria) by two Indians of the distant Cowitchan and Naimo (Nanaimo) tribes, living near the two rivers which flow into the Gulf of Georgia, north of Victoria (31).'

Governor Douglas had come onboard to seek assistance in attending to this matter. Captain Kuper naturally agreed and prompt action was taken:-

> 'Tuesday, 4 January 1853
>
> 06.30 a.m.   Two Lieuts., two mates, 5 midshipmen, one asst. surgeon and 83 seamen with 1 Lieut., I Sergeant, 1 Corporal and 37 Private Marines embarked onboard the H.B. Company Steamer *Beaver* and schooner *Recovery* on an expedition to Cowichin at the request of H.E. The Governor (32).'

Lieut. Moresby was fortunate enough to be selected to proceed ashore and as may be imagined his account of the consequent adventure is fascinating (33). Suffice to say here that, to a great extent owing to the tact and ability of Governor Douglas, backed up as he was by the *Thetis* party, the two guilty men were apprehended and, later, '... a gallows was erected on the island at the entrance of Protection Bay, and there they met their death with steady fortitude.'

At 1 a.m. on Wednesday, 19 January, 'The party of officers, seamen and Marines returned from Cowichin and Nanaimo.' Three days later, at 7.15 a.m. on Saturday, 22 January, *Thetis* weighed and made sail out of Esquimalt for the last time. During the evening of Tuesday, 1 February she anchored off the entrance to San Francisco Bay at Point Reyes, and the following morning shifted in through Golden Gate to anchor within the Bay. Lieut. Moresby relates that, very wisely, from Vancouver's Island they took, 'with us some immense spars to be sold there (at San Francisco) for the benefit of the ship's fund; and a goodly sum they brought, for the city was mainly one of wood in those days, and timber precious.'

Today the twin islands of Thetis and Kuper off the South East coast of Vancouver Island commemorate the presence of *Thetis* and Captain Kuper in those waters in 1852 and 1853.

From San Francisco on 5 February 1853 *Thetis* continued on to the south, passed Guadaloupe Island at midnight on 9 February, and remained at anchor in Cape Lucas Bay at the southern tip of Baja California from 14 to 17 February 1853.

Thetis next proceeded and anchored off Mazatlan on 20 February. For the next three months she was to remain on that Pacific coast of Mexico over the Altata-San Blas range. Within Mexico at the time there was little or no sense of law and order prevailing. One of the results of this breakdown in the normal rules of society was that H.M. Ships frequently were called upon to transport gold and silver, the product of Mexican mines, some of which were English owned, to Panama where this valuable cargo was carried overland to the Caribbean for onward freight to Britain. As will be seen from the following the freight earned by H.M. Ships involved in this trade could be most profitable to some of those involved. At the same time clearly young Lieutenants received no benefit:

> 'The end of this discreditable work was that in two months we had accumulated about GBP 600,000 (worth of bullion), of which the Captain's profit was worth about GBP 8,000, and the

Commander in Chief and Greenwich Hospital received about GBP 1,500 each. Then another ship took our place, and so the practice continued for many a long year (34).'

Via Panama the ship next proceeded on south to return to Valparaiso on 26 September 1853. From there she sailed on 10 October, passed Diego Ramirez on 25 October, and called at Rio de Janeiro from 19 to 26 November 1853. Into the North Atlantic homewardbound, during the afternoon of 12 January 1854 *Thetis* passed Flores in the Azores and at 1.00 a.m. on Friday, 27 January anchored in Plymouth Sound.

Stores and supplies having been landed *Thetis* finally was placed out of commission at Devonport at sunset on Saturday, 4 February 1854 (35).

Commanded *London*, 90, in the Mediterranean for five months from 28 August 1855 to 26 January 1856, this being at the time of the last few months of the war with Russia (36).

By the Treaty of Paris, 30 March 1856, this Crimean War was brought to a conclusion.

Rear Admiral: 29 July 1861.

8 February 1862. Appointed C. in C., East Indies and China Station, in the steam frigate *Euryalus*, 35. At Portsmouth he hoisted his flag in her on Tuesday, 11 February, but only embarked at Plymouth at 4.25 p.m. on Monday, 31 March 1862, an hour before she sailed for Madeira, the Cape and East. On passage then at the Cape she called at Simon's Town from 12 to 24 June 1862.

At this point it is necessary to outline briefly the life of Edward Adolphus Seymour (1805-1885). He was a man with strong Devonian connections having been MP for Okehampton from 1830-1831, and for Totnes from 1834-1855 when he succeeded to the title as Twelfth Duke of Somerset. In addition, from 1859 to 1866 he was First Lord of the Admiralty.

Between 27 August 1862 and 31 October 1864, as a part of their regular exchange of correspondence, he received some eighteen letters from Admiral Kuper from the East.

The first, written in his flagship *Euryalus* from Hong Kong shortly after his arrival at that port, was dated 27 August 1862. This was before he had assumed command and was in reply to, 'your Grace's letter of 10 July'. In this reply Kuper made brief reference to rebel activity in the Shanghai region, spoke of, 'the greatest evil appears to be the wide spread system of piracy going all along the coast and especially in the vicinity of Hong Kong', and mentioned, 'the severe typhoon which committed very serious ravages about three or four weeks ago – the full force of it appears to have been felt in the neighbourhood of Canton where some 30,000 to 40,000 Chinese are said to have lost their lives (37).'

To a great part owing to this activity of the T'ai-p'ing rebels, briefly mentioned above, the domestic situation in southern China, and in the vicinity of the International Settlement at Shanghai, was in a chaotic state. Vacillation within ruling Manchu circles in Peking only served to aggravate this problem.

From the Cape then in his Flagship, Captain John J.S. Josling, he who had served earlier in *Thetis*, he first arrived at Singapore on 29 July 1862. From there on 2 August she proceeded direct across the South China Sea to reach Hong Kong on Monday, 12 August. Finally she reached Yedo Bay on Sunday, 14 September 1862, '6:15 p.m. Stopped and came to in 7.5 fms. off Yokohama (38).'

Quite by chance on that very day the British merchant Charles Lennox Richardson, while out riding with three friends, had been killed near Kanagawa at the village of Namamugi by Satsuma samurai, the escort to their Daimio, Shimazu Hisamitsu. Fortunately the British authorities ashore were able to exert a calming influence over their more excitable nationals who, immediately and without considering possible consequences, had wished to attempt an act of revenge.

On 23 October 1862 he commanded a Naval force led by Captain Josling which participated in the successful expedition against the Taiping rebels at Kahding, near Shanghai (39). Another participant in this affair was Lieut. Edward H. Seymour, then serving in *Imperieuse* (see C. in C., 1897). Ashore much of the successful military activity against the rebels, who were attempting to invest Shanghai, was led by Brigadier Charles William Dunbar Staveley (1817-1896), later to be a General and Colonel of the Worcestershire Regiment. In due course it was he who was to recommend to Viceroy Li Hung Chang that Captain Charles George Gordon, 'Chinese Gordon' and subsequently 'Gordon of Khartoum', be appointed in command of Imperial Chinese troops in that vicinity, the 'Ever Victorious Army'.

Just prior to the Kahding affair *Euryalus* had been anchored off Woosung when early on Tuesday, 21 October a message arrived from Captain Gordon seeking assistance urgently (40). Unfortunately these were the days prior to the removal of the bar in the Whangpoo River at the point at which it meets the Yangtse. However, nothing loath, and with the ship drawing 21' 11" forward and 21' 9" aft, Captain Josling put her at the bar and forced his way through the mud, 'Ship's company sallying the ship' (41). By word of explanation:-

> 'Not an order was heard. All was done by bugle.
> "Everybody aft" – all hands, officers and all.
> "Everyone forward".
> "Everyone port side".
> "Everyone starboard side".
> "Everyone jump up".
> All repeated in succession for about half an hour. The ship was rolling, say, 35 to 40 degrees head up or down, stern up or down, according to the rush of men. She never stopped. If she had stopped we should have been done. The engines were smothered with mud, forced in through the condensers. She came off with a rush, and we were soon up at Shanghai with the city under our guns (42).'

In the event it was at 3 p.m. that day that *Euryalus* moored in seven fathoms off the then rather modest settlement of Shanghai, 'Upon the Sea'.

At 6 a.m. the following morning, 22 October, 'Sent 156 Seamen 60 Marines and 34 officers on shore to assist in capturing Kahding.' The Admiral himself proceeded ashore at 9 a.m., only returning onboard three days later, Saturday, 25 October at 1.30 p.m. (43).

Subsequently at Shanghai on 29 October 1862 he assumed command of the station in succession to acting Vice Admiral Sir James Hope. Also as is recorded in the log book in *Euryalus*:-

> 'Wednesday, 29 October 1862.
> a.m. Sailed H.M.S. *Coromandel* bearing the Flag of Admiral Hope in tow of *Starling* (44).'

In the event, once the situation locally became quiet, *Euryalus* sailed from Shanghai on Sunday, 22 November and returned to Hong Kong on 28 November 1862.

There on 1 December he addressed a letter to The Secretary of the Admiralty which included the following fascinating paragraph:-

> 'For some time past there have been rumours of considerable changes likely to take place in the constitution of the government of Japan which, if carried out, would materially reduce the power of the Tycoon (Shogun), and possibly remove the seat of his executive Government from Yedo to Miako, but I have not as yet been enabled to obtain any reliable information on the subject (45).'

With these comments the C. in C. was just over five years ahead of events for it was only to be on 3 January 1868 that the fifteenth and last of the Shoguns, Tokugawa Yoshinobu, or Keiki, was to resign thus permitting the formal commencement of the Meiji era (see C. in C. 1867).

Also writing from Hong Kong he informed the Duke of Somerset that there in December 1862 he had met the French Admiral Juares:-

> '... who arrived here yesterday (12 December) in the frigate *Semiramis*. He has brought with him an additional force of 500 troops, officers and engineers etc., and expects immediately the guns and machinery for four gunboats which he intends to have built at either Shanghai or Ningpo.

Admiral Juares informs me that he had an interview with the Emperor shortly before leaving France and that it was strongly impressed upon him that it was the Emperor's desire that in all operations in China he was to act entirely in concert with us, and the Admiral expressed to me his earnest wish to maintain the good understanding which has hitherto existed (46).'

Otherwise he wrote about the Russians, 'whose ships have been moving about a good deal lately and they have produced a larger force in these waters than for many years past.'

In closing he anticipated, correctly, future difficulties in Japan:-

'My last letters from Japan state everything to be quiet there, but it is generally believed that this satisfactory state of affairs will not last long (47).'

In the interim, and as was reported at Singapore, it was during the latter months of 1862 that from Suez the French first commenced their commercial steamer service to the Far East:-

'The French mail line of the Messageries Imperiales, as it was then termed, began to run towards the close of the year (-). The first steamer of the company to arrive from Suez, bringing the mails from London of 18 October, was the *Imperatrice* which arrived at Singapore on 21 November 1862 (48).'

With the ship then continuing on to Hong Kong, there it is recorded that, '… the starting of the French Messageries line of mail steamers was celebrated, 22 December 1862, with considerable eclat by a magnificent public ball given onboard s.s. *Imperatrice*.'

In Japan the 'Richardson affair' of 14 September was to lead to a vigorous reaction in Great Britain where the Prime Minister chanced to be Henry John Temple, Third Viscount Palmerston (1784-1865), then approaching the end of his astonishing life. His Secretary of State for Foreign Affairs, Earl Russell (1792-1878), was instructed very clearly and on 24 December 1862 wrote to the British Charge d'Affaires in Japan, Lieut. Colonel Edward St. John Neale. Extracts follow:-

'You are instructed to ask as reparation from the Japanese Government:-

1. An ample and formal apology for the offence of permitting a murderous attack on British subjects passing on a road open by treaty to them.
2. The payment of GBP 100,000 as a penalty on Japan for this offence.

Next you will demand from the Daimio Prince of Satsuma:-

1. The immediate trial and capital execution, in the presence of one or more of Her Majesty's naval officers, of the chief perpetrators of the murder of Mr. Richardson, and of the murderous assault upon the lady and gentlemen who accompanied him.
2. The payment of GBP 25,000, to be distributed to the relations of the murdered man, and to those who escaped with their lives the swords of the assassins on that occasion (49).'

In the event that the Japanese refused to pay then a blockade of the important coastal sea traffic of Japan was suggested. In addition in London it was known that the Prince of Satsuma had a port, 'at the south-west end of the island of Kiu-siu.' Further:-

'The Admiral (-) will be better able to judge than Her Majesty's Government can be, whether it will be most expedient to blockade this port, or whether it will be possible or advisable to shell the residence of the Prince.'

To better understand the meaning of the equivalent of GBP 100,000 in Japan at the time, it may be noted that, '… the indemnity asked for was heavy, amounting to $440,000 (Mexican silver), roughly a third of the Bakufu's (government of the Shogunate or Tycoon) regular annual income (50).'

In these circumstances it is hardly surprising that negotiations dragged on. From the Shogunate point of view matters were not assisted by Imperial pressure from Kyoto being a desire to pursue a policy of, 'joi', or, 'expel the barbarians'.

SOUTHERN DISTRICT.

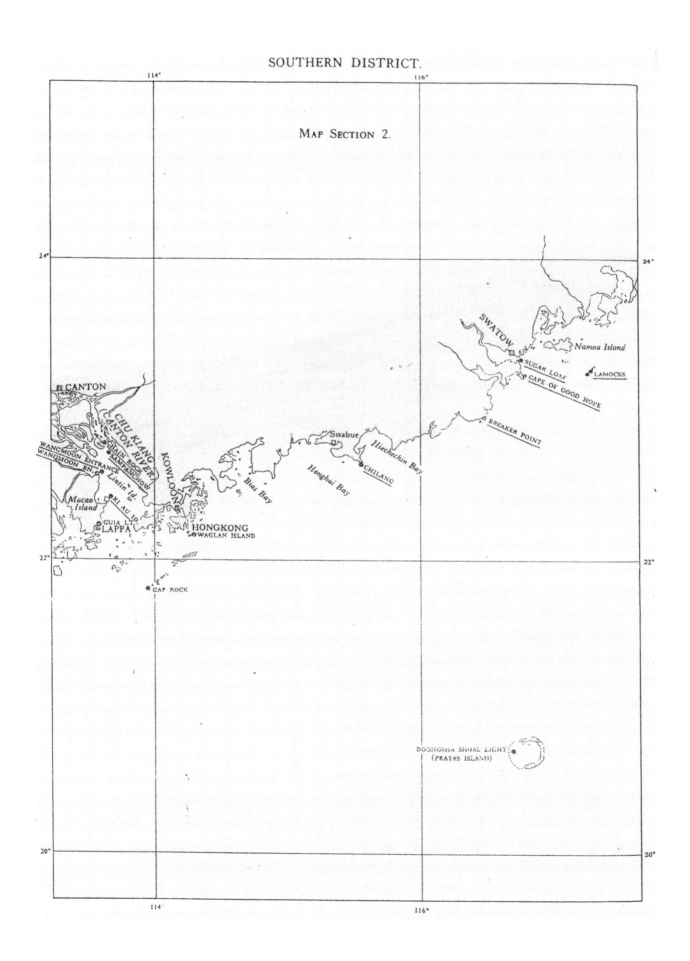

MAP SECTION 2.

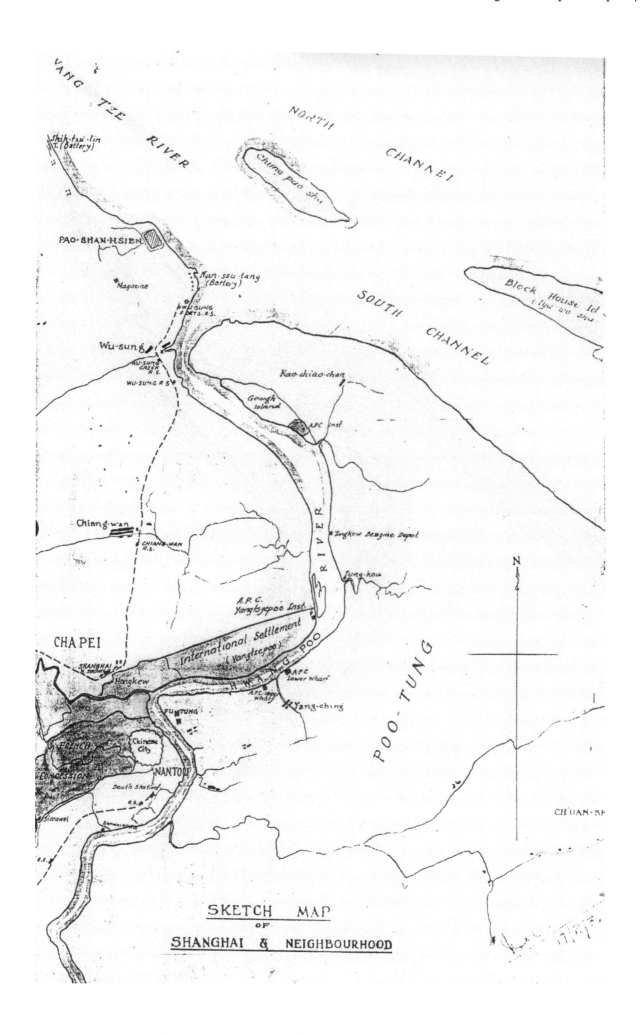

SKETCH MAP
OF
SHANGHAI & NEIGHBOURHOOD

Map of the Far East

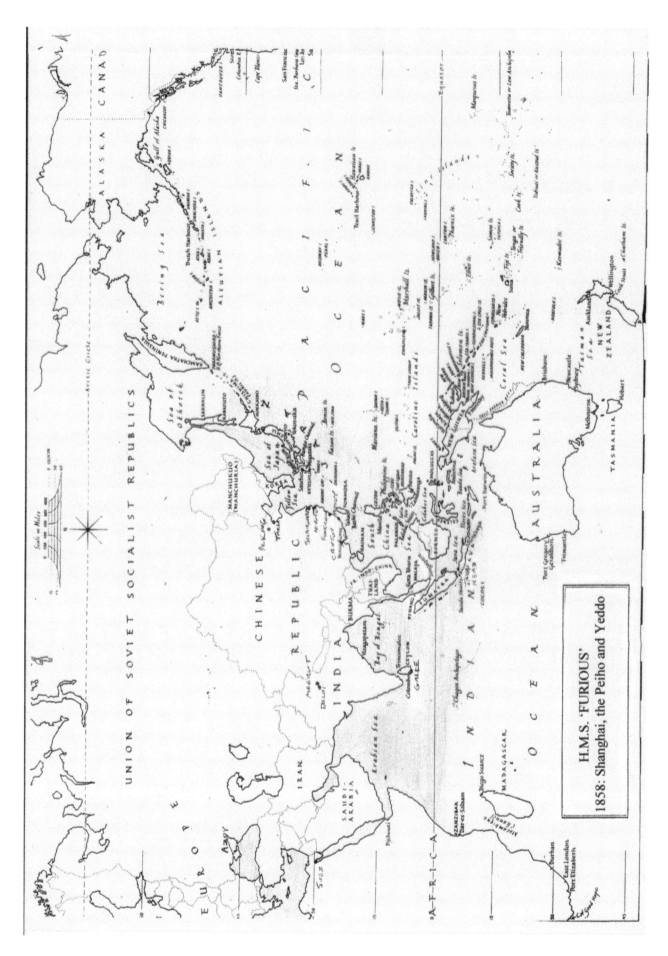

Map of the Far East

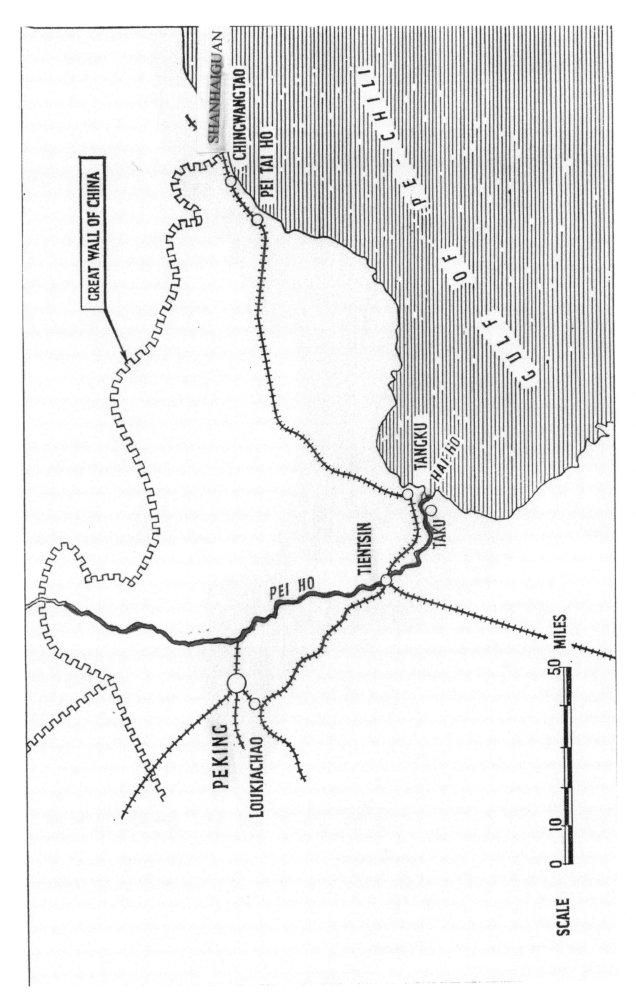

Map of Northern China at the coast, showing the proximity of Peking (Beijing) to the mouth of the Pei Ho at Taku/Tangku.

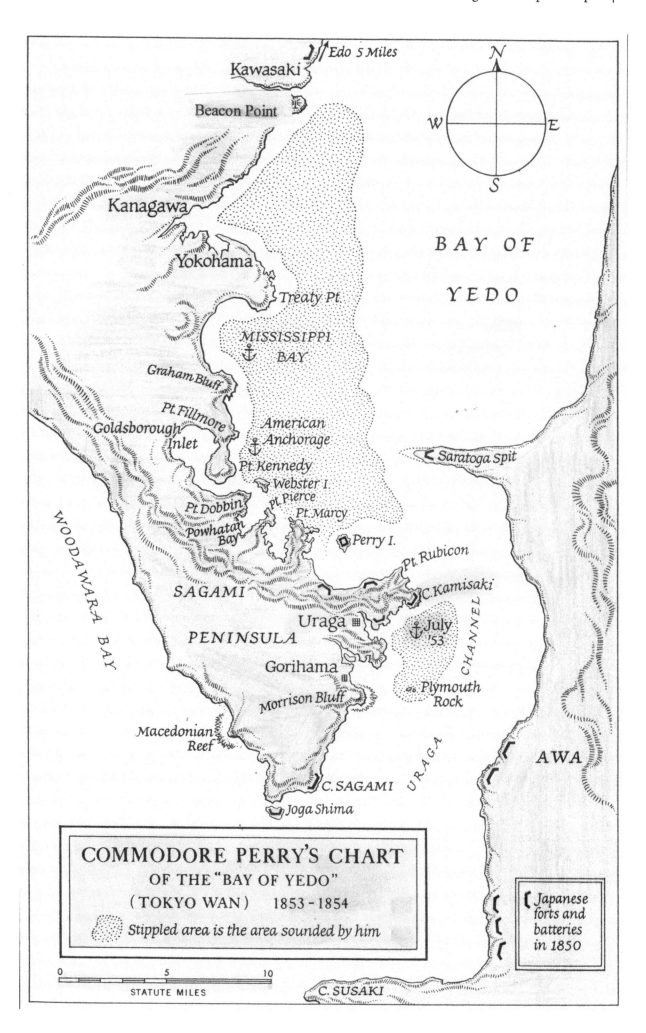

Edo 5 Miles

Kawasaki

Beacon Point

N

W   E

S

Kanagawa

BAY OF

YEDO

Yokohama

Treaty Pt.

MISSISSIPPI
⚓ BAY

Graham Bluff

Pt. Fillmore

Goldsborough
Inlet

American
⚓ Anchorage

Saratoga Spit

Pt. Kennedy

Webster I

Pt. Pierce

Pt. Dobbin

Pt. Marcy

Powhatan
Bay

Perry I.

Pt. Rubicon

WOODAWARA BAY

SAGAMI

C. Kamisaki

Uraga

⚓ July
'53

PENINSULA

Gorihama

Plymouth
Rock

Morrison Bluff

URAGA CHANNEL

Macedonian
Reef

AWA

C. SAGAMI

Joga Shima

COMMODORE PERRY'S CHART

OF THE "BAY OF YEDO"

(TOKYO WAN)   1853-1854

Stippled area is the area sounded by him

{ Japanese
forts and
batteries
in 1850

0   5   10

STATUTE MILES

C. SUSAKI

During this time of uncertainty, while negotiations continued, then rather naturally the mood in the region of Kanagawa/Yokohama was extremely sensitive. On 6 April 1863 the British made their written demand of the Bakufu, with twenty days being allowed for their reply. An American citizen living there on the spot during the period was Francis Hall, to be a founder of the trading and shipping concern, Walsh, Hall & Co. Various excerpts, taken from his diary, follow:-

'14 April 1863. Three weeks since Rear Admiral Kuper, Commanding-in-Chief all her Majesty's naval forces in the China Seas, arrived at Yokohama in *Euryalus*, escorted by three other war steamers. Since that time there have been accessions to the squadron, till now there lie in our harbour eleven men of war, several of which are large and powerful steamers. Several others are daily expected as Admiral Kuper has ordered all the available force on the east Asiatic coast to follow him hither.

25 April 1863. It is officially announced that 15 additional days will be granted the Japanese to consider the English demands.

1 May 1863. The feeling of distrust among the Japanese increases. The merchants are desirous to realize on their goods. Teas are offered ten to twelve dollars a picul cheaper than before the demands, while silk, which has remained firm up to today, has fallen 30 to 50 dollars a picul. In truth, the Japanese seem to be getting ready for a flight. Families at Kanagawa in vicinity of the port have been removed.

4 May 1863. The flight of the Japanese increases. The City Governor of Yedo has advised all the women, children, infirm and aged to retire to the country. The shop keepers grow daily more anxious to realize for their wares and rumours of threatened attack to the foreign settlement grow more frequent.

6 May 1863. Today a regular panic has seized the town; the native population are fleeing in the utmost haste. Everyone believes war is inevitable and is hastening to escape from the vicinity of the sea.

25 May 1863. An envoy from Yedo is here today holding conferences with the French and English Ministers and Admirals relative to the demands. A settlement without war is confidently hoped for (51).'

Fortunately all subsequent meetings were to proceed satisfactorily and eventually the larger penalty of Mexican $440,000 was paid in June 1863. On the other hand the Daimio of Satsuma simply refused to consider making any payment so finally, after giving both the Prince and even the Government of Japan every opportunity to meet British demands, Colonel Neale had no other option than to arrange with the C. in C. for firm steps to be taken against the Shimazu family. Such steps included the possibility of, 'stopping his supplies from the Loo Chew Islands from which a large proportion of his revenue is said to be derived (52).'

In the event the British naval bombardment of Kagoshima, capital of the Satsuma 'han' (fiefdom) took place between 15-17 August 1863. During this engagement, which by no means was one sided, the C. in C. flew his flag in *Euryalus*. Captain Josling, of the flagship, lost his life to the defenders' fire and from 25 August 1863 was succeeded in command of *Euryalus* by Captain John H.I. Alexander (see birth of C. in C., 1925). In addition to considerable damage caused to the batteries defending Kagoshima, British gunfire destroyed much of the industrial capacity of the Prince of Satsuma, and the three of his steamers found in the bay were first captured then destroyed by being set on fire. In addition high winds resulted in the destruction by fire of a part of the city.

During this engagement the British suffered a total of thirteen men killed and forty nine wounded.

Serving in *Euryalus* from 24 June 1862, latterly as Gunnery Officer, was Lieutenant Richard E. Tracey (53).

Present as a member of the Satsuma defending forces was the then very young, but future Admiral of the Fleet Marquis Togo Heihachiro, OM.

Similarly engaged at Kagoshima was the future Admiral of the Fleet Viscount Inoue Yoshika (1845-1929) (see Bridge, C. in C., 1901).

Within the European community in Japan the reaction to the operation at Kagoshima was much as might be expected in that era. Here follows a press extract:-

'The unparalled treachery of those proud misguided orientals, has at last plunged them into trouble in earnest, and before they shall have fairly emerged from the difficulties which they have now deliberately got themselves into, we have no doubt they will be a wiser, and, we hope, a better people than they are at present. Their last act of treachery has cost them dear; and the name of Admiral Kuper and a British fleet will henceforth have a weighty significance in Japan.

We congratulate the British Government for their fortunate choice of Admiral Kuper, who has proved himself to be a naval chieftan well worthy of a first class British fleet; and whose bravery, coolness and skill, under an exceedingly heavy, treacherous fire, accompanied by very trying circumstances of weather, do honour to the great naval power which he worthily represents in the East (54).'

In November 1863 the Prince of Satsuma wisely found himself in a position to settle the British demand for financial compensation to the families of Richardson and the other horsemen of the unpleasant September 1862 incident. Needless to say this was not a straightforward transaction since the Satsuma 'han' Shimazu family first had to threaten the Bakufu with the further assassination of foreigners unless the necessary funds were forthcoming. In turn the Bakufu were only able to obtain such a sum by extortion from the wealthy merchants of the day. One source suggests that this sum of GBP 25,000 was 'borrowed' from the merchant house of Mitsui (55).

Although they were not to maintain their prominent position on the River, it must be recorded that in 1864 of the Western steamship vessel operators on the Yangtse, with five such vessels, the largest was the Shanghai Steam Navigation Company. Founded at Shanghai on 27 March 1862 the firm was managed by the American organisation of Russell and Company, their Edward Cunningham being the imaginative partner. Particularly far sighted had been his earlier selection of well sited wharf properties, especially at Shanghai just below Soochow Creek in Hong Kew thus in close proximity to many Chinese shippers (56).

Another American organisation active for a number of years in the steamship business in Chinese waters was Augustine Heard & Company.

KCB: 25 February 1864 which was awarded as a result of his success in Japanese waters.

19 July 1864. With their successful assault of the rebel capital of Nanking, and with European assistance, the Manchu army, organised by the scholar and military leader, Hunan born Tseng Kuo-fan (1811-1872), brought the Taiping rebellion, which had commenced early in 1851, to a rapid end. However the power and authority of the Manchu Ch'ing dynasty in China had been greatly weakened and never was to be thoroughly regained (see C. in C. 1910-1913).

As mentioned above piracy was always a problem on the Station and, to give an example, on 26 July 1864 the Hong Kong flag, Chinese owned junk *Cum-Shun-Wah* was seized near Macao. Her cargo consisted of 4,850 bags of sugar together with 400 packages of general. Also she was carrying ten passengers, and was manned by a crew of thirty four of whom four were killed during the savage attack (57).

In Hong Kong in July 1864 the first steps were taken which were to result in the founding of the Hongkong and Shanghai Banking Corportation. The guiding light in the creation of this new organisation was Thomas Sutherland (1834-1922), local manager of the P. & O. Steamship Company, and their future Managing Director and Chairman. He was to be knighted in 1891. Amongst the other personalities involved in the founding of this new enterprise were the steamship owner Douglas Lapraik, Francis Chomley of Dent & Co., Albert Farley Heard of the American shipowners and traders, Messrs. Augustine Heard and Co. which had been founded in Canton in 1840, and William Adamson of The Borneo Co. Ltd. (58).

The bank commenced to do business at both Hong Kong and Shanghai on 3 April 1865 (59).

As early as on 29 July 1863 Sir Augustus had commented in a letter addressed to the Duke of Somerset regarding, 'the hostile acts committed by the Prince of Nagato (Choshu) by firing on vessels bearing the French, Dutch and American flags in the Strait of Shimonoseki (60).'

In the meantime the Minister to Japan, Sir Rutherford Alcock, had returned from Britain, reaching Yokohama on 2 March 1864 in the paddle sloop *Argus*, Commander John Moresby. As a Lieutenant, John Moresby had served in *Thetis*, above. Sir Rutherford brought with him, 'a mandate to enforce the treaties and protect British trade (61).' A few days later Colonel Neale, following the success at Kagoshima created a CB, proceeded on leave prior to taking up his next post. This was for a few months at Athens, then from August 1865 to Guayaquil. He was to die on 11 December 1866.

The Allies agreed to work together to restore their right of passage through the Strait of Shimonoseki, and when the Shogunate government proved unable to persuade the Daimio of Choshu to disobey the desire for a policy of 'joi' emanating from His Imperial Majesty in Kyoto, a joint Allied naval action was decided upon.

Alfred Holt (1829-1911) Manager, 1866-1904 (photograph courtesy of Mrs Margaret Anderson)

Although by now it was clear to the Dutch that their previously dominant European trading position in Japan was lost, nevertheless useful assistance was received from their Consul-General, since August 1863 he being Dirk de Graeff van Polsbroek (1833-1916).

Consequently Sir Augustus led the successful Allied attack, British, French, Dutch and American, against Choshu 'han' positions at the Strait of Shimonoseki: 5 – 10 September 1864. The French squadron of three warships was commanded by Rear Admiral Constant Louis Jean Benjamin Jaures (1823-1889), mentioned above, who continued to fly his flag in *Semiramis*. This operation included the landing of forces to destroy forts. Also a good number of captured cannon were removed by the Allies (62).

Writing in *Euryalus* from 'Simone Saki' on 16 September the C. in C. was pleased to be able to inform His Grace, 'that the expedition to the Straits of Simone Saki has met with the most perfect and unqualified success (63).'

Following this operation, in December 1864 Sir Augustus was to be created a Grand Officier de l'Ordre Imperial de la Legion d'Honneur, and in February 1865 he received permission from H.M. The Queen to wear the decoration. Similarly in February 1865 he received the Dutch order, Kommandeure of the Militaire Willems-Orde (64).

Foreign merchants too were hopeful of a positive outcome to this Allied success. Here is Francis Hall once more:

> 'Now that Chosiu has been thoroughly humbled by foreign arms, we wait to see what good shall come of it. If it will lead the Japanese generally to see that trade and intercourse with foreign nations, however disagreeable, is a fixed necessity, and how futile any resistance will be, we may rejoice that the lesson has been taught them with so little bloodshed (65).'

Naturally there were a number of other matters which engaged the attention of the Admiral. These ranged from such subjects as reporting to the Admiralty the existence of some rebel troubles near Amoy, through to him causing to have erected at Yokohama, 'temporary sick quarters in order to treat smallpox cases'.

In the absence of suitable alternative means of transport also he assisted with the requirements of British diplomats. For instance on 24 December 1864 Sir Rutherford Alcock left Yokohama in the screw corvette *Barrosa*, 1,700 tons, Captain Henry Boys, on passage to Shanghai via the Inland Sea and Nagasaki (66). That duty accomplished, from Shanghai *Barrosa* returned to Yokohama, arriving on 11 February 1865.

11 January 1865. Registration in England, by Alfred Holt (1829-1911), of the Ocean Steam Ship Company, in due course for over a century to become widely known throughout the East as The Blue Funnel Line. On 19 April 1866 he was to sail his first steamer from Liverpool to Penang, Hong Kong and Shanghai via Mauritius. Her name was *Agamemnon*, 2,280 grt, Captain Isaac Middleton.

Following the completion of his term of office, on 15 March 1865 H.E. Sir Hercules George Robert Robinson (1824-1897), son of Admiral Hercules Robinson (1789-1864) and a most successful Governor of the Colony through many difficult times, departed from Hong Kong at the commencement of his voyage home. His brilliant career was to continue in Ceylon, New South Wales, Fiji, New Zealand and South Africa. On 11 August 1896 he was to be created Baron Rosmead. A younger brother was Frederick, in due course a Vice Admiral (see C. in C., 1892, but in the East Indies, April 1891).

At Singapore on 22 May 1865 Admiral Kuper handed over the command of the station to his successor, Vice Admiral George St. Vincent King, and on Saturday, 27 May in *Euryalus* sailed for home via Batavia and the Cape.

To illustrate something of the pace of life under sail here follows an outline of the progress of *Euryalus* during her passage home from Yokohama, the C. in C.'s final voyage. As Captain Alexander had been wounded during the engagement at Shimonoseki in September 1864 the ship by now was commanded by Captain William M. Dowell (see C. in C., 1884) :

> 'Sailed from Yokohama: Monday, 13 February 1865.
> Passed Cape Chichakoff (south Kyushu): 17 February.
> Anchored at Nagasaki: Sunday, 19 February.
> Sailed from Nagasaki: Wednesday, 1 March.

Anchored Tinghai, Chusan Island: Monday, 6 March.

Sailed from Tinghai: Tuesday, 21 March.

Anchored at Amoy outer harbour: Sunday, 26 March.

Sailed from Amoy: Thursday, 30 March.

Anchored at Hong Kong: Saturday, 1 April.

Sailed from Hong Kong: Thursday, 27 April.

Anchored at Singapore: Wednesday, 17 May.

> Amongst H.M. Ships in port there found *Princess Royal*.
>
> 'Resigned command of the Station to Admiral King': Monday, 22 May 1865.
>
> 'Dressed Ship and saluted H.M. Queen Victoria's Birthday': Wednesday, 24 May.

Sailed from Singapore: Saturday, 27 May.

Anchored at Batavia: Wednesday, 31 May (67).

Sailed from Batavia: Thursday, 8 June.

Anchored in Simon's Bay, Cape: Sunday, 9 July.

Sailed from Simon's Bay: Sunday, 16 July.

Anchored off James Town, St. Helena between 11.50 a.m. and 6 p.m.: Tuesday, 1 August.

Anchored off Ascension Island and took coals between 1.10 and 8.30 p.m.: Sat., 5 August.

Passed between Flores and Corvo in the Azores at 9 p.m.: Monday, 28 August.

> The log book extract held at Exeter ends on 6 September 1865 with 151 miles remaining to sail to reach England.'

Shortly after his return to Plymouth, *Euryalus* anchoring in the Sound at 5.15 p.m. on Thursday 7 September (68), he received the following welcoming letter dated at the Admiralty, 8 September 1865:-

> 'I am commanded by My Lords Commissioners of the Admiralty to acquaint you that on the occasion of your striking your Flag and coming on shore they have much pleasure in recording the high sense they entertain of the zeal and judgement displayed by you in the performance of your duties as Commander in Chief in China. By your energetic conduct at Kagoshima and at Simonoseki you caused the British flag to be respected in Japan, and were instrumental in establishing relations with that country which afford promise of greater security to the life and prosperity of Europeans, and of an extended commerce with that rich Empire. In the varying circumstances arising out of the distracted State of the Chinese Empire, My Lords consider that you acted with a discretion highly creditable to yourself, and they desire, therefore, on your return from this important command, to convey to you their full approbation of your conduct (69).'

In the event he left the ship at 2.00 p.m. on 8 September with hands, "cheered him on leaving", struck his flag the next day, Saturday, 9 September 1865, and retired the following day (70). He was to see no further active service.

From his service record it may be noted that while on the active list, for earnings purposes, he was on half pay for an extraordinary total of just a month short of twenty eight years.

For many years he resided at Rock Cottage, South Brent, Devon (71). His house also was known as 'The Rock on the Aune', Aune being the ancient name of the village river, Avon (72). This village is to be found on the edge of the moor, less than ten miles from Totnes.

Retired, but not forgotten. In one instance, writing on 30 January 1866, the Admiralty asked for his opinion regarding the construction of a ship, similar to *Gladiator*, to convey 500 troops and armed with six guns, and whether a paddle wheel or screw steamer, in peace and in war, would be the most suitable. *Gladiator*, completed in 1846, was a paddle steamer of six guns, 190' loa and 1,960 tons. In reply, for reasons of lighter draught of water to facilitate the landing and embarkation of troops, together with greater capabilities of stowage, Sir Augustus felt that, 'a paddle wheel steamer would answer the purpose best (73).'

Vice Admiral: 6 April 1866.

In that era foreign travel was not undertaken by great numbers of citizens, nor was a passport a document in booklet form of any kind. Consisting of a single sheet of paper, rather larger than A4 in size, on 6 May 1867, and signed by Lord Stanley, Her Majesty's Secretary of State for Foreign Affairs, the Foreign Office in London issued Passport No. 4166 in the names of:-

> 'Vice Admiral Sir Augustus L. Kuper (British Subject) accompanied by Lady Kuper and one child, travelling on the Continent … (74).'

GCB: 2 June 1869.

Admiral: 20 October 1872.

GSP: 12 November 1874. At the rate of GBP 300 p.a, this supplement to his pension had become available for re-allocation, 'in a vacancy caused by the death of Admiral Sir Robert Smart, KCB, KH (75).'

The announcement of his death appeared in *The Times*, Monday, November 2, 1885:

> 'On the 29th Oct. at The Rock, South Brent, Admiral Sir A.L. Kuper, GCB, aged 76.'

Lady Kuper had died on 19 July 1877, being her sixty fourth year. Sir Augustus himself was laid to rest beside her in the churchyard of St. Petroc's Church, South Brent. Today (July 2008) their gravestone may be made out fairly clearly. His residence, a substantial house, is situated close to the narrow arched Lydia Bridge over the river Aune at a point where it tumbles down from the edge of the moor. After rain and when in spate the stream is a fine sight.

Following his death the gross value of his estate was found to amount to GBP 21,726-7-10. His son, Charles Victor Bremer Kuper, in 1888 a Captain in the Royal Artillery and to be stationed at Agra in the North West Provinces of India, was an executor (76).

In Canada during November 2006 British Columbia Ferry Services Inc. named and launched their new vehicle ferry, *Kuper*, 537 grt, after Kuper Island and Captain Augustus Leopold Kuper.

NOTES

1. William IV. Born in 1765. In 1830 succeeded his older brother HM King George IV.
2. Friends of English Harbour, *The Romance of English Harbour*, (Third edition: Antigua, 1959), 15, 19-22.
3. William R. O'Byrne, *A Naval Biographical Dictionary*, (Reprint in Polstead, Suffolk, 1986), 623. Some slight differences are noted between this record and that under ADM 196/5 as follows as reference (4).
4. National Archives, Kew. NA ADM 196/5. 56. *Record of Service*.
5. O'Byrne.
6. George Smith and successors, *Dictionary of National Biography*, (OUP, 1993). O'Byrne.
7. Ibid. The establishment of the unhealthily situated and to be short lived Port Essington was seen as desirable by the highly esteemed Sir John **Barrow** (1764-1848) at the Admiralty in order to counter perceived French and Dutch interest in Australia. Christopher Lloyd, *Mr. Barrow of the Admiralty*, (London, 1970), 163/4. To give Sir John his due also he was to come out in favour of the subsequent efforts, which were to prove successful, by Sir James Stirling at the Swan River: 'The French having turned their eyes to that quarter makes it absolutely incumbent on us (to) take possession of Swan River… ', Pamela Statham-Drew, *James Stirling*, (Crawley, W. Australia, 2003), 107.
8. Jordan Goodman, *The Rattlesnake*, (London, 2005), 191, 194. **Owen Stanley**. Born: 13 June 1811. Died in Sydney, NSW: 13 March 1850. Commander: 26 March 1839. FRS: 3 March 1842. Captain: 23 September 1844. An officer with considerable scientific interests and background. The Owen Stanley range in New Guinea is named for him. *Australian Dictionary of Biography*.

As an example of the often useful nature of marriage connecting families of potential influence, Owen Stanley's younger brother, Arthur Penrhyn Stanley (1815-1881), latterly Dean of Westminster Abbey, in 1863 married Lady Augusta Elizabeth Frederica Bruce. She was a daughter of Thomas Bruce (1766-1841), 7th Earl of Elgin and 11th Earl of Kincardine thus she was a younger sister of James, the 8th Earl (1811-1863). He, James, as British Plenipotentiary played a most active role in China and Japan in 1858 and 1860. Both James and his son Victor (1849-1917), 9th Earl of Elgin, were to serve as Viceroys of India. In 1874 The Rev. Arthur assisted at the marriage ceremony of HRH Alfred, Duke of Edinburgh (1844-1900), second son of H.M. Queen Victoria, also a serving Naval officer and future Admiral of the Fleet, with Grand Duchess Maria Alexandrovna of Russia (1853-1920), daughter of H.I.M. Tsar Alexander II (1818-1881).

9. Letter from J. Gordon Bremer, Commodore First Class, C. in C., in *Wellesley's* Galley at Sea. Lat. 6.47 N Long. 106.42E (South China Sea between Vietnam and the Natuna Islands). Devon County Council Archives, Exeter. *Box 6232*.

Upon the death of Rear Admiral Sir Frederick Lewis Maitland on 30 November 1839, Commodore Bremer briefly acted as C. in C. (Sir Frederick was he who commanded *Bellerophon* in July 1815 when he took Napoleon Buonaparte from France to England, the commencement of his journey into exile on St. Helena). Similarly when Rear Admiral Hon. George Elliot was invalided home early in 1841 Commodore Bremer again was to act as C. in C. Rear Admiral Sir William Parker (Vice Admiral from 23 November 1841), together with the new Plenipotentiary, Sir Henry Pottinger, only arrived at Macao on 9 August 1841.

10. William Laird Clowes, *The Royal Navy – a History,* Vol. VI, (London, 1901), 284. The C. in C. was Rear Admiral Hon. George **Elliot**, second son of Gilbert, Earl of Minto, Governor-General of India: 1807-1813. Later in November 1840 he became ill and, as mentioned in (9) above, was invalided back home. From 1841 on half pay. Vice Admiral: 13 April 1847. C. in C., The Nore: 9 April 1848 to 23 January 1851. Admiral: 5 March 1853. Retired: 3 October 1855. KCB: November 1862. Died: 24 June 1863. A cousin, Captain Charles **Elliot**, RN, was Chief Superintendent of Trade of British Subjects in China. In his letter dated 21 April 1841 Lord Palmerston, Foreign Secretary, removed Charles Elliot from office. In His Lordship's judgement, following the capture of Canton in May 1840, Elliot had not secured adequate reparations, also in other related matters had acted indecisively. Sir Henry Pottinger replaced Elliot. On 12 September 1865 Charles Elliot was to be promoted Admiral on the Retired List. Prior to that he had served, respectively, as Governor of Bermuda, Trinidad, and then of St. Helena, and in 1856 made KCB. Jasper Ridley, *Lord Palmerston,* (London, 1970), 257/8. *Dictionary of National Biography.* Rear Admiral A.H. Taylor, *Admiral The Hon. Sir George Elliot,* (Mariner's Mirror, Vol. 35, 1949), 316/332. Clagette Blake, *Charles Elliot, RN: 1801-1875,* (London, 1960). Kulangsu is the island on which, in due course, the foreign community at Amoy was to settle.

11. Devon County Archives.

12. O'Byrne.

13. J.R. Jones, *Journal of the Hong Kong Branch of the Royal Asiatic Society,* (Hong Kong, Vol. 12, 1972), 196. Also Geoffrey Robley Sayer, *Hong Kong, 1841-1862,* (Hong Kong University Press, 1980), 93.

14. Devon County Archives.

15. *Record of Service.*

16. NA ADM 53/4336. Log Book *Thetis.*

17. Barrington **Reynolds** (1785-1861) of Penair, Truro. Rear Admiral: 8 January 1848. C. in C., Cape of Good Hope: 3 August 1848, but on 21 June 1849 re-appointed C. in C., S.E. Coast of America. Vice Admiral: 4 July 1855. KCB: 5 February 1856. C. in C., Devonport: 4 May 1857 – 8 June 1860. Admiral: 1 November 1860. *Navy List.* In both Africa and subsequently off the coast of Brazil Sir Barrington was extremely successful in his efforts to eliminate the trade in slaves. 'bm' – builder's measurement.

18. NA ADM 53/4328. Log Book *Thetis.* Noel Salmon correctly is spelt Nowell Salmon.

19. NA ADM 53/4329. Subsequent Log Book *Thetis.*

Fairfax **Moresby** (1786-1877). Captain: 7 June 1814. Rear Admiral: 20 December 1849. C. in C., Pacific: 21 August 1850 – 17 August 1853 when succeeded by Rear Admiral David Price. KCB: 1855. Vice Admiral: 12 November 1856. Admiral: 12 April 1862. GCB: 1865. Admiral of the Fleet: 21 January 1870. *Navy List.*

A younger brother was Robert **Moresby** (1794-1854), of the Bombay Marine and an hydrographer of distinction who rose to be Captain, IN. At the instigation of Sir John Malcolm (1769-1833), Governor of Bombay between 1827 and

1830, then between 1829 and 1833, and as Commander in *Palinurus*, he was responsible for the first accurate survey of the northern waters of the Red Sea, in particular inbetween Suez and Jeddah. As will be appreciated, with the opening of the overland sector between Alexandria and Suez thus this new route from Britain and Europe to India and the East, a thorough knowledge of the dangerous waters of the Red Sea had become vital. L.S. Dawson, *Memoirs of Hydrography, 1,* (Reprint in London, 1969), 127/8. Freda Harcourt, *The High Road to India: The P & O Company and the Suez Canal, 1840-1874,* (International Journal of Maritime History, Vol. XXII, No. 2, December 2010, St. John's, Newfoundland), 22. What was to become the important coaling station at Aden first was occupied in January 1839 by Commander Stafford Bettesworth Haines of the Indian Navy. He remained Political Agent at Aden until 1854.

20. John Moresby, *Two Admirals,* (London, 1913), 96.

 John **Moresby**. Born at Allerford: 15 March 1830. Died at Fareham: 12 July 1922. Commander: 11 December 1858. When in command of paddle sloop *Argus* to fight under Augustus Kuper at Shimonoseki in September 1864. Captain: 21 November 1864. In command paddle sloop *Basilisk*, 1,710 tons: 23 January 1871. In her surveyed many of the waters surrounding New Guinea, this including, in 1873, the discovery and naming, after his father, Fairfax as above, of Port Moresby. The commission ended at Sheerness on 15 December 1874. In command at Bermuda Dockyard: April 1878 – April 1881. Rear Admiral: 26 July 1881. Vice Admiral: 1 May 1888. Retired: 1888. Admiral: 13 May 1893. *Two Admirals. Navy List. Who's Who,* 1922.

21. Ibid. 97.

22. Ibid. 98.

23. NA ADM 53/4330. Log Book *Thetis.*

24. *Two Admirals,* 102.

25. Barry M. Gough, *The Royal Navy and the Northwest Coast of North America: 1810-1914,* (Vancouver, 1971), 132/3. Also see Robert Brown, FRGS, *On the Physical Geography of the Queen Charlotte Islands,* (Proceedings of the Royal Geographical Society, London, Vol. XIII, 1868-1869, 385):-

 'The vein as originally found (in Mitchell Harbour, an anchorage of Gold Harbour, so called) was 7 inches wide, was traced for 80 feet, and contained 25% of gold in many places.'

26. James **Douglas**. Born in British Guiana: 15 August 1803. Died in Victoria, BC: 2 August 1877. As an employee of the Hudson Bay Company first arrived at Fort Vancouver in 1830. As Chief Factor in 1849 he moved the western headquarters of the HBC from Fort Vancouver to Fort Victoria, the site of Victoria, BC. On 30 October 1851 assumed his appointment as Governor of Vancouver Island, at the same time holding his position as HBC Chief Factor. Not always was this new position to be tenable. On 19 November 1858 additionally assumed his appointment as the first Governor of British Columbia, and in that year resigned as HBC Chief Factor. Late in 1863 it was made known from London that his appointments as Governor shortly would cease, when also he received the KCB. Historically regarded as the 'Father of British Columbia'. *Dictionary of Canadian Biography Online.*

27. *Two Admirals,* 105/6.

28. NA ADM 53/4330. Log Book *Thetis.*

29. NA ADM 53/4331. Subsequent Log Book *Thetis.*

30. NA ADM 53/4332. Subsequent Log Book *Thetis.* Paddle wheel steamer *Beaver,* 100.75' in length, built at Blackwall, London and launched on 2 May 1835 for service with the Hudson Bay Company, Western North America. In 1888 to be wrecked near Vancouver, BC.

31. *Two Admirals,* 107.

32. NA ADM 53/4332.

33. *Two Admirals,* 107-114.

34. Ibid. 118.

35. NA ADM 53/4334. Log Book *Thetis.* On Friday, 14 August 2009 at the Annual Conference of the Canadian Nautical Research Society held in Victoria, BC the author read a paper, *Vice Admiral Sir Augustus Leopold Kuper: as a Captain on the Northwest Coast of America, and flying his Flag in China/Japan.*

36. *Record of Service.*

37. Centre for Buckinghamshire Studies, Aylesbury. Ref: *D/RA/A/2A/32/1.*

38. NA ADM 53/ 8353. Log Book *Euryalus.*

39. *Dictionary of National Biography*, 346.

In his letter, No. 409 dated at 'Head-Quarters near Kading', on 24 October 1862, acting Vice Admiral Hope wrote to The Right Honourable Lord Clarence Paget, CB MP, Secretary to the Admiralty, to advise him of the success of the assault against Kahding. In an earlier action against the rebels, 4 April 1862, Admiral Hope had been wounded, '… receiving a ball in the leg'. Andrew Wilson, *The Ever Victorious Army*, (Edinburgh and London, 1868), 83. To give just one example of earlier success achieved by these Taiping rebels, as they swept up from the south, and then to the coast from the west:

> 'Nothing seemed able to resist the advance of the insurgents, and on March 8th (1853) they encamped before Nanking. It was garrisoned by Manchus and Chinese, who, however, made no better defence than their comrades in other cities; in ten days its walls were breached, and all the defenders found inside put to death, including Luh, the governor-general of the province.'

S. Wells Williams, *The Middle Kingdom*, II, (London, 1883), 595/6.

James **Hope**. Born: 3 March 1808. Died: 9 June 1881. Entered the Navy: 1 August 1820. Captain: 28 June 1838. Rear Admiral: 19 November 1857. On 25 January 1859 apppointed C. in C., East Indies and China. Arrived at Singapore on 16 April, there relieving Rear Admiral Sir Michael Seymour. Wounded during the unsuccessful Allied attack on the forts at the mouth of the Peiho: 25 June 1859. In 1860 a subsequent Allied attack was successful which resulted in the signing of the Convention of Peking: 24 October 1860. KCB: 9 November 1860. C. in C., North America and West Indies: January 1864 – January 1867. Vice Admiral: 16 September 1864. GCB: 28 March 1865. C. in C., Portsmouth: February 1869 – March 1872. Admiral: 21 January 1870. Retired: March 1878. Admiral of the Fleet: 15 June 1879. *Navy List. Dictionary of National Biography.*

40. Albert R. Wonham, *Spun Yarns of a Naval Officer*, (Westminster, 1917), 13. Gordon was an engineer officer attached to Brigadier Staveley's force. The statue to Charles G. Gordon, killed at Khartoum on 26 January 1885, may be found in London in the Victoria Embankment Gardens at Horse Guards Avenue.

41. NA ADM 53/8353. Log Book *Euryalus*.

42. Wonham, 14.

43. NA ADM 53/8353.

44. NA ADM 50/287. NA ADM 53/8353: log book *Euryalus*.

Coromandel, 303 tons, builders measurement or bm, paddle despatch vessel. Lieut. and Commander Robert Peel Dennistoun. Built in 1853 as the P. & O. *Tartar* for service out of Hong Kong on local Chinese routes. In January 1855 acquired by the Admiralty. *Starling*, 284 tons, a wooden screw gunboat originally built for the Crimean campaign. One must assume that either *Coromandel* was suffering from engine problems or that she required additional assistance while manoeuvring off Shanghai.

45. NA ADM 1/5790. Letter No. 43, 14. Miyako is 'Imperial City', i.e. Kyoto, thus from Tokyo to Kyoto.

46. Aylesbury, Ref: *D/RA/A/2A/32/2/1*. In *Euryalus* dated 13 December 1862.

Constant Louis Jean Benjamin **Jaures** (1823-1889). French naval officer, and, from 22 February 1889 in Paris, Minister of Marine and Colonies.

47. Ibid.

48. Charles Burton Buckley, *An Anecdotal History of Old Times in Singapore*, II, (Singapore, 1902), 695. BL ref: 9058.c.6. Compagnie des Maritimes Imperiales, from 1 August 1871 to be re-named Compagnie des Messageries Maritimes.

49. *The London Gazette*, Friday, October 30, 1863.

50. Tsuzuki Chushichi, *The Pursuit of Power in Modern Japan*, (OUP, 2000), 47.

51. Ed. F.G. Notehelfer, *Japan Through American Eyes, The Journal of Francis Hall: 1859-1866*, (Boulder, CO, 2001), 329, 331, 332, 334. Francis **Hall**, Born: 27 October 1822. First arrived in Yokohama Bay on 1 November 1859. To leave Japan on 5 July 1866. Died in Elmira, NY on 23 July 1902. Latterly he became a philanthropist of note.

52. Aylesbury, Ref: *D/RA/A/2A/32/3/2*. *Euryalus* at Yokohama, 30 April 1863. The Loo Chew Islands are the Ryukyu chain stretching south from Kyushu towards Formosa/Taiwan.

53. For details of Richard Edward **Tracey** see Willes, C. in C. 1881, reference (28).

54. Devon County Archives. Extra to *The Japan Commercial News*, Kanagawa, Wednesday, 26 August 1863.

55. John G. Roberts, *Mitsui*, (New York and Tokyo, 1989), 55.

'The House of Mitsui began business in the 17th century as a draper and moneychanger with stores in Yedo, Osaka and Kyoto'. Trans. Eiichi Kiyooka, *The Autobiography of Yukichi Fukuzawa*, (Columbia University Press, 1966), 358 (169).

56. Kwang-Ching Liu, *Ango-American Steamship Rivalry in China: 1862-1874*, (Harvard, 1962), 29, 39. Also see, Edward Kenneth Haviland, *American Steam Navigation in China: 1845-1878*, (Salem, Mass., 1956-1958).

    A partner in Russell & Co. between 1840 and 1846, and again between 1861 and 1866, was Warren Delano Jnr., grandfather of Franklin Delano Roosevelt, President of the U.S.A. between 1933 and 1945.

57. NA ADM 1/5877. Kuper to Admiralty, Letter No. 338 dated 4.9.1864.

58. For more information concerning the early and successful American steamship operating activity in Chinese waters see Kwang-Ching Liu as in reference (56). The Borneo Company, first registered in London in June 1856, was a well known agency and trading house in Sarawak, Singapore, Malaya and Siam (Thailand) where, also, they were much involved in the steamship agency business. A non sequitur of interest is the fact that in 1862, while manager of The Borneo Company in Singapore, it was William Adamson who was to facilitate the introduction of Anna to the King of Siam, the widowed Mrs. Anna Harriette Leonowens to H.M. King Somdetch Phra Paramendr Maha Mongkut. Henry Longhurst, *The Borneo Story*, (London, 1956), 38/52.

59. Francis E. Hyde, *Far Eastern Trade 1860-1914*, (London, 1973), 58

60. Aylesbury, Ref: *D/RA/A/2A/32/5/1*. *Euryalus* at Yokohama. The territory of the Prince of Choshu was at the western extremity of Honshu. The Strait of Shimonoseki separates Honshu from Kyushu.

61. Ian D. Ruxton, *The Diaries and Letters of Sir Ernest Mason Satow (1843-1929)*, (Lewiston, NY, 1998), 38. Tsuzuki, 52.

62. Examples of these pieces of captured ordnance may be seen at The Royal Artillery Museum, Woolwich, Ref: LDRAI: GUN 2/248 and 2/249.

63. Aylesbury, Ref: *D/RA/A/2A/32/16/1*.

64. Devon County Archives. Also *London Gazette*, March 3, 1865.

65. Notehelfer, 395.

66. Rutherford **Alcock**. Born: 1809. Died: 2 November 1897. At King's College, London trained for the medical profession. Surgeon of the Marine Brigade of Portugal: July 1833. Deputy Inspector General of Hospitals in the British Auxiliary Legion: 5 May 1835. Consul at Foochow: 30 May 1844. Subsequently served in Shanghai and Canton. Consul General in Japan: 21 December 1858. Envoy Extraordinary and Minister Plenipotentiary to Japan: 30 November 1859. In September 1860 the first foreigner to ascend Mount Fuji, 3,776 metres. KCB: 19 June 1862. Chief Superintendent of British Trade in China: 28 March 1865. Envoy Extraordinary and Minister Plenipotentiary at Peking: 7 April 1865. Retired: 22 July 1871. President of the RGS: 1876, and remained on the Council of the Society until May 1893. First President of the British North Borneo Chartered Company: May 1882. Obituary, *The Geographical Journal*, Vol. 10, 1897. *Foreign Office List*, 1898.

67. Batavia, today Jakarta, founded in 1619 by Jan Pieterszoon **Coen**, born in Hoorn: 8 January 1587 and died in Batavia: 21 September 1629, the capital of the Dutch East Indies as then administered by the VOC – Vereenigde Oost-Indische Compagnie (1602-1796). As the fourth, also sixth Governor General of the VOC in the East, (1619-1623 and 1627-1629), the aggressive and forthright Coen played a vital early role in the establishment of powerful Dutch trading and commercial interests in that part of the world. His fine statue may be found in the Rode Steen Plein, Hoorn. Nearby across the square is the Westfries Museum. From Amsterdam just a short railway journey: a visit is well worth while, in fact on a sunny day a most agreeable outing.

68. *The Times*, 9 September 1865, courtesy Mr. Peter Davis. Also NA ADM 53/8355.

69. Devon County Archives.

70. *Record of Service*.

71. *Census*, 1861.

72. Greg Wall, *The Book of South Brent*, (Tiverton, Devon, 2005), 7, 37.

73. Devon County Archives.

74. Ibid.

75. Ibid. Robert Smart (1796-1874). Rear Admiral: July 1857. C. in C., Channel Fleet: January 1861 – April 1863. Vice Admiral: December 1863. C. in C., Mediterranean: April 1863 – April 1866. Admiral: January 1869. Retired: April 1870. *Navy List*.

76. Ibid.

17 January 1865 to 18 January 1867
Temporary Vice Admiral George St. Vincent **King**

Born on 15 July 1809, the second son of Vice Admiral Sir Richard King (1774-1834), by his first wife, Sarah Anne, only daughter of Admiral Sir John Thomas Duckworth.

He died at Wear House, his residence near Exeter, on 18 August 1891. A memorial to him, and other members of the family, may be seen in St. Margaret's Church, Topsham, Devon (1).

Educated at RNC, Portsmouth where he joined on 8 February 1822. Subsequently:-
> '... embarked in 1824, as **Midshipman**, in *Revenge*, 76, Captain Sir Chas. Burrard, bearing the flag in the Mediterranean of Sir Harry Burrard Neale, with whom he continued until 1827. In 1828 he joined *Java*, 52, flagship of Rear Admiral Wm. Hall Gage in the East Indies, whence he returned to England on the occasion of his promotion (2).'

From his service record it is noted that he was promoted **Mate** on 1 August 1828, the same day as he was appointed to *Java* in which ship he served until 28 January 1830 (3).

Lieutenant: 15 January 1830. From 2 June 1830 served in sloop *Columbine*, 18 guns, Commander John Townshend (1798-1863), from 1855 to be the Fourth Marquess Townshend, Portsmouth and then the West Indies. From 29 December 1831 to 3 December 1833 in frigate *Pallas*, 42, successively commanded by Captain Manley Hall Dixon until January 1832, and then by Captain William Walpole, West Indies Station. From 4 December 1833 to 9 August 1834 in third rate two decker *Ocean*, 80, Sheerness.
Commander: 8 August 1834.

From 25 January 1837 in command sloop *Champion*, 18, West Indies. Paid off at Plymouth on 13 November 1838 (4).

Captain: 28 August 1841.

On 16 December 1847 he married Caroline Mary Dawson-Damer, eldest daughter of Henry, second son of the First Earl of Portarlington, Queens County.
> 'Married by Mr. Wm. Harrison, incumbent at St. Michaels at St. Peter's Church – went to Eaton Square (in London) after, and at 2 started for Worthing where I had taken a house – arrived there at 5 – found cosy (-) comfortable (5).'

They remained at Worthing until 4 March 1848.

Sadly his wife was to die on 5 December 1851, just a few days after the birth of their son Dudley on 28 November 1851.

From 3 June 1852 to 21 November 1854 in command frigate *Leander*, 50, 'Particular Service', Portsmouth/ Devonport, next North America and West Indies, then to the Mediterranean. Great Britain and France declared war on Russia on 28 March 1854, the conflict between Russia and Turkey thereby being extended and becoming known as the Crimean War. In 1854 service during that campaign included in *Leander* at the defence of Eupatoria, just to the north of Sebastopol (6).

From 22 November 1854 in command second rate two decker *Rodney*, 90, Mediterranean, and during the blockade of Sebastopol, Crimea, Black Sea. In one instance he was kind enough to loan the services of a member of his domestic staff to an army family ashore in Crimea:-

> 'We soon fell in with a real Samaritan in Captain King, then commanding the *Rodney*, who lent us his own invaluable servant; but Captain King's subsequent removal to the *St. Jean d'Acre* obliged him to take his cook with him, and we are once more left servant-less, helpless and dinnerless (7).'

Also during this period he, 'Served in the Trenches before Sebastopol from 14 April 1855 to 9 July 1855 (8).' CB: 5 July 1855.

On 7 July 1855 succeeded in command of the ship by Captain the Hon. Henry Keppel (see C. in C., 1867).

Also on 7 July 1855 he was appointed in command of the screw two decker *St. Jean d'Acre*, 101, Mediterranean, 'Particular Service', a continuation of the Crimean campaign.

By the Treaty of Paris, 30 March 1856, the Crimean War was brought to a conclusion.

At Devonport in July 1856 ordered to prepare to convey in *St. Jean d'Acre* a British delegation headed by Granville George Leveson-Gower, second Earl Granville (1815-1891), to St. Petersburg to attend the coronation of Tsar Alexander II (1818-1881). So it was that on 24 July supplies and personnel were embarked and at 6.45 a.m. on Sunday, 27 July he departed for Dover Roads, coast of Kent, where he anchored at 8.00 a.m. the following morning. There at 1 p.m. the small paddle packet *Princess Alice*, Lieut. John Ward, came alongside and Earl Granville and suite embarked, their party including eighteen servants, both male and female as a number of ladies were attached to the delegation, and a photographer. Three hours later, at 4 p.m., *St. Jean d'Acre* proceeded, for much of the passage *Princess Alice* being in company under tow. The Skaw at the most northern point of Denmark was rounded on 31 July and she anchored in Kiel Roads at 6.45 p.m. on Friday, 1 August. There Earl Granville attended to business ashore, only re-embarking at 8.30 p.m. on Sunday, 3 August. The ships sailed an hour later and arrived safely to anchor off Kronstadt at 9 a.m. on Friday 8 August.

A short while later the British party were conveyed ashore to St. Petersburg by a Russian steamer.

During the following eight weeks several visits to the ship were made by Russian, French and other officials and authorities.

The coronation of the Tsar commenced on 26 August and the ceremonies were brought to a magnificent conclusion at the Uspensky Sobor Cathedral in the Kremlin in Moscow on 7 September.

Nevertheless only on Saturday, 4 October did the members of the delegation return to the ship, brought out to her at 1 p.m. by *Princess Alice*. Accompanied by the firing of many salutes she proceeded to sea just over an hour later.

On Wednesday, 8 October the ships returned to anchor at Kiel where Earl Granville and suite disembarked. *St. Jean d'Acre* sailed early on 12 October and at 06.50 a.m. on Friday, 17 October returned to anchor at Spithead. Later during the morning a steamer came alongside to load baggage and horses belonging to the members of the British delegation. The ship sailed for Devonport that evening at 6.50 p.m. and anchored in Plymouth Sound shortly after noon the following day. She shifted alongside on 21 October to decommission, finally paying off on 7 November 1856 (9).

ADC to H.M. Queen Victoria: 12 December 1856.

From 23 April 1857 in command of the three decker *Princess Charlotte*, 104 guns, 4,120 tons, East Indies and China Station. 'Discharged' in Hong Kong on 29 January 1858. At Hong Kong the ship became a floating barracks, however in 1860 her status was to alter to that of Receiving Ship at the port. In 1875 the ship was to be sold in Hong Kong for breaking up.

From the Far East he arrived back in England on 18 April 1858 (10).

At the time, and nearing the end of a most diverse career, H.E. The Governor of Hong Kong was Sir John Bowring (11). In due course, having completed his term of office, he was to leave the Colony on 3 May 1859 in the

Yeh Ming-ch'en, Imperial Commissioner at Canton in the 1850's

Sir John Bowring (1792-1872), appointed Governor of Hong Kong and Chief Superintendent of trade in China in 1854

James Bruce, 8th Earl of Elgin (1811-63) appointed British Envoy to China in 1857

ALBERT GEORGE SIDNEY HAWES,

P. & O. paddle steamer *Pekin*, 1,182 grt. Even his journey home was not to be free of event since the subsequent ship in which he was taking passage, the P. & O. screw steamer *Alma*, 2,164 grt, when passing through the Red Sea on 12 June 1859 grounded on the coral Musejura Reef some seventy miles to the north of Perim. No lives were lost but it was to be three days before His Excellency and the other survivors were rescued (12).

Rear Admiral: 4 April 1862.

C. in C., East Indies and Cape of Good Hope Station: 15 February 1864. Flag in screw ship *Princess Royal*, 73 guns, 3,130 tons. Her Commander was Alexander Buller (see C. in C., 1895).

In succession to Rear Admiral Sir Baldwin Wake-Walker (1802-1876), on 23 July 1864 he assumed command of the Station.

A few months after assuming command at the Cape/East Indies, from 17 January 1865 he was re-appointed C. in C., China, to be promoted temporary Vice Admiral on taking up this new command. He 'resigned command of East India & Cape of Good Hope Station' on 9 April 1865 and proceeded further East in *Princess Royal*. At the Cape the Senior Naval Officer between 17 January and 26 September 1865 was Commodore Frederick Byng Montresor (1811-1887).

From Singapore on 1 June 1865 he wrote to the Secretary of the Admiralty:-

'2. The *Euryalus* bearing the flag of Vice Admiral Kuper left this anchorage in the forenoon of Saturday, the 27 (May) for Batavia and the Cape en route to England (13).'

It was at Singapore that in succession to Admiral Sir Augustus Kuper he had assumed command of the Station with effect from 23 May 1865 (14).

The Governor of the Straits Settlements then was Major General William Orfeur Cavenagh (1821-1891), the last such Governor to be appointed from India prior to the Secretary of State for the Colonies in London assuming the administration of the Colony from April 1867.

Serving in the Flagship from 20 March 1865 as First Lieutenant of Marines, was Albert George Sidney Hawes. From late in 1870 he was to be employed by the fledgling Imperial Japanese Navy as a gunnery instructor. In that capacity also he was to be responsible for the introduction of many Royal Naval systems, routine and concepts of discipline. Today he is regarded by some as a 'father' of the Imperial Japanese Navy (15).

In the United States the Civil War came to an end on 26 May 1865. Just a few weeks later, in July, Commodore Henry Haywood Bell, USN (1808-1868) was appointed in command of the East India Squadron, a very short while later to be re-named Asiatic Squadron (16). During 1866 he was to be promoted Rear Admiral and in May that year was to move the U.S. Navy headquarters from Macao, which was becoming silted up, to Hong Kong.

Sadly he was to drown in a boating accident in heavy seas off Hiogo, Japan on 11 January 1868.

With his flag continuing to fly in *Princess Royal* the C. in C. arrived at Yokohama on 7 August 1865. There he had been preceded by the new British Minister to Japan, Sir Harry Parkes who had arrived from Shanghai a month earlier, on 8 July in the small paddle frigate *Leopard*, 18, Captain Charles Taylor Leckie. Until Sir Harry's arrival the charge d'affaires, Dr. Charles Alexander Winchester, had been attending to British interests (17). Without going into detail it was at this time that Imperial ratification of the 1858 treaties with Japan was being sought by each of the Allies, they being Great Britain, France, The Netherlands and the United States. Accordingly, and in his usual energetic style rapidly having summed up the situation, on 1 November at Yokohama Sir Harry embarked in *Princess Royal* and led an Allied squadron of nine men of war out and around through the Kii and Tomagashima Straits into Osaka Bay where they arrived to anchor off Hiogo (Kobe) during the early afternoon on 4 November.

Sir Harry Parkes took with him three members of his staff, one being Ernest Satow who has left a rather pleasant vignette:-

'Our Admiral was extremely good natured, and had fitted up private cabins for us three civilians on the main deck. I was delighted to find myself onboard with my friend A.G.S. Hawes ... (18).'

While not entirely satisfactory, by the end of November useful agreement had been reached with their Japanese opposite numbers, a considerable British diplomatic achievement (19).

As C. in C. his positive role in the business was not to be disregarded:-

'6 February 1866: Lord Clarendon highly commending him for the valuable assistance rendered by him in the negotiations with the Japanese (20).'

From *Princess Royal* at Hong Kong on 15 March he recorded that on 11 March 1866 the newly appointed Governor, Sir Richard Graves MacDonnell (1814-1881), had arrived in the mail steamer. His Excellency already had had wide experience of colonial Governships, respectively of the Gambia, St. Vincent, South Australia and Nova Scotia (21).

Later in the year a cousin of the new Governor, Francis Brinkley, then a Lieutenant in the Royal Artillery, was to be appointed as his aide-de-camp (also see C. in C., 1871: November 1871).

During April and May at Hong Kong the C. in C. was much involved in negotiations with a number of different suppliers concerning the need for the Admiralty to have recourse to an adequate supply of coal at Shanghai.

Also it may be noted that throughout his term of office in the Far East the inevitable question of piracy was to occupy much of his time and lead to a very considerable amount of correspondence.

Returning to Japanese waters, then accompanied by the British Minister, Sir Harry Parkes, he arrived at Kagoshima on 27 July 1866 (22). Included in the British party was the Aberdonian merchant, Thomas Blake Glover (1838-1911), influential in a number of Japanese circles, particularly those of the Satsuma, Choshu and Saga/Hizen 'han'. Just prior to proceeding to Kagoshima, and before Sir Harry had joined him, at Nagasaki the C. in C. had stayed for some time at Glover House (23). Sir Harry Parkes, himself highly accomplished, on the issue of likely successful opposition to the existing Tokugawa Shogunate regime received much well informed advice from a member of his staff, Ernest Satow (24).

It should be noted that another junior British diplomatic officer on Sir Harry's staff, and who worked with Satow, also was a friend and who held similar political views, was the Japanese scholar, William G. Aston (25).

This official visit to the Prince of Satsuma, Shimazu Hisamitsu, was to have important positive consequences

Sir Ernest Mason Satow, (1843-1929)   *Thomas Blake Glover, (1838-1911)*

SIR HARRY S. PARKES

for Great Britain (26). These consequences were to arise following a time of domestic stress and civil war which was to result in the departure of the last of the shoguns, Tokugawa Yoshinobu (Keiki) on 3 January 1868.

Having sailed from Liverpool on 19 April 1866 the Alfred Holt steamer *Agamemnon*, 2,280 grt, Captain Isaac Middleton, steamed to the East via Mauritius laden with cargo for Penang, Hong Kong and Shanghai. The outward voyage time was estimated at seventy seven days thus giving her arrival at Shanghai early in July 1866. En route outwardbound she made a brief call at Singapore on 20 June (27). Her two sister ships, *Ajax* and *Achilles*, were to follow within months, in this manner establishing the service of the Ocean Steam Ship Company, in due course and for over a century to become extremely well known throughout the Far East as the Blue Funnel Line (28).

By Ishikawajima in Tokyo in mid May 1866, the completion for the Tokugawa Shogunate government of their first Japanese built steam powered man-of-war, *Chiyoda,* 158 tons and four guns. Single screw and of wooden construction, she was 104' loa with a beam of 15'. Her coal fuel capacity was 32,000 kin or 19.2 metric tons and she was capable of five knots. She had been launched on 2 July 1863 but in order to correctly manufacture her propelling machinery first it had been necessary for Engineer Hida Hamagoro to be sent to Holland. From there he returned on 27 January 1866 thereafter construction continuing until the completion of the ship (29).

Statue of Dr. Sun Yat-sen

The future Dr. Sun Yat-sen was born in Choy Hang, a village in the Chung Shan district of Kwangtung Province on 12 November 1866.

A brother, Sun Mei, as a farmer and in business had made a success of his life on Oahu, Hawaii. In due course Sun Yat-sen was to travel to Hawaii where, commencing in September 1879 and under the name Tai Cheong, he was to receive an early education at the Iolani School, Honolulu (30). The Chinese community in those islands was to play an important role in fund raising in order to facilitate Dr. Sun's later political work in China.

1 January 1867. At Shanghai the opening of a new business with their offices on the Bund, that of Messrs. Butterfield & Swire. Their first Eastern manager, and senior Eastern partner from 1869 to 1888, was William Lang (31). On 16 January 1867 this newly established firm despatched their first cargo vessel homeward bound from Shanghai to Great Britain. She was the Ocean Steam Ship, Blue Funnel s.s. *Achilles*, 2,280 grt (32).

Rather rapidly thereafter Butterfield & Swire opened in Japan, their office at Yokohama commencing to operate from 1 August 1867 under the the management of Richard Norman Newby, an expert in woollen goods (33).

Just before midnight on 30 January 1867 the arrival at Hong Kong of the first scheduled trans Pacific mail steamer from San Francisco, s.s. *Colorado*, Captain George Bradbury, of the Pacific Mail Steam Ship Company. She had sailed on 1 January and after a trans Pacific voyage of twenty two days had stopped briefly at Kanagawa (Yokohama) before continuing on across to and down the China coast (34).

As seen above during Admiral Kuper's term in office, in 1864 the Taiping Rebellion finally had been put down. During that long period of unrest many Chinese had sought a new life overseas. Another consequence had been a very considerable transformation of Hong Kong early signs of which were most apparent during Admiral King's term of office:-

> 'In 1867, just three years after the Taiping Rebellion was crushed, the number of Chinese general merchants in Hong Kong had risen to more than seventy from fewer than ten in 1846.
> The combination of the Taiping rebellion and the growth of Chinese communities overseas did more than save Hong Kong from an economic depression; it changed the island's basic reason for being. Hong Kong was transformed from a colonial outpost into the centre of a transnational trade network stretching from the China coast to Southeast Asia and then to Australia and North America (35).'

To a considerable extent secured by their Navy, in Hong Kong the British provided a convenient and safe place in which to do business, and under laissez-faire conditions. The contrast with the chaotic state of affairs then prevailing in their own country, and which was to prevail for several decades to come, was very marked. Great numbers of those Chinese who were able to take advantage of such an apparent utopia took the opportunity.

In *Princess Royal*, with the paddle sloop *Basilisk*, Captain William N. Hewett, VC, in company, on 24 February 1867 the Admiral left Nagasaki and proceeded around to the north of Kyushu and arrived at Fukuoka, seat of the Daimio of the Chikuzen 'han'. There he was most hospitably received by Prince Kuroda. However, of greater importance and influence within the Japanese domestic scene, there next occurred another visit:-

> 'On leaving Chikuzen, the Admiral having, in passing the straits of Shimonoseki, received an invitation from the Prince of Choshiu (Choshu), paid him a visit at Mitageri, about thirty miles down the coast (36).'

As suggested above, within a year the Mori family of the Choshu 'han' were to work successfully with the Satsuma 'han', and the Shimazu family, towards the overthrow of the Tokugawa Shogunate. At the same time already it is clear that in Japan considerable attention was being paid to the ability and performance of western men of war, both at sea and in the influence attached to their mere presence in a port or on the coast. Here follows an extract taken from a letter written by Sir Harry Parkes in Yedo on 17 March 1867. It is addressed to the Foreign Office in London:-

In Japan with Choshu 'han' feudal lords, Daimyo.

'The Japanese are apparently beginning to take great interest in naval matters, and have frequently assured me that they are satisfied that the prosperity of Japan must depend greatly upon its Naval resources (37).'

Vice Admiral: 20 March 1867.

From the northern waters of the Station now he made his way to the south with the intention of in Singapore meeting his successor as C. in C.

There on 5 April 1867 he relinquished command of the station to Vice Admiral The Hon. Sir Harry Keppel, and on Monday, 8 April in *Princess Royal* he sailed for home.

She was to anchor off Plymouth Breakwater at 06:00 on Tuesday, 30 July 1867 with Admiral King leaving her at 10:30, and striking his flag the following day. Also on 31 July powder and shell were discharged to lighters, and at 06:15 on Thursday, 1 August she weighed, then proceeded into harbour to secure alongside in the dockyard. Finally, her de-commissioning complete, the last log book entry of the commission was made on Wednesday, 14 August 1867, 'Hauled down Pendant' (38).

Officially he retired on 1 August 1867. Of his entire time on the active service list a total of twenty five years and 133 days had been spent on half pay (39).

KCB: 24 May 1873.

Admiral: 20 April 1875.

GSP (Good Service Pension valued at GBP 300 p.a.) awarded to him from 19 August 1876.

On 2 November 1887 his brother, Sir Richard, died and he succeeded to the baronetcy as Fourth Baronet. By royal licence on 13 February 1888 he assumed the prefix surname and arms of Duckworth. Now he was to be known as Admiral Sir George St. Vincent Duckworth-King, Bart., KCB.

As mentioned above he died on 18 August 1891, in his eighty third year.

NOTES

1. Today Wear House forms a substantial part of the club house buildings, Exeter Golf and Country Club, established on 30 March 1929. The memorial to the Admiral is prominent to the right of the aisle in the beautiful St. Margaret's Church, Topsham. Both visited by the author: 14 and 15 April 2007.

2. O'Byrne, 613. William Hall Gage (1777-1864). C. in C., East Indies: 1825-1829. Vice Admiral: 1837. Admiral: 1846. C. in C., Plymouth: 1848-1851. KGCB: 18 May 1860. Admiral of the Fleet: 20 May 1862. *Navy List*.

3. NA ADM 195/5, 40. *Record of Service*.

4. Ibid.

5. Caird Library, National Maritime Museum, Greenwich. Ref: *AGC/49*.

6. Eupatoria, N.W. coast of Crimea. Obituary, *The Times*, August 21, 1891.

7. Mrs. Frances Isabella Duberly, *Journal kept during the Russian War*, (London, 1855), Chapter VI: The Fall of Sebastopol, July 11.

8. NA ADM 196/36. *Service Record*.

9. *Record of Service*. Also ADM 53/5375 being the Log Book, *St. Jean d'Acre*.

10. NA ADM 196/36. *Service Record*.

11. John **Bowring**. Born: 17 October 1792. Died in Exeter: 23 November 1872. A cousin of Benjamin Bowring (1778-1846), founder of the Bowring shipping, trading and insurance group. Sir John was a linguist of extraordinary ability, merchant and free trader, and, from 1835-1837 then again 1841-1849, an M.P. Appointed Consul at Canton: 10 January 1849, taking up the position in April 1849. Subsequently Chief Superintendent of British Trade in China. Appointed Governor of Hong Kong: 10 January 1854. Knighted: 16 February 1854. Being on leave at the time of this latter appointment he proceeded out to Hong Kong in *Winchester*, 52, new Flagship of the new C. in C., Rear Admiral Sir James Stirling (1791-1865) who arrived at Hong Kong on 11 May 1854. Proceeded on Special Mission to Siam: 12 March 1855 – also see (22) below. Having left Hong Kong in May, retired: 17 July 1859. On 5 June 1856 he had been elected F.R.S. *Foreign Office List*, 1869. *Dictionary of National Biography*. David Keir, *The Bowring Story*, (London, 1962), 83-85. Pamela Statham-Drew, *James Stirling*, (Crawley, WA, 2003), 466. Gerald S. Graham, *The China Station*, (OUP, 1978), 283.

12. One of the ships involved in the subsequent successful rescue effort in June 1859 was H.M. Paddle Sloop *Cyclops*, 1,862 tons, Captain William John Samuel Pullen (1813-1887). In sharp contrast with Red Sea temperatures Captain Pullen earlier had accomplished much in the Arctic including, during 1852-1854, commanding the store ship *North Star* during the Belcher expedition – see Kellett, C. in C., 1869.

    Also to assist in this Red Sea rescue operation was the P. & O. screw steamer *Nemesis*, 2,018 grt.

13. NA ADM 1/5923.

14. Ibid.

15. Albert George Sidney **Hawes**. Born in Wolborough, Newton Abbot, Devonshire: 9 October 1842. Died in Hilo, Hawaii: 6 August 1897. Joined the Royal Marines as Second Lieutenant, Woolwich Division: 23 December 1859. Appointed to *Severn*, East Indies: 23 July 1862. Promoted First Lieutenant: 15 May 1863. The *Navy List* of July 1870 shows him as a Lieut., RM, Retired List. Left the Japanese service: 31 January 1884. Joined the Consular Service for service in Nyassa in 1885, in Zanzibar in 1889, and then taking up his appointment in the Society Islands in 1890. Promoted Consul-General in the Sandwich Islands: 1 July 1894. Author's notes in respect of his life. *Navy List*. Royal Marines

Museum, Southsea. His grave may be found at the Oahu Cemetery, Nuuanu Avenue, Honolulu: Lot 163, section 2. There respects were paid by the author: 11 July 2005.

16. Department of the Navy: Navy Historical Center, Washington DC.

17. Charles Alexander **Winchester**. Aberdeen, M.D.: 1841. Assistant Surgeon, RN: 13 October 1841. As Medical Officer, Hong Kong, entered the China Civil Service: 4 June 1842. Consular Surgeon, Amoy: 15 October 1843. Acting Vice Consul, Whampoa: 13 April to 24 December, 1854. Subsequent consular service at Amoy, Ningpo and Canton. Consul at Hakodate, Japan: 28 March 1861, then at Kanagawa: 14 December 1862. Charge d'Affaires, Japan: 22 March to 23 May 1862. Consul at Nagasaki: 1 July 1862 to 23 March 1863 then returned to Kanagawa. Again Charge d'Affaires, Japan: 24 December 1864 to 8 July 1865. Thence, and following the promotion of Sir Harry Parkes as Minister to Japan (see (22) below), transferred back to China as Consul, Shanghai. From Shanghai, owing to ill health, retired on pension at age fifty years: 9 June 1870. Died: 18 July 1883. *Foreign Office Lists*.

18. Sir Ernest Satow, *A Diplomat in Japan*, (New York and Tokyo, reprint 2000), 140.

19. Gordon Daniels, *Sir Harry Parkes*, (Richmond, Surrey, 1996), 41-45. John R. Black, *Young Japan*, I, (London and Yokohama, 1880), 389-395.

20. NA ADM 196/36. *Service Record*.
Lord Clarendon: Rt. Hon. George William Frederick **Villiers**, Fourth Earl. Born: 12 January 1800. Died: 27 June 1870. Between 3 November 1865 and 5 July 1866 once again serving as Secretary of State for Foreign Affairs. *Foreign Office List*, 1869.

21. Richard G. **MacDonnell**. For career data see Shadwell, C. in C., 1871, reference (37).

22. Harry Smith **Parkes**. Born in Birchills Hall, Bloxwich: 24 February 1828. Died in Peking: 22 March 1885. 'Arriving at Macao in October 1841, Parkes applied himself to the study of Chinese'. As early as June 1842 attached to Sir Henry Pottinger's suite. Subsequently served with the British Chinese Consular service at Foochow, Shanghai, Amoy and Canton. Under Sir John Bowring, on 18 April 1855 assisted in the negotiation of the first successful European Treaty with Siam. In 1860 attached to the Earl of Elgin's Special Mission to China as Joint Chinese Secretary, then back to England. KCB: 19 May 1862. Following a two year period of long leave in England, in January 1864 left to take up his last Consular post, at Shanghai. Appointed Minister Plenipotentiary to Japan: 28 March 1865. GCMG: 26 November 1881. Minister Plenipotentiary to the Emperor of China: 1 July 1883, and also to the King of Corea: 27 February 1884. *Dictionary of National Biography. Foreign Office Lists*, 1885/6.
Of his appointment to Yeddo one authority writes:-
    'Sir Harry Parkes, imperialist par excellence, represented his country with brilliance.'
John Curtis Perry, Thesis: *Great Britain and the Imperial Japanese Navy: 1858-1905*, (Harvard, 1962), 68. Also see Gordon Daniels, *Sir Harry Parkes*, (Richmond, Surrey, 1996). Pages 12/13 cover the years 1862/64 leading up to his appointment to Japan.
The grave of and memorials to Sir Harry and Lady Parkes may be seen at the Church of St. Lawrence, Whitchurch Lane, Little Stanmore, London (a short distance East of Canon's Park Underground station along B461). The marble memorial bust to Sir Henry Parkes was unveiled in the crypt of St. Paul's Cathedral, London, by Sir Rutherford Alcock in 1887. The author paid respects: 28 June 2012.
There was to be a family connection with Jardine Matheson & Co. as in 1884 James Johnstone Keswick, senior partner from 1889 to 1896, was to marry Marion, a daughter of Sir Harry and Lady Parkes. Her sister Frances married Charles Dickson, senior partner from 1903 to 1906. Dickson was a great grand-nephew of William Jardine. Colin N. Crisswell, *The Taipans*, (OUP, 1981), 133.

23. Alexander McKay, *Scottish Samurai: Thomas Blake Glover 1838-1911*, (Edinburgh, 1997), 93. Today in both Nagasaki and in Aberdeen, Scotland residences named 'Glover House' may be seen, the former being a major visitor attraction in that city. The latter may be visited by appointment.

24. Ernest Mason **Satow**. Born: 30 June 1843. Died: 26 August 1929. Mill Hill. University College, London. Appointed Student Interpreter in Japan: 20 August 1861. Present at the Bombardments of Kagoshima in 1863 and of Shimonoseki in 1864. Second Secretary of Legation, Yedo: 20 July 1876. Consul-General, Bangkok: 16 January 1884. Transferred to Montevideo as Minister: 17 December 1888. Minister Plenipotentiary to the Emperor of Morocco: 1 August 1893. KCMG: 25 May 1895. Minister Plenipotentiary to the Emperor of Japan: 1 June 1895. Transferred to Peking: 26 October 1900. GCMG:

26 June 1902. PC: 28 July 1906. Retired: 26 October 1906. Member of the Permanent Court of Arbitration, The Hague: 30 November 1906 to 30 November 1912. British Plenipotentiary at the Second Peace Conference at The Hague: June-October 1907. *Foreign Office Lists*, 1920 and 1930. *Who's Who*, 1929. Also see Ed. Ian C. Ruxton, *The Diaries and Letters of Sir Ernest Mason Satow (1843-1929)*, (Lewiston, NY, 1998) and Sir Ernest Satow, *A Diplomat in Japan*, (London, 1921). Today his grave and memorial plaque may be seen at the Church of St. Mary of Ottery, Devon. Ottery St. Mary Heritage Society, *The Golden Jubilee Book of Ottery St. Mary*, (Ottery St. Mary, 2002), 112/3, 192.

25. William George **Aston**. Also see Willes, C. in C., 1881, reference (39). Writing of Mr. Aston's Japanese friendships during his very early days in Yedo from the autumn of 1864, one source indicates:-

> 'These contacts gave him a good understanding of the political undercurrents in the turbulent year preceding the fall of the Tokugawa Shogunate, and the advice of Aston and his contemporary at the Legation, Ernest Satow, was instrumental in ensuring that British policy was well informed and responsive during the years of confrontation between the shogunate and its opponents.'

Ed. Hugh Cortazzi and Gordon Daniels, *Britain and Japan, 1859-1991, Themes and Personalities*, (London and New York, 1991), Chapter Three, *William George Aston*, by P.F. Kornicki, 64-75.

26. **Shimazu** Nariakira (1809-1858). He was the far sighted daimio who was amongst the earliest to adopt various western manufacturing and military techniques in his territory. In 1854 these included the construction of the first western type vessel in Japan, *Iroha Maru*. Following his death his son, Tadayoshi, was the titular head of the han however he was overshadowed by both the age and commanding presence of his uncle Hisamitsu (also known as Saburo: 1817-1887), younger half brother of Nariakira. So it was that in practical terms from 1858 Hisamitsu was the han lord. David Chris Evans, *The Satsuma Faction and Professionalism in the Japanese Naval Officer Corps of the Meiji Period, 1868-1912*, (Stanford University, 1978), 21/22.

27. Eric Jennings, *Mansfields*, (Singapore, 1973), 8.

28. Malcolm Falkus, *The Blue Funnel Legend*, (Basingstoke, 1990), 1. Francis E. Hyde, *Blue Funnel*, (Liverpool, 1957), 19, 20, 24.

29. Courtesy of Mr. Masahiko Miyake, 28 April 2003. Also see Hansgeorg Jentschura, Dieter Jung and Peter Michel, *Warships of the Imperial Japanese Navy: 1869-1945*, (London, 1977), 113.

30. Yansheng Ma Lum and Raymond Mum Kong Lum, *Sun Yat-sen in Hawaii*, (Hawaii, 1999), 1.

31. Sheila Marriner and Francis E. Hyde, *The Senior, John Samuel Swire 1825-1898*, (Liverpool, 1967), 22/23.

32. Francis E. Hyde, 33.

33. Grace Fox, *Britain and Japan: 1858-1883*, (OUP, 1969), 315.

34. E. Mowbray Tate, *Transpacific Steam*, (Cranbury, NJ, 1986), 23-25. Note that the first scheduled steam ship service from Europe to Japan was accomplished over the final sector by P. & O. s.s. *Azof*, 700 grt, Captain Gaby. She left Shanghai on 31 August 1859 and arrived at Nagasaki on 3 September. From Nagasaki on 8 September she returned to Shanghai on 11 September 1859. In January 1860 such voyages were extended to Yokohama. At Shanghai connection was made with their Suez service, thence from Alexandria to England. Conversation between the author and Mr. Stephen Rabson, P. & O. Archivist, at Liverpool in September 2002, and subsequent email exchanges.

35. John M. Carroll, *Edge of Empires*, (Harvard, 2005), 50.

36. John R. Black, *Young Japan*, II (London and Yokohama, 1881), 58. Daimio: Mori Takachika (1836-1871).

37. NA FO 391/14. The addressee is the Rt. Hon. Edmund Hammond (1802-1890). Permanent Under Secretary of State for Foreign Affairs from 10 April 1854 to 10 October 1873. PC: 11 June 1866. Baron: 22 February 1874. *Foreign Office List*.

38. NA ADM 53/8880. Log Book *Princess Royal*.

39. *Record of Service*.

18 January 1867 to 31 October 1869
Vice Admiral the Hon. Sir Henry **Keppel**

Born in Earls Court, Brompton, London on 14 June 1809, sixth surviving son of William Charles Keppel, fourth Earl of Albemarle, by his wife Elizabeth Southwell, daughter of Edward, twentieth Lord de Clifford.

Died in London at his residence, Albany Chambers, Piccadilly on Sunday, 17 January 1904, and on 21 January was buried in the churchyard of St. Mary's, Winkfield, Berkshire with naval honours, a memorial service being held in the Chapel Royal, St. James's (1).

Young Henry, or Harry as he was to be more usually known, entered the Royal Naval College, Portsmouth on 7 February 1822. As **Midshipman** appointed to the frigate *Tweed*, 28 guns: 7 February 1824, South America Station. Early in 1825 *Tweed* returned home to refit thereafter ordered to the West Indies. Returned to England in April 1827. Upon re-commissioning again appointed to *Tweed* who sailed for the Cape Station: 8 September 1827. **Mate**: 23 July 1828. **Lieutenant**: 29 January 1829, and from the Cape took passage home in frigate *Rainbow*, 28, arriving at Spithead on 10 August. From 11 February 1830 to May 1831 in frigate *Galatea*, 42, Captain Charles Napier, Portsmouth then West Indies. From 20 July 1831 in *Magicienne*, 24, Captain James Hanway Plumridge, East Indies (2).

> 'The ship sailed from England in November 1831, touched at Rio and arrived at Trincomalee in March 1832 after a passage south of the Cape in which the only land sighted in two months was the desolate St. Paul's Island, half way between Australia and Africa in the Southern Ocean (3).'

In due course, following the arrival of the ship off Malacca on 6 June 1832 quickly he found himself active in Malay waters:-

> 'In the summer of 1832, boat parties from the *Magicienne*, 24, under Lieutenants Frederick Hutton and Hon. Henry Keppel, rendered useful service in the rivers of the Malay peninsula by preventing the passage of supplies by water to the Rajah of Nanning, who, for nearly two years previously, had been at war with the East India Company. The blockade assisted in bringing the war to a satisfactory conclusion (4).'

He paid off out of *Magicienne* on 19 June 1833 (5).

Commander: 30 January 1833. News of his promotion only was received in June 1833. Subsequently returned home in the merchantman, *Claudine*, 117 days from Madras so he only landed at Portsmouth on 20 October 1833.

From 16 May 1834 to 26 May 1838 in command sloop *Childers*, 16 guns, Mediterranean. Off the south coast of Spain co-operated with the forces of the Queen Regent against the Carlists (6).

Subsequently the ship was transferred to the Cape of Good Hope and Coast of Africa Station.

Captain: 5 December 1837. Continued in *Childers* until she paid off at Portsmouth in May 1838.

On 25 February 1839 at St. George's, Hanover Square he married Katherine Louisa, daughter of General Sir John Crosbie (7). They had no children. Sadly she was to die on 5 June 1859.

Admiral of the Fleet The Hon. Sir Henry Keppel in 1894 with H.R.H. Prince Albert Edward, Prince of Wales, and later to be H.M. King Edward VII.

From 30 August 1841 in command *Dido*, 18 guns, 120' loa, East Indies. Via the Cape arrived in Singapore Roads on 6 May 1842. Present in the Yangtse during the campaign and passage upstream which resulted in the Treaty of Nanking: 29 August 1842.

Subsequently ordered as 'Senior Officer in the Straits'. Arrived Penang: 14 January 1843. On 17 March 1843 met Rajah James Brooke of Sarawak in Singapore. Subsequently, both in 1843 and again in 1844, actively engaged on the north coast of Borneo, at sea and up rivers, in suppressing pirates, both their prahus/boats and fortified villages. As one example, with a party from *Dido* under Lieut. James Hunt (1817-1860) manning the Rajah's launch *Jolly Bachelor*, at 03.00 hours on 21 May 1843 off the extreme western point of modern day Sarawak at Tanjong Datu they came up with 'two Lanoon pirate proas' and took them under fire, the engagement ending with, 'the blowing up of one Proa and the destruction of the crew of the other (8).'

As another example in August 1844 he had the Hon. East India Company iron hulled paddle steamer *Phlegethon* under his orders and:-

> '... attacked a large piratical settlement off the island of Borneo where, while the loss of the British amounted to 32 men killed and 30 wounded, the enemy had five of their towns destroyed, 250 men killed, some thousands of houses and 200 or 300 prahus of various descriptions burnt, and 70 brass guns and 13 flags taken (9).'

On her voyage home she sailed from Singapore on 16 October 1844, via the Cape with a fortnight in Simon's Bay, reaching Spithead on 27 January 1845. At the time his wife was at her father's house, some fourteen miles distant, however the ship was ordered immediately to Sheerness.

Nothing daunted:-

> 'He found the Master of the *Dido* who was about his size and build, made him put on his cocked hat, sword and epaulettes, while he donned the Master's oilskin and pea-jacket, accompanied him aboard in the tender, touched his hat to him, and was landed by a waterman at Gosport, while the Master in disguise took *Dido* to Sheerness. (--) The following morning Keppel and his wife started off to post to Sheerness, where he changed clothes with the Master, and all was well (10).'

Paid off at Sheerness: 12 February 1845.

From 1 November 1847 appointed to frigate *Maeander*, 44, East Indies then Pacific Stations. In his capacity as Governor of Labuan, The Rajah of Sarawak, Sir James Brooke, and party, which included Hugh Low, embarked in *Maeander* at Spithead on 24 January 1848 (11). She sailed on 6 February and with calls at Cork, Madeira, Rio de Janeiro, passed through the Sunda Straits on 13 May and reached Singapore during the evening of Saturday, 20 May 1848. At the time Colonel William J. Butterworth, Madras establishment, Indian Army, was Governor of Prince of Wales Island (Penang), Singapore and Malacca.

In *Maeander* again actively involved in assisting Rajah Sir James Brooke to rid his waters of piratical activity.

At nine o'clock in the evening on 14 August 1848 the wood built P. & O. paddle steamship *Braganza*, 855 grt, Captain Potts, dropped her anchor in the bay at Hong Kong (12). One of the passengers to disembark was the botanist, Robert Fortune (1812-1880), who, at the start of what was to prove to be a great enterprise, had sailed from Southampton on 20 June in the iron hulled P. & O. paddle steamer *Ripon*, 1,626 grt, Captain Moresby, I.N. (13). He had been commissioned by the East India Company to secure tea plants and seedlings in China for subsequent shipment to India, the objective being there in the Himalaya regions to establish a tea industry under British control. Successfully overcoming a number of obstacles, by the summer of 1850 the first of some 20,000 such plants were to arrive safely at Calcutta thence to be transferred onwards to the plantation areas (14). Thus was a foundation stone laid for what was to grow into a huge new commercial activity in India and Ceylon.

While on the subject of tea it is appropriate to mention that, with seeds from Japan, as early as in 1820 the Dutch had attempted to establish tea plants in Java. This first attempt failed as during the long sea voyage the seeds had dried out and lost their germinative power. Subsequently however, despatched from Batavia by Governor General Baron Godert van der Capellen, on 23 August 1823 in the ship *De Drie Gezusters*, 535 tons, Captain M.A. Jacometti, the new 'factory' surgeon, German born Dr. Philipp Franz von Siebold (1796-1866), first arrived at the trading outpost of Deshima at Nagasaki. There, in addition to practicing medicine, Dr. Siebold commenced what was to become his well known collection of indigenous plants, herbs, fish, birds, insects, reptiles and mammals. Tea certainly was not forgotten and indeed he was successful with a shipment of seeds packed in iron rich loam being shipped off to the South. The result was that in 1827 there were 3,000 healthy tea plants growing on Java. By 1833 this number had risen to half a million (15).

In June 1849 at Macau a regatta was held in which ships of the USN and those of an RN squadron, including *Maeander*, participated. At the time a British Protestant, and later to take holy orders, James Summers, was being held in gaol in Macau, his crime being one of showing a lack of respect when a Catholic procession, marking Corpus Christi, had chanced to pass him by. The Portuguese governor had refused to release Summers whereupon Keppel, with what may be regarded as typical enterprise, resolved to secure his release. While the regatta was taking place, and thereby engaging the attention of the authorities, this objective was achieved successfully by a party from the ship surreptitiously and safely removing Summers from Portuguese custody. Subsequently Keppel was to receive the personal thanks of Lord Palmerston (16).

In September 1849 received orders to proceed to Port Essington in Australia to, '… remove the garrison and stores and convey them to Sydney (17).'

There he arrived on 13 November 1849, and by 30 November the work of abandoning the Port Essington settlement was completed so bringing to an end the endeavour with which a predecessor on the China Station, Admiral Kuper, had been involved some ten years earlier. Not having in his possession the latest charts covering the Torres Strait, he proceeded around the North of New Guinea to reach Sydney on 7 February 1850. In port was the survey ship *Rattlesnake*, Captain Owen Stanley, FRS, who, alas, was to die in his ship at Sydney on Wednesday, 13 March, in his thirty ninth year. Two days later, with very considerable ceremony, he was buried at the Church of St. Thomas, North Sydney. It was he who had commanded *Britomart* at Port Essington in 1838. Subsequently his name was to be given to the prominent range of mountains in eastern Papua New Guinea.

At Sydney he arranged that the marine artist, Oswald Walters Brierly (1817-1894), be transferred from

I   SIR JAMES BROOKE

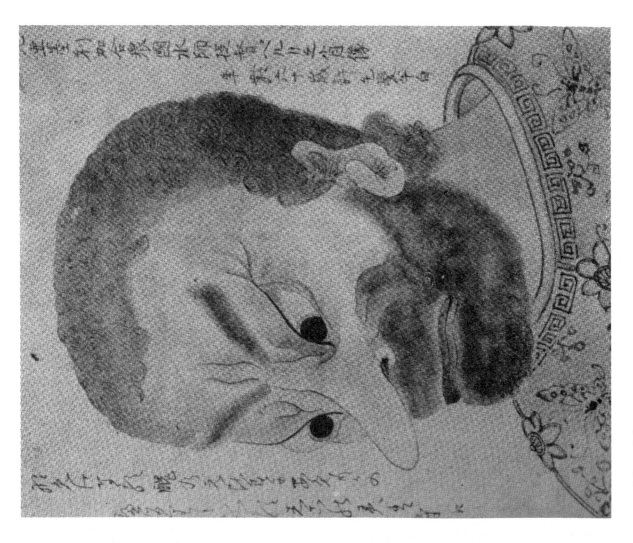

... and through Japanes eyes

Commodore Mathew Calbraith Perry as seen through American eyes...

Rattlesnake to his ship and shortly afterwards he sailed to bring *Maeander* home via South America, so completing his circumnavigation. While rounding the Horn he came up with HMS *Amphitrite*, Captain Charles Frederick, outward bound to the Pacific Station. As is related by one of her grateful young Midshipman:-

> '... we fell in with HMS *Maeander*, homeward bound, commanded by Harry Keppel. Our captain proceeded onboard the *Maeander*, and on his return I was sent for and given part of a hindquarter of beef sent with Captain Keppel's compliments to the "*Amphitrite's* midshipmen's mess". Such an act of attention from a post captain to midshipmen is, I believe, unprecedented. No wonder he was loved by all the service (18).'

Maeander arrived at Sheerness on 30 July 1851 and paid off.

From 21 May 1853 in screw steam ship *St. Jean d'Acre*, 101 guns, in the Baltic during the first year of the Crimean War. Then to the Mediterranean Station and Black Sea. Succeeded in command of the ship by George St. Vincent King (see C. in C., 1865).

In command *Rodney*, 92, Black Sea: 7 July 1855, '... in order to take command of the Naval Brigade on shore before Sevastopol, with which he continued till the fall of the fortress (19).'

GSP: 14 July 1855.

From the Black Sea he returned home in the transport *Orinoco*, 2,245 grt, who arrived at Southampton on 17 January 1856. The ship was a Royal Mail Steam Packet Company steamer taken up for war time service.

Between 25 January and 17 September 1856 in command of the screw second rate *Colossus*, 3,482 tons, this appointment to include the command of a squadron of gunboats and intended for service in the Baltic. However by the Treaty of Paris on 30 March 1856 hostilities against Russia were brought to a conclusion.

In addition to the Baltic and Crimean medals he received the third class of the Medjidie (20).

CB: 4 February 1856.

Also for services rendered during the Crimean War, by the French he was appointed an Officer of the Legion of Honour, and on 2 August 1856 he received permission from Queen Victoria to wear the insignia.

> From 17 September 1856 in command frigate *Raleigh*, 50, East Indies. Near Macao on 14 April 1857 the ship struck an uncharted pinnacle of rock and was lost. Subsequently, '...with his broad pennant flying onboard the *Hong Kong*, a small river steamer chartered by the Admiralty, on 1 June 1857 the attack on the grand fleet of Chinese war junks in the upper reaches of Fatshan Creek was entrusted to him; and under his personal command the whole, some 70 in number, with the exception of two or three, were set on fire and burnt (21).'

Earlier, as *Raleigh* was going down, the French Admiral Guerin chanced to be nearby in *Virginie*. He closed to see if he could be of any assistance whereupon Captain Keppel ordered that the French flag be hoisted and the appropriate salute fired. Later he was to recall:-

> 'The gallant Guerin embraced me exclaiming, '*C'est magnifique!* A British frigate saluting the French flag while she is sinking (22).'

From the Far East returned home in a series of P. & O. steamers including *Formosa*, 675 grt, and *Ripon*, 1,508 grt, and with a stop for a few weeks in India. Eventually he arrived at Southampton early in December 1857.

Rear Admiral: 22 August 1857.

KCB: 12 September 1857.

September 1858: appointed groom-in-waiting to H.M. Queen Victoria (23).

From 10 February 1860 appointed C. in C., Cape of Good Hope with his Flag in the new screw steam frigate *Forte*, 51 guns, Captain Edward Winterton Turnour. "It was understood that some friction or unpleasant feeling between him and the Governor of the Cape Colony led to him being some little time after transferred to the Brazilian command (24)."

At the Cape he was succeeded by Rear Admiral Sir Baldwin Wake Walker (1802-1876), 1st Baronet, with his flag in the screw frigate *Narcissus*, 51 guns.

C. in C., South East Coast of America. To take up this appointment he left the Cape at the end of April 1861 and was only briefly on the South East Coast of America, there in June being succeeded by Vice Admiral Richard Laird Warren (1806-1875).

In the screw frigate *Emerald*, 51, Captain Arthur Cumming, and having sailed from Bahia on 4 July, Sir Henry returned home to Plymouth, arriving on Monday, 5 August 1861.

On 31 October 1861, as his second wife, married Jane Elizabeth, daughter of Martin John West and a sister of Sir Algernon West, private secretary to William E. Gladstone. By her he was to have two children, the future Admiral Sir Colin Richard Keppel, born on 3 December 1862, and who died on 6 July 1947, and Maria Walpole Keppel, born on 6 May 1865, and who died on 20 November 1952. On 3 December 1889 Maria married Admiral Sir Frederick Tower Hamilton (1856-1917).

Lady Jane Keppel, who was born on 25 May 1820, was to die on 21 April 1895.

Vice Admiral: 11 January 1864.

To take up the China command, early in 1867 he proceeded by rail and sea to Alexandria then overland to Suez. He commented as follows on the great French engineering works:-

'Time, money and perseverance will, I believe, complete the great work of the Suez Canal. De Lesseps is sanguine, at no distant period, of being able to pass a ship-of-the-line from the Mediterranean to the Red Sea (25).'

On 9 March he left Suez in the P. & O. *Surat*, 2,578 grt, at Ceylon switched to their *Ottawa*, 1,275 grt, and arrived at Singapore on Sunday afternoon, 31 March 1867.

In China he flew his Flag in *Rodney*, 78 guns, 2,770 tons, a screw steam assisted, second rate. The ship was commanded by that fabulous Victorian eccentric and future Admiral and Commander in Chief, both in the Pacific and then at The Nore, Captain Algernon Charles Fieschi Heneage (1833-1915). For a short period in *Forte* in 1860 he had served as Flag Lieut. to Sir Henry.

Borne in *Rodney* were Commander Richard E. Tracey and Lieutenant Arthur K. Wilson, and party, 'For Instruction of Japanese' (26). The British Minister to Japan, Sir Harry Parkes, had strived successfully to have such a training group ordered to Japan in order both to enhance British standing, and to counter French and Dutch ambitions in that direction. Writing from Osaka to the Foreign Office, Lord Stanley, on 31 December 1867 Sir Harry reported:-

'Captain Tracey, Lieut. Wilson and two men reached Yokohama on 23 October 1867 ... the others followed on 11 November 1867 (27).'

Members of this party, however, were not to undertake their duties in Japan for longer than three or four months from November 1867 as under the conditions of civil unrest between Shogunate and Imperial interests the British felt that the status of the group could not in all fairness be described as neutral. In February 1868 Sir Harry was to feel obliged to write twice to Richard Tracey. Extracts follow:-

'18 February 1868
... enjoining neutrality on all British subjects in the civil contest which has unfortunately broken out in this country...'
29 February 1868
... you discontinue for the present your duties of Naval drill and instruction and to retire to Yokohama... (28)'

The Tracey Mission duly was withdrawn, in 1873 to be replaced by the Archibald Douglas Mission. Shortly thereafter Tracey himself, for a short period of time, was to hold a similar training post with the Chinese Navy.

As the new C. in C., China he actually first hoisted his Flag in the wood paddle despatch vessel *Salamis* at Singapore, 2.20 p.m. on Sunday, 31 March 1867.

It was on 1 April 1867 that government of the Straits Settlements of Singapore, Malacca and Penang was transferred from the authority of the Indian government to that of the Secretary of State for the Colonies. The first colonial governor was His Excellency Colonel Harry St. George Ord, CB, of the Royal Engineers.

Assumed command of the Station on Friday, 5 April 1867. From Singapore his predecessor sailed for home on Monday, 8 April. Then in *Salamis* he sailed for Kuching on 15 April there to meet the acting Rajah of Sarawak, Tuan Muda, Charles Antoni Johnson Brooke, who earlier had served as a Midshipman in *Dido* then under his command. Reached Labuan on 22 April, the acting Governor there being his old friend Hugh Low. On 30 April he arrived at Hong Kong, the Governor there now being Sir Richard Graves MacDonnell (1814-1881), cousin of Francis Brinkley (29).

In respect of one important duty happily the USN, Rear Admiral Henry H. Bell, was to work closely with him:-

> 'Bell soon was on good terms with his opposite number in the Royal Navy, Vice Admiral Keppel, cooperating in the control of pirates. These gentry, Bell wrote Keppel, "… invariably board in calms, light weather, or at anchor, and overpowered by numbers, with stink pots, pistols, and muskets, and frequently in the very entrance of the ports open to trade" (30).'

In his letter of 13 July 1867, Sir Harry Parkes informed Edmund Hammond at the Foreign Office:-

> 'Admiral Keppel arrived at Yokohama on the 5th and came on at once to Yedo where he staid with me for a week (31).'

With the death of Aleksandr Andreyevich Baranov in April 1819 the fortunes of the Russian American Company ebbed, a decline much assisted by an alteration in focus from commercial activity to that of bureaucratic government. So it was that on 18 October 1867 all of Russian America was acquired by the United States. This, the Alaska Purchase initiated by the then Secretary of State, William H. Seward, took place for a consideration of US$7.2 million.

1 January 1868: opening of the port of Hyogo/Kobe to foreign residence and commerce.

On 3 January 1868 the fifteenth and last of the shoguns, Tokugawa Yoshinobu (Keiki) (1837-1913), having resigned the previous November but still with many active supporters, accepted the successful outcome of the palace coup achieved in Kyoto by Satsuma, Choshu and Tosa 'han' interests. Although a short civil war then did occur, Boshin Senso, he worked to restrict such activity thus enabling the Meiji 'Restoration' to take place in a manner relatively free of bloodshed.

This civil war did include what might be regarded as the first Japanese naval engagement of modern times. Off Awaji Island on 28 January 1868 the bakufu *Kaiyo Maru* fought the Satsuma han *Kasuga* in a modest and inconclusive gun battle (32).

As a result of earlier assistance and co-operation received, many of the new leaders of Japan, including, for example, Ito Hirobumi, had good reason to be inclined towards friendship with Great Britain (33).

Together with other British officials, at Osaka on 22 May 1868 he was presented by Sir Harry Parkes to the young Mikado, H.I.M. Emperor Mutsuhito (1852-1912). His reign was to be known as the Meiji, 'enlightened rule', era.

On the following day the C. in C. hosted a reception onboard *Rodney*, with *Ocean* and five other British men-of-war in company. Thirty senior Japanese government officials, together with Sir Harry Parkes, were the guests of the Admiral and, as Sir Harry Parkes was to write to Lord Stanley on 30 May, 'a sumptuous entertainment was served on the poop of the *Rodney*.'

At Singapore on 30 June 1868 the ship chandler and agency house of W. Mansfield & Co., at the time in an unenviable financial position, handled their first vessel of The Ocean Steam Ship Company of Liverpool. She was their *Achilles*, 2,280 grt, Captain T. Russell (34). As with Swires in China and Japan so with Mansfields in the Straits, all were to grow together to attain prominence in their mutually important relationship with Alfred Holt's Ocean Steam Ship, the Blue Funnel Line.

In August 1868 a civil engineer from Scotland, Richard Henry Brunton (1841-1901), arrived at Yokohama. In accordance with treaty obligations his services had been engaged by the Japanese government to survey possible sites and then to construct a number of lighthouses around their dangerous coast as very necessary aids to safe navigation. A number of these fine structures survive today (35).

Even before Brunton had arrived in Japan, the C. in C.'s predecessor, Sir George King, had provided suitable vessels, '... for a survey of the coast to decide on sites for the lighthouses which were to be given top priority.' Likewise it was Sir Harry Parkes who was to ensure that the, '... shogunate implement the terms of the treaties (36).'

Similarly the actual coastlines of Japan were to be surveyed, among other vessels also the small converted gunvessel *Sylvia*, 865 tons, was to be employed in Eastern waters. These waters included the coast of China and in her case *Sylvia* was to be so occupied for the greater part of the several years between 1867 and 1880.

In November 1868 at Anping in Formosa an incident had taken place with the British Consul, John Gibson, consequently requesting the assistance of a gunboat in order that action could be taken as, 'redress for outrages which had been denied to more peaceable efforts'. In a brilliantly handled affair, at night and with odds of twenty to one against, Lieut. and Commander Thornhaugh Philip Gurdon of *Algerine* captured Fort Zeelandia, then in the process of being actively re-fortified by the Chinese. In consequence of this successful feat of arms the local Taiwan officials complied with Mr. Gibson's demands. Further, shortly thereafter the Chinese administration removed the responsible Taotai from his post and subsequently they were to adhere to Treaty obligations.

In his letter of 6 January 1869 the C. in C. outlined the episode in a report to the Admiralty, describing Lieut. Gurdon's role as being carried out with great 'zeal and gallantry' (37).

On 1 June 1869 Gurdon was promoted Commander. He was to retire late in 1873.

Gibson, a Barrister-at-Law and M.A., Edinburgh, had joined the China service in Hong Kong in June 1857. In 1858 he had been appointed Acting Private Secretary to Lord Elgin, Her Majesty's Plenipotentiary during his successful negotiations held that June in Tientsin. Other important appointments had followed but, alas, he was to die of consumption in Amoy on 28 July 1869 (38).

In 1869 the British prime minster was the liberal, William E. Gladstone. Being far removed from the scene of the incident, and being, "utterly ignorant of the manners and customs of the Chinese", the government at home had not appreciated the circumstances surrounding the disagreements with Mr. Gibson and their initial reaction had not been to look with favour upon the successful operation in capturing Fort Zeelandia (39).'

The civil, Boshin, war in Japan referred to above finally was to take the form of the establishment of rebel forces, the Kerais, at Hakodate on Hokkaido, or Yezo. French sympathies were with the rebels who were assisted by six or seven French officers under Jules Brunet. The rebel naval forces were under the command of Enomoto Takeaki (40).

From Hong Kong on 11 January 1869 the C. in C. informed London of this sudden development, the departure of this Tokugawa break-away group, the Kerais, for Hakodate (41).

However just over six months later, writing in *Rodney* at Yokohama on 24 June 1869, he was able to inform the Admiralty:-

'Para. 2. I have the honor to report for the information of the Lords Commissioners of the Admiralty that the attack (by the Mikado's forces) was made on the 4th of June, by five of the Mikado's vessels, but was conducted with so much caution on each side that there was little result.'

'Para. 3. On the 9th instant the attack was repeated by land and sea, the troops covered by the ships. Captain Ross of the *Pearl* reports that they fought with great gallantry not withstanding a brave and vigorous resistance on the part of the Kerais, they were driven out of their entrenchments with considerable loss on each side, and several guns defending the passes were captured by the Mikado's forces. The Kerais still hold the forts, and their fleet appears to be anchored within a line of torpedoes (mines) which the Mikado's vessels are not disposed to pass.'

'Para. 4. By the latest accounts, occasional firing is exchanged between the Mikado's ships and the forts and ships of the Kerais; the resistance of the latter continues with unabated vigor, which is not diminished by the dilatory action of the Mikado's forces. The immense preponderance of the latter can scarcely fail to give them the victory (42).'

The C. in C. quickly was to be proved entirely correct in expressing this opinion as at Hakodate during the afternoon of 23 June 1869 the Mikado's forces were victorious. Enomoto together with some 2,000 followers were captured and held as prisoners, Enomoto himself surrendering on 26 June. Subsequently from the Mikado himself Captain Ross of HMS *Pearl* was to receive the award of a sword as an expression of His Imperial Majesty's thanks, with some smaller presents being given to other members of the ship's company.

Piracy on the coast of China had always been, and was to continue to be a great problem. When British flag junks and shipping were attacked then naturally the C. in C. became involved. In 1868 Admiral Keppel had made certain proposals to the Admiralty, who, desiring to obtain wider approval, so informed the Foreign Office. Politely, on 3 August 1868, the Foreign Office replied:-

'... I am directed by His Lordship to acquaint you, in reply, for the information of The Lords Commissioners of the Admiralty that Lord Stanley fully concurs in Their Lordships proposal to approve Sir Henry Keppel's proceedings in this matter (43).'

To illustrate the significance of this difficulty, in mid 1869 Sir Henry arranged that one of his gunboats, in company with two similar Chinese warships, should engage in joint patrols:-

'HM Gunboat *Bouncer* and the Chinese gunboat *Chen To* have been employed during the month of May cruising in company searching for piratical vessels which have committed depredations in the neighbourhood of Hong Kong (44).'

In just one week, 12 to 18 June 1869 inclusive, *Bouncer* captured sixteen junks, each ranging in size from fifteen to 100 tons, the sixteen carrying a total of seventy six guns and crewed by 424 men, took three prisoners, and released fifty four. The junks themselves were disposed of as follows:-

'Seven were handed over to the Chinese squadron.

Four were destroyed as being unseaworthy.

Five were returned to owners.'

Between them the Chinese gunboats apprehended a total of just seven junks during the week (45).

The services of these Chinese gunboats, to a great extent their navy being ineffective, were supplemented by revenue cutters. These cutters were operated by the ubiquitous, and efficient, Chinese Maritime Customs. From 1863 to 1908 the Inspector-General of Customs was the Northern Irishman, Sir Robert Hart. From Peking on 29 August 1868 Sir Robert wrote to the British Minister at Peking, Sir Rutherford Alcock, to report the ordering in Britain of three armed Customs steamers, primarily for the Customs operated lighthouse service but also:-

'a) to perform the military duties of Customs cruisers for the protection of the revenue.

b) to assist in the suppression of piracy in Chinese waters (46).'

As will be seen throughout this volume these attempts at suppression never were to succeed entirely. Gradually the pirates became bolder and more experienced, in due course tackling European merchant ships including those carrying parties of armed guards.

In the interim at 5.35 p.m. on 8 April 1869 the screw steam gunboat *Opossum*, 284 tons, Lieutenant and Commander John E. Stokes, arrived at Ichang at the foot of the Yangtse Gorges. It was known beforehand that the River was navigable as far as Ichang however, '... *Opossum* was the first (steam powered) vessel that had attempted it (47).'

As has been indicated above, in November 1866 Sir Harry Parkes had reminded the Japanese government of their agreement to a treaty clause whereby Japan should 'provide the treaty ports with such lights as may be necessary to render secure the navigation of the approaches to said ports'. During the months of domestic unrest additional time had been required, but progress had been made. Shortly after the arrival of Richard H. Brunton in August 1868 Admiral Keppel had made available HMS *Manilla*, a merchantman taken up for Admiralty service, and in her Brunton made his first voyage of inspection (48). The following year the first Japanese lighthouse tender was acquired, a barque rigged screw steamer, *Sunrise*, 374 tons, re-named *Tomio Maru* (49). By August 1875 very useful progress was to have been made in establishing an appropriate network of such lighthouses, from Yezo in the north through to Kyushu. Richard Brunton, who had praise for men such as Inoue Kaoru and Ito Hirobumi with whom he had worked at certain times, also had advised the authorities on the construction of telegraph systems and railways, and in 1870 had supervised the construction in Yokohama of the second iron bridge to be built in Japan (50).

Writing in *Rodney* from Yokohama on 12 June 1869 the C. in C. felt able to comment in his letter to the Admiralty:-

> 'As far as British Interests are concerned in China and Japan affairs during the last two years have not been so tranquil as at present (51).'

As another indication of maritime trading enterprise, during the summer season of 1869, thus when water levels in the Yangtse were high, six steamers loaded tea at Hankow, 636 nautical miles upstream from the open sea, direct for the English market. Four of these were owned by Alfred Holt's Blue Funnel Line and one, *Agamemnon*, still commanded by Isaac Middleton, loaded a record breaking 2,516,000 lbs., or 1,123.21 long tons. Her delighted owner later was to write that she brought back the largest cargo ever embarked in one ship and earned the largest freight that he, Mr. Holt, had ever heard of, GBP 28,087. In addition *Agamemnon* made an excellent passage by leaving Hankow on 9 June and passing Gravesend in the River Thames two and a half months later, on 25 August 1869 (52).

Admiral: 3 July 1869.

8 July 1869. In Japan the establishment of the Military Ministry, Hyobusho, to administer the affairs of both the Army and the Navy. Necessarily the army was to receive the greater priority as, to give just one reason, the domestic situation was not to settle down for a number of years. The authorities correctly recognised that once the internal administration of the country was running peacefully then the status of The Emperor's armed forces could be reconsidered.

At this stage in the early development of their armed forces it has been written, 'As an auxiliary force was how many in Japan's new government saw the navy (53).'

Under sail *Rodney* left Yokohama on 25 July 1869 bound for England via the Cape. 'The same day I shifted my flag to *Ocean* (54).'

He was present both in Yedo Bay, and ashore, on the occasion of the first visit paid by a member of the British Royal Family to His Imperial Majesty the Emperor of Japan:-

> 'On the 4 September (1869) His Royal Highness the Duke of Edinburgh had an audience of the Mikado. His Royal Highness was accompanied to the castle by Admiral the Honourable Sir Harry Keppel (55).'

At the conclusion of his very successful visit, on 16 September 1869 HRH sailed for Osaka, thence Nagasaki. With the wooden hulled ironclad steam frigate *Ocean*, 6,535 tons, screw iron troop ship *Adventure*, 1,794 tons, and paddle despatch vessel *Salamis*, 985 tons, in company, Sir Harry Keppel accompanied the steam frigate *Galatea*, 4,686 tons, HRH's command, on her departure from Yedo Bay.

Shortly thereafter the C. in C. returned to Hong Kong.

As has been seen some of Thomas Glover's interests and connections were mentioned in 1866 during the time that Admiral King had served as C. in C. Now on 27 September 1869 Admiral Keppel wrote to the Admiralty on the subject of, 'Purchase of Coal for use of the Navy at Nagasaki'. This supply of coal was offered by Mr. Henry Gribble of Glover & Co. (56).

In due course the export of coal from mines such as Takashima and Miike in Kyushu were to be an important source of foreign earnings used to finance the emerging economy of Meiji Japan.

On 24 October 1869 Sir Harry handed over the Station to his successor, Admiral Kellett.

The ceremony surrounding his departure from Hong Kong on Tuesday, 2 November was without precedent. Amongst other ships in port, but flying the Royal Standard, was the frigate *Galatea*, 26, Captain His Royal Highness The Duke of Edinburgh. HRH and officers of *Galatea* manned the barge, with HRH at stroke and Commodore Challier at the helm, which conveyed the Admiral out from the Government wharf and his guard of honour, to the P. & O. s.s. *Salsette*, 1,491 grt, in which ship he was to take passage home. Appropriate salutes were fired. Waiting onboard *Salsette* at her moorings in Victoria harbour were H.E. the Governor, Sir Richard MacDonnell, and Sir Henry Kellett. Just prior to *Salsette* sailing HRH, 'presented me with a gold watch as a souvenir'.

The event that morning was recorded in the log book of the sloop *Rinaldo*:-

'8.0 a.m. Dressed ship. HMS *Galatea* hoisted Royal Standard: saluted with 21 guns.

Adm. Hon. H. Keppel, KCB left Govt. wharf for Mail ship under a salute of 17 guns from the Fort.

From his service record up to 31 December 1869 it is recorded that he had spent seventeen years and 214 days on half pay (57).

A GSP at the higher rate was awarded to him on 9 April 1870.

On 22 June 1870 at Oxford University, the Chancellor at the time being Lord Salisbury, he received an honorary degree, DCL.

GCB: 20 May 1871.

C. in C., Plymouth: 1 November 1872 to 1 November 1875. Flag in the old three decker *Royal Adelaide*, launched in 1828 and completed in 1835. Here at Devonport once again he was to be served by an old friend and now Flag Captain, Algernon C.F. Heneage (58).

Admiral of the Fleet: 5 August 1877.

First and Principal ADC to H.M. Queen Victoria: 9 March 1878.

Sir Henry enjoyed the close friendship of HRH The Prince of Wales, later HM King Edward VII, but did not always enjoy good fortune at whist. As Vice Admiral Fleet was to record:-

'... I had the honour of dining with His Majesty, then Prince of Wales, at the RN Club, Portsmouth. He came with Prince Louis of Battenberg and Admiral Sir Harry Keppel. (--) Sir Harry Keppel had long retired from the Service, but often came to the club for a rubber of whist, and many I've had with him, but his luck was very bad; he always seemed to lose – money, but not his temper (59).'

In 1899 his memoirs were published in three volumes, *A Sailor's Life under four Sovereigns*. He was the author of two earlier works, *The Expedition to Borneo of H.M.S. Dido for the Suppresion of Piracy*, (1846), and, *A Visit to the Indian Archipelago in H.M.S. Meander* (1853).

On Tuesday, 16 January 1900 the Admiral, then aged ninety and who was paying a visit to those waters of many fond memories, embarked at Singapore in the cruiser *Hermoine*, 4,360 tons, Captain George A. Callaghan. There was another distinguished person also taking passage:-

'At 3.0 (p.m.) His Excellency Hugh Clifford, Governor of Labuan came onboard for passage to Sarawak and then to Labuan.

3.35: pilot came onboard.

3.40: Admiral of the Fleet Sir Henry Keppel came onboard to take passage to Sarawak and Labuan (60).'

As soon as the Admiral had embarked *Hermoine* sailed from Singapore and subsequently stopped off the Sarawak River on 18 January, reaching Labuan on 20 January. Sir Henry did not continue to Labuan but disembarked at Sarawak in order to pay a short visit to his old friend and one time shipmate, the Rajah of Sarawak, H.H. Sir Charles Brooke. After two days at Labuan *Hermoine* returned to anchor briefly off Sarawak on 24 January, reaching Singapore on 25 January 1900.

Following his return from his short visit to Kuching in Sarawak, then in April 1900 there was considerable ceremony when the important new facility at Singapore, Keppel Harbour was named for the Admiral (61).

At the time the acting Governor was Sir James Alexander Swettenham (1846-1933), elder brother of Sir Frank Athelstane Swettenham (1850-1946) who was to govern the colony from November 1901 to April 1904 (62).

From the East he returned home in the P. & O. s.s. *Massilia*, 5,026 grt, who arrived at the Albert Docks, London on 21 May 1900 (63).

Amazingly, at the age of ninety two, he was to return to Singapore once more, travelling out to the East in the P. & O. steamer *Rome*, 5,545 grt, a ship who in 1904 was to be converted and re-named by the company as their 'cruise yacht' *Vectis*. Following this very successful visit an account of his final depature for home follows:-

'When the time came for him to leave for England, Singapore gave Sir Harry Keppel a royal send-off. Escorted by the Governor, Sir Frank Swettenham, in person, with General Doward, the military G.O.C. on his other side, he was led through a guard of honour of seamen, Marines, and soldiers to the P. & O. Wharf in Keppel Harbour, where a large crowd of old friends and new acquaintances had gathered to wave him goodbye. The little old Admiral embarked in the mail steamer under a naval salute, visibly moved by these tributes, and he reached home safely – contrary to his expectations (64).'

O.M.: 26 June 1902. The other naval member honoured on this, the day of the institution of the Order, was Admiral Sir Edward Hobart Seymour (see C. in C., 1897).

At the time of his burial on 21 January 1904, and to accompany her wreath at his grave, HM The Queen wrote:-

'In loving memory of my beloved Little Admiral, the best and bravest of men.

Rest in peace. Alexandra.'

Further:-

'While the funeral was taking place at Winkfield Church, an impressive service was being held at the Chapel Royal, St. James's, which was attended by the King and Queen, who herself chose the hyms that were sung (65).'

He had been nearly eighty two years on the active list, a man of great charm and ability:-

'Keppel's social reputation stood as high as his service character. He was no less remarkable for the charm of his personality than for his love of sport and exuberant vitality. With King Edward VII, especially while Prince of Wales, he was on terms of intimate friendship; and with Queen

Alexandra and the whole royal family his relations were such as are rarely permitted to a subject (66).

Today in St. Mary's Church, Winkfield an attractive brass plaque in memory of both Sir Henry and his wife Jane is to be found at the rear of the church near the central aisle. It was, '... placed here by their son', Admiral Sir Colin Richard Keppel (1862-1947). His grave may be found in the churchyard outside (67).

NOTES

1   *Dictionary of National Biography.*

2.   O'Byrne, 610.

3.   William Jameson, *The Fleet that Jack Built*, (London, 1962), 20.

4.   Clowes, Vol. VI, 270.

5.   NA ADM 196/5, 10. *Service Record.*

6   *Dictionary of National Biography.*

7.   O'Byrne.

8.   Illustration, 'The Attack of Two Lanoon Pirate Proas on the Proa Jolly Batchelor', published in 1845 by Dickinson & Son, 114 New Bond Street, London – a copy in the author's possession.

9.   O'Byrne. The village is Patusan, upstream from the present day Lingga on the left bank of Batang Lupar, Sarawak. Earlier successful adventures undertaken in June 1843 against pirates based up the River Sarebus (Batang Saribas) are described in the reprint of Henry Keppel, *The Adventures to Borneo of HMS Dido*, (OUP, 1991), Vol. 11, 48-71.

10.   Algernon West, *Harry Keppel*, (London, 1905), 48/9.

11.   Hugh **Low**. For career details see Coote, C. in C., 1878, reference (21).

12.   Robert Fortune, *A Journey to the Tea Countries*, (London, 1852), 1.

13.   This is Robert Moresby (1794-1854), he who during the period 1829-1833 first had accurately surveyed the Northern waters of the Red Sea.

14.   Fortune, 340.

15.   Jonathan Parkinson, *Resourceful Tea Hunters in Japan*, (Journal of the Royal Asiatic Society, Hong Kong Branch, Vol. 44, 2004), 143/144. Nederlands Scheepvaartmuseum, Amsterdam. Arlette Kouwenhoven and Matthi Forrer, *Siebold and Japan: his life and work*, (Leiden, 2000), 31.

16.   West, 62/72. James **Summers** (1828-1891) today still is held in regard in Japan being an early Sinologist and pioneer of Japanese newspapers in London, and of English literature in Japan. Ed. J.E. Hoare, *Biographical Portraits*, (Japan Library, Richmond, 1999), 25/37.

17.   Vivian Stuart, *The Beloved Little Admiral*, (London, 1967), 121-127.

18.   John Moresby, *Two Admirals*, (London, 1913), 91.

19.   Obituary, *The Times*, Monday, January, 18, 1904.

20.   *Dictionary of National Biography.*

21.   Obituary, *The Times.*

22.   Stuart, 170.

23.   *Dictionary of National Biography.*

24.   The Governor of the Cape from 1854 to 1859, and re-instated in 1860, was H.E. Sir George **Grey**. Born in Lisbon: 14 April 1812. Died in London: 20 September 1898 and subsequently buried in St. Paul's Cathedral. RMC, Sandhurst. In 1829 joined the 83rd Regiment of Foot. From December 1837 to 1839 led an exploration party in north west Western Australia. Governor of South Australia: May 1841 – 26 October 1845. Governor of New Zealand: 1845 – 1853. KCB: 1848. From the Cape again appointed Governor of New Zealand: October 1861 – 1868, when he returned to England. Retired on pension: 1872. Returned to New Zealand and on 24 March 1875 elected MP for Auckland City West. Prime Minister of New Zealand: 13 October 1877 – 8 October 1879. Thereafter a member of the House of Representatives

for fourteen years. Returned to London in 1894. PC: 1894. Apart from considerable success as a Colonial Governor, especially during his earlier terms of office, a pioneer student of Maori culture. In South Africa presented a valuable collection of Africana to the SA Library in Capetown. Keenly interested in education, he contributed personal funds to assist in the establishment of, for example, the highly respected Grey College in Bloemfontein. *Standard Encyclopaedia of South Africa,* (Capetown, 1972), 344-347. *Colonial Office List,* 1896. Grey's private family life may not have been entirely harmonious. Stuart, 185-194. Also see Fremantle, C. in C., 1892, reference (8).

25. Stuart, 208.

26. For career details covering Richard E. **Tracey** see Willes, C. in C., 1881, reference (28).

27. NA ADM 1/6072. Lord Edward Henry **Stanley** (1826-1893), later Fifteenth Earl of Derby, Secretary of State for Foreign Affairs: July 1866 – December 1868, and again, 1874-1878.

28. Ibid.

29. For career details covering Francis **Brinkley** see Shadwell, C. in C., 1871, reference (29).

30. Rear Admiral Kemp Tolley, USN, *Yangtze Patrol,* (Annapolis, MD., 1987), 28/29.

31. NA FO 391/14. Edmund **Hammond**. Born: 1802. Died: 29 April 1890. Under Secretary of State for Foreign Affairs: 10 April 1854 – 10 October 1873. PC: 11 June 1866. Created a Baron: 22 February 1874. *Foreign Office List,* 1891.

32. David Chris Evans, *The Satsuma Faction and Professionalism in the Japanese Naval Officer Corps of the Meiji Period, 1868-1912,* (Stanford, 1978), 20. The commander of *Kaiyo Maru* was Enomoto Takeaki – see reference (40) below.

33. **Ito** Hirobumi. Born: 14 October 1841. Assassinated in Harbin by a member, Korean independence movement: 26 October 1909. At the time when it was a capital offence for Japanese citizens to leave the country, during the summer of 1863, as one of the group to be known as the 'Choshu Five', secretly travelled to Britain. The scheme was organised by Thomas Glover, and William Keswick of Jardine Matheson & Co. In due course to be Prime Minister of Japan on four occasions, 1885-1888, 1892-1896, 1898, and 1900-1901. In 1889 assisted with the drafting of the Meiji constitution and in 1890 brought about the establishment of a bicameral Parliament, the Diet. Marquis: 1884. Resident General, Korea: 1906-1909. Prince: 1907. Alexander McKay, *Scottish Samurai,* (Edinburgh, 1997), 47-49. *Encyclopaedia Britannica.*

34. Eric Jennings, *Mansfields,* (Singapore, 1973), 14. Francis E. Hyde, *Blue Funnel,* (Liverpool, 1957), 35/36.

35. Dallas Finn, *Meiji Revisited,* (New York, 1995), 40-44. Also see Gordon Daniels, *Sir Harry Parkes,* (Richmond, Surrey, 1996).

36. Lewis Bush, *The Life and Times of the Illustrious Captain Brown,* (Tokyo and Rutland, VT., 1969), 17.

37. NA ADM 1/6094. Written in *Princess Charlotte* at Hong Kong. The Foreign Office were not to approve of Gibson's conduct. See P.D. Coates, *The China Consuls,* (OUP, 1988), 324-326, for a useful account.
    Fort Zeelandia was built by the Dutch VOC, Vereenigde Oost-Indische Compagnie, between 1624 and 1634.

38. *Foreign Office List,* 1869. *China Consuls,* 326.

39. Stuart, 220.

40. **Enomoto** Takeaki. Born in Yedo (Tokyo): 5 October 1838. Died in Tokyo: 26 October 1908. Received early naval training from the Dutch both at Nagasaki and in The Netherlands. Returned to Japan in the Dutch built Shogunate man-of-war *Kaiyo Maru.* Following his surrender at Hakodate on 26 June 1869, and the ensuing three year period under arrest, he was restored to favour subsequently serving HIM Emperor Meiji as envoy to Russia. Then Navy Minister: 1876-1882. Minister to China: 1882-1884. Subsequently held a number of senior government positions at home. Viscount: 1887. *Encyclopaedia Britannica.* Fred T. Jane, *The Imperial Japanese Navy,* (London, 1904), 35. Translation by Eiichi Kiyooka, *The Autobiography of Yukichi Fukuzawa,* (Columbia University Press, 1966), 255/260.

41. NA ADM 1/6094.

42. NA ADM 1/6095. Letter No. *S.214.* Captain John F. Ross commanded *Pearl,* 21 guns, 2,115 tons.

43. NA ADM 1/6072

44. NA ADM 1/6095. The Anglo-Chinese squadron operated under the overall command of the Commodore, Hong Kong, Oliver, J. Jones. *Bouncer,* 284 tons, Lieutenant and Commander Rodney M. Lloyd. *Chen To* was *Chen T'ao,* at times assisted by *An Lan* and *Sui Tsing.* Richard N.J. Wright, *The Chinese Steam Navy, 1862-1945,* (London, 2000), 20.

45. Ibid.

46. NA ADM 1/6072.

47. NA ADM 53/ 9958. Log Book *Opossum.* Robert Swinhoe, *Special Mission up the Yang-tsze-Kiang,* read to Fellows,

9 May 1870. *Journal of the Royal Geographical Society,* 40, 271. Jonathan Parkinson, *The First Steam Powered Ascent Through the Yangtse Gorges,* (Journal of the Royal Asiatic Society Hong Kong Branch, 2006) Vol. 46, 149-174. British Consul Swinhoe himself was a naturalist of note: *The Geographical Journal,* March 1987, 37/47.

48. Richard Henry Brunton, paper *The Japan Lights,* read before The Institution of Civil Engineers, London, 14 November 1876.

49. Lewis Bush, 18.

50. *Dictionary of National Biography.*

51. NA ADM 1/6095. Letter No. 229.

52. Francis E. Hyde, *Blue Funnel,* (Liverpool, 1957), 38.

53. J. Charles Schencking, *Making Waves,* (Stanford, 2005), 12.

54. NA ADM 1/6095. Keppel to the Admiralty, No. 318, *Ocean* at Yokohama, 26 July 1869.

55. John R. Black, *Young Japan,* Vol. II (London, 1881), 269. *Galatea,* of which frigate HRH was in command, had anchored off Yokohama on 25 August 1869. He was Alfred Ernest Albert, second son of HM Queen Victoria.

56. NA ADM 1/6095. Letter No. 422. The Glover mines were at Takashima. After a number of vicissitudes to be acquired by Mitsubishi. Similarly those of Miike were to be acquired by the Mitsui group.

57. *Service Record.*

58. Stuart, 232.

59. Vice Admiral H.L. Fleet, *My Life, and a Few Yarns,* (London, 1922), 319/320.

60. RN Museum Library, Portsmouth. Ref: *MS 216.* Journal kept by Oscar De Satge De Theron, Midshipman in *Hermoine:* 1 August 1899 – 15 January 1901.

   Hugh Charles **Clifford**. Born: 5 March 1866. Died in Roehampton: 18 December 1941. Intended to follow in his father's footsteps into the army but, instead, Cadet, Malay States Civil Service: 1883. Early service in Perak, for a time as private secretary to Hugh Low, and Pahang, and other duties. Governor of North Borneo and Labuan: 1899 – 1901. British Resident, Pahang: 1901. Colonial Secretary, Trinidad and Tobago: September 1903. Colonial Secretary, Ceylon: 3 May 1907. KCMG: 1909. Governor, Gold Coast: 11 December 1912. Governor of Nigeria: 23 July 1919. GCMG: 1921. GBE: 1925. Governor of Ceylon: 1925 – 1927. Governor of the Straits Settlements: 3 June 1927 – 5 February 1930. Author of a number of publications. *Colonial Office List. Who's Who.* Stephanie Williams, *Running the Show,* (London, 2011) – see her chapter seventeen for entertaining biographical anecdotes.

   Captain George Astley Callaghan (1852-1920), later Admiral of the Fleet.

61. *Straits Settlements Government Gazette,* Thursday, 19 April 1900. NA ADM 1/7455.

62. Frank Athelstane **Swettenham**. Born: 28 March 1850. Died in London: 11 June 1946. Dollar Academy and St. Peter's School, York. Cadet, Straits Settlements: July 1870. Spent his working life in Malaya. He was in Perak when the British resident, Mr. James W.W. Birch, was murdered in November 1875. Greatly assisted the British authorities in restoring law and order (see Ryder, C. in C., 1874). British Resident, Selangor: September 1882. Acting British Resident, Perak: March 1884-January 1886. British Resident, Perak, in succession to Sir Hugh Low: 1889. Resident General, Malay States: January 1896. KCMG: 1897. Following his time in office as Governor, he retired in 1904. GCMG: 1909. Chairman, Royal Commission on Mauritius: 1909. CH: 1919. *Colonial Office List.* Obituary, *The Times,* 13 June 1946.

   James Alexander **Swettenham**. Elder brother of Frank Athelstane. Born: 1846. Died: 19 April 1933. Clare College, Cambridge: scholarship May 1867. Ceylon Civil Service: 1868-1883 when appointed Receiver General, Cyprus. Returned to Ceylon as Auditor General: 1891-1895. Colonial Secretary, Straits Settlements: 1895 and where, from time to time, acting Governor. KCMG: 1898. Governor, British Guiana: 1901-1904. Governor of Jamaica: 1904-1907. *Colonial Office List. Who's Who.*

63. Stuart, 244/5.

64. Ibid. 250.

65. *Harry Keppel,* 186.

66. *Dictionary of National Biography,* 394.

67. With kind assistance received from both Ms. Diura Stobart of Bracknell Heritage, and The Rev. Catherine Blundell, Vicar. Visited by the author on Thursday, 17 June 2010.

17 July 1869 to 30 August 1871
Vice Admiral Sir Henry **Kellett**

Born on 2 November 1806, son of John Dalton Kellett of Clonacody, Co. Tipperary, Ireland. Died at Clonacody House, near Clonmel, on Monday, 1 March 1875 at 23:00 hours. Interred at Fethard on Thursday, 4 March 1875.

He entered the Royal Navy on 7 January 1822. From 1823 to 1826 served in sloop *Ringdove*, 18 guns, Commander Edwin Ludlow Rich, West Indies. Later in 1826:-

'... having accompanied a body of troops to Lisbon in *Gloucester*, 74, he joined *Eden*, 26, Captain William Fitzwilliam Owen, under whom he was employed on the coast of Africa for the colonization of Fernando Po, until his return to England in the summer of 1831. He had command during part of that time of the *Cornelia* tender, and was onboard the *Eden* at a period of dreadful sickness, when 46 men were laid up with fever without a surgeon, and only two officers besides himself were left to perform duty (1).'

Lieutenant: 15 September 1828. Continued to serve in *Eden*. From 7 November 1831 appointed to the surveying vessel ship *Aetna*, 6, Coast of Africa, Commander Edward Belcher, in which ship he was to begin to make his name as an hydrographer. From 24 December 1833, as acting Lieut. and Commander, in surveying vessel *Raven*, 4, Coast of Africa.

From 29 October 1835 Lieut. and Commander cutter *Starling*, surveying vessel and sister ship to *Raven*, South America. He was to remain in her for some seven years so it is worth noting her size, a minute 108 tons builders' measurement, 61' loa (length overall) and 20.5' beam. These dimensions will have resulted in her being a slow sailer, not to mention the cramped conditions which will have prevailed onboard. In company with *Sulphur*, Captain Frederick William Beechey (1796 – 1856), he sailed from Portsmouth on 24 December 1835. Survey work on the West coast of the Americas was to follow. However from Valparaiso in mid 1836 Captain Beechey was invalided home so, from Friday, 1 July 1836 at Valparaiso to Monday, 13 February 1837 at Panama, he commanded *Sulphur*. Edward Belcher had been ordered out to replace Beechey and upon him arriving to assume command of *Sulphur* Lieut. Kellett reverted to *Starling*. Usually in company with *Sulphur*, during the next few years *Starling* was to carry out many surveys on the coasts of California and northwest to Russian America (Alaska). Additionally work was undertaken across to the Sandwich Islands where, to take one example, on 27 July 1837 the two ships sailed from Hanalei Bay on the north coast of Kauai.

It was only some fifty nine years earlier, with Captain James Cook's arrival at Waimea, Kauai on 19 January 1778, that the group first had been visited by Europeans.

From the Sandwich Islands during that summer of 1837 the ships continued to Alaskan waters, in August *Sulphur* reaching Port Etches, the northernmost point attained that year. Belcher then turned in a southerly direction and on 5 September he was fortunate enough to obtain a marvellous clear view of Mount St. Elias, 18,008', a short while later coming up with *Starling* (2). In company the two ships continued to the south, in due course entering San Francisco Bay.

Vice Admiral Sir Henry Kellett, C. in C., 1869

Prior to entering the Bay, as they passed Cape Reyes some thirty miles to the northwest of Golden Gate, they were within just a few miles of Drake's Cove within Drake's Estero where, in July 1579 Francis Drake had careened and repaired *Golden Hind* (3).

While in the Bay, on 24 October 1837, members of a small party set off in *Starling* and proceeded some thirty six miles up the Sacramento River, thereafter continuing up the stream in small boats.

Subsequently both ships returned to the waters of Central America.

Having served with him previously Captain Belcher knew the young Lieutenant commanding *Starling* well, and it is clear held him in considerable regard. Two quotations follow:-

'... from Kellett's sanguine temperament ...'

'But trusting the tried caution of Kellett, I felt easier for the *Starling* than if she had been in other hands (4).'

Further work in 1839 included his survey of the bar and entrance to the Columbia River, the border between the present day Washington and Oregon States, the passage across the bar always being a tedious navigational feature (5).

In 1840 he proceeded across the Pacific via the Marquesas, Tahiti, New Hebrides, Solomon Islands and Borneo to China where *Starling* arrived in December 1840 (6). Actively involved during actions against the Chinese such as on 7 January 1841 at the Bogue forts at Chuenpi guarding the head of the estuary of the Pearl River leading up to Canton. As may be seen these efforts were much appreciated:-

'... on 26 February acquired the thanks of Commodore Sir (James) Gordon Bremer for his gallantry and zeal in the action which preceded the capture of the forts at the Boca Tigris (7).'

Again in March 1841 during operations towards Canton itself:-

'... he acquired every favourable consideration for his useful exertions in sounding, cojointly with Lieut. Richard Collinson and Mr. Richard Browne, Master of *Calliope*, the various inlets through which the ships had to pass, and conducting them in safety to an anchorage off that city. In the discharge of these duties Mr. Kellett was indeed indefatigable. At one period, in addition to his own vessel, *Algerine*, and *Young Hebe* and *Louisa* tenders, were simultaneously placed under his orders (8).'

Commander: 6 May 1841. Continued in command of the diminutive *Starling*, now rated sloop. Later in May 1841, '... again found opportunity of distinction,' being much involved with the sounding of safe channels in the approaches to Canton prior to the assault of the city which was captured on 27 May.

The next year, prior to the capture of Chapu on 18 May 1842, again active in the successful survey of those shallow waters so enabling warships of the fleet to close that town in Chekiang Province.

Much of this survey work was carried out in conjunction with *Plover*, Commander Richard Collinson, with whom, again, he was most involved in surveying the passage up the River Yangtse thus enabling the British fleet to proceed upstream prior to the signing of the Treaty of Nanking in *Cornwallis* on Monday, 29 August 1842.

The C. in C. at the time of the successful operation up the Yangtse as far as Nanking was Vice Admiral Sir William Parker (1781-1866), later to be Admiral of the Fleet. The British Plenipotentiary was Sir Henry Pottinger (1789-1856).

Captain: 23 December 1842.

CB: 24 December 1842.

While on passage down the coast towards Hong Kong, together with Richard Collinson responsible for the early detailed survey of Amoy and approaches, especially in the vicinity of Kulangsu, from which in due course Admiralty chart number 1767 was to be prepared.

Returned to England in the summer of 1843.

From 8 February 1845 appointed in command surveying vessel *Herald*, 26 guns, Pacific Station. At Chatham on 19 May 1845 present during the departure down the River Thames of Sir John Franklin in the

Arctic discovery vessel, just recently fitted with auxiliary screw steam propulsion, *Erebus*, with the similarly fitted *Terror* in company. The two were small ships, just 105' and 102' in length respectively. This occasion marked the commencement of Sir John's ill fated North West Passage expedition (9).

Herald left England on 26 June 1845. As was normal he proceeded via Teneriffe, Rio de Janeiro, the Falkland Islands, around Cape Horn and passed Diego Ramirez on 14/15 October, touched at ports in Chile, and finally arrived at Valparaiso on 14 November 1845, some nine months after his appointment to the ship. More hydrographic work followed, in particular along the coast of Colombia and Ecuador between Guayaquil and Panama, but including surveys made in 1846 of the waters of the port of Victoria, Vancouver Island, and other waterways in the vicinity. The need for this latter work arose over the possibility of war with the U.S.A. concerning the question of the Oregon territory (10). Happily by the Oregon Treaty of 15 June 1846 the boundary between British North America and the United States to a great extent was resolved. The summers of 1848, 1849 and 1850 were spent in Arctic waters north of the Bering Strait in the search for Sir John Franklin. Astonishingly, in 1849 at Chamisso Island a party from the ship found and recovered a cask of flour which had been buried on 13 October 1826 by Captain Frederick William Beechey, sloop *Blossom*, in case the flour was required by Franklin during his earlier overland expedition of 1825-1827. With *Plover* and *Nancy Dawson* in company Kellett used this flour to have pies and puddings made for a dinner he gave to the officers of the three ships (11). On 17 August 1849, in about 71.30N 176W, discovered and named Herald Island lying to the East of Wrangel Island (12). Also see Kellett Strait between Melville and Eglinton Islands, North West Territories, and Cape Kellett, SW Banks Island.

In his absence, but placed on his record on 7 November 1849, was a personal commendation from the Board of the Admiralty noting his great zeal and activity (13).

On 31 July 1850 off Cape Lisburne in present day Alaska he came up with the Arctic discovery ship *Investigator*, Commander Robert McClure, on passage towards the western entrance to the NW Passage.

Brought *Herald* home via Singapore and the Cape, arriving in England early during the summer of 1851, anchoring in Spithead on 6 June, and so completing a circumnavigation.

From 10 February 1852 to 1854 in Discovery Ship *Resolute*, 2 guns, again participated in the search for Franklin, on this occasion entering the North West Passage from the East. In Arctic waters during April/June 1853 found, and rescued, Captain Robert McClure and the surviving members of the ship's company, HMS *Investigator* (14). The small rescue party, which he despatched from *Resolute* and which on Wednesday, 6 April 1853 first came up with *Investigator*, stranded in Mercy Bay, Banks Island, was led by Lieut. Bedford Clapperton Trevelyan Pim (1826-1886).

During this Arctic expedition the tender in company with *Resolute* was *Intrepid*, Commander Francis L. McClintock (1819-1907), subsequently to be elected FRS, and to be promoted Admiral.

Also during the less inclement months of 1853 on Dealy Island, off the south coast of Melville Island, he ordered the construction of a storehouse cache in which were placed fuel and supplies sufficient to sustain sixty six men for seven months (15).

The abandonment of *Investigator*, which took place on 3 June 1853, was to have an unexpectedly positive outcome:-

> '…groups of Copper Inuit from western Victoria Island appear to have discovered the ship and for a period of thirty years or more they regularly visited the spot to salvage the large quantities of metal, wood and other goods available (16).'

This expedition of 1852/1854 was led by an officer under whom he had served previously, Captain Sir Edward Belcher. Unfortunately over the years Belcher had tended to become increasingly irascible and now during the early summer of 1854, in contrast to opinions expressed by a number of his officers, including Kellett, he perceived a number of his ships to be iced in. Consequently on 15 May 1854 Sir Edward ordered *Resolute* to be abandoned. Together with members of the companies of other ships in close company Henry Kellett travelled over the ice to Beechey Island then returned home in transports attached to the expedition, including *North Star*, Commander William J.S. Pullen, reaching Cork on 28 September 1854. From there Belcher, Kellett and McClure continued to London by rail.

Subsequently *Resolute* floated clear of the ice, and on 16 September 1855 was salvaged by Captain James M. Buddington (1817-1908) of the American whaler *George Henry*. In due course she was refitted and returned to Great Britain as a gift from the government of the U.S.A., returning to anchor at Spithead on 12 December 1856. Later she was broken up. A desk then was constructed from her timbers and in 1880 shipped to Washington, DC, '... for ceremonial presentation to (President) Mr. Hayes' (17).

As **Commodore**, from 3 August 1855 in the screw steam frigate *Termagent*, 24, served as second in command North America and West Indies Station and Senior Officer, West Indies.

A GSP (Good Service Pension) was awarded to him on 26 February 1857.

From 16 March 1857 Commodore, Jamaica in the Receiving Ship *Imaum*, 72.

Early in 1859 there was some excitement locally on the occasion of yet more domestic trouble in Haiti. Since independence in 1804 the wretchedly poor country had undergone the ordeal of a sequence of many rulers. On this occasion 'emperor for life' Soulouque was overthrown by one of his generals. Fortunately this new dictator would seem to have assumed power with a minimum of bloodshed:-

'I am glad to find that Commodore Kellett has sent you direct a duplicate of his letter of 26 January 1859 by which Their Lordships will be informed of all the leading facts connected with the abdication of the Emperor Soulouque of Hayti, and the establishment of a Republic under the Presidency of General (Fabre) Geffrard (18).'

In the West Indies he had not enjoyed the best of health, on at least one occasion, 'suffering from an attack of Fever', consequently one can imagine that it was with considerable pleasure that he returned to England during the summer of 1860. On his departure he, 'received from the merchants of Jamaica a handsome service of plate in recognition of their estimation of his character (19).' In addition he had got on well with the Colonial authorities on the island. As was to be noted on his record in due course:-

'13 August 1860. Foreign Office enclosing the thanks of the Governor of Jamaica for Captain Kellett's cordial co-operation with him (20).'

Rear Admiral: 16 June 1862.

From 26 November 1864 appointed Admiral Superintendent, Malta Dockyard with his flag in *Hibernia*, 104 guns. She had been launched in 1804, and in 1855 had become guard and receiving ship at Malta. There finally to be sold on 14 October 1902, a service life of ninety eight years.

Led the party of senior Navy and Army officers on the occasion of the opening of the Royal Opera House, Valetta on 9 October 1866.

Vice Admiral: 8 April 1868.

On the news of his promotion being received he left the Mediterranean, striking has flag at Venice on 10 June, and arriving back in England on 27 June 1868.

KCB: 2 June 1869.

To take up his command in the Far East his arrival at Singapore was recorded in the log book of the sloop *Rinaldo*, 951 tons, Commander Frederick Charles Bryan Robinson:-

'Wednesday, 15 September 1869

8.0 a.m. Arrived P. & O. Mail steamer with Red Ensign at the Fore.

9.0 a.m. Hoisted the Flag of Sir H. Kellett, KCB at the Fore and saluted with 17 guns (21).'

He embarked in *Rinaldo* at 11.40 a.m. on Saturday, 18 September and within the hour she weighed and proceeded to Hong Kong. Macclesfield Bank was passed on 26 September and she arrived at Hong Kong and 'came to in 7 fm.' at 3.50 p.m. on Sunday, 3 October 1869.

During the morning of Saturday, 23 October his predecessor, Admiral Sir H. Keppel, arrived in *Salamis*, and there at Hong Kong on 24 October 1869 from him he assumed command of the Station.

The new C. in C. flew his flag in the armour plated screw ship *Ocean*, 24 guns, 6,535 tons, Captain Chandos S.S. Stanhope. From 10 May 1870, when the ship re-commissioned, her Captain was William N.W. Hewett, VC (22), and her Commander, John A. Fisher (23).

During the change of command ceremonies at Hong Kong *Galatea* had been in port.

Subsequently the Sir Henry was to inform the Admiralty:-

'Captain HRH The Duke of Edinburgh left Hong Kong in *Galatea* for Manila and Singapore on 16th inst. after a stay of 16 days, during which the greatest loyalty and enthusiasm was evinced towards him by all classes of society (24).'

The Suez Canal opened on 17 November 1869. This event signalled the commencement of an era of greatly increased European, especially British, mercantile and steam ship owning activity to, from and in the Far East. A variety of examples follow.

Singapore in particular assumed a strategic and dominating position in the trade between Europe and the Pacific. In 1870, which was the first full year of Suez Canal operations, trade at Singapore stood at $70.7 million but by 1890 it had reached $206.7 million (25).

As already noted, having commenced their China service with the sailing of *Agamemnon* from Liverpool on 19 April 1866, in just nine years so by 1875, Alfred Holt's Ocean Steam Ship Company possessed a fleet of fourteen steamers. To illustrate the improved cargo capacity and productivity of these new steamers one authority reminds us:-

'Compared with the famous clipper ships, sailing home from the China coast with approximately 1,000 tons of cargo in a time of 120 to 130 days, the Holt ships with a capacity of 3,000 tons were scheduled to take 77 days on the homeward voyage.

(--) The passage through the Canal reduced the distance by as much as 3,000 miles and thereby cut the sailing time down by (a further) 10-12 days (26).'

In 1867 the German full rigged ship *Etha Rickmers*, 1,160 grt, had carried a large shipment of tea from Shanghai to New York, and the following year the Rickmers barque, *Dr. Petermann*, 750 grt, brought a cargo of tea from Shanghai and Foochow to London at a rate of GBP 4.17.6 per ton. By the turn of the century Rickmers interests were to have expanded considerably in the East including, and together with Norddeutscher Lloyd, the operation of steamers on the Yangtse.

The British Butterfield & Swire organisation was established in Shanghai on 1 January 1867. Their China Navigation Company of coastal and river steamers was to be formed in 1872 in London, with their first two ships being the paddle steamers *Tunsin*, 774 grt, and *Glengyle*, 1,933 grt.

Jardine Matheson & Company, active in a variety of steam shipping interests ever since the short lived venture with *Larriston* in 1852, in the East on 26 October 1872 floated the China Coast Steam Navigation Company, promptly taking up 64% of the shares themselves. Later, in London at the end of 1881 and under the Chairmanship of William Keswick (1834-1912) himself, they formed the Indo-China S.N. Co. Ltd and from 1 February 1882 were to be managing that fleet of twelve ships. One of the first directors of Indo-China was James McGregor, then senior partner of McGregor, Gow & Co., operators of the Glen Line of steamers to the Far East. Even after 1935, with the rescue by Alfred Holt and Company of Glen Line from the Kylsant debacle, Jardine's were to continue to represent Glen Line in, for example, Hong Kong.

7 January 1870: arrival at Nagasaki of the Aberdeen built warship *Jho-Sho Maru,* ordered through Thomas Glover connections by the Higo han (27). In a ceremony on 7 April she was to be handed over to her owners. In turn in May the Daimio would pass her on to the newly formed Imperial Japanese Navy, IJN, by whom she was to be re-named *Ryujo*, a training ship. Similarly during the spring and summer of 1870 nine other Satsuma, Choshu and Hizen/Saga han warships were to be presented to the IJN of the Meiji government. Naturally these gifts were not made without the respective Daimio having their own best interests in mind, "... they donated ships to strengthen the regime and to assure themselves continued influence within it (28)".

In *Jho-Sho Maru* from Aberdeen on 14 August 1869 retired Royal Marine Lieutenant Albert George Sidney Hawes had taken passage to Japan (29).

11 February 1870: opening of the Imperial Japanese Navy Academy at Tsukiji, Tokyo. Two days earlier, but still under the overall auspices of the Army, the Navy had gained a degree of administrative independence under the Satsuma leader Kawamura Sumiyoshi (1836-1904).

1870: foundation by Iwasaki Yataro of the Tosa 'han' of the shipping company Tsukumo Shokai. Also see N.Y.K., the Nippon Yusen Kaisha, to be founded on 1 October 1885, of which the well known steamship company Tsukumo Shokai was a forerunner.

April 1870: Visit to Yedo Bay by a 'Particular Service' Squadron of six warships under the command of Rear Admiral Geoffrey Thomas Phipps Hornby, flag in screw frigate *Liverpool*, 30 guns, 2,656 tons, Captain John O. Hopkins. At the request of Sir Harry Parkes, and intended to positively influence naval opinion in the capital, a party of senior and influential Japanese was invited onboard to witness displays of gunnery drill, target practice, and other evolutions.

12 December 1870. The future Admiral Togo Heihachiro of the Satsuma 'han' was ordered to the training ship *Ryujo* as a cadet officer.

At Versailles in France on 18 January 1871 Kaiser Wilhelm I (1797-1888) was crowned German Emperor thus first marking the union of Germany under Prussian leadership. This event took place during the Franco-Prussian war, just ten days before Paris fell to the besieging forces. The German Imperial Admiralty was to be created on 1 January 1872.
A Sub Lieutenant at the time, on 25 May 1872 Alfred von Tirptiz was to be promoted Lieutenant.

Following the completion of the sector between Singapore and Hong Kong, on 10 June 1871 the C. in C. advised the Admiralty that telegraphic communications between Shanghai and London had been opened.
In the same letter he gave the dimensions of the newly opened drydock at Yokosuka in Yedo Bay (30). Largely constructed by the French under Francois Leonce Verny (1837-1908), from time to time in the future ships of the Royal Navy were to make use of the facility. The dock, naval arsenal and workshops had been opened publicly on 28 March 1871 (31).

With years of experience in China, dating back to the 1840's, from 22 July 1871 Thomas Francis Wade, (1818-1895), was appointed Minister to China (32). At Peking he succeeded Sir Rutherford Alcock (33).

In Japan by Imperial decree during the summer of 1871 the rights of the feudal 'han' daimyo were abolished to be replaced by 'ken', the beginning of the modern Prefectural system of domestic administration of the country.
The leaders of Japan who were responsible for this move were members of those 'han' who had been instrumental in the overthrow of the Tokugawa dynasty, namely Satsuma, Choshu, Tosa and Hizen (34).

Writing to London on 18 September 1871 he reported the sale of an interesting if rather small warship, 'Her Majesty's late ship *Malacca* has been sold to the Japanese government for about Sterling 13,000.'
This sloop, later to be designated a corvette, *Malacca*, 1,034 tons bm, had been launched at Moulmein, Burma in April 1853 but sequently completed in August 1854 at Chatham. Re-engined in 1862 after which she was capable of nine and a half knots. In 1869 she was sold out of the service, later, and as reported by the C. in C., being re-sold to the very young IJN to be their training ship *Tsukuba*. As such to become very well known, she was to remain in service until 1906 (35).

Admiral of the Fleet Marquis Togo Heihachiro, (1848-1934)

William Keswick, (1834-1912), of Messrs. Jardine, Matheson & Co.

Late in November 1871 *Ocean* sailed from Hong Kong homeward bound. While in China Admiral Kellett's health had been adversely affected. Extracts from a letter written by Commander Fisher on 28 November, on passage to Singapore, follow:-

> 'I have just been having a heavy lunch with the admiral. He knows I hate dinners; and so he asks me to lunch and always kills a turkey for the occasion. He certainly is most kind to me. I do pity the old gentleman very much (--) and he is now completely broken down in mind and body and everything else. I sometimes doubt his ever reaching home (36).'

While on the stocks, commencing in June 1861, *Ocean* had been been converted to become an ironclad. Later in life, and in colourful terms, Fisher was to describe the condition of the ship as she existed in 1871:-

> 'She was an old wooden Line of Battleship that had armour bolted on her sides. When we got into heavy weather, the timbers of the ship would open when she heeled over one way, and shut together when she heeled the other, and squirted the water inboard! And always we had many fountains playing in the bottom of the ship from leaks, some quite high (37).'

On completion of his term of office in China Sir Henry left *Ocean* at Singapore to return to England in the P. & O. s.s. *Orissa*, 1,647 grt.

These precise details were recorded in the log book of *Iron Duke*:-

> 'Saturday, 16 December 1871. At Singapore.
> 8.00 a.m. Hoisted Vice Admiral CFA Shadwell's Flag at the Fore as Commander in Chief of China Station.
> Wednesday, 20 December 1871. At Singapore.
> 2.30 p.m. Sailed P. & O. Steamer *Orissa* having onboard Sir H. Kellett late Commander in Chief. Manned rigging and cheered ditto.
> HMS *Ocean* saluted with 15 guns (38).'

Ocean herself reached Plymouth early in June and paid off at Devonport on 22 June 1872.

The Admiral had returned to England rather earlier. Once he had completed outstanding business he retired to his home in Ireland. Unfortunately, and as mentioned above, he had returned from China, 'much debilitated in constitution from the effects of the climate (39).'

On the sad occasion of his death in March 1875 the local press included in their report:-

'His very many friends – and they were numerous and sincerely attached ones – will learn with deep regret of the death of this distinguished naval officer, and most courteous Irish gentleman, which sad event took place at his residence, Clonacody House, in this county, last Monday night. After a lengthened, gallant, and honorable career, the genial, truly fine old Admiral spent the closing years of his life at home, winning from all with whom he came in contact respect, honor and affectionate regard (40).'

Later in 1875 another obituary was published by the Royal Geographical Society. An extract follows:-

'In Henry Kellett we have an admirable example of the scientific officer of our Naval service: a man who combined skill, indomitable energy and seamanship, with frank boldness. It is by such men, working for years laboriously and unostentatiously, and, it is to be feared, but little appreciated beyond the walls of this Society, that the great additions have been made to our nautical knowledge of the world, by which geographical science has been advanced, and ocean navigation made more secure. And it is by the proper use of such men on our Naval and military expeditions that advantages are reaped, in some respects more lasting and beneficial than many of those obtained by the direct force of arms (41).'

Although of greater academic inclination, his successor on the China Station was another man cast from a similar mould.

NOTES

1. L.S. Dawson, *Memoirs of Hydrography,* (London, 1885), Vol. II, 36/7.
2. Ed. R.A. Pierce and J.H. Winslow, *H.M.S. Sulphur on the Northwest and Californian Coasts, 1837 and 1839,* (Kingston, Ontario, 1979), 86/7. Port Etches, Alaska lies at 60.20N 146.33W. Mount St. Elias was sighted by Vitus Bering himself on 16 July 1741. Peter Lauridsen, *Vitus Bering,* (New York, 1969), 140/1. The peak lies on the present day Alaska/ Yukon border.
3. Raymond Aker and Edward Von der Porten, *Discovering Francis Drake's Californian Harbor,* (Palo Alto, CA., 2000). Paper read by Edward Von der Porten on Thursday, 13 August 2009, at Victoria, BC: Canadian Nautical Research Society, Annual Conference.
4. Pierce and Winslow, 12 and 17. Belcher had the reputation of being short tempered and so one can imagine that such praise was not easy to earn.
5. Robin Inglis, *Historical Dictionary: Northwest Coast of America,* (Lanham, MD., 2008), 171.
6. O'Byrne, 601. Also see John Dunmore, *Who's Who in Pacific Navigation,* (Hawaii, 1991), 137/8.
7. Dawson, 36.
8. O'Byrne. Also see Gerald S. Graham, *The China Station,* (OUP, 1978), 156.
9. G.S. Ritchie, *The Admiralty Chart,* (Bishop Auckland, 1995), 279. Sir John died near King William Island on 11 June 1847.
10. Barry M. Gough, *The Royal Navy and the Northwest Coast of North America, 1810-1914,* (Vancouver, 1971), 104. A geographical feature on the west coast of Henry Island in the Haro Strait is Kellett Bluff.
11. Ritchie, 282. Ed. Barry M. Gough, *To the Pacific and Arctic with Beechey,* (Hakluyt Society, 1973), 150. *Plover* was a merchant vessel, *Lady William Bentinck,* purchased in 1842 and subsequently strengthened and fitted out for Arctic

exploration work where used as a storeship. David Lyon and Rif Winfield, *The Sail and Steam Navy List*, (London, 2004), 141.

12. John C. Welch, *John Goodridge – Naval Surgeon*, (Mariner's Mirror, Vol. 90, November 2004), 469.

13. NA ADM 196/36, 743. *Record of Service*.

14. Robert John LeMesurier **McClure**. Born: 28 January 1807. Died: 17 October 1873. Having entered Arctic waters from the west through the Beaufort Sea and, following his rescue from *Investigator* in Mercy Bay, Banks Island in the summer of 1853, and his subsequent departure from those waters through eastern channels such as Lancaster Sound and Baffin Bay, he was to be credited with the first transit of the North West Passage. As one result of this achievement to be knighted in 1854. Ann Savours, *The Search for the North West Passage*, (London, 1999), 229. James P. Delgado, *Across the Top of the World*, (New York, 1999), 130, 140.

There exists evidence that in fact McClure was something of a self seeker, 'ambitious and none too scrupulous'. In contrast, over the questions both of the entrance by *Investigator* into Arctic waters in July/August 1850, and of the rescue of her company in April 1853, Kellett emerged with his reputation enhanced. L.H. Neatby, *Arctic Profiles*, (University of Calgary, ASTIS 32861), 234/5.

On 25 July 2010 an archaeological team despatched by Parks, Canada found the hulk of *Investigator* in thirty six feet of water in Mercy Bay. "You could make out all the planking on the deck, the details on the hull, all the detail of the timber. It's sitting perfectly upright on the floor of the ocean". USNI, Annapolis, *Naval History*, Oct. 2010, 67.

15. In 1978 declared by the Canadian authorities to be a Site of Territorial Historic Significance. Prince of Wales Northern Heritage Centre, Yellowknife. Dealy Island is at 74.57N 108.43W.

16. Clifford G. Hickey and James M. Savelle, *The Mariner's Mirror*, Vol. 68, 1982. 78.

17. Ann Savours, *The Mariner's Mirror*, Vol. 66, 1980. 73. Rutherford Birchard Hayes (1822-1893). From 1877 –1881 the nineteenth President of the U.S.A. A Republican.

Resolute was broken up at Chatham during the summer of 1879. From her timbers Messrs. Morant, Boyd and Blandford of 91, New Bond Street, London manufactured the desk, 6' by 4' in size, at a cost of Sterling Pounds 300. Ritchie, 290*.

18. NA ADM 1/5710. In Haiti between 1834 and 1915 some twenty rulers held power of whom sixteen either were assassinated or overthrown. *Encyclopaedia Britannica*.

19. Dawson, 37.

20. NA ADM 196/36. Between 1857 and 1862 the Governor of Jamaica was Charles Henry **Darling** (1809-1870). RMA, Sandhurst but as an Army Captain retired in 1841. Lieut. Governor of St. Lucia: 1847. Governor, Cape Colony: 1851, and of Newfoundland: 1855. KCB: 1862. Governor, Victoria, Australia: 1863-1866. *Colonial Office List*. Sir Charles was a nephew of an earlier less well known colonial figure, the controversial Sir Ralph Darling (1772-1858).

21. NA ADM 53/9616. Unfortunately the name of the P. & O. steamer is not recorded.

22. William Nathan Wrighte **Hewett**. Born in Brighton: 12 August 1834. Died in Portsmouth: 13 May 1888. Entered the RN: 26 March 1847. For services rendered when serving with the Naval Brigade on 26 October 1854 before Sevastopol in the Crimea, his Victoria Cross was gazetted: 24 February 1857. Captain: 24 November 1862. On the China Station commanded *Basilisk*: 1865-1869. Commodore, Cape of Good Hope and West Coast of Africa Station: October 1873 – October 1876. During the second Ashanti War on 14 November 1873 assumed command of the Naval Brigade from Captain Edmund Robert Fremantle (see C. in C., 1892). For services in West Africa, KCB: 31 March 1874. Rear Admiral: 21 March 1878. C. in C., East Indies: April 1882 – May 1885. Vice Admiral: 8 July 1884. *Navy List*. Clowes, Vol. VII, 259/262. Hewett had been the senior Midshipman in *Spartan* with Edmund Fremantle in 1852. Today his Victoria Cross is held at the National Maritime Museum, Greenwich.

23. John Arbuthnot **Fisher**. Born in Ceylon (Sri Lanka): 25 January 1841. Died in London: 10 July 1920. Joined the Royal Navy at Portsmouth, in *Victory*: 12 June 1854. Captain: 30 October 1874. Rear Admiral: 2 August 1890. KCB: 26 May 1894. Vice Admiral: 8 May 1896. Admiral: 2 November 1901. GCB: 26 June 1902. First Sea Lord: 20 October 1904 – January 1910. OM: 30 June 1905. Admiral of the Fleet: 4 December 1905. Created Baron Fisher of Kilverstone: 9 November 1909. First Sea Lord: 29 October 1914 – May 1915. President of the Board of Invention and Research: 1915-1918. *Navy List*. *Who's Who*. Two more recent biographies include Richard Hough, *First Sea Lord*, (London, 1969) and Ruddock F. Mackay, *Fisher of Kilverstone*, (OUP, 1973). Concerning China it is Richard Hough, page 35, who quotes

from Lord Fisher looking into the future:-

"When by-and-by the Chinese know their power", he wrote at the age of seventy eight, "they have only to walk slowly westwards and, like the locusts in Egypt, no Pharaohs in Europe with all their mighty boats will stop them. They won't want to fire guns or bombs. They'll just all walk along and smother Europe."

Following his death then down The Mall, 'the great funeral procession and service in Westminster Abbey took place three days later.' *First Sea Lord*, 358. His body next was cremated and his ashes subsequently buried adjacent to his wife's grave, St. Andrew's churchyard, Kilverstone.

24. NA ADM 1/6095. No. 50, *Salamis* at Hong Kong, 29 November 1869.

25. Francis E. Hyde, *Far Eastern Trade: 1860-1914*, (London, 1973), 17. K.G. Tregonning, *Home Port Singapore*, (Singapore, 1967), 5/6.

26. Francis E. Hyde, *Blue Funnel*, (Liverpool, 1957), 24.

27. *Ryujo*, a warship of historical note, built in Aberdeen by Messrs. Alexander Hall & Co. Ltd., Yard No. 261, as *Jho-Sho Maru*, a wood screw steamer, barque rigged, of 1,459 grt. Her length was 207.7', breadth 38.5', and depth of hold 30.2'. Messrs. Hall, Russell & Co. supplied her 280 h.p. engines. Her contract price was GBP 46,032. A file is held in the Aberdeen City archives, *Vol. 29 No. HR/1/5/1*, from which it may be noted that she was constructed, '... for the Japanese Navy per Glover Bros., Aberdeen'. Additional data is held at the Aberdeen Maritime Museum. Here it may be noted that her armour belt was 5' in width of 4.5" of iron, outcoat to 6" of teakwood. Her propeller was of brass and could be raised or lowered as required.

28. David Chris Evans, *The Satsuma Faction and Professionalism in the Japanese Naval Officer Corps of the Meiji Period, 1858-1912*, (Stanford, 1978), 48.

29. Albert George Sidney **Hawes**: for career detail see King, C. in C., 1865, reference (15).

30. NA ADM 1/6191.

31. John R. Black, *Young Japan*, (London, 1881), Vol. II, 301.

32. Thomas Francis **Wade**: for career detail see Ryder, C. in C., 1874, reference (44).

33. Rutherford **Alcock**: for career detail see Kuper, C. in C., 1862, reference (66).

34. Tsuzuki Chushichi, *The Pursuit of Power in Modern Japan, 1825-1995*, (OUP, 2000), 63.

35. David Lyon and Rif Winfield, *The Sail and Steam Navy List*, (London, 2004), 213.

36. Admiral Sir R.H. Bacon, *The Life of Lord Fisher of Kilverstone*, Vol. 1 (London, 1929), 43/4.

37. Lord Fisher, *Memories*, (London, 1919), 153/4.

38. NA ADM 53/10352.

39. Dawson, 37.

40. Obituary extract, *Tipperary Free Press*, 5 March 1875. Courtesy Ms Franci Carew.

41. *Journal of the Royal Geographical Society*, Vol. 45: 1875. cxliv/cxlv.

30 August 1871 to 31 August 1874
Acting Vice Admiral Charles Frederick Alexander

Shadwell, FRS.

Born on 31 January 1814, the fourth son of Sir Lancelot Shadwell, last vice-chancellor of England (1779-1850), and his wife Harriet, daughter of Anthony Richardson, merchant of London (1).

He died at 'Meadowbank', Whitley, Melksham on Monday, 1 March 1886.

Educated at the Royal Naval College. Entered the Royal Navy on 3 May 1827. **Lieutenant**: 28 June 1838. From 26 July 1838 in the Chatham built frigate *Castor*, 36 guns, 1,808 tons, Captain Edward Collier, Mediterranean. Present during operations on the coast of Syria against the towns of Caiffa, Jaffa and Tsour, also participated in the bombardment of Acre, then occupied by Egyptians: 3 November 1840. 'At Caiffa he was sent with a flag of truce to demand the surrender of that place to the Sublime Porte (2)'. Off Acre the attacking forces included Austrian and Turkish men of war. Success came in spectacular fashion:-

> 'A most frightful explosion then flung half the town into the air, and shook every ship to her keel, the concussion knocking down the seamen at their guns half a mile away. The grand magazine had blown up, killing, it is believed, upwards of 1,200 people, and absolutely wrecking a space of about 60,000 sq. yds. (3)'.

From 3 December 1841 First Lieutenant in surveying vessel, *Fly*, 18 guns, 485 tons builders measurement, Captain Francis Price Blackwood (1809-1854), East Indies. At the time the Hydrographer of the Navy was Francis Beaufort (1774-1857) who conceived of the science of surveying in a wider sense, also to include, for example, subjects such as natural history, geography and ethnography. So it was that also serving in *Fly* were Joseph Beete Jukes (1811-1869), geologist, John MacGillivray (1821-1867), zoologist, and Harden Sidney Melville (1824-1894), artist. With the cutter *Bramble*, 161 tons, Lieut. Charles Bampfield Yule, in company, the two ships left Falmouth on 11 April 1942. In due course they were to carry out a survey of the waters of the Torres Strait and of parts of the north eastern coasts of Australia, an extraordinarily thorough and comprehensive achievement:-

> 'In the four years Captain Blackwood was thus employed, more than 1,000 miles of sea in length, and 170 in breadth, were surveyed and charted – from Sandy Cape on the east coast of Australia, as far as Latitude 21 deg. S, including the Capricorn Islands, Swain Reefs, and the broad passages between them, a tract of 200 miles in length and 100 miles in breadth; the survey of the coast of the mainland and the adjacent sea, from West Hill to the northern part of Whit-Sunday passage, a distance of 100 miles; the outer line of the Great Barrier Reef from 16.40 S, to its northern limits in 9.20 S, a distance of nearly 500 miles; the survey of Endeavour Strait and of the eastern portion of Torres Strait, from Cape York to the coast of New Guinea, with more than 140 miles of the latter coast, together with the numerous off-lying dangers and wide spread banks of shoal soundings, and the mouths of the numerous rivers and fresh water channels which intersect those shores in

every direction. To mark the most advantageous channel for vessels to pass through the Barrier Chain, the Raine Island beacon was erected by him.

(-) With no anchorage near, and such material as lay at hand, the Tower Beacon was erected 70 feet in height, 30 feet in diameter, and with walls of 5 feet thickness (4).'

By now his reputation seemed well established:-

'Charles Frederick Alexander Shadwell, First Lieutenant in the *Fly*, was an officer whose high scientific attainments and pre-eminence as a navigator and observer were graced by amiable qualities which won the affection of all who served under him (5).'

Fly arrived back in England in February 1846 and paid off at Devonport on 4 July 1846 (6).

Commander: 27 June 1846.

He was, 'specially promoted for surveying service (7).'

'Studied for some time at the Royal Naval College, taking a certificate in 'steam', and devoting himself more especially to nautical astronomy (8).'

On 8 January 1847 elected a fellow of the Royal Astronomical Society (9).

From 2 February 1850 in command paddle wheel steam sloop, *Sphinx*, East Indies. In her participated in the Burmese war: 1852.

Amongst his activities:-

'Commander Shadwell, and the military post at Shouk Shay Khune, assisted by native allies, beat off a Burmese attack with great spirit (10).'

A few days later, on 19 November 1852, a military expedition left Rangoon to proceed upstream the short distance to Pegu:-

'... the naval arrangements being under Commander Shadwell. ... the rest of the troops were put ashore early on the 14th (of December), an advance followed immediately, and being accompanied by Shadwell, with two boat guns and 75 men to drag them. ... By proclamation of 30 December 1852 the province of Pegu was annexed to the Empire (11).'

This was the second war. Rangoon was captured and the annexation by Great Britain of Lower Burma was proclaimed in Rangoon on 20 December 1852.

For his services in Burma, on both 23 October and on 6 December 1852, he received the thanks of the Governor General in Council, Lord Dalhousie (12).

Captain: 7 February 1853.

From the date of his promotion, 'appointed acting Captain of *Winchester* (until) 26 September 1853, discharged to half pay (13).'

CB: 5 December 1853.

From 1 August 1856 to 2 January 1860 in command screw steam corvette *Highflyer*, 21, East Indies and China Station. In her he participated in the capture of Canton, 28-30 December 1857. At the time the acting British Consul at Canton was Harry S. Parkes.

Eighteen months later, during the repulse of the Allied forces at the Peiho in June 1859, severely wounded in an ankle, which rendered him permanently lame, hence his relief in January 1860 by acting Captain William Andrew James Heath as he had been invalided home.

Mentioned in despatches for 'his valuable assistance' (14).

There exists an entertaining account of him dressed for action against this Chinese foe:-

'I saw him go into battle with a tall white hat with a gold stripe on the side of it, a post-captain's uniform tail coat, a yellow waistcoat, white trousers, and a white umbrella which he used to cheer us on to attack the enemy, and we got there all right … He was knocked over and had to be sent home (15).'

During his time in *Highflyer* the future Lord Fisher was serving in the ship as a Midshipman (16). Two of his delightful stories may be recounted:-

'My Shadwell was about the greatest Saint on earth. The sailors called him, somewhat profanely, "Our Heavenly Father". He was once heard to say, "Damn," and the whole ship was upset.'

'… he went in mortal fear of his own steward, who bossed him utterly, he would say, "I think the aroma has rather gone out of this champagne. Give it to the young gentlemen (Midshipmen)". The steward would reply, "Now you know very well, Sir, the aroma ain't gone out of this 'ere champagne", but all the same we got it (17).'

Concerning Captain Shadwell and Fisher, writing in the year 2008 one leading naval historian was to give as his opinion:-

'On his next ship, *Highflyer*, Fisher met one of the navy's leading intellects, Captain Charles Shadwell, FRS. Serving on the China Station, Shadwell taught him navigation, astronomy and advanced mathematics. This was the making of Fisher, who had already displayed a fine intellect, outstanding powers of application, and a talent for exposition (18).'

His 'Pension for Wounds' was granted on 27 August 1860.

From 18 February 1861 in command screw steam ship *Aboukir*, 86 guns, 3,100 tons, Channel Squadron, then, following civil war and changes of government in Mexico, to the North America and West Indies Station.

Elected a Fellow of the Royal Society: 6 June 1861. At the time,when not at sea, he was resident at Slough, near Windsor.

Author of a number of books and pamphlets such as, *Tables for facilitating the approximate prediction of occultations and eclipses for any particular place*, 1847: *Tables for facilitating the determination of the latitude at sea by the simultaneous altitudes of two stars*, 1849: *Formulae of navigation and nautical astronomy*, 1856, and which was revised in 1869: *Tables for facilitating the reduction of lunar observations*, 1860: *Notes on the management of chronometers and the measurement of meridian distances*, 1861: *Notes on the reduction of lunar observations, mathematical and practical. Also various tables for facilitating the computations*, 1881.

Also he was a Fellow of the Royal Geographical Society.

From 8 October 1862 to June 1864 in command screw ship *Hastings*, 50 guns, 1,760 tons, Flagship, Queenstown (today Cork, Ireland), Rear Admiral Sir Lewis Tobias Jones.

Captain-Superintendent of the Royal Clarence Victualling Yard, Gosport, and of Haslar Hospital: from 20 June 1864 to 1 February 1869.

From the Yard correspondence of import is taken the following entertaining item, the letter being addressed to The Secretary to the Admiralty and dated 27 October 1865:-

'Destroyer of Vermin.

George C. Andrews having resigned the situation of 'Rat Destroyer' at this Yard, for which service he received an allowance of GBP 10 per annum, I have the honor to submit that Mr. William Bushnell, engineer of this Yard, may be appointed to the duty, being fully competent to perform the same and under the advantage of residing in the Yard.'

Happily on 1 November 1865 the 'Comptroller of the Victualling' felt able to add his favourable comment to the file:-

'I see no objection thinking it desirable that the Rat Catcher should belong to the Yard (19).'

On 6 September 1867 he addressed the Admiralty on the subject of, 'Staff required at this Yard for Indian Troop Service (20)'.

As will be gathered the nature of the work at Gosport was not entirely exacting however a compensating factor of importance will have been the pleasure of an extended period of life in England with time to pursue academic interests.

Rear Admiral: 15 January 1869 (21).

As a result of the findings of the Shadwell committee of inquiry instituted in 1871, the Royal Naval College at Portsmouth was to be moved to Greenwich. It opened in 1873 in what had been the buildings of the Royal Naval Hospital. 'Shadwell's chief concern was for the advanced training of lieutenants.' Amongst other comments this Shadwell committee had found that at Portsmouth:-

'... the College has not succeeded in imparting to the public service all the benefits such an institution should be capable of conferring (22).'

In September 1871 his Flagship on proceeding to China was the twin screw iron ship, armour plated, *Iron Duke*, 14 guns, 6,010 tons, Captain William Arthur (23).

She sailed from Plymouth Sound on 16 September, was at Gibraltar on 28 September, continued towards the East leaving Suez Roads on 26 October, and arrived at Singapore on 14 December 1871. 'Vice Admiral Kellett transferred to me the command of the squadron on the 16th instant (24).'

It was on assuming command of the station that he became acting Vice Admiral.

In *Iron Duke* at 2.00 p.m. on Saturday, 23 December he shifted out into Singapore Strait ready to proceed to Penang which he did on the following day, Christmas Eve. On 28 December *Iron Duke* anchored at Penang (25). There she dressed ship with masthead flags in honour of the King of Siam who was in port in his yacht. His Majesty departed on 29 December, but it was only in the New Year on 5 January 1872 that *Iron Duke* sailed, spent from 8 to 10 January at Malacca. Then returned to anchor off Singapore on 11 January 1872 (26).

Continuing, he sailed from Singapore on 22 January, called at Labuan on 29 January and at Manila on 8 February, so reaching Hong Kong on 20 February 1872.

Meanwhile on 3 November 1871 Rear Admiral Nakamuta Kuranosuke of the Hizen/Saga han or fiefdom had been appointed superintendent of the Tsukiji Naval Academy, Tokyo (27). He had been assistant superintendent since February. Now, in his new position, he established stricter disciplinary systems. Also he was instrumental, under the then Vice Chief of the Navy Department, Rear Admiral Kawamura Sumiyoshi, in bringing the British 'Douglas Mission' of Instructors to the Academy in 1873. By fortunate chance, Sir Harry Parkes, Minister Plenipotentiary to Japan since 1865, was on leave in England at the time. He ensured that any opposition at home to the formation of such a Mission was overcome.

13 November 1871. Lieutenant Francis Brinkley appointed 'Drill Instructor to the Japanese Troops, Yedo' (28). Lieutenant Brinkley, of the British Army, arrived in Japan in 1867 to take the place of a brother officer in the Ninth Regiment of Infantry and presently became attached to the British Legation in Tokyo (29). By 1 October 1872 his appointment as gunnery instructor had been switched to the School for Gunnery Students, later known as the Marine Military Academy. There he was to remain until 1876 when he was appointed professor of mathematics at the Engineering College, Kobu Daigakko, in due course to be absorbed into Tokyo University.

In addition to other visitors to the training establishment also it is recorded that:-

'His Majesty the Mikado paid a visit to the Naval College, Yedo, in February (1872), but no foreigners save Mr. Brinkley, Lieut., R.A. who was and is still engaged as instructor in scientific artillery in connection with the college, were present (30).'

Together with Albert Hawes, Francis Brinkley was responsible for much of the early training of those who were to become officers in the new Imperial Japanese Navy (31).

From August 1873 their work was greatly augmented by an official Training Mission headed by Commander Archibald Lucius Douglas, RN (32).

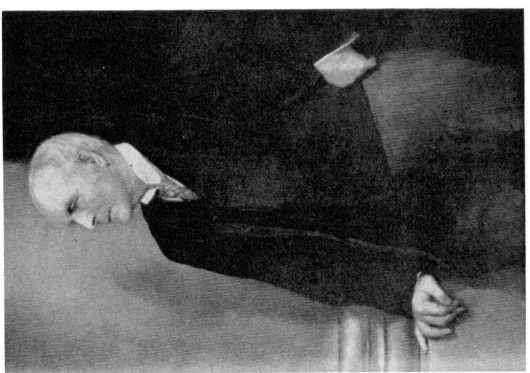

JOHN SAMUEL SWIRE

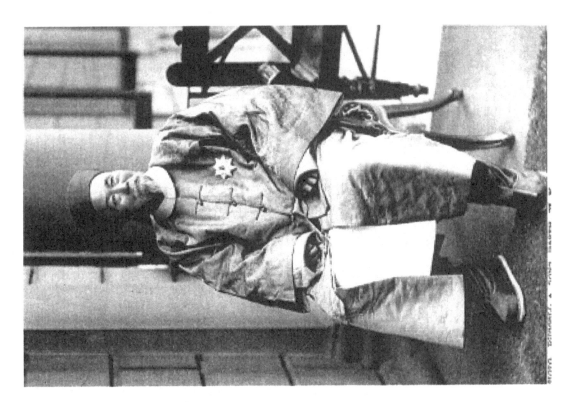

Li Hung Chang in 1896

As has been written:-
> 'The Japanese were sufficiently impressed with British naval power to engage a large educational mission from Great Britain. Hawes and Brinkley were highly successful teachers but they were only two (33).'

In 1872, inspired by John Samuel Swire (1825-1898), the formation in London of The China Navigation Company. As will be seen shortly their first vessel in service was the iron paddle steamer *Tunsin*, 774 tons, built in London in 1863 but acquired on 31 March 1873.

Many of the early steamers acquired for service in Chinese waters had interesting histories and *Tunsin* is no exception. Originally she was built for blockade running into the Confederacy. Then in March 1867 she was purchased from H. Elias and G. Barnet, *Tunsin* being the 'hong' name for George Barnet & Co. Her new buyer was Mr. Francis Arthur Groom of Glover & Co. acting on behalf of a number of Chinese entrepreneurs, and by them she was placed into service on the Yangtse. In due course these owners, the Union Steam Navigation Company but latterly with their operation managed by Olyphant & Co., an American firm, decided to abandon the River trade and so it was that in March 1873 *Tunsin* had become available for acquisition by the Swire organisation (34). In turn in 1878, just over fifty years after being founded in Canton, Olyphant & Company were to cease trading.

5 April 1872: Imperial Japanese Navy Ministry, *Kaigunsho*, founded in Tokyo. Previously the Navy had been a department within the military ministry (35). At least one reason for the establishment of this new Ministry was the perception by Satsuma interests that thereby they would increase their government representation at a Ministerial level (36).

In 1859/1860 a Tsarist Russian naval port had been established at Vladivostok, which translates as 'Rule the East', or 'Power of the East', and by 1872 it had been designated as the headquarters of his Pacific Fleet. During the following year the decision also was to be made to transfer the Eastern seat of government from Nicolaevsk to Vladivostok. In 1903 the Trans Siberian Railway was to connect the settlement with the remainder of the country after which it was to grow rapidly.

In his regular reports to the Admiralty the C. in C. described events of local importance. For example, writing from Hong Kong on 18 April 1872:-
> 'Paragraph 3. (Mentions the grounding of the Douglas Lapraik steamer *Hailoong* and of the protection of both ship and cargo by the prompt arrival of HMS *Elk*). *Hailoong* subsequently refloated and towed to Hong Kong by another Lapraik steamer escorted by *Elk*.'
> 'Paragraph 5. Sir Richard Graves MacDonnell left for England by French Mail on the 11th instant (11 April 1872); and Sir Arthur Kennedy arrived by P. & O. steamer on the 16th and assumed the Government of the Colony (37).'

He was favourably impressed by the manoeuvrability of his Flagship when under steam:-
> 'I take the opportunity of remarking that from her facility of steering and handiness afforded by her twin screws, the *Iron Duke* can be taken safely anywhere if she has but room to turn and depth to float (38).'

On 7 July 1872 a Peruvian barque, *Maria Luz*, arrived off Yokohama. She was on passage from Macao with 232 Chinese coolies onboard. Not only was the ship in a poor state and required a refit to enable her to face the trans Pacific journey home, but it transpired that the coolies were being retained onboard with the practical status of a future as slave labour. Their wretched situation was revealed when two managed to escape and swim across the bay to *Iron Duke*. The British authorities, at the time the acting Charge d'Affaires in Yeddo being Robert Grant Watson, took up their case, to a high level, with the result that finally the coolies all were released and repatriated (39).

The story of this despicable traffic perhaps should be read in conjunction with some of the findings, with especial reference to the behaviour of Peruvians in the Ellice Islands in 1865, made by Captain Bridge when serving in the Pacific in command of *Espiegle* in 1883 (see C. in C., 1901).

Later in 1872, letter dated 4 October, an occasion of his all important contact with the very highest Chinese officials is recorded:-

'... transferred my flag to the *Salamis* on the 11th (September 1872) and arrived at Tientsin on the 13th; where I exchanged visits with His Excellency Li Hung-chang, Viceroy and Governor General of the Province of Chihli.'

'My arrival (at Peking where he stayed with the British Minister, Mr. Wade) having been signified to Prince Kung, His Imperial Highness appointed September 30 as the date to which to receive me. I accordingly paid my official visit on that day, left Peking on the following, and got back to *Salamis* yesterday (40).'

As early as April 1871 the IJN, through the Japanese Consulate in London, had endeavoured to secure the assistance of another Royal Naval training mission. However, it was not before Sir Harry Parkes, who chanced to be on leave in England and was able to place encouraging words in the right quarters, that two years later, in April 1873 and as mentioned above, that the Douglas Mission officially was formed. Commander Archibald Lucius Douglas, from 9 November 1895 to be Rear Admiral, and later Admiral, headed a party composed of officers, petty officers and seamen including gunners and engineers, some thirty four men in all. Members of the Mission arrived in Japan in August 1873. Although Douglas himself, after a period of leave in England, was to be ordered to give up his services to the Mission and on 27 January 1876 was to be appointed in command of the sloop *Egeria* back on the China Station, the work of the Mission was to continue until 1879.

Under the management of Messrs. Jardine Matheson, on 30 October 1872 the China Coast Steam Navigation Company was incorporated. The firm had much experience of operating ships in the East and, as will be seen, in 1881 they would take further steps in that direction.

In December 1872 and at the instigation of Li Hung-chang (1823-1901), Viceroy of Chihli, the Chinese owned China Merchants Steam Navigation Company was founded. One of their first vessels to be acquired was the P. & O. iron, screw steamer *Aden*, 812 grt, built in 1856. Today, in the year 2007, the Taiwan based Yang Ming Marine Transportation Corporation may be regarded as a descendant whereas on the mainland the state owned China Ocean Shipping Company of Beijing also will make a similar claim.

On 10 April 1873 the paddle steamer *Tunsin*, 774 grt, Captain Martin, the first vessel to sail under China Navigation Company (Butterfield and Swire) colours, inaugurated their service on the River between Shanghai and Hankow (41).

KCB: 24 May 1873.

Concerning the drydock facilities at Yokosuka, later to be an IJN base of very considerable importance, writing from *Iron Duke* at Yokohama on 20 October 1873, he gave examples of the use of the facility by HM Ships. Between 14 and 17 October *Frolic* was docked for her copper sheathing to be checked. It was found to be seriously defective. Similarly he commented that *Thistle* was to be docked at Yokosuka as soon as practicable for repairs to her stern gland. Astonishingly she had not been docked for three years.

It is relevant to note that in an earlier letter, 30 July 1873, he had written to the Admiralty giving his opinion of the drydock facilities available to his larger ships, thus those with an appreciable draught, and made it clear that if asked to choose between those at Aberdeen in Hong Kong, or Yokosuka, then definitely he preferred the latter (42).

Between 1 August and 11 September 1873, with corvette *Cadmus*, 2,216 tons, Captain William Henry Whyte, in company, *Iron Duke* cruised extensively across the Sea of Japan and up along the coast of Manchuria into the Gulf of Tartary, prior to returning south to Yezo (Hokkaido), through the Tsugaru Strait, and on to Yokohama. His subsequent report to the Admiralty, dated 8 October 1873, was to run to fifty pages. Visits to such anchorages and bays as Novgorod at 42.38N 130.45E, Nakhodka at 42.49N 132.52E, St. Vladimir at 43.54N 135.27E and Castries at 51.27N 140.53E were mentioned. Shifting to the gunvessel *Dwarf*, 584 tons, Commander Bonham Ward Bax, he even steamed to the north up through the Strait of Tartary, with the island of Sakhalin to starboard, to visit Nicolaevsk on 29 August 1873. Here he heard the news that it was the intention of the Russian authorities to move the seat of government of their possessions on the shores of the Gulf of Tartary from that settlement to Vladivostok. Being frozen in for seven months of the year, the harbour at Nicolaevsk was only of minimal use. Also only vessels of light draught could use the port. Back at the Admiralty the unusual nature of this cruise was to inspire the comment, dated 8 December 1873:-

> 'Interesting – until Sir H. Keppel and Sir C. Shadwell's visits this important part of the China Station was known little of by the C. in C. or his subordinates (43).'

During September 1873 H.M. Ships *Thalia*, a corvette of 2,216 tons, Captain Henry Bedford Woollcombe, and gunvessel *Midge*, 584 tons, Commander John Frederick George Grant, were ordered to patrol the Straits of Malacca in the vicinity of Larut, Perak where piratical activity had been reported.

Also during 1873 in Hong Kong at Wanchai the Royal Navy acquired a property which was renamed Royal Naval Hospital. It stood on a low hill named after the C. in C., Mount Shadwell.

His subsequent presence in Malayan waters proved to be of great assistance to the British authorities in the Straits Settlements:-

> 'As early as January 20, 1874, Sir Andrew Clarke concluded with Perak a treaty in virtue of which the Raja Muda was recognised as Sultan of that long distracted country, and a resident and assistant were appointed to aid him in preserving order in his state (44). Later in the same year residents were also appointed to Selangor and Sungei Ujong. Even that measure of success, however, was not secured until the imagination of the chiefs had been stimulated by naval demonstrations which, owing to the fortuitous presence in that part of the station of Rear Admiral Sir Charles Frederick Alexander Shadwell and a considerable part of the China command, could, when desirable, be carried out on an impressive scale (45).'

June 1874: occurrence of the Japanese punitive expedition against Formosa, at the time under Chinese jurisdiction. The reason given for the expedition was the murder in 1871 of the crew of a Ryukyuan crewed Japanese vessel wrecked on the island. China either was unable to punish the offenders, or was unwilling so to do, so Japan took matters into her own hands. Concurrently Japanese authority over the Ryukyu chain of islands was strengthened. The expedition against Formosa was led by Lieut. General Saigo Tsugumichi of the Satsuma 'han' (46). On this occasion the whole business ended more or less amicably with China paying Japan an indemnity to cover the cost of the affair.

Writing from Hong Kong on 26 November 1874 the C. in C. reported the final demise of *Princess Charlotte*. In December the previous year he had found her to be 'rotten and unsafe':-

> '*Princess Charlotte* to pay off on 30 November and *Victor Emmanuel* to recommission on 1 December to replace her as receiving ship at Hong Kong (47).'

In *Iron Duke* he reached Singapore on 24 January 1875, there to await the arrival of his successor, Vice Admiral Ryder, who was steaming out from England in *Audacious* and was expected on 1 February. In the event all proceeded as planned and *Audacious* anchored in Singapore Roads at 9.50 a.m. on Monday, 1 February.

On 3 February he handed over the command and sailed from Singapore in *Iron Duke* at 11.30 a.m. on 4 February, homeward bound. This was to be a leisurely vogage via Trincomalee on 15 February, Malta on 8 April,

Gibraltar on 21 April, Lisbon on 24 April, finally arriving at Plymouth at 08.15 a.m. on Sunday, 2 May 1875 (48). He disembarked at 2 p.m. that Sunday afternoon.

Vice Admiral: 20 April 1875.
Granted a GSP of Sterling 300 p.a.: 1877.
President of Royal Naval College, Greenwich: March 1878.
Having reached the age of sixty five years, on 1 February 1879 his name was placed on the Retired List (49).

Admiral on the retired list: 2 August 1879.
Continued as President, RNC until March 1881 (50).
In retirement from 1881 he lived at Melksham in Wiltshire. He was unmarried but a nephew, Mr. J. Shadwell, lived with him.
Notice of his death and a short obituary appeared in 'The Times', Thursday, March 4, 1886, and in the 'Wiltshire Times', 6 March 1886.
In their issue of Saturday, 13 March the 'Wiltshire Times' reported:-
> 'The funeral, which took place on Saturday (6 March), was very simple and unostentatious in character. The interment was in the churchyard at Shaw.'

Today in the graveyard of Christ Church, Shaw his headstone easily may be found. It lies adjacent to that of Dorothea Georgina Thomas, nee Shadwell, a relation: born on 12 December 1790, and died on 15 December 1881. The two graves are united within a low railing fence (51).

On 25 June 1888 the Admiralty established the 'Shadwell Testimonial' being, '... a prize in memory of the late Admiral Sir Charles Shadwell, KCB'. The official trustees of the prize fund were the Hydrographer of the Navy, the President of the Royal Naval College, and the Naval Officer at the Board of Trade, and the prize, '... will consist of a pocket sextant, or other instrument of use in navigation or marine surveying (52)'.

NOTES

1. Royal Society, London. Ref: *NA6032*.
2. O'Byrne, 1055.
3. Clowes, Vol. VI, 321.
4. L.S. Dawson, *Memoirs of Hydrography*, Part Two, (Eastbourne, 1885), 23.
   Captain Francis Price Blackwood (1809-1854) was a son of that well known officer of the Nelson era, Vice Admiral Sir Henry Blackwood (1770-1832), the First Baronet.
   Also see Geoffrey C. Ingleton, *Charting a Continent*, (Sydney, 1944), 64/65. Lieut. Commander Ingleton, RAN, states that the height of the circular stone tower erected on Raine Island is forty feet. It seems clear that the actual site of the tower itself is some thirty feet above mean sea level.
5. Ibid. 522/3.
6. Jordan Goodman, *The Rattlesnake*, (London, 2005), 12-14.
7. NA ADM 196/37. *Service Record.*
8. *Dictionary of National Biography.*
9. Obituary, *Royal Astronomical Society*, XLVII, February 1887.
10. Clowes, Vol. VI. 379-384.
11. Ibid. 'By proclamation of 30 December (1852)', presumably in Calcutta.
12. *Service Record. Dictionary of National Biography.* In 1852 the Governor General of India was James Andrew Broun-Ramsay, First Marquis of Dalhousie (1812-1860), another successful product of Christ Church, Oxford.
13. *Service Record.* HMS *Winchester*, 52 gun frigate, at Woolwich Dockyard completed in September 1822. David Lyon

and Rif Winfield, *The Sail and Steam Navy List,* (London, 2004), 104.

14. Obituary, *RAS.*

15. Admiral Sir R.H. Bacon, *The Life of Lord Fisher of Kilverstone,* I, (London, 1929), 9.

16. John Arbuthnot **Fisher**. For career detail see Kellett, C. in C., 1869, reference (23).

17. Richard Hough, *First Sea Lord,* (London, 1969), 28/9.

18. Andrew Lambert, *Admirals,* (London, 2008), 292.

19. NA ADM 1/5930.

20. NA ADM 1/6010.

21. Obituary, *Illustrated London News,* 13 March 1886, 261.

22. Mary Jones, *A Naval Life,* (Dulverton, Somerset, 2007), 70, 81 and 104.

23. William **Arthur**. Born: 4 July 1830. Died in Egham: 15 November 1886. Buried at Atherington, Devon: 19 November 1886. Entered the RN: 1845. In 1860, when in command of the gunboat *Algerine,* 370 tons, discovered the bay towards the tip of the Liaotung peninsula subsequently to be named Port Arthur. Well known during the Russo-Japanese war of 1904/5. Today: Lushun. In Japan known as Ryojun. Captain: 15 April 1867. Following his command of *Iron Duke,* from 26 April 1876 commanded *Vernon,* Torpedo School Ship, Portsmouth. Her Commander was Arthur K. Wilson. From 1 December 1879 to February 1882 Naval Attache in Washington, DC. CB: 24 May 1881. From 28 November 1882 in command *Hector,* 6,710 tons, Coast Guard Service, Southampton Water. Rear Admiral: 31 March 1885. *Navy List. Foreign Office List.* His memorial, erected by his wife Mary Jane, nee Le Mesurier, may be found in St. Ann's Church, Portsmouth.

24. NA ADM 1/6191.

25. Penang. The one time Naval officer, Francis **Light** (1740-1794) who served from 1759 to 1763, subsequently was employed by a firm of merchants in Madras. In 1771 posted to Kedah. By 1786 he was able to report to the Bengal government that from the Sultan of Kedah he had secured the cession of Penang Island to the East India Company. In July 1786 Francis Light was appointed Superintendent of Penang, shortly thereafter re-named Prince of Wales Island. There he died from malaria: 21 October 1794. In due course his second son, William Light, was to found the city of Adelaide, Australia. Australian Dictionary of Biography. See also Nordin Hussin, *Trade and Society in the Straits of Melaka,* (Singapore, 2007), Chapter Eight, *British Urban Administration in Penang,* 237-270.

26. NA ADM 53/10352. Log Book *Iron Duke.*

27. **Nakamuta** Kuranosuke. Born: 24 February 1837. Died: 30 March 1916. In 1856 attended the Nagasaki naval training centre established by the 'bakufu', or Shogunate government, around their *Kanko Maru,* previously the Dutch gunboat *Soembing.* The chief instructor was Dutch Navy Lieut. G.C.C. Pels Rijcken, in due course to be Dutch Navy Minister from 1866 to 1868. In 1859 the bakufu moved the ship/college to Yedo. In 1869 he commanded *Choyo* during the campaign off Hakodate, Hokkaido against Tokugawa loyalists led by Enomoto Takeaki (1836-1908) (see Keppel, C. in C. l867, reference 40). Commander: 14 December 1870. Captain: 5 August 1871. Rear Admiral: 3 November 1871. Vice Admiral: 21 November 1878. 'Although he held many high naval posts in his subsequent career, including that of the chief of the navy staff, some consider his greatest accomplishment the imposition of discipline at the academy'. David Chris Evans, *The Satsuma Faction and Professionalism in the Japanese Naval Officer Corps of the Meiji Period: 1868-1912,* (Stanford, 1978), 74-77.

28. *British Army Lists*: July 1881.

29. Obituary, *Japan Times,* 29 October 1912.

Francis **Brinkley**. Born in Lobinstown, Co. Meath: 9 November 1841. Died in Tokyo: 28 October 1912. In 1860 briefly attended Trinity College, Dublin. In February 1861 Gentleman Cadet at Addiscombe House, Croydon, the military training establishment, East India Company. On 24 August 1861, once this establishment closed, then at Royal Military Academy, Woolwich. Lieutenant: 24 June 1863. With the Royal Artillery to Hong Kong in 1866 where served as ADC to the Governor, Sir Richard Graves MacDonnell, a cousin (see King, C. in C., 1865, and Ref: (37) below). To Japan in 1867. Although seconded to Japanese service promoted Captain on 1 January 1876 and only retired, with a gratuity, on 25 November 1882. In Japanese service he remained principal instructor of Marine Artillery at the Marine Military Academy until 1876, then was appointed Professor of Mathematics at the Engineering College. Retired from this position in 1881. Also in 1881 proprietor and editor, *Japan Mail.* From 1897 to his death in 1912

Japanese correspondent, *The Times*, London. Became well known for his research into, and collections of Japanese, Chinese and Korean porcelain and pottery, Japanese metal work, Japanese pictorial art, Japanese woodblock prints, and for his translation of No and Kyogen plays. J.E. Hoare, *Biographical Portraits*, III (Japan Library, 1999), 99-107.

30. John R. Black, *Young Japan*, (London, 1881), Vol. II, 350.

31. Albert George Sidney **Hawes**. For career detail see King, C. in C., 1865, reference (15).

32. Archibald Lucius **Douglas**. Born in Quebec City, Canada: 8 February 1842. Died at Newnham, Winchfield, Hants: 12 March 1913. Joined *Boscawen*, Flagship, North America and West Indies: 1856. Commander: 1872. Seconded to, and Director, Imperial Japanese Navy College: 1873-1875. Following his service in Japan then in August 1875 returned home on leave. From 27 January 1876 in command sloop *Egeria*, China Station. Captain: 19 July 1880. Rear Admiral: 9 November 1895. C. in C., East Indies: 15 January 1898. Vice Admiral: 15 June 1901. KCB: 1902. C. in C., North America and West Indies: 6 June 1902. C. in C., Portsmouth: 20 October 1904. GCVO: 1905. Admiral: 2 March 1905. Retired: 1907. GCB: 1911. From his obituary it is stated that while a Commander:-

> 'His principal service while in this rank was, however, that of Director of the Imperial Japanese Navy College in Yedo, having been selected by the Admiralty as commander of the Naval Mission to instruct the Japanese Navy. He held this office for two years (1873-1875), and received the thanks of the Emperor of Japan and the approval of the Admiralty while holding the appointment.'

Navy List. Who's Who, 1913. Obituary, *The Times*, Thursday, March 13, 1913.

33. John Curtis Perry, *Great Britain and the Imperial Japanese Navy, 1858-1905*, (Harvard, 1961), 103.

34. Edward Kenneth Haviland, *American Steam Navigation in China: 1845-1878*, (Salem, Mass., 1956-1958), 83-85. Liu Kwang-Ching, *Anglo-American Steamship Rivalry in China: 1862-1874*, (Harvard, 1962), 77.

35. David Chris Evans, 40.

36. Ibid. 41.

37. NA ADM 1/6229. s.s. *Hailoong*, 446 grt, built in Aberdeen and arrived at Hong Kong on 20 November 1871. On passage from Hong Kong to Swatow on 3 April 1872 struck an uncharted rock in a gale. Re-floated and repaired at Hong Kong. Sold out of Lapraik service in July 1887. H.W. Dick and S.A. Kentwell, *Beancaker to Boxboat*, (Canberra, 1988), 136. Gun-vessel *Elk*, 584 tons, Commander Noel Osborn. *Navy List*.

Sir Richard Graves **MacDonnell** (1814-1881). Trinity, Dublin. Irish Bar: 1838. Lincoln's Inn: 25 January 1841. Chief Justice of the Gambia: 1843. Governor of the Gambia: 1 October 1847. Governor of St. Lucia: 1852, and of St. Vincent: 1853, and of South Australia: June 1855 – March 1862. On completion of his term of office in Adelaide, when back in London he applied successfully for a great northward extension of the boundaries of South Australia. The appropriate bill, to colonize the Northern Territories, was placed before the legislature in Adelaide on 1 October 1863. Inhospitable places such as Port Essington, abandoned in 1849 (see Keppel, C. in C., 1867), were situated within this new State. KB: 1856. Governor of Nova Scotia: May 1864 – October 1865. Governor of Hong Kong: March 1866 – April 1872. KCMG: 1871. A cousin of Francis Brinkley – see reference (29) above. *Colonial Office List*, 1879. *Dictionary of National Biography*. Stephanie Williams, *Running the Show*, (London, 2011), 72.

Sir Arthur Edward **Kennedy**. Born: 5 April 1809. Died: 3 June 1883. Trinity, Dublin. British Army: 1827-1847 when sold out. Governor of Sierra Leone: 1852 – 1854, and of Western Australia: 1855 – 1862. Governor of Vancouver Island: 1864 – 1866. KCB: December 1867. Governor of the West African Settlements (Sierra Leone): 1868 – 1872. KCMG: 1871. Governor of Hong Kong: April 1872 – March 1877. Governor of Queensland: 1877 – 1883. GCMG: 1881. On his voyage home to retire died at sea off Aden: s.s. *Orient*, 5,386 grt: 3 June 1883. *Colonial Office List*.

38. Ibid.

39. Harold S. Williams, *Shades of the Past*, (Tokyo and Rutland, VT., 1959), 140/144.

Robert Grant Watson. Appointed Ensign in 2nd Bombay Regiment: 1853. At the close of the Indian Mutiny appointed Attache at Tehran: 18 April 1859. Various other diplomatic appointments followed, both in South America and to Constantinople, until promoted Secretary of Legation at Athens: 27 January 1870. Transferred to Yeddo: 6 March 1872. *Foreign Office List*, 1873.

40. NA ADM 1/6229. For Mr. **Wade** see Ryder, C. in C., 1874, reference (44).

Li Hung-chang (1823-1901). Leading statesman who did much to modernise China. Viceroy of Chihli: 1870-1895. Prince **Kung** (1833-1898), brother of Emperor Hsien-feng who reigned from 1850 to 1861. Succeeded by the child

Emperor T'ung-chih, to whom in 1872 he was co-Regent. Prince Kung did a great deal to modernise China and to stamp out corruption, but by 1884 he was to lose all authority to the corrupt dowager Empress Tz'u-hsi and be banished. *Encyclopaedia Britannica.*

41. *Tunsin*, built by Samuda Bros. at Poplar, London as a blockade runner into the Confederate States during the American Civil War. John Swire and Sons, *The China Navigation Company Limited,* (Hong Kong, 1992), 2.

42. NA ADM 1/6262. Letter dated 20 October 1873, Ref: S.212. That of 30 July 1873 is Ref: S.168.

43. Ibid. Letter Ref: S.184.

    In these waters of the coast of Tartary he was following Jean-Francois de Galaup, Comte de La Perouse (1741-1788) who in *Boussole* and *Astrolabe*, first navigated and charted that coast in 1787, and William Robert Broughton (1762 – 1821) in H.M. Sloop *Providence* and schooner *Resolution* who between 1796 and 1797 carried out a further survey of that entire coast between 35N and 52N. John Dunmore, *Who's Who in Pacific Navigation,* (Hawaii, 1991), 151/154 and 41/43. In those early days neither realised that Sakhalin was an island.

44. Lieut. General The Hon. Sir Andrew **Clarke**, GCMG. Born in Southsea: 27 July 1824. Died in London: 29 March 1902 and was buried at Bath on 3 April. Royal Engineers: 1844. Varied early military career including service in Van Diemen's Land (Tasmania), the Maori Wars of 1848/9 the Governor then being Sir George Grey, and as Surveyor-General of Victoria. In 1858 returned to England. In 1863 on special service to the West Coast of Africa. Director of Works of the Navy: 1864-1873. Governor of the Straits Settlements from November 1873. While Governor initiated the operations which led to the pacification of the Malay peninsula. The treaty of 20 January 1874 is the Treaty of Pangkor. From 1875 to 1880 service in India on the Council of the Viceroy. Between 1876 and 1880 the Viceroy was Edward Robert Lytton Bulwer-Lytton, 1st Earl of Lytton (1831-1891). Subsequently returned to England where active militarily. From 1892 acting agent-general, then agent-general for Victoria and Tasmania. *Colonial Office List,* 1902. *Who's Who.*

45. Clowes, Vol. VII, 269. Sungei Ujong lies on the west coast of the peninsula north of Malacca.

46. **Saigo** Tsugumichi. Born: Kagoshima: 1 June 1843. Died: 18 July 1902. Younger brother of Saigo Takamori but did not join him in the Satsuma Rebellion of 1877. In 1885 to become Navy Minister in the first Ito Hirobumi cabinet. Appointed genro (elder statesman): 1892. Admiral: 1894. Marquis: 1894. *Encyclopaedia Britannica.*

47. NA ADM 1/6300. A screw two decker completed in 1858; in turn in 1899 *Victor Emmanuel* was to be sold.

48. NA ADM 1/6342. Also Log Book *Iron Duke*, ADM 53/10364.

49. *Service Record.*

50. Obituary, *Royal Astronomical Society.*

51. Visited by the writer, Saturday, 5 July 2008. Also with grateful thanks to Mrs. Cathy Berry, Melksham and District Historical Association.

52. NA ADM 125/33.

31 August 1874 to 31 August 1877
Vice Admiral Alfred Phillipps **Ryder**

Born at Wells on 27 June 1820, the eighth son of Hon. Henry Dudley Ryder, latterly Bishop of Lichfield and Coventry, by his wife Sophia, nee Phillipps (1). He was baptised by his father just a few days later, on 1 July 1820. Young Alfred was a nephew of the first Earl of Harrowby, Dudley Ryder (1762-1847).

Died accidentally by drowning after falling into the Thames at the Vauxhall steam boat pier: Monday, 30 April 1888 (2). Buried on Saturday, 5 May 1888 at Hambleden, near Henley-on-Thames in the churchyard of St. Mary the Virgin (3).

Entered the Royal Navy on 6 May 1833. Shortly thereafter at Chatham he joined the survey ship *Thunder*, Commander Richard Owen, bound for Jamaica. As was recorded in the ship's log book, on Monday, 10 June 1833 his father paid a visit to the ship, "The Lord Bishop of Litchfield came onboard." (4). Once *Thunder* was ready to proceed to sea she sailed from Chatham on 20 June, then from Plymouth Sound on Thursday, 4 July 1833.

On passage to Madeira, on 8 July 1833 he wrote to his mother. Extracts follow from which no doubt his loving parent will have noted that her small boy was growing up rapidly:-

> 'I commence writing my first letter from foreign parts. We hope to reach Madeira in 3 or 4 days. I have not been at all sick I am happy to say though we have had a rough sea and all the other youngsters have been as sick as dogs. We set sail from Plymouth on Thursday last. I came up on deck to have my last sight of dear England and was obliged to be at my Station in the mizzen top for about half an hour reefing the sails next morning at half 5 o'clock. (Witnessed his first punishment), … he was sentenced to receive 12 lashes on his back…, (and death at sea), … a nice Irish lad of the name of Martin died this morning. He had a fever for several days… (5)'.

Thunder arrived off the Demerara River (Georgetown, Guyana) on 17 August, subsequently turned in a northerly direction to reach Nassau on 16 December, only finally arriving at her destination of Port Royal, Jamaica on 8 April 1834.

In due course, while serving in frigate *Imogene*, 28, Captain Henry William Bruce, at Valparaiso he passed his examination: 24 July 1839, and the following day was appointed **Mate** (6). *Imogene* returned to England on 6 December 1839, and there at Portsmouth on 10 December 1839 his certificate was signed by the Admiral and C. in C., Edward Codrington (1770-1851), known for his brilliant and aggressive command of *Orion*, 74, at Trafalgar in October 1805. From 1 February 1840 to 1 July 1841 studied at the RNC, *Excellent*, Portsmouth (7). **Lieutenant**: 2 July 1841 and served briefly in the first rate *Royal William*, 120 guns. From 22 September 1841 in frigate *Belvidera*, 38, Captain Hon. George Grey, Mediterranean. She paid off at Portsmouth on 5 March 1845.

Commander: 15 January 1846 and for a few months served in the sloop *Blossom*, lazarette at Sheerness (8). From 3 October 1846 to 7 November 1846 in steam gun vessel *Tartarus*, 560 tons, as additional Commander.

Also in 1846 he had printed privately, *A Pamphlet on the Experimental Cruizes of the Line of Battle Ships in 1845* (9).

From 26 May 1847 in command paddle steam sloop *Vixen*, 6 guns, 1,379 tons, 'Particular Service', then North America and West Indies Station. Following a short cruise with the fleet to the Tagus, this particular service consisted of giving passage to the Portuguese ambassador, the Duke of Palmella, to Madeira, and then of continuing on to Mexico with the newly re-appointed acting British Minister, Percy Doyle. So it was that at Portsmouth on 13 October 1847 the Duke and Mr. Doyle embarked and *Vixen* sailed at 1.20 p.m. Following a very short call made at Plymouth the next day, she continued on to arrive in Funchal Roads at 8.40 a.m. on Wednesday, 27 October. There the Duke and his suite disembarked (10). Two months later, in December and back in Central America, Mr. Doyle proceeded ashore, once again to assume his duties in Mexico (11).

Early in February 1848, following the mistreatment of two British subjects by a local Colonel Salas, thirty miles up the San Juan river in Nicaragua, he was second in command of a Naval Party despatched to reduce the 'Colonel's' fort at Serapaqui:-

> '... employed them (members of the Naval Party) in disabling the guns, in throwing them and captured arms into the river, and in burning the fort and stockades. The party was then re-embarked and taken back to the ships. This little expedition was admirably managed, and deservedly brought a CB to Captain Loch (HMS *Alarm*, 26) and promotion to Commander Ryder (12).'

In a letter written to his mother in February 1848, just about the time of setting off for Nicaragua, he mentioned the unpleasant but ever present problem with fever on the station:-

> 'We, that is the Ship's Company had a smart attack of fever before we left Port Royal (Jamaica) – 38 cases – I thought we should have had some deaths, but fortunately not one (13).'

While at Nicaragua he wrote again on 22 February 1848 to tell his mother of his delight in being under enemy fire for the first time, 'I have at last seen a little real service', and to describe something of the experience:-

> 'We were under a heavy fire from about 200 men for more than an hour – the whizzing and hissing and popping was not pleasant but I was glad to find that I retained my presence of mind and was able to laugh at the shots as they whizzed by me – we had 2 men killed and 13 wounded, one of the last in my boat (14).'

In his subsequent report of proceedings Captain Granville G. Loch wrote generously in respect of his right hand man, 'Ryder was a most admirable second, his temper and judgement were always so correct, a man who you could trust with your in most thoughts (15).'

At the time of the operation at Serapaqui his C. in C., North America and West Indies, was Vice Admiral Sir Francis William Austen (1774-1865), brother of the author Jane and himself to attain, on 27 April 1863, the rank of Admiral of the Fleet. His younger brother was Rear Admiral Charles John Austen (23 June 1779 to 7 October 1852) who, as C. in C., East Indies and China from 14 January 1850, was to die of cholera off Prome, Irrawaddy River during the second Anglo-Burmese war. By nice co-incidence as Captain in *Bellerophon* he had been engaged off Syria in 1840 where also Admiral Ryder's predecessor in China, Charles Shadwell, had fought. Likewise Commander Shadwell had fought under Admiral Austen's orders in Burma in 1852.

Captain: 2 May 1848. On that day the news of his promotion was sent to the family by the First Sea Lord himself, Rear Admiral James Whitley Deans Dundas (1785-1862), in a letter addressed to his sister, Anna Sophia:-

> 'My dear Lady Grey,
> This day your brother was made a Captain and in a few weeks I have no doubt you will see him in England (16).'

Anna Sophia, an elder sister born on 18 January 1805, on 14 August 1827 had married the Rt. Hon. Sir George Grey, Bart. of Falloden, Northumberland. He, born on 11 May 1799, was the grandfather of Sir Edward, born in 1862, to be the first Viscount and long serving Secretary of State for Foreign Affairs, for eleven years between 1905 and 1916.

The news of his promotion to Captain was received in the West Indies only in June. Consequently on 15 June 1848 his period in command of *Vixen* ended, he handed the ship over to Commander Robert Jenner, and returned home to England by mail steamer, arriving on 24 July 1848 (17).

In 1852 the author of, *A treatise on economy of fuel: showing how it may be attained on board men-of-war steamers.*

On 29 June 1852 married his cousin Louisa, daughter of Henry Dawson of Launde Abbey, Leicestershire. They were to have one son, Edward Lisle Ryder, born on 20 April 1853.

From 26 December 1853 in command screw steam frigate *Dauntless*, 33, North Sea, then Mediterranean and Black Sea. A little detail follows.

War between Russia and the Turks had broken out in October 1853, and on 28 March 1854 Britain and France similarly declared war against Russia. Most of the conflict occurred in the Crimea but also Britain exerted pressure in the Baltic, the White Sea and Far East. Ordered in *Dauntless* to the Baltic, where the C. in C. was Admiral Sir Charles John Napier (1786-1860), he appears to have had some disagreement with his superior officer. Fortunately, and as may be seen from the following letter written to him on 4 August 1854 by a Clerk at the Admiralty, Mr. W.S. Gilly, in no manner was this affair to adversely effect his subsequent career:-

'My dear Ryder,

My hands are now untied, and I send you the mysterious document from Sir Chas. Napier. I longed to give you all the information I could but as the correspondence has been carried on in this Department I could not do more than give a hint to Lady Grey. I most sincerely hope and believe that you will get the better of your much respected Commander in Chief. His letter is a mere petulant effusion and I do not think has much weight here. I am very glad that the Admiralty have behaved like gentlemen, and informed you of what is going on… (18).'

From the Baltic by year end he was in *Dauntless* in the Mediterranean. At Malta on 3 December 1854 orders were received from Rear Admiral Houston Stewart to proceed, '… with *Paramatta* No. 52 transport in tow', to Constantinople thence Balaklava (19).

At Constantinople it became necessary for *Dauntless* to receive engine repairs. In these circumstances he had time to pay a visit to the hospital at Scutari. From there on Saturday, 16 December 1854 he wrote home, privately. Extracts follow:-

'It is an enormous place – a square court – it is three stories high and each floor is divided into two passages with double rows of beds. I went through long lines of wounded men, some having their wounds dressed by surgeons and sisters…(20).'

While at Scutari he met a Mrs. Brassbridge and Miss Nightingale. Also he handed over parcels of newspapers, and arranged for the libraries of H.M. Ships ordered home to be first landed at Scutari for the use of the wounded.

Sailing from Constantinople on Thursday, 21 December he took with him to the Crimea a great quantity of beef, together with sheepskins for coats.

Finally having reached Crimea on 29 December 1854, again in a private letter home, he tells something of his feelings:-

'… of how matters are really going on here. It is a subject that I rather shrink from writing about and in fact, as it is impossible for any individual to do anything to mend it, I try to forget it except at those times when one ought to remember all that are miserable and ill and wretched (21).'

Off Sevastopol on 17 February 1855 he received orders from the C. in C., Rear Admiral Edmund Lyons (1790-1858), later to be the first Baron Lyons. These required him to proceed the next morning up the coast to Eupatoria and there to place himself under the orders of the Senior Naval Officer. By May 1855, still in *Dauntless*, he was at Malta, but then by 2 August 1855 he was back in the Black Sea at anchor off Sinope, north coast of Turkey. This had been the scene of the battle of 30 November 1853 during which a Russian squadron had all but annihilated a patrol force of Turkish frigates and corvettes, destroying nine of them and in so doing signalling the active commencement of hostilities.

From Sinope he proceeded north across the Black Sea to Sebastopol on 6 August, then the few miles north again up the coast to anchor back off Eupatoria on 27 August 1855.

By the end of the month, 30 August, *Dauntless* was at anchor off Odessa.

Arrangements now were being made to attack the great fort Kinburn situated at the western tip of the Kinburn peninsula on the south bank of the estuary of the river Dnieper. Thus it was that from the log book in *Dauntless* it may be noted:-

'6 September 1855: Captain and Master went away in *Viper* to sound the entrance to the Dneiper.

12 September 1855: Captain and Master went away in *Viper* gunboat to sound the approaches to Kinburn Fort (22)'.

With *Dauntless* observing the proceedings, during the afternoon on 15 October 1855, 'English and French mortar boats commenced firing on Fort Kinburn'. The main allied attack against the Fort took place two days later, on 17 October, with *Dauntless* participating in company with *Terrible* (23). This was a significant engagement only in that the Allied ironclads, while themselves receiving minimal damage, satisfactorily reduced the Fort. From that moment onwards it was appreciated in the navies of the world that wooden warships now were obsolete.

Very sadly, in the interim, on 16 October, Captain Ryder had written to the C. in C. resigning his command of the ship:-

'... immediately the present operation against the enemy is terminated. My wife who has been ordered to Malta as a last resource, and has just arrived, is dying – I can hardly hope to see her but must not fail to attempt it (24).'

By now the weather had become extremely cold with heavy frosts, and, at intervals, squalls and storms of snow.

As might be expected, from Admiral Lyons he received the necessary permission and on Saturday, 20 October at 1300, 'Captain Alfred P. Ryder left on Admiral's leave'. Lieut. Charles Thomas Dench assumed temporary command of the ship.

It will have been a dreadful business for him as at Malta his wife of only a few months over three years died on 19 October 1855 so rather before he was able to reach her. She was buried there in Malta (25).

He was only able to rejoin *Dauntless* at 4 p.m. on Friday, 1 February 1856, the ship then being at anchor up the Straits of Kertch at the extreme eastern point of the Crimea, the Strait being that body of water leading north into the Sea of Azov.

Happily by the Treaty of Paris, 30 March 1856, the war in the Crimea and against Russia was brought to a conclusion.

In *Dauntless* he cleared the Dardanelles on 11 April 1856 and the following afternoon moored off the Piraeus. By 17 April she had returned to Malta.

The commission was to end when *Dauntless* paid off at Portsmouth on 13 March 1857.

It ought to be recorded, the campaign in the Crimea requiring such a large naval presence, that two of his predecessors in command in China, George St. Vincent King and The Hon. Sir Henry Keppel, also served in those waters against Russia. Likewise a number of successors including Charles Farrel Hillyar, George Ommanney Willes, and William Montagu Dowell, which see accordingly.

In the interim while still in the Mediterranean he wrote several letters to his young son, 'Eddy'. It is clear from these that the boy was back with his late wife's family at Launde Abbey. Captain Ryder had a dog in the ship, 'Sailor', and by relating tales about him, taken together with many sketches and drawings of ports such as Messina and Palermo which he visited, he was able to make a very fine effort to let Eddy know something of his life at sea. The quality of these drawings is high so it is apparent that Captain Ryder was no mean artist (26).

From 2 January 1861 to 22 November 1862, when she paid off at Sheerness, in command screw ship *Hero*, 89 guns, 3,150 tons, Channel Squadron, then North America and West Indies Station. In 1862 the North American Squadron was reinforced following the War of the Reform in Mexico which returned the liberal, Benito Juarez, to power. Subsequently France was to invade Mexico and in June 1863 her forces were to occupy Mexico City.

From 24 November 1862 to 27 April 1863 private secretary to the Duke of Somerset, First Lord of the Admiralty (also see C. in C., 1862).

Also in 1862 he served on, 'Commission of Enquiry into Navigation Schools'.

From 27 April 1863, as **Commodore** First class, served as 'Controller General of the Coast Guard' in screw ship *Pembroke*, 60 guns, 1,760 tons, Coast Guard Service, Harwich.

In 1864 author of, *Heads of enquiry into the state and condition of lighthouses*.

From 23 June 1864 appointed Naval a.d.c. to H.M. Queen Victoria (27).

Rear Admiral: 2 April 1866.

As a newly promoted Rear Admiral, on 9 April 1866 to be succeeded as Comptroller General of the Coast Guard by Captain J.W. Tarleton (28).

In May 1866 he caused to be published his twenty five pages of suggestions, *Remarks on the Three Naval Reserves of Seamen, under the superintendence of the Commodore Controller-General of Coast Guard, with suggestions for their improvement* (29).

From 28 May 1868 he flew his flag in the screw ironclad ship *Bellerophon*, 7,550 tons, as Second in Command, Channel Squadron. His Flag Lieut. was Cyprian A.G. Bridge (see C. in C., 1901).

From 17 July 1868 in the same position but now in the new iron, armour plated, twin screw corvette *Penelope*, 4,368 tons. This appointment ended after just over a year when he hauled down his flag on 4 June 1869 and went on half pay (30).

In 1871 appointed to the Admiralty Committee on Designs. In this connection on 9 March 1871 a report was drawn up and published by Admiral George Augustus Elliot (1813-1901) and Rear Admiral A.P. Ryder, members of the 'Committee on Designs for Ships of War'. This, their minority report, suggested various new alternative designs which the Board decided to accept. The battleship *Temeraire*, 8,540 tons and completed in August 1877, resulted however, 'although the system was entirely satisfactory so far as shooting was concerned', she was not an economic success as regards space and weight and that experiment was not repeated (31).

Also in 1871, through the Royal United Service Institution, he published, *Forms for Registering the Angles of Rolling and Heeling for the information of the Construction Department of the Admiralty*. This was followed by, *The Naval Hammock, its Buoyancy and Use in Saving Life at Sea in Cases of Collision*.

Then during December 1871 he published a paper, *Cork Mattresses (second pattern) for Her Majesty's Navy*. In this he suggested the substitution of cork to replace hair mattresses, '... not only on account of their greater buoyancy, but also owing to their economy in first cost (32).'

Vice Admiral: 7 May 1872.

A turreted, masted, screw steamer warship of new design, *Captain*, 7,760 tons, off Cape Finisterre on 7 September 1870 had overturned and sunk with the loss of some 480 lives. Among those lost was a nephew, Midshipman Edward Dudley Ryder. Admiral Ryder was appointed a Commissioner for the Royal Patriotic Fund, and especially for the *Captain* Relief Fund. Amongst other duties he took it upon himself to seek financial contributions from friends. As one example these included Thomas George Baring, Lord Northbrook, and from

February 1872 to January 1876, Viceroy of India. From Government House, Simla, and dated 29 July 1872, came his generous donation of GBP 50.00 (33).

Also he entered into correspondence with the Dean at St. Paul's Cathedral in London in which the style and phrasing to be employed in the creation of a proposed memorial to the lost members of the ship's company in *Captain* was discussed (34). In due course an appropriate memorial was to be placed in the Cathedral where it may be seen today.

The Committee on Designs for Ships of War, on which he had served in 1871, had been appointed following the loss of *Captain*.

'From 28 February to 1 December 1873 was Naval Attache to H. M.'s Embassies and Missions at the Maritime Courts of Europe (35).'

In the course of carrying out these duties as Naval Attache, on 21 June 1873 he was to commence a journey which took him to Russia, Italy and Austria (36).

Again through the Royal United Service Institution, during 1874 he published two papers. The first, *HMS 'Victor Emmanuel' as an Hospital Ship during the late Ashantee Campaign*, and, secondly, *A Statement to Accompany the Russian Ramming Diagrams Presented by him to the Institution*.

On 31 August 1874 he was appointed C. in C., China Station. Once news of his appointment was announced he received a number of requests for favours to be granted, in other words the placing of friends and/or relatives either in his Flagship or elsewhere on the Station. Of these two senior officers asked that he place Lieut. Herbert J.G. Garbett in his flagship, and a predecessor in China, Harry Keppel, asked that Midshipman Henry N. Thomson similarly be berthed in *Audacious*. The necessary appointments indeed were to take place. Also he entered into correspondence with a well known officer with much earlier experience in China, and also who had served with distinction in the Sea of Azov during the Crimean war. He was Rear Admiral Sherard Osborn (ret'd) who, on 3 July 1874, answered one letter in the following entertaining manner:-

> 'Old Metternich's axiom, 'apres moi le deluge', is the policy of our legislators today, no where more than in Downing Street. To that line you will have to adhere or make a bed of thorns for yourself so take it easy and smoke your pipe in peace as Wade and Shadwell are doing whether they see the storm brewing or not for their successors (37).'

On the following day Sherard Osborn wrote again:-

> 'My dear Ryder. The only book in English or any other language worth reading about China and excellent as a work of reference is, *The Middle Kingdom*, 2 vols. by Dr. Williams, a Yankee missionary who compiled it some years ago and from whose labours everyone has been cribbing ever since … (38)'

His flagship in China, the twin screw armoured ship *Audacious*, 14 guns, 6,010 tons, commissioned at Chatham on 1 September 1874. She was a sister ship to *Iron Duke*. Her Captain was Philip H. Colomb and her Commander, Cyprian A.G. Bridge.

In her at Spithead on Friday, 23 October 1874 his flag was hoisted at 10.30 a.m. The flag of the C. in C., Admiral Sir Rodney Mundy, GCB was saluted with seventeen guns and *Duke of Wellington* returned with thirteen. The following morning *Audacious* weighed and proceeded to Plymouth where she remained from 25 to 28 October. There at the time the C. in C. was a previous C. in C., China, Admiral Sir H. Keppel, now flying his flag in *Royal Adelaide*.

His subsequent voyage East was a gentle affair:-

Gibraltar: 4 – 7 November 1874

Malta: 14 – 22 November

Port Said: arrived on 29 November and made her transit of the canal.

Suez: 3 – 8 December

Aden: 19 – 23 December

Pt. de Galle: 13 – 17 January 1875
Penang: 27 – 28 January
Malacca: 30 – 31 January (39)

Finally he arrived at Singapore. As was recorded in *Iron Duke*:-

'Monday, 1 February 1875
7.0 a.m. Observed HMS *Audacious* Flag of V. Adm. Ryder coming in (40).'

Following his passage out to the East he was to write to the Admiralty to report on one most favourable aspect of his Flagship's behaviour:-

'Whatever objections may have been raised to ships of the *Audacious* class, the longer experience
I have of them the more I am struck with their wonderful steadiness. I have just lately made a
passage, running before a heavy sea and strong wind, all my stern ports barred in, and to my great
surprise the ship did not roll more than 2 deg. to 1 deg. each way (41).'

Having handed over the command on 3 February, his predecessor, Admiral Shadwell, sailed in *Iron Duke* on 4 February, homeward bound.

Sailing from Singapore on 11 February Admiral Ryder proceeded first to visit the French at Saigon, 18 – 21 February, then continued on to reach Hong Kong at 11.25 a.m. on Tuesday, 2 March 1875. There he remained for two months until 4 May when he sailed for Woosung, arriving on 15 May 1875. His term in office had commenced in much the usual manner.

H.I.M. The Emperor Meiji took a keen personal interest in the progress being made at Tsukiji Naval College, Commander Douglas recording a visit which H.I.M. made on 9 January 1875:-

'His Imperial Majesty arrived at ten o'clock … in a gorgeous coach drawn by four American horses.
The school buildings were inspected and luncheon was served after which one of the cadets read
aloud from an account of the life of Lord Nelson, a great hero of the Japanese cadets. The Emperor
then said a few words to the cadets (42).'

In February 1875, by which time it was judged that the relationship between the Treaty Powers and Japan had become sufficiently amicable, the Royal Marine Battalion stationed at Yokohama on garrison duties was withdrawn. Writing of that occasion:-

'Every honour was paid to the battalion on its departure. The Commandant, Colonel Richards,
and his officers were presented to the Mikado by the British Ambassador, Sir Harry Parkes, and
entertained by the officers of the Imperial Marines, whose organisation was the work of Lieut.
Hawes, RMLI, afterwards H.M.'s Consul in Tahiti (43).'

In the event the Marine Battalion embarked in the iron screw troop ship *Adventure*, 2,510 tons, Captain John D'Arcy, on 1 March 1875, arrived at Hong Kong on 13 March, and left four days later for the long voyage to Natal via Singapore and Mauritius.

Following the murder on 21 February 1875 of British consular official Augustus Raymond Margary near the Chinese border with Burma at Manwyne in Yunnan, then, in due course once relevant information came to hand, the British Minister to China, Sir Thomas Francis Wade, was to adopt an uncompromising pose (44). It was to be a year later that first he was to be in a position to write asking the C. in C. to steam north to visit him. As Admiral Ryder informed the Admiralty on 18 March 1876, this he proposed to do in *Vigilant*, leaving Hong Kong on 4 April. In due course an important consequence of the resulting discussions with the Chinese was to be the signing of the Chefoo Convention, 13 September 1876. A clause provided that China should appoint a Minister to the Court of St. James'. The first incumbent, the first in modern times to any western nation, was Kuo Sung-tao (1818-1891) who arrived in London the following year.

In addition a number of ports were opened for both British representation and trade, these including Ichang at the foot of the Yangtse Gorges (45).

Negotiating on behalf of China was the Viceroy of Chihli, Li Hung-chang (46). Advising him was Robert Hart (1835-1911), the British born Inspector General of Chinese Maritime Customs.

With his flag in *Audacious*, Admiral Ryder also was present for the signing of the Convention. In company in port was his yacht, the despatch vessel *Vigilant*, 2 guns, 985 tons, Lieut. and Commander Hugh C.D. Ryder (47).

Writing from *Vigilant* at Shanghai on 12 October 1876 the C. in C. forwarded a copy of the Chefoo Convention to the Admiralty (48).

Meanwhile from Yokohama in a letter to the Admiralty dated 6 July 1875, the C. in C. reported favourably on the service provided at the drydock at Yokosuka:-

> 'The *Audacious* was placed in the Japanese Government Dock at Yokosuka on 18 June with as much method and precision, Captain Colomb informs me, as in a Home Yard. She undocked on 22 June 1875 (49).'

Again, just a few weeks later, from Nagasaki on 18 August he informed the Secretary of the Admiralty of developments within the training Mission to the IJN:-

> 'Commander Douglas having relinquished the superintendence of the Japanese Naval College at Yedo, has left for England via America, – he has received the highest commendation for his services from the Mikado and the Japanese Government. Retired Commander Jones remains as Superintendent of the college on the same footing and pay (50).'

As an example of the manner in which the Flagship could be involved in social activity ashore, in October 1875 a regatta was held by the Shanghai Rowing Club:-

> 'By kind permission of Captain Colomb and the officers, the band of the *Audacious* played in the garden during the afternoon and contributed greatly to the pleasure of the visitors. The apposite introduction of a few bars of "See the Conquering Hero Comes," while the winner of the Ladies Purse was being conducted to receive his prize, was not the least happy of their efforts (51).'

Towards the end of 1875, near Hong Kong, there occurred a piratical attack, on this occasion against a large Hong Kong registered fishing junk. Together with goods being seized three young girls were kidnapped and held for ransom. As will be seen happily not all such wretched deeds were to end with much misery, even murder. To the gunboat survey vessel *Sylvia*, 865 tons, was assigned the task of investigating the business. Her commanding officer, Captain Henry St. John, first made appropriate inquiries and then proceeded:-

> 'Without further incidents I reached the head of the bay, anchored off the village, and at once demanded the three girls. This request, however, was met with blank looks of astonishment, and professions of utter ignorance regarding them. "The three headmen of the village must then return with me to the gunboat," I said. These worthies made all the delay, excuses, and difficulties they could, but ultimately appeared robed in silk, accompanied by a couple of blue jackets, who escorted them to the boat, and then on board. (--) I now made great preparations to hang these three silk robed gentlemen, passing a rope from each masthead, arranging the most elaborate knots, and so on, taking care that they should see and understand what was going on. Their expressions were curious to watch; one, in particular, tried to treat it as a good joke, but with the most evident inward uncertainty. The other two appeared stolid, but grave. All now being ready, one was taken to each mast, and the rope passed carefully over their heads. The effect of the ominous looking noose touching their skin was as if their faculties had received an electric shock. They suddenly remembered, "the girls were there; I should have them at once if only I would spare their lives." The gentleman that laughed at the preparations was so overcome by the excess of his feelings that

he fainted, but came to in a few moments on a little salt water being judiciously applied. Directions were sent to their subordinates in the village, and in a very short time the girls appeared on the beach, escorted by a crowd of men and women: the three rascals were quickly exchanged for the kidnapped fair ones, who were fed with tea and jam, and wrapped up in a sail for the night, and I started on my return to Hong Kong (52).'

It was while he was at Shanghai that on 9 November 1875 the C. in C. first received information regarding the Birch affair in Perak, Malaya. The following extracts are taken from his China Station General Letter written at Hong Kong on 25 November 1875:-

'I received a telegram from Hong Kong repeating one from *Thistle* at Singapore as follows:

"Disturbances in Perak very serious. Mr. Birch murdered on the 1st.

Unsuccessful attack made on stockade yesterday by 60 men of 10th and Rocket party of Seamen. Captain Innes killed and many casualties."

2. The *Modeste* was then on her way to Singapore and instructions were at once sent to Labuan to hasten her. I also despatched the *Ringdove* at once from Hong Kong and ordered the *Egeria* then on passage from Shanghai to Kong Kong to follow the *Ringdove* to Singapore.

3. Subsequent telegrams informed me that there were 13 killed and wounded in the unsuccessful attack on the stockade, which proved afterwards to be 1 killed and 12 wounded, and that the Governor had requested 300 men at once. Further that the Major General Commanding at Hong Kong had started with 300 troops for Singapore.

I accordingly left Shanghai in the *Audacious* and arrived at Hong Kong on the 20th instant (November 1875).

4. The subsequent events of which I have been informed are that on the 16th (November) Commander Stirling (of HMS *Thistle*) telegraphed that he was landing Seamen and Marines and fitting Gun boats. He would probably attack the stockade in three days, and that he knew little of the movements of natives up the river. On the 18th he telegraphed:-

"Three enemy's Stockades carried yesterday by Seamen of *Thistle*, *Fly*, detachments of 10th and artillery. No loss." (53).'

In his capacity as Senior Officer, Straits of Malacca, the Captain of the screw corvette *Modeste*, 14 guns, 1,934 tons, who took a most active part in bringing this unfortunate affair to a successful conclusion, was Alexander Buller (see C. in C., 1895).

Meanwhile the other Naval reinforcements ordered to the scene by the C. in C. were arriving in those waters off Perak.

In the interim the C. in C. himself was under some pressure to remain where he was:-

'Mr. Wade (the British Minister to China, Sir Thomas Wade) has informed me that though there is a temporary lull in China it will be a great relief to him to learn that I do not consider it necessary to go further South than Hong Kong.'

Fortunately with the success of the operation, in which too Commander Stirling played an important role, matters in Malaya commenced to calm down. By 23 December Admiral Ryder was able to report to the Admiralty, again from Hong Kong:-

'... I telegraphed to the Governor of the Straits Settlements to ask if he wanted any more naval aid and offering to come down in *Audacious* if he did but he telegraphed back that he did not require any more naval aid (54).'

A summary of the Birch business may be given as follows.

The successor to Sir Andrew Clarke, and for two years from May 1875 the Governor of the Straits Settlements, was that distinguished Royal Engineer and colonial administrator, Lieut. General Sir William

Francis Drummond Jervois, GCMG, CB, FRS (1822-1897). At the time an ex Midshipman, RN, James Wheeler Woodford Birch (1826-1875), was serving as the first British resident in Perak (55). As already seen above, British protection over that state, vice that of Siam, had been agreed on 20 January 1874. On 2 November 1875 a local Malay chief murdered Birch. Sir William ordered prompt and vigorous action, 'to stimulate the imagination of the chiefs', subsequently the murderers being tried and hung. Others found guilty of complicity were exiled to the Seychelles. As one noted colonial authority was to write:-

'(These actions) did more in six months to bring order and good government to Malaya than could have been achieved by twenty years of peaceful persuasion (56).'

Rather to the west of Chefoo on 10 November 1876 the twin screw gunvessel *Lapwing*, 774 tons, had the misfortune to ground on the Island of Chang-shan. Fortunately after considerable effort and ingenuity she was got clear on 4 December (57). Having been towed to Shanghai a survey showed that she had been too badly damaged to risk passage on to Hong Kong therefore, as the C. in C. reported on 18 January 1877, at a cost of GBP 4,600.00, she was docked and repaired at Shanghai. In due course her Captain, Commander Sir William Wiseman, Bart., and the Navigator, and officer of the watch who had chanced to be the gunner, were all sentenced, 'to be severely reprimanded'.

Six weeks later on Kyushu the Satsuma rebellion broke out.

Following the demise of the Shogunate era in January 1868 there had been, 'a succession of abortive uprisings of disaffected shizoku (former samurai) (58).' In this instance the element of unrest resulting from the loss of status by samurai had been aggravated in 1873 by disagreements between Korea and Japan. The Satsuma general, Saigo Takamori had lost face over the Korean question as the government had not been prepared to back his warlike approach. Subsequently in Kagoshima Saigo had taught, 'ethics and military science to the would-be young samurai'. On 29 January 1877, while Saigo was away on a hunting trip, a group of his followers attacked government facilities in Kagoshima. Returning home, and although dismayed by this insurrection, reluctantly Saigo agreed to become their leader, the vague thought being that a march should be made on Tokyo to present grievances. The government, however, reacted promptly and their forces blocked the dissidents at Kumamoto, western central Kyushu. By May the rebels were on the defensive. Shortly thereafter they suffered a series of defeats and by September 1877 plans were made for a last stand on a hill overlooking Kagoshima. There on 24 September Saigo was badly wounded and, by prior arrangement in the event of such a situation, beheaded by a loyal supporter (59).

'When he (Saigo) was defeated and killed, it was a clear demonstration of the power of the government and all attempts to oppose it by force disappeared (60).'

Professor Tsuzuki too is another to stress this important stage in Japanese history which, as has been seen, took place during the early days of Meiji:-

'The fact that an army of conscripts had defeated the picked forces of Satsuma samurai was an eloquent demonstration of the exit of the samurai from the scene of history (61).'

As British Minister Sir Harry Parkes fully understood the importance of the above but initially, until the outcome became known, it was necessary to ensure the safety of foreigners. On 1 March 1877 Admiral Ryder advised the Admiralty that Sir Harry Parkes had informed him of the Satsuma Rebellion in Kyushu. Immediately he had ordered *Modeste* to Kagoshima, '... to carry away foreigners residing there as the Government intends to attack that place by sea immediately (62).' *Thistle* already was at Nagasaki and he ordered *Egeria* there too.

A fortnight later, to the Admiralty in his general letter of 15 March, the C. in C. quoted at length from a missive received from Sir Harry in which details of the rebellion were given. By then, in Sir Harry's opinion, although government troops had not achieved a decisive victory, there were clear signs that they were gaining the upper hand. In the meantime *Modeste* had brought away from Kagoshima all those foreigners who desired to leave, and conveyed them to Nagasaki.

On 2 April, by now writing from Yokohama, the C. in C. was able to let the Admiralty know that:-
'Troops are being sent down (to Kyushu) almost daily and numbers of wounded arrive from the scene of the conflict around Kumamoto. The Government appears to be acting with much vigour.'

On 10 April Admiral Ryder informed London that the rebellion continued but that, 'government troops and equipment pour into Kyushu where it was estimated that from 30-40,000 government troops were fighting 10-12,000 rebels'.
With the demise of Saigo Takamori the rebellion collapsed and later, from Hakodate, so the C. in C. informed the Admiralty in London.

Meanwhile at Shanghai on 23 January 1877 a great Victorian age traveller, Captain William J. Gill, Royal Engineers, embarked in the steamer *Hankow* at the beginning of his splendid adventure which was to take him across China to Burma (63). Initially he travelled with Mr. Baber of the British Chinese Consular service, appointed as the first such official at Chungking (64). From Hankow to Ichang and then on up through the Gorges they were to engage the services of a local junk or kwa-tsze owner and arrive safely at Chungking on 8 April.
Early in November Captain Gill was to reach Bhamo on the Irrawaddy above Mandalay.

Admiral: 5 August 1877.
Alas, he was not to enjoy celebrating his promotion for more than just a few weeks as on 24 September 1877 his son, Edward Lisle, died. Amongst the many communications of commiseration which he received was a charming and touching letter dated 9 October 1877 from H.E. John Pope Hennessy (1834-1891), Governor of Hong Kong (65).
It was during His Excellency's term in office that the Surveyor General of the Colony, Mr. J.M. Price, prepared a plan covering the proposed Observatory to be built on Mount Elgin in Kowloon. Not only was it suggested that in consequence storm warnings could be issued, but also that other meteorological observations would be undertaken. 'On 30 October 1877 Admiral Ryder wrote a letter warmly supporting Mr. Price's suggestions and adding the recommendation that the observation of tides and currents should be included in the scheme (66).'

Early on Sunday, 4 November 1877 his successor arrived at Hong Kong in the P. & O. s.s. *Gwalior*, 2,733 grt. Amongst his last official acts before leaving to return home, on that same day he wrote to the Colonial authorities strongly supporting the construction of the proposed new breakwater at Causeway Bay on Hong Kong Island (67). Finally to be completed in 1883 this was to form the first small craft typhoon shelter in the Colony.
From Hong Kong on 8 November 1877, and having on that day transferred command of the station to the new C. in C., Vice Admiral Charles F. Hillyar, he sailed for home in the P. & O. s.s. *Nizam*, 2,726 grt (68). He was to arrive back in England on 29 December 1877 (69). Finally he returned home on 18 January 1878 (70).

From 14 August 1877 up until the advent of the second Gladstone premiership from 28 April 1880, the First Lord of the Admiralty was William Henry Smith (1825-1891), 'Pinafore' Smith.
On his return from the East it is clear that the Admiral, then only fifty eight years of age, still wished to be employed elsewhere should a suitable opportunity arise. He set wheels in motion and on 22 September 1878 received the following reply from the First Lord:-
'My dear Admiral,
    I shall not fail to bear in mind so long as I continue at the Admiralty that you are still willing to
    serve and it will give me very great pleasure if it is within my power with due regard to the claims
    of other officers, to offer you employment (71).'

During October 1879 at Swansea a 'Church Congress' was held at which one of the selected speakers was Admiral A.P. Ryder who spoke on *Religious Duties in Men-of-War* (72).'

His successor in the East, Admiral Charles F. Hillyar, only returned home in February 1879. Once the announcement of Admiral Ryder's forthcoming appointment to Portsmouth was made then amongst the many letters of congratulation was one, dated 21 October 1879, which he received from Admiral Hillyar:-

'Allow me to offer you my sincere and hearty congratulations on your being nominated future Chief at Portsmouth... (73).'

He succeeded Admiral Edward Gennys Fanshawe, CB as C. in C., Portsmouth: 27 November 1879, his Flag flying in *Duke of Wellington*, 6,070 tons. He occupied that important post until 28 November 1882 when in turn he was succeeded by Admiral Sir Geoffrey Thomas Phipps Hornby, KCB (1825-1895), from 1 May 1888 to be promoted Admiral of the Fleet.

From Portsmouth on 7 February 1880 he wrote to congratulate Dudley Francis Stuart Ryder, Viscount Sandon (1831-1900), from November 1882 to be the Third Earl of Harrowby, on an election victory in Liverpool. This letter also contains remarks in respect of the Far East, from which comments it is clear and of interest that he knew Sir Harry Parkes well, and held his opinions to be of great value (74).

Also while at Portsmouth it is recorded that in their issue of *The Lifeboat*, dated 2 August 1880, the National Life-Boat Institution confirmed him as a member of their committee (75).

Subsequently he lived for the most part at Torquay. An uncle, being his mother's youngest brother, Commander Henry Cranmer March Phillipps (1793-1880), had died on 22 January 1880 and left him Wellswood House (76).

KCB: 24 May 1884.

The last paper which he appears to have published again was through the auspices of the Royal United Service Institution. Dated 1884 the subject was, *Collision of Ships in Fogs*.

Admiral of the Fleet: 29 April 1885.

The Ryder family connection with Hambleden, Buckinghamshire may be explained, at least in part by the fact that one of the Admiral's sisters, Harriet Amelia, sometimes known as Emily but more intimately in the family as Minnie, and who had remained unmarried, died there on 31 October 1885, aged seventy seven years. She had been resident in the village for forty seven years, her house, which still stands, being positioned just across behind the churchyard close to the position in which in due course Sir Alfred himself was to be buried (77).

On 13 May 1886 he was, 'approved by War Office additional Commissioner of the Patriotic Fund (78).'

Above it has been noted that Mr. W.H. Smith had been First Lord of the Admiralty from 1877 to 1880. Subsequently he was to hold other high offices of state including that of Secretary of State for War and Chief Secretary for Ireland. His final position, from 14 January 1887 until his death on 6 October 1891, was as First Lord of the Treasury. While holding this latter office, on 16 November 1887 at Hambleden, where in the early 1870s he had acquired a substantial property, his eldest daughter, Mabel Danvers Smith, married John Herbert Dudley Ryder. On the occasion of the death of his father on 11 December 1900, he was to become the Fifth Earl of Harrowby. So, although somewhat tenuous, in can be seen that towards the end of his life, Admiral of the Fleet Sir Alfred P. Ryder was to become related to his one time civilian superior.

To describe in part the sad circumstances surrounding his death on 30 April 1888, here follows an extract taken from *The Times*, Wednesday, May 2, 1888:-

'... the Admiral, who resided at Wellswood House, Torquay, was on a visit in London to his brothers in Pall Mall, and, as he had been in rather indifferent health, he thought a trip on the river would do him good. On Monday afternoon he accompanied his brothers to the Vauxhall pier, where three tickets for Battersea were purchased. As an up-boat had only that moment left the pier, the gentlemen were informed that they had nearly a quarter of an hour to wait, and after a few seconds conversation the Messrs. Ryder retired to the small waiting room, leaving the Admiral on the pier.'

In the next few seconds it appears that he misjudged his step and unfortunately fell into the river where the fast flowing water, judged to be making about four knots, rapidly moved him out of reach of assistance. Quickly boats were sent to his aid but, alas, too late to effect a rescue. Subsequently at the inquest it was found that, 'the deceased dropped into the water while suffering from an epileptic fit (79).'

His two brothers who witnessed this unfortunate and sad event were William Dudley Ryder, born: 13 October 1813, and Richard Calthorpe Whitmore Ryder, born: 22 July 1822.

Obituary notices regarding the death of Sir Alfred appeared in national and regional newspapers throughout England, and also, in their issue of June 1888, in *The Church Pennant*, the monthly magazine of 'The Naval Church Society'.

That he was a God fearing man there is no doubt. The Parish Magazine at Hambleden, for example, contains evidence of many regular donations made over the years in respect of such requirements as the Church Choir, Church Warming and Lighting, and Sunday School (80).

A Memorial to Sir Alfred may be seen on the south wall of St. Ann's Church, HM Dockyard, Portsmouth.

Subsequently the 'Ryder Memorial Prize' was to be, 'Founded by Deed of 12 July 1889 to perpetuate the memory of Admiral of the Fleet Sir Alfred Phillips Ryder KCB.' The prize was funded by a sum of GBP 160 invested in government securities and was to awarded to:-

> 'Sub Lieutenant who shall take the first place at the examination in French held by the Examiner in French at the Royal Naval College, Greenwich, but a colloquial knowledge of the language shall be deemed necessary (81).'

NOTES

1. There were ten sons and three daughters. An elder brother, Charles Dudley, when serving as a Midshipman in the frigate *Naiad*, 44, Captain Hon. Robert Spencer, together with five of his crew had drowned off Civitavecchia on 28 May 1825 when their boat upset in disturbed seas. He was buried in the Protestant cemetery, Rome. Family tree, Sandon Hall: visit by the author on 3-4 July 2008. Courtesy Mr. Michael J. Bosson. Dates of birth and baptism kindly confirmed by Mr. Philip Nokes, Deputy Diocesan Secretary at Wells: 21 October 2008.
2. *Illustrated London News*, 12 May 1888, 510.
3. *Dictionary of National Biography.*
4. NA ADM 53/1443.
5. Sandon Hall. *Harrowby Mss.* Vol. 1118.
6. Ibid.
7. O'Byrne, 1016. Also *Harrowby Mss.* Vol. 1076, document 33.
8. It was in *Blossom* between 1825 and 1828 that Captain Frederick William Beechey (1796-1856) had carried out his splendid voyage of discovery. Barry M. Gough, *To the Pacific and Arctic with Beechey*, (Cambridge, 1972).
9. *Harrowby Mss.* Vol. CIII, document 456.
10. NA ADM 53/ 3371. Log book *Vixen*.
11. Percy William **Doyle** (1804-1887). Following earlier service in Washington, Madrid and Constantinople, from 6 December 1842 had been appointed Secretary of Legation to the Mexican Republic. Subsequently Charge d'Affaires at that place. From 24 December 1851 to 19 February 1858, when he retired, Minister Plenipotentiary to the Mexican Republic. CB: March 1858. *Foreign Office List*, 1883.
12. Clowes, Vol. VI, 350/1.

13. *Harrowby Mss.* Vol. CIV, document 23.

14. Ibid., documents 29 and 30.

15. *Harrowby Mss.* Vol. 1118. Granville Gower **Loch** (1813-1853). From 16 March 1852 to command frigate *Winchester*, 50, in the East Indies and on 4 February 1853 to be killed up the River Irrawaddy during the second Burma War. *Navy List.*

16. Ibid.

17. *Harrowby Mss.* Vol. 1076, document 33.

18. *Harrowby Mss.* Vol. 1118.

   Charles John **Napier.** Born near Falkirk: 6 March 1786. Died: 6 November 1860 and was buried at All Saints, Catherington, Hampshire. Entered the Navy in 1799 and, especially as a younger officer, won a great name for himself. However as a Captain in the Levant in 1840 he had behaved, although successfully militarily, in an insubordinate manner, on this occasion this misbehaviour being overlooked by his superior. KCB: 4 December 1840. Between 1841 and 1847, and again between 1855 and 1860, MP for Marylebone and Southwark respectively. Technically a progressive officer, and privately wealthy. Rear Admiral: 9 November 1846. Vice Admiral: 28 May 1853. C. in C., Baltic: February – November 1854. Frequently brilliantly competent, unfortunately also he was inclined to interpret facts to show himself to avantage, and to criticize his superiors. Admiral: 6 March 1858. The phrase employed by Gilly, 'petulant effusion', is most appropriate and indeed, from the Baltic, Napier was not to be employed again. Conversely, in Parliament, he was to work towards better treatment of seamen and an improvement in their conditions.

   Also at All Saints, Catherington is to be found a monument to Rear Admiral Sir Christopher G.F.M. Cradock, killed during the Battle of Coronel, 1 November 1914.

19. Ibid.

20. Ibid.

21. Ibid.

22. NA ADM 53/5560. *Viper*, 586 tons, Lieut. and Commander Henry Wandesford Comber. One of the six *Arrow* class especially ordered for service in the shallow waters encountered both in the Baltic and Black Seas in the war against Russia. David Lyon and Rif Winfield, *The Sail and Steam Navy List,* (London, 2004), 218/9.

23. Ibid. Paddle wheel *Terrible*, 3,190 tons, Captain James Johnstone McCleverty (1810-1863). *Navy List.*

   Surgeon Edward Hodges Cree, *Odin*, 16 guns, 1,326 tons, was present off Kinburn. Extracts taken from his diary of 17 October 1855 follow:-

   '7.30 a.m. the Russians opened fire from the large fort on the French troops. We got the mortar vessels into position again and sent our shell into the large fort. In the meantime three French floating batteries had arrived (-). It was strange to see the shot striking their iron sides and flying off again, generally split into pieces. By 9.40 the batteries had steamed into position asnd then opened a terrible fire, in volleys, which brought down the outer wall of the fort in cartloads at each volley. It was a fine sight for us, but not to the poor Russians, the volleys from the heavy guns crumbling away the wall by tons, our shells bursting in the fort.'

   Ed. Michael Levien, *The Cree Journals,* (Exeter, Devon, 1981), 263.

24. *Harrowby Mss.* Vol. 1118.

25. With his communication of 11 September 2008, kindly confirmed by Mr. Michael Bosson, Archivist, Sandon Hall.

26. *Harrowby Mss.* Vol. 1118.

   Also see Lisle Ryder, *Letters to Eddy – The Letters of Admiral Sir Alfred Ryder,* (Woodbridge, Suffolk, 2014). The author is a great-great-nephew of Sir Alfred. The ninety six page volume is beatutifully produced and illustrated.

27. *Harrowby Mss.* Vol. 1076, document 19.

28. Ibid., document 20.

29. Caird Library, National Maritime Museum, Greenwich. Ref: *MLN/199/82*.

30. NA ADM 196/37. *Service* Record.

31. *Harrowby Mss.* Vol. 1069, document 191.

   Oscar Parkes, *British Battleships,* (Annapolis, MD., 1990), 222/223, 226.

32. *Harrowby Mss.* Vol. CV, document 315.

33. Ibid., document 323.

34. Ibid., documents 332 and 334.

35. *Foreign Office List,* 1884.

36. *Harrowby Mss.* Vol. CV, document 340.

37. Ibid., document 369. Wade is Thomas Francis Wade (1818-1895), then British Envoy Extraordinary and Minister Plenipotentiary to Peking – see reference (44) below. Shadwell is his immediate predecessor on the China Station.

38. Ibid., document 371. A later edition, also in two volumes, Dr. S. Wells Williams, *The Middle Kingdom,* (London, 1883).

39. NA ADM 53/11014A.

40. NA ADM 53/10364. Log Book *Iron Duke.*

41. Oscar Parkes, *British Battleships,* (Annapolis, MD., 1990), 155.

42. John Curtis Perry, *Great Britain and the Imperial Japanese Navy, 1858-1905,* (Harvard, 1961), 109.

43. Colonel C. Field, *Britain's Sea Soldiers,* II (Liverpool, 1924), 150.

44. Thomas Francis **Wade**. Born in London: 25 August 1818. Died at Cambridge: 31 July 1895. Trinity College, Cambridge: graduated in 1837. Ensign 81st Regiment: 2 November 1838. Various other Regiments. Lieutenant: 16 November 1841. Landed in Hong Kong: June 1842. Participated in the attack on Chinkiang and in the advance upon Nanking. In 1843 appointed Interpreter to the Garrison at Hong Kong. Assistant Chinese Secretary: 30 March 1847. Sold out: 22 June 1847. Vice Consul at Shanghai: 1852. In 1853 the native Chinese city of Shanghai fell to the Taiping rebels. With the encouragement of the local Ch'ing authorities from 12 July 1854 appointed Collector of Customs, Shanghai. (From May 1859 this position was to evolve into Inspector-General of the Chinese Maritime Customs). From 6 July 1855 Chinese Secretary at Hong Kong. Was attached to the Earl of Elgin's Special Missions to China in 1857/8 and 1860. Chinese Secretary to the British Mission in China: 19 August 1859. Together with Messrs. Harry Parkes and Henry Loch, captured outside Peking and held prisoner by the Manchu: 18 September – 8 October 1860. CB: 13 May 1861. Secretary, Chinese Secretary and Translator to the Legation in China: 27 January 1862. Acting Charge d'Affaires at Peking: 23 June 1864 – 30 November 1865. (On 7 April 1865 Sir Rutherford Alcock was appointed Minister to Peking). Again Acting Charge d'Affaires: 2 November 1869 – 22 July 1871 when appointed Envoy Extraordinary and Minister Plenipotentiary and Chief Superintendent of British Trade in China. KCB: 25 November 1875. Retired: 1 July 1883. Elected as the first Professor of Chinese at Cambridge University: 1888. Developed the Wade-Giles system of romanizing the Chinese language. GCMG: 24 May 1889. As Professor of Chinese, in 1897 succeeded by Herbert Allen Giles (1845-1935). *Foreign Office List,* 1869 and 1896. *The China Year Book,* 1919. *Encyclopaedia Britannica.* Ian C. Ruxton, *The Diaries and Letters of Sir Ernest Mason Satow (1843-1929),* (Lewiston, NY, 1998), 438.

    See P.D. Coates, *The China Consuls,* (OUP, 1988), 303-305 for more on Margary.

45. On 9 November 1877 the first British consular official to be posted to Ichang was Walter Edward **King**. The unappealing circumstances surrounding him taking up the post, up river from Hankow in HMS *Kestrel,* are described in *The China Consuls,* 273/4. Owing to ill health King was to retire on pension on 21 August 1878, but he lived to 13 November 1917. *Foreign Office List.*

46. **Li** Hung-chang. Born: 15 February 1823. Died in Peking: 7 November 1901, but the following year, in considerable state, his body was returned to his family at Ho-fei, Anhui. For twenty five years from 1870 the Viceroy of the capital province, Chihli. Keenly interested in, and the driving force behind many of China's efforts made during this era to modernise her economy, industry and military ability. In 1872 initiated the founding of China Merchants Steam Navigation Co. In 1895 the leader of the Chinese delegation which resulted in the treaty of Shimonoseki, his opposite number being Ito Hirobumi. It must be added however that much of Li's enterprise was made with a view to personal financial gain. *Encyclopaedia Britannica.* Alicia Helen Neva Little, *Li Hung-chang: His Life and Times,* (London, 1903). For a career précis of Ito Hirobumi see Keppel, C. in C., 1867, reference (33).

47. *Navy List.* An entertaining account of the Convention, as witnessed by an onlooker, may be seen in William John Gill, *The River of Golden Sand,* (London, 1883), 8-10.

48. NA ADM 1/6378.

49. NA ADM 1/6343.

50. Ibid.

51. *North China Herald,* 28 October 1875, 430-432.

52. Captain H.C. St. John, RN, *The Wild Coasts of Nipon,* (Edinburgh, 1880), 324/5.

53. NA ADM 1/6343. Gun vessel *Thistle*, 4 guns, 584 tons, Commander Francis Stirling. *Navy List*.

54. Ibid.

55. James Wheeler Woodford **Birch**. After leaving the Navy first entered the Colonial service in Ceylon, there rising to be Government Agent of the Eastern Province. In 1870 appointed Colonial Secretary, Straits Settlements. Following the signing of the Treaty of Pangkor in 1874, selected, '... for the difficult post of adviser to the Sultan of Perak.' Ed. William R. Roff, *Stories and Sketches by Sir Frank Swettenham*, (OUP, 1967), 74.

56. Sjovald Cunyngham-Brown, *The Traders*, (London, 1971), 159. The author is quoting Sir Frank Swettenham (1850-1946). See also (55) Ed. William R. Roff, 74-87.

57. The cruise is described by Hon. Henry Noel Shore, *The Flight of the Lapwing*, (London, 1881).

58. Tsuzuki Chushichi, *The Pursuit of Power in Modern Japan, 1825-1995*, (OUP, 2000), 69/70.

59. **Saigo** Takamori. Born in Kagoshima: 7 February 1827. Died near Kagoshima: 24 September 1877. Played an important role in the overthrow of the Tokugawa Shogunate. By 1871 in command of the Imperial Guard, a disciplined force with the backing of whom the Meiji authorities felt able to abolish the feudal han administrative regions of the country, to replace them by prefectures. In this manner the remaining troops of the han daimio were rendered powerless. It was in part the reaction to this tactic which had resulted in samurai unrest. Tsuzuki, 53, 56, 61. *Encyclopaedia Britannica*. Today in Ueno Park, Tokyo a bronze statue to Saigo Takamori may be seen. Saigo Tsugumichi (1843-1902) was a younger brother.

60. Trans. Eiichi Kiyooka, *The Autobiography of Fukuzawa Yukichi*, (Columbia University, 1966), 363/4.

61. Tsuzuki, 70.

62. NA ADM 1/6411. General Letter. *Audacious* at Hong Kong, 1 March 1877.

63. *The River of Golden Sand*. The account of Captain Gill's travels on the Yangtse, and then overland, are related between pages 44 and 318. Paddle steamer *Hankow*, 3,073 grt. Built in Glasgow for China Navigation (Butterfield and Swire) and during March 1874 placed in service on the Lower River. One of their first vessels in the East. In 1886 transferred to their Hong Kong – Canton service. At Hong Kong on 14 October 1906 gutted by fire, a disaster during which 130 lives were lost. Subsequently used as a godown hulk cum pontoon wharf at Hankow, Shasi, and finally from 1938, at Ichang. Destroyed during WW2. *The China Navigation Co. Ltd.*, 15.

64. *The China Consuls*, 307. Edward Colborne Baber, FRGS. Born: 30 April 1843. Christ's Hospital and Magdalene College, Cambridge. Appointed Student Interpreter in China: 28 July 1866. Acting Vice Consul at Kiukiang: 1 September 1871 to 9 May 1872. Similarly at Tamsui: 6 June 1872 to 30 September 1873. Interpreter: 14 November 1876. Following his expedition with Gill and posting to Chungking, then Chinese Secretary at Peking: 22 October 1879. Between 23 October 1885 and 24 November 1886 acting Consul General in Corea. Died at Bhamo, Burma: 16 June 1890. *Foreign Office List*, 1891. A traveller of note.

65. *Harrowby Mss*. Vol. CV, document 457.

   John Pope Hennessy (1834-1891). MP: 1859-1865. Governor of Labuan in 1867 and there on 4 February 1868 married Catherine Elizabeth Low, 'Kitty', (1850-1923), daughter of Sir Hugh. Subsequently, in relatively quick order, Governor of the Gold Coast, Sierra Leone, Bahamas and Barbados. Arrived in Hong Kong: 22 April 1877. KCMG: 22 April 1880. Left Hong Kong: 7 March 1882. Governor of Mauritius: 1883-1889. E.J. Eitel, *Europe in China*, (London and Hong Kong, 1895), Chapter XXI. As appears to have been usual in all the colonies over which he held administrative sway, His Excellency's term in office was controversial.

66. Eitel, 540. John Macneile Price, Surveyor General between 1873 and 1889.

   In the event the Observatory was to be established in 1883 during the gubernatorial service of Sir George Bowen. As will be appreciated an important function was that of typhoon forecasting and reporting.

67. Ibid. 538.

68. NA ADM 1/6411.

69. *Service Record*.

70. *Harrowby Mss*. Vol. 1976, document 33.

71. *Harrowby Mss*. Vol. CV, document 471.

72. Ibid., document 484.

73. Ibid., document 498.

74. *Harrowby Mss.* Vol. XLIV, documents 205/7.

75. *Harrowby Mss.* Vol. CV, document 500.

76. Information kindly made available by Canon Lisle Ryder, great-great-nephew of the Admiral: 9 May 2015. Canon Ryder is the author of that delightful volume – reference (26) above.

77. *Extract from the Parish Register*, a copy of which kindly was supplied by Mr. Charles Gray. Also information kindly supplied on 11 September 2008 by Mr. Michael Bosson, Sandon Hall.

78. *Service Record.*

79. *Harrowby Mss.* Vol. 1118. Various newspaper cuttings reporting post inquest.

80. Courtesy Mr. Charles Gray, Hambleden.

81. NA ADM 1/22835.

31 August 1877 to 26 September 1878
Vice Admiral Charles Farrel **Hillyar**

Born on 24 July 1817 and baptised at Berry Pomeroy near Totnes, Devon on 19 December 1817, son of Rear Admiral Sir James Hillyar, KCB, who died suddenly at Torre House on Sunday, 9 July 1843, and his wife Mary, nee Taylor (1).

Died suddenly of heart disease at his residence, Torre House, Torpoint, aged seventy one years: 14 December 1888 (2).

A brother was Rear Admiral Henry Shank Hillyar (1819-1893).

Entered the Royal Navy on 18 March 1831. Passed his examination on 17 March 1837, and served for a time on the South America Station as Mate in *President*, 50, Captain William Broughton (3). His Captain was the son of William Robert Broughton (1762-1821), the well known surveyor of the west coast of Asia from latitude 35 deg. N up to 52 deg. N in the sloop *Providence* and her tender, especially during the years 1796 and 1797.

Lieutenant: 24 March 1842. From 13 May 1842 appointed to and served for several months in the old first rate three decker *Caledonia*, 120, Captain Alexander Milne, flagship at Plymouth of Admiral Sir David Milne (1763-1845) (4).

From 12 May 1843 in frigate *Tyne*, 26, Captain William Nugent Glascock, Mediterranean.

From 4 September 1846 continued in the Mediterranean but now in *Amazon*, Captain James John Stopford, until she paid off on 6 April 1848 (5). She had been a frigate, forty two guns, but had re-entered service in January 1845 but by now razeed to become a corvette of just twenty six guns (6).

Commander: 15 May 1848. From 1 January 1849 in the steam frigate *Centaur*, 6 guns, flagship, West Coast of Africa, Commodore Arthur Fanshawe. From her in West Africa he paid off on 1 July 1851 and, a month later, on 5 August joined the small paddle frigate *Penelope*, 16 guns, 2,766 tons, Commodore Henry William Bruce (7). There on the Coast during the latter part of 1851 he was involved in attacks against Cocioco, (also see Coote, C. in C., 1878). As a consequence, ' 26 December 1851: severely wounded at the successful attack on Lagos (8).'

> 'In the course of 1851, Cocioco, a usurping king of Lagos, then one of the chief centres of the slave trade, became troublesome and intractable... Mr. Beecroft (John Beecroft: 1790-1854), British Consul at Fernando Po, determined to seek another interview with the king; and, in order that Cocioco should be under no misapprehension concerning the seriousness and solemnity of the British demands, he arranged that armed boats of the squadron should accompany the mission under a flag of truce...'

This first approach on 25 November 1851 was thwarted. Reinforcements assembled and on 24 December an attack was launched:-

'... and the boats were under Commanders Robert Coote, Alan Henry Gardner, and Charles Farrel Hillyar.'

By the end of December 1851 Cocioco had abandoned the town and fled (9).
Following his successful endeavours in West Africa he was to receive early promotion.

Captain: 20 February 1852.
In passing it should be recorded that British trade to and from West Africa had become increasingly important during the early years of the nineteenth century. So it was that with his first sailing from England on 24 September 1852, Macgregor Laird of the Liverpool and Birkenhead shipbuilding family, founder of the African Steam Ship Company, was able to commence operating successfully the first line of steamships between Britain and that region (10).

On 28 March 1854 Great Britain and France declared war on Russia and the Crimean War, initially revolving around a dispute between France, Russia and Turkey concerning control of the Holy places in Jerusalem, grew considerably in stature.
From 15 December 1854 until 28 March 1855 in command of steam sloop *Malacca*, 17 guns, 'Particular Service' (11).
From 6 June 1855 in command of the paddle wheel steam frigate *Gladiator*, 6, Mediterranean. Some friends of his who were involved with the Army in the Crimea recorded:-

'In the vicinity of Sebastopol, Monday, August 6, 1855.
The first evening that we arrived, Captain Charles Hillyar came on board, but only to say 'good-bye', as he left the next morning in the *Gladiator* for Corfu, where he was sent to fetch up troops and guns.'
'Wednesday, August 22.
The *Gladiator* came up from Balaklava yesterday, where she had discharged the products of her trip to Corfu; she brought, in addition to eight mortars, 2200 shells and a couple of hundred artillerymen. I dined onboard with Captain Hillyar (12).'

Also during the Crimean War, on 17 October 1855 at the Liman of the Dnieper he participated in the bombardment of the fort at Kinburn which led to its capture by the Allies. During this engagement the practical value of armour plated men of war was demonstrated most clearly (see also Ryder, C. in C., 1874).
By the Treaty of Paris the Crimean War was brought to a conclusion on 30 March 1856.
Lying some thirty five kilometres off the coast at the mouth of the River Danube near Sulina is Serpent Island. Against the wishes of the Allies, in 1856 the Russians endeavoured to land forces on this minute piece of land. He was ordered to attend to the matter, and later was to receive due recognition of his success:-

'18 August 1856: Admiral Lord Lyons commending his prudent and active conduct on the occasion of the Russians attempting to take possession of the Isle of Serpents (13).'

Gladiator paid off in Devonport on 22 May 1857.
For his services in the Crimea, '... he received the Crimea and Turkish medals, the Sebastopol Clasp, and the fourth class of the Order of the Medjidie (14).'
From 18 November 1859 in command of the screw steam ship *Queen*, 3,249 tons, Channel Squadron. His Commander in the ship was John J.S. Josling (1838-1863). Unfortunately there appear to have been problems with discipline in *Queen*. The consequences of these difficulties would seem to have had little or no effect on his subsequent career nevertheless two relevant entries, which were noted in his record, are repeated herewith:-

'2 January 1861: severely admonished for inflicting corporal punishment on a first class Man.'
'25 January 1862: the Board much dissatisfied with the want of discipline and good conduct in the Crew of *Queen*.'

In mid 1861 *Queen* had been transferred to the Mediterranean, only paying off in Portsmouth on 15 December 1863.

> 'In the Mediterranean, during the revolutionary troubles in Greece, Captain Charles Farrel Hillyar, of the *Queen*, 74, screw, had occasion more than once to land Marines, especially in July (1863) when a force under Lieut. James Woodward Scott, RM, undertook the protection of the British Legation at Athens (15)'.

In correspondence with the Admiralty, on 10 July 1863 the C. in C., Vice Admiral Smart, was to praise his, Captain Hillyar's, conduct in respect of these disturbances at Athens, 'calling his measures very judicious (16)'.

Clearly by 1863 disciplinary problems in the ship had been resolved.

From 14 June 1865 in command of the screw frigate *Octavia*, 39 guns, 3,161 tons, East Indies Station. The ship had been launched in 1849 as a sailing frigate, but was converted, and lengthened, in 1861.

From 26 September 1865 as **Commodore** Second Class in command of the Station in *Octavia*.

Rear Admiral: with seniority from 24 May 1867.

It is of interest to note that, precisely as usual, the latter part of his certificate of commission was phrased in the following manner:-

> 'Given under our hands and the Seal of the Office of Admiralty this 31st day of May 1867. In the thirtieth Year of Her Majesty's Reign (17)'.

At the conclusion of his term of duty, on 29 July 1867 being succeeded by Commodore Leopold George Heath (1817-1907), he returned from the East Indies by Packet, reaching England on 8 September that year (18).

CB: 2 June 1869.

From 9 July 1872 appointed C. in C., Pacific with his Flag in the armour plated screw ship *Repulse*, 12 guns, 6,190 tons. She was commanded by Captain Charles Thomas Curme who, on 19 February 1892 and as a Vice Admiral, was to die in office as C. in C., The Nore.

In the event, via Madeira and Rio de Janeiro, *Repulse* arrived at Valparaiso on 27 October and there he actually assumed command of the station on 1 November 1872. Leaving Valparaiso in February 1873 he cruised up the west coast of South America with calls at Coquimbo, Arica, Callao and Paita, in June visited the Sandwich Islands, finally arriving at Esquimalt, BC on 26 July 1873. It is of interest to note that in 1855 a predecessor, the then C. in C., Pacific Station, Rear Admiral Henry William Bruce, under whom he had served on the West Coast of Africa in *Penelope* in 1851, first had initiated the construction of base facilities ashore at Esquimalt.

Vice Admiral: 29 May 1873.

On 15 September 1873 at Esquimalt succeeded on the Pacific Station by Rear Admiral The Hon. Arthur A.L.P. Cochrane, who had been appointed on 6 June 1873 (19).

He arrived back in England on 21 October 1873.

To take up his command in China he sailed from England in the P. & O. screw steamer *Gwalior*, 2,733 grt, and arrived at Hong Kong on 4 November 1877. At 1.0 p.m. that afternoon first hoisted his flag in the steam paddle despatch vessel *Vigilant*, 985 tons.

From Admiral Ryder he assumed command of the station on 8 November 1877 (20). His Flagship was the ironclad *Audacious*, 6,010 tons, Captain Francis Durrant.

Early in the new year he advised the Admiralty that on the subject of 'Pirates in China Seas', both German and English Ships of War were to co-operate in the common cause of endeavouring to control this great problem (21).

Concerning a future C. in C., as he was to be from 1895, but otherwise purely a routine change of senior personnel on the Station, in March 1878 he informed London that, '... Captain Alexander Buller, CB on being superseded (as SNO, Japan), will return to England via America.'

There exists an amusing insight into the hospitality afforded to his guests by the C. in C. A newly appointed Lieutenant, George Fowler King-Hall, joined *Audacious* on Sunday, 24 March 1878. He had sailed out from England, leaving Southampton on 7 February 1878 in the P. & O. steamer *Pekin*, 3,777 grt, and in her had travelled to Galle. There he had switched to their smaller *Kashgar*, 2,621 grt. In his diary he records the detail of his arrival onboard the Flagship at Hong Kong, and of dinner that evening:-

'I joined on Sunday morning whilst Church was going on, a launch being sent for me. Found Willoughby (the Flag Lieut.) all ready to welcome me, and after Church made acquaintance with Admiral and others. Tho' after all it was not making acquaintance as I knew all before. (Later in the day). Came onboard and dined with the Admiral, a very good dinner. He manages to stow a good deal of liquor away under his jacket and tries to make everyone else do the same (22).'

Meanwhile, in transit through Japan and about to take passage back to England across the Pacific, Alexander Buller had carried out a little modest intelligence work of his own:-

'Captain Buller wrote to the Admiral from Yokohama. He had lately dined with the Russian Admiral. They keep a sharp look out for the English ships. Buller also sent a plan of the Outrigger Torpedoes the Russians had constructed at Yokohama (23).'

Although they carefully watched each other's movements, at that stage the day to day relationship between the British and Russian fleets was perfectly amicable. Here follows an extract from Lieut. King-Hall's diary entry made at Kobe on Sunday, 28 April 1878:-

'Came in here last Wednesday (24 April). Found the Russian squadron in here.
Coaled ship Thursday. That evening the Admiral gave a large dinner to the Russians.
The dinner went off very well not withstanding the fact that neither Admiral could communicate with each other, ours speaking English and French, and the Russian his own language and German.
We drank the Queen's and Czar's health together standing, band playing (24).'

Indeed the C. in C. paid especial attention to the movements of Russian men-of-war, and in keeping the Admiralty informed. As one example he wrote to inform London that the Russian squadron, flag in the screw corvette *Bayan*, had arrived at Yokohama on 3 May 1878. Again, writing from Nagasaki three days later, '… the movements of the Russian Squadron are kept as secret as possible but Their Lordships may rest assured that I keep a close watch on them. Had war been declared …'.

By 17 June clearly matters had become more serious and from Nagasaki, in response to, '… the telegrams received at Hong Kong announced the possibility of England being involved in war…', he described how he concentrated the vessels under his command at Yokohama, Nagasaki, Hong Kong and Singapore, '… for the protection of British shipping (25).'

Fortunately, following the Congress of Berlin, 13 June to 13 July 1878, tensions between the powers, including the Ottoman Empire, relaxed and in the East by August 1878 the C. in C. found himself in a position to disperse his ships. These peaceful arrangements included the return of the armoured cruiser *Shannon*, 5,450 tons, Captain William B. Grant, and wooden screw corvette *Diamond*, 1,934 tons, Captain George S. Bosanquet, to England, and the transfer of the composite screw corvette *Ruby*, 2,120 tons, Captain Robert H.M. Molyneux, to Trincomalee.

Meanwhile on 22 May 1878, having been absent from Japan since May 1871, the future C. in C., Combined Fleet, IJN, Togo Heihachiro returned to Yokohama in the ironclad corvette *Hiei*, 2,248 tons, recently completed at Milford Haven. In addition to intervals of academic study at Cambridge and at Greenwich, his maritime training in England had included a period, from August 1873 to December 1874, in H.M.S. *Worcester*, a frigate on loan from the Navy to the Worcester Mercantile Training School, Captain Henderson Smith, and moored in the River Thames off Greenhithe. Also, between February and September 1875 he had completed a circumnavigation via Australia in the sailing ship *Hampshire*, 1,214 grt, Captain Robert Ridgers.

On his return home he was appointed first class sub-lieutenant, initially remaining in *Hiei* (26).

In June 1878 s.s. *Orduna*, 729 grt, arrived at Yokohama from England. She had been acquired by the Mitsui organisation who were to use her to transport coal from the state owned Miike mines near Nagasaki, to Shanghai. The new owners re-named her *Hideyoshi Maru*. From this beginning grew the Mitsui ship owning arm of what is today, in 2008, the huge operation of Mitsui OSK Lines Ltd (27). Subsequently acquired by the Mitsui organisation, the Miike mines were to cease operation as recently as in March 1997.

Admiral: 26 September 1878.

As his short term of office drew to a close, in *Audacious* he left Hong Kong on 23 October 1878 and arrived at Singapore on 1 November. On 15 November, that day having handed over command of the station to Admiral Coote, he sailed in *Audacious* bound for Trincomalee, Aden, Suez, Malta and Gibraltar. The ship grounded briefly when making her transit of the Suez Canal otherwise she proceeded satisfactorily. Finally leaving her last port of call, Gibraltar, at daylight on 28 January 1879, she anchored back in Plymouth Sound at 4.10 p.m. on Sunday, 2 February 1879. At sunset the following evening his flag was hauled down for the last time.

Subsequently the ship herself was to proceed around to Chatham where she paid off on Saturday, 22 February 1879 (28).

He retired on 9 June 1882, just short of his sixty fifth birthday. In retirement his pension was at the rate of GBP 870.00 per annum (29).

KCB: 21 June 1887.

His funeral in the churchyard at Anthony took place on 19 December 1888 and was attended by numerous relatives and friends including the newly appointed C. in C., Devonport, Admiral Sir William Dowell (see C. in C., 1884) (30).

> 'Around the coffin was a silken flag, presented to the deceased by the officers and crew of the *Audacious* on the occasion of his promotion to the rank of full Admiral whilst on the China station. This flag and the wreaths were lowered into the grave with the coffin. The breast plate bore the simple inscription: "Admiral Sir Charles Hillyar, KCB, died 14 December 1888; aged 71 years." The bearers were 14 petty officers from the *Cambridge*, gunnery ship, who carried the coffin on their shoulders from the car to the church (31).'

NOTES

1. Sir James Hillyar (1769-1843) being well known, when in command of HMS *Phoebe*, 38, for his capture of USS *Essex*, 46, Captain David Porter, off Valparaiso on 28 March 1814.

2. *Illustrated London News*, 29 December 1888, 787. Further detail from his Obituary, *The Times*, Monday, December 17, 1888. Also letter to the author from Torpoint Archives: 14 February 2007. Devon Record Office: Ref. GM2007-1711 dated 23 March 2007. Actually baptized Charles Ferrell Hillyar – Berry Pomeroy, Parish of St. Mary, entry 191, 1817.

3. O'Byrne, 517.

4. Captain Alexander **Milne** (1806-1896). To be promoted Rear Admiral: 20 January 1858 and Vice Admiral: 13 April 1865. Admiral: 1 April 1870. GCB: 1871. Baronet: 1876. Admiral of the Fleet: 10 June 1881. Admiral David Milne (1763-1845), father of Alexander, had been promoted Admiral on 23 November 1841. On completing his term of office at Plymouth he was to die at sea on 5 May 1845 while on passage back to his native Scotland. *Navy List*.

5. James John **Stopford** (1817-1868). Joined the Navy: 1829. Captain: 14 May 1841. Rear Admiral: 4 June 1861. His father was Admiral The Hon. Sir Robert Stopford (1768-1847), and grandfather James Stopford (1731-1810), Second Earl of Courtown, Co. Wexford, Ireland. For many years the Stopford's were a well known Naval and military family. *Navy List*. NA ADM 196/36. *Service Record*.

6. *Amazon*: David Lyon and Rif Winfield, *The Sail and Steam Navy List*, (London, 2004), 116.

7. *Service Record*. Henry William Bruce (1792-1863). From West Africa to be promoted Rear Admiral: 30 July 1852. C.

in C., Pacific: November 1854 – July 1857. Vice Admiral: 2 October 1857. C. in C., Portsmouth: March 1860 – March 1863. KCB: 28 June 1861. Admiral: 27 April 1863. *Navy List.*

8. Ibid. Also, obituary, *The Times.*

9. Clowes, Vol. VI, 367/371.

    John Beecroft (1790-1854). Born at Sleights, near Whitby, Yorks. Died in West Africa, today a forgotten but at the time a well recognised figure in the campaign to suppress the slave trade. K.O. Dike, *Journal of the Historical Society of Nigeria,* Vol. 1, No. 1, December 1956.

10. Peter N. Davies, *The Impact of Improving Communications on Commercial Transactions: Nineteenth Century Case Studies from British West Africa and Japan,* (International Journal of Maritime History, Vol. XIV, No. 1, June 2002), 227. The African Steamship Company subsequently was to be acquired by Elder, Dempster & Co.

11. *Malacca,* launched at Moulmein, Burma: 9 April 1853. Engined and fitted out at Chatham: 17 August 1854. Sold out of the service in June 1869 and later that year acquired by the recently established Imperial Japanese Navy as their *Tsukuba.* Broken up ca. 1906. *The Sail and Steam Navy List,* 213.

12. Frances Isabella Duberly, *Journal Kept During the Russian War,* (London, 1855), VI, The Fall of Sebastopol.

    The Lord High Commissioner to the Ionian Islands between 1849 and 1855 was Sir Henry George **Ward** (1797-1860), subsequently Governor of Ceylon. At Corfu in 1855 he was succeeded by Sir John **Young**, First Baron Lisgar (1807-1876), later Governor of New South Wales, then Governor General of Canada. British protection over the Ionian Islands was to end on 21 May 1864, the islands then becoming Greek.

13. *Service Record.* Serpent Island, or Ostriv Zmiinyi, is at 45.15N 30.12E. Today, 2008, the island falls within the boundaries of Ukraine.

14. Obituary, *The Times.*

15. Clowes, Vol. VII, 189/190. Otto I, King of Greece was forced to give up his throne in 1862. In 1863 he was replaced by Prince William of Denmark (1845-1913), brother of HM Princess Alexandra who was to become Queen of England. As George I he reigned from 1863 to 1913. He gave Greece a more democratic form of government. *Encyclopaedia Britannica.*

16. *Service Record.*

    Robert **Smart** (1796-1874). Captain: 10 January 1837. Rear Admiral: 9 July 1857. C. in C., Channel Squadron: January 1861 to April 1863. Vice Admiral: 3 December 1863. C. in C., Mediterranean from April 1863 to April 1866. KCB: 28 March 1865. Admiral: 15 January 1869. *Navy List.*

17. Caird Library. Ref: *MS 89/037.*

18. *Service Record.*

19. Ibid. Arthur Auckland Leopold Pedro **Cochrane**. Born: 24 September 1824. He was the fourth child and third son of the Tenth Earl of Dundonald, Admiral Sir Thomas Cochrane (1775-1860). Died: 20 August 1905. Entered the RN: April 1839. Captain: 29 August 1854. Rear Admiral: 1 April 1870. C. in C., Pacific: June 1873 – April 1876. Vice Admiral: 12 November 1876. Admiral: 1 December 1881. KCB: 25 May 1889. *Navy List.*

20. NA ADM 1/6411. Admiral Ryder to the Admiralty, 8 November 1877.

21. NA ADM 1/6450. *Letter No. 11. Audacious* at Hong Kong, 7 January 1878.

22. RN Museum Library, Portsmouth. King-Hall Ref: *2000.53.* Diary Vol. 1, 28 March 1878.

23. Ibid. Entry dated 7 April 1878. At Sea from Hong Kong to Nagasaki.

24. Ibid.

25. NA ADM 1/6450. *Letter No. 259.*

26. R.V.C. Bodley, *Togo,* (London, 1935), 63-65. Also The Nelson Legacy Conference Series Ltd.

27. Mitsui OSK Lines Ltd., *The First Century of Mitsui OSK Lines Ltd.,* (Japan, 1985), 22. *Lloyds Register,* 1878-1879 and 1879-1880.

28. NA ADM 53/11017.

29. *Service Record.*

30. *Western Morning News,* Thursday, December 20, 1888.

31. *Naval and Military Record,* 27 December 1888.

26 September 1878 to 3 January 1881
Vice Admiral Robert **Coote**

Robert was born in Geneva on 1 June 1820, fourth son of Sir Charles Henry Coote, ninth Baronet of Ballyfin House, Queen's County, Ireland who died on 9 October 1864, and brother of the tenth Baronet, Sir Charles Henry Coote who died, unmarried, on 15 November 1895. In turn the eleventh Baronet was their brother Rev. Sir Algernon Coote who was to die on 20 November 1899. Their mother was Caroline, daughter of John Whaley of Whaley Abbey, Wicklow.

After a long illness he died at 'Arden', College Road, Dulwich on 17 March 1898, and was buried in Brookwood Cemetery, Woking, Surrey (1).

In Ireland the local press rued his passing:-

> 'The deceased gentleman possessed extensive property in Tullamore and district, as well as in Westmeath and Roscommon, and was distinguished by a most benevolent and charitable disposition (2).'

From September 1829 he attended Eton College (3).

Subsequently he entered the Royal Navy on 18 August 1833 and in due course saw early service in the 100' brig sloop *Pelican*, 18 guns, West Coast of Africa. Passed his examination on 5 February 1840. **Mate** in corvette *Daphne*, 18, Captain John Wyndham Dalling, Mediterranean and in particular on the coast of Syria where in 1840 he participated in operations subsequently receiving both the Syrian and Turkish medals (4). These operations included, in November, the bombardment of Acre, at the time occupied by the Egyptians (also see Shadwell, C. in C. 1871-1874). During 1842 and 1843 served in the Royal Yachts *Royal George*, ship rigged and 103' loa, and then in the new paddle vessel *Victoria and Albert*, 1,034 tons bm, both, consecutively, being commanded by Lord Adolphus FitzClarence (5).

Lieutenant: 25 September 1843. From 24 November 1843 served in the wood paddle frigate *Cyclops*, 1,862 tons, Captain William Frederick Lapidge, 'Particular Service' which was on the Irish station during Repeal disturbances.

From 11 March 1845 appointed to the wood paddle frigate *Vulture*, 1,960 tons, Captain John McDougall. The ship was completed at Pembroke Dockyard on 7 June that year and after working up proceeded to the East Indies Station.

Early in April 1847, from *Vulture*'s pinnace he commanded a division of boats during operations in the Canton River. In the main military operations ashore were carried out by the officers and men from various regiments, the whole exercise being rather successful with, as will be seen below, much of the enemy artillery being rendered useless. As SNO, from Hong Kong on 9 April 1847 Captain McDougall wrote his report, an extract from which follows:-

> 'Before daybreak of the 9th, the expedition left Whampoa, on return to Hong Kong, and when passing the Bogue forts, between 8 and 9 a.m., observed them full of troops, and the tompions out

of the guns; we reached this anchorage about 3 p.m. after having spiked eight hundred and seventy nine guns within the Bogue forts, and destroyed all their ammunition, with the exception of the fort in Tiger island which owes its salvation to the ebbing of the tide, and the Major General's and my anxiety to be at Canton on the night of the 2nd for the protection of British life and property (6).'

In succession to Sir Henry Pottinger, from May 1844 to March 1848 the second Governor of Hong Kong was H.E. Sir John Francis Davis (1795-1890). Owing to his considerable linguistic abilities, as far back as 1816 Sir John had been attached to Lord Amherst's Embassy to the Manchu Emperor Chia Ch'ing (1760-1820) in Peking (7). This was only the second such diplomatic attempt by Great Britain.

Commander: 25 June 1847. He received this early promotion especially for services in China.
Continued to serve in *Vulture* until 23 March 1848 (8).
From 21 April 1851 in command of the wood paddle sloop *Volcano*, 5 guns, West Coast of Africa Station. He led her boats in two attacks on, and in the destruction of Lagos:-
'In the course of 1851, Cocioco, a usurping king of Lagos, then one of the chief centres of the slave trade, became troublesome and intractable. …
Mr. Beecroft, British Consul at Fernando Po, determined to seek another interview with the king; and, in order that Cocioco should be under no misapprehension concerning the seriousness and solemnity of the British demands, he arranged that armed boats of the squadron should accompany the mission under a flag of truce. … (Amongst the boats engaged were) from *Volcano* 5, paddle, Commander Robert Coote, whaler under Cmdr. Coote.'

This first approach of 25 November 1851 was thwarted. Reinforcements assembled and on 24 December 1851 an attack was launched:-
'… and the boats were under Commanders Robert Coote, Alan Henry Gardner, and Charles Farrel Hillyar (see C. in C., 1877).'

The affair continued until Monday, 29 December. Meanwhile, on Saturday, 27 December:-
'An hour later, Coote, with some gunboats and a rocket boat, was sent forward to fire a few rounds at Cocioco's house.'
'On the Sunday however Cocioco abandoned the town and fled to the woods. … Only a small British party, under Coote, was that day landed. On Monday, the 29th, Gardner landed with Coote and a larger party, which embarked or destroyed fifty two guns of one kind or another (9).'

At the end of the commission the ship paid off at Woolwich on 30 January 1854 (10).

On 14 February 1854 at Charlton Church he married Lucy, daughter of the naval officer and Arctic explorer Rear Admiral Sir William Edward Parry (1790-1855) (11). She was to pass away on 7 February 1906.
Their son, Stanley Victor Coote was born on 30 May 1862. On 26 October 1889 Stanley was to marry Louisa Bathurst. For a number of years resident at 109 Sloane Street in London, he died on 3 May 1925.
Following Stanley's birth their daughter, Caroline Maud Coote was born twenty one months later, on 22 February 1864. In due course she was to marry Cecil William Park (1856-1913), later Major General, Devonshire Regt. She died on 4 September 1927.

Captain: 29 April 1854.
For three years from 1 March 1860 in command of *Victory*, 101, Flagship, Portsmouth. From the same date, also until 1 March 1863, the C. in C. was Vice Admiral Henry William Bruce (1792-1863), to be created a KCB on 28 June 1861.
There at Portsmouth Robert Coote, 'organised the new naval police (12).'

From 26 November 1864 in command of the screw two decker *Gibraltar*, 81 guns, 3,729 tons, Mediterranean. Early in 1867 she paid off at Devonport.

From 1 June 1867 in command of the screw frigate *Arethusa*, 35 guns, 3,141 tons, Mediterranean. This is the same ship who in 1874 was to be loaned to the Shaftesbury Homes as a training ship at Greenhithe. Only in 1933 was she to be sold, and to be broken up the following year (13).

As is to be expected clearly he and his officers ensured that a high standard was maintained in *Arethusa*. From his Service Record it may be seen that:-

'6 Oct.1868: Board approve state of Efficiency of *Arethusa* on Inspection.

22 Dec. -do-: again complimented on inspection by Snr. Off. at Sheerness.'

Awarded a GSP (Good Service Pension): 1 January 1869.
On 7 January 1869 *Arethusa* paid off.

Rear Admiral: 1 April 1870.
CB: 24 May 1873.
From 1 January 1874 served as Senior Officer, Coast of Ireland with Flag in the screw ship *Revenge*, 52 guns, 5,260 tons.

Vice Admiral: 18 June 1876.

His Flagship on the China Station was to be *Iron Duke*, 6,010 tons. Following a refit she re-commissioned at Devonport on 5 July 1878, Captain Henry F. Cleveland, who took her East. She arrived at Singapore on 19 October, there to await the arrival of the new C. in C. To join her he travelled out from England in the P. & O. packet who arrived at Singapore:-

'... on the 10th (November 1878) instant, two days before he was due, and hoisted his flag onboard the *Iron Duke* (14).'

In the customary manner the exchange of command was accomplished with many salutes being fired, on this occasion an additional seventeen guns by *Iron Duke* early in the evening on Monday 11 November following a visit paid to the ship by the Governor of the Straits Settlements, His Excellency Sir William Cleaver Francis Robinson (1834-1897).

From his predecessor, at Singapore on 15 November 1878 he assumed command of the Station. Admiral Hillyar in *Audacious*, a sister ship to *Iron Duke* so also of 6,010 tons and with a main armament of ten 9" guns, sailed for England that day at 5.45 a.m. (15).

A short while later, in *Iron Duke* on 18 November, he sailed from Singapore on his first cruise around and up into the Strait of Malacca arriving at Malacca the following day. Local business having being attended to next he proceeded further up the Strait and anchored off The Dindings on 21 November 1878, only remaining there for the day before continuing to Penang where he arrived on 22 November (16). He returned to Singapore on 2 December 1878 with the intention of leaving on 5 December for Hong Kong via Sarawak, Labuan and Manila.

Indeed this next cruise took place precisely as planned as on 5 December, with the gun vessel *Lapwing*, 805 tons, in tow, he departed from Singapore and early on 9 December anchored off the mouth of the Sarawak River. In *Lapwing* he proceeded upstream to Kuching, the capital and seat of H.H. Rajah Sir Charles Brooke, second of the Brooke family Rajahs of Sarawak and who ruled from 1868 to 1917, where he spent the day. His visit concluded, that same evening *Lapwing* was ordered to Hong Kong via Manila while *Iron Duke* continued to Labuan where she remained from 12 to 13 December, and coaled 125 tons. Continuing up the coast of Borneo towards the Philippines he arrived at Manila on 19 December, eventually crossing the China Sea and anchoring at Hong Kong in the New Year on 4 January 1879 (17).

Meanwhile in Lorain, Ohio on 23 November 1878 was born the future Fleet Admiral Ernest Joseph King, USN (1878-1956). After the USA entered WW2, at the time when finally command of the seas gradually was to be assumed by the USN vice the RN, in Washington, DC he was to be C. in C., US Fleet and Chief of Naval Operations. Necessarily a huge proportion of the United States conduct of this future war at sea was to be involved with the Pacific campaign against Japan (18).

Far off in Zululand on 22-23 January 1879 the battles of Isandhlwana and Rorke's Drift were fought, the former being a disaster to British arms. Consequently, from Hong Kong on 29 March 1879, the C. in C. wrote to the Admiralty:-

'In view of the grave aspect of affairs at the Cape of Good Hope I deemed it adviseable to inform their Lordships by telegram that the *Juno* was at Hong Kong and available for the Cape, if desireable (19).'

During the summer of 1879 considerable excitement was caused by the loss of a China coasting steamer. Onboard had been an important passenger. From Yokohama Admiral Coote wrote:-

'On the 17 June Commander Douglas of H.M.S. *Egeria*, then senior officer at Shanghai, received intelligence of the total wreck of the steamer *Shun Le* on the south east point of the Shantung promontory, the vessel having onboard Sir Thomas Wade, H.M. Minister in China... (20).'

Needless to say Commander Douglas had proceeded to sea immediately but fortunately on his arrival at the scene, '... found Sir Thomas Wade and the rest of the passengers had been taken off the previous night by a coasting steamer.'

From Japanese and the northern waters of the station, by early 1880 the C. in C. was back at Singapore. In the paddle despatch vessel *Vigilant*, 985 tons, he returned up the Strait of Malacca to satisfy himself that, 'the miners and opium farmers at Laroot', were behaving themselves as there had been some restlessness during the previous year. Laroot is Larut in Perak. There on a number of occasions, and following the discovery of tin in 1848, feuding had taken place. Chinese merchants therefore had requested British assistance in their quest to bring an element of peace and stability to the region. One positive result had been the signing of the Pangkor Treaty of January 1874.

Admiral Coote personally investigated:-

'I ascended the Laroot River shortly after daylight on the 9 February (1880) and visited the Resident, Mr. Low (21).

From this gentleman, a contemporary of the 1st Rajah Brooke in Sarawak, I gained much valuable information and I was glad to hear that my visit would have the effect of materially strengthening his administration. Mr. Low informed me that popular excitement had quite subsided, and that the Chinese miners had, after their fantastic creed, burned and otherwise destroyed the gods whose evil spirits had betrayed them into unwarrantable and foolish acts; and that the settlement was again healthy in tone and active in enterprise (22).'

As usual during his time on the Station epidemics of cholera took place, especially during the summer months. Less frequently his men suffered from malaria.

In addition acts of piracy, and attempts at the prevention thereof, required considerable attention.

Admiral: 3 January 1881.

In 1881 in London Messrs. Jardine Matheson & Co., and their interests, formed the Indo China Steam Navigation Co. Ltd., '...with the object of running steamers on the Coast and Rivers of China to the Straits Settlements and Calcutta (23).'

As seen above Messrs. Jardine Matheson already had considerable earlier experience of operating merchant vessels and trading in Eastern waters.

Although with earlier experience in Far Eastern waters, dating back to 1859, also by 1881 Messrs. William Thomson and Company of Edinburgh, Managers of The Ben Line Steamers Ltd., were advertising their service to China and Japan as being maintained by 'The Ben Line of London and China Clippers'. Steamers to operate on this line included *Benarty*, 1,734 grt and built in 1876, *Bengloe*, 1,854 grt and built in 1878, and *Benalder*, 2,054 grt and built in 1880 (24).

By February 1881 the C. in C's term in office was drawing to a close.

His successor, Admiral Willes, arrived at Singapore on 26 February and at noon that day hoisted his flag in the corvette *Modeste*, 1,934 tons.

From Singapore on 28 February Admiral Coote, who had embarked in her at 2 p.m. that afternoon, sailed for home in the P. & O. mail steamer *Zambezi*, 2,431 grt. From that date, and with his flag being hoisted in *Iron Duke* at 4.20 p.m., Admiral Willes assumed command of the China Station (25).

At the end of his voyage home he reached England on 7 April 1881 (26).

Upon reaching the age of sixty five years he retired on 1 June 1885. In retirement his annual pension was GBP 830.00 (27).

He was a Fellow of the Royal Geographical Society.

In retirement served as a JP for Hampshire. For such a duty he had been sworn in at Winchester as early as on Saturday, 10 September 1870.

In 1865 he had bought his house, 'Shales', West End Road, South Stoneham, Hampshire from his brother, Charles Henry, and lived there until about 1888 (28).

Following his death in March 1898, then in his memory his son, Stanley Victor Coote, caused a stained glass window to be placed in St. Catherine's Church, Tullamore (29).

NOTES

1. Obituary, *The Times*, Friday, March 18, 1898. *Illustrated London News*, 26 March 1898, 433.
2. *Midland Tribune*, 26 March 1898.
3. Courtesy of the College Archivist, 14 December 2006.
4. Obituary, *The Times*. O'Byrne.
5. Ibid. At the end of 1854 *Victoria and Albert* was to be re-named *Osborne* and be replaced by the new *Victoria and Albert*, 2,470 tons, who was to be broken up only in 1904. David Lyon and Rif Winfield, *The Sail and Steam Navy List*, (London, 2004), 169/170.
   Lord Adolphus **FitzClarence**. Born: 18 February 1802. Died: 17 May 1856. An illegitimate child of Prince William, Duke of Clarence and later King William IV, and his mistress, Dorothy Jordan. Entered the RN in 1813. In command Royal Yachts from 1830 to 1853 when promoted Rear Admiral. *Dictionary of National Biography*.
6. NA ZJ1/256. *London Gazette*, 25 June 1847.
7. **Chia** Ch'ing Emperor, fifth son of Ch'ien Lung Emperor who had reigned from 1735 to 1796, the first forty years of his reign being one of considerable success and resulting in great expansion of the Empire. Chia Ch'ing himself, neither a popular nor effective Emperor, was to die of heat stroke at the summer palace, Jehol, on 2 September 1820. Ann Paludan, *Chronicle of the Chinese Emperors*, (London, 2005), 196, 198, 204/5. *Encyclopaedia Britannica*.
8. NA ADM 196/36. *Service Record*.
9. Clowes, Vol. VI, 367/371. In 1861 Docemo, a later king of Lagos, ceded the island and port to Great Britain. In exchange until his death he received an annual pension.
   John Beecroft died at Fernando Po on 19 June 1854. *Foreign Office List,* 1882.
   Commander Gardner commanded *Waterwitch*, 10 guns and 324 tons bm. She had been ordered as a yacht for the

Duke of Belfast but in 1834 had been purchased on the stocks at Cowes and completed as a small gun boat. *The Sail and Steam Navy List*, 128.

10. *Service Record.*

11. Obituary, *The Times. Illustrated London News.*

12. Ibid.

13. *The Sail and Steam Navy List,* 206.

14. NA ADM 1/6450. Admiral Hillyar to The Admiralty, *General Letter No. 476*, Singapore, 13 November 1878.

15. NA ADM 53/11722. Log Book *Iron Duke.*

16. NA ADM 1/6450. Coote to The Admiralty, 28 November 1878.
    The Dindings were ceded to Great Britain by the Pangkor Treaty of 1874. The minute territory consists of a few islands and small area of mainland at the mouth of the Perak River. It was to prove to be an unimportant acquisition.

17. NA ADM 1/6485. *Letter No. 79.* Hong Kong, 18 January 1879.

18. Thomas B. Buell, *Master of Sea Power,* (Boston, 1980), xiii/xv.

19. NA ADM 1/6485. *Letter No. 160.* Wood screw corvette *Juno*, 2,216 tons, Captain James A. Poland. *Navy List.*

20. Ibid. *Letter No. 304.* Written in *Iron Duke* at Yokohama, 14 July 1879. s.s. *Shun Le* is *Shun Lee*, 1,712 grt, owned by China Coast Steam Navigation Co. (Jardine Matheson & Co.). On 14 June 1879 when bound from Shanghai to Chefoo grounded in fog. Total loss. H.W. Dick and S.A. Kentwell, *Beancaker to Boxboat*, (Canberra, 1988), 24.
    Archibald Lucius **Douglas**: see Shadwell, C.in C., 1871, reference (32).
    Thomas Francis **Wade**: see Ryder, C. in C., 1874, reference (44).

21. Hugh **Low**. Born in London: 10 May 1824. Died in Alassio: 18 April 1905. Visited Sarawak and in 1845 became known to the first Rajah, Sir James Brooke (1803-1868). Acquired a degree of botanical knowledge. Joined the Colonial Service: Secretary of the Government of Labuan: 1848. To take up this position, on 1 February 1848 sailed from England as a member of HH Rajah Sir James Brooke's party in HMS *Maeander*, Captain The Hon. Sir Henry Keppel (see C. in C., 1867). In 1851 the first European to scale Mount Kinabalu, 4,101m. Appointed British Resident, Perak: April 1877. This was the post occupied earlier by James W.W. Birch, murdered on 2 November 1875. Working with Henry J. Murton of the Singapore Botanical Gardens, in October 1877 he planted nine rubber seedlings, Hevea Brasiliensis, in his Residency garden at Kuala Kangsar. As recently as 2005 one of these seedlings continued to survive as a well tended historic monument, and no doubt remains so at Kuala Kangsar near the police station. His record as an early Colonial administrator is held in great regard. KCMG: 24 May 1883. GCMG: 2 January 1889. Retired: 1889. *Who's Who, Colonial Office Lists.* Steven Runciman, *The White Rajahs*, (Cambridge, 1960), 92. John Loadman, *Tears of the Tree*, (OUP, 2005), 96-99.

22. NA ADM 1/6527. *Letter No. 59.* HMS *Vigilant* at Singapore, 17 February 1880.

23. Ed. Maggie Keswick, *The Thistle and the Jade*, (London, 1982), 142.

24. George Blake, *The Ben Line*, (Edinburgh, 1956), 57/8. Also 52, 190-194.

25. NA ADM 1/6575. Admiral Willes to the Admiralty, letter dated 2 March 1881. Also ADM 53/11723: Log Book *Iron Duke.*

26. *Sevice Record.*

27. Ibid.

28. Copy of document provided by Hampshire County Council in January 2007.
    Details regarding 'Shales' courtesy of Mr. Peter Baker, Bitterne Local History Society.

29. Visited by the author on Tuesday, 12 May 2009. Courtesy The Revd. Gerald Field. The church is beautifully and prominently sited on a natural hillock to the east of the town. The window may be found to the right of the centre aisle well up towards the altar.

3 January 1881 to 3 January 1884
Vice Admiral George Ommanney **Willes**

Born at Hythe, Hants. on 19 June 1823, son of Captain George Wickens Willes, RN, (1785-1847) by his wife Anne Elizabeth, a daughter of Sir Edmund Lacon of Great Yarmouth, the first Baronet and M.P. (1750-1826) (1).

After a very short illness he died at his residence, 73, Cadogan Square, London, on Monday, 18 February 1901 (2).

The family motto: Tenax Propositi or 'Firm of Purpose'.

Entered the Royal Navy on 9 February 1836. **Mate**: 12 September 1842 and, 'served first in the *Cornwallis*, flagship of Sir William Parker, and afterwards in *Childers*, brig, on the East Indies and China Station (3)'. *Childers* was commanded by Commander George Greville Wellesley, a nephew of Arthur, first Duke of Wellington. At the end of the commission she paid off at Portsmouth on 11 July 1844. **Lieutenant**: 11 December 1844. From 4 March 1845 in *Hibernia*, 104, Captain Peter Richards, Flagship, Mediterranean, Vice Admiral Sir William Parker (4). Lieutenant and Commander paddle steam vessel *Spitfire*, 140 h.p., 3 guns, Mediterranean: 30 April 1848. While in command of this ship he received some well deserved recognition:-

'27 Nov. 1848. Earl Grey approving of his conduct in rendering assistance to the
Ionian government during some disturbances in the Island of Cephalonia (5).'

During 1849 he was transferred in command of another small paddle steam vessel *Volcano*, 140 h.p., 4 guns. While in her he had one unfortunate experience as on 8 September he was, 'reprimanded and admonished to be more careful in future on occasion of collision between *Volcano* and *Eliza*.' Paid off out of *Volcano* on 3 October 1849.

From 8 August 1850 served in the paddle wheel steam frigate *Retribution*, 28, Captain Frederick Warden, 'Particular Service', and then in the Mediterranean as on 28 March 1854 Britain and France declared war on Russia. Thereafter the Crimean War became widespread:-

'... he was appointed to *Retribution* and as senior Lieutenant of that vessel was present at the bombardment of Odessa in 1854 (6).'

This bombardment took place on 22 April 1854 however in the interim he had received his promotion so shortly thereafter returned home, however only for a very short period of time. Clearly Captain Warden had greatly appreciated his ability as First Lieutenant since on 6 July 1854 he gave his 'strongest testimony' to 'the highly efficient state of *Retribution*.'

Commander: 17 April 1854. From 1 June that year Commander in *Britannia*, 120, Captain Thomas Wren Carter, Flagship, Mediterranean, Vice Admiral James Whitley Deans Dundas. Earlier, between July 1847 and

February 1852, the Admiral had served as First Sea Lord. To join his new ship he took passage from Marseilles to Malta in the P. & O. paddle steamer *Valetta*, 832 grt. Onboard on 12 June wrote a few lines, mostly of thanks for his congratulations on his promotion, to a very great friend and brother officer, the future Admiral Sir Augustus Phillimore (1822-1897) (7).

In due course in his new ship, '… when serving in the *Britannia* he assisted in the bombardment of Fort Constantine, Sevastopol.'

Following that campaign he was to receive the Crimean and Turkish medals, the clasp for Sevastopol, the Fifth class of the Medjidie, and was made a knight of the Legion of Honour (8).

On 13 March 1855 he paid off out of the ship (9).'

On 16 May 1855 he married Georgiana Matilda Josephine, daughter of William Joseph Lockwood who sadly had died just eight months earlier, on 16 September 1854. The Lockwood seat was Dews Hall at Lambourne in Essex. On 13 June 1816 William had married Rachel, daughter of Sir Mark Wood of Gatton Park, Surrey.

Georgiana's brother George, born on 16 June 1818, and serving as a Captain, 8th Hussars, had been killed at Balaklava on 25 October 1854. As can be seen 1854 had been a bad year for the family so one can only hope that Georgiana's wedding the following May brought her mother much joy.

As Lady Georgiana Willes she was to die in 1912.

From 8 October 1855 served in the screw steam ship *Duke of Wellington*, 131 guns, Flagship, Baltic, Rear Admiral The Hon. Richard Saunders Dundas, who had been appointed to that command in succession to Sir Charles Napier. On this front of the war with the Russians Sir Charles had not enjoyed amicable relations with Their Lordships at the Admiralty. As Hon. Sir Richard Dundas, KCB the new C. in C. subsequently was to be First Sea Lord on two occasions, firstly and briefly between November 1857 and March 1858, then secondly and as a Vice Admiral, between June 1859 and the time of his unfortunately early death, aged only fifty nine, of heart attack on 3 June 1861.

Captain: 10 May 1856.

At the end of 1858 and into early 1859 he and his wife were in Paris. In January 1859 he wrote to Augustus Phillimore, clearly unimpressed by the appearance of Napoleon III:-

'We were at the Tuileries Ball last Tuesday – what a scrubby common looking man the Emperor looks in his evening costume (10).'

On 12 February 1859 appointed in command screw steam frigate *Chesapeake*, 51, Flagship, East Indies and China Station, Rear Admiral James Hope (11).

Early in April 1859, while on passage East per P. & O., from south Ceylon at Galle he addressed yet another letter to, 'My dear Phillimore':-

'We arrived here yesterday and found Lord Elgin who has been awaiting Mr. Bruce's arrival about a fortnight. He will now hasten on to Suez in the *Furious*. Osborn tells me that he has written to be superceded …(12).'

Mr. Bruce is Frederick William Adolphus Bruce (1814-1867), younger brother of Lord Elgin who is James Bruce, the Eighth Earl, returning to England following the successful signing of his treaties with China in June 1858, and with Japan in August 1858. During much of his time in the East His Lordship had used the steam frigate *Furious* to convey him from place to place. Her Captain, Sherard Osborn, indeed was to be succeeded in command of the ship, but by Captain Oliver Jones so unfortunately for Phillimore there was no opening for him there on that occasion.

Frederick Bruce was returning to North China with the object of exchanging the ratifications of his brother's Treaty of Tientsin of 1858. In the interim the Chinese had decided to resist such impertinent behaviour by the barbarians. As follows here, Willes was to be closely involved with subsequent efforts to overcome this reluctance on the part of Manchu China to ratify the Treaty.

H.M.S. 'Furious' 18 April 1857

Captain Sherard Osborn (25 April 1822 – 6 May 1875). In command of 'Furious' during that Voyage East in 1857-1858

In the flagship at the Peiho on 24 June 1859:-

'There were three booms or obstructions … . That night three boats, under Captain George Ommanney Willes, of the *Chesapeake*, passing through or circumventing the first boom, pulled up to the second, and cut one, and blew away with powder two, of the cables forming part of it. … Before the return of the party, Willes examined the third or inner boom; and, in consequence of his report on it, the Rear Admiral concluded that he would not be able to pass the works and attack them from above, but must attack them, if at all, from the front, and, upon silencing them, endeavour to carry them by storm (13).'

On behalf of the Allies on 25 June 1859 Admiral Hope led this attack against the Taku forts at the Peiho. In that shallow water he switched his Flag from *Chesapeake* to the gunboat *Plover*, Lieut. and Commander William H. Rason who was killed during the action, his ship being sunk by Chinese fire. The attack continued but was repulsed by the Chinese. Among the wounded in this affair were both the Admiral, hit in the thigh, and Captain Shadwell of *Highflyer* (see C. in C., 1871).

With both the Admiral and his senior, Captain Shadwell, wounded it will be noted that:-

'The management of the retreat devolved upon the able flag captain, G.O. Willes – a most trying and anxious duty; for the enemy opened a perfect *feu-de-joie* from all sides, upon vessels and boats, and for a while threatened total destruction to the force (14).'

Subsequently his wife Matilda was to write to Phillimore:-

'Thank you very much for your kind congratulations on the Peiho affair. George had indeed a most merciful escape and I feel I can never be sufficiently grateful to God for sparing him in the midst of such great dangers. Your appreciation of his services on the occasion are no doubt like my own, very partial, for friendship and affection will give a bright colouring to every circumstance but I really think without departing from a sober view of matters, we may feel certain my Husband had great opportunities of usefulness, and that he did not fail to do all in his power towards the relief and assistance of his comrades. I continue to receive excellent accounts from China, Admiral Hope's recovery seems to be complete and George's accounts of some of their long walks together almost surprise me (15).'

Although in June 1859 the attack at Taku had been unsuccessful he personally was to receive considerable recognition:-

'16 September 1859: gazetted with high praise for his conduct in the unsuccessful action in the Pay-Ho.

27 September 1859: commended by the Board for his exertions in recovering the sunken vessels (16).'

At the Peiho in August/September 1860 wiser tactics were employed and the Allies secured their delayed victory thus leading to the ratification of the Treaty of Tientsin of 26 June 1858. In addition the Manchu were forced to agree to the terms of a new treaty, that of Peking, 24 October 1860. As in 1858, also again in 1860 the British Plenipotentiary was James Bruce, Eighth Earl of Elgin.

Amongst his duties in 1860 at Taku:-

'In August the following year (1860) he commanded the rocket boats in the operation against the Taku forts.'

'For these services he received the China medal with the Taku clasp (17).'

Be under no illusions regarding the characterless nature of the endlessly flat countryside in the vicinity of Taku and Tientsin: rich farming country certainly, but of no scenic value. Here follows an extract taken from comments made by the botanist, Robert Fortune, writing following a visit which he made in September 1861.

In the small vessel *Fee-loong* he steamed to Taku from Chefoo:-

> '... and on the following morning we were nearing the far famed Taku forts and the mouth of the Peiho, the scene of our disasters and subsequent triumphs a short time before. The view on approaching the mouth of this river has often been described by writers on China from Lord Macartney's embassy downwards, and therefore I need say nothing about it here further than it was the most unprepossessing one which it had ever been my lot to look upon (18).'

From 9 May 1861 in command screw steam frigate *Imperieuse*, 51, the new Flagship, East Indies and China Station, acting Vice Admiral Sir James Hope.

CB: 16 July 1861.

Late in 1861 the Taiping rebels took Ningpo swiftly and relatively easily. The British, who had assisted the Imperial Ch'ing forces in making plans for the defence of the city, were disappointed. However, as Admiral Hope was to explain:-

> "Everything had been done to assist the Imperialists in the defence of the town, except the use of force, in their favour ... '. His dismay led him to observe, '... how utterly useless such measures prove, in consequence of the cowardice and imbecility of the Mandarins (19)."

'In 1862 he, Captain Willes, was employed in investigating the creeks preliminary to operations against the Taiping, near Shanghai, and in July of that year was relieved and came home (20).' (see Kuper, C. in C., 1862). Once again he had distinguished himself:-

> '3 June 1862: Rear Admiral Sir James Hope commending him for good services against the Chinese Rebels (21).'

From 14 March 1863 borne in *Royal Adelaide*, 'Addl. for service in *Prince Consort*'. The latter ship was undergoing conversion from being a wooden screw ship of the line to become an ironclad frigate. Then from 12 January 1864 he served actually in command of *Prince Consort*, 35 guns, 6,430 tons. Her conversion was complete by 6 February after which she was assigned to the Channel Squadron.

From 10 April 1866 in command second rate *Indus*, 80, Flagship, Admiral Superintendent, Devonport, Rear Admiral The Hon. James Robert Drummond (22).

From 26 January 1869 appointed to *Fisgard*, 42, Woolwich: 'Additional for Service at Whitehall', then, from October 1870, 'Chief of Staff'. Also from April 1870 Aide de Camp to H.M. Queen Victoria.

'There was at this date no Second Sea Lord, and the duties of the Chief of Staff included a large share in the business of manning the fleet (23).'

Whilst in *Fisgard* on three short occasions, during the summers of 1869, 1870 and 1871 respectively, he served as 'Commodore of the 1st Class' while participating in exercises with the Coast Guard Squadron. In 1870 and 1871 his ship so involved was *Achilles*, 9,820 tons, guard ship at Portland.

From 1 June 1872, 'discharged from *Fisgard* to half pay'.

Rear Admiral: 11 June 1874.

From 14 March 1876 acting as Admiral Superintendent, Devonport, *Cambridge*, 'during sick leave of Rear Admiral (William Charles) Chamberlain'.

From 1 May 1876 confirmed as Admiral Superintendent, Devonport.

Subsequently on his service record was to appear the annotation, '30 Jan. '79: Praised for services as Adml. Supt.'

At the Admiralty between 6 November 1877 and 12 August 1879 the First Sea Lord was his one time Commander in *Childers* in 1844, now Admiral George Greville Wellesley (1814-1901). During that period the First Lord was Mr. W. H. Smith.

Vice Admiral: 1 February 1879.

For a few months early in 1879 he fulfilled the role as Chairman of Seamen Gunners Committee.

Intimation of his next appointment was received in November 1880, and on 24 November in the following manner he wrote from St. James's Street, SW to his great friend:-

> 'My dear Phillimore,
>
> Lord Northbrook sent this morning to say that he wished to see me and I have just left the Admiralty.
>
> Lord Northbrook told me that he had submitted my name to the Queen for the China command and that it was approved. Did I want it – of course I could not just say that I was willing (24).'

In the event to take up his new command he left London on Thursday, 20 January 1881 for Paris with the expectation of leaving the French capital on the Monday for Brindisi. His voyage East involved a call at Bombay, 8-9 February 1881, thence around to Bengal, '... five days at Calcutta which I enjoyed'. Subsequently another letter to Augustus Phillimore and dated 23 February 1881 is headed, 'Opium Steamer *A. Apcar*, 100 miles from Penang'. She was the iron screw steamer *Arratoon Apcar*, 2,153 grt., built in Newcastle in 1873, Captain McTavish, registered in London and owned by Apcar & Co. of Calcutta (25). In her:-

> 'This evening we anchor at Penang – this will recall our *Cornwallis* days and the fun we had there (26).'

His voyage proceeded smoothly and he arrived in Singapore on 26 February 1881. That morning at 11.58 a.m. his flag was hoisted in *Modeste* (27).

On assuming the command of the China Station on 28 February, at 4.20 p.m. his Flag was broken in *Iron Duke*, 6,010 tons, Captain Richard E. Tracey (28). Her main armament consisted of ten 9" and four 6" guns. His Flag Lieutenant was Egerton Bagot Byrd Levett who, in 1884, was to marry Mabel Desborough, a daughter of Sir Harry and Lady Parkes.

His predecessor, Admiral Coote, had sailed for England that morning in the P. & O. iron, screw mail steamer *Zambezi*, 2,431 grt.

His first cruise took place between 3 and 11 March 1881 and consisted of a short voyage up the Straits of Malacca to The Dindings and Penang before returning to Singapore via Malacca.

At the time the Governor of the Straits Settlements was Sir Frederick Aloysius Weld (1823-1891), who previously, between November 1864 and October 1865, had served as the 6th Prime Minister of New Zealand. On 6 August 1880 His Excellency had opened the new Town Hall in Penang.

When the Chinese trade figures for 1880 became available he reported to the Admiralty that during that year:-

> 'British ships had made almost 12,400 entries and clearances at China ports carrying over 9.6 million tons of trade. The total value of foreign and coastal trade carried in British vessels was over GBP 665 million (29).'

Clearly the C. in C. believed in some of the advantages of proceeding under sail. From Chefoo on 6 June 1881 he included the following remarks in a letter to the Admiralty:-

> 'Captain Tracey has endeavoured to work the ship as much under sail as possible and though it was next to useless so far as making a passage, it gave good work to the young hands; and the time on the voyage has been well spent in the various drills and exercises, which have promoted discipline and efficiency as well as health (30).'

At anchor at Yokohama on 6 July 1881 he received visitors from the British Legation. The writer is Ernest Satow, then Japanese Secretary:-

> 'Went to Yokohama with Buchanan to call on Admiral Willes, who was very gracious (31).'

However, although there may have been some advantages in endeavouring to cruise under sail, as far as his flagship was concerned the C. in C. was not impressed by either of her means of motive power. Here he is just two and a half months later, writing to London on 16 August 1881:-

'As their Lordships are aware she cannot sail and consumes a vast quantity of coal (32).'

Off Yokohama on 21 October 1881, with his flag in screw corvette *Encounter*, 1,970 tons, Captain George Robinson, present on the occasion of the arrival at anchor of the iron screw corvette, cased with teak wood, *Bacchante*, 4,130 tons, Captain Rt. Hon. Lord Charles T.M.D. Scott. Serving as Midshipmen in the ship were T.R.H. Prince Albert Victor, later Duke of Clarence, and Prince George of Wales, later H.M. King George V. Also serving in the Gunroom were a number of other young officers of whom, in due course, more would be heard. These included Hugh Evan-Thomas, Arthur H. Limpus, Arthur H. Christian and Rosslyn E. Wemyss.

On 31 October 1881:-

'At 10.30 a.m. we all manned yards, and every ship of the two British squadrons, the American, Russian and Japanese, fired in turn a Royal salute of twenty one guns as the Mikado left the shore (33). A quarter of an hour afterwards he came alongside the *Bacchante*; and was received at the gangway by Admiral Willes, Captain Lord Charles Scott and Captain Robinson; and the Japanese Royal Standard was hoisted at the *Bacchante*'s main (34).'

A few days later, writing to the Admiralty from Woosung on 8 November 1881, the C. in C. expounded on the subject of H.I.M. The Emperor Meiji's visit to *Bacchante*:-

'His Imperial Majesty the Mikado of Japan expressed a wish to visit the *Bacchante* and communicated his intention of going onboard that ship on the morning of 31 October. This proceeding was one very unusual on the part of a Japanese Monarch who is accustomed to live in majestic seclusion at his capital. I took care therefore to mark his embarkation by every honor due to a Sovereign.

Onboard *Bacchante* he was received by myself and the Captains of H.M. Ships present, the Vice Admiral Commanding the Detached Squadron being too unwell to attend.

After going round the ship, and inspecting her arrangements with much interest and intelligent attention to details, His Majesty was entertained at luncheon by Captain Lord Charles Scott, the two Princes of Wales being present. Prince Albert Victor, with much grace, proposed the Mikado's health and welcomed him, in appropriate terms, on his first visit to a British man of war. I also took the opportunity of expressing my great pleasure in seeing His Majesty on board one of the Queen's ships which I looked upon as a high compliment to the Navy and assured His Majesty that his friendly visit to the sons of the Prince of Wales would tend to cement the cordiality and good will which already existed between Japan and the British Empire. The occasion called for some remarks of this nature (35).'

Following the cruise of the ship in Far Eastern waters, on 20 December 1881 *Bacchante* arrived at Hong Kong. The C. in C. was in port in *Iron Duke* and on Christmas Day was pleased to be able to entertain the two Royal Princes to tea ashore. Subsequently, on the eve of their departure from Hong Kong, on 30 December the two Princes attended a ball given in their honour at the City Hall:-

'The splendid building was decorated with long festoons of lanterns, bright with bunting. Dent's fountain gaily splashing in the courtyard, the lights of the Assembly Rooms reflected on the waters of the harbour, Beaconsfield Arcade presenting a brand new façade across the way. Hosts and guests arriving from all sides. A cavalcade in the Ewo livery swings in magnificently from East Point. Prominent businessmen drop down from the middle levels. The red uniforms of the Government House chair carriers are streaming along Garden Road. Military officers stroll over from the mess at Murray Barracks. A venturesome civilian bowls up in one of the new rickshaws, the latest novelty from Japan. At the landing steps behind the Hall the stately barges manoeuvre with a flourish of boat hooks, discharging one by one the naval captains resplendent in cocked hat and gold lace.'

'The floor was in first rate order, and there was plenty of room, and it was altogether a great success (--). We got away at 2 a.m. (36).'

As early as in 1878 Alfred Dent (1844-1927) had formed a syndicate to investigate the potential of North Borneo. Then in August 1881, and for the purpose of developing various interests on the island of Borneo, the British North Borneo Chartered Company was formed. From May 1882 the first president of the company was Sir Rutherford Alcock, one time British Minister to both Japan and China (37).

In June 1882 the C. in C., guided by instructions from London, followed the United States Navy C. in C., Commodore Robert Wilson Shufeldt (1822-1895), in negotiating an initial form of treaty with Corea (38). During these discussions he was assisted by William G. Aston of the British Japanese Consular service (39). In November 1883 Mr. Aston and Sir Harry Parkes were to take this arrangement a stage further and organize a more detailed treaty document. However never during that era ending with the outbreak of WW2, also bearing in mind that from 1910 the country was to be the Japanese colony of Chosen, were British trading or other interests in Korea to amount to a very great deal.

During July 1882 anti-Japanese feeling prevailing within Corea manifested itself in the flight of the Japanese Minister, and of His Excellency and his party taking refuge in one of HM Ships, the sloop survey vessel *Flying Fish*, 950 tons. Her Lieut. and Commander, Richard Frazer Hoskyn, reported to the C. in C. in his letter of 30 July advising that the Japanese Minister to Corea, a Mr. Hanabusa together with a party of twenty four, having been driven from Seoul on Wednesday, 26 July 1882 by the locals, took flight in a junk and were received onboard *Flying Fish* then at anchor off the Whittall Group. They were taken onboard 'for protection'. Apparently a mob had attacked the Delegation in Seoul and in making their escape three Japanese were killed and two still were missing. Hoskyn conveyed the party of diplomat refugees to Nagasaki and from there communicated with both the C. in C. and with Sir Harry Parkes (40).

As might be expected the Japanese reaction to this Korean behaviour was prompt. Early in August, writing from Vladivostok, the C. in C. informed London accordingly:-

'I learn from Sir Harry Parkes that the Japanese Minister at Seoul had returned to Inchuen (Inchon) with a force of two war vessels, 200 marines and 300 regular troops. The Chinese appear also to have despatched a force to the same port, including troops. I hope that no contretemps may occur (41).'

In Elizabeth, NJ on 30 October 1882 the future Fleet Admiral, USN, William Frederick Halsey Jr., was born. He was to make his name in the Pacific campaign against Japan during WW2.

It was about this time that Japan and the Meiji Navy commenced to spread their wings into waters which were to become especially well known during the Pacific War of 1941-1945:-

'During a cruise from late 1882 to the early autumn of 1883, the corvette *Ryujo*, with the entire tenth class of the Naval Academy aboard, stopped at Kusaie and Ponape in the eastern Carolines; it was the first Japanese warship to enter Micronesian waters (42).'

Meanwhile arrangements had been made to exchange Flagships on the Station accordingly *Iron Duke* sailed from Hong Kong on 7 December 1882.

Audacious, who had commissioned at Devonport on 5 September 1882, was brought out from England by Captain H.C. St. John and anchored off Singapore at 11.00 a.m. on Wednesday, 13 December (43).

Even with the effect of the North East monsoon behind her *Iron Duke* only arrived at 1.30 p.m. on 16 December, nine days on passage. On 18 December the two Captains exchanged ships leaving Captain St. John to return home with *Iron Duke* while Richard Tracey assumed command of her sister ship, *Audacious*. On 20 December *Iron Duke* coaled in New Harbour and at 5.10 p.m. that evening sailed for England.

In turn *Audacious* coaled on 21 December and sailed at 8.40 a.m. on 23 December for Labuan where she anchored in Victoria Harbour at noon on 28 December. In due course, and via Manila, she was to reach Hong Kong and secure to the Flagship's buoy at 2.50 p.m. on Thursday, 18 January 1883. Her rate of progress at sea from Singapore had averaged six knots, and she was 105 days out, England to Hong Kong.

By proceeding from Singapore up along the north coast of Borneo and Palawan Island the worst of the direct force of the NE Monsoon across the China Sea was avoided.

As will be appreciated in that era when ships were slow and frequently proceeded under sail much movement around the Station was governed by the monsoon. This blew, frequently powerfully, across the China Sea from the North East between the months of November and April, otherwise from the South West. At the same time it is obvious that at times it would be necessary for warships to proceed against the monsoon when perhaps some disturbance or other matter requiring attention took place. The quality of his ships was such that this was not always possible. To illustrate his point, already hinted at above when describing the behaviour of *Iron Duke* when under sail or steam, at the end of 1882 the C. in C. sent to the Admiralty a printed table in which were shown the various characteristics of the twenty four ships under his command.

A few details follow.

In *Iron Duke* herself the boiler pressure on her safety valves, originally twenty five, now was only fifteen lbs./sq. in. She could not attain the modest speed of ten knots, in fact of all the ships in the squadron only nine could manage that speed. Even then, at eight knots, the Flagship consumed the astonishing total of sixty tons of coal per day so her endurance was limited to 8.8 days. Five of his ships could not even attain eight knots. On the subject of 'Efficiency under Sail' only *Encounter* was rated as 'Good', the remainder varying between 'None' as is the case of the Flagship, to 'Fair'. Further, in answer to the heading, 'Can she make direct passage under steam against Monsoon', between Singapore and Hong Kong he reckoned that only one ship, *Swift*, would be capable of making such a passage (44).

It will be apparent that in times of emergency the fleet as then constituted would have only a very limited capability. His table presented this fact to the Admiralty in a succinct manner.

It was by 1883 that freighters of Alfred Holt's Blue Funnel Line were maintaining a regular weekly service between Nagasaki and Europe, the principal cargoes on offer being the export of tea and silk. True their *Ajax* had called at Yokohama as early as in 1870, and their *Achilles* at Nagasaki in December 1872, but otherwise their sailings to and from Japan previously had been intermittent. This service was to prosper until by 1888, 'Japanese ports became regular terminals for the main Far Eastern service (45).'

From correspondence originated by the C. in C. it is clear that at times during this period Captain Richard Tracey of the Flagship, together with Commander Henry B. Lang who was promoted from Lieutenant on 14 January 1883, and Lieut. (G) Henry E. Bourchier then serving in the steel corvette *Curacao*, 2,380 tons, were all under orders to attempt to act in a training capacity to some units of the Chinese Navy (46). In this connection a naval academy had been opened in 1881 at Tientsin and by 1885 some 120 students were under training there (47).

During May 1883 it became apparent that relations between China and France were becoming unpleasantly strained over the Annam question. Naturally the C. in C. reported accordingly to the Admiralty, adding:-

> 'The advent of Li Hung-chang to Shanghai has caused a little excitement. It is reported that he has been appointed Viceroy of the Southern Provinces of China bordering Annam, made Generalissimo of land and Sea Forces, and ordered to take command of the Southern Army and "settle the Annam question". If this be true, one of two things must happen – a successful termination of the Annam difficulty favourable to China, or the disgrace of the great Li. Under such circumstances the action taken by Li will have grave significance and importance (48).'

In common with most if not all all European authorities the C. in C. held Viceroy Li Hung-chang in considerable regard: 'He appears to possess high intelligence and a strong will, accompanied by health and vigour.'

However naturally the Viceroy attended to this problem with France in his own way and by 7 August 1883, writing from Nagasaki, Admiral Willes was able to report:-

'... even the Franco-Tonquin difficulty which once threatened the quietude of some of the ports having almost dropped out of discussion. Li Hung-chang has resumed his post of Governor General of Chihli in order, it is said, that he may be near the Tsungli Yamen to direct the policy of the Foreign Office in its correspondence with the French Minister. Li's present pacific attitude seems to have allayed the apprehension of the timid inhabitants of our Settlements as well as the martial blustering of the Chinese soldiery.'

As may be seen below, during the time that his successor Admiral Dowell was C. in C., then an actual Sino-French conflict was to take place.

Meanwhile on 1 July 1883, in succession to Sir Thomas Wade, Sir Harry Parkes was promoted to be Envoy Extraordinary and Minister Plenipotentiary to the Emperor of China, Kuang-hsu (1871-1908).

These were 'interesting times' in China as the unscrupulous Empress Dowager Tz'u-hsi was the actual power behind the throne.

On leaving Japan to proceed to China, on 22 August 1883 Sir Harry was given a farewell luncheon by none other than H.I.M. The Emperor Meiji himself who spoke most graciously of his high regard for the departing British Minister. From Tokyo Bay he took passage in the wooden paddle steamer *Tokyo Maru*, 2,217 grt (49).

Happily by now and regarding the matter of health, progress had been made in Japan. Writing from Yokohama on 22 October 1883 the C. in C. informed the Admiralty:-

'Smallpox, the scourge of Japan during my last visit in 1861, and from which our officers and men suffered so much is now unheard of at the Treaty Ports (of Japan) (50).'

Finally on 4 March 1884 he was able to inform the Admiralty that as his term in command came to an end the following arrangements had been made. Here he is, writing from Hong Kong:-

'Sir William Dowell appeared on 2 March which has given me ample time for transacting official business with him and I consequently propose sailing in the P. & O. steamer *Ganges*, hauling my Flag down on my departure tomorrow (51).'

Indeed, *Ganges* sailed from Hong Kong at 6.00 a.m. on Wednesday, 5 March and he arrived back in England on 11 April 1884 (52).

His services while in the Far East had been valued by both the Admiralty and HE the Governor of Hong Kong:-

'12 Apr. 84: Satisfaction expressed at zealous and efficient conduct of his duties as Comm. in Chief, China, and appreciation of care and attention in regard to Squadron cruising and exercises at sea: copy forwarded of letter from Gov. of Hong Kong Colony (Sir G. Bowen) testifying to benefits from cordial relations maintained with him (53).'

KCB: 24 May 1884.
Also during 1884 he became a justice of the peace for Middlesex.

Admiral: 27 March 1885.

Writing from St. James's, London on 12 June 1885 he gave his friend Phillimore an interesting and relevant piece of service gossip concerning China:-

'I tell you that the following nominations of Flag officers have been approved by H.M. Vesey

Hamilton, China – vice Dowell (and then he included other information relating to other Stations) (54).'

In succession to Admiral Sir Geoffrey Thomas Phipps Hornby (1825-1895), he served as C. in C., Portsmouth from 28 November 1885 to 20 June 1888. Flag in *Duke of Wellington*, 6,070 tons.

With his Flag in the twin screw turret ironclad *Inflexible*, 11,400 tons, he had the honour of commanding the Fleet on the occasion of the Jubilee Review, HM Queen Victoria: 23 July 1887.

By many junior officers the person of the C. in C. was regarded with considerable awe, however not by all. Here follows an entertaining story related by the future Admiral Sir Frederick William Fisher, brother of the well known Admiral of the Fleet Lord 'Jacky' Fisher of Kilverstone:-

'If ever there was a martinet, Sir George Ommanney Willes was one.

One day my brother Jack – who had served with him – sat at Sir George's table, his host said:-

"Fisher, I can't understand why you look so young, while Clayton, who is about your age, gives me the impression of being an old man."

Obviously not a bit afraid, my brother answered:-

"Don't you know the reason sir? I was only with you for six months, but Clayton was with you for two years (55).

Succeeded in command at Portsmouth on 20 June 1888 by Admiral Sir John Edmund Commerell, VC, GCB (1829-1901). While commanding the iron paddle gunvessel *Weser*, 6 guns, he had been awarded the Victoria Cross following a deed ashore at the Sea of Azov, Crimea on 11 October 1855.

On reaching the age of sixty five years Admiral Willes himself had retired the previous day, 19 June 1888, his retirement pay being at the rate of GBP 930.00 per annum (56).

On 2 February 1889 he suffered an injury in an accident with a horse and expected that it would be some three months before he was restored to good health (57).

From his correspondence in retirement it is apparent that he followed the custom of the day in 'taking the waters at Homburg'. This small town, Bad Homburg vor der Hohe, is a few miles north of Frankfurt, Germany.

He was a Member of the Council of the Royal United Service Institution and took an active part in their affairs.

GCB: 24 May 1892, the Birthday of H.M. Queen Victoria.

His friend Admiral Phillimore had retired to Shedfield House in Hampshire. On 28 June 1893 when writing to him from 73 Cadogan Square he offered these sage words regarding the sinking of *Victoria* in the Mediterranean a few days earlier, on 22 June (see Winsloe, C. in C., 1910):-

'My dear Phillimore,

From the accounts one reads of the disaster the ships must have been performing a manoeuvre not laid down in the signal Book – the columns could not have been 8 cables apart when the signal alluded to was made. However we shall hear all about that when Markham's despatch arrives. The Admiral or Senior Officer who orders a manoeuvre not laid down by authority incurs a great responsibility (58).

Following his death on 18 February 1901, at noon on Thursday, 21 February his funeral service was held at Holy Trinity Church in Sloane Street, London.

Subsequently no less than four plaques or memorials were to be placed there in his memory. Firstly within the church building itself the main plaque on the right interior wall. Later, placed parallel to Sloane Street outside the church, Lady Willes donated:-

'... a magnificent forged iron strapwork screen festooned with scrolling vines picked out in gold.

(-) Its aesthetic importance has long been recognised and, even during the darkest days of the

Second World War, when park railings were being ripped up and misguidedly melted down to help the war effort, it was given official protection (59).'

Thirdly and fourthly this generous act in turn is commemorated by a small plaque over on the left wall inside the church building, dated Easter Day, 1903, also by an appropriately phrased inscription on the exterior wall to the right of the front entrance to the church (60).

NOTES

1. *Dictionary of National Biography.* While serving in command of the second rate ship of the line *Vanguard*, 80, his father died at Malta on 26 October 1847.

2. Obituary, *The Times,* Tuesday, February 19, 1901.

3. *Dictionary of National Biography.*

4. William **Parker**. Born: 1 December 1781. Died: 13 November 1866. Entered the RN early in 1793. Captain: 9 October 1801. Rear Admiral: 22 July 1830. KCB: 16 July 1834. On 10 August 1841 at Hong Kong assumed command of the East Indies and China Station. Vice Admiral: 23 November 1841. With his flag in *Cornwallis*, 72, also with Captain Peter Richards in command, captured Amoy, Ningpo, Woosung and Shanghai and on 21 July 1842 closed the Grand Canal at Chinkiang. The Treaty of Nanking was signed onboard *Cornwallis* on 29 August 1842, the British Plenipotentiary being Sir Henry Pottinger (1789-1856). GCB: 18 May 1843. Appointed C. in C., Mediterranean in February 1845, to which, in May 1846, was added the command of the Channel Fleet. Admiral: 29 April 1851. Finally struck his flag on 28 April 1852. C. in C., Devonport: May 1854 to May 1857. Admiral of the Fleet: 27 April 1863. *Navy List.* George Pottinger, *Sir Henry Pottinger*, (Stroud, 1997), 99-101. *Dictionary of National Biography.* Andrew Lambert, *Admirals*, (London, 2008), 203-243.

    Peter Richards (1787-1869). Third Naval Lord: 3 June 1854 – 2 April 1857, thus during the Crimean War. Rear Admiral: 6 June 1855. Retired Vice Admiral: 12 April 1862. KCB: 7 June 1865. Retired Admiral: 12 September 1865. *Navy List.*

5. NA ADM 196/37. *Service Record.* Earl **Grey** is Henry George, the Third Earl (1802-1894). From 1846 to 1852 he was Secretary of State for War and the Colonies. The Ionian Islands were administered by Great Britain between 1815 and 1864. In 1848 the High Commissioner was John **Colborne**, First Baron Seaton (1778-1863).

6. Obituary.

7. Caird Library, National Maritime Museum, Greenwich. Their collection of correspondence from Willes to Phillimore is held under reference *PHL/2/92-114*. The letter of 12 June 1854 is in file *PHL/2/93*.

    Admiral Sir Augustus Phillimore was not to hold high office in the Far East. Instead, from second in command of the Channel Fleet in January 1876, later he commanded the Royal Naval Reserve. Promoted Admiral in October 1884 he was C. in C., at Plymouth: 1884-1887, and then retired. A son, Richard Fortescue Phillimore (1864-1940), was to become Admiral Sir Richard, GCB, KCMG.

8. *Dictionary of National Biography.*

9. ADM 196/37. *Service Record.*

10. Caird. *PHL/2/94.* Letter dated 17 January 1859.

11. James **Hope**. Born: 3 March 1808. Died at Carriden House in Scotland: 9 June 1881. Entered the RN College at Portsmouth in 1820. In June 1822 was appointed to frigate *Forte*. Captain: 28 June 1838. Rear Admiral: 19 November 1857. C. in C., East Indies and China: 1859 – 1862 until relieved by Rear Admiral A.L. Kuper, which see. KCB: 9 November 1860. C. in C., North America and West Indies: 1863-1867. Vice Admiral: 16 September 1864. GCB: 28 March 1865. C. in C., Portsmouth: 1869-1872. Admiral: 21 January 1870. Admiral of the Fleet: 15 June 1879. *Navy List. Dictionary of National Biography.*

12. Caird. *PHL/2/94.* Letter dated 7 April 1859.

13. Clowes, Vol. VII, 124/5.

14. *Blackwood's Edinburgh Magazine*, Vol. LXXXVI, December 1859, 664. Among the warships lost as a result of that engagement at the Peiho in June 1859 was the gunvessel *Cormorant*, 860 tons, who had been in the van during the successful attack the year before, on 20 May 1858.

15. Caird. *PHL/2/94*. Letter from Rome dated January 29, 1860. At the time Captain Augustus Phillimore was commanding the screw steam frigate *Curacao*, 31 guns, on the S.E. Coast of America Station. *Navy List.*

16. *Service Record.*

17. *Dictionary of National Biography.*

18. Robert Fortune (1812-1880), *Yedo and Peking*, (London, 1863), 307. On 2 May 2008 the writer visited a national monument at the mouth of the Peiho, being the fort of Dagukou on the South bank. In recent years considerable land reclamation has taken place on the flats out to sea to both North and South of the muddy estuary. Today the scene of much maritime and industrial activity, indeed it is a dreary spot. However from the fort, with their collection of an assortment of artillery, then looking out from the ramparts it requires little imagination to visualise the situation with Allied forces approaching in the years 1858, 1859 and 1860.

   George, Lord Macartney (1737-1806) and party first embarked in small craft to proceed in across the bar at the mouth of the Peiho on Monday, 5 August 1793. George Staunton, *An Historical Account of the Embassy to the Emperor of China*, (London, 1797), 250. His Lordship took passage to and from the East in *Lion*, 64, Captain Sir Erasmus Gower.

19. Stephen Uhalley, *The Taipings at Ningpo*, (Journal of the Hong Kong Branch of the Royal Asiatic Society, II, 1971), 18.

20. *Dictionary of National Biography.*

21. *Service Record.*

22. In 1856 the then Captain The Hon. James Drummond (1812-1895) of the Strathallan family married Catherine Francis Elliot, daughter of Admiral The Hon. Sir George Elliot (1784-1863). Between July and November 1840 Sir George had been C. in C. in Chinese waters during an early volatile period. See Kuper, C. in C., 1862 for a brief reference.

23. *Dictionary of National Biography.*

24. Caird. *PHL/2/105*. Lord Northbrook is Thomas George Baring, second Baron. Born: 22 January 1826. Died at Stratton Park: 15 November 1904. Christ Church, Oxford. Liberal MP for Penryn and Falmouth: 1857. As a Liberal held a number of senior government positions. Viceroy of India: 1872-1876. Created an Earl: 1876. First Lord of the Admiralty: 12 May 1880 – 30 June 1885. *Who's Who.* From July 1882 the Junior Naval Lord with him on the Board was Rear Admiral Sir Frederick William Richards, see C. in C., 1890.

25. Lloyds Register, 1880/1. In March 1912 the Apcar fleet was acquired by British India S.N. Co. George Blake, *B.I. Centenary*, (London, 1956), 171/2.

26. Caird. *PHL/2/106*.

27. NA ADM 50/299.

28. Richard Edward **Tracey**. Born: 24 January 1837. Died in London: 7 March 1907. Lieutenant: 28 June 1859. Borne in *Euryalus* from 24 June 1862 and served in her during the engagement at Kagoshima: 15 – 17 August 1863. Commander: 21 November 1864. Appointed to *Rodney*, 78, flagship, Vice Admiral The Hon. Sir Henry Keppel: 5 March 1867. In Japan the last Shogun, Tokugawa Yoshinobu, resigned on 3 January 1868 and the Imperial Meiji era commenced. While borne in *Rodney* Commander Tracey led the British Mission sent to train officers of the fledgling Imperial Japanese Navy. Captain: 29 December 1871. Appointed to *Iron Duke*, Flag Captain to Vice Admiral Willes: 3 January 1881. Rear Admiral: 1 January 1888. Superintendent Malta Dockyard: 12 January 1892 – 20 January 1894. Vice Admiral: 23 June 1893. President, Royal Naval College: October 1897. KCB: 21 May 1898. Admiral: 29 November 1898. Retired: 24 January 1901. *Navy List. Dictionary of National Biography.*

29. Ed. Richard Harding, Adrian Jarvis and Alston Kennerley, *British Ships in China Seas*, (Liverpool, 2004), Chapter 2 by Eric Grove, 8. Quoting, *Naval Force for the China Station*.

30. NA ADM 1/6575. Writing in *Iron Duke*.

31. NA 30/33/15/6 being the Satow diaries. Eventually Buchanan was to equal Satow in his achievements.

   The Rt. Hon. Sir George William **Buchanan**. Born in Copenhagen: 25 November 1854. Died: 20 December 1924. Early service in Vienna and Rome. Second Secretary at Tokio: 12 November 1879. Transferred to Vienna: 19 September 1882, then to Berne in December 1889. Later served in Rome and Berlin. Consul-General to Bulgaria: 14 November

1903. KCVO: 8 March 1905. Minister to the Queen of the Netherlands and Grand Duke of Luxembourg: 1 May 1909. GCVO: 3 June 1909. KCMG: 25 June 1909. PC: 7 November 1910. Ambassador at St. Petersburg: 23 November 1910. GCMG: 3 June 1913. GCB: 3 June 1915. Transferred to Rome: 21 October 1919. From Rome retired on pension: 25 November 1921. *Foreign Office List*, 1920. *Who's Who*.

It is of interest to note that while in Russia during the tense months of 1917 his close relationship with Tsar Nicholas II was such that he felt able to advise him, directly and forcefully, to grant a degree of constitutional reform. Alas for the Imperial family's fortunes this sound advice was not to be heeded.

32. NA ADM 1/6576. Writing in *Iron Duke* from Vladivostok.

33. His Imperial Majesty Emperor Mutsuhito, Meiji Tenno. Born: 3 November 1852. Died: 30 July 1912. Reigned from 1867 to 1912.

34. Prince Albert Victor and Prince George of Wales, *The Cruise of HMS Bacchante: 1879-1882*, (London, 1886), Vol. II, 68/69.

35. NA ADM 1/6576.

36. Ewo is Jardine, Matheson & Co. *The Cruise of HMS Bacchante: 1879-1882*, II, 266. Geoffrey Robley Sayer, *Hong Kong: 1862-1919*, (Hong Kong, 1975), 48/9.

37. Rutherford **Alcock**. See Kuper, C. in C., 1862, reference (66).

38. J.E. Hoare, *Embassies in the East*, (Richmond, Surrey, 1999), 171.

39. William George **Aston**. Born near Londonderry: 9 April 1841. Died at The Bluff, Beer, Devon: 22 November 1911. Classics, modern languages and history scholar and gold medallist of Queen's University, Belfast. MA: 1863. Appointed Student Interpreter in Japan: 16 August 1864, and arrived in Yedo that autumn, some two years after Ernest Satow. Interpreter and Translator to the Legation at Yedo: 6 October 1870. In 1872 one of the founding members of the Asiatic Society of Japan. In attendance on the Iwakura Mission while in England: 8 August to 16 December 1872. Assistant Japanese Secretary at Yedo: 1 April 1875 to 1 April 1882. Also served at Nagasaki and Hiogo. Provisional Consul-General for Korea: 17 March 1884. Japanese Secretary at Tokio: 20 May 1886. Retired on pension: 1 June 1889. 'Both to their contemporaries and to several generations of successors, Aston, Satow and (Basil Hall) Chamberlain (1850-1935) had no equals as scholars of Japan.' A number of his works are consulted by scholars to this day. Owing to ill health unfortunately he had no option but to retire early. *Foreign Office List*. Sir Hugh Cortazzi and Gordon Daniels, *Britain and Japan: 1859-1991*, (London and New York, 1991), 64-75. *Dictionary of National Biography*, (OUP, 1976), 67/68. Also see King, C. in C., 1865, reference (25).

40. NA ADM 1/6618. Commander Hoskyn to the C. in C., Nagasaki, 30 July 1882.

41. Ibid. Writing in *Iron Duke*, 18 August 1882.

42. Mark R. Peattie, *Nanyo*, (Hawaii, 1988), 7.

43. NA ADM 53/12575. Log Book *Audacious*.
Henry Craven **St. John**. Born: 5 January 1837. Died: 21 May 1909. Mate: 5 January 1857. Lieutenant: 10 August 1857. Commander: 12 April 1866. Appointed in command survey ship *Sylvia*, 865 tons, China Station: 7 October 1869. Most of the following seven years were occupied in surveying the coasts of Japan following which, in Edinburgh in 1880, was published his, *Notes and Sketches from the Wild Coasts of Nipon, with Chapters on Cruising After Pirates in Chinese Waters*. Being a talented amateur botanist and zoologist it is worthy of note that much of his collection of crustacea and mollusca subsequently was to be added to the collection at the British Museum. Captain: 18 September 1873. Continued in *Sylvia* to 31 January 1877. After taking *Iron Duke* home he paid off on 15 March 1883. Rear Admiral: 13 August 1889. Vice Admiral: 19 January 1896. Admiral and retired: 15 June 1901. *Navy List*. NA ADM 196/14.

44. NA ADM 1/6618. 'China Station, 1882. Efficiency of Her Majesty's Ships under Steam and Sail.' Composite screw gunvessel *Swift*, 788 tons, 11.8 knots. Completed in 1880. *The Sail and Steam Navy List*, 295.

45. Malcolm Falkus, *The Blue Funnel Legend*, (Basingstoke, 1990), 30/1.

46. NA ADM 1/6673. File S.193 dated 9 April 1883.

47. Richard N.J. Wright, *The Chinese Steam Navy 1862-1945*, (London, 2000), 30/31.

48. NA ADM 1/6673. Letter dated 30 May 1883.

49. *Tokyo Maru*. Built in 1864 and the following year acquired from Cornelius Vanderbilt by the U.S. flag Pacific Mail S.S. Company as their *New York*. In 1875 sold by them to the Mitsubishi S.S. as their *Tokyo Maru*. In 1885 the Mitsubishi

Steam Ship Co., or Mitsubishi Jokisen Kaisha, was to become a constituent of Nippon Yusen Kaisha. In 1886 she was sold by N.Y.K.

50. NA ADM 1/6674.

51. NA ADM 1/6713. Screw steamer *Ganges,* 4,168 grt. Built in 1882.

52. *Service Record.*

53. Ibid.

George Ferguson **Bowen**. Born in County Donegal: 2 November 1821. Died in Brighton: 21 February 1899. Charterhouse, and Trinity College, Oxford. 1st class, Classics: 1844. Fellow of Brasenose College, and member of Lincoln's Inn. Chief Secretary to the government of the Ionian Islands: 1854-1859. KCMG: 1856. Governor of Queensland: 1859-1868. GCMG: 1860. Governor of New Zealand: 1868-1873. Governor of Victoria: 1873-1879. Governor of Mauritius: April 1879 – December 1880. Governor of Hong Kong: 30 March 1883 – 6 October 1887. PC: 1886. Commissioner for delimitation of electoral districts, Malta: January 1888. *Colonial Office List.*

54. Caird. *PHL/2/108.* Indeed Vice Admiral Richard Vesey Hamilton was appointed from 1 September 1885 to succeed Admiral Dowell as C. in C., China – which see below .

55. Admiral Sir Frederick William Fisher, *Naval Reminiscences,* (London, 1938), 196.

56. *Service Record.*

57. Caird. *PHL/2/112.* Written from 73 Cadogan Square at the end of 1890.

58. Caird. *PHL/2/114.*

59. Peyton Skipworth, *Holy Trinity Sloane Street*, (London, 2006), 23.

60. The author is grateful to the Assistant Priest at Holy Trinity, Revd. Graham Rainford, who, during a visit on Thursday, 5 May 2011, most kindly assisted in making available all relevant information.

3 January 1884 to 1 September 1885
Vice Admiral Sir William Montagu **Dowell**

Born on 2 August 1825, second son of Reverend William Dowell, Vicar of Holme Lacy in the Wye valley near Hereford (1). His mother was Charlotte, a daughter of Reverend William Yonge, Chancellor of Norwich and for sixty five years, between 1779 and 1845, Vicar of St. Peter and St. Paul Parish Church at Swaffham in Norfolk (2).

He died at Ford, near Bideford, Devon on Friday, 27 December 1912, aged eighty seven years.

William entered the Royal Navy on 27 April 1839, 'passing' onboard *Royal Adelaide* in which ship he was to hoist his flag as C. in C., Devonport some fifty years later (3). Subsequently present at Amoy and Canton during the China War: 1841-1842. Received the China medal and clasp. While serving on the China coast it seems possible that a unique honour came his way:-

> 'Hongkong was ceded to Great Britain by China, as a result of the first China war, in 1841; and in January of that year the British Ensign was hoisted on Possession Point by Midshipman Dowell (now Admiral Sir William Dowell, KCB) (4).'

Promoted **Mate** on 2 July 1845, serving his first month in that rank in the brig *Racer*, 16 guns (5). Appointed to the large frigate *Eagle*, 50, Captain George Bohun Martin, south east coast of America: 5 August 1845. Naval Brigade, Montevideo: 1846-7. **Lieutenant**: 12 April 1848. Supernumerary Lieutenant in *Excellent*, Gunnery Ship, Portsmouth: 21 April 1848. Thereafter his promotion to Lieutenant was ante-dated to 25 October 1847. Confirmed as Lieutenant in *Excellent*: 13 June 1849. From 30 May 1850 appointed Gunnery Lieut. in the second rate *Albion*, 90, Captain William J.H. Johnstone, Mediterranean. In her saw service in the Black Sea also with the Naval Brigade, Crimea: 1854. He was to serve in the ship for some five years (6). In the Crimea he may have been fortunate to escape with his life:-

> '7 Nov. 1854 – gazetted as having been severely wounded.
> 20 Feby. 1855. Rear Admiral Sir E. Lyons commending his zeal and gallantry in offering to serve in the trenches before Sebastopol though on half pay (7).'

For services with the Naval Brigade at the Crimea he received accelerated promotion. Also he received the Crimean and Turkish medals with Sebastopol clasp, and was awarded the fifth class of the Medjidie.

Commander: 13 November 1854.

Later during 1855 he married a cousin, Caroline Johnna, daughter of Captain John Pyke, RN, JP of Ford, North Devon (8). She was born on 16 April 1829 and died on 2 September 1922, a long life of ninety three years. They were to have three sons of whom two, Arthur John William and George William, were to become officers in the Army, and two daughters. Their eldest son, Frank, died in London a few months before the death of the Admiral himself.

ADMIRAL SIR WILLIAM MONTAGU DOWELL, K.C.B.

On 18 November 1890 a daughter, Ellen Caroline Charlotte, was to marry Walter Basset Basset (1863-1907), one time Lieutenant, RN. She died on 5 March 1945. His other daughter, Miss Annie Teresa Dowell, in due course was to be the Admiral's sole executor. Annie Dowell:-

> '... had been his constant companion and had practically devoted her life to the care of her father (9).'

From 24 January 1856 in *Rodney*, 90, Portsmouth, then for a short period of seven months engaged in 'Particular Service'. This was to assist in bringing troops home from the Black Sea after the Crimean War.

For services rendered during the Crimean War, by the French he was appointed Knight of the Legion of Honour, and on 2 August 1856 received permission from HM Queen Victoria to wear the insignia.

From 15 August 1857 appointed in command screw steam sloop *Hornet*, 17 guns, 1,045 tons. East Indies and China Station, assuming command ten days later, on 25 August. While serving in her he was assigned to the Naval Brigade in the operation leading to the capture of Canton, of which city the bombardment commenced on 28 December 1857. Subsequently to be, 'gazetted for his gallant conduct at the assault of Canton.'

It was during this affair that on 5 January 1858, while endeavouring to make his escape over the wall at the rear of his yamen, that Viceroy Yeh Ming-ch'en was captured by a British party which included Consul Harry Parkes (10). Subsequently sent into exile, Viceroy Yeh was to die in Calcutta on 6 April 1859.

Captain: 26 February 1858.

Following his promotion he was succeeded in *Hornet* on 31 July 1858, her new Commander being Richard James Meade, Viscount Gilford, later to be Admiral of the Fleet The 4th Earl Clanwilliam (1832-1907).

From 24 September 1862 in command screw corvette *Barrosa*, 21 guns, 1,700 tons. East Indies and China Station. Commanded her at Shimonoseki: 5 – 10 September 1864. During that successful affair the C. in C., Vice Admiral Sir Augustus Kuper, flew his Flag in *Euryalus*.

Prior to the actual engagement at Shimonoseki *Barrosa* had been selected to carry two members of the 'Choshu Five', just returned from England, to warn their Daimio of the inevitable consequences of the attack about to take place against his batteries. These two were Ito Hirobumi and Inoue Kaoru, and from their experiences in Britain both were very well aware that Japan, only then about to emerge from feudal conditions, was in no position to tackle any western power, either militarily or commercially (11). One member of the British Legation at Yedo who was nominated to accompany this small party as an interpreter was Ernest Satow who recorded:-

> '21 July 1864. Our Captain Dowell is a very jolly old brick, but with a most quixotic phiz, quite a Knight of sorrowful countenance. Very good set of fellows in his wardroom (12).'

During the operation at Shimonoseki the steam sloop *Perseus*, 17, Commander Augustus J. Kingston, took the ground and Captain Dowell was ordered to get her off. He allocated the task to *Argus* whose Commander, John Moresby, subsequently was to write:-

> 'My old friend and shipmate Sir William Dowell was in command of the work, and with the disinterestedness which has distinguished all his brilliant career, he officially gave me the credit of the successful result (13).'

At Shimonoseki on 6 September 1864 the Captain of *Euryalus*, John Hobhouse Inglis Alexander, was wounded in the foot during an attack on the stockade behind Choshu shore Battery No. 5. Consequently from 14 September 1864 Captain Dowell was appointed in command of the ship, and to take her home at the end of her commission. She paid off at Portsmouth on 23 September 1865.

In the interim, on 18 November 1864 he had been, "Gazetted for Service at Attack on Batteries in Simono Seki Strait, Japan."

CB: 30 November 1864.

For five months from 23 January 1866 in command of the screw frigate *Topaze*, 31 guns, 2,659 tons, prior to her proceeding to the Pacific Station. Then between 16 June and 17 October 1866 he commanded the frigate *Leander*, 39 guns, 2,760 tons, on her return from the Pacific and prior to her paying off at Sheerness.

With his pendant in the screw corvette *Rattlesnake*, 19 guns, 1,705 tons, in command West Coast of Africa and Cape Station from 9 September 1867 to 26 April 1871 when she paid off in the Cape (14).

From 1 December 1867 he was a **Commodore** second class in this post. The West African slave trade gradually was coming to an end. Here follows an extract taken from his letter written from Loanda on 4 June 1868 and addressed to Sir Alexander Milne, First Sea Lord:-

'Since I last wrote to you I have visited all the places on the Southern division of this station, and I have been most particular in obtaining all possible information about the slave trade, and the conclusion I have come to is that as a permanent business it is entirely at an end; the slave dealers have all, with one exception, become legal traders, principally as agents to other Europeans. (--) Of course it is impossible for me to state positively that no more cargoes would be run if the blockade were entirely raised, an occasional cargo might of course be shipped, but I do not think that even that is probable; certainly I do think that the time has arrived when the expense of a regular Naval squadron might be saved, and vessels enough only kept to protect legal trade ... (15).'

A month later, on 4 July *Rattlesnake* now being at Lagos, he brought up another subject, also related to an economy which might be made. Specifically he made mention of a saving should the Admiralty Coal Depot, 'at Loanda be done away with and a contract entered into to supply coal instead. I feel sure that it would be a saving to the government as the waste in our coal store is always large (16).'

From 1870 to 1875 a.d.c. to H.M. The Queen (17).

From 4 January 1872 to 5 June 1874 in command of the armour plated iron screw ship *Hercules*, 14 guns, 8,677 tons, Channel Squadron. In honour of her Naval Constructor, Sir Edward James Reed (1830-1906), the ship, completed at Chatham in November 1868, was known as 'Reed's Masterpiece'.

Rear Admiral: 11 December 1875.

Meanwhile, between September 1875 and February 1876 he sat on a, 'Committee on Supply of Engineers and Engine Room Artificers (18).'

Second in command Channel Squadron with his Flag in *Black Prince*, 28 guns, 9,137 tons: 16 May 1877. Her sister ship was *Warrior*, today the museum ship at Portsmouth.

A keen boat sailer here he is from *Black Prince* having challenged a brother officer to a race:-

'Admiral Dowell sailed in his six-oared galley, which carried a private rig of two dipping lugs. I (Lord Charles Beresford) was confident of beating him but the admiral knew better. (--) At first I went away from him but when I was just inside the breakwater (at Portland), a puff came, over went the boat, and it went down under me. Dowell, seeing that I was swimming safely and that the boats of the Fleet were coming to pick me up, went on and won the race (19).'

Based at Queenstown, his next appointment was as Senior Officer, Coast of Ireland with his Flag in the screw two decker *Revenge*, 28 guns, 5,260 tons: 28 September 1878 – 15 April 1880, latterly as Vice Admiral.

Vice Admiral: 20 January 1880.

In April 1880 succeeded in command on the Coast of Ireland by Rear Admiral Richard Vesey Hamilton, (see C. in C., 1885).

With his Flag in the screw armoured iron frigate *Minotaur*, 10,690 tons, from 17 April 1882 in command Channel Squadron but temporarily in the Mediterranean. The Egyptian War took place during 1882 but *Minotaur* did not participate in the bombardment of Alexandria. However members of his Flagship's company were to participate ashore:-

'On September 19 and 20 (1882), Vice Admiral Dowell, who lay meanwhile in Aboukir Bay, landed a force of Marines, under Major Arthur French, RMA, of the *Minotaur*, and occupied the forts there. ... and a few days later the last sparks of Arabi's rebellion had flickered out (20).'

'26 October 1882. Thanked by Parliament for operations in Egypt (21).'

KCB: 17 November 1882.

His flag in *Minotaur* was struck on 1 December 1883.

His appointment as C. in C., China having been announced on 3 January 1884, then two days later his flag was hoisted at Devonport.

In China his Flagship was to be *Audacious*, Captain Hugo L. Pearson (22). By now in the Navy List she is described as being a second class battleship. In the event to take up his duties as the new C. in C. he took passage East and arrived at Hong Kong on 2 March 1884. Following the departure of Admiral Willes on 5 March, then he assumed command of the Station. As was recorded in the log book in *Audacious* at Hong Kong on Sunday, 2 March 1884:-

'12.30 p.m. Arrived P. & O. mail steamer *Clyde*.

1.30 p.m. H.M.S. *Cleopatra* hoisted flag of Vice Admiral Sir W.M. Dowell (23).'

4 April 1884. As Takano Isoroku, the future Admiral of the Fleet Yamamoto Isoroku, was born in Nagaoka, Honshu. At the outbreak of the Pacific War in 1941 he was to be C. in C., Combined Fleet, IJN. As a young officer he was to serve in the U.S.A. on two occasions, the first between May 1919 and July 1921. Secondly, now as Naval Attache, he was to serve in Washington, DC between January 1926 and March 1928.

In May 1884 it seemed possible that France and China might reach peaceful agreement over the question of Annam but by July the situation had altered for the worse. The following extract is taken from his long letter written from Shanghai on 24 July 1884 in which he informed the Admiralty:-

'On reaching Tientsin I learnt by telegram from H.M. Minister at Peking (who was Sir Harry Parkes) that the French had, on the 12th instant, sent an ultimatum to Peking demanding an indemnity of 50 millions of dollars, and threatening to seize territory if the terms were not accepted within 7 days. I was informed that the Chinese Government has replied that they would pay nothing (24).'

While still at Tientsin, the C. in C. exchanged official visits with Viceroy Li Hung-chang, by whom he was received with every civility.

Then on 16 July he received the normal instructions from the Admiralty, 'to prepare to afford assistance to Europeans at the Treaty ports.' On 18 July, by now at Taku, he received news from his SNO (Senior Naval Officer) at Shanghai concerning French fleet movements together with other information, 'from which I gathered that Foochow would be the probable point of attack.'

The C. in C. now made his dispositions accordingly, these including the continual presence of Royal Naval guardships a short distance down the coast from Foochow at Amoy. He himself in the gunboat *Vigilant*, 985 tons, steamed to the Min River and on 28 July 1884 anchored below Foochow in the historic Pagoda Anchorage. From there he visited the French C. in C. who, 'renewed his assurance to me that due notice should be given before hostilities were commenced.'

From Foochow on 2 August Britain commenced to evacuate any foreign citizens who desired to leave. Also early in August the French occupied Keelung in Formosa, on a temporary basis, as earlier the Chinese authorities there had refused to allow the warships of the French squadron to be supplied with coal.

In the event, further discussions between China and France not producing satisfaction to either side, on 23/24 August 1884 the Mawei naval dockyard at Foochow was taken under fire by the French, and received considerable damage. Also in the River Min in the vicinity of Pagoda Anchorage a number of Chinese warships were sunk by a French squadron under the command of Vice Admiral Amedee Courbet (1828-1885).

Great Britain remained neutral throughout this affair. However it seems clear that in one important instance private feelings reflected a certain bias:-

'... the British admiral was an old friend of the (French) Far East squadron. The British gunboat *Vigilant* had been one of several foreign warships anchored near Foochow on 23 August 1884, and Dowell had been an interested spectator of the destruction of China's Fukien Fleet by Courbet's ships. On the night before the battle Courbet had sent a Midshipman to *Vigilant* to notify Dowell that he intended to attack the Chinese fleet on the following afternoon, and Dowell had produced a bottle of whisky and offered a toast to a French victory (25).'

It was on 6 April 1885, when at Nagasaki, that finally the C. in C. was to hear better news:- 'H.M. Minister at Tokio informed me that he had received a telegram from Peking announcing that a protocol of peace between France and China had been signed (26).'

In the interim unfortunately the hope expressed by Admiral Willes in August 1882 that no further contretemps would arise between Corea and Japan was not to be realised. From Hong Kong on 12 January 1885 Admiral Dowell informed the Admiralty:-

'I gather that the Japanese had landed about 2,000 troops at Chemulpo and marched towards Seoul and that they had stated that they would treat with the Coreans first and with the Chinese subsequently. The energetic measures taken by the Japanese have had immediate effect on the Corean Government for I now learn by telegram that the difficulties between Japan and Corea have been settled, a treaty having been signed on the 9th instant (January 1885). The Chinese question had not been touched and the Japanese troops remained. A Chinese squadron consisting of the *Yung Wei, Chao Yung, Wei Yuan* (two gunboats and a sloop), and a transport were at Masampo (present day Masan near Pusan) on 25 December (27).'

Both the Corean and Chinese governments were to call for mediation by Great Britain, Germany and the USA in an attempt to resolve their differences.

The future Fleet Admiral Chester William Nimitiz, USN was born in Fredericksburg, Texas on 24 February 1885. During the Pacific War of 1941-1945 against Japan he was to serve with outstanding ability and success as C. in C., Pacific Fleet and Pacific Ocean Areas (28). In succession to Fleet Admiral Ernest J. King, on 15 December 1945 to become Chief of Naval Operations.

Today the U.S. National Museum of the Pacific War may be visited in Fredericksburg.

Although not immediately to be of much interest or concern to those Navies of the world operating coal fired steamships, it was in 1885 near the east coast settlement of Pangkalan Brandan in North Sumatra that oil in commercial quantities first was struck in the East Indies. The successful entrepreneur was the Dutchman, Aeilko Jans Zijklert (1840-1890), originally a tobacco planter, and his well was known as Telaga Tunggal No. 1. To exploit this achievement, in June 1890 he and his backers were to form the 'Royal Dutch Company for the Working of Petroleum Wells in the Dutch Indies.' By the turn of the century further oilfields were to have been discovered in South Sumatra, Central and Eastern Java, and in East Kalimantan, Borneo.

Meanwhile in 1897 the Shell Transport and Trading Company was to be founded in England by Marcus Samuel, later Viscount Bearsted (1853-1927). He, with his steamer *Murex*, 3,564 grt and completed in 1892, Captain John R. Coudon, earlier had commenced to develop a bulk oil transport tanker business. On 24 February 1907 the Royal Dutch Shell group was to be formed, a combination of British and Dutch interests in that rapidly expanding field. By that date an ever increasing number of both merchantmen and warships were to be burning oil.

Meanwhile in Peking:-

'Worn out by overwork and restless mental activity, Sir Harry Parkes succumbed, after a brief illness, to Peking fever, 22 March 1885, at the age of fifty seven. His body, after every mark of honour and respect had been paid by the foreign communities and both the Chinese and Japanese governments, was brought to England and buried at Whitchurch. In 1887 a memorial bust was unveiled in St. Paul's Cathedral by his old chief, Sir Rutherford Alcock (29).'

Passed Midshipman Chester W. Nimitz and his "wonderful white-bearded grandfather," Charles Henry Nimitz, Texas, February 1905.

At the time the Japanese Minister to China was Enomoto Takeaki, none other than he who had helped to lead the Tokugawa supporters during the short lived Boshin War of 1868/1869. Acting quickly he assisted with the arrangements for both Counts Ito Hirobumi and Saigo Tsugumichi to cross over from Japan in order to attend, and to pay appropriate respects, on the occasion of Sir Harry's funeral which took place in the chapel of the British Legation to Peking at 11.00 a.m. on 30 March (30). From 23 March acting as Charge d'Affaires in the British Legation was Nicholas R. O'Conor of whom more will be heard.

In the course of the long journey home the remains of the late Sir Harry Parkes first reached Tientsin on 5 April 1885 from where Sir Harry's daughter, Marion Plumer, now Mrs. James Keswick, wife of the Jardine Matheson Taipan, had arranged onward transport to Shanghai in their steamer *Kow Shing* (31). Owing to the troubles with Russia Sir William was unable to do more than to order the gunboat *Merlin*, Lieut. and Commander Reginald O.B.C. Brenton, who was in Peiho waters, to pay befitting respects and to provide an escort to *Kow Shing* where possible. At the time *Merlin* was rather busily occupied in watching a Russian gunboat, nevertheless once the Jardine steamer cleared the Peiho and entered the Gulf of Chihli *Merlin* was able to carry out her orders. The relevant log book extract reads as follows:-

'Saturday, 11 April 1885. Off Taku.

8.15 a.m. Observed s.s. *Kow Shing* with body of Sir H. Parkes.

8.45 Stopped to speak to steamer.

8.55 Proceeded. Fired 15 minute guns.

Shaped course to rejoin Russian gunboat (32).

Carried home from Hong Kong in the Blue Funnel steamer *Anchises*, 2,021 grt, eventually Sir Harry's body was to reach England. There at St. Lawrence Church, St. Lawrence Close off Whitchurch Lane, Canons Park, London he was buried next to his wife Fanny Hannah, nee Plumer, who sadly had died some five and a half years previously, in November 1879. The couple had married there at St. Lawrence Church on 1 January 1856. The church building itself is a remarkable structure, built between 1714 and 1716 by James Brydges, 1st Duke of Chandos.

On 30 March 1885 Russian forces clashed with those of Afghanistan at Panjdeh (today known as Serhetabat) in present day Turkmenistan south of the River Oxus. Known in Russian as the Battle of Kushka, this was yet another aspect of the Anglo-Russian 'Great Game' concerning India. Naturally regarded very seriously at the time, in London the Gladstone government of the day resolved to apply pressure against Russia in the Baltic, the Black Sea and in the Far East. Thus in April 1885 Great Britain occupied a small group of islands lying thirty six miles north east of Quelpart Island off the south coast of Korea. This new base was known as Port Hamilton, at about 34N 127.20E (33). At a cost of GBP 85,000 the Admiralty even went to the expense of laying a submarine cable between Port Hamilton and Woosung.

As Port Hamilton, or Geomun-do, is only some 700 miles from Vladivostok this move by Britain was to have an additional advantage in that also it gave Russia cause to reflect over possible evil intentions which she might have been contemplating against Korea.

In the event in September 1885 the Russo-Afghan border question was settled by arbitration. Concerning Russia's territorial interest in Korea, upon the necessary guarantees being received it was only to be some eighteen months later, on 27 February 1887, that Britain felt that she was able to commence removing much military equipment from Port Hamilton.

As will be obvious, early in 1885 the C. in C. was closely involved with making all the arrangements necessary to secure, establish and equip, and also with the construction of the necessary defences at Port Hamilton. Starting from scratch he moved quickly to reinforce the new base with stocks of coal, the chartered steamer *Thales* assisting with that process from Nagasaki (34). Amongst other necessary requirements were the placing of provisions suitable for 1,000 men for a month, these including live bullocks, huts for the detachment of Royal Marines and other members of the garrison, and timber for the construction of booms across the two entrances to the anchorage. Also shallows adjacent to the entrances needed to be blocked. From Hong Kong HM Sloop

Flying Fish, 949 tons, Captain John F.L.P. Maclear, was ordered up to Port Hamilton with mines and mining gear and subsequently the Flagship's Torpedo Lieutenant, Gerald L. King Harman, proceeded to the island especially to supervise the laying of these mines together with the necessary electrical firing arrangements (35). In addition:-

> 'It will probably be desireable to build some tanks to receive rain water, springs appearing to be scarce on the island (36).'

Further, merchant ships such as Donald Currie's steel screw steamer *Pembroke Castle*, 3,946 grt, the fifteen knot Glen Line *Glenogle*, 3,748 grt, and the P. & O. *Rosetta*, 3,411 grt, were taken up for cruiser and transport duties. At Hong Kong these ships were fitted with guns and the appropriate Naval personnel were embarked to attend to their operation. In respect of *Rosetta* for example, the officers and men from HM paddle despatch vessel *Vigilant* were transferred across to assist in manning her in her new role (37).

The movements of Russian men-of-war were watched, likewise those of Russian merchant vessels, the latter frequently laden with emigrants and convicts bound for Vladivostok.

In *Audacious* on 3 June 1885 the C. in C. himself was at Port Hamilton to inspect the defences, 'necessary to render it secure from hostile attack (38).'

The base arrangements were maintained in readiness for war until later in 1885 when, in the light of the arbitration mentioned above, it proved possible to remove the mines and boom defences for storage ashore on the island.

In the interim considerable correspondence was taking place between Mr Nicholas Roderick O'Conor (1843-1908), then acting British Charge d'Affaires at Peking, and Mr Byron Brenan (1847-1927), Consul at Tientsin where he was in close communication with Viceroy Li Hung-chang (1823-1901). The matter of Port Hamilton received attention but in reality China already had lost to Japan any influence which earlier she had held in Corean affairs. However, on 18 June 1885, Mr. O'Conor brought up the question of the Chinese Navy:-

> 'I think it is important to encourage as far as may be Li's wish to put the Naval Reorganisation under the superintendence of Englishmen, and I have written to the F.O. generally supporting any application that may be made by Marquis Tsing, and also saying that Captain Lang's return to China under proper engagement, would be desireable. If we do not come to blows with Russia I daresay we should be glad and able to comply with all Li wants, tho' what he understands by the "loan of some ship" is not very clear (39).'

Events were to show that within China there lacked a cohesion of purpose and desire and so, especially when compared with the competent progress made in Japan, no properly concerted effort was to be made to seek foreign assistance with the objective of modernising of their Navy.

Meanwhile in Marshalltown, Iowa on 29 April 1885 the future Admiral Frank Jack Fletcher, USN was born. From the outbreak of the Pacific War in 1941, therefore before time had permitted the later enormous increase in the manufacture and supply of war materials from the U.S.A., so necessarily and wisely making do with what was available, he was to achieve wonders in those early days of the Naval war against Japan. Perhaps only in more recent years have his great achievements in 1942 at the Coral Sea, Midway, and in the Solomon Islands come to be correctly appreciated.

Admiral: 1 July 1885.

As usual during the summer months cholera made its appearance again, in particular at Nagasaki, Shanghai, Foochow, Ningpo and Chefoo.

During 1885 Hugh Low, the Resident at Kuala Kangsar, Perak, Malaya and a great friend of Sir Henry Keppel (see C. in C., 1867), went on leave (40). To act in his place Frank Swettenham was appointed (41).

Amongst other duties he supervised the collection of 400 seeds of *Hevea Braziliensis*, taken from seedlings first planted by Mr. Low in the Residency garden in 1877, and planted them out. In this manner was most useful practical assistance given to what was to become, from 1895 onwards, the huge rubber industry in Malaya. The first commercial rubber from Malaya was to reach London in 1899 and be sold for 3s. 10d., in today's money just over 19P, a pound (42).

Continuing to exercise all his, 'talents as a colonial adminstrator', was H.E. the Governor, Sir Frederick A. Weld, in 1885 to be created GCMG.

1 October 1885. Commencement of operations of the merchant shipping company N.Y.K., Nippon Yusen Kaisha. The earlier Tsukumo Shokai, and successors, now were amalgamated with Kyodo Unyu Kaisha to form Nippon Yusen Kaisha. The first President of the N.Y.K. was Morioka Masazumi of the Satsuma 'han'. A Scot, Captain Albert Richard Brown, was appointed General Manager (43). The affairs of N.Y.K. were always to be greatly influenced by the Mitsubishi concern.

Their founder, Iwasaki Yataro of the previous Tosa 'han' on Shikoku, had died that February so now the fortunes of the firm were guided by his younger brother, Iwasaki Yanosuke (1851-1908).

Until such time as Japan was able to introduce the necessary maritime education systems then in early years the Masters of N.Y.K. vessels tended to be British. In fact, and maybe somewhat surprisingly, the last British Master with N.Y.K., Francis Cope, only was to retire in 1920.

The Aberdonian Scot, Thomas Blake Glover, was closely involved with the Iwasaki family and early Mitsubishi development. Two further connections were the Takashima coal interests and Nagasaki Dockyard of Kosuge, both originally inspired by Glover in 1867/1868, and in due course both to come within the Mitsubishi fold. Warships such as the great battleship *Musashi*, 67,100 tons and commissioned in 1942, and *Kirishima*, first commissioned in 1915 as a battlecuiser of 27,500 tons, were to fight against the Allies during the Pacific War of 1941-1945. Both were to be built at the Mitsubishi Nagasaki Yard.

Particularly following the Sino-Japanese war of 1894/5, with the Navigation Encouragement Law of 1896, the Japanese were to take great steps to increase the size and number of trade routes served by their merchant marine.

Again concerning maritime matters, the Japanese government was to adopt a cohesive policy of training manpower, developing their shipbuilding abilities, and increasing the importance and size of both their Navy and merchant marine. Their success in this direction was in complete practical contrast to Manchu Chinese efforts.

Nevertheless during October 1885 the Manchu in China did create their Hai-chun Yamen or Navy Office. This was the first of many new official military projects, a direct result of the conflict with France, which had brought about an increased awareness within China of the need for self strengthening military power. Similarly within China in some important circles there was a growing realization that military power was an adjunct of industrial power and that arsenals and shipyards called for a wide range of supporting industrial and communications projects (44). Unfortunately from on high, particularly in the person of the Empress Dowager Tz'u-hsi, no support for these efforts ever was to be evident. Sadly for China the latter years of the Ch'ing dynasty, in miserable contrast to the early years, were notable for nepotism, corruption, and a general lack of progressive zeal within the administration (45).

Also in October 1885 another piracy took place. Writing from *Audacious* at Hong Kong on 19 October 1885 the C. in C. gave details of the unpleasant affair:-

> 'The British steamer *Greyhound* pirated on 17 October 1885 within 70 miles of Hong Kong on
> passage to Hoihow and Pakhoi (down the coast to the south west). Some of the 100 passengers
> were pirates who rushed the ship, murdered the Master and threw his body overboard. Later met
> by three junks and disappeared with their booty, allowing *Greyhound* to return to Hong Kong on
> 18 October.
>
> The Viceroy at Canton sent 3 gunboats to assist HMS *Midge* in co-operating in the hunt to find
> the culprits (46).'

A fortnight later, on 3 November, he was able to give the Admiralty his homeward bound travel plans. Admiral Hamilton arrived at Hong Kong in the English mail late on 4 November 1885, and at sunset on 10 November the flag of the C. in C. was struck in *Audacious*. He himself had sailed that afternoon at 4.30 p.m. in the P. & O. *Hydaspes*, a screw steamer of 3,083 grt.

On leaving *Audacious* for the last time H.M. Ships in port manned yards and salutes were fired, these honours also being paid by the French cruiser *Primauguet*.

Admiral Hamilton succeeded to the command of the China Station on 11 November 1885.

Sir William returned to England on 21 December 1885, on the following day to begin a period of some three years on half pay (47).

However for a brief interval between 31 December 1885 and 16 January 1886 he was appointed President of a Committee for the revision of Signal Book and Manual of War Manoeuvres.

In October 1888 he was appointed as one of three members of an Admiralty committee, the other two being Admirals Sir Frederick Richards and Sir Vesey Hamilton, the latter having returned from the East earlier in the year, to report on the lessons learned during the naval manoeuvres held that year. (See Admiral Richards, C. in C., 1890-1892, 'Blockade Committee'). Their findings were to lead to the adoption by the government of the 'Two Power' standard.

C. in C., Devonport: 15 December 1888 – 4 August 1890. Flag in his old ship *Royal Adelaide*. During this time, during the early summer of 1890, additionally he was appointed an umpire for the manoeuvres of that year. At Devonport in 1890 he was succeeded by Admiral HRH The Duke of Edinburgh (48).

Amongst his charitable interests in Devonport was that of the Royal British Female Orphan Asylum, an institution with close naval connections:-

'In 1890 the Patron was H.M. Queen Victoria with Admiral Sir William Dowell, KCB
as President (49).'

On 2 August 1890 he had reached the retirement age of sixty five years.

From 5 August 1890 he retired to live at Ford, near Bideford. Although he had joined the Navy in 1839, some fifty one years earlier, his actual time on full pay on the Active List had amounted to thirty four years and eight days, his basic retirement pay entitlement then being at the rate of Sterling 930.00 p.a. (50).

In retirement he was extremely involved and active in local affairs including the County Bench of Magistrates, the Bideford Amateur Athletic Club, Naval Brigade and, another important maritime interest, the Appledore Lifeboat (51).

In 1891 he acted as the Chairman of the Committee of the Royal Naval Exhibition which was held at Chelsea, London between 2 May and 24 October that year. This was a huge affair with well over 5,000 exhibits, the whole brought together to demonstrate to the public how their Navy had developed over the centuries.

Also in 1891, on 19 August, he was awarded one of the ten Good Service Pensions, GSP, then available. This was worth Sterling 300 p.a.

GCB: 25 May 1895.

After his death in December 1912 his wife was in receipt of a telegram:-

'The King is so grieved to hear of the death of dear Sir William Dowell, whom he had known for
so long, and he offers you and family his heartfelt sympathy in your great loss (52).'

In addition to family members, and many others who desired to pay their last respects, his funeral, which took place on Wednesday, 1 January 1913, was attended by Captain Alexander Duff, RN (see C. in C., 1919), representing HM The King, and Admiral Sir William May, C. in C., Devonport. In addition in Bideford, of which town he had been a Freeman since 1904:-

'Throughout the town flags flew at half mast, blinds were drawn at shops, and everywhere signs of
mourning were evident (53).'

In 1931 a memorial to both the Admiral and his wife was erected on the north wall within All Saints' Chapel, a side chapel entered to the left immediately prior to proceeding through into the Bideford Parish Church, St. Mary's (54).

Still today the small village of Ford , outside Bideford, remains a quiet, unspoilt community just off the A39 highway which continues on around Barnstaple Bay and off to the West.

NOTES

1. Admiral of the Fleet Sir Arthur Knyvet **Wilson**, VC (1842-1921) was a cousin, Admiral Wilson's mother being Agnes Mary Yonge, Charlotte's sister. In addition another sister was to become Mrs. Pyke, a daughter of whom, and therefore also a cousin, was to marry William in 1855. Admiral Sir Edward E. Bradford, *Life of Admiral of the Fleet Sir Arthur Knyvet Wilson*, (London, 1923), 3. Also see Reference (8) below.
2. *Who Was Who: 1897-1916*. Courtesy: Plymouth Library Services.
3. Ibid. *Royal Adelaide*, 4,122 tons, completed in July 1835. Flag/guard ship at Plymouth: May 1859. Transferred to Chatham: September 1891. Sold on 4 April 1905 and subsequently broken up at Dunkirk. *The Sail and Steam Navy List*, 91.
4. William Legge, *A Guide to Hong Kong with some Remarks on Macao and Canton*, (Hong Kong, 1893), 2. Courtesy of The Librarian, Royal Asiatic Society, London. The British flag first was hoisted at Hong Kong on Tuesday, 26 January 1841. Frank Welsh, *A History of Hong Kong*, (London, 1997), 105. It should be noted that in his relevant volume Captain Edward Belcher makes the flag hoisting claim for himself. (Unfortunately in the National Archives at Kew no log book covering the movements of *Sulphur* during January 1841 is available.)
5. NA ADM 196/1. 530/534. *Service Record*.
6. Ibid.
7. NA ADM 196/36. *Service Record*
8. *Who's Who*, 1912. His mother, Charlotte, nee Yonge, had several sisters of whom Caroline Sarah married the then Lieutenant John Pyke, RN on 18 May 1827. By amusing co-incidence another sister, Agnes Mary Yonge, married Rear Admiral George Knyvet Wilson. They were the parents of Admiral of the Fleet Sir Arthur Knyvet Wilson, VC (1842-1921). Also see Reference (1) above.
9. Obituary, *North Devon Journal*, 2 January 1913.
10. Gerald S. Graham, *The China Station: War and Diplomacy: 1830-1860*, (OUP, 1978), 338/9.
11. **Inoue** Kaoru (1836-1915). During the Meiji era, in 1878 to be Minister of Public Works, and in 1878 Minister of Foreign Affairs. Also from Eiichi Kiyooka, *The Autobiography of Yukichi Fukuzawa*, (Columbia University, 1966), 368, it may be noted, '... he was a powerful friend and co-worker of Ito (Hirobumi).'
12. NA 30/33/15/1 being the Satow Diaries.
13. John Moresby, *Two Admirals*, (London, 1913), 195.
14. Concerning the trans Atlantic slave trade from West Africa, by now diminishing:-

    'Also, on September 30, 1866, our Commissioner, Synge, at Havana reported that "the Cuban slave trade is virtually at an end".

    J. Holland Rose, *The Royal Navy and the Suppression of the West Africa Slave Trade*, (The Mariner's Mirror, Vol. 22, 1936), 171. As one result of changing times, from the Navy List of July 1869 the Station first is shown as being named 'Cape of Good Hope and West Coast of Africa.' Prior to that date West Africa was a station with separate identity. The Cape too had been a separate command under a Commodore.

    Subsequent events were to show that in writing as he did in 1866 Commissioner William Webb Follett Synge (1826-1891) was a little premature in his judgement of the situation nevertheless the trend was clear.
15. Caird Library, National Maritime Museum, Greenwich. Ref: *MLN/165/3*. Admiral of the Fleet Sir Alexander **Milne**, First Baronet (1806-1896). Twice First Naval Lord: July 1866 – December 1868, and again, November 1872 – September 1876. *Navy List*.

16. Ibid. Loanda is Sao Paolo da Assuncao de Loanda, present day Luanda, capital city of Angola.

17. *Who's Who.*

18. *Service Record.*

19. Lord Beresford, *The Memoirs of Admiral Lord Beresford,* (London, 1916), 506.

20. Clowes, Vol. VII, 346.

21. *Service Record.*

22. Hugo Lewis **Pearson**. Born: 30 June 1843. Died: 12 June 1912. Rear Admiral: 1 January 1895. C. in C., Australia Station: 1 November 1897 – 1 November 1900. Vice Admiral: 13 March 1901. From 1 January 1904 C. in C., The Nore with his Flag in *Wildfire*. KCB: 24 June 1904. Admiral: 20 October 1904. Continued at The Nore until succeeded, on 1 January 1907, by Admiral Sir Gerard Noel (see C. in C., 1904). Retired: summer 1908. *Navy List.*

23. NA ADM 53/12576. s.s. *Clyde*, 4,124 grt. Built in 1881 at Dumbarton, and to be sold in 1901 to Indian interests for the Mecca pilgrim service. Capable of fifteen knots. Small cruiser *Cleopatra*, 2,380 tons, completed at Govan in 1880. *The Sail and Steam Navy List*, 273.

24. NA ADM 1/6713. Para. 7. Written in *Vigilant*.

25. David Wilmhurst, translation from the French, Maurice Rollet de L'Isle, *Hong Kong During the Sino-French War (1884-85)*, *Journal of the RASHKB*, Vol. 50, (Hong Kong, 2010), 160. *Vigilant*, 985 tons, in fact was a paddle despatch vessel.

26. NA ADM 1/6757.

27. Ibid.

28. E.B. Potter, *Nimitz*, (Annapolis, MD, 1987), 26, 471.

29. *Dictionary of National Biography,* 304. Sir Harry Parkes. Not in fact interred at Whitchurch but in the graveyard at the Church of St. Lawrence, Whitchurch Lane, London HA8 7QQ (a short walk East from the Canon's Park underground station on the Jubilee Line). In St. Paul's his memorial bust is to be found in the crypt in location 'J1'. The author paid his respects at the former on 29 June 2008, and in the crypt at the latter on 28 June 2012.

30. NA FO 17/979. At the time the Foreign Secretary was Granville George, the Second Earl Granville.

31. *Kow Shing*, 2,134 grt. Built in 1883 for the Shanghai/Tientsin trade. In July 1894 again to feature in the news.

32. NA ADM 53/14541. *Merlin*, 430 tons. 125' in length. Launched in 1871, and to be sold in February 1891. Reginald Brenton was to be promoted Commander on 30 June 1885. *Navy List.*

33. Port Hamilton first was surveyed on 16 and 17 July 1845 by Captain Sir Edward Belcher in *Samarang*:-
    '… and proceeded to the examination of this new group. It was found to be composed of three islands, two large and one small, deeply indented and forming a most complete harbour within, as well as a very snug bay without. The ship was anchored in the outer bay and the day following (this being 17 July) devoted to the survey of the island.'
    Captain Sir Edward Belcher, *Narrative of the Voyage of H.M.S. Samarang During the Years 1843-1846*. I, (London, 1848), 352. BL reference: V.10013. Indeed, as may be seen from the ship's log book survey operations had commenced early on 16 July 1845:-
    'Wednesday, July 16, 1845
    9.30 a.m. Hove to – Captain left the ship in 3rd Gig – with 2nd Gig, 1st Cutter and Jolly.
         (All day the ship manoeuvred off the coast of these islands)
    7.10 p.m. Shortened sail and came to with SB in 7 fthms. Furled sails.
         Captain and surveying officers came onboard. Up boats.
    Thursday, July 17, 1845
    At anchor on the North side of an island at Lat. 34.4N and Long. 127.21E
    6 a.m.   Captain and surveying officers left the ship.
         Crew employed dredging and as most requisite.
    7.40 p.m. Captain came onboard in gig.
    Friday, July 18, 1845
    4.15 a.m. Weighed and made all plain sail.'
     NA ADM 53/3105 being the log book, H.M.S. *Samarang*.
    He named the port for Captain William Alexander Baillie Hamilton (1803-1881), between September 1841 and

January 1845 private secretary to a relation, Thomas Hamilton, Ninth Earl of Haddington and who was First Lord of the Admiralty between September 1841 and January 1846, Sir Robert Peel being Prime Minister. In succession to Sir John Barrow (1764-1848), between January 1845 and May 1855 Captain Hamilton was Second Secretary to the Admiralty. *Navy List – Civil Dept. of the Navy.*

In *Saracen* in 1855 John Richards, Master, made additions to this earlier survey. Dawson, II, 120.

For twenty six years between 1829 and 1855 the Hydrographer of the Navy was Rear Admiral Sir Francis Beaufort (1774-1857). Alfred Friendly, *Beaufort of the Admiralty,* (London, 1977).

34. Iron screw steamer *Thales,* 1,199 grt. To be named *Kentucky,* built in Dumbarton in 1865 as a blockade runner into the Confederacy. Subsequently acquired for Eastern service. In 1885 owned by Douglas S.S. Co., Hong Kong. After an astonishing career with many different owners, latterly Japanese, on 6 April 1945 to be mined and sunk off Yawata, north Kyushu. *Lloyd's Register,* 1865. H.W. Dick and S.A. Kentwell, *Beancaker to Boxboat,* Canberra, 1988), 138. In October 1892 she was to assist with the rescue of survivors, P. & O. s.s. *Bokhara.*

35. NA ADM 1/6757.

36. NA ADM 1/8610.

37. NA ADM 1/6757. In 1906 *Pembroke Castle* was to be sold to the Turkish government and in August 1914 to be sunk by Russian warships in the Black Sea. In 1904 *Glenogle* was to be sold to owners in Rangoon and eventually be broken up in 1920. In 1900 *Rosetta* was to be sold to Japanese owners and then in July 1907 to be disposed of for scrap in Japan.

38. Ibid.

39. Archives Centre, Churchill College, Cambridge. Ref: *OCON 5/1/1.*

40. Hugh **Low**. See Coote, C. in C., 1878, reference (21).

41. Frank Athelstane **Swettenham**. Born: 28 March 1850. Died: 11 June 1946. Cadet, Straits Settlements: July 1870. Served in Malaya for his entire early working life. In 1896 appointed as the first Resident-General, Malay States. KCMG: 1897. Governor of the Straits Settlements and High Commissioner to Malaya: 1901-1904. Chairman, Royal Commission to investigate the finances of Mauritius: 1909. GCMG: 1909. During the early years of the Great War served as assistant director, then director of the Press Bureau. CH: 1917. *Colonial Office List.* Obituary, *The Times,* June 13, 1946.

42. Daniel Green, *A Plantation Family,* (Ipswich, 1979), 133. The seedlings were shipped East by Sir Joseph Dalton **Hooker** (1817-1911), Director, Royal Botanic Gardens, Kew. Between 1875 and 1879 the Superintendent of the Singapore Botanical Gardens was Mr. Henry James Murton who had worked with Mr. Low on this pioneering project. The story of natural rubber is in itself a fine tale. John Loadman, *Tears of the Tree,* (OUP, 2005), 99.

43. NYK Corporate profile: www.nykline.co.jp. Lewis Bush, *The Illustrious Captain Brown,* (Tokyo and Rutland, VT, 1969), 83. During 1867 Mr. Brown first had arrived in Japan as First Officer in the P. & O. s.s. *Malacca,* 1,709 grt. Also see Ed. Hugh Cortazzi, Chapter 23 by Takeno Hiroyuki, *Britain and Japan, Biographical Portraits, Vol. V,* (Folkestone, Kent, 2005), 247-251. N.Y.K. in full, Nippon Yusen Kabushiki Kaisha, or Japan Mail Shipping Line.

44. Edward LeFevour, *Western Enterprise in Late Ch'ing China,* (Harvard, 1968), 73/4.

45. The three especially active and capable Manchu Emperors early in the Ch'ing era were the understanding and energetic K'ang Hsi who ruled from 1661 to 1722, then Yung Cheng from 1722 to 1735, followed by the remarkable, in particular initially, reign of Ch'ien Lung between 1735 and 1796. Ann Paludan, *Chronicle of the Chinese Emperors,* (London, 2005), 191-203. In respect of K'ang Hsi also see Jonathan D. Spence, *Emperor of China,* (London, 1974).

46. Iron screw steamer *Greyhound,* 372 grt. Built: 1880. Owned by F.H. Bell and registered in London. *Lloyd's Register.* Her Master who was murdered was a Captain Lyder. *Beacon* class twin screw gun vessel *Midge,* 4 guns, 603 tons, Commander Edwin Hotham. *Navy List.*

47. *Service Record.*

48. Ibid.

49. *The Encyclopaedia of Plymouth History.*

50. *Service Record.* Also *London Gazette,* August 5, 1890.

51. *North Devon Journal,* 2 January 1913. *Bideford Gazette,* 7 January 1913. The lifeboat station continues to remain active with their new 'Tamar' class boat, *Molly Hunt,* first arriving in the river on 22 March 2010.

52. *The Times,* Tuesday, December 31, 1912, 9.

53. *Bideford Gazette,* 7 January 1913.

54. Memorial No. CM046 – North Devon Record Office. Also a communication dated 23 December 2009 kindly sent to the author by the Parish Administrator, Ms. M. Bray. Visited by the author on Saturday, 19 June 2010: the attractive memorial is immediately apparent to the left inside the Chapel. Actually inside the Church, to one's right on entering, is another memorial, this one to Rear Admiral Bedford Clapperton Trevelyan **Pim**, born in Bideford on 12 June 1826. As a young Lieutenant, Pim was to serve under Henry Kellett (see C. in C., 1869) in the Arctic in *Resolute* during the expedition of 1852/1854. It was Pim who was given command of a small party who, on Wednesday, 6 April 1853, came up with Commander Robert John LeMesurier McClure (1807-1873) of *Investigator*, stranded in the ice since the early winter of 1850. The subsequent rescue of the ship's company in *Investigator* was to take place just in time as starvation had been imminent.

1 September 1885 to 17 December 1887
Vice Admiral Richard Vesey **Hamilton**

Born in Sandwich, Kent on 28 May 1829, younger son of Reverend John Vesey Hamilton, vicar of St. Mary's Church, Sandwich, by his wife, Frances Agnes Malone.

Aged eighty three he died at his home, 'The Elms', Chalfont St. Peter, Bucks. on Tuesday, 17 September 1912, and his funeral took place at Eltham, Kent on Monday, 23 September (1).

Educated at the Royal Naval School, Camberwell and he entered the Royal Navy in July 1843. Much early service in the Mediterranean in the paddle sloop *Virago*, 1,590 tons, Commander George Graham Otway, later Second Baronet, and then for a year in the brigatine *Bonetta,* 319 tons bm, Commander Thomas Saumarez Brock. The latter service included 'learning the theory and practice of marine surveying'. Subsequent service in the small frigate *Spartan*, 26, Captain Thomas M.C. Symonds. **Mate:** 1 August 1849. From that date until 2 March 1850 served in *Excellent* (2). From 2 March 1850 in 'Discovery Ship' *Assistance*, Captain Erasmus Ommaney, during the Arctic expedition of 1850/51 searching for Sir John Franklin. It was now, in the Arctic, that he began to make a considerable name for himself. In *Assistance* for example, he surveyed two islands to the north of Prince of Wales Island, these being Lowther and Young (3). Among the Lieutenants senior to him in the ship were Francis Leopold McClintock and George F. Mecham (4). **Lieutenant:** 11 October 1851. From 16 February 1852 served in *Resolute*, 2, Captain Henry Kellett (see C. in C., 1869), and with Commander Francis L. McClintock in *Intrepid*, this being the Belcher expedition of 1852-1854, again searching for Franklin. In this ship he continued to enhance his reputation by discovering the northern end of Melville Island, the Sabine peninsula, and two off-lying islets, Vesey Hamilton and Markham. These are to be found at approximately 110 deg. W 77 deg. N. During these journeys his sledge was named 'Hope', and his sledge flag was white with a rising sun (5).

Also throughout the severe Arctic winters when it was impossible to venture abroad he was actively involved in the provision of entertainment onboard:-

> 'During the three winters that he spent in the Arctic Hamilton acted as prompter and stage manager to the companies of the Royal Arctic Theatre (6).'

In the course of these and other Arctic duties he had achieved two most useful sledge journeys, one of 168 miles in sixteen days and another, mentioned above to the Sabine peninsula, of 663 miles in fifty four days (7).

Resolute was iced in in Melville Sound for the winter of 1853/54. Once the temperatures moderated he travelled over the ice to the expedition depot ship, *North Star* at Beechey Island. Thomas C. Pullen, Master of *North Star* recorded:-

> '19 March 1854: 4.30 p.m. Lieut. Hamilton with a dog sledge from *Resolute* arrives alongside from the *Resolute* and *Intrepid* lying S 34 deg. W from Cape Cockburn, 27 miles. Mr. Nares, Mate, is of this party (8).'

It was during this early spring of 1854 that the commander of the expedition, Captain Sir Edward Belcher in *Assistance*, ignoring opinions expressed by his officers, decided that his ships were trapped in the ice and ordered all four of them to be abandoned. In *Resolute* Captain Kellett so informed his officers and crew on Sunday, 30 April. On Monday, 8 May, Hamilton, with one man and five dogs, left with records for deposit at Dealy Island, and also with orders for western travelling parties from the ship. *Resolute* herself was abandoned on 15 May, a sad business. Subsequently Hamilton re-joined the ship's company at Beechey Island. All members of the expedition, embarked in *North Star, Talbot* and *Phoenix*, left for England on 27 August 1854 (9). On returning home he was to pay off on 17 October 1854 (10).

In passing it is worth noting that the Commander in *Pioneer*, tender to *Assistance* during this expedition, was another well known officer of the period, Sherard Osborn (1822-1875), later Rear Admiral. This unfortunate man had suffered much under the irascible Belcher.

From 16 January 1855, during the Crimean War against Russia, served in the screw steam sloop *Desperate*, 8 guns, 1,628 tons, Commander Richard Dunning White, Baltic Sea.

In addition to a number of engagements and skirmishes carried out earlier during 1855, the historian and author, William Clowes, mentions another two active little affairs with which the ship was involved, taken together all first rate experience:-

'In the Gulf of Riga, on July 23rd, Arensburg, in the island of Osel, was taken possession of by a landing party from *Archer*, 13, screw, Captain Edmund Heathcote, and *Desperate*, 8. (--) On August 6th, the *Archer* and *Desperate*, landing a detachment near Dome Ness, destroyed a sloop and government buildings, and repulsed a body of cavalry.'

He paid off out of *Desperate* on 4 March 1856 and immediately took up his next appointment.

From 5 March 1856 Lieut. and Commander in 60 h.p. gunboat *Haughty*, China where, amongst other duties, he was very active during the engagement at Fatshan Creek, 1 June 1857. That was to prove a spirited business:-

'Presently, to the disgust of the gallant commanders of those vessels, the gunboats, with the exception of *Haughty*, grounded; so now came our turn. The boats shoved off, and with a rattling cheer made a dash for the junks under a terrific fire of round shot, grape, canister, scrap iron, and bags of nails. Fortunately for us, the space to be traversed was only a few hundred yards, otherwise not a soul could have lived through it. As it was, every boat was struck in several places, and many a poor fellow lost the number of his mess in those few minutes. The water was ploughed up by the storm of shot, and the air whistled with the hail of grape and canister. However, before the Chinaman could reload we were alongside. Without waiting to drop the netting and spear us like eels in the meshes, they jumped overboard on one side as we clambered up on the other, and the first lot of eighty junks was ours. Meanwhile the Marines had done their work in gallant style, and captured the fort without any serious opposition (11).'

For services at Fatshan he received early promotion.

Commander: 10 August 1857.

On promotion he returned from the East, arriving in England on 6 December 1857.

From 4 June 1858 in command paddle wheel steam sloop *Hydra*, 6 guns, 1,096 tons, West Coast of Africa. Then in 1859 he took her across to the North America and West Indies Station. On the latter station, '... had opportunities of collecting much geographical information, both in the ascent of the Orinoco as far as Bolivar, and on the coast of Labrador (12).'

The civil war between the Union and the Confederate States of America took place between April 1861 and April 1865.

Captain: 27 January 1862. Remained in *Hydra* on the North America and West Indies Station until 15 July 1862 when she paid off at Woolwich.

On 18 December 1862 he married Julia Frances Delme Murray, born on 1 April 1839, a daughter of Vice Admiral James Arthur Murray (1790-1860) of the Atholl family, and Julia Delme, she being the Admiral's second wife. They were to have two sons and two daughters (13). Still relatively young, and by then Lady Hamilton, most unfortunately she was to die on 4 June 1897 and be buried at Eltham on 9 June.

From 16 July 1862 appointed in command paddle sloop *Vesuvius*, 6 guns, 970 tons, fitting out for the North America and West Indies Station. Much of the commission was spent in the region of the Newfoundland fisheries. Paid off at Portsmouth on 8 November 1864.

From 27 April 1865 in command paddle sloop *Sphinx*, 6 guns, 1,061 tons. North America and West Indies Station. Having at least one pressing matter which was of concern to him at the onset of his new command, the following month, at Plymouth, he addressed the following request to the C. in C., Admiral Sir Charles Fremantle, KCB. Sir Charles was an uncle of Edmund Robert Fremantle, see C. in C., 1892:-

> 'I have the honor to represent to you that a five oarded whaler would be a much more serviceable boat for a ship of this class (having so few boats) than a five oared gig which is properly allowed; and to request that you will be pleased to allow me to draw a whaler in lieu of the gig (14).'

In *Sphinx*, and in company with the paddle frigate *Terrible*, 21 guns, 1,850 tons, Captain Gerard J. Napier, an early duty was to escort Brunel's great creation, s.s. *Great Eastern*, Captain James Anderson, now converted to be a cable layer, across from Fiolhommerum Bay, Valentia Island, Ireland towards Trinity Bay, Newfoundland. The cable laying exercise commenced on 23 July 1865 but on 31 July, when only some 600 miles from Trinity Bay, unfortunately the cable broke (15). Subsequently, amongst other duties, much survey work was undertaken in the waters of this, the North America and West Indies Station. To assist he was assigned the services of Commander Peter A. Scott, borne in the Flagship *Duncan*, 81, Vice Admiral Sir James Hope, but 'additional for surveying service'. Earlier Admiral Hope (1808-1881) had been C. in C., China (see C. in C., 1862).

From May 1864 to October 1865 the Governor of Nova Scotia, wherein lies the important naval base of Halifax, was Richard Graves MacDonnell, subsequently to be Governor of Hong Kong (see C. in C., 1865).

On 21 May 1868 he was succeeded in command of the ship by Captain John E. Parish, thereafter returning home to arrive on 1 June 1868 (16).

Member of the Ordnance Select Committee: 10 June to 31 December 1868.

In 1869 he became a Fellow of the Royal Geographical Society and in due course on several occasions was to serve on their Council.

From 21 April 1870 to 25 April 1873 in command iron screw ship *Achilles*, 6,121 tons, 'Ship of the First Reserve', Coast Guard Service, Portland.

From 24 May 1873 to 14 March 1875 in command *Indus*, 3,653 tons, Flagship of Admiral Superintendent, Devonport, Rear Admiral Sir William King-Hall (17).

Meanwhile from 11 January 1875 granted a GSP valued at Sterling 150.00 p.a.

From 15 March 1875 Captain Superintendent, Pembroke Dockyard in *Nankin*, 28 guns, 2,540 tons. The ship, built as a fifty gun frigate and completed in 1855, had been the receiving ship at Pembroke since 1867.

CB: 29 May 1875.

Rear Admiral: 27 September 1877.

Continued in *Nankin* until 15 October 1877.

Through the Royal United Service Institution in 1878 he published, *Facts Connected with the Naval Operations during the Civil War in the United States*.

Director of Naval Ordnance: 5 June 1878 to 5 April 1880.

From 6 April 1880 to 16 April 1883 Senior Officer on the Coast of Ireland in *Revenge*, 28 guns, 5,260 tons, Flagship, Queenstown. In this position he succeeded his future predecessor in the Far East, Vice Admiral William

Dowell. *Revenge* was commanded by Captain Charles Mathew Buckle who held few illusions concerning the value of the ship to the fleet:-

> 'This was a harbour appointment pure and simple as the ship had ceased to be considered a sea going ship altho' the fiction was nominally kept up. She had become gradually unfit for anything but a harbour Guard Ship and it did not suit the Admiralty to replace her with a better ship, but they often talked of it. (-) Whenever she is removed it can only be to be broken up, or converted into a Training Ship. (-) The crew of *Revenge* was small, only 200 men, and their duties were very various both onshore at Haulbowline Dockyard as well as onboard (18).'

Vice Admiral: 17 February 1884.

To take up his appointment in the Far East he left England on 23 September 1885.

Following his arrival at Hong Kong at 9.40 p.m. on Wednesday, 4 November 1885 in the P. & O. s.s. *Ravenna*, 3,385 grt, that night at 11.45 p.m. his flag was hoisted first in the turret ironclad *Agamemnon*, 8,500 tons.

Audacious was in port however the exchange of command only took place on Tuesday, 10 November when Admiral Dowell left the ship at 3 p.m. and sailed for home in the P. & O. steamer *Hydaspes* at 4.30 p.m. that afternoon.

As suggested the Flagship continued to be *Audacious*, still commanded by Hugo L. Pearson, and, on assuming command in China, his flag was hoisted in her at 8 a.m. on Wednesday, 11 November 1885.

Immediately on taking up command his attention was drawn to a state of affairs of which evidence frequently occurred in the East during that era. From the British Consulate in Taiwan, an island nominally under the control of China, an example of, so to speak, carelessness in backing the wrong horse, is quoted. The writer is the highly regarded Consul William Donald Spence (19):-

> '... the foreign community and myself had to depend for protection during the continuance of the (French naval) blockade on Lui Taotai (senior administrative official) and the local executive. I am happy to say that no effort was spared by him, or his civil and military subordinates, to enable us to live in safety and even in comfort, and their efforts were completely successful. (-) Our gratitude to the Taotai was expressed in an address signed by every member of the foreign community at this city, at Amping, and at Takow, which I had the pleasure of presenting to him in May last, after the suspension of hostilities. Lui Taotai's subsequent fortunes have been of the bitterest kind. His patron, the late Governor General Tso Tsung-tang and he himself were unsparing critics of the Chinese defence in the North and they accused the Commander in Chief Lui Ming-chwang of incompetence and cowardice. On the restoration of peace Lui Ming-chwang brought brought an accusation against him of embezzling Tls. 60,000 of the public funds, stripped him of his rank, and took him to Tamsui for trial. The death of his patron completed his ruin. He has been found guilty of this grave charge and his property has been confiscated to the State, and his wives and family turned into the street. He is now in custody at Foochow awaiting trial on other charges and I should not be surprised if he were beheaded (20).'

As C. in C. any local difficulty of this nature certainly could result in anxious requests being made for gunboat protection so at all times it was necessary for him to be aware of such potential problem areas on the Station.

Writing to the Admiralty at the end of November he forwarded information received from *Cleopatra* at Yokohama where the German gunvessel *Nautilus* had arrived on 29 November, '... reports the annexation by Germany of the Marshall Islands (21).'

Just a few days later, on 8 December 1885 and having received word from the British Charge d'Affaires in Peking, Nicholas O'Conor, that affairs in Corea looked anything but peaceful, he advised the Admiralty that he had ordered *Cleopatra* to Chemulpo, 'to afford protection to Europeans should the necessity arise.'

In the interim HM Consul in Batavia reported that three Russian warships were there in port for minor repairs but were homeward bound. No doubt the C. in C. will have been happy to receive this additional confirmation of an easing of Tsarist pressure in the East, and on 22 November 1885 he had passed this piece of intelligence on to London.

In Japan during December 1885 Saigo Tsugumichi became Navy Minister (22). This position was in the first cabinet formed by Ito Hirobumi on 22 December 1885, he being the first prime minister in modern Japan. Early in September 1886 the new Navy Minister was to arrive in England where Captain Richard E. Tracey, as a Commander in 1867 then the head of the first official RN mission to Japan, was to escort the Japanese party during their stay in the country (23). One useful result was to be the appointment of Captain Ingles, RN (see below) to Japan as a consultant.

Writing from *Audacious* at Hong Kong on 17 April 1886 he issued standing order No. 7 covering the question of landing armed parties to assist, '… British Subjects actually in danger from violence which otherwise cannot be controlled.' As will be appreciated this was an action requiring careful and strict control since the British authorities always held the view, '…that landing an armed force in a foreign country is looked on as a serious matter (24).'

At the time this instruction was especially appropriate as a form of reminder of existing Admiralty regulations since Consuls at places as far apart as Chemulpo, Canton and Chinkiang from time to time did request the presence of gunboats to protect British interests, also to be on hand in case disturbances ashore required that 'Subjects' be evacuated.

On the other hand it is clear from other correspondence during the era that many Commanders in Chief felt that such Consular requests on occasion were difficult to justify.

As always in China during that period the line between a local protest gathering, and an out and out uncontrollable riot was a thin one.

The future Admiral Raymond Ames Spruance, USN, was born in Baltimore, MD on 3 July 1886. An extremely talented but self-effacing officer, especially as Fifth Fleet Commander he was to become a household name during the latter part of the Pacific War against Japan. When promoted Admiral in February 1944 he was the youngest naval officer, USN, to have attained that rank. Also that month, February 1944 at Majuro Lagoon, Marshall Islands, he was to shift his flag to the magnificent *New Jersey* BB-62, 45,000 tons (25).

Although the tense Russian situation in the East had eased, at Port Hamilton during July the C. in C. caused precautions to be taken. As has been seen above the necessary equipment first had been placed on the island in 1885 by his predecessor. The following extract is taken from his letter of 15 July 1886, written at Port Hamilton:-

> 'During our stay here the ships have been employed laying down a minefield for the defence of the
> main entrance to the harbour, and placing booms across the other two.'

The following month he was in Russia, on 27 August 1886 writing from Vladivostok. There at Possiette Bay on 19 August he met a General Baranoff, Governor General of Eastern Siberia, who, on the following day, returned his official visit and was saluted with nineteen guns (26).

In 1882 Vice Admiral Willes had reminded the Admiralty of the wretched inability of the ships under his command to cope with adverse weather conditions such as the monsoon. The following extract serves to stress this point. Lieut. and Commander Charles K. Hope, gunboat *Zephyr*, 4 guns, 438 tons, is writing from Singapore on 16 September 1886, reporting to his Senior Officer, Commander Edmund H.M. Davis, sloop *Daring*, 950 tons.

With the Assistant Colonial Secretary at Singapore, Mr. Arthur Philip Talbot, embarked, on 11 August 1886 in *Zephyr* Hope had left Singapore, coaled at Batavia between 14 and 16 August, and reached the Cocos Islands on 20 August 1886.

'On Tuesday, 24 August, the Proclamation transferring the Cocos Islands from the Government of Ceylon to that of the Straits Settlements was publicly read by Mr. Talbot, Assistant Colonial Secretary, and the deed transferring the fee-simple to Mr. George Ross was handed over to Mr. Charles Ross (George Ross being absent in England), and at the same time the colours were hoisted … '

That piece of business being completed, on 28 August *Zephyr* sailed for the Sunda Strait and Singapore but was swept by the current up the west coast of Sumatra. 'With Muara (Labuan) coal burning twice as rapidly as the Welsh', Hope decided to call at Benkoelen. Arrived at Benkoelen, 'having to sweep the bunkers out to enable the ship to reach the anchorage.' There the Dutch colonial officials were most helpful and obliging but no coal could be obtained so procured wood. On 4 September he sailed from Benkoelen but it was found that the wood burned so rapidly that during the afternoon of 5 September he anchored at Sampat Bay. 'Arranged with some Malays to cut wood, landed a working party, and on the 7th instant (September), having filled the bunkers and taken a considerable amount of wood on the upper deck, I left for Batavia, but was again obliged to anchor at 8.40 p.m. on 9 September about 17 miles from Batavia, the wood being all burnt. I arrived and anchored at Batavia at sunset on the following day, a light fair wind having enabled the ship to make this distance under sail.'

Fortunately at Batavia he was able to coal satisfactorily. He sailed on 13 September and eventually returned safely to Singapore at 11 p.m. on 16 September 1886 (27).

Back in Singapore it is with some amusement that one can imagine Mr. Talbot subsequently dining out with tales of his recent experiences at sea.

In Osaka, Japan on 25 September 1886 the future wartime C. in C., Second Fleet and Admiral, Kondo Nobutake, IJN, was born. As head of his class he was to graduate from Etajima in November 1907, and subsequently to specialise in gunnery. (Also see September 1941 under Layton, C. in C., July 1940).

Captain John Ingles, RN, the last of a line of British executive officer advisers to the IJN, arrived in Japan early in 1887. His leave of absence was granted for three years to enable him to act as a consultant to the Japanese Ministry of Marine. Subsequently, and at the request of the IJN, this period was to be extended for another three years to October 1893.

Clearly concern continued to exist regarding possible Russian intentions. The intentions of others too. Writing from *Audacious* at Hong Kong on 2 January 1887 he included this comment in his letter to the Admiralty, '… calling on me to report, in the event of war with Russia or France, the disposition of the Naval force at my command … (28).' His reply was comprehensive and, once again, it is seen that the weather exerted an important influence since the work was prepared under two main headings, N.E. Monsoon, and S.W. Monsoon (29).

Writing once more from *Audacious* at Hong Kong, on 12 April 1887 he gave the Admiralty some details concerning British flag vessels then engaged in the trans Pacific trade to and from the U.S.A., and continued:-

'… is at present carried on in powerful steamers averaging over 10 knots on the passage, and who, if chased could at least go 12 knots, (-) a speed very unlikely to be approached by a Russian cruiser who would be nearly 1,000 miles from Vladivostok (30).'

Other subjects covered included the usual matter of supplies of coal on the station, also he mentioned the adverse effect to the officers and men under his command when paid at a fixed rate of exchange whereas in fact on the station at a variety of ports the value of currency fluctuated greatly.

Then on 20 April 1887 he wrote to H.E. Sir Frederick A. Weld, Governor of the Straits Settlements, commenting on a paper, 'The Defences of Singapore', prepared by His Excellency in November 1880 and added to in February 1887, thus towards the end of his term in office (31).

Also to the Admiralty he gave some detail relating to the British flag merchant shipping trade between

Japan/China/Malaya and Australia which then was operated by three companies, Eastern and Australian S.S. Co., China Navigation (Butterfield and Swire), and the Gibb Line. For example on this service China Navigation used ships such as the sisters *Whampoa* and *Woosung*, each of 1,734 grt, and both built by Scott & Co., Greenock in 1882, together with the slightly smaller but newer, *Soochow*, 1,572 grt, built in 1885.

Meanwhile at Hillsboro, Wisconsin on 26 January 1887 the future Admiral Marc Andrew Mitscher, USN, had been born. In due course in many informed circles he was to be regarded as the 'preeminent carrier force commander' to emerge from the future Pacific conflict during WW2.

At Craigellachie, BC on 7 November 1885 the two ends, East to West, of the Canadian trans continental railway finally had united. A logical consequence was a trans Pacific steamship service to and from Vancouver. Initially this service was performed by three old Cunard Line steamers who had become available. The first to sail, from Hong Kong on 17 May 1887, and Yokohama on 31 May, was *Abyssinia*, 3,651 grt, Captain Alexander Marshall. She arrived at Vancouver on 14 June 1887 in this manner commencing the Canadian Pacific Railway steamship service which was to be of considerable importance in the Far East (32). In the Orient the agents for this new steamship line were Messrs. Adamson, Bell and Company, predecessors to an agency house to become widely known in the East, Dodwell & Co. Ltd. of London.

In June 1887 at Yokosuka dockyard, launching of the first steel warship constructed in Japan, the gunboat *Atago*, 612 tons.

KCB: 21 June 1887.
Admiral: 18 October 1887.
Following a visit to north China, during which he had called on 'Li Hung Chang, the Viceroy of Shantung and Pechili', from *Alacrity* at Shanghai on 2 November 1887 he wrote to the Admiralty, including the following illuminating and sometimes entertaining remarks:-

'He (the Viceroy) asked me if we could take any of his young men training for the Navy into our Ships on the Station. I told him it was a matter on which I could give no opinion, and that he must apply through the Foreign Office, when the matter would be settled between that office and he Admiralty. If the necessary consent was obtained I thought we might accommodate six on the Station. He stated he should telegraph to the Chinese Minister in London on the subject, and considerable desultory conversation on Navies occurred, and on his returning my visit some days after, he expressed his surprise at not having received a favourable reply, and it appeared to me that the idea he entertained was that, instead of receiving a favour, China was rather conferring one on us, by allowing her students to enter our service.'

'In point of fact, except as a matter of foreign policy, I am averse to our receiving Chinese into our Service, for many reasons; the principal one is, I think it more than probable for a good many years to come the Chinese will probably be the beaten party in any war, and if so, a considerable part of the discredit will attach itself to us. The Russians say "the Chinese are getting out fine ships for us to take".'

'At present, as I gather from various sources, there is really no Chinese Navy, but several local Navies. First and best is Li Hung Chang's – the Northern Navy. (--) A Board of Admiralty has recently been established, but it is, so far, only in name. (--) It is to be remembered that, in China, Naval and Military rank carries no social status. Admiral Ting, Lang's coadjutor last year, was originally a coolie, and on shore has no rank; every petty civil Mandarin looks down on a Naval or Military officer.'

'--- but it is certain that China will not have a Navy, however many ships she may have, for at least two generations (33).'

Meanwhile on 6 October 1887 the new Governor of Hong Kong, Sir George W. Des Voeux, had arrived in the steamer *Abyssinia*, just mentioned above, from Vancouver via Japan (34).

At Government House on Friday 6 January 1888 His Excellency received two visitors, his notes made on the occasion rather tending to confirm the sad state of the Chinese Navy of that era:-

> 'In the afternoon Admirals Ting and Lang of the Chinese Navy called, the former being the Commander in Chief of the Chinese fleet, and the latter an English naval captain, who acts as a kind of dry nurse to the other. Ting is a big, coarse Chinaman, with a manner more hearty, but less dignified, than that of the ordinary mandarin. This is probably to be accounted for by the fact that he is a soldier – a profession which the civilian potentates regard as distinctly inferior. He has risen to his present position of dignity, not because of any proficiency in naval matters (of which, I am told, he knows very little except what has been taught him by Captain Lang), but simply because of his exceptional bravery and his services on shore (35).'

In January 1888 the Chinese Imperial Customs Return for 1886 became available and from Hong Kong on 5 January the C. in C. sent a copy to the Admiralty. A few figures are taken from which it is seen how prominent was the British involvement. The total value of foreign and coastal trade amounted to GBP 116,158,159.00 of which the value carried in British bottoms totalled GBP 77,980,036.00 or some 67%. Chinese flag carried GBP 28,410,851.00 worth or rather over 24% however of the Chinese total only GBP 908,609, or under 1% of the total China trade, consisted of foreign traffic, the remainder being coastal. Of the remaining foreign carriers the Germans were the greatest with a total value of GBP 5,309,447, or 4.57% (36).

In the interim Captain Ingles, as mentioned above, on secondment to the IJN, had been touring extensively, and reporting regularly to his Navy Minister, Saigo Tsugumichi. Amongst other suggestions he recommended that during training less emphasis be placed on work with sails and more on subjects such as mathematics and physics and the handling of vessels under steam. Of interest, perhaps the more so in view of aspects of the Selborne Scheme still to come in the Royal Navy, in February 1888 he suggested to Minister Saigo that:-

> 'The new engineering skills, demanding a degree of specialization "almost to approach the medical profession", should be entrusted, he said, to a small elite corps of men educated solely with a view to this object (37).'

Captain Ingles was impressed by much that he found. Two examples follow.

Firstly: for Kure he had nothing but admiration; it had just been decided that a naval base should be built at this Inland Sea town. "I have not much to remark on this magnificent establishment. The site is all that can be desired; and it will no doubt become the great Naval Station of the Empire."

Secondly: he liked the "good order, discipline, and cleanliness at the training establishments", and was most favourably impressed with, "… the active and prompt manner in which the sailors go about their drills and their routine as I know so well that without these it is impossible to have an efficient Navy (38)."

Naturally he found room for improvement, perhaps more so at sea than in respect of the shore facilities, nevertheless it is clear that in the short time that had passed since the commencement of the Meiji era giant strides had been made, and, importantly, that a most positive will existed that such progress should continue.

Just prior to returning home, on 20 January 1888 Sir Richard wrote to the Admiralty submitting a report headed, 'Russian Eastern Siberian Ports' (39).

In order to hand over command of the station to his successor, Vice Admiral Salmon, in *Audacious* he arrived at Singapore at 6.57 p.m. on Friday, 17 February 1888. There he found in port H.M. Ships *Orion* and *Audacity*. Admiral Salmon came onboard the following morning to visit him but it was only on Tuesday, 21 February 1888 that the command was transferred. During that afternoon Admiral Hamilton proceeded onboard the P. & O. s.s. *Ballarat*, 4,890 grt, who sailed at 5 p.m. At sunset in *Audacious* Admiral Hamilton's flag was hauled down and that of Admiral Salmon broken (40).

The central battery ram *Orion*, 4,870 tons, mentioned above, originally had been built on the Thames for the Turks as *Buruc-i-Zaffer*, but had been purchased by the Admiralty in February 1878 during a Russian war scare (41). Following the Penjdeh Incident of March 1885 (see C. in C., 1884) she had shadowed a Russian warship to the East but on reaching Singapore had remained there as a guardship.

He arrived back in England on 31 March 1888 (42).

In October 1888 appointed as one member of a small Admiralty committee consisting of, besides himself, Sir William Dowell and Sir Frederick Richards, to report on the lessons taught by the naval manoeuvres of that year. (See Richards, C. in C., 1890-1892, 'Blockade Committee').

Next he was appointed a Lord of the Admiralty, being Second Naval Lord from 7 January 1889, and First Naval Lord from 24 October 1889 to 30 September 1891.

It was during his time as First Naval Lord that on 1 July 1890 the Anglo-German Agreement, or Heligoland-Zanzibar Treaty, was signed. (See also Fremantle, C. in C., 1892). Personally he was not to approve of all the terms of the Agreement however, before consulting him, the British Cabinet, the Prime Minister being Lord Salisbury (1830-1903), already had committed themselves (43).

President, Royal Naval College, Greenwich: 1 October 1891 to 30 September 1894.

Meanwhile officially, owing to his reaching the age of sixty five years, he had retired on 28 May 1894 (44).

From 25 March 1895 in receipt of a Good Service Pension (GSP) valued at GBP 300.00 p.a.

GCB: 25 May 1895.

From its first foundation he took a keen interest in the Naval Records Society. Also he was an active member of the Royal United Service Institution.

The author of a number of naval publications (45). These include, through the Naval Records Society in 1898, 1901 and 1903, the editing of three volumes, *The Letters and Papers of Admiral of the Fleet Sir Thos. Byam Martin, GCB, (1773-1854)*. Earlier, in 1896, he had completed his book, *Naval Administration*.

Although retired he was keen to remain involved and these interests rather naturally included a number of the activities of the Royal Geographical Society:-

> 'Sir Vesey took a deep interest in the progress of Antarctic discovery. Indeed he was the first to bring the subject forward, by a paper and discussion on the apocryphal voyages of Captain Morell. It was at the time when Captain Davis was proposing Sabrina island for observing the transit of Venus. The admiral served on the Executive and Ship Committees of the Society's Antarctic Expedition, when his advice and help were invaluable. He was extremely well read, and had plenty to occupy and interest him in his retirement… to the last he was eager to help any old shipmate whose needs were brought to his notice (46).'

On 23 September 1912 his funeral service at Eltham commenced at 12.30 o'clock. Among the many mourners there present was the representative of H.M. The King, Captain E.F.B. Charlton, RN, and Admiral Sir Cyprian Bridge, (see C. in C., 1901) who also represented The Naval Records Society. The Board of the Admiralty was represented by Rear Admiral Arthur William Waymouth, Director of Naval Equipment (47).

His executor was The Revd. Edmund Horace Fellowes (1870-1951), clergyman and a musical scholar of note. Also at Eltham on 23 September Revd. Edmund, at the time Minor Canon of St. George's Chapel at Windsor Castle, had conducted the Admiral's funeral service (48). On 12 January 1899 he had married one of Sir Richard's daughters, Lilian Louisa.

The Antarctic peak, Mount Hamilton, 1990 m, at 80.40S 158.17E is named for him (49).

NOTES

1. *Dictionary of National Biography*. Obituary, *The Times*, Thursday, September 19, 1912. *Who's Who.*

2. NA ADM 196/1. *Service Record.*

3. Obituary, *The Geographical Journal*, Vol. XL, 1912. 570-572.

4. Francis Leopold **McClintock**, FRS. Born: 8 July 1819. Died: 17 November 1907. Well known Arctic explorer, his name being closely associated with various Franklin search expeditions. Captain: 21 October 1854. Commodore at Jamaica: 1865-1868. Rear Admiral: 1 October 1871. Superintendent, Portsmouth Dockyard: 1872-1877. Vice Admiral: 5 August 1877. C. in C., North America and West Indies Station: 27 November 1879 – 1882, with his Flag in *Northampton*, Captain J.A. Fisher. Admiral: 7 July 1884. KCB: 30 May 1891. *Who's Who. Navy List.*

   George Frederic **Mecham**. Born in Cork, Ireland: 1828. Entered the RN: 1 September 1841. Mate: 19 November 1847. Lieutenant: 8 March 1849. Also sailed with Kellett in *Resolute* in the expedition of 1852. It was Mecham who found McClure's message at Winter Harbour which was to result, during the summer of 1853, in the timely rescue of the ship's company, HMS *Investigator*. As recorded above this rescue party was led by Lieut. Bedford C.T. Pim – see Kellett, C. in C., 1869, also Dowell, reference (54). Commander: 21 October 1854. From 1 November 1855 Mecham commanded *Salamander*, West Coast of Africa. On 3 February 1857 in command paddle wheel steam sloop *Vixen*, Pacific Station. Following an attack of bronchitis died at Honolulu, aged thirty: 17 February 1858. Buried at the Oahu Cemetery, Nuuanu Ave., Honolulu. *Navy List.* The writer paid respects at his grave on Oahu: Monday, 11 July 2005. *Dictionary of Canadian Biography Online.*

5. Obituary, *The Geographical Journal.*

6. Obituary, *The Times.*

7. *Dictionary of National Biography.* Also see Ann Savours, *The Search for the North West Passage,* (London, 1999), 256/7.

8. Scott Polar Research Institute, Cambridge. MS 274: *The Pullen Records,* 53.

   George Strong **Nares**. Born: 24 April 1831. Died: 15 January 1915. Explorer and navigator of note. Captain: 10 December 1869. FRS: 1875. KCB: 1876. Retired as Rear Admiral: 1 January 1887. Vice Admiral: 1892. Professional Officer of the Harbour Department, Board of Trade: March 1879 – 1896. Conservator of the Mersey: December 1896 – October 1910. *Navy List. Who's Who.* Obituary, *The Times,* January 16, 1915.

9. NA ADM 53/4553. Log Book *Resolute.* Also see Kellett, C. in C., 1869.

10. *Service Record.*

11. Vice Admiral Sir William R. Kennedy, *Hurrah For The Life of a Sailor,* (Edinburgh and London, 1900), 87.

12. Obituary, *The Geographical Journal.*

13. *Dictionary of National Biography.* Sadly their second daughter, Violet Julia Delme Hamilton, born on 25 April 1873, was to die on 7 February 1886, shortly before her thirteenth birthday. The author is grateful to Ms Margaret Taylor, Honorary Archivist, Eltham Parish Church, for her kind assistance with items of information.

14. Caird Library, National Maritime Museum, Greenwich. Ref: *VHM 1.* Vice Admiral Sir Charles Howe **Fremantle** (1800-1869). C. in C. Plymouth: October 1863 – November 1866. Ann Parry, *The Admirals Fremantle,* (London, 1971), 137/8. The port of Fremantle in Western Australia is named for Sir Charles. That colony was founded in June 1829, the first Lieutenant Governor being another naval officer, Captain James **Stirling**. As Rear Admiral Sir James, from January 1854 to February 1856 he was to be C. in C., East Indies and China. At Nagasaki on 14 October 1854 he reached a seven point agreement with the bakufu, 'Convention for Regulating the Admission of British Ships into the Ports of Japan', this being the first agreement between Great Britain and Japan since that signed very early during the Tokugawa Shogunate era, in 1613. NA FO 93/49/1. Also see Pamela Statham Drew, *James Stirling,* (University of Western Australia, 2003), 479.

15. Ibid. Letter dated at St. Johns, Newfoundland, 21 August 1865. *Navy List.* Fortunately on 27 July 1866 *Great Eastern* arrived safely at Trinity Bay with another cable and on the following day telegraphic contact was made with England. By 7 September the broken cable, lost the previous year, had been recovered. Once the necessary repairs were made the laying of this cable was completed successfully so giving two working trans Atlantic cables. By then *Sphinx* was engaged in duties elsewhere.

16. *Service Record.*

17. Rear Admiral Sir William **King-Hall**, KCB (1816-1886), who, as a Captain, from 3 March 1856 had commanded *Calcutta*, 84, flagship of Rear Admiral Sir Michael Seymour, C. in C., East Indies and China Station from 1856 to 1859. Sir William later served as C. in C., The Nore: 1877-1879, and was promoted Admiral in 1879. *Navy List.*

18. West Sussex Record Office. *Buckle Papers: MS 7.*

19. 'Spence, considered by (Minister) O'Conor one of the best men in the service...'. P.D. Coates, *China Consuls,* (OUP, 1988), 344. William Donald Spence (1848 – 25 June 1890). Following service in Taiwan then from 1 March 1886 on loan from the Foreign Office to Messrs. Jardine Matheson & Company.

20. NA ADM 1/6757. Written on 10 November 1885 and addressed to Captain Adams, RN, HMS *Espoir,* then at Takow, but for forwarding to the C. in C.

21. Ibid. Written in *Audacious* at Hong Kong, 30 November 1885. The German commercial headquarters in the central Pacific were to be on Jaluit Atoll. After the outbreak of WW1 then on 3 October 1914 to be occupied by units of the IJN (see Jerram, C. in C., 1913). Mark R. Peattie, *Nanyo,* (Hawaii, 1992), 42. Francis X. Hezel, *Strangers in Their Own Land,* (Hawaii, 2003), 45. Papal mediation fomalised this early transfer of authority from Spain.

22. **Saigo** Tsugumichi. For detail see Shadwell, C. in C., 1871, reference (46).

23. John Curtis Perry, *Great Britain and the Imperial Japanese Navy, 1858-1905,* (Harvard, 1961), 143.

24. NA ADM 125/30.

25. USS *New Jersey* BB-62. As a museum ship today it is possible to visit her at her berth at Camden, NJ in the Delaware River close to the position in which first she was commissioned on 23 May 1943. (Written in 2011).

26. NA ADM 1/6809.

27. NA ADM 1/6810.

28. Caird Library. Ref: *VHM/2.*

29. NA ADM 125/31. Letter No. 3.

30. Caird Library. Ref: *VHM/2.*

31. Ibid. Frederick Aloysius **Weld**. Born at Bridport: 9 May 1823. Died at Chideock: 20 July 1891. Stonyhurst. University of Fribourg. In 1843 emigrated to New Zealand and invested in a sheep station. Elected to the House of Representatives: 1853. Prime Minister of New Zealand: November 1864 – October 1865. Governor of Western Australia: September 1869 – January 1875, and of Tasmania: January 1875 – 1880. KCMG: 1880. Governor of the Straits Settlements: March 1880 – 1887. GCMG: 1885. *Encyclopaedia Britannica. Colonial Office List.* His Excellency was to leave Singapore on 17 October 1887 to proceed home to retirement in Chideock, Dorset. Today his grave may be found within the beautiful Church of Our Lady, Queen of Martyrs, & St. Ignatius, family built and consecrated in 1874. Through the kind offices of Mrs. Gaby Martelli visited by the author on 7 May 2016.

32. W. Kaye Lamb, *Empress to the Orient,* (Vancouver, 1991), 11/12.

33. NA ADM 1/6881.

34. s.s. *Abyssinia.* See reference (32) above. Built in 1870 for the Cunard Line service Liverpool/New York. In February 1887 placed on the new Canadian Pacific Railways trans Pacific service while their own new ships were being built. To make her final Pacific voyage in 1891, the year in which the first of the CPR *Empress* liners commenced their Pacific service.

35. Sir G. William Des Voeux, *My Colonial Service,* (London, 1903), 213.

36. NA ADM 125/33.

37. John Curtis Perry. 159.

38. Ibid. 159/160.

39. Caird Library. Ref: *VHM/2.*

40. NA ADM 53/12582. Log Book *Audacious.*

41. David Lyon and Rif Winfield, *The Sail and Steam Navy List,* (London, 2004), 252.

42. *Service Record.*

43. *Dictionary of National Biography.*

44. *Service Record.*

45. *Dictionary of National Biography.*

46. Obituary, *The Geographical Journal.*

47. *The Times,* Tuesday, September 24, 1912.

48. Information kindly given to the author on 6 May 2011 by Ms. Margaret Taylor, Honorary Archivist, Eltham Parish Church.

49. Australian Antarctic Data Centre: *SCAR Gazetteer Reference No. 5931.*

17 December 1887 to 29 November 1890
Vice Admiral Sir Nowell **Salmon**, VC

Born at Swarraton, Hampshire, son of Reverend Henry Salmon, Rector of the parish, on 20 February 1835. His mother, Emily, was the daughter of Vice Admiral William Nowell who had died at Iffley, Oxford on 19 April 1828, aged seventy three years.

He died, 'owing to an attack of bronchitis', at 44 Clarence Parade, Southsea on Wednesday, 14 February 1912, and is buried in St. Peter's Churchyard, Curdridge, Hampshire. In the church the South Sanctuary window, of St. James and St. John, was placed by his wife in his memory (1).

Marlborough College. Entered the Royal Navy on 10 May 1847. In 1851 saw early service as a **Midshipman** in frigate *Thetis*, Pacific Station, Captain Augustus L. Kuper (see C. in C., 1862) (2). **Mate**: 1 March 1854. From 18 March 1854 to 4 January 1856 in screw steam ship *James Watt*, 91 guns, Captain George Augustus Elliot, Baltic Sea (3). This was during the Crimean War. **Lieutenant**: 5 January 1856. From 6 March to 15 September 1856 standing by the new gunboat *Ant*, 100' loa, Devonport Dockyard (4). From 16 September 1856 in screw steam frigate *Shannon*, 51, Captain William Peel, East Indies and China Station (5). During the Indian Mutiny, which broke out at Meerut on Sunday, 10 May 1857, served with Peel's Brigade. His Victoria Cross was gazetted: 24 December 1858:-

> 'For conspicuous gallantry at Lucknow, on 16 November 1857, in climbing up a tree, touching the angle of the Shah Nujeeff (mosque), to reply to the fire of the enemy, for which most dangerous service the late Captain Sir William Peel, KCB, had called for volunteers (6).'

Also on this occasion, 16 November 1857 at Lucknow, another Victoria Cross was awarded to Leading Seaman John Harrison (1832-1865). Today his medal may be found at the National Maritime Museum, Greenwich, reference MED 2081.

While in the tree close to the wall of the mosque Lieut. Salmon was wounded in the thigh.

Today the Memorial to the Naval Brigade, HMS *Shannon* in 1857, may be seen on Clarence Parade, Southsea.

Commander: 22 March 1858. For services in India he received this early promotion.

Returned home from India on 4 November 1858 (7).

From 19 November 1859 to 27 January 1864 in command of the new screw steam sloop *Icarus*, 11 guns, 861 tons, commencing on the North America and West Indies Station. While in command of *Icarus* in 1860 he captured the filibuster Walker, subsequently receiving a gold medal from the Central American States (8).

Briefly, on arrival at Trujillo, Honduras on 20 August 1860 he, '... found Mr. W. Walker, filibuster, in possession of Trujillo'. Two days later, Wednesday, 22 August: 'Found that Mr. Walker and party had decamped'. Having ascertained Walker's whereabouts then during the afternoon of 3 September he despatched an armed party in boats up the Black River, the mouth of which is only a short distance down the coast, to obtain the surrender of Walker. Merely three hours later the boats returned with Walker and companions, some seventy three in number. *Icarus* then returned to Trujillo and on Wednesday, 5 September 1860:-

> '5 p.m. Landed Mr. Walker and party. Delivered ditto over to the Honduras Govt. (9).'

As a consequence of that satisfactory achievement, in December 1860 he was to receive official thanks from the Colonial Office, the Foreign Office and from Their Lordships, the latter, "expressing their gratification at his zealous and humane conduct" during that time when also members of his own ship's company were, "attacked with fever".

From the West Indies he brought *Icarus* home for service during 1861 with the Channel Squadron and then, from February 1862, in the Mediterranean.

Captain: 12 December 1863.

At Upwey in Dorset on 11 January 1866 he married Emily Augusta, daughter of Erasmus Saunders of Westbrook, Dorset, and born on 26 August 1846. They were to have two sons, John Nowell born about 1869, and Geoffrey Nowell born in Naples on 26 November 1871. Geoffrey subsequently was educated at Sherborne and in due course was to serve in the Rifle Brigade.

Their eldest child was their daughter, Eleanor Nowell, born in 1867.

Lady Salmon was to die on 14 February 1915, exactly three years to the day after her husband.

From 25 March 1869 in command iron screw ship, armour plated, *Defence*, 18 guns, 3,720 tons, Channel Squadron. Subsequently to North America and West Indies Station, then Mediterranean. Early in 1870 while in the West Indies he participated in an action against insurgents endeavouring to capture Port au Prince, Haiti, being slightly wounded during the engagement. Subsequently to be thanked by the Foreign Office for this success (10). She paid off at Devonport on 2 August 1872.

From 23 March 1874 attended a short torpedo course.

From 29 April 1874 to 31 March 1876 in iron screw ship *Valiant*, 18 guns, 6,713 tons, (Ship of First Reserve), Coast Guard Service, Foynes, River Shannon.

CB: 29 May 1875.

Appointed ADC to H.M. Queen Victoria: 12 December 1875.

From 28 November 1877 to 4 October 1878 in iron screw ship, armour plated, *Swiftsure*, 14 guns, 6,910 tons, Mediterranean. She had been designed for service in the Pacific and sailed well.

Early in 1877 Russia had declared war against Turkey and her forces advanced across the Danube in a southerly direction towards Adrianople (today: Edirne) in west Turkey. While the powers engaged in diplomatic procedure Great Britain took the precaution of positioning a fleet, under the command of Vice Admiral Geoffrey Thomas Phipps Hornby (1825-1895), in the Dardanelles and Sea of Marmora. *Swiftsure* lay off Gallipoli, 'to hearten the Turks there'. Fortunately by 3 March 1878 peace negotiations were entered into and conflict averted. In October 1878 the ship paid off at Devonport.

From 2 April 1879 attended 'Senior Torpedo Course'.

Rear Admiral: 2 August 1879.

Dating back to his time as a Midshipman in *Thetis* a delightful tale may be re-counted which relates to their boatswain at that time, a certain Mr. Tonge:-

> 'Years passed on, and Nowell Salmon had hoisted his flag at Plymouth as C. in C., Cape Station. Mr. Tonge, the boatswain, then long retired, went on board to visit his old shipmate, by whom, needless to say, he was generously entertained. Then they both came up on deck, where Admiral Salmon, attended by his flag-captain and staff, bade him good bye. But Mr. Tonge could not forget the little Midshipman, his protégé, in the Commander in Chief, and putting his hand on the Admiral's shoulder, he said, with all the well remembered severity:-
> 'Look you here my boy: you mind what I've been a-telling on ye, and ye'll do well in this here ship,' and thus saying, with a roll of his swivel eye, he departed (11).'

C. in C., Cape of Good Hope and West Coast of Africa Station: 10 January 1882 – 15 May 1885. On 11 April 1882 he succeeded Commodore Sir F.W. Richards (see C. in C., 1890). Flag in iron screw corvette, cased in wood, *Boadicea*, 16 guns, 4,140 tons.

Also serving in *Boadicea* from 4 October 1883 was Midshipman Robert Falcon Scott, in due course to be the well known Antarctic explorer. This young gentleman held his Admiral in considerable awe, '... a rather stern figure and a strict disciplinarian (12).'

Another Midshipman was Charles F. Sowerby. On 31 May 1916 at the Battle of Jutland, and as a Captain commanding the battlecruiser *Indefatigable,* 18,800 tons, to lose his life when she blew up, being destroyed by gunfire received from SMS *Von Der Tann,* Captain Hans Zenker.

A Sub Lieutenant appointed to the ship from 31 August 1883 was Alexander L. Duff, from 1919 to be C. in C., China.

At the time in Natal, and following the Zulu War campaign of 1879, the colonial authorities were endeavouring to keep the peace between various Zulu tribal factions. As Naval C. in C. early in 1883 he was able to assist, and subsequently:-

'Colonial Office, 6 Apr. '83: Governor of Natal expresses his thanks for readiness in undertaking all the arrangements for the conveyance of Cetewayo to Port Durnford (13).'

Later there was a short period of some excitement which took place in March 1885, the Penjdeh Incident between Russian and Afghan forces. For a while there was some danger of war between Great Britain and Russia:-

'Foreign stations were warned that hostilities were imminent, and Russian ships were being watched and shadowed by our own in all parts of the world (14).'

Also at this latter time the telegraphic cable to the Cape was interrupted. Anticipating problems, quite conceivably with Tsarist Russia, he called up the Reserves, also took up two Union Line mail steamers to be fitted out as auxiliary cruisers. These were *Mexican*, 4,661 grt, and *Moor*, 3,688 grt. The Union Line and their then rival steamship operator, the Castle Line, were to amalgamate only in 1900.

Subsequently Their Lordships were to express their approval of his prompt action in this matter.

At the completion of his period of service at the Cape, when in May 1885 he was succeeded by Rear Admiral Sir Walter James Hunt-Grubbe (1833-1922), he returned to England in *Boadicea*, arriving at Spithead on 3 July 1885. His flag was struck at sunset the following day.

Vice Admiral: 1 July 1885.

KCB: 21 June 1887, the occasion of H.M. Queen Victoria's Golden Jubilee.

Looking ahead, and knowing that in due course she was to become his future flagship in the East, from his diary may be noted an entry dated Thursday, 17 November 1887:-

'Went down to Portsmouth. Lunched with Willes and had a look at *Imperieuse* (15).'

In his diary there are frequent references to him out with various hunts so, as befits the era, obviously he was keen on the sport of riding to hounds.

From 17 December 1887 to 10 January 1888 a Member of a Royal Commission investigating the system of purchase of stores for H.M. Forces.

To take up his command in the East he travelled out with the P. & O. From his diary the details follow, included here so as to give an example of such a journey:-

'Thursday, 12 January 1888: Embarked in the P. & O. s.s. *Nepaul* in Albert Docks.

Fog prevented her starting. Landed and went with E to Poplar – put up with Nowells (16).

Friday, 13 January: Re-embarked at 9 o'clock – hauled out of dock and started down the river.

Weather muggy but smooth. Landed pilot off I. of W. (Isle of Wight) at 2 a.m.

Saturday, 14 January: 280' (miles run). Passed Ushant at 7 p.m.

Sunday, 15 January: 315'.

Monday, 16 January: 288'. Rounded Cape Finisterre about 4 a.m.

Tuesday, 17 January: Passed Cape St. Vincent. Rainy day.

Wednesday, 18 January: Arrived at Gibraltar at 0730. Saw friends. Sailed 1030.

Thursday, 19 January: 290'. Passed Algiers at 9 p.m.

Friday, 20 January: 301'

Saturday, 21 January: Arrived Malta 7.30 p.m. Went to Opera and Club with H.R.H. (17)

Sunday, 22 January: Left Malta at 4.30 a.m.

Monday, 23 January: 301'.

Tuesday, 24 January: 297'.

Wednesday, 25 January: Arrived Port Said at 9.30 a.m. Entered Canal at 11.

Thursday, 26 January: Night moored at Suez end of the Bitter Lakes.

Friday, 27 January: Suez at 10 a.m. Received mail and passengers from Brindisi and went on.

Saturday, 28 January: 268'.

Sunday, 29 January: 297'.

Monday: 30 January: 304'.

Tuesday, 31 January: 308'. Arrived Aden at midnight.

Wednesday, 1 February: Left Aden at 7 a.m.

Thursday, 2 February: 270'. Head wind and sea.

Friday, 3 February: 260'.

Saturday, 4 February: 262'.

Sunday, 5 February: 288'.

Monday, 6 February: 281'. Concert in evening went well.

Tuesday, 7 February: 259'. Passed Minikoi.

Wednesday, 8 February: 258'. Sighted Cape Comorin.

Thursday, 9 February: Arrived Colombo at 7 a.m. Received telegram to take over at Singapore. (A guest from the shore lunched with him.) Started at 3.30 p.m.

Friday, 10 February: 225'.

Saturday, 11 February: 293'.

Sunday, 12 February: 259'.

Monday, 13 February: 263'.

Tuesday, 14 February: Got into Penang early. Breakfast with Mr. (William Edward) Maxwell, Resident (18).

Wednesday, 15 February: Steaming through Straits of Malacca.

Thursday, 16 February: Arrived at Singapore at 8. Hoisted flag in *Alacrity*. Called upon Governor Sir Cecil Clementi Smith and took up quarters at Government House.

Friday, 17 February: Went onboard *Alacrity*. Sent *Mutine* to North Borneo. Played tennis in afternoon. *Audacious*, *Constance* and *Heroine* arrived with Flag (19).

Saturday, 18 February: Met Hamilton onboard *Audacious*.'

Although the date on which he had switched ships was not especially indicated in his diary, in fact he had arrived at Singapore in the P. & O. s.s. *Ganges*, 4,124 grt. It is most likely that the transfer of passengers bound for the Straits and Far East took place at Colombo after which *Nepaul* would have continued her passage up through the Bay of Bengal to Calcutta. Between October 1874 and April 1885 the south west breakwater had been built at Colombo which thereafter became a safe port, so replacing Galle. In fact however, the advantages being readily apparent, vessels of the P. & O. had commenced to use Colombo a few years before final completion of this new feature.

He assumed the China Command on 21 February 1888, also continuing with *Audacious* as his Flagship. That same day, after Admiral Hamilton had embarked in the mail steamer for home, he, '... landed and played tennis'.

On Wednesday 22 February he attended a official dinner at Government House held in honour of French visitors, the Prince and Princess Henri de Bourbon and their staff.

During these few days at Singapore several official calls were made and returned, in addition on Thursday, 1 March 1888 he, '... went in *Alacrity* to Johore and lunched with the Sultan.'

Finally, while still in the Straits, on 5 March he proceeded across to Sarawak, but H.H. The Rajah was absent, and therefore he continued his voyage eventually to arrive at Hong Kong. There at the time the Governor was H.E. Sir George William Des Voeux (1834-1909).

Between 17 and 20 April 1888 he paid a visit to Canton.

At Shanghai in *Alacrity* on Thursday, 17 May 1888 he had two most interesting guests to dinner. Together with Captain Henry H. Boys of the cruiser *Cordelia*, 2,380 tons, these were the 'Archibald Littles (20)'.

Meanwhile the new flagship, *Imperieuse*, Captain William H. May, had been making her way out from England via Simon's Bay, Mauritius, and Christmas Island to Singapore where she arrived at 5 p.m. on Sunday, 10 June 1888 (21). The reason for calling at Christmas Island was to expand the Empire by a very modest acreage. Captain May subsequently was to report that Admiralty and Foreign Office wishes had been complied with and that on 6 June 1888 :-

'I took possession of Christmas Island in the name of Her Majesty (22).'

Subsequently she proceeded to Yokohama where the change of flagship took place, at 8 a.m. on Saturday, 21 July 1888 the flag of Vice Admiral Sir Nowell Salmon, VC, KCB being hoisted in *Imperieuse*.

In the interim at Tokio on Tuesday, 10 July 1888 he 'interviewed Mikado', still at the time he being H.I.M. Emperor Mutsuhito, Meiji Tenno (1852-1912).

On 24 July *Audacious* sailed from Yokohama on passage home. It is an interesting reflection both on the centralised control exerted by the Admiralty, even in those days, and on the very slow cruising speeds of major warships in that era, that as early as 22 March 1888 the Admiralty had written to Admiral Salmon giving clear instructions as to how best *Audacious* should proceed home. Extracts follow:-

'Hong Kong to Singapore. 1450 miles. The S.W. Monsoon is at its strongest in July and August, but by keeping well over on the coast of Cochin China it would not be felt so much, and *Audacious* could make this passage at any time of the monsoon.

Singapore to Batavia. 550 miles.

Batavia to Seychelles. 3,150 miles. *Audacious* stows about 470 tons of coal in her bunkers, and with 100 tons in her lower battery, she would carry 570 tons. With her weather screw only working, she would burn about 15 tons a day, and this ought to give her an average run of 150 miles a day (6.25 knots), at least, across the Indian Ocean.

15) 570 (= 38 days consumption. She would probably only require 150) 3150 (= 21 days consumption, but even allowing the very low average of 100 miles a day (4.17 knots), she would then cover 3,800 miles.

Seychelles to Cape Guardafui. 1,020 miles. After leaving the Seychelles she would soon steam into a fair wind and favourable current (23).'

In the interim by means of an official letter dated 30 June 1888 and addressed to Commodore William H. Maxwell in Hong Kong, the Secretary of the Dock Yard Company, Mr. D. Gilley, advised, '... that the New Dock (at Kowloon) is ready from this date to receive any of H.M. Ironclads (24).'

On the Station the facilities for the docking and maintenance of H.M., and of other ships, steadily were improving.

On 1 August 1888 the Imperial Japanese Naval Academy moved into new buildings at Etajima near Kure. As seen above the first training school had been established on 22 October 1869 in Tsukiji, Tokyo, and opened on 11 February 1870, but the facilities there no longer were adequate.

Meanwhile, although much of the material used in their construction had been imported, the first four small gunboats to be built in Japan, with the use of iron and or steel being incorporated into their hulls, were completed between 1887 and 1889. Of 622 tons and a length of 154', they were *Maya*, *Chokai*, *Akagi* and *Atago*.

A start had been made (25). As will be seen, a later warship also named *Akagi,* 'Red Castle', was to become very well known following the outbreak of the Pacific War in 1941.

As already has been seen on numerous occasions, formal etiquette was very important in those far off days of Imperial splendour. Here is Governor Cecil Clementi Smith writing from Government House in Singapore on 21 August 1888 to the Senior Naval Officer, Straits of Malacca, Captain Henry J. Carr in *Orion,* '... on any occasion that the Rajah of Sarawak may visit this Colony he should receive a salute of 17 guns.'

As would be expected the passing of foreign shipping intelligence and information between the Commanders in Chief on the various Stations was a matter which received attention, the more so during times of tension between nations. Writing to Admiral Salmon from *Boadicea* at sea on 8 July 1889, a future C. in C., China, but then C. in C., East Indies, Rear Admiral Edmund R. Fremantle, gave details of how such information would be passed to the China Station from his Senior Officers at Aden and East Coast of Africa, and from the Navy Agent, Colombo. In turn Admiral Fremantle asked that such information, of use to him in the East Indies, be sent to Aden, if of an urgent nature then by telegraph (26).

In October 1889, being at Hankow, he proceeded further upstream in a civilian paddle river steamer, s.s. *Kiang Tung,* 566 grt, owned by China Merchants S.N. Co. Ltd. This journey from Hankow to Ichang and return occupied just a few days, 1 to 8 November 1889. From Ichang on 5 and 6 November he went away in a local craft, just a short distance above the first rapid, and then returned. The wind was such that they were able to sail when proceeding upstream but necessarily were forced to track over the rapid itself (27).

On 20 January 1890, the formation in Singapore of the Straits Steamship Company. The founder was Theodore Cornelis Bogaardt of W. Mansfield & Company together with Tan Jiak Kim of Kim Seng & Company and other prominent Chinese merchant friends. Initially their fleet consisted of five small ships.'

It is relevant to note that in the twenty years since the opening of the Suez Canal in 1869 Singapore's trade had just about tripled in value, from Straits $70.7 million to $207.6 million (28).

From *Imperieuse* at Hakodate on 22 July 1890 in a letter to his wife, who, amusingly, invariably was addressed as "Dearest Old Chappie', and who at the time was staying at the Club Hotel in Yokohama, he made reference to some tension with the U.S.A., 'I don't want to go to war at all, least of all with America (29).'

It seems likely that this dispute was to do with the Bering Sea fur seal controversy which in due course was to be resolved peacefully.

All during the summer of 1890 in much of his correspondence he made reference to outbreaks of cholera at a variety of places on the station.

In Tokyo on 29 November 1890 H.I.M. Emperor Meiji proclaimed the opening of the Diet, the first such occasion. The prime minister then was Yamagata Arimoto (1838-1922), of Choshu 'han' upbringing and later to be a Field Marshal, the father of Japanese militarism. Opposition to his policies was epitomized by Ito Hirobumi, also Choshu by birth, on 22 December 1885 to have been his country's first prime minister and the man who, perhaps more than any other, had arranged that a constitution be adopted and the Diet be proclaimed.

An age old problem on the coast of China, the following is another example of the piracy of a British coastal steamer by a relatively new method. Disguised as ordinary deck passengers a group of these desperadoes embarked at Hong Kong to take passage up the coast in the Douglas Lapraik & Co. s.s. *Namoa,* 1,375 grt. On 10 December 1890, just a few hours out of port, the ship was seized. Her Master, Captain Thomas Guy Pocock, was shot dead and the ship was forced to proceed the short distance to an inlet which was to become notorious, Bias Bay (30). There junks ready waiting took off the pirates and their loot, whereupon the ship was permitted to return to Hong Kong. Fortunately in this instance the local Chinese authorities were to take swift action and it appears that some thirty two pirates subsequently were caught, tried and beheaded. An account of such an exercise follows:-

'The Chinese mode of decapitation is simple and expeditious. A dozen or more of the condemned are taken to the execution ground, which at Canton is a small open space within the city. They are made to kneel down, their hands are then secured behind them, and the executioner goes along the line and arranges their heads and necks. I remember one poor wretch who shrunk up whenever the executioner approached, drawing his head into his shoulders, as if the very touch or nearness of the man was too much for him. The executioner tried to explain how much easier it would be for him to take his head off cleanly and neatly if he kept it well out, and thereupon gave it a good pull, and bared the unfortunate wretch's neck once more. Going to one end of the line he walks along, at each step with one blow severing a head from the body. The implement used is a sort of heavy half-sword half-butcher's cleaver, and is used with both hands (31).'

Over the years piracy on the China coast always was to occupy much time and to continue to require much attention from the various Commanders in Chief.

The fouling of ships' bottoms was, and remains, an important subject and the C. in C. looked into the possibility of using substances such as Japanese lacquer for this purpose. In that regard in May 1890 the Admiralty notified him that, '… as now applied the material in question would not fulfil the requirements of H.M. Ships'. By November 1890 the decision seems to have been reached that Rahtjen's Compositions were the approved product for this purpose. The C. in C. followed this up on 5 January 1891 with a clear instruction to Commodore, Hong Kong:-

'It is my direction that Sim's Anti-Fouling Compositions are not to be used, in future, for coating the bottoms of sea going ships (32).'

Imperieuse being due for docking at Hong Kong, in order to proceed to Singapore, there to be relieved by his successor, on Saturday, 17 January he hoisted his flag in *Alacrity*, Commander Charles Henry Adair, and sailed from Victoria Harbour at 2.15 that afternoon.

She arrived at Singapore on Friday, 23 January 1891, that afternoon saluting H.E. The Governor, who continued to be Sir Cecil Clementi Smith (1840-1916), with the customary seventeen guns.

In *Alacrity* at 8 a.m. on Tuesday, 27 January:-

'8 a.m.   Saluted the flag of Vice Admiral Sir Nowell Salmon with 15 guns.

Hoisted the flag of Vice Admiral Sir Frederick Richards, KCB (33).'

Admiral Richards assumed command the following day: 28 January 1891.

On 23 April 1891 Sir Nowell communicated with the Admiralty reporting his return to England.

Admiral: 10 September 1891.

For just a few days, from 27 December 1892 to 17 January 1893, he flew his flag in his old command, *Swiftsure*. This was on the occasion of the court martial of Vice Admiral Henry Fairfax, C. in C., Channel Squadron. When entering Ferrol harbour on 2 November 1892 the battleship *Howe*, 10,300 tons, had grounded on an uncharted rock. Her salvage proved to be a lengthy business but in due course she re-entered service, to be sold only in October 1910. Once the circumstances were ascertained Admiral Fairfax naturally was acquitted, and in due course, as an Admiral from 10 May 1897, from 10 June 1899 was to be C. in C., Devonport in succession to Sir Edmund Fremantle.

C. in C., Portsmouth: 22 June 1894 to 3 August 1897. However he only succeeded his predecessor, Admiral Hon. Earl of Clanwilliam, on 18 September 1894, also with his flag in *Victory*. In turn on 31 August 1897 he was to be succeeded by Admiral Sir Michael Culme-Seymour.

GCB: 22 June 1897.

In the Solent he commanded the Fleet during the occasion of H.M. Queen Victoria's Diamond Jubilee Review: 26 June 1897 (34). He flew his Flag in the new battleship *Renown*, 12,350 tons, Captain Arthur W.

Moore (see C. in C., 1905). Amongst the foreign men-of-war present was the new British built battleship HIJMS *Fuji*, 12,320 tons.

From August 1897 to January 1899: First and Principal Naval ADC to HM Queen Victoria.

Admiral of the Fleet: 13 January 1899.

On 15 December 1904 he was granted permission to travel in Algeria for six months, and on other occasions similarly authorised to proceed to the Continent during the winter of 1908/1909, and subsequently to visit India (35).

He retired from the active list on 20 February 1905, his seventieth birthday. However his pay of sixty seven shillings a day as an Admiral of the Fleet continued in full until his death some seven years later (36).

For many years he lived at Curdridge Grange, near Botley, Hants. On 10 January 1866 the land on which the Grange stands had been transferred to Erasmus Saunders, Nowell Salmon, and Emily Augusta Saunders, the lady who was to marry Nowell Salmon on the following day (37). He and Lady Salmon sold the Grange in 1911 and moved to Southsea where, as mentioned above, the Admiral died a year later (38).

His funeral service took place on Saturday, 17 February 1912 in the Dockyard Church at Portsmouth, his body afterwards being taken by rail, and accompanied by family mourners, to Curdridge for interment that afternoon at 3.30 p.m. At his funeral service H.M. The King was represented by Admiral Sir Lewis A. Beaumont. In addition to his widow and members of his family the mourners included the C. in C., Portsmouth, Admiral Sir. A Moore (see C. in C., 1905), Admiral Sir E. Fremantle (see C. in C., 1892), and Captain F.C.T. Tudor (see C. in C., 1917). 'The service was conducted by The Rev. A.W. Plant, Dockyard Chaplain. The roads from the church to the South Railway Jetty, where, after the service, the coffin was entrained for Botley Station, were lined by 1,600 bluejackets (39).' Then at Botley the gun carriage, on which rested his coffin, was drawn to Curdridge Church by a party of men from HMS *Excellent*.

On the north wall of the nave there is a memorial to him in St. Ann's Church, HM Dockyard, Portsmouth.

NOTES

1. Also as may be seen in the attractive parish booklet produced by the village historian, John Hogg, on page 36 is shown the precise location of his grave. Extract, *Hampshire Chronicle & General Advertiser for the South and West of England*, Saturday, 17 February 1912. Courtesy Mr D.H. Stokes, Botley and Curdridge Local History Society.

2. John Moresby, *Two Admirals*, (London, 1913), 93.

3. George Augustus **Elliot** (1813-1901). Entered the Navy in 1827. Captain: 3 June 1840 and commanded *James Watt*: January 1854 – May 1856. Rear Admiral: 24 February 1858. Vice Admiral: 12 September 1865. Admiral: 1 April 1870. C. in C., Portsmouth: 1 March 1875 – 1 March 1878. KCB: 1877. *Navy List*. His father, the second son of Gilbert, 1st Earl of Minto (1751-1814), was Admiral Sir George Elliot (1784-1863) who briefly served as C. in C., East Indies and China: July – November 1840.

    Also see Ryder, C. in C., 1874, reference (31), 'Committee on Designs for Ships of War'.

4. NA ADM 196/16. 155. *Service Record*.

5. William **Peel**. Born: 2 November 1824, third son of Sir Robert Peel (1788-1850). As a Midshipman entered the Navy on 7 April 1838. Commander: 27 June 1846. Captain: 10 January 1849. For courageous conduct during the Crimean War his Victoria Cross was Gazetted: 24 February 1857. Appointed in command of the screw steam frigate *Shannon*, 51 guns, 2,667 tons: 13 September 1856. Under the orders of James Bruce, Eighth Earl of Elgin (1811-1863) at the commencement of his first Special Mission to China, shortly after the outbreak of the Indian Mutiny he reached Calcutta in August 1857. A Naval Brigade was formed under the command of Captain Peel. Left the ship on 14 August 1857. Before Lucknow and Cawnpore conducted himself with great courage. KCB: 21 January 1858. In India died of smallpox: 27 April 1858. *Illustrated London News*, 12 June 1858. *Navy List*.

6. Sir O'Moore Creagh and E.M. Humphris, *The VC and DSO*, (London), 48.

7. *Service Record.*

8. William **Walker**. Born: Nashville, Tenn.: 8 May 1824. Executed at Trujillo, Honduras: 12 September 1860. Early adventures in lower California were overcome in 1854 by Mexican resistance. From 1855 involved in much unethical conduct, but military success, in Nicaragua where president from 12 July 1856 to 1 May 1857. Following other unsuccessful escapades in Central America, in 1860 landed in the Honduras where he was captured by the Royal Navy. Subsequently turned over to the Honduran authorities. *Encyclopaedia Britannica.*

   A more elaborate account of the affair may be seen in Clowes, Vol. VII, 152/155.

9. NA ADM 53/7888. Log book *Icarus.*

10. NA ADM 196/37. *Service Record.*

11. *Two Admirals*, 95/6.

12. Bulletin, *Simon's Town Historical Society,* (Simon's Town, July 2008), 17.

13. *Service Record.* In 1883 the Governor of Natal was Sir Henry Ernest Gascoyne Bulwer (1836-1914). Following their defeat at Isandlwana on 22 January 1879, the British eventually were to win the Zulu War of 1879 and depose the Zulu king, Cetewayo (ca. 1826-8 February 1884), who was exiled to London. He was permitted to return to Natal in 1883. Port Durnford is in Zululand, just south of the present day port of Richards Bay. There on 10 January 1883 he was met by Sir Theophilus Shepstone (1817-1893). It is likely that Cetewayo died by being poisoned by a rival.

14. Admiral Sir Edward E. Bradford, *Life of Admiral of the Fleet Sir Arthur Knyvet Wilson,* (London, 1923), 101.

15. Caird Library, National Maritime Museum, Greenwich. Ref: *SAL/1/25.* Willes is Admiral Sir George O. Willes, C. in C., Portsmouth from 28 November 1885, and, earlier, C. in C., China, 1881-1884.

16. Caird Library. Ref: *SAL/1/26.* E is his wife, Emily. s.s. *Nepaul*, 3,536 grt. Built in Glasgow in 1876 for the India service. Off Plymouth on the Shagstone Reef in foggy conditions to be wrecked at around 7 p.m. on 10 December 1890. Service speed of twelve knots.

17. Admiral His Royal Highness The Duke of Edinburgh. C. in C., Mediterranean from 5 March 1886. *Navy List.*

18. William Edward Maxwell. Born: 5 August 1846. Died at sea: 14 December 1897. Repton. Employed in Supreme Court, Penang and Singapore: 1865-1869. Various appointments as a magistrate in Malaya. Acting Resident Councillor of Penang: 1884-1889. British Resident Selangor: 1889. Called to the bar, Inner Temple: 1891. Colonial Secretary, Straits Settlements: 1892. Acting Governor of the Straits Settlements: 30 August 1893 – 1 February 1894. Governor of the Gold Coast: April 1895 – 6 December 1897. There he successfully oversaw the campaign and arrangements whereby in 1897 Ashanti became a British Protectorate. KCMG: 1896. *Colonial Office List*, 1896.

19. Sloop *Mutine*, 1,130 tons, Commander John H. Martin. *Audacious*, Captain John B. Warren, expected to pay off at Devonport on 10 January 1889. Cruiser *Constance*, 2,380 tons, Captain Leicester C. Keppel. Cruiser *Heroine*, 1,420 tons, Captain Charles J. Balfour. *Navy List.*

20. Captain Henry Boys, in command of *Cordelia* from 25 January 1887. *Navy List.*

    Archibald John **Little** (1838-1908) and his wife, Alicia Helen Neva Bewicke Little (1845-1926). Archibald first went out to China in 1859, in the tea business based at Kiukiang. In 1883 established his own business at Ichang. Married to Alicia in 1886. Between 15 February and 9 March 1898, in his especially constructed steam launch *Leechuen*, to be the first to navigate in a steamer up through the Yangtse Gorges from Ichang to Chungking. Jonathan Parkinson, *The First Steam Powered Ascent Through the Yangtse Gorges,* (Journal of the Royal Asiatic Society Hong Kong Branch, Vol. 46, 2006), 149-174. (See Seymour, C. in C., 1897).

21. NA ADM 53/14079. Log Book *Imperieuse.* William Henry May (1848-1930), from 20 March 1913 to be promoted Admiral of the Fleet. *Navy List.*

22. NA ADM 125/33. In turn his success was reported by the C. in C. to the Admiralty. Letter No. 234 dated 30 June 1888. The island was to become an important source of phosphate rock.

23. Ibid. Admiralty letter No. 113.

24. Ibid.

25. Fred T. Jane, *The Imperial Japanese Navy,* (London, 1904), 68. Hansgeorg Jentschura and others, *Warships of the Imperial Japanese Navy: 1869-1945,* (London, 1977), 115.

26. NA ADM 125/35.

27. Caird Library. Ref: *SAL/1/27.*

28. Eric Jennings, *Mansfields,* (Singapore, 1973), 21.

29. Caird Library. Ref: *SAL/2/18.*

30. Harry Miller, *Pirates of the Far East,* (London, 1970), 153. H.W. Dick and S.A. Kentwell, *Beancaker to Boxboat,* (Canberra, 1988), 136. In due course when on passage from Amoy to Foochow, on 3 October 1897 *Namoa*, Captain Thomas Philip Hall, was to strike an unmarked rock and become a total loss. Of the seventy seven passengers and crew in the ship eleven lives were to be lost by drowning.

31. Captain H.C. St. John, RN, *Notes and Sketches from the Wild Coasts of Nipon with Chapters on Cruising after Pirates in Chinese Waters,* (Edinburgh, 1880), 287.

32. NA ADM 125/37.

33. NA ADM 53/12349. Log Book *Alacrity.*

34. H.M. Queen Victoria had ascended to the throne on 20 June 1837.

35. *Service Record.*

36. Ibid.

37. Information kindly supplied in July 2008 by Mrs. Olga Furby, mother of the present owner.

38. Obituary, Lady Salmon: *Hampshire Chronicle & General Advertiser for the South and West of England*, 20 February 1915. Courtesy of Mr D.H. Stokes.

39. Ibid. 24 February 1912.

29 November 1890 to 16 February 1892
Vice Admiral Sir Frederick William **Richards**

Born at Ballyhally, Co. Wexford on 30 November 1833, the second son of Captain Edwin Richards, RN, and his wife Mary Anne, nee Kirwan (1).

He died at Horton Court, Chipping Sodbury, Gloucestershire on 28 September 1912.

Educated at the Naval School, New Cross, London and entered the Royal Navy on 6 February 1848 (2). Served for several years on the Australia Station and there promoted **Mate**: 8 January 1854, and from that date in sloop *Fantome*, 12 guns, also on the Australia Station. Traces of gold had been found in Australia earlier, but it was in 1851 that the gold rushes had commenced, a very lively era for the authorities to endeavour to control.

Lieutenant: 31 October 1855. From 29 June 1857 to 8 February 1860 in the two deck second rate *Ganges*, 84, Flagship, Pacific Station. The ship had been built of teak in Bombay, there being launched in 1821. At the time the C. in C. in the Pacific was Rear Admiral Robert Lambert Baynes (1796-1869). While serving in *Ganges* latterly he was Flag Lieut. to the C. in C.

Today just off Vancouver Island to the north of Victoria, BC, the village of Ganges on Saltspring Island, today a popular recreational boating centre, is named for the flagship of that commission.

Commander: 9 February 1860 and from that date appointed in command paddle wheel steam sloop *Vixen*, 6, Pacific Station. Her previous commanding officer, Commander Lionel Lambert, had been murdered and robbed at Lima on 8 February 1860, being buried ashore on 11 February. Temporarily in command of the ship was Lieutenant Lewis J. Moore (3).

To bring her home from Callao, the port of Lima, he sailed south, departing from Valparaiso on 10 January 1861, called at Punta Arenas on 1 February, then continued on through the eastern Straits of Magellan, leaving Punta Dungeness to port, to eventually reach the River Thames and pay off at Woolwich on 20 April 1861(4).

From 8 March 1862 – 5 January 1866 in command screw gunvessel *Dart*, 5, West Coast of Africa. One minute affair slightly enlivened the routine:-

'Early in 1865, while the *Dart*, 5, screw, Commander Frederick William Richards, lay at Akatoo, on the West Coast of Africa, a rumour arose to the effect that the natives were about to plunder the British factories (trading stores). One factory, indeed, had been actually looted, and a schooner had been stripped and set adrift.

Richards therefore landed some men from his gun vessel, and, also a small detachment from the *Lee*, 5, screw, Lieutenant Oliver Thomas Lang. Several boats were capsized in the surf, and two people drowned; and, in a subsequent collision with the natives, one seaman was wounded (5).'

Captain: 6 February 1866.

Now followed a period of four years on half pay, an entirely normal state of affairs in that era.

On 30 October 1866, in the Newton Abbot district of Devon, he married Lucy Lucinda, born on 20 March 1818, daughter of Fitzherbert Brooke of Horton Court, and his wife, Theresa Frances Acland, daughter of Sir Thomas Dyke Acland (1752-1794), ninth Baronet. Lucy was the widow of Rev. Edwin King Fayle whom she had married on 23 June 1845 but who had died in 1855. They had no children, indeed she had no children by either husband.

In her will she bequeathed Horton Court and all the Manor property to Frederick Richards.

The founder of the branch of the Brooke family known as 'Brooke of Horton' was Thomas Brooke, a lawyer, (1735-1813). The estate had come into his hands, seemingly in somewhat dubious circumstances, on the death of Mary Isabella Paston in 1794 (6). Horton Court itself was built over many years between the twelfth and eighteenth centuries but with most of the work being undertaken in Tudor times. In about 1884 Admiral Richards, as he then was, was to appoint an architect, F.W. Penrose, to take charge of various renovations.

From 6 February 1870 to 30 June 1873 in command iron screw Indian troop ship *Jumna*, 3 guns, 6,200 tons, Bombay and Portsmouth.

From 3 October 1873 to 11 May 1877 in command of the first sea going turret ship *Devastation*, 9,190 tons. She was twin screw and, for the first time in a ship of this class of early battleship, the provision of sails was entirely omitted. Following the loss of *Captain* in heavy weather on 7 September 1870, exhaustive tests were carried out to ensure the stability of the very low freeboard type of vessel in all states of sea. His able reports on these tests, 'completely satisfied the authorities and allayed public anxiety (7).' At the conclusion of these trials in 1874 he took her to the Mediterranean for the remainder of the commission.

FRGS: 1874.

From 1 January 1878 'Captain of the Steam Reserve' in *Pembroke* at Chatham. She was an old third rate launched in 1812, but in 1855 converted to screw steam power and subsequently serving for several years as a coast guard depot ship at Leith and Harwich. By 1878 she was doing duty as 'Barracks at Chatham (8).'

Commodore Second Class and C. in C., Cape of Good Hope and West Coast of Africa Station: 31 October 1878 – early in April 1882. Pennant in iron screw corvette, cased with wood, *Boadicea*, 16. Unfortunately on arrival at the Cape early in 1879 smallpox was found to have broken out in the ship and so he was not able to land men immediately.

Having crossed from Natal to invade Zululand on 11 January 1879, a British force, poorly led by Chelmsford, on 22 January was defeated at Isandlwana by Zulu forces cleverly led by Ntshingwayo.

However in Natal by 18 March 1879 the C. in C. was able to land a Naval Brigade consisting of ten officers and 218 men under Commander Francis Romilly. During the latter part of these Zulu Wars, especially on the occasion of the British victory at the Battle of Ginginhlovo, 2 April 1879, this party, 'had a conspicuous share as the Navy held the corners of the British square, and its guns rendered excellent service (9).'

Not only were men of the Naval Brigade employed in the fighting which took place but they rendered much other assistance to the Army. To take another example:-

'… in three weeks' time over 2,000 tons of commissariat and ordnance stores had been landed on the open beach, to the entire relief of the land transport (10).'

On 7 May 1879, 'Gazetted for services with Naval Brigade at Ginginhlovo (11).'

CB: 27 November 1879.

Sadly his wife Lucy died at Admiralty House, Simon's Town on 14 June 1880. She is interred in 'The Old Burying Ground at Seaforth' (12).

Surveyed the Zululand coast where the port of Richards Bay, today much used for the bulk export of coal, is named after him.

During the Boer War of 1881 he landed 120 men, a Naval Brigade under Commander Francis Romilly once again, who were engaged at Laing's Nek: January – February 1881. Sadly Romilly himself was mortally wounded at Majuba, fought on 27 February, and died on 2 March 1881.

For his services in South Africa on 24 May 1881 he was made KCB.

His successor in command of the Africa Station, Rear Admiral Nowell Salmon (see C. in C., 1887), was appointed on 10 January 1882 and he assumed the command on 11 April that year.

Rear Admiral: 9 June 1882.

From 25 July 1882 to May 1885 a Junior Lord Commissioner of the Admiralty.

Appointed C. in C., East Indies: 18 May 1885, and assumed command on 4 June 1885. Flag in iron screw corvette, cased with wood, *Bacchante*, 14 guns, 4,130 tons, Captain Arthur Moore (see C. in C., 1905). She had commissioned at Portsmouth on 14 April 1885.

On a voyage from Calcutta to London, on 8 November 1885 the P. & O. steamer *Indus*, 3,462 grt, was wrecked on a Muliavattu reef sixty miles to the north of Trincomalee. He was in a position to render prompt assistance and fortunately no lives were lost. Subsequently the official thanks of the P. & O. Steamship Company were to be received at the Admiralty.

The Burma Annexation or third Burmese war took place during 1885/6, Upper Burma being annexed on 1 January 1886. In *Bacchante* he arrived at Rangoon on 19 November 1885. With invaluable assistance provided by river craft of the Irrawaddy Flotilla Company, both soldiers and men of the Naval Brigade, Captain Robert Woodward, RN, moved upstream towards Mandalay. British forces reached that place at 0900 hours on 28 November 1885. The King surrendered on 29 November, and on the following day:-

> 'So Thebaw, last King of Burma, left his palace in Mandalay with Supayalat, his Queen, and was
> conducted onboard the Flotilla steamer *Thooreah* (Captain Patterson). They arrived in Rangoon
> on 10 December and were transferred to HMINS *Clive* to be taken into exile in India (13).'

For his services in Burma he was to be officially thanked by the government of India '... for admirable organisation and equipment of Naval Brigade, Burma 1885 (14).'

In April 1888 his successor arrived at Bombay:-

> 'Rear Admiral the Hon. E.R. Fremantle having arrived in the mail steamer *Assam* on the 14th inst.
> I am this day (20 April) transferring the command of the East Indies Station to him (15).'

From the East Indies he arrived back in England on 13 May 1888 in the P. & O. steamer *Ganges*, 4,168 grt (16).

Later in 1888 together with Admirals William Dowell and Vesey Hamilton (respectively Cs. in C., 1884, 1885), appointed to examine "the feasibility or otherwise of maintaining an effective blockade" – 'Blockade Committee'. The members of the Committee first met at the Admiralty on 16 October 1888. Their subsequent report:-

> '... was a masterly document which extended far beyond its terms of reference.
> Besides criticizing the performance of various classes of ships, it formulated the principles of
> British sea power and definitely affirmed the absolute necessity for establishing and maintaining a
> Two-Power Standard. It reported that the Fleet was "altogether inadequate to take the offensive in
> a war with only one Great Power," and that "supposing a combination of two Powers to be allied
> as her enemies, the balance of maritime strength would be against England." The gravity of this
> Report could not be ignored, although the Board attempted to mitigate its effect before publishing
> it as a White Paper (17).'

Soon after the publication of this report the government introduced the Naval Defence Act, 1889, which was to result in the construction of seventy ships to be completed by 1894 at a cost of some sterling pounds twenty one and a half million. These included the successful *Royal Sovereign* class of seven battleships, each 14,150 tons and with a main armament of four 13.5" guns.

To pay for this huge programme one prominent authority has written:-

> 'On the financial side Lord George Hamilton was exceedingly fortunate in having Mr. W.H. Smith
> as First Lord of the Treasury and Mr. Goschen as Chancellor of the Exchequer, both having held

office as First Lord and quite ready to provide the necessary funds to put the Fleet upon an effective footing (18).'

Following the naval manoeuvres of 1888 he was appointed a member of the committee to consider the results. Initially the members met at the Admiralty on 16 October 1888.

Vice Admiral: 25 October 1888.

Already from June 1888 he had been serving on the Hartington Commission on Naval and Military Administration, and this duty was to continue until November 1890. Nevertheless he found time to proceed overseas:-

'20 February 1890: granted 3 months foreign leave to go to Cape of Good Hope (19).'

On 29 November 1890 he was appointed C. in C., China Station and subsequently took passage to the Far East:-

'H.M.S. *Caroline* at Singapore. Tuesday, 27 January 1891.

08:00   Arrived P. & O. Mail *Bengal*. Vice Admiral Sir Fredk. Richards hoisted his flag onboard *Alacrity* (20).'

His new flagship, the twin screw first class armoured cruiser *Imperieuse*, 8,400 tons, Captain Edmund S. Poe who had joined her there on 6 January 1891, was about to enter drydock in Hong Kong. So it was on the following day, 28 January 1891 at Singapore at 08.00 hours, that the flag of Admiral Salmon was hauled down in the despatch vessel *Alacrity*, 1,700 tons, and Sir Frederick's flag as C. in C. was saluted with fifteen guns.

In her he proceeded on his initial cruise, sailing from Singapore on 12 February bound to the south to reach Batavia on 14 February. At the time the Governor General of the Dutch East Indies was Cornelis Pijnacker Hordijk (1847-1908). Compliments having been paid to the Dutch, on 23 February he sailed to return in a northerly direction around the west coast of Borneo and on Thursday 26 February reached Sarawak. There the following day His Highness Rajah Sir Charles Brooke visited the ship, on both his arrival onboard, and subsequently on his departure, receiving a salute of twenty one guns (21).

Alacrity next proceeded up the coast of Borneo with calls at Labuan on 4 March and the Muara Anchorage for Brunei on 6 March, then Kudat on 8 March and Sandakan, also in North Borneo, on 10 March, before steaming to Manila where she arrived, with appropriate salutes to the Spanish flag, on Tuesday, 17 March. From Manila on 24 March the new C. in C. arrived in Hong Kong harbour and secured to his buoy at 12.28 hours on Saturday, 28 March 1891.

During a cruise undertaken to the East the Tsarevich of the Russias, accompanied by his cousin Prince George of Greece, arrived at Hong Kong on 4 April 1891. While in the Colony he stayed in Government House as a guest of Sir George William Des Voeux. Also:-

'... and went on that perennially favourite occupation of visitors to Hong Kong, a shopping trip.

This was made incognito, the future Tsar heavily disguised in a billycock hat and tan shoes (22).'

In addition the Tsarevich and his party visited Canton from where he returned on 8 April, and two days afterwards sailed on up the coast of China. Ten days later and by then well up the Yangtse River, on 20 April at Hanyang (Wuhan) they were entertained at luncheon by the Viceroy, Chang Chih-tung.

Three weeks afterwards, during his official visit to Japan, at Otsu near Kyoto on 11 May 1891 an assassination attempt, fortunately unsuccessful, was made on him. From 1894 to 1917 Tsarevich Nicholas Alexandrovich was to be Tsar Nicholas II. Early in the twentieth century, as the war clouds gathered between Russia and Japan, it was thought by many observers that the Tsar's attitude towards Japan was to be coloured by this unhappy experience in May 1891.

By now with his flag in *Imperieuse*, and leaving Nagasaki early on Wednesday 8 July 1891, the C. in C. undertook a summer cruise around the Empire of Japan. Through the Shimonoseki Strait into the Inland Sea, first he called at Kobe from 10-13 July. Thence through the Kii Strait and around to Yokohama where he remained for a fortnight to 29 July before steaming up the east coast of Honshu to anchor at Hakodate in Hokkaido at 10.00 on Saturday, 1 August 1891. He crossed south into Mutsu Bay on 13 August to anchor off Awomori that afternoon. A day and a half later he steamed to Vladivostok where he anchored at 11.35 on Tuesday, 18 August. There he remained for four days, until 22 August 1891. A few days later he wrote to The Admiralty , his report including the following paragraph:-

> 'My reception by the Governor and the Admirals was quite cordial, but the regulations of the Port
> and Fortress are just now especially stringent (23).'

From that centre of Russian interests in the East he continued to Goshkevitch Bay, 23-27 August; Olga Bay in North Sakhalin, 29 August – 2 September; Barracouta Harbour in the Gulf of Tartary, 4 – 9 September; before returning to Hakodate on 14 September. While at sea during various passages then in the usual manner a great variety of exercises were carried out and practiced.

From Hakodate he cruised in *Alacrity* to visit small ports in the vicinity.

In due course in his flagship he visited Port Lazaref, Fusan (Pusan or Busan), Tsushima, and Port Hamilton on 28 October 1891. From this small island he proceeded across the Strait to anchor back at Nagasaki at 15.42 hours on Saturday, 31 October.

Again he embarked in *Alacrity* to cruise in Chinese waters. *Imperieuse* spent Christmas and New Year back in Hong Kong where he re-joined her on Tuesday 5 January 1892 (24).

Also during 1891, commencing at Wuhu in May where the French Jesuit establishment was attacked and burnt, and spreading further up the Yangtse in July and August, various outbreaks of anti-missionary and anti-foreign activity took place. This necessitated the positioning of a number of warships at Treaty ports in the River. H.M. Cruiser *Archer*, 1,770 tons, Commander John Ferris, gunvessel *Swift*, 756 tons, Commander Robert D.B. Bruce, cruiser *Caroline*, 1,420 tons, Captain William R. Clutterbuck, and gunboat *Peacock*, 755 tons, Lieut. and Commander Thomas F.W. Ingram, and others as necessary, were involved. Working in the common interest in an effort to minimise the effect of this tension much co-operation was received from both the French and German Navies. They positioned their river gunboats in conjunction with the movements of the British men-of-war (25).

In addition to the above mentioned visit, also during 1891 in his correspondence quite frequent references are made to the continued use of Port Hamilton. For example on 10 November that year he specifically included the following paragraph in his General Letter to the Admiralty:-

> '*Imperieuse* having completed her prize firing and other exercises at Port Hamilton I left in her
> with *Alacrity* on the 30th and arrived at Nagasaki on the following day (26).'

Early in 1892 he sent the protected cruiser *Pallas*, 2,575 tons, '... to report upon the state of affairs in Formosa'. Extracts follow which are taken from Captain Angus MacLeod's reply dated 17 February 1892. From this will be gathered something of the difficulties experienced in attending to matters in regions administered by the Manchu authorities, also an insight into the quality of some of their officials. By no means were the following failings unique:-

> '... I now have the honour to inform you of the results of my visits to Formosa and the Pescadores.
> Both Mr. Holland, acting Consul at Tamsui and Mr. Warren, Consul at Taiwan complain of their
> difficulties with the new Governor of Formosa in regard to their relations with him, and with his
> subordinates, in important everyday concerns.
> Several cases have occurred locally requiring settlement but no satisfaction can be obtained,
> either from the Governor at Taipei or from the Taotai at Taiwan. Consular representatives are
> habitually disregarded or ignored by those officials to such an extent that the Consuls have felt

bound to report to Peking, but, failing to obtain either directions or advice from thence, matters are practically at a dead-lock.

Whatever may be the cause, the effect is evidently prejudicial to our trade interests in Formosa and to the business of our countrymen who have taken advantage of treaty rights to reside in the island; I respectfully submit that a visit from an officer from the British Legation would be very opportune just now, if directed to investigate the reasons for this unsatisfactory condition of public service.

The Governor (Shao-yu-lien) has the reputation of being a good financier and he is dealing energetically with an accumulation of liabilities left by his predecessor (Liu-ming-chuan) who seems to have been open to everyone, and ready to take up their schemes and suggestions of improvements to such an extent that he handed over an empty treasure chest, although it is broadly hinted that he quite provided for his own private purse out of the numerous contracts made (27).'

Just as he will have been hoping for a peaceful end to his period of command in the East, on 10 April 1892, while at Hong Kong in *Imperieuse*, he received a telegram from Captain Robert William Craigie, Senior Officer, Straits of Malacca informing him of a rising at Pahang. Apparently two Englishmen, Messrs. Stewart and Harris of the Pahang Exploration Company, had been murdered, and the capital of Pakan was being invested. In response he ordered Captain Craigie in the cruiser *Hyacinth*, 1,420 tons, to proceed to Pahang, and also telegraphed the Governor, Cecil Clementi Smith (1840-1916), to request his opinion on the matter (28). Fortunately also available in those waters was the screw gunboat *Rattler*, 715 tons, Lieut. and Commander John G. Heugh.

Formally on 27 April 1892, once again writing from Hong Kong, he was able to inform the Admiralty that his successor had arrived on the Station:-

'Vice Admiral The Hon. Sir E.R. Fremantle arrived by packet on the 22nd inst. and after transferring the command of the China Station to him I propose leaving tomorrow in s.s. *Oceanic* for England via America (29).'

Actually he wrote his last China Letter on the day he handed over the command, 28 April (30). Naturally several remarks were included especially for the information of Admiral Fremantle. One enclosure, No. 4, was entitled 'Missionaries in China' and from this as Appendix IV is an 'Abstract of Mission Statistics in China Proper.' Since at all times, and has been seen above, xenophobia was likely to rear its head in China it is of interest to see the numbers of missionaries involved in that huge country during that era, and something of the success, or otherwise, that they enjoyed:-

'Catholics   530 Foreign Missionaries
                 525,000 Native Christians
Protestants   589 Men
                 391 Wives
                 316 Single Women
                 1,296 Foreign Missionaries
                 37,287 Native Christians.'

For Sir Edmund's guidance he included some remarks covering the anti Missionary activity in the Yangtse basin in 1891 which, 'made it necessary to position from 5 – 7 gunvessels to help keep the peace.' Then he continued in a more general manner:-

'While the state of affairs on the North China Division has called for much constant care and watchfulness during the past year the South China Division, as Their Lordships will have learned from the periodical reports furnished by Commodore Church in Hong Kong, and myself, has not been without its excitement, and it has been necessary all through to keep at least two vessels at the Commodore's disposal to meet the ever recurring demands for the presence of gunboats especially as coming from Canton and Foochow.

While the state of affairs on China Divisions is such as to demand so large a strain on the available force at the disposal of the C. in C., the requirements of the Straits of Malacca Division are also increasing (and here he concluded by mentioning the then current problem in Pahang, and the requirements by the hydrographer's department on the Borneo coast).'

Having returned to Britain then on 23 May 1892 he was appointed Second Lord Commissioner of the Admiralty, the intention being that in the latter part of 1893 he would become Senior Naval Lord. Serving with him as a Lord Commissioner was Rear Admiral John A. Fisher.

Admiral: 1 September 1893.

Senior or First Sea Lord from 1 November 1893 to August 1899. His appointment to this, the highest office, was made in succession to Admiral Sir Anthony Hiley Hoskins.

'This period was marked by a great development of the shipbuilding programme begun under the Naval Defence Act of 1889, and, at Richards's particular instigation, by a series of big naval works carried out under the Naval Works Acts of 1895 and subsequent years. The result was that the naval ports and dockyards at home and abroad were renovated and brought up to date to meet the requirements of the modern navy.

(--) In carrying out his naval programme Lord Spencer (Fifth Earl, First Lord) had to contend with a most formidable opposition from Sir William Harcourt (Chancellor of the Exchequer) and from Mr. Gladstone (Prime Minister) himself, and it was only the unwavering determination of Richards and his other colleagues on the board that enabled him to succeed – a success which had no little to do with Mr. Gladstone's final decision to retire from office (in March 1894) (31).'

In his inimitable style Lord Fisher writes of Sir Frederick during this time in office:-

'I was Controller of the Navy when Lord Spencer was First Lord of the Admiralty and Sir Frederick Richards was First Sea Lord. Mr. Gladstone, then Prime Minister, was at the end of his career. I have never read Morley's "Life of Gladstone", but I understand that the incident I am about to relate is stated to have been the cause of Mr. Gladstone resigning – and for the last time. I was the particular Superintending Lord at the Board of Admiralty, who, as Controller of the Navy, was specially responsible for the state and condition of the Navy; and it was my province, when new vessels were required, to replace those getting obsolete or worn out. Sir Frederick Richards and myself were on the very greatest terms of intimacy. He had a stubborn will, an unerring judgement, and an astounding disregard of all arguments. When anyone, seeking a compromise with him, offered him an alternative, he always took the alternative as well as the original proposal, and asked for both. Once bitten, twice shy; no one ever offered him an alternative a second time (32).'

GCB: 28 June 1895.

Also in 1895 the extremely able George Joachim Goschen (1831-1907) was appointed First Lord in Lord Salisbury's coalition cabinet of 1895-1902. This was Mr. Goschen's second period of service as First Lord. Previously he had held the post between 1871 and 1874.

'He (Goschen) and Richards worked together with remarkable unity of purpose during the next four years. The sending of the fleet to the Dardanelles in 1895 brought the Turkish government to a sense of its responsibility for the Armenian massacres; the commissioning of the flying squadron in 1896 indicated clearly to the German Emperor the dangerous consequence of his ill advised telegram to President Kruger; in 1897 and 1898 it was the action of the British fleet which at length restored order in Crete; the vigorous handing of the naval situation in the Fashoda crisis in 1898 was the chief preventive of war with France over that incident (also see Moore, C. in C., 1905); and, finally, the firm attitude of the government based on the readiness of the fleet stopped any interference by European powers in the Spanish-American war. There was thus a universal and well founded feeling in the naval service that its interests were safe in the hands of Richards (33)'.

On Thursday, 27 January 1898 the cruiser *St. George*, flagship of Rear Admiral Harry Holdsworth Rawson (1843-1910), returned from a commission on the Cape and West Africa Station and berthed at Portsmouth. Amongst other activities, in particular in February 1897, her Naval Brigade had landed and played a leading role in the destruction of Benin City in present day Nigeria, a punitive exercise. H.M. Queen Victoria wished to inspect a party of her officers and men who had carried out this operation so successfully and so on Wednesday, 2 February this group of thirty seven officers and some 300 seamen and Royal Marines, under the command of Commander Henry H. Torlesse, travelled across to Osborne House to be inspected. Among the senior Naval officers in attendance on The Queen on this rather special occasion was Sir Frederick himself, also Admiral Sir Michael Culme-Seymour, C. in C., Portsmouth (34).

Admiral of the Fleet: 29 November 1898.

This promotion was arranged by the future Viscount Goschen so that he could remain as First Sea Lord for a short while after reaching the normal retirement age of sixty five years. In the event:-
'Ceased to be 1ˢᵗ Naval Lord at his own desire: 20 August 1899 (35)'.

His successor was Vice Admiral Lord Walter Talbot Kerr (1839-1927), to be promoted Admiral in March 1900 and Admiral of the Fleet in June 1904. In turn, in October 1904 he was to be succeeded at First Sea Lord by Admiral Sir John Arbuthnot Fisher (1841-1920). As mentioned above Sir John knew Admiral Richards well as they had served together on many an occasion. Here follows a few more amusing tales recorded by the future Lord Fisher. The first relates to William Harcourt when serving as Chancellor of the Exchequer:-

'Sir William Harcourt always started the conversazione by insulting Lord Spencer (in quite a friendly way); then he would say to Sir Frederick Richards, "I always thought that one Englishman was equal to three Frenchmen, and according to this table of ships required, which has been presented to the Prime Minister, it takes three Englishmen to manage one Frenchman." Old Richards would grow livid with anger; he wanted to say, "It's a damned lie!" but he couldn't get the proper words out.'

'He had an ungovernable temper. I heard him once say to one of the principal officers in his ship: 'Here, don't you look sulky at me, I won't have it!'

'There was a famous one-legged cabman at Portsmouth whom Sir Frederick Richards hired at Portsmouth railway station by chance to drive him to the Dockyard. He didn't recognise the man, but he was an old ship-mate who had been with him when Sir Frederick Richards commanded a brig on the coast of Africa, suppressing the Slave Trade – he led them all a dog's life. The fare was a shilling and ample at that; and as old Richards got out at the Admiral's door he gave the cabman five shillings, but the cabby refused it and said to old Richards: "You drove me for nothing on the Coast of Africa, I will drive you for nothing now, " and he rattled off, leaving old Richards speechless with anger (36).'

The great value of his services to his country was to be summarised at the time of his death in 1912:-
'During the long period Sir Frederick Richards acted as the First Naval Adviser of the government remarkable progress was made in all branches of naval administration and equipment (37).'

Having reached the age of seventy years, on 30 November 1903 'Placed on Retired List (38).'

In retirement, and in addition to his residence at Horton Court, he maintained a flat in London, 34 Hurlingham Court, S.W. Earlier his London residence had been at 121 Victoria Street, SW.

In 1904, shortly after the election of Lord Goschen as Chancellor, he received the honorary degree of D.C.L. from the University of Oxford.

In addition:-

> 'After the successful struggle over the naval programme in the Cabinet of 1893-1894, the officers of the fleet had Richards's portrait painted by Sir Arthur Cope, R.A., and presented it "from the navy to the nation" (39).'

Following his death on 28 September, his funeral took place on Friday, 4 October 1912 and he was interred in the graveyard of the Parish Church at Horton, immediately adjacent to his house (40). In addition to the members of his family the mourners included Admiral Sir Hedworth Meux (see C. in C., 1908) who represented H.M. The King, Admiral of the Fleet Sir Edward Seymour (see C. in C., 1897), Admiral Sir Gerard Noel (see C. in C., 1904), Admiral Sir Arthur Moore (see C. in C., 1905) and several other naval officers. Among the many wreaths was one sent by Lord and Lady Goschen (41).

Amongst other bequests he left Horton Court to his nephew, Alan Stack.

A local weekly newspaper, *Dursley, Berkeley and Sharpness Gazette*, in their issue of Saturday, October 5, 1912, reminded their readers of the late Admiral's political interests:-

> 'The deceased Admiral was an ardent politician, and did good work for the Conservative cause.
> He had frequently travelled long distances to record his vote in the Thornbury Division (42).'

At the Royal United Service Institution in London on 13 November 1912 the 'Sir Frederick Richards Memorial Fund' was established by a large representative meeting of Admirals, friends and admirers, the Trustees of which make charitable grants to Naval and Marine officers and their dependants. In 1947, in an article by Admiral Sir Percy L.H. Noble (see C. in C., 1938), then the Chairman of this Fund, and headed 'A Great Naval Victorian and His Memorial', readers of the RUSI Journal were reminded of Sir Frederick's great contribution to the safety of the Empire and Nation (43).

A memorial tablet to him may be found in the crypt of St. Paul's Cathedral near the tomb of Lord Nelson on the wall of the alcove wherein are situated the graves of Earls Jellicoe and Beatty.

NOTES

1. Strangely his gravestone indicates that his date of birth was 29 November 1833 whereas all other sources state 30 November 1833. Churchyard of St. James the Elder, adjacent to Horton Court.
2. *Dictionary of National Biography.* Today (written in 2008) the Richard Hoggart Building, Goldsmiths' College, University of London.
3. Lewis James Moore. Promoted Commander: 6 August 1860. From August 1862 in command paddle wheel steam sloop *Argus*, 1,630 tons, and in her participated in the bombardment of Kagoshima: 15-17 August 1863 (see Kuper, C. in C., 1862). Captain: 9 January 1863. *Navy List.*
4. NA ADM 196/16. 182. *Service Record.* Also ADM 53/6708 and 6709, being log books *Vixen*.
5. Clowes, Vol. VII, 209.
6. Gilbert Edward Brooke, *Brooke of Horton in the Cotswolds,* (Singapore, 1918). The author is greatly indebted to Mrs Jill Martin of the Sodbury and District Historical Society for photographs and detail relating to Horton Hall, and information concerning Sir Frederick's wife Lucy. Correspondence during February, March and April 2009.
7. *Dictionary of National Biography.*
8. David Lyon & Rif Winfield, *The Sail and Steam Navy List,* (London, 2004), 46 and 197.
9. Clowes, Vol. VII, 307.
10. Ibid., 308. While not as hazardous an operation as landing through the surf on the coast of West Africa in the Bight of Benin, the open coast of Natal on the Indian Ocean still can be anything but calm and smooth.

11. NA ADM 196/37. *Service Record.*

12. Simon's Town Historical Society, *Chronicle,* No. 58, October 2005. Visited by the author on 15 October 2010. Enter from Queen's Road and Lucy's grave is on the left a short distance up the slope in the recently restored Garden of Remembrance section. Gravestone location information courtesy of Mrs. Cherry Dilley.

13. Clowes, Vol. VII, 379-383. Alister McCrae and Alan Prentice, *Irrawaddy Flotilla,* (Paisley, 1978), 111.

    The Viceroy of India then was Frederick Temple Hamilton-Temple-Blackwood, First Marquis of Dufferin and Ava (1826-1902). The Secretary of State for India was Lord Randolph Churchill (1849-1895).

14. *Service Record.* Gazette: 22 June 1886.

15. NA ADM 1/6917. Letter No. 200 to the Admiralty. P. & O. s.s. *Assam,* 3,038 grt, built in 1873.

16. *Service Record.*

17. Oscar Parkes, *British Battleships,* (Annapolis, 1990), 352.

18. Ibid., 350. Lord George Hamilton (1845-1927) was First Lord: briefly in 1885/6, and then from 9 August 1886 to 25 August 1892, this being Lord Salisbury's government. For Mr. W.H. Smith see Ryder, C. in C., 1874.

    George Joachim **Goschen**. Born in Stoke Newington: 10 August 1831. Died: 7 February 1907. Rugby. Oriel College, Oxford. First in Classics. Banker. On 22 September 1857 married Lucy, nee Dalley. Sadly she was to die on 21 February 1898. At age twenty seven appointed a Director of the Bank of England. MP, initially for City of London: 1863. Paymaster General: 1865-1866. Chancellor of the Duchy of Lancaster: 1866. First Lord of the Admiralty: 1871-1874. Chancellor of the Exchequer: January 1887-August 1892. Rector of the University of Edinburgh: 1890-1893. First Lord of the Admiralty: June 1895 – October 1900, being succeeded by the Earl of Selborne. Created Viscount Goschen of Hawkhurst: 1900. Chancellor of the University of Oxford: 1903-1907, being succeeded by George, Baron Curzon of Kedleston. *Who's Who.* A brilliant and most capable man. Within St. Augustine's Church, Flimwell, East Sussex on the North side adjacent to the pulpit, may be found a beautiful stained glass window placed there in his memory. His grave stone is to be found outside to the South of the church some seven grave positions down the slope from the East end of the building. There on 26 July 2016 the writer received much kind guidance and hospitality from Church Warden, Mrs Jaye Hughes and her husband Alan.

    His younger brother, Sir William Edward Goschen (1847-1924), Rugby and Corpus Christi, Oxford, was a diplomat and sportsman of distinction. British Ambassador to Berlin at the outbreak of the Great War.

19. *Service Record.*

20. NA ADM 53/12973. Log Book *Caroline.* P. & O. s.s. *Bengal,* 4,344 grt. Single screw. Construction completed in January 1886.

21. Rajah Sir Charles **Brooke** (1829-1917). In succession to his uncle, H.H. Rajah Sir James Brooke, Rajah from 1868 to 1917. As a young naval officer he had served under Captain Hon. Henry Keppel in both *Dido* and *Maeander* (see C. in C., 1867). NA ADM 1/7066.

22. Frank Welsh, *A History of Hong Kong,* (London, 1997), 299.

23. NA ADM 1/7066. Letter No. 300.

24. NA ADM 53/14082. Log Book *Imperieuse.*

25. NA ADM 1/7066.

26. Ibid. Letter No. 402.

27. NA ADM 1/7108. Captain MacLeod's full report was forwarded to the Admiralty as an attachment to Letter No. 99 dated 18 February 1892.

    Angus **MacLeod**. Born: 11 June 1847. Died in London: 29 April 1920. Captain: 30 June 1888. In command battleship *Empress of India*: December 1895. Rear Admiral: 11 August 1901. CVO: 1904. Vice Admiral: 4 December 1905. Director of Naval Ordnance: Senior Naval Officer, Coast of Ireland: 1904-1906. Admiral and Retired: 1910. *Navy List. Who's Who.*

    William **Holland**. Born: 27 May 1851. Appointed Student Interpreter in China: 16 July 1872. Various posts then acting Consul at Tamsui: 26 February 1890 to 18 May 1892. Subsequently Vice Consul at Shanghai: 1 December 1893. Consul at Ichang: 24 January 1895, and at Swatow: 5 April 1902. Retired: 22 September 1902. *Foreign Office List,* 1912. He died in Birmingham on 5 March 1924.

    Pelham Laird **Warren**. Born: 22 August 1845, son of Captain, later Admiral Richard Laird Warren and his wife

Eleanor. Died at Sidmouth: 21 November 1923. Appointed Student Interpreter in China: 2 February 1867. Various postings in China and Taiwan. Consul at Taiwan: 19 July 1886. Transferred to Hankow: 1 December 1893. Promoted Consul General at Hankow but instead transferred to Shanghai, acting there: 1 July 1899. Of this latter period, the Boxer troubles of 1899-1901, it was to be written of him, 'It was a very difficult time and he never lost his head'. KCMG: 26 June 1902. Retired: 20 January 1911. *Foreign Office List. Who's Who. The China Consuls*, 225.

28. Ibid. General Letter No. 224, dated 13 April 1892, para. 13. Also NA ADM 125/43.

Robert William **Craigie**. Born: 25 July 1849. Died: 21 August 1911. Entered RN: 1863. Captain: 30 June 1886. Rear Admiral: 10 August 1900. Superintendent, Chatham Dockyard: 1902-1905. Vice Admiral and retired: 24 February 1905. Admiral: 2 July 1908. The father of Robert Leslie Craigie, born on 6 December 1883, and from 1937 to 1941 to be HM Ambassador to Tokyo. *Navy List. Who's Who.* Also see Tudor, C. in C., 1917.

29. Ibid. General Letter No. 255, para. 8. His voyage home would be via Yokohama and San Francisco, where he disembarked, then he travelled up to and across Canada.

s.s. *Oceanic* was chartered from the British White Star Line by the Occidental and Oriental Steamship Company of California. She and her two sisters offered competition to the earlier established Pacific Mail Steamship Company. *Oceanic* first arrived in San Francisco at the end of June 1875. E. Mowbray Tate, *Transpacific Steam*, (Cranbury, NJ, 1986), 30. *Oceanic*, 3,808 grt, built in 1870, registered: Liverpool. *Lloyd's Register.*

30. NA ADM 1/7109. Letter No. 257.
31. *Dictionary of National Biography.*
32. Admiral of the Fleet Lord Fisher, *Records,* (London, 1919), 50.
33. *Dictionary of National Biography.*
34. NA ADM 53/15533, log book *St. George. Daily News,* Thursday, 3 February 1898.
35. *Service Record.*
36. *Records,* 51-52.

William George Granville Venables Vernon **Harcourt** (1827-1904). Trinity College, Cambridge. Lawyer, journalist and politician. Knighted: 1873. PC: 1880. Home Secretary: 1880-1885. Chancellor of the Exchequer in 1886 and again, 1892-1895. Leader of the Liberal Party and Opposition: 1896-1898. *Who's Who.*

37. Obituary, *The Times,* Monday, September 30, 1912.
38. *Service Record.*
39. *Dictionary of National Biography.*
40. Courtesy of Jill and Mike Martin, on 2 February 2010 the author visited the house below the Cotswold Edge. As might be imagined the building, parts of which date back to Norman times, is largely constructed of the characteristic Cotswold stone. It is a National Trust property, however then the house was neither furnished nor open to the public. Maintenance worked was being carried out. The house, rather wisely perhaps, is situated close behind the church which in this way provides much shelter from the westerly winds to which otherwise it would be rather exposed. Three fish ponds, a fish stew, lie behind the house and church which are positioned in a small valley within the Edge. It is some three miles from Chipping Sodbury. Sir Frederick's grave is within the adjoining churchyard immediately on the left of the drive as one approaches the house from the main gate.
41. *Bristol Times and Mirror,* Saturday, October 5, 1912.
42. Thornbury is in South Gloucestershire.
43. RUSI Journal, Vol. XC11, Feb.-Nov. 1947, 232/3.

16 February 1892 to 28 May 1895
Vice Admiral Sir Edmund Robert **Fremantle**

Born at Swanbourne, Buckinghamshire on 15 June 1836, fourth son of Thomas Francis Fremantle, first Baron Cottesloe (1798-1890), by his wife, Louisa Elizabeth whom he had married on 24 November 1824, she being the eldest daughter of Field Marshal Sir George Nugent.

Thomas Francis, first Baron, at various times held many high government positions including Secretary to the Treasury, Secretary at War, Chief Secretary for Ireland, and Chairman of the Board of Customs and Excise being associated with this Board from 1846 to December 1873.

Sir Edmund died in London on Sunday, 10 February 1929, and was buried at Swanbourne (1).

This estate had been purchased in 1798 by his grandfather, Vice Admiral Sir Thomas Francis Fremantle (1765-1819).

Sir Edmund's sister, Augusta Mary, who was to die on 1 June 1903, on 25 October 1853 married William Brodrick, in 1870 to succeed his father as the Eighth Viscount Midleton (1830-1907). A son, so a nephew of the Admiral, William St. John Fremantle Brodrick (1856-1942), in 1920 was to be created Earl of Midleton. Between 1900 and 1903 he was Secretary of State for War, and from 1903 to 1905, Secretary of State for India.

This somewhat elaborate preamble is included purely to illustrate how in that era powerful family connections might well be useful to any career, in the services or otherwise.

His grandfather, Sir Thomas Francis Fremantle mentioned above, had been a friend of Horatio Nelson, and he had two uncles who were then post Captains in the navy, so that as, '… my three elder brothers had preferred civil life, accordingly I thought it my duty to "follow the sea," especially as I had no great taste for classics though I liked mathematics (2).'

Early education at Cheam. In due course he received a nomination from the First Sea Lord, Sir James Whitley Deans Dundas, and entered the Royal Navy in 1849 in *Queen*, "a three decker of 116 guns, at Plymouth (3)". She flew the flag of Admiral Sir William Parker.

He served in her in the Mediterranean for three years, leaving her in 1852. Appointed to frigate *Spartan*, 26, Captain Sir William Hoste, Bart.: 8 June 1852. She participated in the Burmese war of 1852 following which he was to be a recipient of the India General Service Medal of 1854, with the Pegu clasp. **Mate**: 15 June 1855. Acting Lieutenant in *Spartan*, East Indies and China: 11 March 1856. Although in March 1854 Perry had signed his Treaty of Kanagawa with the bakufu these continued to be times when the presence of foreigners on their sacred land was viewed with considerable doubt by most Japanese. Later in life he was to describe briefly a short visit ashore which he made at Hakodate during this time when still he was a very junior officer:-

> '… while they had been allowed considerable freedom ashore at Hakodate, the Japanese looked upon us with some suspicion and we were generally escorted at a respectable distance by armed retainers with two swords (4).'

Lieutenant: 14 January 1857. The ship paid off at Devonport on 13 November 1857. From 20 July 1858 to 10

October 1860 Flag Lieutenant to his uncle, Rear Admiral Sir Charles H. Fremantle, C. in C., Channel Squadron in the screw steam ship *Royal Albert*, 121 guns. Then between 7 November 1860 and 12 August 1861 he served in the screw steam ship *Neptune*, 90, Mediterranean. From February 1861 she was commanded by Captain Geoffrey Thomas Phipps Hornby.

Commander: 9 July 1861.

While on half pay, in January 1862 he attended the Royal Naval College at Portsmouth to study for his steam certificate.

Appointed in command of the first class gunvessel/despatch boat *Eclipse*, 4 guns, a steam ship capable of a maximum of eleven knots: 16 February 1864. To join her in New Zealand was to be a lengthy journey. He started off overland to Marseilles from where, on Sunday, 28 February 1864, having just joined the 'Massilia Packet', she being the P. & O. steamer of 1,640 grt, he wrote to inform his mother: 'You will be glad to hear that I have got here and on board with all my luggage, myself and boxes not much the worse for wear (5)'.

The trans Mediterranean leg to Alexandria accomplished, and then overland to Suez, from the latter port he continued in P.& O. s.s. *Bengal*, 2,185 grt, to Galle, then on in the P.& O. s.s. *Madras*, 1,185 grt, to Sydney where he arrived on 17 April. To cross the Tasman Sea he travelled in the small London registered steamer *Otago*, 645 tons, and in her arrived at Auckland on 24 April 1864.

On 26 April 1864 at Onehunga, seven miles from Auckland, but today a suburb of the city, he relieved Richard C. Mayne who had not only been wounded earlier, but also promoted to Captain on 12 February 1864, thereby assuming command of *Eclipse* (6).

During this service on the Australia Station, for much of the commission he remained in New Zealand waters during the Maori Wars.

Concerning these wars in a letter dated at Sydney, 4 November 1865, he addressed the following remarks to his sister Augusta:-

> 'There has been a good deal of fighting going on which has been very successful and I hope it may finish the war. At last they seem to be carrying on the war in earnest pushing on with small bodies of troops or volunteers assisted by friendly natives instead of having an absurd regular campaign in the European fashion which the Maori only laughed at saying that it required 10 soldiers for one Maori. Now they find that man for man we are their superiors and that poor fellows they have no chance with their wretched arms and powder against our Enfield rifles (7).'

During his last year in New Zealand he saw a great deal of the Governor, Sir George Grey. In due course he was to modify his personal opinion of Sir George however it appeared that, in general, His Excellency did not enjoy an enviable reputation:-

> 'In a life time of official dealings Sir George Grey had acquired a reputation for deviousness which was not undeserved (8).'

Meanwhile he underwent a somewhat daunting experience which fortunately does not seem to have adversely affected his subsequent career.

> 'In consequence of *Eclipse* running onto a sunken rock about 2 miles to the northward of Wharariki, East Coast of New Zealand, on 13 July 1865, whereby she sustained considerable damage', then naturally he was court martialled. Happily there were extenuating circumstances:-

> 'And the Court doth adjudge the said Commander Edmund Robert Fremantle, in consideration of the urgent service upon which he was employed, only to be reprimanded and cautioned to be more careful for the future (9).'

The explanation in respect of the grounding affair follows:-

> 'On this last trip *Eclipse* touched on an uncharted rock. Fremantle was not even onboard at the

time. He had gone ashore to supervise the disembarking of the militia, and returning onboard was horrified to hear that the First Lieutenant had moved the ship nearer to the shore to pick up the boats and in doing so had struck (10).'

On the completion of the commission then to bring *Eclipse* home he sailed from Auckland on 4 October 1866, rounded the Horn, touched at the Falkland Islands and Rio de Janeiro, and reached Spithead on 25 January 1867, thereby completing a circumnavigation.

She paid off at Sheerness on 13 February 1867.

While on the Australia Station, in Sydney on 31 August 1866 he had married Barberina Rogers Isaacs, eldest daughter of Hon. Robert McIntosh Isaacs. She was known in his family as Cici. They were to have six sons, the fourth of whom died as a child (11). Their eldest son, Sydney Robert, born on 16 November 1867, in due course also was to become full Admiral, GCB, KCB. Their second son, Selwyn Howe, born on 11 August 1869, attended Eton and Magdalen College, Oxford, then in 1890 joined the Indian Civil Service. He was knighted in 1925.

Lady Fremantle was to die in 1923.

Captain: 15 April 1867.

During this period, while on half pay, he and his wife lived at Swanbourne where he became a County Magistrate, and also established a village Cooperative for the benefit of many in that small country community.

Professionally he arranged to return to the RNC, Portsmouth and there during 1871 and 1872 studied gunnery, mathematics and nautical astronomy. His success was formally recorded:-

'9 September 1871. Passed satisfactory voluntary exam. in Gunnery at RNC (12).'

Appointed to the Australia Station in paddle wheel steam sloop *Barracouta*, 6 guns: 10 March 1873. From Sheerness early in April she proceeded to Portsmouth, reached Vigo on 15 April, and arrived at Gibraltar on 26 April 1873. Here fate was to take a hand.

First, on 29 April she was able to save the Italian barque *Vittoria* who had been blown ashore on the east coast of the Rock. In this respect, being a successful salvage, subsequently the Admiralty were to receive an unsolicited offer of GBP 300 which in due course was to be distributed as salvage money amongst the officers and men in the ship (13).

Secondly, and to be of far greater consequence, the natives on the Gold Coast had become restless consequently in May he was ordered from Gibraltar to Lisbon. From there he transported a party of one hundred and ten Royal Marines, including Lt. Col. Francis W. Festing, to the Gold Coast (Ghana) as reinforcements for the garrison at the start of the second Ashanti war (14). To rendezvous at Lisbon this party of Royal Marines was brought out from England in the paddle frigate *Valorous*, 2,300 tons.

On the Coast the first fracas with which he was involved took place in the native town of Elmina. The tribal Fante territory, in which is situated the Cape Coast Castle, is to the east and adjacent to that of Elmina. At Elmina troops and Royal Marines were landed but, first, due warnings were given to the rebel Ashanti natives who were invading from the north:-

> 'Then at noon on June 13 (1873) a bombardment of their town began both from the boats and from the castle. In ten minutes Elmina was on fire in several places, and the natives, leaving it, took to the bush, whither they were pursued by (Lt. Col., R.M.) Festing, Fremantle, with most of the blue jackets, also landing to assist (15).'

In his subsequent report, dated 18 June 1873, Colonel Festing was to include the following relevant remarks:-

> 'From the moment we took the field, and any of his own men were landed, Captain Fremantle, RN, without any hesitation, most unreservedly placed them under my orders, at the same time coming himself and adding his valuable services; this step put matters on a good footing and allowed of no divided directions.'

'I beg leave to express my best thanks to Captain Fremantle and to his officers and men for the great assistance they have rendered in these engagements, and may I venture to add my admiration of the personal gallantry displayed by him when cheering on his men within pistol shot of the enemy (16).'

Naval vessels also were much occupied in blockading any likely landing places so as to prevent the Ashanti from receiving supplies of arms and powder. It will be appreciated that the heavy surf which runs along that stretch of coast was an added hazard.

Reinforcements came out from England and an advance was made inland towards Kumasi in Ashanti territory. The thinking behind this move was that by taking the conflict to the Ashanti then the hinterland in the vicinity of both Elmina and Cape Coast Castle would be rendered secure (17).

From August to November 1873 he was in command of the Naval Brigade. In *Barracouta* from Elmina on 2 August 1873 he wrote his sister Augusta. Extracts follow in which he describes something of the health hazards likely to be experienced on the Coast, and also indicates that the conduct of the civilian Administrator of the Gold Coast, Colonel Robert William Harley, CB did not meet with his entire approval:-

'Fancy our having landed 104 men in good health at Cape Coast Castle on 9th of June, and since then 2 have died and no less than 67 of the remaining 102 are sick. I cannot quite account for it all by climate, as we are fairly healthy onboard and there cannot be that enormous difference between living onboard and on shore. My belief is that the Marines on shore were not half looked after as our men are, and 'trade gin' or rum are wretched compounds only too plentiful and not conducive to health or longevity. I am very well and our sick list is only 9 today so we cannot complain much.'

'... but as for Colonel Harley CB he is simply the most incompetent Governor I ever had to deal with, always interfering in details which do not concern him and never minding his own business. (--) I can well believe that Midleton is busy with H of Lords and other work. Please tell him not to believe a word Lord Kimberley may say of Harley, who ought to be recalled at once as the most egotistical, pompous, officious, incompetent, impolitic and offensive Governor that ever stepped in shoe leather (18).'

Lord Kimberley is John Wodehouse (1826-1902), the First Earl, and at the time Colonial Secretary during this, the latter part of W.E. Gladstone's first term as prime minister.

Fortunately shortly thereafter Fremantle was to amend his opinion of the Colonel:-

'Colonel Harley went home in *Volta* on October 6th, and I saw him off. We had got on capitally of late, and we parted very good friends, though we had certainly had difficulties at times, and I could not think that he was equal to the situation (19).'

The gun running fraternity clearly hoped to benefit from this state of hostilities in West Africa but, as mentioned, a blockade had been instituted and Captain Fremantle's orders in this connection gave no room for misinterpretation. An example follows, being his directive of 8 October 1873 addressed to Lieut. Edward F. Day in the gunboat *Merlin*, 4 guns, 408 tons:-

'As you are well acquainted with the political aspect of affairs on the coast, it is unnecessary to give you more detailed instructions as to supporting King Blay and opposing those in arms against Her Majesty.

I am informed that several English vessels are at Assinee and Grand Bussam, and, at your earliest opportunity, you are directed to visit these places acquainting all vessels of the blockade and warning English ships, that, when discharging powder in these places they are supplying the Queen's enemies.

Should any flagrant case come under your notice, such as an English vessel discharging munitions of war at Assinee in defiance of your warning, you are directed to seize her and send her to Cape Coast (20).'

On 14 October 1873, during a Naval Brigade operation ashore, "on the Ashantees and Essamon", he was wounded severely, sustaining a gun shot in his upper right arm, and a month later was superceded as Senior Naval Officer by Commodore William Nathan Wrighte Hewett, VC (21). Subsequently he recuperated at St. Helena and Ascension, only returning to the Gold Coast on 9 January 1874.

On 17 January 1874, from *Barracouta* at Cape Coast, he wrote to his brother-in-law, Viscount Midleton. An extract follows:-

> 'My reign is over, and I am not allowed to go to the front which is a great disappointment to me. The Naval Brigade had started before I came here, and we have to do all the dirty work at Cape Coast; coaling and provisioning transports, carrying about coolies to do the transport work ashore and so on. It is the fortune of war I suppose and it is always one's duty to take these disappointments philosophically... (22).'

On this occasion the ship never did continue to Australia. At the end of the commission she anchored in Spithead on 6 May 1874. Subsequently he took her to Sheerness to refit, 'for Foreign Service'. There she paid off on 22 June 1874 (23).

CB for services in West Africa: 31 March 1874. Clearly his efforts on The Coast had been much appreciated.

Appointed to frigate *Doris*: 22 September 1874, 'Detached Squadron', South Atlantic. From Gibraltar on 15 July 1875 she proceeded to Bombay on the occasion of the Royal visit paid by HM The Prince of Wales to India in the Indian troopship *Serapis*, 6,211 tons, Captain Hon. Henry C. Glyn, CB. In due course the Royal party arrived at Bombay on 8 November 1875 and, following what was generally agreed to have been a most successful visit, sailed from Bombay on 13 March 1876, homeward bound.

From Indian waters *Doris* returned home via the Cape and in due course paid off at Devonport on 4 September 1876.

Between 4 September 1876 and 4 April 1877 he attended, '*Vernon* for torpedo course (24).'

From 8 May 1877 to 27 November 1879 in command screw ship, armour plated *Lord Warden*, 18 guns, 7,842 tons, (Ship of the First Reserve), Coast Guard Service, Queensferry (25).

For service in the Mediterranean, on 28 November 1879 at Plymouth he was appointed in command of the twin screw iron ship, armour plated *Invincible*, 6,010 tons. The ship was in poor order, her previous Captain having been dismissed by the C. in C., Admiral Sir Geoffrey T. Phipps Hornby. However, '... her new Captain soon had the ship in first-class order (26).'

Here follows an example of another side to his great character and abilities:-

> 'While in command of these ships he saved life on two occasions. When leaving Plymouth Sound in June 1877 he jumped overboard after a boy who had fallen from aloft, and in Alexandria harbour in February 1880, his ship being underway, he dived off the bridge and rescued with great difficulty, and nearly at the cost of his own life, a man who had fallen overboard. For the first of these acts he received the bronze medal of the Royal Humane Society, and for the second the Stanhope gold medal for 1880, the silver medal of the Royal Humane Society, and the gold medal of the Shipwrecked Fishermen and Mariners' Royal Benevolent Society (27).'

In 1880 he was awarded the gold medal of the Royal United Service Institution for a prize essay on 'Naval Tactics' (28). The full title of the paper was, *Naval Tactics on the open sea with existing types of Vessels and Weapons*.

In connection with his two recent awards, and other matters, from *Invincible* at Malta on 28 March 1880 he wrote to his sister Augusta:-

> 'Enough has been made of my successes I think. Of course I am much prouder of my Prize Essay than of the saving life – the latter was an impulse ... Admiral Sir B. (-eauchamp) Seymour has been very civil though he has not said much merely jerking out in his curious way, "Pon my soul! Pluckiest thing I ever heard of, it was really". We are to have a month here now I believe which suits me very well as I want to (set?) the ship to rights thoroughly and my new Commander (who from

25 February 1880 was William McC. F. Castle) is equally anxious to do all that is possible to make *Invincible* the smartest ship in the Mediterranean.'

From the same letter is seen family influence at work. Naturally Fremantle hoped to return to Australia but, alas for his plans and hopes, it was the Liberals under Gladstone who were returned in 1880. As follows, he had hoped otherwise. Mr. Smith is he who was First Lord of the Admiralty from 1877 to 1880, William Henry Smith (1825-1891):-

'I am pretty sanguine that the Conservatives will come in again and in that case I think Mr. Smith must give me a nomination for Sydney. Many thanks to both Midleton and yourself for your help with Mr. Smith (29).'

It is useful and of interest to consider one opinion he expressed in his prize winning paper of 1880. In this he made reference to the size of warships and expressed the view that, 'it cannot be too frequently repeated that the object of any real naval war must be maritime supremacy. (--) To do this we require large vessels which can cruise and keep the sea, and of such ships our war fleet must mainly consist (30).'

Needless to say there was another point of view such as had been expressed in his prize winning RUSI essay of 1876 by the future C. in C., China in 1904, but in 1876 still just a Commander. Here he is, Gerard Noel:-

'The cost of our present sea-going ironclads is so vast, that of necessity it greatly limits their number. By a reduction in their size and in the complications of their build, we should find ourselves possessed of a considerably larger number of really efficient ships for the same sum now expended on a few monsters (31).'

As is well known the view as expressed by the future Admiral Fremantle was to prevail and stand the test of time during the 'big gun' era.

From *Invincible* he was relieved at Gibraltar on 8 January 1881 and assumed command of that important base the next day. Up until 7 February 1884, when he arrived back in England, he served as Senior Officer, Gibraltar.

While holding that command, on 16 July 1882 he received two Royal visitors, T.R.H. Prince Albert Victor and Prince George of Wales who were on passage home at the end of their long cruise in *Bacchante*, 'in the evening landed at the dockyard and went up to call on Captain the Hon. E.R. Fremantle, senior naval officer.'

Between 1876 and 1883 the Governor of Gibraltar was General Lord Napier of Magdala who, in August 1860, had played an important part in the attack on the Taku forts at the time of the successful Allied advance and eventual capture of Peking.

Appointed in command turret ship *Dreadnought*, 10,886 tons: 23 August 1884 to 28 April 1885. On 14 October 1884 she commissioned out of Reserve at Portsmouth only then proceeding to the Mediterranean where she was to remain for the next ten years.

Rear Admiral: 7 April 1885. 'He was then, with the exception of the Duke of Edinburgh, the youngest officer on the flag list (32).' His age was just a few weeks short of forty nine years.

Through the Royal United Service Institution in 1886 he published another paper, the title of this work being *Naval Tactics*.

From 9 August 1886 to 18 August 1887 second in command, Channel Squadron: Flag in iron ship, armour plated, *Agincourt*, 10,690 tons. In her in a prominent position he participated at the head of a line of battleships at the Fleet Review held in Spithead on 23 July 1887 to celebrate H.M. Queen Victoria's Golden Jubilee.

In 1888 at the R.U.S.I. he delivered a lecture entitled, *Speed as a Factor in Naval Warfare*.

Appointed C. in C., East Indies: 25 February 1888. To take up this position he left England on 23 March in the P. & O. s.s. *Britannia*, 6,525 grt. At Aden he transferred to the P. & O. s.s. *Assam*, 3,038 grt, and arrived at

Bombay on 14 April 1888. Initially he flew his flag in *Bacchante* who was ordered home, then, from 23 July 1888, in the second class cruiser *Boadicea*, 4,140 tons, Captain The Hon. Assheton G. Curzon-Howe (33).

From 1 December 1888 to 30 September 1889 he directed a blockade of the Zanzibar littoral, on behalf of Great Britain, Germany, Italy and Portugal, principally to aid in the suppression of slavery on the coast. An additional benefit, to Germany, was the attempt thereby to restrict the landing of arms at some of the coastal towns and intended for those in revolt against German rule. This activity was inspired by Arab slave traders.

Between 1888 and 1891 the German Governor, or Reichskommissar, of their East African Protectorate was the soldier and explorer, Hermann von Wissman (1853-1905).

As may be seen from the following extracts this blockade was very active. The Admiral, in *Boadicea* off Mombasa, is writing to the Admiralty on 13 February 1889:-

> 'The work done by the Blockaders of the British squadron is best shewn by a return which I ordered to be kept of all vessels boarded, which shews that during the month of January no less than 637 vessels or dhows were boarded by our ships or boats (34).'

No slaves were found in January 1889 which it was felt was owing to the fact that in 1888 a number of slaves had been released and vessels confiscated. Secondly the time to run slaves to Arabia was during the south west monsoon season which blew from April to October. As the following examples taken from three of these months in 1889 indicate, the blockading squadrons were active during the period:-

> 'In April 1889:   1,232 vessels/dhows were boarded
> May 1889:   505 boarded
> June 1889:   497 boarded'

Between 30 December 1888 and 15 June 1889 Captain Albert George Sidney Hawes, RM (ret'd) was employed on special duty at Zanazibar as his predecessor, always a problem in those territories, had had to return to England for health reasons (35). Accidentally awarding him rapid promotion, in his memoirs the C. in C. mentions meeting him:-

> '... when I arrived at Zanzibar on the evening of April 27 (1889), as soon as I anchored, Colonel Hawes, formerly of our marines, our acting Consul-General, came onboard (36).'

KCB: 25 May 1889.

In a private letter dated in *Boadicea* at Zanzibar on 25 September 1889, and addressed to Admiral Sir Richard Vesey Hamilton (see C. in C, 1885), who from the following month was to be First Naval Lord, Sir Edmund commented on what he perceived to be a locally held opinion, and also on another anti slavery success. Extracts follow:-

> '... and that we English are decidedly popular while the Germans are the reverse. The latter have been rather a good foil to us in some ways.'
> '*Reindeer*'s boats made a capture of a slaver with 130 slaves at Pemba a few days ago. We must continue to watch that coast well at all events. Prices of slaves are very high there now. I have 2 ships and 12 boats there and that is none too many (37).'

Vice Admiral: 30 August 1890.

On 1 July 1890 the Anglo-German Agreement had been signed in Europe. This document generally clarified the issue of British zones of interest in East Africa in return for handing Heligoland over to Germany. Prior to this Agreement, one result of which was that Kenya came under the protection of Great Britain, German interests had been actively trading in that region. On 15 September 1890, and over the following few days, some nine Germans were killed at Vitu. It was only about the time of these incidents that news of the Agreement first reached East Africa and that the German and British authorities became conscious of the fact that now Vitu lay within British jurisdiction. Somewhat naturally it was perceived in Europe that action was necessary. Consequently in October 1890 the C. in C. personally led the Royal Naval Brigade in an attack ashore:-

'It fell to the lot of Vice Admiral Sir Edmund Robert Fremantle to conduct the expedition, and on October 18, 1890 orders to do so reached him from the Admiralty (38).'

Between 24 and 27 October he commanded a considerable British force ashore, the Naval Brigade being formed from parties supplied by HM Ships *Boadicea* herself, and also from *Turquoise, Conquest, Cossack, Brisk, Kingfisher, Redbreast, Pigeon* and *Humber*. After landing his force he advanced upon Vitu and destroyed the Sultan's dwelling and the village.

In due course it was to transpire that previously the Germans had acted in a provocative manner, especially a certain Herr Kuntzell, and that it was not impossible that in fact the Sultan had reacted reasonably towards those Germans then behaving badly in his territory (39).

Following this successful operation ashore, in November he reported to the Admiralty, including the following lines:-

'A fine tusk was found in the Palace of the late Sultan when the town was captured.' (Subsequently gratefully accepted by H.M. Queen Victoria).

During the same expedition a fowling piece was found, a gift from His Imperial Majesty the German Emperor to the Sultan. In due course the Emperor requested that this gun:-

'... should be handed over to Admiral Fremantle as a token of His Majesty's acknowledgement of the bravery displayed by the Admiral and his troops under his command during the recent expedition against Witu (40).'

His three year period of command was concluded at the end of April 1891 when he was relieved at Trincomalee. From Aden he returned home in the P. & O. s.s. *Mirzapore*, 3,891 grt. reaching England on 21 May 1891, and then going on half pay.

In the following manner in April 1891 had he reported his transfer of the East Indies Station to his successor:-

'On the morning of the 24th inst. Rear Admiral Frederick C.B. Robinson arrived at Trincomalee in the B.I. steamer *Manora*, and in accordance with my orders HMS *Marathon* hoisted the Rear Admiral's flag, the usual salutes being interchanged.

Having turned over all the records of the station to my successor, I left Trincomalee in HMS *Boadicea* on the morning of the 25th inst. arriving at Colombo on the following day. Having coaled and received a mail from England, I sailed from Colombo yesterday morning (27 April), and I expect to arrive at Aden on the 7 May when I propose to haul down my flag and to proceed to England in the P. & O. steamer *Mirzapore*, the *Boadicea* continuing her voyage to Malta, to pay off, in compliance with their Lordships' orders (41).'

Again at the R.U.S.I., in 1892 he delivered a lecture entitled, *The Training of our Seamen*.

A little later in the year, having been appointed to China, he took passage East and arrived at Hong Kong in the P. & O. steamer *Surat*, 2,578 grt, at 10.30 on Friday, 22 April 1892.

As was recorded in *Imperieuse*:-

'12:25   Vice Admiral Sir Edmund Fremantle hoisted his flag in *Alacrity* and saluted C. in C. with 15 guns. *Imperieuse* returned the salute with 13 guns.

14:00   Vice Admiral Fremantle visited the ship.

Saturday, 23 April 1892. At Hong Kong.

11:00   Vice Admiral Fremantle visited the Governor (Sir William Robinson, KCMG). Shore battery saluted him on leaving with 13 guns.

Thursday, 28 April 1892. At Hong Kong.

a.m.   Discharged Captain Poe, Mr Carlisle and Lt. Nicholson to mail steamer. 13:30 Vice

Admiral Sir F. Richards hauled down his flag on leaving the station.
Joined Captain J.M. McQuhae

Friday, 29 April 1892. At Hong Kong.
08:00   Broke flag of Admiral Sir Edmund Fremantle. Salutes etc. (42).'

As is clear from the above at Hong Kong on 28 April 1892 he relieved Admiral Richards and on the following day his flag was broken in the twin screw first class armoured cruiser *Imperieuse*, 8,400 tons, Captain John M. McQuhae.

In his general letter of 9 May 1892 he confirmed to the Admiralty that Admiral Richards indeed had sailed in *Oceanic*, 'at 1.30 p.m. on 28th inst.'.

Also he was able to give Their Lordships an indication of the current situation on the east coast of the Malay peninsula where, 'the state of affairs at Pahang remained unsettled but no outbreak was anticipated (43).'

In the despatch vessel *Alacrity*, 1,700 tons, he sailed from Hong Kong on 9 May and steamed up the coast of China while on passage visiting Swatow, Amoy, the Pagoda Anchorage below Foochow, and Ningpo, to arrive at Shanghai on 20 May 1892. Then writing from *Alacrity* at Wuhu on 30 May he gave the Admiralty encouraging news concerning Malaya:-

'The Governor of the Straits Settlements (Cecil Clementi Smith) appears satisfied that matters will be settled in Pahang as the Sultan has taken the field and is acting vigorously against his disaffected subjects... (44).'

Later in 1892, writing from *Imperieuse* at Hakodate on 4 August, this call being made during a Vladivostok cruise, he was in the fortunate position of being able to inform the Admiralty that during the spring and summer of that year, 'there have been no disturbances recently.' In September, likewise, he wrote that in Pahang the Sultan had driven the rebels out of his territory.

Following more first hand experience of calling at a variety of Chinese ports, in his letter dated 4 November 1892 he made the following comment:-

'I have to express my appreciation of the courtesy invariably shown me by the Chinese Viceroys and Officials with whom I have come in contact, and I have been especially anxious to pay complimentary visits to all high Chinese authorities in view of the importance attached by all Orientals to ceremonious observances.'

About this time he received a charming and chatty letter from Harry Keppel, no less than he who had been C. in C. on the China Station between March 1867 and October 1869, so a quarter of a century previously, and who now was Admiral of the Fleet Hon. Sir Henry Keppel, GCB. Sir Henry, in his own hand, asked Sir Edmund to look out for a youngster in whom he was interested, then added, somewhat feelingly as always he had loved the East:-

'The happiest Command I ever had was that you are now enjoying ... (45).'

Also on 4 November, writing from *Alacrity* at Shanghai just before setting off up the Yangtse once more, he described a recent visit which he had made to Seoul and Tientsin. To visit the former he had arrived at Chemulpo (Inchon) on 3 October 1892. Then, together with a staff of four in his steamboat, he ascended the sixty miles from Chemulpo to Mapu up the 'shallow and tortuous river', thence, '... 3 miles of bad road from Mapu to Seoul, so that it was 7.30 p.m. before we reached the town gates which were closed and the only resource was to climb the 30 foot wall by means of a rope'.

Subsequently he was well received by both the King and President of the Foreign Office. From the former he obtained permission to visit Port Hamilton whenever he so desired (46).

The sight of the C. in C. scaling the city wall must have been memorable.

At Tientsin on 14 October he was received by Viceroy Li Hung-chang, '... a fine man, 6'4" in height, and was extremely courteous.' Further:-

'He is certainly a very intelligent, well informed man, and he asked me an infinity of questions the interview lasting quite half an hour. He was anxious to show his own shrewdness and some of his questions were not easy to answer. He was especially anxious about my visit to Vladivostok and what the Russians, who he was evidently afraid of, were doing there, also about my visit to Corea of which he had certainly heard a good deal from other sources, and he expressed very friendly sentiments towards Great Britain hoping that our maritime strength would be maintained.'

From *Alacrity* 'on the Yangtsze', he wrote to his sister Augusta on 13 November 1892. It is apparent that he was enjoying the experience:-

'We are steaming 12 knots up the Yangtsze, and shaking a good deal so excuse writing.
We left Shanghai on the 11ᵗʰ and I am bound for Hankow looking up the Treaty Ports of Chingkiang, Wuhu and Kiukiang on my way. I was at Chingkiang yesterday and now we are going on again. The river has its shallows of course but it is a grand stream, and with a good Pilot onboard we go on night and day, and of course it saves a great deal of time to be able to go on at night (47).'

Towards the end of the year, on 8 December he visited Sand Island, Pescadores, the site of the wreck of the P. & O. steamer *Bokhara*, lost two months previously, there to satisfy himself concerning the graves of the numerous victims, passengers and crew, the former including members of the Hong Kong cricket team who had been returning from Shanghai. Also he wished to inspect such cargo salvage arrangements as were possible. 'Nothing whatever could be seen of the ill fated ship, but her position was clearly shewn by her masts which were washing to and fro, moored by their rigging to the hull (48).'

At the Hong Kong College of Medicine for Chinese on 23 July 1892 the Dean, Dr. James Cantlie, who held that post from 1889 to 1896, awarded Dr. Sun Yat-sen his graduation diploma. A brilliant student, Dr. Sun had passed nine out of the eleven subjects with honours. A member of this, the first class to graduate, he had studied there since 1887. As will be seen by no means was all of Dr. Sun's future to be medically inclined (49).

Today, 2007, the College is the Faculty of Medicine at the University of Hong Kong.

Writing in *Alacrity* from Hong Kong on 8 May 1893, he touched on a Franco-Siam border dispute problem and, paragraph eleven, also mentioned an outbreak of student unrest to the north of Amoy, apparently anti-missionary in character.

He does not appear to have been unduly concerned by either:-

' ... reports of the state of affairs in Siam where there is considerable excitement in consequence of French demands and their action in seizing...'
'I attach little importance to this riot (near Amoy) which is of the normal character occurring during the annual examinations, but it tells the usual tale of troubles caused by the student class which the Government are too weak or supine to prevent (50).'

Nevertheless, concerning the problem in Siam, it was necessary to send the protected cruiser *Pallas*, 2,575 tons, Captain Angus MacLeod, to watch over British interests. On 21 August 1893 Captain MacLeod was to report that on 13 August the, 'French Blockading Squadron departed from the Menam delta downstream from Bangkok'. Happily matters continued to progress satisfactorily and a little over a month later, on 26 September, MacLeod was able to inform the C. in C. that:-

'Everything is quiet at Bangkok and Franco-Siamese negotiations are progressing slowly (51).'

As noted above, in 1892 at Tientsin, he had met Viceroy Li Hung-chang. Now on three occasions during May 1894, at Port Arthur, Ta-lien-whan and Wei-Hai-Wei, he exchanged further visits with the Viceroy. These latter series of meetings occurred just prior to the outbreak of the Sino-Japanese war. Certainly it is apparent from his subsequent report to the Admiralty that by May 1894 he felt some degree of rapport with that notable servant of the Emperor:-

'... the Viceroy looked upon me, to some extent, as an old friend, and was prepared to be very frank and open in his conversations. He does not speak English, but his secretary is a first rate interpreter, while Mr. H. Cockburn of the Chinese Consular Service, whom Mr. O'Conor had allowed to accompany me, and who was present on all three occasions, is a very good Chinese scholar... (52).'

Having had, during these latter exchanges of visits, the opportunity to inspect units of the Chinese Navy he recorded his impressions from which two extracts follow:-

'When speaking of the Chinese Navy, I am referring to the Pei Yang (Northern) Squadron under Li Hung-chang; the other Chinese men-of-war had really no pretensions to the name.'

'... and the men were intelligent, the system of keeping captains in command who had vested rights, and who were allowed to farm the coal, oil and paint, was so rotten, that any efficiency was only spasmodic, and soon rusted out. It was even said that the greater part of the crews were got rid of, somebody getting their pay, and that coolies were put onboard to complete the complement on occasions of inspection, which I think is true; while keeping the ships in harbour saved coal and wear and tear, so that little cruising took place (53).'

From 14 April 1894 his new Flagship was the battleship *Centurion*, 10,500 tons, first commissioned at Portsmouth two months previously, on 14 February. *Centurion* and the armoured cruiser *Undaunted*, 5,600 tons, Captain John S. Hallifax, were sent East in response to Russian naval reinforcements being ordered to Vladivostok (54). At the time Britain had to consider all possible consequences arising from the Franco-Russian Alliance, concluded in January 1894. This alliance had been formed to counter the Triple Alliance of Germany, Austria-Hungary and Italy.

The exchange of flagships occurred at Singapore where *Imperieuse* arrived on 10 April and *Centurion* the following day. Thereafter *Imperieuse* continued on her voyage home. She was to return to Pacific waters as Flagship, Pacific Station for just over three years between March 1896 and August 1899. On 14 April *Centurion* sailed for Hong Kong where she arrived on 21 April 1894.

The C. in C. meanwhile remained at Hong Kong in *Alacrity*.

The screw gunboat *Redpole*, 805 tons, Lieut. and Commander Charles G. May, on 16 April 1894 was despatched from Hong Kong to Hakodate, and then on to Commander and Robben Islands in the western Bering Sea on 'sealing patrol duties' (55).

16 July 1894. Prime Minister Ito Hirobumi signed the agreement with Great Britain whereby in 1899 in Japan extraterritorial arrangements would cease (56).

In part resulting from an increased sense of Japanese national pride arising from their successful programme of industrialisation which had commenced early in the Meiji era, but largely over the question of Korea, for centuries regarded by China as a vassal state, the Sino-Japanese war was declared on 1 August 1894. However, already on 25 July the Japanese cruiser *Naniwa* (57), Captain Togo Heihachiro, had stopped and then sunk the British s.s. *Kow Shing*, Captain Thomas Ryder Galsworthy, chartered to transport Chinese troop reinforcements from Tientsin to Asan, west coast of Korea (58).

Even earlier, as may be seen from the following extract from a letter dated in the British Legation, Peking on 21 June 1894, the British Minister to China had written to give the C. in C. examples of provocative Japanese behaviour in Corea:-

'The Japs have been trying to set the house on fire and doing everything most calculated to irritate

China – buying 10 to 15 steamers, bidding for all the Cardiff coal, sending over 500 men to Seoul and about 4,000 to Chemulpo while order in both places was not disturbed and by the last accounts hectoring some British subjects at Chemulpo … (59).'

Following the outbreak of hostilities, on 17 September 1894 the Imperial Japanese Navy under the command of Vice Admiral Ito Yuko, flag in *Matsushima*, 4,277 tons, defeated the Chinese under Admiral Ting Ju-chang in the Battle of the Yalu (60).

Shortly after this engagement, on 1 October 1894 Captain Wilmot H. Fawkes, commanding the cruiser *Mercury*, 3,730 tons, visited Admiral Ito at Chefoo. The French built *Matsushima* had been damaged during the recent battle so the Admiral now flew his flag in the new armoured cruiser *Hashidate*, 4,220 tons. Built at Yokosuka to the same French plans as *Matsushima*, she was the first armoured ship to have been built in Japan. The goodwill then still existing between the RN and IJN, and to continue to exist for many more years, is readily apparent from the following extracts:-

'I went onboard *Hashidate*, bearing the flag of Vice Admiral Ito, and was most courteously and kindly received by him. I presented your compliments to him, and stated that I was sent to find out in the interest of naval science, the results of the late action. I congratulated him on having been in command in the first fleet action since the battle of Lissa (20 July 1866) and said that the results of the modern weapons employed in it would be of great interest to our navy. He said that he was very glad to tell me anything about it, and to let me see anything that was of interest to me. The officers, though showing no undue elation, were proud of their victory, and said several times to the officers with me that they owed it to our teaching (61).'

At the outbreak of the Battle of Yalu, mentioned above, Admiral Ting, with his flag in the German built battleship *Ting Yuen*, 7,144 tons, had been injured by blast from the opening fire of his own forward guns. Later Sir Edmund had sent him a letter expressing his condolences to which, on 3 October 1894, the Chinese C. in C. replied:-

'Dear Admiral Fremantle,

I thank you sincerely for your kind sympathy – am improving slowly but unable to be about yet.

I regret our loss of ships deeply: the damaged are being put in order as fast as possible… (62).'

The C. in C. himself, at Tientsin on 21 October 1894, once more visited Viceroy Li Hung-chang. It is not surprising to read that he found the Viceroy, 'depressed by Chinese inability to oppose Japan in Corea.' A further Viceregal comment was recorded:-

'The Japanese Fleet is practically in full command of the sea, their transports pass freely, unconvoyed between Japan and Corean ports, while they have now made a descent on the coast of China without being molested by the Chinese ships (63).'

From the Chinese point of view worse was to come.

The important Chinese fortified harbour and naval base of Port Arthur fell to Japanese land forces on 21 November 1894. The British were to learn that the Japanese Army carried the town from the land, 'after five hours fighting.' Admiral Fremantle was to comment:-

'Practically, the (Japanese) Fleet took no part. Admiral Ito informed me that he had been asked by General Count Oyama not to fire at the Forts for fear of injuring Japanese attacking parties. Practically the fine sea Forts did nothing though at one time their fire drove the Japanese out of one of the redoubts on the land side, which they had captured. They had probably short supplies of provisions and water, and when the town fell, the Chinese deserted the Sea Forts, though they commanded the town and harbour (64).'

Meanwhile from Japan Count Inouye Kaoru had been appointed to Korea as 'Special Commissioner' but even he was unable to make headway against the overall feeling of hatred by Koreans towards Japan (65). For the moment the war continued. The European powers were to intervene however and on 17 April 1895 the Chinese and Japanese envoys signed the Treaty of Shimonoseki which brought hostilities to an end. The cost to China was considerable. In addition to the payment of an indemnity, China conceded the independence of Korea, gave extraterritorial rights to Japan at a number of cities within China including as far up the Yangtse River as Chungking, granted Formosa to Japan, also granted to Japan the southern part of the Liaotung peninsula in Manchuria, including Port Arthur. This latter concession concerned Russia, France and Germany who were to pressure Japan into giving up this territory. Not only did the war clearly reveal China's overall weakness, but by subsequently forcing Japan to return their award of territory in the Liaotung peninsula those European powers concerned rather naturally incurred the bitterness of Japan.

In the interim, following the Battle of Yalu and prior to the Treaty of Shimonoseki, the IJN at first watched the situation, and then had taken further action, specifically against the sheltered Chinese anchorage at Wei-Hai-Wei on the north coast of the Shantung peninsula. This place is just a short distance to the East from Chefoo. As the following extracts show, Admiral Fremantle kept the Admiralty well informed, and added comments of his own:-

'Letter of 8.1.1895. Written in *Centurion* at Chefoo.

The Japanese Fleet is still about Ta-lien-whan Bay, a few ships being refitted at Port Arthur, with occasionally, but rarely, a few cruisers out towards Wei-Hai-Wei where the Chinese Fleet remains at anchor. I am informed that the *Chen Yuen*, though temporarily repaired, is not fit to go to sea, and that her guns could not be fired with safety. Admiral Ting, who has recently been ordered to Peking, still retains the nominal command of the Fleet, but is said to have little power, and to be much shaken in health. The moving spirit in the Chinese Fleet now is a Scotchman – Captain McClure, who is well known as the Master of a tug boat at Shanghai and Tientsin. He has been given the rank of Vice Admiral in the Chinese Navy and is credited with considerable energy and intelligence, though his antecedents will scarcely have qualified him for his present position.'

'Probably the Japanese have taken a just measure of their opponents in assuming that they will make no attempt to put to sea, or to harass their transports and commerce, in which case Admiral Ito is justified in saving his ships the wear and tear of cruising, but it is evident that we have little to learn in Naval warfare, either from a belligerent who keeps his ships in port, or from one who can safely assume that his opponent will act in this innocuous manner (66).'

'Letter of 21.1.1895. Written in *Centurion* at Chemulpo (Inchon). There appears to be little news of importance here; the King of Corea has reluctantly agreed to accept the Japanese reforms forced upon him, and has sworn at the tombs of his ancestors to renounce all allegiance to or dependence on China. The Tonghak insurrection (peasant movement against over taxation and injustice) appears to be subsiding, but the persistent and often unnecessary interference of the Japanese with Corean customs cannot fail to keep alive the hatred of the Coreans for their traditional enemies, and all changes, improvements and reforms introduced will have to be forced on a reluctant people (67).'

Inevitably, in order to secure Wei-Hai-Wei, on 20 January 1895 the Japanese army commenced landings on the Shantung peninsula and by 30 January had secured all the Chinese forts situated to the east of Wei-Hai-Wei itself thus overlooked both the bay and the remaining Chinese facilities on the island of Liukungtao. Warships of the IJN also took the Chinese under fire. By telegram from Chefoo Sir Edmund informed the Admiralty:-

'3 February. Japanese have taken all forts on the mainland Weihaiwei – guns apparently rendered unserviceable – Chinese still hold island and sundry ships are intact. Part of the Japanese fleet is engaged with island forts this morning.'

'9 February. I returned from near Weihaiwei last night. Successful attack torpedo boats by Japanese night February 5th. *Ting Yuen* torpedoed grounded shallow water and deserted. *Lai Yuen* (and) *Wei Yuen* sunk. Japanese lost two torpedo boats. One wrecked. Chinese Squadron still held out.

Thirteen Chinese torpedo boats attempted to escape February 7 – all driven ashore or captured.'
'22 February. Just returned from Weihaiwei. Island Lewkungtan (Liukungtao) occupied 17
February. Officers and foreigners sent Chefoo in Chinese ships. 4000 soldiers 2000 seamen
prisoners landed and sent home. Ships captured *Chen Yuen*, *Tsi Yuen*, *Ping Yuen*, *Kwang Ping* and
six gunboats – remainder sunk or destroyed all quiet here improbable Chefoo will be occupied at
present. Japanese fleet now at Weihaiwei. Am proceeding Shanghai in *Alacrity* (68).'

The island of Formosa was captured by Japanese forces on 23 and 24 March 1895. Already on 7 March he
had written to the Admiralty indicating that Formosa was likely to be ceded to Japan during the forthcoming
peace talks, and proposing that the Pescadores group be occupied by Great Britain. In making this suggestion
the C. in C. had in mind the protection of British trade and shipping passing through the Formosa Strait.
There was a precedent in that between 1884 and 1885 the islands had been occupied by France. However Their
Lordships showed no interest in taking the matter further. In the event, along with Formosa itself, the group
was to be ceded to Japan.

The very next day, 8 March, Sir Edmund informed London of the important movements of an old
acquaintance:-

'Li Hung-chang has left Peking and will, it is stated, proceed direct to Hiroshima shortly, to
endeavour to arrange terms of peace (69).'

Following the signing of the relevant Treaty at Shimonoseki on 17 April then the necessary ratification duly
took place at Chefoo:-

'On the 7th (May 1895) the Japanese delegates arrived in the s.s. *Yokohama Maru* from Port Arthur,
and the Treaty of Shimonoseki was ratified and exchanged late on the night of the 8th (70).'

With future nationalistic Japanese behaviour to consider it is important to understand what this victory
over China really meant to Japan. In this connection a useful opinion follows:-

'Japan's victory over China in the Sino-Japanese War of 1894-95 was a watershed in Japan's modern
emergence. Success on the battlefield, at sea, and at the negotiating table left a tangible imprint
on the Japanese nation materially, politically, and psychologically. To Japan's elder statesmen,
defeat of East Asia's historically dominant country and civilization further validated the oligarchs'
centrally directed state-building and westernization programmes launched soon after the Meiji
Restoration. For the Japanese people, many of whom wholeheartedly supported mobilization and
the war effort, victory further strengthened the bond between citizen, subject, Emperor, and state,
and heightened a sense of national pride not previously witnessed in modern Japan (71).

One consequence of the peace settlement was the payment by China to Japan of a huge indemnity, the
equivalent of 7.45 million kg. of silver. This sum was to be used by Japan to fund very considerable development.
Not surprisingly the IJN was to receive much benefit from their share of this expenditure, and from their new
found popularity at home. To take just one example, an important new warship was to be the future fleet
flagship, the battleship *Mikasa*, 15,200 tons, her armament including four 12" and fourteen 6" guns, launched
at Barrow in November 1900.

Another clause in the peace treaty had ceded the Liaotung peninsula to Japan however, as mentioned above,
Russia, Germany and France quickly objected, demanding that Japan give up this territory. Unable, then, to
contemplate a war with Russia, reluctantly Japan acceded to this request, a national 'humiliation'. However in
accepting the adjusted peace terms the indemnity to be paid by China to Japan was increased still further.

Russian and Japanese ambitions in Korea, not always openly discussed, added spice to international
diplomatic negotiations throughout the above mentioned peace proceedings.

Before leaving the subject of this particular Sino-Japanese war there was to be another longer term advantage
to Japan in the cession of Formosa (Taiwan) to her, and of her subsequent colonisation of the island. Looking

ahead, as will be seen in due course the military were to assume great power in the administration of Japan and her Empire. As early as in 1922, after the imposition of naval limitations as a result of the Washington Naval Conference, it was to be appreciated in Tokyo that although the navy as such now had to exist within the bounds of the treaty clauses:-

'... the construction of modern, distant water fishing fleets could effectively compensate for this deficiency. Since such fleets were equipped with modern telecommunication devices and were suitable for long distance navigation (--) they could also be used for military purposes. (--) In 1936, Kobayashi Seizo, a Japanese Naval Reserve Admiral, was appointed Taiwans's Governor General. (--) The activities of the navy directly encouraged the southward development of the fishing industry. The navy expected fishing vessels to collect all sorts of intelligence, and Japanese fishers willingly cooperated (72).'

In the interim, in October 1894 Dr. Sun Yat-sen had arrived in Honolulu where, as a youth, he had attended school. Following the outcome of the Battle of Yalu, which had been fought only a month earlier, then clearly news from China was not good. In a number of Chinese circles in Hawaii it was felt that funds should be raised to help finance and organise uprisings at home against the occupying Manchu regime, the Ch'ing dynasty. Together with several friends, in Honolulu on 24 November 1894 the Revive China Society, Hsing Chung Hui or Xingzhonghui was founded, Dr. Sun himself being the first to swear their agreed oath to:-

'...drive away the Tartars, recover China for the Chinese, and establish a republic (73).'

At Nagasaki on 28 May 1895 Admiral Fremantle handed over command of the Station to Admiral Buller and sailed for home via Yokohama, then to Victoria, BC in the CPR s.s. *Empress of Japan*, 5,940 grt, Captain George A. Lee. In 1891 the three purpose built new liners, *Empress of India, Empress of Japan,* and *Empress of China* had replaced the earlier, ex Cunard Line, ships who had initiated the CPR trans Pacific service. After arriving in North America he visited Esquimalt briefly before crossing to Vancouver to continue his travels by train to Montreal. While there at Esquimalt he had the opportunity to meet the C. in C., Pacific Station, Rear Admiral Henry F. Stephenson in his flagship, the screw cruiser *Royal Arthur*, 7,700 tons (74). Admiral Stephenson was a nephew of Sir Henry Keppel (see C. in C., 1867). En route from the west coast he stopped over in Banff for two days. Finally he made his way to New York where he embarked on 29 June, and returned to Liverpool in the Cunard s.s. *Campania*, 12,950 grt, Captain H. Walker, arriving on 5 July 1895.

From 6 July 1895 to 9 June 1896 he was on half pay at the rate of thirty two shillings and six pence a day (75).

During 1896 at the R.U.S.I. he spoke on the subject of *Naval Aspects of the China-Japan War*.

C. in C., Devonport from 10 June 1896 to 16 June 1899. Flag in *Vivid*. In that position he succeeded Admiral Sir Algernon McLennan Lyons, then in turn in 1899 was relieved by Admiral Sir Henry Fairfax.

Admiral: 10 October 1896.

While at Devonport for those three years it chanced that in 1898 one of the ships under his command was the cruiser *Crescent*, 7,700 tons, Captain HRH the Duke of York later to be H.M. King George V. In the Fremantle family archives is a delightful letter written in HRH's own hand. Extracts follow as it seems that he had transgressed somewhat, at the same time being conscious of his delicate personal position in command of one of His Grandmother's men of war:-

'H.M.S. *Crescent*, Portland to Kirkwall. July 14, 1898

My dear Sir Edmund: I am going to put in tomorrow at Larne, on purpose to send you these lines, to tell you how grieved I was that through negligence the signal "Permission to proceed in execution of previous orders" was not hoisted this morning and that therefore I left the Sound without your permission. I much regret that this should have occurred, more especially so as the movements of the *Crescent* may be more severely criticized than those of other ships. I hope you will forgive what might appear an act of rudeness on my part. (--)

Please thank Lady Fremantle very much for so kindly sending me that beautiful and most acceptable basket of flowers and also for the tent which she has given to our little boy, and for her nice letter. Believe me very sincerely yours, George (76).'

From Devonport in December 1898 he offered to provide a Royal Naval launch to take out to the P. & O. steamer *Arabia*, 7,930 grt, Lady Mary Curzon and party who were to embark there and sail in her to Bombay. On 8 December Lord Curzon himself, the new Viceroy and who was to embark in her at Marseilles a few days later, wrote to the C. in C. gratefully accepting this offer (77).

GCB: 3 June 1899.

At times between 1899 and 1905 he corresponded with the well known naval and maritime author of that era, Sir Archibald Spicer Hurd (1869-1959).

At the time Sir Edmund's address was 44, Lower Sloane Street in London.

In one such letter to Hurd, dated 21 October 1899, he explained that he had agreed to such an exchange of corrspondence as, 'I quite believe you have the good of the service at heart (78).' Rather over a year later, in reply to a query from Hurd, on 31 December 1900 he gave his opinion on two important matters, however tending to carefully hedge his bets:-

> 'As to submarine boats I am not disposed to put much faith in them, but we ought to try a couple, and they may prove to be of value.'

> 'The submarine boats are wonderful so is the Brennan torpedo. The latter I am sure has no military value, and I doubt whether the former has, but one ought not to be too sure.'

In Victorian times certainly there had been a period when in some Naval circles the physical appearance of a man of war was of prime importance, it being alleged that in some instances, rather than foul the paintwork or spoil the beautiful picture of the ship, then during the quarterly dispersal for gunnery practice some ships merely disposed of such ammunition by throwing it all overboard.

On this subject, on the matter of feeding rations, and on the question of carrying out the inspection of warships, on 1 January 1901 Sir Edmund again replied to Hurd:-

> 'On the gunnery question for instance there is no doubt that too often efficiency has been sacrificed to appearance and it is well that public opinion should check this.'

> 'As to the ammunition being thrown overboard (--). In 1877 I was made to join *Lord Warden* (--). A gun boat under my orders was temporarily commanded by a Lieutenant whose name I cannot remember and she was sent to Newcastle to drill Reserve men I think. She was most unsatisfactory and on returning to my station at Queensferry I had the Lieutenant removed and he shortly afterwards left the service. It reached my ears afterwards that he had actually thrown overboard his quarterly allowance of ammunition to expend it without going to sea. From his log I was inclined to think this might be true, but the Lieutenant had left and I could not well prove it – I never heard of its being done on any other occasion.'

> Rations: 'It is clear enough that they need reform as not only are the times unsuitable, but there is really only one meal, dinner, a day (--).'

> 'One other hint – no doubt it is a good thing that the Admiral should inspect a ship while she is firing at a target occasionally, but a man who knows his job can see whether guns are carefully laid and drills carried out thoroughly without actually firing the guns. Personally I preferred to see ships at odd times, going onboard occasionally in a friendly way, to supplement the formal inspection which can be more or less prepared for. They never knew at Devonport when I might turn up and I fancy that they had much more effect than any number of formal inspections.'

He retired on 15 June 1901, his pension then being valued at GBP 950.00 per annum.

From 13 November 1901 this was augmented by a GSP (Good Service Pension) at the rate of GBP 300 per annum, a useful benefit. However between 14 November 1901 and 31 March 1919 his Admiral's pension did drop to GBP 922.15.0 p.a. (79).

Meanwhile on 26 July 1901 he had been, 'Granted Office of Rear Admiral of Great Britain and Ireland and of the Admiralty.'

In retirement he was much involved with bodies such as the Naval Records Society and Royal United Service Institution. Also he was Vice President of the Missions to Seamen and an Associate of the Institution of Naval Architects. As has been seen above over the years he had become well known at the R.U.S.I. In retirement, and as just mentioned, this close association was to be maintained. Amongst other activities he was responsible for a further four fine efforts:-

'*A Reserve for the Navy from the Navy*, a lecture delivered in 1902.
Admiral Rodjestvensky's voyage to the Far East, a letter in 1910.
Naval War Past and Present, article in 1915.
Sea Power and the American War of Independence, article in 1917 (80).'

In addition to the above, and to his own autobiography which appeared in 1904, in 1899 he contributed passages covering the lives of Hawke and Boscawen in Sir John Laughton's volume, *From Howard to Nelson*.

In correspondence with Archibald Hurd during 1902, on a number of occasions he expressed his concern at the lack of cruisers in the Navy.

Again in 1905, as the German naval building programme took very obvious effect and tension between the two countries increased, on 16 January 1905 he gave Hurd his views on the subject:-

'Of course I am not hostile to Germany, and my relations with German officers have been uniformly friendly, also I don't approve of our making attacks on Germany in the papers, or of our complaining of them increasing their Fleet. But I have a profound mistrust of German policy. All the Prussian history has shown a special disregard of anything but their own interests. They have fished in troubled waters and always are looking out for the opportunity of doing so. The Japanese with their usual cuteness have Christened them "fire thieves".'

GCVO: 3 July 1926.

His death on 10 February 1929 was reported in *The Times* on the following Tuesday:-

'... died in London on Sunday at the age of 92. In him the Navy loses the senior officer of his rank on the retired list, and the oldest, for he was the only flag officer remaining who was born in the reign of William IV (81).'

On Thursday, 14 February his funeral took place at Swanbourne at 2.30 p.m. This followed a service which was held at St. Michael's, Chester Square at 11.00 that morning. As was reported in *The Times* the following day:-

'The family of Admiral The Hon. Sir Edmund Fremantle have received a message of sympathy from the King and Queen. The funeral took place at Swanbourne, Buckinghamshire yesterday. The service in the Parish Church was conducted by the Vicar, the Rev. J.R.C. Forrest, and the Bishop of Buckingham officiated at the graveside (82).'

Amongst those who attended the funeral at Swanbourne was Admiral Sir Arthur Leveson (see C. in C., 1922). The huge congregation present at St. Michael's included the representative of H.M. The King, Admiral Sir Richard Phillimore, also The First Sea Lord who by then was Admiral of the Fleet Sir Charles Madden, Admiral of the Fleet Earl Jellicoe, Admiral Sir Arthur Moore (see C. in C., 1905), and a great many other distinguished mourners.

In the *Dictionary of National Biography* his entry was prepared by a well known brother officer and academic, Admiral Sir Herbert W. Richmond (1871-1946). In February 1934 Sir Herbert was appointed Professor of Naval

History at Cambridge to be followed, from November 1936 until his death, as the elected Master of Downing College.

At Swanbourne the Admiral's grave and that of Lady Fremantle do not lie in the churchyard immediately surrounding the Church of St. Swithun, but instead within the new cemetery down the hill the entrance to which is off the street, Nearton End. Inside the church on the right hand wall, however, may be found his memorial plaque (83).

NOTES

1. Ann Parry, *The Admirals Fremantle, 1788-1920,* (London, 1971), 199-252.
2. Admiral The Hon. Sir Edmund R. Fremantle, *The Navy as I have Known it, 1849-1899,* (London, 1904), 2.
3. Obituary, *The Times,* Tuesday, February 12, 1929.
4. Hugh Cortazzi and Gordon Daniels, *Britain and Japan: 1859-1991,* (London, 1991), 26.
5. Caird Library, National Maritime Museum, Greenwich. Ref: *FRE/107.*
6. NA ADM 196//36. *Service Record.*
7. Surrey History Centre, Woking. Ref: *5295.*
8. Parry, 205. Sir George **Grey** – also see Keppel, C. in C., 1867, reference (24).
9. Caird Library. Ref: *FRE/108.*
10. Parry, 207.
11. *Dictionary of National Biography.*
    Robert Macintosh Isaacs. Born in Tortola, BVI in 1814. Educated in England, Middle Temple and called to the Bar: 12 January 1839. Migrated to Sydney in 1843. Acquired a reputation placing him 'among the leading Sydney counsel'. In February 1857 appointed to the Legislative Council. Solicitor-General: January 1866. Lost his seat in November 1869. Spent a year in Tasmania: 1871/2 when returned to Sydney. Weakened by typhoid fever, died in Sydney: 26 March 1876. *Australian Dictionary of Biography.*
12. *Service Record.*
13. Caird Library. Ref: *FRE/103.*
14. Francis Worgan **Festing**. Born: 24 July 1833. Died: 21 November 1886. Royal Naval College, New Cross. Entered the Royal Marines, 2nd Lieut: 3 July 1850. Saw action in the Baltic and in the Black Sea during the Crimean War: 1854-1855. Further action in China: 1857-1859. Distinguished himself in West Africa: 1873-1874. Brevet Colonel: 1874. KCMG: 8 May 1874. Colonel Commandant, RMA: 3 September 1886. *Encyclopaedia Britannica.*
15. Clowes, Vol. VII, 251/2.
16. *The London Gazette,* 15 July 1873, 3330.
17. The castle at Elmina was built in 1482 by the Portuguese, Diogo de Azambuja (1432-1518), and in early days known as the Castle of St. George the Mine, Sao Jorge da Mina. Included in his party was Bartholomew Dias, in 1488 to be the first European to round Cape Agulhas into the Indian Ocean. A simple lodge on the site of the Cape Coast Castle first was built by the Swedes in 1653. The two castles are some ten kilometres apart.
18. Surrey History Centre.
19. Fremantle, 215/6. Steamer *Volta,* 1,477 grt.
20. Caird Library. Ref: *FRE/101.* Lieut. Day was to be promoted Commander a few months later: 31 March 1874.
21. William Nathan Wrighte **Hewett**. Born: 12 August 1834. Died: 13 May 1888. Cadet in *Ocean:* 22 April 1847. As Acting Mate in *Beagle* served ashore at Sevastopol during the Crimean campaign and there on 26 October 1854, while in command of a Battery, handled a difficult situation with much forthright courage. Again most courageous at Inkerman on 5 November. Subsequently awarded the Victoria Cross. Commander: 13 September 1858. Captain: 14 November 1862. KCB: 31 March 1874. Rear Admiral: 21 March 1878. C. in C., East Indies: 15 April 1882. Vice Admiral: 8 July 1884. C. in C., Channel Squadron: 18 March 1886 to April 1888. *Navy List.*
22. Surrey History Centre. Cape Coast in West Africa, not to be confused with The Cape, South Africa.

23. *Service Record.*

24. Ibid.

25. Ibid.

26. Andrew Lambert, *Admirals,* (London, 2008), 277.

    Geoffrey Thomas **Phipps Hornby**. Born: 20 February 1825. Died at Lordington House: 3 March 1895. Entered the Navy in March 1837. Captain: 18 December 1852. Rear Admiral: 1 January 1869. Vice Admiral: 1 January 1875. C. in C., Mediterranean: January 1877 – March 1880. KCB: Aug. 1878. Admiral: 15 June 1879. C. in C., Portsmouth: November 1882 – November 1885. GCB: 19 December 1885. Admiral of the Fleet: 1 May 1888. *Navy List.*

27. *Dictionary of National Biography.*

28. Ibid.

29. Surrey History Centre.

30. Sir Thomas Brassey, *The British Navy,* III, (London, 1883), 90.

31. Ibid., 88.

32. *Dictionary of National Biography.*

33. *Service Record.*

34. NA ADM 1/6967. File Sa.78.

35. Albert George Sidney Hawes. See King, C. in C., 1865, reference (15).

36. Fremantle, 350.

37. Caird Library. Ref: *FRE/139.* Screw sloop *Reindeer,* 6 guns, 970 tons. Commander Henry B. Lang until 31 August 1889 when Commander Hon. Edward T. Needham was appointed to the ship. *Navy List.*

38. Edward Fraser and L.G. Carr-Laughton, *The Royal Marine Artillery, 1804-1923,* II, (RUSI London, 1930), 607.

39. Vitu today is Witu in Kenya. Then the Sultan of Vitu was the local ruler, nominally under the jurisdiction of the Sultan of Zanzibar. Admiral of the Fleet Sir Roger Keyes, *Adventures Ashore and Afloat,* (London, 1939), 84-89. J. Forbes Munro, *Maritime Enterprise and Empire,* (Woodbridge, Suffolk, 2003), 445 and elsewhere. Clowes, Vol. VII, 394/6. Kevin Patience, *Zanzibar: Slavery and the Royal Navy,* (Bahrain, 2000), 32-36. The British Foreign Office official who negotiated with Germany the terms of the Anglo-German Agreement of 1 July 1890 was Sir Henry Percy Anderson, KCB, KCMG (1831-1896). Of interest today is the fact that between 1852 and 1854 his career in the Foreign Office had commenced as, "a Clerk in the Slave Trade Department." *Foreign Office List,* 1897, 233.

40. NA ADM 1/7065. Letter 499 dated 3 November 1890.

41. Ibid. Letter 185 dated 28 April 1891. British India *Manora,* 4,696 grt, built in 1884.

    Frederick Charles Bryan **Robinson** (1836-1896). Rear Admiral: 7 July 1887. Vice Admiral: 2 September 1892. He was the younger brother of the Colonial Governor Sir Hercules Robinson (see C. in C., 1862). *Navy List.*

    P. & O. steamer *Mirzapore,* 3,763 grt, built at Greenock in 1871. Twelve knots, iron hull.

42. NA ADM 53/14083. Mr. Carlisle is John Carlisle, Secretary, and Lt. Nicholson is Douglas R.L. Nicholson, Flag Lieutenant, both having completed duty on Admiral Richards's staff. *Navy List.*

43. NA ADM 1/7108. Letter No. 24.

44. Ibid. Letter No. 57.

45. Caird Library. Ref: *FRE/141d.* A letter dated Sep. 20, but with no year given.

46. NA ADM 1/7109. Letter No. 286/1112.

47. Surrey History Centre.

48. NA ADM 1/7109. Letter No. 372 written from Hong Kong on 22 December 1892. s.s. *Bokhara,* 2,944 grt, had been caught by a typhoon on 8 October 1892, and driven ashore. Only twenty three were to survive from a total of 148 passengers and crew. Norman L. Middlemiss, *Merchant Fleets, P. & O. Lines,* (Gateshead, 2004), 114. Only two members of the cricket team had been saved from the disaster. G.B. Sayer, *Hong Kong: 1862-1919,* (Hong Kong, 1975), 73.

49. In Hong Kong at the end of 2006 the Sun Yat-sen Museum was opened at 7 Castle Road, Mid-levels. Better viewing is his old home in Shanghai in the previous French Settlement at 29, Rue Moliere, now 7 Xiangshan Road. There a good museum is maintained. Best is his mausoleum outside Nanking/Nanjing in the Purple Mountain. See Waistell, C. in C., 1929.

50. NA ADM 1/7150. General Letter No. 237.

51. NA ADM 1/7151.

52. NA ADM 1/7199. *Alacrity* at Shanghai, 25 May 1894.

   Li Hung-chang. Born: 15 February 1823. Died in Peking: 7 November 1901, but the following year, in considerable state, his body was returned to the family at Ho-fei, Anhui. For twenty five years from 1870 Viceroy of the capital Province of Chihli. Keenly interested in, and the driving force behind much of China's effort made during this era to modernise her economy, industry and military ability. In 1872 he initiated the foundation of China Merchants Steam Navigation Company. Leader of the Chinese delegation resulting in the Treaty of Shimonoseki of 1895, his opposite number being Count Ito Hirobumi. The following year, representing the Ch'ing dynasty, he travelled to Russia, first arriving at Odessa on 28 April 1896, then travelling on to attend the Coronation of Tsar Nicholas II which took place in Moscow on 14 May. Thereafter he continued his great journey through Western Europe, Great Britain, where Queen Victoria created him KCVO, and the U.S.A., finally returning home in October. It must be remembered, however, that unfortunately much of Li's enterprise also was made with a view to personal financial gain. *Encyclopaedia Britannica.* Alicia Helen Neva Little, *Li Hung-chang: His Life and Times,* (London, 1903).

   Henry **Cockburn**. Born in Calcutta: 2 March 1859. Died: 19 March 1927. Student Interpreter in China: 30 March 1880. Service in Canton and Chungking. Assistant in the Chinese Secretary's Office at Peking: 4 May 1893 to 27 October 1896 when promoted Chinese Secretary. CB: 2 January 1899. China Medal, Defence of the Legation at Peking: 1900. Secretary of Legation: 26 June 1902. Charge d'Affaires in Corea: 23 November 1905 to 1 April 1906 when promoted Consul-General, Corea to reside at Seoul. Retired: 16 July 1909. *Foreign Office List.*

53. Fremantle, 423.

54. At the time a Midshipman serving in *Undaunted* was Alfred DPR Pound, to be First Sea Lord during the early years of WW2. *Navy List.*

55. NA ADM 1/7199. In August 1991 a party of Russian and Danish archaeologists were to locate the grave of Vitus Jonassen **Bering** (1681-1741) in the Commander or Komandorski Islands. Once the identity of these remains were confirmed they were re-buried there on 15 September 1992. Nearby is a steel cross, in June 1966 erected in honour of Bering. Robin Inglis, *Historical Dictionary of the Discovery and Exploration of the Northwest Coast of America,* (Lanham, MD., 2008), 82.

56. Similar agreement to end extraterritoriality in China would not be reached until 11 January 1943.

57. HIJMS *Naniwa*, 3,727 tons. Launched at Elswick: 18 March 1885. Two 10.2", six 5.9" plus smaller guns. 18.5+ knots. Peter Brook, *Warships for Export,* (Gravesend, 1999), 58.

58. *Kow Shing,* 2,134 grt. Built at Barrow-in-Furness in 1883 for Indo-China S.N. Co. (Jardine Matheson & Co.) for the Shanghai/Tientsin trade. First arrived at Shanghai: July 1883. On 25 July 1894 while on charter to the Chinese government and bound for Korea with 1,500 troops, she was intercepted by *Naniwa* in Asan Strait and sunk by gunfire. H.W. Dick and S.A. Kentwell, *Beancaker to Boxboat,* (Canberra, 1988), 25.

   As early as 14 July Japanese Intelligence had become aware of the charter for the purpose of transporting Chinese troops to Korea. In fact only carrying 1,100 troops however certainly they were more than sufficient in number to seize the ship once it was perceived by them that Captain Galsworthy intended to follow the instructions received from Captain Togo that *Kow Shing* follow Japanese orders. As soon as Captain Togo observed that *Kow Shing* no longer was under the control of her British officers, and concerned that the Chinese fleet might appear, he sank *Kow Shing* by gunfire. Also he fired one torpedo which missed. Although war was not to be declared until 1 August it was clear to all observers that well before this date hostile acts had been taken by both China and Japan against each other. In her sinking of *Kow Shing* later it was established that 'Japan was inside her legal rights.' Fred T. Jane, *The Imperial Japanese Navy,* (Portsmouth, 1904), 110-112. H.W. Wilson, *Battleships in Action,* I, (London), 96-98.

59. Caird Library. Ref: *FRE/141b.* From 1 April 1892 the Envoy Extraordinary and Minister Plenipotentiary to the Emperor of China, and also to the King of Corea, was Nicholas Roderick **O'Conor**. Born in Dundermott, Co. Roscommon: 3 July 1843. Died in office in Constantinople: 19 March 1908. Stonyhurst. Munich. Nominated an Attache: 28 March 1866. Earlier service in Berlin, Washington, Madrid, Rio de Janeiro and Paris. Previous service in China from 7 December 1883 until transfer back to Washington: 14 December 1885. Thence Bulgaria prior to returning as Minister to China in April 1892. KCB: 25 May 1895. Ambassador to Russia: 24 October 1895. GCMG: 27 February 1896. PC: 6 March 1896. GCB: 22 June 1897. Transferred to Constantinople: 1 July 1898. *Foreign Office List,* 1909. At the time of

his death he was serving as British Ambassador to the Ottoman Empire.

60. **Ito** Yuko, also known as Sukeyuki (1843-1914). C. in C., IJN during the Sino-Japanese war of 1894-1895. Chief of Naval Staff: 1895-1905. Dr. John Curtis Perry writes about Ito:-

    'There was not much pepper in Ito's character. He was supremely cautious, deeply concerned with husbanding Japanese resources; his leadership inspired loyalty but not enthusiasm.'

    The Battle off the Tayang, 17 September 1894, (Mariner's Mirror, Vol. 50, No. 4, 1964), 245/6.

61. NA ADM 1/7201. Captain Fawkes to Admiral Fremantle, letter dated 2 October 1894. Included in the party accompanying Captain Fawkes was the Japanese interpreter and, from 1886 to 1926, a member of the British Consular staff in Japan, Ralph George Elliott Forster. *Foreign Office List,* 1927.

62. Caird Library. Ref: *FRE/141d.*

63. NA ADM 1/7201. General Letter No. 464 written in *Centurion* at Chefoo, 30 October 1894.

64. Ibid. Letter 516/4090 written in *Centurion* at Chefoo, 27 November 1894.

65. **Inouye** Kaoru. Born: 16 January 1835. Died: 1 September 1915. A boyhood friend of Ito Hirobumi and another member of the 'Choshu Five' of 1863. Following the commencement of the 'Meiji Restoration' he was an influential member of the oligarchy that ruled Japan. Held important positions in the ministries of finance, industry, and foreign affairs. Once Ito Hirobumi became prime minister then to serve at times as foreign minister, minister of the interior, and minister of finance. Associated with Mitsui interests. He retired from active politics in 1898 however continued to exert influence as an elder statesman or genro. *Encyclopaedia Britannica.* John G. Roberts, *Mitsui,* (New York and Tokyo, 1989), 75, 95.

66. NA ADM 1/7248.

67. Ibid.

68. Ibid. For an account of the war see Wilson, I, 90-111. In respect of the last stand by the Chinese on Liukungtao, on page 110 Wilson relates:-

    'The bombardment continued until February 12, when Ting surrendered, himself committing suicide. His body was sent by the Japanese to Chefoo in great state.'

69. Ibid.

70. Ibid. s.s. *Yokohama Maru,* 2,305 grt. Owned by N.Y.K., Tokio. Built in Glasgow in 1884. *Lloyd's Register.*

71. J. Charles Schencking, *Making Waves,* (Stanford, 2005), 78.

72. Henry T. Chen, *Research in Maritime History No. 39. Taiwanese Distant-Water Fisheries in Southeast Asia: 1936-1977,* (St. Johns, Newfoundland, 2009), 8. Also by the same author, *Birth of Takao's Fisheries in Nanyo,* (International Journal of Maritime History, XX, No. 1, St. Johns, June 2008), 137.

73. Yangsheng Ma Lum and Raymond Mun Kong Lum, *Sun Yat-sen in Hawai'i,* (Honolulu, 1999), 7.

74. Fremantle, 448.

75. *Service Record.*

76. By kind permission, Commander Charles Fremantle, RN (ret'd). 30 July 2011. 'Our little boy' is HRH Prince Edward, born on 23 June 1894, and subsequently to be King Edward VIII, then Duke of Windsor.

77. Ibid. In the event *Arabia* arrived at Bombay on 30 December 1898 and there the Viceregal party disembarked to 'cheering crowds'. George Nathaniel Curzon, first Marquess Curzon of Kedleston (1859-1925).

78. Archives Centre, Churchill College, Cambridge. Ref: *Hurd 1/20.*

79. *Service Record.*

80. Robin Higham and Mrs. Karen Cox Wing, *The Consolidated Author and Subject Index to "The Journal of the Royal United Service Institution 1857-1963",* (Ann Arbor, Michigan, 1964).

81. *The Times,* Tuesday, February 12, 1929.

82. *The Times,* Friday, February 15, 1929.

83. Through the kind offices of the Clerk to the Parish Council, Anthony Hilton who very thoughtfully made the arrangements, visited by the author on Tuesday, 17 May 2011. Also he was good enough to introduce the author to Commander John Tapling Fremantle, 5th Baron Cottesloe who generously hosted luncheon that day in the village hostelry, 'The Betsy Wynne'. Lord Cottesloe remembers that in the family Sir Edmund was known as Uncle Eddy.

21 March 1895 to 12 December 1897
Vice Admiral Alexander **Buller**

Born in Bodmin, Cornwall on 30 June 1834, the second son of the Reverend Richard Buller, Rector of Lanreath, Liskeard and his wife Elizabeth, daughter of John Hornby of Hook House, Titchfield in Hampshire (1). He was baptised by his father just a few months later, on 21 September. His grandfather, James Buller (1772-1830), was a Lord of the Admiralty from 1807 to 1812.

In respect of his death on Saturday, 3 October 1903:-

'(The Admiral)… of (Erle Hall) Plympton, Devon and (Belmore House) West Cowes, Isle of Wight,' died suddenly, '… while hunting with the Devon and Somerset staghounds in the neighbourhood of Exford' (2).

He entered the Royal Navy as a **Cadet** in June 1848. Promoted **Mate** (Sub Lieutenant): 12 January 1854 and served in the packet brig *Star*, just 95' in length, until 5 July that year (3). Then he was transferred to the huge three decker *Royal Albert*, 121 guns: 6 July 1854. On the stocks since 1844, in 1852 her conversion to be steam power assisted had been approved, and as such she had been launched shortly before he joined her, on 13 May 1854 (4). In her he proceeded to the Mediterranean and:-

'… in the Black Sea during the Crimean War, was present at all the operations before Sevastopol, and as Lieutenant in the *Princess Royal* took part in the attacks on Kertch and Yenikale and in the capture of Kinburn (5).'

Promoted **Lieutenant** on 10 April 1855. As just noted, served in *Princess Royal*, 91 guns, Captain Lord Clarence Edward Paget, from 2 April 1855 until 7 August 1856. For services in Crimea received the Crimean and Turkish medals, and Sebastopol clasp (6). From 8 August 1856 to 24 August 1858 served in the screw steam ship *Royal Albert*, 5,520 tons, initially Flagship, Mediterranean. From 5 February 1859 in *Excellent*, Gunnery Ship, Portsmouth. From 15 July 1859 in new building screw steam ship *Donegal*, 101, Liverpool. From 15 February 1860 appointed to the screw steam frigate *Forte*, 51, Flagship, Cape of Good Hope, Rear Admiral Hon. Sir Henry Keppel (see C. in C., 1867). In the end he did not proceed to the Cape. Instead from 28 April 1860 to 27 October 1860 he was Flag Lieutenant to Vice Admiral William Fanshawe Martin, C. in C., Mediterranean in the screw steam ship *Marlborough*, 131 (7). From 24 May 1861 to 10 July 1862 Lieutenant (G) in screw steam ship *Edgar*, 89, Flagship, Channel Squadron.

Received the Royal Humane Society's bronze medal for bravery on 18 September 1861 after jumping overboard to assist in the rescue of two seamen who fell from the main rigging of *Edgar* at Queenstown (8).

From 28 February 1863 to 25 March 1863 in *Excellent*, Gunnery Ship, Portsmouth. Then followed further very short periods of service, first in *Marlborough* and next in the small paddle frigate *Magicienne*, 14 guns, 2,300 tons.

Commander: 10 June 1863. From 11 February 1864 Commander in his old ship *Princess Royal*, now 73 guns, 3,129 tons, Flagship East Indies and Cape of Good Hope, Rear Admiral George St. V. King (see C. in C., 1865). With her to China. Paid off at Devonport on 14 August 1867 (9).

From 1 April 1868 to 20 December 1869 Commander in *Royal Adelaide*, 2,446 tons. Flagship, Devonport, Admiral Sir William F. Martin, Bart., KCB.

Captain: 10 December 1869.

In 1870 he married Emily Mary, daughter of Henry Tritton of Beddington, Surrey and born on 20 July 1840. They were to have a family of one daughter and five sons, two of whom followed their father into the Navy. One Naval son, Henry Tritton Buller, born on 30 October 1873, was to be promoted Rear Admiral on 21 November 1921 and to command the Royal Yachts from April 1922 until 1931. KCVO in 1925 and GCVO in 1930. He was to be promoted Admiral on 1 April 1931 and to retire. His long life only was to end on 29 August 1960 (10). The other Naval son, Francis Alexander Waddilove born in 1879, was to retire from the Navy in 1922, on 27 May 1929 to be promoted Rear Admiral on the retired list, and to die on 14 July 1943.

Lady Emily Buller died on 6 April 1921.

From 11 December 1874 to 28 May 1878 in command screw corvette *Modeste*, 14 guns, 1,934 tons, China Station. He travelled East by mail steamer and joined her on 23 February 1875 (11).

Later that year he commanded the Naval Brigade during operations against the Malays in the Strait of Malacca: 29 November 1875 to 5 January 1876. This activity in Perak had become necessary following the murder on 2 November 1875 of Mr. James Wheeler Birch, the first British Resident (see Ryder, C. in C. 1874). Received the Perak medal and clasp.

CB: 25 March 1876.

He remained in *Modeste* when she re-commissioned at Hong Kong 11 May 1877, only leaving her from Japanese waters in March 1878, then to return home across the Pacific via America, finally to end that period of duty on 28 May 1878 (12).

From 19 December 1878 to 22 August 1880 in command screw iron ship *Agincourt*, 8,492 tons. She was the flagship, second in command, Channel Squadron.

From 23 August 1880 to 24 August 1883 in command *Cambridge*, Gunnery Ship, Devonport. Immediately following this service then until 28 September 1883, still at Devonport, he sat on a 'Committee on Torpedo Instruction'.

From 22 January 1884 to 27 March 1885 in command iron screw ship, armour plated, *Achilles*, 16 guns, 9,820 tons, Channel Squadron.

ADC to HM Queen Victoria: July 1884 to January 1887 (13).

From 28 March 1885 to 31 December 1886 in command *Pembroke*, Flagship, Admiral Superintendent, Chatham.

Rear Admiral: 1 January 1887.

There followed a brief period, between 13 July and 21 August 1888 when he filled the role of Umpire during manoeuvres, otherwise he remained on half pay at the rate of twenty five shillings a day until 9 January 1889 when his next appointment was announced. To take up this position in the Mediterranean he sailed from England on 31 January and arrived at Malta on 9 February.

Officially this new appointment as Admiral Superintendent, Malta Dockyard, had commenced on 10 January 1889 and only was to be concluded on 20 February 1892. His flag was flown in the old first rate *Hibernia*, now the receiving ship at that place (14).

Vice Admiral: 26 March 1892.

His half pay now rose to thirty two shillings and six pence a day.

Also during 1892 he served for some eight months on a committee to consider the design of propelling machinery and boilers in H.M. Ships.

Appointed C. in C., China: 21 March 1895, and he travelled East in the P. & O. *Ravenna*, 3,385 grt, a screw steamer built in 1880. In her he arrived on the station at Singapore on 11 May, and remaining in her, left the next day for Hong Kong.

On Friday, 19 May 1895 at Hong Kong:-

'1.15 p.m. Vice Admiral Buller hoisted flag onboard *Alacrity* (15).'

From Hong Kong on 20 May he sailed in *Alacrity*, Commander Francis G. De Lisle, and reached Nagasaki on 25 May. From Admiral Fremantle he assumed the command in China on 28 May 1895 (16). His flag was flown in *Centurion*, 10,500 tons, Captain Spencer Henry Metcalfe Login. Her Commander was George J.S. Warrender (17).

Following the conclusion of the recent Sino-Japanese war then rather naturally the authorities in England were anxious to learn more, specifically as regards the damage caused to sunken Chinese warships by the IJN torpedo attack at Wei-Hai-Wei. Following a visit to that place then writing from *Centurion* at Chefoo on 7 June 1895 the C. in C. included much data. Extracts follow:-

'The island of Liu-Kung-Tau (in the bay opposite the town of Wei-Hai-Wei which is situated on the mainland) remains in the possession of the Japanese under the direction of a Captain and 400 soldiers and sailors. The forts are dismantled and the work of removing guns, ammunition, electric light, and valuables to Japan by contract is nearly completed. The sunken Chinese ships, four in number, are not considered worth the expense of raising, and their guns have been removed. I was informed by the Japanese officers that the Government intended having some experiments against the armoured side of *Ting Yuen* (18).

In order to ascertain the full extent of the damage done to the hull of *Ting Yuen* and other ships which were sunk by torpedoes at Wei-Hai-Wei an examination was made by *Centurion*'s divers. (The diver in charge of this operation was Lieut. (T) R.K. Arbuthnot (19) who wrote):-

'... examined by diving the holes made by the torpedoes in *Ting Yuen*, *Lai Yuen*, *Wei Yuen* and an iron tug which were all sunk in February last during a night attack by Japanese Torpedo Boats. (-) The torpedoes used were 14 inch Schwartzkoff carrying a charge of about 120 lbs. of guncotton. (There follows very considerable detail, then his conclusion):-

'I beg to submit that the enormous size of the holes made in all ships that have been sunk by Whitehead torpedoes is worthy of the most serious consideration (20).'

In London having been introduced to the new Under Secretary of State for Foreign Affairs, and future Viceroy of India, George Nathaniel Curzon, on 29 June 1895 Sir Ernest Satow left England for New York. As the new Minister to Japan, from Vancouver he arrived at Yokohama in s.s. *Empress of China*, Captain Rupert Archibald, on 28 July 1895.

He was delighted to meet many old friends. One, Ito Hirobumi, again was prime minister but nearing the end of his second term in that office.

On 20 September 1895 the C. in C., Admiral Buller himself, came to Tokyo:-

'In comparing the characters of China and Japan, he and Satow agreed, "that China is hopeless in the matter of reform, that a Chinaman does not know what patriotism is, the government system is thoroughly rotten. Japanese per contra full of loyalty and fighting power, able to make war on a minimum of provisions (21)."

Not only on a minimum of provisions. In January 1896 Prime Minister Ito Hirobumi submitted to the Diet the largest military expansion budget in the history of Japan. With little or no dissent, on 4 February the lower house endorsed this plan. The total cost was 280 million yen of which the naval portion amounted to 200 million yen to be spent over the next ten years (22). To better understand this large figure, between 1873 and 1889 total naval expenditure had amounted to less than 91 million yen (23).

Eventually, with supplementary votes, between 1890 and 1905 naval expenditure was to total 469,985,000 yen, this total excluding the extraordinary war expenditures incurred during the 1894-1895 campaign against China and of 1904-1905 against Tsarist Russia (24).

In London during the Liberal administrations of William Gladstone and Lord Rosebery, between 1892 and 1895 the First Lord of the Admiralty had been John Poyntz, Fifth Earl Spencer (1835-1910), and whose father, Frederick, the Fourth Earl (1798-1857), had served as a Naval officer for several years (25). As will be appreciated John Poyntz is the Lord Spencer who had sided with his Admirals during the Navy scare during the time that Admiral Richards, as seen above, was First Sea Lord. In addition he had been First Lord at the time of the recent Sino-Japanese war.

On 24 March 1896 Lord Spencer arrived at Nagasaki from Hong Kong in the CPR liner, *Empress of Japan*, 5,940 grt, Captain Henry Pybus. Through Sir Ernest Satow, who had made many of the necessary arrangements with none other than Mr. Thomas B. Glover, it had been arranged that His Lordship, in an unofficial capacity, would inspect the IJN installations both at Sasebo and Kure, and later at Yokosuka. Naturally the C. in C. made appropriate dispositions and in readiness at Nagasaki was the small cruiser *Porpoise*, 1,770 tons, (26). Accompanied by Mr. Glover, in her Lord and Lady Spencer proceeded that same Tuesday to Sasebo, a very short distance to the north. There they remained for just an hour and forty five minutes before returning to Nagasaki that same day (27).

Subsequently he visited Kure in the Inland Sea.

Following His Lordship's visit to Japan then on 16 April Sir Ernest wrote to London. His letter ended on an amusing yet prophetic note:-

'Lord Spencer also (in addition to Sasebo and Kure) saw the dockyard at Yokosuka.

At none of these places were there any signs of getting ready for active operations … the peaceful attitude of Japan seems to indicate a settled determination not to oppose Russian action in Corea.'

'Yet Satow compared the Japanese to, "… a conjuror, who displays to his audience an empty box, and then shortly proceeds to draw from it an incredible quantity of articles that he had concealed in his sleeve all the while " (28).'

The twin screw gunvessel *Swift*, 756 tons, Commander Robert K. McAlpine, sailed from Hong Kong on 11 April 1896 for Yokohama en route to the Komandorski (Commander) Islands to carry out the Seal Fishery Patrol (29). The need for such a patrol had arisen following the purchase by the United States in 1867 of Russian territorial rights in Alaska and adjacent islands. Subsequently Congress enacted laws prohibiting the foreign slaughter of fur seals in certain of those waters. A dispute arose, largely as a result of poor phrasing of the law and no clear understanding of the precise territory and surrounding waters acquired by the United States from the Russians. British and Canadian interests were adversely effected. Finally agreeing to a process of arbitration, in Paris on 15 August 1893 a conclusive agreement was reached, the findings being in favour of Britain. At the same time happily regulations were established for the preservation of these animals. Naturally these regulations required enforcement.

KCB: 24 May 1896, the Birthday Honours List.

Writing to the Admiralty from Kure on 11 June 1896 he made mention both of Port Hamilton, and of the use by the RN of Japanese drydocking facilities, '*Immortalite* left Nagasaki on 6 June for Port Hamilton to carry out prize firing, and returns to Nagasaki to be docked'. It is clear from other correspondence that use was made of the anchorage at Port Hamilton whensoever the C. in C. saw fit. Later in the same General Letter he mentioned a somewhat unusual duty:-

'*Humber* is at Hong Kong and is to arrive at Yokohama on 1 July to be in readiness to convey to Kushiro the first detachment of the Astronomer Royal's party to observe the total eclipse of the sun on 8 August (30).'

A month later, 11 July 1896, he described two aspects of a recent visit paid to the IJN naval base at Sasebo:-

'The Japanese are anxious to keep foreigners in the dark respecting their works at this place as well

as Kure, but by special request the Government gave *Alacrity* permission to visit this place.
… it is astonishing to see the energetic and systematic manner in which they are building up their
arsenals and dockyards without one European to assist them (31).'

There was at least one other useful result of this visit to Kure. As has been seen relations between the RN
and IJN were good however naturally on such occasions visitors were encouraged to keep their eyes open. In
this instance, and following a visit to the Torpedo Store at Kure, the British were to record:-

'… that the Store covered both mines and Whitehead Torpedoes. The Whitehead store contained
about 150 torpedoes, nearly all Schwartskoff, and apparently in excellent order. Everything was
scrupulously clean in these stores, not a speck of dust anywhere (32).'

Accompanying the report was a layout map of the base, drawn from memory and with all the facilities
detailed as best possible. One may be sure that whenever the circumstances were reversed then members of the
IJN reciprocated these observant honours.

The first class cruiser *Grafton*, 7,350 tons, Captain Edward P. Jones, and flying the flag of his Second in
Command, Rear Admiral Charles L. Oxley, arrived at Vladivostok on 15 September 1896, there to come up with
an officer who was to feature greatly in future Anglo-German relations:-

'I found in the harbour the German men of war *Kaiser* (Flag of Rear Admiral Alfred Tirpitz) and
Irene (33).'

In 1896 the summer cruise of the China Squadron drew to an end when he wrote to London on 3 October from
Port Lazareff in Yonghung Bay just north of Gensan or present day Wonsan. Commencing with their departure
from Yokohama on 6 June, then through the Inland Sea and Strait of Shimonoseki, he had ordered many exercises,
tactics, sending away of landing parties, gunnery drills and so on, in the meantime the ships of the squadron
calling at many ports along the south and east coasts of Korea, the Sea of Japan, even north into the Gulf of Tartary.

10 October 1896. In London Dr. Sun Yat-sen was kidnapped and held prisoner in the Chinese Legation. By that
time Dr. James Cantlie, who had completed his tour of duty in Hong Kong earlier in the year, was back in London
and Dr. Sun was able to smuggle a message to him. The effect of the resulting furore reached the highest level, Lord
Salisbury himself requesting the Chinese Minister to release the prisoner. As was reported on 24 October:-

'Sun Yat Sen, the Chinaman who had been under detention at the Chinese Legation in Portland
Place, was set at liberty yesterday afternoon in accordance with the demands of the British
government (34).'

In the Spanish possession of the Philippine Islands in 1896, and on into 1897, insurgent activity had
caused the Spanish authorities many problems. The British C. in C. made available the services of, amongst
other warships, the sloops *Phoenix*, 1,050 tons, Commander Reginald P. Cochran, and *Daphne*, 1,140 tons,
Commander Arthur A.C. Galloway, in support of British subjects then living in the vicinity of Manila.

In his reports to the Admiralty, and concerning an apparent lack of Spanish resolve, from time to time he
was to comment much as indicated in the following two examples:-

'November 1896: Troops are arriving from Spain, raw and undisciplined recruits, and no decisive
action is expected.'
December 1896: Affairs at Manila are unchanged, and the Royal troops do not seem to make
much progress (35).'

To give a small insight into secretarial progress within the Navy, it was from December 1896 that General
Letters written from the East by various of the Commanders in Chief began to be prepared in typewritten form.
Prior to this all correspondence had been submitted in long hand.

Later into 1897, as far as the British could tell, in their efforts to restore law and order in the Philippines the Spanish continued to perform poorly. Here follows an extract dated 24 March 1897 taken from another report to the Admiralty:-

'The news from Manila is not reassuring. The royal troops had captured some important outposts belonging to the rebels, and on 3 March were within three miles of Imus, the principal stronghold. An attack was to have been made on Imus but General Polivieja has now changed his plans, withdrawn the troops, and the advantage gained during the last six weeks has now been lost. The rebels have been re-armed with Mauser rifles and ammunition; over 10,000 are reported to have been imported, but it is impossible to get the correct number. The Germans have the credit of shipping the rifles and ammunition from Shanghai in junks and landing them on the coast of the Philippine Islands. The rains will shortly set in and the floods will stop all operations. The royal troops are badly clothed, poorly fed, and there is much sickness amongst them (36).'

The withdrawal referred to above must have been purely tactical as by April the Spanish military at last had achieved the upper hand. On 7 April 1897 the Admiralty were advised:-

'The royal troops have captured Imus, Rosario, Noveleta, Binayacun and Cavite. The insurgents are coming in under the amnesty granting a free pardon, and the rebellion may be considered drawing to a close. The military object has been successfully attained but there still remains work for the Civil guards in the country and suburbs (37).'

Until reasonably satisfied that the relatively peaceful state of affairs in Manila in fact would continue, *Phoenix* remained in those waters for several more weeks, only leaving on 20 May to proceed to Hong Kong.

Early in November 1897, being one result of machinations by the Russian Consul General to Seoul, the Commissioner of Korean Customs and protégé of Sir Robert Hart, John McLeavy Brown, an Ulsterman, was removed from his post (38).

Also during the latter part of 1897 in Korea, the Russians made clear their desire to secure a coaling station on Deer Island off Pusan. To add weight to their demands, early in December a Russian squadron of nine warships anchored off Chemulpo (Inchon). When the news was received in London prompt and firm decisions were taken with Sir Alexander being ordered to take appropriate action. On 29 December he arrived off Chemulpo with a squadron of eight ships. This, and other similar moves, proved to be effective. Korean resolve was strengthened and not only was the demand for the coaling station resisted but some sixty Russian advisers to the Korean government were dismissed. In addition the mischievous Tsarist Consul General to Korea was transferred to Brazil.

As mentioned above, at the time the British Prime Minister was Lord Salisbury.

Admiral: 11 December 1897.

Port Hamilton continued to be of use to warships of the Royal Navy. Here follows an extract from the letter of 3 January 1898 written by the C. in C. to the Admiralty:-

'... arriving at Port Hamilton on 25 December 1897 where I found in port (six of H.M. Ships including the twin screw first class armoured cruiser *Immortalite*, 5,600 tons, Captain Edward Chichester) (39).'

At Singapore at the time the Senior Naval Officer was Lieut. and Commander Ion P. Barton in the torpedo boat destroyer *Whiting*, 360 tons. He noted that on 30 January 1898 *Orlando*, flying the flag of Rear Admiral Cyprian A.G. Bridge, arrived from Batavia. The Admiral had just relinquished his post as C. in C., Australia and was proceeding home. After a long stay at Singapore *Orlando* only was to continue her voyage on 8 March 1898. As will be seen shortly, in 1901 Admiral Bridge was to be appointed C. in C., China.

Also on 30 January the new C. in C., Admiral Seymour, arrived at Singapore on passage through to Hong Kong in the P. & O. mail steamer *Coromandel*, 4,652 grt.

Arriving at Hong Kong on 4 February, the next day Admiral Seymour hoisted his flag in *Alacrity* and on 8

February sailed for the north. At Tinghai, Chusan Archipelago, on 13 February he hoisted his flag in *Centurion* while Admiral Buller hoisted his in *Alacrity* for passage back to Hong Kong there to join the mail steamer for passage home.

At Hong Kong officialy relieved by Admiral Seymour on 19 February 1898, '6.0 p.m. Flag of Adm. Sir A. Buller, KCB struck onboard *Alacrity* on his being superseded in command of the China Station (40).'

It was on that day, 19 February 1898, that Admiral Buller and his staff finally sailed from Hong Kong bound for England in the P. & O. mail steamer *Ganges*, 4,196 grt (41).

As a reminder of the size of the Fleet on the China Station during that era here follows the Disposition list of the Squadron of twenty eight men-of-war as it existed on 1 January 1898:

'Chemulpo:	*Centurion* (Flag)	Port Arthur:	*Immortalite*
	Pique		*Iphigenia*
	Undaunted	Tongku:	*Rattler*
	Narcissus	Nagasaki:	*Redpole*
	Rainbow	Hankow:	*Pigmy*
	Algerine	Ichang:	*Esk*
	Phoenix	Hong Kong:	*Grafton*
	Daphne		*Tamar*
North Borneo:	*Plover*		*Archer*
Singapore:	*Powerful*		*Linnet*
	Fame		*Peacock*
	Whiting		*Humber*
Bound for Hong Kong:	*Edgar*		*Hart*
			Handy and
			Alacrity
			(42)'

Following his return to England on 22 March then from 23 March 1898 he went on to an Admiral's half pay of forty two shillings a day.

Retired: 30 June 1899, his retirement pay being GBP 950.00 p.a. (43).

An uncle, Charles Reginald Buller who had spent many years in Kandy, Celyon, and who had died on 22 April 1879 aged seventy two years, had left him Erle Hall at Plympton, Devon. Between 1899 and 1900 Sir Alexander was to have the building extended.

In retirement he took a keen interest in local affairs, for many years being a JP, and was especially involved in educational affairs, for example being a governor of Plympton Grammar School and a foundation manager of Plympton St. Maurice National School. Earlier, in 1894, he had presented the Grammar School with a bell. Also he was a vice president of the Plympton Agricultural Association.

GCB: 26 June 1902.

The following charming entry appears in a local history:-

'Admiral Sir Alexander Buller, GCB, who died 3 October 1903, gave by his will GBP 50.00 free of legacy duty to the poor of the parish of Plympton St. Maurice.

This has been invested by the Charity commissioners, and the income is devoted to the purchase of blankets and serge for distribution among the poor (44).'

On 5 October 1903 in London *The Times* reported that, 'it is believed that heart failure was the cause of death'. Two days later, on Wednesday, 7 October, a further news item stated that the following telegram has been received at the Admiralty from His Majesty:-

'The King greatly regrets to hear of the sad death of that distinguished officer the late Admiral Sir Alexander Buller (45).

He was buried at Plympton St. Maurice Church on Saturday, 10 October 1903, the service commencing at 3 o'clock and with his coffin being borne to the graveside by workmen on his estate (46). Around the coffin:-

'... was wrapped the late Admiral's silk flag which was presented in 1898 by the wardroom officers of the *Centurion*, his flagship on the China Station (47).'

Amongst the great many mourners who attended his funeral was his successor on the China Station, Admiral Sir Edward Seymour, now C. in C. at Devonport.

He had been a wealthy man, the gross value of his estate amounting to GBP 158,541-8-0.

In 1926 the family home, Erle Hall, was to be acquired by the Sisters of Charity and by them be known as St. Elizabeth's. Today (the year 2010) it is an hotel. One suite in this hotel remains known as the Alexander Buller Room.

Sir Alexander's grave, together with that of Lady Buller, at Plympton St. Maurice Parish Church is to be found at the rear of the churchyard off to the left hand corner (48). Just behind the churchyard is a knoll or hillock, tree covered and dominated by the ruined remains of a small Norman fortification.

NOTES

1. Some documentation indicates that Alexander was born on 30 January 1834. On his gravestone and on his baptismal certificate the correct date is confirmed as being 30 June 1834. County of Cornwall, Baptismal Records. Lanreath in 1834, page 50, entry No. 397.

   John Hornby had been born in Bombay on 5 July 1764 as his father, William Hornby (1723-1803) had entered the East India Company in 1740 and finally attained rather high office serving as Governor of Bombay from 26 February 1771 to 1 January 1784. On his retirement to England then between 1786 and 1790 William built Hook House. John Hornby himself, Harrow and St. John's Cambridge, and who in Bath on 13 January 1794 married Jane Wynne, died in London on 7 May 1832 and was buried at Titchfield on 16 May.

   Elizabeth Buller, nee Hornby, was born at Hook House on 26 September 1802 and died on 25 May 1875.

   The Revd. Richard Buller was to die at Pounds House, Plymouth on 19 June 1883, aged seventy eight years.

2. Obituary, *The Times*, October 5, 1903. Also from *Transactions of the Devonshire Association*, 1904.

3. NA ADM 196/13. 461 and 529. *Service Record*.

4. David Lyon and Rif Winfield, *The Sail and Steam Navy List*, (London, 2004), 183.

5. Obituary, *The Times*. Also *Transactions of the Devonshire Association*.

6. *Naval and Military Record*, 28 May 1896.

7. William Fanshawe **Martin**. Born: 5 December 1801. Died in Winchfield: 24 March 1895. Entered the Navy: 15 June 1813. Lieutenant: 15 December 1820. Commander: 8 February 1823. Captain: 5 June 1824. Rear Admiral: 28 May 1853. Superintendent of Portsmouth Dockyard: 1853-1857. Vice Admiral: 13 February 1858. Lord Commissioner of the Admiralty: 8 March 1858 – 28 June 1859. C. in C., Mediterranean: 19 April 1860 – 20 April 1863. KCB: 28 June 1861. Admiral: 14 November 1863. C. in C., Devonport 26 October 1866 – 1 November 1869. Retired: 1 April 1870. GCB: 24 May 1873. Of him Admiral Sir Cyprian Bridge (see C. in C., 1901) in *Some Recollections*, (London, 1918), 195, was to write:-

   '... the greatest flag officer of the 19th century after the close of the Napoleonic War. The Navy of the present day is to a great extent the offspring of the reforms which he introduced into its organisation, its interior economy, and its method of discipline.'

8. Obituary, *Naval and Military Record*, 8 October 1903. Also, *Transactions of the Devonshire Association*, 1904.

9. *Service Record*.

10. *Who's Who*, 1903 and 1960. As a Captain when commanding the battleship *Malaya*, 27,500 tons, in January and February 1921 Henry Tritton Buller had the honour of taking her to a selection of ports in Malaya as a form of post Great War 'thank you' to the the Sultans and citizens of the Federated Malay States for their gift of the ship to the Royal

Navy. NA ADM 53/80249 and Imperial War Museum Ref. Buller 66/19/1.

11. *Service Record.*

12. Ibid. To return home he left the East on 6 April 1878, his last position of that tour of duty being as SNO Japan. NA ADM 1/6450. Letter No. 149, dated 20 March 1878.

13. Obituary, *Naval and Military Record.*

14. *Service Record.*

15. NA ADM 50/378.

16. NA ADM 1/7248. Letter to the Admiralty dated 7 June 1895. Written from *Centurion* at Chefoo.

17. George John Scott **Warrender**, Seventh Baronet. Born in Edinburgh: 31 July 1860. Died in London: 8 January 1917. Captain: 13 May 1899. Rear Admiral: 2 July 1908. Commanded 2CS, Home Fleet: 1910-1912. KCVO: 1911. Vice Admiral: 4 June 1913. KCB: 1913. At the outbreak of the Great War he was VA 2BS with his flag in *King George V,* 23,000 tons. C. in C., Plymouth: 20 March 1916. *Navy List. Who's Who.*

18. *Ting Yuen,* 7,144 tons. Steel battleship built at Stettin, Germany. Launched: 28 December 1881. Main armament of four 12". 14.5 knots. Richard N.J. Wright, *The Chinese Steam Navy: 1862-1945,* (London, 2000), 50.

19. Robert Keith Arbuthnot, Baronet. Commander: 1 January 1897. Captain: 26 June 1902. Rear Admiral: 13 July 1912. From 29 October 1913 to fly his flag as R/A 2BS in the battleship *Orion,* 22,500 tons, Captain Frederic C. Dreyer. To be killed in action at the Battle of Jutland, 31 May 1916 when his 1CS flagship, the armoured cruiser *Defence,* 14,600 tons, Captain Stanley V. Ellis, was taken under heavy enemy fire. There were to be no survivors. *Navy List.*

20. NA ADM 1/7249. By specifying Whitehead torpedoes Lieut. Arbuthnot stresses that the damage was not caused by static mines. In London the relevant file, 13/4090, was received at the Admiralty on 22 July 1895. Clearly Their Lordships were grateful as the following annotation in due course was to be affixed thereon:-

    'I am to acquaint you that they consider this report of the diving operation to be very interesting, (-) and I am to desire that you will convey to this officer the expression of their Lordships appreciation of his proceedings of report.'

21. Ian C. Ruxton, *The Diaries and Letters of Sir Ernest Mason Satow (1843-1929),* (Lewiston, NY, 1998), 200 and 211. At the time China was administered by the Manchu Ch'ing dynasty, this dynasty being decadent and shortly to end its period of rule which had commenced in 1644. Japan had just defeated China in the war of 1894-1895.

22. J. Charles Schencking, *Making Waves,* (Stanford, 2005), 87/8.

23. Ibid., 47.

24. Ibid., 104.

25. Another Spencer family connection with the Royal Navy was George John Spencer, Second Earl (1758-1834), father of Frederick, Fourth Earl, and grandfather of John Poyntz, Fifth Earl. George John was First Lord of the Admiralty between 1794 and 1801 so it was that John Poyntz was, to a degree, following in family footsteps.

26. Brian Burke-Gaffney, *Nagasaki: The British Experience, 1854-1945,* (Folkestone, Kent, 2009), 138/9.

27. NA ADM 53/15135. Log book, *Porpoise.*

28. Ian C. Ruxton, 226/7.

29. NA ADM 1/7291.

30. 30) Ibid. Kushiro is situated SW of the Easternmost point of Hokkaido. Screw Storeship *Humber,* 1,640 tons, Commander Frank W. Wyley. *Navy List.*

31. Ibid. Written in *Centurion* at Hakodate.

32. NA ADM 1/7261. Letter from Captain Spencer H. Login to the C. in C., written in *Centurion* at Port Hamilton on 27 June 1896. As mentioned above, the reference to Whitehead torpedoes indicates self propelled torpedoes in the modern sense rather than static mines.

33. NA ADM 1/7291. Alfred Peter Friedrich **Tirpitz**. Born: 19 March 1849. Died: 6 March 1930. Entered the Prussian Navy in 1865. Commissioned in 1869. As a Captain in 1892 became Chief of Naval Staff. Rear Admiral: 1895. In command Asian Squadron: 1896-1897. Secretary of State, Imperial Naval Office: 1897-1916. Created a noble, hence 'von': 1900. With the enthusiastic support of Kaiser Wilhelm II, and numerous Fleet Acts, greatly enlarged and improved the quality of the German Navy. Admiral: 1903. Grand Admiral: 1911. After WW1 broke out gradually he was to fall out of Imperial favour. Resigned: 15 March 1916. *Encyclopaedia Britannica.*

SMS *Kaiser*, armoured frigate, 7,320 tons, first commissioned in 1875.

SMS *Irene,* third class cruiser, 4,224 tons, completed in 1888. T.A. Brassey, *The Naval Annual,* (Portsmouth, 1905), 277.

34. *The Times,* Saturday, October 24, 1896, 6. An extensive report is carried.

Dr. James **Cantlie**. Born in Banffshire: 17 January 1851. Died: 28 May 1926 and was buried at Cottered, Herts. Aberdeen University and Charing Cross Hospital, London. Proceeded to China in 1887, and between 1889 and 1896 was Dean of College of Medicine for Chinese, Hong Kong. In London he ensured government interest in this business. In 1907 founder of the Royal Society of Tropical Medicine and Hygiene. During the Great War active with ambulance services. KBE: 1918. *Who's Who.* The late Admiral Sir Colin Cantlie (1888-1967) was one of his sons.

35. NA ADM 1/7291.

36. NA ADM 1/7332A. Letter No. 139 written in *Alacrity* at Hong Kong.

The Spanish monarch who reigned from 1886 to 1931 was Alfonso XIII (1886-1941). He was only to rule after he came of age in 1902.

Camilo Garcia de Polavieja y del Castillo (1838-1914), Governor General of the Philippines from 13 December 1896 to 15 April 1897 when he returned to Spain.

37. Ibid. Letter No. 157.

38. John McLeavy **Brown**. Born: 27 November 1835. Died: 6 April 1926. Queens' College, Belfast and Trinity College, Dublin. Appointed Student Interpreter in China: 26 July 1861. Acting Chinese Secretary at Peking: 1 January 1871 to May 1872 when he resigned from the Consular Service to join the Chinese Maritime Customs under Sir Robert Hart. By 1874 Deputy Commissioner of Customs at Canton. Subsequently Chief Commissioner of the Corean Customs and Financial Adviser to the Corean government. Knighted: 30 June 1906. From December 1913 Councillor of the Chinese Legation, London. *Who's Who,* 1926. *Foreign Office List,* 1920.

39. NA ADM 1/7371. Letter No. 9 written in *Centurion* at Chemulpo.

40. NA ADM 50/378.

41. NA ADM 1/7371.

42. NA ADM 50/378.

43. *Service Record.*

44. The quote kindly was passed to the author by Local and Naval Studies, Central Library, Plymouth. Taken from J. Brooking Rowe, *A History of the Borough of Plympton Erle.*

45. *The Times,* Wednesday, October 7, 1903. Apart from other connections, a friend of H.M. The King, dating back to the years during which he had been Prince of Wales, was Mr. Richard Cory of William Cory and Son, and of Langdon Court at Wembury, South Devon. On a number of occasions HRH had been pleased to accept invitations from Richard Cory to Langdon Court. Sir Alexander often had been included in such shooting parties. *Plymouth and West Devon Record Office*: references 1132/12-14.

46. *The Times,* Monday, October 12, 1903.

47. *Naval and Military Record,* 15 October 1903.

48. Visited by the author on 13 May 2011, and there made most welcome by churchwarden, Geoff Easterbrook and historian Sally Luscombe. From inscriptions on the gravestone it may be noted that Sir Alexander and Lady Buller's son, Richard Edward, was born on 14 January 1874 and sadly died just three months before his mother, on 6 January 1921. Their youngest son, Edward Maxwell Buller, died on 27 August 1931.

Seperately it is recorded that another son, Herbert Cecil Buller, born in 1882, as a Lieut. Colonel was to die during the Great War, on 2 June 1916. Although of the Rifle Brigade, at the time he was attached to the Princess Patricia's Canadian Light Infantry and during the Battle of Mount Sorrel fell while directing the defence of Sanctuary Wood. This is just south of Hooge, two miles to the east of Ypres, Belgium.

12 December 1897 to 10 April 1901
Vice Admiral Sir Edward Hobart **Seymour**

He was born at Kinwarton, Warwickshire on 30 April 1840, the second son of Rev. Richard Seymour, Rector of Kinwarton and Canon of Worcester Cathedral, by his wife Frances Smith. Young Edward was a grandson of Rear Admiral Sir Michael Seymour (1768-1834), first baronet, and nephew of Admiral Sir Michael Seymour (1802-1887). Thus it is not surprising to read:-

'As soon as I had sense enough to form a real wish, it was to go to sea.'

He died at his home, Hedsor View, Maidenhead Court at Maidenhead, on Saturday, 2 March 1929. He was unmarried (1).

Educated at Radley, and later for two months at Eastman's Naval Academy, Southsea. Then he entered the Royal Navy on 11 November 1852 as a **Cadet** in the screw corvette *Encounter*, 14 guns. In her he remained until 8 July 1853 (2). On 9 July 1853 at Woolwich joined paddle wheel frigate *Terrible*, 1,847 tons. In the presence of HM Queen Victoria, on 11 August 1853 he participated in her Review of her Navy at Spithead. In October 1853 his ship was ordered to the Mediterranean. Following the outbreak of the Crimean War, on 22 April 1854 present in *Terrible*, Captain James Johnstone McCleverty, during the bombardment of Odessa. Similarly before Sevastopol on 17 October 1854. **Midshipman**: 11 November 1854. Paid off at Sheerness on 2 August 1856. Immediately appointed to *Calcutta* so in September 1856 at Portsmouth joined sloop *Cruiser*, 1,045 tons, Commander Charles Fellowes, for passage to China. Her speed of passage was hindered by virtue of her escort of three gunboats being repositioned to the China Station. Of the three, *Haughty* was commanded by Lieutenant Richard Vesey Hamilton (see C. in C., 1885). The other two of these diminutive men of war were *Forester* and *Staunch*. Finally *Cruiser* arrived at Hong Kong on 29 April 1857. Joined *Calcutta*, 84 guns: 30 April 1857, flagship of the C. in C., his uncle, Rear Admiral Sir Michael Seymour. Following the *Arrow* affair, 8 October 1856, he participated in the battle of Fatshan Creek: 1 June 1857. In December 1857 took part in the assault and occupation of Canton. The British and French subsequently took the conflict North. On 20 May 1858 participated in the forcing of the Taku forts at the Peiho, he being in command of a pinnace during that affair. Owing to sunstroke, from China on 10 July 1858 invalided home in the frigate *Pique*, 40. Paid off on 16 February 1859 (3). From 21 March 1859 in screw steam frigate *Mersey*, 40, Channel Squadron. **Mate**: 4 May 1859. From 8 October 1859 in screw steam frigate *Imperieuse*, 51, Flagship of the second in command, East Indies and China, Rear Admiral Lewis Tobias Jones. As just one example of the lengthy passages regarded as being quite normal in that era, between the Cape Verde Islands and Java Head they were out of sight of land for some seventy days (4). Then:-

'In Rhio Straits (south of Singapore island), on the way out, he went overboard to rescue a seaman in waters infested with sharks, and for this exploit he received the silver medal of the Royal Humane Society (5).'

Lieutenant: 11 February 1860. From 26 March 1860 in screw steam frigate *Chesapeake,* 51, East Indies and China. She was commanded by Captain George O. Willes (see C. in C., 1881). Although not to participate in the actual action, in her he was present during the capture of the Taku forts during the allied engagement with the Chinese in July/August 1860. The C. in C., Rear Admiral James Hope, subsequently was to receive his knighthood, KCB: 9 November 1860.

Early in 1861 Admiral Hope resolved to proceed up the Yangtse to Hankow, and possibly beyond. In due course in the paddlewheel steam vessel *Coromandel,* of only 150 h.p., Lieut. Edwin John Pollard, at 6 p.m. on 15 March 1861 he was to reach Yochow at the junction of the River and Tung Ting Lake, some 150 sea miles above Hankow thus a most successful venture. To assist in surveying the channel the gunboat *Bouncer,* 232 tons, Commander John Ward, was in company (6). The C. in C. had departed from Shanghai on 12 February 1861. Lieut. Seymour, temporarily appointed executive officer of *Cowper,* a merchant vessel taken up for service, was fortunate enough to be able to accompany this expedition upstream but only as far as Poyang Lake, a short distance below Kiukiang (7). This town, in due course to become an important tea trading centre for Western interests, is situated on the right bank some 251 nautical miles above Nanking and 143 nautical miles below Hankow/Wuhan. In due course Lieut. Seymour was to recall that as *Cowper* had accommodation available the Admiral decided that, 'we should take up several merchants representing the British firms at Shanghai, who were of course most anxious to go (8).'

From 11 June 1861 borne in *Princess Charlotte,* Receiving Ship, Hong Kong, 'For Service in *Waterman,* Tender'. He joined her at Shanghai and took her down to Hong Kong. Then followed a period of rather unusual service in the paddlewheel sloop *Sphinx,* 6, acting Commander Ralph A.O. Brown, ordered to the Caroline Islands to search for the crew of the wrecked barque *Norna,* 460 tons, Captain J. Ray. While on passage from Australia to Hong Kong with coal she had had the misfortune to ground on St. Augustine reef near Ponape. Fortunately, and having been away for four and a half months, the Naval party was able to rescue the few survivors. On their return to Hong Kong, '... we heard of the beginning of the great Civil War in America (9).'

From 25 October 1861 in screw frigate *Imperieuse,* 2,358 tons. In the vicinity of Shanghai the Taiping rebels were active. Later, in October 1862, he participated in the successful expedition to retake Kahding, close to Shanghai, from these Taiping rebels (see Kuper, C. in C., 1862). On 29 October 1862 Admiral Hope was succeeded in command of the station by Admiral Kuper. In November from Hong Kong *Imperieuse* was 'Ordered Home' and after a voyage of nearly four months via The Cape, arrived at Portsmouth and paid off early in March 1863.

From 9 March 1863 he was appointed Flag Lieutenant to his uncle, Vice Admiral Sir Michael Seymour, C. in C., Portsmouth, alternately in *Victory* and *Duke of Wellington.*

Commander: 5 March 1866. On 19 March 1867 he left Peterhead in the whaler *Mazinthien,* 397 grt, on something of a busman's holiday in Arctic waters. His intention was gain experience of the ice as he proposed to volunteer for a projected Arctic expedition (10). On his return he was to venture the opinion, and it is sad to read that this was as early as in 1867:-

'... and it seems possible that the right whale will become extinct before very long (11).'

From 11 January 1868 in the Coast Guard service at Queenstown (Cork). 'This was at a time when Coast Guard officers had an allowance to keep two horses so that they might rush off to any part of their coast in case of emergency'.

From 25 June 1869 in command of the new gunvessel *Growler,* 464 tons, Cape of Good Hope and West Coast of Africa. Early the following year he was to see some action:-

'On January 28, 1870, when the twin screw gun vessel, *Growler,* 4, Commander Edward Hobart Seymour, was lying in the mouth of the Congo, she was boarded by some men belonging to the British schooner *Loango,* who reported that their vessel had been attacked by pirates on the previous afternoon. The *Growler* weighed at once, and steamed up to the scene of the outrage (12).'

Prompt action was taken against the village and people of a local chief, the suspect. Looted goods were recovered, and gunpowder blown up, also two hostages were recovered successfully. However amongst the wounded were Seymour himself, seriously in the right leg, in consequence of which some weeks later he was invalided home, taking passage from Ascension Island to Southampton in the Cape mail steamer *Roman*, 1,282 grt of the Union Line. At the time the Commodore, West Africa was William M. Dowell (see C. in C., 1884).

As is recorded:-

> 'The wound was severe and he was invalided: consequently, when he applied in 1875 for the command of the *Discovery* in the Polar expedition under (Sir) George Nares, he was rejected on medical grounds.
>
> An enforced leisure of 18 months on half pay was used by Seymour to improve his French by visiting France and Switzerland (13).'

From 15 May 1872 in command paddle despatch vessel *Lively*, 2 guns, 940 tons, Channel Squadron.

Captain: 13 February 1873. Attended the Royal Naval College at Greenwich, 'and then travelled in France and Italy.'

From 11 January 1876 to early 1879 in command iron screw troop ship *Orontes*, 5,600 tons. On his first voyage he conveyed the new Viceroy, Lord Lytton (1831-1891), his wife and party to Bombay where he arrived on 7 April 1876. Other trooping voyages were made to South Africa, to Cyprus on the occasion of the British occupation in July 1878, to Canada, and to the West Indies.

The occupation of Cyprus followed the secret agreement, the Cyprus Convention of 4 June 1878, between Great Britain and the Ottoman Empire. The first British High Commissioner in Nicosia was a well known Army officer, Lieut. General Sir Garnet Joseph Wolseley (1833-1913).

From 27 April 1880 in command despatch vessel *Iris*, 10 guns, 3,735 tons, the first all-steel cruiser in the R.N., Mediterranean Station. Although not to participate in the bombardment of Alexandria, 11 July 1882, he was to be involved in subsequent operations in Egypt:-

> 'At Port Said no difficulties were experienced. At 3.30 a.m. on that day (20 August 1882) a party of 216 seamen and 276 Marines with two Gatling machine guns, landed in silence under Captains Fairfax (*Monarch*) and Edward Hobart Seymour (*Iris*). The Egyptian troops in the barracks were surrounded, and seamen were posted right across the isthmus, from Lake Menzaleh to the sea. The troops surrendered immediately.
>
> Captain Seymour then seized the (Suez) Canal Company's offices, so as to prevent the alarm from being transmitted thence to other stations (14).'

About this time he relates in his memoirs that at Port Said he, '... was employed with Captain Gill, Royal Engineers, to find out things connected with the canal (15).' On 11 August 1882 out in the Sinai desert, Gill and his two companions were to perish at the hands of the Arabs.

This is William John Gill, the author of an important work, *The River of Golden Sand, A Journey Through China and Eastern Tibet to Burmah*, published posthumously in London in 1883. This journey up the Yangtse and through China had commenced at Shanghai on 23 January 1877.

From 9 November 1882 in command of the twin screw iron turret ship, armour plated, *Inflexible*, 11,880 tons, Mediterranean. She had distinguished herself during the bombardment of Alexandria, and during the subsequent landing of parties to attend to matters ashore. Her Captain, John A. Fisher, then had become extremely ill and on 9 November 1882 left to return to England.

At the end of the commission *Inflexible* paid off at Portsmouth in February 1885.

When war threatened with Russia, one of the consequences of the Panjdeh Incident, from 27 May 1885 until the end of the summer he was in command of the iron single screw armed merchant cruiser, and Cunard liner, *Oregon*, 10, Channel and Combined Squadron.

From 30 May 1886 Flag Captain to Admiral Sir George O. Willes (see C.in C., 1881) in *Duke of Wellington*, 6,071 tons, Flagship, Portsmouth.

From 1 January 1887 Naval ADC to H.M. Queen Victoria.

CB: 21 June 1887.

While continuing as Flag Captain in *Duke of Wellington* he commissioned *Inflexible* for Queen Victoria's Jubilee Review, she being the Flagship of Sir George Willes during that splendid occasion on 23 July 1887.

From 20 December 1887 borne in *President*, West India Docks, 'For Service with Naval Reserves', which was as assistant to the Admiral Superintendent of these Reserves (16).

Rear Admiral: 14 July 1889.

> 'A long period of half pay was then employed in again visiting foreign countries: he travelled in France, Russia, the West Indies, and United States (17).'

From 21 July 1892 Flag in *Swiftsure*, 6,910 tons, as Second in Command, summer manoeuvres.

Second in Command, Channel Squadron: 16 September 1892 – 24 April 1894 with Flag at first in the battleship *Anson*, 10,600 tons, Captain George T.H. Boyes, then from the date of her first commissioning, 4 September 1893, in *Empress of India*, 14,150 tons.

At Ferrol on 2 November 1892 *Howe*, Captain Alexander P. Hastings, CB, sister ship to *Anson*, grounded. He was appointed to supervise her salvage which was carried out by the Neptune Salvage Co. of Stockholm, *Howe* finally being re-floated on 30 March 1893.

Writing of his appointment in *Empress of India*, one naval officer makes reference to Rear Admiral Seymour, '… who was surely one of the Great Gentlemen of the Navy'. The same author continues with a lovely description of the First Lieutenant in the ship:-

> '… Robert Bourchier Wrey was a famous magnifico. His nickname indeed was "the Duke of North Devon", and he was a law unto himself in matters of uniform as in everything else. He wore a stiff cap with an almost straight up-and-down peak like a guardsman and tight trousers strapped under his boots. In the Ward Room he took complete charge of everything. He scrapped all the ugly admiralty crockery and replaced it at his own expense by a more elegant dinner service of his own design.
> Old brandy and port wine of his own choosing were kept for his special use, and so it was with cigars and cigarettes. (--) After dinner Wrey retired to his cabin and changed his mess jacket for a magnificent smoking jacket of crimson silk brocade (18).'

From 25 April 1894 – May 1897 Superintendent of Naval Reserves with Flag in battleship *Alexandra*, 9,490 tons, Portland.

Vice Admiral: 9 November 1895.

Continued in *Alexandra*.

KCB: 22 June 1897.

To assume command on the China station he and his future Flag Captain, John Rushworth Jellicoe, left England at the end of 1897 and in the P. & O. mail steamer *Coromandel*, 4,359 grt, duly arrived at Hong Kong (19). There on 5 February 1898 he hoisted his flag in the twin screw despatch vessel *Alacrity*, 1,700 tons, Commander Arthur H. Smith-Dorrien, and proceeded to Chusan Island, there relieving Admiral Sir Alexander Buller on 19 February 1898 (20). Flag in the small battleship *Centurion*, 10,500 tons.

In Japan from 1898 to January 1906 the Navy Minister was Vice Admiral Yamamoto Gonnohyoe (1852-1933), born in Kagoshima but distinguished by his reluctance to promote only Satsuma interests. Rather, while having favourites, he promoted those officers whose ability would be of overall benefit to the Navy (see C. in C., 1910 and 1933). In addition his tact and understanding of the parliamentary process was to result in the

Diet making funds available for the expansion of the Imperial Japanese Navy (21). Both China and Russia were perceived as likely future opponents.

Also in Japan, between November 1898 and October 1900 the Prime Minister was Choshu born Field Marshal Yamagata Arimoto (22). In 1900 he was to ensure passage of the necessary ordinance whereby only officers on the active list could fill the posts of War and Navy Ministers. As will be appreciated unfortunately this was to result in the armed forces having a power of veto over the formation of future civilian governments, and, 'be a crucial factor in the development of Japanese imperialism (23)'. Concerning this development, in a similar vein another authority was to write:-

> 'Now the military brought another, potentially more formidable source of instability into the system. From May 1900, the army and navy ministers had to be officers on the active list (24).'

6 March 1898. Treaty of Kiaochow between Germany and China. The former acquired the lease of some 200 square miles of territory in Shantung Province. There, on the south coast of that promontory, the port of Tsingtao was to be developed in impressive style, and be fortified.

Just a month earlier, 10 February 1898, the German authorities had awarded their first local mail contract to a German owner, the Michael Jebsen steamship interests. His first vessel placed on that new service was the steamer *Apenrade*, 696 tons, who sailed from Shanghai on 13 April 1898. However in 1901 these interests were to be acquired by the Hamburg-Amerika Linie and were to be retained by them until the outbreak of WW1 in 1914 (25).

While on the subject of German merchant shipping interests in the East then obviously, with the outbreak of the Great War, then also to the south and operating out of Singapore, especially to Bangkok and to Borneo, there too the interests of the North German Lloyd, Norddeutscher Lloyd of Bremen, were to be lost to them. The Straits Steamship Company, with the support of Alfred Holt & Co. of Liverpool, the Blue Funnel Line, were to gain from that development at Singapore (26).

Later in March 1898 Sir Edward was involved with the reaction from London to the Russian demand that China agree to a twenty five year lease of Port Arthur for their use as an ice free port. To counter this move Britain negotiated with China for the lease of a base on the north coast of the Shantung peninsula at Wei-Hai-Wei. In London at the time fortunately the Under Secretary of State for Foreign Affairs continued to be George Nathaniel Curzon who well appreciated the reasoning behind a number of various Tsarist moves. The appropriate Sino-British Convention was signed in Peking on 1 July 1898.

One version of these negotiations covers the astute British handling of the situation:-

> 'The Chinese were very bitter indeed against the Russians when they took Port Arthur, which was not to be wondered at. When Sir Claude Macdonald at the Tsung-li Yamen asked for Wei-hai-wei, Li Hung-chang turned to him and said: "You are as bad as the rest." Sir Claude replied: "No. The case is this: you have given one of two men who stand opposite each other a gun. Now you must give a gun to the other. Directly Russia gives up Port Arthur we will evacuate Wei-hai-wei. We can't go so far as to go to war with Russia on your account, but giving us Wei-hai-wei will neutralize her action, which is the next best thing."
> Whereupon the Chinese consented to Sir Claude's proposal (27).'

Neither Wei-Hai-Wei nor the island in the bay, Liukungtao on which were constructed the modest base facilities, they being largely recreational in nature, ever were to be fortified by Great Britain.

1 May 1898. In Manila Bay in USS *Olympia*, 5,870 tons, Captain Charles Vernon Gridley, Commodore George Dewey achieved his victory over Spain (28). On that occasion the Spanish flagship, *Reina Christina*, 3,042 tons, Rear Admiral Don Patricio Montojo y Pasaron, together with other warships of his squadron were at anchor off Sangley Point and Cavite in the shallow waters of the bay.

Sadly Captain Gridley only had a few more weeks to live:

'HMS *Immortalite* at Manila, Saturday, 11 June 1898.

    11 a.m. Halfmasted colours in consequence of the death of Captain Gridley, late of USS *Olympia*
        (29).'

However all was not to be peaceful within the Philippine Islands.

In due course, facilities not being available in Manila, on 29 August *Olympia* was to arrive at Hong Kong for docking between 31 August and 2 September. She sailed on 3 September 1898, bound back to Manila.

Earlier the Spanish colonial power had experienced difficulties in those islands. These unsettled conditions within the new American colony were to continue. For example in October 1898 Captain Hedworth Lambton in *Powerful* was at Manila to watch over British interests. Writing on 13 October the SNO, Hong Kong, Rear Admiral C.C. P. Fitzgerald, wrote to inform the C. in C.:-

'On the 7th inst. I informed *Powerful* that if *Rattler* was no longer required in the Philippines, she was to be sent to Hong Kong, but Captain Lambton reported that affairs were still unsettled at Ilo Ilo, and so she will remain there for the present (30).'

In the interim at Wei-Hai-Wei on Monday, 23 May 1898 the Japanese garrison peacefully withdrew in s.s. *Gaisen Maru* and other transports, with the battleship *Fuji*, 12,530 tons, also in attendance, and the British took up their lease (31). Acting for Great Britian was Captain George F. King-Hall in the armoured cruiser *Narcissus*, 5,600 tons, with the British Consul from Chefoo, Mr. L.C. Hopkins, also present (32). Two days later, Wednesday, 25 May, the C. in C. arrived in *Centurion* to inspect the facilities.

H.M. The Queen's Birthday took place on 24 May and so locally the festivities held to mark the occasion were particularly memorable to those participating, both Chinese and British (33).

Writing to the Admiralty on 14 July 1898, the C. in C. referred to H.M. Ships *Archer*, a small cruiser of 1,770 tons, Commander Charles E. Kingsmill, and the screw gunboat *Redpole*, 805 tons, Lieut. and Commander Ernest H. Grafton, being on 'Seal Patrol'. This activity took place to the north of the Station off the east coast of the Kamchatka Peninsula in the vicinity of Komandorski Island (34).

In passing, initially as a Rear Admiral, to which rank he was to be promoted on 12 May 1908, then between 1908 and 1920 the Canadian born Charles Kingsmill was to be Director of Naval Services of Canada, the future Royal Canadian Navy. He was to be promoted Admiral on 3 April 1917 and to be knighted in 1918.

During October 1898, over the incident in the Sudan provoked by Captain Marchand, the Fashoda affair, there was a considerable risk of war between Britain and France. In London it was thought likely that in the event of hostilities breaking out then, 'in all probability Russia would side with France (35).' To meet any possible combination of a Franco-Russian fleet Sir Edward concentrated his forces at Hong Kong.

Fortunately after a fortnight the crisis passed.

Centurion, with the C. in C. onboard, spent Christmas 1898 at Hong Kong. A German squadron under Prince Henry of Prussia in *Deutschland* was in port over the holiday season. As was always the case in those days a very considerable and agreeable social activity took place between the ships and men of the two nations (36).

Leaving Hong Kong on 16 January 1899 he visited Manila, there meeting Admiral Dewey in U.S.S. *Olympia*. The C. in C. proceeded ashore on a short journey to see for himself how the Americans were managing the affairs of their new colony. After a stay of four days he returned to Hong Kong in *Centurion*.

17 July 1899. Extraterritoriality in Japan came to an end.

In South Africa on 11 October 1899 war was declared between the Boer forces and those of Great Britain. Although finally to be victorious, for the British the war was to be an humiliating and expensive experience, the latter both in lives and treasure.

Sir Claude MacDonald

To see the hazard for himself, prior to the ascent being attempted the following spring, on Friday, 27 October 1899 in *Woodcock* he visited the Ichang Gorges in the Yangtse River.

Subsequently, during 1900 the 126 ton river gunboat *Woodcock*, Lieut. Hugh Dudley Richards Watson (1872-1954), with *Woodlark* in company, successfully made an important steam powered ascent through the Yangtse River Gorges above Ichang, reaching Chungking on 7 May 1900. Although preceded during February/March 1898 by Mr. Archibald Little's small steam launch *Leechuen* of seven tons, these were the first steamships of appreciable tonnage ever to have made this ascent up through those most difficult waters. *Woodlark*, Lieut. Henry E. Hillman, accomplished this feat with no shore assistance being provided by trackers, a very fine achievement (37).

Also this was the time of the Boxer Rebellion in northern China, 1899-1901. While at Wei-hai-wei, on 28 May 1900 by telegram from the British Minister, Sir Claude MacDonald, he received the first warning of impending trouble at Peking. 'Not liking the turn of events, on the 31st took all the ships to Taku so as to be prepared for any eventuality (38).'

On 10 June he led a small relief party up the Peiho then by train from Tientsin. This force was inadequate and was rebuffed prior to reaching Peking. On 14 August 1900 a military force, augmented by a Naval Brigade, successfully relieved the foreign legations at the capital.

Elsewhere the Boxer business in North China has been written about widely and therefore is not covered in any detail here. However, amongst the great numbers of officers who were to take part, invariably in operations in the vicinity of Taku and who were to go on to great things, were the Flag Captain himself, John Jellicoe, together with David Beatty, Commander in the second class battleship *Barfleur*, 10,500 tons, sister ship to the Flagship, Christopher Cradock, now in command of the despatch vessel *Alacrity*, and Roger Keyes, in command of the TBD *Fame*, 340 tons. During operations ashore Captain Jellicoe was wounded after which the services of Captain Guido von Usedom, later to be an Admiral in the Imperial German Navy, were to be especially useful to Sir Edward (39).

Xenophobic by nature, missionaries being a particular target, latterly the Dowager Empress T'zu-hsi had given the Boxer movement much encouragement.

Fortunately in the Yangtse valley Viceroys Liu K'un-yi (1830-1902) at Nanking, and Chang Chih-tung (1837-1909) at Wuchang/Wuhan, did not follow this lead given by the Dowager Empress thus limiting the excesses of the Boxer troubles to the North of China. During those anxious times, in June 1900 especially, instrumental in reaching an understanding with these two Viceroys was the British Consul General in Shanghai, Pelham L. Warren, son of Admiral Richard Laird Warren (1806-1875) (40).

In addition to overcoming this problem in north China itself, Britain was conscious of her need to act firmly with a view also to attempting to limit Russian ambitions in Manchuria.

He, his officers and men of *Centurion*, subsequently caused to be erected in Victoria Park, Portsmouth, a granite memorial to those from the ship who lost their lives in the Naval Brigade, North China, 1900.

Meanwhile in the Philippine Islands the new colonial power, the United States, had resolved to attempt a new technique in an effort to stabilise the domestic situation. Writing from *Centurion* at Wei Hai Wei on 22 May 1900 the C. in C. advised the Admiralty:-

'2. The islands are still under Military Governorship and are also under martial law, but the military government is shortly to be superseded by Civil Government which is to be vested in a commission of five members who are now on their way out. The head of this commission is Judge William H. Taft, a very eminent lawyer.

3. There are now in the Philippines about 65,000 U.S. troops distributed in the islands of Luzon, Samar, Leyte, Mindanao, Panay, Negros and Cebu. The lines round Manila are 17 miles long, and American action now is limited to the defensive, no offensive operations being undertaken as the Authorities hold that in the end the Filipinos will be able to manage their own internal affairs under a paternal U.S. government.

7. By far the greatest part of the commercial interests is in the hands of British merchants; Americans have not yet taken to investing their money in the Philippine Islands, although with a good and secure government there should be a great opening for trade (41).'

Staff Paymaster F. C. Alton Secretary   Flag-Lieutenant F. A. Powlett   Flag-Captain J. R. Jellicoe

Vice-Admiral Sir Edward Hobart Seymour, K.C.B., and Staff.

During this difficult time, towards the latter part of the summer of 1900, the sloop *Daphne*, 1,140 tons, Commander Charles Winnington-Ingram, was stationed as guardship off Wuhu, fifty miles above Nanking. A brief description of the prevailing conditions is worth including:-

'Lying at Wuhu in the middle of the summer was anything but enjoyable. It was stiflingly hot; we had no amenities such as ice, the strained relations between the Chinese and ourselves restricted us to the small foreign settlement, and in order to save coal we had to use the river water for washing. Although chlorine was used it always stank, was tepid, and of a rich brown colour, thick and muddy, and altogether most uninviting. Also one could not but remember the numerous corpses, animal and human, that continually floated past the ship, the result of the summer floods (42).'

Shortly afterwards *Daphne* was ordered up to Hankow to be guardship through the low water winter season. The extract is included as giving therein is an interesting view of the Viceroy mentioned above, Chang Chih-tung:-

> 'During our stay Sir Edward Seymour came up the river to thank Chang Chih-tung for the attitude he had taken over the Boxer rising, and for this purpose we took him over to Wuchang. Subsequently the Viceroy returned the visit and came onboard in great state and with a curious blending of ancient and modern. All the trappings of medieval China, peacock's feathers, fan and umbrella, contrasted with very smartly turned out officers in the latest modern equipment, wearing shocking yellow boots.
>
> The Viceroy himself was an old gentleman, very dignified, with a long white beard, and intelligent quick eyes which had a glint in them which made it easy to understand why his orders were carried out (43).'

The above comments regarding prevailing weather conditions during the summer in the Yangtse Valley are corroborated by extracts taken from the Journal of Midshipman De Thoren then serving in the cruiser *Hermoine*, 4,360 tons. No doubt members of her company were upset at not being present at the scene of the action up at Taku, nevertheless at the same time they were fulfilling an important role as guardship at Nanking. On both 18 and 19 July 1900 this young Midshipman refers to the siege of the Legations at Peking and of the action at Tientsin. Then on 22 July the ship dressed and at noon, 'Fired a salute of 21 guns in honour of the Chinese Emperor's Birthday'. One can only wonder as to the process by which the decision to fire such a salute was reached, the country then being at war with forces purporting to be those of the Emperor. On 27 July 1900 the temperature on board in the shade at noon was noted by him as being 105 deg. F. However the associated wretchedly high humidity was not specifically mentioned (44).

Also then serving as a Lieutenant in *Hermoine* was the future Admiral Sir William Goodenough. Subsequently he was to write of this period, and with one amusing anecdote:-

> 'We in *Hermoine* were stationed in the Yangtse during the Boxer troubles. (--) In the Yangtse we saw nothing of the fighting further north, and we lay there, sweating – physically, morally, mentally – not knowing what had become of our people inside Peking, nor very much of those going to their rescue. Mostly we were at Nanking, and there the Taotai said he was able to communicate with Peking itself, and from time to time we did get a sort of vague message that all was well. But there were also messages that all was over, and obituary notices appeared of Sir Claude MacDonald, Sir Robert Hart and Dr. Morrison. As Morrison said afterwards, his obituary notice was worth a lot to him, for no one could go back on the wonderful things that had been said of him (45).'

From Nanking *Hermoine* returned to Shanghai on 30 September 1900. A few days later, on 9 October 1900, Midshipman De Thoren noted:-

> 'At 4 p.m. *Snipe* hoisted flag of Sir Ernest Satow the British Minister who is going to relieve Sir Claude MacDonald at Peking. He is going down to Wusung in *Snipe* and will then go on to Taku in HMS *Undaunted* (46).'

At Shanghai on 8 and 9 November 1900 *Hermoine* was inspected by the C. in C.

Then a short while later, and in absolute contrast to the temperatures suffered off Nanking in the summer, at Shanghai on 8 December 1900:-

> 'We started to scrub decks as usual this morning but had to give it up owing to the water freezing immediately on the decks.'

GCB: 9 November 1900.

Not to be ignored consequent to this time of the outbreak of the Boer War on 12 October 1899, and of the Boxer activity mentioned above, taken together both stretching British ability to meet their world wide obligations, were German naval ambitions:-

'On 14 June 1900, further influenced by the Boer War and the Boxer rebellion in China, the Reichstag passed the Second Navy Bill. This called for nothing less than a doubling of the fleet... (47).'

For the sake of the record, also which serves to indicate the size of the fleet under his command, on 1 January 1901 his men of war were distributed as follows:-

' Ship	Place	Ship	Place
Phoenix	Sinho	Britomart	Hong Kong
Arethusa	Liautung Gulf	Barfleur	Hong Kong
Plover	Liautung Gulf	Undaunted	Hong Kong
Isis	Wei-Hai-Wei	Terrible	Hong Kong
Bonaventure	Wusung	Endymion	Hong Kong
Alacrity (C. in C.)	Shanghai	Dido	Hong Kong
Wallaroo	Shanghai	Humber	Hong Kong
Rosario	Shanghai	Waterwitch	Hong Kong
Snipe	Shanghai	Otter	Hong Kong
Woodcock	Shanghai	Taku	Hong Kong
Whiting	Wusung	Sandpiper	Hong Kong
Hart	Wusung	Lizard	Canton
Centurion	Wusung	Robin	West River
Goliath	Wusung	Bramble	Manila
Aurora	Wusung	Brisk	Singapore
Orlando	Wusung	Algerine	Singapore
Peacock	Wusung	Pigmy	Singapore
Pique	Chinkiang	Hermoine	Nanking
Linnet	Wuhu	Redpole	Kiukiang
Daphne	Hankow	Esk	Ichang
Woodlark	Hankow	Astraea	Hong Kong
Mohawk	Pagoda Anchorage	Argonaut	Amoy (48).'

Still as Midshipman De Thoren, but shortly to be promoted Sub Lieutenant, one of his last Journal entries contains both good news and bad. It is dated 4 January 1901 and *Hermoine* once again is back at Nanking:-

'We have news today that Peace is declared between China and the Foreign Powers but no details as yet.

Affairs in South Africa seem to be getting worse, De Wet being still at large causing us considerable trouble. The guerrilla warfare in a country like the Boers have to operate in must be very trying to our leaders.'

22 January 1901: death at Osborne, Isle of Wight of H.M. Queen Victoria.

The battleship *Glory* had arrived at Hong Kong on 18 January. As was recorded in her:-

'January 23. We received the news of Queen Victoria's death by cablegram at 9.10 a.m. Royal Standard half-masted on flagships, and ensigns of every ship half-masted.

January 25. Ships fired a requiem salute of eighty-one minute-guns as a last token of respect to Her late Majesty the Queen. Then the fleet fired a salute of twenty-one guns in honour of the accession to the throne of King Edward VII (49).'

During 1901 in north Kyushu at the state owned Yawata Iron Works the first firing took place. In such a manner was initiated the huge Japanese iron and steel industry. Looking ahead, and to give just one example of the success of such enterprise, already by 1913 domestic production of merchant ships, of metal construction, was to equal those of imports (50).

In the Aoyama Palace, Tokyo on 29 April 1901, the birth of Prince Michi, the future Showa Tenno, H.I.M. Emperor Hirohito.

Admiral: 24 May 1901.

On 26 June 1901 at Wei-Hai-Wei he turned over command of the Station to his successor, Vice Admiral Sir Cyprian Bridge, who flew his flag in *Glory*, and sailed for home in *Centurion*. On passage naturally he spent a few days at Hong Kong, only sailing from the colony on 3 July 1901. While in port he was the guest of honour at a number of farewell banquets, one of which was hosted by HE The Governor, Sir Henry Blake (51).

On passage, while the ship coaled at Colombo he paid an interesting call:-

'At Mount Lavinia I visited our Boer prisoners of war, and talked to many who spoke English; mostly they said they still expected to win in South Africa (52).'

Finally the ship arrived at Portsmouth on 19 August 1901.

'On the 21st I left the ship, and my flag was hauled down: such leave takings are things not easily forgotten. These endings of the chief phases of our lives are the milestones of our existence (53)!'

In London on 30 January 1902, during the last few months of Lord Salisbury's third and final period of service as Conservative Prime Minister, the Anglo-Japanese Alliance was signed. At the time the Foreign Secretary was Henry, Fifth Marquess of Lansdowne who, between 1888 and 1894 had served as Viceroy of India so was very well aware of both the perceived and real dangers from territorially ambitious Tsarist Russia. However in many circles the prime mover, if not the creator of the Alliance was regarded as being the Japanese Minister to the Court of St. James's, Hayashi Tadasu (1850-1913).

A few weeks later, from Gibraltar on 6 April 1902, Sir Edward wrote to his successor in China, Sir Cyprian Bridge:-

'I am delighted with our Anglo-Japanese agreement. Nothing in the world is without possible drawbacks; there may be some here; but fancy if instead Japan had made such an agreement with Germany or Russia. When should we have come in (54)?'

In the spring of 1902, in the Royal Yacht *Victoria and Albert* via Bilbao, he was the Naval representative in the Duke of Connaught's suite on the occasion of his visit to Madrid to confer the Order of the Garter upon H.M. King Alfonso XIII (1886-1941). On 17 May 1902, his sixteenth birthday, H.M. took the oaths of office.

At sea on 24 May 1902, during the return voyage to England, he wrote a few chatty lines to Sir Cyprian Bridge in China:-

'I am on my way back to England, from Madrid where I have been in the suite of the Duke of Connaught for the occasion of the King of Spain coming of age. The life of a Courtier is one to which I am least of all suited, and certainly do not like.

It has however been interesting to meet the people one has met, and get the view of affairs that belongs to doing so (55).'

Also during 1902, 'In the same year he served on Sir Edward Grey's committee on the manning of the navy (56).'

O.M.: 26 June 1902. The other Naval member on this, the day of the institution of the Order, was Admiral of the Fleet The Hon. Sir Henry Keppel (see C. in C., 1869).

From 3 October 1902 First and Principal Naval ADC to H.M. King Edward VII.

During this period in London he resided at 9 Ovington Square, SW.

C. in C., Devonport: 28 March 1903 – 20 February 1905 with his Flag in battleship *Temeraire*, 8,540 tons, the Depot Ship for Fleet Reserve.

In June 1903 at the University of Cambridge he was conferred with the degree of LL.D.

Admiral of the Fleet: 20 February 1905.

Subsequently he undertook a number of duties such as, in May 1905, being attached to HRH Prince Arthur of Connaught's suite to Berlin to attend the wedding of the Crown Prince of Prussia.

Later in the year he travelled to Boston, Massachusetts to represent the Navy at the centenary of the Battle of Trafalgar celebrations, 21 October 1905. There in the Tremont Temple he relates that the main speaker was the well known historian, Captain Alfred Thayer Mahan, USN (1840-1914):-

> 'Those who have read the illuminating works of Mahan can imagine how he did justice to his subject (57).'

11 January 1906. Again attached to HRH Prince Arthur of Connaught's suite, on this occasion in Japan to invest H.I.M. The Emperor Mutsuhito, Meiji, with the Order of the Garter. To undertake this mission the party left London by rail for Marseilles. Then from Marseilles on 12 January they continued to the East in the P. & O. *Mongolia*, 9,505 grt, arriving at Colombo on Saturday, 27 January. Continued in P. & O. s.s. *Dongola*, 8,038 grt, to Hong Kong where the ship arrived on 9 February 1906. On 13 February they sailed on from Hong Kong in HMS *Diadem*, 11,000 tons, Captain Herbert W. Savory, arriving at Yokohama on 19 February 1906. In Japan he met Admiral Togo on a number of occasions. From Japan on 16 March he returned home across the Pacific in the Canadian Pacific s.s. *Empress of Japan*, 5,940 grt, Captain Henry Pybus, by rail across Canada, and from Halifax to Liverpool in the Allan Line s.s. *Victorian*, 10,629 grt, arriving home early in May. Thus, in considerable style, he completed a circumnavigation.

GCVO: 15 May 1906.

PC: 1909.

On 1 September 1909 appointed, and on 16 September 1909 hoisted his Flag, as an Admiral of the Fleet a rare occurrence, in the new battlecruiser *Inflexible*, 17,250 tons, Captain Henry H. Torlesse, to proceed to New York to attend the 'Hudson-Fulton' celebrations. This was an extravagant affair held to honour the 300th anniversary of Henry Hudson's arrival, and the centennial of Robert Fulton's river steamboat *Clermont*. On 29 September and 4 October a part of the celebrations included the spectacle of flights by Wilbur Wright over New York harbour.

From *Inflexible* on 6 October 1909 he wrote, rather charmingly, to the First Lord of the Admiralty, Mr. Reginald McKenna:-

> 'It may interest you to hear from us here. So far all has gone off well I consider. New York has gone mad over the affair, which resembles a great national fete, not a municipal one (--) This ship has been an immense success, the one great vessel to see and visit, and I am much obliged to you for giving her to me as Flag Ship. Her illuminations were declared by all to be the best here …… (58).'

Returned to Portsmouth on 19 October 1909.

Retired: 30 April 1910.

On 1 July 1911 he was the principal host at a dinner in London given by the Royal Navy Club to Admiral Count Togo Heihachiro. Their guest of honour commencing his speech of thanks, 'Admiral Sir Edward Seymour and Gentlemen (also see Noel, C. in C., 1904).'

On Wednesday, 6 March 1929 the local press reported his death. Short extracts follow:-

> 'We regret to announce the death on Saturday, after influenza, of the Rt. Hon. Sir Edward H. Seymour, O.M., Admiral of the Fleet, at his residence at Hedsor View, Maidenhead Court, in his 89th year – one of the grandest of 'grand old men' of Maidenhead and a great friend and supporter of the best local movements.'

'Many times he was chosen to represent the nation or the navy on special occasions at home or abroad, where his courtesy and tact were always displayed to good purpose. Tall, and of fine physique, with his handsome presence he added dignity to many State ceremonies in various countries.'

'Although a good man to hounds he was not specially keen on sport (59).'

He was buried at Cookham Parish Church, Holy Trinity, on Thursday, 7 March 1929, the service being conducted by the vicar assisted by two of the late Admiral's nephews, Rev. R. Seymour and Rev. A.G. Seymour. One of the pall bearers was Admiral of the Fleet Earl Jellicoe (1859-1935), and amongst those present in the huge congregation was the second Lord Fisher of Kilverstone, and many senior Naval officers. 'The service at the cemetery was brief, the Vicar reading the burial service. A firing squad fired over the grave three times; and then rang out the solemn refrain of the 'Last Post' by a bugler of H.M.S. *Pembroke*. The cortege then dispersed.'

Also on the Thursday a memorial service was held at Westminster Abbey where H.M. King George V was represented by Admiral Sir Richard Phillimore, and H.M. The Prince of Wales by Admiral Sir Lionel Halsey. The First Sea Lord, Admiral of the Fleet Sir Charles Madden (1862-1935), was among those in the Abbey congregation. Also present were several foreign Naval Attaches.

Subsequently within Holy Trinity Church at Cookham an appropriate memorial plaque was to be placed:-

'To the beloved memory of the Right Honourable Sir Edward Hobart Seymour, Admiral of the Fleet, GCB OM GCVO LLD who died on the 2nd March 1929 in his 90th year. For many years a regular worshipper in this Church. From boyhood to old age a brave and devoted servant of his country (60).'

In the *Dictionary of National Biography* his entry was prepared by Admiral Sir Herbert Richmond, Master of Downing College, Cambridge. In recent editions this entry has been revised by Professor Andrew Lambert.

NOTES

1. *Dictionary of National Biography.*
2. NA ADM 196/14. 840. *Service Record.*
3. Ibid.
4. E.H. Seymour, *My Naval Career and Travels,* (London, 1911), 83.
5. *Dictionary of National Biography.*
6. NA ADM 53/7556. Log Book, *Bouncer.*

    In the tow of *Coromandel* as far as Yochow was a junk which had been chartered by Captain Thomas Wright Blakiston (1832-1891) of the Royal Artillery, and party, to convey them upstream as far as Ichang. They were to reach Ichang on 31 March, and from there engage the services of a smaller junk in which, up through the Gorges, they were to reach Chungking, 1,352 nautical miles from the open sea, on 28 April 1861. The author's notes, *Yangtse Gorges: Early Steamship Passages – The First Moves.* Lyman P. van Slyke, *Yangtze,* (Stanford, CA, 1988), 158. Obituary, *Proceedings of the R.G.S.,* N.S. 13, 1891, 728/9. Alfred Barton, *Journal of the R.G.S.,* 32, 1862, 32-41. Captain Thomas Wright Blakiston, *Five Months on the Yangtse,* (London, 1862).
7. Wooden paddle steamer *Cowper,* 342 grt, in April 1860 built for Hong Kong owners, Lyall, Still & Co., for the Canton route, but in May 1860 acquired by the RN. In November 1861 sold by the RN to Douglas Lapraik & Co. and in Hong Kong re-named *Fei Seen.* In September 1862 acquired by Hong Kong Parsee owners for their Macao service. Subsequently served a number of other owners. H.W. Dick and S.A. Kentwell, *Beancaker to Boxboat,* (Canberra, 1988), 134.
8. Seymour, 92.
9. Ibid. 108. With the Confederate attack on Fort Sumter, SC, the U.S. Civil War commenced on 12 April 1861.

10. *Dictionary of National Biography.*

11. Seymour, 130.

12. Clowes, Vol. VII, 228.

13. *Dictionary of National Biography.*

14. Clowes, Vol. VII, 342.

15. Seymour, 223. Gill and his companions were 'treacherously and cruelly slain' on 11 August 1882.

16. *Dictionary of National Biography.*

17. Ibid.

18. Captain A. MacDermott, RN, *Some Naval Characters I Have Known,* (Mariner's Mirror, Vol. 45, 1959), No. 4, 282. Sir Robert Bourchier Sherard Wrey (1855-1917), in 1900 to succeed his father as the Eleventh Baronet.

19. Admiral Sir Reginald Bacon, *The Life of John Rushworth, Earl Jellicoe,* (London, 1936), 74. P. & O. s.s. *Coromandel,* 4,359 grt. Built: 1885. Sold: 1905. Scrapped: 1908.

20. Seymour, 320/1.

21. J. Charles Schencking, *Making Waves,* (Stanford, 2005), 73/77. To better appreciate the great importance of the influence and leadership exerted by Yamamoto Gonnohyoe (Gombei) see David Chris Evans, *The Satsuma Faction and Professionalism in the Japanese Naval Officer Corps of the Meiji Period, 1868-1912,* (Stanford, 1978), Chapter VI, 177-231. The Admiral's career resume is given under Bridge, C. in C., 1901, reference (68).

22. **Yamagata** Aritomo. Born in Hagi: 14 June 1838. Died in Tokyo: 1 February 1922. In 1869 visited Europe, there being much impressed and influenced by Prussian military and political thought. War Minister: 1873. The father of Japanese militarism thus his beliefs were in direct contrast to those of Ito Hirobumi, also of Choshu origin. Twice prime minister of Japan, on the first occasion between December 1889 and May 1891. OM: 1906. Koshaku (Prince): 1907. *Encyclopaedia Britannica.*

23. Hugh Cortazzi, *The Japanese Achievement,* (London, 1990), 213.

24. Tsuzuki Chushichi, *The Pursuit of Power in Modern Japan 1825-1995,* (OUP, 2000), 164.

25. Paper presented at IMEHA, 2008, Greenwich, England by Dr. Bert Becker, University of Hong Kong.

26. K.G. Tregonning, *Home Port Singapore,* (OUP, 1967), 45/6.

27. Bacon, 75/6. For Viceroy Li Hung-chang see Fremantle, C. in C., 1892, reference (52).

28. USS *Olympia.* Today (year 2007) still open to visitors at her berth in the River Delaware at Philadelphia, PA.

29. NA ADM 53/14062.

30. NA ADM 1/7371. Written in *Barfleur* at Hong Kong.

31. s.s. *Gaisen Maru,* 1,791 grt. Built in 1886 for German owners but acquired by Japanese owners in 1895. Registered at Osaka. *Lloyd's Register.* HIJMS *Fuji,* British built, launched on 31 March 1896. The first Japanese battleship. Four 12" and ten 6" main armament. Capable of 18.5 knots. Regarded as an improved *Royal Sovereign* type. Fred T. Jane, *The Imperial Japanese Navy,* (London, 1904), 168, 172 and 174.

32. Lionel Charles **Hopkins**. Born: 20 March 1854. Died at Haslemere: 11 March 1952. Appointed Student Interpreter in China: 13 January 1874. Early service in Ningpo, Chinkiang, Canton, Amoy, Pakhoi and Kiukiang. Acting Consul at Tamsui: 9 November 1893 to 14 September 1895. Subsequently Shanghai, Chefoo, Hankow and Wuhu. Consul at Chefoo: 27 September 1897. Consul-General at Tientsin: 22 March 1901. Retired: 1 September 1908. *Foreign Office List,* 1953.

33. RN Museum Library, Portsmouth. Ref: *2000.53.* King-Hall Diaries.

34. NA ADM 1/7371. Letter No. 342.

Charles Edmund **Kingsmill**. Born: Guelph, Ontario: 7 July 1855. Died: Grindstone Island, Ontario: 15 July 1935. Captain: 31 December 1898. Vice Admiral: 17 May 1913. In many respects the father of the RCN. Richard H. Gimblett, *Admiral Charles E. Kingsmill: Forgotten Father,* pub. in Michael Whitby et al, Eds. *The Admirals, Canada's Senior Naval Leadership in the Twentieth Century,* (Toronto, 2006).

Ernest Humbert **Grafton**. Captain: 30 June 1905. Commanded battleships *Victorious*: 4 October 1910, and *London*: 14 May 1912. Captain of Chatham Dockyard: 15 September 1913. Rear Admiral and retired: 15 June 1916. Vice Admiral: 25 November 1920. *Navy List.*

35. Bacon, 80.

36. Bacon, 82/3.

37. Jonathan Parkinson, *The First Steam Powered Ascent Through the Yangtse Gorges*, (Journal of the Royal Asiatic Society Hong Kong Branch, Vol. 46, 2006), 162-168.

38. Bacon, 93.

39. Seymour, 349. Ernst Adolf Julius Guido von Usedom. Born: 2 October 1854. Died: 24 February 1925. Joined the German Navy: 1871. For his services in China during the Boxer Rebellion to be awarded the Pour le Merite: 15 April 1902. Rear Admiral: 14 March 1905. In 1910 retired as a Vice Admiral but was recalled for WW1 service. Appointed Commander, Dardanelles Defences: 19 August 1914. Admiral: 27 January 1916. Until the end of WW1 he remained in Turkey with the Ottoman forces.

40. Pelham Laird **Warren**. Born: 22 August 1845. Died at Sidmouth: 21 November 1923. Appointed Student Interpreter in China: 2 February 1867. Following several junior appointments promoted Consul at Taiwan: 19 July 1886. Transferred to Hankow: 1 December 1893. Acting Consul-General at Shanghai: 1 July 1899 to 6 October 1900, then Special Service at Shanghai: 7 October 1900 to 17 April 1901. CMG: 1 January 1901. Consul-General at Shanghai: 1 July 1901. KCMG: 26 June 1902. Retired: 20 January 1911. *Foreign Office List*.

41. NA ADM 1/7455. Extracts taken from letter No. 339/3513. William Howard **Taft** (1857-1930). Governor of the Philippines: 1901-1904. Republican President of the USA: 1909-1913.

42. Admiral of the Fleet The Earl of Cork and Orrery, *My Naval Life*, (London, undated), 41.

    Appointed in command of *Daphne* from 7 March 1901 was Commander William C. Pakenham. On 30 June 1903 to be promoted Captain and from 14 April 1904 to Tokio as Naval Attache – see Noel, C. in C., 1904.

43. Ibid. 43.

44. RN Museum Library, Portsmouth. Ref: *MSS 216*. Journal kept by Oscar De Satge De Thoren.

45. Admiral Sir William Goodenough, *A Rough Record*, (London, 1946), 46/47. From 7 April 1898 he served as Lieut. (G) in *Hermoine*. Promoted Commander: 30 June 1900. On being relieved then from Nanking he left the ship on 22 September 1900. *Navy List*. Also *MSS 216* as immediately above, reference (44).

46. *MSS 216*. Armoured Cruiser *Undaunted*, 5,600 tons, Captain Arthur C. Clarke. *Navy List*.

47. Holger H. Herwig, *Luxury Fleet – The Imperial German Navy, 1888-1918*, (London, 1980), 42.

48. RN Museum Library, Portsmouth. Ref: *MSS 182*. Admiral Sir Edward Hobart Seymour: Journal as Commander in Chief of the China Squadron, 1898-1901.

49. A.E. Butterworth, *The Commission of HMS Glory: 1900-1904*, (London, 1904), 6.

50. Francis E. Hyde, *Far Eastern Trade, 1860-1914*, (London, 1973), 139.

51. Henry Arthur **Blake**. Born in Limerick: 18 January 1840. Died in Youghal: 23 February 1918. Joined the Irish Constabulary: 1859. Special Resident Magistrate: 1882. Governor of the Bahamas: 1884-1887, and of Newfoundland: 1887-1888. KCMG: 1888. Governor of Jamaica: 1889-1897. GCMG: 1897. Governor of Hong Kong: November 1898 – July 1903. Governor of Ceylon: 1903-1907. FRGS. *Who's Who*. *The Times*, 25 Feb. 1918.

52. Seymour, 375/6.

53. Seymour, 376.

54. Caird Library, National Maritime Museum, Greenwich. Ref: *BRI/19*.

55. Ibid.

56. *Dictionary of National Biography*.

57. Seymour, 389.

58. Archives Centre, Churchill College, Cambridge. Ref: *MCKN 3/9*.

59. *The Maidenhead Advertiser*, 6 March 1929. Copy courtesy Mr. T.O. Mayhew.

60. Enter the church and turn right. Sir Edward's memorial may be seen on the right hand wall between the third and fourth pews from the back under a memorial to The Revd. Ralph Leycester. Visited by the author on Thursday, 6 January 2011.

10 April 1901 to 15 January 1904
Vice Admiral Sir Cyprian Arthur George **Bridge**

Born in St. Johns, Newfoundland, the eldest son and where his father, Ven. Thomas Finch Hobday Bridge, then was Rector, and later to be the Archdeacon: 13 March 1839 (1). His mother was Sarah Christiana, daughter of John Dunscomb, an aide-de-camp to the Governor of Newfoundland (2)

He died at his residence, 'Coombe Pines', Kingston Hill, Surrey on 16 August 1924.

He left Newfoundland for England in January 1851 and:-

'On reaching London he was taken to see the opening of the Great Exhibition where he saw the arrival of Queen Victoria and the Prince Consort, and also the Duke of Wellington. He was sent to Walthamstow House School, kept by Dr. Greig, who did not spare the rod, and Sir Cyprian said he had a taste of it every day except Sunday, but in spite of that he and the other boys liked the Doctor (3).'

With a nomination given by Admiral Sir Thomas John Cochrane (1789-1872), as above governor of Newfoundland from 1825 to 1834, he entered the Navy, Portsmouth Royal Naval College on 12 January 1853. As a **Naval Cadet** on 27 January 1853 he joined the paddle wheel sloop *Medea*, Commander John Crawshay Bailey, thence to the North America and West Indies Station.

'Early in February *Medea* sailed for the West Indies station, where young Bridge had a hard time, the captain being a brute who was subsequently tried by court martial for tyranny and deprived of his command (4).'

At Halifax on 14 September 1853 he was transferred to the third rate *Cumberland*, 70, 'Flagship of his father's friend, Admiral Sir George Seymour'. Next on 21 February 1854 at Bermuda he transferred into the screw steam sloop *Brisk*, 14 guns, commanded by the C. in C.'s nephew, Commander Frederick Beauchamp P. Seymour (5). During the Russian or Crimean War, in 1854 served in the White Sea, *Brisk* being a member of the squadron blockading Archangel. When the sea iced over she returned to Portsmouth to refit. Here, on the promotion of Commander Seymour to post rank, Commander Alfred J. Curtis assumed command: 20 October 1854. Promoted **Midshipman** on 13 January 1855 and in that same month, via the Straits of Magellan and still in *Brisk*, proceeded to the Pacific Station (6). When on the Station at first the ship proceeded to Kamchatka via the Sandwich Islands, then returned across the Pacific to Vancouver Island. In his memoirs Sir Cyprian was to recall that at the time the British Consul at Honolulu was, 'General (William) Miller, the former companion-in-arms of the celebrated Bolivar'. Subsequently at Guaymas, Mexico she loaded a cargo of silver later to be landed at Panama for transport by railway across the isthmus, then to be shipped in the steamers of the Royal Mail Company for England:-

'... the total value of the treasure which we took onboard amounted to two million and seven hundred thousand dollars, or rather more than GBP 540,000. The 'freight', as it was called, on this was about GBP 5500; of which one half was paid to the Captain, one quarter to Greenwich Hospital, and one quarter to the Admiral, Commander in Chief of the Station (7).'

On 14 June 1857 at Devonport he joined Captain Frederick Beauchamp P. Seymour, who from 16 July 1857 was in command of the screw steam corvette *Pelorus*, 21, East Indies and China. In her he continued to serve in the Bay of Bengal during the Indian Mutiny, and with the Naval Brigade in Burma. **Mate**: 15 March 1858. Thence in *Pelorus* to Australia. **Lieutenant**: 28 June 1859. Home from Sydney in the P. & O. screw, barque rigged, *Bombay*, 1,186 grt, to Suez, overland to Alexandria, then in the new paddle wheel steamer *Delta*, 1,618 grt, to Southampton arriving on 15 September 1859 (8). From Sydney he was fifty four days on passage. Attended *Excellent* for examinations. In these he did well, '... it turned out that I had passed first of all and had obtained marks only ten short of full numbers.'

From 22 February 1860 in screw steam ship *Algiers*, 91, Channel Squadron, and then to the Mediterranean. At the time in the Mediterranean the C. in C. was Admiral Sir William F. Martin (9). Paid off at Portsmouth on 12 December 1862. From 24 January 1863 in screw ship *Hawke*, 60 guns, 1,754 tons, Coast Guard Service, coast of Ireland. At various times on the Irish coast seconded in command of the steam screw gunboats *Griper*, then *Blazer*. Both displaced 284 tons being wooden 'Crimean' gunboats of the *Albacore* class of which ninety eight originally had been ordered. From 1 July 1864 to 18 February 1867 First Lieut. in screw sloop *Fawn*, 17 guns, 751 tons, North America and West Indies (10). The American Civil War then was in progress. At Nassau on one occasion he counted thirty six blockade running steamers in port. On receiving the news of his next appointment then from Saint John, New Brunswick he took passage home in a Nova Scotia barque of just 450 tons. She was heavily laden with timber and boxes of fish and, being winter, not only did they experience a number of storms so in consequence their passage took twenty one days, but 'the weather was intensely cold'. In addition, 'the captain, seeing that I had my sextant on board, asked me to do the navigating work, which I did until the day before we arrived at Greenock.'

From 19 February 1867 to 26 May 1868 in *Excellent*, Gunnery Ship, Portsmouth. In addition to studying gunnery later he was to claim that, 'I was the first officer in the Navy to be examined in submarine mining, counter mining, and torpedo work.'

Next, from 27 May he was appointed Flag Lieutenant to Rear Admiral Alfred P. Ryder (see C. in C., 1874), Second in Command, Channel Squadron. First, for a short period, the Admiral flew his flag in the iron clad *Bellerophon*, who was 'very unhandy', then from 17 July 1868 in the new iron, twin screw corvette, armour plated *Penelope*, 10 guns, 4,368 tons.

Commander: 15 February 1869. From 1 June 1869 to 22 August 1871 Commander in the armour plated, screw ship, *Caledonia*, 30 guns, 4,125 tons, Mediterranean.

From 7 March 1872 Commander in *Cambridge*, 29, Gunnery Ship, Devonport.

In 1873 through the R.U.S.I. he published a paper, *Fleet Evolutions and Naval Tactics*.

From 15 April 1873 to 31 August 1874 in command *Implacable*, 16, Training Ship for Boys, Devonport.

From 1 September 1874 to 7 March 1877 Commander in *Audacious*, 14, Flagship, China, the C. in C. being Vice Admiral Alfred P. Ryder, and with Captain Philip Howard Colomb (1831-1899) in command of the ship.

Clearly his services in the Flagship were held in high regard:-

'Sept. '76: very strongly recommended by Capt. Colomb and Vice Adml. Ryder (11).'

In 1876 he visited Peking. Amongst his experiences there he met Prince Kung, then Regent to the infant Emperor Kuang Hsu (1871-1908). In fact the real power in the land was the Empress Dowager, T'zu-hsi (1835-1908), on her death bed to have Kuang-Hsu poisoned. Also:-

'... we started for the Great Wall, going up the pass on foot. Both going up and coming down we passed long strings of camels on the way to Manchuria and Siberia.

We estimated the number seen at three thousand. (--) Nearly all the camels which we saw going up the pass were loaded with brick tea.'

Naturally the Flagship visited Japan:-

'I found it extraordinarily fascinating, and was greatly delighted with its charming and courteous people. In later years I was brought into frequent contact with the highest authorities in Japan, and my recollections of my intercourse with them are especially pleasant. I found these great officials not merely consistently courteous and dignified in bearing, but also thoroughly upright and honourable. I can never forget my first voyage in the *Audacious* through the inland sea of Japan. It was at the best time of year, and the scenery was enchanting. (--) I was one of a party of officers who had the honour of being presented to the Emperor in his palace in Tokio (12).'

Having now picked up an ailment of some kind, owing to his poor state of health in March 1877 from China he was invalided home, arriving back in England on 30 April 1877. Fortunately by 21 July 1877 he was found to be fit once more for further active service (13).

During 1876 and 1877, for the R.U.S.I., he translated a number of papers which originally had been published in French or German or Italian.

In 1877 he married Eleanor Thornhill, daughter of George Thornhill of the Indian Civil Service, however there were to be no children.

Captain: 17 September 1877.

'His attention now was drawn to the beginnings of the German Navy, a subject on which he wrote two papers in the *Journal* of the Royal United Service Institution, *Estimates for the German Navy for the financial year 1877-1878* (vol. xxi, 1877) and *On the Organisation and Strength of the German Navy* (vol. xxii, 1878). His close study of foreign affairs led him to foresee by many years the menace of this new maritime power, and also the need for that redistribution of the British Fleet which it ultimately brought about (14).'

In addition to the above, also published in the *Journal* in 1878 were, firstly, *Experiences of a New System of Lighting H.M. Ships*, and, secondly, *On the Adoption of the Naval and Military Systems of Europe by China and Japan* (15).

Appointed to War Office Committee on Heavy Guns: 11 May 1878. Also he served on an 'explosive committee'.

Served on the New Ordnance Committee: 1 April to 18 October 1881.

From 19 October 1881 in command of the screw sloop *Espiegle*, 6 guns, 1,130 tons, Australia Station. From Plymouth he took her out via Simon's Bay, thence via Fremantle and other Australian ports to Sydney.

'In that appointment he was a deputy commissioner for the Western Pacific, and rendered a series of reports on conditions in the islands which covered every field of activity and interest, political, social, ethnological, and commercial, and testify to the breadth of his mind and the acuteness of his perception (16).'

At the time in various South Sea islands cannibalism was not unknown. As he was to write in his memoirs:-

'My own belief about cannibalism – which must be taken for what it is worth and for no more – is, that it is not and never was very common, even amongst undoubted cannibals. (--) It was generally advisable when you landed on a cannibal island not to let a native get behind you. As long as they were kept in front, where their movements could be seen, I often found them pleasant and even merry fellows.

When we landed on an island the disposition of the inhabitants of which was not well known, we always approached the shore with two boats. From one we disembarked on the beach. The other remained about seventy or eighty yards off as a covering boat, the crew keeping their loaded rifles ready. If, when we landed on an island, there were no women and children about, it was necessary to be extremely cautious. The savages rarely attacked strangers until the women and children of the neighbourhood had been sent or had stayed away (17).'

As a excellent example of the duties which Commanders of H.M. Ships could be called upon to perform it is worth reading the entire account of the following cruise undertaken, largely under sail, in 1883 (18). A précis follows.

Espiegle left Sydney on 24 April 1883 bound for Norfolk Island, where she spent the day on 5 May 1883, and then on to arrive at Fiji on 11 May (19). There at the time the High Commissioner for the Western Pacific High Commission was Sir George Des Voeux (20). Also at Fiji the Judicial Commissioner, G. Ruthven Le Hunte, embarked on 18 May 1883 (21). Subsequent calls were made at Rotumah, the Ellice Islands, Gilbert Islands, Marshall Islands, Caroline Islands, Pelew (Palau) Islands, Yap, and at other islands on return passage to Sydney which beautiful harbour she reached on Wednesday, 3 October 1883 (22).

At Majuro in the Marshalls where they arrived on Saturday, 16 June 1883, Bridge proposed a peace treaty between two factions:-

'Later that same day the chiefs from both factions, unarmed and accompanied by British officers, cautiously left their defences and proceeded to a point midway between the two enemy camps. As the hostile parties slowly approached one another, several persons broke into a run and rushed into one another's arms. Jebrik (leader of one faction), trembling with emotion, embraced his daughter, married to a warrior on the enemy's side and whom he had not seen in three or four years. Families that had been divided by the struggle were reunited and there were tears in almost everyone's eyes. (--) When Bridge and his officers left them to return to their ship, the people who had been shooting at one another the day before were gathered in little groups absorbed in conversation as if there had never been a war at all (23).'

In addition to bringing about an element of inter-factional peace in the Marshalls, on 11 August 1883 he rendered a similar service at Palau, western Caroline Islands:-

'After a ceremonious greeting Captain Bridge had the short treaty read out in Palauan and English. (Then) one by one the chiefs stepped forward to put their mark on the document while the British officers looked on approvingly (24).'

During the cruise numerous calls were made at islands where no other warship previously had visited. On a number of occasions he had cause to investigate examples of misbehaviour perpetrated by 'traders', inevitably either fiscal in nature or involving labour. In addition he came across evidence of such extraordinary misdeeds as the kidnapping by Peruvians in 1865 of many hundreds of the inhabitants of the Ellice Islands. In this latter connection Mr. Le Hunte recorded:-

'The population is very small now, owing to the havoc committed by the Peruvian vessels, but the population of children is enormous, which gives us good hopes of their recovering, unless some dreadful epidemic is carried to them (25).'

Father Hezel, however, reminds us that the acquisition of the services of labour in this unpleasant manner was not confined to Peruvian entrepreneurs:-

'For years labour recruiters – blackbirders as they were popularly called – had been intermittently calling at Pacific islands to find natives to work in the copper mines of Peru, the coffee plantations in Central America, and the cotton and sugar fields of Queensland (26).'

Other Pacific cruises were carried out in 1884 and early in 1885. Then, when homeward bound in 1885, owing to strained relations with Russia, in *Espiegle*:-

'I was stopped by Admiralty order for several weeks at Singapore, in view of foreign complications and the desireability of retaining our squadrons in the Far East at full strength (27).'

This difficulty with Tsarist Russia arose over the Penjdeh affair of March 1885, another aspect of the 'Great Game' between Russia and Great Britain, largely over India and particularly in the North West Frontier/ Afghanistan region.

Finally he reached home to pay off at Devonport on 22 September 1885 (28).

Following his most successful commission in *Espiegle* it is gratifying to read in his 'Service Record' the numerous expressions of approval and thanks received from Their Lordships, the Colonial Office and the Foreign Office. In addition, following various inspections of the ship by senior officers, phrases such as, 'A precise and correct man of war', and, 'ship in very good order – gunnery good', similarly appear.

From 13 April 1886 to 10 November 1888 in command twin screw steel armour plated ship *Colossus*, 9,150 tons. Initially at Portsmouth, 'Fitting Out for Particular Service', then to the Mediterranean. At the commencement of the commission her Lieut. (G) was John R. Jellicoe. The ship completed at Portsmouth on 31 October 1886 (29). *Colossus* was the first British battleship to carry breech-loaders, being four 12". Also the first in which steel was used for general construction, and the first in which compound armour was used generally in place of iron.

Having relinquished command of *Colossus* he arrived back in England on 7 December 1888.

A month later followed his appointment as Director of Naval Intelligence, initially from 1 January 1889 but, for his first period, to be through to 7 July 1891.

GSP or Good Service Pension granted on 18 November 1889. This was one of only twelve so granted and paid Sterling 150 p.a.

During the summer of 1891 he was appointed in command of the ironclad *Sans Pareil*, 10,470 tons, for a month, to 4 August, during manoeuvres.

Then on 5 August 1891 returned to his duties as Director of Naval Intelligence.

Rear Admiral: 25 February 1892.

Continued as Director of Naval Intelligence to 31 August 1894.

C. in C., Australia Station: 1 November 1894 to 10 January 1898, flag in the first class armoured cruiser *Orlando*, 5,600 tons. The ship was commanded by Captain F.W. Fisher, younger brother of the future Admiral of the Fleet Lord Fisher. The new C. in C. travelled out from England by P. & O. steamer and joined her at Sydney, assuming command of the Station on 14 January 1895 (30).

While in command of the Station he prepared a paper, *Precis of existing and proposed Coast Defences of Australia*, for which he received the thanks of the authorities.

In 1898 succeeded by Rear Admiral Hugo Lewis Pearson and proceeded home in *Orlando*, on passage spending February 1898 at Singapore. While at Singapore the ship's bottom was cleaned in a rather unusual manner:-

> 'Cruising, and still more lying at anchor, in tropical waters lead to a rapid fouling of ships' bottoms, which seriously diminishes their speed when under way and increases steamers' consumption of coal. There was no dock at Singapore large enough to take in *Orlando*, and yet her bottom had to be cleaned somehow. Our diver reported that it was covered with marine growths. A party of Malays offered to clean it for a sum of money which, compared with that which docking would have cost, had it been possible to dock the ship, was almost ridiculously small. I directed the captain to make a contract with them to scrub the ship's bottom. All that they asked for was that a plank should be suspended from the ship's side, so as to be just above the surface of the water, and that it might be shifted from place to place as their work proceeded. This was done. The Malays simply jumped into the water, dived under the bottom, scrubbed vigorously at the fouling, and came to the surface again for a short rest on the plank. The party was not large, about nine or ten men and lads. The jumping in and diving under the ship was of course repeated many times by each individual. The whole operation was completed in a surprisingly short time, and was so thoroughly done that on the voyage from Singapore to England the ship was easily able to proceed at her best speed without undue consumption of coal (31).'

From the Straits he continued his passage to England, on 16 April 1898 arriving in Portsmouth in *Orlando*, and paying off three days later, on 19 April.

From 20 April to 28 November 1898 on half pay as a Rear Admiral which amounted to twenty five shillings a day.

Vice Admiral: 29 November 1898.

His half pay as a Vice Admiral from 29 November 1898 to 9 April 1901 was thirty two shillings and six pence a day.

While on half pay, as a serving officer, he was given leave to travel abroad for one month from 5 May 1899. On his return he was appointed Umpire for the 1899 manoeuvres.

KCB: 3 June 1899.

Prior to proceeding to the East to take up his appointment as C. in C. he communicated with his predecessor, Admiral Seymour, who wrote to him accordingly. Excerpts follow:-

1) From *Centurion* at Hong Kong on 29 March 1901.

   'About expenses out here; the pay et al covers them. Such of my private income as I have spent while out here has not been on the necessities of command. An admiral can quite live within his professional income here. I consider this all round the most preferable one we have; and personally, independent of expense, I would rather be here than in the Mediterranean.'

2) Homeward bound in *Centurion*, Indian Ocean, 14 July 1901.

   '... have talked to the Governor. He is a good fellow, but has many worries at Hong Kong. I commend you to my friend Sir Thomas Jackson, whose opinion on financial things in China, and love of the Navy are alike great (32).'

To assume command on the China Station he departed, '... in the Packet leaving England on 8 May (1901) for New York.' She was s.s. *Oceanic*, 17,274 grt, who arrived in New York on 13 May. From there he continued his journey via Buffalo, Chicago, Minneapolis and Moose-Jaw to Vancouver. A short visit was paid to Victoria then he sailed across the Pacific to Yokohama in the CPR s.s. *Empress of India*, 5,943 grt, Captain O.P. Marshall, arriving on 10 June 1901 (33). There he joined *Glory*, 12,950 tons. She had commissioned at Portsmouth in November 1900 as the new Flagship, China Station. After a short visit to Kobe, he arrived at Wei-Hai-Wei on 25 June and took up his appointment the following day, 26 June 1901, Sir Edward Seymour sailing for home immediately.

It being necessary to confer with the British ambassador, Sir Ernest Satow, next he took passage in *Alacrity* to Chingwangtao, thence by train via Tientsin to Peking.

To bring the Boxer uprising to an end the Boxer Protocol was signed at the Spanish Legation in Peking on 7 September 1901. Li Hung-chang, with just two months to live, signed for China.

It is relevant to note that between May 1900 and November 1901, in the absence of Mr. Jordan on home leave, the British Charge d'Affaires in Korea was John Harrington Gubbins, a Japanese scholar of distinction. Mr. Gubbins would have liked to have remained in Korea although he did hold a poor view of the country, 'an oriental state in complete decay'. However, to be of greater significance in just nine years, was a comment he made at this time:-

   'He observed the actions of the Japanese and found them to be active in all the aspects of Korean affairs: "The Japanese legation has the best information in regard to all matters in the peninsula" (34).'

Early during Sir Cyprian's term of office in the East the Admiralty brought up the question of coal supply for his men-of-war. Steam coal from Wales was of the best quality, and their mining industry well developed, but concern was expressed that in the event of war then possibly supplies might be interrupted. An alternative source was thought to be Westport, South Island, New Zealand. To this day (written in 2008) that region, which includes Stockton, remains an important source of this fuel.

In *Glory* he anchored at Yokohama in November 1901. Purely as a reminder of the era an indication follows of the number and frequency of salutes that were fired on these occasions:-

'1 November: 21 (guns) to The Emperor (Mikado) of Japan, these being returned by the Japanese cruiser *Kasagi*.

German Rear Admiral saluted the C. in C. with 15 guns. We returned the salute.

He paid an official visit to the C. in C. and we saluted him on his leaving the ship with 13 guns.

3 November: ships in harbour dressed ship at 8 a.m., Japanese flag at main, in honour of the Mikado of Japan's birthday. Men-o'-war fired a Royal Salute of 21 guns at noon.

4 November: American flagship *Brooklyn* (Rear Admiral) arrived at 10 a.m., first saluting port, and then saluting C. in C. with 15 guns. We returned the salute.

7 November: HBM Minister for Japan, Sir Claude MacDonald, paid an official visit to the C. in C. We saluted him on his leaving the ship with 15 guns.

9 November: dressed ship in commemoration of HM King Edward VII's birthday.

All men-o'-war fired a Royal Salute of 21 guns at noon, and played the National Anthem (35).'

In London the Anglo-Japanese Alliance was signed: 30 January 1902. From the British point of view the objective was largely one of thwarting Russian ambitions in the Far East. However Japan placed emphasis elsewhere:-

'It is noteworthy that the central issue for Japan was Korea. "The policy which Japan must always maintain", it read, "is to place Korea outside the scope of foreign countries' expansion policies, whatever dangers that may involve, however great the price." (36).'

The signing of the Alliance brought another benefit to Japan:-

'The boost which the alliance gave to Japanese national pride was immense. Japan was at last regarded as a fully privileged member of the international community (37).'

The First Lord of the Admiralty at the time was William Waldegrave Palmer, Second Earl Selborne (1859-1942). Once the Anglo-Japanese Alliance had been signed he sought Sir Cyprian's opinion concerning the new strategic conditions which now would prevail. On 22 April 1902 the C. in C. replied to His Lordship. An extract follows:-

'I would say that the Anglo-Japanese Agreement has profoundly modified them as regards the Far East. Japan was certain to join with some occidental state and it would have been deplorable if we had sat still and seen her combine with those who would be against us instead of getting her to combine with us. The bellicose character of the governing class in Japan is not to be denied; and, no doubt, there are many valiant warriors in the Japanese Army and Navy who are spoiling for a fight. Nevertheless I think that this need not make us very apprehensive of being dragged into unnecessary quarrels (38).'

Following the ratification of the terms of the Alliance, then on 14 May 1902 at the Yokosuka Navy Base a conference took place during which details were discussed. Amongst those attending was the C. in C. himself, Sir Claude Maxwell Macdonald (1852-1915) then the British Minister to Tokyo, together with the Navy Minister or Minister of Marine, and subsequent prime minister, Satsuma born Vice Admiral Yamamoto Gonnohyoe (1852-1933), General Terauchi the army minister, and Rear Admiral Saito Makoto, Vice Minister of Marine.

The next day Admiral Bridge wrote to the Admiralty giving an outline of the future practical arrangements for co-operation at sea between Great Britain and Japan (39).

Similarly on 19 May Sir Claude wrote to the Foreign Office, the Marquess of Lansdowne, however he ended his report with the following fascinating paragraph:-

'A somewhat interesting commentary on the day's proceedings was the fact that Vice Admiral Baron Inoue, Superintendent of the Yokosuka Dockyard, who presided at the lunch and proposed the King's health, was as a young man severely wounded by a British shell in the Batteries at Kagoshima in 1863 (40).'

Shortly after this conference, at 1.50 p.m. on Tuesday, 20 May 1902, a Japanese Squadron including the British built battleship *Hatsuse*, 14,850 tons and flying the flag of the Vice Admiral, with the British built battleship *Asahi*, the German built armoured cruiser *Yakumo*, American built cruiser *Chitose*, and other warships in company, entered harbour and anchored. The usual great numbers of salutes were fired, including twenty one guns to each respective country (41).

Subsequently *Glory*, flying the flag of the C. in C., sailed from Tokyo Bay at 7.40 a.m. on 23 May bound for Wei-hai-wei.

To the Admiralty, together with his letter of proceedings dated 29 July 1902, the C. in C. enclosed a copy of a report submitted to him by Captain Alfred W. Paget who in his cruiser *Endymion*, 7,350 tons, had visited the Etajima Naval Academy earlier that year, on 19 April (42). In view of the problems to come regarding the ever increasing trend towards Japanese militarism the following extract is relevant:-

'All religions, including the national Buddha and Shinto Faiths, are purposely ignored, instead a sentiment of intense loyalty to Emperor and Country is fostered (43).'

June 1902: departure from Japan of the British built cruisers *Asama*, 9,670 tons, and *Takasago*, 4,160 tons, to participate in the Coronation Naval Review, Spithead on 16 August.

HM King Edward VII was crowned on 9 August 1902. That day the Flagship *Glory* was at Wei-hai-wei where the fleet dressed at 0800 hours and at 1215 the Captain read out the King's message to his people. At 1230 followed a twenty one gun Royal salute fired by all men-o'-war there present.

The Christmas holidays in 1902 were spent at Hong Kong, and in the New Year the C. in C. cruised to Saigon, Singapore, Sarawak, Labuan, Brunei, British North Borneo, and Manila before returning to Hong Kong on 21 February. At the time the American Governor of the Philippine Islands was the one time judge and future Republican President of the U.S.A., the most competent and far sighted William Howard Taft (1857-1930).

Between November 1898 and July 1903 the Governor of Hong Kong was Sir Henry Arthur Blake (1840-1918). His distinguished career in the Colonial service was to end in 1907 when he retired to County Cork, his final position being to serve as Governor of Ceylon.

In January 1903, Lord Selborne, continuing in office as First Lord of the Admiralty, wrote in reply to two of Sir Cyprian's earlier letters. A few particularly relevant extracts follow. In one remark he refers to the Eastern business community:-

'... and owing to the clamour of those most short-sighted merchants which are the bane of our diplomacy in the Far East.'

'We had ear-marked the Yang-Tse as our sphere of interest, not our exclusive sphere of interest, because that would have been contrary to our policy of the open door, but as the sphere in which historically we had a special interest and therefore were not prepared to see any foreign nations obtain exclusive interests to our disadvantage as the Russians had done in Manchuria and the Germans in Shantung. There is no doubt that the foreigners were and are very jealous of our position on the Yang-Tse, knowing that with equal opportunities we could derive the greater advantage.'

'The importance of naval influence on our position in the Yang-Tse becomes greater and not less, and I was very glad to be able to promote Lieutenant Watson at the New Year as a mark of my sense of the admirable work he had done in *Woodcock*.'

He ended his communication with general comments concerning the expansion of shore establishments, and the new system of entering Naval officers. The latter arose from the perceived need to draw such officers, including the ever increasing requirement for engineers and technical men, from a wider social source:-

'As regards the general principle, I have no hesitation in saying that we regard the increase to the shore establishments as an evil; an evil which in some cases is necessary, but we rely upon the Commanders in Chief to assist us in checking it with all the means in their power.'

'I hope you will in the main approve of the new scheme for the entry and training of naval officers. The general principles of that scheme have been very deliberately adopted and will not of course be departed from, but in all matters of detail we shall welcome the suggestions and observations of all those who know the Service and have its welfare at heart (44).'

On the question of the short sighted merchants one cannot but wonder if His Lordship, a civil servant, might have paused to reflect that it was the taxes and duties generated by such trade and commerce which helped to cover the overheads and cost of running of both his department and those of his colleagues? Also there remains the question that without the activity of such merchants would there have existed the same need for diplomatic activity?

'The new scheme for the entry and training of naval officers' is a reference to the 'Selborne Scheme' of which much was heard from early in 1902. Admiral Sir John Fisher was one who fully recognised the importance of engineering officers in the technical Navy that had been developing at an ever increasing pace, and also felt that it was necessary to widen the net so that future officers, both deck and engine, were attracted to the service from a wider social scale than had been the case during the Victorian era. Lord Selborne generally concurred with the overall proposals. In due course the scheme was to come into effect in September 1903. By no means did all the ideas contained therein stand the test of time but:-

'Its two undeniable merits were that it produced a better and more fully educated naval officer, and a diminution of class prejudice in the service. Both led to greater efficiency, and this, as in all Fisher's reforms, had been his first aim (45).'

It is most apparent from the files of his private correspondence held at the National Maritime Museum at Greenwich that Sir Cyprian maintained an extraordinarily large correspondence with a great number of brother officers, colonial Governors and officials, government Ministers in England, and a host of other friends and family.

On 8 April 1903 in *Glory* he arrived at Kobe in order to participate in an Imperial Japanese Naval review:-

'A fine array of Japanese men-o'-war were at anchor here, comprising nearly the whole of their fleet, which were formed up in four lines. They presented a magnificent spectacle of Japan's great naval power. The foreign line consisted of *Glory* and *Blenheim* (British), *Hansa* (German flagship), *Calabria* (Italian), *Askold* (Russian), and *Pascal* (French). We dressed ship at noon in honour of the Emperor of Japan's arrival at Kobe. Fired a Royal Salute of 21 guns at 4 p.m., taking time from the Japanese flagship. Undressed ship at sunset.

April 10th (Good Friday). This day was chosen by the Mikado of Japan to hold the naval review. The morning opened rather dull and misty but luckily soon cleared. Fleet dressed with bunting at 8.20 a.m. (late owing to fog). The Mikado left the shore in a steam launch at 9.50 a.m., a gun being fired from shore as a signal to denote he had embarked. He stepped onboard *Asama* at 10 a.m., when she weighed, this being the signal for the fleet to commence the salute of 21 guns. *Asama*, preceded by a destroyer, and followed by the cruisers *Chihaya* and *Miyako*, commenced her tour through the long line of men-o'-war, coming first between the foreign line and first line of Japanese.

Each ship was manned, and the men gave three hearty cheers as the Emperor's ship passed, it being very amusing to hear the different nationalities cheer. *Asama* continued on through the lines, and finally anchored close to us. *Idzumo* fell out of line and anchored with *Asama*. All officers of the fleet were invited onboard *Idzumo* to lunch, as guests of the Emperor (46).'

Leaving Woosung on 29 April, from 7 to 10 May 1903, under the command of Captain Arthur W. Carter, *Glory* was at Hankow, 600 miles up the Yangtse River. Draft: fwd: 26' 7": aft: 26' 9". On passage upstream the size of the ship had caused some excitement:-

'At one place, Wuhu, I was told that every male inhabitant of the city able to walk had gone to the river front to gaze at the spectacle. It was an astonishing sight. There were tens of thousands of Chinese standing in close ranks along some two or three miles of river frontage.'

As may be imagined at Hankow too it was to be an especial occasion. As *Glory* steamed up river, on 4 May 1903 the British Consul, Mr. Everard D.H. Fraser, wrote to give Sir Cyprian an outline of some of the details in respect of his forthcoming visit:-

'The acting Viceroy will be happy to receive you at 3 p.m. on Thursday, May 7, and will return your call on board without delay. This means that you should land at the Cotton Mill at 2.30 p.m. Will you please telegraph if the hour does not suit. I told the Viceroy's secretary that you would salute the Chinese flag if they had a ship there to return the compliment – as this is what Commanders in Chief have done hitherto.

My wife and I hope you will dine with us one night of your visit and should be grateful if you would telegraph the evening that suits you from Kiukiang; and also, if you will grant the community the pleasure of hearing your band, we should like to issue invitations to a Garden Party to meet you on Saturday.

I hope you will not mind my making these requests: a visit from a Commander in Chief in his flagship is a great event in Hankow.

The Viceroy will provide vehicles for the party if you will telegraph the number of officers who will accompany you (47).'

His visit brought to a successful and happy conclusion then during the afternoon of Saturday, 9 May at Hankow the C. in C., accompanied by his staff, embarked in the despatch vessel *Alacrity*, Commander Osmond de B. Brock. In her, and with several stops en route, he returned downstream to reach Shanghai on Friday, 15 May 1903 (48).

At Wei-Hai-Wei during the afternoon of 5 August a sailing race for the cup presented by *Glory* took place with two of her boats covering the ship with glory by coming in first and third.

The C. in C. gave a ball onboard that evening, the guests including Mrs. Evans, the wife of the C. in C., Asiatic Fleet, Rear Admiral Robley Dungliston 'Fighting Bob' Evans, USN (1846-1912). With his flag in *Connecticut* BB-18 on 16 December 1907 he was to lead the 'Great White Fleet' out through the Virginia Capes at the start of that very considerable undertaking around the world.

In order that she could attend this social occasion at Wei-Hai-Wei, Sir Cyprian had given Mrs. Evans passage the short distance along the coast from Chefoo. Admiral Evans was most grateful, also in his subsequent letter of thanks adding remarks concerning the current political situation in Manchuria:-

'*Kentucky* at Chefoo. 4 August 1903.

I can never tell you how much I appreciate your courtesy and kindness in giving passage to Mrs. Evans to Wei-Hai-Wei in *Alacrity* ...

Manchuria matter seems to be more quiet during the past week and it looks as if the crisis may have passed but the Japanese are much excited and no one can say how far they may go. Russia grows stronger every day and seems confident (49).'

Returning from leave to his post as Minister to China, and writing from Government House in Hong Kong, where he was staying as a guest of Sir Henry Blake, on 8 August 1903 Sir Ernest Satow explained his movements and mentioned how much he was looking forward to meeting Sir Cyprian prior to returning to Peking:-

'... and shall go straight to Shanghai in the P. & O. steamer *Sumatra* by which I came here from Penang. From Shanghai I can get to Wei-Hai-Wei by one of the Butterfield & Swire steamers, for I want greatly to see you and hear what the state of international politics really is (50).'

All proceeded smoothly and in due course, on 16 August 1903, Sir Ernest recorded in his diary the substance of a conversation with Sir Cyprian which they had held together at Wei-Hai-Wei. Far from steaming north with China Navigation, Sir Ernest had arrived that Sunday morning from Shanghai in the cruiser *Eclipse*, 5,600 tons, Captain Robert H.S. Stokes. Excerpts follow:-

'He (the Admiral) considers that our people at home have not played the game as regards the Japanese alliance, and ought to have done much more. (--).

We both agree that it would be very bad policy to allow Russia to crush Japan, and that we should favour her trying to resuscitate China, also that Japan would not attack Russia about Manchuria, but would fight for Corea (51).'

Admiral: 30 August 1903.

On the day of his promotion he was flying his flag in *Glory* on passage from Wei-Hai-Wei to Vladivostok and already had rounded the southern coast of Korea and had entered the Sea of Japan. The news of his promotion was received in the ship on 8 September by which time he had completed his visit to the Russians and the ship was at anchor off Hakodate, Hokkaido.

On the following day the French C. in C., Vice Admiral C.J. Bayle, and a great friend of Sir Cyprian, arrived in his flagship, *Montcalm* (52).

During his cruise in these northern waters of the Station clearly the C. in C. had written to the Governor in Hong Kong mentioning increased signs of tension between Japan and Russia. From Government House in Hong Kong on 1 September 1903 Sir Henry replied privately in his own hand. His Excellency was well aware of at least one Japanese characteristic. Extracts follow:-

'Your letter was the first intimation that I have had of any especial strain; but it is certain that public opinion in Japan is in favour of a war, and the question is whether the Government can withstand it. Apparently Russia thinks not. I quite agree with you that it is a time for incessant vigilance. I question if even you will hear any thing from the Japs if they intend to strike, until the bolt has been shot, for secretiveness is their dominant inspiration.

If the Japs want to fight they must begin before the Russian naval reinforcement arrives (53).'

Earlier in the commission his Second in Command on the station had been Rear Admiral Harry Tremenheere Grenfell (1845-1906) but, owing to ill health, on 3 July 1903 from Yokohama in a CPR liner via Canada, he had been invalided home. In England he had undergone further medical treatment. From his home in Northampton on 24 September 1903 he wrote to Sir Cyprian. Apart from describing aspects of his recovery he added other remarks, a few of which follow, the first and last paragraphs being especially entertaining, the last also being a sad reflection:-

'I was very well taken care of on the journey home but it is a trip to take your time over to enjoy it. The Rockies are really very grand but rushing through one loses a great deal. I was very much struck with Vancouver – last time I saw it was in 1875 when it did not exist (if that is not Irish).

They are sending out Nathan as Governor to Hong Kong – he was a Captain of Engineers with the Inspector General of Fortifications.

No one seems to know that there are such animals as Russians in the Far East in this part of the World (54).'

As second in command of the China Station, in August 1903 Admiral Grenfell was succeeded by Rear Admiral The Hon. Assheton Gore Curzon-Howe (1850-1911).

At Singapore between 10 and 13 October Sir Cyprian held talks with two brother Admirals, Vice Admiral Arthur Fanshawe, C. in C., Australian Station and Rear Admiral George Lambart Atkinson-Willes, C. in C., East Indies. The latter was a nephew of the late Sir George Willes, C. in C., China in 1881.

GCB: 9 November 1903.

With his flag in *Glory*, when he arrived at Kobe on 6 November 1903 the American flagship *Kentucky* BB-6, continuing to fly the flag of Admiral Robely D. Evans, was found in port.

Off Kobe on 28 November 1903 the C. in C. transferred from *Glory* to *Alacrity* as it was in the latter ship that he was to make his farewell round to various ports on the station. *Glory* herself returned to Hong Kong to refit.

As the tension between Russian and Japan gradually moved towards breaking point it was on 11 January 1904 that Lord Selborne again wrote to Sir Cyprian. Included in his letter was confirmation of the clear policy to be followed by Great Britain: 'We shall observe the letter and spirit of our duties as allies according to the treaty with Japan. We shall keep the ring clear.' Nevertheless, as may be seen from the following, it was equally clear where sympathy rested. The two battleships referred to were no longer required by Chile and so had come onto the market:-

> 'I did all I could to get the Japanese to buy those two Chilean battleships but they made a sad mess of the business and we had only just time to step in and buy them out of the very mouth of the Russians which alone was no mean service to Japan (55).'

6 February 1904. Japan severed relations with Russia and two days later the Russo-Japanese war commenced with a successful Naval attack at Port Arthur. There Vice Admiral Togo Heihachiro, IJN gained the advantage over the Tsarist fleet, Vice Admiral Oskar Stark.

This operation off Port Arthur covered the Japanese landings which commenced on 8 February at Chemulpo, an important objective and which eventually was to result in the successful Japanese occupation of Korea. On 9 February the proceedings at Chemulpo were witnessed by HMS *Talbot*, Captain Lewis Bayly. There two Russian men of war, *Varyag* and *Korietz*, the former having received considerable damage by 8" gun fire from HIJMS *Asama*, the cruiser mentioned earlier, were scuttled during the afternoon of 9 February. *Talbot* received onboard some 300 Russian survivors of whom one officer and twenty four men were wounded. Additional medical assistance was provided by the surgeon from the Alfred Holt cargo vessel *Ajax*, 7,043 grt, who chanced to be at anchor nearby (56).

In *Talbot* clearly the British were impressed by the Japanese staff work. On 17 February, in addition to 'a good fall of snow' onboard, it was recorded that:-

> 'The Japanese, in all their movements about here, seem to show remarkable thoughtfulness and planning in all arrangements for disembarking the troops, horses, guns and stores. All the transports bring a number of large sampans for landing the troops, and the larger transports have brought several harbour tugs. Each tug tows four, six, or eight sampans laden, and they are on the move day and night. No difficulties are encountered entraining for Seoul or in housing the troops there (57).'

Naturally the composition of the Japanese Fleet was of the utmost importance to that country. In this connection one authority has written:-

> 'The prime concern of all governments and the parties in this period in Japan, except for a handful of socialists, was the acquirement of larger and more modern armaments. This was achieved mainly with the help of the British. Out of 44 naval vessels of 194,473 tons in total, launched between the end of the Sino-Japanese War and 1904, as many as 27 (133,367 tons in all, 66% of the total) were built in Britain. All six battleships of 13,500 to 15,000 tons were British made. Four out of six armoured cruisers were also built in Britain. Home made vessels, mostly small cruisers, destroyers and communication ships, launched from the Yokosuka and Kure naval yards, formed only 8.5% of the total naval strength. "As far as major warships were concerned, the Japanese navy was a sub species of the British navy" (58).'

It goes without saying the the progress of the Russo-Japanese conflict was of interest to a great many diplomats, officals, and to other observers of all nations. As one example on 25 February 1904 from Peking Sir Ernest Satow wrote to Sir Cyprian. Firstly he was concerned about the danger to any British subjects in Manchuria, and then continued as follows, his next point being that, in common with most European commentators, he too thought that the outcome of the war was certain. Finally he gave his opinion regarding the matter which to this day is regarded as being questionable. It is held by some that the niceties were not observed in that although Japan indeed broke off diplomatic relations with Russia on 6 February, she did not actually declare war prior to their attack at Port Arthur on 8 February:-

> 'I cannot learn anything about the movements of Japanese troops, but infer that the only landing that has hithero taken place is in Corea, perhaps at Wonsan as well as Chemulpo. Nechida tells me the navy has established a provisional base somewhere south of the latter point, on the west coast of Corea (-).
>
> My colleagues think the Russians will certainly crush the Japanese land forces when they come to close quarters, and I cannot myself say that I have confidence in any other result. It may take a long time for Russia "to strike a blow worthy of her might", but she has enormous reserves in the way of men (-).
>
> The outcry against Japan for treachery seems unjustified. On the 6th the Japanese Minister at Petersburg delivered notes breaking off relations, announcing that Japan would take all measures to protect her interests and that he was to withdraw. They thus had forty eight hours notice, and ought to have warned Alexeieff to be on the look out... (59).'

With his successor arriving at Hong Kong on 11 March, it was just three days later, on Monday, 14 March 1904 that indeed he was relieved by Vice Admiral Sir Gerard Noel.

Prior to leaving the ship and proceeding home to retire he received a number of letters of good wishes from many friends and brother officers. One, dated 1 March 1904, was addressed to him by the Captain of *Glory*, Arthur William Carter:-

> '... like to feel that I am something more than 'somebody you've served with' to a man to whom I owe so much as I do to you – I therefore hope that you will for once relax your usual rule and accept the small silver plate which accompanies this as a token of goodwill from, yours sincerely, ... (60).'

On 15 March 1904 Captain Lewis Bayly, a future Admiral, wrote to him from *Talbot* to offer:-

> '... sincere gratitude for all you have taught me by word and example, during the many years that I have had the honour of knowing you, (--)... thoroughly good officer, and a kind and courteous gentleman (61).'

He returned to England from Yokohama to San Francisco via Honolulu, arriving home on 8 May 1904 (62). To join his trans Pacific liner he steamed up from Hong Kong in the armoured cruiser *Leviathan*, 14,150 tons, Captain Francis G. Kirby, who arrived at Yokohama on 20 March.

Concerning some of the officials in Japan whom he had come to know he later was to write:-

> 'I met many of the most prominent personages in Japan – ministers, generals, admirals, and other high officials. I look back with unalloyed pleasure to my intercourse with them. I invariably found them honourable and high-minded men, on whose word I could implicitly rely (63).'

Officially however, he had retired on 15 March 1904, according to Admiralty records that day being his sixty fifth birthday (64).

On receipt of the senior officers' GSP of GBP 300.00 p.a. from 22 August 1911, then his Admiral's retirement pay of GBP 950 p.a. was reduced to GBP 922-15-0 p.a., only reverting to the higher figure from 31 March 1919 (65).

Meanwhile on 6 June 1904 Togo Heihachiro, IJN had been promoted full Admiral. Sir Cyprian wrote to congratulate him and, writing from HIJMS *Mikasa*, on 1 August 1904 Admiral Togo replied:-

'I have the great pleasure to acknowledge your letter dated June 9; I feel much flattered to have your congratulation of my promotion.

Our nations feel much proud to have such allies as Great Britain especially at the time of present trial.

I myself feel sincerely honoured to have friendship with you, we had so far a good work with Russians; I am happy to assure you that our forces are quite healthy and willing to serve this war. Yours very truly, H. Togo (66).'

Later in 1904 he presided over the North Sea Inquiry Commission. The need for the inquiry had arisen over the wretchedly irresponsible behaviour of the Russian Fleet against British fishing trawlers on Dogger Bank during the night of 21/22 October 1904.

At Chelsea on Saturday, 29 October 1904, at the Chapel of the Royal Hospital, he was a Pall Bearer on the occasion of the funeral of the soldier and Colonial Governor, Field Marshall Sir Henry Wylie Norman who had died just three days previously. They had been old acquaintances since, at the end of 1894, on taking up his appointment as C. in C., Australia Station, Sir Henry was just commencing his final year as Governor of Queensland (67).

In retirement he continued to take an interest in and to correspond with friends in the East. The Russo-Japanese war of 1904-1905 was only to be brought to a final conclusion by the Treaty of Portsmouth: 5 September 1905. However prior to the actual signing of this treaty he had written to friends in the Imperial Japanese Navy and in reply on 31 August 1905 the Naval Attache at the Japanese Legation wrote:-

'I am instructed by Baron Yamamoto, The Minister of Marine, to transmit to you that, "to offer his most sincere thanks for your kind congratulation for the peace concluded" (68).'

Admiralty Representative on Royal Patriotic Fund Corporation: 1906-1912.

A member of the Mesopotamia Commission of Inquiry: August 1916.

Proficient in Latin, French, German and Swedish, he was the author or editor of many works on naval and military history including *The Art of Naval Warfare* (1907), *Sea Power and Other Studies* (1910), and *Some Recollections* (1918). Earlier in 1899, as a Vice Admiral, he had edited, *History of the Russian Fleet During the Reign of Peter the Great, by a Contemporary Englishman (1724)*. In addition in 1910 he was a founding committee member of the Society for Nautical Research. On 16 June 2010 this Society celebrated their centenary with a gathering at the RUSI, Whitehall.

His Funeral took place at Putney Vale Cemetery on Wednesday, 20 August 1924, the service being conducted by a cousin, The Rev. H.F. Waller-Bridge. Among the mourners were his wife and many members of his family. Also among those present to pay their last respects were Admiral Sir Reginald Custance (1847-1935), Paymaster Rear Admiral Sir Francis Harrison-Smith who had been his secretary in China, and the Assistant Naval Attache to the Japanese Embassy, London (69).

On his death the gross value of his estate amounted to GBP 16,116-16-7 (70).

In the Dictionary of National Biography his entry was written by a distinguished brother officer, Admiral Sir Herbert W. Richmond (1871-1946), latterly Master of Downing College, Cambridge. Amongst other remarks, in describing aspects of Sir Cyprian's life and career Sir Herbert was to include:-

'His social gifts were considerable. Very courteous, he was both a good listener and a good talker with a ready and sometimes caustic wit. He sought information at all times and was quick to discern those who possessed it.'

NOTES

1. 'According to the positive statements of both my parents I was born on 13 March 1839.' 'The old rector by whom I was baptised, in noting the date of birth either put '15th' in the register by mistake for '13th', or made his 3 so like a 5 that the Admiralty insisted on 15 March being officially counted as my birthday'. Admiral Sir Cyprian Bridge, *Some Recollections,* (London, 1918), 25.

   There was a Naval background as his father, Thomas Finch Hobday Bridge (1807-1856), was the second son of Captain Thomas Bridge, RN. Health problems however, prevented his father from going to sea. Charterhouse and Christ Church, Oxford. Having taken Holy Orders then in 1832 he 'went to Newfoundland in 1832 as chaplain to (H.E. The Governor, Captain Sir Thomas John, RN) Cochrane and tutor to his son.'

   Thomas John Cochrane (1789-1872), cousin of the well known 10th Earl of Dundonald, was to leave Newfoundland in 1834 and subsequently continue with his Naval career, and most successfully. Admiral of the Fleet: 12 September 1865. With his appointment on 16 April 1825, Sir Thomas had become the first resident Governor of Newfoundland. *Dictionary of Canadian Biography Online.*

2. *Dictionary of National Biography.* John Dunscombe (1777-1847). Born in Bermuda. In Newfoundland from 1808 to represent a group of Bermuda businessmen. Member of the Executive Council of Newfoundland: 1833-1842. Subsequently moved to Montreal but eventually was to die in Liverpool, England. *Dictionary of Newfoundland and Labrador Biography.*

3. Obituary, *The Surrey Comet,* 20 August 1924.

4. Ibid. John Crawshay **Bailey** (1818-1896). Lieutenant: 27 August 1844. Commander: 3 December 1851. Appointed in command of *Medea,* indeed his last ship: 18 December 1852. *Navy List.*

5. Obituary, *The Times,* Monday, August 18, 1924. The obituary gives his date of birth as 13 March 1839.

6. NA ADM 196/14. 796. *Service Record.* Also in ADM 196/36.

7. *Some Recollections,* 129-133. For another account of this remarkable 'freight', also see Barry M. Gough, *The Mariner's Mirror,* Vol. 69, 1983, 419-433. As a Captain in 1853 Augustus Kuper also received similar benefit – see C. in C., 1862.

8. *Service Record.*

9. William Fanshawe **Martin** (1801-1895). For career detail see Buller, C. in C., 1895, reference (7).

10. *Service Record.* During that commission in the West Indies he served under, firstly, Commander Charles Joseph Wrey, then Commander Walter Cecil Chetwynd-Talbot (1834-1904), son of the Earl of Shrewsbury but in 1868 to assume the surname Carpenter thus in due course to be Admiral The Hon. Walter Cecil Carpenter. Finally under Commander Basil Sidmouth De Ros Hall.

11. Ibid.

12. *Some Recollections,* 223/4. HIM Emperor Mutsuhito reigned from 1868 to 1912, the Meiji era.

13. *Service Record.*

14. *Dictionary of National Biography.*

15. Higham and Cox Wing.

16. *Dictionary of National Biography.*

17. *Some Recollections,* 233. HMS *Espiegle* was manned by 13 officers, 28 petty officers, 66 seamen, 10 boys and 24 Royal Marines to give a total of 141 men. NA ADM 53/12233.

18. NA ADM 1/6676. 11-20.

19. NA ADM 50/326.

20. George William **Des Voeux.** Born in Baden-Baden, Germany: 22 September 1834. Died in London: 15 December 1909. Charterhouse. Balliol College, Oxford and University of Toronto. Called to the Bar of Upper Canada: 1861. Magistrate, British Guiana: 1863-1869. Administrator, St. Lucia: 1869. Acting Governor of Trinidad: January 1877 – January 1878. Acting Governor of Fiji: June 1878 – September 1879. Governor of the Bahamas: 1880. Governor of Fiji and High Commissioner, Western Pacific: 1880 – 1885. KCMG: 1883. Governor of Newfoundland: 1886 – 1887. Governor of Hong Kong: October 1887 to May 1891 when he retired. GCMG: 1893. *Colonial Office List,* 1909. *Who's Who,* 1908. In 1875 he married Marion Denison Pender (1856-1955), younger daughter of the submarine cable pioneer, Sir John Pender (1816-1896). Aged twenty nine he, Des Voeux, had first arrived in Georgetown, British

Guiana just before Christmas 1863. The quite astonishing story of a number of the great many difficulties which he was to overcome as a young man are recounted in Stephanie Williams, *Running the Show*, Chapter Three. Also see his autobiography, *My Colonial Service*, II, (London, 1903).

21. George Ruthven **Le Hunte**. Born in Co. Wexford: 20 August 1852. Died in Crowborough: 29 January 1925. Eton. Trinity College, Cambridge. Barrister, Inner Temple: 1881. Between 1875 and 1887 held a variety of posts in Fiji including, from May 1883, that of Judicial Commissioner for the High Commission to the West Pacific Islands. President of Dominica: 1887-1894. Colonial Secretary, Barbados: 1894-1897. Colonial Secretary, Mauritius: 1897. Lieutenant Governor, Papua: 1898-1903. KCMG: 26 June 1903. Governor of South Australia: 1 July 1903 to 18 February 1909. Governor of Trinidad and Tobago: 11 May 1909 to January 1916. GCMG: 1912. *Colonial Office List*, 1924. *Who's Who*, 1925. *Australian Dictionary of Biography*.

22. NA ADM 1/6676. Report No. 7 addressed to Commodore Erskine.

    James Elphinstone **Erskine**. Born in India: 2 December 1838. Died: 25 July 1911. Entered the Navy: 1852. Captain: 4 November 1868. As Commodore Second Class, C. in C., Australia: 21 January 1882 to 23 January 1885 when succeeded by Rear Admiral George Tryon. Rear Admiral: 18 January 1886. Vice Admiral: 14 February 1892. C. in C., North America and West Indies: 5 March 1895 to 15 September 1897 when succeeded by Vice Admiral Sir John A. Fisher. KCB: 22 June 1897. Admiral: 23 August 1897. Admiral of the Fleet: 3 October 1902. *Navy List*. Rear Admiral C.C. Penrose Fitzgerald, *Sir George Tryon, KCB*, (Edinburgh and London, 1907), 196.

23. Francis X. Hezel, *The First Taint of Civilization*, (Hawaii, 1983), 295/6. J. Ruthven Le Hunte, *Six Letters from the Western Pacific*, (Colombo, 1883), Letter No. 4, 23-34. The latter courtesy of Professor Donald R. Shuster, University of Guam.

24. Hezel, 281. Le Hunte, Letter No. 6, 43-63.

25. Le Hunte, Letter No. 2, 15.

26. Hezel, 236.

27. *Some Recollections,* 304

28. *Service Record.*

29. Oscar Parkes, *British Battleships*, (Annapolis, 1990), 288.

30. *Service Record.*

31. *Some Recollections,* 309. *Orlando* was 300' in length and 56' in beam. In addition to the Straits it may be noted that the waters of Ceylon (Sri Lanka) also are especially notorious for rapid marine growth. Apart from hindering the progress of the ship, such marine growth also tends to block intake pipes such as of cooling water.

32. Caird Library. Ref: *BRI/19*. HE The Governor was Sir Henry A. Blake.

    Thomas **Jackson**. Born in Carrigallen, Co. Leitrim: 4 June 1841. Died in London: 21 December 1915. In Hong Kong in 1865 he joined the Hongkong and Shanghai Banking Corporation. Early service as an accountant in Shanghai and Yokohama, latterly as Manager in Yokohama from 1870-1874. In 1876, when only thirty five years of age, appointed Chief Manager, the most senior executive position in the bank. With two intervals in charge of the London office to retain that position until his retirement in 1902. Baronet: 25 July 1902. Maurice Collis, *Wayfoong: The Hongkong and Shanghai Banking Corporation*, (London, 1965).

33. A.E. Butterworth, *The Commission of HMS Glory*, (London, 1904), 15.

34. Ed. Ian Nish, *Britain and Japan: Biographical Portraits, Vol. II,* (Richmond, Surrey, 1997), Chapter Eight, 113.
    John Harington **Gubbins**. Born in Agra, India: 24 January 1852. Died in Edinburgh: 23 February 1929. Harrow. Appointed to Tokyo as a Student Interpreter: April 1871. 'Gubbins became highly proficient in the language and in 1889 published, *A Dictionary of Chinese-Japanese words in the Japanese Language*.' With the Japanese naturally desiring to bring to an end the era of extraterritoriality, it was he who, for Britain, negotiated the terms of the new commercial treaty of 16 July 1894. CMG: 1898. Following service in Korea he proceeded to Britain on leave: 1902-1903. Promoted Secretary of Legation: 26 June 1902. Returned to Japan for a further five years, until 1908. Officially retired: 10 September 1909. Subsequently Lecturer in Japanese at the University of Oxford following which, in 1911, was to be published his, *The Progress of Japan:1853-1871*. A close friend both of Chamberlain and of Satow. Great War service in postal censorship. In 1922 another major work of his was published, *The Making of Modern Japan*. *Foreign Office List*, 1929.

35. *The Commission of HMS Glory*, 25.

Leaving Tokyo on 28 May 1901 in s.s. *Hongkong Maru*, 6,185 grt, for San Francisco on the start of his voyage home, Sir Claude MacDonald was away in England for some three months and during this time, 'there is evidence that he was fairly frequently consulted', on the matter of the proposed Anglo-Japanese Alliance. Hugh Cortazzi, *British Envoys in Japan: 1859-1972*, (Folkstone, Kent, 2004), 96. Ian C. Ruxton, *The Diaries and Letters of Sir Ernest Mason Satow: 1843-1929*, (Lewiston, NY, 1998), 306. Sir Claude returned to Tokyo late in October 1901. Cortazzi, 97.

36. Tsuzuki Chushichi, *The Pursuit of Power in Modern Japan: 1825-1995*, (OUP, 2000), 168.

37. John Curtis Perry, *Great Britain and the Imperial Japanese Navy: 1858-1905*, (Harvard, 1961), 202.

38. Ed. D. George Boyce, *The Crisis of British Power: The Imperial and Naval Papers of the Second Earl of Selborne, 1895-1910*, (London, 1990), 143.

39. NA ADM 116/1231B.

40. Ibid. The future Admiral of the Fleet Viscount **Inoue** Yoshika. Born in Kagoshima: 3 November 1845. Died in Tokyo: 22 March 1929. The British bombardment of Kagoshima took place between 15 and 17 August 1863 – see Kuper, C. in C., 1862. Admiral Inoue was C. in C., Yokosuka between 20 May 1900 and 20 December 1905.

41. NA ADM 53/21328. Log Book *Glory*.

42. Alfred Wyndham **Paget**. Born, a son of General Lord Alfred Henry Paget: 20 March 1852. Died: 17 June 1918. Entered the RN: 1865. Egyptian War: 1882. Eastern Sudan: 1884-1885. Suakim: 1888. Captain: 30 June 1896. Naval Attache respectively at Paris, Petrograd and Washington: 1896-1899. China Station: 1900-1902. KCMG: 1905. Rear Admiral: 1 October 1906. Senior Officer Coast of Ireland: 1908-1911. Vice Admiral: March 1911. KCB: June 1911. Admiral: December 1913. Retired: September 1914. RNR during WW1. *Who's Who*.

43. NA ADM 1/7590. Letter No. 692.

44. Caird Library. Ref: *BRI/15*. Between 5 April and 7 May 1900 Lieut. Hugh Dudley Richards **Watson** (1872-1954) had ascended the Yangtse Gorges from Ichang to Chungking, only the second such ascent in a steam powered ship, and the first in a ship of appreciable tonnage. Promoted Commander: 1 January 1903. Jonathan Parkinson, *The First Steam Powered Ascent Through the Yangtse Gorges*, (Journal of the Royal Asiatic Society, Hong Kong Branch, Vol. 46, 2006), 149-174.

45. Richard Hough, *First Sea Lord*, (London, 1969), 156. Ruddock F. Mackay in *Fisher of Kilverstone*, (OUP, 1973), 284:-
    'However, what with the new education scheme for officers together with improved training and prospects of ratings, there can be no question that Fisher had swiftly achieved a number of much needed reforms.'

46. H.I.M. Emperor Mutsuhito (1852-1912). 1868 to 1912, the Meiji era.
    Armoured cruiser *Asama*, 9,670 tons, built at Elswick in 1899. Recently she had returned from the Coronation Review at Spithead. To receive considerable damage from Russian gunfire at Tsushima, 27/28 May 1905. Sold for scrapping in August 1946.
    Chihaya, 1,250 tons, built at Yokosuka in 1901, and *Miyako*, 1,800 tons at Kure in 1901.
    Armoured cruiser *Idzumo*, 9,750 tons, built at Elswick in 1900. Yard No. 681. Also to play an active role in the Russo-Japanese war of 1904-1905. In May 1905 at Tsushima the Second Fleet flagship of the Satsuma born Vice Admiral **Kamimura** Hikonojo (1849-1916). Between 1932 and 1942 frequently to be positioned at Shanghai as flagship. See C. in C., 1936 for the 14 August 1937 affair at Shanghai, and C. in C., 3-10 December 1941 for the sinking of HMS *Peterel* at Shanghai: 8 December 1941. Scrapped in 1947. Peter Brook, *Warships for Export*, (Gravesend, Kent, 1999), 109-114.

47. Caird Library. Ref: *BRI/17*. Everard Duncan Home **Fraser**. Born in Duddingston, Edinburgh: 27 February 1859. Died in office in Shanghai: 21 March 1922. Appointed Student Interpreter in China: 30 March 1880. Early service in Foochow, Kiukiang, Ichang, Chemulpo, Chungking and Canton. Consul, Chinkiang: 13 May 1899. Acting Consul-General, Hankow: 24 January 1900. Consul-General, Hankow: 1 July 1901. Transferred to Shanghai: 20 January 1911. KCMG: 14 June 1912. *Foreign Office List*. Describing his service at Shanghai it has been written:-
    '… after an incumbency so distinguished that the leading local 'paper, not given to praising the service, declared that Shanghai would not look upon his like again.'
    P.D. Coates, *The China Consuls*, (OUP, 1988), 444.

48. NA ADM 53/16793. In due course de Brock was to reach the highest rank, promoted Admiral of the Fleet: 31 July 1929. *Navy List*.

49. Caird Library. Ref: *BRI/18*. USS *Kentucky* BB-6, 11,520 tons. Commissioned on 16 May 1900. Under the terms of the

Washington Naval Treaty to be sold for scrap in January 1924. Participated in the around the world cruise of the 'Great White Fleet': 1907-1909. *Dictionary of American Naval Fighting Ships.*

50. Ibid. s.s. *Sumatra*, 4,607 grt. Built in 1895, sold out of P. & O. service in 1914.

51. Ed. Ian C. Ruxton, *The Diaries and Letters of Sir Ernest Mason Satow (1843-1929),* (Lewiston, NY, 1998), 323.

52. Butterworth, 101.

53. Caird Library. Ref: *BRI/18*. In due course considerable Russian Naval reinforcements for the Far East, designated Second Pacific Squadron under the command of Vice Admiral Zinovy Petrovich Rozhestvensky, were to leave the Baltic in October 1904.

54. Ibid. Ref: *BRI/17*.

55. *The Crisis of British Power,* 168. The two small battleships acquired by the RN were to be named *Swiftsure* and *Triumph*, each 11,800 tons. At the outbreak of the Great War *Triumph* was to operate in cooperation with the IJN against the enemy at Tsingtao – see C. in C., 1913.

56. W.A. May, *The Commission of HMS Talbot: 1901-1904,* (London, 1904), 142-150.

57. Ibid. 153. The greatest range of spring tides at Chemulpo/Inchon is thirty three feet, and some of the channels are narrow and difficult, thus adding spice to landing operations from ships at anchor in the bay.

58. Tsuzuki, 169.

59. Caird Library. Ref: *BRI/17*. Alexieff is Viceroy of the Far East, Vice Admiral Alexieff, 'who compensated for his lack of sea going experience by his position as protégé of the Grand Duke Alexei Alexandrovich and as rumoured illegitimate son of the Tsar Alexander II.' David Walder, *The Short Victorious War,* (London, 1973), 55.

60. Ibid. Ref: *BRI/14*.

61. Ibid.

62. *Service Record.*

63. *Some Recollections,* 316.

64. *Service Record.*

65. Ibid.

66. Caird Library. Ref: *BRI/19*.

67. Ibid. Ref: *BRI/17*. Henry Wylie **Norman**. Born: 2 December 1826. Died in Chelsea, London: 26 October 1904. At age seventeen joined the Indian Army. Made his name during numerous Frontier campaigns, and during the Mutiny. Mentioned in Despatches on no less than twenty five occasions. In May 1870 appointed Military Member of the Viceroy's Council, The Viceroy then being Richard Southwell Bourke, 6th Earl of Mayo (1822-1872). KCB: 1873. General: 1 April 1882. Governor of Jamaica: 1883-1889. GCMG: 1887. GCB: 1887. Governor of Queensland: 1889-1895. Field Marshall: 26 June 1902. *Who's Who.*

68. Ibid. **Yamamoto** Gonnohyoe. Born in Kagoshima: 26 November 1852. Died: 8 December 1933. Satsuma born but, once he attained high Naval rank, credited for ensuring the promotion of able officers from other han. Rear Admiral: 1895. Vice Admiral: 1898. Baron: 1902. Admiral: 1904. Count: 1907. Twice Prime Minister: February 1913 to April 1914, and September 1923 to January 1924. As Minister of Marine during the Russo-Japanese war of 1904-1905 it was he who appointed Togo Heihachiro as C. in C., Fleet. *Encyclopaedia Britannica.*

69. *The Surrey Comet,* 23 August 1924.

70. *Service Record.*

15 January 1904 to 6 December 1905
Vice Admiral Sir Gerard Henry Uctred **Noel**

Born on 5 March 1845, the second son of The Reverend Augustus William Noel (1816-1884), Rector of Stanhoe, Norfolk, and his wife Lucy Elizabeth, nee Tonge.

Died on Thursday, 23 May 1918 at his residence, 'The Moat', Fincham, Downham, Norfolk.

Joined the Royal Navy and as a **Naval Cadet** served in *Illustrious* for a fortnight: 14 to 31 December 1858. Thereafter in *Britannia* from 1 January to 18 May 1859 (1). Appointed to the converted second rate *Hannibal*: 19 May 1859 and while serving in her promoted **Midshipman**: 17 August 1860. Remained in *Hannibal* until 24 December 1861 when, on Christmas day 1861, appointed to *Shannon*. **Sub Lieutenant**: 7 March 1864. Continued in screw frigate *Shannon*, 2,667 tons, Captain Oliver J. Jones, North America and West Indies, until 11 April 1865 (2). Between 12 April and 23 May 1865 briefly attended the gunnery school *Excellent*. From 18 September 1865 in paddle sloop *Basilisk*, 1,031 tons, Captain William N. W. Hewett, VC, China. **Lieutenant**: 21 April 1866. From 10 May 1866 in *Princess Royal*, Captain William Gore Jones, Flagship, China Station. She flew the flag of temporary Vice Admiral George St. V. King (see C. in C., 1865), and her Commander was Alexander Buller (see C. in C., 1895). From 30 June 1866 in screw sloop *Rattler*, 1,280 tons, China. Prior to the opening of Kobe and Osaka to foreign trade, 1 January 1868, a party from the British Legation at Yedo took passage in her from Yokohama. Excerpts from the Satow memoires follow:-

'We anchored off Ozaka in the afternoon (of 2 December).'

'The same afternoon (13 December) we returned to Ozaka by boat, accompanied by Noel, first lieutenant of the *Rattler*. There we found the whole population occupied with festivities in honour of the approaching opening of the city to foreign trade.'

'That evening (16 December) we, that is, Mitford, Noel and I, devoted to a *diner en ville* in the Japanese fashion at a sort of 'Trois freres' called Tokaku, and about half past six we started forth.'

'Noel returned next day (17 December) to his ship (3).'

On 24 September 1868 *Rattler* was wrecked on a previously unknown reef in the La Perouse Straits which runs between Hokkaido and Sakhalin. At the time of this unfortunate accident she was commanded by Commander Henry Frederick Stephenson (1842-1919), the future Admiral and a nephew of the C. in C., the Hon. Sir Henry Keppel. Fortunately there was no loss of life.

From 4 October 1869 in *Excellent*, Gunnery Ship, Portsmouth. Here he received instruction in a gunnery course, 'through which he passed with marked distinction (4).' On 21 December 1870 he received his, '1st class certificate in Gunnery (5).' From 14 February 1871 as Lieut. (G) he served in the screw iron ship, armour plated, *Minotaur*, 6,621 tons, Flagship, Channel Squadron. A Midshipman then serving in her was Alfred L. Winsloe (see C. in C., 1910). Paid off at Portsmouth: spring 1873. From 26 June 1873 borne as 'Additional' in *Excellent*. Then from 2 October 1873 to the West Coast of Africa in the corvette *Active*, 3,078 tons, Captain William N.W. Hewett, VC, with whom earlier he had served in *Basilisk* in China. This was during the time of war with the

Ashanti. Commanded the Naval Guard at Cape Coast Castle, landing with this Naval Brigade on 27 December 1873. Mentioned in Despatches for services in West Africa. Also on 7 March 1874:-

'Gazetted as commanding a wing of the Naval Brigade at Battle of Amoaful, Ashanti War (6).'

Commander: 31 March 1874.

'In 1874 he was awarded a prize for an essay on naval tactics which was published under the title of *Gun, Ram and Torpedo*, and in 1875 he received the Gold Medal of the Royal United Service Institution (7).'

From 27 July 1874 in screw frigate *Immortalite*, 3,984 tons, 'Detached Squadron'. He joined her at Portsmouth during the morning of Wednesday, 29 July 1874. Subsequently vessels of the squadron cruised to Vigo, Lisbon, Gibraltar, Madeira, St. Vincent in the Cape Verde Islands, Montevideo, Falkland Islands, Cape of Good Hope, Simon's Bay, St. Helena, Ascension Island, St. Vincent again, finally returning to Gibraltar on 20 June 1875. From Gibraltar on Tuesday, 13 July 1875 he disembarked in order to take passage home in the P. & O. mail ship *Lombardy*, 2,723 grt. Arrived back in England on 20 July 1875.

In England on 11 August 1875 he married Charlotte Rachel Frederica Cresswell, whose mother was a member of the Calthorpe family. By her he had a son, Francis Arthur Gerard Noel (1880-1955), later Lieut. Colonel, and two daughters, Charlotte Ida Frederica (1878-1961), and Ida Constance Diana Mary (1879-1953) (8).

Lady Noel was to die on 15 July 1927.

From 15 September 1875 re-appointed as Commander in *Immortalite*, 'Detached Squadron'. In due course at Mauritius on 25 January 1877 Captain Francis Alexander Hume went ashore to be invalided home. As acting Captain, Noel was ordered home with *Immortalite*. On passage she entered Simon's Bay on 16 February and eventually returned to Spithead on 11 May, finally paying off in Portsmouth on Monday, 21 May 1877 (9).

22 May to 4 June 1877, '*Vernon* for short course of Whithead Torpedo (10).'

Reverted to Commander, and from 11 January 1878 he served in the Royal Yacht *Victoria and Albert*, 2,470 tons.

Also during 1878 through the R.U.S.I. he published, *Great Britain's Maritime Power, how best Developed as regards Fighting Ships*.

Captain: 11 January 1881.

Studied at RNC, Greenwich from 1 October 1881 to 16 June 1882.

From 18 July to 16 October 1883, '*Vernon* for special torpedo course.' On 21 October 1883 he passed, 'Good exam. in Torpedo (11).'

Consequently on 28 January 1884: 'Appointed Member of Committee on Torpedo Instruction.'

Meanwhile he continued to submit articles to the R.U.S.I. and in 1883 was published, *On Masting of Ships of War and the Necessity of still employing Sail Power in Ocean Going Ships*.

Then on 26 November 1884 at the R.U.S.I., and with Admiral Sir Edward G. Fanshawe, KCB in the chair, the following subject was debated by those present: 'What are the most urgent measures that should be taken for increasing Her Majesty's Navy'. It was on this occasion that Captain Noel employed the phrase which subsequently has been quoted elsewhere, and which is equally true today (written in 2010):-

'... for the last 14 years the Navy has been starved (12).'

Clearly numbers of senior officers present at this debate were most concerned at the sorry state of affairs prevailing. As one other example Admiral Vesey Hamilton (see C. in C., 1885) is quoted as stating, 'In my opinion, whenever the Navy fails to protect our commerce, the Navy fails in its Mission and I for one should be ashamed of belonging to it.'

From 21 September 1885 to 1 November 1888 in command iron screw corvette *Rover*, 3,460 tons, 'Training Squadron'.

At the R.U.S.I. in 1889 he delivered a lecture entitled, *The Training of the Executive Branch of the Navy*.

On 18 July 1889 appointed to the new protected cruiser *Narcissus*, 5,600 tons, for the summer manoeuvres.

From 26 October 1889 to 19 June 1891 in command of the battleship *Temeraire*, 8,540 tons, Mediterranean. While holding this command it is related that in May 1891 he astonished the entire fleet by his brilliant feat of bringing *Temeraire* under sail in to Suda Bay, North West Crete. At the entrance to the bay he stopped engines and sailed in, fourteen tacks over a period of five hours in order to progress the necessary five miles up the bay to the anchorage.

From 30 June 1891 in command battleship *Nile*, 11,940 tons, Mediterranean. She was not involved in any way but in *Nile* he was present at the scene on 22 June 1893, the occasion of Vice Admiral Sir George Tryon's disastrous manoeuvre in the eastern Mediterranean off Tripoli when his Flagship *Victoria* came into collision with *Camperdown*. This resulted in the loss of *Victoria*, together with Sir George's own life and those of twenty two officers and 336 men.

His time in *Nile* was completed when, his services being urgently required, he was ordered home on 17 October, 'without awaiting arrival of successor'. He arrived in England on 28 October 1893.

From 1 November 1893 a Lord Commissioner of the Admiralty. He was the Junior Naval Lord with Admiral Sir Frederick William Richards (see C. in C., 1890) being First Naval Lord.

From 1 January 1894 appointed ADC to H.M. Queen Victoria.

Rear Admiral: 8 May 1896.

Continued in the Admiralty as a Lord Commissioner.

From 12 January 1898 to 9 February 1900 served as second in command, Mediterranean with his Flag in the battleship *Revenge*, 14,150 tons. At the time the C. in C. was Admiral Sir John Ommanney Hopkins (1834-1916). To take up his command he proceeded from England by Packet and hoisted his Flag in *Revenge* on 4 February 1898.

Together with French, Russian and Italian allies he was closely involved in successful negotiations with the Turks which resulted in their departure from Crete by 5 December 1898. Turkey had held Crete since 1669. Earlier rioting had adversely affected the British community at Candia (Heraklion) on the north coast of the island. To overcome this problem he had demanded that the authorities ashore act firmly, one source stating that, 'the Admiral interviewed him (the Turkish governor) and gave him an ultimatum that unless the murderers were on the quay by 6 p.m. his palace would be blown to smithereens'. Thus persuaded the Governor duly acted and in short order:-

> '… the ringleaders were delivered up, were tried by Court Martial and hanged (13).'

KCMG awarded for services in Crete: 25 November 1898.

In London on 22 December 1898 *The Times* stated that, 'To England, more than any other Power, the liberation of Crete has been due.'

Lord Salisbury too was well pleased:-

> 'Suffice it to say that Lord Salisbury, then Foreign Minister, is reported to have said that the best ambassador he knew was Sir Gerard Noel and his flagship, *Revenge* (14).'

At the conclusion of this period of service, from February 1900 he was authorised, 'To remain abroad for 3 months after being superseded in appointment in Med.'

From 21 May 1900 Admiral Superintendent of Naval Reserves in battleship *Alexandra*, Portland.

In June 1900 the future Admiral Sir Reginald Bacon was promoted Captain, RN. Writing of the period he was to include the following remarks in his memoirs:-

> 'At that time there were several of the more junior officers who were greatly disturbed at the want of preparation of the Navy for war. The Navy was quite efficient, the ships in good order,

and the men well trained, but there was no authoritative information as to how they would be employed in battle or in what formation they would fight the enemy. As an illustration of this I recall that Rear Admiral Gerard Noel, one of the finest of the pure, as differentiated from war applied, tacticians we had, while temporarily in command of the Fleet, carried out some unique manoeuvres and had asked for two officers from each ship to forward to him any remarks on them that they might wish to make. Lieutenant Richmond and I tried to twist these manoeuvrings to fill a war time frame, and sent them along. They were kindly acknowledged; but Sir Gerard at the same time replied that they were purely for peace use and had no connection with naval warfare. This was a great blow. We sent in no more remarks (15).'

Vice Admiral: 2 November 1901.

Continued as Admiral Superintendent of Naval Reserves, now once again with his flag in the battleship *Revenge*, who also was 'Coast Guard Ship', Portland.

KCB: 26 June 1902.

From 1 October 1902 continued as Admiral Superintendent of Naval Reserves, but also, on the occasion of various manoeuvres, as Vice Admiral Home Fleet. His flag remained in *Revenge*, 14,150 tons, Captain Frederick William Fisher, brother of the well known Lord Fisher.

On 21 May 1903 command of the Home Fleet was assumed by Vice Admiral Sir Arthur K. Wilson, KCB, VC, also Sir Gerard went on half pay, the 'office of Adl. Supt. of Naval Res. becoming non existent'.

Meanwhile on 28 April 1903 he had been appointed a member of the Royal Commission, 'to inquire into the supply of food and raw material in time of war (16).'

Towards the end of 1903 the news of his forthcoming appointment as C. in C., China Station was announced. Many were pleased. In the Far East the incumbent, Admiral Sir Cyprian Bridge, received the following few lines, dated 7 November 1903, from Mr. John Newell Jordan, British Minister Resident at Seoul:-

'I had seen the notice of Sir Gerard Noel's appointment, and if you are to relinquish the command, it is satisfactory to learn that the reins will be in such strong hands. I know of Admiral Noel chiefly by his Cretan record where he seems to have played the double role of sailor and diplomatist with marked success (17).'

To take up his appointment as C. in C., China he arrived at Hong Kong at 11.00 a.m. on Friday, 11 March 1904 in the P. & O. s.s. *Simla*, 5,884 grt. (18). He assumed command of the station on 14 March 1904, with his flag in the battleship *Glory*, 12,950 tons, Captain The Hon. Walter George Stopford (1855-1918), son of James, Fourth Earl of Courtown.

At the time of the change of command *Glory* was in Kowloon Dry Dock therefore, following his arrival at Hong Kong, the new C. in C. first hoisted his flag in *Alacrity*, 'at 2 p.m. on Friday, 11 March'. Then, 'at 3 p.m. on Monday, 13 March', having handed over the Station to his successor, Admiral Bridge sailed for Japan in the armoured cruiser *Leviathan*, 14,150 tons, (19).

In due course, and after carrying out exercises in Hong Kong waters, the C. in C. eventually hoisted his flag in *Glory* on 9 May 1904 and on the following day proceeded up the coast to Amoy, thence to Woosung and Nanking in the Yangtse River.

Of the Admiral at the time it has been written:-

'Sir Gerard Noel (vulgarly known as 'Sharky Noel') had a great reputation in the Navy for ability and determination, and had come before the public for his firm handling of the difficult international situation in Crete during the Allied occupation in 1898. He was the right man in the right place in China at that particular time, for he had the complete confidence of his own command, and in addition the presence and personality to impress those who felt inclined to question British rights in the Far East (20).'

Between July 1904 and April 1907 the Governor of Hong Kong was H.E. Sir Matthew Nathan, KCMG, (1862-1939) a one time Royal Engineer and previously Governor of the Gold Coast. In due course he was to go on to be Governor of Natal (1907-1910), the latter being the year of the Union, and then of Queensland (1920-1925). To take up his post in Hong Kong he arrived by P. & O. liner on 29 July 1904.

Once he had completed his first voyage of inspection up the Yangtse the C. in C. wrote to the Admiralty on 14 July 1904. First he mentioned the great commercial competition he found taking place, and then touched on the desireability of Britain exerting political as well as commercial pressure in an effort to secure Chinese railway construction contracts. In reality though it is apparent that he would have liked to receive more ships on the Station. No doubt over the years The Admiralty had become well acquainted with such requests received from the Commanders of many Stations around the world:-

> 'The number of foreign war vessels in the Yangtse has very much increased of late years, and the German flag is now much too frequently seen, considering that they have so strong a hold on another part of China in the Shantung province, which should occupy, one would think, most of their commercial interests; it is therefore all the more important that the British Squadron should be well represented. There is no doubt that our flag is thoroughly respected, and its presence has a quieting and beneficial effect. This is not the case with the flags of other nations, which are in some cases feared rather than respected.
>
> As regards the vessels employed in the river, we are at present well off, on account of the Japanese Division of the Station having been withdrawn, but when the present war is over, I should be glad of some reinforcement… (21)'

On the Station news of the Russian fleet's sortie from Port Arthur, and subsequent engagement with the Japanese on August 1904, the Battle of the Yellow Sea, was reported by the C. in C. to the Admiralty in the following manner. At the time *Glory* was at Wei-Hai-Wei:-

> 'On 10 August from about noon until late in the evening, and in the early hours of the next day, heavy firing was heard to seaward. News was received next day that the Japanese Fleet had engaged the Russian Fleet, an action ensuing, which resulted in the dispersal of the Russians. Since then distant firing had been heard now and again, but nothing of importance has been seen from Wei-Hai-Wei.
>
> On 12 August the Commanding Officer of the Russian torpedo boat destroyer *Burni* came onboard and surrendered himself and crew, reporting that his vessel had run on Shantung Promontory and that he had marched into Wei-Hai-Wei along the coast with his crew (22).'

During this affair, in which in terms of their ships the two sides were rather evenly matched, the Russian C. in C., Rear Admiral Vilhelm K. Vitgeft, who flew his flag in the French built battleship *Tsarevitch*, 12,900 tons, was killed. Vice Admiral Togo Heihachiro, with his flag in the British built battleship *Mikasa*, 15,200 tons, had the day and thereafter never again were the Russian warships in Port Arthur to attempt to offer battle.

Indeed Japanese destroyers had cut off *Burni*, Lieut. and Commander Tirkov, and, although not able to sink her, in foggy conditions on 11 August 1904 had forced her ashore on the Shantung peninsula which for all practical purposes had a similar final result (23). Subsequently the members of her ship's company were sent to Hong Kong and there interned by the colonial authorities.

One readily apparent consequence of this Russo-Japanese war was the disruption of Eastern trade beyond Hong Kong. This affected at least two well known British steamship companies in very different ways.

McGregor, Gow and Co.'s Glen Line for example, 'suffered a series of setbacks, including substantial losses during the Russo-Japanese war of 1904 (24)'. Indeed during that year they were to dispose of four of their ships, *Glenogle*, 3,749 grt to owners in Rangoon, but three to Japanese owners who made good use of the tonnage for supply purposes during the conflict. These ships were *Glengarry*, 3,034 grt who became *Koto Maru*, *Glengyle*, 3,455 grt who became *Miyoshino Maru*, and *Glenshiel*, 3,455 grt who became *Kotohira Maru*.

On the other hand Alfred Holt's Ocean Steam Ship appears to have received benefit:-

'The war between Russia and Japan in 1904 provided a timely boost to Blue Funnel trade at a time of depression, with the temporary withdrawal of Japan's merchant fleet and a booming demand in Japan for war goods (25)'.

In similar terms another source describes the benefit received by Alfred Holt & Co. as a result of this Russo-Japanese war:-

'The combined effect of war in the Far East, causing the temporary withdrawal of Japan as a carrier, and a general upward movement in trade, was to provide more abundant cargoes at more remunerative rates (26)'.

Examples follow which may serve to illustrate something of the considerable variety of activities which received the attention of the C. in C. or with which he was involved. First on 26 November 1904 he reported to London:-

'3. On 8 October H.I.M. The Emperor of China and the Dowager Empress received myself and Staff, and Captain H.M.T. Tudor of HMS *Cressy* in audience. We were accompanied and introduced to Their Majesties by Sir Ernest Satow.

22. s.s. *Inveric* with the sections of the River Gunboat *Widgeon* arrived at Shanghai on 24 September, and the work of discharging the sections and bolting them together was commenced on the 26th and completed by noon on the 28th. The work of reconstruction is now completed and it is expected that the vessel will be commissioned about 30th instant (27).'

Later, during her trials off Woosung on 22 November 1904, *Widgeon* achieved, 'about 13 knots'. This was the minimum necessary for safe navigation through the Gorges of the Upper River without having to seek the assistance of shore trackers.

Secondly, enclosed with this letter was a report in respect of a Naval Court of Inquiry held in HMS *Fearless*, Commander Price Vaughan Lewes, at Shanghai on 24 August 1904. The British flag steamer *Hipsang* had sailed from Newchwang on 15 July 1904 bound for Chefoo and Canton with a cargo of beans and general, and a crew of sixty seven hands as well as one European and twenty two Chinese passengers. At 38.55.30N 120.57.30E (Gulf of Chihli just west of the southern tip of the Liaotung peninsula) at 0415 on 16 July 1904 a Russian destroyer, name unknown but No. 7, had opened fire on her, had fired a torpedo, and had sunk her at 4.40 a.m. The weather conditions at the time were good with no fog and sufficient light, and with the visibility fair. The facts having been established the whole file subsequently was forwarded to the Board of Trade in London (28).

In addition during the latter part of 1904 the Admiralty ordered that he and his brother Commanders in Chief in the East Indies and Australian Stations should confer at Singapore to discuss the arrangements which it would be necessary to carry out should war develop between Great Britain and 'another maritime power or powers'. This conference was scheduled for 3 November 1904 but as a consequence of the North Sea outrage, the C. in C., East Indies was delayed until 6 November. Vice Admiral Sir Arthur Dalrymple Fanshawe (1847-1936) commanded in Australian waters and Rear Admiral George Lambart Atkinson-Willes in the East Indies. They met in *Glory* and by the evening of 7 November 1904 had completed their discussions (29).

The 'North Sea outrage' came about when a very nervous Russian Fleet, the Second Pacific Squadron under the command of Vice Admiral Zinovy Petrovich Rozhestvensky (1848-1909), on passage from the Baltic to reinforce their fleet in the Far East, shortly after midnight on 22 October 1904 mistook a number of British fishing vessels on the Dogger Bank in the North Sea for Japanese torpedo boats, and had opened fire causing some death and destruction. Following this episode relations between London and St. Petersburg, already tense, rather naturally deteriorated even further.

Meanwhile ashore, from their positions surrounding Port Arthur from the north, the Japanese Army continued to attack Russian defences. A crucial success, brought about with grim determination and the expenditure of a great number of lives, took place on 5 December 1904 when an all important feature, 203 Metre Hill, was captured. From this vantage point the remaining units of the Russian fleet in Port Arthur could be seen clearly, and taken under fire. There could be only one result:-

> 'Vainly the Russian crews tried to position their vessels in places of protection or reinforce the
> decks with sandbags and the like. It was all a waste of time. At short range, 11 inch howitzer shells
> falling from a considerable height at a steep angle dropped like aerial bombs on the ships, tearing
> through the decks and exploding well inside the hulls (30).'

One of the Russian battleships sunk on this occasion, *Pobieda*, 12,700 tons and completed at St. Petersburg in 1902, subsequently was to be raised and during 1908 was to be reconstructed and subsquently to enter IJN service as *Suwo*, now of 13,500 tons. As such, after the Great War commenced in 1914, she was to see action as the Japanese flagship during the successful operations against Germany at Tsingtao, Shantung peninsula.

In their issue of Monday, 16 January 1905, in London *The Times* printed a news item dated in Tokio the previous day:-

> 'The British steamer *Lethington* laden with 6,500 tons of coal for Vladivostok, was seized by a
> Japanese torpedo boat in the Tsu Shima Strait on the 12th inst.'

In due course this ship was to serve in the IJN Fleet as the seaplane tender *Wakamiya Maru* (31). For her successful WW1 operations against Germany see Jerram, C. in C., 1913.

Subsequent to their rather disastrous passage through the North Sea the previous October, by April 1905 the Russian Second Pacific Squadron had reached Eastern waters. Naturally wishing to keep an eye on their slow and ponderous progress, on 7 April 1905 the C. in C. ordered the armoured cruiser *Sutlej*, 12,000 tons, Captain W.L. Grant (see C in C., 1915), to proceed from Hong Kong to Singapore. On passage he was to report any sighting of the Russian Fleet. In turn on 12 April from Singapore Captain Grant was to follow up his signalled reports by letter:-

> 'At 5 a.m. on the 11th the Russian Second Pacific Squadron was sighted and passed at a distance of
> about two and a half miles in Lat. 8N, Long. 108.28 E (some 170 nautical miles S.E. of the Mekong
> delta).
> They were steering N.E. by North at a varying speed of from five to eight knots, the battleships in
> single line ahead at irregular intervals of about three cables.
> All the ships of that squadron as published by the Naval Intelligence Dept. were present with the
> exception of two destroyers making a total of 44 vessels, i.e. 15 warships, 8 destroyers, 5 volunteer
> fleet and 16 transports ...(32).'

That tension between Russia and Great Britain continued to be great is readily apparent from the tone of the Admiralty telegram, No. 78, sent to the C. in C. on 20 April 1905:-

> 'Very secret indeed. There is a possibility of the Russian Fleet attacking you unawares, though
> possibility very remote, yet the information received must not be ignored. Use your own discretion
> respecting taking your squadron to sea in vicinity of Hongkong ostensibly for a cruise, if you
> consider this will make you better prepared. Inform Governor in strict secrecy, and also state to
> him that the Prime Minister attaches utmost importance that no outward indication be given
> that such an event is conceived possible. H.M. Government does not wish ships to move up from
> Singapore in order to avoid any further risk of meeting Russian fleet at sea, which has already
> caused provocative telegram from Russia. You can move all vessels from the North to Hong Kong.
> Report any action you take and any movements of our ships from the North to Hongkong.

Impress the Governor of the necessity of the utmost secrecy and caution in order to avoid indication of our suspicions. Acknowledge receipt of this by telegraph (33).'

Between 27 and 28 May 1905 Admiral Togo Heihachiro, IJN achieved his greatest victory, known as the Battle of Tsushima, over the Russian Tsarist Fleet.

No attack against Britain took place. As will be seen in the next few lines these Russian men of war, on passage towards Vladivostok and having coaled where possible, were to meet their fate off Tsushima towards the end of the following month.

Admiral: 24 May 1905.

On 27/28 May 1905 Admiral Togo Heihachiro, IJN, still with his Flag in the battleship *Mikasa*, 15,200 tons, Captain Ijichi Hikojiro, achieved his overwhelming victory over the Russians off Tsushima and in the Sea of Japan (34). On this momentous occasion serving as Chief of Staff to the C. in C. was a future prime minister of his country, Rear Admiral Kato Tomosaburo.

During the battle an observer in HIJMS *Asahi* was Captain William Christopher Pakenham, RN. In London his subsequent report was to be highly regarded:-

'Pakenham's report on Tsushima further proved the superiority of long range firing and heavy guns. It arrived (at the Admiralty) just before the *Dreadnought* was laid down (35).'

While that most significant engagement was taking place *Glory* was at anchor in Tolo Harbour, Hong Kong. In correspondence with the Admiralty from Wei-Hai-Wei, on 13 June 1905 the C. in C. mentioned the great Japanese victory:-

'... as they (the Russian fleet) reached the Corean Channel by the morning of the 27th (May). On the two following days telegrams were received at Hong Kong reporting the total defeat of the Fleet (36).'

Following the Battle of Tsushima, on 16 June President Theodore Roosevelt (1858-1919) wrote from The White House to his friend Cecil Spring-Rice, a future British Ambassador to the U.S.A. The following extracts include a number of the President's perceptive, far-sighted remarks:-

'Well, it seems to me that the Russian bubble has been pretty thoroughly pricked. I thought the Japanese would defeat Rozhdestvensky; but I had no conception, and no one else had any conception (-) that there would be a slaughter rather than a fight, and that the Russians would really make no adequate resistance whatever.

What wonderful people the Japanese are! They are quite as remarkable industrially as in warfare. In a dozen years the English, Americans and Germans, who now dread one another as rivals in the trade of the Pacific, will have each to dread the Japanese more than they do any other nation. In the middle of this war they have actually steadily increased their exports to China, and are proceeding in the establishment of new lines of steamers in new points of Japanese trade expansion throughout the Pacific. (-) The industrial growth of the nation is as marvellous as its military growth.

It is now a great power and will be a greater power.

My own policy (towards Japan) is perfectly simple (-). I wish to see the United States treat the Japanese in a spirit of all possible courtesy, and with generosity and justice.

At the same time I wish to see our navy constantly built up, and each ship kept at the highest possible point of efficiency as a fighting unit. If we follow this course we shall have no trouble with the Japanese or any one else. But if we bluster; if we behave rather badly to other nations; if we show that we regards the Japanese as an inferior and alien race, and try to treat them as we have treated the Chinese; and if at the same time we fail to keep our navy at the highest point of efficiency and size – then we shall invite disaster (37).'

In London on 12 August 1905 the second Anglo-Japanese Alliance was signed. Under the terms of article three Britain recognised Japan's 'political, military and economic interests in Corea' (38).

From the west coast of Korea the C. in C. had left Chemulpo on 2 August 1905 and in *Alacrity* called at various ports, including Port Hamilton, as he proceeded around and along the south coast towards Pusan. At a very short distance before Pusan:-

'At Sylvia Basin I unexpectedly found at anchor a detachment of the Japanese Fleet, consisting of the battleships *Shikishima* and *Fuji*, a small cruiser, and some destroyers. Admiral Togo's flag was flying in *Shikishima*, and I exchanged visits with that Officer. With a view to avoiding publicity and possible misinterpretation by the European Press, I cautioned the ships under my command present to refrain from mentioning this meeting with the Japanese ships, and asked the Japanese Commander in Chief to consider my visit as quite unofficial (39).'

If only speaking professionally, one can imagine how delighted he will have been to be able to personally congratulate Admiral Togo on his splendid achievement in May.

The British Minister at Seoul continued to be Sir John N. Jordan and at this time he was the C. in C.'s guest in *Alacrity*. On 14 August he addressed a few lines to the Assistant Under Secretary of State for Foreign Affairs in London, Mr Francis A. Campbell (40). Relevant extracts follow:-

> 'Admiral Noel's (meeting with Admiral Togo) took place on the 8th inst. in Sylvia Basin, the great sheet of water which had served as so convenient a hiding place for the Jap. Fleet for months before the Battle of the Sea of Japan. (-) Togo speaks English with difficulty, the other two (Chief of Staff Rear Admiral Kato and his Flag Lieutenant) quite fluently, but all three were reserved and not very communicative about recent events. I think they felt a natural reluctance to talk about their own exploits.
>
> The Chief of the Staff, who looked as if he had passed thro' a great strain, said they had had 100 ships in Sylvia Basin for some 5 months before the Battle and that they were all sick to death of the place. He himself had only been twice ashore since the beginning of the war and the men had only had such exercise on land as was necessary for health purposes. (-) Alluding to the inferiority of the Russian gunnery he mentioned that he had asked Rozhdestvensky's Chief of the Staff if the Russian Ships had done much firing practice on the way out. The answer was that they had not – they had been too fully occupied with coaling and victualling. (-) Admiral Togo is a very small, well proportioned man with a most kindly face and the modesty of a girl. Somehow I thought of him rather as the Captain who startled us all by sinking *Kowshing* than as the hero of the present naval campaign (41).

The Russo-Japanese war was brought to a conclusion by the Treaty of Portsmouth, New Hampshire, 5 September 1905, the senior delegates being Serge Witte for Russia and Komura Jutaro for Japan (42). However the terms of the peace treaty were received badly in Japan it being perceived that Russia had escaped lightly. In addition, and in important contrast to the Japanese victory over China ten years earlier, no indemnity was paid by Russia to Japan.

At the same time, to a great extent forgotten today, rather over one century later, was the astonishment felt in most informed Western circles that the forces of any Asian country could so convincingly defeat those of a European power.

As noted above Theodore Roosevelt mentioned the rapid expansion of Japanese foreign steamship services. To stress this point two examples may be considered:

a) Nippon Yusen Kaisha. As early as 1896 they had opened their London office, and from Yokohama in March that year, with *Tosa Maru*, 5,789 grt, Captain John B. McMillan, had commenced a liner service to Europe. Also in 1896 other services were introduced to Australia and Seattle. By 1902 they were to be members of both the Outward and Homeward Far East/European Conferences. When first constituted the Conference members had consisted of just one French and six British steamship companies (43).

b) Osaka Shosen Kaisha, since 1963 a constituent of Mitsui OSK Lines Ltd. Immediately after Port Arthur fell in 1905 they commenced their Osaka/Dalien service, followed in 1906 by Osaka/Tientsin and Nagasaki/Dalien sevices. In July 1909 their *Tacoma Maru*, 6,178 grt, sailed from Hong Kong to commence their trans Pacific service to Tacoma (44).

Following that great event off Tsushima in May Sir Gerard was to dispute Admiralty orders of 6 June 1905 that he send home the five battleships then on the China Station. These were the four sisters, *Albion*, *Glory*, *Ocean*, *Vengeance*, plus *Centurion*. The Admiral regarded their removal as an, 'indignity to the C. in C.' (45).

The First Sea Lord at the time was Admiral Sir John Fisher. Following the demise of the Russian fleet in the Far East clearly there existed no further threat to Britain from that source.

During the summer of 1905 the C. in C. transferred his Flag to the protected cruiser *Diadem*, 11,000 tons, Captain Herbert W. Savory.

Meanwhile, in Tokyo on 20 August 1905 Dr. Sun Yat-sen and a number of colleagues came together to unite various Chinese underground revolutionary movements, including his Revive China Society founded in Honolulu in 1894. This new United Allegiance Society, T'ung-meng Hui or Tongmengui, was, in August 1912, to become the Kuomintang, Nationalist Party.

Concerning the terms of the Treaty of Portsmouth of September 1905, to which reference has been made, in a letter dated 11 November 1905 the C. in C. reported to the Admiralty:-

> 'The disappointment of the nation as a whole at the terms of peace concluded with Russia was undoubtedly great, and was the cause of riots at Tokio (46).'

Nevertheless, in order to celebrate the outstanding Japanese victory over Tsarist Russia, during the previous month a great Naval Review had taken place in Tokyo Bay. *Diadem* was accorded a place of honour during these proceedings. Extracts taken from her log book follow:-

> 'Wednesday, 11 October 1905. *Diadem*. Arrival off Yokohama.
>
> 10:24   Anchored at Yokohama.
> 12:15   HIJMS *Iwate* saluted C. in C. with 17 guns.
>
> Friday, 20 October 1905. At Yokohama.
> 08:00   Japanese fleet arrived and anchored.
>   Saluted Admiral Togo: 17 guns.
>   HIJMS *Shikishima* returned ditto.
>
> Saturday, 21 October 1905.
> 09:30   Manned ship.
> 10:00   Admiral Togo (and party) from Japanese squadron visited C. in C.
> 10:30   Saluted Admiral Togo: 17 guns.
> 11:30   HIJMS *Shikishima* saluted C. in C. 17 guns.

Diadem was fitted with an electrical circuit for illuminations. These were switched on each evening during her stay at Yokohama.

> Monday, 23 October 1905.
>   *Diadem* shifted to take up billet for Review by His Imperial Majesty (Emperor Mutsuhito) in *Asama*.
> 09:35   Saluted H.I.M. with 21 guns.
>   Later C. in C. received onboard *Asama* by H.I.M. (47).'

On 19 October H.I.M. The Emperor had awarded Admiral Noel with the Order of the Rising Sun, First Class.

The review and magnificent associated spectacle ended on 24 October and early the following morning *Diadem* sailed for Kobe. However Admiral Noel embarked in *Alacrity* first to visit Yokosuka and Osaka.

His tour of Japanese ports, made both to celebrate the renewal of the Anglo-Japanese Alliance and Japan's recent great victory over Tsarist Russia, ended at Nagasaki and from there on 11 November *Diadem* returned to Woosung, arriving on Monday, 13 November 1905.

His visit with his staff to Nagasaki had provided their kind hosts with the chance to mark the occasion in considerable style:-

> 'The officers and crew received received an enthusiastic welcome from the people of the city, who came out by the thousands to the waterfront and filled a reception ground established for the occasion near Nagasaki Railway Station. In his speech to the visitors and participants, Mayor

Yokoyama Toraichiro expressed joy at the opportunity to welcome the squadron to Nagasaki and commented as follows on the significance of the visit:-

"Our two Island Empires, one the most powerful in the West and the other having just emerged victorious from a great conflict, are geographically widely separated from each other, but in heart and mind they are knit together as brothers. We feel that we owe a great deal to our Western brethren for the rapid develoment and improvement of our country.

Moreover, the conclusion of the new treaty of alliance not only strengthens the initimate relations already existing between the two nations but ensures the peace of the Far East."

On the evening before departure, the bankers and merchants of Nagasaki hosted a party for Noel and the other officers (-). The party began with still another round of congratulatory speeches on the renewal of the alliance and a musical presentation by teams of geisha using the Rising Sun and Union Jack to colourful effect. (-) When the squadron steamed out of Nagasaki harbour the following day the waterfront was packed with Nagasaki school children waving the Union Jack, and the harbour itself was dotted with the boats of local officials and other citizens out in untold numbers to bid their friends farewell (48).'

In the form of a brief summary of the IJN planning and approach to their recent most successful campaign against Tsarist Russia, on 15 December 1905 Sir Gerard included the following few lines in his report of that date addressed to the Admiralty:-

'As regards the general conduct of the war operations by the Japanese, everything seems to have been thoroughly well prepared and organised from the beginning: the ships were in a splendid state of readiness, and the officers and men only too anxious to engage the enemy, caring little for what personal risks they ran (49).'

Briefly reverting to their merchant navy it was only in 1906, with the appointment by N.Y.K. of their Captain Murai Mamoru, that command of one of their steamships on the presitigous European service first was given to one of their own Japanese citizens (50). Nevertheless numbers of foreign Masters, many British, were to continue to command several of the vessels in their continually expanding fleet.

In London the decision had been made to create H.I.M. Emperor Mutsuhito, Meiji Tenno, a Knight of the Garter. On 23 February 1906 from *Alacrity* at Hong Kong in his General Letter to the Admiralty in London the C. in C. wrote:-

'HRH Prince Arthur of Connaught and suite arrived at Hong Kong in the P. & O. s.s. *Dongola* on the 9th instant and Prince Arthur and suite embarked in *Diadem* on the night of the 13th, the Royal standard being saluted when hoisted in that ship, and the *Diadem* sailed at once for Yokohama, where she arrived on the morning of the 19th (February 1906) (51).'

A member of HRH Prince Arthur's suite on this rather grand occasion was Admiral of the Fleet Sir Edward Seymour (see C. in C., 1899).

As has been seen at the time Japan and Great Britain enjoyed an especially amicable relationship:-

'In 1906, too, when the Garter Mission arrived in Japan, there were almost incredible demonstrations of enthusiasm up and down Japan, the Union Flag being seen on an equality with the Rising Sun in remote mountain villages (52).'

At Hong Kong Vice Admiral Sir Arthur Moore succeeded in command of the station on Friday, 16 March 1906, whereupon in *Diadem*, that morning at 1015, Sir Gerard slipped and proceeded to Yokohama, there to join the CPR steamer across the Pacific to Vancouver, and home. On passage, and having just passed through the Straits of Shimonoseki to enter the Inland Sea on 20 March, thick fog was experienced which forced her to anchor until it lifted. However all went well and *Diadem* later continued to anchor off Yokohama at 1826 hours on Thursday, 22 March 1906, his Flag being struck at noon the following day (53).

C. in C., The Nore: 1 January 1907 – 2 December 1908.

During his time at The Nore opposition to the person of the First Sea Lord, then Admiral Sir John (Jack) Fisher, was expressed by a number of officers. Indeed Fisher's methods frequently had been, and with additional seniority tended to remain, both controversial and divisive. Most senior naval officers of the era were either in the 'Fishpond' or out. Sir Gerard corresponded, carefully, with a number who were out. Two examples follow.

The first is an extract taken from a letter dated 4 January 1907 which he received from Admiral Charles C.P. Fitzgerald:-

> 'I appreciate your approval. It is refreshing and encouraging to find that there are a few of one's contemporaries left who have refused to bow the knee to Baal, or to help to drag in the mud that professional dignity and reserve of which we used to be proud, before the present cheap-Jack, advertising business was established at Whitehall. I hear from several of my friends that there is about to be a reaction and that the great imposter is being found out at last ….

Secondly, in response to a letter from Admiral Lord Charles Beresford, C. in C., Channel Fleet in the battleship *King Edward VII*, 16,350 tons, and which was dated 16 May 1907, he replied on 17 May:-

> 'Our duties as Commanders in Chief are clear enough to me, and we have to carry them out to the best of our abilities. Thank goodness I have a clear conscience as regards all the abominable scheming that has been going on of late, and I do not allow it to influence my determination to run my part of the business as far as I can to the benefit of the service (54).'

As will be seen from the following, a letter dated 3 July 1908 and written from Admiralty House, Chatham, he was happy to give his opinions to the First Lord himself. These pointed remarks, expressed to Reginald McKenna, are aimed at Sir John Fisher:-

> 'I and others never saw the need for building *Dreadnoughts*, but as they are built, and are increasing in number, docks must be provided for them, and the sooner this is done the better: employment of labour does no harm, and if this rich country wishes to safeguard its riches, it had better spend freely on <u>essentials</u> to its naval efficiency (55).'

At the same time he was rather conscious of his own position in life. A month later, 10 August 1908, again he wrote to Mr. McKenna:-

> 'I see that the *Times* of the 6th inst. has made a full list of the appointments of Admirals and others for the next six months, which announcement if not with your sanction and the King's approval, is a gross bit of impertinence – the Naval correspondent is evidently in close touch with the Admiralty. With reference to the Nore command, I am expecting to hold it for 3 years, unless advanced to Admiral of the Fleet (56).'

Admiral of the Fleet: 2 December 1908.

Relieved at The Nore by Admiral Sir Charles C. Drury.

In 1911 Admiral Count Togo Heihachiro of the Imperial Japanese Navy was a member of the Japanese Imperial party who travelled to England in the NYK liner *Kamo Maru* to attend the Cornonation of HM King George V and Queen Mary at Westminster Abbey on 22 June (57). A few days later, on 1 July 1911, he was the guest of honor at the Royal Navy Club Dinner. Sir Gerard was one of the senior hosts at this gathering. Admiral Togo's speech on that splendid and glittering occasion was brief, and is quoted below. The warm feelings that existed at that time between the RN and IJN once again will be apparent:-

> 'I feel it a great honour and privilege to meet at this Banquet the Members of the Royal Navy Club,

which is a historical and famous Institution, and has traditional association with Lord Nelson. Gentlemen, it is a well known fact that our Japanese Navy owes much to the British Navy. For my own part, I am proud to declare that, if I have done any services to my country, it has been in a great degree due to the education which I received in this country more than thirty years ago.

When two dear friends meet and shake hands, they are strongly affected by the upwelling of strong emotion. Now, standing before you in this Banquet Hall, words fail me to express my deep and sincere feeling. I am profoundly moved. I can only say that I firmly believe that there is nothing to be afraid of in the accomplishment of our task for our respective native lands, when we stand shoulder to shoulder and hand in hand.

Gentlemen, the kind hospitality which you have shown me this evening is too great to be monopolized by me alone, and I beg to be allowed to take it as an expression of the goodwill and sympathy of the British Navy towards the Navy of her Ally. I cordially thank you therefore, not only for myself, but also on behalf of the Japanese Navy.

I drink to the ever-increasing prosperity of the British Navy in the name of the Navy of Japan (58).'

Prior to the outbreak of the Great War many navies in Europe and elsewhere were expanding. Necessarily much of the thinking behind and consequences of such an expansion remained not only controversial but confidential. As mentioned above in Great Britain the First Sea Lord between 1904 and 1910 had been Admiral of the Fleet Lord Fisher. Between 1900 and 1905 the First Lord of the Admiralty was William Waldegrave Palmer, Second Earl Selbourne (1859-1942).

On 14 July 1912 Sir Gerard wrote to Lord Selbourne, making reference to an interview held some eight years previously:-

'... (an interview) I had with you at the Admiralty before I left to take up the China Command in 1904. I firmly believe that had you listened to the protest I then made against Fisher's coming to the Admiralty as First Naval Lord – a protest which was backed by the opinions of practically all the most reliable men in the upper ranks of the navy – we should not have been brought into the deplorable and even perilous position we now hold in the world.'

Lord Selbourne replied, succinctly, on 16 July 1912:-

'I am much obliged for your letter and for the enclosure, but the truth is that we are in hearty disagreement in many aspects of naval policy. Yours sincerely (59).'

GCB: 1 January 1913.

On reaching the age of eighty years he retired on 5 March 1915, his pay when retired being sixty seven shillings a day (60).

Following the Battle of Jutland on 31 May 1916 he was to receive an amusing letter of commiseration from an old friend, Admiral Charles C.P. Fitzgerald:-

'Jellicoe's despatch will be interesting. Some of us old buffers got born twenty years too soon, but it wasn't our fault (61).'

Likewise following the Battle of Jutland he had written a letter to the commander of the battlecruiser squadron, Vice Admiral Sir David Beatty. Replying from *Tiger* on 12 July 1916 Sir David wrote:-

'My dear Sir Gerard,

Thank you very much for your kind note and congratulations. The approbation of the senior officers of our grand old Service is indeed appreciated by me more than I can say, especially of those who have done so much to forge and prepare the weapon which it is our great good fortune to have the privilege and honour of using.

Yours very sincerely, David Beatty (62).'

Having passed away on 23 May, on Saturday, 25 May 1918 in the churchyard at Fincham, 'the funeral was of the quietest possible character, and a request had been made that no floral offerings should be forwarded, though in spite of this some beautiful emblems were in evidence (63)'.

In addition to members of the family the principal mourners included Admiral Sir Reginald Neville Custance, GCB, KCB, KCMG (1847-1935) (64).

NOTES

1. NA ADM 196/15. 459. *Service Record.*
2. Ibid.
3. Sir Ernest Satow, *A Diplomat in Japan,* (New York and Tokyo, 2001), 281-287. An extraordinary experience accompanying the British diplomats ashore at this very disturbed time immediately prior to the conclusion of the Shogunate era and the commencement of the Meiji period in January 1868.
4. Obituary, *The Times,* London, Friday, 24 May 1918.
5. NA ADM 196/37. *Service Record.*
6. *Service Record.* Under the overall command of Sir Garnet Wolseley, the Battle of Amoaful was fought on 31 January 1874. Amoaful is near Bekwai to the south of Kumasi, Ashanti, Gold Coast (Ghana).
7. Obituary. *The Times.*
8. Ibid. *Who's Who.*
9. NA ADM 53/10711. Log Book *Immortalite.*
10. *Service Record.*
11. Ibid.
12. *Journal of the Royal United Service Institution,* Vol. XXVIII, (London, 1885), 1024.
13. Obituary, *The Times.* Also see Admiral Sir Reginald Bacon, *From 1900 Onward,* (London, 1940), 86.
14. *From 1900 Onward,* 86. Lord Salisbury: Robert Arthur Talbot Gascoyne-Cecil, Third Marquess of Salisbury (1830-1903), then also Prime Minister for his third period of office in that role. He presided over a wide expansion of Great Britain's colonial empire. *Encyclopaedia Britannica.*
15. Ibid. 23. Lieutenant Richmond is the future Admiral Sir Herbert Richmond (1871-1946), latterly Master of Downing College, Cambridge. Also see Arthur J. Marder, *Portrait of an Admiral, the Life and Papers of Sir Herbert Richmond,* (London, 1952).
16. Obituary, *Lynn News.* Courtesy of the editor, Mr. Malcolm Powell. *Service Record.*
17. Caird Library, National Maritime Museum, Greenwich. Ref: *BRI/17.*
   John Newell **Jordan.** Born: 5 September 1852. Died: 14 September 1925. Queen's College, Belfast then Cork. Appointed Student Interpreter in China: 10 March 1876. Early service in Canton, Kiungchow, Amoy and Peking. Promoted Consul-General for Corea: 27 October 1896. Minister resident at Seoul: 15 July 1901. KCMG: 24 June 1904. The Legation at Seoul was withdrawn on 1 February 1906. Minister Plenipotentiary to the Emperor of China: 31 May 1906, but from 28 November 1910 to the Republic of China. KCB: 25 June 1909. GCIE: 12 December 1911. PC: 10 June 1915. Retired on pension: 14 August 1920 thereafter GCMG. Delegate to the Washington Naval Conference: 1921/22. Succeeded at Peking by Beilby Francis **Alston** (1868-1929). *Foreign Office List.*
18. W.A. May, *The Commission of H.M.S. Talbot: 1901-1904,* (London, 1904), 172. Also NA ADM 53/21330, Log Book *Glory.*
19. NA ADM 53/21330.
20. Admiral of the Fleet The Earl of Cork and Orrery, *My Naval Life,* (London, 1942), 50.
21. Caird Library. Ref: *NOE/20C: Affairs in the Yangtse.*
22. NA ADM 1/7728. Letter No. 993 dated 26 September 1904.
23. Caird Library. Ref: *NOE/20C.*
24. Malcolm Falkus, *The Blue Funnel Legend,* (Basingstoke and London, 1990), 228.

25. Ibid. 138.

26. Francis E. Hyde, *Blue Funnel*, (Liverpool, 1957), 128.

27. NA ADM 1/7728. Letter No. 1178. Captain Henry M.T. Tudor, twin screw armoured cruiser *Cressy*, 12,000 tons. s.s. *Inveric*, 4,387 grt, Captain W.R. Kennedy. Andrew Weir & Co., Glasgow. Built: 1901. *Lloyd's Register*. In 1921 she was to be sold to Japanese interests. The Journal of Commerce and Shipping Telegraph, *Seventy Adventurous Years*, (Liverpool, 1956), 97.

    Gunboat *Widgeon*, 195 tons. Commissioned at Shanghai: 28 November 1904. Lieut. Christopher P. Metcalfe. *Navy List*.

28. Ibid. Twin screw cruiser *Fearless*, 1,580 tons. *Navy List*. s.s. *Hip Sang*, 1,659 grt, built in 1899 and by 1900 owned by Indo-China S.N. Co. (Jardine Matheson). Russian torpedo boat named as *Raztorpni*. H.W. Dick and S.A. Kentwell, *Beancaker to Boxboat*, (Canberra, 1988), 29.

29. Ibid.

30. David Walder, *The Short Victorious War*, (London, 1973), 233.

31. *His Imperial Japanese Majesty's Ship Wakamiya and Some Developments.* Paper read by the author at the Fourth ICMH, Corfu, June 2004.

32. NA ADM 1/7804. Of his sighting of the Russian Fleet at 0710 on 11 April Captain W.B. Fair in the cruiser *Iphigenia*, 3,600 tons, similarly reported that, 'The formation was very irregular'.

33. Caird Library. Ref: *NOE/20C*. The Prime Minister from 11 July 1902 to 5 December 1905 was the Conservative, Arthur James Balfour.

34. **Ijichi** Hikojiro. Also of Satsuma heritage. Born: 14 December 1859. Died: 4 January 1912. Cadet: 20 October 1874. Captain: 25 September 1900. Appointed in command of HIJMS *Mikasa*: 26 September 1903. Rear Admiral: 22 November 1906. Vice Admiral: 1 December 1910. *Russo-Japanese War Research Society*.

    HIJMS *Mikasa* today is a Memorial Ship berthed at Yokosuka. Visited by the author: 15 April 2015.

35. Arthur J. Marder, *From the Dreadnought to Scapa Flow*, I, (OUP, 1961), 60. John Curtis Perry, 228.

36. NA ADM 1/7804. Letter No. 514.

37. Ed. Stephen Gwynn, *The Letters and Friendships of Sir Cecil Spring Rice*, I, (London, 1929), 472/3.

    Cecil Arthur **Spring-Rice**. Born: 27 February 1859. Died in Ottawa after being re-called from Washington, DC: 14 February 1918. Eton. Balliol College, Oxford. Early Foreign Office career in various British embassies. KCMG: 1906. Minister to Persia: 1906-1908. GCVO: 1908. Minister to Sweden: 1908-1912. Ambassador to the USA: 1912-1918. PC: 1913. GCMG: 1916. *Who's Who*.

38. Tsuzuki, 175/6.

39. NA ADM 1/7804. Letter No. 645. HIJMS *Shikishima*, 14,850 tons, battleship built in Britain in 1899. HIJMS *Fuji*, 12,320 tons, battleship built in Britain in 1897. T.A. Brassey, *The Naval Annual*, (Portsmouth, 1905), 286.

40. Francis Alexander **Campbell**. Born: 2 May 1852. Died: 28 December 1911. Wellington. Clerk at the Foreign Office: 24 November 1871. Between June 1877 and July 1887 Private Secretary to, respectively, the Duke of Richmond and Gordon, and Lord Pauncefote. In June 1889 Joint Secretary to the British Delegates to the Anglo-Dutch Borneo Boundary Commission. Private Secretary to Lord Currie, Under Secretary of State for Foreign Affairs: August 1892 to December 1893. Senior Clerk: 25 July 1896. CB: 1 January 1901. Assistant Under Secretary of State for Foreign Affairs: 1 August 1902. KCMG: 9 November 1906. *Foreign Office List*, 1912.

41. NA FO 350/3. In fact, following seven youthful years spent in British company, both at sea and ashore, Admiral Togo both understood and spoke English well.

42. Sergei Yulyevich **Witte**. Born in Tiflis (Tbilisi), Georgia: 29 June 1849. Died: 13 March 1915. A brilliant man, with service as Minister of Transport, then as Minister of Finance: 1892-1903. Largely responsible for the successful construction of a great number of railway systems within Russia. Selected by Tsar Nicholas II to act as his Plenipotentiary at Portsmouth, NH. Created a Count: 1905. Chairman of the Committee of Ministers: 1903-1906. *Encyclopaedia Britannica*.

    Komura Jutaro. Born: 16 September 1855. Died: 25 November 1911. Following university in Tokyo, in 1875 selected to continue studies abroad. Graduated from Harvard Law School: 1878. Ministry of Justice: 1880. Ministry of Foreign Afairs: 1884. Minister for Foreign Affairs: September 1901 – 1906. Ambassador to Great Britain: June 1906 – August 1908. Minister for Foreign Affairs: 1908 – 1911. *Encyclopaedia Britannica*.

43. Eric Jennings, *Cargoes*, (Singapore, 1980), 25.0

44. *The First Century of Mitsui OSK Lines Ltd.,* (Tokyo, 1985), 43.

45. Arthur J. Marder, I, 85.

46. NA ADM 1/7804. Letter No. 875.

47. NA ADM 53/19557. HIJMS *Asama,* 9,700 tons. Armoured cruiser completed in Britain in 1899. Brassey.

48. Brian Burke-Gaffney, *Nagasaki, The British Experience, 1854-1945,* (Folkestone, Kent, 2009), 178-180.

49. NA ADM 1/7804. Letter No. 966.

50. Nippon Yusen Kaisha, *Nanatsu no umi de isseiki (A Century on the Seven Seas),* (Tokyo, 1985), 22/3. Sadly further information is not available. In March 2010 NYK in Tokyo were kind enough to advise the author:-
    '... our museum isn't in possession of log book, the sailing schedule and crew lists in those days as they were lost due to damages by floods and wars in the past.'

51. NA ADM 1/7869. s.s. *Dongola,* 8,038 grt, twin screw, built 1905. HRH had travelled by rail from London on 11 January 1906 to Marseilles where he and his suite had joined the P. & O. s.s. *Mongolia* for passage East, subsequently transferring to *Dongola. The Times,* 10 and 11 January 1906.

52. Sir Hugh Cortazzi and Gordon Daniels, *Britain and Japan: 1859-1991,* (London, 1991), 124.

53. NA ADM 53/19558. Log Book *Diadem.*

54. Caird Library. Ref: *NOE/5.*

55. Archives Centre, Churchill College, Cambridge. Ref: *MCKN 3/8.*

56. Ibid.

57. Steamer *Kamo Maru,* 8,524 grt. Built: 1908. In position 32.24N 128.46E, near Fukue Jima to the west of Kyushu, to be torpedoed and sunk on 3 July 1944 by USS *Tinosa* SS-283, Lieut. Commander D.F. Weiss. Theodore Roscoe, *United States Submarine Operations in WW2,* (Annapolis, 1988), 560.

58. Caird Library. Ref: *NOE/5.*

59. Ibid.

60. *Service Record.*

61. Caird Library. Ref: *NOE/5.* Charles Cooper Penrose **Fitzgerald**. Born: 30 April 1841. Died: 11 August 1921. Joined the RN in *Victory*: 1854. Second in Command, China Station: 1898-1899. *Who's Who.*

62. Ibid.

63. Obituary, *Lynn News.* As related he had died at his home, 'The Moat', Boughton Road, about half a mile South and East of the village. On Friday, 27 March 2015 the author paid respects at his grave. This may be found in the church yard of St. Martin, N.E. of the Eastern part of the building. Courtesy of historian, Mr. Stewart Waterston.

64. As Midshipman Custance he had served in *Euryalus* and been present in her at the action at Kahding in 1862, at Kagoshima in 1863, and at Shimonoseki in 1864. See Kuper, C. in C., 1862. *Who's Who.*

6 December 1905 to 1 January 1908
Vice Admiral Sir Arthur William **Moore**

Arthur was born on 30 July 1847, the third son and fourth child of Reverend Edward Moore, Honorary Canon of Canterbury, and vicar and squire of Frittenden, Kent from 1842 to 1864, and his wife, Lady Harriet Janet Sarah Montagu-Scott, daughter of Sir Charles William Henry, Fourth Duke of Buccleuch. He had four sisters and seven brothers but sadly two of his sisters, 'died in an epidemic of diphtheria which swept the village (1)'.

A major landowner, The Revd. Edward was responsible for practically the entire rebuilding of the Parish Church, and of its rededication in 1848. In addition he and his wife created much in the village including a school, bank, Provident Society, and numerous buildings.

In due course Lady Harriet, who had married The Reverend Edward on 29 March 1842, was to die on 16 February 1870.

Arthur's great-grandfather, John Moore, had been Archbishop of Canterbury from 1783 to 1805.

Arthur himself died in London on 3 April 1934, and his funeral took place at Frittenden Parish Church of St. Mary's on Friday, 6 April 1934.

Initially educated at Eton, he entered the Royal Navy on 11 December 1860, **Cadet** in *Britannia* at the time moored off Haslar Creek, Portsmouth. Appointed to screw frigate *Tribune*, 23 guns, 1,570 tons, Captain The Lord Gilford, for the Pacific Station: 3 April 1862 (2). **Midshipman**: 30 June 1862. Next served briefly in new screw sloop *Camelion*, 17 guns, 1,365 tons, Commander Edward Hardinge, and then in the Flagship, screw frigate *Sutlej*, 35 guns, 3,066 tons, Captain Matthew Connolly, flying the flag of Rear Admiral John Kingcome. From the Pacific subsequently he returned home in *Tribune*. She paid off at Portsmouth on 16 May 1866.

There exists a most pleasant tale in respect of his return home after his first long commission abroad. Naturally his parents and family had missed him a great deal:-

> 'Lady Harriet arranged that on his arrival at the Staplehurst railway station a runner came ahead of
> his party so that the bell ringers at St. Mary's could begin ringing a Peel of Welcome (3).'

From 29 July 1866 served in iron clad *Caledonia*, 30. Owing to Fenian troubles in Ireland she was used to transport a battalion of Royal Marines to Queenstown. **Sub Lieutenant**: 1 April 1867. Continued in *Caledonia* until 21 August 1867. Next followed short gunnery and navigation courses at Portsmouth. From 9 September 1867 in the screw gun vessel *Jaseur*, 5 guns, 427 tons, West Coast of Africa. From 5 November 1868 in *Rattlesnake*, 1,705 tons, West Coast of Africa. Her Captain was William M. Dowell (see C. in C., 1884). From 11 October 1869 to 15 November 1870 in screw frigate *Liverpool*, 30 guns, 2,656 tons, Captain John O. Hopkins, and flying the flag of Rear Admiral Geoffrey T.P. Hornby. He joined her at Simon's Bay thence proceeded across the Indian Ocean to Australia. At Sydney on Christmas Day appointed acting Lieutenant. Continued on to New Zealand. Left Auckland on 9 February 1870 and arrived at Yokohama on 6 April 1870. From that place *Liverpool* visited Yedo to be inspected by HIM Emperor Mutsuhito, subsequently returning the short distance across the bay to Yokohama together with Sir Harry Parkes who took passage in the ship. From Yokohama on 19 April she proceeded home via Esquimalt, Honolulu, Valparaiso and Bahia to arrive at Plymouth on 15 November 1870. At Esquimalt promoted **Lieutenant**: 19 May 1870.

From 24 May 1871 in screw frigate *Glasgow*, 28 guns, 3,037 tons, Captain Theodore M. Jones, East Indies. Off the Hoogly on 24 January 1872 embarked the Viceroy, Richard Southwell Bourke, Sixth Earl of Mayo (1822-1872) and party as His Lordship wished to visit Burma and the Andaman Islands. At Port Blair on 8 February The Viceroy was murdered by a convict, Sher Ali Afridi. Returned to the Hoogly. Subsequently *Glasgow* carried the coffin to Suez from where the Admiralty Yacht *Enchantress* conveyed His Lordship's remains to England. At Suez on Monday, 8 April the new Viceroy, Lord Northbrook, and staff embarked and were conveyed via Aden to Bombay, arriving on 26 April 1872.

From 14 February 1872 *Glasgow* was the flagship, East Indies, Rear Admiral Arthur Cumming (1817-1893). In 1874 extra personnel were borne in the ship, 'Transit of Venus Expedition'.

Also in 1874 an accident took place during which he acted with great courage:-

'The Royal Humane Society's Bronze Medal was awarded to Lieutenant Moore for his gallant conduct in saving the life of W. Read, Ordinary Seaman, who fell overboard from aloft at sea in shark infested waters, 7 October 1874 (4).'

Vice Admiral Sir Arthur William Moore

At the end of the commission *Glasgow* paid off at Portsmouth in July 1875.

During 1876 he attended gunnery and torpedo courses. On 9 February 1877 appointed first Lieutenant in screw corvette *Charybdis*, 17 guns, 2,187 tons, China. To take up this appointment then between 5 March and 5 May 1877 he travelled from out from England to Hong Kong in troopship *Tamar*, 4,857 tons, Captain William H. Liddell. From 1897 *Tamar* was to be the receiving ship at Hong Kong where eventually she was to be scuttled in December 1941 at the time of the Japanese attack on the colony. *Charybdis*, Captain Charles Frederick Hotham, re-commissioned at Hong Kong on 9 May 1877. At the end of her commission the ship returned home via the Cape and on 9 November 1880 paid off at Devonport.

From 15 January 1881 he served in the twin screw armour plated iron ship *Invincible*, 14 guns, 6,010 tons, Captain Robert O'Brien Fitzroy, Mediterranean.

Commander: 31 December 1881. From 24 June 1882 Commander of the armour plated twin screw corvette *Orion*, 4,870 tons, Captain Robert O'B. Fitzroy, Mediterranean. Served in the Egyptian War although *Orion* herself did not engage at Alexandria in July 1882. Instead:-

> 'He was present at the occupation of Ismailia, and was afterwards in command of the Naval Flotilla on the Sweet Water Canal, which was organised for the transport of stores to the front and for the conveyance of sick and wounded to the base. He was also present at the battle of Tel-el-Kebir (5).'

Also on 20 August 1882 from Ismailia he commanded a successful naval bombardment onto Arabi's forces at Nefiche, range 4,200 yards. Following the engagement at Tel-el-Kebir, which was fought on 13 September, he was much involved in transporting supplies to the front and in taking down sick and wounded to the rear. Members of their Naval Brigade returned to *Orion* on 4 October, thence to Alexandria where the ship remained until March 1883.

From 8 March 1883 in command twin screw gun vessel *Beacon*, 4 guns, 603 tons. From Suez he brought her home. It was a memorable voyage:-

> '… being then 30 miles to the east of Algiers. For three days the gale lasted, and it did blow. We could no nothing, but the ship just bobbed about like a cork and made good weather, though if land had been to leeward she must have gone aground and broken up. It was the heaviest gale I have known in the Mediterranean. At last, at 10.00 p.m. on 1 May during a lull, we managed to creep into Algiers. The whole harbour was an extraordinary sight with wrecked craft everywhere (6).'

The ship, 'could neither sail nor steam unless wind was fair', consequently it was only after a voyage of three months from Suez that *Beacon* arrived at Chatham on 11 June and paid off on 30 June 1883.

From 7 July 1883 in command twin screw gun vessel *Frolic*, 4 guns, 619 tons, Cape of Good Hope and West Coast of Africa. Relieved on the station on 20 June 1884, and returned home to England by mail steamer on promotion, arriving in England on 16 July 1884 (7).

Captain: 27 June 1884.

From 14 April 1885 in command corvette *Bacchante*, 14 guns, 4,130 tons, Flagship, East Indies, the C. in C. being Rear Admiral Sir Frederick W. Richards (see C. in C., 1890). At the conclusion of the commission, on 29 April 1888 he was relieved on the station by Captain R. Henderson and returned home by mail boat, arriving on 24 May.

From 20 June 1888 at Chatham in command battleship *Rodney*, 10,300 tons. The ship was in commission temporarily for manoeuvres. Paid off at Chatham on 31 August 1888.

Between 28 May and 14 September 1889 for trials he commanded of the first of a new type of protected cruiser, *Medea*, 2,800 tons. This involved taking her to Gibraltar and return, a trial run for speed and to ascertain rates of coal consumption. Afterwards she participated in manoeuvres.

Subsequently, on 6 November 1889, 'Appointed a British Delegate to the Slave Trade Conference at Brussels (8).'

After this experience he was to leave some thoughts, pleasantly dry. Excerpts follow:-

'The conference lasted eight months and as we got two guineas a day for expenses and were received everywhere in Brussels, I thought it better fun than serving on the west coast of Africa (--).

It was all very interesting, but with the exception of England and Belgium, I do not think the Powers taking part were really in earnest although all signed and ratified the results arrived at (9).'

During the early summer 1890 commanded cruiser *Mersey*, 4,050 tons, during manoeuvres which continued up to 22 July (10).

For six weeks from 30 August 1890 he accompanied Admiral Sir Geoffrey Phipps-Hornby to Germany as the guests of the Kaiser to witness their naval and military manoeuvres. Neither he nor the Admiral appear to have been impressed by the former.

Member of the Australian Defence Committee: 1890-1891. This had been formed, by Australia, to inspect and report on their local defences and, from Britain, he was the nominated naval officer. Joining the P. & O. s.s. *Rome*, 5,013 grt, at Brindisi, he arrived at Albany on 23 November 1890. Members of the committee subsequently inspected the defences of various Australian coastal cities, including those in Tasmania. In January 1891 he undertook a similar service in New Zealand. He returned to Sydney in March to join in the inspection of the defences of east coast ports and cities. Between 8 and 12 May at Melbourne the committee drew up their reports for the Minister of Defence, Mr. F.T. Sargood. Then from Adelaide on 13 May he returned to Europe in the P. & O. s.s. *Britannia*, 6,525 grt, who arrived at Brindisi on 12 June and where he disembarked. Seizing the opportunity he spent the next few days visiting Turin, Aix-les Bains, Chamonix and Geneva, finally returning to London on 24 June 1891.

From 14 November 1891 in command battleship *Dreadnought*, 10,820 tons, Mediterranean.

For services recently rendered in Australasia he was made CMG on 1 January 1892.

In company with other ships of the Fleet, on 4 February 1892 assisted in re-floating the Flagship *Victoria*, aground at Snipe Point, Platea.

Off Tripoli, Lebanon on 22 June 1893 *Victoria* was lost in collision with *Camperdown*. The C. in C., Sir George Tryon, had erred. In *Dreadnought* not only did he witness the whole wretched affair but skilfully manoeuvred his ship in order to avoid further damage. Then he ordered boats away to assist in the rescue of survivors.

In 1893, then a young Cadet, the future Admiral Hugh Tweedie served in *Dreadnought* for a few months. He has left a brief account of his first Captain at sea:-

'Arthur Moore must have been as fine a captain as a youngster could possibly have, a mixture of severity and kindness. (--) We had, if the "old Man" was in sight, always to be running; he could not bear to see a midshipman (cadet) walking. I was his doggie or A.D.C. for a year. He used to start me off on a message and when I had gone a few yards call me back, and, waving a large hand at me in a peculiar way he had, would say, "always run my boy when you are given an order", but as long as one ran, and ran fast, all was well (11).'

From 17 April 1894 to 21 April 1897 in command *Britannia*, 'Training Ship for Naval Cadets', Dartmouth. There he was responsible for several most necessary reforms:-

'Bullying and fagging had evidently got beyond a joke while 'the punishment system for trivial offences was inhuman'. Much of this changed with the arrival of Captain Moore in 1894 who started the term Lieutenant system, abolished ship's corporals and put discipline in the hands of a gunner and four gunner's mates. Training was improved … Because the old hulks were wearing out, Captain Moore's final effort was to persuade the Admiralty to build the college on the hill above the Dart (--), the go ahead was given in 1898 (12).'

Indeed he did attend to and supervise the application of these most necessary reforms however this still was the Victorian age. The future Admiral Sir William Milbourne James (1881-1973) joined *Britannia* in 1895. Later he was to write:-

'There were two Captains in my time – Moore and Curzon-Howe – both tall, very handsome men – god-like creatures to us – at whom we gazed during Sunday parade and saw occasionally watching a cricket or football match. Forty years later when visiting the college at Dartmouth I asked a cadet if he had seen the Captain recently; he replied that the Captain was playing racquets with a cadet. Nothing could illustrate better the great changes that had taken place since my day; Moore or Curzon-Howe in flannels, playing a game with a cadet, was inconceivable (13).'

Additionally from 9 November 1895 appointed, 'Naval Aide de Camp to the Queen'.

From 8 June 1897 appointed for two months to the battleship *Renown*, 12,350 tons. She was preparing as Flagship for the North America and West Indies Station, Vice Admiral Sir John Fisher.

CB: 22 June 1897.

On 31 December 1897 appointed as a Lord Commissioner of the Admiralty and Fourth Sea Lord, the First Lord being the Rt. Hon. George J. Goschen. The First Sea Lord was Admiral Sir Frederick William Richards (see C. in C., 1890), his previous Admiral in the East Indies from 1885.

The Fashoda Incident between Britain and France occurred in the Sudan on 18 September 1898. Britain made, 'all preparations for war (14)'. Fortunately the matter was to be resolved peacefully.

Rear Admiral: 13 January 1899.

Continued as a Lord Commissioner of the Admiralty and as Fourth Sea Lord, 4SL.

Following the commencement of the second Boer War on 11 October 1899, as 4SL his responsibilities now included all transport and coaling arrangements for the conveyance of troops to South Africa.

In succession to Vice Admiral Sir Robert Harris, he was to serve as C. in C., Cape of Good Hope and West Coast of Africa: 11 February 1901 – 11 April 1904. Flag in the cruiser *Gibraltar*, 7,700 tons, Captain Arthur H. Limpus (15). He took up his command at the Cape on 15 April 1901.

In August 1901 The Duke and Duchess of York arrived in South African waters in HMS *Ophir*, Commodore Alfred Winsloe (see C. in C., 1910).

The Boer War was to end on 31 May 1902.

KCB: 26 June 1902.

Vice Admiral: 8 December 1903.

He gave up his command at the Cape on 20 April 1904. In his service record in August 1902 the following words of appreciation had been noted:-

> 'Despatch from War Office stating Lord Kitchener greatly indebted to Admiral Moore for kind manner in which he has always endeavoured to meet requirements of army in field in S. Africa, and TLs (Their Lordships) satisfaction expressed.'

In South Africa he was relieved, 'by my friend Rear Admiral John Durnford and returned to England in *Gibraltar*,' arriving on 17 May 1904 (16). His flag was struck at sunset two days later, 19 May 1904.

From 9 May 1905 appointed Second in Command, Channel Fleet with his Flag in the battleship *Caesar*, 14,900 tons, Captain Archibald P. Stoddart.

KCVO: 11 August 1905, this honour being awarded to him by HM King Edward VII as a consequence of the visit paid that month by a French Naval Squadron to Portsmouth. Following the signing of a convention in April 1904, Great Britain and France had become closer, the 'Entente Cordiale'.

On 18 November 1905 Prince Carl of Denmark, who on 22 July 1896 had married Princess Maud, youngest daughter of the future King Edward VII, was offered, and accepted, the throne of Norway. Shortly thereafter the Admiral proceeded in *Caesar* to Christiania (Oslo) to represent Great Britain during the accession celebrations. His Majesty took the Norse name of Haakon. As King Haakon VII he was to be crowned at Trondheim on 22 June 1906 and was to reign until his death on 21 September 1957. To mark the occasion of the accession of His Majesty, Sir Arthur was conferred with the Grand Cross of the Norwegian Order of Saint Olaf.

On his return from Norway his flag in *Caesar* was struck on 5 December 1905.

The next day, 6 December 1905, he was appointed C. in C., China Station.

Out in the China command he flew his flag in the twin screw armoured cruiser *King Alfred*, 14,100 tons, Captain Cecil F. Thursby (17). The ship completed commissioning at Portsmouth on 2 January 1906. In her he sailed on 19 January 1906 and, via Suez from where he departed on 17 February, reached Colombo on 28 February, and finally Hong Kong on 14 March. As was recorded in *Diadem*:-

> 'At Hong Kong, Wednesday, 14 March 1906
>
> 08:30   H.M.S. *King Alfred* flying flag of Vice Admiral Moore arrived and saluted
>
> C. in C. with 17 guns. *Alacrity* returned ditto with 15 guns (18).'

Two days later, 16 March, he assumed command of the station from Admiral Noel.

The Governor of Hong Kong from July 1904 to April 1907 was that most talented administrator, and bachelor, Sir Matthew Nathan (19), and from July 1907 to March 1912 was Sir Frederick Lugard (20). To take up his post Sir Frederick arrived in the colony on 28 July 1907 and assumed office the following day.

Writing from *King Alfred* at Sasebo, 21 June 1906, Sir Arthur informed the Admiralty that on 10 May the twin screw protected cruiser *Astraea*, 4,360 tons, Captain Charles L. Vaughan-Lee, had arrived at Shanghai from Nanking, 'having onboard Sir Ernest Satow who was on his way to England. I was fortunate in being afforded this opportunity of meeting Sir Ernest and discussing with him the general situation in China (21).'

Over the ever-present matter of piracy, on 11 May the sloop *Clio*, 1,070 tons, Commander Henry D. Wilkin, DSO, was despatched to Wei-Hai-Wei to, 'enquire into a case of piracy in that locality.'

Subsequently the C. in C. reported to London that he had arrived at Kure on 23 June 1906 and on the following day been shown around the Arsenal and dockyard as a guest of Vice Admiral Yamanouchi:-

> '... very complete and well organised establishment, which employs 26,000 men, and is capable of
>
> building and completing for sea the most powerful modern battleship (22).'

From ports in the Inland Sea Admiral Moore continued around to Tokyo Bay anchoring off Yokohama on 7 July 1906:-

> 'On the 9 July, accompanied by my Staff and all Commanding Officers, I proceeded to Tokio by
>
> rail and was graciously received by Their Imperial Highnesses The Emperor and Empress and
>
> afterwards entertained at luncheon at the Palace, at which the Emperor was present. A series of
>
> entertainments was organised for the Officers and men of the squadron and free passes issued to
>
> Tokio and adjacent stations on the railway. In fact at every port visited nothing could exceed the
>
> kindness and cordiality of our welcome (23).'

One rather unpleasant feature concerning cruising in Japanese waters at the time, and a point frequently mentioned by Admiral Moore in his various General Letters, was the presence of, 'many floating mines still remaining.' Clearly since their recent conflict with Russia there had not been adequate time to thoroughly complete the sweeping process.

From *King Alfred* at Chemulpo (today: Inchon) on 12 September 1906 he proceeded, 'with my staff to Seoul to pay an official visit to the Resident General, the Marquis Ito, by whom I was very cordially received (24).'

King Alfred continued on to Dalny on 17 September, and then on 19 September next door into Port Arthur, one scene of the great success at sea, but especially on land by Japanese forces in their recent war against the forces of Tsarist Russia:-

> '... and having called on the Governor General I was entertained at luncheon by Admiral Tamari
>
> and afterwards shewn around the fortifications. Beyond collecting the debris the Japanese have
>
> done nothing to the forts since the capitulation, and apparently have no intention at present of
>
> rebuilding them (25).'

It being that season of the year, on 18 September a powerful typhoon hit Hong Kong and caused considerable damage:-

'The European community lost, by drowning, its Anglican bishop, Dr. C.J. Hoare, on board a mission vessel with trainees, and the Chinese counted their dead by thousands. Shipping in the harbour suffered particularly and the decision was forthwith taken at all costs and without delay to build an adequate harbour of refuge (26).'

The C. in C., continuing his cruise in the northern waters of the station, now crossed the Gulf of Chihli to the coal exporting port of Chinwangtao, just south-west of the point at which the Great Wall of China reaches the sea. On occasion visiting ships could berth alongside but even if this was not possible the anchorage was far more convenient than the alternative at Taku. From there:-

'On the 24 September I proceeded to Peking by rail from Chinwangtao and was accommodated at the Legation by Sir John Jordan. The following morning, accompanied by my staff and by the principal members of the British Legation, I was received in audience by the Empress Dowager and the Emperor at the Summer Palace.

(-) While in Peking I had an excellent opportunity of discussing with Sir John Jordan and Sir Robert Hart many matters of interest and the general situation in China (27).'

From China Sir Arthur cruised on to visit the Americans at Manila, and the Dutch at Batavia and Buitenzorg, reaching Singapore shortly before Christmas 1906.

Between April and September 1906 the Governor of the Philippine Islands had been Henry Clay Ide who then had been succeeded by the Army General and Judge, James Francis Smith (1859-1928). Behind both appointments had been the wise and steady hand of the first civilian American Governor of the Philippines, William Howard Taft (1857-1930), from 1909 to 1913 to be President of the U.S.A.

In the Dutch East Indies the Govenor-General then was Johannes Benedictus van Heutsz (1851-1924). To him is due credit for the establishment of Dutch authority throughout the archipelago, also to the fact that he worked to improve the welfare of the population at large and to organise education. In addition he endeavoured to ban the indigenous customs of headhunting and suttee (28).

15 November 1906. Launch at Yokosuka of the battleship *Satsuma*, at 19,400 tons briefly the largest battleship in the world. Even though she took nearly five years to complete the mere fact that she had been constructed in Japan, be it with several items of equipment supplied from England, served to confirm the extraordinarily rapid growth and capability of the domestic ship building industry in that country.

On his return from the Dutch East Indies, then from Singapore the C. in C. steamed up the Straits of Malacca to pay a return visit to Selangor, rich in tin and rubber:-

'On the 22 December (1906) I transferred my flag to the *Alacrity* and left in that ship for Port Swettenham in Selangor arriving the following afternoon, and proceeding by train to Kuala Lumpur on the 24th to visit Sir W. Taylor, the Resident General. I was much struck with the evidences of prosperity and progress in Kuala Lumpur and the surrounding country. What was, some 20 to 25 years ago, nothing but thick jungle, has now resolved itself into vast rubber plantations and tin workings. Kuala Lumpur itself has sprung up in the same period and is now a prosperous town with handsome buildings, electric light everywhere, and motor cars much in evidence (29).'

Christmas Day was spent as the guest of the Resident General in Kuala Lumpur and then from Port Swettenham (today: Port Kelang) on 26 December, Sir Arthur returned to Singapore on 27 December. There he transferred his flag to *King Alfred* immediately and thereafter visited Bangkok. Next he returned to Singapore to attend a conference, 'in connection with war arrangements', and which was held during the latter part of January 1907. His brother Commanders in Chief on that occasion were Vice Admiral Sir Edmund Poe, East Indies, and Vice Admiral Sir Wilmot Fawkes (1846-1926), Australia. Immediately the conference ended he proceeded across the South China Sea to visit the French at Saigon, from there returning to Hong Kong.

By 15 April 1907 he was back at Kure there to witness the launch of the battleship *Aki* who, during the previous June, he had seen under construction.

In Japan, after George Sansom had been promoted Second Assistant on 30 January 1907, then the British Ambassador, Sir Claude Macdonald, appointed him to be his Private Secretary. For Great Britain this was to prove to be a most valuable appointment. In due course his wife, Katharine Sansom, was to record:-

> 'He often said that there had been a great advantage in being the Ambassador's private secretary, for in that way as a young man he met all the prominent men of the period, with many of whom he became intimate. He wrote later of having played billiards with the Japanese Prime Minister, and of being on extremely easy terms with most of the admirals and generals, who, with relish, used to attend Embassy parties. He was also fortunate in knowing their young attaches and secretaries, for as they went up the ladder and a generation later became prominent he remained, as it were, one of them; so that precious friendships grew out of those early contacts (30).'

With their victory over China in the Sino-Japanese War of 1894/5 the Japanese had gained many rights including that of operating steamship services on the Yangtse. Intially their efforts in that direction had proved unsatisfactory, even fragmented, however in 1905 the decision was taken to merge all their national shipping interests in order to compete as a single unit. So it was that in March 1907 the Nisshin Kisen Kaisha, or Japan-China Steamship Company, was formed. The two major shareholders were Osaka Shosen Kaisha with 46% and Nippon Yusen Kaisha with 41%. Aided by a substantial government subsidy, and by efficiently operating a fleet of modern ships, soon the new company's sevices were to gain a prominent place on the River (31).

On 31 May 1907 the C. in C. received orders from the Admiralty that *Monmouth* was to proceed across the Pacific to embark and convey Prince Fushimi Sadanaru (1858-1923) back to Japan. He was returning home at the conclusion of a long journey which had included a visit to England, such was one aspect of the spirit of the Alliance with Great Britain. Accordingly Captain J.A. Tuke completed with coal at Yokosuka and on 6 June 1907 sailed for Esquimalt, arriving on 19 June having averaged thirteen knots on his crossing. There when he completed with coal he took a further 100 tons on deck. Once Prince Fushimi and his suite had embarked *Monmouth* departed early on 25 June and arrived at Honolulu on 2 July, 'where the ship was berthed alongside the United States Navy wharf.' There she loaded a further 800 tons of coal and at 3.00 p.m. on 3 July she continued on to Yokohama arriving at 1.00 p.m. on 14 July. No doubt members of the ship's company will have enjoyed most thoroughly their cruise of just over five weeks.

Even so long after the events of 1885, Port Hamilton still received some attention:-

> 'I detached *Kent* to Port Hamilton with instructions to effect any repairs to the British Naval Cemetery there and to rejoin on 26 May.'

During the summer of 1907 Admiral Moore also visited the Russians at Vladivostok, arriving there in *Prince Alfred* on 20 August. As usual there was much mutual entertainment arranged. He sailed five days later, on 25 August, 'in heavy rain and squally weather.'

By 22 September he was back at Chinwangtao where he landed and proceeded to Peking by train. Together with Chinese authorities in Peking on 24 September he attended a conference to discuss the question of piracy in the waters around Canton, and of the need for its suppression. Next came a journey overland. 'On the night of the 25 (September) I proceeded by rail from Peking to Hankow arriving there on the morning of the 27 (September).' Following a visit to meet the British Consul General he embarked in the gunboat *Kinsha* for passage upriver to Ichang (32). The river level was high consequently the current was strong and so they only arrived at Ichang at noon on 1 October. As at that place the river level was found to be twenty feet above normal he was delayed at Ichang until such time as the level dropped and the current through the gorges and over the rapids above Ichang eased. Happily the C. in C. was in experienced hands:-

> 'I had the benefit of the advice of Mr. Plant, an Englishman, the Upper Yangtse Pilot for the French gunboat *Orly*, who is an expert in the navigation of the rapids, and who had asked permission to take passage up in the *Widgeon*, and as he considered a start might be made the next morning, if the river continued to fall, I transferred my flag to the *Widgeon* (Lieutenant and Commander Spicer-Simpson) on the evening of the 6 October (33).'

Indeed the following morning conditions were good and *Widgeon* sailed from Ichang at 7.30 a.m. on 7 October 1907. Nevertheless, as an example of the strong current which was flowing, when steaming through the 'Witches Mountain Gorge' at Wushan she required, 'three and a half hours steaming at 14 knots to accomplish 20 miles'.

At Chungking, where they arrived late in the afternoon on 11 October, Sir Arthur, 'the first Admiral to visit Chungking', paid calls on the Taotai and Military Commandant, 'both of whom expressed their satisfaction at my visit'. Other duties attended to, he left on 13 October reaching Ichang two days later, on 15 October. There he re-embarked in *Kinsha* to continue on downstream. At the time the railway from Shanghai had not been completed through to Nanking therefore he boarded the train at Chinkiang, in that manner reaching Shanghai on 21 October. In his subsequent report to the Admiralty he stressed:-

> 'I may here remark too that throughout the voyage the advice and assistance of Mr. Plant in navigating the more dangerous rapids was invaluable.'

Admiral: 10 October 1907.

Bearing in mind the repercussions which had followed the *Arrow* incident of October 1856, during which that lorcha, Chinese owned but registered in Hong Kong and flying the British ensign, off Canton had been boarded by the local authorities and her crew arrested, then rather over fifty years later the following does appear to be most relevant:-

> 'Sir Arthur Moore himself speaking to me on the 25th January (1908) said that he was 'ashamed and humiliated' to find how few of the forty nine launches on the Canton river flying the British flag were genuine British owned and entitled to our protection. One man named Fisher had twenty launches registered in his name yet knew nothing about their movements and could not tell the Admiral even the names of the places to which they plied. The scandal was so bad that our Chief Justice was sent specially to Canton to draft new regulations that would prevent such an abuse of the British flag (34).'

As if confirmation was required regarding the rapid growth of the Japanese shipbuilding capability, it was to be during 1908 that for the first time the tonnage completed domestically exceeded the tonnage of those ships imported.

Admiral Lambton assumed command of the station on 21 March 1908 and from Hong Kong that evening Sir Arthur sailed for home in the twin screw P. & O. s.s. *Marmora*, 10,509 grt, arriving in England on 24 April. On passage home the ship called at Bombay where he dined with the governor, Lord Sydenham (35).

On 7 September 1908 he was granted permission to proceed on a private visit to New Zealand. Following that journey it was on 2 April 1909 that he was to report his return to England.

GCB: 19 June 1911.

In succession to Admiral Sir Assheton Curzon-Howe, he served as C. in C., Portsmouth: 18 March 1911-31 July 1912 with his Flag in *Victory*. In her his Flag Captain was Edwyn Alexander-Sinclair (see C. in C., 1925). His Flag Lieutenant in the ship was Lieutenant Commander Francis George Gillilan Chilton who, between 1933 and 1935 was to be Rear Admiral, Yangtse.

As a Commodore Second Class, the Captain of the Royal Naval Barracks at Portsmouth from 25 October 1910 was Alexander L. Duff (see C. in C., 1919), yet another connection with the China Station.

On Saturday, 24 June 1911, two days after the Coronation of H.M. King George V:-

'His period (in command at Portsmouth) coincided with the Coronation festivities, and he hoisted his flag in the battleship *Lord Nelson* as C. in C. of the Fleet assembled for review by King George, when there were 165 war vessels at Spithead, in addition to 18 foreign warships (36).'

The occasion of this Review was the time at which HM King George promoted him GCVO. Also promoted on that day was Admiral Sir Francis Bridgeman, C. in C., Home Fleet.

There exists an amusing story concerning this Review. Rather naturally the Admiralty had ordered that from 0800 that morning, 'no vessels other than those flying the White Ensign are allowed to approach or enter the lines of warships'. However the Chairman of the Department of Customs and Excise, Sir Laurence Guillemard, from 1919 to be Governor of the Straits Settlements, was able to remind the Admiralty that his Department held a charter from King Charles II which in Home Waters gave his Department authority over even that of the Royal Navy. Consequently in his Revenue Cutter *Vigilant*, at an appropriate time and without fear of repercussion, he was able to sail down the lines of warships and anchor at their head (37).

A few months later another important ceremonial occasion took place.

On Saturday, 11 November 1911 in the new P. & O. s.s. *Medina*, 12,350 tons, Rear Admiral Sir Colin R. Keppel, KCIE, KCVO, CB, DSO and Captain Alfred E.M. Chatfield, HM King George V and Queen Mary sailed from Portsmouth to India and the great Durbar at Delhi. While building at Greenock the ship especially had been fitted out for use as a Royal Yacht. In due course Their Royal Highnesses were to return to anchor in Spithead on Sunday, 4 February 1912, berthing at Portsmouth the following morning. At the time in India the Viceroy was Charles, Baron Hardinge of Penshurst (1858-1944). It was during this Durbar that on 12 December 1911 H.M. King George first proclaimed the news of the transfer of the seat of the Government of India from Calcutta to the ancient capital of Delhi.

On 12 January 1912 at Portsmouth the keel of the battleship *Iron Duke*, 25,000 tons and future Flagship, Grand Fleet, was laid down. His sister Evelyn Isabella (1856-1923), one time Maid of Honour to HM Queen Victoria, performed this pleasant duty.

At the end of July 1912 succeeded in command at Portsmouth by Admiral Lambton, by now known as Meux.

Having reached the age of sixty five years, on 30 July 1912 he was placed on the Retired List.

Following his retirement he mentioned to a niece that:-

"I want to go out to New Zealand to look up the relations there, and then I want to run out to the Cape to see how the new docks which I started have got on. I have been all over the world but I don't know my own country, and I want to see the west country and Scotland and visit all the cathedrals and abbeys."

The Admiral eventually carried out most of these plans, beginning with New Zealand.

On his return he bought a charming Georgian house in Cadogan Street, to which he brought the treasures which he had collected during the travels of a lifetime. (--) With the outbreak of war in 1914 most of the Admiral's naval friends were on active service. They kept him informed of their engagements at sea, notably the Battle of Jutland (38).'

In succession to Admiral Sir J.O. Hopkins, from 31 July 1916 he was in receipt of a Good Service Pension at the rate of GBP 300.00 p.a. (39).

On 1 October 1926 the Frittenden Parochial Council formally thanked Sir Arthur for his donation of GBP 250.00 for investment in government securities in order to ensure a permanent income to a fund for the maintenance of the churchyard and other Church expenses. Still in 1935 this investment was producing GBP 8-3-0 p.a. (40).

His residence in London, referred to above, was at 55 Cadogan Street, SW3.

Following his death on 3 April 1934, having remained unmarried, then in writing of his funeral, which took place at Frittenden on Friday, 6 April, the local press mentioned that:-

'Sir Arthur had not lived at Frittenden since he was a boy, but he frequently visited the village and was a generous friend to the Parish Church. His benefactions included a capital sum for the maintenance of the churchyard and a generous donation towards the repair of the church tower. His last visit was about two years ago when he climbed the belfry to inspect the bells which were re-cast at his expense. The funeral service was marked by the utmost simplicity, attended by members of the family and his household staff. Those present included the Squire, the villagers and the choir (41).'

The bells mentioned above, which he had had retuned and rehung in 1928, were the very same which had welcomed him home early in his career nigh on sixty eight years previously, in 1866.

NOTES

1. E. Marjorie Moore, *Adventure in the Royal Navy,* (Liverpool, 1964), 16. This diptheria epidemic struck the village in 1859. The sisters who died were Harriet Anne, aged sixteen years, and Helen Mary, aged fifteen months. Of the two remaining sisters Alice married Revd. Sydney Phillips but Evelyn Isabella remained unmarried. Of the Admiral's brothers Edward Marsham entered the Priesthood and became Archdeacon of Oakham, Charles Henry (1846-1924) also remained unmarried, then the three, Henry, Walter and Francis, all married and emigrated to New Zealand. In due course Walter became a sheep farmer in the Chatham Islands. Revd. Herbert Octavius, having been chaplain to the Bishop of Calcutta later became chaplain at Windsor Great Park. He remained unmarried and died in 1931. Finally, William Francis in 1880 married Alice Rathbone of Liverpool and died there in his 90th year, on 6 February 1940. On 16 May 2011 the author visited Frittenden and had the great pleasure of meeting historian Roy Latham who most kindly made available much family and other relevant information.

2. Richard James **Meade**. Born: 3 October 1832. Died at Henley-on-Thames: 4 August 1907. Known as Lord Gilford until October 1879 when he succeeded his father as the Fourth Earl of Clanwilliam. Eton. Joined the RN in 1845. He chanced to be serving in *Raleigh* when she was wrecked near Macao: 14 April 1857 – see Keppel, C. in C., 1867. Captain: 22 July 1859. Rear Admiral in 1876, and Vice Admiral: 26 July 1881. Between 1880 and 1882, with his flag in *Inconstant*, commanded the Flying Squadron which included *Bacchante* in whom the Royal Princes were serving – also see reference (15) below. KCMG: 1882. C. in C., North America and West Indies: August 1885 – September 1886. Admiral: 22 June 1886. KCB: 1887. C. in C., Portsmouth: June 1891 – June 1894. There succeeded by Admiral Sir Nowell Salmon – see C. in C., 1887. Admiral of the Fleet: 20 February 1895. GCB: May 1895. Retired in October 1902. *Navy List. Who's Who.*

3. Courtesy Mr. Roy Latham, Frittenden Historical Society, 22 February 2011.

4. Moore, 40.

5. Obituary, *The Times,* Tuesday, April 10, 1934. Captain Robert O'Brien Fitzroy to be promoted Rear Admiral on 14 May 1888. *Navy List.*

6. Moore, 62/3.

7. NA ADM 196/39. *Service Record.*

8. *Foreign Office List,* 1913

9. Moore, 76.

10. *Service Record.*

11. Admiral Hugh Tweedie, *The Story of a Naval Life,* (London, undated), 22/23.

12. John Wells, *The Royal Navy: An Illustrated Social History 1870-1982,* (London, 1999), 40/1. As might be expected, with the introduction of the Selborne Scheme late in 1902 powerful impetus towards the construction of the RN Colleges at Osborne and Dartmouth was to be given by the then Second Sea Lord, Admiral Sir John Fisher. At Dartmouth the foundation stone was laid by HM King Edward VII on 7 March 1902 and the College opened at the end of 1905. Richard Hough, *First Sea Lord,* (London, 1969), 151. Ruddock F. Mackay, *Fisher of Kilverstone,* (OUP, 1973), 273. By

way of some comparison the USN Academy at Annapolis, Fort Severn, had opened on 10 October 1845, and the IJN College at Etajima had opened on 1 August 1888. As an aside, the first superintendent at Annapolis was the future Civil War Confederate Admiral, Franklin Buchanan (1800-1874).

13. Admiral Sir William James, *The Sky was Always Blue*, (London, 1951), 25.

14. Moore, 124.

15. Arthur Henry **Limpus**. Born: 7 June 1863. Died: 3 November 1931. As a Midshipman, on 15 July 1879 appointed to iron, screw corvette *Bacchante*. Fellow Gunroom messmates were HRH Prince Albert Victor and HRH Prince George, the latter in due course to be HM King George V. As Commander in *Terrible*, Captain Percy M. Scott, during November and December 1899, and in to 1900, second in command of the Naval Brigade during operations, especially with Naval 4.7" and twelve pounder guns, leading up to the relief of Ladysmith on 28 February 1900. Captain: 2 May 1900. Rear Admiral: 23 January 1909. Head of British Naval Mission to Turkey: April 1912 – Sept. 1914. Vice Admiral: 14 September 1914. Admiral Superintendent, Malta: 20 September 1914 – October 1916. KCMG: 1916. In 1917 appointed President of the Shell Committee at the Admiralty. Admiral: 30 January 1918. Retired: January 1919. *Navy List. Who's Who.* George Crowe, *The Commission of HMS Terrible*, (London, 1903).

16. Moore, 148. John **Durnford**. Born: 6 February 1849. Died: 13 June 1914. Eton. Entered the RN: 1862. Commander during the Burma War of 1885-6 where awarded the DSO. Captain: 30 June 1888. As a Rear Admiral, C. in C., Cape: 1904-1907. Vice Admiral: October 1906. President, RNC, Greenwich: March 1908 – March 1911. Admiral: 1910. Retired: May 1913. GCB: 1913. Obituary, *The Times*, Monday, 15 June 1914.

17. Cecil Fiennes **Thursby**. Born: 17 January 1861. Died: 28 May 1936. Entered RN: 1874. Midshipman in *Amethyst* during her engagement with Peruvian *Huascar*: 29 May 1877. Captain: 31 December 1901. Rear Admiral: 17 July 1911. Dardanelles: 1914-1915. Commanded British Adriatic Squadron: 1915-1916. KCMG: 1916. Vice Admiral: 10 April 1917. C. in C., Eastern Mediterranean: 1917. KCB: 1918. C. in C., Devonport: 1 August 1918. Admiral: 3 April 1919. Retired to Great Ryton, Shropshire: 1920. *Navy List. Who's Who.*

18. NA ADM 53/19558.

19. Matthew **Nathan**. Born in Paddington, London: 3 January 1862. Died in West Coker, Somerset: 18 April 1939. Sandhurst. Entered Royal Engineers: 1880. Sudan Expedition: 1885. Lushai Expedition (hills east of Chittagong on the India/Burma border): 1889. Captain: 1889. Colonial Defence Committee: 1895-1898. Major: 1898. Administered government of Sierra Leone: 1899. Governor of the Gold Coast: 1900-1903. KCMG: 1902. Appointed Governor of Hong Kong: 21 September 1903 and served in that position from 29 July 1904 to 20 April 1907. Lieut. Colonel: 1907. Governor of Natal: 2 September 1907 – 23 December 1909. GCMG: 1908. Secretary to the Post Office: 1909-1911. Chairman of the Board of Inland Revenue, and member of the Pacific Cable Board: 1911-1914. Under Secretary for Ireland: 1914-1916. London Defences: 1916. Secretary to the Ministry of Pensions: 1916-1919. Chairman Special Grants Committee: 1919. Governor of Queensland: 3 December 1920 – 17 September 1925. Chairman Civil Research Sub-Committee on Geophysical Surveying: 1927. Member of Special Commission on Constitution of Ceylon: 1927-1928. Chairman Colonial Secretary's Advisory Committee on Rubber: 1926-1928. Chairman Civil Research Sub-Committee on Irrigation Research: 1928-1930. On his retirement to Somerset much involved with local societies. *Colonial Office List*, 1940. *Who's Who.* His papers are held at The Bodleian. His grave is to be found within the Jewish Willesden cemetery, London, section A, row E, number 52.

20. Frederick John Dealtry **Lugard**. Born in Madras: 22 January 1858. Died at Abinger, Surrey: 11 April 1945. Rossall. Sandhurst. Commissioned Ninth Foot: May 1878. Afghan War: 1879/1880. Sudan: 1885. Captain: August 1885. Burma: 1886/7. DSO: 1887. Commanded expedition against slave traders, Lake Nyassa: February 1888. (As British Consul to the 'territories of the African Kings and Chiefs in the districts adjacent to Lake Nyassa' Albert G.S. **Hawes** (see King, C. in C., 1865, reference 15) had departed from Nyassa just a few days previously). East Africa: November 1889 – October 1892 during which administered Uganda. Acting for Sir George Goldie made treaties on behalf of Royal Niger Company: 1894/5. Similarly for British West Charterland to Lake Ngami in Bechuanaland: 1896/7. Major: August 1896. H.M. High Commissioner, and Commandant, West African Frontier Force: August 1897. Lieut. Colonel: July 1899. High Commissioner, Northern Nigeria: December 1899 – September 1906. Temporary Brigadier General: 1900-1907. KCMG: 1901. On 11 June 1902 at Funchal he married the influential and extremely well connected writer and journalist, Flora Louise Shaw (1852-1929). In succession to Sir Matthew Nathan, Governor of Hong Kong: 29 July

1907 – 16 March 1912. Created the University of Hong Kong: 1911. GCMG: 1911. Appointed Governor, Northern and Southern Nigeria: March 1912. Governor-General of Nigeria: Dec. 1913 – 1919. PC: 1920. British Member, Permanent Mandates Commission, League of Nations: 1922-1936. Gold Medallist, RGS. Created Baron Lugard of Abinger: 1928. Honorary degrees at Cambridge, Oxford, Glasgow, Durham and Hong Kong universities. *Colonial Office List,* 1940. *Who's Who.* His papers are held at The Bodleian. His body was cremated at Woking Crematorium.

21. NA ADM 1/7869. Sir Ernest Satow was returning to England to retire to Ottery St. Mary, Devon. Twin screw protected cruiser *Astraea,* 4,360 tons, Captain Charles L. Vaughan-Lee. *Navy List.*

22. Ibid. Letter No. 5 written in *King Alfred* at Hakodate, 31 July 1906. At the time the battleship *Aki,* 20,100 tons, was under construction at Kure. Launched: 15 April 1907. Completed 11 March 1911. Finally to be used as a target ship and sunk in Tokyo Bay: 2 September 1924. Hansgeorg Jentschura, Dieter Jung, Peter Michel, *Warships of the Imperial Japanese Navy 1869-1945,* (London, 1977), 24.

23. Ibid.

24. Ibid. The Marquis Ito Hirobumi.

25. Ibid. Today Dalny is Dalien. During the Russian occupation named Dairen. Similarly today Port Arthur is Lushun, but in Japan is known as Ryojun.

26. Geoffrey Robley Sayer, *Hong Kong: 1862-1919,* (Hong Kong, 1975), 94.

27. Ibid. Sir John Newell **Jordan**. Born: 5 September 1852. Died: 14 September 1925. Appointed Student Interpreter in China: 10 March 1876. Served in the China Consular Service in a variety of cities being promoted as Consul General for Corea, at Seoul: 27 October 1896. Promoted Minister Resident at Seoul: 15 July 1901. KCMG: 24 June 1904. The Legation at Seoul was withdrawn on 1 February 1906 when the offices of Japanese Resident General and Residents in Corea were opened under the agreement of 17 November 1905 between Japan and Corea. In succession to Sir Ernest Satow, Envoy Extraordinary and Minister Plenipotentiary to the Emperor of China: 26 October 1906. KCB: 25 June 1909. GCIE: 12 Dec. 1911. PC: 10 June 1915. Retired: 14 August 1920. *Foreign Office List,* 1920.

Empress Dowager **Tz'u-hsi**. Born: 29 November 1835. A concubine of Emperor Hsien-feng who ruled from 1850 to 1861. Her name is associated with many years of much ruthless intrigue within Manchu ruling circles, she dominating those circles for close to fifty years. Died in Peking: 15 November 1908. Ann Paludan, *Chronicle of the Chinese Emperors,* (London, 2005), 209-216.

Robert **Hart**. Born: 20 February 1835. Died: 20 September 1911. Queen's College, Belfast. Entered Consular Service in China: 1854. Served at Ningpo and Canton. In 1859 appointed Deputy Inspector of Chinese Customs. On 30 November 1863 succeeded Mr. Horatio Nelson Lay as Inspector General of the Customs Service. KCMG: 17 April 1882. GCMG: 24 May 1889. First Baronet: 20 July 1893. In May 1908, his office having been made subordinate to Chinese appointees, returned on leave to the British Isles. Under Hart the Service not only collected duties but charted the coastline, managed a number of port facilities, supervised the lighting of the coastal and many inland waterways, and even, by 1896, managed the first modern national postal service. *Who's Who. Encyclopaedia Britannica. Foreign Office List,* 1912. Concerning Hart it has been written:-

> 'Hart, autocratic towards his subordinates in his highly efficient Customs organisation, was the supple and trusted adviser to his Chinese employers on many matters and died wealthy and loaded with honours. He took with him to the Customs contemporary Foreign Office concepts of patronage and over the years offered Customs berths to numerous sons and relations of his former consular colleagues.'

P.D. Coates, *The China Consuls,* (OUP, 1988), 137.

28. Kees Zandvliet, *The Dutch Encounter with Asia: 1600-1950,* (Rijksmuseum, Amsterdam, 2002), 95.

Suttee is the custom of the burning of a widow on her husband's funeral pyre. In India too the British endeavoured to eliminate this traditional procedure.

29. NA ADM 1/7929. General Letter No. 1, 1907. Written in *King Alfred* at Mirs Bay, 31 January 1907.

Sir William Thomas **Taylor** (1848-1931). From 1904 to 1910 Resident General of the Federated Malay States.

30. Katharine Sansom, *Sir George Sansom and Japan,* (Tallahassee, Fla., 1972), 5. In 1907 the Japanese Prime Minister was **Saionji** Kinmochi (1848-1940), a personal friend of HIM Emperor Musuhito, Meiji Tenno, and in due course to be the last surviving genro; an honoured statesman of the 1920s and 1930s. In Japan in that era it would be hard to imagine a more influential or important billiards opponent.

George Bailey **Sansom**. Born in London: 28 November 1883. Died while on a visit to Tucson, AZ: 8 March 1965. Appointed Student Interpreter in Japan: 28 October 1903. Served in Tokyo, Yokohama, Chemulpo. Promoted First Assistant: 20 July 1912. Employed in the Admiralty, London: 26 July 1915 – 30 June 1917. Intelligence Directorate, War Office: 1 July 1917 – 30 October 1919. Acting Japanese Counsellor: 1 January – 23 November 1920. Thereafter Consul at Shimonoseki, then Yokohama, and Osaka. Commercial Secretary to the Embassy, Tokyo: 2 September 1923. KCMG: 3 June 1935. Retired: 8 September 1940. Visiting Professor at Columbia University, New York: 1935-1936 and 1940-1941. Adviser, Far Eastern Mission, Ministry of Economic Warfare, and Civilian Member, Far Eastern War Council, Singapore and Java: 1941-1942. Adviser to HM Ambassador at Washington DC, with local rank as Minister Plenipotentiary: 14 September 1942. United Kingdom Member, Allied Far Eastern Commission: 1946-1947. GBE: 1947. Professor, 1947-1953, and Director, East Asian Institute, Columbia University, New York, NY: 1949-1953. Member of Japanese Academy: 1951. Author of a number of books and papers on Japanese language, literature and history. *Who's Who. Foreign Office List,* 1945. *Dictionary of National Biography.*

31. H.W. Dick and S.A. Kentwell, *Beancaker to Boxboat,* (Canberra, 1988), 165.

32. The Consul General at Hankow from 1900 to 1911, and where he had established a good relationship with Viceroy Chang Chih-tung, was Everard Duncan Home **Fraser**. Born: 27 February 1859. Died in office in Shanghai: 21 March 1922. Aberdeen University. First appointed to China as a Student Interpreter: 30 March 1880. Transferred to Shanghai: 20 January 1911. KCMG: 14 June 1912. From his obituary:-

> 'No British subject in the history of our dealings with China has commanded greater respect and affection than Sir Everard Fraser, whom 'The North China Daily News' rightly describes as head and shoulders above all his contemporaries in every respect.'

Foreign Office List. The Times, March 25, 1922. It is clear that Sir Ernest Satow held Everard Fraser in very high regard and had recommended him for early promotion to Hankow – see *China Consuls,* 376/377.

At the time *Kinsha* was under the command of Lieut. Alan Dixon of *Cadmus.* Lieut. and Commander Crabtree was ill. *Navy List.*

33. NA ADM 1/7929. General Letter No. XII. Written in *King Alfred* at Mirs Bay, 1 November 1907. Addressed to the Secretary of the Admiralty.

Samuel Cornell **Plant**. Born at Framlingham, Suffolk: 8 August 1866. Died at sea in s.s. *Teiresias* on passage from Shanghai to Hong Kong: 26 February 1921. First went to sea at age fourteen. Obtained his Second Mate's certificate: 30 October 1886. Gained experience of river navigation on the Tigris and Euphrates in Mesopotamia/Iraq, and on the Karun in Persia/Iran. In June 1900 took Archibald Little's paddle wheel steamer *Pioneer* up to Chungking, indeed a pioneering voyage. The doyen of European service navigators and pilots on the Yangtse upstream from Ichang. From 1910 employed by the Chinese Maritime Customs as Senior River Inspector on the Upper Yangtse. Retired: 1919. Acquired by the Admiralty then *Pioneer* in Naval service was re-named *Kinsha. The Journal of the Hong Kong Branch of the Royal Asiatic Society,* Vol. 41, 407-416, and Vol. 43, 185-200. *South China Morning Post,* 3 March 1921. Family papers kindly made available to the writer by Mr. Michael Gillam. Today, written in 2008, the memorial oberlisk to Captain Plant may be seen on the left bank of the Yangtse River approximately ten nautical miles above the great new dam at Sandouping. Thoughtfully the Chinese authorities have repositioned it well above flood water level. For more recently ascertained data covering the Plant children see Polly Shih Brandmeyer, *Journal of the Royal Asiatic Society, Hong Kong Branch, Vol. 54, 2014,* 101/129.

34. Ed. Lo Hui-min, *The Correspondence of G.E. Morrison, Vol. 1, 1895-1912,* (Cambridge University Press, 1976), 450. George Ernest Morrison (1862-1920), Australian born and for many years Peking correspondent for *The Times.* From 1 August 1912 Political Adviser to the President of the Republic of China, Yuan Shih-K'ai (1859-1916). The extract is taken from his letter of 14 April 1908 written from Peking to Sir Ignatius Valentine Chirol (1852-1929), a prominent author, historian and journalist of the day, an inimate of many men of power.

The Morrison volumes made available to the author courtesy of the British Library.

35. Moore, 172. In this volume it is stated that he travelled home in s.s. *Morea,* an error as she only made her maiden voyage that December. Also see *Service Record.*

Lord Sydenham: Sir George Sydenham **Clarke** (1848-1933). Joined the Royal Engineers: 1868. Secretary, Colonial Defence Committee: 1885-1892. KCMG: 1893. FRS: 1896. Governor of Victoria: 1901-1903. GCMG: 1905. Governor of Bombay: 1907-1913. GCIE: 1907. GCSI: 1911. GBE: 1917. Raised to the peerage on his retirement in 1913. M.N. Lettice, *Australian Dictionary of Biography,* (Melbourne, 1981), Vol. 8, 13-14.

36. Obituary, *The Times*. Battleship *Lord Nelson,* 16,500 tons. Launched: 4 September 1906. The Review of the Fleet by HM King George V took place on 24 June 1911, two days after his Coronation. *Lord Nelson* then was commanded by Captain Alfred A.E. Grant. *Navy List.*

37. Kindly related to the author on 16 May 2011 by Mr. Roy Latham.

38. Moore, 197-199. One of the letters, dated 24 June 1916, was written from *Galatea* by Commodore Edwyn S. Alexander Sinclair (see C. in C., 1925).

39. *Service Record.*

40. Courtesy of Mr Roy Latham, Frittenden Historical Society.

41. Moore, 214/5. Extract from *The Maidstone Gazette.*

1 January 1908 to 25 January 1910
Vice Admiral The Hon. Sir Hedworth **Lambton**

Hedworth was born in London on 5 July 1856, the third son and child of George Frederick D'Arcy Lambton, the Second Earl of Durham, by his wife, Lady Beatrix Frances, second daughter of James Hamilton, first Duke of Abercorn. His two elder brothers, in due course respectively to become third and fourth Earls, were twins born on 19 June 1855.

An aunt, Lady Mary Louise Lambton, on 7 November 1846 had married, as his second wife, James Bruce, Eighth Earl of Elgin and Twelfth Earl of Kincardine (1811-1863). It was he who in 1858 had negotiated two British treaties, the first in June at Tientsin with China, and the second in August at Yedo with the Tokugawa Shogunate of Japan (see C. in C., 1862, 1865 and 1867).

He died of cardiac failure and cerebral thrombosis on 20 September 1929 at Danebury, his estate near Stockbridge, Hampshire and was buried in the churchyard of St. Mary's, Cheshunt, Hertfordshire (1).

As a youngster he attended Cheam School, then entered the Royal Navy as a **Naval Cadet** on 15 January 1870. He remained in *Britannia* until 20 December 1871 (2). On the very next day, 21 December, transferred to *Endymion*. **Midshipman**: 21 March 1872. Continued to serve in the screw frigate *Endymion*, 22 guns, 3,200 tons, from 24 April commanded by Captain Edward Madden, training ship for cadets then, latterly, Detached Squadron, Devonport until 31 July 1874 when she paid off at Sheerness. From 1 August 1874 in screw iron ship, armour plated, *Agincourt*, 28 guns, 10,630 tons, Flagship, Channel Squadron, the C. in C. then being Rear Admiral Frederick Beauchamp Paget Seymour (1821-1895), later Lord Alcester. Acting Sub Lieutenant: 20 September 1875, then from 22 October 1875 to 28 December 1876 studying at the Royal Naval College, Greenwich. Confirmed as **Sub Lieutenant** with seniority dating from 20 September 1875, then from 29 December 1876 in *Alexandra*, 12 guns, 9,500 tons, Captain Robert O'Brien Fitzroy, Flagship, Mediterranean, Vice Admiral Geoffrey T.P. Hornby. Admiral Hornby's Flag Lieutenant was Alfred L. Winsloe (see C. in C., 1910). **Lieutenant**: 27 February 1879. He left the Mediterranean on 11 March 1879 and arrived back in England a fortnight later, on 26 March. Then followed a period on leave on full pay until 7 May 1879 (3). From 28 June 1879 in *Lord Warden*, 18 guns, 7,850 tons, ship of First Reserve temporarily employed with Channel Squadron, Captain Hon. Edmund R. Fremantle (see C. in C., 1892). From 5 February 1880 Flag Lieut. to his Admiral who had commanded in the Channel in 1874, but by now had been promoted to be Vice Admiral Sir F. Beauchamp P. Seymour, C. in C., Mediterranean with his flag in *Alexandra*. She re-commissioned at Malta on 12 March 1880, Captain Lord Walter T. Kerr. In her during the bombardment of Alexandria which commenced early on 11 July 1882. However personally he was able to play a more active role:-

> 'At nearly the same hour (2 p.m. on 11 July), it being seen that the gunners in the lower battery of
> Mex had abandoned their guns, a party of twelve volunteers (including Lieutenants Richard Poore,
> and Hon. Hedworth Lambton, and Midshipman Edward Ernest Hardy), under Lieut. Barton
> Rose Bradford, landed through the growing swell and breaking surf, spiked six smooth-bores, and

disabled two 10" rifled muzzle loaders by exploding charges of guncotton in their muzzles.

This was done without casualty, though it cost the loss of *Bittern's* dinghy (4).'

On 29 July 1882, and on occasion subsequently, accompanied Captain John A. Fisher on a railway reconnaissance in the vicinity of Alexandria in one of the armoured trains first devised by Captains Fisher and Arthur K. Wilson.

By mail steamer he left the Mediterranean on 3 February 1883, returning to England a week later, on 10 February.

Commander: 10 March 1883. Returned to study briefly at RNC, Greenwich. Subsequently a.d.c. in Dublin to the Lord Lieutenant, the Fifth Earl Spencer. He was John Poyntz Spencer (1835-1910) a Liberal party politician who, from 1892 to 1895, was to be First Lord of the Admiralty.

From 16 July 1886 to 15 February 1888 in command sloop *Dolphin*, 4 guns, 925 tons, Mediterranean.

From 16 February 1888 in command Royal Yacht, *Osborne*, 1,850 tons, a paddle steamer.

Captain: 30 June 1889.

Continued in command of *Osborne* until 30 November 1889 (5).

From 4 February 1890 in command armoured cruiser *Warspite*, 8,400 tons, Flagship, Pacific Station.

'... on February 19 (1891), while trying to arrange an armistice between the belligerent Chileans at Iquiqui, Captain the Hon. Hedworth Lambton, of the *Warspite*, flagship of Rear Admiral Charles Frederick Hotham, had narrowly escaped death, one bullet having passed through the bottom, and another through the awning of his gig as he went ashore to conduct the negotiations (6).'

He paid off out of *Warspite* on 24 June 1893.

Private Secretary to successive First Lords: 3 July 1894 – 25 April 1897. The first was John Poyntz Spencer, mentioned above in Dublin. In 1895 the noble Earl was succeeded by George Goschen (7).

From 8 June 1897 in command cruiser *Powerful*, 14,200 tons, China Station.

Towards the end of 1897, in order to take up his appointment in command of the armoured cruiser *Narcissus*, 5,600 tons, Captain George King-Hall took passage from England to the East in the cruiser *Edgar*, 7,350 tons, Captain William C.C. Forsyth. On arrival at Hong Kong he went onboard *Powerful* as a guest of Captain Lambton, *Narcissus* then being at Chefoo. As seen above, from his appointment between 1894 and 1897 Captain Lambton had acquired a first rate knowledge of the inner workings of the Admiralty, and of aspects of international relations. In view of the slowly worsening relationship betwen Great Britain and Germany the following entry recorded by Captain King-Hall in his diary in January 1898 is of interest, and also was to be especially relevant in 1914. A little gossip also was noted:-

'Lambton told me a good deal about the inner workings of the Admiralty, and generally critcised the whole Flag List, coming to the conclusion that there were not many able men on it. Noel he did not consider clever. He told me also that when Lord Salisbury and the Czar had their meeting, the Czar said the German Emperor had said this and that of England. He (the German Emperor) said that Russia was thwarting us (Great Britain) in Egypt, whereupon the Czar said to Salisbury, "What a perfidious fellow he is". The German Emperor is a very dangerous man and not to be trusted (8).'

At the time the Czar was Nicholas II (1868-1918), and the German Emperor by then was Wilhelm II (1859-1941).

Amongst other duties, and following the American seizure of the Philippines from Spain, on Friday 9 September 1898 *Powerful* anchored at Manila, there to succeed *Immortalite* in her duties as guardship over British citizens and interests.

The Boer War commenced on 11 October 1899 and so on passage home *Powerful* was ordered 'temporarily' to the Cape of Good Hope and West Africa Station.

Prior to the actual declaration of war, but perceiving that it would be as well to position military reinforcements in South Africa, after sailing from Singapore on Sunday, 24 September 1899 *Powerful* first was ordered to Mauritius where she anchored off Port Louis at 0955 hours on Tuesday, 3 October. There she coaled on 4 and 5 October. Then at 11:30 on Friday, 6 October:-

'Commenced embarking Second Battalion King's Own Yorkshire Light Infantry
Regt.: 12 officers, 437 men and 3 horses for passage (9).'

These men were embarked by 14:00 hours whereupon he weighed and proceeded at 14:35.

Four days later, at 12:20 on Tuesday, 10 October 1899 he anchored off Durban where this army party disembarked into lighters immediately. He weighed again at 14:30 and continued on to Table Bay where he anchored at 08:27 on Friday morning, 13 October 1899.

Subsequently from the Cape he brought up and landed at Durban two 4.7", four 12 pounder, and four maxim guns (10). With the guns and ammunition he proceeded inland from Durban, arriving at Ladysmith on 30 October, by happy chance just in time. Subsequently, during the siege by the Boer forces, he commanded the Naval Brigade from 2 November 1899 until the relief of the town on 28 February 1900. These Naval guns kept down the Boer artillery throughout this siege (11).

In connection with the above some further details follow. As may be seen at the Cape in October 1899, and once Boer army intentions in Natal had become apparent, no time was wasted:-

'H.M.S. *Powerful* at Simon's Bay. Thursday, 26 October 1899.

5:15 p.m.	Ship commenced to drag. Let go port anchor and veered to six on starboard. Stopped coaling there being too much sea for lighters, having received 910 tons. Hoisting in 4.7" guns, ammunition and mountings.
10:55 p.m.	Weighed and proceeded out of Simon's Bay.'

The arrival of *Powerful* from Simon's Bay to anchor off Durban was accompanied by other activity. Also no time was lost in landing reinforcements. As may be seen from her log book:-

'H.M.S. *Powerful* to Durban. Sunday, 29 October 1899.

10:10 a.m.	Stopped and came to off Durban. Found here H.M.S. *Tartar* and Dutch s.s. *Maria*.
10:30 a.m.	Arrived H.M.S. *Magicienne* who boarded and seized s.s. *Maria* for carrying contraband of war. Employed hoisting out into lighters field service guns and ammunition.
5:00 p.m.	Landed two 4.7" guns (together with 12 pounder and maxim guns, and a total of 282 men, 'for active service on shore all fully equipped,' including Captain Lambton and a Lieut. Egerton). They proceeded the same night by train to Ladysmith (12).'

Although Ladysmith was about to be invested word still came through to the ship as on 31 October, 'Landed a further two 12 pdr. guns and 1,120 rounds ammunition per telegraphed orders from Captain Lambton, Pietermaritzburg (13).'

On 4 November news was received in the ship that Lieut. Egerton had died of his wounds received during the siege.

Powerful weighed off Durban at 10.55 a.m. on Monday, 6 November 1899 and returned to anchor in Simon's Bay on 8 November.

Once the siege of Ladysmith was lifted by General Redvers Buller on 28 February 1900, then a fortnight later the men of their Naval Brigade returned to the ship, still at anchor in Simon's Bay. The whole Boer War was to be marked by very considerable loss of life due to illness. Already this aspect of that long drawn out campaign was to be becoming apparent:-

'Monday, 12 March 1900.

10:15 a.m.	Arrived transport *Columbian* with *Powerful*'s Naval brigade who had been part

of Ladysmith's garrison during the siege.

Captain Hon. H. Lambton rejoined the ship.

1:20 p.m.   Naval Brigade returned onboard from transport *Columbian* having lost
Commander Egerton and 5 men killed in action and 23 men from disease during
the siege of Ladysmith. Lieut. Heneage and 18 men were left behind sick unable
to travel. Lieut. Hodges, Mr. Sims, Gunner, and 3 men were discharged to
hospital on arrival (14).'

Indeed, writing to the Fourth Sea Lord at The Admiralty, also on 12 March, he elaborated a little concerning this aspect of poor health and sickness at Ladysmith:-

'My officers and men behaved admirably during the siege. It is very sad having lost so many from dysentery and enteric. The food was so meagre that the sick and convalescents had not much chance, but thank goodness none of our little middies succumbed, though three or four of them had very narrow squeaks (15).'

CB: 13 March 1900.

Powerful sailed from Simon's Bay on Thursday, 15 March 1900, called at St. Helena from 22 to 24 March, at Ascension for the day on 27 March, and at Las Palmas from 3 to 4 April. Finally, at 4.15 p.m. on Wednesday, 11 April 1900, she secured to the Southern Railway Jetty at Portsmouth.

It was on Wednesday, 2 May 1900 at 8.30 a.m. that the men of the ship's Naval Brigade left by special train for Windsor to be inspected by H.M. The Queen (16).

Finally he paid off on 8 June 1900 and after a month of leave went on half pay until 31 March 1901.

Later in 1900 in the 'Khaki' general election, as a Liberal, he stood unsuccessfully for Newcastle-upon-Tyne.

From 1 April 1901, as **Commodore** Second Class, commanded the Royal Yacht, *Victoria and Albert*, 4,700 tons (17). He enjoyed, then, the confidence and friendship of HM King Edward VII.

Rear Admiral: 3 October 1902.

He continued in command of *Victoria and Albert* until 23 April 1903.

Commencing with her sailing from Portsmouth on Tuesday, 31 March 1903, naturally this period in command of the Royal Yacht had included the triumphal tour and series of visits paid by His Majesty to Portugal, Gibraltar, Malta, Italy and, especially, to Paris, the latter marking the occasion of the 'clearing of the ground' by King Edward ahead of the Anglo-French agreements, the 'Entente Cordiale', which were to be signed in London on 8 April the following year (18).

From 5 June 1903 second in command Channel Fleet, Flag in battleship *Magnificent*, 14,900 tons until 1 February 1904 when, after her refit at Chatham, he shifted his flag to the sister ship *Victorious* and remained in her until 25 June 1904.

From 10 November 1904 to 1 December 1906 served as RA 3CS in cruiser *Leviathan*, 14,100 tons, Mediterranean. Of this period later a brother officer was to write:-

'Rear Admiral the Hon. Sir Hedworth Lambton was at that time in command of the cruisers in the Mediterranean. He was certainly one of the most able officers I have ever known who held high command in the Navy. Unfortunately, he was a man of many preoccupations, and the Navy never absorbed the whole of his energies. He was, however, an Admiral of broad vision, and one whose views were always listened to with respect (19).'

These 'many preoccupations' may have had a disagreeable side. At the time unfortunately much unpleasantness existed within high ranks in the Navy. Cliques had formed, one with Admiral Lord Charles Beresford as its spokesman, and it was to this group that he allied himself. A biographer of the then Rear Admiral Prince Louis of Battenberg has elaborated. Brief extracts follow:-

'Hedworth Lambton was as tireless and unremitting an opponent to Louis as was Beresford.

Lambton was a spoilt, handsome, lazy patrician who had the ear of the Prince of Wales but like Beresford had lost the confidence of the King. (--) Lambton loathed Louis's vigour, the importance he attached to success, and his manifest delight in success when he achieved it. 'How very German!' we can hear him saying in his slurred, fruity voice (20).'

In 1906 elected as a member of the Jockey Club, Newmarket, the body which governs horse racing in Britain (21).

KCVO: 16 April 1906.

Vice Admiral: 1 January 1907.

Appointed C. in C. China on 1 January 1908 and to take up his command he sailed out to the Far East with the P. & O.:-

'I arrived at Hong Kong in P. & O. s.s. *Malta* on 20 March and hoisted my flag in H.M.S. *King Alfred* on 21 March, taking over command of the China Station from Admiral Sir Arthur W. Moore, KCB KCVO CMG, who left the same day for England (22).'

By now *King Alfred* was commanded by Captain Lewis Clinton-Baker (23).

A Lieutenant then serving in the ship, and through the change of command, later was to write of one aspect of the rather different style which now prevailed on occasion onboard:-

'Sir Hedworth entertained lavishly and to cope with his bigger parties, with the help of the ship's carpenter, a horse-shoe shaped table was designed that went right round the after part of the quarter deck. I think we could seat seventy. The table was made with a wooden framework on which sheets of plate glass were laid. At night we ran an electric circuit under the table with pink tinted bulbs, which showed through the glass and tablecloth and produced a light which the ladies voted most becoming. (--)

Hedworth Lambton had caused to be made a red and white striped awning, to go under the main canvas awning – quite a familiar sight now, but was certainly the first seen out East. He also had a very fine collection of plate with the Ascot Gold Cup for a centre piece. The whole business, laid out and lit up, looked well. Many distinguished visitors fed at that table. Amongst others, the King and Queen of Siam, The Crown Prince and Princess of Japan, ambassadors and governors galore (24).'

In his General Letter dated 20 April 1908 he reported to London that, 'the new railway between Shanghai and Nanking was opened on 28 March 1908.'

In the customary manner in April 1908 he arranged appropriate transport on the Yangtse during a visit paid to that region by the British Minister to Peking, Sir John Jordan:-

'... to place HMS *Clio* at His Excellency's disposal for the purpose of conveying him from Nanking to Hankow, calling at such places en route as H.E. might wish."

Between 7 and 10 April 1908, with his flag in *Alacrity*, Sir Hedworth proceeded up to Canton to make an official call upon the Viceroy. Possibly as a result of earlier representations being made in Peking by his predecessor, subsequently he was able to remark:-

'The patrol of Canton River and Delta appears to be efficiently maintained by the Chinese Government. No acts of piracy or other items of especial interest have been reported (25).'

Even nearly a year later the situation in the river leading up to Canton remained good. On 25 March 1909 he reported:-

'Conditions on the West River have continued to be satisfactory, and the Chinese patrol has been effectively maintained (26).'

Unfortunately though such was not the situation existing right around the China coast in that era. The author of the following was at the time the Coast Inspector at Shanghai. He is describing an occasion when an act of piracy had been committed against the Saddles Island lighthouse off the entrance to the Yangtse River:-

'At Woosung we wakened the captain of a war junk whose nominal duty was pirate hunting. We told him to come with us. He came reluctantly – it looked too much like the real thing. We wanted him for his authority, such as it was. It was a seventy miles' journey to the Saddles, and on the way the Lieutenant and I made the war junk captain talk. He had been in them all his life and had risen from the ranks. How many pirates had he caught? None; not only so, he had never seen one – and he did not want to. He did his duty; he took his periodic cruise among the islands and showed the flag; and he drew his pay, and doubtless the pirates supplemented it. It was a pleasant life; he did not wish it marred. And in all this there was no dereliction of duty; he was supposed – on paper – to hunt for pirates, but he was not expected to.

I am sorry but this story ends quite lamely. By the time we arrived at Saddles, the pirates had left some hours before. They had not touched our station; they had held the village up to ransom – a few hundred dollars – and carried off some girls (27).'

From 1 March 1908 the new British Naval Attache in Tokio was Captain Charles Dundas of Dundas, to be promoted Rear Admiral on 22 July 1910. He was fortunate in that from 1906 to 1914 the Navy Minister was Vice Admiral Baron Saito Makoto, on 16 October 1912 to be promoted Admiral (28). Clearly as WW1 approached much intrigue existed. Later Captain Dundas was to recollect as follows, and naturally the C. in C. will have agreed fully with the manner in which he handled the situation:-

'I will never forget the courtesy and kindness I received at the Japanese Admiralty from Admiral Baron Saito and all the officers of his staff. They simply couldn't do enough for me and my work was made very easy. I was very loyal to the (Anglo-Japanese) Alliance and I think they liked me for that. Never once during my stay in Japan did I give anything away to the other foreign naval attaches, though I was approached over and over again (29).'

KCB: 26 June 1908.

Here follows an extract taken from his letter of 24 July 1908 written to the First Lord, Reginald McKenna, *King Alfred* then being at Wei-Hai-Wei. It reveals a most kind and thoughtful side to Sir Hedworth. Also, concerning the Battle of Tsushima fought in May 1905, he relates findings which are directly opposed to those reported by Captain Pakenham who actually was present during that engagement (see C. in C., 1904). HMS *Dreadnought* herself, launched in February 1906, was armed with ten 12" and twenty seven 12 pounder guns. The following class of three *Bellerophon* battleships were all launched in 1907, and were armed with ten 12" and sixteen 4" guns:-

'I did not know you well enough to congratulate you on either your becoming our First Lord or on your marriage, but I hope both ventures will be happy and prosperous.

The writer of enclosed is evidently one of the world's unfortunates – and I trust you will do something for the poor fellow even if red tape puts obstacles in the way. The officers and men stationed at the 4.7" guns at Ladysmith had a very hard time of it and although they bore the strain well at the time several of them have broken down and died since.

When I was private secretary to Lords Spencer and Goschen it was the custom of C. in C.s to occasionally write privately to the First Lord and I presume you would like that procedure to continue. (--).

During my squadron's stay in Japan we received every civility from the authorities and I saw a good deal of their leading Admirals including the great Togo, Kato, Ito and Baron Saito, Minister of Marine. The former is the nicest, gentlest and most modest of men and idolised by Japanese – he is also a most silent man – hardly ever speaks even to his own countrymen.

At the many luncheons and dinners I had to eat either he or Sato were generally alongside of me and as Japanese have no general conversation there was nothing we could discuss except professional matters.

They, and they ought to know, attribute great importance to a secondary battery and consider we have made a very grave mistake in our *Dreadnought* armament of only 12 inch guns. Of course there is one nation that ought to know even better than the Japanese, for the defeated can have no doubt as to what caused their defeat, and as the Russians also apparently refuse the *Dreadnought* single type of armament it seems to me that our theorists are accepting a most audacious and dangerous responsibility in opposing the views and neglecting the experiences of the only two nations that have a practical experience of modern sea warfare. It was the endless stream of six inch shell that demoralized the Russians at Tsushima – the 12 inch finished them. After passing my seamanship examination at Trincomalee in 1875 I was given a few days shooting leave and one morning disturbed a large python. As it glided away I let it have a charge of small shot in the tail, and then polished it off with a rifle bullet through the head. This is more or less what happened at Tsushima and will I believe re-occur in future naval engagements.

(He ended his letter with comments regarding the new American battleships, also mentioned how suitable and pleasant was Wei-Hai-Wei for gunnery and torpedo exercises) (30).'

15 November 1908. The death in Peking of the Manchu Empress Dowager, Tz'u-hsi. Initially secretly, she had given support to the xenophobic Boxer movement of 1899-1901 which however had caused great disruption only in the north of China. A concubine of Emperor Hsien-feng, who ruled from 1850 to 1861, her name is associated with many years of much ruthless intrigue in Manchu ruling circles. It was to be nearly a year before her actual funeral took place (31). From Hong Kong on 16 December 1909 the C. in C. informed the Admiralty:-

'On November 9, the day appointed for the funeral of the late Dowager Empress of China, H. M. Ships at Hong Kong, Wei-Hai-Wei, and in Chinese ports half-masted their Colours, and hoisted the Chinese Ensign at half mast.'

A few days earlier, on 26 October 1909 at Harbin in Manchuria, the victim of a political assassination, Ito Hirobumi died. He had been one of the 'Choshu Five' of 1863 who had been to Britain, and subsequently was four times prime minister of Japan. Following the feudal era of the Tokugawa shoguns Ito had played a crucial role in the building of modern Japan. In addition he was a great personal friend of the Emperor Meiji.

Meanwhile, by the Anglo-Siamese treaty signed in Bangkok on 10 March 1909, four Malay states situated in the north of the peninsula in the vicinity of Thailand were transferred to the British zone of influence as Protectorates, later to be Unfederated Malay States. Two of these states, Kelantan contiguous to Thailand, and Terengganu just south, are situated on the east coast. Perlis and Kedah, to the north of Butterworth and Penang Island, are on the west coast.

To assist with the appropriate ceremonies he made available the sloop *Cadmus*, 1,070 tons, Commander Hugh L.P. Heard, to the H.E. Governor at Singapore, Sir John Anderson (1858-1918) to enable him to, '... personally take over the new territories, ' of Kelantan and Terengganu from Siam.

On 19 July 1909 *Cadmus* arrived at Kuala Kelantan and from there a party, and Guard of Honour of thirty men from *Cadmus*, proceeded to Kota Bharu. The celebrations concluded she sailed on 24 July, and arrived just down the coast at Kualu Terengganu on the following day.

In due course, on 7 and 8 August 1909, Kedah also was to be visited (32).

From *Alacrity* at Wuhu on 11 November 1909 he wrote to Reginald McKenna who still had another eleven months to serve as First Lord at the Admiralty. He ended a chatty letter with a comment on life as the C. in C. in China, also wondered if at some time in the future Mr. McKenna might return to the Admiralty:-

'Two years out here is quite long enough for the annual rounds of visits and feasts are almost unbearable.'

'However, like Lord Goschen you will perhaps return at a future date. When I went Private secretary to him he told me how happy he was to return to the Admiralty as it was the one post all politicians loved as there never was any friction in the office and Naval Lords always protected their chief (33).'

As the final few days of his term of office in command in China drew closer, writing from Singapore on 4 March 1910 he reported to the Admiralty:-

'I left Hong Kong in the *King Alfred* on 24 February and arrived at Singapore on 1 March. HMS *Minotaur* is expected on the 5th, and the command of the Station will be transferred to Vice Admiral Sir Alfred Winsloe on the 6th – I propose to leave on that date, calling at Malacca and Penang (34).'

Indeed *Minotaur* arrived at Singapore at 10.00 a.m. on 5 March. As was recorded:-

'Sunday, 6 March 1910. At Singapore.

11:00 a.m. Vice Admiral Sir A.L. Winsloe took over command of the China Station.

5:10 p.m. *King Alfred* sails for England with flag of Vice Admiral Hon. Sir H. Lambton (35).'

As may be seen from the following extract taken from her log book *King Alfred* proceeded back to England according to a leisurely schedule:-

'Left Singapore on Sunday, 6 March 1910 at 17:00 hours.Malacca between 03:43 and 20:00 on 7 March 1910.

Penang from 23:45 on 8 March to 11:35 on Friday, 11 March.

Colombo from early morning on 15 March to 08:00 on Saturday, 19 March 1910.

Aden from 05:34 to 10:23 on Friday, 25 March.

Suez: 05:42 – 10:30 on Tuesday, 29 March and through the Canal.

Port Said from 01:10 on 30 March to 05:50 on Friday, 1 April 1910. Here she coaled 1,910 tons.

Malta from 13:36 on Sunday 3 April to 17:10 on Monday, 4 April.

Gibraltar: 10:31 on Thursday, 7 April to 15:15 on 8 April 1910.

Portsmouth and anchored off Spit Fort at 19:35 hours on Monday, 11 April 1910 and shifted into Harbour the following morning.

During the afternoon on Friday 15 April 1910 he and his staff left the ship and his flag was struck (36).'

'A few days after hauling down his flag he married the Hon. Mildred Cecilia Harriet, third daughter of the first Baron Alington and widow of Viscount Chelsea, eldest son of the fifth Earl Cadogan', who had died in 1908. They were to have no children (37).'

At Buckingham Palace in London H.M. The King Emperor Edward VII died on Friday, 6 May 1910 at fifteen minutes before midnight.

Admiral: 2 March 1911.

H.M. The King Emperor George V was crowned on 22 June 1911.

From October 1911, and with a change of surname in the previous month so now as The Hon. Sir Hedworth Meux, appointed 'Extra Equerry to the King'. (38).

In succession to Admiral Sir Arthur W. Moore (see C. in C., 1905), appointed C. in C., Portsmouth with Flag in *Victory*: 1 August 1912. On appointment his Flag Captain was Edwyn S. Alexander Sinclair (see C. in C., 1925).

GCB: 3 June 1913.

Royal Naval reserves were called up on 10 July 1914 in order to conduct summer manoeuvres for a fortnight. Over the weekend of 25/26 July, as the situation in Europe rapidly became worse, Prince Louis of Battenberg, then First Sea Lord, took the decision to retain these reservists in their ships. So it was that when war broke out on 4 August 1914:-

'... every vessel of the Navy's vast armada was stationed according to the contingency plans long since prepared (39).'

With the movement of British army units to France the C. in C. and naval staff at Portsmouth were to be greatly involved in ensuring the safety of such convoys:-

'On the outbreak of the European War, Meux's principal duty was to secure the safe passage of the transports conveying the British Expeditionary Force to France, and to guard the army's main line of communication from Southampton to Havre. This anxious work was carried out with complete success (40).'

Together with Admiral Sir George A. Callaghan, on 9 September 1914 he was called upon by The Admiralty to enquire officially into the failure of Rear Admiral Ernest C.T. Troubridge (1862-1926) to engage the German battlecruiser *Goeben* in the Mediterranean before she escaped successfully into Turkish waters in early August 1914 (also see C. in C., 1931). In respect of this Court of Inquiry, in which he sat as President, the relevant paragraph of explanation reads as follows:-

'My Lords are not satisfied with the explanation given by Rear Admiral Troubridge as to his failure to carry out his clear duty in declining to attack the enemy or heading him off and driving him back on to the superior force with the Commander in Chief. They have therefore decided to order him to haul down his Flag and return home. On his arrival home he will be informed that his conduct is to be enquired into by a Court of Enquiry at Portsmouth and he will be directed to report himself to you for this purpose.'

This stage of the whole unfortunate affair was brought to a conclusion in their report to the Admiralty dated 23 September 1914 and which was signed by both Admirals Meux and Callaghan (41). Neither Troubridge nor his Flag Captain, Fawcet Wray, emerged well however, following the subsequent court martial, 'the Court found the charge against Troubridge not proved, and fully and honourably acquitted him.' In addition, 'Wray's career was by no means ruined', in due course he rising to Vice Admiral on the Retired List. Troubridge himself, although never again employed afloat, was to be promoted Admiral in 1919 and retire from the Navy in 1921 (42).

Continued as C. in C., Portsmouth until 17 February 1916 when succeeded by Admiral The Hon. Sir Stanley Cecil James Colville.

Admiral of the Fleet: 5 March 1915.
M.P., Portsmouth: 1916-1918. He did not stand in the post war elections of 1918.
Retired: 5 July 1921, aged 65 years (43).
He was always very interested in the turf and as early as 1882 had started breeding blood stock.
Having been elected to the Jockey Club in 1906, and on inheriting Theobald's Park where Lady Meux had a racing stable, and, incidentally, also being a member of the National Hunt Committee, he continued to breed with many most successful results.

'He was a very shrewd judge of racing and breeding and of all turf matters, and would have been an even more successful owner had he not been too fond of his horses to part with them (44).'

As Captain Lambton his racing colours were white with green sleeves, but later he adopted sea green with a turquoise cap, later again to be a purple cap. Amongst his many successes the following examples will have given him particular pleasure:-

1905   with *Ruy Lopez*, the Grand Military Gold Cup at Sandown Park, and in the same year with the same horse, the Stand Steeple Chase at Kempton Park (45).

1919   with *Sir Douglas*, the Hardwicke Stakes at Ascot, and in the same year with the same horse, the Newmarket Three Years Old Handicap, and the Wiltshire Stakes at the Bibury Club meeting.

1920   with *White Surrey*, both the Penshurst Moderate Handicap Steeple Chase at Folkestone and, again, the Grand Military Gold Cup at Sandown Park.

1922   with *Torelore*, the Manchester November Handicap.

1923   with *Chosroes*, again the Hardwicke Stakes at Ascot.

1924   again with *Chosroes*, once more the Hardwicke Stakes at Ascot, and with the same horse in the same year, the Manchester Cup (46).

Following his death on 20 September 1929, in Hertfordshire the county press reported that:-

'The funeral took place at the Cheshunt Parish Church on Tuesday (24 September) morning, when there were hundreds of people present (47).'

One of the pall bearers at his funeral was the C. in C., The Nore, Admiral Sir Edwyn Sinclair (see C. in C., 1925).

NOTES

1. NA ADM 196/19. *Service Record.*

2. Ibid.

3. Ibid.

4. Clowes, Vol. VII, 330. Mex was a fort ashore lying half way around the bay with Alexandria town and harbour a short distance to the East.

5. *Service Record.*

6. Clowes, Vol. VII, 401/2.
    Admiral Charles Frederick **Hotham**. Born in York: 20 March 1843. Died in London: 22 March 1925. As a junior officer participated in both the New Zealand and, subsequently, the Anglo-Egyptian Wars. C. in C., Pacific between February 1890 and May 1893. KCB: 1895. Subsequently C. in C., The Nore, and then, between November 1900 and September 1903, C. in C., Portsmouth. GCVO: 1901. GCB: 1902. Admiral of the Fleet: 30 August 1903. *Navy List.*

7. In 1894 the First Sea Lord was Admiral Sir Frederick W. Richards (see C. in C., 1890). The Third Sea Lord was Rear Admiral Sir John Fisher, and the Fourth was Captain Gerard Noel (see C. in C., 1904). *Navy List.* Lord Salisbury formed a government on 25 June 1895 following which the position of First Lord was filled by George Joachim Goschen (1831-1907), from 1900 to be the First Viscount Goschen. This was his second period in office as First Lord as earlier he had held that position between 1871 and 1874 – also see Richards, C. in C., 1890, Ref. (18).

8. RN Museum Library, Portsmouth. Ref: *2000.53*. Diary extract from the time when King-Hall was serving in command of *Narcissus*.

9. NA ADM 53/15143: log book *Powerful.*

10. Ibid.

11. *Dictionary of National Biography.*

12. NA ADM 53/15143. Third class cruiser *Tartar*, 1,770 tons, Commander Frederick R.W. Morgan. Steel screw steamer *Maria*, 3,649 grt, built in 1898 and registered at Rotterdam. Owners: Holland Gulf Stoomvaart Maats. (J. de Poorter, Mngr.). Third class cruiser *Magicienne*, 2,950 tons, Captain William B. Fisher. *Navy List. Lloyd's Register*, 1899/1900.

13. NA ADM 53/15143.

14. Ibid. s.s. *Columbian*, 5,088 grt, built in 1890 and registered at Liverpool. Owners: F. Leyland & Co. Ltd. *Lloyd's Register*, 1899/1900. Lieutenant Frederick Greville Egerton, son of Admiral Francis Egerton, severely wounded by a Boer shell on 2 November 1899, and died later that day. Captain Lambton and the ship's company of *Powerful* subsequently caused a memorial tablet to be placed in St. Anne's Church, Portsmouth in his memory, and to those with him of the

Naval Brigade, 1899-1900, who also died.

15. E. Marjorie Moore, *Adventure in the Royal Navy,* (Liverpool, 1964), 125.

16. NA ADM 53/15144. Subsequent Log Book *Powerful.*

17. A Lieutenant then serving in *Victoria and Albert* was Hubert G. **Brand**. From 9 October 1912 to be Naval attaché to Tokio and in 1914, after the commencement of WW1, to spend some three months embarked in various ships of the IJN during the Allied assault against German positions based on Tsingtao, Shantung peninsula. *Navy List.* Author's notes, *HIJMS Wakamiya and Some Developments.*

18. Gordon Brook-Shepherd, *Uncle of Europe: The Social and Diplomatic Life of Edward VII,* (New York and London, 1976), Chapter VII, 'A Royal Triumph', 165-186 and 206*.

19. Admiral Sir Reginald Bacon, *From 1900 Onward,* (London, 1940), 125. Early in 1906 in the Mediterranean Captain Bacon had assumed command of the battleship *Irresistible*, 14,685 tons.

20. Richard Hough, *Louis and Victoria, the First Mountbattens,* (London, 1974), 238.

21. British Horseracing Authority, London. Visit on 8 May 2009. Courtesy Ms. Kelly Sutton and Mr. Owen Byrne.

22. NA ADM 1/7984. General Letter dated 20 April 1908 written in *Alacrity* at Hong Kong.

23. Lewis **Clinton-Baker**. Born: 16 March 1866. Died: 12 December 1939. Captain: 30 June 1906. Appointed in command cruiser *Berwick*, 9,800 tons: 16 May 1911. In her in September 1914 captured the German merchant vessel *Spreewald*, Hamburg Amerika Linie. In 1916 she was to be converted to the submarine depot ship *Lucia* (see Layton, C. in C., 1940). From 23 April 1915 in command battleship *Hercules,* 20,000 tons, and participated in the Battle of Jutland: 31 May 1916. Rear Admiral: 19 August 1917. RA 2BS: 1919-1920. Admiral Superintendent, Chatham: 1920-1921. C. in C., East Indies: 1921-1923. KCVO: 1922. Vice Admiral: 1 July 1922. Admiral Commanding Reserves: 1925-1927. KCB: 1926. Admiral: 8 November 1926. Retired: 1927. *Navy List. Who's Who.*

24. Admiral Hugh Tweedie, *The Story of a Naval Life,* (London, undated), 91/92.

25. NA ADM 1/7984.

26. NA ADM 1/8039.

27. William Ferdinand Tyler, *Pulling Strings in China,* (London, 1929), 211.

28. **Saito** Makoto. See Kelly, C. in C., 1931, reference (30).

29. Admiral Sir Charles Dundas of Dundas, *An Admiral's Yarns,* (London, 1922), 205.

30. Archives Centre, Churchill College, Cambridge. Ref: *MCKN 3/8.*

31. NA ADM 1/8118.

32. NA ADM 1/8039. Written from *King Alfred* at Wei-Hai-Wei, 27 August 1909.

33. Churchill College, Cambridge. Ref: *MCKM 3/22.* Alas, his successor at the Admiralty in 1911 was to create a new less trusting and amicable atmosphere.

34. NA ADM 1/8118.

35. NA ADM 50/ 383.

36. NA ADM 53/22740.

37. *Dictionary of National Biography.*

38. The widow of the wealthy brewer, Sir Henry Bruce Meux, in turn made Lambton her heir on the sole condition that he changed his name to Meux. A very considerable fortune came his way. *Dictionary of National Biography.*

39. Richard Hough, *The Great War at Sea, 1914-1918,* (OUP, 1983), 53/4.

40. *Dictionary of National Biography.*

41. Ed. E.W.R. Lumby, *Policy and Operations in the Mediterranean: 1912-1914,* (Naval Records Society, 1970), 244 and 270/1.

42. Ibid. 242/3.

43. *Service Record.*

44. *Dictionary of National Biography.*

45. The *Dictionary of National Biography* errs in mentioning the former victory as taking place in 1895.

46. The British Horseracing Authority, London. With much gratitude for the keen interest and assistance received from their most helpful staff.

47. *The Hertfordshire Mercury*, Friday, 27 September 1929.

25 January 1910 to 25 January 1913
Vice Admiral Sir Alfred Leigh **Winsloe**

Vice Admiral Sir Alfred Leigh Winsloe, C. in C., 1910

He was born at Pitminster, Somerset on 25 April 1852, second son of Richard Winsloe, chemical merchant of Liverpool, and Maria Louisa, nee Jack, of Mount Nebo, Taunton. These, his parents, had married at Old Church, St. Pancras, London on 1 May 1849. Baptised at Pitminster: 7 September 1852 in the Church of St. Mary and St. Andrew, the same church in which his mother had been Christened on 17 March 1818. Both his parents died in Liverpool in 1895, his father aged seventy four and his mother seventy seven years.

Sir Alfred died, a bachelor, at Biarritz: 16 February 1931.

At not quite fourteen years of age young Alfred entered the Royal Navy on 23 January 1866. In *Britannia* he obtained a first class certificate (1). **Midshipman**: 16 April 1867 with service for rather over three years in the wooden screw frigate *Liffey*, 3,900 tons, Captain John Ormsby Johnson, and then, from 30 November 1870, in *Pembroke*, flagship at Sheerness. Finally he joined *Minotaur* on 28 April 1871. **Sub Lieutenant**: 15 October 1871, remaining in *Minotaur*, 10,627 tons, Flagship, Channel Squadron. From 16 May 1873 served in *Agincourt*, 10,627 tons, a sister ship to *Minotaur* and the new Flagship, Channel Squadron. **Lieutenant**: 30 September 1874. Studied at RNC, Greenwich. From 5 July 1876 in screw corvette *Encounter*, 14 guns, 1,934 tons, Captain Richard Bradshaw, North American and West Indies Station.

From 17 January 1877 Flag Lieut. to Vice Admiral Geoffrey T.P. Hornby in *Alexandra*, 9,492 tons, Flagship, Mediterranean. In February 1878, once again being in conflict with Turkey, the Russian army advanced close towards Constantinople. To assist in keeping the peace Admiral Hornby was ordered to take the fleet up through the Dardanelles. So it was that at an early age his young Flag Lieutenant was to learn something of the positive and successful use of the mere presence of warships of the Royal Navy in such potentially awkward circumstances.

From 3 September 1880 Flag Lieut. to Rear Admiral The Rt. Hon. Earl of Clanwilliam in *Inconstant*, 16 guns, 5,780 tons, Flagship, Detached Squadron. This was the occasion, between 1880 and 1882 with *Inconstant* as Flagship, of the Royal cruise undertaken by Midshipmen T.R.H. Prince Albert Victor and Prince George of Wales in the iron screw corvette *Bacchante*, Captain Lord Charles T.M.D. Scott. From Australia the ships arrived at Yokohama on 21 October 1881, and after visiting other ports in Japan, and in China, plus Hong Kong, departed from Singapore on 15 January 1882. Naturally, as Flag Lieutenant, frequently he moved in exalted company which during a visit to Tokyo on 25 October had included the pleasure of being a member of the party accepting H.I.M. The Mikado's kind hospitality.

From 29 August 1882 Lieutenant and Commander, Paddle Despatch Vessel, *Helicon*, 2 guns, 1,000 tons, Mediterranean. Served in the Egyptian war of 1882. *Helicon* was not involved in the bombardment of Alexandria in July, but instead:-

> 'The Canal having been secured, the gun vessels *Beacon*, Commander William Frederick Stanley
> Mann, and *Falcon*, Commander John Eliot Pringle, the dispatch vessel *Helicon* Lieut. Alfred Leigh
> Winsloe, and the special service vessel *Stormcock*, entered it to undertake patrol and other duties;
> and on August 21, the waterway was temporarily closed to all vessels save those under the orders
> of the British government (2).'

However, in addition in Egypt from the Canal, '... being landed with the Naval Brigade, took part in the battle of Tel-el-Kebir (3).'

Commander: 30 June 1885.

Continued in *Helicon*. Then returned home to reach England on 15 August 1885, and next:-

> '... served for a time on a committee for the revision of Naval signals (4).'

On half pay from 22 October 1885 to 19 March 1888.

From 20 March 1888 he commanded the twin screw, third class cruiser *Brisk*, 6 guns, 1,770 tons. Cape of Good Hope and West Coast of Africa Station. Subsequently transferred in her to the East Indies Station. In East Africa in 1890 he served in the Naval Brigade during the Expedition against the Sultan of Vitu, today Witu in Kenya (5).

The following year an unusual task came his way:-

> 'In 1891 he went to Massikessi as Commander to draw a boundary between Portuguese territory
> and that of the Chartered Company (6).'

To return home he left the East Indies Station on 1 November 1891 and arrived in England by mail steamer on 27 November 1891 (7).

Captain: 30 June 1892.

From 29 June to 20 July 1892 he served on a 'Committee on Uniformity of Signalling'.

Then from 21 July to 6 September 1892 he served in the small protected cruiser *Barham*, 1,830 tons, during summer manoeuvres.

Between 17 and 27 July 1893 at Malta he was given the unenviable task of acting as prosecutor at the court martial to try the surviving officers and men of the battleship *Victoria*, sunk in collision in the eastern Mediterranean on 22 June 1893. While undertaking this duty at least he did receive the benefit of being on full pay from 6 July to 7 August.

Also the experience was to enhance his reputation in something of an unusual manner. The ship who had come into collision with *Victoria* was the battleship *Camperdown*, Captain Charles Johnstone, so naturally Johnstone was amongst those questioned by Winsloe. An example follows of the latter's ability in this unaccustomed role:-

> 'It was not until an hour later, for Winsloe spaced his questions as cleverly as an experienced barrister, that Johnstone contradicted himself (8).'

Regardless, it was to transpire that the C. in C., Vice Admiral Sir George Tryon, with his flag in *Victoria* and who was one of those drowned in the accident, had given orders of such a nature that the manoeuvre which apparently he had intended to carry out was impossible to execute.

From 16 January 1894 he commanded the second class twin screw cruiser *Spartan*, 8 guns, 3,600 tons in the Mediterranean. In 1895 she was transferred to the China Station. Between 1894 and 1895 the Sino-Japanese War took place however he arrived on the Station too late to become involved in any way. Instead, in case of troubles in Formosa, for a time he stood by off Tamsui.

10 May 1894: a cousin, Emma Alice Margaret Tennant (1864-1945), married Herbert Henry Asquith, later first Earl of Oxford and Asquith. Her mother, also Emma, nee Winsloe (1821-1895), on 2 August 1849 had married Sir Charles Tennant (1823-1906).

Asquith's first wife had died of typhoid fever in 1891.

His commission in *Spartan* ended on 5 May 1897.

Between 15 June and 29 July 1897 he commanded the new cruiser *Juno*, 5,600 tons, this being from the day of her completion and then briefly during the summer manoeuvres.

On 23 August 1897 his half pay increased by the sum of two shillings a day to fourteen shillings and six pence (9).

From 14 April 1898 he was appointed in command of the twin screw cruiser *Blake*, 9,000 tons, Channel Squadron. Off Gibraltar assumed command on Monday, 2 May 1898 (10). Ordered to West Africa where troubles had arisen in the Karene district of Northern Sierra Leone, the so-called 'Hut Tax War'. With assistance in the form of the small cruisers *Phoebe* and *Blonde*, together with the gunboat *Thrush*, 805 tons, all three to join him within six days, he arrived off that place at 1.30 p.m. on Wednesday, 11 May 1898. Naval parties sent ashore exerted a calming influence until, a little later, troops were landed and the insurrection was quelled (11). Sailed from Sierra Leone on Monday, 6 June 1898 (12).

Continued in command of *Blake* until 5 December 1898.

From 6 December 1898 commanded the twin screw cruiser *Niobe*, 11,000 tons, Channel Squadron. However between 25 November 1899 and 23 August 1900 she was present in South Atlantic waters during the Boer War. In detail, as an example of possibly the more tedious aspects of naval service, *Niobe* arrived at Simon's Bay at 3.12 p.m. on Saturday, 25 November 1899 (13). In December she cruised briefly to St. Helena Bay and Table Bay, then in February 1900 visited Walvis Bay in South West Africa (Namibia) (14). This latter cruise arose since the German governor at Swakopmund feared an attack by 600 Boers in his territory. At Walvis Bay a landing party from *Niobe* were successful in apprehending two Boer spies and the danger of attack faded away (15). Finally on

4 April 1900, 'to the relief of everyone on board', she sailed from Simon's Bay for the island of St. Helena where she anchored off Jamestown on 10 April. From the Cape she convoyed:-

'... five hundred of the Boer prisoners amongst whom were Cronje (16).'

Guardship at St. Helena, where were held a rather considerable number of Boer prisoners, until 23 August 1900.

Subsequently she returned to Devonport, England on 10 September 1900, but the commission only was to end at Portsmouth on 1 October. Captain J. Denison assumed command on Tuesday, 2 October 1900 and Captain Winsloe left the ship on appointment to *St. George* (17).

For just three days, 2 – 4 October, he was borne in *Duke of Wellington*, 'to avoid half pay'.

In the interim at Windsor Castle on 9 July 1900 H.M. Queen Victoria had signed the document establishing the Commonwealth of Australia. At the subsequent inauguration of the Commonwealth on 1 January 1901 Her Majesty was represented by the first Governor General, John Adrian Louis Hope (1860-1908), seventh Earl of Hopetoun, and later to be the first Marquis of Linlithgow.

From 5 October 1900, as **Commodore** second Class, in the cruiser *St. George*, 7,700 tons. Training Squadron. From 19 June 1900 her Commander was Alexander L. Duff (see C. in C., 1919).

From 26 February 1901, still as Commodore second class, served in *Ophir*, 6,910 grt and built in 1891, chartered from the Orient Line but to a considerable extent manned by the Royal Navy. 'Special Service'. Her Commander was Rosslyn E. Wemyss. The occasion was the Royal Tour to Australia, New Zealand, South Africa and Canada carried out between 16 March and 1 November by the Duke and Duchess of Cornwall and York, later HM King George V and Queen Mary. HM Queen Victoria had died at Osborne House on 22 January 1901 which naturally caused the departure of the ship to be delayed, indeed the tour nearly was cancelled.

In the event, escorted by the cruisers *Niobe* and *Diadem*, he sailed from Portsmouth at 4 p.m. on Saturday, 16 March and took *Ophir* to the antipodes with calls at Gibraltar: 20 to 22 March, Malta: 25 to 27 March, Port Said: 30 to 31 March, Suez: 1 April, Aden: 5 April, Colombo: 12 to 16 April, Singapore: 21 to 23 April, Albany: 3 to 4 May, and Melbourne: 6 to 18 May.

On 9 May 1901 in the Exhibition Building at Melbourne, an important Royal engagement was, '... the opening of the first Parliament of the Commonwealth (18).'

The first prime minister of the Commonwealth was Sir Edmund Barton (1849-1920).

Ophir continued to Sydney: 20 to 24 May, Hawkesbury River: 24 to 27 May, Sydney: 27 May to 6 June, Auckland: 11 to 16 June, Wellington: 17 to 21 June, Lyttleton: 22 to 27 June, Hobart: 2 to 6 July, Adelaide: 8 to 15 July, Albany: 20 to 22 July, Fremantle: 23 to 26 July, Mauritius: 4 to 8 August, Durban: 13 to 15 August, Simon's Town: 18 to 23 August, St. Vincent, Cape Verde Islands: 3 to 5 September, Quebec: 15 to 21 September, Halifax: 23 September to 21 October, St. Johns: 23 to 25 October, then home, returning to Portsmouth on Friday, 1 November 1901.

During the cruise *Ophir* was coaled on many occasions. It is as well to be reminded of the days when the carrying out of that vile task was the norm. Here is her Commander, with feeling:-

'How I loathe the very word Coal. It plays the very deuce with the appearance of the ship and I always have so little time to do it in (19).'

Subsequently he rceived the C.V.O. and was created C.M.G.

At the conclusion of the Royal Tour, on 7 November 1901 he returned to *St. George*, Cruiser Squadron, and remained in her until 15 November 1902.

Next followed a short period of three months on half pay, now at the rate of sixteen shillings and six pence a day.

He commissioned the new battleship *Russell*, 14,000 tons, at Chatham on 19 February 1903 and took her out to the Mediterranean. She was one of six of the *Duncan* class, the first to be capable of steaming at nineteen knots. A Lieutenant then serving in the ship was Percy L.H. Noble.

In addition from 12 August 1903 he was appointed Naval ADC to HM The King.

On 6 April 1904 he returned to England in *Russell* on the occasion of her transfer to the Home Fleet. In due course, during the Great War and off Malta on 27 April 1916, *Russell* was to be mined and lost together with 126 lives.

The next day, 7 April 1904 at Devonport, he commissioned the new battleship *Queen*, 14,160 tons, and took her out to the Mediterranean. In command of her until 9 December that year. *Queen* was to see WW1 service in the English Channel and Mediterranean, for much of that latter time as base ship Taranto, was to surive the war, eventually to be sold in 1920.

Rear Admiral: 26 November 1904.

Upon his promotion he paid off out of *Queen* and proceeded home, arriving on 12 December 1904. On leave until 30 December 1904.

As the Commander of Torpedo and Submarine Flotillas from 31 December 1904, he served on Admiral Fisher's Committee on Designs which contributed greatly to the configuration of the new battleship *Dreadnought*, 17,900 tons. She was laid down on 2 October 1905.

During this period he flew his Flag in the cruiser *Sapphire*, 3,000 tons, attached to Chatham, but in 1905 based at Portland, 'Training Ship'.

From 2 January 1907 served in *President*, London: 'miscellaneous duties' which consisted of service on a 'Committee on Design of H.M. Ships'.

From 8 February 1907 until 24 January 1910 Fourth Sea Lord thus a Lord of the Admiralty during Their Lordships' successful stand at the time of the pre Great War German Dreadnought building scare which dragged on from 1907 to 1909. At the time of this scare the First Sea Lord was Admiral Sir John Fisher. In addition, and most fortunately for much of this period, the First Lord of the Admiralty was the very able Reginald McKenna (1863-1943). Asquith was the Prime Minister.

As an example to illustrate the reason behind Sea Lords' determination to make this stand here follows an excerpt taken from a note prepared for the First Lord and signed by the four Sea Lords, J.A. Fisher, W.H. May, J.R. Jellicoe and A.L. Winsloe. Unfortunately it is undated but as will be seen from the text it seems likely that it was prepared during the late spring of 1909. The copy is with the then Prime Minister's papers:-

'We think it right to inform you that in our judgement the situation is so serious that we could not regard it as consistent with our duty if we did not inform you at once of our conviction that the orders for the four ships for April 1st, 1910 must be made absolute in July next and the tenders should be invited at once. (--) The fact that the new German Dreadnoughts are vessels of 22,000 tons with a speed of not more than 19 to 20 knots points conclusively to a far heavier armament than that carried by our Dreadnoughts. The fact that one hundred 12 inch and 11 inch guns have been counted in Krupp's works together with the evidence of the immense facilities which exist for manufacture indicates the ease and rapidity with which their ships can be equipped.

Then there is also the striking evidence of the rapid advance in construction of the German Dreadnought at Schichau's works in Danzig. Although we knew that the materials for this vessel had been ordered, we were under the impression that she was not to be commenced till next month: yet at the time when these officers observed her she was actually four months advanced in building. (--) (20).'

In connection with the above naturally it was important that the Sea Lords presented a united front when dealing with the Cabinet. Sir John Fisher clearly spoke to Winsloe on the subject, and on 19 December 1908 wrote to Reginald McKenna in the following positive manner. It is amusing to consider something of the likely nature of the earlier conversation between the First and Fourth Sea Lords:-

'It has been arranged for Winsloe to be at Admiralty soon after 11 a.m. today and after seeing us he will send you a note to the Cabinet stating his views which you can safely anticipate as being in perfect accordance with the other Sea Lords (21).'

Vice Admiral: 5 November 1908.

KCB: 25 June 1909.

By coincidence in China his new flagship was another *Minotaur*, this one being a twin screw armoured cruiser of 14,100 tons, completed in March 1908. She re-commissioned at Chatham on 4 January 1910, Captain George C. Cayley, '… big and genial and a very popular Captain (22).' An important member of his staff was the Flag Lieutenant, Percy L.H. Noble (see C. in C., 1938). In her, leaving England on 25 January 1910, he steamed to the East.

In respect of wireless telegraphy these were early days and, as may be seen from the following, on passage he had been ordered to attempt to carry out certain exchanges of signals:-

> 'After leaving Colombo communication was established with *King Alfred* (his predecessor's flagship) at a distance of 1,200 miles, but I was unable to get in touch with Hong Kong before reaching Singapore although when abreast of Penang the distance is only about 1,350 miles. I was in communication with a German mail steamer in the Indian Ocean and she has been the only merchant steamer I have so far met with a Wireless Telegraphy installation of any sort (23).'

Minotaur arrived at Singapore at 10.00 hours on 5 March 1910 and there he assumed command of the Station the following day, Sunday, 6 March 1910. That evening Admiral Lambton sailed for England in *King Alfred*.

By pleasant chance at the time the Governor of the Straits Settlements was Sir John Anderson (1858-1918), an old friend dating from the time of the Royal cruise in *Ophir* in 1901. During that cruise Sir John had been appointed to the staff of H.R.H. as Colonial Office representative. Following service in the Straits then on 8 June 1911 he was to be appointed permanent under Secretary of State for the Colonies and subsequently, late in 1915, Governor of Ceylon. There, while still in office and suddenly from cancer, on 24 March 1918 he was to die in Nuwara Eliya, up in the beautiful hills of the tea growing region.

HM King Edward VII died in London just before midnight on Friday, 6 May 1910.

When Sir Alfred received this sad news he was on passage to Yokohama but immediately altered course to return to Wei-Hai-Wei, 'recalling all ships to meet me there.' Next he decided, together with the Consul-General at Shanghai, Sir Pelham Laird Warren, that the appropriate Memorial Service should be held at Shanghai, there also being an ulterior motive. These, and other subjects were covered in his letter of 24 May 1910, written "in the Yangtse" and addressed to Mr. Reginald McKenna, First Lord of the Admiralty:-

> 'Thinking things over I determined to go personally to Shanghai: as I daresay you know there is keen competition in that most cosmopolitan town to be top dog. A new German Consul has lately gone there, and he does everything in his power to set one nation against another.'
> 'The Cathedral (in Shanghai) is a very fine one, and there were nearly 2,000 people inside, besides all overflow on the grass outside the door. As you will see from the enclosed cutting out of the Shanghai daily paper the British community were very pleased that such a memorable service should have been held in Shanghai. Perhaps you would be good enough to send the paper to Sir Arthur Bigge for the information of the King. He was at Shanghai in '81 and therefore I have no doubt takes an interest in the place which since his day has quadrupled in size.'

In the same missive he expounded on the tendency for Consuls to over play their hand when requesting the presence of a gunboat to be anchored in the River off their Consulate:-

> 'The Consul at Nanking is now asking for a ship to be there all the time a certain exhibition is open. (The Minister at Peking) said he considered the presence of a ship of war during the whole time was unnecessary but I feel sure that will not prevent the consul sending telegrams all the time making out that something really desperate is about to happen.
> I am going to Hankow to put it quite straight to the Consul General that *Astrea* is no longer required here and to get her to Wei-Hai-Wei for gunnery. I have been left such a legacy of good

shooting by Lambton that I cannot expect to live up to it especially if my ships are kept in the River (24).'

During the Russo-Japanese war of 1904-1905 the Japanese Army had achieved an astonishing if bloody success in advancing upon Port Arthur overland, the more so as the nature of the terrain gave the defenders much advantage. Clearly inspired by the experience of a visit to the scene of the Japanese success, on 20 July 1910 Sir Alfred wrote to Reginald McKenna from *Alacrity*, then at anchor at Wei-Hai-Wei:-

> 'I lately went over to Port Arthur in this ship taking the Captain of the Squadron with me. We were most hospitably received and taken all over the Battlefields. So much were we impressed by the strength of the positions that on the invitation of the Japanese Governor and Admiral I am taking all the fleet over so that the young officers may have a chance of seeing them. Standing on the top of the hills on which the forts stood, it looks impossible that troops could take them if defended even without the miles of wire entanglements they were protected with (25).'

With effect from 29 August 1910. Korea was annexed formally by Japan to become their colony of Chosen. Then the capital city of Seoul was re-named Keijo. General Terauchi Masatake (1852-1919), also to be a future prime minister of Japan, was appointed as the first Governor-General.

'Both Russia and Britain had agreed to Japan's proposal to annex Korea (26).'

From as few as 835 Japanese residents in Korea in 1880, by 1910 this number had grown to 171,543. As has been related, '… treaty port merchants were "the shock troops of Japanese economic penetration" (27).

Early in October 1910 Sir Alfred visited Japan. As mentioned above, in 1881 as a young Lieutenant he had visited the country for the first time. Now, these years later, his opinion of one of the hazards of such a visit were given in a private letter written to the First Lord, by now Mr. Winston Churchill, which he wrote a year later, from Nanking on 30 December 1911:-

> 'I would like to tell you that the reason I do not go to Japan more often that I can help is because when I do so with the squadron the occasion is taken to make life horrible by one long succession of lunches and dinners. Every day of your visit is mapped out; there is lunch in one place and dinner in another, all meals are very long and heavy. I generally find myself sitting between the same two Admirals at every meal, and it becomes more than an ordinary person's internal economy can stand to go through a ten days visit to Yokohama unless necessity demands it. I went there in October 1910, and I have promised to take as many ships as I can there in May next (1912), so I did not think it necessary to go this year (1911) (28).'

From Shanghai on 17 October 1910 he steamed up the Yangtse in *Alacrity*, commanded by a future C. in C., China, acting Commander P.L.H. Noble, CVO, only very recently appointed to the ship. Being the winter season the river level had dropped very appreciably therefore, following short visits to Chingkiang and Nanking, he arrived off Kiukiang on 13 November. It being a risky business to proceed further, especially over the 'Red Bluffs Bar' just a short distance above Kiukiang, there he remained until 21 November then returned, carefully, to Shanghai where he arrived on 7 December (29).

From a platform erected over the foredeck of the light cruiser U.S.S. *Birmingham*, 3,750 tons, then at anchor off Hampton Roads, VA., on 14 November 1910 the first successful take off by an aircraft from a ship took place. The pilot was Eugene Burton Ely (1879-1911) in a Curtiss Model D pusher.

By 13 December 1910 he was back in Hong Kong and that morning once again his flag was broken in *Minotaur*.

The Admiral's administration of the squadron naturally included the preparation of War Orders. On 22

December 1910 these confidential instructions were circulated to the ships and establishments under his command (30). No enemy is mentioned, indeed the opening paragraphs, under 'General Arrangements', read as follows:-

> 'In the case of war with any country except Japan the object of the China Squadron will be to localize the hostile men-of-war and bring them to action before reinforcements can reach them.
> As the Japanese Alliance will hold good until 1915 war with that country is improbable.
> No definite offensive operations could be undertaken against Japan with the squadron at its present strength.'

His preamble continues with remarks concerning the difficulty of giving definite instructions prior to knowing with which country Great Britain might be at war. Under paragraph four he does elaborate at some length on the question of, 'merchantmen being converted into armed cruisers on the high seas'. A very large merchant fleet sailed under the German flag. At home tensions between Germany and Britain, to a great extent resulting from German naval ambitions, were considerable. Although left unsaid Germany was the enemy in mind.

The question of the renewal of the Anglo-Japanese Alliance was bound up with the matter of Anglo-German naval rivalry. Should the alliance with Japan not be renewed then it would be necessary for Britain to greatly reinforce her fleet in the East. However that could not be contemplated as then Britain would be left weak in Home waters. In the event the Agadir crisis in Morocco, made critical by the arrival of the German gunboat *Panther*, 962 tons, on 1 July 1911, helped to concentrate minds in London most wonderfully. The Anglo-Japanese Alliance was renewed on 13 July 1911 and was to be valid for a further period of ten years, therefore to 1921.

Also on 22 December 1910 in Sarawak, Miri Oil Well No. 1 struck light crude oil at the modest depth of 425 feet. Inspired by the earlier exploratory work carried out by Dr. Charles Hose, a servant of H.H. Rajah Sir Charles Brooke, in 1909 the Royal Dutch Shell Company geologist Dr. Josef Theodor Erb travelled out from Europe to Miri, together with Dr. Hose, to investigate further (31). Very useful quanties of oil were to be discovered and important developments, including the construction of a refinery nearby at Lutong, subsequently were to take place. The Admiralty in London was to become an important customer.

24 April 1911. Sloop *Rosario*, 980 tons, commissioned at Hong Kong for service as 'Depot Ship for Submarines'. On that day, and with Lieut. and Commander Nicholas E. Archdale in command,
'And for Command of Hong Kong Submarine Flotilla', was instituted the first such command on the China Station. Also on 24 April 1911 the three submarines commissioned:-

> *C36*: Lieut. Godfrey Herbert
> *C38*: Lieut. John R.A. Codrington
> *C37*: Lieut. Athelstan A.L. Fenner

H.M. The King Emperor George V was crowned on 22 June 1911.

Here follows a charming description of an official luncheon greeting at Anking, some one hundred miles above Wuhu on the left bank of the Yangtse, late in September 1911. The Governor is welcoming his guests, three officers of the gunboat *Bramble*, Lieutenant and Commander Basil George Washington, who have been conveyed in sedan chairs from the River to the front steps of his Yamen. These days were about to disappear forever:-

> 'At the top we see our host, a dear old man in a beautiful but simple robe, with the long thin beard and moustache which has been the fashion in old China for thousands of years. With him are his staff, courteous and urbane. He shakes hands and welcomes us to an ample repast and through an interpreter gives an unconscious and perfect demonstration of hostmanship and how to put one's guests at their ease, an experience the memory of which I have always treasured (32).'

Inspired by the leadership of Dr. Sun Yat-sen (1866-1925) the Chinese revolutionary movement against their Manchu occupational government achieved success at Wuchang on 10 October 1911, the 'Double Tenth'. At the Admiralty the first news of this outbreak was from a telegram sent by Sir Alfred and received in London at 6 p.m. on 12 October 1911:-

> 'Serious outbreak Wuchang foreign drilled troops responsible wrecked yamen Viceroy escaped he is in man-of-war Have sent ships Hankow ready should trouble spread across river also some Nanking where there are a good many of these troops Have ordered *Newcastle* to Wusung Trouble at present time anti-dynastic not anti-foreign.
> There are 4 British 5 Chinese 3 foreign men-of-war at Hankow, quite sufficient to deal with any outbreak (33).'

Dr. Sun himself was abroad at the time but duly returned home and in due course, with his capital at Nanking, briefly held office as the first President of the Republic of China: nominally from 1 January to 1 April 1912. Then, in the interests of united China, he resigned in favour of the military leader, Yuan Shih-kai in Peking. In the interim the last Manchu Emperor, Hsuan T'ung (Pu-yi) abdicated on 12 February 1912 and on 14 February Yuan Shih-kai was elected Provisional President.

With the end of the Ch'ing dynasty, in Peking on 25 August 1912 the various revolutionary groups, previously dedicated to the overthrow of the Manchu, and including Dr. Sun's United Allegiance Society, were retitled Kuomintang, or Nationalist Party.

Dr. Sun was an unusual man in that always he placed the interests of a united and democratic China before any personal considerations.

Here the opportunity is taken to give another example of the sad times and circumstances then prevailing within China. A young Sub Lieutenant then serving in *Monmouth*, on 6 July 1912 wrote to his mother from Wei-Hai-Wei:-

> 'The flotilla rushed off to Chefoo the other day to preserve order. The military had mutinied for a few years back pay, and the government had ordered the merchants to pay them. The merchants protested and so the troops attacked the merchants – eventually the latter paid up (34).'

Even far away in the East on the China Station clearly the future of naval aviation, or 'aeroplaning', was discussed amongst officers in the ships of the squadron. On 30 August 1912 the same young officer ventured an aeronautical opinion in writing to 'Dear Mother':-

> 'I think there can be no doubt that it is just as much a coming branch of the service as were submarines ten years back (35).'

Late in 1911 USS *Cincinnati* C-7, Captain Samuel Shelburn Robison, joined the Asiatic Squadron. Serving as Engineer officer in the ship was Raymond Ames Spruance (1886-1969). Earlier, as a Midshipman, he had served in *Minnesota* BB-22 during the world cruise of the Great White Fleet and in her first had visited Japan in October 1908. Amongst other experiences, '... and saw the immortal Admiral Togo at an afternoon garden party.'

'On 1 April 1913 Lt. (j.g.) Raymond A. Spruance (was appointed) in command', of the destroyer *Bainbridge* (36). He only remained in the East until May 1914 when he returned to the USA. In this manner did the future Admiral and Fifth Fleet Commander during the Pacific War of 1941-1945 first experience the Orient.

During the same cruise of the Great White Fleet the future Fleet Admiral William Frederick Halsey, USN (1882-1959), then an Ensign, had been serving in *Kansas* BB-21. This too was his first experience of the waters of the future Pacific battlegrounds.

It is good, and useful, to see that the First Lord in London maintained a private correspondence with his Commanders in Chief around the world. In this instance from China on 9 February 1912, and in response to another letter from Mr. Churchill, Admiral Winsloe replied to thank him for arranging for reinforcements to be sent out to the East, on this occasion the armoured cruiser *Defence*. Also he wrote about the difficulties facing Yuan Shih-kai in Peking, mentioned the need to defend the southern boundaries of Wei-Hai-Wei where an insurrection had broken out, touched on the subjects of new crews coming out for his river gunboats, and piracy on the West River, also briefly discussed War Staff matters within the Admiralty.

All in all it was a pleasant method of supplementing dry official reports and letters. The First Lord encouraged such mail:-

'I hope you will communicate to me your ideas on all questions connected with your command. A free exchange of thought does much towards solving problems which occur from time to time (37).'

This free exchange of ideas, as may be seen from a letter to, 'My dear Mr. Churchill', dated at Wei-Hai-Wei on 25 June 1912, also could include private subjects:-

'I am writing to you about a personal matter, to ask that I may be considered when the appointment of C. in C. at Devonport is made.

Rumour says it is to be given to Admiral (--) but this if true seems very hard because he has not nearly as much service in command of a man of war at sea as myself as a Captain or as an Admiral, and he is junior to me.'

After continuing with a few more lines to stress this point, also in the same letter he mentioned a recent visit to Japan, '... where our Allies were particularly civil and they gave me the official house of the Miniser of Marine to live in during my stay in Tokio and we had a good many entertainments.'

In addition he added the following comments concerning the sad state of affairs then prevailing in China:-

'I went to Peking and had a long talk with Sir John Jordan who is very pessimistic on the subject of China and the chances of the Republic lasting any time. Yuan Shih-kai has no power outside the immediate precincts of Peking and the government by the Republic a farce. Canton proclaims itself openly as ag(g)rieved at so few Cantonese getting appointments as Ministers, and bands of discharged soldiers are roaming every Province robbing, murdering and plundering anyone who has anything to steal (38).'

Meanwhile on 2 May 1912 from a temporary platform constructed over the foredeck of the battleship *Hibernia*, 16,350 tons, Captain Ernest Humbert Grafton, in Weymouth Bay Lieut. Charles Rumney Sampson (1883-1931), flying a Short S.38 aircraft, achieved the first take off from a ship underway. She was steaming at ten and a half knots at the time, and in smooth seas.

From 4 July 1912 the new Governor of Hong Kong was His Excellency Sir Francis H. May (39).

At Wei-Hai-Wei in July 1912, and, as will be seen below, again at Saigon in January 1913, the C. in C. was engaged in discussions with the French Rear Admiral H. de Kerillis, the object being to consider ways in which any future confrontation against Germany in the Far East best could be arranged (40).

HIM Emperor Mutsuhito died and the Meiji era ended on 29 July 1912. In Tokyo his funeral took place during the evening of 13 September 1912. Great Britain was represented by HRH Prince Arthur of Connaught, third son of HM Queen Victoria. Attached to HRH's suite was Admiral Sir Edmund S. Poe (41). Through the British Ambassador, Sir Claude MacDonald who then was nearing retirement, Admiral Winsloe had offered to land a party to be present during the funeral ceremony, an offer which was accepted by the Japanese authorities:-

'I therefore landed 375 seamen and 125 Marines with arms; Captain Cayley in command, and they marched in the procession as a Guard of Honour between two portions of the Japanese Guard of Honour bringing up the rear of the procession (42).'

As will be appreciated the death of H.I.M. Emperor Meiji marked, in an especial manner, the end of that astonishing era through from the end of the feudal Tokugawa Shogunate in January 1858 to a Japan who had defeated an important European power in war. Also she was Allied with the greatest Empire the world had ever seen, and herself had grown to become an economic power of very considerable significance.

Amongst the men of war at Yokohama on the occasion of the late Emperor's funeral was the armoured cruiser *Monmouth,* 9,800 tons, Captain Brian H.F. Barttelot. The Sub Lieut. in the ship was Hugh C. Arnold-Foster who, from the Admiralty buildings in Tokyo where the funeral commenced at 8 p.m., witnessed the funeral procession. This lasted for two and a half hours. A few days later he wrote a most descriptive letter to his mother. Excerpts follow:-

> 'Everything was absolutely silent and for hours on end the whole city might have been dead. No lights were lit save those actually on the route. Round the corner the troops in a great quadrant held Japanese lanterns. It was very uncanny, and I confess that for most of the time I felt almost frightened – so I think did the crowds. Suddenly the gun from the palace rang out and shattered the silence of the city – Mutsuhito, the Emperor Meiji had started on his last silent drive. A long time passed before the head of the procession reached us. The roads were laid with soft sand so that the sound of the tramp of feet was quite inaudible even as they passed one. The far off sounds of the Beethoven march and the minute guns was all I could hear. Suddenly I looked up and saw that troops were slowly gliding by in the dim light. It was most uncanny to see them move past at the slow march without a sound. It seemed as if the troops would never cease. The minute guns at the palace must have fired fifty times before the naval and military guards of honour had passed silently by. Then came the most curious part of all – the ritualistic part. All now were dressed in ancient Shinto robes, very quiet in colour but not black – grey or violet or blue. Many of the more important wore headgear such as Gilbert's Mikado wears and carried great double-handed swords. (--) Then the Chief Ritualist in green robes walked in front of the sacred banner of the Rising Sun – in gold – and then, surrounded by men whose names one knew so well, Togo and Oyama and others who had helped to create the Meiji dynasty – the great Samurai – came the coffin. Drawn by five sacred white bullocks, so draped that one could scarcely see them at all, creaked the great funeral car. (--) The wheels creaked and groaned (intentionally) as it passed.
>
> That, the distant sound of the reed pipes and the occasional boom of a minute gun, was all one heard. The light of the torches made everything even more indefinite and shadowy. It was very 'creepy' and incomprehensible. The car passed and Prince Fushimi walked alone in gorgeous old state robes, then the Princes of the blood. After this the procession was dull and 'civilized' (43).'

H.R.H. Prince Henry of Prussia, younger brother of the Emperor, Wilhelm II, had represented Germany at the funeral after which, at noon on 17 September, he left in SMS *Scharnhorst.* However Prince Arthur of Connaught remained on in Tokyo as on 18 September he invested H.I.M. Emperor Yoshihito with the insignia of the Garter (44). Admiral Winsloe and his staff witnessed these proceedings:-

> 'After the investiture His Majesty entertained every one who had been present at the ceremony at luncheon, after which we were each in turn presented to him. His Majesty through an interpreter was good enough to thank me for sending the officers and men to march in the Funeral Procession (45).'

There is no doubt that the senior officers of the Imperial Japanese Navy, and Ministers and officials of the Japanese government had greatly appreciated the British presence on the occasion of the funeral of the late Emperor. The following extract is taken from a letter written on 16 September 1912 to Admiral Winsloe by the Navy Minister, Admiral Saito Makoto:-

> 'This particular act of courtesy shown by Your Excellency can not but be the testimony of the profound sympathy of the British nation towards its ally, and it is a source of great satisfaction

to me to be able (to) confirm to Your Excellency that I myself personally and the Imperial Navy together with the whole nation, we are highly sensible of this delicate mark of friendship (46).'

On this, the occasion of the funeral of the Emperor Meiji, Sir Alfred was decorated with the First Class Order of the Rising Sun (47).'

Admiral: 20 September 1912.

In *Minotaur* and with *Monmouth* in company he left that same morning, 20 September, for Vladivostok where he arrived on 24 September. It was at Reval (Tallinn) in Estonia on 10 June 1908 that H.M. King Edward VII had made H.M. Tsar Nicholas II an honorary Admiral of the Fleet in the Royal Navy and, by chance on that illustrious occasion, the Tsar's new flag first had been hoisted in *Minotaur* (48). To mark the occasion later the Tsar presented the ship with a suitably engraved cup. Rather neatly, on 26 September, Admiral Winsloe was able to introduce this subject when speaking to a large assembled company of Tsarist officers:-

'I made a short speech telling them of the occasion on which the cup was given to the ship and saying that as this was the first occasion on which we had met our friends of the Russian Army and Navy we took the opportunity to invite them onboard to Christen the cup.
Russian military officers seldom talk anything but Russian so this was interpreted to them by the Consul, I then proposed the health of the Tsar and the band played the Russian Hymn.'

As might be supposed the Russian officers' response was one of great delight. Better was to come:-

'On the morning of 27 September the ships sailed at 9.30 a.m. and after getting outside the inner harbour we saw on Point Novosilski, Russian Island, some 10-15,000 men massed on the top of the Point and also in double lines down to the landing place. The General and his staff were there, also a Regimental band; I altered course to go as close as possible and slowed down when passing, the band onshore and the band of *Minotaur* played the others National Anthem and the cheering from this large mass of troops and also from the crews of H.M. Ships was loud and prolonged as long as we were in hearing of each other, finally the fort fired a salute of 17 guns which I returned. This expression of good feeling was quite unexpected and was one of the most impressive sights I have seen for many years (49).'

From *Monmouth* at Wei-Hai-Wei on 14 October 1912 Sub Lieut. Arnold-Foster also wrote a few lines in which he described aspects of this Russian visit:-

'Vladivostok was good. We arrived there intoxicated – no, not with sake or vodka, but with the air of the place which is electrifying. The harbour of course is amazing, rivalling Sydney, I believe, and very pretty.
An odd incident happened as we were leaving the harbour. Of course it is magnificently fortified, and there are enormous garrisons stationed along the banks of the great harbour. We had left the town, when we noticed on one of the banks an army drawn up in review order, with massed bands in front and generals galloping about in an important way. There must have been nearly 10,000 men in the ranks. Suddenly the band struck up 'The King' and we realized that this was all for us. Then they began to cheer. Cheering isn't the right word; they roared – not just three cheers, but one long steady roar which made the air shake (50).'

As a sign even of those times, in the same letter of 14 October 1912 Arnold-Foster warned his mother, 'Don't write any confidential matter "via Siberia", as very systematic tampering of English mails is going on at present.' The alternative mail by sea through Suez naturally was secure, however tended to be slower than the rail postal service across Siberia.

During 1912 the first seaplanes to enter Naval service in Japan arrived in the country, the suppliers being Glenn Curtiss of the USA and Farman of France. The first actual flight took place on 6 November 1912 when Lieutenant Yozo Kaneko, who had received earlier training in France, ascended in a Farman from Oppama near the IJN base at Yokosuka in Tokyo Bay (51).

On 12 and again on 14 November 1912 H.E. The Governor of the Straits Settlements and High Commissioner to the Malay States, Sir Arthur Young, advised the Secretary of State for the Colonies that, "… the Rulers and the people of the Federated Malay States desire to offer to His Majesty's government a first class armoured ship … (52)". In this manner was born the gift to Britain of the *Queen Elizabeth* class battleship *Malaya*, 27,500 tons. At Elswick, Newcastle upon Tyne, she was laid down on 20 October 1913 and completed in February 1916, in time to participate in the Battle of Jutland when she was commanded by Captain The Hon. Algernon Douglas Edward Harry Boyle (1871-1949). Hit by German shell fire she sustained casualties amounting to thirty three wounded and sixty three dead. Also during the battle, in addition to the usual British flags she flew the Naval Ensign of the Federated Malay States, those being Selangor, Perak, Negeri Sembilan and Pahang. Following further service in WW2, on 12 April 1948 this great ship was to arrive at Faslane in Scotland for scrapping.

In Tokyo on 20 February 1913 Count Yamamoto Gonnohyoe formed a government as the first Admiral to serve as Prime Minister of Japan. Following the Siemens scandal of 1914, in which he appears not to have been involved, he was to resign on 16 April 1914. He was succeeded by Okuma Shigenobu (1838-1922), founder of Waseda University, and who, later in 1914, was to lead Japan into the Great War on the side of the Allies.

Such was his stature that between September 1923 and January 1924 Admiral Yamamoto again was to serve as Prime Minister of his country.

In the New Year, from 22 to 28 January 1913 in *Minotaur* Sir Alfred was at Saigon paying a farewell visit to the French (53). In addition to exchanges of hospitality and expressions of goodwill, there was another reason for the visit. Subsequently from Hong Kong on 13 February 1913, he was to express himself as follows in another of his regular private letters addressed to Mr. Churchill at the Admiralty:-

'During the time there the arrangements for the two powers acting in concert were fully talked over, and it has now been arranged that the two first class cruisers should at once join our Fleet in the north thus putting the British C. in C. at once in a position to deal with the German Fleet. There could of course be some minor difficulties of joining their ships up with ours as the French senior officers are old and very timid. Still I am of opinion that with an exchange of Lieutenants, or even a Commander for the Flagship, and a couple of our signalmen in each French ship that we could work the whole with our signal books. It certainly is the proper policy to concentrate all our force so as to be able to attack him at once (54).'

He returned to Hong Kong on 31 January 1913.
From Friday, 21 to Sunday, 23 February he was away from his Flagship in *TB 036*.
On Saturday, 29 March 1913 at Hong Kong succeeded by Admiral Jerram. Returned home from the East in the P. & O. s.s. *India*, 7,911 grt, who reached England on 3 May 1913 (55).
Once home he inquired about further possible appointments, for example in October 1913 regarding the Mediterranean, but finally decided to retire (56). From his obituary it may be noted:-

'In company with certain other Admirals who had reached the top of their profession, Sir Alfred decided, in December 1913, to retire voluntarily in order to accelerate the promotion of younger officers. He was then 61, and could have remained for over three years longer on the active list had he wished (57).'

Indeed, he retired on 12 December 1913.
For many years in London he resided in Piccadilly.

On 17 August 1924 he was made a recipient of the GSP, Good Service Pension, then valued at Sterling 300 p.a. This pension, one of a limited number, had become available upon the death of Admiral Sir Cyprian Bridge (see C. in C., 1901).

In London on 23 February 1931, the day of his funeral, 'The Times' published this appreciation of his life:-
'Those who had the privilege of serving under 'Jimmy Winsloe', as he was affectionately called, and who knew him intimately will remember him with gratitude as a lovable man and a firm friend who always had a happy ship. He possessed a remarkable power to instil in his subordinates the desire for the ship to excel both at work and play. An untirable sportsman, may he rest in peace.'

NOTES

1. NA ADM 196/18. *Service Record.*

2. Clowes, Vol. VII, 343. Donald Featherstone, *Victorian Colonial Warfare – Africa,* (London, 1992), 148/9.

3. Obituary, *The Times,* Wednesday, February 18, 1931. British forces under Sir Garnet Wolseley (1833-1913) landed at Ismailia, Suez Canal on 21 August 1882. Subsequently, and rapidly, they advanced in a Westerly direction. The important victory over the army of Arabi Pasha took place at Tel-el-Kebir early on 13 September 1882. Sir Garnet entered Cairo on Friday, 15 September. *Encyclopaedia Britannica.* Admiral Lord Beresford, *The Memoirs of Admiral Lord Beresford,* (London, 1916), 182/3.

4. Obituary.

5. Also see Fremantle, C. in C., 1892.

6. Obituary. Massikessi is Macequece, Mocambique, just over the border from Rhodesia on the route down from Umtali (Mutare) to Beira. The Chartered Company is Cecil Rhodes' British South Africa Company. Robert I. Rotberg, *The Founder,* (Johannesburg, 1988), 306, 321. By the Anglo-Portuguese Treaty of 11 June 1891 the borders of various nations were agreed and the colony of Portuguese East Africa/Mocambique was founded.

7. *Service Record.*

8. Richard Hough, *Admirals in Collision,* (London, 1973), 144. Charles Johnstone (1843-1927). Retired as a Captain: 19 October 1898.

9. *Service Record.* 14/6 a day equates to the present sum of 72.5P a day.

10. NA ADM 53/12748. Log Book *Blake.*

11. Clowes, Vol. VII, 454.

12. Log Book *Blake.*

13. NA ADM 53/14746. Log Book *Niobe.*

14. St. Helena Bay, a short distance to the north of the present day iron ore export facility and South African Naval base at Saldanha, was first discovered on 7 November 1497 by Vasco da Gama, then outward bound on his pioneering voyage to India. He anchored there the following day and spent the following, '… eight days, careening the vessels, repairing the sails and taking in firewood.' Eric Axelson, *Vasco da Gama: The Diary of his Travels Through African Waters: 1497-1499,* (Somerset West, Cape, 1998), 23.

15. Admiral Sir William James, *A Great Seaman, the Life of Admiral of the Fleet Sir Henry Oliver,* (London, 1956), 91.

16. Lady Wester Wemyss, *The Life and Letters of Lord Wester Wemyss,* (London, 1935), 50.
    Boer General Pieter Arnoldus Cronje (1836-1911), on 27 February 1900 had surrendered to Field Marshal Lord Roberts at Paardeberg.
    St. Helena, where on 17 October 1815 in the ship of the line *Northumberland,* 74, Captain Charles Bayne Hodgson Ross, and flying the flag of Rear Admiral Sir George Cockburn, Napoleon Bonaparte had landed to commence his period of exiled imprisonment which he was to endure until his death there on 5 May 1821.

17. NA ADM 53/14747. Log Book *Niobe*: 28 November 1899 to 14 November 1900.

18. Obituary.

19. Lady Wester Wemyss, 62. Commander Wemyss is writing at Simon's Town, 21 August 1901.

20. Bodleian Library, Oxford. Ref: *MS Asquith 21, fol. 163.*

    The four battleships of the *Helgoland* class had a designed displacement of 22,800 tons, a speed of 20.8 knots and were laid down between October 1908 and March 1909. Their main armament was twelve 12" guns. They were *Helgoland* herself, plus *Ostfriesland, Thuringen* and *Oldenburg.* The last named was built by Schichau in Danzig. Indeed, she was laid down on 1 March 1909, launched on 30 June 1910 and commissioned on 1 May 1912. *Encyclopaedia Britannica.* Richard Hough, *Dreadnought,* (London, 1965), 249.

21. Archives Centre, Churchill College, Cambridge. Ref: *MCKN 3/4.*

22. Richard Bell Davies, *Sailor in the Air,* (Barnsley, England, 2008), 56.

    George Cuthbert **Cayley** (1866-1944). Entered the Navy: 15 January 1880. Captain: 31 December 1905. Rear Admiral: 28 April 1917. In charge at Harwich: July 1917 – March 1918, subsequently Area Commander R.A.F. Retired at his own request: 18 July 1919. Vice Admiral: 3 May 1922. Admiral: 8 November 1926. *Navy List.*

23. NA ADM 1/8118.

24. Churchill College. Ref: *MCKN 3/10.* H.M. King George V had visited Shanghai on 25 November 1881 in *Bacchante.* At the time he was Midshipman HRH Prince George of Wales. Prince Albert Victor and Prince George of Wales, *The Cruise of HMS Bacchante, 1879-1882,* (London, 1886), II, 140/1. Sir Arthur Bigge, from 1911 to be Lord Stamfordham (1849-1931), was Private secretary to His Majesty. Sir Pelham Laird Warren (1845-1923) continued as Consul-General at Shanghai until retirement: 20 January 1911. *Foreign Office List.*

25. Ibid.

26. Tsuzuki, 181.

27. Ibid., 170.

28. Churchill College. Ref: *CHAR 13/11.*

29. Proceeding downstream from Hankow in 1858, on 19/20 December Captain Sherard Osborn in his steam paddle frigate *Furious,* 1,287 bm, carefully trimmed and drawing some 15' 6", found himself in the unenviable position of having to force his way through this bar at Red Cliffs. James Bruce, Lord Elgin was embarked at the time. His secretary recorded:-

    'There is a scrape and a lurch; the paddles revolve helplessly; the order, "Stop her", is reluctantly given, and the next process of hawsers, stream cables, and anchors, in all sorts of directions, is vigorously entered upon. By dint of dextrously bringing the ship broadside onto the current, she was converted into a species of dredging machine, and, during upwards of twelve hours, we dragged steadily through the mud, shifting our anchors whenever our altered position rendered this operation necessary.'

    Laurence Oliphant, *Narrative of the Earl of Elgin's Mission to China and Japan in the Years 1857, '58, '59,* (New York, 1860), 587. Proceeding upstream on Wednesday, 23 April 2008 in *Victoria Prince,* 4,587 grt, Captain Xie Shou Gui, the author noted that today the channel at this point is carefully buoyed with it being necessary for the ship to alter course very noticeably opposite the Red Bluffs from close in to the right bank diagonally across towards the left bank of the River.

30. NA ADM 116/3132.

31. Charles Hose. Born: 12 October 1863. Died: 14 November 1929. Felsted. Jesus College, Cambridge. Sarawak cadet: March 1884. He progressed rapidly in the Rajah's service. Officer in Charge, Baram District (in which area Miri is situated): 1888. Resident, Third Division and a member of the Supreme Council: May 1904. Retired in 1907 but revisited Sarawak in 1909 and 1920. Between 1916 and 1919 he was Superintendent of H.M. Explosives Factory, Kings Lynn. He maintained his Sarawak connections, and was the author or co-author of a number of books concerning Sarawak and Borneo. Courtesy: Cambridge University Library. An uncle, Rt. Revd. George Frederick Hose (1838-1922), in 1881 had been appointed Bishop of Singapore, Labuan and Sarawak.

32. Patrick Beesly, *Very Special Admiral,* (London, 1980), 11. The officer who made these notes was Lieutenant John Henry Godfrey (1888-1971), later Admiral.

    Basil George Washington (1877-1940). A grandson of Rear Admiral John Washington, FRS, Hydrographer of the Navy from 1855 to 1863. To return to the China Station in 1922 in command of the light cruiser *Durban.* Rear Admiral, retired: 6 April 1931. As a Commodore of Convoys drowned on 25 August 1940 when s.s. *Harpalyce,* 5,169 grt, was torpedoed by *U-124,* Wilhelm Schulz, to the north of the Hebrides. The ship was on passage from Baltimore, MD and

Halifax, NS to Hull laden with 8,000 tons of steel. She must have gone down in seconds. Author's notes covering the life and times of HMS *Durban*: 1921-1944.

33. NA ADM 116/1150.

34. RN Museum Library, Portsmouth. Ref: *2006.69*. Papers of Commander H.C. Arnold-Foster.

35. Ibid.

36. Thomas B. Buell, *The Quiet Warrior*, (Annapolis, 1988), 23, 28-32. *DANFS "Bainbridge".*

37. Churchill Archives Centre, Cambridge. Ref: *CHAR 13/8*. Letter from the First Lord, 28.2.12.

38. Ibid. Ref: *CHAR 13/9*.

    Correspondence with Mr. Churchill: as seen above, Prime Minister Asquith's wife was a cousin of Sir Alfred. From an extract taken from a letter, dated 1 July 1912, an example of one opinion of Sir Alfred as held in high places may be noted. The P.M. was writing to the First Lord, Winston Churchill:-

    'Winsloe is a cousin of Margot's: I saw something of him when he was (in) the Admiralty, and he is a hardish able man.'

    Ref: *CHAR 13/8*.

    C. in C., Devonport from 20 March 1913 was to be Vice Admiral Sir George Le Clerc Egerton (1852-1940). A Rear Admiral on 2 March 1905, and promoted Vice Admiral on 2 January 1909. Admiral: 21 March 1913. *Navy List*.

39. Francis Henry May. Born in Dublin where his father was Lord Chief Justice: 14 March 1860. Died at Clare, Suffolk: 6 February 1922. Harrow. Trinity, Dublin. First Honourman and Prizeman in Classics and Modern Languages. Hong Kong Cadet: 1881. Assistant Colonial Secretary: 1891. Captain Superintendent of Police: 1893-1902. Colonial Secretary 1902. Administered the government on a number of occasions. KCMG: 1909. Governor of Fiji and High Commissioner, Western Pacific: 9 January 1911. Appointed Governor of Hong Kong: 9 March 1912. He was the first cadet in the Hong Kong service to become Governor. GCMG: 1919. Owing to ill health retired in September 1919. *Colonial Office List*. H.J. Lethbridge, *Hong Kong Cadets: 1862-1941*, 53 (19). In Hong Kong the Helena May Foundation is named after his wife. The Hong Kong Jockey Club was founded in 1884 and he was an early member and jockey. Also subsequently he was to be a keen owner.

40. I.H. Nish, *The Mariner's Mirror*, Vol. 56, 1970. 413.

41. Edmund Samuel **Poe**. Born: 11 September 1849. Died: 1 April 1921. Entered the Navy: 1862. Captain: 30 June 1888. Rear Admiral: 9 September 1901. Second in Command Home Fleet with flag in the battleship *Empress of India*, 14,150 tons: 8 May 1903. In command, ICS, Channel Fleet with flag in cruiser *Good Hope*, 14,100 tons: 2 November 1904. C. in C., East Indies and Cape of Good Hope with flag in cruiser *Hyacinth*, 5,600 tons: 20 August 1905. (Her Commander from 21 July 1903 was William A.H. Kelly: see C. in C., 1931). Vice Admiral: 20 February 1906. KCVO: 19 March 1906. In the East Indies from 1 February 1907 succeeded by Commodore Sir George J.S. Warrender. C. in C., Cape of Good Hope: 1907-1908. KCB: 1908. Admiral: 30 April 1910. C. in C., Mediterranean: 1910-1912. GCVO: 1912. Retired: 15 September 1914. *Navy List. Who's Who.*

42. NA ADM 1/8267.

43. RN Museum Library, Portsmouth. Ref: *2006.69*. Letter dated 19 September 1912, the First Year of Taisho. **Oyama** is Field Marshal Oyama Iwao. Born in Kagoshima: 10 October 1842. Died in Tokyo: 10 Dec. 1916.

44. H.I.M. Emperor Yoshihito, the Taisho or 'Great Righeousness' era. Born: 31 August 1879. Died: 25 December 1926. Always an unwell man, in 1921 his son, Crown Prince Hirohito, was to be appointed Regent.

45. NA ADM 1/8267.

46. Ibid.

47. NA ADM 196/41, 1412. *Service Record*.

48. *Minotaur*, Captain William O. Boothby, on that occasion in the Baltic she had been one of H.M. Ships escorting the Royal Yacht *Victoria and Albert*, the other being *Achilles*, Captain Henry F. Oliver. *Minotaur* anchored off Reval at 11.06 hours on Tuesday, 9 June 1908. Royal and other Salutes fired that day were to total 231 guns. The Tsar was present in his yacht *Standart*. Subsequently *Minotaur* weighed at 03.00 hours on Thursday, 11 June 1908 to return with *Victoria and Albert* to Kiel. NA ADM 53/23723: Log Book *Minotaur*.

49. NA ADM 1/8267. General Letter No. 7, written in *Alacrity* at Shanghai, 8 October 1912.

50. RN Museum Library. Ref: *2006.69*.

51. The author's notes in respect of 'H.I.J.M.S. *Wakamiya*: early IJN Air Power'. Paper read at the Fourth International Congress of Maritime History, Corfu, 26 June 2004.

52. NA ADM 1/8284, No. 555.

Captain Sir Arthur Henderson **Young**. Born: 1854. Died: 20 October 1938. Edinburgh Academy, Rugby and Sandhurst. 27th Inniskillings. Entered the Colonial Service in 1878. All his early service was in Cyprus where in 1894 he attained the position of Chief Secretary. Special mission to St. Vincent: November 1902. Colonial Secretary, Straits Settlements: June 1906. KCMG: 1908. Governor, Straits Settlements: 2 September 1911 – 17 February 1920, when retired. GCMG: 1916. KBE: 1918. *Colonial Office List.*

53. NA ADM 53/23732. Log Book *Minotaur.*

54. Churchill Archives. Letter marked: *The Chartwell Trust*, dated Feby 13th.

55. s.s. *India*. In 1914 to be taken up and converted as an AMC – Armed Merchant Cruiser. On 8 August 1915, while investigating a suspected blockade runner, torpedoed and sunk off the coast of Norway near Bodo by *U-22*, Bruno Hoppe. 160 lives were lost but fortunately 141 survivors were rescued by small craft and landed at Narvik. At the time she was serving with the Tenth Cruiser Squadron, Rear Admiral Dudley Rawson Stratford de Chair (1864-1958), and was under the command of Commander W.G.A. Kennedy. On 20 August 1900 *India* had been the first P. & O. liner to enter Fremantle. Boyd Cable, 131.

56. Alfred Winsloe was born in the same year as Sir George Callaghan, namely 1852. At the outbreak of WW1 in 1914 one of the reasons given for the replacement of Sir George as C. in C., Home Fleet by Sir John Jellicoe was that Jellicoe was a younger man, born in 1859 so then only 55 years of age. In January 1915 Sir George was promoted to C. in C., The Nore, and then, on 2 April 1917, to Admiral of the Fleet.

57. Obituary. Additionally the somewhat devious and unscrupulous political behaviour by the First Lord in November 1913 rather put him off the idea of seeking further employment at home. As an example, concerning the Poore affair at The Nore, he was to write to Admiral Jerram on 1 February 1914:

'During the time this was on Winston sent for me and said the C. in C. at Nore will haul down his flag on a certain day, will you take the Nore. Of course directly the Sea Lords heard I had been sent for they told me of the trouble and so when offered the job I declined for I had no ideas for mixing myself up in the sort of jobs Winston always seems to have on hand.'

Caird Library. Ref: *JRM/15*. Also see the following, Jerram, C. in C., 1913.

25 January 1913 to 28 July 1915

Acting Vice Admiral Thomas Henry Martyn

Jerram

Born, second son of Reverend Samuel John Jerram, sometime Vicar of Chobham, by his wife Grace, daughter of Thomas Hunt of Hermitage, Co. Waterford: 6 September 1858.

He died at his residence 7a, The Crescent, Alverstoke on 19 March 1933.

Entered the navigating branch of the Royal Navy through *Britannia*: 15 January 1871. **Midshipman**: 21 December 1872. Service in HM Ships *Hercules* and *Monarch*, Channel Squadron. **Sub Lieutenant**: 6 September 1877, studying navigation at RNC, Greenwich. Once qualified then appointed as Sub Lieut. (N) to the brig *Seaflower*, 454 tons, Training Ship for Boys, Portland: 6 May 1879. **Lieutenant**: 1 January 1881. Appointed to the Troop and Store Ship *Tyne*, 3,560 tons: 1 December 1881. At this time he maintained a diary from which may be noted an outline of her subsequent passage East:-

	Days	Hours
'Plymouth/Malta	9	0.5
Malta/Port Said	4	3
In Suez Canal	3	
Suez/Colombo	15	7.5
Colombo/Singapore	7	7

While crossing the Bay of Bengal, on 2 February 1882 he noted:
'One advantage of teetotalism, you have more money at the end of the month.'

Singapore/Hong Kong	8	2

From Singapore, on 7 February 1882 he recorded:-
'Sailed at 9 a.m. filled up with the 'Buffs'.'

Hong Kong/Singapore	6	2
Singapore/Penang	1	23
Penang/Singapore	1	22
Singapore/Hong Kong	7	22 (1)'

At Hong Kong on 24 March 1882 he was transferred to *Iron Duke*, flagship of the C. in C., Vice Admiral George O. Willes. *Tyne* was sailing the next day and he visited her briefly:-

'Went onboard *Tyne* in the morning for an hour to see the fellows before she started. A tremendous

Acting Vice Admiral Thomas Henry Martyn Jerram | 297

crowd onboard seeing the Inniskillings off. *Tyne* sailed at 11.45. Wishing much I was in her but no such luck.'

On 6 April 1882 an entry in the diary reads:-
'Dined with Admiral Willis at Morrison Hill. Rather slow and very shoppy conversation. Levett, McQuhae and Madeley besides myself (2).'

On 18 April the ship sailed at 6 a.m. for Manila but after sailing their destination was altered to Handcock Bay, Loo-choo (Ryukyu) Islands.
Then on 16 May:-
'Arrived at Nagasaki at 10 a.m. Entrance and harbour almost the most beautiful I've ever seen in the way of sea and land scape.'

His diary contains little of interest until on 7 December 1882 they left Hong Kong at 6 a.m. for Singapore and England. On the station *Iron Duke* was replaced as flagship by *Audacious*.

After arrival in England, and some foreign service leave, then on 1 April 1883 he was appointed Lieut. (N), again in the training brig *Seaflower*.

Early in February 1884 he left England in command of the torpedo boat *Childers*, sixty tons and only 113' in length. She was on her delivery voyage from her builders, J.I. Thornycroft, to the Colonial Navy of Victoria, Australia (3). Her coal capacity was only ten tons so it is not surprising to read that while steaming on her own from Portsmouth to Gibraltar when off Cadiz supplies ran short and he accepted the offer of a tow from the steamer *Pathan*. Subsequently she proceeded via Malta, Suda Bay, Suez Canal, Suakin in the Red Sea, Aden, Colombo, Sunda Strait, then through the Java and Arafura Seas to the Torres Strait, North Queensland. As the ships approached Thursday Island foul weather was experienced subsequently causing him to record that, 'I never spent such an awful time in all my life and I hope I never shall again'. For much of the voyage *Childers* was towed by the gunboat *Victoria*, 530 tons. With *Albert*, 350 tons, in company, the squadron reached Melbourne on 25 June 1884 (4).

Lieutenant in sloop *Reindeer*, 970 tons, East Indies: 4 December 1884. Attended Gunnery Short Course: January 1889. Appointed Lieut. (G) in *Conquest*, 2,380 tons, East Indies: 1 February 1889. Commanded a party of seamen during the Vitu Expedition of 1890 in East Africa.

In April 1891 the Captain of the gunboat *Pigeon* was taken ill. Here follows an extract taken from the report addressed by the C. in C., Rear Admiral Fremantle (see C. in C., 1892), to the Admiralty:-
'On the 23rd inst. I was informed by telegraph from Zanzibar that Lieutenant and Commander Henry R. P. Floyd, commanding HMS *Pigeon*, had been invalided and Captain Henderson, as Senior Officer, had appointed Lieut. Thomas H.M. Jerram, 1st Lieut. of HMS *Conquest*, to take his place. This appointment I confirmed. Lieut. Jerram is a very good officer, thoroughly competent for the command should Their Lordships think fit to confirm him in the appointment (5).'

Also he acted as Vice Consul at Beira, Mocambique on the occasion of negotiations with Portugal which continued from 9 to 26 June 1891:-
'.... while the coast road to Mashonaland (eastern region of Southern Rhodesia) was being begun, and received from the Foreign Office, 'high appreciation and thanks for his services (6).'

The road in question was through from the coast to the interior. The Royal Navy was much involved in this small example of diplomacy with Portugal, Captain John Pakenham Ripon of HMS *Magicienne* being positioned at Beira as HBM Consul. Also Commander Alfred Leigh Winsloe (see C. in C., 1910) was temporarily employed to survey the boundary between Mashonaland, Rhodesia and Mocambique. Jerram himself was stationed at Mopanda in order to keep an eye on, and if necessary, 'prevent anyone going to the interior (7)'. The relevant Anglo-Portuguese Treaty was signed on 11 June 1891, and, writing on 8 June to Jerram, Captain Ripon gave instructions accordingly:-
'The route to the interior is to be declared open at 8.0 a.m. on Thursday the 11th inst.'

On 12 July 1892 at Hampstead, London he married Clara Isabel, second daughter of Joseph Parsons, brush manufacturer of Ennox, Somerset, and Fanny Elizabeth nee Jones. Clara was born in Wells, Somerset on 28 May 1861. They were to have two sons (8). The elder, Roy Martyn Jerram was born on 10 November 1895 and, as a Brigadier, Royal Tank Regiment, was to die on 6 April 1974. The younger, Nigel Martyn Jerram, to be a cricketer of some note, was born on 9 March 1900 and died on 19 December 1968. In 1923 he played in the Minor Counties Championship, for Bickley Park in 1926, and for the RAF in the 1930s.

Lady Clara Jerram died several years before her husband, in 1926 and at only sixty four years of age, and was buried in Harpsden cemetery, the Church of St. Margaret, on 11 February.

Senior Lieut. in *Ruby*, 2,120 tons, Training Squadron: 14 October 1892.

Commander: 1 January 1894. Appointed to *Northampton*, 7,630 tons, 'Sea Going Training Ship for Boys on the Home Station': 14 June 1894.

In command of the training ship *Curacao*, 2,380 tons: 2 June 1896. Writing of his time in the ship one young officer, in due course to become well known, later was to remark:-

'My Captain, Commander Martyn Jerram, was a fine sailorman, who hunted me a good deal to start with, taught me much, and became a warm friend for the rest of his life (9).'

Captain: 1 January 1899.

In command of training ship *Boscawen*, 4,579 tons: 1 September 1899.

From 4 March 1902 appointed in command battleship *Albion*, 12,950 tons, Flagship RA, China Station who was Harry Tremenheere Grenfell. Since 26 June 1901 the C. in C. had been Vice Admiral Sir Cyprian Arthur George Bridge (1839-1924).

A Lieutenant then serving in the ship was Hugh Justin Tweedie, from 19 October 1927 to assume the position of RAY (Rear Admiral, Yangtse). In his memoirs he tells of an impressive occasion in *Albion* at Nanking which took place shortly after the turn of the century when the Viceroy paid an official call on the Admiral:-

'He came complete with yellow jacket, jade button and peacock feather, carried in a highly ornamental chair, preceded by bannermen and surrounded by a personal bodyguard in the viceregal uniform carrying spears. As he emerged from the gates and passed through the crowded villages, which lay outside the wall and between the city and the river, everyone went down on their knees, noses to the ground, in a deep kowtow. Here was the height of the Manchu dynasty so shortly after to disappear, after some three hundred years (10).'

Between 1 February and 7 May 1904 studying at RNC, Greenwich, 'War Course' (11).

In command battleship *Russell*, 14,000 tons, Channel Fleet: 8 May 1904 to 5 December 1905.

In command Royal Naval Engineering School *Vivid*, Devonport: 6 December 1905 to 29 July 1908 (12).

Rear Admiral: 30 June 1908.

Flag in the battleship *Magnificent*, 14,900 tons, Chief of Staff to the Vice Admiral commanding Third and Fourth Divisions, Home Fleet: 17 February 1909.

H.M. King Edward VII died just before midnight on 6 May 1910.

The first indication he received that he was to participate in the funeral arrangements was from a telegram sent by the C. in C., Home Fleet, Admiral Sir William Henry May, on Thursday, 12 May. This was addressed to his Vice Admiral, Sir George Neville:-

'Urgent Admiralty telegraph that Rear Admiral Jerram has been appointed to take command of Officers and men of Royal Navy who will take part in funeral ceremony on Tuesday and Friday 17th and 20th inst. and that he is to attend Admiralty tomorrow Friday for instructions as to general arrangements stop please acknowledge receipt by wire (13).'

On 20 May the route from Westminster Hall to Paddington Station, from where the special train to Windsor departed, was lined by 2,000 men of the Naval Brigade, Rear Admiral T.H.M. Jerram, Commanding, together with thousands of troops. All proceeded smoothly, on 21 May the Admiralty expressing their satisfaction:-

> 'My Lords desire to take the opportunity of expressing to Rear Admiral T.H.M. Jerram their complete satisfaction with the arrangements made by him for the officers and men of the Royal Navy and Royal Marines who participated in the ceremony (14).'

Early in June 1910 he was offered an important new position, and on 10 June 1910 wrote to the First Lord, Mr. Reginald McKenna, gratefully accepting:-

> 'In reply to your letter I am proud to accept the appointment of second in command of the Mediterranean Fleet, to relieve Sir George Callaghan after the manoeuvres, and hope soon to have an opportunity of thanking you personally for this further mark of your confidence in me (15).'

9 August 1910 to 31 July 1912: Second in Command, Mediterranean Fleet with his Flag in the battleship *Duncan*, 14,000 tons. The C. in C., Mediterranean at the time was Admiral Sir Edmund S. Poe with his flag in the sister ship, *Exmouth*.

In their issue of Tuesday, October 24, 1911 a news item had appeared in *The Times*:-

> 'Cabinet Changes. Rearrangement of Offices. Mr. Churchill at the Admiralty.'

CB: 27 September 1912.

Following his return from the Mediterranean he had been made aware that his next appointment would be to the Far East. While conscious of this, in December he received a letter from the First Lord at the Admiralty, Mr. Winston S. Churchill, instead offering him command of the Second Battle Squadron:-

> 'I therefore propose to offer you this most important appointment instead of the command in China which you have already had assigned to you (16).'

For financial reasons Jerram felt unable to accept this new offer and so at the Admiralty it was decided that, '.. you should proceed to China as originally arranged.'

In his stead, from 16 December acting Vice Admiral Sir George J.S. Warrender was appointed to the Second Battle Squadron with his flag in the new battleship *King George V*, 23,000 tons.

To take up his command in China he travelled across the Atlantic and Pacific arriving at Hong Kong in the CPR steamer *Empress of India*, 5,943 grt, Captain A.W. Davison, on 14 March 1913. There he,'... remained ashore unofficially until 28 March, the day before Admiral Sir A. Winsloe sailed for England when, according to Admiralty orders, my flag was hoisted in *Monmouth* (17).'

Indeed at Hong Kong at 1.00 p.m. on 29 March 1913 he assumed command in China. Flag now in the armoured cruiser *Minotaur*, 14,600 tons, Captain Edward B. Kiddle (18). Later the same day his predecessor, Admiral Winsloe, sailed for England in the P. & O. s.s. *India*.

From 7 to 9 April 1913 *Minotaur* exercised in Mirs Bay then on Saturday, 19 April, with *Monmouth* in company, he sailed for Yokohama where he arrived on 24 April, amongst other warships finding in port SMS *Scharnhorst*, the German flagship (19). Here discussions with the IJN took place:-

> 'After an exhaustive study of Japan's naval power he told the Admiralty that, 'if the Japanese Alliance can be safely calculated on, we have an overwhelming superiority (against Germany) and there is no more to be said'. But he had two mental reservations. One was that he did not take seriously the prospect of Japan taking an active part in any war against Germany; when she eventually did so, it came as a last minute surprise to most European observers. The other was that he found the Japanese were interfering in China – in ways which were an anathema to Britain, and he felt that there might come a time when the two allies would be at daggers drawn over China (20).'

From Yokohama on 5 May he proceeded to Kobe where he remained from 6 to 7 May, then continued on to Wei-Hai-Wei where he arrived on 9 May 1913.

Vice Admiral: 4 June 1913.

5 November 1913: arrival at Yokosuka of the battlecruiser *Kongo*, 26,230 tons, the last warship of appreciable size to be completed in Great Britain for the IJN. She had been laid down on 17 January 1911 and completed on 16 August 1913, so under construction for thirty one months. She was to be reconstructed between September 1929 and March 1931, and again between June 1935 and January 1937, so emerging as a fast battleship for service during WW2, the Pacific War. During the sortie of *Prince of Wales* and *Repulse* from Singapore in December 1941 (see C. in C., 3-10 December 1941) she was to be attached to the IJN Second Fleet, Vice Admiral Kondo Nobutake, in support up until the rapid demise of these two British heavy ships by IJN air attack.

In Tokyo on 21 November 1913 at 4.10 p.m. the last of the shoguns, Prince Tokugawa Yoshinobu, died (see C. in C., 1867). During the afternoon of 30 November his funeral took place, '... at the Kan'ei-ji in Ueno, the Tokugawa family temple (21).' In addition:-

'An Imperial envoy attended the funeral, along with over three hundred of the former daimyo. There were many mourners from the defunct hatamoto families, but what struck everyone most of all was the large number of representatives of foreign countries in attendance. From their perspective, the funeral marked the passing of a former head of state, and they were paying the proper respect.'

KCB: 1 January 1914.

Following receipt of this honour a number of relatives and friends wrote. As might be expected Lord Fisher was brief and to the point:-

'My dear Jerram,
One line of sincere congratulations on your well deserved KCB.
Yours truly,
Fisher
6.1.14
Don't trouble to answer (22)'

His predecessor in the China command, Alfred Winsloe, also sent congratulations as did Arthur Christian, RA 5CS, both these adding various items of news. A particularly current item concerned the Churchill/Poore affair of November 1913. This is mentioned since inclusion is relevant to a letter of explanation, which follows in due course, written by Jerram to his wife after the outbreak of the Great War.

As mentioned above, on the occasion of his appointment, indeed the First Lord of the Admiralty between October 1911 and May 1915 was Winston Churchill, on 30 November 1911 to turn thirty seven years of age so then a rather young man. Although clever, persuasive and energetic, not all his methods met with general approval. Shortly after his appointment as First Lord, in their issue of 28 October 1911 the 'Spectator', and many would have agreed, summed up the man as follows:-

'He has not the loyalty, the dignity, the steadfastness, and the good sense which make an efficient head of a great office. He must always be living in the limelight, and there is no fault more damning in an administrator (23).'

The new First Lord commenced his term of office with the rather unsatisfactory Bridgeman business, the appointment by him from 9 December 1911 of Admiral Sir Francis Bridgeman as First Sea Lord. Naturally there are arguments in support of both men, and certainly the young First Lord brought much energy and a fresh viewpoint to Naval activity in a time of rapid development in preparation for possible war.

However, far from being an easily coerced dupe, Sir Francis possessed a mind of his own and a number of disagreements took place. As has been written, 'The brash young politician obviously rubbed him up the wrong way (24)'. The long and the short of it all was that on 28 December 1912 Bridgeman, who at times during his year in office had been unwell, resigned and was succeeded as First Sea Lord by Admiral Prince Louis of Battenburg.

Then in November 1913 there erupted an affair which derived from Churchill again ignoring established patterns of behaviour in the services, of which he of all people, as an ex Army officer, was well aware. Basically, concerning a matter of Naval Air, he listened to the views of a young Naval Lieutenant, was impressed, then instructed the Captain of the ship that these ideas were to be followed. That was bad enough but then the young Lieutenant overstepped the mark. The Captain complained to his C. in C., Admiral Sir Richard Poore at the Nore. Quickly the whole affair grew out of proportion, the conflagration being increased in temperature by Churchill's dubious methods and poor judgement. The First Lord went so far as to threaten to remove Poore from his post, even offering that position at the Nore to Winsloe. Naturally the Sea Lords in turn, horrified at Churchill's appalling attitude, indicated that they would all resign. Once he knew the facts of course Winsloe declined the offer of the Nore (25).

Rear Admiral (Arthur Henry) Christian, in his letter to Jerram dated 22 January 1914, included the phrase:-

> 'Vivian (the Captain involved) wrote a very strong letter to Poore who supported him for all he
> was worth, and I believe characterized Churchill's conduct as "extremely subversive to discipline".'

Fortunately sense was to prevail and a short while later once more the seas were to become calm. However it is hardly surprising, with the youthful Churchill as First Lord, that senior serving Naval officers of the era made an extra effort to protect themselves and their reputations from the effects of any future unscrupulous and unethical behaviour from on high.

19 May 1914. Announcement in London of the proposed amalgamation of the interests of two great British steamship companies with historic involvement in the waters of the East, P. & O. and British India. The first Chairman of the combined group was to be James Lyle Mackay (1852-1932), Lord Inchcape, later the first Earl.

Between 12 June and 16 June 1914 the C. in C. visited the German East Asiatic Cruiser Squadron at Tsingtao, Vice Admiral Count Maximilian von Spee, Flag in SMS *Scharnhorst*, 11,600 tons. The Governor of Tsingtao also was a Naval officer, Captain Alfred Meyer-Waldeck (1864-1928). As was recorded by a German source, the writer being a Naval officer, between 23 and 30 June a similar visit was to take place in Europe:-

> 'An English squadron was expected at Kiel, and both there and here (in Tsingtao) we were glad
> to be able to welcome our comrades of the sea; all of us had enjoyed much hospitality in English
> harbours (26).'

4 August 1914: commencement of the Great War, WW1. On that day SMS *Scharnhorst* and *Gneisenau* were at Ponape in the Caroline islands (today: Pohnpei in Micronesia). After coaling from the chartered collier *Fukoku Maru* the two armoured cruisers were to sail on Wednesday, 6 August, eventually to meet the British off Coronel in Chile in November, then at the Falkland Islands on 8 December 1914 (27).

Immediately prior to the outbreak of war the C. in C. had been at Wei-hai-wei in *Minotaur* and with *Hampshire* in company. At the end of July:-

> 'All being ready I raised steam and was on the point of weighing to proceed to a line to the
> southward of Tsingtau, my recognized first rendezvous in the War Orders submitted by me and
> approved by the Admiralty. To my horror I just then received a telegram from Admiralty (dated
> 30 July) to concentrate at Hong Kong of all places in the world just over 900 miles from where I
> wanted to go. I was so upset I very nearly disobeyed the order entirely. (--) My position blockading

Tsingtau would have prevented German merchant ships from going there either to seek refuge or to load ammunition and stores and coal for the big German cruisers or to be converted into armed merchant cruisers; would prevent exit of any there; would bottle up *Emden*, and would ensure coming to action with the two big cruisers should they endeavour to return to Tsingtau (28).'

Events were to prove the C. in C. to have been at least partially correct in his anticipation of German activity. SMS *Emden* cast off from her berth at Tsingtao at 1900 on 31 July 1914. On 4 August she captured the Russian passenger freighter *Rjasan* in the Tsushima Strait and two days later brought her safely to Tsingtao. Immediately the German authorities commenced investigating her suitability for conversion to an armed merchant cruiser.

In due course they were to re-name her after the gunboat *Cormoran* and initially to use her as an auxiliary cruiser escort for their squadron supply train.

As has been written in more recent times:-
'Vice Admiral Martyn Jerram's plans to deploy his squadron against Tsingtao were thrown into confusion by Admiralty orders to concentrate on Hong Kong, Churchill being anxious that Jerram had *Triumph* with him before he gave battle. This assisted German shipping, including the light cruiser *Emden*, to escape (29).'

With the light cruiser *Newcastle*, 4,800 tons, Captain Frederick A. Powlett, in company, on 12 August 1914 and with his flag still in *Minotaur*, he bombarded and destroyed the German wireless and communication facilities at Yap in the Caroline Islands (30).

On 23 August 1914 Japan declared war against the Central Powers. He ordered the small battleship *Triumph*, 11,800 tons, and the destroyer *Usk*, 590 tons, to assist the IJN, Vice Admiral Kato Sadakichi (1861-1927), during Allied operations against German positions at Tsingtao. Admiral Kato flew his flag in the old battleship *Suwo*, 13,500 tons. As *Pobieda* she had been captured from the Russians at Port Arthur in 1904.

After a siege of seven weeks, on 7 November 1914 the Governor of Tsingtao had no option but to surrender his forces to those of the Japanese Army. It was during this siege that, from early in September, Farman seaplanes attached to the tender *Wakamiya Maru*, Commander Tsunataro Iyama, were to provide the first example of the use of Naval sea borne air power in war against facilities ashore (31). Her aircraft carried out reconnaissance patrols and bombing attacks against German positions (32).

In Germany the Kaiser, '.. was very depressed by the news reported to him yesterday evening of the fall of Tsingtau (33).'

To be of considerable consequence during the future Pacific War of 1941-1945, in October 1914 units of the IJN occupied the Marshall, Caroline, Palau and most of the Mariana Islands. As one example, on 3 October Vice Admiral Yamaya Tanin (1866-1940) put ashore a permanent landing party at Jaluit in the Marshalls, German commercial headquarters in the central Pacific (34).

This Naval activity quickly was followed, in Japan in January 1915, by the founding of Nan'yo Kyokai, South Seas Society, the objectives of which were to study and then disseminate information about the region, also to train the necessary manpower to enable Japanese business activity to take place in that part of the world. Already, for instance, in 1889 Japan had opened their consulate in Singapore. Now in 1916 Nan'yo Kyokai established an office in that city. Under their auspices, and from 1919 onwards, their *Nan'yo Economic Bulletin* was to be issued regularly. So comprehensive and valuable was much of the data gathered that in Japan by 1935, 'some of it was distributed to government agencies and business circles as classified information (35).' This is not to say that Japanese investment in the Malayan peninsula had not occurred earlier. In 1911 in Johore some 13,000 acres of rubber had been planted by the Nan'a K.K., however the activity of Nan'yo Kyokai was to prove an important catalyst so that by 1938 Japanese planters with some 800,000 acres controlled almost one quarter of the entire Malay rubber industry. To give additional meaning to this figure, in the 1930s Malayan production of natural rubber amounted to between one half and two thirds of the total world production, 57% of which was exported to the U.S.A. (36).

In contrast, although by 1932 at least the Japanese mandated territories of the Marshall, Caroline, Palau and Mariana Islands were to be paying their way, the total value of their exports to the homeland, principally of sugar, was to be relatively miniscule.

Also in October 1914 he established his headquarters ashore in Singapore. The reason was communications which could not be adequately handled and supervised while he was at sea. As he pointed out to the Admiralty in a letter sent from Singapore on 16 October 1914, '... the difficulties of maintaining communication by wireless (while at sea) were insuperable due to the great distances and atmospheric disturbances.' Further, '... my position requires me to keep in close and direct telegraphic communication with the Admiralty and with the Japanese and Australian naval authorities.' Also, '... I am engaged in controlling the operations of a number of small detached squadrons or single ships of four nationalities (British, French, Russian and Japanese) and also acting in concert with the Australian Fleet.' In addition he mentioned the large geographical area involved, '... area to be covered is immense, comprising practically the whole of the Pacific Ocean and the eastern portion of the Indian Ocean.'

Intially he had considered using Hong Kong but instead selected Singapore, '... as the latter place is much more centrally situated under the present circumstances (37).'

On his staff at Singapore, for four months until December 1914, was Commander Yamanashi Katsunoshin, IJN who assisted with liaison matters, a duty which was especially important while the German cruiser *Emden* remained at large (38). To assist in the hunt for this raider the IJN had provided the services of their armoured cruiser *Ibuki*, 14,650 tons. Other IJN warships operated out in the Pacific in the search for the main units of the German Pacific Squadron who, as shortly was to be learned most emphatically, were steaming towards the coast of Chile.

9 November 1914: SMS *Emden*, Commander Karl von Muller, the last effective member of the German East Asiatic or Pacific Squadron in Eastern waters, was destroyed off the Cocos Islands by HMAS *Sydney*, Captain John C.T. Glossop (39).

A few days previously, on 28 October 1914, von Muller had entered Penang harbour and in a brilliant exercise destroyed the Russian protected cruiser *Zhemchug* together with the small French torpedo boat destroyer *Mousquet*.

Meanwhile on 1 November 1914, when some fifty miles to the West of Coronel in Chile, units of the German East Asiatic/Pacific Squadron, with Vice Admiral Maximilian Graf von Spee continuing to fly his flag in *Scharnhorst*, came up with and overwhelmed a lesser British squadron under Rear Admiral Sir Christopher G.F.M. Cradock with his flag in *Good Hope*, 14,100 tons.

In turn, just to the south of the Falkland Islands on 8 December 1914, a Royal Naval Squadron with Vice Admiral Sir Frederick Charles Doveton Sturdee (1859-1925) flying his flag in *Invincible*, 17,250 tons, gave battle to that same German Squadron who, early that morning, very conveniently had appeared off the Islands with the intention of bombarding and destroying communications and other facilities. The subsequent British victory was most convincing.

The First Sea Lord at the outbreak of war had been Admiral Prince Louis of Battenburg (1854-1921) who resigned that position on 28 October 1914. On the following day he was succeeded by Admiral of the Fleet Lord Fisher, then in his seventy fourth year. From his firm hand had come the dispositions which had resulted in this success of 8 December in the South Atlantic.

As suggested above, after the outbreak of the Great War Admiral Jerram felt obliged to write a seven page letter to his wife. From the entry dated 4 August 1914 above, one sees clearly that in the East his hands were somewhat tied. Therefore in this missive he gives detailed reasoning behind several of his wishes concerning the deployment of the ships available to him. To explain his motive an excerpt follows:-

'.... I can give you some idea of what has been going on. You must not make it public, but it might be useful if I happen to be knocked out, from an historical point of view and also in case my reputation was at any time unfairly attacked (40).'

18 January 1915. Taking advantage of China's weak situation, and also of the fact that European powers were fully occupied in Europe, Japan under prime minister Okuma Shigenobu (1838-1922) of the Hizen 'han', presented China with the infamous 'Twenty One Demands'. President Yuan Shih-kai had little option but to accept the terms proposed by Japan. This date was 9 May 1915, the affair being regarded by many as being a, 'national disgrace for the Chinese.'

At Singapore on Monday, 15 February 1915 a number of Indian and Malay troops mutinied, killing three British officers. At the Tanglin Barracks one group attempted to recruit assistance from the 309 Germans interned there, including members of the ship's company of *Emden*. However, apart from a mere seventeen men, they refused to participate in such dishonourable behaviour. From HMS *Cadmus* a detachment of Marines and seamen landed to join other garrison troops in bringing the matter under control. Much assistance also was received from men from the French cruiser *Montcalm*. On 20 February British troops arrived from Rangoon, thereafter order rapidly being restored. Subsequently the officer commanding troops, Straits Settlements, wrote to Admiral Jerram:-

'The whole of the Troops here owe a great deal of gratitude to Your Excellency and Staff for the prompt measures which were taken by the Navy on the 15 February 1915 (41).'

Later in 1915 the C. in C. asked the Admiralty for a more active role in the war. Consequently he was recalled home on 19 September, some time before the previously intended end of his term in command of the Station (42).

In due course his successor, Vice Admiral W.L. Grant, reported his assumption of command:-

'... my flag was hoisted at Singapore on 24 September, and on the same day I took over command of the China station from Vice Admiral Sir T.H.M. Jerram (43).'

Back in home waters, from 16 December 1915 to 28 November 1916 he was placed in command of the 2BS, Grand Fleet, the very command which he had felt unable to accept in 1912. Furthermore his flagship was *King George V*, 23,000 tons, Captain Frederick L. Field. This service included his participation in the Battle of Jutland, 31 May 1916. Following the battle Admiral Sir John Jellicoe, C. in C., Grand Fleet, included Sir Martyn in a list of senior officers whom he felt had, '.. acted throughout with skill and judgement (44).'

For his services at Juland then later in 1916 he was appointed KCMG.

At the end of 1916 various changes took place at The Admiralty. Admiral Sir Henry Jackson (1855-1929), who resigned on 3 December 1916, was replaced as First Sea Lord by Sir John Jellicoe and, in turn, command of the Grand Fleet passed to David Beatty. The whole affair took place amicably.

Jerram also left the Grand Fleet at the end of November 1916. He was not considered, even momentarily, for the position as the new C. in C. as, '.. his lack-lustre performance at Jutland was enough to ruin any chance he might have had (45).' Jellicoe, in praising his 'skill and judgement' during Jutland, may have lacked judgement himself in so wholeheartedly and undeservedly, although kindly, supporting him and indeed a number of other senior officers of the Grand Fleet.

Admiral: 10 April 1917, 'and retired at his own request a few months later (46).'

For his war services he received Japanese, French, Russian, Italian and Chinese decorations.

Well before the end of the Great War it had become most apparent that Naval rates of pay required considerable adjustment. On 6 January 1919 he was appointed President of a Committee to review the matter (47). Subsequently he was to act as President of a Welfare Committee.

He may have hoped to retire in 1917 but this wish was not to be granted immediately:-

'To cease duty on 20 May 1919 and to revert to Retired List on expiration of any leave due to him (48).'

GCMG: 1919.

In July 1919 a Victory march took place through the streets of London, a route of seven miles in length. Naturally much thought was given to the method by which senior officers of all three services should proceed but Lord Beatty decreed that Naval officers should walk. In due course the senior officers of the Navy assembled and a number of enthusiastic young officers from *Excellent,* the training establishment wherein such matters were taken extremely seriously, suggested to them that when marching then the distance between fours was so much, and between individuals such and such, and that keeping in step was of importance. The senior Admirals were unimpressed, it being recorded that:-

'Young man', said Admiral Jerram, 'if I get round these seven miles on a hot day without falling out, I shall have done very well (49).'

Also in 1919 he was elected a Councillor of the Society for Nautical Research, then in 1924 a Vice President. In 1925 he became president of the Naval Prize tribunal.

Even with due allowance being made for the era the Admiral may have been fortunate to have achieved high rank:-

'Nor did the commander of the 2nd Battle Squadron, the colourless Vice Admiral Sir Martyn Jerram, possess much initiative or dash. He was a reliable, reasonably competent officer with no frills (50).'

Another opinion follows:-

'While not, perhaps, an outstanding leader of men, he was one in whose sympathy, fairness, and understanding of their needs in the difficult matters of their pay and conditions of service the men of the navy had full confidence (51).'

'Jerram was twice commended for jumping overboard and saving life at sea, in 1881, when Lieutenant of the *Seaflower,* for which he received the bronze medal of the Royal Humane Society, and in 1902, when Captain of the *Albion* (52).'

At the time of the death of his wife in February 1926 they were living at Chobham Rise, St. Andrews Road, Henley-on-Thames. Subsequently he moved to Alverstoke near Gosport, Hampshire.

From 11 February 1929, vice Admiral Fremantle deceased, he was in receipt of a GSP (Good Service Pension) at the rate of GBP 300.00 p.a. (53). This Admiral Fremantle was Sir Edmund Robert, none other than his C. in C. in East Africa, 1889-1891.

On the day following his death on 19 March 1933 at Alverstoke, rather naturally the local press published an account of aspects of his life. An extract follows which covers a part of his latter years:-

'Upon his retirement he took up residence at Alverstoke, and was created a Justice of the Peace for Hampshire in 1918. He did not sit regularly on the Bench however, until 1926, as he resided for some time at Henley-on-Thames. He returned to Alverstoke in 1926, and until his health began to fail was a regular attendant at the Gosport Court. He also associated himself with the Boy Scout Movement, and for a short period was Chairman of the Gosport Association.

The funeral will take place at Harpsden Church, Henley-on-Thames at 2 p.m. on Thursday (23 March) (54).'

On 24 March *The Evening News* reported that indeed his funeral had occurred, "yesterday at Harpsden, where Lady Jerram was interred several years ago." At the same time as his funeral was taking place then at the Alverstoke Parish Church of St. Mary a Memorial Service was held. Present at both services were members of his family together with several Naval officers and a number of dignitaries.

The grave of the Admiral and Lady Jerram may be found in the 'new' cemetery a short distance further along Woodlands Road from the church, St. Margaret, towards the village of Harpsden. The lich-gate entrance is situated there at a sharp bend precisely at the point where the road divides to the left and right (55).

NOTES

1. Caird Library, National Maritime Museum, Greenwich. Ref: *JRM/2*. The 'Buffs' are the East Kent Regiment.

2. Ibid. Flag Lieutenant Egerton B.B. Levett. Lieutenant John M. McQuhae, Lieut. and Commander Gunboat *Foxhound*, 455 tons. Staff Surgeon George H. Madeley, Sloop *Albatross*. *Navy List*. At the time, well before the subsequent Praya East land reclamation, Morrison Hill stood adjacent to the shore of the bay.

3. *Dictionary of National Biography*.

4. Colin Jones, *Colonial Torpedo Boat*, (The Mariner's Mirror, Vol. 94, No. 1, February 2008), 92. Screw steamer *Pathan*, 2,709 grt, 340' loa, built in Glasgow in 1883 for Gellatly, Hankey, Sewell & Co. Registered: Rochester. Captain J. Rowley. *Lloyd's Register*, 1884.

5. NA ADM 1/7065. letter No. 185 dated 28 April 1891, para. 6.

6. *Foreign Office List*, 1892. Obituary, *The Times*, Tuesday, March 21,1933.

7. Caird Library. Ref: *JRM/12*. Letter from Ripon to Jerram, 3 June 1891.

8. *Dictionary of National Biography*. Also a communication with the writer from a relative, Ms. Kathy Matsuo, dated 19 December 2003.

9. Admiral of the Fleet Sir Roger Keyes, *Adventures Ashore and Afloat*, (London, 1939), 143.

10. Admiral Hugh Tweedie, *The Story of a Naval Life*, (London, 1939), 76. The Manchu Ch'ing dynasty: 1644-1911.

11. NA ADM 196/19. *Service Record*.

12. Ibid.

13. Caird Library. Ref: *JRM/14*.

14. Ibid.

15. Archives Centre, Churchill College, Cambridge. Ref: *MCKN 3/10*.

16. Caird Library. Ref: *JRM/16*. Churchill to Jerram, 5 December 1912.

17. NA ADM 125/62. Letter dated 8 April 1913.

18. Edward Buxton **Kiddle**. Born in Gosport: 2 November 1866. Died in Alverstoke: 29 April 1933. Captain: 30 June 1907. At the Battle of Jutland, 31 May 1916, commanded the battleship *Revenge*, 27,500 tons. Commanded the battleship *Marlborough*, 25,000 tons: 1917-1918. Rear Admiral: 28 October 1918. RA 2BS: 1920-1921. Admiral Superintendent, Chatham Dockyard: 1921-1923. Vice Admiral: 19 July 1924. Retired: 1924. KBE: 1926. Admiral on the Retired List: 22 February 1928. *Navy List. Who's Who*.

19. NA ADM 53/23732. Log Book *Minotaur*.

20. I.H. Nish, *The Mariner's Mirror*, Vol. 56, 1970, 414/5.

21. Shiba Ryotaro, *The Last Shogun, The Life of Tokugawa Yoshinobu*, (New York and Tokyo, 2004), 246.

22. Caird Library. Ref: *JRM/15*.

23. Arthur C. Marder, *From the Dreadnought to Scapa Flow*, I, (OUP, 1972), 252.

24. Richard Hough, *Louis and Victoria*, (London, 1974), 259.

25. Caird Library. Ref: *JRM/15*. Winsloe to Jerram, letter dated 1 February 1914. In the event Sir Richard Poore was to see out his full term only being succeeded on 1 January 1915 by Admiral Sir George A. Callaghan. For a further account of the 'Poore affair' see Richard Hough, *Former Naval Person*, (London, 1985), 45-47.

26. Captain Hans Pochhammer, *Before Jutland*, (London, 1931), 16/17.

27. s.s. *Fukoku Maru*, 4,763 grt. In 1895 built at Port Glasgow for British owners as *Langbank*. Her new Japanese owners had registered her at the Manchurian port of Dairen, today Luta. *Lloyd's Register*.

28. Nish. 417/8.

29. Ed. Richard Harding, Adrian Jarvis and Alston Kennerley, *British Ships in China Seas*, (Liverpool, 2004): Eric Grove,

*The Century of the China Station: The Royal Navy in Chinese Waters, 1842-1942,*11.

30. NA ADM 1/8365/7. Letter No. 533.

31. *Nihon Kaigun Koku Shi – History of Japanese Naval Air,* 4, (Tokyo, 1969), 22.
The 'Cuxhaven Raid' by RN air power against that German airship base situated at the mouth of the Elbe only was to take place on 25 December 1914.

32. *His Imperial Japanese Majesty's Ship Wakamiya and Some Developments,* Paper read by the author at the Fourth ICMH, Corfu, June 2004.

33. Ed. Walter Gorlitz, *The Kaiser and His Court,* (London, 1961), 42/3.

34. Mark R. Peattie, *Nan'yo,* (Hawaii, 1992), 42.

35. Ed. Akashi Yoji and Yoshimura Mako, *New Perspectives on the Japanese Occupation in Malaya and Singapore: 1941-1945,* (Singapore, 2008), Chapter One being, Akashi Yoji, *The Nan'yo Kyokai and British Malaya and Singapore, 1915-1945,* 21/22.

36. Ibid. 115, 121, 126.

37. NA ADM 1/8365/7.

38. Hugh Cortazzi and Gordon Daniels, *Britain and Japan: 1859-1991,* (London, 1991), 204. In this volume, chapter sixteen, pages 198-213, Haruko Fukuda describes the life of Admiral Yamanashi Katsunoshin.
Yamanashi Katsunoshin. Born into the Date clan in Sendai, Miyagi Prefecture (ken): 26 July 1877. Died: 17 December 1967. Graduated from Etajima: 1897. As a young officer in 1901/2 served in *Mikasa* during her final year of construction and subsequent delivery voyage from Great Britain. Commander: 1 December 1912. Captain: 1 December 1916. Rear Admiral: 1 December 1921. Vice Admiral: 1 December 1925. Vice Minister of the Navy: 10 December 1928. C. in C., Sasebo: 1 December 1930. C. in C., Kure: 1 December 1931. Admiral: 1 April 1932. Counsellor to H.I.M. The Emperor, Showa Tenno: 1 December 1932. Retired: 11 March 1933. From 1939 and well into post war years to be closely involved with education and the Imperial Family. Prior to WW2 he was one of the group of officers to be saddened by Japan's increasingly militaristic attitudes which were to lead up to the Pacific War. Other such officers included Kato Tomosaburo, Hori Teikichi, Yamamoto Isoroku, Taniguchi Naomi, Sakonji Seizo, Yonai Mitsumasa, Koga Mineichi and Inoue Shigeyoshi. Hiroyuki Agawa, *The Reluctant Admiral: Yamamoto and the Imperial Navy,* (Tokyo and New York, 1979), 29.

39. The fighting top and mast of HMAS *Sydney* today (written in 2005) may be seen prominently situated on a promontory on the North shore of Sydney harbour, Bradley's Head.

40. Caird Library. Ref: *JRM/16/4.* The copy, undated, is titled: 'Copy of a letter from Father to Mother outlining events on the China Station at and after the outbreak of war.'

41. Letter from Brigadier Dudley Ridout and dated 23 September 1915. Caird Library. Ref: *JRM/16.*
Sloop *Cadmus,* 1,070 tons, Commander Hugh D. Marryat. *Navy List.* At the time the Governor of the Straits Settlements was Sir Arthur Henderson Young (1854-1938). *Colonial Office List.*

42. Nish. 421.

43. NA ADM 125/63. Letter dated 14 October 1915.

44. Admiral Viscount Jellicoe of Scapa, *The Grand Fleet, 1914-1916,* (London, 1919), 491.

45. Marder, III, 286.

46. *Dictionary of National Biography.*

47. Lady Wester Wemyss, *The Life and Letters of Lord Wester Wemyss,* (London, 1935), 412. In the same volume, page 427, it may be noted that by the end of April 1919:-
'.. the Jerram Committee had produced a scheme of pay for officers and men on an ample and generous scale, though by no means more than their deserts. The Board had approved – the Cabinet hesitated.'
Not for the first time in history did the First Sea Lord indicate that he would have to resign if the government failed in their duty. Fortunately the Cabinet did not let down the Service and country.

48. *Service Record.*

49. Admiral Sir William Goodenough, *A Rough Record,* (London, 1945), 103.

50. Marder, III, 39.

51. *Dictionary of National Biography.*

52. Ibid.

53. *Service Record.*

54. *The Evening News*, Portsmouth and Southsea, Monday, March 20, 1933.

55. Visited by the author on Thursday, 6 January 2011. On entering the graveyard proceed straight ahead up the path in front of you and their substantial granite gravestone, surmounted by a cross, is to be found some thirty yards up on the left, 'The finger of God touched them and they slept'. With thanks to Ms. Susan Hunt, churchwarden.

28 July 1915 to 20 July 1917
Vice Admiral William Lowther **Grant**

William was born in Southsea, Hants. on 10 November 1864, son of Mr. William Grant, J.P. (1838-1912) of Witley, Surrey, and his wife Sophia (1).

He died at his residence, 'New Barn', West Malling, Kent on Wednesday, 30 January 1929.

On 15 July 1877 new entry Grant, William, joined the Royal Navy in *Britannia*, since March 1869 the training ship moored in the river at Dartmouth. She replaced an earlier *Britannia*, training ship since 1859, first at Portsmouth, then briefly at Portland, but at Dartmouth from 1863. In view of his fine academic achievements to come it is of interest to note that in the examination for Cadet entry he was placed just twenty third out of the successful number of entrants, forty six.

Midshipman: 24 August 1879. Meanwhile for most of the period between 25 July 1879 and 6 April 1880 served in the steam frigate training ship *Newcastle*, 51, Captain Edward Kelly. From 7 April 1880 appointed to armoured iron frigate *Northumberland*, single screw, 10,780 tons, and served in her until September. Then from 9 September 1880 in corvette *Tourmaline*, 12 guns, 2,120 tons, Captain Robert P. Dennistoun, 'Detached Squadron', first to the Mediterranean for the Egyptian War, then to the East Indies. **Sub Lieutenant**: 10 November 1883. Studying in *Excellent*. He passed such a good examination that he received rapid promotion. **Lieutenant**: 10 May 1884. From 2 April 1885 in brig *Nautilus*, 501 tons, tender to *Impregnable*, Training Ship for Boys, Devonport. From 31 October 1885 in turret ship *Monarch*, 8,320 tons, Channel Squadron. From 1 October 1886 in *Vernon*, Torpedo School Ship, Portsmouth, Captain Samuel Long, undergoing a course in torpedoes. From 22 June to 31 August 1888 in the new iron clad turret battleship *Rodney*, 10,300 tons, for the summer manoeuvres. Then from 1 September 1888 to 18 November 1889 returned to *Vernon*, now as a Lieut. (T) instructor. From 19 November 1889 to 29 July 1891 Lieut. (T) in cruiser *Australia*, 5,600 tons, Captain Martin J. Dunlop, Mediterranean. However from the Mediterranean, where he had become ill, on 13 July 1891 he joined the storeship *Humber*, 1,640 tons, to take passage home to hospital, between 30 July and 20 August 1891 being borne in *Victory* on 'full pay leave' (2). From 21 August to 24 March 1892 followed a period on half pay at the rate of six shillings a day.

On 12 January 1892 he married Mabel Emily Brodrick, daughter of Reverend The Hon. Alan Brodrick (1840-1909) and his wife Emily Hester Melvill. Mabel's father, The Rev. Alan, was the youngest son of Rev. William John Brodrick, seventh Viscount Midleton (1798-1870). Rev. Alan's elder brother, also William (1830-1907), was to become the eighth Viscount. On 25 October 1853 he had married Hon. Augusta Mary Fremantle (see C. in C., 1892).

Lady Mabel Grant was to die on 24 December 1956. They had two sons, Alan Lowther born on 12 July 1896, and Richard Brodrick born in 1907, and one daughter, Marjorie Harriet born in 1898. After marrying she was to become Mrs. A.N. Gosselin. His son Alan followed his father into the Navy, being a Midshipman from 15

January 1914, and from that date serving in the battle cruiser *Queen Mary*, 27,000 tons. Later, unfortunately suffering from rheumatic fever, he was invalided out.

Again, between 25 March and 24 August 1892, he returned to *Vernon* as a Staff Officer. From 25 August 1892 Lieut. (T) in *Defiance*, Torpedo School Ship, Devonport. From 12 March 1895 Lieut. (T) in cruiser *Crescent*, 7,700 tons, Captain Francis Powell, Flagship, North America and West Indies Station. The C. in C. was Vice Admiral James E. Erskine, in October 1902 to be promoted Admiral of the Fleet.

While serving in *Crescent* he did have a short period of just over a month from 2 March 1897 in acting command of the third class protected cruiser *Tartar*, 1,770 tons.

Commander: 22 June 1897. Remained in *Crescent* until 15 October 1897 as Commander (T). From 30 November 1897 to 12 February 1899 in *President*, West India Docks, 'For Service in Department of Director of Naval Ordnance'.

Then between 13 February and 8 September 1899 he served in *Trafalgar* during a time of 'special mobilization' and 'summer manoeuvres from 11 July' (3).

Next on 9 September 1899 he took passage out to the Cape to join the cruiser *Doris*, 5,600 tons, Captain Reginald C. Prothero, Flagship, Cape of Good Hope and West Coast of Africa, as Commander in the ship (4). Between 8 June 1898 and 15 April 1901, when he was succeeded by Rear Admiral Arthur W. Moore (see C. in C., 1905), the C. in C. was Rear Admiral Sir Robert H. Harris.

In October the second Boer War of 1899-1902, commenced. On 29 January 1900 two 4.7" guns were landed from *Doris* and under his command they proceeded up to the front in time to participate at Paardeberg and the capture of Boer General Cronje on 27 February. Next they assisted in the capture of Bloemfontein.

> 'Landed in command of a detachment which became known as 'Grant's Guns', operating in the Orange River Colony. Commander Grant was mentioned in Lord Roberts's dispatch of March 31, 1900 and for his arduous and gallant services was promoted to Captain (5).'

The capital of the of the Boer Orange Free State was, and remains, Bloemfontein. The town had surrendered to Lord Roberts on 13 March 1900, hence the reference to the dispatch just mentioned above. Unfortunately the new occupying power neglected the local sanitary arrangements and there the men of the Naval Brigade were to suffer severely from enteric fever, typhoid, with no fewer than eighty nine officers and men being taken ill.

Continuing north into the Transvaal his guns rendered further assistance at the capture of Johannesburg, and then of Pretoria on 5 June 1900.

Subsequently he and his party returned to *Doris* on 6 October 1900 (6).

They had done very well:-

> 'Grant's two 4.7's too, had been in all the actions, and had marched over a thousand miles, once covering 250 miles in fifteen consecutive days. One march of 37 miles was done in thirteen hours. The men were splendid (7).'

In due course, on 27 February 1904 at Devonport Park, a memorial was to be unveiled by the C. in C., Admiral Sir Edward H. Seymour (see C. in C., 1897). Vice Admiral Sir Robert H. Harris also was present. This memorial was in the form of a gun which had been captured from the Boer forces at Paardeberg in February 1900 and was erected in memory of the Officers and Men from *Doris* who had lost their lives during the campaign.

Captain: 21 October 1900.

As indicated above, he was, 'especially promoted for services during the Boer War.'

On his return from Africa he proceeded on leave until 23 June 1901 and then endured a period on half pay, at the rate of twelve shillings and six pence per day, until 5 January 1902.

Between 6 January and 4 May 1902 he attended a course at RNC, Greenwich.

From 5 May to 6 October 1902 in command of the old battleship *Monarch*, 8,845 tons and first commissioned at Chatham in May 1869, Port Guard Ship, Cape of Good Hope.

Under the auspices of the Colonial Defence Committee, served as Naval Adviser to the Inspector-General of Fortifications, Army Council: 7 October 1902 – 18 November 1904.

From 19 November 1904 in command cruiser *Sutlej*, 12,000 tons, China. Then the C. in C. was Vice Admiral Sir Gerard Noel. At the end of the commission, while on passage home, from Gibraltar he was given the task of escorting the two small Torpedo Boat Destroyers, *Myrmidon*, 356 tons, and *Bat*, 447 tons, back to England. These ships had a limited steaming range, especially if sea conditions were poor, therefore after leaving Gibraltar on Monday, 16 April 1906 it proved necessary to call first at Peniche, a small fishing village some ninety kilometres north of Lisbon, and then at Ferrol in N.W. Spain. Next the ships coaled in West Brittany at Douarnenez Bay and finally reached Plymouth at 1725 on Friday, 27 April, a somewhat tedious voyage of eleven days. From Plymouth on 28 April *Sutlej* herself steamed on to Portsmouth and then between 10 and 11 May on to Chatham Basin where eventually she paid off on Monday, 14 May 1906 (8).

From 15 May 1906 in cruiser *Hawke*, 7,350 tons, In Reserve, Chatham.

From 14 January 1907 – 3 June 1908 in command battleship *Cornwallis*, 14,000 tons, Atlantic Fleet. During the first five months of 1908 she underwent a refit at Gibraltar.

Assistant to Director of Naval Intelligence: 25 June 1908 – 19 December 1909. For a part of this time the Director was Rear Admiral Edmond Slade.

From 12 September 1908 appointed ADC to H.M. The King.

Rear Admiral: 26 October 1909.

Between 20 December 1909 and 8 August 1910 on half pay.

From 9 August 1910 borne in battleship *Bulwark*, 15,000 tons, Home Fleet, but Flag flown ashore at Sheerness, 'Rear Admiral for Special Service with Vice Admiral commanding Third and Fourth Divisions, Home Fleet.'

CB: 19 June 1911.

With tension in Europe increasing rapidly it seems odd that from 28 October 1911 to 12 July 1914 followed another period on half pay at the rate of twenty five shillings a day.

RA, 6CS: 13 July 1914, with Flag briefly in *Good Hope*, then from 27 July in *Drake*, 14,100 tons. Great Britain's involvement in the Great War commenced on 4 August 1914. A leading authority has written:-

> 'Rear Admiral William L. Grant, a mediocrity, in the sense of a man of middling ability, commanded the Sixth Cruiser Squadron, which was intended for the Grand Fleet but was soon scattered in all directions for commerce protection.
> His appointment made no sense (9).'

RA, 3CS: 13 March 1915 to 27 July 1915 with Flag in *Antrim*, 10,850 tons.

Vice Admiral: 15 July 1915.

His predecessor having requested a more active wartime role in home waters, from 28 July 1915 he was appointed C. in C., China and took passage to the East.

Writing to the Admiralty on 14 October 1915 he duly reported that at Singapore his flag had been hoisted on 24 September. In the same letter he touched on a variety of subjects including German efforts to create political trouble in India, and also their efforts at gun running. In addition there arose the question of illegal shipments of strategic commodities such as rubber taking place, mentioning shipments to Amsterdam in 'neutral' Holland (10).

The matter of shipments through Holland was serious. From the diaries kept by the Chief of the German Naval Cabinet, Admiral Georg Alexander von Muller (1854-1940), an entry dated 23 January 1916, reads:-

> '... statistically it was difficult to estimate the imports to date, and he assessed the daily amount of goods taken from Holland to be valued at five million marks (11).'

In 1916 the rate of exchange was approximately DM5.5 to USD1.00 therefore that daily rate amounted to some US\$ 331,818,170 per annum, a most appreciable trade, the more so in that era when money still held some value.

Meanwhile in Tokyo on 25 October 1915 Dr. Sun Yat-sen married Soong Ching-ling (1893-1981), his second wife. As was the custom in many instances during the era, his first, to Lu Muzhen, had been an arranged marriage.

Ching-ling's eldest sister, Soong Ai-ling, married K'ung Hsiang-hsi, or H.H. Kung (1881-1967), an extremely wealthy banker and politician. Her youngest, Soong May-ling, in Shanghai on 1 December 1927 married General Chiang Kai-shek.

Throughout the remainder of his term of office in the Far East much of the considerable correspondence with London was concerned with the subjects of illegal trade with the enemy, real and possibly imagined enemy shipping movements, and, certainly, German inspired rebel activity in India, Burma and Malaya, the latter supported by local dissident movements (12).

Although the wartime headquarters were at Singapore there also was a base ship at Hong Kong being the sloop *Rosario*, 980 tons.

6 June 1916. From uraemia, the death in Peking of Yuan Shih-kai, political rival of Dr. Sun Yat-sen and self proclaimed founder of a new but extremely short lived Chinese Imperial line.

At Penang in June 1916 he met Rear Admiral Sir Rosslyn Erskine Wemyss (1864-1933), C. in C., East Indies and Egypt Station, and a future First Sea Lord, for discussions.

To keep this appointment he and his staff embarked in the armed merchant cruiser *Laurentic*, 14,892 grt, Captain Victor G. Gurner, at Singapore at 2.15 p.m. on Monday, 19 June 1916, weighed ten minutes later, and arrived at Penang the following afternoon at 3.38 p.m. In the armoured cruiser *Euryalus*, 12,000 tons, Rear Admiral Wemyss arrived the following morning, Wednesday, 21 June, at 0605 hours.

Meetings and discussions complete, both ships weighed early on the Saturday morning, 24 June, *Euryalus* to return to Colombo and Egypt, and *Laurentic* to Singapore where he arrived and disembarked at 16:00 the following afternoon, Sunday, 25 June 1916 (13).

In a subsequent letter to his wife Admiral Wemyss has left a short account of his visit to Penang:-

> 'We have had great talks and the meeting has been of great mutual benefit. It has been a pleasant meeting, for he (Grant) is a nice creature, and it is amusing talking of old times; moreover, he was in the North Sea until nine months ago and has been able to relate much to me. I am delighted at having been able to visit this place. I am surprised at the prosperity, even wealth. Tin, rubber and coco-nuts are no doubt as desirable commodities as any place may wish for (14).'

Naturally with the German Asiatic Squadron disposed of he was left with only a small Allied fleet under his overall command. Patrol duties were their prinicipal function. From the following example, the disposition of his ships on 31 August 1916, the general situation may be appreciated:-

'*Diana*   RN. Cruiser, 5,600 tons, Captain George B. Hutton.
            Left Singapore 30 August to patrol off Bangkok first then South Cambodia, to examine especially traffic between South China and Siam ports.

Cornwall RN. Cruiser, 9,800 tons, Captain Walter M. Ellerton.
            Cruising in Java Sea. While at Singapore her picket boat patrolled Singapore Strait to examine all traffic passing through without calling at Singapore. Nothing of importance was found, but examination will be repeated shortly.

City of London   British Armed Merchant Cruiser, 8,956 grt, Captain George M. Keane.
            At Singapore.

Psyche	RAN. Light cruiser, 2,135 tons, Commander Henry J. Feakes.
	After patrolling off Swatow on Manila and Bangkok routes, returned to Hong Kong for replenishment and is now patrolling the approaches to Swatow from Shanghai and Japan. She will continue on this service for the present, calling at Hong Kong when necessary and sending ships there for examination of mails etc.
Fame	RN. Torpedo Boat Destroyer, 340 tons.
	Arrived Singapore 27 August from patrolling north of Banka Straits.

Cadmus	RN. Sloop, 1,070 tons, Commander Hugh D. Marryat.
Fantome	RAN. Sloop, 1,070 tons, Commander Lewis T. Jones.
Warrego	RAN. Torpedo Boat Destroyer, 700 tons, Commander Arthur G.H. Bond.
Huon	RAN. Torpedo Boat Destroyer, 700 tons, Lieut. Commander Charles F. Stow.
	These four ships were occupied, "cruising from Sandakan as base, on trade routes etc., especially Sibutu and Palawan passages."

Torrens	RAN. Torpedo Boat Destroyer, 700 tons
Swan	RAN. Torpedo Boat Destroyer, 700 tons.
	These two ships left Sydney 28 August for Sandakan, calling at Cairns and Thursday Island and due Sandakan 12 September. On their arrival *Warrego* will exchange Commanding Officer with *Swan* and then return to Australia.

Tone	IJN. Cruiser, 4,100 tons. Flagship of Vice Admiral Nomaguchi Tadashiro.
	Singapore.
Niitaka	IJN. Cruiser, 3,370 tons.
	Colombo.
Tsushima	IJN. Cruiser, 3,370 tons. Sister ship to *Niitaka*.
	Penang.
Akashi	IJN. Cruiser, 2,760 tons.
	Sandakan.

Sugi	IJN. All destroyer sister ships of the *Kaba* class, 665 tons.
Matsu	Several of this class were to serve in the Mediterranean in 1917-1918,
Kashiwa	and a further twelve were built in 1917 for the French Navy, the first warships
Sakaki	built in Japan for a European navy. Engaged in the 'Brothers' Patrol and Malacca Straits (15).'

KCB: 1 January 1917.

By now in European waters the German U-boat campaign was proving to be most effective. The Allies desired any and all assistance to meet this threat. Consequently, and after much negotiation, under the command of Rear Admiral Sato Kozo (1871-1948), with his flag in the light cruiser *Akashi,* 2,750 tons, it is recorded that:-

> 'In 1917 the Japanese navy dispatched to the Mediterranean a fleet consisting of two cruisers, one seaplane ship, and 12 destroyers to co-operate with the allies in dealing with German submarines. This was undertaken after assurances from the allies that they would support Japanese claims to the former German interests in East Asia and the Pacific at a future peace conference (16).'

This IJN Second Special Service Squadron left Singapore on 11 March 1917 and, via Colombo, Aden and Port Said, arrived at Malta on 16 April. Quickly they earned for themselves an excellent reputation. Warships of the Squadron carried out a great number of convoy escort duties, their only near loss being on 11 June 1917 off Cerigo island (Kithira) when the destroyer *Sakaki* was torpedoed and badly damaged by the Austro-Hungarian *U-27.* Fortunately she could be beached at Suda Bay in Crete and subsequently was salved.

Bearing in mind this IJN experience in the Mediterranean during WW1, but looking ahead to the Pacific War of 1941-1945, the following fact has been noted:-

'Thus, the important principles of the convoy system and the lessons of anti-submarine warfare, learned at the cost of much strenuous effort by a handful of Japanese officers and men on a distant station, were quickly forgotten. This oversight undoubtedly played some part in the disastrous failure of the Japanese navy to develop an effective counter to the ravages of American submarines in the Pacific War (17).'

His successor in command of the Station, Admiral Tudor and his staff, arrived at Singapore on 2 October 1917 and he himself arranged to leave the island, 'by the first opportunity about 10 October, via Hong Kong, Japan and Canada (18).'

Officially his term of office on the China Station came to an end on 25 October 1917. Between 26 October and 7 December 1917 he was on passage returning to England (19).

In succession to Vice Admiral Sir Montague Browning (1863-1947) served as C. in C., North America and West Indies: 7 January 1918 – 9 February 1919. In those waters for a part of the time he flew his Flag in the cruiser *Highflyer*, 5,600 tons.

Admiral: 1 September 1918.

During the latter part of 1918 he worked with the Canadians in securing assistance from the U.S.N. in the provision of additional patrol craft.

In February 1919 he was succeeded in command of the station by Vice Admiral Sir Morgan Singer (1864-1938) and on 17 February he returned to England having taken passage from American waters with his flag in the sloop/survey ship *Mutine*, 980 tons (20).

On two occasions later in 1919 he was appointed to *President* for very short periods of 'special service'.

Retired: 24 March 1920 (21).

On 18 August 1920 in Wellington, New Zealand, the Board of Trustees to administer the 'Flock House' fund were appointed. This was a post Great War scheme for helping the children of British Seamen who had died in the conflict. The Admiral was appointed to represent the Royal Navy on the London Advisory Committee of this unusual body.

Rear Admiral William Sowden Sims, USN (1858-1936), who during the Great War had commanded U.S. Naval forces in European waters, visited Europe in 1921. At the time he was serving as President of the Naval War College, Newport, Rhode Island. On 15 June he left London to return to New York. The Admiral was one of those who saw him off:-

'A large crowd of friends assembled at Waterloo Station this morning to bid farewell to Admiral and Mrs. William S. Sims as they left to embark on the liner *Olympic* at Southampton (22).'

As has been mentioned in retirement he resided at West Malling in Kent where, on 22 October 1925, he was appointed a Justice of the Peace for the Malling Division. In addition at various times he was chairman of the West Malling conservative association and vice president of the local branch of the British Legion. Other interests included the Amateur Operatic Society, and the Kent County Opthalmic and Aural Hospital at Maidstone (23).

Following his death on 30 January 1929, his funeral took place in the Parish Church at West Malling. Unfortunately his wife was indisposed so was unable to attend. However among the mourners were the C. in C., The Nore, Admiral Sir Edwyn Sinclair (see C. in C., 1925), also Admiral Sir William Goodenough, and the Earl of Midleton (24).

NOTES

1. NA ADM 196/20. *Service Record.*

2. Ibid.

3. Ibid.

4. Reginald Charles Prothero. To take passage out to the Cape to join the ship Captain Prothero had travelled in the Union liner *Norman*, 7,537 tons. Also taking passage in the ship was a future Admiral of the Fleet, then Cadet Andrew B. Cunningham, who has left an amusing account of one aspect of this voyage from Southampton on 21 May 1898:-

    'All through this voyage, though we did not realize it, we were under the steely eye of Captain Prothero.

    He was a most intimidating man, nearly six feet tall and immensely broad, with a heavy jet black beard.

    We heard later he was known as "Prothero the Bad",

    Admiral of the Fleet Viscount Cunningham of Hyndhope, *A Sailor's Odyssey*, (London, 1951), 18/19.

5. Obituary, *The Times*, Thursday, January 31, 1929.

6. *Service Record.*

7. *A Sailor's Odyssey*, (London, 1951), 30.

8. NA ADM 53/27127. Log Book *Sutlej*.

9. Arthur J. Marder, *From the Dreadnought to Scapa Flow*, II, (OUP, 1966), 13/4.

10. NA ADM 125/63. General Letter No. 1.

11. Ed. Walter Gorlitz, *The Kaiser and His Court*, (London, 1961), 128.

12. NA ADM 125/65.

13. NA ADM 53/46292: log book *Laurentic*. In peace time owned and operated by the White Star Line. Entered service with them on the Canada run in 1908. On 25 January 1917 to be mined and sunk off Malin Head, North Ireland. NA ADM 53/41220: log book *Euryalus*.

14. Lady Wester Wemyss, *The Life and Letters of Lord Wester Wemyss*, (London, 1935), 310.

15. NA ADM 125/64. *Navy List.* Jentschura, Jung and Mickel, *Warships of the Imperial Japanese Navy, 1869-1945*, (London, 1977).

16. Tsuzuki Chushichi, *The Pursuit of Power in Modern Japan, 1825-1995*, (OUP, 2000), 188. Rear Admiral **Sato** Kozo. Born: 15 May 1871. Died: 23 March 1948. Vice Admiral: 1 December 1920. Retired in 1938.

17. David C. Evans and Mark R. Peattie, *Kaigun*, (Annapolis, 1997), 169. The authors quote Nomura Minoru, *Kaisenshi ni manabu*, 138-166.

18. *Service Record.*

19. NA ADM 137/717. Letter No. 434, written from Singapore on 4 October 1917.

20. *Service Record.*

21. Ibid.

22. *New York Times* 16 June 1921. The White Star s.s. *Olympic*, 46,439 grt.

23. Obituary notice: *Kent Messenger*, Saturday, 2 February 1929.

24. Ibid. Saturday, 9 February 1929.

20 July 1917 to 24 July 1919

Acting Vice Admiral Frederick Charles Tudor

Tudor

Born to Harrington Rogers Jones, Admiral's secretary, and Henrietta Augusta, nee Tudor at 7 Napier Street, Stoke Damerel, Devon on 29 March 1863 (1).

He died at 'Dennistoun', Park Road, Camberley on Sunday, 14 April 1946.

As Frederick C.T. Jones he entered the Royal Navy as a **Cadet**: 15 January 1876.

Midshipman: 21 December 1877. From 10 January 1878 in iron screw frigate, sheathed with wood, *Raleigh*, 5,200 tons, Captain Charles T. Jago, Mediterranean. The ship was present during operations early in 1878 to aid the Turks against the Russians before Constantinople. Following the Cyprus Convention of 4 June 1878 also she was present at Kyrenia at the time of the Turks handing over the administration of the island to Great Britain (2). Thereafter:-

> 'End 1879: *Raleigh* ordered home, refitted for Australia with relief crews, went out via the Cape of Good Hope and entered Sydney harbour in June 1880 as the largest man of war that had ever visited Australia. Returning via Cape Horn *Raleigh* paid off (at Devonport): 8 January 1881 (3).'

Next he served for a few months in *Northumberland*, Channel Fleet. Then from 27 July 1881 in the iron plated armoured ship *Nelson*, 7,320 tons, Captain James Elphinstone Erskine, Australia Station. She sailed from Devonport on 1 October 1881, via the Cape to arrive at Sydney on 1 January 1882. There Captain Erskine (1838-1911), in due course to become an Admiral of the Fleet, acted as Commodore of the Station. **Sub Lieutenant**: 29 March 1882. From that date in sloop *Cormorant*, 1,130 tons, Acting Commander Thomas E. Maxwell, 'On Passage Home to Portsmouth'. She sailed from Australia on 13 April 1882, via Cape Horn, to arrive at Plymouth in September. In this manner he completed his second circumnavigation. From October 1882 to December 1883 studying at RNC, Greenwich, and attending courses in *Excellent* and *Vernon*, obtaining four First Class certificates and one second (4). **Lieutenant**: 29 March 1884. From 1 April 1884 Lieut. (N) in sloop *Liberty*, 447 tons, tender to *Lion*, 'Training Ship for Boys', Devonport. From 16 September 1884 Lieut. (N) in gunboat *Zephyr*, 438 tons and only 125' loa, China. In due course and having been ordered home, early in August 1886 he left China on passage, arriving in England on 3 September. From 30 September 1886 in *Excellent*, Gunnery Ship, Portsmouth, 'Qualifying for Gunnery Officer'. Passed first in his batch and awarded the Gunnery Prize (5). From 24 August 1888 continued in *Excellent* as Lieut. (G) on the Staff. From 7 November 1889 Lieut. (G) in battleship *Collingwood*, 9,500 tons, Captain Charles C.P. Fitzgerald, Mediterranean. With, on 26 December 1890, his surname altered to Tudor, from 31 July 1891 served in cruiser *Shannon*, 5,390 tons, Captain Arthur

E. Dupuis, Coast Guard Service, Bantry. From 22 February 1892 Lieut. and Commander (G) in *Kite*, 254 tons, tender to *Excellent*, Portsmouth.

'Held this appointment for two years which were contemporaneous with the great change over to QF (quick firing) guns and the modern type of hydraulic mounting (6).'

Vice Admiral Fredrick Charles Tudor Tudor, C. in C., 1917

From 5 January 1894 Lieut. (G), 'Senior Staff Officer' in *Excellent*. From 1 January 1896 Lieut. in *President*, West India Docks, 'For Service in Department of Director of Naval Ordnance.'

Commander: 31 December 1896. Remained in the Department of Naval Ordnance. From 10 May 1898 to May 1901 commissioned then served in the new battleship *Hannibal*, 14,900 tons, Captain Sir Baldwin W. Walker, Bart., Channel Squadron, and one of nine battleships of the *Majestic* class, the most numerous class ever built (7).

From 28 February 1902 to 12 January 1903 in command cruiser *Prometheus*, 2,135 tons, Channel Squadron.

Captain: 31 December 1902.

From 30 September 1903 to *President* to attend 'War Course' which was completed on 30 January 1904 and for which he obtained a '1st Class'. Thereafter he attended short courses covering Signals, Senior Officers' Gunnery, and Senior Officers' Tactical (8).

From 3 May 1904 to 22 March 1906 in command cruiser *Challenger*, 5,800 tons, Australia Station.

'On arrival in Fremantle was ordered to recruit Australians, New Zealanders and Tasmanians to train them to replace Imperial Ship's Company. Was relieved in May 1906 having replaced 240 of the original Ship's Company (9).'

From 24 September 1906: Assistant Director of Naval Ordnance. Up until September 1908 the Director was Captain, later Rear Admiral John R. Jellicoe, during that month to be succeeded by Captain Reginald H.S. Bacon (1863-1947). Of that appointment in due course in his memoirs Bacon was to write:-

'In the gunnery division I had a most excellent assistant DNO in Captain F.C.T. Tudor, who relieved me of the majority of the work in connection with the gunnery exercises and gunnery schools (10).'

From 22 May 1909 in command of the new battleship *Superb*, 18,600 tons, ten x 12" and sixteen x 4" guns, Home Fleet. She commissioned at Portsmouth on 29 May 1909.

In succession to Captain Reginald Tupper, from 16 August 1910 to 29 May 1912 in command *Excellent*, Gunnery School, Portsmouth.

From 12 June 1912 Director of Naval Ordnance and Torpedoes.

Rear Admiral: 25 January 1913.
Continued as Director of Naval Ordnance and Torpedoes until August 1914.
CB: 3 June 1913.

At Beaconsfield, Buckinghamsire on 12 June 1913 he married Henrietta Isabella, 'Netta', nee Dinnis, widow of Admiral Robert William Craigie who had died on 21 August 1911.

A Lord Commissioner of the Admiralty being Third Sea Lord and Controller of the Navy: 11 August 1914 – 1 June 1917, '.... thus he was responsible for all the materiel of the Navy in the first part of that War (11).'

Considering this, and his preceding appointment as Director of Naval Ordnance, an observer might be forgiven for inquiring if it was he who ultimately was responsible, in the early years of WW1, for the wretched tendency of British naval shells to break up on the occasions when they struck armoured enemy warships at an oblique angle.

In addition to much other work, certainly one task was undertaken with results which were outstanding and to be far reaching. As may be seen from the relevant 'Tudor' records held at King's College, it is clear that on the subject of 'Development of the Tank', it was the Navy, specifically the department of the Director of Naval Construction, Eustace H.T. D'Eyncourt (1868-1951), who was responsible for the successful creation of the first 'Land Ship'. Extracts follow, taken from notes prepared by Sir Eustace on 18 September 1916:-

'Page 3. At this stage the big wheel type was entirely abandoned and it was approved in June 1915 that I should complete one caterpillar machine for trial.
Page 5. By 12 February 1916 (following satisfactory trials of the one machine contributed by the Royal Navy) the Ministry of Munitions authorised the construction of 100 tanks.
Page 6. From the above it is clear that the Admiralty committee was alone responsible for the design and construction of the first complete machine, which was the exact model for all the tanks subsequently constructed.'
The notes conclude with an appropriate annotation by the Third Sea Lord:
'Concur that this correctly represents the history of the initiation and construction of the tanks.
F.C.T.T. 18.9.16 (12).'

As might be expected his duties also brought him in touch with that new arm of Naval warfare, the air. For example during August and September 1915, Admirals Beatty and Hood had been working to develop the idea of balloon operating vessels being used with the fleet in the North Sea, in part to counter the perceived German advantage in their use of zeppelins for reconnaissance purposes. At that time the Admiralty felt that there were other priorities in making available, and then having to modify, a suitably fast ship. As it so happened in due course the old Cunard liner *Campania*, taken up for war service, was to be modified to fill this role, in part. In the interim, although his suggestion was not to be taken up, he had put forward a proposal:-

'... Rear Admiral Frederick Tudor, the Third Sea Lord, had advanced a compromise proposition

– that the existing balloon ships be used as depot vessels to supply balloons to light cruisers (13).'

From late in May 1917 as Controller of the Navy he was succeeded by the forty one year old Sir Eric Geddes, a successful railway operator, and, from 17 July 1917, to succeed Sir Edward Carson as First Lord. Rear Admiral Lionel Halsey assumed his duties as Third Sea Lord.

Thus, after five years at Whitehall, Tudor returned to sea as C. in C., China.

As the late Professor Marder makes clear these changes, and others, were instigated by Prime Minister Lloyd George (1863-1945) (14). Fortunately the informed and sensible opinions of Sir Maurice Hankey (1877-1963) can be seen behind the scene, especially as regards coping with the submarine menace (15).

On 20 July 1917, having been appointed C. in C., China Station, and as an acting Vice Admiral, he proceeded to the Far East and at Singapore his flag was hoisted on 4 October 1917 (16). As with his predecessor, at least initially, he was to fly his Flag ashore.

Between 22 May 1917 and 7 December 1918 the C. in C., Asiatic Fleet was Admiral Austin Melvin Knight, USN (1854-1927). Amongst other duties naturally he was to direct U.S. naval operations during the Russian civil war when the Allies intervened at Vladivostok. His flagship was the armoured cruiser *Brooklyn* CA-3, 9,215 tons.

Vice Admiral: 23 October 1917.

KCMG: 1 January 1918. This appointment was made for services as C. in C., China Station however the actual investiture was only to take place, 'at Buckingham Palace on 22.4.20 (17).'

Following the Russian revolution of 1917 then from June 1918 onwards Allied troops, primarily Japanese, occupied Vladivostok. These forces were not to be withdrawn until the departure of the last of the Japanese troops on 25 October 1922, thereafter the Bolsheviks assuming authority.

The Great War, WW1, ended on 11 November 1918.

On 6 April 1919, and included as just one example of the extraordinary adventures which took place during those chaotic times during the Russian civil war, the departure of a Naval Party, Captain Thomas H. Jameson, RMLI, westward from Vladivostok on their journey of 4,350 miles to Perm on the River Kama, just west of the Ural range. There assistance was given to White Russian forces in their conflict with the Bolsheviks (18).

Meanwhile the C. in C. was much involved with other post Great War activity. Extracts taken from his letter of 9 January 1919, written from Singapore and addressed to the Admiralty, will serve to elaborate.

'Anamba Islands Base for Minesweepers. In conjunction with the Dutch, as usual with the supply of coal for use by minesweepers being a great consideration. The question of using volunteers or non-volunteers for this purpose was complex.

Various changes to the composition of the Squadron bearing in mind, 'complicated arrangements for demobilisation and reorganisatin of Fleet'.

Austro-Hungarian Ships. 'It is desireable that the allocation of the ships among the Allied nations should be made as early as possible and the nations concerned should then be fully responsible for getting vessels ready for sea.'

Three submarines at Hong Kong to be scrapped.

IJN. After consultation the Japanese Navy Department, 'agreed that the 1ˢᵗ Detached Squadron should leave Singapore on 31 January, leaving one cruiser and the four destroyers behind to continue minesweeping…'.

Affairs on the Yangtse. 'News of the Armistice was received here (by the SNO, presumably in Shanghai) on the night of 11 November. This news has caused a considerable change among the Chinese who are now outwardly most enthusiastic Allies and are very anxious to make peace in their own country. (-) I think now that there is every prospect of peace in Europe shortly, that the trouble in China will be greatly reduced, and that peace will be patched up between the North and South. I cannot say that I anticipate a lasting peace or much improvement in the Government, but do not expect any further trouble on the Yangtse for some time, except on the Upper River…'

Canton and the West River. 'The political situation in the South was in its usual chaotic state up to the receipt of the news of the European Armistice.' Other developments consisted of the validity or otherwise of the credentials in respect of the delegate from the Southern Government, as distinct from the country of China, to the Versailles Peace Conference .

China Coast Ports Visited. *Cadmus*, Commander Ronald H. Hilliard, had visited seven such ports, 'her visit cannot but have beneficial results and in some cases these ports have not been visited by one of HM Ships since the commencement of War.'

German Ships in Dutch East Indies (The Netherlands were neutral in WW1). The Admiralty required answers to four questions concerning each such ship. These were:-

a. General state of readiness for sea.

b. Do they require docking, coal or stores.

c. Number and nationality of crews.

d. Authority handling ship's business in port.

As far as was known 17 such ships were involved but the Dutch already had taken a number into their service (19)'.

In view of the trouble which he was to assist in causing in China from June 1921 onwards (see C. in C., 1919), the following is of interest. Together with his report to the Admiralty dated 23 January 1919, the C. in C. enclosed a letter dated 1 January which he had received from Mr. J.V.A. Ruston, British Consul in Batavia. In this Mr. Ruston told of an Islamic uprising at Semarang (north coast, central Java), and discussed some of the activities of the Javanese Revolutionary Party, mentioning Sneevliet (later also to be known as Maring) by name as a socialist (20).

Actually Hendricus Sneevliet (1883-1942) already had been deported by the Dutch in 1917. At the time of the C. in C.'s letter he will have been close to joining Comintern. Clearly though the effect of his subversive work in Java had lingered on.

On the relevant file the Director of Naval Intelligence in London, Captain William M. James, added his comments. Dated 7 March 1919, these include the following:-

'The state of unrest in the NEI (Netherlands East Indies) is chronic. It is largely due to weak and
· bad Dutch administration. (-) The progress of events requires watching because owing to its strong Islamic complexion unrest may spread to British Dominions or Protectorates.'

From Singapore on 30 January 1919 the C. in C. made a reference to another sad result of the Russian Revolution, briefly mentioned above, '…. evacuation of 3,000 sick and wounded Czechoslovaks from Western Siberia'.

This matter of refugees and evacuees, an effect of the Russian civil war, was to remain a problem for three more years. By then, White Russians themselves, the majority as stateless persons, were to arrive in Shanghai in considerable numbers.

The centenary of Singapore was celebrated on 6 February 1919. Following the Great War the city was enjoying a period of 'unexampled commercial prosperity', the population stood at more than 300,000, and her total value of trade was Straits $1,000 million.

Early in February 1919 he transferred the China Station headquarters back from Singapore to Hong Kong. In addition to the above his letter to the Admiralty, No. 173 dated 31 March 1919, mentions a number of other matters. These included IJN spying activity and intelligence gathering at Amoy, '.. the officers from these destroyers had landed in plain clothes and distributed themselves over the island of Kulangsu (the international settlement) making sketches and photos of beaches and other objects as if for a Naval intelligence report.'

Just down the China coast at Swatow the situation was quiet. Nevertheless many unfortunate Chinese suffered, a sad state of deja vu:-

'The Southern Authorities continue to allow extortion to be practiced by their Water Police and other minor Officials, and this evil is growing worse. Piracy of native junks along the coast is also frequent, so much so that many native junks are flying Japanese flags in the hopes of evading this plague (21).'

In the interior again the unfortunate people suffered:-

'The Province of Hunan (in which is situated Tung Ting Lake, south of the Yangtse) has been quiet for the last month or two but the Northern soldiers, especially the 7th Division, have been behaving very badly and looting and terrorising the inhabitants.'

As anticipated by the SNO in January 1919, conditions could be lively on the Upper River:-

'The river is generally quiet and travelling from Ichang to Chungking is once more fairly safe although there are still a good many brigand bands about, but there (they) are always fairly prevalent in Szechuan (Chungking being the inland port of Szechuan Province, 1352 nautical miles from the sea) (22).'

As may be seen below the C. in C. himself shortly was to have first hand experience of this brigand activity.

At Shanghai in February 1919 'The Bureau of Repatriation of Enemy Subjects' was established. Of the two senior Chinese officials active in the Bureau one, 'appeared to be very pro-British and also to be very keen on the repatriation scheme, and a straight forward, honest Chinaman'. Of the other, '.. but he is greatly handicapped by General Lu who is pro-German, is reported to accept bribes, and is generally a stumbling block to the whole scheme'.

Fortunately for him on a day to day basis the C. in C. was not directly involved in the activity of this Bureau.

The C. in C. was under no illusions concerning a well known trait of Chinese officialdom in that era. This comment relates to railway construction:-

'.... the other one was originally started by the Chinese about 1910, but made little progress owing to lack of knowledge and the "squeezing" of the funds (23).'

Much work was being undertaken to improve navigation on the Yangtse. While hoping that Great Britain might participate in such a business also he held an interesting point of view, maybe somewhat in advance of his time:-

'A British survey of the river, control of navigation aids, and if possible, conservancy, would do much to revise (revive) our prestige and help towards regaining our sphere of influence on the Yangtse, if spheres in China are not out of date (24).'

As may be seen from the following example, with much justification Chinese military discipline could be severe. In February 1919 on the West River HBM's Vice Consul at Wuchow was assaulted by some unruly soldiers. The British Consul-General was brought up from Canton in the gunboat *Moorhen*, Lieutenant A.K. Watson, RNR. Together with local Chinese officials the affair was investigated and he:-

'.... obtained complete satisfaction for the assault which was committed by a Chinese Sergeant who called to his assistance some soldiers; this Sergeant has been executed; the death punishment of the remaining soldiers having been commuted to extreme imprisonment; ten thousand dollars have been paid to the Consul and the Consular Constable; a written and personal apology has been made... (25).'

Happily by the time of this report the minesweeping activity in the vicinity of the Anamba Islands had been brought to a satisfactory conclusion by acting Commander P.G. Russell, RN.

Finally his letter ended with the news that:-

'The services of s.s. *Hang Sang* as a Station Collier will be finished when the Admiralty stock has been brought from Penang to Hong Kong (26).'

At the end of March 1919 Sir Frederick again touched on the matter of the repatriation of German citizens, clearly a subject which occupied much of his time if not his direct involvement.

Also he mentioned his need to visit the Yangtse which, '.. was last visited by the C. in C. of the China Station in 1907.' In fact, as seen above, in the interim Admiral Lambton had steamed well up the Yangtse so he must be making reference to the last visit to Chungking, that made by Vice Admiral Moore between 11 and 13 October 1907.

The fears he had expressed just a short while previously were completely justified as lasting peace in China certainly was not a feature of life on the Station. 'The situation at Foochow was quiet and no further fighting has been reported between the Northern and Southern forces in (the Province of) Fukien.' He must have wondered for how long that state of affairs would endure.

Additionally and naturally the civil war situation in Russia required close attention. In that connection in April he mentioned that Canadian troops under Major General J.H. Elmsley, who had gone ashore in Russia at Gornostai, had commenced to leave from Vladivostok on 21 April 1919. By 5 June they had completed their embarkation in the Canadian Pacific steamer *Monteagle*, 5,468 grt, and sailed for home (27).

At Kobe in April 1919 there took place the founding of Kawasaki Kisen Kaisha, the organisation to be better known today as the Japanese merchant shipping company, 'K' Line. By the beginning of WW2 they were to own thirty six ships.

As will be seen, prior to the outbreak of the Pacific War in December 1941 their motorship *Kamikawa Maru*, 6,853 grt, built in 1937 for service on their prestigious New York route, was to be taken up for war service in the IJN.

From Hong Kong on 17 April 1919 the C. in C. addressed a private letter to Mr Walter Hume Long (1854-1924), since January that year the new First Lord in succession to Sir Eric Geddes. He had heard that his successor, due out later in the year, was to have as his flagship a cruiser, *Hawkins*. Sir Frederick made a case, particularly valid in that era when prestige counted for much, requesting that if at all possible such a ship could be made available to him, '.. to move about the Station in as soon as possible after the Armistice was concluded'. He was especially concerned with relations with Japan:-

'.... both Lady Tudor and I have done everything in our power to improve relations – none too good out here – with the Japanese generally.

Both they (the IJN) and I have looked forward to the time when my Flagship would arrive to enable me to visit them this autumn in Japan with – I had hoped – a Fleet.'

Alas it was not to be. On 8 June 1919 Mr. Long replied in a letter expressing great appreciation for, 'the splendid work that you have done in very difficult circumstances,' but, concerning the possibility of sending a suitable flagship East, at the same time making it clear that, 'I am sorry to say it is absolutely impossible (28),'

4 May 1919. Once terms of the Treaty of Versailles became known riots occurred in Peking as Japan was to be awarded the previous German concession in Shantung centred upon Tsingtao. There was considerable student involvement in this, 'The May Fourth Movement', a fact taken advantage of by Dr. Sun in an effort to broaden the appeal of his party.

Also the Movement:-
'... added new impetus to the growing nationalist fervour in China. The British Minister to China, Sir John Jordan, was sufficiently impressed to write, "This is the first time in China's history that public opinion has been fully stirred and the consciousness of its strength has been fully realised". Japan's aggressive actions also subjected her trade to the full strength of the Chinese boycott, a traditional Chinese weapon used by guilds, merchants, and peasants in previous centuries. The effect of the 1919 boycott was described by Jordan as "devastating", with Japan's export trade being reduced from roughly four million pounds per month to one million (29).'

At Ichang on Monday, 26 May 1919, accompanied by his staff, he shifted his Flag from *Kinsha* to *Widgeon*. *Widgeon*, Commander Edward G. de S. Jukes-Hughes, weighed at 0435 on Tuesday, 27 May 1919 and, with overnight stops, proceeded up through the Gorges to Chungking where she arrived at 12:40 on Friday, 30 May 1919. His business complete, on Tuesday 3 June 1919 she weighed and returned downstream with an overnight stop at Wanhsien. On the next day:-
'Wednesday, 4 June 1919
05:10   Weighed and proceeded downstream.
10:00   Wushan – under fire for 5 minutes from right bank.
10:05   Recv'd one hit on chart table.
15:30   Anchored at Ichang.
        Kinsha, *Gnat*, and *Scarab* in company (30).'

He was present in the chart house when the bullet struck, however fortunately was uninjured.
At that time the British Consul at Ichang was another of those delightful characters occasionally produced in the East, John L. Smith (31). Of him the following year it was to be be written:-
'Called officially on the British Consul, an interesting antiquarian. He is a collector of fossils, Buddhas, and old books, and is known up and down the River as 'Fossil' Smith. I found him an interesting old bird (32).

From Europe and centred around the cruiser *Nisshin*, 7,700 tons, on 18 June 1919 a small squadron of IJN warships arrived at Yokosuka. They had escorted home seven surrendered German U-boats which had been awarded to Japan at Scapa Flow the previous December.
'Five of these boats were of the latest German design. These vessels, thoroughly tested and studied by Japanese technicians, provided vital data from which to design new and formidable classes of submarines (33).'

On 8 November 1919 his successor, Vice Admiral Sir Alexander Duff, with his flag in the cruiser *Hawkins*, assumed command of the Station.
Following his return home, and a period of leave, then from 15 November 1920 to 15 November 1922 he served as President of RNC, Greenwich.

Admiral: 16 May 1921.
KCB gazetted on 4 June 1921.
The signing of the Washington Naval Treaty on 6 February 1922 will have been of great interest to him, indeed to all Naval officers.
From Greenwich on 15 November 1922 he retired voluntarily, aged only fifty nine years.
From that October, Trafalgar Day 1922, and under the auspices of The Society for Nautical Research, he was to play an active role in the raising of the necessary funds for restoration work to be carried out on HMS *Victory*. Under the Chairmanship of Admiral of the Fleet Sir Doveton Sturdee he was a member of the General Committee of the 'Save The *Victory* Fund' (34).

He was the stepfather to a future British Ambassador to Japan, Sir Robert Craigie (1883-1959), who was to occupy that post during the vital years from 1937 to 1941.

In retirement in Camberley, and to support the Camberley Town Football Club, as President of their Supporters Club in 1925 he led the appeal to raise funds for their new grandstand and other improvements at the ground (35).

Following the death of Admiral Sir Lewis Bayly, from 17 May 1938 he was awarded the GSP of GBP 300.00 p.a. which then had become available.

On Friday, 19 April 1946 his obituary was published in the local press (36). In addition to his enthusiasm for the town Football Club, just mentioned, it is clear that in retirement he had done much work for the British Legion and for the Camberley branch of the National Conservative Association.

With a large congregation of family and friends present, on Wednesday, 17 April his funeral service had taken place at St. Paul's Church, Camberley, and this had been followed by his actual interment nearby at St. Peter's Parish Church in Frimley:-

> 'Members of the Camberley British Legion were pall bearers, and Lieut. Colonel R.D. Beadle recited the Legion Exhortation. A firing party of 24 men was supplied by H.M.S. *Excellent* under Lieut. A. Archibald. Among those present were Lady Tudor (widow), Sir Robert Craigie (stepson), (--) Vice Admiral F.C. Fisher (son-in-law), and a great many others (37)'.

NOTES

1. King's College, London. Ref: *GB99 KCLMA Tudor 4*, being a family biographical note.
   'Son of Mr. H.R. Jones of Harwich and he assumed his mother's maiden name of Tudor, in place of Jones, in December 1890'.
   Obituary, *The Times*, Monday, April 15, 1946.
2. Ibid.
3. Ibid.
4. NA ADM 196/42. *Service Record*.
5. Obituary, *The Times*.
6. Ibid.
7. Oscar Parkes, *British Battleships*, (Annapolis, 1990), 382.
8. *Service Record*.
9. Kings College: biographical notes.
10. Admiral Sir Reginald Bacon, *From 1900 Onward*, (London, 1940), 161.
11. Obituary, *The Times*.
12. Kings College. Ref: *GB99 KCLMA Tudor*. This is not to say that the tank was entirely a Navy idea. For example as early as November 1914 such a machine, 'the Caterpillar', was being spoken about by Maurice Hankey. Stephen Roskill, *Hankey, Man of Secrets*, I, (London, 1970), 146/7.
13. R.D. Layman, *Naval Aviation in the First World War*, (London, 2002), 122.
14. Arthur J. Marder, *From the Dreadnought to Scapa Flow*, 4, (OUP, 1969), 174.
15. *Hankey, Man of Secrets*, I, 383/4.
16. NA ADM 125/66.
17. *Service Record*.
18. Thomas Henry Jameson, *Expedition to Siberia – 1919*, (Royal Marines Historical Society, 1987).
   Thomas Henry **Jameson**. Born: 10 December 1894. Died as a Major General, RM: 28 February 1985. Monkton Combe School. Commissioned into the Royal Marines: 1913. DSO: 1919. Major: 18 January 1932. OBE: 1937. Lieut. Colonel: 15 March 1939. Commandant General, Portsmouth Division: 1944-1946 and retired. CBE: 1946. From 11 June 1918

was Major, RM in cruiser *Kent*, Commodore John D. Edwards. *Navy List.*

From his obituary in *The Times,* Thursday, March 7, 1985 it may be noted:-

'In 1919 he led a unique expedition of Royal Marines and sailors with 6" and 12 pdr. guns, from Vladivostok to the Kama River some 300 miles from Moscow, where they supported the White Russian forces under Admiral Kolchak. They mounted the guns on a tug and barges and fought a number of successful engagements against the Red Army.'

En route to Perm late in April 1919 a stop was made at Ekaterinburg where they saw the house in which the Imperial family had been murdered on 16 July 1918. On the their return East left Perm on 29 June, just ahead of the Bolsheviks who occupied the town on 1 July 1919. Finally returned to Vladivostok on 18 August 1919.

19. NA ADM 116/1878. Sloop *Cadmus,* 1,070 tons. Six 4" and four 3 pdr. guns. *Navy List.*
20. Ibid. General Letter No. 166. In the Foreign Office List during that period no such person as J.V.A. Ruston is shown. At the time the British Consul-General to the Netherlands East Indies was William Norman Dunn. *Foreign Office List,* 1920. Joseph Victor Anthony Ruston later is shown as Vice Consul at Samarang, Java for a very short period, 20 November 1923 to 26 April 1924. *Foreign Office List,* 1925. As her second husband, between 1926 and 1939 Ruston was married to a Dutch lady, Ella, Baroness van Heemstra. Their daughter, Audrey Kathleen Ruston, better known as Audrey Hepburn, was born in Brussels in 1929.
21. Ibid.
22. Ibid.
23. Ibid.
24. Ibid.
25. Ibid. The unfortunate Vice Consul was Stanley Wyatt **Smith** (1887-1958). Happily in due course he was to retire in 1945 at age 57, his last position being as Consul General in Honolulu. The Consul-General who came up from Canton was James William **Jamieson** (1867-1946), KCMG: 1923. In December 1926 he was to be transferred to Tientsin, and to retire on 8 September 1930. For an account of the Wuchow incident see P.D. Coates, *The China Consuls,* (OUP, 1988), 414/5. *Foreign Office List. Who's Who.*
26. Ibid. *Hang Sang,* 2,343 grt. Built in Glasgow in 1901 for Indo-China SN Co. (Jardine Matheson). In 1939 to be sold to Chinese owners. In October 1950 sold in Hong Kong for breaking up. H.W. Dick and S.A. Kentwell, *Beancaker to Boxboat,* (Canberra, 1988), 29.
27. Canadian Army Historical Section, *Report No. 83,* 20 October 1959, 22.
28. Wiltshire and Swindon Record Office. Ref: *Long Collection: 947/711.*
29. Christopher J. Bowie, *Great Britain and the use of Force in China, 1919-1931,* (Ph.D thesis, Oxord, 1983), 28. The author is quoting from the Minister's letters of 15 June 1919 and 23 September 1919 to the Foreign Office in London. NA FO 371/3695/3696.
John Newell **Jordan**: see Moore, C. in C., 1905, reference (27).
30. NA ADM 53/68612. Log Book *Widgeon.* From the relevant Foreign Office file held in the National Archives at Kew, FO 371/3694, it is clear that this was merely one in a series of incidents against foreign shipping carried out by 'troops' under the command of 'general' Li T'ien-t'sai who, during this period, had a record of unruly behaviour locally.
31. John Langford Smith. Born in Ceylon on 19 January 1877, the son of a tea planter. Died: 13 December 1928. Appointed Student Interpreter in China: 18 March 1897. Served at Tientsin, Hangchow, Shanghai, Chengtu, Chungking and Yengyueh. Called to the Bar at the Middle Temple: 28 June 1911. Next served at Tsinan, Hangchow and Chengtu. Briefly attached to the Consulate-General at Marseilles: 13 May to 24 August 1917. Subsequently transferred to Ichang. Consul at Chefoo: 1926 and 1927. *Foreign Office List,* 1930. *The China Consuls.* Indeed he carried out much pioneering work finding and collecting fossils from the Gorges region:-
'A large collection of well preserved fossils from the Ordovician of the Yangtse region has been sent to the survey by HBM Consul, J. Langford Smith of Ichang.'
Bulletin American Museum of Natural History, Vol. XLVI, (New York, NY, 1922), 729.
32. Ed. Dennis L. Noble. Glenn F. Howell, *Gunboat on the Yangtze,* (Jefferson, NC., 2002), 66. Diary entry dated at Ichang, 17 September 1920.
33. David C. Evans and Mark R. Peattie, *Kaigun (Strategy, Tactics and Technology in the Imperial Japanese Navy: 1887-*

1941), (Annapolis, MD., 1997), 215. Naturally all the victorious Allies similarly were to benefit from their studies of captured U-boats awarded to their respective Navies.

34. Hugh Murphy and Derek J. Oddy, *The Mirror of the Seas,* (The Society for Nautical Research, London, 2010), Chapter 2, 31.

35. Courtesy Surrey Heath Museum, Ms Sharon Cross.

36. Ibid. *Camberley News,* Friday, April 19, 1946.

37. Frederick Charles Fisher. Born: 16 December 1877. In 1918 he had married Ella, daughter of Admiral R.W. Craigie. *Who's Who.*

24 July 1919 to 10 September 1922
Vice Admiral Sir Alexander Ludovic **Duff**

He was born on 20 February 1862, the fourth son and seventh child of Colonel James Duff (1820-1898) of Knockleith House, Turriff, Aberdeenshire by his wife, Jane Bracken, nee Dunlop, of Edinburgh but born in Calcutta on 7 December 1829.

Sir Alexander died in London on 22 November 1933.

He entered the Royal Navy in *Britannia* as a **Naval Cadet**: 15 July 1875. **Midshipman**: 27 October 1877. Already from 28 July 1877 he had been serving in the new iron, armour plated, steam ship *Temeraire*, 8,412 tons, Mediterranean, and continued in her until 27 October 1881. *Temeraire*, completed on 31 August 1877, was the first barbette ship in the Navy and was to spend most of her active service in the Mediterranean (1). **Sub Lieutenant**: 27 October 1881. From January 1882 studying at RNC. From 13 March 1883 in corvette *Opal*, 2,120 tons, Cape of Good Hope and West Coast of Africa Station. From 31 August 1883 same station, appointed to *Boadicea*, 4,140 tons, Flagship of the C. in C., Rear Admiral Nowell Salmon, VC, CB (see C. in C., 1887). In October 1883 while on the West African coast:-

> 'There having been trouble with the natives of Igah and Aboh, on the river Niger, Captain Arthur Thomas Brooke, of the *Opal*, left his corvette at the mouth of the stream. .... The *Opal*'s steam cutter, under Sub Lieutenant Alexander Ludovic Duff, and one of her pulling boats were also with the expedition. Brooke met the chiefs on October 25. The natives, however, showed hostility, and the chiefs, upon being required to disperse them, refused, whereupon the British officer withdrew to his ship. The natives then opened fire on the vessels, which retaliated by beginning a general bombardment. Later, bluejackets … and a body of Marines landed and completely destroyed Igah. On the day following the three ships steamed to Aboh, where a British subject had been ill treated; and Brooke ordered the local chiefs to assemble for a palaver. The chief who was specially implicated refused to attend. (…)
>
> The chief still refused (to attend), and, moreover, expressed his willingness to fight.
>
> On the 29th indeed, about four or five thousand natives assembled on the shore, and attacked the various parties which had been landed. After a smart action they were driven back with heavy loss, but not until two seaman of the *Opal* had been killed and two officers wounded, Midshipman Edward Hay fatally (2).'

From 20 May 1884 in Royal Yacht *Victoria and Albert*, 2,470 tons, Portsmouth. **Lieutenant**: 3 September 1884. From 16 September 1884 in Turret Ship *Agamemnon*, 8,510 tons, China Station. Ordered home from China and on 10 August 1885 took passage in *Pembroke Castle* (3). Then from 30 September 1885 in *Vernon*, Portsmouth, 'Qualifying as Torpedo Lieutenant.' As a Torpedo Lieutenant, or (T), in April 1887 he was to obtain a First Class certificate. At the time being qualified as a Torpedo officer included an ability with other underwater weapons such as mines, also in the generation and distribution of electricity in ships (4).

On 8 July 1886 he married Janet Douglas, third daughter of Garden William Duff of Hatton Castle, Aberdeenshire. They were to have two daughters. Sadly his wife was to die when still rather young, on 21 February 1908 (5).

Their younger daughter, Dorothy Alexandra (1890-1971), on 18 January 1915 was to marry, as a Commander, the future Admiral Sir William Milbourne James (1881-1973), the well known author, M.P., and C. in C., Portsmouth between June 1939 and October 1942.

From 22 September 1887 as a qualified Lieut. (T) continued in *Vernon* as a Staff Officer.

From 1 March 1888 Lieut. (T) in cruiser *Imperieuse*, 8,400 tons, Flagship, China Station, Vice Admiral Sir Nowell Salmon, VC, KCB. Subsequently, from 26 August 1891, Lieut. (T) in battleship *Camperdown*, 10,600 tons, Flagship, Channel Squadron. From 16 December 1891 to 4 June 1895 Lieut. (T) cruiser *Blake*, 9,000 tons, Flagship, North America and West Indies Station. Returned to *Vernon* from 26 August 1895, then from 10 September 1895 transferred as Lieut. (T) in Special Torpedo Vessel Depot Ship, *Vulcan*, 6,620 tons, 'Particular Service'.

Commander: 1 January 1897. From 14 January 1898 in command Torpedo Boat Destroyer *Bat*, 360 tons, Tender to *Vivid*, Flagship, Devonport. The C. in C. was Admiral The Hon. Sir Edmund R. Fremantle (see C. in C., 1892).

From 26 March 1900 he attended a Senior Officers' Gunnery Course and then from 19 June 1900 to 15 November 1902 served as Commander in cruiser *St. George*, 7,700 tons, 'Training Squadron.' While in the ship a duty during 1901 was to, '…. escort *Ophir* during the Empire Tour by King George and Queen Mary, then the Duke and Duchess of Cornwall and York (6).'

Captain: 31 December 1902.

Between 30 September and 12 November 1903 attended a 'War Course' and at the conclusion of which he obtained a First Class pass (7).

From 12 November 1903 to 16 November 1905 in command of the new battleship *Albemarle*, 14,000 tons, Flagship of the Rear Admiral, Mediterranean, he being Sir Richard Poore, Bt. During January 1905 she transferred to the Channel Fleet, remaining as Flagship of the Rear Admiral.

From 20 December 1905 to 5 January 1909 Naval Assistant to the Controller of the Navy who was the Third Sea Lord, Captain Henry B. Jackson.

From 5 January 1909 to 24 October 1910, Home Fleet in command of the new *Dreadnought* type battleship *Temeraire*, 18,600 tons, but with a powerful secondary armament of sixteen 4" guns.

From 25 October 1910, as **Commodore** Second Class and in succession to Christopher G.F.M. Cradock, appointed Captain of Royal Naval Barracks, *Victory*, Portsmouth, and, 'took over command at Portsmouth Bks. 28/10/10'.

Director of Naval Mobilization, Naval Staff: 3 October 1911 – October 1914.

CB: 27 September 1912.

Rear Admiral: 2 March 1913.

Continued as Director of Naval Mobilization, Admiralty War Staff until 22 October 1914.

Of him as a Rear Admiral at the commencement of WW1 one historian of note was to write:-

'Among the outstanding rear-admirals at the outbreak of war were the very gifted Duff,… (8).'

From 22 October 1914 he flew his Flag in the new battleship *Emperor of India*, 25,000 tons, 4BS, Grand Fleet. These four ships of the *Iron Duke* class were the last coal burning British battleships.

On 20 October 1914 the British s.s. *Glitra*, 866 tons, bound from Leith to Stavanger with a cargo of coal, had been boarded by a party from *U-17*, Johannes Feldkirchner, and sent to the bottom, but only after all her crew had been given time to board the ship's lifeboats. She was the first merchant vessel ever to be sunk by a submarine. In this gentlemanly manner did Germany's underwater offensive commence. Few Naval authorities in Britain could foresee the future danger. So much so that even he on 11 February 1915 was to comment in his diary:-

'With submarines alone she (Germany) cannot hope to inflict any serious damage on our merchant shipping (9).'

At the Battle of Jutland, 31 May 1916, he served as RA, 4BS with his Flag in *Superb*, 18,600 tons, Captain Edmond Hyde Parker. She was a sister ship of his earlier command, *Temeraire*.

In the interim in London the government, David Lloyd George (1863-1945) then being Prime Minister, had become increasingly concerned at the apparent inability of those responsible to deal with the increasing menace of U-boat attacks on merchant and other shipping. Certain moves were proposed with a view to tackling this problem energetically. From the Grand Fleet flagship *Iron Duke* on 27 November 1916 Admiral Jellicoe signalled him as follows. Excerpts follow:-

'My dear Duff,

I don't know if you quite understand the position. I go as 1ˢᵗ S.L. Beatty as C. in C.

(--). I am being taken to Admlty as it is considered the S/M menace is so serious. I feel that I want a Flag Officer to deal with the problem under me and I therefore asked you. I propose Dreyer to help you, with some younger talent.

The idea is to get you to consider new methods of dealing with them offensively and also defensively. Until I get south I can't really settle any more than that. But you may like to reconsider your acceptance on further knowledge. Hence this letter (10).'

In consequence of the above he struck his flag on 30 November 1916.

At the Admiralty, Director Anti-Submarine Division: 1 December 1916 to 31 May 1917.

Concerning much of his war service, at the time of his death the following was to be written:-

'At the outbreak of the War in 1914 he was Director of the Mobilization Division of the Naval Staff, but in October of that year hoisted his flag in the *Emperor of India* as RA 4BS of the Grand Fleet. In addition to his ordinary duties he was, with Rear Admiral Leveson (see C. in C., 1922), placed in charge by Sir John Jellicoe of experiments with appliances to defend ships from mines, out of which tests the paravanes evolved.'

Also:-

'When Jellicoe was recalled from the Grand Fleet as First Sea Lord in December 1916, he brought Rear Admiral Duff with him as head of the Anti Submarine Division, which it was then decided to form to coordinate the efforts against the enemy's underwater campaign (11).'

A Lord Commissioner of the Admiralty and Assistant Chief of Naval Staff, especially concerned with the Atlantic convoy system: 31 May 1917 to 23 July 1919 (12). On being appointed to the Admiralty in December 1916 it must be noted, however, that in addition to Jellicoe and his brother Lords, initially he was opposed to the overall re-introduction of the convoy system.

It is to their discredit that initially Their Lordships were inclined to doubt this lesson of history.

Happily well before the end of the war it seems clear that that successful aspect of the maritime past had been re-learnt:-

'In the area of convoy, however, the principal decisions in 1918 were not to do with whether convoy worked, but to do with how far it should be extended across the world (13).'

On Christmas Eve 1917 Jellicoe received word from the First Lord of the Admiralty who, since the summer of 1917 had been a fomer railwayman, Sir Eric Campbell Geddes (1875-1937), that he was to be replaced as First Sea Lord by acting Admiral Sir Rosslyn Erskine Wemyss. This was a controversial move within naval circles. Admiral Duff was one of those who had views on the subject, and made these known. The following week was difficult within the highest circles of the Admiralty administration. Admiral Duff later was to note:-

'I was kicked out of the Admiralty on account of opinions I expressed re Jellicoe's dismissal, and then asked to remain (14).'

Without elaborating further, Geddes rather rapidly did change his mind and indeed Admiral Duff was to remain, as has been noted above, at his Admiralty post as Assistant Chief of Naval Staff until the summer of 1919, thus until well after the end of the Great War. At the same time, and looking ahead a little, it is pleasant to be able to record that his war time efforts at the Admiralty were to be much appreciated by Lord Wemyss who, at the end of October 1919, was to resign as First Sea Lord. At that time Lord Wemyss was to write to him in China, both to express his appreciation, and to say that he was recommending him for a decoration:-

> 'If I may be allowed to say so, it is at least a recognition on my part that your work has been equal to that of any officer commanding a Battle Squadron. Really such work as you have done cannot be weighed by such baubles, but there are some of us who realized what you went through during the war and how triumphantly you emerged (15).'

In the interim he had been knighted. KCB: 1 January 1918. The investiture took place at Buckingham Palace on 23 January 1918.

Vice Admiral: 15 January 1918.

Appointed C. in C., China with effect from 24 July 1919 and at Chatham on that day at 09:00 hours his flag first was hoisted in the cruiser *Hawkins*, 9,750 tons, Captain Reginald G.H. Henderson (16). In due course, in June 1921, Reginald Henderson was to be succeeded in command of the ship by the C. in C.'s son-in-law, Captain William James (17).

To take up his command in the East in *Hawkins* he left Plymouth on Saturday, 6 September 1919, passed Gibraltar three days later, and arrived at Penang on Tuesday, 14 October 1919. Thereafter, in *Alacrity*, he continued in a southerly direction down the Strait (18). From Singapore on 20 October, and once again in *Hawkins*, he reached Hong Kong on 26 October, and finally anchored at Wei-Hai-Wei at 23:57 hours on Thursday, 6 November 1919. There the following morning at 08:00 the flag of Vice Admiral Sir F.C. Tudor was saluted with fifteen guns which the sloop *Cadmus*, 1,070 tons, returned.

To enable Admiral Tudor to take his farewell of the Imperial Japanese Navy at Moji, it was arranged that he would transfer to *Hawkins* for a few days.

Accordingly, after he, Admiral Duff, had assumed command of the station on Saturday, 8 November 1919, he shifted his flag to *Cadmus* and at 1808 that evening *Hawkins* departed for Moji. There, at Moji on Tuesday 11 November, Admiral Tudor shifted his flag to the light cruiser *Carlisle* and *Hawkins* returned to Wei-Hai-Wei where, at noon on 13 November, the new C. in C. re-embarked. Wasting no time Admiral Duff then returned in a southerly direction to Shanghai from 15 to 17 November, thence to Hong Kong where at 15:50 on Wednesday 19 November 1919 *Hawkins* secured to 'Flag moorings'.

The six submarines comprising the China Station Submarine Flotilla, boats *L1, 3, 4, 7, 9* and *15*, arrived at Hong Kong on Sunday, 30 November 1919. Leaving Malta at the end of September they had been escorted East by the coal fired Depot Ship *Ambrose*, 6,480 tons, Commander Cecil Ponsonby Talbot, DSO*. He had been assisted in these duties by *Marazion* and *Moonshine*, a rather slow and tedious, although fortunately successful voyage via the Suez Canal, Aden, Bombay, Colombo, Singapore and Manila (19).

From 1 March 1920 the new British Minister Plenipotentiary to Peking, in succession to Sir John Jordan, was Beilby F. Alston. From July 1918 to March 1919 he had been Deputy High Commissioner at Vladivostok, and then had acted as Charge d'Affaires at Tokyo. He was to end his diplomatic career as HBM Ambassador to Brazil: 1925-1929 (20).

On 1 April 1920 the status of H.I.J.M.S. *Wakamiya* was altered from that of a coast defence ship seaplane tender to that of an aircraft carrier, 'koku bokan', and in June a flying off platform, some twenty metres in length, was fitted over her fo'cstle. It was from this temporary structure that on 22 June 1920 Lieutenant Kuwabara Torao, at the time an instructor at Yokosuka, achieved the first successful take off by a Japanese pilot from any ship (21). *Wakamiya* was underway at the time, be it at a modest nine knots, and the aircraft used was an 80 h.p. British built Sopwith Pup.

Generally speaking in the years following the Great War a perception gradually was to form in London that possibly in the future Japan might become difficult. Slowly steps were taken to improve the significance of Singapore to wider British interests. These included the construction of a causeway linking the island with the mainland of the Malay peninsula. Here follows an extract taken from the letter of 13 August 1920, ref. 38479/20, written to the Admiralty by the Under Secretary of State, Colonial Office:-

> 'A contract was signed between the Crown Agents for the Colonies and Messrs. Topham, Jones and Railton on the 30 June 1919 for the construction of a Causeway with lock, lock gates, lifting bridge, machinery, guide walls, dredging and other works between Johore Bahru and Woodlands, Singapore Island, the causeway to be 60' wide at formation level and to carry a roadway on the western side (22).'

Work on the causeway had commenced immediately.

Although in slightly out of date sequence, here it may be mentioned that as regards speed of construction it was to be a vastly different story with regard to the building of the proposed new Naval Base. Nevertheless as early as 22 June 1921 at the Admiralty the DCNS wrote to inform the CNS (Chief of Naval Staff) that by the end of June 1921 the Cabinet had decided to proceed with the development of Singapore Base, 'when funds admit'(23).

'Captain Plant Country'. The Yangtse Gorges upstream towards Chungking.

25 November 1920. Commissioning of HIJMS *Nagato*, Captain Iida Nobutaro, the first battleship in the world to be equipped with 16" guns, and capable of over twenty six knots.

On Tuesday, 1 March 1921 in Hong Kong the *South China Morning Post* informed their readers:-
'The Blue Funnel steamer *Teiresias* arrived yesterday from Shanghai with the body of Captain Plant, an old China hand. Captain Plant left Shanghai for home with Mrs. Plant, and when two days out from Shanghai died rather suddenly from double pneumonia. He was one of the best known skippers in China. For many years he navigated the Yangtsze River ...'

Sadly Mrs. Plant died on 1 March so joining her husband, and on Wednesday, 2 March being interred together at the Happy Valley cemetery. Included amongst the many wreaths placed on the grave was one from the C. in C. and his wife. There today, the year 2008, their gravestones still stand in good condition (24).

Also to this day, again written in the year 2008, in the Gorges about ten sea miles above the great new dam at Sandouping and on the left bank of the River may be seen the obelisk erected in memory of Captain Samuel Cornell Plant (1866-1921). Recently the obelisk was re-positioned well above the maximum height of the waters which now flood the gorges above the dam. Even after the dam filled happily the scenery upstream and through the Gorges continues to remain extremely impressive.

In the old British built battleship *Katori*, 15,950 tons, and with her near sister HIJMS *Kashima*, 16,400 tons, as escort, from Yokohama on 3 March 1921 Crown Prince Hirohito sailed on his Royal visit to Great Britain. At Malta on 25 April he visited the Royal Naval cemetery there to pay his respects to those Japanese members of the IJN who had lost their lives on 11 June 1917 when the destroyer *Sakaki*, 850 tons, had been torpedoed and so badly damaged.

At the conclusion of a most successful tour, which included visits to France, Begium, Holland and Italy, at Naples on 18 July he re-embarked in *Katori* to return home via the Indian Ocean, finally arriving back at Yokohama on 3 September 1921 (25).

At Penang from 7 March 1921 onwards a conference was held in *Hawkins* to discuss: 'The Higher Command of the Pacific and its Headquarters'. In addition to the C. in C. himself, his brother Commanders in Chief , East Indies and Australasian Stations, respectively Rear Admirals Tothill and Sir Edmund Percy F.G. Grant attended (26). After eliminating alternatives the conclusion was reached, "... that Singapore is the only site suitable for the location of the 'Higher Command' as well as for the main fleet base." Further, "The loss of Singapore would be 'disastrous to the British Empire' and the Conference therefore has assumed (when selecting Singapore as the main fleet base and for the Higher Command) that it will be made impregnable. No alternative to Singapore is seen from which the fleet could operate successfully (27)."

In connection with this conclusion also see C. in C., 1938.

16 April 1921. The first members of the British Civil Air Mission, or 'Sempill Mission', to the IJN arrived at Yokohama as passengers in the N.Y.K. steamer *Suwa Maru*, 10,672 grt. Although in London care had been taken to ensure the unofficial nature of the group in Japan it was noted:-
'The British Air Ministry superficially pretended to be indifferent, but they gave not a few conveniences and made it easy to form the Mission.'

In London on 7 June 1921 the Oversea Sub-Committee of the Committee of Imperial Defence produced a summary headed, 'Singapore, Development of as Nave Base, Memorandum'. The CID agreed with an important conclusion reached by the three Commanders in Chief mentioned above. A relevant extract follows:-
'That it is impracticable, under existing conditions, to maintain in time of peace at Hong Kong a sufficient military garrison to secure for certain its safety in the early stages of a war with Japan; and that, consequently, of Hong Kong and Singapore the latter must be regarded as the most

suitable for use as the rendezvous and main repair and supply base of any British fleet which may be sent to operate in the Pacific.'

However the members of the CID sub committee, although mentioning the subject, hardly placed as much emphasis as did the Admirals on the need to render Singapore impregnable:-

'That, unless the defences of Singapore are strengthened, there would, under existing conditions, be every inducement to a Japanese commander in the early stages of a war to attack the fortress .... (28).'

Also in June 1921 the Soviet Comintern agent, the Dutchman Hendricus Sneevliet (Maring) (1883-1942), arrived in Shanghai. He recognised that Dr. Sun Yat-sen's Kuomintang was a unifying force in the country and ought to be infiltrated by the communists. Once he met Dr. Sun then shortly thereafter communist infiltration of Kuomintang (Nationalist party) was to follow.

In so doing Dr. Sun had few options since all the western powers had shunned his organisation. In fairness to him it should be emphasised that rather than permitting his party to become a communist tool Dr. Sun's policy was more one of, 'allying with Russia and tolerating the communists.'

Admiral: 1 July 1921.

21 July 1921. Off the Virginia Capes the captured German battleship *Ostfriesland*, 22,400 tons, was sunk by air attack. Latterly as a Commander, IJN, between 5 April 1919 and 10 August 1921 Yamamoto Isoroku had been posted to the U.S.A. as Assistant Naval Attaché in the Japanese Embassy, Washington DC. For much of the period he was studying at Harvard. Also during this overseas assignment, at his own expense, he visited the Mexican oil fields. These, and other related experiences, were to assist him in developing his ideas concerning the future of Naval air power, and the use of oil fuel to replace coal.

End July 1921. At Kasumiga Ura, sixty kilometres north east of Tokyo, the official opening by the IJN of the Central Training School of their Naval Air Service. Much of the work carried out by the British Sempill Mission was centred on this station.

25 November 1921. As his father, HIM Emperor Yoshihito, Taisho Tenno, was not a well man Crown Prince Hirohito was proclaimed Regent.

6 February 1922. Washington Treaty signed in Washington, DC. The British Empire, U.S.A., Japan, France and Italy agreed to a tonnage ratio in respect of battleships and battlecruisers, then the Capital Ships of the Fleet. Also similar agreement was reached concerning aircraft carriers.

At this Washington Conference it is of interest to note that the Japanese plenipotentiary was Admiral Baron Kato Tomosaburo (1861-1923) who at the Battle of Tsushima in May 1905, and as a Rear Admiral, had served as chief of staff to Admiral Togo Heihachiro in *Mikasa*. Between June 1922 and his unfortunate death from cancer on 24 August 1923 he was to serve as prime minister of Japan. His successor as prime minister was another naval officer, serving on his second occasion, Admiral Count Yamamoto Gonnohyoe, or Gombei (1852-1933).

In addition in February 1922 a nine power agreement was concluded whereby Britain, the USA, Japan, France, Italy, Belgium, Holland, Portugal and China agreed to respect Chinese sovereignty, independence, territorial preservation, and also for equality of trade opportunities. Dr. Sun and the Nationalists were unimpressed:-

'Sun had always thought of the Western democracies as models for his country, but recent events had shaken his faith in their sense of justice, and the Nine Power Treaty was the greatest disappointment of all; though it cancelled out a good deal of the Japanese threat it did little to lessen exploitation by other nations. Worse, in his opinion it substituted Britain and America for Japan in the role of exploiter (29).'

31 March 1922. Outward bound from Great Britain HMS *Renown*, 26,500 tons, Captain The Hon. Herbert Meade, arrived at Singapore. Taking passage was HRH The Prince of Wales on his Royal Tour of the Far East. Although London intended to allow the Anglo-Japanese Alliance to lapse an important objective of the Tour was to reassure Japan of Great Britain's continued desire for amicable relations. In *Renown* HRH arrived off Yokohama on Wednesday, 12 April 1922. Subsequently, and following his most successful visit, from Kagoshima Bay he left Japanese waters on 9 May 1922.

The arrival of *Renown*, escorted by the light cruiser *Durban*, Captain Casper B. Ballard, into Tokyo Bay on 12 April was witnessed from the air by Major H.G. Brackley of the Sempill Mission:-

> 'What a glorious sight! In the clear morning sun, and deep blue water, was the glorious *Renown* surrounded by a cruiser squadron in perfect formation and led by our *Durban*, a light cruiser. It was a grand sight from the air to watch them wending their way smoothly to Yokohama. Arriving off Yokohama we were met by the whole Japanese Navy and Air Service! Ye Gods, what a sight! There was the *Mutsu, Kongo, Haruna, Ise, Kiso* – Japan's latest battleships, and a whole squadron of cruisers and destroyers and submarines, all lined up in perfect formation, through which the *Renown* and *Durban* passed majestically to enter harbour. Never shall I forget that sight! (30)'

Always believing in and working towards the unification of China, by 1922, and supported by the local war lord, Ch'en Chiung-ming (1875-1933), Dr. Sun Yat-sen had become president of a somewhat shaky government based in Canton. However that summer he fell out with Ch'en who drove him from the city. Although the western powers did not actively support Dr. Sun neither did they all dismiss his ideals and intentions. Immediately following his defeat by Ch'en he applied to the British Consul-General in Canton, Mr. J.W. Jamieson, for assistance in leaving the city safely (31). Mr. Jamieson acted promptly and on 9 August passage to Hong Kong was arranged in the river gunboat *Moorhen* (32). The following day in the Canadian Pacific liner *Empress of Russia* Dr. Sun left Hong Kong for Shanghai. There he arrived on 14 August and took up residence in the French Settlement at 29, rue Moliere (33).

KCVO: 8 April 1922.

Superceded in command in China on 10 September 1922 but, following the arrival of his successor, only struck his flag on 7 November 1922. From the log book in *Hawkins*, who then was refitting alongside the camber in the Dockyard at Hong Kong, it may be noted:-

'Tuesday, 7 November 1922

08:00   Flag of Admiral Sir Arthur Leveson hoisted in *Durban*.

17:40   Flag of Admiral Sir Alexander Duff hauled down.'

Wednesday, 8 November 1922.

09:40   Cleared lower deck to cheer Admiral Sir Alexander Duff (34).'

On 10 January 1924, as his second wife, he married Marjorie, daughter of Charles Hill-Whitson of Parkhill, Perthshire. They were to have no children.

GBE: gazetted on 3 June 1924, and he was invested a month later, on 9 July.

At his own request he retired on 1 July 1925 and settled in Copdock outside Ipswich (35). Also he and his wife spent time at Senwick House, Brighouse Bay, Kirkcudbright.

GCB: gazetted on 1 January 1926 and he was invested at Buckingham Palace a month later, on 4 February.

Following his death his body was cremated at Golders Green Crematorium, Hoop Lane, London NW11, on 24 November 1933, with his ashes subsequently being scattered at sea off Harwich.

NOTES

1. Oscar Parkes, *British Battleships*, (Annapolis, 1990), 222/229.

2. Clowes, Vol. VII, 349. Corvette *Opal*, 12 guns, 2,120 tons. From 13 March 1883 commanded by Captain Arthur T. Brooke. *Navy List*.

3. NA ADM 196/42. *Service Record*.

4. Alastair Wilson and Joseph F. Callo, *Who's Who in Naval History*, (Abingdon, Oxford, 2004), 89.

5. *Dictionary of National Biography*.

6. Obituary, *The Times*, Thursday, November 23, 1933.

7. *Service Record*.

8. Arthur J. Marder, *From the Dreadnought to Scapa Flow*, I, (OUP, 1961), 408.

9. Richard Hough, *The Great War at Sea, 1914-1918*, (OUP, 1983), 169. The author is quoting from, 'Diary, 11 February 1915: Duff MSS.'

10. Caird Library, National Maritime Museum, Greenwich. Ref: *DFF/1*.

11. Obituary, *The Times*.

12. *Service Record*.

13. Nicholas Black, *The British Naval Staff in the First World War*, (Woodbridge, Suffolk, 2009), 223/4.

14. Caird Library. Ref: *DFF/14*. Pencilled annotation, *MS 63/061*. It seems clear that Geddes was well justified in dismissing a possibly exhausted Jellicoe. Stephen Roskill, *Hankey, Man of Secrets*, 1, (London, 1970), 447, 472. Lady Wester Wemyss, *The Life and Letters of Lord Wester Wemyss*, (London, 1935), 364. One paragraph may be quoted in which is described the prevailing atmosphere at the Admiralty after his arrival in September 1917:-

    'To dispel the pall of fatalistic gloom which seemed to envelop the Admiralty appeared as impossible as to try and rouse them to accept new ideas.'

    John Winton, *Jellicoe*, (London, 1981), 262. The author, though appalled by the method of Jellicoe's dismissal, also does remark:-

    'Of course, Geddes sincerely believed that Jellicoe was no longer fit for the duty and was no longer the right man for the job, and almost certainly he was right. He very probably did Jellicoe a kindness in the long run, to relieve him of a burden that was crushing him.'

15. *The Life and Letters of Lord Wester Wemyss*, 449.

16. NA ADM 53/43950. Log book *Hawkins*.

17. He wrote entertainingly of his Eastern experiences. Admiral Sir William James, *The Sky was Always Blue*, (London, 1951), 115-130.

18. NA ADM 125/67.

19. NA ADM 53/33515. Log book *Ambrose*.

20. Beilby Francis Alston. Born in Enfield: 8 October 1868, second son of Sir Francis Alston, KCMG, Foreign Office. Died in London: 28 June 1929. Clerk at the Foreign Office: 1 December 1890. Subsequent service in Copenhagen, Paris, Buenos Ayres, and Brussels. Senior Clerk: 1 July 1907. Was in attendance on H.I.H. Prince Zai Suun of China during his visit to England with the Chinese Naval Mission: November/December 1909. Secretary to H.S.H. Prince Alexander of Teck's Special Mission to attend the Coronation of the King of Siam: October/December 1911. Acting Counsellor at Peking: January-July 1912. Foreign Office from 30 September 1912. CB: 3 June 1913. Acting Counsellor at Peking: 3 May 1913, and Charge d'Affaires: 6 June to 24 November 1913. Again acting Counsellor: 17 June 1916, and Charge d'Affaires: 16 November 1916 to 7 October 1917. Deputy High Commissioner at Vladivostok: July 1918 to March 1919. Charge d'Affaires at Tokyo: 6 April 1919 to 1 April 1920. Minister Plenipotentiary from 8 September 1919. Appointed Envoy Extraordinary and Minister at Peking: 1 March 1920. KCMG: 3 June 1920. Transferred to Buenos Aires: 1 September 1922. Ambassador at Rio de Janiero: 12 October 1925. PC: 16 December 1925. GBE: 3 June 1929. *Foreign Office List*, 1930. *Who Was Who: 1929-1940*.

    The author thought twice about including the following quote regarding Mr. Alston, but then decided that, if a trifle unkind, it was too entertaining to omit. Here is George Morrison, from 1 August 1912 Political Adviser to the President of the Chinese Republic, Yuan Shih-kai (1859-1916), writing from London on 2 August 1914 to Laurence John Lumley

Dundas (1876-1961), second Earl of Ronaldshay, later Governor of Bengal, Secretary of State for India, and second Marquess of Zetland.

> 'He (Alston) is a pleasant society man, but if he has any capacity he has on both occasions of his being Charge d'Affaires in Peking been careful to conceal it. (--) I believe it was the universal opinion, even among the Legation people, that he was the most incompetent noodle that had ever been given a post of responsibility in a Legation at Peking.'

Ed. Lo Hui-min, *The Correspondence of G.E. Morrison, Vol. II, 1912-1920,* (Cambridge University Press, 1978), 714.

21. Author's notes, 'H.I.J.M.S. *Wakamiya*: early IJN Air Power'.

    Kuwabara Torao. Born: 26 October 1887. Died: 5 June 1975. Graduated from Etajima: November 1909. Appointed air instructor at Yokosuka: July 1918. Lieut. Commander: December 1922. Kasumiga Ura air corps: August 1923. Commander: December 1926. Commander, Yokosuka air corps: December 1928. Commander, aircraft carrier *Kaga*, 29,600 tons: November 1929. Captain: December 1932. Captain, aircraft carrier *Ryujo*, 8,000 tons: October 1933 to November 1934. In Command at Kasumiga Ura Air Station: June 1935. Rear Admiral: November 1938. Thereafter held a number of senior positions with air groups and at the outbreak of the Pacific War in December 1941 was in command, No. 3 Air Squadron. In command at Tsingtao: April 1942. Vice Admiral: May 1942. Retired: December 1943 but re-called for service in command of Niigata Supply Administration Dept. In Command, Hokuriku Supply Administration Dept.: April 1944. In Command, Air Weapon Bureau: February 1945. Released from service: September 1945. *Military History Department, Tokyo.*

22. NA ADM 116/2100. The lock installation was constructed at the northern or Johore end of the causeway.

23. Ibid.

24. Respects paid by the author on Monday, 5 May 2008.

25. Ed. Ian Nish, *Biographical Portraits,* II, (Richmond, Surrey, 1997), Chapter Fifteen, 205-215.

26. Rear Admiral Sir Hugh Henry Darby **Tothill** (1865-1927). Rear Admiral: 17 April 1917. C. in C., East Indies from 1 August 1919. Vice Admiral: 15 June 1921.

    Rear Admiral Sir Edmund Percy Fenwick George **Grant** (1867-1952). Rear Admiral: 17 January 1919. At the time just completing duty as First Naval Member, Australian Commonwealth Naval Board. *Navy List.*

27. NA ADM 116/3100 ff. 4-18. Also see: Ed. Nicholas Tracy, *The Collective Naval Defence of the Empire, 1900- 1940,* (Naval Records Society, 1997), 279.

28. NA CID 143-C, CAB 5/4. Tracy, 287.

29. Emily Hahn, *China Only Yesterday,* (London, 1963), 272.

30. RAF Museum, London. Ref: *X001-2315.* Frida Brackley, *Brackles: Memoirs of a Pioneer of Civil Aviation,* (London, 1952), 142.

31. James William **Jamieson**. Born: 11 September 1867. Died: 8 January 1946. FRGS. Joined the Chinese Consular Service: 1886. Superintendent of Chinese Labour in the Transvaal: 1905-1908. Consul-General, Canton: 1909-1926. KCMG: 1923. Consul-General, Tientsin: 1927-1930 then retired. *Who's Who.*

32. NA ADM 1 8630/143. China Station Letter No. 203. HMS *Moorhen*, 180 tons. Lieut. Commander Victor P. Alleyne. *Navy List.*

33. NA FO 228/3291. Today the address in Shanghai is 7 Xiangshan Road. His house is a beautifully maintained and tended museum, well worth visiting.

34. NA ADM 53/78590. The light cruiser *Durban*, 4,850 tons, by now commanded by Captain Basil George Washington (1877-1940).

35. *Dictionary of National Biography.*

10 September 1922 to 10 September 1924
Admiral Sir Arthur Cavenagh **Leveson**

Born in Kensington, London on 27 January 1868, the third son of Edward John Leveson and his wife Mary, nee Iveson (1).

He died suddenly at Contrexeville, Vosges, France on Wednesday, 26 June 1929.

In January 1881 Arthur entered the Navy as a **Cadet** in *Britannia*. **Midshipman**: 15 January 1883. From 9 January 1883 serving in the iron ship, armour plated, *Alexandra*, 9,490 tons, Flagship, Mediterranean. From 2 March 1886 in corvette *Emerald*, 2,120 tons, Captain Richard Horace Hamond, North America and West Indies Station. From 1 November 1886 in corvette *Rover*, 3,460 tons, 'Training Squadron', Captain Gerard H.U. Noel (see C. in C., 1904). **Sub Lieutenant**: 27 January 1887. Studying at RNC, Greenwich. Passed a very good examination achieving five 'firsts' and, 'Awarded Beaufort Testimonial for 1888', 'Awarded Goodenough Medal, 1888', and 'Promoted to Lieutenant and awarded prize for examination (2)'. **Lieutenant**: 27 July 1887, aged nineteen and a half years. From 27 November 1888 in battleship *Iron Duke*, 6,010 tons, Captain Rodney M. Lloyd, Channel Squadron. From 30 September 1889 in *Excellent*, gunnery school ship, Portsmouth, 'Lieutenant Qualifying for Gunnery'. The Commander of the ship was Percy M. Scott. His brilliant academic performance continued:-

'Passed for Gunnery Lieut., June 1891. 1st Class Cert. (3).'

From 17 August 1891 in *Excellent* as a Lieut. (G), 'Staff Officer'. From 1 April 1893 Lieut. (G) in battleship *Victoria*, 10,470 tons, Flagship, Mediterranean, Vice Admiral Sir George Tryon, KCB. The Commander of the ship was John R. Jellicoe. Safely survived the sinking of the ship after the collision with *Camperdown*, 22 June 1893. From 17 October 1893 Lieut. (G) in battleship *Ramilles*, 14,150 tons, Captain Francis C.B. Bridgeman-Simpson, Flagship, Mediterranean. Again, the Commander in the ship was John R. Jellicoe. From 31 December 1895 Lieut. (G) in *Excellent*, 'Senior Staff Officer'.

In 1896 he was elected a Fellow of the Royal Geographic Society.

Commander: 1 January 1899. From 24 August 1899 Commander of the new battleship *Canopus*, 12,950 tons, Captain Wilmot H. Fawkes. She commissioned at Portsmouth on 5 December 1899 for the Mediterranean. Remained with the ship for her entire first commission. Paid off: 24 April 1903.

At Valetta, Malta on 3 March 1902 he married Jemima Adeline Beatrice Blackwood, born on 23 March 1880, daughter of Francis James Lindesay Blackwood (1849-1892), he being a member of the well known Naval family. To take one example his father, Captain Francis Price Blackwood (1809-1854), by nice co-incidence had commanded *Fly* between 1841 and 1846 with Charles Shadwell (see C. in C., 1871) as his First Lieutenant.

Arthur and Jemima were to have a son, Arthur Edmund Leveson (1908-1981), who served in the Navy during WW2 achieving the rank of Acting Commander, RNVR, and three daughters. After marriage one of these daughters was to become Mrs. Derek Stephens. Her sisters were Mary and Pamela.

Lady Leveson died in April 1964. Previously, on 26 January 1899, she had been married to Edward Henry Stuart Bligh, Seventh Earl of Darnley, who had died on 31 October 1900.

Captain: 30 June 1903. Naval Assistant to the Controller of the Navy and Third Sea Lord, Rear Admiral William Henry May who was to be knighted in January 1905 and promoted Vice Admiral just six months later, on 26 June.

From 3 January 1905 to 5 March 1907 Flag Captain in battleship *King Edward VII*, 16,350 tons, Flagship, Atlantic Fleet, Vice Admiral Sir William H. May (4).

Following the 'Entente Cordiale' agreement with France of April 1904, then between 10 and 17 July 1905 Admiral May took his Fleet to Brest. The press reported enthusiastically:-

'The Atlantic Fleet, under the command of Sir William May, arrived at Brest today in circumstances that must be most gratifying to both nations.'

'Admiral May and 100 British officers arrived by special train from Brest in Paris today (13 July), accompanied by Sir Francis Bertie, British Ambassador (5).'

1905: received the Croix d'Officier of the Legion of Honour.

From 3 January 1908 in command battleship *Bulwark*, 15,000 tons, Flagship, Rear Admiral, Home Fleet.

From 13 June 1908 to June 1910 in command battleship *Africa*, 16,350 tons, Channel Fleet, then in Home Fleet.

In command of the new battlecruiser *Indefatigable*, 18,750 tons, name ship of Lord Fisher's second class of 'Greyhounds': 17 January 1911. Commissioned at Devonport: 24 February 1911, First Cruiser Squadron, Home Fleet. While holding this command between 15 December 1911 and 5 January 1912 also he served as, 'Vice President of Gunnery Conference at Admiralty.'

In January 1913 the 1CS was to become 1BCS (Battle Cruiser Squadron).

CB: 27 September 1912.

ADC to H.M. King George V: 25 January 1913.

From 8 March 1913 in *President*, London, 'Miscellaneous'.

As **Commodore**, First Class, during the summer of 1913 he served in armoured cruiser *Euryalus*, 12,000 tons, on the staff of the Umpire in Chief, Admiral of the Fleet Sir William Henry May, during Naval Manoeuvres (6).'

Rear Admiral: 1 December 1913.

From 1 May 1914 Director of Operations Division, Admiralty War Staff. One noted naval historian described something of him at the time of this appointment:-

'The D.O.D. under him ('him' being Sturdee, Chief of the War Staff) was Rear Admiral Arthur Leveson, a stocky, broad shouldered figure who walked with such a pronounced nautical roll that his youngest daughter refused to walk with him because it made her feel seasick! Leveson had a good brain, plenty of ability, and a powerful personality. But he was a 'driver', even a bully, and not a leader – the sort of man who shouted down opposition. Actually, his bullying manner was in part a pose. Beneath his ferocious exterior there was a kind heart. Unfortunately, only those near him appreciated this, with the result that few were keen to serve under the domineering 'Levi', whether at the Admiralty or at sea (7).'

Following the outbreak of war, on 4 August 1914, at the Admiralty the fighting of a modern war in itself involved much adjustment in thinking and of daily practice. Here follows a brief opinion of the situation as recorded at the time by a member of the Operations Division staff:-

'Neither the Chief of the War Staff (Sturdee) nor the Director of Operations Division (Leveson) seemed to have any particular idea of what the War Staff were supposed to be doing, or how they should make use of it; they had been brought up in the tradition that the conduct of the operations of the fleet was a matter for the admiral alone, and that he needed no assistance in assimilating the whole situation in all its ramifications, and in reaching a decision, probably instantaneously, upon what should be done and what orders should be issued in order to get it done (8).'

This critique would seem to be corroborated:-

'In February 1913 Richmond was appointed Assistant Director of Operations, Naval Staff, a post for which his long study of naval strategy and history had eminently qualified him. It was, however, an increasingly disagreeable billet once war broke out.

His superior (Leveson), failing to understand the importance of careful staff work, refused to give the junior officers any real responsibility and isolated them from all work of importance. He was compelled to stand by helplessly as 'errors of preparation' and 'errors of execution' piled up (9).'

Once war had broken out then initially some setbacks were experienced. These included, on 22 September 1914, the loss to submarine torpedo attack in the North Sea of the three old armoured cruisers, *Cressy*, *Aboukir* and *Hogue*, together with great loss of life, 1,459 souls in total. The successful German commander was Otto Weddigen in *U-9*.

Vice Admiral Count Maximilian von Spee's victory off Coronel on 1 November 1914 was another shock to British arms. However here follows an account of the view from the Admiralty of the subsequent Battle of the Falkland Islands, 8 December 1914:-

'Well I remember the excruciating anxiety of the evening when Admiral Leveson came into my room and, calling me outside, told me of the receipt of the first of Sturdee's cables, 'I am engaging German ships', and then we had to wait. Leveson and I both found we could not do any work. The excitement was too great. It must be remembered that we had had our bad times. There had been a goodish number of losses during those first four months of war.... We were in a state, therefore, of peculiar tension; but presently the blessed news came in that we had sunk all the enemy's ships but one, and the relief was tremendous, and the feeling of elation glorious (10).'

Following the return of Lord Fisher as First Sea Lord from the end of October 1914, then from 17 January 1915 he was appointed RA, 2BS, Grand Fleet, with his Flag in battleship *Orion*, 22,500 tons, Captain Oliver Backhouse, one of a class of four, the first all centreline British Dreadnoughts. Ten 13.5", sixteen 4" plus smaller guns. In her in command of the squadron and Second Division at the Battle of Jutland: 31 May 1916. On that occasion an opportunity presented itself for him to act in what might be described as with a 'Nelsonic touch' but unfortunately he did not take advantage of the situation. A squadron of enemy battleships had been sighted but in spite of his staff urging him to give chase he declined to disobey Fleet orders and thus remained in line.

After this battle then on 4 June Admiral Jellicoe appointed a number of committees to look into the question of materiel and associated problems. Rear Admiral Leveson was made responsible for investigating the protection of battleships (11).

During the years of the Great War necessarily many warships were based at Scapa Flow, watching, waiting, exercising and patrolling. In that frequently inhospitable part of the world great efforts were made to keep officers and men provided with outside interests and these included much sport and other activity ashore. Light heartedly one officer subsequently was to write:-

'Some made gardens. Some looked on while their coxswains made gardens for them.

One made a sundial and put an inscription on it half in Latin, half in Greek. I pointed this out to him one day and asked him why he did that. With ready wit – it was Arthur Leveson – he replied that it was to give asses like myself the opportunity of asking stupid questions (12).'

From 10 January 1917 RA, 2 BCS in battlecruiser *Australia*, 19,200 tons, Captain Oliver Backhouse. In due course, in 1919, she was to become Flagship of the Royal Australian Navy. *Australia* was a sister ship of his earlier command, *Indefatigable*, who had been sunk on 31 May at Jutland during her engagement with SMS *Von der Tann*, 19,100 tons, Captain Hans Zenker.

Early in 1918 *Australia* was used to continue the experiments with aircraft which had begun elsewhere. On both 8 March and 14 May 1918 these resulted in the successful launching of a Sopwith 'One and a Half' Strutter from a platform which had been erected over her starboard side 'Q' twin 12" gun turret. At the time the ship was based at Rosyth (13).

He spent the month of September 1918 in the Admiralty, *President* 'additional for Special Service'.

As an acting Vice Admiral from 1 October 1918 flew his Flag in battleship *Barham*, 27,500 tons, as VA, 5BS, Captain Richard Horne. She was one of a class of five very successful British battleships, in the R.N. the first to mount 15" guns and first big warships to be oil fired.

'From the bridge of *Barham* he witnessed the surrender of the High Seas Fleet in November 1918 (14).'

Vice Admiral: 1 January 1919.

KCB: 1 January 1919.

Retained his Flag in *Barham*, from 8 April 1919 to 1 October 1920 as VA, 2BS, Atlantic Fleet, however on 15 April 1919 his Flag was transferred to sister ship *Warspite*. Between 1 and 18 May 1919 at Scapa Flow briefly supervised the interned warships of the surrendered German Fleet, the latter being under the nominal command of Vice Admiral Ludwig von Reuter (1862-1943) (15).

While holding this command as VA, 2BS clearly the Admiralty recognised that in the course of his duties he would have to offer much hospitality:-

'To be paid Table Money at rate of Sterling 3.10.0 a day while holding appt. (16).'

Admiral: 1 June 1922.

31 October 1922: Benito Mussolini was named Premier of Italy.

Appointed C. in C., China on 10 September 1922 (17)

At Hong Kong he assumed command on 7 November 1922. Flag in the cruiser *Hawkins*, 9,750 tons. Flag Captain Argentine Hugh Alington.

On assuming command of the ship from Captain James, and concerning the future need for continued competent staff work on the station, of Captain Alington it has been written:-

'On that my successor looked very gloomy. He was certain that his Admiral, Arthur Leveson, would never consult anyone before issuing orders to his ships; Admirals required obedience, not advice, was his dictum. The next three years on the China Station were not the happiest in its history (18).'

15 November 1922 at Shanghai, the opening of their new office building, Jardine Matheson & Co. at 27, The Bund (19). Their previous office, and their first Shanghai building had dated back to 1850.

In Tokyo Bay on 27 December 1922 HIJMS *Hosho*, 7,470 tons, first was commissioned by Captain Jiro Toyoshima. She was the first aircraft carrier in any Navy of the world to be designed, laid down, launched, completed, and to enter service as such. In view of the forthcoming importance of aircraft carriers in the Navies of the world comparable RN and USN information follows:

HMS *Hermes* frst commissioned at Devonport on 6 August 1923. Captain The Hon. Arthur Stopford (1879-1955).

USS *Ranger* CV-4 first commissioned at Norfolk, VA on 4 June 1934. Captain Arthur LeRoy Bristol (1886-1942).

On 23 April 1923, and following a cruise to Japan, *Hawkins* sailed from Hong Kong to Singapore, arriving at that port on Saturday, 28 April. At 0800 on Monday, 30 April the old P. & O. steamer *Syria*, 6,660 grt, arrived from England carrying in her the new members of her ship's company. *Hawkins* paid off at 1400 that afternoon and, 'discharged ship's company to s.s. *Syria* (20)'. On Saturday, 5 May, and with her new company beginning to feel familiar in the ship, she sailed from Singapore and, with brief calls at Labuan and Jesselton, returned to Hong Kong on 13 May 1923.

From Liverpool on 9 June 1923 the maiden voyage of the Alfred Holt Blue Funnel Line twin screw turbine steamer *Sarpedon*, 11,321 grt. One of a class of four carrying 155 passengers in first class, they were to become well known in the East. Only she and her sister *Antenor* were to survive WW2. Of the other two on 3 November 1940 *Patroclus* was to be torpedoed and sunk off the west coast of Ireland by *U-99*, Otto Kretschmer. In Colombo harbour *Hector* was to be sunk by IJN air attack during Vice Admiral Nagumo's raid on 5 April 1942.

On 17 August 1923 the terms of the Washington Conference, November 1921 – February 1922, were ratified. The Anglo-Japanese Alliance, first signed on 30 January 1902, lapsed. At the time the British Ambassador to Tokyo was that champion of a close Anglo-Japanese relationship, the brilliant linguist and scholar Sir Charles Norton Edgcumbe Eliot (1862-1931). However, rather in contrast, in 1924 at the Foreign Office in London one important opinion held that:-

> 'The fact is Japanese interests and British interests in the Far East do not harmonise while the American and ours are identical. It is this which makes co-operation with the Japanese so difficult and forces us more and more to co-operate with the Americans. Close contacts with America has become the only right policy for this country to pursue (21).'

1 September 1923. The occurrence in Japan of a great earthquake which resulted in the death of some 140,000 persons in the Tokyo/Yokohama region, the Kanto plain. In *Hawkins* first he steamed to Shanghai to embark doctors and to load medical supplies, then he proceeded to Yokohama, arriving on 10 September 1923.

Serving as Lieut. (E) in *Hawkins* at the time was the future Engineer Rear Admiral George Campbell Ross. Written at Yokohama here follows some extracts taken from his account of the after effects of the earthquake:-

> 'It was a miserable rainy day when we anchored outside the breakwater, much of which had disappeared. When I looked shorewards it was unrecognizable. On the Bund there had been a row of prominent buildings, the Grand and Oriental hotels, the Yokohama Club, the Hong Kong and Shanghai Bank. They were there no longer.
> At the rear of the Bund was the Bluff – a high piece of land where the foreign community lived. The Naval hospital on the Bluff was a building clearly seen from the harbour. Like other buildings it too had disappeared and all that remained was a leaning flagstaff flying the White Ensign. The Surgeon Commander of the hospital was our first visitor (22). He arrived with his son Robert in a most dishevelled state. I asked him what happened and he told me that he was in his living room with his wife and son when the floor suddenly lifted under their feet and the whole building shook and came down on them. They were buried under a pile of masonry. It was some time before a rescue squad dug them out. They were unscathed but, when they found his wife, she was dead.'
> 'On the following day, 11 September, I went ashore. The city was a shambles. The streets had disappeared beneath the rubble. In the middle of a huge pile of bricks, which I took to be the Grand Hotel, was a row of burnt out motor cars, the hotel garage. Along the Bund from which the tumbled down masonry had been cleared were wide splits in the road. One could see the way in which the shock waves had travelled as the road had developed an undulating surface (23).'

On 16 October 1923 Rear Admiral David M. Anderson assumed command as RAY, Rear Admiral, Yangtse. Both on the River, and subsequently in the Navy and then the Colonial service, he was to achieve a great deal during a life of considerable variety (24).

At year end and into 1924 in the Yangtse Upper River the local war lord situation was to prove extremely difficult to follow with, for example in Chungking, a town at times under 'siege conditions', 'the generals, British

Consul Henry Archer said, were changing sides almost from day to day (25)'. Also, rather naturally, shipping on the River encountered difficulties:-

's.s. *King Wo* was shot at near Wanhsien and H.M.S. *Teal* was despatched to lodge a protest in January 1924. The gunboat's commander discussed the situation with the offending Chinese commander, a subordinate of Yang Sen, and discovered that he had been detailed to shoot at any passing steamer that refused to stop. The *Teal*'s commander received the Chinese officer's promise to stop this shooting; the negotiations were aided by a $500 bribe paid by the owners of *King Wo* (26)'.

In Canton between 20 and 30 January 1924 the First National Congress of the Kuomintang was held. Earlier the Soviets had sent their Lithuanian born agent, Michael Grusenberg or Borodin, to assist Dr. Sun Yat-sen in his reorganisation of the Kuomintang. The necessary ratification of the new political direction of the Party was agreed to during this Congress. In the meantime Dr. Sun had sent Chiang Kai-shek to Moscow to learn what he could of the Soviet leadership. Chiang saw clearly that the Soviet leadership was not to be trusted and recorded that:-

'The Russian Communist Party, in its dealings with China, has only one aim, namely to make the Chinese Communist Party its chosen instrument.'

Dr. Sun, by now thoroughly under the influence of the charming and apparently sincere Borodin, and receiving no material assistance from the west, paid little heed to this and to similar opinions expressed by Chiang. Instead Dr. Sun chose as his policy:-

'Allying with Russia and tolerating the Communists.'

From Ceylon on passage to Australia, early in February 1924 the warships of the Empire Cruise divided with the light cuisers visiting Penang and the battlecruisers, *Hood* and *Repulse*, Port Swettenham. The two squadrons subsequently united as they steamed down the Strait of Malacca to anchor at Singapore in heavy rain at 1630 hours on Sunday afternoon, 10 February. Flying his flag in *Hood* was Vice Admiral Sir Frederick L. Field. At Singapore Admiral Leveson was lying at anchor in *Hawkins* (27).

At the time the Governor of the Straits Settlements was Sir Laurence Nunns Guillemard (1862-1951). With imperial pomp and circumstance on the Monday salutes and calls were exchanged. On Friday, 15 February a Ceremonial March of the Naval Brigade took place through the streets of Singapore, then after this short visit of just a week, the Cruise was resumed in a southerly direction through the Sunda Strait towards Christmas Island then Fremantle.

16 June 1924. The new Whampoa Military Academy was opened by Dr. Sun Yat-sen. Chiang Kai-shek was appointed as the first superintendent. His chief of staff was a Russian, General Vasili Konstantinovich Bluecher, known as Galen (1889-1938). The political commissar was Liao Chung-kai, and his deputy was a man later to become very well known, Chou En-lai, aged 26 years (28).

The new Causeway between Singapore island and the mainland of the Malay peninsula at Johore officially was opened on 28 June 1924 by H.E. The Goveror, Sir Laurence Guillemard, and H.H. The Sultan of Johore. By happy co-incidence three aircraft, being used for aerial survey purposes and from the tender *Pegasus*, Commander Henry C. Rawlings, were able to add an extra dimension to the affair by flying overhead in formation at the appropriate moment. For all but a very few this was their first sight of aircraft overhead (29).

3 November 1924: arrival at Hong Kong of the seaplane tender *Pegasus*, 3,300 tons, just mentioned. She was the first such vessel ever to serve with the Royal Navy in the waters of the Far East.

As just one example of the domestic troubles then prevailing in China, and to continue to prevail during the war lord era, writing from *Hawkins* at Hong Kong on 10 November 1924 the C. in C. touched on the subject:-

'War outside Shanghai ended when Ho Feng Lin and his associates fled to Japan on 13/10 in *Shanghai Maru* (30). Chi Hsieh Yuan was the victor (31). Foreign Settlement untouched.'

On the China Station he struck his Flag on 15 November, and Vice Admiral Everett assumed the command on the following day, 16 November 1924. From the log book in *Hawkins* at Hong Kong the details are clear, including those in respect of his passage home:-

'Saturday, 15 November 1924

    08:00   *Diomede* broke flag of Vice Admiral Everett and saluted flag of Admiral Leveson with 17 guns. *Hawkins* returned salute with fifteen guns.

    11:10   Admiral Leveson, Captain Alington and staff left ship for s.s. *Malwa* for passage to England.

    17:30   Struck flag of Admiral Leveson.

Sunday, 16 November 1924

    08:00   Broke flag of Sir Allen F. Everett, C. in C., China station (32).'

Appointed first and Principal Naval ADC to H.M. King George V on 4 October 1926.

A member of both the Naval Records Society and the Society for Nautical Research.

Younger Brother of Trinity House.

GCB: gazetted on 3 June 1927.

On Tuesday, 24 January 1928 he represented HM King George V on the occasion of the funeral of Admiral of the Fleet Sir John de Robeck who had died at his home in London just a few days earlier, on 20 January (33).

He was placed on the Retired List on 22 February 1928.

For many years his home was at 'Bridgelands', Midhurst, Sussex, he being associated with the district for over twenty years. Latterly, however, he had moved to 'Park Cottage' in Easebourne, a village lying on the western border of Cowdray Park.

Following his death in France his body duly was brought home and his interment took place at St. Mary's Church, Easebourne, near Midhurst, on Monday, 1 July 1929. The church itself lies immediately adjacent to the historic Easebourne Priory:-

'No such funeral has been witnessed at Easebourne in living memory (34).'

To elaborate a little, his funeral procession was headed by a Royal Marine band which was followed up by a firing party. The pall bearers included Admirals of the Fleet Earl Jellicoe and Sir Charles Madden, together with Admiral Sir Sydney Fremantle. In addition to members of his family among the mourners were Admiral Sir Martyn Jerram (see C. in C., 1913), the C. in C., The Nore, Admiral Sir Edwyn Sinclair (see C. in C., 1925), Vice Admiral Sir Hugh Watson (1872-1954), and Vice Admiral and Mrs. F.C. Dreyer (see C. in C., 1933). There were 150 wreaths.

An obituary notice was published in The Geographical Journal in 1929. Excerpts follow:-

'He was endowed with brains of an exceptional character, with great power in the acquisition of all sorts of knowledge and information. Those who partook of his ever ready hospitality would be sure to find the map and book relating to the latest topic of interest laid on his table, and would listen to his incisive judgements with pleasure and interest.

It was indeed remarkable that one whose life had been largely spent in the study of the more material side of an exacting profession should have found time to assimilate a knowledge of history and geography combined that was far above the average. His genial presence will be greatly missed. W.E.G. (35).'

NOTES

1. Arthur's father had been born in Manchester and was Christened Edward John Levyssohn in the Cathedral on 28 May 1832, second son of Edward Henry Levyssohn and Sarah Ashworth who had married at St. Mary's, Radcliffe, Lancashire on 12 December 1825. Edward Henry himself, born in Rotterdam in 1795 was naturalised British on 29 July 1831. *Journal of the House of Lords.* Vol. 63. Subsequently he was to arrange for his surname to be altered to Leveson. Sadly he died when just fifty three years of age, at Uxbridge in January 1849.

   Mary Iveson was born in Halliford, Middlesex on 12 October 1837. As Edward John Leveson, merchant of 10 Upper Gloucester Place, Dorset Square, London, he and Mary Iveson were married at Christchurch, Savernake, Wiltshire on 4 July 1860 and shortly thereafter left for Singapore where their eldest son, also Edward John, was born the following year, 5 May 1861. This son, the Admiral's eldest brother, in due course was to return to business in Singapore, and, later in England, to become a member of the London Stock Exchange. Subsequently he moved to Vancouver, BC where he died on 22 December 1933.

   Between 1859 and 1867 the Governor of the Straits Settlements was His Excellency Major General William Orfeur Cavenagh (1820-1891), Bengal Staff Corps. Among other interests His Excellency chaired the Agri-Horticultural Society of Singapore of which, by 1866, E.J. Leveson was the Honorary Secretary/Treasurer. From this and no doubt other friendly connections it would seem clear that it was from this source that the Cavenagh as one of the Admiral's names was derived.

   It is most apparent, during that period in Singapore, that Edward John Leveson was a prominent citizen, also that later in life he was to retain Eastern connections. For example, as early as 1850, aged eighteen, he had travelled back to Singapore where he had joined the firm of Apel & Co. Later, together with George Adolph Reme, he was a partner in the firm of insurance and shipping agents, Reme, Leveson and Company, established in 1857 and with offices at 33 Raffles Place and Collyer Quay. In addition by 1867 he was a committee member of the Singapore Club, was District Grand Junior Deacon in the Masonic Lodge, and was a Justice of the Peace for the Straits Settlements. Together with George Reme they were Italian Consuls. After returning to England by 1872 he was a committee member of the Straits Settlements Association, 21 St. Swithin's Lane, Cannon Street, London. Aged sixty seven years, of heart failure he died at home, 'Cluny', 101 Anerley Road, Penge, London on 6 January 1900. Suffering from influenza his wife Mary died the following day. *The Straits Calendar and Directory,* 1867. *The Straits Times,* 7 February 1900. Wiltshire and Swindon History Centre. National Library, Singapore. The author is grateful to the researchers, Mrs. Cecelia Boylan and Mr. Richard Leveson for enthusiastic assistance received.

2. NA ADM 196/42. *Service Record.*

3. Ibid.

4. William Henry **May**. Born: 31 July 1849. Died: 7 October 1930. Captain: 9 May 1887. In 1888 Flag Captain to Sir Nowell Salmon – see C. in C., 1887. Rear Admiral: 28 March 1901. Vice Admiral: 29 June 1905. Admiral: 5 November 1908 and latterly C. in C., Devonport: 11 April 1911 to 20 March 1913. Admiral of the Fleet: 20 March 1913. *Navy List.* As with Arthur Leveson, Admiral May's family also had some roots in The Netherlands.

5. *The Times,* special correspondent. As befits the occasion, one of importance in the jockeying for position amongst European powers which took place prior to the outbreak of the Great War, the daily reports filed were lengthy and phrased in an appropriately eloquent style. In August a French Fleet paid a return visit to Portsmouth.

   Francis Leveson Bertie (1844-1919). Eton. Entered the Foreign Office in 1863. Assistant under-secretary: 1894. At the Foreign Office 'he was instrumental in promoting the idea of an Anglo-Japanese alliance as a means of containing Russian ambitions in the East.' KCB: 1902. GCVO: 1903. Ambassador to Italy: 1903, and to France: 1905. He was to remain in Paris for thirteen years. There he was most closely identified with the creation of a positive working relationship covering the Entente Cordiale. GCMG: 1904. GCB: 1908. Created Baron Bertie of Thame: 1915. Viscount: 1918. *Dictionary of National Biography.*

6. *Service Record.*

7. Arthur J. Marder, *From the Dreadnought to Scapa Flow,* II, (OUP, 1965), 10.

8. Ibid., 37.

9. Arthur J. Marder, *Portrait of an Admiral: The Life and Papers of Sir Herbert Richmond,* (London, 1952), 21. Herbert

William **Richmond** (1871-1946). At the time Richmond was a Captain, RN. KCB: 1926. Admiral: 1929. From 1934 until his death in 1946 to be Master of Downing College, Cambridge.

Subsequently, in the same volume by the late Professor Marder, Richmond's views and opinions are detailed.

10. Obituary, *The Times,* Friday, June 28, 1929. The account was given by Rear Admiral Sir Douglas Brownrigg, Chief Naval Censor. SMS *Dresden* escaped but at Mas a Tierra, Juan Fernandez Group, on 14 March 1915 was disposed of by HM Ships *Glasgow* and *Kent.*

11. *From the Dreadnought to Scapa Flow,* III, (OUP, 1966), 213.

12. Admiral Sir William Goodenough, *A Rough Record,* (London, 1946), 94.

13. Much information kindly supplied, and other details confirmed by Sea Power Centre, RAN, Canberra. Ref: 2011/1000829/5 dated 27 June 2011.

14. Obituary, *The Times.*

15. *From the Dreadnought to Scapa Flow,* V, (OUP, 1970), 273.

16. *Service Record.*

17. No doubt Sir Arthur will have been amused to reflect that in taking up this position in the Far East not only was he returning to waters well known to his parents, those of Singapore, but also to those of Nagasaki.

   As seen above the Admiral's father was Edward John Levyssohn/Leveson (1832-1900). He was a son of Edward Henry Levyssohn (1795-1849). A brother of Edward Henry was Joseph Henry Levyssohn, born in Rotterdam on 26 July 1800. Joseph Henry was at least partially educated in England but subsequently joined the Dutch East Indian service and arrived in Batavia on 8 October 1823. In due course, at Deshima, Nagasaki, he was to be opperhoofd from November 1845 to October 1850. He returned to the Netherlands in 1851 and subsequently died at Arnhem on 6 March 1883. Therein is the family connection, the Admiral's great uncle Joseph at Deshima. (At Deshima Joseph was succeeded by Frederick Colnelis Rose: 1 November 1850 to 31 October 1852, and then by Janus Henricus Donker Curtius from 2 November 1852 until the expiry of the post on 28 February 1860. The Tokugawa Shogunate era, greatly weakened by 1858, with the resignation of Tokugawa Yoshinobu was to end in January 1868).

   The author is most grateful to Doctor Manon Osseweijer, The International Institute for Asian Studies at Leiden, for her kind assistance in confirming certain family connections.

18. Admiral Sir William James, *The Sky was Always Blue,* (London, 1951), 128.

19. 27, The Bund. Still standing today and visited by the writer on 17 April 2008. Apparently unoccupied but with a guard on duty, the entrance hall still impresses in the old style of solid architecture in which dark heavy wood, marble and granite appeared to predominate. Fortunately today the authorities regard the historic buildings lining the Bund as National Monuments.

20. NA ADM 53/78591. The P. & O. twin screw triple expansion *Syria,* completed in June 1901 for the Indian service and for trooping charters. Some service during WW1 as a hospital ship. In June 1924 sold for breaking up in Italy.

21. NA FO 371/10244 dated 13 September 1924.

22. Surgeon Commander William Perceval Hingston (1879-1950), appointed to the position on 15 December 1922. *Navy List.* For his great efforts in Japan on 30 November 1923 his CB was to be gazetted. His wife who so sadly had lost her life was Myfanwy Dora, nee Marsden.

23. Imperial War Museum, London. Ref: *86/60/1* – chapter 11. Lieut. Ross was appointed to *Hawkins* on 9 May 1921. *Navy List.*

24. NA ADM 196/43. 242. David Murray Anderson. Born: 11 April 1874. Died in office as Governor of New South Wales: 30 October 1936. For career detail see Admiral Alexander-Sinclair, C. in C., 1925, reference (21).

25. P.D. Coates, *The China Consuls,* (OUP, 1988), 405. Consul Henry Allan Fairfax Best **Archer.** Born: 5 August 1887. Died in Capetown: 19 September 1950. Rugby. Appointed Student Interpreter in China: 26 February 1912. Service in Tsinanfu, Tsingtao, briefly in 1922 back in the Foreign Office in London, then to Chungking. OBE: 3 June 1924. Next in Shanghai, Peking, Wei-Hai-Wei, Changsha and Hankow. Promoted Consul General: 1 July 1940 and on 14 January 1941 appointed to Harbin where detained by the Japanese occupying power from the beginning of the Pacific War in WW2 in December 1941 through to 25 September 1945. Retired: 16 September 1946. He was a Freeman of the City of London. *Foreign Office List,* 1951.

26. Christopher J. Bowie, *Great Britain and the use of Force in China: 1919-1931,* (Ph.D thesis, Oxford, 1983), 115/116. The

author is quoting from NA FO 371/10249.

King Wo, 617 grt. Owned by Indo-China SN Co. Ltd. (Jardine Matheson & Co.).

Yang Sen. Born: 20 February 1884. Died: 15 May 1977. Szechwan war lord. Played an active Nationalist role in WW2 and in 1949 participated in the exodus to Taiwan.

27. V.C. Scott O'Connor, *The Empire Cruise*, (London, 1925), 97-112.

28. **Chou** En-lai. Born: 5 March 1898. Died: 8 January 1976. In August 1925 to escape unharmed at the time that Liao Chung-kai had been assassinated by right wing interests. On 1 October 1949, following the Communist party victory in the civil war, to become the first Premier of the People's Republic of China, a post he held until his death. Additionally, between 1949 and 1958, Foreign Minister. He was a skilled and able diplomat. *Encyclopaedia Britannica*.

29. G.E. Livock, *To the Ends of the Air*, (London, 1973), 81.
Although officially opened in June 1924 goods trains had been operated across the Causeway since 17 September 1923, and passenger trains since 1 October 1923.

30. *Shanghai Maru*, 5,252 grt. Built in 1923 for N.Y.K., Tokyo by W. Denny Bros., Dumbarton. Twin screw turbine powered steamer. *Lloyd's Register*.

31. **Chi** Hsieh Yuan. *China Year Book,* 1925. A Peking supporter and from 10 October 1922 a full General. He was victorious in that Kiangsu/Chekiang war of October 1924 but subsequently he too was defeated. He fled to Japan where he arrived on 20 December 1924, shortly thereafter retiring in Beppu, the resort on Kyushu. It goes without saying that both he, and Ho, will have extorted adequate funds with which to ensure comfortable retirement.

32. NA ADM 53/78593. P. & O. steamer *Malwa*, 10,883 grt. Built in 1908. Twin screw. During the latter part of the Great War she had served as a troopship. Returned to commercial service in September 1920. Late in 1932 to be sold for breaking up in Japan.

33. *The Kildare Observer*, 28 January 1928.

34. *Midhurst Times,* Friday, 5 July 1929. The author visited his grave on 18 May 2011. It is situated just a short distance directly towards the church from the prominent headstone marking that of Lord Cowdray. There is no headstone, the low stone outline of the double grave being appropriately inscribed along the two longer sides:

> 'To the memory of Admiral Sir Arthur Leveson, GCB, died 26 June 1929, aged 61, and his wife Jemima, died 29 April 1964, aged 84.'

A parishioner kindly mentioned to the author that the low steel railings which at one time surrounded his grave site were removed as scrap during WW2 when the demand for all metals was very high.

35. *The Geographical Journal*, Vol. LXXIV. July to December 1929, 512. W.E.G. is Admiral Sir William E. Goodenough, also FRGS.

10 September 1924 to 22 April 1925
Vice Admiral Sir Allan Frederic **Everett**

He was born on 22 February 1868, the fourth child and son of Colonel John Frederic Everett, J.P. of Greenhill House, Sutton Veny, Warminster and Upton Lovell Manor (1). In October 1863 the Colonel had married Mary Florence, daughter of the Rev. Henry Fowle. They were to have six sons. The Colonel, who for many years was Master of the South and West Wiltshire Hounds, died in May 1903.

Sir Allan died on 22 January 1938 at his home, 24 Morpeth Mansions, London, S.W.

In July 1881 he entered the Royal Navy as a **Cadet. Midshipman**: 14 May 1884 (2). From 4 January 1884 served in the iron ship, armour plated *Invincible*, 6,010 tons, Captain Claude Edward Buckle, China Station. From 11 January 1886 in the iron ship, armour plated, *Sultan*, 9,200 tons, Channel Squadron. From 26 May 1887 in cruiser *Volage*, 3,080 tons, 'Training Squadron.' **Sub Lieutenant**: 14 May1888. Studying at RNC, Greenwich. From 9 November 1889 in battleship *Collingwood*, 9,500 tons, Captain Charles C.P. Fitzgerald, Mediterranean. Also serving in the ship was Lieut. Frederick C.T. Jones (see C. in C., 1917). **Lieutenant**: 30 June 1891. From 18 December 1891 in cruiser *Amphion*, 4,300 tons. Mediterranean. From 31 March 1894 Flag Lieut. to Rear Admiral, Mediterranean, Compton E. Domville, in battleship *Trafalgar*, 11,940 tons. From 26 June 1896, 'appointed on Committee for revision of Signal Books (3).' From 7 June 1897 Flag Lieut. to the C in C., Channel Squadron, Vice Admiral Henry F. Stephenson, in battleship *Majestic*, 14,900 tons, Captain Prince Louis of Battenberg.

On 13 June 1899 in Salisbury Cathedral he married Michaelangela Kattrine, daughter of Captain G. Lyon-Carr, RN. At the time of his death in one obituary notice it was to be mentioned that:-

> 'Before her marriage Lady Everett was well known as a singer, and as Miss Lina Carr she was at one time one of the members of the D'Oyly Carte Opera Company (4).'

Sadly she was to die in 1931. Their son, Robert Norman, born on 23 May 1913, was to follow his father into the Navy. Midshipman: 1 September 1931. Subsequently he was to serve in the Fleet Air Arm and, as a Commander, to retire on 8 May 1955. He died in November 1992.

From 12 November 1900 in *Victory*, Portsmouth, 'For charge of Signal School.'

Commander: 30 June 1901. Remained in charge Signal School, *Victory*, until 31 December 1903.

From 1 January 1904 in command Torpedo Boat Destroyer *Myrmidon*, 370 tons, Tender to TBD Depot Ship *Orion*, 4,870 tons, Mediterranean. To join her he took passage out in the P. & O. s.s. *Malacca* and on 5 February 1904 assumed command at Malta (5).

Subsequently the Depot Ship was *Leander*, 4,300 tons.

In *Myrmidon*, during exercises being undertaken while some of the warships of the Mediterranean Fleet were on passage from Malaga to Gibraltar, at 0815 hours on 28 May 1904 he, '.. fouled *Coquette* in turning astern. Side plates abreast Standard Compass torn on water line. Placed collision mat (6)'. Fortunately this small incident was accepted as a part of the normal risk of conducting operations in such circumstances, also the damage was not serious. He brought *Myrmidon* safely to Gibraltar and, after he had left her, repairs were carried out up the dockyard slip between 3 and 8 June 1904.

Between 1902 and 1905 the C. in C., Mediterranean was Admiral Sir Compton Edward Domville (1842-1924), an Admiral whom he had served earlier.

On 1 June 1904, at Gibraltar, he assumed command of the TBD *Exe*, 550 tons, tender to TBD depot ship *Leander*, Atlantic Fleet. Subsequently he took *Exe* to China where she was the tender to TBD depot ship *Hecla*, 6,400 tons. On the China coast during the late summer of 1905 he underwent an unenviable experience:-

> 'I regret to say that HMS *Exe* is temporarily *hors de combat*. When we shall be able to take to the high sea again is doubtful. Twenty miles off the Saddles it was obvious that a typhoon was imminent. I tried to push on to make landfall but I was forced to heave to. For 18 hours I had to keep my vessel bow to the wind. --- I fetched up here on Sunday after an experience which I trust will never fall my lot again. I have two plates where the rivets went, my provision room flooded, two large cowls were unshipped, electric lights failed, charts went, log went until I hoped the end would soon be over. --- I would like some of the b**** construction people who cavil about minor defects to have been aboard (7)'.

Captain: 31 December 1905. Brought *Exe* home from China.

From 1 August 1906 in *Victory*, 'For Charge of Signal School at Portsmouth, and for duty as Superintendent of Signal Schools'. He was a great signal enthusiast, often carrying out experiments with new equipment, making proposals for amending signal books, and indeed writing many of the books himself.

From 22 April 1908 to 6 June 1910 in command cruiser *Cumberland*, 9,800 tons, 'Training Ship for Naval Cadets.'

From 9 August 1910 in command battleship *King Edward VII*, 16,350 tons, Flagship of Vice Admiral Commanding Second Division, Home Fleet, Vice Admiral Sir George A. Callaghan. From 24 July 1911 to 5 December 1911 similarly as Flag Captain to Sir George Callaghan in the new battleship *Hercules*, 20,225 tons (8).

From 5 December 1911 in command battleship *Neptune*, 19,900 tons, Flagship, C. in C., Home Fleet, acting Admiral Sir George A. Callaghan. The First Lieutenant in *Neptune* for some of this period was the future Admiral Sir William Milbourne James (1881-1973). In due course, writing of his short time in the ship, Sir William was to include the following remarks:-

> 'The Captain, Everett, talked and moved lazily and never took any exercise, but he was a good Captain and much respected by all hands. He rose rapidly, but his career was cut short by illness when he was Commander in Chief, China (9).'

From 9 May 1913 appointed Captain of the Fleet and **Commodore** First Class, first continuing in *Neptune*, then in the new battleship *Iron Duke*, 25,000 tons, Flagship of C in C., Home Fleet, Admiral Sir George A. Callaghan. This class of four were the last coal burning battleships in the Royal Navy. *Iron Duke* was completed in March 1914.

CB: 1 January 1914.

Continued as Captain of the Fleet and Commodore First Class in *Iron Duke*, from 4 August 1914 the C. in C. being acting Admiral Sir John R. Jellicoe.

From 15 June 1915 to December 1916 Naval Assistant to the First Sea Lord, Admiral Sir Henry Jackson. This period included the time during which the Battle of Jutland was fought, 31 May 1916. Quite by chance at that very moment he was acting as the Chief of the War Staff, temporarily standing in for Rear Admiral Oliver, and subsequently it was to be revealed within the Admiralty that certain important intelligence signals relating to German movements that fateful evening of 31 May had not been forwarded to the C. in C., Grand Fleet, Sir John Jellicoe. As the late Professor Arthur Marder was to write:-

'The Room 40 men also said that Captain A.F. Everett, the Naval Secretary to the First Lord, was temporarily acting for Oliver. Jackson, the D.O.D., would have been the natural person to take over, and if he, too, were resting, it would be one of the duty captains. Why, then, Everett? We simply do not know. Now Everett was a very level headed, capable officer, whose lazy way of speaking disguised a great deal of common sense. But, having had little or no experience of German operational signals and naval procedure, he was not aware of the vital significance of such signals as the one ordering an air reconnaissance and for all destroyer flotillas to be assembled off Horns Reef.

They were accordingly just put on file. I state this as a possibility. Admiral James writes, "If it is true that Captain Everett was the recipient of these vital signals, he surely would not have put them on the file without discussing them with the Operations staff, some of whom must have been present. All that is certain is that they were put on the file and none of them passed to Jellicoe. None of the officers who were in the Operations room during those fateful hours are alive and so it will never be known if there was a division of opinion about passing the information to Jellicoe and who decided to take no action." (10).'

In recent times another historian has suggested, especially with relation to the remark above that Captain Everett had, 'no experience of German operational signals and naval procedure', that Professor Marder may have erred in stressing this aspect:-

'Yet this (again) was not true. Everett had spent his entire naval career immersed in the world of signals, both visual and wireless. In addition, his posting immediately prior to that at the Admiralty was in (on) HMS *Iron Duke* and so he would have been well versed in Jellicoe's methods and approach to battle (11).'

By and large it certainly does seem most unlikely that an officer with Captain Everett's exposure to Home/Grand Fleet procedure at sea at a high level, and there in the North Sea in both peace and war, also with his very considerable experience of signalling activity, could possibly not have appreciated the significance of enemy signals ordering air reconnaissance and for the assembly of destroyer flotillas at such a position as Horns Reef, this Reef being situated just to the East of the area in which the Battle of Jutland was being fought.

When Jellicoe became 1SL, on 5 December 1916, then from 16 December 1916 he was appointed Naval Secretary to the First Lord of the Admiralty, Sir Edward Carson. Here follows another quote taken from Arthur Marder:-

'The Naval Secretary to the First Lord was a good choice: Commodore Allan F. ('Ev') Everett, a genial, level headed, hard working officer of independent mind and considerable professional attainments (12).'

Indeed, while holding this appointment as Naval Secretary to the First Lord then, by order in council approved on 22 December 1916, he was promoted **Commodore** first class, 'such temporary rank, however, to carry with it no benefits of a financial nature (13).'

Rear Admiral: 28 April 1917.

Continued as Naval Secretary to the First Lord. From July 1917 Sir Edward was succeeded by Sir Eric Geddes.

From 26 October 1918 RA, 4LCS, Grand Fleet with Flag in the light cruiser *Calliope*, 3,750 tons, Captain Percy L.H. Noble (see C in C., 1938). In *Calliope*:-

'.... present at the surrender of the German Fleet off Rosyth on November 21, 1918 (14).'

KCMG: 1 January 1919. The investiture took place at Buckingham Palace just six weeks later, on 15 February 1919 (15).

From March 1919 Flag in *Calcutta*, 4,190 tons, Captain Percy L.H. Noble, as RA, 8LCS, North America and West Indies.

Later that year the ship was able to provide useful assistance in an important sugar, asphalt and oil producing colony:-

> 'Colonial Govt. of Trinidad expresses thanks for valuable service rendered during and after disturbances at Port of Spain and Tobago (16).'

As far as the ship was concerned this exercise had commenced at 13:45 hours on Saturday, 6 December 1919 when she had, '… landed 'B' Company for protective measures at Port of Spain'. Immediately after landing these men then at 1410 hours she had weighed for Scarborough, where she had arrived three hours later and there, 'At 18:45 landed 'A' Company to protect life and property at Scarborough, Tobago'.

Subsequently at Tobago:-

> 'Tuesday, 9 December 1919
>
> 10:00   17 ratings from 'A' Company re-embarked. 15 prisoners, natives (male and female) embarked for passage to Port of Spain.
>
> 12:50   Weighed and proceeded (passage made at twenty two knots).
>
> 16:30   Anchored off Port of Spain.
>
> 17:10   Discharged 15 prisoners (natives) under police escort (17).'

At Port of Spain at various times during December 1919 she had, '… landed armed party to visit outlying districts'.

From the end of 1919 until his sad death on 30 July 1920, and subsequent burial at the Bermuda Royal Naval Cemetery, the C. in C. on the North America and West Indies Station was Vice Admiral Sir Trevylyan Dacres Willes Napier.

KCVO: 2 October 1920 for services rendered during H.R.H. The Prince of Wales's tour of Newfoundland and Canada, which also included a brief visit to the U.S.A. To undertake the tour H.R.H. had left Portsmouth in the battlecruiser *Renown*, 26,500 tons, on 5 August 1919.

Between 21 February 1919 and 3 February 1920 Admiral Lord Jellicoe undertook his World Cruise in the battlecruiser *New Zealand*, 18,800 tons. The last port of call was at Port of Spain where he arrived on 17 January 1920, and:-

> 'Here the 8th Light Cruiser Squadron was met, under the command of Rear Admiral Sir Allan Everett, KCMG, CB. Lord Jellicoe then called on HE the Governor, Major Sir John Chancellor, KCMG, DSO… (--) In the evening a large dinner was given in honour of Lord Jellicoe and Sir Robert Borden (18).'

At the end of the commission, and accompanied by Captain Noble, he returned home from New York in s.s. *Aquitania* who sailed on 12 April 1921. By that time the C. in C. on the Station was Vice Admiral Sir William Christopher Packenham (1861-1933), none other than he who from the decks of HIJMS *Asahi* in May 1905 had witnessed proceedings during Admiral Togo's overwhelming victory at Tsushima.

From 15 September 1921 appointed First Naval Member of the Australian Commonwealth Naval Board. His ship sailed for Australia on 15 October and his term of office commenced on 24 November 1921.

Vice Admiral: 3 May 1922.

Continued as First Naval Member in Australia, actually in Australia until 29 August 1923, and then subsequently:-

> 'He attended the Imperial Conference in London in the autumn of 1923 as Chief Naval Adviser to the Australian prime minister (19).'

Only on 18 December 1923 did he cease to be First Naval Member of the Australian Naval Board. Next, in September 1924, he was appointed C. in C., China Station. To take up this appointment he travelled to the Far East in the P. & O. liner *Mantua*, 10,946 grt, who was due at Hong Kong on 14 November.

At Hong Kong, Admiral Leveson and his staff having embarked the previous day in the homeward bound P. & O. liner *Malwa*, a sister ship to *Mantua* and of 10,883 grt, he assumed command as C. in C. on Sunday, 16 November 1924. His Flagship was the cruiser *Hawkins*, 9,750 tons, Captain W.J.C. Lake.

Almost immediately he proceeded on his first cruise, in *Hawkins* leaving Hong Kong on 19 November for Taku Bar at the mouth of the Peiho where he arrived on Sunday, 23 November 1924. Subsequently he continued the cruise by retracing his course to Wei-Hai-Wei, and then onwards in a southerly direction to Shanghai (20).

On Monday, 1 December 1924 Sir Reginald Stubbs became the first Governor of Hong Kong to inspect his territory from the air. That morning, in Fairey 3D seaplane 'Z', seaplane tender *Pegasus*, he made a short flight from Tolo Harbour (21).

Meanwhile at the end of November 1924, sailing from Shanghai in the NYK steamer *Shanghai Maru*, 5,252 grt, Dr. Sun Yat-sen paid a short visit to Nagasaki and Kobe. In a speech delivered in Kobe he raised the relevant point, whether Japan as she appeared to be developing was to adopt the policies as he perceived were practiced by the West, that 'might is right', or whether she would retain what he regarded as being the desireable Oriental characteristic of 'rule of right'. Dr. Sun regarded right as, 'seeking a civilization of peace and equality, and the emancipation of all races'.

From Japan Dr. Sun continued to on to north China. There, suffering from inoperable liver cancer, sadly he died in Peking on 12 March 1925. Until the time of the Japanese invasion in 1937 his wife, Soong Ching Ling (1893-1981), was to continue to live at their house in Shanghai, 29 rue Moliere in the French Settlement (today: 7 Xiangshan Road). As his second wife she had married Dr. Sun in Tokyo on 25 October 1915.

Of her two sisters, Soong Ai-ling married the wealthy K'ung Hsiang-hsi or H.H. Kung, long time finance minister and governor of the Central Bank of China, and Soong May-ling married Chiang Kai-shek. A brother was Soong Tzu-wen or T.V. Soong (1894-1971), yet another prominent businessman and politician within the broader Kuomintang leadership.

In a sense it was after his death that Dr. Sun was to become more powerful politically. His ideas and beliefs became a focal point around which his supporters could and did rally.

All during this period the question of the desireability of constructing a naval base at Singapore was the subject of considerable argument in Britain. Well into the 1930s the controversy continued to exist.

Remember that in 1918 the 'war to end all wars' had been fought and won however Great Britain, and many other countries for that matter, had been left exhausted by the conflict. Money was extremely tight. Many viewed the construction of such a base as an extraordinary waste which smacked of sabre rattling, if not worse. Nevertheless as has been seen above, during the time of Lloyd George's coalition in June 1921 the project had been approved in Cabinet. Later work began, slowly. In 1924 the first Labour government, that formed by James Ramsey MacDonald, decided to halt construction. Money, that scarce commodity, was required for pressing social expenditure. This Labour government, however, lasted only a few months and at the end of 1924 the Conservative, Stanley Baldwin, was returned to office and within a month Cabinet approved in principle that work should resume.

It is worthwhile recording that Winston Churchill was Chancellor of the Exchequer in Baldwin's government. With the need for strict economy in mind he had opposed the project, a courageous stand but, after all, as Chancellor, he was responsible for all national financial matters. Within fifteen years, in the greatly differing circumstances which then would prevail, there was to be no greater exponent of the virtues of the supposed 'Fortress' of Singapore.

Although continuation of work on the base may have been approved the actual pace of construction was to remain very slow.

While on the subject, and looking ahead, when the Labour party was returned to power in June 1929 then

MacDonald, in part due to considerable pressure from the Dominions of Australia and New Zealand, was to agree that the work should continue. Still by no means was it all to be plain sailing. The very next year at an international naval conference held in London, and as a result of various decisions taken, once more work on the project was to be in danger of ceasing.

Procrastination followed procrastination. British politicians of a pacifist frame of mind being aided by the infamous and self perpetuating Ten Year Rule, that there would be no war for another ten years. Even as late as 1933 the question was not to be firmly resolved, neither stopped nor started, just pottering along. At last in 1934, with MacDonald still in power as leader of a coalition government, but with tension around the world clearly becoming greater, the pace of work was to be accelerated and funds made available in order to have a base of some use ready by 1938.

The above on the subject of the Naval base at Singapore, in due course to be named *Sultan,* also serves to illustrate another difficulty faced by many British authorities throughout the East during this period. The chaotic domestic situation in China, with very real communist undertones, was beginning to come to a head. It was they on the spot who had to propose and recommend to London various courses of action. Huge social and other problems existed in each country in Europe including Britain. As already stressed there was little spare cash. Naturally a Labour government and MacDonald had a quite different set of priorities to those of the Conservatives and Baldwin. Almost invariably Ministers, Governors, Administrators, Admirals and Generals in the East, seeking some form of a continuous and firm policy direction from their political masters in London were to find it an uphill task.

At Shanghai between 11 and 22 January 1925 the Chinese Communist Party held their Fourth National Congress. In the words of the author of a subsequent volume:-

> '.... in which the leadership of the proletarian class over the democratic revolution was raised and resolutions to develop the revolution were worked out, thus preparing for the oncoming revolutionary upsurge. In February, workers in a Japanese owned cotton mill held a big strike to maintain their work and political rights (22).'

During the spring of 1925 the C. in C. was, '.. obliged to relinquish his command owing to ill health (23).'

In fact at Singapore at 18.11 hours on Sunday, 12 April 1925 his flag in *Hawkins* was struck and transferred to the C. in C's yacht, *Petersfield.* In turn at noon the following day his flag was struck in *Petersfield* who then returned to Hong Kong. There in Victoria Harbour at 0800 on Wednesday morning, 22 April 1925 she broke the flag of Rear Admiral D. Murray Anderson as acting C. in C., China Station (24).

He returned home and retired on 12 August 1925, 'medically unfit' (25).

Admiral on the Retired List: 8 November 1926.

Subsequent to his death on 22 January 1938 then two days later it was announced that his funeral service was to take place at St. Jude's Church, Southsea on Wednesday, 26 January 1938 at 2 p.m. This was to be followed by a private interment at the Highland Road Cemetery, Portsmouth (26).

NOTES

1. Extract from the *Wiltshire Gazette* in May 1924 under the heading, 'New Admiral for China Station'.
2. NA ADM 196/43. *Service Record.*
3. Ibid.
4. Obituary, *Wiltshire Gazette,* 27 January 1938.
5. NA ADM 53/ 23906. Log Book *Myrmidon.*
   P. & O. s.s. *Malacca,* 4,045 grt. The Russo-Japanese war of 1904-1905 broke out in February 1904. During her next

voyage, steaming from Europe to the East, on 13 July 1904 in the Red Sea *Malacca* was to be apprehended by a Tsarist warship as it was suspected by Russia that she was carrying cargoes which could be of use to Japan in their prosecution of the war. Not surprisingly subsequent inter governmental discussions were to reach the highest level. After a short delay the Russians were to release *Malacca* who continued her voyage. In 1909 her owners were to dispose of her for scrapping.

6. NA ADM 53/ 23908. Later log book, *Myrmidon.*

7. Letter of 4 September 1905 reporting to his commanding officer. Frank Urban, *Ned's Navy,* (Shrewsbury, 1998), 110/111. The Saddles are a small group of islands off the southern approach to the Yangtse River estuary.

8. *Service Record.*

9. Admiral Sir William James, *The Sky was Always Blue,* (London, 1951), 75.

10. Arthur J. Marder, *From the Dreadnought to Scapa Flow*, III, (OUP, 1966), 154.
Room 40 then was occupied by the Admiralty Intelligence and Decrypting organisation.
Oliver is the subsequent Admiral of the Fleet Sir Henry Francis Oliver (1865-1965). 'Oliver was taking the first opportunity since the fleet had sailed to retire for a badly needed rest.' However Professor Marder also writes, page 153:-

> 'In the second place, the organization of the Operations Division was not as efficient as it should have been, because it was really a one man show. Oliver, the Chief of the War Staff, virtually conducted all operations single handed. (--) A fundamental reason, then, for the failure to pass on the vital signals was that everything was in the hands of one man – an able man, no doubt, but no one person could conduct four or five campaigns and cope with the U-boat warfare without a strong staff to help him.'

Another authority is in general agreement with the above: Richard Hough, *The Great War at Sea: 1914-1918*, (OUP, 1983), 282/3.
Jackson is the subsequent Admiral Sir Thomas Jackson (1868-1945). Then a Captain, shortly after Jutland he was to be promoted Rear Admiral.
Admiral James is Sir William Milbourne James (1881-1973). In his biography, *A Great Seaman, The Life of Admiral of the Fleet Sir Henry Oliver,* (London, 1956), pages 153/155, Admiral James makes no mention of any role performed by Captain Everett during the time of the Battle of Jutland.

11. Nicholas Black, *The British Naval Staff in the First World War,* (Woodbridge, Suffolk, 2009), 162/3.

12. *From the Dreadnought to Scapa Flow*, IV, (OUP, 1969), 56.

13. *Service Record.*

14. Obituary, *The Times,* Monday, January 24, 1938.

15. *Service Record.*

16. Ibid.

17. NA ADM 53/36613. Log Book *Calcutta.*

18. Admiral Sir Reginald Bacon, *The Life of John Rushworth Earl Jellicoe,* (London, 1936), 422.
Later Lt. Colonel. Sir John Robert **Chancellor** (1870-1952). One time Royal Engineer. Previously Governor of Mauritius: 1911-1916. Governor of Trinidad and Tobago: 1916-1921. Subsequently Governor of Southern Rhodesia, and later the High Commissioner in Palestine. *Colonial Office List.*
Robert Laird **Borden** (1854-1937). Prime Minister of Canada: 1911-1920. *World Book Encyclopaedia.*

19. Obituary, *The Times.* The Australian prime minister was Stanley Melbourne **Bruce** (1883-1967), in 1947 to be created a Viscount.

20. NA ADM 53/78593. Log Book *Hawkins.*

21. NA ADM 53/81599. Log Book *Pegasus.*

22. Ed. Bai Shouyi, *An Outline History of China: 1919-1949,* (Beijing, 1993), 36.

23. Obituary, *The Times.*

24. NA ADM 53/78594. Log Book *Hawkins.* Unfortunately at the National Archives, Kew there is no log book available covering the movements of *Petersfield* herself during this period.

25. *Service Record.*

26. *The Times,* Monday, January 24, 1938.

22 April 1925 to 8 November 1926

Vice Admiral Sir Edwyn Sinclair **Alexander-**

Sinclair

He was born in Malta at 14 Strada Scozzese, Valetta on 12 December 1865, second son of Captain John Hobhouse Inglis Alexander, commanding officer *Euryalus* at Shimonoseki, 5-10 September 1864 (see Rear Admiral Augustus L. Kuper, C. in C., 1862), and his wife Isabella Barbara, daughter of Thomas Cochrane Hume of Halifax, Nova Scotia (1).

He died on Tuesday, 13 November 1945 at 'his residence, Dunbeath Castle, Dunbeath (2).'

Twyford School, then as Edwyn S. Alexander he entered the Royal Navy as a **Naval Cadet** on 15 January 1879. From 5 January 1881 served in iron ship, armour plated *Iron Duke*, 6,010 tons, Flagship, China Station, Vice Admiral George O. Willes (see C. in C., 1881). The ship was commanded by Captain Richard Edward Tracey who had served under his father in *Euryalus* at Shimonoseki in 1864. **Midshipman**: 24 August 1881. Continued to serve in *Iron Duke*. From 15 December 1882 in the new China Station Flagship, iron ship, armour plated *Audacious*, 6,010 tons. Admiral Willes continued as C.in C.

Having completed his time in the Far East he was discharged from the ship on 29 March 1884 and took passage home in the twin screw gunvessel *Kestrel*, 610 tons.

From 25 July 1884 in iron ship, armour plated *Sultan*, 9,200 tons, Captain Richard E. Tracey, Channel Squadron.

Between September 1884 and April 1885 ill suffering from, and recovering from, an attack of typhoid fever (3).

From 23 September 1885 in corvette *Active*, 3,080 tons, 'Training Squadron'. Acting Sub Lieutenant: 6 January 1886. Studying at RNC, Greenwich. **Sub Lieutenant**: 6 May 1886. Studying in *Excellent*, Portsmouth. Writing of activities about this time a brother officer was to record:-

> 'Jack Alexander, now Admiral Sir E.S. Alexander-Sinclair, drove a yellow dog cart, with a horse called Bendigo, round Southsea to the danger of himself and his companion and the delight of the onlookers. Football and boxing at the 'Hat in Hand' kept us fit (4).'

By no means was his academic record outstanding as he failed at College in February 1887 but fortunately passed two months later, in April.

While in *Excellent*, from 16 January 1888 'ordered to commence a Pilotage Course'. This he passed with a third class certificate. However it is clear from his service record that he excelled at Signals, also impressed senior officers with his zealous approach, sound judgement, tact and sense of discretion. Invariably he was, 'strongly recommended for promotion'.

From 16 March 1888 in cruiser *Fearless*, 1,580 tons, Commander Reginald O.B. Carey Brenton, Mediterranean.

Lieutenant: 1 January 1890. From 18 February 1890 Flag Lieutenant to Rear Admiral Richard E. Tracey, second in command, Channel Squadron, in battleship *Anson*, 10,600 tons. On 12 January 1892 appointed to continue as Flag Lieutenant to Rear Admiral Richard Tracey on his appointment as Admiral Superintendent, Malta Dockyard in *Hibernia*. In this position he was to gain an early knowledge of both administrative and dockyard work.

Meanwhile on 26 January 1892 at St. Mary's Cathedral in Edinburgh he married Julia Margaret, twenty one year old daughter of Colonel Charles Vereker Hamilton-Campbell of Netherplace, Ayrshire. Sadly she was to die in 1930. They had three children, their daughter, Stroma Grisell, born in 1899, and two sons (5). Their elder son, Mervyn Boyd (1894-1979), was to follow his father into the Navy and attain the rank of Commander. He retired from the RN after WW2. Similarly their younger son, Roderick Ian (1911-1985), also was to join the RN from which he retired as a Lieut. Commander.

From 17 October 1893 he served in the new battleship *Ramilles*, 14,150 tons, Flagship, Mediterranean, Admiral Sir Michael Culme-Seymour.
On 2 May 1894, on succeeding as twelfth laird, he assumed the additional form of Sinclair of Freswick (6).
From 3 August 1897 Flag Lieutenant to Admiral Sir Michael Culme-Seymour on his new appointment as C. in C., Portsmouth in *Victory*. The Flag Captain was Francis Charles Bridgeman (1848-1929), in November 1911 to be appointed First Sea Lord.
At the time Lieut. Rosslyn Wemyss was serving in the Royal Yacht wherein the duties were not unduly onerous. There was time for other maritime activity to be arranged:-
> 'With another of his friends, now Admiral Sir E. Alexander-Sinclair, then Flag Lieutenant to Admiral Sir Michael Culme-Seymour at Portsmouth, he shared a Solent one-design yacht, *Margaret*, which they sailed together all summer.. (7).'

Commander: 11 January 1901. From 1 April 1902 in command torpedo boat destroyer *Albatross*, 430 tons, initially at Chatham then to the Mediterranean. From 19 January 1904 in command despatch vessel, *Surprise*, 1,650 tons, Mediterranean.
In succession to Captain Rosslyn Wemyss, from 1 May 1905 in command R.N. College, Osborne, borne in sloop *Racer*, 970 tons.

Captain: 30 June 1905. Continued in command of RNC, Osborne to 5 August 1908.
From the spring of 1907 a pupil at the College was H.M. Prince Edward (1894-1972), later to be King Edward VIII and subsequently Duke of Windsor.
MVO: 1 October 1908.
From 5 January 1909 in command cruiser *Sapphire*, 3,000 tons, commanding Second Destroyer Flotilla, Home Fleet.
From 8 February 1910 to 7 February 1911 in command cruiser *Bellona*, 3,350 tons, continuing to command 2DF, Home Fleet.
From 28 March 1911 Flag Captain to Admiral Sir Arthur W. Moore (see C. in C., 1905), C. in C., Portsmouth in *Victory*.
From 30 July 1912 continued in *Victory* as Flag Captain to Admiral The Hon. Sir Hedworth Meux (see C. in C., 1908), C. in C., Portsmouth.
From 1 September 1913 in command battleship *Temeraire*, 18,600 tons, 4BS, Home Fleet/Grand Fleet.
The Great or First World War commenced on 4 August 1914.
From 8 February 1915 as **Commodore** Second Class, 1LCS, in *Galatea*, 3,500 tons. This Squadron formed a part of the Battle Cruiser Fleet, later Force, and was commanded by Vice Admiral Sir David Beatty in *Lion*, 26,350 tons. The Force remained an integral portion of the Grand Fleet and naturally operated in the waters of the North Sea.
On 4 May 1916 he was to enjoy, for that era, an unusual success:-

'At 10 a.m. a Zeppelin, *L7*, was sighted by the 1ˢᵗ Light Cruiser Squadron and attacked by gunfire by *Galatea* and *Phaeton*. She was damaged sufficiently to cause her to descend near submarine *E31* in the vicinity of the Vyl Lightship. *E31* completed her destruction and rescued seven survivors (8).'

Subsequently he was to be awarded the CB for his part in this affair with the Zeppelin, the investiture being made in person by H.M. The King in the battlecruiser *Princess Royal*, 26,350 tons, on 26 June 1917 (9).

At 1420 hours on 31 May 1916, as Commodore 1CS in *Galatea*, in the North Sea first sighted and reported the presence of German warships. Fifteen minutes later he reported further:-

'... a large amount of smoke "as from a fleet" bearing E.N.E. followd by a report that the vessels were steering north (10).'

These ships, 'as from a fleet', proved to be the five German battlecruisers, with escorting destroyers, under Vice Admiral Franz Hipper (1863-1932) with his Flag in SMS *Lutzow*, 26,180 tons. The Battle of Jutland resulted, being fought that afternoon and evening.

Rear Admiral: 26 April 1917.

From 11 July 1917 Flag in cruiser *Cardiff*, 4,190 tons.

'Promoted to Rear Admiral in 1917, he was transferred to command of the 3LCS, with his flag in the *Cardiff*. In this vessel, flying a kite-balloon aloft, he had the honour of leading in the surrendered German Fleet to its anchorage off Rosyth on November 21, 1918 with the Grand Fleet forming two columns on either side (11).'

Here follows a selection of extracts taken from his private correspondence, dated 21 November 1918:-

'I suppose this has been a wonderful day. If anyone had told me two months ago that such a thing could happen I'd have put him down as a raving lunatic. That the pick of the G. (German) Fleet should be brought in here surrounded by our Fleet still seems impossible – and one still is dazed but it has happened. (--) I am sorry the Squad. was not with me, we have been through so much together but it was very good of the C. in C. to give me the job especially to a Light Cruiser. We all arrived feeling no elation, if anything a bit depressed as one can't keep wondering what their feelings must be. There must be very gallant men among them but it was impossible to imagine what one's feelings would be were the position reversed. I'm sure I couldn't do it (12).'

Various extracts taken from the log book in *Cardiff* confirm the bald details covering these memorable and historic events:-

'Monday, 11.11.1918 at Rosyth.

11:00   Ceased hostilities against Germany on their signing the armistice (13).'

'Thursday, 21.11.1918

01:35   Slipped from Rosyth

07:26   Sighted German fleet. Led in *Seydlitz* and 14 battleships (14).

13:23   Parted company from German fleet. German fleet anchored.'

The next day, 22 November 1918, up in the Baltic Sea region the Russian Bolshevik army attacked Narva, an Estonian city ten miles up river from the Gulf of Finland and close to the Russian border, thus marking the commencement of the Estonian War of Independence. Britain and Finland immediately came to the aid of the Estonians. Indeed at Rosyth as early as on Monday, 25 November in *Cardiff*, "... hands employed hoisting in small arms and ammunition."

The following evening, with his flag continuing to fly in *Cardiff*, he sailed from Rosyth and after a short call at Copenhagen, anchored off Libau (Liepaja), on the Baltic coast of Latvia at 15:10 on Sunday, 1 December 1918 with, "… ship ready for action, 2 guns' crews closed up."

Meanwhile, while at Copenhagen, from the British Naval Attache he had received a copy of a message from the Admiralty addressed to the RA 6LCS, who in due course after just a short interval was to be his successor, Walter Cowan, that gave clear instructions. Extracts follow:-

'British interests in the Baltic may be generally summed up as follows: To prevent the destruction of the Esthonian and Livonian provinces by external aggression, and the only external aggression which at present threatens them is that by Bolshevik invaders. You should support Esthonian resistance to Bolsheviks by sea, but military operations should be avoided. (-).

Whenever we are in a position to resist by force of arms Bolshevik attacks on friends of Allies we should unhesitatingly do so. A Bolshevik man-of-war or armed auxiliary of any kind operating off the coast of the Baltic Provinces should be assumed to be doing so with hostile intent and should be treated accordingly (15).'

Over the next few days he returned quickly to Copenhagen then by Thursday, 12 December was at anchor off Reval (Tallinn) on the north coast of Estonia where, "… representatives of Estonian Provisional Government came onboard", and the ship, "… landed party to instruct Estonians in Machine Guns" (16). Other activities included, with *Caradoc* in company, on Saturday, 14 December, "… opened fire on supposed position of Bolsheviks", and, that afternoon, "… shifted position three miles to eastward to shell bridge in rear of Bolshevik positions".

The activity of his ships may be summarised as follows:-

'A British Naval squadron under Admiral Alexander-Sinclair delivering 6500 rifles, 200 machine guns and two field guns to the Estonian army. In addition on 26 December 1918 his light cruisers *Calypso*, Captain Bertram S. Thesiger, and *Caradoc*, Captain William M. Kerr, with four destroyers in company, captured the Bolshevik destroyers *Spartak* and *Avtroil*, each of 1,350 tons, while they were engaged in bombarding Reval (Tallinn). These two men-of-war were transferred to Estonia to become the nucleus of their Navy as *Vambola* and *Lennuk*. Subsequently he was to blockade Kronstadt.'

His maritime conflict in the Baltic had not all been one sided however as at 0050 hours on 5 December 1918 in the approaches to the Gulf of Finland the light cruiser *Cassandra* had struck a mine, very probably of German origin, and subsequently had sunk.

As has been seen his appointment to the Baltic had only been on a temporary basis and at Copenhagen on 19 January 1919 he was succeeded by Rear Admiral Walter Cowan (1871-1956) (17). His successful efforts in Scandinavian waters were much appreciated in London.

KCB: gazetted on 15 February 1919.

From 8 April 1920 Admiral Superintendent, Portsmouth Dockyard.

Vice Admiral: 4 April 1922.

Continued as Admiral Superintendent, Portsmouth Dockyard until 30 September 1922.

From 14 October 1922 to September 1924 VA, 1BS, Atlantic Fleet with his Flag in *Barham*, 27,500 tons. Flag Captain Percy L.H. Noble (see C. in C., 1938).

About this time a brother officer, recently promoted Rear Admiral and in May 1924 appointed to the Atlantic Fleet with his flag in *Resolution*, rather amusingly was to write:-

'I was at one time supposed to have a great resemblance to Admiral Alexander-Sinclair, and presumably that was so, for many people have greeted me in the belief that I was he. I have often noticed a look of disappointment appear on people's faces when they discovered their mistake. I can hardly flatter myself that he has suffered in the same way (18).'

To take up his next appointment in the Far East he took passage out from England in the P.& O. s.s. *Mantua*, 10,946 grt, 'sailing 22 May 1925', and in her arrived at Shanghai on Monday, 29 June 1925. At 0800 that same morning at Woosung his flag was hoisted in the cruiser *Hawkins*, 9,750 tons, 5CS. Flag Captain W.J.C. Lake (19). However it was only at 1740 the following afternoon that from *Petersfield* he came alongside his new Flagship and embarked (20).

In the interim and as mentioned above, following the departure of Admiral Everett owing to ill health, RAY, David Murray Anderson, had acted as C. in C. (21)

Also in the interim there had been a very considerable domestic upset following an incident at Shanghai which had taken place in May 1925. This affair had commenced earlier in the year when workers at a Japanese owned cotton mill went on strike. Then on 15 May a guard had shot and killed one of these men. Unsurprisingly further anti-foreign protests and strikes took place however when, on 30 May, a student protest occurred in the vicinity of Nanking Road itself then rather naturally the Shanghai Municipal Police arrested the ringleaders, some fifteen in number. That same afternoon demonstrators massed at the police station where these youths were being held and, prior to matters becoming completely out of control, and in spite of police warnings of the action that they would be forced to take, the mob did not disperse and it became necessary for the greatly outnumbered police detachment there present to open fire. Some nine demonstrators were killed instantly or died shortly thereafter. Within a month, on 23 June at Shameen, Canton, this had been followed by another somewhat similar affair although on this latter occasion it seems possible that actually the agitators had been the first to open fire. A great communist inspired anti British boycott had resulted. This was to endure until well into 1926, with serious financial consequences for British trading and commercial interests.

As may be gathered from the following example the flames were there to be fanned:-

> 'On 31 July (1925) the Royal Marine platoon from the light cruiser *Durban* was landed to protect life and property at the premises of the International Export Company, Nanking where there was some labour trouble. In the course of removing the mob a detachment of Chinese police injured some coolies. With a xenophobic bias rather typical of the time, quite unthruthfully it was reported in an element of the local press that Royal Marines had killed the men (22).'

10 August 1925. First arrival at Hong Kong of the first purpose built aircraft carrier to serve in the Royal Navy, *Hermes*, 10,950 tons, Captain Cecil Talbot, DSO and bar (23).

On Saturday, 31 October 1925 the outgoing Governor, Sir Reginald Stubbs (1876-1947), left Hong Kong to proceed on leave prior to taking up his next appointment in Jamaica. His successor, Mr. Cecil Clementi, arrived the following day from Ceylon in the P. & O. steamer *Kalyan*, 9,144 grt. In much the same manner as had Sir Reginald been escorted from Hong Kong, Mr. Clementi's ship too was escorted in to her buoy in Victoria harbour by aircraft flown off *Hermes*.

As may be imagined much pomp and circumstance, with salutes being fired and bands playing, surrounded these gubernatorial movements.

In passing, and in connection with Sir Reginald, there exists a gorgeous story which is too good to omit. In Hong Kong each Thursday His Excellency had found that his traditional schedule called for him to preside over a meeting of the Colony's Executive Council in the mornings, and over that of another official body in the afternoons. As he put it to some of his friends and senior officials:-

> 'Well, if have to listen to tripe every Thursday morning, and more tripe every Thursday afternoon, then we shall have tripe for lunch on Thursdays, and you shall come to Government House to eat the tripe with me.'

In this manner was founded the exclusive Thursday luncheon group which came to be known as, 'The Victoria Tripehounds'.

During December 1925 the new Governor of Hong Kong, Mr. Cecil Clementi, informed the Secretary of State for the Colonies that:-

> 'The forces of the 'Red' Canton government are mainly under the control of General Cheung (Chiang) Kai-shek who is said to be a professional soldier and not a politician. I can get no reliable information concerning him, and I do not know how far he is under Bolshevik influence. His troops certainly have been drilled and equipped by Russians (24).'

However in a report dated 22 January 1926 The Governor was in a position to advise London:-

> 'Number of Russian Bolsheviks presently in Canton is 144 men. No trace of active women agents. Each Chinese regiment has two Russian military instructors. The Head of the Soviets in South China is named Borodin.'

20 March 1926. Uneasy at the direction in which the Kuomintang appeared to be moving, and well aware of the real motives of the Soviet Russians, in Canton at 03:00 hours Chiang Kai-shek acted. Twenty five communists were arrested and all the Soviet advisers were confined to their places of residence. The coup was a brilliant success since it was entirely unexpected. At a stroke Chiang became the undisputed leader of the Kuomintang. However he did not overplay his hand. He was conciliatory enough to continue a close relationship with Borodin. The Soviet Communists simply were put back in their place as advisers. At the same time Chiang took the precaution of establishing a secret service to keep an eye on the activities of both left and right.

Having consolidated his position in the South, and desiring to fulfil Dr. Sun's dream of uniting the country, in mid 1926 he started his armies to the North.

To emphasise the difficult economic times it is worth mentioning that in Great Britain at midnight, 3/4 May, the General Strike of 1926 commenced. To politicians in London, with such grave problems there on their doorstep, China and difficulties in the East will have seemed very far distant.

For a few days from 27 August 1926, in the Yangtse Gorges below and in the vicinity of Wanhsien, there occurred an incident involving aggressive behaviour by men of the local war lord, Yang Sen, in boarding also in seizing ships of the China Navigation Company. Their ships involved were *Wanliu, Wantung* and *Wanhsien*. The British Consul from Chungking, Arthur E. Eastes, refused to consider any ransom conditions (25). In the requisitioned Indo-China river steamer *Kia Wo*, Captain Albert Robert Williamson (1891-1995), a Royal Naval force arrived on 5 September to effect the rescue of ships and men. Sadly this proved to be a somewhat bloody affair with three British naval officers, including Commander F.C. Darley of HMS *Despatch*, and four ratings being killed. The Chief Engineer of *Wantung* also was drowned while attempting to escape from his ship which was occupied by brigands/troops, however the Master and Mate survived (26).

It may be that in handling the affair Britain was not best represented by their Consul however Yang Sen had refused to negotiate with anyone other than Eastes. Of the latter it has been written,

' .. that Eastes lacked the happy knack of settling cases by tact and personal influence'. The same writer recording this opinion happily continues with a most entertaining quote from the relevant Foreign Office file held in London:-

> 'A despatch reporting that he (Eastes) had exploded in a vigorous oral protest against a damnable outrage on the British flag had attracted the anonymous marginal comment, "quite in the style of the good old days of Sir Harry Parkes." (27)'

Yang Sen himself, in contrast to many of his peers, was to prove to be one of life's great survivors. Born in Szechwan in 1884, in due course he was to ally himself with Chiang Kai-shek including the flight to Taiwan during the exodus of Nationalists in 1949. Always a busy man, in addition to numerous wives, concubines and children he was active in the Republic of China's Olympic organisation and was a keen mountaineer. He died as recently as in May 1977.

Admiral: 4 October 1926.

7 October 1926. Wuhan, the important tri-city on the Yangtse in central China, fell to the advancing Kuomintang forces of Chiang Kai-shek.

At Wuhan international commercial interests were based in Hankow on the north bank of the River immediately downstream from the point at which the tributary River Han enters the main stream. In 1920 at least one Naval gunboat commander had written of Hankow:-

> 'The port is one of the best laid out in China, with a handsome and dignified Bund, wide streets and stately buildings (28).'

At Yokosuka on 12 November 1926 the dedication took place of HIJMS *Mikasa* as a memorial ship. In Britain HMS *Victory* is held in much the same high regard, as is USS *Constitution* in the U.S.A.

At the end of 1926 an offer, to be much appreciated by Commanders in Chief in the future, was made by the executors of the estate of Sir Paul Chater, Kt., CMG, who had died on 27 May 1926. On 23 November the Governor, Sir Cecil Clementi, by now a KCMG, wrote indicating that, subject to Lady Chater vacating the house, then by the terms of Sir Paul's will it was to be offered for use by the C. in C. on the station. The house, 'Marble Hall', was a palatial dwelling. Admiral Sinclair relayed this gratifying information to the Admiralty by letter on 2 December, and on 14 March 1927 the generous offer was to be accepted by the Treasury (29).

In Japan on 25 December 1926, the ascension to the throne of H.I.M. Emperor Hirohito (29 April 1901 – 7 January 1989), Showa Tenno.

Having been succeeded by Admiral Tyrwhitt, who assumed command on 7 January 1927, Sir Edwyn sailed for home in the P. & O. s.s. *Malwa*, 10,941 grt. Just a week later, on 14 January, *Malwa* called at Singapore before continuing on up the Strait of Malacca homeward bound. He seems to have been anxious to return to the British Isles quickly as towards the end of his journey home we see that his request, 'to proceed overland from Marseille approved (30).'

In succession to Admiral Sir William Edmund Goodenough, C. in C., The Nore from 16 May 1927 to 16 May 1930 when succeeded by Admiral Trywhitt.

First and Principal ADC to H.M. King George V: 23 May 1930.

GCB: 3 June 1930 and invested a month later, on 5 July.

Having reached the age of sixty five, on 12 December 1930 placed on the Retired List.

On 7 November 1933 he married Maud Kathleen Davenport, younger daughter of Captain Samuel Yates Holt Davenport of the Forty Seventh Loyal North Staffordshire Regiment, and widow of Major William Robinson Campbell, DSO, Fourteenth Hussars. She was to die on 12 January 1969.

In 1939 at Caithness he was appointed to the National Service Committee.

Unfortunate man, with only a few months to live it was not to be of great value to him, but on 6 March 1945 he was awarded a GSP of GBP 300 p.a. in succession to Admiral Sir Reginald Godfrey Otway Tupper (31).

In Great Britain victory over Japan, VJ-Day, was declared on 15 August 1945.

For many years, as Laird of both Freswick and Dunbeath, he lived in Freswick House, Caithness. Today the estate and castle, the latter spectacularly situated on a cliff top promontory, are open to the public thereby providing an opportunity for those so inclined to hunt and fish.

Dunbeath Castle, where he died on 13 November, remains a private residence.

He was interred on Friday, 16 November 1945 at Berriedale Cemetery, where his first wife is buried, the funeral being private. Among the mourners were his wife, both sons, Commander Mervyn Alexander-Sinclair and Lieut. Commander Roderick Alexander-Sinclair, and his daughter, Miss Stroma Alexander-Sinclair (32).

NOTES

1. *Dictionary of National Biography.*

2. *John O'Groat Journal,* 16 November 1945. Courtesy of Mr Robert Bain, Wick Carnegie Library.

3. NA ADM 196/42. *Service Record.*

4. Admiral Sir William Goodenough, *A Rough Record,* (London, 1943), 27.

5. The author is grateful to Ms. Fiona Sinclair for the confirmation of this data.

6. *Service Record.*

7. Lady Wester Wemyss, *The Life and Letters of Lord Wester Wemyss,* (London, 1935), 44.

8. Admiral Viscount Jellicoe of Scapa, *The Grand Fleet: 1914-1916,* (London, 1919), 292/3.
    H.M.S. *Phaeton,* Captain John E. Cameron, also of 1LCS, and in 1925 to be RA, Yangtse. The Vyl Lightship was anchored off Esbjerg. Submarine *E.31,* Lieut. Commander Ferdinand Feilman.

9. *Service Record.*

10. Admiral Viscount Jellicoe of Scapa, 322.

11. Obituary, *The Times,* Wednesday, November 14, 1945.

12. Maritime Museum of British Columbia Society. No. 0474L – one item, three leaves, marked 'Private'.

13. NA ADM 53/37063. The entry of 11 November 1918 was written in red ink.

14. Nine battleships and five battlecruisers constituted the head of the German line of surrendered warships. They were followed by seven light cruisers and forty nine destroyers. Rear Admiral W.S. Chalmers, *The Life and Letters of David Beatty,* (London, 1951), 347. Indeed *Seydlitz* was in the van.

15. NA ADM 116/1864.

16. NA ADM 53/37064. Subsequent log book, *Cardiff.*

17. Lionel Dawson, *Sound of the Guns,* (Oxford, 1949), 152.
    It was to be during the night of 16/17 June 1919 that Lieut. Augustus **Agar** (1890-1968) launched his successful attack against the Bolshevik cruiser *Oleg,* 6,645 tons, then at anchor off Kronstadt. The waters in which this splendid affair took place were viewed by the author on 7 September 2015.

18. The Earl of Cork and Orrery, *My Naval Life,* (London, 1942), 135.

19. NA ADM 116/2289. Letter No. 890/2301 dated 9 August 1925.

20. NA ADM 53/78594. Log Book *Hawkins.*

21. David Murray **Anderson**. Born: 11 April 1874. Died in office in Sydney: 30 October 1936. Joined the RN, *Britannia*: January 1887. Brass River Expedition for which services especially promoted Lieutenant on 23 February 1895. Appointed to light cruiser *Blonde*: 3 August 1895. Captain: 11 August 1911. Appointed Flag Captain in cruiser *Hyacinth,* 5,600 tons: 11 February 1913. In her participated during 1915 in the successful operation in the Rufiji delta to destroy SMS *Konigsberg.* His C. in C., Africa Station during that successful operation was Rear Admiral Herbert Goodenough King-Hall (1862-1936). In command battleship *Ajax,* 23,000 tons: 21 March 1918. Rear Admiral: 6 April 1922. RAY: October 1923 – April 1925. Acted as C. in C., China: April-June 1925. Vice Admiral: 24 January 1927. C. in C., Africa Station: February 1927 – February 1929. Admiralty representative at the League of Nations: April 1929 – April 1931. KCB: 1930. Admiral: 20 April 1931. Retired: July 1932. Governor of Newfoundland: 1933-1936. KCMG: 1936. Governor of New South Wales where sworn in in Sydney: 6 August 1936. *Navy List. Who's Who. Colonial Office List. Australian Dictionary of Biography.*
    Admiral **King-Hall** was appointed C. in C. at the Cape on 28 December 1912. Vice Admiral: 5 March 1915. KCB: 1 January 1916. Admiral: 25 August 1918. *Navy List.*

22. NA ADM 1 8705/193. China Station letter No. 2 dated 4 September 1925. Report of 14 August 1925 received from RAY, David M. Anderson.

23. Cecil Ponsonby **Talbot**. Born: 31 August 1884. Died in Penberth, Cornwall: 17 March 1970. Bedford School. Midshipman: 15 September 1900. From 1 November 1900 in *Glory,* China Station. Lieutenant: 15 November 1904, subsequently specialising in submarines (together with Geoffrey Layton – see C. in C., 1940). Slightly senior to them in the Submarine service was Charles Little (see C. in C., 1936). Commander: 21 October 1914. When in command of HM Submarine *E.16* on 26 July 1915 torpedoed and sank enemy T.B.D. *V.188.* DSO gazetted: 13 September 1915.

Two days later torpedoed and sank *U-6*. From 19 September 1918 in command Submarine Depot Ship *Ambrose* and i/c China Station Submarine Flotilla. Captain: 31 December 1919. Remained in the Submarine service until appointed in command aircraft carrier *Hermes*: 15 July 1925. Rear Admiral: 1 July 1932. RA(S): 10 December 1934. Vice Admiral: 17 February 1936. Retired: 10 December 1936. Rejoined the active list in 1937 for wartime service as Director of Dockyards and in Anti Submarine Warfare Division. KBE: 1939. KCB: 1947. *Navy List.* Author's notes, *The Life and Times of HMS Hermes: 1923-1942.*

24. Rhodes House Library, Oxford. Clementi Papers. Ref: *MICR.IND.OCN.5.*
Between 1924 and 1929 the Secretary of State for the Colonies was the Conservative, Leopold Charles Maurice Stennett Amery (1873-1955). Harrow and Balliol.

25. Arthur Ernest **Eastes**. Born: 10 November 1877. Died: 6 June 1948. Vice Consul: 1 September 1916. As Consul-General he retired on 1 August 1933, his final post being at Mukden in the Japanese occupied territory of Manchuria. *Foreign Office List.*

26. Gregory Haines, *Gunboats on the Great River,* (London, 1976), 58-63. Rear Admiral Kemp Tolley, USN, *Yangtse Patrol,* (Annapolis, 1987), 140-143. P.D. Coates, *The China Consuls,* (OUP, 1988), 467/8. Captain A.R. Williamson also gives his account of this affair in *Eastern Traders,* (Jardine Matheson & Co., 1975), 209/10.

27. P.D. Coates, *The China Consuls,* (OUP, 1988), 468.

28. Ed. Dennis L. Noble. Glenn F. Howell, *Gunboat on the Yangtse,* (Jefferson, NC., 2002), 69.
Lieut. Commander Glenn Fletcher Howell, USN, commanded USS *Palos* PG-16, during 1920 and 1921. This diary entry extract is dated at Hankow, 27 September 1920.

29. NA ADM 1/8738/113.

30. *Service Record.*

31. Ibid.

32. *John O'Groat Journal,* 23 November 1945.

8 November 1926 to 1 February 1929
Vice Admiral Sir Reginald Yorke **Tyrwhitt**

He was born on 10 May 1870, fifth son of The Rev. Richard St. John Tyrwhitt, Vicar of St. Mary Magdalene, Oxford. His first wife, who produced a son, Walter, sadly had died in childbirth. By his second wife, Caroline, daughter of John Yorke of Bewerley Hall, Yorkshire, he had four sons and two daughters, Reginald being their youngest son.

After a short illness he died at his home, 'Ellerslie House', Hawkhurst, Kent on Wednesday, 30 May 1951.

He was educated at Dragon School, Oxford and then, to prepare him for a Naval career, Burney's Naval Academy at Gosport. **Naval Cadet**: 15 July 1883. From 7 August 1885 served in iron ship, armour plated *Alexandra*, 9,490 tons, Flagship, Mediterranean, Admiral the Rt. Hon. Lord John Hay. **Midshipman**: 15 December 1885. Remained in *Alexandra*. From 5 February 1886 the C. in C. was Vice Admiral His Royal Highness The Duke of Edinburgh. From 14 November 1888 in cruiser *Calypso*, 2,770 tons, 'Training Squadron'. Acting Sub Lieutenant: 14 December 1889 and from 25 February 1890 studying at RNC (1). **Sub Lieutenant**: 14 March 1890. From 28 October 1891 in cruiser *Aurora*, 5,600 tons, Captain Arthur Dalrymple Fanshawe (1847-1936), Channel Squadron. On 30 April 1910, having completed his term of duty as C. in C., Portsmouth, Sir Arthur Fanshawe was to be promoted Admiral of the Fleet.

From 2 February 1892 transferred briefly to the protected cruiser *Blake*, 9,150 tons, then to the training ship *Impregnable,* and even, for barely two months between 1 July and 25 August 1892, to the Royal Yacht *Victoria and Albert* (2). **Lieutenant**: 25 August 1892. From 21 September 1892 to December 1895 in cruiser *Cleopatra*, 2,380 tons, Captain The Hon. Assheton G. Curzon-Howe, North America and West Indies Station. In February 1894 a Naval Party from the ship landed in Nicaragua. The explanation follows:-

> 'Great Britain had long exercised a nominal protectorate, and, since 1860, a benevolent though informal guardianship over the strip of coast land which had been assigned as a reservation to the Mosquito Indians in the republic of Nicaragua. On February 12, 1894 the republic saw fit to land troops in the reserve, to occupy Bluefields, the capital, to hoist the Nicaraguan flag, and to arrest the British Vice-Consul. Early on February 25 the cruiser *Cleopatra* reached the spot from Greytown with the British Consul onboard. On the 26th the representative of the Nicaraguan government was informed that the Mosquito flag must be re-hoisted, alone, or side by side with that of Nicaragua, and that a written guarantee must be given for the lives of the chief and the other people who had been arrested. In the meantime the cruiser landed a detachment of blue-jackets and Marines. The most pressing of the British conditions were eventually complied with (3).'

From 14 January 1896 Lieut. and Commander torpedo boat destroyer *Hart*, 260 tons, tender to cruiser *Gibraltar*, 'Particular Service Squadron', subsequently tender to *Victory*, Portsmouth. From 18 August 1896 Lieut. and Commander TBD *Ranger*, tender to *Victory*. From 18 November 1896 First Lieut. in despatch vessel *Surprise*, 1,650 tons, Mediterranean: Commander Hon. Hugh Tyrwhitt, a distant cousin. *Surprise* was used by the C. in C. as his yacht. From Malta ordered home on 24 November 1899. Proceeded overland via Syracuse and Rome, arriving in England on 28 November 1899.

On 12 December 1899 he was appointed First Lieut. in the cruiser *Indefatigable*, 3,600 tons, Captain Frederick L. Campbell, North America and West Indies Station. She re-commissioned at Bermuda: 1 January 1900.

In the northern part of the French island of Martinique, Mount Pelee erupted on 8 May 1902, destroying the town of St. Pierre. In addition, the violence of the eruption being so great, on neighbouring islands much loss of life and damage was incurred. *Indefatigable* was despatched from Trinidad with relief supplies and provisions. Although at anchor at Fort de France, fifteen miles away, she was to undergo an unusual experience following a subsequent eruption:-

> '... it was a perfectly calm and clear morning, when suddenly an enormous mushroom shaped cloud shot upward from the crater and spread rapidly. Tyrwhitt ordered the crew to their fire stations, furled awnings and drenched the upper deck --- By the time the lava (ash) reached the ship it was comparatively cool, though since it covered the deck to a depth of several inches it was as well that the hoses had been kept going. ---
>
> By now the land was completely covered by grey ash and not a single leaf was left on the trees, though beyond this no further harm had been done (4).'

Vice Admiral Sir Reginald Yorke Tyrwhitt, (1870-1951)

Commander: 1 January 1903. Once the news of his promotion was received, from the West Indies in January he left *Indefatigable* and returned home by passenger steamer, arriving in Britain on 31 January 1903.

From 22 April 1903 to January 1904 Commander of cruiser *Aurora*, 5,600 tons, tender to RNC, *Britannia*, 'Engaged in the Torpedo Craft Manoeuvres'.

Also in 1903, on 24 February, he married Angela Mary Corbally of Rathbeale Hall, Swords, Co. Dublin. They were to have two daughters and a son.

Their elder daughter Dame Mary Joan Caroline Tyrwhitt joined the army and in 1949 became director of the Women's Royal Army Corps. His son, St. John Reginald Joseph, born on 18 April 1905, joined the Navy and in due course became Second Sea Lord but sadly was to die young, in 1960. Their second daughter, Patricia Angela Mary, was born in 1913 and in due course was to marry and thereby become Mrs. Patricia Lacy (5).

From 15 April 1904 in command TBD *Arun*, 550 tons, Devonport: Home Fleet.

From 29 August 1904 in command TBD *Waveney*, 550 tons, Portland.

From 2 January 1906 in command scout *Attentive*, 2,670 tons, In Reserve, Chatham.

From 2 January 1907 in command scout *Skirmisher*, 2,895 tons, Home then Channel Fleets.

Captain: 30 June 1908. From 6 August 1908 to 5 August 1910 commanded the cruiser *Topaze*, 3,000 tons, as Captain (D), 4DF, Home Fleet.

Between 22 August and 26 September 1910 attended a Signals Course (6).

From 26 September 1910 in command cruiser *Bacchante*, 12,000 tons, Flagship of RA 6CS, Mediterranean, Sir Douglas Gamble. Between 27 February and 1 June 1912 transferred to the new Flagship, cruiser *Good Hope* (7).

From 10 August 1912 in command cruiser *Bellona*, 3,350 tons, and as Captain (D), 2DF.

From 28 August 1913 in command cruiser *Adventure*, 2,670 tons and as Captain (D), 2DF.

From 1 December 1913 to August 1914 in light cruiser *Amethyst*, 3,000 tons, commanding destroyers of First Fleet. With a speed of twenty three knots her Captain reckoned her, 'damned slow' (8). From 27 April 1914 he held this position as **Commodore** second class.

The Great War/WW1 commenced on 4 August 1914.

On 5 August 1914 ships under his overall command were the first to engage the enemy, sinking the minelayer *Koningen Louise* (9).

From 26 August 1914 with his pendant in the new light cruiser *Arethusa*, 3,500 tons and capable of twenty eight knots, and as Commodore first class from 4 December 1914, he continued in command of his destroyers. Unfortunately off Felixstowe the ship was mined and sunk on 11 February 1916. Continued from 15 February 1916 in the light cruisers *Cleopatra*, 3,750 tons, *Conquest*, *Carysfort* and *Centaur* until, finally, *Concord* from February 1917 to January 1918. Acting Rear Admiral from 8 January 1918 and remained, but now as Rear Admiral Commanding Harwich Force, until 1 May 1919. From 27 June 1918 he flew his Flag in *Curacao*, 4,190 tons (10).

CB: gazetted 23 October 1914.

As has been seen above, as Commodore destroyers in the North Sea he was well known for his vigorous prosecution of the war against Germany during WW1. Much has been written elsewhere describing his great achievements. One gentle but no doubt rhetorical tale is worth repeating:-

> '... on a Sunday morning his ships hoisted the church pennant and the crews went to divine service.
> A zeppelin came out to attack. It did not disturb the Sunday worship; but Tyrwhitt sent up a small
> aeroplane which mounted to a great height in a very short time. The zeppelin was soon seen falling
> in flames. Then Tyrwhitt made a general signal to his ships, "Sing hymn No. ---", which each ship
> did and hundreds of British sailors sang:
>> "O happy band of pilgrims
>> Look upward to the skies.
>> Where such a light affliction
>> Shall win you such a prize (11)."

As just sensed above, but perhaps rather unusually for that era, was his ready appreciation of possibilities in the air:-

'Noteworthy was his pioneer work in sea-air co-operation, in which he showed real vision and enterprise (12).'

DSO: 3 June 1916.
KCB: 15 July 1917 and invested by HM King George V on 29 August.
On 14 November 1918, just three days after the armistice, in *Curacao* he steamed to Rosyth to participate in meetings with German officers concerning the surrender of ships of their fleet.

During 1918 in the Canadian Rocky Mountains, Mount Tyrwhitt, 9,429', was named for him. The peak is in Alberta, 50.34.55N in the Elk Range on the continental divide.

On 9 January 1919 awarded a Good Service Pension.
Between 1 June and 4 July 1919 appointed to *President*, The Admiralty, 'Special Service'.
From 5 July 1919 Senior Naval Officer, Gibraltar, and assumed command on 10 July.
'Lady Tyrwhitt, 3 children and 2 maids left London 25 July by s.s. *Margha* for Gibraltar (13).'

The issue of Hansard dated 5 August 1919 announced proposed grants to be considered by Parliament. These were monetary awards to be made to certain officers who had served His Majesty during the Great War. That sum marked against the name of Commodore Sir Reginald Y. Tyrwhitt was GBP 10,000.

Rear Admiral: 2 December 1919.
On 13 December 1919 created a Baronet: Tyrwhitt of Terschelling and of Oxford.
Continued to serve at Gibraltar.
From 18 January 1921 RA 3LCS with Flag in *Cardiff*, 4,190 tons, Mediterranean.
From 30 June 1923 to 30 June 1925 Admiral Superintendent Rosyth Dockyard, and Commanding Officer, Coast of Scotland.

Vice Admiral: 18 January 1925.
Continued holding the Scotland Command until superceded on 30 June 1925.

H.I.M. Emperor Yoshihito died on 25 December 1926 and the short Taisho era ended. Succeeded by his son, Crown Prince Hirohito. However Emperor Hirohito only was to be enthroned at Kyoto on 10 November 1928.

From 8 November 1926 appointed C. in C., China Station. To take up this appointment in China he, Lady Tyrwhitt and their daughters travelled to the East in the P. & O. s.s. *Morea*, 10,954 grt, and arrived at Hong Kong on 6 January 1927. There the following day he assumed command of the Station. Leaving his wife and children in the Colony, his flag was hoisted in the light cruiser *Despatch*, 4,850 tons on 8 January 1927 and he sailed for Shanghai immediately. Arriving at Shanghai on 11 January he:-

'.. was soon in consultation with the British Consul-General, Sir Sidney Barton, a very experienced and competent man who was to become a firm friend (14).'

Initially his Flagship was the cruiser *Hawkins*, 9,750 tons. Flag Captain L.W. Braithwaite.
Something of the difficult political nature of the situation in China may be sensed by the following extract taken from some memoirs written of the time:-

'My duty was to be Senior Naval Officer in Southern China (based at Hong Kong) and to be ready for action against Canton should hostilities be forced upon us. I use that term advisedly, for the attitude prescribed from Whitehall was a very long- suffering one, and went much against the grain of the British officials and community on the spot who had to bear the brunt of Chinese hostility, and stand by while their business was being ruined (15).'

As a first step towards ending extraterritoriality, which arrangement at five coastal ports first had been entered into in 1842, the British concessions at Hankow and Kiukiang were rendited on 19 February and 4 March 1927 respectively, this being a result of the Ch'en/O'Malley Agreement. This diplomatic activity followed violent Chinese mob activity which had occurred at Hankow early in January 1927. As informed foreigners were well aware, the concession area in that city in any case was in no position to withstand any really positive attack by a determined Chinese force.

On 24 March 1927 the Nationalist Sixth Army of Chiang Kai-shek captured Nanking. Unruly elements attacked and looted foreign property, Consulates and Roman Catholic missions, six foreigners were killed, and others subjected to gross indignities. It was no accident that the British cruiser *Emerald*, Captain Hugh T. England, and the American destroyers *Noa* DD-343 and *William B. Preston* DD-344, Lieut. Commander George Bancroft Ashe, were at anchor off the city. Modest fire from these warships served to calm extreme elements in the city. The British contribution to this affair has been described in the following delightful manner:-

'H.M.S. *Emerald*'s 6-inch 100-pounders added a touch of *basso profundo* to the orchestration. All told she fired seventy six rounds (16).'

At the time Lieut. Commander Roy C. Smith commanded USS *Noa*. Naval officers serving today will appreciate the following excerpt describing the occasion when it became necessary for him to order his gunnery officer to open 4-inch fire at carefully selected targets in the city:-

'The modesty of the action in no way lessens a claim to naval immortality for his order to Lieut. Benjamin Franklin Staud:-

"Well, I'll either get a court martial or a medal out of this.

Let her go Bennie" (17).'

Here follows an excerpt taken from an account of the most fortunate positive effect of this gunfire from warships lying off Nanking during those very difficult few days:-

'It was from the (British) consulate the British party eventually escaped to the house of the manager of the Standard Oil Company, situated close to the wall of the city, and where they were closely besieged; the doors being at the point of being battered in when the first shell from the cruiser *Emerald* in the river screamed overhead and the besiegers fled. That same shell saved the life of a Mr. Jack who had managed to get out of the city with the hope of guiding the relief party on their way from the ship; he had not gone far when he was caught by a roving band of soldiers, and was actually facing a firing squad when the shell passing over, the squad took to their heels, and so did Jack; and as he showed me the wall he had managed to get over, he said: "If any one had told me I could go over that wall with one jump, I should have said 'impossible', but I did it" (18).'

Chiang was no lover of the foreign presence in China but neither was he willing to tolerate this poor behaviour by his men. Subsequently arriving at Nanking he restored discipline ruthlessly by having a number of ringleaders executed.

At the time of these troubles at Nanking and elsewhere in China the C. in C., Asiatic Fleet was Admiral Clarence Stewart Williams, USN (1863-1951). Later in the year, on 9 September 1927 he was to be succeeded by Admiral Mark Lambert Bristol, USN (1868-1939).

From USS *Noa* later it was Lieut. Commander Smith's son who was to tell of one less desireable feature of being at anchor in a small ship on the River:-

'There were a few bad points to life on the Great River, among them the 'floaters', human or animal corpses bloated from long immersion that continually drifted downriver, occasionally catching in the anchor chain or under a propellor guard to hang there until dislodged. One caught on *Noa* just after sunset and wasn't found until the next dawn when a search party discovered the cause of a foul smell that had permeated the ship. It took two days to get rid of the aroma in the below decks compartments (19).'

25 March 1927. The future Flagship, First Air Fleet, IJN, the aircraft carrier *Akagi*, 'Red Castle', commissioned at Kure, Captain Kaizu Ryutaro. Her third commanding officer, from 10 December 1928 to 1 November 1929, was to be Yamamoto Isoroku, later to be the well known Admiral and early wartime C. in C., Combined Fleet.

In connection with the advance by the Nationalist armies northwards from Kwangtung, foreign interests, in particular Great Britain, had had the necessary foresight to reinforce their garrison in the International Settlement, Shanghai. By 4 April 1927 these allied forces, known as SHAFORCE, amounted to some 28,000 men.

To his great credit immediately following his arrival at Shanghai in January the C. in C. quickly had appreciated the need for Great Britain to take vigorous action to send out reinforcements to the garrison in Shanghai. He had so informed London and happily it came about that the conservative government of Stanley Baldwin (1867-1947) had not only agreed but, as recorded above and as will be seen below, had acted promptly:-

'The British government had no intention of allowing Shanghai's international settlement to go the way of the Hankow concession. To secure it against possible attack they sent troops in massive strength, far exceeding the contribution to the settlement's defence made by any of the other powers who shared responsibility for its status (20).'

Amongst those ships especially chartered to carry military equipment from Britain to the East were the twin screw coal-fired Blue Funnel *Bellerophon*, 8,954 grt, together with the P. & O. steamer *Karmala*, 9,128 grt, and the Aberdeen Line *Herminius*. To give one example, it was in February 1927 that *Bellerophon*:-

'... loaded troops, horses and supplies at Birkenhead for Hong Kong and Shanghai.
She carried 750 horses and their troopers. *Bellerophon* made full speed all the way stopping only to refuel for 12 hours at Port Said (21).'

Also *Bellerophon* carried a number of armoured cars. So urgently were these required that following arrival in China then during the evening of 22 March they were discharged by a working party supplied by the light cruiser *Durban*, 4,850 tons, Captain Guy L. Coleridge.

Troops too were moved East extremely rapidly. Again to give just one example, on 22 January 1927 the second Battalion, Coldstream Guards, Lt. Col. P.R.B. Lawrence, MC, received orders to stand by to proceed from England. Only a week later the men left Wellington Barracks and at Southampton embarked in the especially chartered s.s. *Kinfauns Castle*, 9,656 grt, built in 1899 and now at the end of her working life. By 10 March they had reached Shanghai and disembarked. Taking into consideration the distance and era by no means was that a slow deployment.

12 April 1927. Chiang Kai-shek finally broke with the Communists by having great numbers arrested and their labour organisations suppressed. Despite occasional appearances to the contrary this split between the communists and their Kuomintang supporters on the one hand, and Chiang Kai-shek and his Kuomintang supporters on the other, was to be final. Chiang's supporters, it should be noted, included triad gangsters and underworld leaders who had long backed him.

It is apparent that Communist methods had not been guided wholly by idealism. From Shanghai in his political report for the period ending 30 June 1927 Sir Sidney Barton mentions:-

'Although the strength of the communist Labour Union and of the 'Workers Supervisory Corps' was broken, so thoroughly had the fear of them been instilled into the labouring classes that the latter allowed themselves to be influenced by it even after the power of these bodies to do them harm had gone.'

In a later paragraph in the same report Sir Sidney gives an indication of another aspect of Comintern's subversive work. Here he described attempts which were made to produce a feeling of discontent and of class hatred amongst the rank and file of the British military. In addition to the distribution of communist propaganda amongst British troops, men of the British Indian Army received especial attention:-

'Cases have occurred where Indian troops were approached direct by their fellow countrymen.'

Sadly, and much as usual, it was the unfortunate Chinaman in the street who, regardless of who was in power, bore much of the financial load. Again from Sir Sidney:-

'The energies of such civil administration as can be said to exist are concentrated on the collection of revenue. Forced loans, blackmail and increased taxation in every form have been in evidence since the arrival of the Nationalist authorities (22).'

In London in May 1927 the premises of the Soviet Trade Delegation were raided and various incriminating documents were found. This, the Arcos House affair, was to lead to a break in relations between Great Britain and the Soviet Union. As mentioned above, at the time the British prime minister was Stanley Baldwin.

As has been seen domestically within China at the time there were two main factions, the Kuomintang on the one hand, and, then far smaller, the communists on the other. Neither was powerful enough to exert anything approaching overall control throughout the huge country. Into this vacuum slipped numbers of warlords together with smaller groups of bandits. There was a further complication. At all times numbers of individuals appearing to belong to any single one of these groups, Kuomintang included, were by no means averse to seizing any opportunities which might from time to time present themselves for self enrichment.

In short such was the degree of chaos ashore in China, frequently with it being difficult to distinguish between the antics of bandits or armies, that from *Hawkins* at Hankow on 18 May 1927 the C. in C. felt it wise to issue the follow memorandum. He was addressing the commanding officers of all of HM Ships on his Station, with copies being sent to all senior British authorities and Consular officials:-

'Retalitory action.

As HM Government have delegated to me certain discretionary powers, I wish to impress upon all Commanding Officers of HM Ships the urgent necessity of achieving successfully, the local retaliatory measures required to punish and prevent the recurrence of hostile action by the Chinese, with the smallest possible expenditure of ammunition and other resources.

2. The expenditure of a large amount of ammunition with indifferent results is undesirable from both a political and economical point of view, since it tends to diminish the moral effect of such gunfire and may encourage the Chinese to go to greater lengths.

3. While therefore, HM Ships have authority to return fire which has been directed at them or at any other vessel flying the British flag, using the main armament and manoeuvring the ship as requisite, such action should only be taken when the target is definitely located and where the gunfire can be really effective.

4. In cases where the target cannot be located or where for any other reason no effective retaliatory action can be taken at the time, I am to be informed immediately of the circumstances, giving sufficient detail to enable other units of HM Navy to proceed to that point particularly to deal with the culprits as ordered by me.

5. Commanding Officers are to note that the instructions contained in para. 4 above apply equally to any circumstances in which the lives of British Nationals are endangered, or their property is suffering actual, deliberate, and wanton destruction. In cases where the lives of British Nationals are in imminent peril, and there is no time to refer to me, Commanding Officers may open fire to save life. In every case I am to be immediately and fully informed of the details.

The report should contain, as far as possible, the exact position of the culprits and scene of the outrage, and the suggested local punitive action with forces required for its successful and speedy execution if ordered by me (23).'

To take one small example of the prevailing circumstances a short while later *Durban*, especially around her bridge additionally protected against casual light arms fire by the appropriate positioning of mattresses and light steel plating, steamed upstream from Woosung to Hankow, arriving on Tuesday, 31 May. While on passage from time to time she did experience sniper fire from the shore but received no injuries, and Captain Coleridge had had no occasion to return the fire.

As seen the C. in C. had authorised retaliatory action but his farsighted orders had insisted on a policy of tolerant patience. This approach to the difficulty worked wonders as neither Borodin's men, nor those of Chiang, were able to use 'wicked Imperial bullying' as an excuse for whipping up excitement amongst members of the general populace. At the same time both they and the man in the street knew that if pushed too far then the warships, by now anchored off many treaty ports, would open fire as they had done at Nanking in March.

It required great effort and much tolerant patience to maintain this delicate balance.

In the face of this aggressive action by various groups ashore also it became necessary for merchant shipping to be escorted over certain sectors on the River. To fulfill this role armed parties were provided both by the larger warships and by gunboats. Men from the United States Navy naturally shared in the performance of these escort duties. It was an Allied effort, in the face of considerable provocation, to help preserve law, order, trade and commerce. Not only European interests received the benefit from such outstanding and patient work. Domestic Chinese commerce too only could thrive under relatively peaceful conditions.

The pirates on the coast remained active. On 30 August 1927 Jardine's steamer *Yat Shing*, 2,284 grt, was seized near Swatow and forced to steam to Bias Bay. There she was thoroughly looted and the ship then was released. She returned to Hong Kong on Wednesday, 31 August. The British authorities were not amused.

That very evening from his study in Government House His Excellency wrote to the Commodore, Hong Kong, J.L. Pearson:-

> 'In view of the piracy of the British s.s. *Yat Shing* by the Bias Bay gang, news of which outrage has reached me this evening, I have the honour to request that a naval punitive expedition, according to the plan already arranged, may be undertaken forthwith against the pirate lairs in Bias Bay.
>
> I have the honour to be,
> Sir,
> Your most obedient servant,
> (Sd.) C. Clementi
> Governor (24)'

No time was wasted with the allocated warships steaming off at 04:15 on 1 September to carry out operation "H.K. 02". The following morning the landing force, consisting of twenty six officers and 450 men accompanied by eighteen members of the Hong Kong police, proceeded ashore. Seaplanes supplied by *Hermes* flew overhead whilst on the ground some forty houses were burned and eight or ten large houses destroyed. These were known to be owned by pirates such as Lam Tsoi Sau. At Fan Lo Kong harbour five sampans and five junks were destroyed. Naturally the pirates themselves had long since departed so no lives were lost on either side. The British warships departed the scene that evening.

From 19 October 1927 to 22 October 1929 RAY with his flag in *Bee*, 645 tons, Commander C.A.G. Hutchison, was Hugh Justin Tweedie, CB (1877-1951). His predecessor as RAY was Rear Admiral J.E. Cameron.

Also on 19 October 1927 another piracy took place when the steamer *Irene*, 1,343 grt and of 1890 vintage, was seized at sea off Hong Kong. This incident is especially mentioned only as on the next day she was intercepted in rather an unusual manner, by submarine. HM S/M *L4* came up with her near Bias Bay but initially the pirates refused to obey her orders to heave to. To make her point the submarine placed a few rounds into her engine room. Unfortunately some fourteen lives were lost in the ensuing fracas. However during the subsequent rescue operations crew members from *L4* were able to save some 224 survivors who packed her deck. A sister submarine, *L5*, who also had participated in the operation, rescued a few more. On 21 October the steamer, whilst under tow to Hong Kong, was abandoned and sank. Among the survivors were a number of pirates who were indentified back in Hong Kong, then tried and hanged (25).

Meanwhile on 16 November 1927 the first of the two large and fast aircraft carriers to join the United States Navy, *Saratoga* CV-3, 38,500 tons, was commissioned by Captain Harry E. Yarnell. Her sister *Lexington* CV-2, Captain Albert W. Marshall, was to follow on 14 December.

The pedigree of both was similar to that of HIJMS *Akagi* in that originally all three had been laid down as battlecruisers.

Although their cause had been badly damaged by Chiang's coup in April, the Chinese Communists remained active. Encouraged by messages from Moscow, on 11 December they established their 'Canton Commune'. However the move had been badly timed and was poorly planned. Quickly the Nationalists overcame this effort. In his subsequent report the British Vice-Consul, John F. Brenan, included the following paragraph:-

> '15 December 1927. Five more Russians implicated in communist uprising were publicly executed yesterday after being paraded through the streets. Russian Consul General with staff and family all arrested. Consulate searched and documents seized. Terrible revenge has been taken on all suspected of helping Communists. I saw over 100 corpses in a short drive but it is credibly stated that 2000 people have been killed, and search is continuing (26).'

To look ahead briefly to the Japanese air raid over the Hawaiian Islands on 7 December 1941, it was in April 1928 that in the central Pacific the US Navy carried out their annual fleet exercise, Fleet Problem VIII. Rear Admiral Joseph M. Reeves flew his flag in *Langley* CV-1, Commander John H. Towers (27). Her aircraft successfully scouted for their "Blue Fleet" battleships as they closed on Hawaii. Then in June Admiral Reeves ordered *Lexington* CV-2 to run at near full power from San Pedro to Pearl Harbour, a distance of 2,225 miles. This she achieved in a passage of seventy two hours and thirty four minutes, arriving at Pearl on 12 June having attained an average speed of close on thirty one knots, an outstanding achievement. Next he transferred his flag to her and at night steamed in to exercise against Army defences at Pearl Harbour. Very successfully his dawn air attack over various bases in Oahu took these defences completely by surprise, this in spite of the fact that the 'attack' had been made at the request of the Army (28).

Passing through Yokohama in May 1928 the late Vice Admiral Sir Hector MacLean, then a Midshipman serving in the light cruiser *Durban*, described in amusing style one aspect of a dinner kindly hosted by the Mayor of Yokohama. The food, mostly raw fish, was not especially appreciated, however:-

> 'We did each have our own geisha girl but these were not what I imagine our mothers would have thought them to be. We each had a little table with backs to the wall, and kneeling in front of each table was a little geisha who was there to wait on you, help with chopsticks and so on.'

Admiral MacLean left Japan with other most pleasant memories, '... laughing, smiling people, and overrun with laughing, smiling children (29).'

The new Flagship, China Station, the heavy cruiser *Kent*, 10,000 tons, commissioned at Chatham on 25 June 1928. From 29 August 1928 his Flag Captain in her was James Wolfe-Murray, DSO (30). At Chatham *Hawkins* paid off into dockyard hands on 12 November 1928.

As may be imagined, following the great experience gained during WW1, it was not only the Navies of the world that were becoming more and more internationally air minded.

In late 1927 the Far East Flight of the RAF, using four Supermarine 'Southampton' class flying boats, with open cockpits, successfully flew from England to Melbourne. The range of these machines was limited, '… about 500 sea miles was a safe maximum in still air', so this had been a lengthy exercise (31). A side trip then was made from Singapore to Hong Kong and return, this requiring from 1 November to 11 December 1928. To take advantage of prevailing wind conditions it is worth noting the route: Singapore/Kuching/Labuan/ Puerto Princesa on Palawan Island/Manila/ Salomargue Bay/Hong Kong/Da Nang/Saigon/Bangkok/North Malaya/ Singapore. At Singapore with effect from 18 January 1929 this Far East Flight was re-named 205 (Flying Boat) Squadron. More will be heard of this Squadron in late 1941.

4 December 1928. With his Flag in *Kent*, and with *Suffolk* and *Berwick* in company, off Yokohama Sir Reginald was present on the occasion of the review of his ships by the newly enthroned, HIM Emperor Hirohito from the battlecruiser *Haruna*, 27,500 tons.

Later in *Haruna*:-

> '… taken below for a long talk with Admiral Togo, the great Japanese naval hero and victor of the battle of Tsushima in the Russo-Japanese war, who was now 83 but, 'a very fine old man and very much alive' (32).'

At Mukden (today: Shenyang) in North China on 29 December 1928 the local warlord supporter of Chiang Kai-shek, the 'Young Marshal', Chang Hsueh-liang, caused the Nationalist flag to be hoisted. To a casual observer China appeared to be united. It seemed that at last the hopes and dreams of Dr. Sun Yat-sen might have come to pass. Not quite. In this act of defiant bravado Chang had acted against the wishes of Japanese interests. It was these powerful interests who, on 4 June 1928, had arranged for the railway carriage in which Chang's father, Chang Tso-lin, was travelling to be blown up outside Mukden. This influential war lord had died three days later. Informed observers knew very well that Japan had further ambitions in Manchuria.

To better appreciate one aspect of the duties performed by HM Ships in the Far East in this era it is useful to consider the importance of British flag mercantile shipping in those waters. As an example here follows figures in respect of mercantile traffic at the Port of Shanghai for 1928:-

'(a) Number of ships by Nationality as classified under certain regulations which in general specify larger ships rather than native junks and similar.

Chinese	4472	40.16%
British	3054	27.42%
Japanese	2210	19.85%
American	648	5.82%
Norwegian	277	2.49%
German	156	1.40%
French	105	0.94%
Others	214	1.92%
	11136	

(b) By tonnage however, there emerges a rather different pattern:-

British	32%
Japanese	27%
American	15%
German	8%
Chinese	5%

Norwegian	3%
Others	10% (33)'

The extraordinarily complicated domestic situation in the Yangtse Valley at the time may be summarised further by the following extract taken from a report prepared at Shanghai in January 1929 by Major General Alexander Ernest Wardrop, Commanding North China Command. During December 1928 and January 1929 he and Colonel J. McD. Haskard, especially with the evacuation of British subjects in mind, had undertaken a tour of inspection as far upstream as Chungking to see for themselves something of the nature of the difficulties which would need to be overcome in any such an eventuality. Between Wanhsien and Chungking RAY, Rear Admiral Hugh J. Tweedie, had arranged for this army party to be escorted by the gunboat *Tern* (34).

'3. The Yangtze River from the sea to Chungking is divided for navigation purposes into three sections.

Lower – Sea to Hankow
Middle – Hankow to Ichang
Upper – Ichang to Chungking

The sections do not coincide with the present political partitioning of the country (January 1929). The Nationalist government of Nanking, now recognised by our government as the Government of China, does not control more of the Yangtze valley than the section from the sea to Kiukiang. Kiukiang to Ichang is nominally under the control of the Hankow regime. Actually, between Chenglin and Ichang a sort of No Man's Land exists, the country being given over to small independent generals, robbers and pirates. Above Ichang the province of Szechuan is independent as regards military forces, revenue and provincial government. This province nominally subscribes to the tenets of the Nanking government and their ideals but it is almost certain that its own local interests predominate and would outweigh any directions from Nanking (35).

Meanwhile from Hong Kong on Wednesday, 19 December 1928, and with his flag still in *Kent*, he undertook his final Eastern cruise which was to take him around the island of Borneo:-

'Port	Arrived	Departed
Hong Kong	–	Wed., 19 December 1928
Sandakan	Sunday, 23 December	Thursday, 27 December
Macassar, Celebes	Saturday, 29 December	Tuesday, 1 January 1929
Surabaya, Java	Wed., 2 January	Sunday, 6 January
Tanjong Priok, Batavia	Monday, 7 January	Friday, 11 January
Labuan	Monday, 14 January	Friday, 18 January
Kudat	Saturday, 19 January	Sunday, 20 January
Hong Kong	Thursday, 24 January 1929	– (36)'

During the morning on 9 January 1929 the flagship of the Dutch East Indies Squadron, H.Nl.M.S. *Java*, a light cruiser of 7,000 tons, had arrived in Hong Kong on an official visit.

Also on 9 January the Governor, Sir Cecil Clementi had returned from leave, arriving back in Hong Kong in s.s. *Empress of France,* 18,452 grt (37). His Excellency had travelled in her from Vancouver to Yokohama and then on down the coast of China. From Yokohama to Shanghai and Hong Kong the precaution was taken of placing onboard an anti-piracy guard consisting of a detachment of men from the Northamptonshire Regiment (38).

Having completed his term of duty in the East, from Hong Kong on 2 February 1929 the C. in C. returned home to England in the P. & O. s.s. *Morea,* 10,895 grt.

His successor, Vice Admiral Waistell, assumed command in China on 1 February 1929.

Admiral: 27 February 1929.

GCB: 30 July 1929.

C. in C., *Pembroke*, The Nore: 16 May 1930 – 16 May 1933.

From 10 October 1932 – 31 July 1934: First and Principal ADC to HM King George V.

At Chatham on 6 March 1934 Lady Tyrwhitt launched the new light cruiser *Arethusa*, 5,220 tons. She commissioned on 21 May 1935, Captain William G. Tennant, for initial service with 3CS, Mediterranean.

Admiral of the Fleet: 31 July 1934.

'In May 1936 became one of the trustees of the National Maritime Museum, then
just founded (39).'

Retired List: 31 July 1939.

As an Admiral of the Fleet restored to the active list on 6 February 1940 (40).

May 1940: An early volunteer into the Home Guard, 'in command of 3rd Kent Battalion'.

At that time it was written of his service during WW1:-

> 'Right up to his death at the age of 81 the officers and men of the Harwich Force continued to meet
> for their annual dinners, bound together by the extraordinary personality of the man under whom
> they had served over thirty years before (41).'

Following his death on Wednesday, 30 May 1951 then two days later it was announced that:-

> 'The Funeral Service for Admiral of the Fleet Sir Reginald Tyrwhitt will take place privately at All
> Saints Church, Hawkhurst tomorrow at 9.30 a.m. and will be followed by cremation at Charing. A
> memorial service will be held in London later (42).'

Subsequently, 'his ashes were consigned to the sea off Harwich, the sea which he had kept so well, from the destroyer *Opportune* (43).'

As may be imagined his subsequent memoral service, held in Westminster Abbey on Friday, 22 June 1951 and where the Dean of Westminster officiated, was attended by many members of his family and in addition H.M. King George VI was represented. Among the many Naval officers of distinction there present were Admiral Sir Percy Noble (see C. in C., 1938), Admiral Sir W.A. Howard Kelly (see C. in C., 1931), Vice Admiral and Mrs. R.V. Holt (RAY during 1937-1939), Admiral Sir William G. Tennant, and Admiral of the Fleet Lord Fraser of North Cape (44).

Just a few days later Admiral Sir Howard Kelly was to write to *The Times*. An extract follows:-

> 'Modesty and integrity were the two basic qualities in the formation of the characters of the two
> best loved naval leaders in my generation, John Jellicoe and Reggie Tyrwhitt (45).'

Today (2008) in Britain the Ex-Services Mental Welfare Society provides for the welfare and treatment of post traumatic stress disorder. Their Tyrwhitt House was acquired in 1946 and named for an earlier President of the Society, Admiral of the Fleet Sir Reginald Yorke Tyrwhitt.

NOTES

1. NA ADM 196/43. *Service Record.*
2. Ibid. Another young officer selected to serve in *Victoria and Albert*, 'for Queen Victoria's summer cruise', was David Beatty. William Jameson, *The Fleet that Jack Built*, (London, 1962), 247. Concerning Midshipman, then Lieutenant Tyrwhitt, in the same chapter Admiral Jameson also recounts a number of youthful experiences.
3. Clowes, Vol. VII, 430. The President of Nicaragua from 1893 to 1909 was Jose Santos Zelaya. Today Greytown is San

Juan del Norte. The British Consul from Greytown was Mr. Herbert Frangopulo Bingham, appointed: 12 November 1881. Later San Jose, Costa Rica also was to come under his jurisdiction. Died, 'at his post': 12 January 1911. *Foreign Office List,* 1912.

4. A. Temple Patterson, *Tyrwhitt of the Harwich Force,* (London, 1973), 28.
5. Ibid. 35, 36, 291, 334.
6. *Service Record.*
7. Ibid. H.M.S. *Good Hope,* armoured cruiser, 14,100 tons. To be lost with all hands, including Rear Admiral Sir Christopher Cradock, at the Battle of Coronel, 1 November 1914.
8. Temple Patterson, 41.
9. Alastair Wilson and Joseph F. Callo, *Who's Who in Naval History,* (London, 2004), 316/7.
10. *Service Record.* The 'C' class light cruiser *Curacao* was to be sunk in collision with RMS *Queen Mary* on 2 October 1942. The position was 55.50N 08.38W, off the north west coast of Ireland. David Brown, *Warship Losses of World War Two,* (London, 1996), 70.
11. Paymaster Rear Admiral W.E.R. Martin, *The Adventures of a Naval Paymaster,* London, 1924), 291/2. The tale is told in a rather different manner in *Tyrwhitt of the Harwich Force,* 203/204. The zeppelin in question was *L-53,* shot down by Flight Sub Lieutenant Stuart Douglas Culley in his Sopwith Camel, N6812, on 11 August 1918. The aircraft had taken off from a lighter being towed into Heligoland Bight by the destroyer *Redoubt,* Commander Reginald Vesey Holt, from 21 December 1937 to be the last Rear Admiral, Yangtse. The aircraft itself today may be seen in the Imperial War Museum, London.
12. Arthur J. Marder, *From the Dreadnought to Scapa Flow,* II, (OUP, 1966), 15.
13. *Service Record.* B.I. steamer *Margha,* 8,278 grt, entered service late in 1917 for the UK-Calcutta service. Twin screw, 13 knots. Accommodation for forty five passengers in first class and twenty five in second class. To be sold in 1934 for breaking up.
14. William Jameson, *The Fleet that Jack Built,* (London, 1962), 277.
Sidney **Barton**. Born: 26 November 1876. Died: 20 January 1946. St. Paul's School. Entered HM Consular Service in China as a Student Interpreter: 24 September 1895. Service in Wei-Hai-Wei, Peking, Tientsin, Shanghai. Called to the Bar at the Middle Temple: 17 November 1910. Chinese Secretary, British Legation, Peking: 12 May 1911. Counsellor of Embassy: 18 October 1919. Consul General, Shanghai: 21 March 1922-1929. KBE: 5 June 1926. Envoy Extraordinary and Minister Plenipotentiary at Addis Ababa: 21 May 1929 – 29 November 1936. KCVO: 30 October 1930. GBE: 1 January 1936. Retired: 22 May 1937. *Who's Who. Foreign Office List,* 1938.
15. The Earl of Cork and Orrery, *My Naval Life,* (London, 1942), 142. The Governor of Hong Kong then was Sir Cecil Clementi (1875-1947).
16. Rear Admiral Kemp Tolley, USN, *Yangtze Patrol,* (Annapolis, 1987), 159.
17. Ibid.
18. Admiral Hugh Tweedie, *The Story of a Naval Life,* (London, undated), 236.
19. Roy C. Smith III, *The Last Powder Monkey,* (American Heritage, USNI, July/August 1996), 88.
20. P.D. Coates, *The China Consuls,* (OUP, 1988), 476.
21. Duncan Hawes, *Merchant Fleets: The Blue Funnel Line,* (Burwash, 1986), 71.
22. NA FO 228/3640.
23. NA FO 228/3635.
24. NA ADM 116/2502.
25. s.s. *Irene,* built in Glasgow as a heavy lift ship for the China coast. Owned by J. Whittall & Co., London but sold by them in 1895 to the China Merchants S.N. Co. H.W. Dick & S.A. Kentwell, *Beancaker to Boxboat,* (Canberra, 1988), 199. Harry Miller, *Pirates of the Far East,* (London, 1970), 176.
26. NA FO 228/3586. John Fitzgerald **Brenan**. A background in China where his father had been with the Chinese Maritime Customs. Also his uncle, Byron Brenan (1847-1927) had served with the British China Consular Service. Born: 29 July 1883. Died: 11 January 1953. Student Interpreter in Siam: 1903. Transferred to China: 1905. Second Class Assistant: 1910. Called to the Bar, Middle Temple: 1913. Served at Tientsin, Foochow and Peking. With Chinese Labour Corps in France: 1917. Returned to China: 1918. Nanking: 1919-1920. Thence Peking and Shanghai. Canton:

1926-1929. A very able man, 'His performance at Canton gave much satisfaction…'. Subsequently Consul General, Shanghai: 1929-1937, a position held by his uncle Byron between 1898 and 1901. KCMG: 3 June 1932. Foreign Office as adviser on Chinese Affairs: 1937-1943. *The China Consuls*, 478 and 530. *Foreign Office List. Who's Who.*

27. Joseph Mason **Reeves**. Born in Illinois: 20 November 1872. Died in Maryland: 25 March 1948. As Lieut. (j.g.) served in *Oregon* BB-3, Captain Charles E. Clark, off Santiago, Cuba in 1898 during the Spanish-American War. Commanded *Jupiter* AC-3: April 1913 – April 1914. Only between March 1920 and March 1922 was she to be converted and become *Langley* CV-1. Subsequently during WW1 to hold other commands including that of *Maine* BB-10. Post war duties included two years as Naval Attache in Rome. Here is developing a true member of, as they were referred to in the USN, the 'Gun Club'. However, after first arriving at Pensacola, Fla. on 1 June 1925, subsequently qualified as a Naval Aviation Observer and in October 1925 appointed Commander Aircraft Squadrons, Battle Fleet. He sported a goatee hence was known irreverently as 'Billy Goat'. He was instrumental in causing to be developed such tactics as dive bombing, also in increasing the ability of carriers to handle aircraft, and in greatly increasing the pace of flight deck aircraft handling procedure. Rear Admiral: 16 August 1927. As has been written about him:-

> 'Reeves more than any other single figure, pointed the way to making carrier aviation an indispensable part of the fleet. He was a far sighted man who did more to shape the future role of carrier aviation than any other officer in the Navy.'

As a full Admiral on 15 June 1934 to hoist his flag in *Pennsylvania* BB-38 as C. in C., US Fleet. Retired: 1 December 1936. Recalled to active service: 21 May 1940. During WW2 held a number of senior posts, usually logistical in nature. Retired again: 23 December 1946. Thomas Wildenberg, *All the Factors of Victory, Admiral Joseph Mason Reeves and the Origins of Carrier Airpower,* (Washington, DC, 2003). 268 and elsewhere. *Naval Historical Center,* Washington DC. John Henry **Towers**. Born: 30 January 1885. Died: 30 April 1955. Ensign: 12 February 1908. In *Kentucky* BB-6 participated in the around the world cruise of the 'Great White Fleet': 1907-1909. Reported to the Curtiss plant, Hammandsport, NY to be taught to fly: 27 June 1911. Qualified as Aero Club Aviator No. 62: 14 September 1911. Recognised by the USN as Naval Aviator No. 3: 22 March 1915. At Annapolis on 11 October 1912 took Lieut. Ernest J. King up on his first flight. Selected for promotion to Captain: 6 June 1930. In California relieved Captain William F. Halsey in command *Saratoga* CV-3: 9 June 1937. Chief of the Bureau of Aeronautics: 1 June 1939. Rear Admiral: 29 December 1939. On 14 October 1942, now a Vice Admiral, arrived at Pearl Harbour as Commander, Air Force, Pacific Fleet. From February 1944 Deputy to Admiral Chester W. Nimitz as C. in C., Pacific Fleet and Pacific Ocean Areas. Admiral: 8 November 1945. C. in C., Pacific Fleet: 1 February 1946. Retired: 1 December 1947. Admiral Towers always was a most erudite and forceful advocate for both the use of, and administration of, increased Naval air power. Clark G. Reynolds, *Admiral John H. Towers,* (Annapolis, 1991). *Naval Historical Center,* Washington, DC. Thomas B. Buell, *Master of Sea Power,* (Boston, 1980), 36.

28. Adolphus Andrews Jnr., *Admiral With Wings,* (Princeton University, 1943), 131/2. Courtesy Seeley G. Mudd Manuscript Library.

29. Correspondence with the author. Letter dated 5 January 1997. Sir Hector died on 19 February 2003 and was buried at St. Mary's, Burnham Deepdale on 28 February. Respects paid by the author: Thursday, 26 March 2015. His grave, together with that of his wife, is to be found at the East end of the graveyard adjacent to the boundary wall.

30. James **Wolfe-Murray**. Born: 1880. Died: 16 November 1930. Entered *Britannia* as a Cadet: July 1894. Specialised in Gunnery. Lieut. Commander (G) in *Cornwall*, 9,800 tons, at the Battle of the Falkland Islands: 8 December 1914. Together with *Glasgow* sank SMS *Leipzig*. From May 1917 acting Captain of *Suffolk*, 9,800 tons, flying the pennant of Commodore, Vladivostok. In 1919 Head of the British Naval Mission at Perm (see Tudor, C. in C., 1917, Ref: (18). Captain: 30 June 1920. From 8 December 1920 to 14 February 1923 Naval Attache to Scandinavian countries, resident in Copenhagen. Owing to ill health relinquished command of *Kent* and retired in 1929. Aged fifty died suddenly at Mentone. *Navy List. Foreign Office List.* Obituary, *The Times,* Tuesday, November 18, and Wednesday, November 19, 1930.

31. G.E. Livock, *To the Ends of the Air,* (London, 1973), 137.

32. A. Temple Patterson, 271. In fact Admiral Togo was born on 27 January 1848.

33. NA FO 228/4287. The Port of Shanghai then was administered by the Whangpoo Conservancy Board. These figures covering 1928 are taken from their 1929 Year Book.

34. Hugh Justin **Tweedie**. Born: 5 April 1877. Died: 20 August 1951. Entered *Britannia*: 1891. Captain: 31 December 1914. Rear Admiral: 2 March 1926. RAY: 19 October 1927 – 22 October 1929. Vice Admiral: 24 May 1930. C. in C., Africa Station: 26 February 1931 – 9 March 1933. KCB: 1933. C. in C., The Nore: 16 May 1933 – 3 December 1935. Admiral: 8 May 1935. *Navy List*. Obituary, *The Times*, 22 August 1951. *Who's Who*.
   Tern, 262 tons, built 1927. From 21 November 1927 Lieut. Commander C.C.L. Mackenzie. Oil fired steam turbines for fourteen knots. Scuttled in Deepwater Bay, Hong Kong: 19 December 1941. *Navy List*.

35. GOC, North China Command to The Under Secretary of State, War Office, London. Ref: *N.C.C./S/132 (G)*, dated 23 January 1929. A copy kindly made available to the writer from a private source.

36. NA ADM 53/79406. Log book *Kent*. After leaving Tanjong Priok on 11 January, that night between 2224 and 2355 hours *Kent* anchored off Discovery East Bank. In 1903 the Dutch authorities first had positioned a lighthouse on this reef in the north western waters of the Java Sea at the southern entrance to Karimata Strait. By nice coincidence in Java at the time the Governor General of the Dutch East Indies was Jonkheer Andries Cornelis Dirk de Graeff (1872-1957), son of Dirk de Graeff van Polsbroek, Dutch Consul General in Japan during the last years of the Shogunate – see Kuper, C. in C., 1862.

37. *Empress of France*, launched at Glasgow: 22 March 1913 as the Allan Line *Alsatian*. Saw much Great War service as the AMC Flagship of the Tenth Cruiser Squadron, Rear Admiral Dudley de Chair, on the Northern Patrol, an important sector of the German blockade. On 16 July 1917 transferred to her new owners, Canadian Pacific Railways. Post war refitted at Glasgow then on 26 September 1919 placed on their Liverpool/Quebec service. On 31 October 1928 left Southampton for just a year of service on the trans Pacific route. Laid up in the Clyde: September 1931. Sold for breaking up: 20 October 1934. Duncan Haws, *Merchant Fleets: Canadian Pacific*, (Hereford, 1992), 74/5. Frederick Emmons, *Pacific Liners: 1927-1972*, (Newton Abbot, 1973), 29. Admiral Sir Dudley de Chair, *The Sea is Strong*, (London, 1961), 188 and thereafter.

38. Clementi papers, Rhodes House Library. Ref: *MICR.IND.OCN.5*.

39. Obituary, *The Times*, Thursday, May 31, 1951.

40. *Service Record*.

41. *The Fleet that Jack Built*, 286.

42. A. Temple Patterson, 292.

43. *The Times*, Friday, June 1, 1951. In recent years the church has become redundant and no longer is in use.

44. *The Times*, Saturday, June 23, 1951.

45. *The Times*, Wednesday, June 27, 1951.

1 February 1929 to 28 February 1931
Vice Admiral Arthur Kipling **Waistell**

He was born on 30 March 1873, son of Mr. Charles Rowland Waistell (1835-1911) of Northallerton, Yorkshire, and his wife Margaret Ida, nee Toyne. Arthur had an elder brother, and sister who sadly died when very young, and two younger brothers and another sister. The Admiral's father, who practiced as a solicitor, was prominent in local affairs in Northallerton and district for over forty four years. Charles Waistell died on 2 February 1911 and was buried on the following Monday, 6 February. Being in home waters at the time fortunately Arthur, together with his brothers and other members of the family, was able to attend the funeral (1).

Sir Arthur died at Old Mead, Freshwater, Isle of Wight on Monday, 26 October 1953.

Young Arthur entered the Royal Navy as a **Cadet** on 15 July 1886. **Midshipman**: 15 August 1888. From 29 November 1888 to the summer of 1892 in cruiser *Cleopatra*, 2,380 tons, south east coast of America. During this commission and while in the Falkland Islands:-

'To be paid surveying pay at 2/6 a day for period 15 Jan. to 2 Feb. '91 surveying Port Stanley (2).'

Sub Lieutenant: 14 August 1892. Studying at Royal Naval College, Greenwich, where he obtained three 'firsts'. From 14 March 1894 Sub Lieut. (N) in the sailing brig. *Sealark*, 311 tons, attached to *Caledonia*, 'Training Ship for Boys', Queensferry, Firth of Forth. **Lieutenant**: 14 August 1894. From 1 April 1895 in cruiser *Archer*, 1,770 tons, China. While on the China Station:-

'May '96 – Selected to qualify for Torpedo duties and ordered to be home by middle of Sept. 16 Sept. '96 – Arrived in England (3).'

From 30 September 1896 in *Vernon*, Portsmouth, 'Qualifying as Torpedo Lieutenant'. From 28 September 1898 Lieut. (T) in Torpedo Boat Depot Ship *Vulcan*, 6,620 tons, 'Particular Service'. From 18 April 1899 Lieut. (T) in battleship *Royal Oak*, 14,150 tons, Mediterranean. From 28 January 1900 Lieut. (T) in battleship *Ramilles*, 14,150 tons, Flagship of RA, Mediterranean. From 1 May 1902 Lieut. (T) on the staff in Torpedo School Ship *Vernon*, Portsmouth. From 1 January 1903 Lieut. and Commander (T) in *Devastation*, 9,330 tons, Tender to *Vernon*, Portsmouth.

Commander: 31 December 1903. From 12 February 1904 in command of the one time China Station flagship *Audacious*, 6,010 tons, now a Depot Ship for Torpedo Boats and Torpedo Boat Destroyers, Felixstowe. In April 1904 she was re-named *Fisgard* and from 1 January 1906 was used as a training hulk. In 1914 to be re-named again, now at Scapa Flow as the repair ship cum receiving hulk *Imperieuse*. In March 1927 finally to be sold for breaking up, a life of some fifty seven years.

Also during 1904 he married Madelaine E. Winter-Fisher. Sadly she was to die some five years before her husband, on 10 October 1948 (4).

On the Mediterranean Station between 22 February and 14 October 1905 in command of TBD *Albatross*, 430 tons.

From 14 October 1905 in command TBD *Stag*, 320 tons, Mediterranean.

From 4 June 1906 in command TBD *Foam*, 310 tons, Mediterranean.

From 28 February 1907 for duty in 'War Course College', Portsmouth, later described as, 'Royal Naval War College.'

From 2 February 1910 in command scout *Pathfinder*, 2,940 tons, 'Attached to 1DF, Home Fleet.'

Captain: 31 December 1910.

Continued in command of *Pathfinder* until 16 January 1911.

Between 12 August and 8 November 1912 he attended short courses covering, respectively, Navigation, Gunnery, and Torpedoes (5).

From 7 December 1912 in command *Vindictive*, 5,750 tons, tender to *Vernon*, Portsmouth.

From 1 September 1913 to 18 September 1917 in command submarine depot ship *Maidstone*, 3,600 tons. 8 S/M Flotilla, Portsmouth, then at Harwich. This flotilla:-

'.... was composed of the latest types of 'oversea' boats of the 'D' and 'E' classes (6).'

A number of boats under his command were to enjoy success in operations against the enemy. For example Commander Cecil Ponsonby Talbot, in command of *E.16*, on 26 July 1915 in the German Bight torpedoed and sank the destroyer *V. 188*, 650 tons. Then, just over six weeks later off Stavanger on 15 September 1915, he torpedoed and sank *U-6*, Rheinhold Lepsuis (7).

CB: 25 October 1916.

From 28 September 1917 to 21 February 1919 in command battleship *Benbow*, 25,000 tons, Grand Fleet. She was of the same class as *Iron Duke*, the other two such battleships being *Emperor of India* and *Marlborough*.

From 1 March 1919 in command *Vernon*, Torpedo School Ship, Portsmouth.

From 6 April 1920 at the Admiralty, 'Director of Torpedo Division'.

On 26 November 1920 appointed Naval adc to HM The King.

Rear Admiral: 1 July 1921.

Continued as 'Director of Torpedo Division' until 6 April 1922.

On 24 April 1922 appointed to a Committee to consider the question of the retirement of Captains.

From 15 July 1922 to 19 April 1923 Flag in light cruiser *Coventry*, 4,190 tons, as RA (D), Commanding Destroyer Flotillas, Atlantic Fleet.

From 15 May 1923 to 9 October 1924 Assistant Chief of Naval Staff and a Lord Commissioner of the Admiralty.

At the time the First Sea Lord was Admiral of the Fleet Earl Beatty.

From 9 October 1924, with his Flag in the light cruiser *Frobisher*, 9,750 tons, he served as RA, 1CS. Mediterranean. When ashore in Malta he lived in Villa Guardia Mangia at Pieta.

Vice Admiral: 6 August 1926.

Continued as VA, 1CS until 9 September 1926.

From 28 November 1928 appointed C. in C., China.

He assumed command at Hong Kong on 1 February 1929, at 0800 that morning his flag being hoisted in *Cornwall*. The next morning at 0800 his flag was hoisted in the heavy cruiser *Kent*, 10,000 tons, who, following a cruise, had arrived from Kudat, North Borneo on Tuesday, 24 January 1929.

Two hours later, at 1000 hours, hands cheered ship on the departure of Admiral Tyrwhitt.

Inititially in *Kent* his Flag Captain was J. Wolfe-Murray however, from Nanking on 31 May 1929, he was to leave the ship for passage back to England. Captain A.L. Snagge joined her and assumed command at Wei-Hai-

Wei on 8 June 1929. In turn, and again from Wei-Hai-Wei, he was to leave the ship on 4 September 1929 (8).

On 25 April 1929 HRH The Duke of Gloucester arrived at Hong Kong in the P. & O. s.s. *Morea*, 10,895 grt. *Kent* was in Hong Kong at the time and, as may be imagined, in honour of the occasion she dressed ship and the appropriate Royal salutes were fired. From the Colony HRH continued on to Japan in the heavy cruiser *Suffolk*. There he was to invest the newly crowned Emperor Hirohito with the Order of the Garter.

Appointed in command of *Kent* from 27 July 1929, and to join her at Wei-Hai-Wei on 19 September, was Captain B. H. Ramsay, the future Admiral Sir Bertram Home Ramsay (1883-1945). Writing of the time, Ramsay's biographer was to stress two points. Firstly concerning the C. in C.'s involvement with the overall problems of the day, and secondly how Ramsay and his C. in C. held many similar ideas, an agreeable state of affairs:-

> 'The Commander in Chief was fully occupied with political and strategical problems, most of which concerned the British Ambassador, who sometimes came for a cruise in the flagship.'
> 'I can't recall a single instance in which I found myself at variance with your view point and I've been able to go ahead all the time knowing I was working with you on a common basis (9).'

In June 1944 Admiral Ramsay was to command Operation 'Neptune' during the Allied liberation landings in Normandy.

As a further indication of the constantly fluctuating domestic situation in China here follows an extract taken from his letter of proceedings addressed to the Secretary to the Admiralty on 14 June 1929:-

> 'The strained situation between Generals Chiang Kai-shek and Feng Yu-hsiang, which has been in evidence since the defeat and dispersion of the Wuhan forces at Hankow, has become acute and developed into the preliminary stages of what may be another civil war of the first magnitude. General Feng has concentrated his main forces in a strong strategical position in North Central China and has cut railways to ensure isolation on three fronts, keeping his Western front open. The attitude of General Yen Hsi-shan, controlling the province of Shansi and the Peking-Tientsin areas, is an unknown factor which will most probably have a decisive effect on the course of events in the near future.
> Chiang Kai-shek has ordered extensive mobilisation, which is proceeding apace, involving heavy troop traffic on the Yangtse River, and the Nationalist government have issued a Mandate denouncing Feng as a rebel.
> Negotiations and manoeuvres continue, and no contact between the opposing forces has yet been reported (10).'

Apropos this situation within China, on 8 May 1929 H.E. the Governor of Hong Kong, Sir Cecil Clementi, wrote to his son, his letter including the following two extracts:-

> 'I shall not be sorry to see Chiang Kai-shek disappear, but I shall regret the advent to power of Feng Yu-hsiang supported, as he is pretty sure to be, by Russian influence and by the Radicals of Kuomintang.'
> 'Poor unfortunate merchants and peasants of China! What terrible sufferings they have to endure (11).'

Historically the seat of Nationalist/Kuomintang power was the southern province of Kwangtung. At the same time as Chiang Kai-shek was involved with Feng in central/northern China, there arose strife between the province of Kwangtung and its neighbour, Kwangsi, the objective being control of Kwangtung and the important city of Canton. The war lord era always was one of considerable treachery and untrustworthiness.

Although Dr. Sun Yat-sen had died in Peking in March 1925 it was not until 1929 that his mausoleum, which was situated a short distance outside Nanking in the hills, was complete. Naturally his burial in the late spring of 1929 was an event of very considerable importance. Admiral Waistell described the ceremonies as follows:-

'Diplomatic representatives of 20 foreign nations assembled with their staffs at Nanking for the funeral ceremonies connected with the interment of the body of Doctor Sun Yat-sen. (--) These ceremonies commenced on 28 May and culminated on 1 June with the actual interment at 11 a.m., followed at noon by a salute of 21 guns by all ships in the harbour.

The British delegation to the funeral consisted of the British Minister, Sir Miles Lampson, and staff, Consul General Hewlett, myself and personal staff, Rear Admiral Tweedie and Captain Arbuthnot of *Suffolk*. On Friday, 31 May, the whole of the foreign delegations assembled at 7 a.m. and, after a wait of one hour, were received by the President of the Chinese Republic – General Chiang Kai-shek. All then proceeded to the Kuomintang headquarters where the body of Sun Yat-sen was lying in state, and each foreign Minister in turn laid a wreath beside the coffin and bowed to the corpse, the various delegations filing in turn past the coffin (which had a glass lid and showed the fully dressed figure of Sun Yat-sen with uncovered face).

On Saturday, 1 June the 20 foreign delegations assembled at the Kuomintang headquarters at 3.15 a.m. and, one and a quarter hours later, the funeral cortege started on the seven mile walk to Purple Mountain. The foreign delegations left the cortege at 6 a.m., rejoining at 9.30 a.m. at the foot of the 365 steps up to the Mausoleum, which was reached at 10 a.m. The 'service' inside the Mausoleum and in the inner tomb consisted of the reading of Sun Yat-sen's will; there was no religious ceremony of any kind. The proceedings terminated at 11.30 a.m. (12).'

The British Consul General, Mr. Hewlett, relates that the C. in C. took advantage of this wonderful opportunity:-

'The day ended with a dinner on board H.M.S. *Kent*, Admiral Waistell's flagship at which fifty sat down to dinner, including all the Diplomatic Body and every member of the Chinese Government. It was a tremendous success (13).'

At Singapore on Wednesday, 14 August 1929 the new floating drydock at H.M. Navy Base was officially opened, with considerable ceremony, by H.E. The Governor Sir Hugh Clifford (14). As will be imagined this was an important development in the slow but gradual improvement of facilities at the base.

In New York on 24 October 1929 the great crash in share prices on the Stock Exchange took place, 'Black Thursday'. Around the world there was great concern and financial uncertainty as the effects of the Great Depression began to take hold of the entire global economy.

As just one more example of attacks carried out by pirates, in the very early hours of 8 December 1929, while on passage from Swatow to Hong Kong, the British s.s. *Haiching*, 2,182 grt, suffered from such an ordeal when a group of some twenty five men, travelling amongst the total of 300 deck passengers, attempted to seize the ship. Fortunately her officers were alert and although the ship was set afire by the rogues, were able to defend themselves, and even launch a counter attack, until assistance arrived in the form of the destroyers *Sterling* and *Sirdah*, each 1,075 tons. Sadly it was a bloody business. The Third Officer, one Indian guard, five Chinese passengers and five pirates were killed or drowned, and some twenty pirates and passengers wounded. Later in Hong Kong numbers of the captured pirates were tried and executed (15).

Haiching herself, built in Port Glasgow in 1898 for the Douglas Steam Ship Company, subsequently was repaired and re-entered service. In December 1941 she was to escape from Hong Kong to India where she was placed under B.I. management until 2 October 1943 when, eighty miles W.S.W. of Bombay, she was to be torpedoed and sunk by *U-168*, an impressive commercial life of some forty five years (16).

Although his award of the KCB had been gazetted on 3 June 1929 it was in the New Year's Honours List, 1930, that it was proclaimed. Accordingly during a special ceremony in Government House, Hong Kong on 3 January he was invested by Sir Cecil Clementi.

In another letter to his son, dated 28 January 1930, Sir Cecil included the the following telling remark, 'The whole Chinese administration today is one large piece of bluff, and their main instrument is propaganda.'

Two days later, on 30 January Sir Arthur, as he now was, hosted Sir Cecil at a Farewell Fleet Dinner held in *Kent*. All of his Captains who were available attended this splendid gathering. Then on 1 February Sir Cecil proceeded on transfer to the Straits Settlements where he was to succeed Sir Hugh Clifford as Governor. To travel to Singapore he took passage in the P. & O. s.s. *Mantua*, 10,946 grt, Captain A.H. Hignett. Sir Arthur gave him an impressive escort from the waters of the Colony. Here is Sir Cecil writing from Singapore on 6 February 1930:-

> '*Mantua* was escorted from Hong Kong by *Bruce* ahead, and *Serapis* and *Thracian* on each side (17). Out through Lyemun Pass. Also in the ship was Sir James Jamieson once Consul-General at Canton but who was returning to England from his last post at Tientsin having suffered a stroke. We also had onboard Group Captain Cave-Browne-Cave who is in command of the Air Force at Singapore, and Colonel J.G.R. Halland who is on his way home from Shanghai. He originally came out with the SHAFORCE in 1927, and has been since then on intelligence work connected with Communism and the Indian seditionists of whom there are some in Nanking. This summer he will take up a police job at Delhi. He considers the Indian outlook very menacing and expects plenty of trouble this year and next (18).'

In passing, Colonel Halland was to prove quite correct with his forecast. From late 1931 in India the civil disobedience campaign was to gather increasing momentum. By May 1932 there were to be 36,000 members of the Congress party in gaol, these numbers including Ghandi.

Between 1931 and 1936 the Viceroy was Freeman Freeman-Thomas, Viscount Willingdon (1866-1941), in 1936 to be created Marquess.

Between the two world wars a number of naval conferences were held in London, Washington and Geneva. The principal objective was to attempt to reach agreement on restricting the numbers and tonnage of warships owned by the major powers, especially in respect of the then capital ships of the fleets, battleships. In London between 21 January and 22 April 1930 another in the series was held. In this instance the effort was particularly important owing to the effect of the Great Depression and resulting financial constraint throughout the world. The major change resulting from this conference was slightly in favour of Japan as the ratio of battleship tonnage allowed to Great Britain, the USA and to Japan was altered from 5:5:3 to 10:10:7, France and Italy excusing themselves from the new arrangement. All five countries agreed to halt battleship construction until the next conference scheduled for 1935. There were other restrictive clauses in particular effecting aircraft carriers and submarines.

From Kobe on 13 May 1930 the maiden voyage of the N.Y.K. passenger/cargo liner, m.v. *Hikawa Maru*, 11,622 grt, to Seattle via Yokohama, Honolulu, Los Angeles and San Francisco. Restored and re-opened in April 2008, today the ship may be visited at her berth at Yokohama, an impressive reminder of a bygone era.

Admiral: 23 May 1930.
From Hong Kong on 7 August 1930, the maiden trans Pacific voyage sailing of the Canadian Pacific steamer *Empress of Japan*, 26,032 grt, Captain Samuel Robinson. Steaming via Shanghai, Kobe and Yokohama she arrived at Vancouver on 22 August. After Japan's entry into WW2 to be re-named *Empress of Scotland*, she was to be the last of the Pacific 'Empress' passenger liners.

On 1 October 1930 the territory of Wei-Hai-Wei formally was returned to China (19).
However at the same time the facilities on Liukungtao, largely recreational in nature, were leased back to Great Britain for continued use by the Royal Navy.

14 November 1930 at Tokyo railway station a right wing assassin, Sagoya Tomeo, shot prime minister Hamaguchi Osachi (1870-1931). The unfortunate man was to linger on but eventually to die of his wounds

several months later, on 26 August 1931. His government, already resented in some quarters by acceptance of the terms of the London Naval Conference, January – April 1930, also had sought to curtail military activists and their powers.

Also in Japan, on 1 December 1930, Yamamoto Isoroku, who had been promoted Rear Admiral on 30 November 1929, and who also had attended the Naval Disarmament Treaty Conferences in London earlier in the year, was appointed Director of the Technical Section in the Department of Naval Aeronautics.

In *Suffolk* at Hong Kong on Thursday, 26 February 1931 Vice Admiral Sir W.A.H. Kelly came onboard preparatory to assuming command of the China Station.

Two days later in *Suffolk*:-

'Saturday, 28 February 1931. At Hong Kong.

08:00   Saluted flag of Admiral Sir A.K. Waistell: 17 guns. *Kent* returned 15 guns.

               Hoisted flag of of Vice Admiral Sir Howard Kelly, C. in C., China Station.

09:30   C. in C. called on Admiral Waistell.

10:15   Admiral Waistell left *Kent* for s.s. *Malwa*. Cheered ship (20).'

With his Flag in *Victory*, on 18 June 1931 he succeeded Admiral of the Fleet Sir Roger Keyes (1872-1945) as C. in C., Portsmouth. In turn on 18 February 1934 he was to be succeeded by Admiral Sir John Kelly (1871-1936). Sir John, elder brother of his successor in China in 1931, was to be promoted Admiral of The Fleet on 12 July 1936, just a few months before his death that November.

On 11 February 1934, at his own request, he was placed on the Retired List (21).

Following his retirement he lived in Winchester, Hampshire where he was especially involved with the affairs of the Royal Hampshire County Hospital, for some time being a member of their Court of Governors and chairman of the management committee. Also he was President of the Winchester Sea Cadet Corps (22).

At the outbreak of war in 1939, in Hampshire he was appointed to a position on the National Service Committee.

Unfortunately between 21 May and 21 September 1945 he was to spend time in the Royal Naval Hospital, Haslar, and recuperating at Osborne, suffering from the ailment which eventually was to lead to his death, cerebral thrombosis (23).

A year after his wife died in 1948, being an invalid, he moved to the Isle of Wight. There he was 'devotedly cared for by his sister, Miss I. Waistell, ARRC'.

Following his death on 26 October 1953, then during the morning of Friday, 30 October his funeral service took place at the Yarmouth Parish Church, Isle of Wight. In addition to members of the family, among the mourners was the C. in C., Portsmouth, Admiral Sir John Edelsten, and the Flag Officer, Submarines, Rear Admiral George W.G. Simpson (24). Subsequently his coffin was borne to the motor torpedo boat *Pathfinder* and then, in Yarmouth Roads, transferred to the destroyer *Finisterre*, 2,325 tons. In her his remains were brought to Southampton. Later that day his interment took place at the Winchester Cemetery, Magdalen Hill, next to his wife, a short service being conducted by the chaplain of the Royal Hampshire County Hospital (25).

NOTES

1. Information kindly supplied by Mr Jim Sedgwick, Northallerton and District Local History Society, February 2009. Charles Roland Waistell's obituary: *Darlington and Stockton Times*, 10 February 1911. Today in the High Street the Main Post Office occupies the site of the old Waistell family dwelling.
2. NA ADM 196/43. *Service Record*. Two shillings and sixpence a day, or twelve and a half P.
3. Ibid.
4. Obituary, *The Isle of Wight County Press*, Saturday, October 31, 1953. Courtesy of The County Press and of Mr. Terence

Blunden, Isle of Wight Branch, The Historical Association.

5. *Service Record.*

6. Obituary, *The Times,* Wednesday, October 28, 1953.

7. Cecil Ponsonby Talbot, DSO and bar, a knighted Vice Admiral (1884-1970). See also the author's *Life and Times of HMS Hermes: 1923-1942.* Also Vice Admiral Sir Edwyn Alexander-Sinclair, C. in C., 1925. Ref. (23).

8. NA ADM 53/79406/7 being consecutive log books *Kent.*

9. Rear Admiral W.S. Chalmers, *Full Cycle,* (London, 1959), 37, 38. Admiral Ramsay sadly died on 2 January 1945 when his aircraft crashed after take off from Toussus-le-Noble airport SW of Paris near Versailles.

10. NA ADM 116/2694. **Feng** Yu-hsiang (1882-1948). In 1928 Feng together with the Shansi warlord, Yen Hsi-shan, had occupied Peking and in 1929 declared their independence of Chiang's Nationalists or Kuomintang authority. However in 1930 Chiang overcame their opposition and they were both exiled. By and large this affair was yet another example of the flow of fortune experienced by most of the warlords. Earlier for example, Feng had received military aid from the Soviet Union. Japan also backed various 'generals'. Such outside aid was made purely with the perceived interests of the donor country in mind.

11. Clementi Papers, Rhodes House Library, Oxford. Ref: *MICR.IND.OCN.5.*

12. NA ADM 116/2694. Rear Admiral Hugh Justin Tweedie, from 19 October 1927 RAY (Rear Admiral Yangtse) with his flag in the river gunboat *Bee,* 645 tons. *Navy List.*
Representing the United States was Admiral Mark Bristol, flag in USS *Isabel* PY-10.
Miles Wedderburn **Lampson**. Born: 24 August 1880. Died: 18 September 1964. Eton. Clerk in the Foreign Office: 23 March 1903. Appointed to Tokio: 1 September 1908. Returned to the Foreign Office: 31 December 1910. Sofia: 18 October 1911. Foreign Office: 4 January 1912. Peking: 18 September 1916. Acting High Commissioner in Siberia: 8 November 1919 – 1 February 1920 when returned to Peking. Foreign Office: 30 April 1920. Attached to the British Delegation, Washington Conference on the Limitation of Armaments: October 1921 to February 1922. Envoy Extraordinary and Minister Plenipotentiary at Peking: 22 October 1926. KCMG: 1 January 1927. High Commissioner for Eygpt and the Sudan: 16 December 1933. Ambassador Extraordinary and Plenipotentiary at Cairo: 22 December 1936. GCMG: 1 February 1937. PC: 12 June 1941. Raised to the Peerage as Baron Killearn: 1 January 1943. Special Commissioner in South East Asia: 1946-1948. *Foreign Office List.*
Today, written in 2008, the Sun Yat-sen mausoleum outside Nanjing is a beautifully maintained memorial much frequented by Chinese citizens and foreigners, all visiting to pay their respects.

13. Sir Meyrick Hewlett, *Forty Years in China,* (London, 1943), 226/7.
William Meyrick **Hewlett**. Born: 1 July 1876. Died: 16 March 1944. Harrow. Appointed Student Interpreter in China: 6 August 1898. Served during the defence of the Legations at Peking: 1900. Following numerous appointments within China, commissioned as Consul: 1 March 1922. Served in Peking and Nanking. Consul-General: 3 January 1928. Nanking: 1928-1931. KCMG: 1 January 1931. Hankow: 1931-1935. Retired: 2 September 1935. *Foreign Office List. Who's Who.*

14. Hugh Charles **Clifford**. Born in Roehampton, London: 5 March 1866. Died in Roehampton: 18 December 1941. Cadet, Malay States Civil Service, Perak: 1883. All of his early service in Malaya. Resident, Pahang: 1896-1899. By the Colonial Office but under the Chartered Company, nominated Governor of North Borneo and Labuan but resigned in 1900 and returned as Resident, Pahang: 1901. Colonial Secretary, Trinidad and Tobago: 1903-1907, and of Ceylon: 1907-1912. KCMG: 1909. Governor, Gold Coast: 1912-1919. Governor, Nigeria: 1919-1925. GCMG: 1921. Governor, Ceylon: 1925-1927. GBE: 1925. Governor, Straits Settlements: 3 June 1927 to 5 February 1930, when succeeded by Sir Cecil Clementi. FRGS. The author of numerous volumes: well known in literary circles of the day. *Who's Who. Colonial Office List.* Sir Frederick Weld, Governor of the Straits Settlememts between 1880 and 1887, was a cousin of Sir Hugh's father.

15. NA ADM 116/2706. 12 January 1930. Also Harry Miller, *Pirates of the Far East,* (London, 1970), 178/181.

16. It is of interest to note that at the time *U-168,* Helmut Pich, was on passage from Lorient to operate out of Penang. Her success in Eastern waters was to be very modest. Having left Batavia on 5 October 1944 sunk early the following morning by the Dutch submarine *Zwaardvisch,* Lt. Cmdr. Hendrikus Abraham Waldemar Goossens. Kapitanleutnant Pich was amongst the twenty seven survivors. He died as recently as 18 March 1997.

17. *Bruce*, a destroyer flotilla leader of 1,800 tons. Captain (D) W.P. Mark-Wardlaw, DSO. *Serapis* and *Thracian*, each 1,075 tons. Respectively Commander J.M. Porter and Commander N.L. Veresmith. *Navy List*.

18. Clementi Papers.

19. Ed. Greg. Kennedy, *British Naval Strategy East of Suez, 1900-2000*, (Abingdon, Oxon, 2005), 27.

20. NA ADM 53/86453. Log Book *Suffolk*. P. & O. s.s. *Malwa*, 10,883 grt.

21. *Service Record*.

22. Obituary, Courtesy of *The Isle of Wight County Press*, and The Historical Association.

23. *Service Record*.

24. John Hereward **Edelsten**. Born: 12 May 1891. Died: 10 February 1966. Captain: 30 June 1933. Whilst in command heavy cruiser *Shropshire*, between March 1940 and March 1941 was SNO in operations against Italian Somaliland. During 1941 and 1942 Chief of Staff to Admiral Sir Andrew Cunningham, C. in C., Mediterranean. Rear Admiral: 6 February 1942. From 1942 to 1944 a Lord Commissioner of the Admiralty and Assistant Chief of Naval Staff – U- boat Warfare and Trade. Thereafter R/A Destroyers, BPF: 1945. Vice Admiral: 25 September 1945. KCB: 1946. Lord Commissioner of the Admiralty and Vice Chief of Naval Staff: 1947-1949. Admiral: 3 February 1949. C. in C., Mediterranean: 1950-1952, thence C. in C., Portsmouth: 1952-1954. GCB: 1 January 1953. GCVO: 1953. Retired: 24 November 1954. *Who's Who. Navy List*.

George Walter Gillow **Simpson**. Born: 6 June 1901. Died in New Zealand: 2 March 1972. Joined the submarine service in 1921. Well known as Commander (S), then Captain (S) from 10 January 1941 to 22 January 1943 with Tenth Submarine Flotilla at Malta. Captain: 30 June 1941. Commodore (D), Western Approaches, Londonderry: 26 April 1943 to mid 1945. First Naval Member and Chief of New Zealand Naval Staff: 1947-1950. Rear Admiral: 7 July 1950. Flag Officer, Germany: 1951. Flag Officer, Submarines: 1952-1954. Retired: 30 March 1954. *Who's Who. Navy List*.

25. *The Isle of Wight County Press*, Saturday, 31 October 1953. This cemetery is to be found to the East of Winchester on the Alresford Road on the south side of this road. Courtesy: The City of Winchester Trust. On 18 May 2011 the author visited his grave in the rather large and beautifully maintained cemetery, location reference Z2/48. Enter through the main gate and walk up the drive taking the second road which bears off to the left. Their grave is some eighty yards along on the left, well before one reaches the prominent hedge, and is to be found seven yards off this road on the left.

28 February 1931 to 11 March 1933
Vice Admiral Sir William Archibald Howard **Kelly**

Born on 6 September 1873, the third son of Lieut. Colonel Holdsworth Kelly, Royal Marine Artillery, of South Beach House, Florence Road, Southsea (1).

An elder brother was the future Admiral of the Fleet Sir John Donald Kelly (1871-1936).

Sir William died on Sunday, 14 September 1952.

Naval Cadet: 15 January 1886. From 10 January 1888 in battleship *Temeraire*, 8,540 tons, Channel Squadron. **Midshipman**: 15 May 1888. Remained in *Temeraire*, the ship subsequently being 'Temporarily Attached to the Mediterranean.' From 22 August 1891 in cruiser *Ruby*, 2,120 tons, 'Training Squadron'. **Sub Lieutenant**: 6 September 1892: studied at the RNC, Greenwich, where his speciality was to be in Navigation.

From 22 December 1893 to 13 July 1894 Sub Lieutenant (N) in gunboat *Firefly*, 455 tons, then in gunboat *Onyx*, 810 tons, tender to *Mersey*, Coast Guard ship, Harwich (2). From 9 October 1894 Sub Lieut. (N) in gunboat *Hebe*, 810 tons, Mediterranean. **Lieutenant**: 31 December 1894. Remained in *Hebe* as Lieut. (N). From 1 May 1896 Lieut. (N) in sailing sloop *Cruiser*, 1,130 tons, 'Training Ship for Ordinary Seamen', Mediterranean. From the Mediterranean he arrived home on 27 June 1898. From 1 August 1898 Lieut. (N) in cruiser *Iris*, borne in *Victory*, Portsmouth. From 24 January 1899 Lieut. (N) in cruiser *Calliope*, 2,770 tons, 'Particular Service': attached to *Northampton*, 7,630 tons, 'Training Ship for Boys on the Home Station'. From 28 January 1902 Lieut. (N) in cruiser *Ariadne*, borne in *Duke of Wellington*, Depot Ship, Portsmouth. From 26 March 1902 Lieut. (N) in cruiser *Spartiate*. Again borne in *Duke of Wellington*. Just a few months later, from 1 July to 5 December 1902 transferred to the pre-dreadnought battleship *Hood*, Mediterranean. At the end of this commission *Hood* was to undergo a long refit at Chatham. On 27 December 1902 he was, 'allowed to go abroad for 4 months to study French'. On 23 May 1903 he passed the necessary examination so qualified as an interpreter in French therefore additionally an Interpreter Lieutenant, (I). Meanwhile from 20 May 1903 he had been appointed Lieut. (N) in cruiser *Hyacinth*, 5,600 tons, Flagship, East Indies, Rear Admiral George L. Atkinson-Willes and Flag Captain Hon. Horace L.A. Hood. She commissioned at Devonport on 21 July 1903. In *Hyacinth*:-

> '.... he served during the campaign in Somaliland and received the General East Africa Medal, with Somaliland 1902-1904 clasps (3).'

Commander: 31 December 1904. Remained in *Hyacinth* until 6 April 1906 as Commander (N)(I). From 20 August 1905 the new C. in C. was Rear Admiral Edmund Poe (4).

From 21 April 1906 to 22 January 1907 Commander (N)(I) in battleship *Russell*, 14,000 tons, Channel Fleet. The ship was commanded by Captain Robert S. Lowry. However, between 2 December 1906 and 2 March 1907, when he was found to be fit again, he was granted sick leave to undergo an operation for variocele in the King Edward VII Hospital, and afterwards to convalesce at Osborne. Thereafter until May he attended courses.

On 14 May 1907 he married Grace Mary Leonora, generally known as Nora, the daughter of Vice Admiral Sir Edmund Poe. She was to die in 1951. They were to have one son, later to be Colonel D.H. Kelly, and one daughter, in due course to marry thus to become Mrs. C.F. Hammill (5).

From 11 June 1907 Commander (N)(I) in battleship *Nile*, 11,940 tons, Home Fleet, Devonport.

Then followed a period of just over two years, from 28 December 1907 to February 1910, at the Admiralty, Naval Intelligence Department. The Director of the Department was Captain Edmond J.W. Slade, none other than he who in 1912/4 was to be closely involved with the far sighted inquiries which were to result in the purchase of 51% of the Anglo-Persian Oil Company by the British government (6).

In January 1910 he was granted a gratuity in the sum of GBP 25.00 on passing as Interpreter in French (Higher) – previously he had passed Lower (7).

From 19 February 1910 in command cruiser *Barham*, 1,830 tons, Mediterranean.

From 16 February 1911 Naval Attaché to France, Belgium, Spain and Portugal, resident in Paris.

Captain: 31 December 1911.

Continued as Naval Attache, resident in Paris, until 15 March 1914 (8).

> 'On the occasion in June 1913, of the state visit to King George V of M. Poincare, the French President, to whose suite he was attached, Kelly was made MVO (9).'

MVO: 30 June 1913.

From 21 March 1914 in command light cruiser *Gloucester*, 4,800 tons, Mediterranean. The Commander in Chief was Admiral Sir Archibald Berkley Milne (1855-1938) with his flag in the battlecruiser *Inflexible*, 17,290 tons, Captain Arthur N. Loxley. In November 1912 he had succeeded Admiral Sir Edmund Poe, the appointment being influenced by Sir Archibald's personal friendship with the late H.M. King Edward VII, and Queen Alexandra (10). The Great War commenced and on 4 August 1914 Great Britain declared war against the Central Powers, principally Germany and Austria-Hungary. At the time present there in the Mediterranean were SMS *Goeben*, a fast battlecruiser of 22,640 tons, flag of Rear Admiral Wilhelm Anton Souchon (1864-1946), accompanied by the light cruiser *Breslau*, 4,550 tons. Admiral Milne made dispositions in order to bring these German warships to action. Naturally *Gloucester* was included in these arrangements:-

> 'HMS *Gloucester* located the *Goeben* and *Breslau* at Messina on the afternoon of August 5, 1914. At 5 p.m. on August 6 the German ships steamed out of harbour, expecting to encounter one or more British battlecruisers, but they were otherwise engaged. Kelly in the little *Gloucester*, a 4,800 ton ship with two 6" and ten 4" guns, shadowed the *Goeben*, a ship of 22,640 tons with ten 11" and twelve 5.9" guns, all that night and until late in the afternoon of the next day. The *Goeben* could have caught and sunk her at any time had she dared to turn upon her, but she was apparently deterred by the boldness of the *Gloucester* which gave the impression of support close at hand. In spite of the danger, Kelly hung on to the heels of the *Goeben* for over 24 hours, and only relinquished the chase under the direct orders of the C. in C. The German ships, it will be recalled, fled to the shelter of the Dardanelles where their arrival was a primary cause of the entry of Turkey into the war against the Allies (11).'

The escape of *Goeben* to Turkish waters was aided by a sadly notable lack of aggression in the handling of the four warships of the First Cruiser Squadron.

End December 1914: *Gloucester* returned to home waters and was ordered to 2LCS (Second Light Cruiser Squadron), Grand Fleet.

CB: 10 April 1915.

Resulting from the *Goeben* affair the award of his CB was well justified:-

> 'The combination of audacity with restraint, unswerving attention to the principal military object,

namely, holding on to the *Goeben* without tempting her too much, and strict conformity to orders, constitute a naval episode which may justly be regarded as a model (12).'

The contrast between the brilliant handling of *Gloucester*, and the timid handling of the First Cruiser Squadron, flag in the armoured cruiser *Defence*, 14,600 tons, (see C. in C., 1908), is glaringly apparent.

He was superceded in command of *Gloucester* on 8 January 1916 (13).

From 8 January 1916 served for a few months in *President*, the Admiralty, temporarily attached to Intelligence Division. Then, from May 1916 until August 1917, transferred for duty as Naval Liaison Officer in Paris between the Admiralty and the French Ministry of Marine (14).

CMG: 28 September 1917.

From 25 September 1917 **Commodore** 8LCS, then as Commodore First Class in light cruiser *Lowestoft*, 5,440 tons, commanding British Adriatic Force. She paid off on 15 April 1919.

From 1 June 1919: 'Head of British Naval Mission to Greece with rank of Vice Admiral in the Royal Hellenic Navy'. During the Great War Greece had fought on the Allied side and at the conclusion of hostilities had obtained much territory from both Bulgaria and the Ottoman Empire, especially western Thrace or Thraki.

ADC to H.M. King George V: 17 June 1921.

From September 1921 in command of battleship *Emperor of India*, 25,000 tons, Mediterranean.

GSP (Good Service Pension): 27 September 1921. As it had for a great many years, as a Captain this still paid only GBP 150 p.a.

Rear Admiral: 3 May 1922.

From 3 May 1923 to 3 May 1924 RA, 1BS (First Battle Squadron) with his Flag in *Revenge*, 27,500 tons. His Flag Captain was Gilbert O. Stephenson.

From 2 June 1924 in *President*, 'For Miscellaneous Services at Admiralty'. These duties were with the Signal Book Committee to 're-edit and bring up to date the fleet signal books.'

From 15 May 1925 to 16 May 1927, with his Flag in light cruiser *Curacao*, 4,190 tons, RA 2CS, Atlantic Fleet. Flying his flag in his old ship, the battleship *Revenge*, the C. in C. at the time was Admiral Sir Henry F. Oliver (1865-1965), a future Admiral of the Fleet.

Shortly after taking over this command, 2CS, in *Curacao* he undertook a most agreeable summer cruise into the Baltic:-

Port	Arrived	Departed
Rosyth	–	5 June 1925
Copenhagen	8 June	13 June
Helsingfors (Helsinki)	15 June	22 June
Reval (Tallinn), Estonia	22 June	24 June
Riga, Latvia	25 June	1 July 1925
Oslo	4 July	10 July
Torquay 1	3 July 1925	-

Vice Admiral: 2 July 1927.

From 30 September 1927: 'Admiralty Representative on League of Nations Permanent Advisory Commission', Geneva. On the conclusion of this term of office in Geneva in April 1929 he was succeeded by an earlier Rear Admiral, Yangtse, Vice Admiral David M. Anderson.

From 26 April 1929 returned to *Revenge* as VA, 1BS, and also as Second in Command, Mediterranean Fleet. With his flag in the battleship *Warspite*, 27,500 tons, the C. in C. was Admiral Sir Frederick Lawrence Field (1871-1945), in 1930 to be promoted First Sea Lord.

His appointment in the Mediterranean ceased at Marseilles on 10 October 1930 when he was superceded by Vice Admiral Sir William Wordsworth Fisher (1875-1937).

Appointed C. in C., China on 26 December 1930, flag in the 'County' class heavy cruiser *Suffolk*, 10,000 tons, 5CS. Flag Captain Geoffrey Layton (see C. in C., 1940).

KCB: 1 January 1931.

To take up his appointment as C. in C., China Station he took passage East in the P. & O. steamer *Rawalpindi*, 16,697 grt, and at Hong Kong disembarked, 'during forenoon of 26/2/31.' Later that same Thursday morning, at 11:05 hours, he visited *Suffolk*, 'preparatory to assuming command of the China Station'.

Captain Geoffrey Layton assumed command in *Suffolk* at 0800 on Friday, 27 February, and Captain G.S. Arbuthnot left the ship at 13:35 that afternoon.

From Admiral Sir Arthur K. Waistell he assumed command of the Station on Saturday, 28 February 1931, his flag being hoisted in *Suffolk* at 08:00 hours.

The obligatory official call on H.E. The Governor, Sir William Peel, was made at 10:45 after which, at 11:40, His Excellency returned the call, being saluted with nineteen guns. Sir William had joined the Malayan Civil Service in 1897 and, until his appointment to Hong Kong in 1930, had spent his working career in that peninsula.

It was only on Wednesday, 1 April 1931 that as C. in C. he steamed from Hong Kong on his first cruise up the coast to Amoy where he anchored from 2 to 4 April. Thereafter he visited Nanking between 7 and 15 April then returned to Shanghai for the remainder of the month (15).

At Hankow, in Hupeh Province some 636 sea miles from the River mouth, on 27 July 1931 during the height of the summer waters great floods occurred when the banks of the River burst. Especially to the west of the city much land lay well below river level so when the enormous dyke was breached many hundreds of square miles of countryside were flooded and many thousands of people drowned.

Serving as a Paymaster Midshipman in the heavy cruiser *Cumberland*, Captain L.F. Potter but on 22 August 1931 to be succeeded by Captain T.B. Drew, at the time was the late Commander (S) C.H.A. Harper, always known as Peter. Well did he remember the floods:-

> 'We were guardship at Hankow for two extremely hot Augusts, the first in 1931 when the Yangtse had flooded with enormous loss of life. Great sheets of water, as far as the eye could see, and hundreds of miles inland. On one occasion we took a party to the Race Club by motorboat through the back streets of Hankow, and stood at the bar in seaboots (16).'

In an effort to assist China in overcoming this disaster an International Relief Commission was established. Naturally Great Britain was much involved and warships of her China squadron likewise. However, being China in that war lord era, no activity was straightforward. Unless it particularly suited them there was a general disinclination by the Hupeh authorities to obey any instructions received from the government at the capital of Nanking. Always allowance had to be made for a variety of especial local interests. Writing to the C. in C. on 6 October 1931, the Vice Admiral and Senior Naval Officer, Yangtse, Colin MacLean, summed up the situation:-

> 'The Hupeh Provincial authorities do not, in my opinion, care a rap for Flood Relief.
>
> To them the floods are a merciful dispensation in disposing of a surplus population and the only use they have for Flood Relief is to fill their own pockets from the funds (17).'

Nearer Shanghai too, the flooding was appalling in extent. In due course to be a director of Jardine's, here is Sir John Keswick describing the view from the air during the latter stages of a flight made from Peking during the summer of 1931:-

> '... he sent me down to Shanghai in his tri-engined Ford aeroplane. For 250 miles we flew over the flat countryside without once seeing dry land, only occasional rooftops and trees: six million people died in the floods that year. It was a frightening way to realize the problems of China (18).'

During the late evening of 18 September 1931 at Mukden in Manchuria the Japanese Kwantung Army, Lieut. General Honjo Shigeru, staged the event used by them to justify the commencement of their occupation of that Chinese Province (19). In that region at the time the local war lord was a protégé of Chiang Kai-shek, Chang Hsueh-liang, the 'Young Marshal'. It was his father, Chang Tso-lin, the 'Old Marshal', who had been assassinated by the Japanese in June 1928.

As a consequence of his internal conflict with the Chinese communists, Chiang Kai-shek had decided on a policy of first conquering the bandits and rebels, his euphemism for the communists. He reasoned that with these left wing groups eradicated then later he would be able to deal with the foreign, or Japanese, invaders. So it was that in order to limit the extent of what he saw as being merely an incident, he ordered the 'Young Marshal' not to actively resist the Japanese moves in Manchuria. In short order the Japanese army went on to occupy the remainder of that large and rich Province. Thus was established the region later to become their puppet state of Manchukuo. There were two important results.

First, by their action in Manchuria which had not been sanctioned by the civilian government of Japan, the army confirmed itself as a force within that government. No longer was each aspect of government always under civilian control. Sadly this independence of the armed forces arose as a result of a fault in the Japanese constitution.

Secondly within the country her people saw that China, as represented by Chiang Kai-shek, had permitted Japan to occupy a sizeable portion of their land. By not attempting to eject the Japanese forces, and in doing so thereby endeavouring to rally all of China behind him, Chiang had made an important error.

Meanwhile in England the Labour government of Ramsay MacDonald had not been able to cope with the problem of rapidly rising numbers of unemployed. His government had resigned in August 1931 and been replaced, from 25 August, with a coalition administration however with him continuing as Prime Minister. Financial stringency was necessary, one method which was adopted being the reduction in pay of civil servants and the members of HM Forces. Unfortunately within the Royal Navy the matter was poorly handled by the Admiralty and, to a lesser extent, by the senior officers in the Atlantic Fleet. So it was that early in September 1931 the distressing affair at Invergordon had resulted (20).

In China too all was not easy.

As the C. in C. was to comment drily:-

> 'Even for the China Station, where dull moments are unusual, the month of September has been one of considerable excitement.
>
> The assumption of office by the new Government of the United Kingdom and consequent economy measures, the advance of the Cantonese forces against Nanking with the prospects of increased unrest in the Yangtse valley, the commencement of the fall of the River, when trouble in Hankow might be expected, the unrest in the Atlantic Fleet, the Japanese aggression in Manchuria, and the change of Sterling from a gold basis, with its serious effect on ships' companies paid in silver, were events all calling for the closest attention (21).'

Admiral: 6 October 1931.

In November 1931 the C. in C., together with his wife and daughter, proceeded from Shanghai south to Foochow and Swatow in the twin screw minesweeper *Petersfield*, 710 tons, Commander Douglas Cuthbert Lang. As was the case on this occasion, in the normal course of events the ship was used as the C. in C.'s yacht. Being of shallow draft one great advantage was that she could visit ports with draught restrictions. Without elaborating at length, Sir Howard was well known for his possession of a somewhat arrogant, superior nature. Undoubtedly this impression was countered by a kind heart towards those who had the courage to stand up to him, but few were so inclined, the more so in view of his high rank. The long and the short of it was that the C. in C., as has been seen a Navigator by specialization, one evening had assisted in laying off the course the ship should steer that night. Unfortunately she grounded on Tung Yung Island at 03:00 the following morning, 12 November 1931, shortly thereafter becoming a total loss, fortunately without loss of life. In response to the S.O.S. message sent out by *Petersfield*, ships who responded, and who were to assist with the rescue of survivors, included the Canadian Pacific steamer *Empress of Asia*, 16,909 grt, and the North German Lloyd steamer *Derfflinger*, 9,060 grt.

The result of the subsequent court martial decided against the Captain of the ship. Suffice to say that feeling on the Station ran very high at the time as the unfortunate man was dismissed his ship, in fact by January 1935 was on the Retired List. Also severely reprimanded as a result of this accident was the navigating officer, Lieut. G.A.H. Pratt (22).

However the C. in C., for whom at one stage even greater heights were forecast, was not to be employed again in peace time (23).

On 16 November 1931 he switched flagship to a sister ship, *Kent*, 10,000 tons, Flag Captain T.B. Drew, his flag being hoisted in her at 08:00 hours that morning. At 09:30 he and his staff, including Flag Lieut. Commander L.A.H. Wright, '.. transferred to *Kent* after saying "good bye" to the officers of *Suffolk*' (24).

Kent had been brought out from England by Captain John H. Godfrey who arrived at Hong Kong on 9 October 1931 (25). Godfrey then took over the command of *Suffolk*. As Commodore Second Class, Geoffrey Layton also transferred across to *Kent* as Chief of Staff.

> 'This was a troublous time in the Far East, culminating in the Sino-Japanese dispute and landing of Japanese marines and troops at Shanghai in January 1932. A small and inconclusive war was waged, without any declaration of hostilities, between Japan and China in the area north of Shanghai, and the International Settlement was endangered. Comparative quiet was restored early in March, and armistice proposals were made at a conference onboard Sir Howard Kelly's flagship, HMS *Kent*, although peace was not signed until May 5 (26).'

This Japanese landing in Shanghai and vicinity in fact had been a considerable operation. Reinforcements arrived in February and at that time Captain Godfrey noted as follows:-

> 'Disembarkation of Japanese Division at Shanghai and Woosung: 14-16 February 1932.
>
> It was given as an opinion that about 10,000 men and equipment were landed at Shanghai, and about 2,000 ditto at Woosung. Also at Shanghai about 60 guns, anti-aircraft guns, mortars, 15 tanks, about 12 crated aeroplanes, field kitchens, 25 light landing craft, lorries and vehicles.'

The peace treaty arrangements, which were to reach that fortunate conclusion on Thursday, 5 May 1932 at Shanghai, were complicated by assassination attempts and mob violence, a sad feature of much political life during that era in the Far East:-

> 'In spite of forebodings caused in the first instance by the Korean Bomb Outrage, and in the second instance by the attack on Mr. Quo Tai-chi, Political Vice Minister of Foreign Affairs and Chief Delegate at the Sino-Japanese discussions over the cessation of hostilities, the Sino-Japanese Peace Treaty was signed at 1100 a.m. (27).'

'Korean Bomb Outrage' refers to the bomb attack made on the Japanese Minister to China, Shigemitsu Mamoru, in Shanghai on 29 April 1932 (28).

In the second instance Mr. Quo had been beaten by a nationalist mob who had not approved of his decision to sign the armistice with Japan (29).

Mr. Shigemitsu in fact signed the necessary treaty papers from his bed in Foomin hospital just shortly before his right leg was amputated. He was to walk with an artificial leg and to use a cane for the remainder of his life. Looking ahead to the end of WW2, he was to be Minister of Foreign Affairs and as such, on behalf of Japan, was one of the delegates who was to sign the instrument of surrender onboard USS *Missouri* BB-63 in Tokyo Bay on 2 September 1945.

Playing an important role during the latter part of these Sino-Japanese treaty discussions was the British Minister to China, Sir Miles Wedderburn Lampson, later Baron Killearn (1880-1964), and in many instances the chosen venue in which negotiations took place was the British Consulate-General on the Bund in Shanghai.

In the interim across the Pacific on Sunday, 7 February 1932, while positioning his carriers in readiness for the US Navy exercises, Fleet Problem XIII, Rear Admiral Harry E. Yarnell carried out a surprise attack on Pearl Harbour. This mock raid, which again was a great success, bore a resemblance to that carried out by Admiral Reeves in 1928. However on this occasion Admiral Yarnell was able to use both the large and fast fleet carriers, *Lexington* CV-2, Captain Ernest J. King, and *Saratoga* CV-3, Captain Frank McCrary. In planning the operation Admiral Yarnell, who flew his flag in *Saratoga*, had been assisted by his Chief of Staff, Captain John H. Towers, the pioneer naval aviator and a previous Captain of *Langley*, CV-1.

In February 1932 Rear Admiral Yamamoto Isoroku, IJN was still in his post as Director of the Technical Section in the department of Naval Aeronautics. As will be seen, in October 1933 he was to receive his next appointment back at sea, Commander of the First Aviation Squadron with his flag in *Akagi*.

The proclamation of the new state of Manchukuo took place on 18 February 1932. The installation of P'u-i (1906-1967), last Emperor of the Ch'ing dynasty in China, occurred just a few days later, on 9 March 1932. Japan at first named him president, but then from 1934 to 1945 he was to be emperor of their puppet state of Manchukuo, previously Manchuria.

In Japan on 15 May 1932 Prime Minister Inukai Tsuyoshi was assassinated. His government opposed actions taken by the army in Manchuria. This sad event, carried out by a group of young ultranationalist officers, finally marked the end of civilian government control over the desires of the military. As seen above, since the previous September any such pretence of civilian authority already had received one severe blow. This situation was not to change until the last months of WW2, during the summer of 1944, with the conquest of the Marianas and reoccupation of Guam by the U.S.N. Fifth Fleet, Admiral Raymond A. Spruance.

A compromise Prime Minister was appointed, the moderate Admiral Saito Makoto (30). Unfortunately however, the ultranationalist General Araki Sadao remained as War Minister.

As an indication of the value of money in that era, in an issue of the *North China Post* in August 1932 a First Class return passage from Shanghai to Yokohama per P. & O. passenger liner was advertised as costing just Sterling pounds fifteen.

The façade of the official recognition by Japan of their occupied puppet state of Manchukuo took place on 15 September 1932, and in due course their 'Embassy' was to be opened at the new capital city of Changchun (Hsinking). As might be expected, Germany and Italy also were to recognize Manchukuo, and later also the puppet state of occupied China under Wang Ching-wei.

At Changchun the Japanese did their best to emulate, perhaps co-incidentally, New Delhi, completed by the Raj in 1931:-

> 'The grand Army Building on Changchun's wide main street reflected the majestic appearance of the Japanese military, and the newly completed Building of Justice displayed a degree of splendour unsurpassed even in their homeland. The area around the station resembled bustling Japanese streets, and the adjoining pleasure district of Yoshino was better even than similar areas at home. Department stores flourished and in the colourful streets one could find eating and drinking stalls and all sorts of entertainment. (--) Nowhere outside Japan could one feel more proud of being a Japanese. In these grand buildings, power and prestige paired with a never ending energy in the buoyant shopping streets full of Japanese (31).'

There was another most lucrative side to the Japanese occupation of Manchuria:-

> 'With the establishment of Manchukuo, opium traffic was legalized and put into official colonial hands (32).'

> 'Opium was an important source of revenue for the Manchukuo government, through the Opium Monopoly Bureau set up by Hoshino (33).'

Historically the subject of opium was, and remains, controversial. Here follows two opinions expressed on the subject, the writer being a Taikoo merchant who worked in China for many years, and at Chungking between 1932 and 1936:-

'When one went riding up into the hills there were the opium poppies hidden from the sight of the casual observer from the river all growing away, all banned, all strictly controlled and collected by the military and taxed here, taxed there and taxed the other place. You got shot if you attempted to smuggle it, not because the authorities were against opium but because they were against any breach of their monopoly which magnified the price. It was smoked all over the place.

A lot of rot is talked about opium: its real evil was that it was so expensive that it could ruin you, if you were not near the source, as you were in Chungking. It was like alcohol and I rated it about the same, as a vice. Several Chinese I knew of had been smoking six pipes of opium every day for years and years. it seemed to be as controllable by will and as harmless or harmful as alcohol. Just as there are some people who start by drinking a couple of shorts a day and end up beggared alcoholics so there are people who ruin themselves with opium but others for whom it seemed almost a social drug (34).

W. Somerset Maugham too suggests that not all opium parlours were dens of iniquity:-

'I was introduced to a neat enough room, brightly lit, divided into cubicles the raised floor of which, covered with clean matting, formed a convenient couch. In one an elderly gentleman, with a grey head and very beautiful hands, was quietly reading a newspaper, with his long pipe by his side. In another two coolies were lying, with a pipe between them, which they alternately prepared and smoked. They were young men, of a hearty appearance, and they smiled at me in a friendly way. One of them offered me a smoke. In a third four men squatted over a chess board. (--) It was a cheerful spot, comfortable, home-like, and cosy. It reminded me somewhat of the little intimate beer houses of Berlin where the tired working man could go in the evening and spend a peaceful hour (35).'

At 2200 hours on 9 November 1932, with his flag in *Kent*, Sir Howard returned to Hong Kong.

Returning from leave, on Thursday morning, 17 November, The Governor, Sir William Peel, arrived back in Hong Kong in the P. & O. steamer *Ranpura*, 16,688 grt.

On 11 December 1932 at Canton the members of the Naval Club gave a dinner in honour of the C. in C. Among the guests was the Minister of Foreign Affairs in the Canton government, Chu Chao-hsin. Mr. Chu, a graduate of Columbia University in New York City and a one time Charge d'Affaires at the Chinese Legation in London, was well known in the West. It will have been brought home to the guest of honour that such pleasant social gatherings could be hazardous as during the banquet Mr. Chu died:-

'Snakes were served at the dinner, and it is presumed that Chu's death was due to snake poisoning (36).'

Further to the north in China winter conditions were severe and on the Yangtse River the water level vastly different from that which prevailed in summer. Once the headwaters froze then the water level dropped considerably, as did the temperature. To assist in visualising the scene here follows a few lines written in January 1933 by Lieut. E.H. Chavasse, then serving as First Lieutenant in the gunboat *Scarab*. The ship is bound upstream from Wuhu:-

'The stretch of river was very different from the one I had seen a mere three months before, in October. Then it had been almost 'high river' and in places the green banks were only a foot or two higher than the level of the water; this time the banks were steep and thirty feet high so that from the bridge you could only just see over the top into an unbroken wilderness of snow. It was really rather an eerie sensation for the day was calm and clear and both sky and river were almost pure white so that one felt as though the ship were gliding through nothing. Almost the only definable objects were trees, houses, navigational beacons, and, in the distance, snow covered mountains. In silence we slipped through a world of white (37).'

On 30 January 1933 Adolf Hitler was named Chancellor of Germany.

Over the matter of the international dispute arising from her occupation of Manchuria, and having been condemned by the League of Nations, on 24 February 1933 Japan withdrew from the League. At Geneva on that occasion their delegation was led by a future Foreign Minister, Matsuoka Yosuke (1880-1946).

As if any confirmation is required here is H.E. Sir William Peel, Governor of Hong Kong, giving a brief comment covering one aspect of this period of domestic chaos within China:-

'On one occasion I and other officers lunched on a very smart and clean Chinese Flagship and were shown a most excellent exhibition of gymnastics and sword drill, together with a short play given by the officers and crew. The Chinese Admiral was a pleasant man but fell from grace shortly after his visit and was removed from his post. I do not know what became of him. Tenure of office was very precarious among the Chinese in those days (38).'

Before leaving China the C. in C. entertained some friends to dinner in Hong Kong where the restaurant menu was written in Chinese. By chance he counted the courses and at the end noted that they appeared to have consumed one fewer than those marked on the menu. Both the head waiter and manager assured him that the full number of courses had been served but, determined not to be cheated, he summoned the services of an interpreter. One can only wonder if he was amused as when translated the final few lines read:-

'This is for the British Commander-in-Chief. Treat him well and charge him accordingly (39).'

As his tour of duty in the Far East drew to an end his secretary, Paymaster Captain E.H. Wethey, prepared a report headed, 'Incidents which have occurred during C. in C.'s period of command of the China Station when Naval assistance has been asked for and/or given'. There were a total of fifty four such incidents. Purely as an indication of such occasions a random selection follows:-

'a) s.s. *King Wo* ashore at mile 40, Upper River. 27.1.31 to 31.1.31.
Armed guard despatched from Ichang.
b) Grounding of s.s. *Wai Shing* in Namkwan harbour. 1.8.31 to 15.8.31.
H.M.S. *Sepoy* sent from Hong Kong and placed armed guard onboard as protection from pirates.
c) Piracy of s.s. *Hangyang*. 20.11.31 to 3.12.31.
H.M.S. *Sterling* sent to Namoa Island and effected recapture of some cargo.
d) Nanking. s.s. *Changsha* boarded by Chinese soldiers demanding free passage. 22.2.32.
Armed guard from *Sandwich* ejected soldiers.
e) Transport of Argyll and Sutherland Highlanders from Shanghai to Hong Kong. 18.4.32 to 20.4.32.
H.M.S. *Kent* transported this battalion from Shanghai to Hong Kong.
f) Civil war in Shantung province – Chefoo. 14.9.32 to 22.12.32.
One Captain's command of H.M. Ships at Chefoo from 19.9.32 to 7.10.32. One sloop from 7.10.32 to 27.12.32.
g) Kidnapping of Mrs. Pawley and Mr. Corkran at Newchwang. 8.10.32 to 20.10.32.
H.M.S. *Sandwich* sent to Newchwang and remained there the whole period giving active assistance in recovery.
h) Attempted hold up of s.s. *Luen Ho* twenty miles above Chinkiang by members of Opium Suppression Bureau. 3.1.33.
H.M.S. *Cricket* sent armed guard to *Luen Ho* and handed over Chinese offenders to

Chinese authorities at Chinkiang.
i) Grounding of Chinese s.s. *Tai Lee*. 6.1.33.
Ship was towed off Mahning bar by H.M.S. *Cicala* (40).'

At Hong Kong on Saturday, 11 March 1933 he embarked in the P. & O. s.s. *Ranpura*, 16,585 grt, to return to England.

This P. & O. steamer was one of a class of four built in 1925 originally for the UK/Bombay direct service. Only she and her sister *Ranchi* were to survive WW2. On 23 November 1939 another sister, as an AMC therefore HMS *Rawalpindi*, Captain Edward C. Kennedy, RN, was to be sunk in the North Atlantic off Iceland during the well known, brave engagement with the large armoured cruisers *Scharnhorst* and *Gneisenau*, Vice Admiral Wilhelm Marschall (1886-1976).

On the same day, 11 March 1933, his successor, Admiral Sir Frederic Dreyer, assumed command in China.

Back home once more, on Wednesday, 4 October 1933 he delivered a lecture at the Royal United Service Insitution in London. In the chair was Admiral Sir Reginald Y. Tyrwhitt (see C. in C., 1926). Sir Howard, who entitled his talk, 'British Interests in China', described some of his recent experiences in the Far East and ended with a few words under the heading, 'The Future'. Today few persons would disagree with his general economic forecast:-

'What of the future? In China, life is lived from day to day; nobody but a madman attempts to prophesy what the future may bring forth; but a future there must be. The future of China depends on security; security for life and property, and security for capital. Given security, it is hard to set any limits to the possibilities of this vast country, whose riches are unlimited and almost untouched. For security a united country and a stable government are required; the federal system of government would seem to be the most appropriate, with wide autonomy for the provincial governments (41).'

GBE: 1 January 1934
He retired on 19 June 1936.
In retirement he maintained a variety of interests for example, 'By decree dated 12 February 1937 elected to the Academie de Marine as foreign associate member.'

Following the outbreak of WW2 in Europe, on 2 May 1940 he was recalled to active service, thence to be appointed British Naval Representative in Turkey. There he remained until July 1944. In Turkey:-
'He was one of the few persons, and certainly the only foreigner, who had free access to the unapproachable Field Marshal Fevzi Chakmak, former chief of the Turkish general staff, and he became very popular with the Turkish public (42).'

On 12 August 1944 he returned to England but only on 11 December was his final appointment officially terminated and he re-retired the following day, 12 December 1944 (43).
His home in London was at 51 Ashley Gardens, SW1.
By 1950 he was Chairman of both the Anglo-Hellenic League, and of the Royal Central Asian Society (44).
Following his death on 14 September 1952 his subsequent funeral was private. However at St. Martin-in-the Fields, London on Thursday, 25 September 1952 a memorial service was held. During this service a lesson was read by Admiral Sir Geoffrey Layton (C. in C., China, 1940/1) and amongst the large congregation of family members, Naval officers, and dignitaries who attended was Admiral Sir Charles Little (C. in C., in China, 1936-1938) (45).

NOTES

1. *Who's Who*, 1951.

2. NA ADM 196/43. *Service Record.*

3. Obituary, *The Times*, Monday, September 15, 1952.

   The Somaliland Affair was a religious rebellion led by Mohammed Abdullah Hassan (1864-1920), the 'Mad Mullah'. Between 1900 and 1904 four major British, Ethiopian and Italian expeditions were carried out against him. *Encyclopaedia Britannica.*

4. Edmund Samuel **Poe**. Born: 11 September 1849. Died: 4 April 1921. Entered the RN: 1862. Captain: 30 June 1888. Rear Admiral: 9 September 1901. Second in Command, Home Fleet, flag in the battleship *Empress of India*, 14,150 tons: 8 May 1903. In command ICS, Channel Fleet with flag in cruiser *Good Hope*, 14,100 tons: 2 November 1904. C. in C., East Indies and Cape of Good Hope: 20 August 1905. Vice Admiral: 20 February 1906. KCVO: 19 March 1906. KCB: 26 June 1908. Admiral: 30 April 1910. C. in C., Mediterranean with flag in battleship *Exmouth*, 14,000 tons: 30 April 1910 to 26 November 1912. GCVO: 1912. Retired in September 1914. *Navy List. Who's Who.*

5. *Who's Who. Service Record.*

6. Edmond John Warre **Slade**. Born: 20 March 1859. Died: 20 January 1928. Eton. Entered the Navy: 1872. Captain: 31 December 1899. Director of Naval Intelligence: 1907-1909. Rear Admiral: 5 November 1908. With his flag in *Highflyer*, 5,600 tons, C. in C., East Indies: 3 March 1909 – 4 February 1912. KCIE: 1911. KCVO: 1912. This far sighted and important move by the Admiralty then took place:-

   'On his return to England in 1912 the Admiralty appointed him for special service in connexion with oil fuel supplies, and when, some two years later, an agreement was made with the Anglo-Persian Oil Company by which the Admiralty became a large shareholder in the undertaking with the right to nominate a director, they selected Vice Admiral Slade, as he had then become, as their nominee, and at his death he was Vice Chairman.'

   Extract from his obituary, *The Times*, Monday January 23, 1928.

   Between October 1913 and February 1914 he was head of the four man British Government Expedition to Persia to investigate the oil prospects. To Mr. Winston Churchill, First Lord of the Admiralty between 1911 and 1915, must go great credit for initiating this most successful move.

   Vice Admiral: 25 April 1914. Admiral: 18 August 1917. Retired: 1 September 1917. Subsequently and until his death to be a government nominated director of the Anglo-Persian Oil Company, in 1935 to be re-named Anglo- Iranian Oil Company, and in 1954 the British Petroleum Company. *Navy List. Who's Who.*

7. *Service Record.*

8. *Foreign Office List*, 1920.

9. Obituary, *The Times.*

10. Of Admiral Milne it has been written, 'He was an officer of inferior calibre, utterly lacking in vigour and imagination, whose appointment to the Mediterranean command in 1912 had largely been due to Court influence.' Arthur J. Marder, *From the Dreadnought to Scapa Flow*, (OUP, 1966), II, 21. In making the appointment the First Lord, Mr. Winston Churchill, would appear to have submitted to this oft mentioned Court influence.

11. Obituary, *The Times*. SMS *Goeben*, completed by Blohm and Voss in Hamburg in August 1912, later in August 1914 was transferred to the Turkish Navy as *Yavuz Sultan Selim*. The longest lived of the Dreadnoughts of that era, only in 1971 was she to be disposed of for breaking up.

12. Ibid.

13. *Service Record.*

14. *Foreign Office List. Service Record.*

15. NA ADM 53/86455.

16. Correspondence with the author between May and July 2001.

17. NA ADM 116/2843. Report 0702/204 written at Hankow.

18. Ed. Maggie Keswick, *The Thistle and the Jade*, (London, 1982), 208.

19. **Honjo** Shigeru. Born: 10 May 1876. Died by committing suicide: 30 November 1945. Graduated from the Imperial

Japanese Army Academy: 1897. Future Generals Araki Sadao and Matsui Iwane were class mates. Served with distinction during the Russo-Japanese war of 1904/5. Major General: 1922. Lieut. General: 1927. From Manchuria in 1932 returned home, a national hero. Supreme War Council: 1932-1933. Baron: 1932. Chief adc to HIM Emperor Hirohito: April 1933 – April 1936. *Encyclopaedia Britannica.*

20. The C. in C., Atlantic Fleet at the time was Admiral Sir Michael Hodges who unfortunately chanced to be ill with pleurisy. The First Sea Lord was Admiral Sir Frederick Laurence Field. *Navy List.*

21. NA ADM 116/2843. China General Letter No. 7 covering the period 1-30 September 1931.

22. Caird Library, National Maritime Museum, Greenwich. Ref: *KEL/37.*

23. Commander Geoffrey L. Lowis, *Fabulous Admirals,* (London, 1957), 219/222.

24. Caird Library. Ref: *KEL/37.*

25. Royal Naval Museum, Portsmouth. Godfrey papers, Ref: *MSS 319.*
    John Henry **Godfrey**. Born: 10 July 1888. Died: 29 August 1971. Captain: 30 June 1928. In command of *Suffolk*: 1931-1933. Rear Admiral: 22 February 1939. Vice Admiral: 15 September 1942. Flag Officer, Indian Navy: 22 February 1943. Admiral: 25 September 1945 and retired. *Navy List. Who's Who.* Also see Patrick Beesly, *Very Special Admiral,* (London, 1980).

26. Obituary, *The Times.*

27. Caird Library. Ref: *KEL/37.*

28. **Shigemitsu** Mamoru. Born: 29 July 1881. Died: 26 January 1957. At Shanghai the bomb attack had been carried out by a Korean independence activist, Yoon Bong-Gil. Since 1910 Korea had been the Japanese colony of Chosen. Vice Minister of Foreign Affairs: 1933-1936. Ambassador to the Soviet Union: 1936-1938. Ambassador to the Court of St. James': 1938-1941. Minister of Foreign Affairs: 1943-1945 and again, 1954-1956.

29. **Quo** Tai-chi. Born: 1888. Died: 29 February 1952. Graduated from the University of Pennsylvania in 1911. Career diplomat and active Kuomintang member. Minister/Ambassador to the Court of St. James': 1932-1940. Foreign Minister from April 1941 until shortly after the Pearl Harbour attack on 7 December 1941 when succeeded by T.V. Soong. At the formation of the U.N. in San Francisco in 1946 he represented the Republic of China, and in New York in March presided over the first security council session.

30. **Saito** Makoto. Born: 27 October 1858. Died: 26 February 1936. Entered the Naval Academy, Tsukiji: October 1873. This was early during the Douglas era (see Shadwell, C. in C., 1871, Ref: 32). Graduated: July 1879. As a Midshipman served in *Fuso*: May 1880. From 1884 served as the first IJN Attache to Washington, DC. At the end of 1885 accompanied Navy Minister Saigo Tsugumichi (1843-1902) to England and Europe, his first visit, then returned to the U.S.A. Returned to Japan in October 1888 and appointed to the Navy General Staff. Subsequent service in *Takao*, 1,750 tons, and Flagship *Takachiho*, a protected cruiser of 3,650 tons. Returned to the Naval Staff. Further service in *Takao*, then promoted Lieut. Commander and in December 1893 appointed to Naval Affairs Bureau, Navy Ministry. Naval member of the committee formed to inquire into the circumstances surrounding the sinking of the British steamer *Kow Shing* by HIJMS *Naniwa* on 25 July 1894. Captain Togo Heihachiro was exonerated (see Fremantle, C. in C., 1892). In 1897 a member of the party sent to England to bring home the new battleship *Fuji*, 12,500 tons, the first IJN battleship. In her attended the Naval Review on 26 June 1897 held in honour of HM Queen Victoria's Diamond Jubilee. Subsequently promoted Captain and commanded cruisers *Akitsushima* then *Itsukushima*. Rear Admiral: 20 May 1900. At the start of the Russo-Japanese war of 1904/5 was Vice Navy Minister. On 16 April 1914 the government, the first formed by Admiral Yamamoto Gonnohyoe, fell as a result of the Siemens and Vickers scandals so forced to resign as Navy Minister. Governor General of Korea: 1919- 1927 when credited with promoting a civilian rather than a militaristic administration. Viscount: 29 April 1925. At Geneva as Commissioner Plenipotentiary participated in the Disarmament Conference of 1927. Thereafter, before returning home, in England met old friends Admirals Moore and Meux (see C.s in C., 1905 and 1908). Subsequently privy councillor to the Emperor. Again Governor General of Korea: August 1929 but, following a mild stroke, resigned in June 1931. Following the right wing assassination of Prime Minister Inukai Tsuyoshi on 15 May 1932 an attempt was made by genro Saionji Kinmochi to prevent a continuation of the move towards the right and, as a compromise, Saito, in his 74th year, was made Prime Minister. Following the Teijin Silk Company scandal the entire cabinet resigned: 8 July 1934. Lord Keeper of the Privy Seal: 26 December 1935. Assassinated during the 26 February 1936 right wing army fracas, sadly yet another relative moderate

removed by that extreme element. *Encyclopaedia Britannica.* Ed. J.E. Hoare, *Biographical Portraits,* III, (Japan Library, 1999), 182-194 by Tadashi Kuramatsu.

31. Henry Frei, *Guns of February,* (Singapore, 2004), 34.

32. Barbara J. Brooks, *Japan's Imperial Diplomacy,* (Hawaii, 2000), 113.

33. John G. Roberts, *Mitsui,* (New York and Tokyo, 1989), 312. Hoshino Naoki (1892-1978), '.. who had managed the puppet empire's finances for many years.', 311.

34. Christopher Cook, *The Lion and the Dragon*, (London, 1985), 119.

35. W. Somerset Maugham, *On a Chinese Screen,* (OUP, 1985), 60/1. Mr. Maugham visited China twice between the years 1919 and 1921.

36. *The Times,* Monday, December 12, 1932.

37. E.H. Chavasse, *Up and Down the Yangtse,* Chapter 21, (Privately printed). In June 1999 a copy kindly loaned to the author by his nephew, Mr. Tim Chavasse. River Gunboat *Scarab,* 625 tons, mean draught of 4.5'. 14 knots. In 1917 she had seen Great War service upstream from Basra. Wilfred Nunn, *Tigris Gunboats,* (London, 2007), 277/8.

38. Rhodes House Library, Oxford. Ref: *S.208.*
    William **Peel**. Born: 27 February 1875. Died: 24 February 1945. Silcoates School and Queen's College, Cambridge. In October 1897 joined the Straits Settlements service as a Cadet. Spent practically his entire working life in Malaya. Chief Secretary to the Government, Federated Malay States: 1926-1930. KBE: 1928. Governor of Hong Kong: 9 May 1930 – 17 May 1935. KCMG: 1931. *Who's Who. Colonial Office List.*

39. *Fabulous Admirals,* 212.

40. Reading Room, Imperial War Museum, London. Ref: *99/42/1.*
    a) Jardine Matheson steamer *King Wo,* 617 grt.
    b) Jardine Matheson steamer *Wai Shing,* 1,865 grt. Blown ashore when sheltering from a typhoon. Namkwan Bay is near Wenchow, Chekiang province, roughly half way between Foochow and Ningpo. She refloated on 20 August. Destroyer *Sepoy,* 905 tons.
    c) Destroyer *Sterling,* 905 tons. Namoa Island lies to the N.E. of Swatow a short distance up the coast.
    d) China Navigation (Butterfield and Swire) steamer *Changsha,* 2,482 grt. Sloop *Sandwich,* 1,045 tons.
    e) Heavy cruiser *Kent,* 10,000 tons, Flagship on the Station.
    f) Chefoo lies on the north coast of the Shantung peninsula. Frequently used by the USN as a summer base.
    g) Newchwang in Fengtien province, Manchuria. A port on the Liao river.
    h) Jardine Matheson steamer *Luen Ho,* 2,868 grt. River gunboat *Cricket,* 645 tons.
    i) River gunboat *Cicala,* 645 tons, was stationed on the West River.

41. *The Journal of the Royal United Service Institution*, Vol. LXXVIII, November 1933, 679/696.

42. Obituary, *The Times.* Fevzi Cakmak (1876-1950). Soldier and politician. Prime Minister: January 1921 – July 1922. Chief of Staff of the Turkish Army: July 1922 to January 1944. *Encyclopaedia Britannica.*

43. *Service Record.*

44. *Who's Who.*

45. *The Times*, Friday, September 26, 1952.

11 March 1933 to 11 January 1936
Admiral Sir Frederic Charles **Dreyer**

Born at Parsonstown, Ireland on 8 January 1878, the second son of Dr. John Louis Emil Dreyer, PhD, DSc (1852-1926). He, born a Dane, between 1869 and 1873 studied astronomy and related subjects at Copenhagen University. In 1874 he took up an astronomical position at Birr Castle. There in Ireland in November 1875 he married Katherine Hannah, daughter of John Tuthill of Kilmore, Co. Limerick. In 1885 he became a British citizen. As an astronomer of international repute he was awarded the Gold Medal of the Royal Astronomical Society in 1916 and served as the Society's President from 1923 to 1925. Frederick Charles' grandfather once had served as Danish Minister for War and the Navy. The Admiral's elder brother, John Tuthill Dreyer (1876-1959), became a Major General in the Royal Artillery.

Died at his home in Winchester on 11 December 1956. A memorial to Sir Frederic may be found in Winchester Cathedral.

Royal School, Armagh, and entered *Britannia* on 15 July 1891 (1). **Midshipman**: 15 July 1893. From 12 September 1893 in battleship *Anson*, 10,600 tons, Mediterranean. From 7 September 1896 in battleship *Barfleur*, 10,500 tons, Mediterranean. **Sub Lieutenant**: 15 January 1897. From 29 April 1897 studying at RNC, Greenwich. Achieved four 'Firsts'. From 8 June 1898 in TBD *Ferret*, 280 tons, Devonport. **Lieutenant**: 15 July 1898. From 5 August 1898 in battleship *Repulse*, 14,150 tons, Channel Squadron. From 30 September 1899 in *Excellent*, Portsmouth, 'Lieutenant qualifying for gunnery officer'. At *Excellent*:-

> 'Having passed with honours the advanced course he became a fully qualified gunnery Lieutenant in 1901 at the age of 23 (2).'

In 1900 the author of *How to get a First Class in Seamanship*.

On 26 June 1901 at Bishop's Tachbrook near Leamington in Warwichshire he married Una Maria Hallett (1876-1959), daughter of Rev. John Thomas Hallett, vicar of Bishop's Tachbrook, Leamington, and by her was to have a family of three sons and two daughters.

His second son was Desmond Parry Dreyer, born on 6 April 1910. Vice Admiral: 27 January 1961, and Flag Officer, Far East: 6 November 1962. Thus he was in command in 1963 at the outbreak of the conflict between Indonesia and Malaysia, or Konfrontasi. Britain was to play a most active role in this affair. KCB: 1963. Admiral: 5 June 1965. GCB: 1967. Sir Desmond died on 15 May 2003.

From 9 July 1901 to 12 August 1902 served in *Wildfire*, Flagship, Sheerness as Lieut. (G), 'for duty in the Gunnery School'. Spent the remainder of the year as Lieut. (G), first briefly in *Hawke*, then for three months in the pre-dreadnought battleship *Hood*, 14,150 tons, in the Mediterranean. In *Hood* at the time Howard Kelly was serving as Lieutenant (N). From 13 January 1903 Lieut. (G) again in cruiser *Hawke*, 7,350 tons, 'Special Service', which consisted of two trooping voyages to the Mediterranean. Between 12 March and 1 June 1903 he returned to serve in *Excellent* to qualify in advanced Gunnery. Then from 2 June 1903 appointed Lieut. (G) in battleship *Exmouth*, 14,000 tons, Mediterranean. She re-commissioned at Chatham on 18 May 1904. Remained in the ship, now Flagship, Channel Fleet, Admiral Sir Arthur K. Wilson, VC. Following his time in *Exmouth* Admiral Wilson, no easy man to impress, was to write of him:-

> 'Extremely able (G) officer, practically and scientifically, with great powers of imparting his knowledge to those under him and evoking their enthusiasm. His methods have been largely copied in all ships that have done best in Battle Practice. I trust Their Lordships will see their way to promote him shortly (3).'

From 7 January 1907 Lieut. (G) in the new battleship, and name ship for the future style of great battleships, *Dreadnought*, 17,900 tons. She had completed at Portsmouth on 11 December 1906. Captain Reginald H.S. Bacon commanded her during her extensive trials which included voyages to the Mediterranean and trans Atlantic to the Gulf of Paria, Trinidad. Later Bacon was to write:-

> '(Admiral) Fisher most wisely had arranged for Lieutenant F.C. Dreyer, the most accomplished gunnery Lieutenant of that time, to be appointed to the ship for the cruise; he was of the greatest assistance in carrying out the gunnery trials (4).'

From 29 April 1907 in *President*, the Admiralty, Naval Ordnance Department. At the time Rear Admiral Jellicoe was Director of Naval Ordnance and Torpedoes. Also in 1907:-

> 'Later in that year he was concerned in experiments with Mr. Pollen's aim corrector, an instrument designed to improve the control of fire of a ship's armament (5).'

Commander: 31 December 1907. Remained in the Naval Ordnance Department.

From 15 December 1909 Commander of the new building battleship *Vanguard*, 19,250 tons, Home Fleet. She commissioned at Devonport: 1 March 1910.

In *Vanguard* developed his 'Fire Control Table'. In due course this equipment, with subsequent modification, was to be adopted widely in the Fleet.

From 20 December 1910 Flag Commander to acting Vice Admiral Sir John R. Jellicoe, C. in C., Atlantic Fleet in battleship *Prince of Wales*, 15,000 tons. From 19 December 1911 Flag Commander to Vice Admiral Jellicoe, now commanding Second Squadron, Home Fleet, in the new battleship *Hercules*, 20,000 tons, main armament of ten 12" guns. She had completed to full crew at Portsmouth on 31 July 1911.

From November 1912 in command new light cruiser *Amphion*, 3,440 tons, 'Completing at Pembroke Dock'. She commissioned at Devonport on 2 April 1913 for 1LCS.

Captain: 30 June 1913. Continued in command of *Amphion*.

From 28 October 1913 in command battleship *Orion*, 22,500 tons, main armament of ten 13.5" guns, Flagship RA 2BS. The Rear Admiral was Sir Robert Keith Arbuthnot, Bart., born on 23 March 1864, a strict disciplinarian, and who was to lose his life at Jutland on 31 May 1916 when flying his flag in the armoured cruiser *Defence*, 14,600 tons, Captain Stanley V. Ellis.

CB: 22 June 1914.

24 October 1915: in command Grand Fleet Flagship *Iron Duke*, 25,000 tons, main armament of ten 13.5" guns.

16 March 1916: 'Awarded GBP 5,000 for Gunnery Inventions; during war he handed over this sum to the War Pensions Statutory Committee (6).'

At the Battle of Jutland: 31 May 1916, Flag Captain to the C. in C., Grand Fleet, Admiral Sir John R. Jellicoe in *Iron Duke*.

From 29 November 1916 in *President*, The Admiralty, for 'Miscellaneous or Special Service' which was Assistant Director, Anti-Submarine Division, Naval Staff. This appointment was just one resulting from Jellicoe's promotion to be First Sea Lord, a position which he assumed on 5 December 1916. The Director of this new Anti-Submarine Division was Rear Admiral Alexander L. Duff (see C. in C., 1919).

From 1 March 1917 to 20 June 1918 at The Admiralty as Director of Naval Ordnance:-

'In that capacity he saw to the introduction of a new design of armour piercing projectile, with a new type of burster and an altered fuse, for heavy guns (7).'

Towards the end of the Great War this title was augmented and so from 20 June 1918 to 1 February 1919 he served as Director of Naval Artillery and Torpedoes (8).

From 11 February 1919, as **Commodore** Second Class, Chief of Staff to Admiral of the Fleet Viscount Jellicoe of Scapa in battlecruiser *New Zealand*, 18,800 tons. This was the occasion of Lord Jellicoe's Empire Mission to India, Australia, New Zealand and Canada. Returned to Spithead on 2 February 1920.

From 15 April 1920 Director of Gunnery Division, Admiralty Naval Staff. By this time perceptive naval officers were well aware that naval aviation had an important future role to play in the Fleet. Although a gunner, through and through, Frederic Dreyer possessed a lively mind and at least one brother officer, then the Head of the infant Naval Air Section, credited him with considerable perception:-

'Under his leadership the Gunnery Division was even more of a hive of industry than it usually was and for a while I was alarmed lest it should swallow the Naval Air Section. Captain Dreyer put this right very early in the discussions on the observers. Calling me into his room one morning he remarked, "Look here, Bell Davies, don't imagine I intend to put any spokes into the Naval Air wheel. It seems to me much more likely Naval Air will be able to put spokes into the Gunnery wheel before long. Let us work together in this." (9)'

In command battlecruiser *Repulse*, 26,500 tons: 18 April 1922 to 21 November 1923.

Good Service Pension or GSP: awarded from 1 November 1922 at the rate of GBP 150.00 p.a.

Also between 24 March and 12 December 1923 he was appointed ADC to H.M. The King Emperor George V.

Rear Admiral: 12 December 1923.

From 7 January 1924 attending 'Senior Officers' Technical Course' at Portsmouth.

From 8 March 1924 attending 'Senior Officers' War Course' at Royal Naval War College, Greenwich.

About this time an important development, with which he was closely involved, took place at Portsmouth:-

'The Tactical School was founded at Portsmouth Dockyard in 1924 (it was the proposal of Admiral Sir Frederic Dreyer) to promote a more scientific study of naval tactics. It expounded the *Battle Instructions* (--) with a well organised demonstration of Jutland on the big tactical board as the high spot. This was laid on to bring out the lessons to be learned. For the rest the officers did convoy exercises and staged imaginary fleet actions (10).

From 9 October 1924 – 21 April 1927 to serve as a Lord Commissioner of the Admiralty and Assistant Chief of Naval Staff. In this post he succeeded Rear Admiral A.K. Waistell (see C. in C., 1929).

On 22 October 1924 in London he attended the funeral of Admiral Sir Percy Scott, an outstanding Naval Gunnery Officer of the era.

Commanded the Battle Cruiser Squadron, Atlantic Fleet, with Flag in *Hood*, 41,200 tons, for a period of exactly two years, from 21 May 1927 to 21 May 1929.

Meanwhile through the auspices of the R.U.S.I. in London in August 1927 he published, *History and Leadership in War*, and then in February 1928, *The Birth of a Staff System* (11).

Vice Admiral: 1 March 1929.

From 12 August 1929: attended the 'Senior Officers' Technical Course' at Portsmouth.

From 30 June 1930 to 9 January 1933, Lord Commissioner of the Admiralty and Deputy Chief of the Naval Staff. The First Sea Lord was Admiral Sir Frederick Field.

The Invergordon Mutiny occurred in September 1931, an affair which was not well handled by many of those officers in authority at the Admiralty. To Admiral Dreyer was apportioned a degree of the blame.

KCB: 3 June 1932.

He knew well beforehand that on the China Station he would be succeeding Admiral Kelly, and in April so informed an old friend, Admiral Sir Lionel Halsey. On 21 April 1932 Sir Lionel replied as follows. The quote is included here as reference is made to an unfortunate consequence of Invergordon:-

'I was pleased – very – to get your most charming letter, and although you said I was not to reply I am most certainly going to ignore that request. I am more pleased than I can say that you have accepted the appointment of C. in C., China and I do congratulate you most heartily on the splendid way in which you have taken what must really to you be a very bitter disappointment and rightly so. You, with your marvellous service and wonderful record, I suppose second to none ever known throughout one man's service, had every right to suppose you should have gone to the Main Fleet or at least one of them, and the sole reason you are not going is that of pure bad luck – namely the repercussion due to Invergordon … (12).'

In addition on 22 April 1932 he wrote to Captain Algernon Willis in the hope of securing his services in the East:-

'I am going out as C. in C. in China early next year and write to ask whether you will come as my Flag Captain. I need not tell you what a tremendous adventure it all is, and of course there are great responsibilities connected with the station (13).'

Also on 22 April 1932 Admiral Hubert G. Brand wrote from Admiralty House, Devonport, 'I wish all officers who had suffered over Invergordon had accepted it in the same spirit you have. Splendid.' On the envelope containing this letter Admiral Dreyer himself pencilled in the following comment:-

'Having been a member of Board of Admiralty when Tomkinson foolishly let the men get out of hand and mutiny at Invergordon – it was thought best not to appoint me as C. in C., Home Fleet as had been intended. I think that was perfectly right (14).'

Officially his, 'Appointment as C. in C., China in succession to Admiral Sir W.A. Howard Kelly,' was dated 21 July 1932, letter M.1943/32 from the Secretary of the Admiralty. The appointment was effective from 9 January 1933.

Admiral: 31 December 1932.

He took passage to the Far East in the P. & O. s.s. *Ranpura*, 16,688 grt, Captain Furlong, arriving at Hong Kong on 9 March 1933. At the time the Governor of that Colony was the delightful Sir William Peel (1875-1945). Assumed command in China on 11 March 1933, Flag in the heavy cruiser *Kent*, 9,850 tons, Flag Captain Algernon U. Willis.

Almost immediately he was introduced to that one tedious facet of life on the China Station, the matter of piracy. While at anchor off the mouth of the Liao River leading up to the treaty port of Newchwang in Manchuria, on 29 March 1933 the China Navigation Company steamer *Nanchang*, 2,488 grt, Captain Robinson, was boarded by pirates who took four of her European officers as hostages. Matters were complicated by the fact that although the Japanese were in military occupation of Manchuria they adopted a policy, when it suited them, of suggesting that domestic problems within the country were in the hands of the local Manchukuo authorities. Britain did not recognize the Japanese puppet state of Manchukuo, and the Chinese officials, rather naturally, would not act without Japanese authority.

To act as a calming influence the sloop *Cornflower*, 1,175 tons, Commander C.F. Hammill, was ordered to the scene and arrived very shortly afterwards. However on this occasion it was to be left to others to attempt to deal with the various parties ashore.

Without going into detail it will be understood that great patience and tact were required by British diplomatic personnel during their subsequent negotiations. Only after six months were the hostages to be released, alive, and the matter resolved. Assistance rendered by Japanese officials had proved to be most beneficial (15).

As will be seen from the following, subsequent to the Invergordon debacle the Admiralty thought it necessary to take certain steps in HM Ships. These extracts are taken from the 'Secret' letter dated 16 July 1933 which the C. in C. wrote to London from *Kent* at Wei-Hai-Wei:-

'Since taking over the command of the China Station on 11 March 1933 I have been onboard every ship in the Fleet except a few of the Gunboats which have not yet been in company, and have inspected and addressed the ships' companies. From these inspections, from what Commanding Officers have told me and from what I have seen of the men ashore and in my Flagship, I have formed the opinion that the discipline, bearing and spirit of the men on this station are of a very high order. In consequence I venture to suggest to Their Lordships the discontinuation of the system of obtaining information as to the feeling of the Lower Deck by means of security agents, which was introduced after the events at Invergordon in October 1931 .... (--).

I consider that agents should only be employed to spy on ratings when the authorities have cause to suspect that subversive activities are in progress ... (16).'

It is possibly of rather more than just passing interest to read one opinion formed by a Special Correspondent of *The Times*, London, who, during the latter part of the summer of 1933 was fortunate enough to be granted an interview by the emerging Chinese leader, General Chiang Kai-shek. This took place at Kuling, the hill resort behind Kiukiang. The cooler temperatures there at some 4,000' afforded a welcome relief from the great heat prevailing down at River level.

'He (the General) came into the room quietly, and stood quite still, looking at us. (-)

His eyes were the most remarkable thing about him. They were large, handsome, and very keen – almost aggressive. His glances had a thrusting and compelling quality which is very rare in China, where eyes are mostly negative and non-committal, if not actually evasive. We stood up and bowed. Chiang Kai-shek motioned us to sit down. I was conscious of his eyes. The interview began. I got through the essential courtesies as quickly as possible. The Marshall replied to them with business like and un-Oriental brevity. (-) It was obvious that Chiang Kai-shek enjoyed the sound of his own voice far less than most politicians, in China and elsewhere. He was not the usual type of glib and rather impressive propaganda-monger; he did not cultivate salesmanship. He was moreover a busy man in the middle of a busy morning. I decided that we should make a better impression if we emulated his laconic methods and anticipated his wishes by cutting our interview as short as possible. I therefore asked him only one more question: When might we expect a rapprochement between China and Japan?

"On the Manchurian issue, never," said Chinang Kai-shek firmly.

We rose and took our leave, with many expressions of gratitude. As we parted I received once more one of those formidable glances – we trooped down the garden path feeling very small.

(-) Here was a man with a presence, with that something incalculable to him to which the herd instinctively defers. He was strong and silent by nature, not by artifice (17).'

In Japan on 3 October 1933 Rear Admiral Yamamoto Isoroku was appointed Commander of the First Aviation Division. He flew his flag in HIJMS *Akagi*.

8 December 1933: death in Tokyo of Admiral Count Yamamoto Gonnohyoe. As a senior Naval officer, especially from 1893, under his patron Navy Minister Saigo Tsugumichi, and prior to the end of his own first term as Prime Minister in April 1914, he was to prove most influential in modernising the procedure whereby able Naval officers were selected for promotion. Although himself of Satsuma heritage it is written:-

'Yet the Yamamoto faction differed from what had preceded it. Yamamoto chose his followers for their ability. He eliminated the old Satsuma based regionalism and, while he showed special favour to some, established a new kind of leadership for the navy (18).'

At Singapore between 23 and 27 January 1934 Sir Frederic hosted a Naval Conference which was held in *Kent*. Those participating included Vice Admiral Martin E. Dunbar-Nasmith, V.C, C. in C., East Indies, Vice Admiral Sir George Francis Hyde (1877-1937), Australian Naval Board, and Rear Admiral F.B. Watson, Commanding New Zealand Squadron (19).

At the time the Governor of the Straits Settlements was Sir Cecil Clementi (1875-1947).

Following the conference, on 29 January Admiral Dunbar-Nasmith returned to his Station in his flagship *Hawkins*, Captain T.S.V. Phillips (see C. in C., Eastern Fleet, December 1941).

Then on 1 February in *Suffolk*, Captain Errol Manners, Sir Frederic sailed on a cruise of two months' duration to visit Batavia, Sourabaya, Bali, Ende, Port Darwin, Banda, Menado, Sandakan, Jesselton and Manila, finally arriving at Hong Kong on 31 March (20).

As usual at sea all ships and navies always were ready to assist each other. As an example, bound from Hong Kong to Foochow, and shortly after sailing from Hong Kong during the afternoon on 14 March 1934, a serious engine room fire developed in the American gunboat *Fulton* PG-49, 1,410 tons, Commander Harry D. McHenry. *Tsinan*, 2,994 grt, of China Navigation took off a number of her crew members and then the destroyers *Wishart*, 1,140 tons, Commander P. Todd, and *Whitshed*, 1,120 tons, the former in a , 'fine display of seamanship and courage', assisted further, with *Whitshed* managing to get the fire partially under control. By extraordinary good fortune no lives were lost and subsequently the badly damaged hulk of *Fulton* was towed back to Hong Kong by the British naval tug *Poet Chaucer*, arriving in Junk Bay the following afternoon, 15 March (21).

Admiral of the Fleet Marquis Togo Heihachiro, OM died in Tokyo on 30 May 1934.

When the news was received the C. in C. was at Tsingtao. With his Flag still in the heavy cruiser *Suffolk*, 10,000 tons, he steamed across to Yokohama, where he arrived, 'in the evening of June 3rd in foggy wet weather,' to represent the Royal Navy and British Empire at Admiral Togo's State funeral on 5 June 1934. As was recorded in *Suffolk* at the time:-

'On the following Tuesday the funeral of Fleet Admiral Marquis Togo took place. It was attended by the Commander-in-Chief and officers and a detachment of 40 ratings and Royal Marines from *Suffolk*. The smartness of the detachment in the procession called forth much favourable comment. The ceremony was simple but impressive, the Chief Ritualist being the son of the deceased. The Shinto religion does not lead to overwhelming grief for the loss of so great a leader, because the belief is that his spirit lingers still to guide and direct the nation even as he did when in the flesh. Offerings of various kinds of food and delicacies and a prayer of petition were made to the departed, after which a sprig of the sacred tamakushi tree was laid before the shrine by every one of the mourners.

The attendance of so many Japanese and foreign officers and diplomats in full dress made a colourful and unforgettable picture (22).'

During a previous visit to Japan, on 4 October 1933 the C. in C. had been invited to meet Admiral Togo at his home in Tokyo.

The China Navigation steamer *Shuntien*, 1,758 grt, on passage from Shanghai to Tientsin and when off Chefoo, was boarded by pirates on 17 June 1934. At the time serving as a Pilot in the carrier *Eagle*, 22,600 tons, Captain L.V. Wells, was Lieut. Douglas C.V. Pelly. In addition to the passengers and crew being robbed of money and jewellery, hostages, including two RN officers, were taken. *Eagle* was a short distance down the coast at Wei-Hai-Wei at the time and, from his aircraft, Lieut. Pelly participated in the successful rescue operations. In a private letter to England dated 22 June 1934 he has left some interesting, and sometimes amusing, comments:-

'The pirates, about thirty of them, all disguised as passengers, attacked at eleven o'clock at night, locked the Captain and officers down below, seriously wounded one who resisted, and then steamed the ship for twenty hours, beached her, and landed the loot and captives in junks.

It all seems so incredible that these things can really happen these days. Piracy is the only well organised business in China, and is usually worked out to the last detail months before, and is usually controlled by some master mind in Shanghai.

(After an engagement from the air two men were rescued). These two had been released by the pirates on the arrival of the aircraft and told to take the letters demanding the ransom to a British consul. They had had an awful time of it; all were starving including the pirates who were Chinese soldiers who had deserted because they had not been paid this year, their general having pinched the lot!

The next step was to rescue the others, and the first thing we did was to drop an ultimatum to say that unless they guaranteed to place the remaining prisoners in a sampan, and send them down the river, we would bomb them out of existence, - of course we couldn't really do this as it would have meant killing the prisoners too – but the threat was successful, and they soon made the sign we had demanded, and the aircraft left, first dropping their bombs a quarter of a mile away to show them that we really had got some. All night our boats armed to the teeth sat at the mouth of the river searching every junk that passed, and sure enough a sampan was eventually discovered with all the captives in it, and now they are all onboard sleeping peacefully.

The Chinese Navy arrived this morning, and we turned over to them the job of finally destroying the pirates, but as they were quite content to have their position within the nearest fifty miles it is obvious that they will never find them, and have no intention of doing so (23).'

16 October 1934. From Kiangsi Province, southern China, Communist forces, in total some 100,000 men and women, broke out through the surrounding armies of Chiang Kai-shek and commenced their 'Long March'.

29 December 1934. In Washington the Japanese government gave the required two years notice that from 31 December 1936 they would no longer be bound by the terms of the Washington Treaty of 6 February 1922 limiting naval armament.

Early in the new year piratical activity continued when, at 18:00 hours on Tuesday, 29 January 1935, a dozen of these desperadoes seized the China Navigation steamer *Tungchow*, 2,104 grt, Captain J.G. Smart, at the mouth of the Yangtse, in the process killing a White Russian guard. She had sailed from Shanghai that morning bound for north China. The affair attracted particular attention at the time as amongst her passengers were seventy three British school children returning from their Christmas holidays to the China Mission School at Chefoo.

The pirates had prepared themselves thoroughly as the ship was immediately altered in character to become the Japanese flag *Toya Maru*. In addition to repainting her name, to the black funnel were added two white bands. So it was that although the hunt was on, she was undetected and brought south towards Bias Bay, arriving off Chilang Point at 13:00 on 1 February 1935. Happily that same afternoon, hearing search aircraft which had flown from *Hermes*, then near Hong Kong, the pirates became most concerned and hastened to leave the ship, the long and the short of it being that at 20:20 that same evening the destroyer *Dainty* came up with *Tungchow* and the day was saved (24). As the C. in C. later was to write:-

'... the mere presence of the aeroplane had a most excellent result.'

'It was one of her (*Hermes*) aircraft which alarmed the pirates and caused them to land and bolt inland without taking any hostages and with practically no loot ...(25).'

At Hong Kong on Monday, 11 February 1935 HM ships dressed overall in honour of Japanese Empire Day. Although these courtesies were observed punctiliously it did not mean that eyes were closed. Just a week later, on 18 February, an Observer Lieutenant then serving in *Hermes* made a note in his diary:-

Wei-hai-Wei "Hermes" anchored

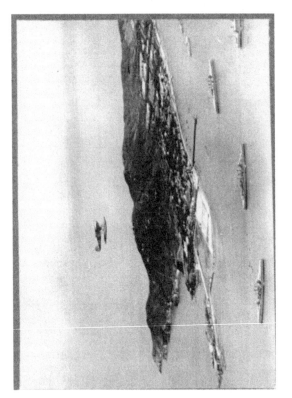

Wei-hai-Wei with 'Dorsetshire', "Berwick," & "Kent" & other ships in foreground

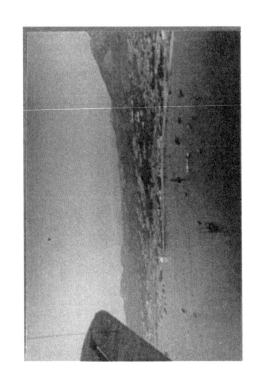

Wei-hai-Wei The mainland

H.M.S. Hermes

'Word came that Japanese ships were inspecting the islands outside Hong Kong. The Wing Commander and Senior Observer were sent up in a Seal. They did sight them steaming eastward, but from their position it was obvious that for an hour or two they had been doing something unethical (26).'

That intelligence was being gathered was a well known fact. Here is Sir William Peel himself:-

'The Japanese indulged freely in espionage and were probably acquainted with many military dispositions in the Colony (27).'

16 March 1935. Arrival at Hong Kong of the Flagship, United States Asiatic Fleet, the heavy cruiser *Augusta* CA-31, 9,050 tons, Captain Chester W. Nimitz (28).

As a Midshipman, Chester Nimitz first had sailed to the Far East across the Pacific in 1905 in the new battleship *Ohio* BB-12, Captain Leavitt C. Logan. In Tokyo at the conclusion of the Russo-Japanese hostilities HIM The Emperor gave a garden party with Admiral Togo as chief guest. Young Nimitz was one of the officers detailed to represent *Ohio*.

'Towards the end of the party, the Americans saw Admiral Togo coming down the path to take his departure. Somewhat flushed with wine, they decided to intercept him, and it was Midshipman Nimitz whom they selected to step forward and invite the Admiral to their table. Togo smilingly accepted the invitation and came over.

He shook hands all round, took a sip of champagne, and chatted briefly in English, a language he spoke fluently, for he had spent seven years in England, first as a student and later as overseer of the building of a light cruiser. The Admiral made a deep impression upon Nimitz, who never again saw him alive but was repeatedly involved over the years in honouring the old sea dog's memory (29).'

During the early summer of 1935 he became severely unwell with an attack of dysentery (30). So much so that it became necessary for RAY, Rear Admiral F.G.G. Chilton, on occasion to act on his behalf (31). Happily by 14 July he was sufficiently recovered and able to resume his duties, at 09:00 on 17 August his flag once again being hoisted in *Kent*. She was then at Wei-Hai-Wei.

On Sunday, 25 August the sloop *Falmouth*, 1,060 tons, Commander F.J. Walker, and frequently used by the C. in C. as a yacht, arrived at Wei-Hai-Wei with the British ambassador to China, Lord Cadogan, onboard (32).

3 October 1935: Italy commenced her invasion of Abyssinia. At the time the British Minister Plenipotentiary to Addis Ababa was Sir Sidney Barton (1876-1946), from 1922 to 1929 British Consul General at Shanghai, and now on excellent personal terms with Emperor Haile Selassie. Spare a thought for the unfortunate position in which now he found himself, having to explain to the Emperor the attitude both of the toothless League of Nations and of his own people in London.

As a precautionary measure the Admiralty previously had ordered certain dispositions which involved warships around the world. As just one example on the China Station these included the small aircraft carrier *Hermes* who weighed at Wei-Hai-Wei at 20:10 hours on 12 September, her destination being secret. In poor weather, and maintaining radio silence, she steamed at eighteen knots in a southerly direction around the coast of China. Her log book entry at 03:00 on 16 September reads:-

'Estimated passing fifty miles West of typhoon centre. Force 12'

The day before Captain The Hon. George Fraser had given an address:-

'The Captain spoke to the ship's company telling us that all ships were now on their way to their war stations, that a formal declaration of war might be the next move, and that he believed we should all give a good account of ourselves (33).'

Hermes arrived at Singapore at 01:58 hours on 19 September, and oiled and stored immediately. In the event no effective action was taken by the League of Nations against Italy.

Towards the end of October 1935 the 8,000 or so remaining members of the communist 'Long March' arrived in Yenan, Shensi Province in the north of China, there to join with local communist forces. Centred on Yenan the region became the Chinese communist headquarters during their forthcoming war against Japan, 1937 to 1945, and subsequently against the Nationalists over whom they were to be victorious in 1949.

Admiral of the Fleet The Earl Jellicoe of Scapa died at his home in England on 20 November 1935. As has been seen above Admiral Dreyer had known him very well and he was most moved by the sad news. In each and every ship of the China Fleet a memorial service was held.

On 2 December 1935 Vice Admiral Yamamoto Isoroku was appointed Chief of the Naval Aeronautical Department, IJN. This followed previous appointments, earlier in the 1930s, in Naval 'air'. Under his influence, and with his very positive guidance, the IJN successfully promoted the development of such aircraft as the land based Navy type 96 bomber, 'Nell', and was to ensure the development of the 'Zero' fighter, and Navy type 1 bomber, 'Betty'.

By virtue of his previous experience, such experience including his years as an Attache in the U.S.A., it has been seen that Admiral Yamamoto was extremely air minded. As if any confirmation of his viewpoint is required, just over a year previously, when writing to an assistant on 10 November 1934, he had included the following remark, 'For the navy, the most urgent task of all is to make rapid strides in the field of aviation… (34).

Within the IJN in December 1935 no more appropriate appointment could have been made.

In the P. & O. s.s. *Carthage* early on 12 December 1935 the new Governor of Hong Kong, Sir Andrew Caldecott (1884-1951), arrived and was escorted in through the Lye Mun Pass to Victoria Harbour by the heavy cruiser *Dorsetshire*. Her Captain later recorded in his diary:-

> 'C. in C. made a signal, "Manoeuvre well executed", to us, referring to the whole business, which was very gratifying. Then at 09.50 all Captains mustered at the Pier the Governor was to land at, with a whole host of Legislative Council, Army, Air Force etc. and we were all introduced in turn (35).'

In this manner did the charming and talented Sir Andrew arrive in the Colony. During the early years of WW2 he was to occupy a similar position in Ceylon.

On 19 January 1934 Hon. Sir Alexander Cadogan had been appointed Minister Plenipotentiary at Peking (36). Unsurprisingly by the latter part of 1935 he had reached certain conclusions concerning the position of Japan in the Far East, and of her relationship with China. Excerpts taken from his diaries certainly make it clear that although the precise timing remained unknown, the likelihood of future Japanese aggression against China had been anticipated by the British Foreign Office:-

> 'Japan's policy, he wrote, had changed since the success of the aggression against Manchuria; she aimed to dominate the Far East and ultimately, perhaps, Asia; the Japanese military might at any moment become impatient of purely economic penetration and occupy Chinese territory, to which step China could offer little resistance in the military sense. It seemed that the Chinese Government had stiffened against Japan's intention to set up an 'autonomous' regime in the North and it would be a mistake for the British to identify themselves with Japanese policy. If this was a correct reading of it, and if the more irresponsible elements took control in Tokyo:
>
> > "We should not be able to defend our position out here without a trial of strength, which we should wish to avoid at all costs and which only in the most exceptional circumstances could turn out in our favour."

'As for Great Britain, her trade with China would not warrant the running of vital risks for its protection, nor, perhaps, would the loss of the very large British investment. But an abandonment of those interests, "if it had the appearance of a retreat before the Japanese, might have the gravest repercussion on our position and prestige throughout the whole of Asia." This view (--) found general acceptance in the Foreign Office. Sir Robert Vansittart, sending the paper on to Eden, minuted simply:-

"We shall get no consideration from the Japanese till we are stronger. It will then be less worthwhile to offend us. Japan certainly cares nothing about 'her moral position in the eyes of the world'. Whose morals anyway? Ours. Not hers (37)." (38)'.

The following extract, which gives an opinion concerning the work habits of the C. in C., is taken from a private diary. The entry is dated Thursday, 9 January 1936:-

'Admiral Little arrived in the harbour today, and has been onboard *Kent*. His first business was to tell the Chief of Staff to make the best arrangements he could for giving Dreyer a good send off, leaving all the details to him. FCD would have seen to every detail himself, and the contrast fills the staff with hope.'

Saturday, 11 January 1936. Having handed over command of the station to Admiral Little, from Hong Kong Admiral Dreyer sailed for home in the P. & O. s.s. *Carthage*, 14,283 grt, Captain Jack. Having steamed across the South China Sea, which no doubt at times was a boisterous voyage with the winds of the N.W. monsoon behind her, she arrived at Singapore on 15 January. Then at 11:00 hours on Friday, 17 January she sailed from Keppel Harbour. Both the carrier *Hermes* and the heavy cruiser *Cornwall* were lying off and as *Carthage* drew near all hands manned and cheered ship, a farewell to their homeward bound Admiral. Exactly at that moment twenty nine aircraft flew overhead in another cleverly timed salute.

On passage home sad news was received in the ship:-

'On 20 January 1936, while in the Indian Ocean, we were deeply grieved to hear of the death of H.M. King George V. A memorial service was held onboard (39).'

After returning home, from his service record it may be noted that he was granted permission to proceed to Switzerland between 3 and 17 May 1936, a well deserved holiday.

GBE: 11 May 1937.

Retired List: 15 May 1939.

Although retired, on 16 September 1939 he was recalled, initially for war time duty as a Commodore of Convoys.

Then from 28 May 1940 he was borne in *President* for 'Special service for duty with General Officer, C. in C., Home Forces'.

Just a few weeks later, from 7 September 1940 he was recalled to the Admiralty as 'Chairman, U-Boat Assessment Committee' (40).

The following year, from 10 April 1941 he was appointed Inspector of Merchant Ship Gunnery, and eleven months later, from 6 March 1942 to this responsibility was added that of, 'Advisor on Small Ships (Royal Navy) Gunnery'.

Then, from 11 July 1942 his focus switched to the air as Temporary Chief of Naval Air Services. Finally, between 14 January and 11 March 1943 came his appointment as Deputy Chief of Naval Air Equipment (41).

With effect from 1 April 1943 he reverted to retired pay.

He continued to take a keen interest in the conduct of those various aspects of the war with which he was familiar. Of particular concern to him, and to many others, was the lack of adequate air power at sea. To many it seemed that there was an over emphasis on using large aircraft to bomb targets in Germany. A number of knowledgeable men felt that a necessary balance in the use of limited resources was required by using a few more such large aircraft in support of the vital campaign against enemy submarines in the North Atlantic. One such person was the extremely well informed Lord Hankey, a man with great and long experience of the inner workings and machinations at a high level within Whitehall (42). From the Privy Council Office on 27 March 1943 he wrote to Sir Frederic:-

'Your experience is identical with mine. When in office I was profoundly concerned with the same subject as you. I had just written a Six Monthly Appreciation of the whole war, and it stood out a mile that the Navy was being neglected. As the P.M. (Prime Minister Churchill) won't read long appreciations I pulled out the naval part and put it into the shape of two short and pithy Memoranda. While I was preparing them I received a letter from the P.M. giving me the sack, for no reason except that he wanted my place for a labour man owing to an internal row in the Labour Party. I had no grievance because I was dissatisfied with the conduct of the war at sea and I could not get anything done from inside.

I sent my Memoranda next day and had some correspondence (quite civil) but nothing was done, so, very reluctantly and against the grain, I kicked up a row in the House of Lords, stirred up the whole press and got a little done – but a year too late (Napoleon!).

Winston does not understand the war at sea (43).'

On 11 June 1943 Lord Hankey again wrote to Sir Frederic. The letter is worth quoting in full since it indicates the important grasp of the Naval situation held by both men as regards the North Atlantic, and also the lengthy, even convoluted, steps which it was necessary to take to endeavour to secure a correct and balanced utilisation of aerial forces. G.M. is 'Great Man', i.e. the Prime Minister, Winston Churchill:-

'Several times it has been in my mind to write to you, but something told me you would write in your own time. Your letter of June 8 therefore was most welcome.

I agree with you that your action has had a good effect. The dates you give confirm that.

The great man gave you pretty much the same reply as he had given me a year before.

Here are my dates:-

4 March 1942: Sent two Memoranda to the G.M. the second was a strong plea for the diversion of a large number of bombers "to support the war in the N. Atlantic".

7 March 1942: G.M. acknowledges with thanks. Promises to have them examined.

17 March 1942: Ismay, with authority of G.M., shows me the replies of C.N.S. and C.A.S. Both thoroughly unsatisfactory.

18 March 1942: My second letter to G.M. contains the following:-

"All I propose is that a large proportion of our bomber aircraft should be drawn from their present unremunerative targets and used offensively against naval targets in order to strengthen our sea power and reduce shipping losses, which is the greatest need of the Allies at the present time."

21 March 1942: G.M. replies in five lines ending:-

"I have taken note of what you say."

Adds in manuscript: "I could reassure you a good deal I think."

23 March 1942: I acknowledge with thanks.

24 May 1942: I return to the charge at some length, giving first hand evidence of the proven value of aircraft against submarines; emphasising that the military operations already announced for 1943 will need a lot of shipping; "whether on a short view or a long view of the war, shipping, as ever in our history, is the primary requirement."

"at this stage of the war the concentration of as many aircraft as can be spared to support our sea power by attacking enemy submarines, wherever they are present in the greatest strength, is the outstanding requirement."

27 May 1942: G.M. replies, "You may be sure that this question is under continuous study and review from month to month."

(We know now that the Battle of the Atlantic Committee was meeting only at long intervals).

That ended the correspondence. Dissatisfied, I raised a public agitation, speeches in House of Lords, articles and letters in the press, stirring up interest in parliamentary, scientific and other circles. Much private supprt from Navy, F.A.A. (Fleet Air Arm) and Coastal Command. In November and December I received assurances that action was being taken on my lines.

Then came your powerful and independent move, which gave a well timed impetus. (--).

My information on the present position, most of it from the inside, is that a lot has been done to strengthen the position, especially in the supply of Liberators, but there are not yet enough; the Americans keep too many on their West coast, where there are now no U-boats; in March losses were very heavy – about 706,000 gross tons of shipping; April and May together were about the same as March, with a falling tendency; June, so far, V.G.; many more U-boats being bagged.

On the whole I think that between us we have done a lot of good, but I am watching the situation with an eagle eye, and shall return to the charge if necessary.

But I think the G.M. has the wind up and will not dare again to forget the Navy (44).'

In his memoirs, published in 1955, Sir Frederic makes no mention of his private correspondence with Lord Hankey. In his capacity as Chief of Naval Air Services however, and as suggested above, he indicates that he did fight hard to secure a proper proportion of air patrol resources for the RN:-

'The Admiralty clamoured for long range bomber aircraft in 1942. I knew that the bombing of Germany in 1940 and 1941 had been most inaccurate. Although our Merchant Navy losses and those of our Allies were approaching the figure beyond which we should starve and have no petrol for the R.A.F., etc., yet the Admiralty could not get a fair share of aircraft production for the rapid expansion of our Fleet Air Arm. So on 4 January 1943, I suggested borrowing and converting some hundreds of very long range bombers for Coastal Command and setting up more shore bases, from which the long range bombers could cover the convoys. In order to win the battle of priorities in the War Cabinet I used strong words to the effect that while I was all for the bombing of Germany, this must not also be with the blood of the Merchant Navy. The truth of this would not allow my proposal to be sidetracked (45).'

After WW2 much was to be written about all aspects of the war. One well respected Naval author is Richard Hough. In a volume published in 1986, and writing of the above mentioned difficulty, he was to include remarks such as:-

'But the worst misallocation of weaponry was in long range patrolling aircraft.'

'Sittings of the Atlantic Convoy Conference led to the transfer of, for a start, one of the American Army (Antisubmarine) Squadrons to Newfoundland. It became operational on 19 April (1943). Before this, RAF Coastal Command VLRs had begun a shuttle service from Iceland to Newfoundland. Forty one VLRs were operating in the North Atlantic by mid April 1943. The 'Air Gap' which had permitted the U-boat crews to work so freely in mid-Atlantic had been closed (46).'

At the front line, so to speak, as C. in C., Western Approaches, Admiral Sir Max Kennedy Horton (1883-1951) was to write with similar feeling. The following extract is taken from a letter dated 23 March 1943:-

'The Air, of course, is a tremendous factor, and it is only recently that the many promises that have been made show signs of fulfilment, so far as shore based stuff is concerned, after three and a half years of war (47).'

It is fair to state that to Sir Frederic must go at least a small share of the credit for such an advance, eventually, in long range air patrol activity over the North Atlantic.

In due course about him it was to be written:-

'Throughout his Service life Dreyer was a completely dedicated man, supremely efficient in all he undertook and sparing no pains to equip himself professionally to the highest pitch of knowledge and skill. He was an austere man in his personal life and a stern disciplinarian, with little sense of humour (48).'

In retirement he lived at Freelands, Winchester, Hampshire.

Following his death on 11 December 1956 his funeral service was held in Winchester Cathedral on Saturday, 17 December. Subsequently his body was to be cremated and his ashes scattered at sea from the frigate *Dundas* off Portsmouth (49). On 4 January 1957 a Memorial Service was held at St. Martin in the Fields, London (50).

Within Winchester Cathedral his memorial is inscribed horizontally in stone beneath a stand from which, rather appropriately, hangs the ship's brass bell, *Iron Duke*. The words read as follows:-

'In memory of Admiral Sir Frederic Dreyer, GBE, KCB. Born 1878. Died 1956.

Who in a Naval Career of over fifty years made an outstanding contribution to the gunnery of the Fleet and of the Merchant Navy. Also Una Maria his devoted wife for 55 years. Born 1876. Died 1959 (51).'

NOTES

1. Obituary, *The Times,* Wednesday, December 12, 1956. Also NA ADM 196/44: *Service Record.*

2. Ibid.

3. *Service Record.*

4. Admiral Sir R.H. Bacon, *The Life of Lord Fisher of Kilverstone,* I, (London, 1929), 266/7.

   Concerning the desire to promote the interests of gunnery in the Navy, Bacon was to go further in comparing the approach of that somewhat abrasive though extremely competent and able exponent, Percy Scott, with that of Frederic Dreyer:-

   'The homilies of Percy Scott did a world of good, but unfortunately he was rather like the Old Testament seers, who rubbed those in authority the wrong way. Officers of high standing did not appreciate being told that for years they had neglected gunnery training, and that they should now repent and do better. (--) Lieut. Dreyer was entirely different; he carried his knowledge less aggressively, and, therefore, did just as good work in the cause of gunnery without raising factious opposition.'

   Admiral Sir Reginald Bacon, *From 1900 Onward,* (London, 1940), 155.

5. Obituary, *The Times.*

6. *Service Record.*

7. Obituary, *The Times.*

8. NA ADM 196/96.

9. Richard Bell Davies, *Sailor in the Air,* (Barnsley, England, 2008), 194.

   Richard **Bell Davies**, VC. Born: 19 May 1886. Died: 26 February 1966. Entered the Navy in 1901. In 1911 learned to fly privately, Claude Grahame-White's Flying School at Hendon. Royal Flying Corps, Naval Service: 1913. Following a raid into Bulgaria on 19 November 1915, on 1 January 1916 awarded the Victoria Cross. Captain: January 1928. From March 1933 commanded heavy cruiser *Cornwall*, China Station. On 11 January 1938 became the first air officer to be promoted Rear Admiral. RA, Naval Air Stations: 24 May 1939. Vice Admiral and retired: 29 May 1941. Subsequently held a number of war time positions. *Navy List.*

10. Arthur J. Marder, *From the Dardanelles to Oran,* (OUP, 1974), 35/6.

11. Higham and Cox Wing.

12. Archives Centre, Churchill College, Cambridge. Ref: *Dryr 9/1.*

    Lionel **Halsey**. Born: 26 February 1872. Died: 26 October 1949. Joined *Britannia*: 1885. Participated in the defence of Ladysmith: 1899-1900. Captain: 30 June 1905. Commissioned the battlecruiser *New Zealand*, 19,100 tons: 23

November 1912, and commanded her during the Dominion and World Cruise between February and November 1913. Remained in command early during WW1. Captain of the Fleet in *Iron Duke* at Jutland: 31 May 1916. Rear Admiral: 26 April 1917. Third Sea Lord: 1917-1918. KCMG: 1918. Commanded RAN: 1918-1920. KCVO: 1919. GCVO: 1920. Vice Admiral: 5 July 1921. KCIE: 1922. Comptroller/Treasurer to the Prince of Wales: 1920-1936. Retired List: 1922. GCMG: 1925. Admiral: 4 October 1926. *Navy List. Who's Who.*

13. Ibid. Ref: *Wlls 4/3.*

14. Ibid. Ref: *Dryr 9/1.*

   Hubert George **Brand**. Born: 20 May 1870. Died: 14 December 1955. Entered RN: 1883. Captain: 31 December 1907. Naval Attache at Tokyo: 1912-1914 and present with the IJN during the Tsingtao siege in 1914 (see Jerram, C. in C., 1913). Chief of Staff to Sir David Beatty, Battle Cruiser Fleet: 1916. Captain of the Fleet: 1916 – 1919. KCMG: 1919. Rear Admiral: 12 February 1919. Commanded HM Yachts: 1919-1922. KCVO: 1922. Vice Admiral: 1 October 1924. Second Sea Lord: 1925-1927. KCB: 1927. C. in C., Atlantic Fleet: 1927-1929. Admiral: 11 June 1928. C. in C., Devonport: 8 October 1929 – 10 October 1932, then retired. GCB: 1932. *Who's Who. Navy List.*

   Wilfred **Tomkinson**. Born: 15 December 1877. Died: 7 October 1971. Captain: 30 June 1916. Commanding Officer, battlecruiser *Hood*, 45,200 tons, when she first commissioned: 15 May 1920. Rear Admiral: 2 August 1927. Owing to the sudden illness of the C. in C., Admiral Sir Michael Hodges, temporarily was in command of the Atlantic Fleet, ironically with his flag in *Hood*, prior to the manoeuvres which were due to commence from Invergordon on Tuesday, 15 September 1931. Vice Admiral: 15 February 1932. Retired List: 1935. *Navy List.* Alan Coles, *Invergordon Scapegoat*, (Stroud, 1993).

15. For a full account of the episode see J.V. Davidson-Houston, *The Piracy of the Nanchang*, (London, 1961).

16. Churchill College. Ref: *Dryr 8/1.*

17. Peter Fleming, *One's Company, A Journey to China*, (London, 1934), 225-227. Peter Fleming (1907-1971), Eton and Christ Church, Oxford, was to estabish a considerable reputation as an adventurer, journalist and author.

18. David Chris Evans, *The Satsuma Faction and Professionalism in the Japanese Naval Officer Corps of the Meiji Period: 1868-1912*, (Stanford, 1978), 184-208.

19. Chaplain W.E. Rea, *Nil Desperandum*, (Privately, 1935), 285.

20. R.G. Howard and others, *H.M.S. Suffolk, Third Commission*, (Privately printed at Hong Kong, 1935), 26, 28, 29. In respect of the visit to Batavia, between 1931 and 1936 the Governor General of the Dutch East Indies was Bonifacius Cornelis de Jonge (1875-1958).

21. USNI, *Naval History*, (Annapolis, October 2008), 13. *Warship International*, Vol. No. 47, issue number 1, 2010, 68-75.

22. *H.M.S. Suffolk, Third Commission*,, 62. The Chief Ritualist in fact was Admiral Kato Hiroharu (1871-1939).

23. Interview kindly granted by Commander Douglas Pelly, RN (ret'd) at his home near Hook on 4 April 1997. By co-incidence serving as Lieut. Commander (G) in *Eagle* at the time was the officer later to become the well known Naval historian and author, Stephen W. Roskill. *Navy List.*

24. NA ADM 116/3037. Report No. HK 530. The guard killed was Sgt. Tihrivoff. Also murdered was an engineer, Mr. McDonald. Enid Saunders Candlin, *The Breach in the Wall – a Memoir of the Old China*, (London, 1974), 138/141. *Dainty* was commanded by Commander R.S. Lovatt. As a Captain, RN to lose his life on 24 November 1941 when in command of the light cruiser *Dunedin*, torpedoed in the South Atlantic by *U-124* (Johann Mohr). *Navy List.* In Lloyd's Register for 1935 and 1936 there is no such vessel as *Toya Maru* listed.

25. NA ADM 116/3074. China General Letter No. 24 dated 10 March 1935.

26. The late Commander Richard Phillimore. By kind invitation, papers seen by the author at Shedfield: 13 and 20 April 1996. The 'Seal' was a Fairey biplane of which some ninety one machines were constructed for FAA (Fleet Air Arm) service. Basically they were Fairey 3F machines fitted with a 525 h.p. Armstrong Whitworth Panther radial engine. The type of aircraft first flew on 11 September 1930.

27. Rhodes House Library, Oxford. Ref: *S.208.*

28. Chester William **Nimitz**. Born: 24 February 1885. Died: 20 February 1966. The brilliant and delightful Chester Nimitz saw much early service as a submariner. Captain: 2 June 1927. In command USS *Augusta* CA-31: 16 October 1933 – 12 April 1935. Rear Admiral: 23 June 1938. At Pearl Harbour on 31 December 1941 on the deck of USS *Grayling* SS-209 his four star flag as a full Admiral was hoisted and he assumed command as C. in C., Pacific Fleet. From 3 April 1942

additionally C. in C., Pacific Ocean Areas. As such during WW2 to oversee the entire Pacific campaign. Fleet Admiral: 19 December 1944. In Tokyo Bay on 2 September 1945, for the U.S.A., signed the peace documents while in USS *Missouri* BB-63, 45,000 tons, Captain Stuart S. Murray. On 15 December 1945 to succeed his wartime superior, Fleet Admiral Ernest Joseph King, as CNO (Chief of Naval Operations) the most senior professional post in the USN. Naval Historical Center, Washington, DC. E.B. Potter, *Nimitz*, (Annapolis, 1987). Today in Fredericksburg, TX the Admiral Nimitiz Museum is an important constituent of the National Museum of the Pacific War.

29. *Nimitz*, 57. The champagne was Russian, captured at Port Arthur. As one example of his respect for Admiral Togo, in 1945 at Yokosuka after visiting *Mikasa* immediately following the Japanese surrender formalities, and in accordance with a decision reached earlier by the Staff of the CNO, Admiral E.J. King, USN, and as instigated by Rear Admiral Charles M. 'Savvy' Cooke, USN, he was to have the pleasure of ordering a permanent Marine guard aboard the ship to prevent her from being further damaged or looted. Information kindly confirmed and details provided by Dr. David Kohnen, US Naval War College, at a conference at Greenwich, London in June 2016. Today, in a somewhat similar manner to *Victory* at Portsmouth, and *Constitution* at Boston, Mass., *Mikasa* is a beautifully restored and maintained Memorial Ship. Visited by the author, 15 April 2015.

30. NA ADM 196/96. Telegram to The Admiralty dated 15 June 1935.

31. Frances George Gillilan **Chilton**. Born: 8 July 1879. Died: 23 March 1964. Rear Admiral: 1 June 1931. RAY: 23 October 1933. Vice Admiral: 2 January 1936, and retired. Rejoined for service during WW2. *Navy List*.

32. Frederic John **Walker**. To become very well known during WW2 in the North Atlantic as the most successful hunter and destroyer of U-boats. His name particularly was to be associated with the sloop *Starling*, 1,430 tons. As a Captain, CB, DSO and three bars, he was to die on 9 July 1944 from cerebral thrombosis brought on by strain, overwork and exhaustion. Terence Robertson, *Walker R.N.*, (London, 1956) and, Alan Burn, *The Fighting Captain*, (London, 1993). The Hon. Sir Alexander Montagu George **Cadogan**. Born: 25 November 1884. Died: 9 July 1968. Eton. Balliol College, Oxford. Foreign Office: 18 June 1908. Constantinople: 8 January 1909. In Vienna at the outbreak of the Great War. Subsequently Foreign Office, London. KCMG: 1 January 1934. Envoy Extraordinary and Minister Plenipotentiary to Peking: 19 January 1934. Elevated to Ambassador: 15 June 1935. Deputy Under Secretary of State in the Foreign Office: 1 October 1936. Permanent Under Secretary of State for Foreign Affairs: 1 January 1938 – February 1946. GCMG: 1939. KCB: 1941. PC: 1946. Permanent Representative to the United Nations: 1946 – 1950. OM: 1951. Government Director, Suez Canal Company: 1951 – 1957. Chairman, BBC: 1952 – 1957. *Foreign Office List. Who's Who*.

33. Diary entry dated 15 September 1935. Courtesy of the late Commander Richard Phillimore, then a Lieutenant (O) serving in *Hermes*.

34. Agawa Hiroyuki, *The Reluctant Admiral*, (Tokyo and New York, 1979), 38, 105/6. Mark R. Peattie, *Sunburst*, (Annapolis, MD, 2001), 81 and 86.

35. Diary entry dated 12 December 1935. Captain Arthur J.L. Murray.

36. Alexander Montagu George **Cadogan**. See reference (32) above.

37. NA FO 371/20241. Minute dated 4 February 1936.
    Sir Robert Gilbert **Vansittart**. Born: 25 June 1881. Died: 14 February 1957. Eton. Entered the Foreign Office: 1902. Permanent Under-Secretary for Foreign Affairs: 1930-1938, when succeeded by Alexander Cadogan.
    Eden is Robert Anthony **Eden**. Born: 12 June 1897. Died: 14 January 1977. Eton. Foreign Secretary: 1935-1938, and again 1940-1945, 1951-1955. Prime Minister: 1955-1957. Created Earl Avon: 1961.

38. Ed. David Dilks, *The Diaries of Sir Alexander Cadogan: 1938-1945*, (London, 1971), 11/12.

39. Admiral Sir Frederic Dreyer, *The Sea Heritage*, (London, 1955), 330.

40. NA ADM 196/96.

41. Ibid.

42. Maurice Pascal Alers **Hankey**. Born: 1 April 1877. Died: 26 January 1963. Rugby. Joined the Royal Marines Artillery: 1895. Mediterranean Fleet then Naval Intelligence: 1899-1906. Assistant Secretary, then Secretary, Committee of Imperial Defence: 1908-1938. KCB: 1916. War Cabinet: 1916. Imperial War Cabinet: 1917-1918. GCB: 1919. Cabinet: 1919-1938. Clerk of the Privy Council: 1923-1938. GCMG: 1929. Colonel RM (ret'd): 1929. GCVO: 1934. Minister without Portfolio in the War Cabinet: 1939-1940. PC: 1939. First Baron: 1939. Chancellor of the Duchy of Lancaster: 1940-1941. Paymaster General: 1941-1942. Served on numerous other government committees. Author of a number

of publications. *Who's Who.* Stephen Roskill, *Hankey: Man of Secrets,* (London, 1970, 1972, 1974), 3 vols. Roskill, himself a retired Naval officer, as a Midshipman as early as 1921 had served at sea on the China Station in the light cruiser *Durban.*

43. Churchill College. Ref: *Dryr 11/2.*

    'Winston does not understand the war at sea'. Also see Arthur J. Marder, *From the Dardanelles to Oran,* (OUP, 1974), 120/121. Here the author discusses one of Churchill's thoughts on the subject of the U-boat war and concludes, 'Churchill never completely grasped the nature of maritime war.'

44. Ibid.

45. *The Sea Heritage,* 410.

46. Richard Hough, *The Longest Battle,* (London 1986), 270/1. A number of other weapons and aids such as radar, 'Leigh Light' aircraft, escort aircraft carriers, improved depth charges and launching technique, and 20mm cannon guns also were to most beneficial. Taken together all were to result in an eventual Allied superiority in and over the North Atlantic.

47. Rear Admiral W.S. Chalmers, *Max Horton and the Western Approaches,* (London, 1954), 188.

48. *Dictionary of National Biography,* (OUP, 1971).

49. *The Times,* Monday, 19 December 1956.

50. *The Times,* Saturday, 5 January 1957.

51. The magnificent Cathedral visited and memorial inspected by the author on Wednesday, 18 May 2011. The guides within the Cathedral are extremely obliging.

11 January 1936 to 5 February 1938
Vice Admiral Sir Charles James Colebrooke **Little**

Born in Shanghai: 14 June 1882. There his father, Louis Stromeyer Little, FRCS, BA, FRAS (1840-1911), a most distinguished physician with a number of pioneeering methods of procedure to his credit, for thirty years practised as a surgeon in the General Hospital. Also while in Shanghai he had initiated the foundation of an observatory from where he photographed the transit of Venus.

An uncle was Archibald John Little (1838-1908), known for the first steam powered ascent of the Yangtse Gorges in his launch *Leechuen* of some seven tons. In her he had departed from Ichang on 15 February 1898 and arrived at Chungking the following month, on 9 March (1).

Another uncle was Robert Little, for many years editor of the *North China Herald*.

He died at home, 'The Old Mill', Ashurst, Sussex on Wednesday, 20 June 1973.

Together with the two future Admirals of the Fleet, Andrew Browne Cunningham and James Fownes Somerville, he entered *Britannia* on 15 January 1897.

Midshipman: 15 July 1898. Already, from 15 May 1898 as a **Cadet**, he had been serving in the cruiser *Hermoine*, 4,360 tons, Captain George A. Callaghan, China Station. In May 1900 she was present at Shanghai for H.M. Queen Victoria's birthday celebrations, and then afterwards proceeded up river.

In an entry made in his Journal on Sunday, 24 June 1900, a brother Midshipman then serving in the ship remarked on an aspect of the river gunboat service, also made a reference to a recent Naval success in ascending through the Yangtse Gorges. This voyage by Lieut. Hugh Watson in *Woodcock*, with *Woodlark* in company, was only the second steam powered ascent nevertheless was the first in ships of an appreciable size. As just mentioned above, Archibald Little had preceded Watson with his fine achievement in *Leechuen*. On 24 June 1900 *Hermoine* was at Wuhu. Extracts follow:-

> 'At 3.20 p.m. H.M. River Gunboat *Snipe* arrived. She displaces about 80 tons and was sent out a little while ago for service on the Yangtse kiang river. She was 'put together' at Shanghai having been sent out in pieces as she is not capable of weathering even a slight sea. Her armament consists of two 6 pounders and four maxim guns. Her boiler, part of which is necessarily above water owing to her extremely shallow draft of 2 ft., is protected by armour 3/8 of an inch thick, her sides being 3/16", thick enough only to withstand bullets. She carries 30 tons of coal. Her sister gunboats are *Woodcock* and *Woodlark* which are in the river now. They have just returned from a successful trip up as far as Suifu having been over the Gorges (2).'

From *Hermoine* he paid off on 15 August 1901 and returned home in s.s. *Tabor*, 2,406 grt (3). From 3 October 1901 to 15 January 1902 served in the battleship *Jupiter*, 14,900 tons, Channel Squadron. **Sub Lieutenant**: 15 January 1902. '11 February 1902: Joined College'. Studying at RNC, Greenwich where he was outstanding in achieving five 'Firsts' for which fine effort he was awarded the prize of ten pounds sterling, and rapid promotion. **Lieutenant:** 15 January 1903. As now will be seen already he had made his decision regarding his future speciality. In most naval circles in that era his was regarded as being a brave selection:-

'Little describes his own promotions as "fortuitous", helped by service in submarines; "a new branch in its infancy, much frowned upon by the Service in general, which later turned up trumps" (4).'

From 28 April 1903 in cruiser *Latona*, 3,100 tons, then from 20 July 1903 in *Thames*, 4,050 tons, Captain Reginald H.S. Bacon, 'Inspecting Captain of Submarine Boats'. 'For (service with) Submarine Boats'. From 27 October 1905 to 2 January 1907 in cruiser *Forth*, 4,050 tons, 'For Command of Submarine Boats' (5).

From 2 January 1907, regarded by some as being a rather more respectable appointment, he served for a year in new battleship *Hibernia*, 16,350 tons, Captain Cecil F. Lambert, Flagship of the second in command, Channel Fleet. He was Vice Admiral Sir Reginald N. Custance. On that day, 2 January, she commissioned at Devonport, one of eight of the "King Edward VII" class of pre dreadnoughts.

From 14 January 1908 in Depot Ship for Submarines *Mercury*, 3,730 tons, Portsmouth: 'For Command of Submarines', 'And for Instruction of Officers and Men'. From experience he had a clear message for his pupils:-

'Minute attention to and knowledge of every detail is essential for the best results in a submarine where, more than in any other vessel, awkward situations and rapid decisions are so frequent (6).'

On 29 February 1908 he married Rothes Beatrix Leslie, daughter of Colonel Sir Charles Leslie, seventh Baronet. They were to have one daughter. Sadly his wife was to die on 9 May 1939.

Secondly, in Westminster Abbey on 1 January 1940, he married Mary Elizabeth Little, JP, a cousin and daughter of Ernest Muirhead Little, FRCS.

April 1909: remained in *Mercury*, additionally shown in command of submarine *D.1* (submerged displacement of 600 tons, and, hard to credit, powered by a single 850 h.p. petrol engine). From 3 May 1910 to 8 November 1911 in new battleship *St. Vincent*, 19,250 tons, Captain Douglas R.L. Nicholson, Flagship of the RA Home Fleet, he being Frederick C.D. Sturdee. The Admiral was to be the victor at the Battle of the Falkland Islands, 8 December 1914.

From 23 November 1911 Lieut. and Commander in *Hazard*, 1,070 tons, Patrol Flotillas, Portsmouth, 'For Duty with Submarines.'

Commander: 1 January 1913. Remained in *Hazard* at Portsmouth until 3 August 1914, in command Fourth Submarine Flotilla.

From 3 August 1914 in command light cruiser *Arrogant*, 5,750 tons, 'and in command of Submarines'. His command consisted of several 'C' class boats. From 13 October 1914 *Arrogant* also became the Flagship of Rear Admiral The Hon. Horace L.A. Hood. 'Dover Patrol'. Sadly the Admiral was to lose his life at the Battle of Jutland when flying his flag in the battlecruiser *Invincible*, 17,350 tons, at the time when she was destroyed by enemy gun fire.

From 10 February 1915 in *Dolphin*, Portsmouth, 'Assistant to Commodore (S) and for duty in Submarines'. The Commodore was Captain Sydney S. Hall.

From September 1916 in command *Fearless*, 3,440 tons, Depot Ship for Submarines. From 15 November 1916 Lieut. Commander Geoffrey Layton (see C. in C., 1940) served in the ship.

Captain: 30 June 1917. Continued in command *Fearless*. In the Firth of Forth on 31 January 1918 naturally he was to become involved with the outcome of the unfortunate affair during which a number of the large 'K' boats were in collision resulting in the loss of two, and the lives of 103 officers and men (7).

Between 4 March and 22 December 1919 in command light cruiser *Cleopatra*, Flagship, Rear Admiral Sir Walter H. Cowan (1871-1956). In the Baltic ships of the Admiral's command were actively involved in hostilities against the Bolsheviks and, under the enthusiastic and energetic Sir Walter, one can be sure that no stones were left unturned in the pursuit of these duties.

CB: 11 June 1919.

From 23 December 1919 appointed to the Admiralty as Assistant Director of the Trade Division, but from 24 May 1920 until 2 May 1922 as Director of Trade Division.

In 1921 a member of the British delegation to the Washington DC Naval Conference.

From 16 June 1922 to 20 August 1924 Captain of the Fleet in the Mediterranean Fleet Flagship, battleship *Iron Duke*, 25,000 tons. The C. in C. was Vice Admiral Sir Osmond de B. Brock (1869-1947), in July 1929 to be promoted Admiral of the Fleet.

From 27 October 1924: Royal Naval War College as Senior Staff Officer.

From 30 July 1926 to 8 August 1927 battleship *Iron Duke*, Flag Captain, 3BS, Atlantic Fleet. The RA 3BS was a future First Sea Lord and Admiral of the Fleet, Roger Roland Charles Backhouse (1878-1939).

From 14 November 1927 Director, Royal Naval Staff College.

In February 1929 through the R.U.S.I. and their *Journal* he published, *Naval Bases and Sea Power* (8).

Rear Admiral: 27 February 1929.

Continued as Director, Royal Naval Staff College until 28 February 1930.

From 26 April 1930 to 25 April 1931 RA 2BS, Atlantic Fleet with Flag in battleship *Warspite*, 27,500 tons.

From 4 May 1931 attended the Senior Officers' Tactical Course, then from 2 September 1931 to 10 December 1932 served as RA, Submarines in *Dolphin*, Portsmouth.

On 12 December 1932 to *President*, the Admiralty.

From 9 January 1933, in succession to Admiral Dreyer who had been appointed C. in C., China, a Lord Commissioner of the Admiralty and Deputy Chief of Naval Staff.

Vice Admiral: 1 September 1933.

Continued to 29 October 1935 as a Lord Commissioner of the Admiralty and Deputy Chief of Naval Staff.

While a Lord Commissioner, and commencing in October 1934, he was a member of the British team in London negotiating with Japan and the U.S.A. over the question of a new agreement on naval limitation. During these discussions the Foreign Office Counsellor was a future British ambassador to Japan, Sir Robert Craigie. An important member of the Japanese delegation was their chief naval representative, Yamamoto Isoroku, from 15 November to be Vice Admiral. From a diplomatic point of view the notice of Japan's withdrawal from the Treaty, which had originated in Washington on 6 February 1922, was given in Washington at noon on Saturday, 29 December 1934, the relevant Note being received by the U.S. Secretary of State, Cordell Hull (1871-1955). Thus it was to be that from two years thence, 31 December 1936, that the terms of the Treaty no longer would be binding. In this connection it may be noted that in November 1937 at Kure the IJN were to lay down the keel of their first super-dreadnought, *Yamato*, subsequently to be of some 72,000 tons at full load.

Also early in October 1935, from the Admiralty and following many years of great austerity one result of which had been the imposition of severe fuel restrictions throughout the Fleet, then at the time of the Italian invasion of Abyssinia, '... I lived to see the start of the Abyssinian affair through the pleasure of ordering ships to proceed at more than economical speed once more! (9).'

KCB: 3 June 1935 and invested the following month, on 9 July.

On 8 November 1935 appointed C. in C., China Station.

Taking passage from England, he arrived at Hong Kong in the P. & O. s.s. *Chitral*, 15,555 grt, on 9 January 1936. Assumed command of the Station on 11 January 1936. Flag in the heavy cruiser *Kent*, 9,850 tons, Flag Captain I.B.B. Tower.

At 07:58 in the morning on Tuesday, 21 January 1936, Hong Kong time, H.M. King George V died. Colours were half masted and H.M. Ships went into mourning. Commencing at noon, and to correspond with his age, seventy minute guns were fired.

The following day marked the accession of King Edward VIII. With a large Naval and military guard present, together with a great crowd of officials and spectators, the Royal Salute was fired at noon and from the steps of the Law Courts at 3 p.m. H.E. The Governor read the appropriate Proclamation. Immediately afterwards bands played the National Anthem and H.M. Ships fired a Royal Salute. At the conclusion of these formalities the guard marched off.

26 February 1936. Revolt by younger army officers in Japan during which numbers of senior government officials were murdered, an unfortunate, and violent, example of Japanese militaristic extremism. The Prime Minister, Admiral Okada Keisuke (1868-1952), was fortunate to escape when in error the attackers murdered his brother-in-law secretary, Colonel Matsuo Denzo. Amongst those murdered was the ex Prime Minister and moderate, Admiral Viscount Saito Makoto (10).

> 'Three months later the new Imperial Defence Policy was approved which included Britain as Japan's hypothetical enemy for the first time (11).'

It was in March 1936 that British civil air services, which gradually were being established throughout the Empire, first were extended through to Hong Kong. On 18 April 1936 the C. in C. was to report to the Admiralty as follows:-

> 'Following trials which have been carried out since November 1935, Imperial Airways inaugurated the Hong Kong/Penang air service on 23rd March 1936. Hong Kong now is linked up with the Australia to London service and is within ten days of England (12).'

In conjunction with Australian interests onwards from Koepang in Timor, the first Imperial Airways trial mail flight from London to Sydney had taken place between 4 and 29 April 1931.

To help to bring these achievements into perspective two other air services will be mentioned.

Firstly the Dutch operation between Amsterdam and Batavia. As early as during the months of October and November 1924 KLM Royal Dutch Airlines, under the inspirational leadership of Dr. Albert Plesman (1889-1953), had carried out this route survey flight. Then, from 12 September 1929 from Amsterdam, a regular fortnightly mail service had been inaugurated to the capital of their Eastern territories. Subsequently passengers too would be carried. As might be expected, initially on this route KLM used Fokker aircraft.

Secondly the U.S. trans Pacific operation from San Francisco to Hong Kong via Hawaii, Midway, Wake, Guam, Manila and Macau was to commence with the Pan American World Airways flying boat *Hong Kong Clipper* who arrived in Victoria Harbour on 28 April 1937. This Pan Am service as far as Manila first had commenced with *China Clipper* from San Francisco on 22 November 1935. As will be appreciated distances across the Pacific were a great barrier to early air transport. Over this route, for example, the shortest leg is Midway/Wake at 1080 nautical miles. During this first flight *China Clipper*, Captain Edwin Musick, had required twenty hours and thirty three minutes flying time to cover the 2,074 nautical miles from San Francisco to Honolulu (13).

Between June 1933 and his departure from Japan on 17 July 1936, the Assistant Naval Attache in the British Embassy to Tokyo was Commander (E) George C. Ross (14). A gifted linguist, in Japan he not only learned to speak the language but also, to an unusual extent, identified with the life and customs of the people and in particular with many senior officers of the IJN. His memoirs give a useful insight into aspects of life in Japan during this time. An extract follows:-

> 'I feel I should clarify the situation of the Emperor of Japan as it played an important part in the life of the nation during the time that I was there. An atmosphere of divinity surrounded the throne and this was instilled into the fighting services, into all children from a young age and, by propaganda, it was never forgotten. This love or worship of the Emperor took the place of leadership so that every officer was taught to serve him personally and directly. (This cult even spread to factories). As the fighting services were thus the personal forces of His Majesty, they were in no way subservient to the State. An insult to a member of the armed forces was an insult to the Emperor himself.

The services could also act independently and engage in hostilities without the knowledge of the Foreign Office. To complicate matters further, the Army and Navy were not on speaking terms, being bitter rivals.

During my first two months in Tokyo, the Army simulated air attacks on the city by day and night, dropping tear gas bombs. All buildings were blacked out and, if one ventured onto the streets, it was advisable to wear a gas mask. Why should they do this if they were not preparing for war? One had the impression of sitting on top of a volcano which was bound to erupt before long.

One felt that the Army was taking control of the country, led by the 'Young Officer' movement. The word 'jijoji – crisis' cropped up everywhere and was the excuse for any unpleasant sacrifices that the people might have to suffer.

To pay for the build up of the armed forces, salaries were cut, taxes increased, import quotas introduced and substitute materials developed. Even pine needles were tried as substitutes for wooden matches but proved useless. Small towns subscribed to pay for military aircraft for the Army and Navy; almost each week the newspapers announced a presentation ceremony, the accompanying photograph depicting a fuselage with the donor town's name painted on its side.'

Meanwhile at a tea and tennis party held by the C. in C. at Wei-Hai-Wei on Sunday 21 June 1936 an interesting revelation is made concerning the appalling financial circumstances in which some of the peasants of China found themselves in those days of chaotic domestic conditions under a variety of war lords:-

'Met Mr. Clarke of Clarke and Lavers, the mainland bankers – an interesting man who has been out here for 40 years (--). As to the Japs. general intentions he feels sure that they will be in general control of these five provinces up here before long – though perhaps indirectly – partly because the Chinese would prefer a settled stable administration to the present under which there are places where the land tax has been extracted in advance up to 1983 already (15).'

At Keelung, the island of Formosa then being in Japanese occupation, during the night of 7/8 October 1936 the *Medway* incident occurred ashore. To sum up this business, on 9 October Captain C.G.B. Coltart of *Medway*, 14,650 tons, the submarine depot ship, wrote to H.B.M. Consul at Tamsui, Mr. Clement Archer. Relevant excerpts follow:-

'Three rating assaulted on night 7/8 October 1936 by the Japanese police at Keelung:-
Stoker John J. Turner of HM S/M *Odin* who had suffered a fracture of
his left lower jaw.
AB G.R. Harrison of HM S/M *Rover*.
AB Harry J. Smith of HM Destroyer *Bruce*.
It was alleged that a taxi fare had not been paid, however a witness, Supply
Petty Officer S. Allgood of *Bruce* had seen them pay.
After approximately six hours of argument and of being insulted their release was secured
by Lieut. T.A. Pack-Beresford of *Bruce* at 0700 on 8.10.36 (16).'

To an extent the whole affair probably was complicated by the question of photography about which the Japanese were most sensitive. Earlier the Paymaster Commander in *Medway* had been seen on deck taking photographs, an offense for which in person later he had apologised to the Fortress Commander, and after the film had been removed by the Japanese. Be that as it may, concerning the behaviour of the police no satisfactory apology was to be forthcoming from Japan consequently it was decided that henceforth no courtesy visits by ships of the Royal Navy were to be made to that country (17). This policy was reciprocated by Japan with the single exception of the voyage undertaken by the heavy cruiser *Ashigara*, Captain Moriji Takeda, to England to attend the Coronation Naval Review in May 1937.

HBM Ambassador to Japan at the time was Sir Robert Henry Clive, GCMG (1877-1948). As has been written:-

'Clive was outraged in October 1936 when a number of Royal Navy ratings visiting the port of Keelung in Formosa were arrested and then beaten by Japanese police.

Clive believed that this incident was symptomatic of Japanese arrogance and its lack of respect for British interests and was therefore convinced that Britain should push hard to achieve a satisfactory settlement of this incident, which he hoped would bring the Japanese to their senses (--).

Clive's increasingly tough stance towards Japan had both its admirers and detractors. Among the former was the Commander in Chief, China station, Admiral Sir Charles Little, who noted approvingly to the First Sea Lord, Admiral Sir Ernle Chatfield, on 6 July 1936 that Clive recognized that the only language that the Japanese understood was force (18).'

At Hong Kong on 15 November 1936 for the first time the C. in C. hoisted his flag in his new Flagship, the heavy cruiser *Cumberland*, 10,000 tons, Captain John C. Leach. The ship had re-commissioned at Chatham on 13 May, and had arrived at Hong Kong on 19 October. However at that time the Admiral had been otherwise engaged in attending to the consequences of the *Medway* incident (19).

In Berlin on 25 November 1936 Germany and Japan signed their Anti-Comintern pact.

During 1936 a leading Japanese news agency quoted as follows, these words being taken from a speech delivered to a group of Osaka industrialists by Admiral Takahashi Sankichi (1882-1966) who between November 1934 and December 1936 was C. in C., Combined Fleet:-

'Japan's economic advance must be directed southward, with either Formosa or the South Seas Island Mandate as a foothold. In this case the cruising radius of the Japanese Navy must be expanded suddenly as far as New Guinea, Borneo and Celebes (20).'

Following upon the abdication of his brother, HM King Edward VIII on 10 December, in Hong Kong on 12 December 1936 the accession of the King Emperor, H.M. King George VI, was proclaimed.

The Governor of Hong Kong then was H.E. Sir Andrew Caldecott (21).

7 to 25 December 1936. Chiang Kai-shek, during a visit to Sian, was arrested by Chang Hsueh-liang (1898-2001), son of an earlier north China warlord, Chang Tso-lin. As recorded earlier he, Chang Tso-lin, had been murdered by the Japanese near Mukden on 4 June 1928. Chang led a group keen to persuade Chiang to alter the emphasis of his campaign against the Chinese communists and rather to place greater stress on ridding China of the invading Japanese. Cleverly Chiang did not commit himself nevertheless, once released, it appeared that he was inclined to adjust his ideas and to place greater stress on handling the Japanese problem. In any case, in short order and as will be seen below, the Japanese were to go a long way toward uniting, be it uneasily, the Kuomintang and communists against themselves, the common enemy.

In Tokyo in an entry in his diary made on 1 January 1937 the U.S. Ambassador to that country, Joseph C. Grew, summed up the general Far Eastern situation as follows:-

'The New Year for Japan, so far as her international relations are concerned, opens in an ominous key. Not only has her reputation in the world suffered an important deterioration during the past year, but her relations with Great Britain, Soviet Russia and China are on a far from satisfactory footing and recently have been growing worse. With the Dutch East Indies relations have improved. Only with the United States, among her nearer neighbours, can it be said that the *status quo* has been maintained, but with the expiration of the Washington Naval Treaty, due to Japan's intransigeance, and the risk of a race in sea power and fortifications, the long future as contrasted with the immediate present holds out no evident grounds for optimism.

For this unhappy situation Japan herself is primarily to blame, for she has played her cards unwisely and is now reaping the logical results. It is the old story of the defects arising out of a dual control of foreign policy wherein the civil authorities of the Government, including the Prime Minister and the Foreign Office, are overridden by the military and are subject to the behests of the Army and Navy, which know or care little about developing good relations with foreign countries but without whose support the cabinet could not long survive. We saw very much the same thing working out in Germany in 1914 (22).'

February 1937: appointment of the new Navy Minister, IJN, Vice Admiral Yonai Mitsumasa (1880-1948). He was to serve until 1939 and then, for a few months, January to July 1940, to be prime minister. A moderate himself, Yonai possessed a down to earth attitude (23). In a generally tense atmosphere, to a great extent arising from right wing pressure and their unpleasant habit of selected political assassinations, towards the end of his term as Navy Minister one of his final acts in August 1939 was to ensure the relative safety of his assistant, and another political moderate, Vice Admiral Yamamoto Isoroku, by appointing him back to sea as C. in C., Combined Fleet.

On 16 April 1937 His Excellency the Governor of Hong Kong, Sir Andrew Caldecott, left in s.s. *Empress of Japan*, 26,313 grt, to proceed on leave prior to taking up his next position as Governor of Ceylon (24).

Coronation Day, 12 May 1937. To assist in the celebrations surrounding the Coronation of H.M. The King Emperor, George VI, the C. in C. was present in his Flagship *Cumberland* at Shanghai. The day, '…. itself was worthily celebrated. There were services onboard and ashore in the forenoon, a children's fete in the afternoon at which a number of *Cumberland*'s sailors assisted, and the tattoo in the evening. (-) On the next day the Commander in Chief, the Captain and Officers gave a ball onboard, which was a great success. Admiral Little, it will be remembered, had particular associations with Shanghai; he himself had spent his early youth there… (25).'

In London on 1 June 1937 there took place another official gathering, one objective of which was to maintain the faith of the Australasian Dominions in Britain's defence intentions in the Far East, and to be re-assured as to her ability so to perform. Before a group which included Mr. N.J. Savage, Prime Minister of New Zealand, and Sir Archdale Parkhill, Minister for Defence, Australia, Admiral of the Fleet Lord Chatfield, First Sea Lord, clarified and confirmed the British policy of a seventy day reinforcement of Singapore by the Fleet (26). In other words seventy days after perceiving that hostilities were about to break out in the Far East then heavy units of the Fleet would arrive to reinforce the 'fortress' at Singapore.

Admiral: 25 June 1937.

Certain naval officers were to play an important role in the forthcoming war which on 7 December 1941 was to break out across the Pacific. On 7 July 1937, the significance of which date follows, they were employed as is shown here:-

United States Navy:

Ernest J. King	Rear Admiral, commanding Aircraft, Base Force. Flag in *Langley* AV-3 at Seattle, WA.
Chester W. Nimitz	Captain, Assistant to the Chief, Bureau of Navigation, Washington, DC.
William F. Halsey	Captain, Commandant of the Naval Air Station, Pensacola, Fla.
Raymond A. Spruance	Captain, serving at the Naval War College, Newport, R.I.
John H. Towers	Captain in command *Saratoga*, CV-3.
Marc A. Mitscher	Commander, serving at the Bureau of Aeronautics, Washington, DC.
Alexander A. Vandegrift	Colonel, USMC, Military Secretary to the Major General Commandant, Washington, DC.

特別フォト・ドキュメント

「海軍中攻隊」大陸を翔る

★未発表秘蔵アルバム

昭和12年10月27日、浙韶線（中国の鉄道）黄渡鎮付近にある散兵壕攻撃に向かう途中、上海上空をゆく鹿屋空の九六式陸攻（中攻）。

Navy Type 96, over Shanghai, in 1937.

Japanese bomber over Shanghai

Royal Navy:

    Bruce A. Fraser   Captain in command aircraft carrier *Glorious*.

    H. Bernard Rawlings Captain, Naval Attache, British Embassy, Tokyo.

Imperial Japanese Navy:

    Yamamoto Isoroku   Vice Admiral, Vice Minister of the Navy.

    Kondo Nobutake   Rear Admiral, Director of the First Division, Naval General Staff.

    Nagumo Chuichi   Rear Admiral, Commander of the First Destroyer Squadron.

    Ozawa Jisaburo   Rear Admiral, Instructor, Naval War College.

Outside Peking, on 7 July 1937, the Japanese army staged the Marco Polo bridge 'Incident' used by them to justify the initial stages of their subsequent assault of China. Both Peking and Tientsin were occupied very rapidly. Shortly thereafter their forces were to attack other regions of the country including Shanghai, the Yangtse valley, and Canton. Thus it was that for great numbers of people in the East, what was to become better known as the Second World War, may be said to have commenced on 7 July 1937.

It was on Friday, 13 August 1937 that the Japanese assault of the Chinese city at Shanghai commenced. Somewhat to the astonishment of most Western observers, Chinese forces fought bravely and with determination, so much so that the defending armies were able to resist until late October. By then, with Japanese Army reinforcements landing at Hangchow Bay, Lieut. General Yanagawa Heisuke, in the south, and others in the north at Paimou on the Yangtse delta, Lieut. General Nakajima Kesago, thus with every danger of being encircled from the rear, the Chinese military were forced to retreat in the general direction of Nanking.

The following extract gives merely one example of the subsequent commercial rape of the country:-

'Of particular value to Japanese business was the great industrial city of Shanghai. As soon as the invaders had it under control, zaibatsu 'carpetbaggers' began grabbing major industries, such as the public utilities, cotton mills, and silk filatures. By taking over the textile mills they were able to eliminate Chinese competition, which until then had been fierce. The damage to Shanghai's industrial and private property as a result of the invasion was approximately eight billion dollars, and most local businessmen were ruined. Those whose factories were operable could not reopen them without permission from the Japanese consulate; but a condition for receiving that approval was the acceptance of Japanese partners or 'technical assistance', which amounted to surrendering control (27)'.

At Shanghai the Chinese aerial response to the Japanese presence both on land and on the river unfortunately proved to be wildly erratic. Those who were able did their best to take precautions. As the future chairman of Jardine Matheson and Co., Sir John Keswick, wrote on 27 August 1937:-

'We are now working in a veritable fortress. Ground floor windows to the front are sandbagged and upper floor rooms which are in use have the windows protected by timber and bullet proof sheeting (28)'.

These safeguards taken by most foreign firms rather naturally included the evacuation of families. For example, also on 27 August 1937, the managers in Hong Kong of Butterfield & Swire reported to London:-

'Evacuation from Shanghai:

127 dependants of Staff Members were sent from Shanghai (29)'.

Amongst those ships used to assist with the evacuation of refugees from Shanghai was the Canadian Pacific *Empress of Asia*, Captain George Goold, on 18 August with 1,329 refugees for Hong Kong, also the P. & O. *Rajputana*, 16,644 grt, and Blue Funnel *Patroclus*, 11,314 grt.

Indeed, in order to assist with this evacuation, such was the perceived dire nature of the situation, that at Hong Kong the British authorities had commandeered the services of *Empress of Asia* for the round trip, Hong

Kong/Shanghai/Hong Kong, with military reinforcements being carried North (30). From Commodore, Hong Kong on 16 August Captain Goold had received his orders:-

> 'Having embarked the 1st Battalion Royal Ulster Rifles you are to proceed with utmost possible despatch to Shanghai today, August 16. On arrival at Shanghai you are requested to place your ship at the disposal of the British Naval Commander in Chief for the evacuation of refugees for passage to Hong Kong (31).'

Admiral William Fredrick Halsey Jnr., USN (1882-1959)
Commander, South Pacific Area in 1942, then in 1943 until war end to be in command of the Third Fleet, USN.

Admiral John Henry Towers, USN (1885-1955)
A pioneer of naval aviation, Chief of the Bureau of Aeronautics from 1939-1942, then commander of naval air forces in the Pacific region.

In the Yangtse at a safe anchorage near the Blockhead Buoy, some six miles below Woosung therefore some twenty miles from Shanghai itself, all the refugees embarked from destroyers *Duncan*, Captain Harold Hickling as Captain (D), 8DF, *Delight*, Commander J.R.N. Taylor, and *Duchess*, Lieut. Commander W.T.W. Curtis, each 1,375 tons, who had brought them all down River to *Empress of Asia* (32). These destroyers then embarked the troop reinforcements for passage back up to Shanghai.

Subsequently Captain Goold was able to state, 'by 7 p.m. on August 21 we had every man, woman and child safely ashore at Hong Kong.' These passengers included one boy born at sea during the voyage South, and Christened onboard, Michael Asia Rowland.

Ironically, and sadly, earlier when *Empress of Asia* had arrived at Yokohama on 3 August then being outward bound from Canada to the East, she had embarked Chinese refugees, some 650 in number, fleeing from Japan and with the greater number bound for Shanghai. One can only wonder as to the eventual fate of these most unfortunate people, a miserable confirmation of the old saw, 'out of the frying pan into the fire'.

Earlier, at Shanghai on 14 August and with the cruiser *Idzumo*, 9,520 tons, together with the Japanese Consulate as targets, units of the Chinese Air Force had attempted to destroy them by bomb attack. Hopelessly inaccurate, a number of the bombs landed on the other side of Soochow Creek killing 1,740 and wounding 1,873 entirely uninvolved persons. In mitigation it may be added that at the time the weather was poor, with low cloud, thus giving the aircraft pilots no option other than to launch their bombs from a very low altitude which made it difficult to be sure of their position.

Early that Saturday morning of 14 August the first Chinese attack was witnessed from Holt's Wharf at Pootung:-

> 'The Whangpoo was crowded with shipping. Ships lay at the wharves and buoys busily loading or discharging, others were just arriving or leaving, river steamers, tugs, lighters, sampans and junks – all going about their normal business, while in the city streets, offices, hotels, and shops the crowds were carrying on as usual.
>
> Suddenly there was a roar of aircraft as a half dozen or so low-flying planes appeared from nowhere and flew down the river from the direction of the Bund, dropping a number of bombs which sent up great fountains of mud and water but did not appear to hit any ships.'

It was the attack in the afternoon of 14 August which caused the dreadful loss of civilian life mentioned above:-

> 'One got the impression that the Chinese airmen were not very skilful, either at identifying their targets or at aiming their bombs. In this same attack one plane dropped its bombs on the Palace Hotel in Nanking Road, while another, trying to escape from the Japanese flak, shed its load on to a crowded square in Avenue Edward VII outside the Great World Theatre. (-) In both cases the death toll of harmless and unprepared civilians, mostly Chinese, was enormous. Days later the piles of shattered corpses were still being sorted out and taken away for burial (33).'

Rather naturally, from both sides, Chinese and Japanese, much anti aircraft fire took place, and on 20 August this anti aircraft fire was to result in the first American naval casualty. One such shell missed its target and quite by chance landed on USS *Augusta*, Captain Harold V. McKittrick, and unfortunately there exploded. Killed outright was Seaman Frederick J. Falgout.

The erratic performance by Chinese aviators may be seen again from the following news extract:-

> 'The inexperience of Chinese airmen was once more demonstrated on August 30 (1937) when bombs were aimed by a Chinese 'plane at the *President Hoover*, monster Dollar Company luxury Trans-Pacific liner, as she approached Woosung on her way to Shanghai from Hongkong. One of the bombs struck so near the ship that seven members of the crew and two passengers were injured, one of the former since dying from his wounds. The Chinese Government, which immediately assumed full responsibility for this untoward incident, stated that it was an accident, the bomber having believed *President Hoover* to be a Japanese transport carrying troops to Shanghai (34).'

Also during August 1937, in an effort to restrict enemy traffic on the Yangtse, the Chinese authorities sank a number of steamers and other vessels, such as junks filled with stone, across the channel. In this manner they did their best to create a boom at Kiangyin which lies approximately half way between Woosung and Nanking. That was a good point to select as, proceeding upstream, it is at Kiangyin that one encounters the first point at which the width of the River is relatively narrowly restricted by natural rocky formations on both banks.

Similarly another boom was laid across the Whangpoo just above Shanghai between Nantao and Pootung across on the opposite bank.

Off to the south another effect of the Japanese invasion of China in 1937 was the subsequent increase in the Chinese population of Hong Kong, occasionally by as many as 5,000 people a day. To the advantage of the colony among the new immigrants were prosperous Shanghai businessmen who established factories in Hong Kong thereby providing employment for thousands (35).

A further important consideration in respect of this Japanese invasion of China, and perhaps an aspect overlooked at the time, follows. The writer was a retired member, highly experienced, of the British Chinese Consular service. This far sighted comment was published in 1943:-

'Since this was (first) written has come war with Japan. The great event has occurred which will bind China as one, and from which she will emerge a united country. In previous foreign wars only localities in this huge country have been involved, either the South were opposing the attempts of foreigners to gain a footing and the North was uninterested, or the North, as in 1900, were deeply involved and the South rather thought a corrupt Court had brought calamity on themselves. But now East, West, North and South are all involved and the whole of China is suffering. Nothing could possibly have occurred so calculated to lay the foundation of a strong united China, a permanent block to Japanese Imperialistic expansion, than the 'Incident' so callously undertaken by the Japanese Military Party. (-) Japan by her actions has created a new and united China, a China which will rapidly take her place as a world Power, and this gives food for thought (36).'

Also in the commercial world men of much experience in the East, old 'China hands', were to expound along similar lines. The following extracts are taken from the memoirs of a Scot, for many years before WW2 resident in Shanghai where he was engaged in the insurance business:-

'It may be that, in the long run, this Japanese invasion will prove to be a decisive turning point in the long history of China. It may well mark the moment when China first felt herself as one nation, and the first emergence of a patriotic Chinese man. Hitherto China had been a compound of separate elements, loosely bound together by a common, spiritual allegiance to a God-like Emperor. The component parts that made up the Chinese nation were as different, and often as antagonistic to each other, as are the nations of Europe. (--)
The armies of western powers which had invaded China, as after the Boxer Rebellion, had found no difficulty in recruiting willing labourers to man their supply lines. A full rice bowl was of more importance to a Chinese coolie than any amount of posthumous honours for offering resistance. The Japanese did not fill any rice bowls. On the contrary, they starved, tortured and massacred thousands of farmers and peasants as they advanced through the country. Thus they alienated a population which might have co-operated with them, or at least offered no active antagonism. (--) Japanese arrogance and senseless persecution changed the attitude of a whole nation and, for the first time in their long history, the Chinese people, widely separated by language and custom, united in one common aim – to drive the 'piratical dwarfs' from their land (37).'

On 31 August 1937 the forces of Japan made it clear that they intended to take their undeclared war against China right across that country including the South. Early that morning their first air raid against Canton took place, the aircraft being land based Navy Type 96 twin engined bombers, Mitsubishi G3M 'Nell'. One eye witness was a Lieutenant then serving in the river gunboat USS *Mindanao* PR-8, 560 tons, who was at anchor off the Shameen Bund:-

'... not yet sunup. The Japanese bombers were between us and the bright sky in the east. There were 9 of them, wheeling around in perfect formation, at about 10,000 ft. We could hear a great sustained roar, like the sound of the surf, as the Chinese in the city charged around the streets in panic. Sampans by the thousands cut their moorings and drifted down on the American gunboat, hoping it would not be a target. Chinese AA batteries meanwhile were filling the sky with pretty pink puffs of smoke that were nowhere near the planes (38).'

Amongst the ships blown ashore by the powerful typhoon which hit Hong Kong on 2 September 1937 were the China Navigation vessels s.s. *Kalgan*, 2,655 grt, s.s. *Hunan*, 2,827 grt, and s.s. *Shuntien*, 3,059 grt. At the time the latter was undergoing repair at the Group's Taikoo Dockyard. The same owner's s.s. *Kwangchow*, 2,626 grt, was so badly damaged by grounding that she was declared a constructive total loss. Another unfortunate victim was the B.I. liner *Talamba*, 8,018 grt, to remain for many months fast on the rocks at Lye-Mun Pass before finally being re-floated. Yet another was the beautiful m.v. *Asama Maru* of N.Y.K. (39). In all some thirty ships were driven ashore, in addition to innumerable junks being damaged and destroyed. 11,000 lives were lost, to a great part owing to the huge tidal surge.

Meanwhile, and as briefly mentioned above, at Shanghai Japanese military pressure had been building rapidly and from 26 October the expected Chinese retreat commenced. One aspect of this withdrawal was recorded in *Cumberland* at her moorings off The Bund astern of the U.S. flagship *Augusta* CA-31:-

> '... in the morning there were no Chinese forces left north of Soochow creek except for a rearguard whose duty was to set fire to everything they could lay hands on and so hamper the Japanese advance. By the afternoon the whole of Chapei was in flames and we witnessed a fire such as few have ever seen or are ever likely to see again. A pall of smoke many hundreds of feet high blotted out the sun, and the roar of the flames could be heard from the International Settlement (40).'

At the same time at sea it is clear that many Chinese were suffering from uncalled for attention, and much worse, at the hands of warships of the IJN. Here follows a number of extracts taken from a report written by the Commodore in Hong Kong to the C. in C. on 14 October 1937:-

> 'Japanese war vessels have passed through Hong Kong territorial waters on several occasions in connection with hostile operations against Canton. In one case some evidence was forthcoming that a Japanese destroyer opened fire on a Chinese Maritime Customs vessel whilst actually within such waters.
>
> A Japanese cruiser boarded an Admiralty Tug (flying Admiralty Blue Ensign) whilst re-victualling Gap Rock Light House.
>
> Complaints have been received by the Hong Kong Police at various times from fishermen that their junks had been fired on, boarded and masts cut and gear destroyed or that other ill treatment had been received at the hands of Japanese men-of-war in the vicinity of Hong Kong, but outside territorial waters.
>
> Reports that burnt out junks dangerous to navigation are met with up and down the China Coast confirm that these poor fishermen are subject to barbarous treatment (41).'

In the P. & O. steamer *Ranchi*, 16,738 grt, on 28 October 1937 the new Governor of Hong Kong, Sir Geoffry A. S. Northcote (1881-1948), arrived to assume office. For the previous two years he had governed British Guiana so no doubt will have been well pleased with his new climatic environment. In addition during the post World Depression era there had been much labour unrest in British Guiana and other British West Indian territories. Leaving those difficulties behind him nevertheless His Excellency will have been well aware of the different nature of many of the problems that now he was to face in the East.

Appropriately *Ranchi* was escorted into port by destroyers *Thracian* and *Duchess*, a seventeen gun salute was fired by *Tamar*, and all warships in harbour were dressed overall.

From the British Embassy in Tokyo on 30 October 1937 a circular to Consuls was despatched. This letter covered aspects of the new Japanese 'Law for the protection of Military Secrets' (42). As will be seen from the following extract, domestically within that country there could have been be little doubt concerning the direction in which their leaders were steering the nation:-

> 'Then, in October, the Japanese government promulgated the 'national spiritual mobilization movement' to enhance unity among the Japanese people and to galvanize wartime attitudes. The nationwide effort to strengthen defence systems resulted in an order for the organization of civilian guards and the compulsory establishment of neighbourhood groups called *tonarigumi* that assisted as a kind of peer-police in weeding out slackers and dissenters. It also precipitated the 'New Military Secrets Protection Law', which gave authorities far reaching powers to arrest and imprison anyone suspected of collecting sensitive information or leaking military secrets to outsiders (43).'

Also in Japan in November 1937 a supreme war council, "dai honei", was set up to co-ordinate the army and navy general staffs and to prepare for an expanding war (44).

The man destined to be the last Rear Admiral, Yangtse, Reginald V. Holt, accompanied by his staff, arrived at Hong Kong in the P. & O. s.s. *Rajputana* on 11 November 1937 (45). From Victoria Harbour the small party took passage to Woosung in the heavy cruiser *Dorsetshire,* Captain Francis Reginald Barry, arriving at 0932 hours on 16 November. There they disembarked into the tug *St. Breock* to proceed further upstream towards Shanghai.

In the interim in England one of the C. in C.'s friends, Vice Admiral Sir Geoffrey Blake, unfortunately had had to retire early owing to ill health (46). On 25 November 1937 Sir Charles wrote a letter of commiseration which included the following two extracts relating to the China Station: first his pleasant relations with the USN, and, secondly, rather less pleasant with the Japanese:-

> '*Augusta* is a beautiful ship, very well arranged and very well finished. I get on very well with their C. in C., Admiral Yarnell. He is our senior Admiral but of course British interests are far greater than anyone else's so most awkward questions are mine and he supports me most loyally.'
>
> 'My time out here has been rendered less pleasant than it should be as I have been continually up against the Japs. – first the Keelung Incident and now the Sino-Japanese conflict (47).'

As the year of 1937 progressed this new and increasingly disagreeable atmosphere in the Far East naturally also was noted in the Merchant Navy. Serving as Chief Officer in the P. & O. steamer *Carthage*, 14,304 grt, at the time was D.G.O. Baillie. The following excerpts are taken from his autobiography:-

> 'We met Japanese transports packed solidly with troops crossing the Inland Sea, Japanese cruisers in the Woosung River; whole armies, it seemed, were on the move once more.
>
> In Shanghai the tension increased perceptibly with every voyage, although the Concessions still existed and the port was still nominally an International one. On the few occasions when I had time to go ashore, there were far too many Japanese officers for my liking, reeking of scent and swaggering about the streets, too many strutting little Japanese soldiers herding wretched looking Chinese prisoners through the city. (-)
>
> We had one good Japanese friend, the P. & O. Choice Pilot for the Inland Sea. His name was Yokoyama, and he had occupied this post for years, discharging with skill and efficiency the exacting pilotage of that stretch of water, liberally bestrewn with islands, swept by terrific tides, noted for typhoons in summer and for fog and snowstorms in winter, which lies between Moji and Kobe. An excellent golfer, Yokoyama usually took the Captain of *Carthage* ashore for a round of golf on the links at Kobe. Then, sometime in 1938, came the black day when the invitation was no longer forthcoming, and he had to confess that he had been forbidden to play golf with an Englishman (48).'

Near Wuhu on the Yangtse on Sunday, 12 December 1937 Japanese aircraft attacked and sank the river gunboat, USS *Panay,* Lieut. Commander J.J. Hughes, USN. In the same vicinity on the previous day the British river gunboat *Ladybird,* Lieut. Commander H.D. Barlow, had been taken under fire by Japanese shore based artillery with the loss of one life.

Just fifty nautical miles down stream other Japanese forces assaulted the southern capital, Nanking, which fell on 13 December 1937. The infamous massacre, which was to continue into January 1938, now took place. Still today (the year 2008) the extent of the horror of murder, rape and destruction perpetrated by the Japanese army is a subject of considerable debate (49). One relatively recent Chinese account, for example, reads as follows:-

> 'On the 13th Nanjing fell. The Japanese invaders launched a 'competition' to kill, rape and loot, which lasted six weeks. Over 300,000 Chinese were massacred , and one third of the houses in the city were burned to ruins (50).'

Shortly before Christmas 1937 the C. in C. fell ill with pleurisy. For several weeks he was compelled to lie up in Admiralty House, from 21 December his place being filled on a temporary basis by Vice Admiral Crabbe who had just relinquished his post as Rear Admiral, Yangtse (51). As mentioned above, Admiral Crabbe's successor as RAY, Reginald V. Holt, was to be the last officer to hold that post.

Concerning the Japanese economy during this era it is relevant to comment briefly. The following data is taken from a statistical table for 1937. Formosa (Taiwan) supplied much sugar, Chosen (Korea) useful quantities of rice, and Manchukuo (Manchuria) was the source of good quantities of beans, maize, coal and iron ore. However, as moves continued to be made towards an expansion of the misery of WW2, this extract serves to illustrate how dependent Japan was on distant overseas sources for the supply of just three of the most basic raw materials which she required:-

> 'Raw cotton came from India and the United States, and about half of Japanese iron ore and scrap iron was obtained from America. About 80% of her crude oil also came from America (52).'

On 5 February 1938 Sir Charles officially was succeeded on the Station by Vice Admiral Sir Percy L.H. Noble. In practical reality the arrival of Sir Percy at Hong Kong resulted in Vice Admiral Crabbe ceasing his temporary command of the Station.

Following his bout of pleurisy, then subsequent to his return to England in the P. & O. steamer *Comorin*, 15,116 grt, on 12 April 1938 Sir Charles was admitted to the Royal Naval Hospital, Haslar for medical examination. Fortunately he was discharged the following day, 'to 90 days sick leave'. Happily on 11 July 1938 he was, 'found fit for duty' (53).

From 2 September 1938 he was appointed to *President* for duty in the Admiralty and, just a few days later, from 30 September 1938 for a period which was to endure to February 1941, to be a Lord Commissioner of the Admiralty and Chief of Naval Personnel, so Second Sea Lord.

From April 1941 to August 1942 Sir Charles was stationed across the Atlantic as Head of the British Joint Staff Mission in Washington, DC. In due course, from there in the USA, he was to be relieved by his one time *Britannia* classmate of 1897, Admiral Sir Andrew Browne Cunningham (1883-1963).

From April 1940 his friend Geoffrey Blake had been offered, and had accepted, the post as Additional Assistant Chief of Naval Staff and as a wartime Lord Commissioner of the Admiralty. On 18 January 1942 Admiral Blake wrote to him in Washington. Extracts follow:-

> 'I am afraid you will be waving across the Atlantic for a long time yet as it is going to be a slow and hard task to round up those nasty Japs who have sprawled themselves all over the Pacific. There is little to disturb them at present ....'
>
> 'It was sad about *PoW* (*Prince of Wales*) and *Repulse* – poor little Tom (Phillips: see C. in C., 3-10 December 1941) and Jack Leach – I remember Dudley (Pound) saying that Tom was a fire-eater; he certainly got the fire – he should never have been sent there without an aircraft carrier – in any case, I think he underestimated the efficiency of the Japanese T.B. (torpedo) bombers who from all accounts made most determined attacks (54).'

GBE: 11 June 1942.

C. in C., Portsmouth: 1 October 1942 – 28 September 1945, then retired. However according to his service record he was placed on the retired List on 15 April 1945. Be that as it may, at Portsmouth he had succeeded Admiral Sir William M. James who in turn was to be succeeded by Admiral Sir Geoffrey Layton (see C. in C., 1940).

The funeral of the First Sea Lord, Admiral of the Fleet Sir Dudley Pound, took place in Westminster Abbey at 15.15 on Tuesday, 26 October 1943. As 1SL he was succeeded in office by Admiral of the Fleet Sir Andrew Browne Cunningham, later to be Viscount Cunningham of Hyndhope (1883-1963).

The Allied landings in Normandy commenced on 6 June 1944. Naturally the role played by the Allied Navies operating from Portsmouth was vital.

In Tokyo Bay on 2 September 1945, onboard USS *Missouri* BB-63, representatives of Japan signed the surrender documentation. Thus, from being on the spot in the East at the time of the invasion of China by Japan in July 1937, here at Portsmouth, Britain's premier naval base, he continued to be on active service at the time of her surrender just over eight years later.

GCB: 27 February 1945, 'for distinguished service as Commander in Chief, Portsmouth'.
Trustee of the National Maritime Museum.
Vice President, Royal United Service Institution.
Vice President, Navy Records Society.

Following his death on 20 June 1973 a notice in the London press stated, simply:-
'Loved husband of Bessy and father of Elizabeth Mansfield-Robinson. Funeral private (55).'

NOTES

1. Jonathan Parkinson, *The First Steam Powered Ascent Through the Yangtse Gorges,* (Journal of the Royal Asiatic Society Hong Kong Branch, 2006), Vol. 46.
2. RN Museum Library, Portsmouth. Ref: *MSS 216* being the Journal by Oscar De Satge De Thoren, from 7 April 1898 Midshipman in *Hermoine.* She sailed from Devonport on 17 April 1898 and reached Singapore on 23 May. River Gunboat *Snipe,* 85 tons. Commissioned at Shanghai: 19 October 1899, Lieut. and Commander Arthur H. Oldham. *Navy List.* Although still very small men of war, at 126 tons each, *Woodcock* and *Woodlark* in fact were rather larger than *Snipe.*
3. NA ADM 196/47. *Service Record.*
4. S.W.C. Pack, *Cunningham the Commander,* (London, 1974), 19.
5. *Service Record.* In 1920 *Thames* was to be sold out of the service then in March 1922 be re-commissioned as the South African Training Ship *General Botha.*
6. Richard Compton-Hall, *Submarines and the War at Sea, 1914-1918,* (London, 1991), 73.
7. Ibid. 297-299.
8. Higham and Cox Wing.
9. Caird Library. Ref: *BLE/7.* Letter to Vice Admiral Sir Geoffrey Blake, 25 November 1937.
10. **Saito** Makoto: see Kelly, C. in C., 1931, reference (30).
11. Ed. J.E. Hoare, *Biographical Portraits,* (Japan Library, 1999), Chapter 16, Tadashi Kuramatsu, 194. Following the assassination of Admiral Saito his wife Haruko was to write:-
    '... it was an unfortunate morning, the beginning of the cursed era for Japan.'
12. NA ADM 1/8862. China Station letter 602/2301, para. 42.
13. Robert L. Gandt, *China Clipper,* (Annapolis, 1991), 103.
14. George Campbell **Ross**, latterly Rear Admiral. Born: 9 October 1900. Died: 30 July 1993. Memoir at the Imperial War Museum, London. Ref: *86/60/1,* chapter 18.
15. Extracted from a private diary kindly loaned to the writer. The sums involved may have been minimal nevertheless for most of us happily it is almost impossible to imagine being forced to pay taxes for forty seven years in advance.
16. NA FO 262/1954 'Keelung Incident'. Clement Hugh **Archer**. Born: 19 February 1897. Joined the British Consular Japan service: 27 June 1919. Consul at Tamsui, Formosa: 5 December 1934. *Foreign Office List.* He was a keen mountain walker with several Korean and Japanese peaks to his credit.
    Odin, 1,475 tons, Lieut. Commander R. McP. Jonas. *Rover,* 1,475 tons, from 2 October 1936 Lieut. Commander H.G. Bowerman. Destroyer *Bruce,* 1,530 tons, Commander E.M. Loly. *Navy List.*

17. Arthur J. Marder, *Old Friends, New Enemies,* I, (OUP, 1981), 24.

18. Ed. Hugh Cortazzi, *British Envoys to Japan: 1859-1972,* (Folkestone, Kent, 2004), 143. Chapter 14 by Anthony Best who is quoting from the Chatfield Papers, Caird Library, Ref: *CHT 4/8.*

19. *Commission of HMS Cumberland: 1936-1939,* (Chatham, 1939), 5/6.

20. William Henry Chamberlin, *Japan Over Asia,* (London, 1938), 148.

    Mr. Chamberlin (1897-1969) was a long time correspondent with the *Christian Science Monitor.* In this volume he gave as his his opinion that in that era, 'the army is the patron of Manchoukuo, the consistent advocate of continental expansion, so the navy is the sponsor of Japan's southward advance.'

    As early as 1 April 1928 Rear Admiral Takahashi had been appointed as the first commander of the newly formed First Carrier Division, IJN where his two carriers were the very different *Akagi*, Captain Kobayashi Seizaburo, and *Hosho*, Captain Kiyoshi Kitagawa. By no means was he to hold the 'big gun' opinions so common amongst senior naval officers in the navies of the world prior to WW2.

21. Andrew **Caldecott**. Born: 26 October 1884. Died: 14 July 1951. Uppingham and Exeter College, Oxford. Joined the Civil Service, Malaya: 1907. Chief Secretary, Government of the Federated Malay States: 1931-1933. Colonial Secretary, Straits Settlements: 1933-1935. KBE: 1935. Governor of Hong Kong: 12 December 1935 – 28 October 1937. KCMG: 1937. Governor of Ceylon: 1937 – 1944. GCMG: 1941. John O'Regan, *From Empire to Commonwealth,* (London, 1994). *Colonial Office List,* 1951. *Who's Who.*

22. Joseph C. Grew, *Ten Years in Japan,* (London, 1944), 172.

23. Yonai Mitsumasa. Born in Morioka, North Honshu: 2 March 1880. Died of pneumonia: 20 April 1948. Agawa Hiroyuki, *The Reluctant Admiral,* (Tokyo and New York, 1979), 143. Mr. Agawa also writes:-

    'The minister, Yonai, had a temperamental aversion to the Germans. A stay of two and a half years in Germany had convinced him that it was excessively dangerous for any country to ally itself to that nation.'

    At the time the U.S. Ambassador to Tokyo was Mr. Joseph **Grew**. In his memoires he makes it clear that not only was Admiral Yonai to be trusted but that had he, and those of similar inclinations, had their way Japan never would have formed a Tripartite Alliance with Germany and Italy. Joseph C. Grew, *Ten Years in Japan,* (London, 1944), 245/6, 271, 281. Another authority confirms:-

    'The cabinet led by Admiral Yonai Mitsumasa, then in office (early 1940), was opposed to this (joining the Alliance) and was overthrown.'

    Tsuzuki Chushichi, *The Pursuit of Power in Modern Japan: 1825-1995,* (OUP, 2000), 289.

24. NA ADM 116/3682.

25. *HMS Cumberland: 1936-1939,* 14.

26. NA CAB 53/7, 231. Ironically, also in attendance at this 209th meeting of the Committee of Imperial Defence, Chiefs of Staff Sub Committee, was the Director of Plans in the Admiralty, Captain T.S.V. Phillips.

27. John G. Roberts, *Mitsui,* (New York and Tokyo, 1989), 317.

28. Alan Reid, *The Mariner's Mirror,* Vol. 75, 1989, 94.

29. Courtesy of Messrs. Butterfield and Swire. Library, School of Oriental and African Studies, London. *Box 51.*

30. *Vancouver Daily Province,* August 16, 1937. Courtesy Mr. Nelson Oliver.

31. Commodore, Hong Kong at the time was Edward Bernard Cornish Dicken. Born: 18 January 1888. Died: 3 April 1964. Joined the RN in 1902. Lieutenant: 15 July 1909. During WW1 saw much service in the Dardanelles. Commander: 30 June 1922. Captain: 31 December 1929. In command light cruiser *Durban* in the Mediterranean: March 1934 – September 1936. In command *Tamar*, Hong Kong: 1937-1939. Rear Admiral, Retired List: 25 June 1940, however War service in the Admiralty as an Assistant Controller. Author's notes, *Life and Times of H.M.S. Durban: 1921-1944. Navy List.*

32. *Vancouver Daily Provnce,* September 11, 1937. Courtesy Mr. Nelson Oliver. Harold Hickling (1892-1969), to retire to New Zealand as a Vice Admiral. His partial autobiography relates most interesting experiences in both World Wars: *Sailor at Sea,* (William Kimber, London, 1965).

33. Captain W.J. Moore, *Shanghai Century,* (Ilfracombe, 1966), 34-36.

34. *The China Journal,* Vol. XXVII, September 1937.

35. John M. Carroll, *Edge of Empires,* (Harvard, 2005), 57.

36. Sir Meyrick Hewlett, *Forty Years in China*, (London, 1943), 255/6.

William Meyrick **Hewlett**. Born: 1 July 1876. Died: 16 March 1944. Harrow. Student Interpreter in China: 6 August 1898. Service in Peking, Tientsin, Hankow, Changsha, Ichang, Newchwang and Shanghai. Acting Consul-General, Chengtu: 1916. Other postings. Acting Chinese Secretary at Peking: 11 December 1922 to 31 January 1923. Consul-General in China: 3 January 1928. Thence Nanking: 1928-1931. KCMG: 1 January 1931. Consul-General, Hankow: 1931-1935. Retired: 2 September 1935. *Foreign Office List*, 1936. *Who's Who*.

37. James R. Paton, *Wide Eyed in Old China*, (Edinburgh, 1974), 161/2.

38. *South China and Yangtze Patroller*, (Port St. Lucie, FL, 1 September 1997), frontpiece. However that day units of the Chinese Air Force, 29th Independent Pursuit Squadron, did manage to shoot down one of the IJN aircraft.

39. *Asama Maru*. Quadruple screw motorship of 16,975 grt. Built by Mitsubishi at Nagasaki and completed in 1929. Main engines by Sulzer. Registered: Tokyo. *Lloyds Register*. On 1 November 1944 in the waters to the south of the Formosa Strait, to be torpedoed and sunk by USS *Atule* SS-403, Commander J.H. Maurer. Theodore Roscoe, *United States Submarine Operations in WW2*, (Annapolis, 1988), 411/2.

40. *HMS Cumberland: 1936-1939*, 25.

USS *Augusta*, 9,050 tons, was flying the flag of Admiral Harry Ervin **Yarnell**. Born: 18 October 1875. Died: 7 July 1959. From the Naval Academy, graduated with distinction: 2 June 1897. As a Cadet served in USS *Oregon*, BB-3, Captain Charles E. Clark, at the Battle of Santiago (Cuba): 3 July 1898. Ensign: 1 July 1899. Subsequent service on the Asiatic Station included with the China Relief Expedition during the Boxer rebellion: 1901. Senior Engineer Officer, USS *Connecticut* BB-18: June 1908 – April 1909. During the US involvement in WW1 served in command of USS *Nashville*, then as USN base commander at Gibraltar, and latterly as an aide to Admiral William S. Sims. Awarded the Navy Cross for services rendered in European waters during WW1. Much destroyer time followed, then from June 1922 to June 1924 commanded Naval Air Station, Hampton Roads, VA., and subsequently served as Commander Aircraft Squadrons, Scouting Fleet. To qualify as a Naval Observer attended NAS, Pensacola: July 1927. From September 1927 at Camden, NJ stood by new building USS *Saratoga* CV-3: commissioned her: 16 November 1927. Rear Admiral: 17 August 1928 when appointed Chief of the Bureau of Engineering. Additionally between January to April 1930 in London as Naval Adviser to the US representatives at the London Naval Conference. In June 1931 appointed Commander Aircraft, Battle Force. Early in February 1932, just prior to further exercises as Fleet Problem XIII, and operating from *Saratoga* and *Lexington* CV-2, he achieved his far sighted surprise attack on Hawaii. C. in C., Asiatic Fleet: 30 October 1936 to 25 July 1939. Retired in 1939 but in November 1941 was recalled for WW2 service. Admiral: 16 July 1942. Retired: December 1944. Navy Office of Information, Washington, DC. Clark G. Reynolds, *Admiral John H. Towers*, (Annapolis, 1991), 237/8.

41. NA ADM 1/9561.

42. NA FO 796/199. *Circular to Consuls: No. 20*.

43. Brian Burke-Gaffney, *Nagasaki: The British Experience, 1854-1945*, (Folkestone, Kent, 2009), 212.

44. Tsuzuki, 285.

45. Reginald Vesey **Holt**. Born: 26 May 1884. Died: 9 December 1957. Eton. *Britannia*. Captain: 1925. Captain i/c Bermuda DY: 1928-1930. Chief of Staff, The Nore: 1931-1933. Commanded heavy cruiser *Shropshire*: 1933-1934. Captain, Royal Naval College, Dartmouth: 1934-1936. Rear Admiral: 22 June 1936. Assumed command as RAY: 21 December 1937. Vice Admiral: 15 December 1939. Retired: May 1940. Re-employed as Flag Officer, Humber, HMS *Beaver*: October 1940 to 1942. Commodore, L.S.T.: 1942-1943. Senior British Naval Officer, Azores: 1943-1944. Naval Officer i/c, Newhaven (for the D-Day landings): April-October 1944. Flag Officer, Denmark: 1945. *Who's Who. Navy List*.

46. Geoffrey **Blake**. Born: 1882. Died: 18 July 1968. Winchester. Entered the RN in 1897. Captain: 31 December 1918. Naval Attache to the USA: 1919-1921. Director, RN Staff College: 1926-1927. Commodore, New Zealand Station: 1929-1932. Rear Admiral: 2 April 1931. Fourth Sea Lord: 1932-1935. Vice Admiral: 17 September 1935. KCB: 1937. Retired: 1938. Rejoined for war service as additional Assistant Chief of Naval Staff: 1940. Flag Officer Liaison, USN in Europe: 1942-1945. Gentleman Usher of the Black Rod: 1945-1949. *Navy List. Who's Who*.

47. Caird Library. Ref: *BLE/7*.

48. Captain D.G.O. Baillie, *A Sea Affair*, (London, 1957), 120/1. As a senior Master in the P. & O., thus as Captain D.G.O. Baillie in *Himalaya*, 27,955 grt, he was to end his service at sea at Tilbury Docks on 2 February 1955.

49. After the end of WW2 Generals Matsui Iwane and Tani Hiseo were to be executed for their respective roles in this revolting affair. However, possibly in their eagerness to sentence those perceived to be guilty, the members of the Tribunal may have been somewhat over zealous concerning their decision regarding General Matsui. Rather naturally today 'The Rape of Nanking' is regarded in one light in China, and in another in Japan. For a recent study: Takashi Yoshida, *The Making of the "Rape of Nanking"*, (OUP, 2006). Professor Tsuzuki, 287, quotes, '.. the number of victims of the Nanking atrocities at 200,000 on the basis of available evidence...'. In Nanking/Nanjing today a memorial to the victims of this ghastly business may be seen.

50. Ed. Bai Shouyi, *An Outline History of China: 1919-1949*, (Beijing, 1993), 159.

51. *HMS Cumberland: 1936-1939*, 27.
Lewis Gonne Eyre **Crabbe**. Born: 19 January 1882. Died: 2 July 1951. Captain: 30 June 1922. SNO, Persian Gulf: 16 May 1930 to 20 April 1933. Rear Admiral: 28 February 1934. RAY: 22 October 1935 to 20 December 1937. Vice Admiral: 5 November 1937. Retired: 1938. Flag Officer, Liverpool: 1939-1940. Commodore of Convoys: 1941- 1945. *Navy List. Who's Who.* ADM 196/46: *Service Record.*

52. Tsuzuki, 234/235.

53. *Service Record.*

54. Caird Library. Ref: *BLE/8.*

55. *The Times*, Friday, June 22, 1973.

5 February 1938 to 10 July 1940
Vice Admiral Sir Percy Lockhart Harnam **Noble**

He was born at Bahrouch, or Bahraich, in Oudh, India, today Uttar Pradesh N.E. of Lucknow towards the Nepali border, on 16 January 1880. His father was Colonel Charles Simeon Noble, 'late Bengal Staff Corps (1)'. His mother was Annie Georgina Noble.

Died, 'suddenly, in his 76th year', at his home, 66 Ashley Gardens, London, SW1, on Monday, 25 July 1955.

Entered the Royal Navy: 15 January 1894. As a Cadet from 15 January 1896 appointed in cruiser *Immortalite*, 5,600 tons, Captain Sir Edward Chichester, Bt., China Station. To join her sailed from Tilbury on 25 January 1896 in the P. & O. s.s. *Shanghai*, 3,503 grt (2). From her, and at Hong Kong, he joined his ship on Monday afternoon, 9 March 1896. **Midshipman**: 15 July 1896. Remained in *Immortalite*. Following the naval victory by the United States over Spain in Manila Bay on 1 May 1898, in order to protect British interests *Immortalite* arrived off Cavite on 7 May. On the following morning, Saturday, 8 May, she shifted to be nearer the shore. Then:-

'10.55 a.m.	Let go and veered to 5 shackles. Saluted Commodore Dewey's broad pendant with 11 guns. U.S.S. *Olympia* returned ditto. Observed wreck of one Spanish cruiser, one mail steamer ashore and one launch ashore.
1 p.m.	American Commodore visited ship (3).'

Following a few weeks of negotiation, and some exchange of fire with the Spanish Fort Malati, largely a gesture to save Spanish 'face', then during the late afternoon of Saturday, 13 August 1898 the Spanish surrender to the forces of the U.S.A. took place, 'Hauled down Spanish flag ashore and hoisted American colours. USS *Olympia* and rest of fleet saluted ditto (4).'

In Manila Bay on 9 September 1898 *Powerful* arrived as guardship and at 1.15 p.m. on Saturday 10 September 1898 *Immortalite* weighed and sailed for Hong Kong. There she arrived on Tuesday, 13 September 1898.

Early in the New Year, from Hong Kong on 16 January 1899, *Immortalite* commenced her voyage home. She proceeded via Labuan from 22 to 24 January, and arrived at Singapore on Saturday 28 January 1899.

There on Tuesday, 7 March 1899 he was one of those who received a rather special invitation:-

'Myself, Hay, Fforde and Lieutenant Seymour went to dine with Sir J.A. Swettenham and slept the night there (5).'

Finally *Immortalite* sailed from Singapore on Saturday, 15 April 1899. At Colombo from 23 to 26 April he noted that at the time only the South breakwater protecting the harbour had been built, the North breakwater being 'proposed'. Via Aden, the Canal, Malta and Plymouth, the ship eventually reached Sheerness on 7 June 1899 and paid off at Chatham a month later, 7 July 1899. He, however, on 17 June had transferred to *Cleopatra* in the Training Squadron for a cruise to Norway and Scotland subsequently, at Devonport on Monday, 30 October 1899, switching ships to join cruiser *Cambrian*, 4,360 tons, also Training Squadron, Home Waters (6).

During the following spring, and from Gibraltar:-

'Arrived in England on May 19, 1900 from *Cambrian* per P. & O. *Victoria* (7).'

Sub Lieutenant: 15 January 1900. As seen above he arrived back in England on 19 May and then on, '1 June 1900 joined college.' Studying at the Royal Naval College, Greenwich.

H.M. Queen Victoria died at Osborne House, Isle of Wight, on 22 January 1901, aged eighty one years. The story of the Naval party hauling the gun carriage bearing her coffin at Windsor on 2 February 1901 has been related on numerous occasions. Here is Sir Frederick Ponsonby:-

'.... the sailors swarmed round the horses and took off the traces. In an incredibly short time they had got into a compact group and were ready to start (8).'

Percy Noble was a junior officer with this party (9).

MVO: 19 March 1901.

From May 1901 in Torpedo Boat Destroyer *Albatross*, 430 tons, Chatham. From 20 August 1901 in battleship *Hannibal*, 14,900 tons, Channel Squadron. Amongst his young charges in the Gunroom in *Hannibal* was Midshipman Andrew B. Cunningham, the future First Sea Lord and Viscount. **Lieutenant**: 1 April 1902. Remained in *Hannibal*. From 19 February 1903 in battleship *Russell*, 14,000 tons, Mediterranean. Her Captain was Alfred L. Winsloe (see C. in C., 1910). From 7 April 1904 in battleship *Queen*, 15,000 tons, Mediterranean. Eight months later he left the ship:-

'Left Malta overland: 21/12/04. 14/1/05: lent *Firequeen* for instruction in Signals (10).'

From 2 January 1905 Flag Lieutenant to Rear Admiral Alfred L. Winsloe in cruiser *Sapphire*, Chatham. *Firequeen*, 446 tons, had been a private yacht, *Candace*, however in 1882 the Admiralty had acquired her for 'special services' (11). It would appear that at the time also she was being used for Signals purposes. Eventually his actual signals course was to commence in *Victory* on 25 September 1905 and from which, on 23 January 1906, he was to emerge with a first class certificate. As mentioned earlier, in *Sapphire* Admiral Winsloe commanded torpedo craft and submarine flotillas. As a young Flag Lieutenant one can only surmise that his exposure to those aspects of life afloat may have served to confirm to Percy Noble that he had made a good choice in selecting Signals as his specialization.

From 1 January 1907 Lieut. and Commander in TBD *Ribble*, 590 tons, Tender to *Sapphire*.

From 29 October 1907 Lieut. and Commander in TBD *Peterel*, 370 tons, tender to *Hecla*, Depot Ship for TBDs, Home Fleet, Portsmouth. From 14 January 1908 in *Victory*, Portsmouth, 'For Signal School'. From 2 June 1908 temporarily appointed, for a period of just over four months, in HM Yacht *Victoria and Albert*, 4,700 tons. Just a few days later, 9/10 June, he was present on the occasion of the most successful visit paid by H.M. King Edward VII to Reval (Tallinn) in order to meet and confer with Tsar Nicholas II. Included in the Royal party was Admiral of the Fleet Lord Fisher (12).

Between 24 March and 15 December 1909 Lieut. and Commander in TBD *Angler*, 335 tons, Mediterranean, tender to *Orion*, Base Ship for TBDs, Malta.

From 25 January 1910 Flag Lieutenant to Vice Admiral Sir Alfred L. Winsloe, C. in C., China in *Minotaur*, 14,600 tons. This period of service in the Far East was to end as follows:-

'9 August 1911. Ordered by telegram to be sent home from *Minotaur* so as to arrive by 9 October 1911, having been selected for the Royal Yacht – 17/9/11 arrived home (13).'

From 5 October 1911 First Lieutenant in HM Yacht *Victoria and Albert*, 4,700 tons, Portsmouth.

On 18 February 1913, as his second wife, he married Celia Emily Kirkman Hodgson, daughter of Robert Kirkman Hodgson, JP and Lady Honora Janet, nee Boyle, daughter of Sir Richard Edmund St. Lawrence Boyle, Ninth Earl of Cork and Orrery (1829-1904). They were to have one son, Charles Patrick Cay Noble (1914-1988), who made his career in the City but always held a passion for the Navy. As a Lieutenant, RNVR, Charles was to commence his WW2 Naval career in the light cruiser *Calcutta*, ending as a Lieut. Commander assisting in the escort of surrendered U-boats into safe custody in Scottish waters. An extract taken from his obituary follows:-

> 'When the RNVR became the RNR, Noble was London Division Commanding Officer and in 1958 became its first Commodore (14).'

Sadly, after just two years of marriage, Percy Noble's first wife, Diamantina Isabella Campbell, had died in 1909. Her parents, Allan Campbell and Adelaide Diamantina Bourne, had married in Mauritius on 24 July 1879. He had married her in St. Peter's, Eaton Square on 16 July 1907. On retiring from the Navy, their son, Commander Sir Allan Herbert Percy Noble (1908-1982), was to enter parliament as conservative member for Chelsea and between 1956 and 1959 was to be Minister of State for Foreign Affairs (15).

Commander: 31 August 1913. Continued to serve in *Victoria and Albert* until October 1913.

From 28 December 1913 Commander of cruiser *Achilles*, 13,550 tons, 2CS. Captain Arthur L. Cay, Grand Fleet (16). From 9 September 1916 Commander of the new building, 'large light cruiser', *Courageous* (17).

Captain: 30 June 1918. From 15 October 1918 in command cruiser *Calliope*. She flew the Flag of Rear Admiral Allan F. Everett, CB (see C. in C., 1924).

From 10 March 1919 Flag Captain *Calcutta*, 8LCS America and West Indies Station, Rear Admiral Sir Allan F. Everett, KCMG. During November 1919 the services of parties from the ship were called upon to help control some restless colonial subjects:-

> 'Colonial Government of Trinidad expressed thanks for valuable services rendered during and after disturbances at Port of Spain and Tobago (18).'

At the end of the commission accompanied Admiral Everett homewardbound leaving New York on 12 April 1921 in the well known and popular Cunard Line s.s. *Aquitania*, 45,647 grt. Having proceeded on her maiden voyage in 1914, and following service in both World Wars, it was only in 1950 that *Aquitania* was to be scrapped.

From 17 October 1921 he attended a Technical Course in *Victory* and then, early in 1922 for seven months to July, served as Chief of Staff to the Rear Admiral, Coast of Scotland, Sir John Frederick Ernest Green (1866-1948).

From 14 October 1922 served as Flag Captain to Vice Admiral Sir Edwyn S. Alexander-Sinclair (see C. in C. in 1925) in the battleship *Barham*, 27,500 tons, 1BS, Atlantic Fleet.

CB: 1923.

From 15 May 1925 in command *Ganges*, Boys' Training Establishment, Shotley. These duties included those of, 'Admiralty Representative on the Harwich Harbour Conservancy Board'.

From 2 May 1927 similiarly in command of the Boys' Training Establishment at Gosport, *St. Vincent*.

Director of Operations Division at the Admiralty: 1 March 1928. The Deputy Director was Captain G. Layton (see C. in C., 1940).

Rear Admiral: 10 October 1929.

In March and April 1930 attended the Senior Officers' War Course at Greenwich.

From 22 September 1930 attending Tactical Course, Royal Naval War College, Greenwich.

From 19 January 1931 at the Admiralty, Director of Naval Equipment.

From 15 December 1932 to 14 December 1934 RA 2CS, Home Fleet. Initially Flag in the heavy cruiser *Dorsetshire*, 9,900 tons, Captain Arthur J. Power, himself a future WW2 commander of the Eastern Fleet and later to be an Admiral of the Fleet, then in the light cruiser *Leander*, 7,140 tons.

From 15 February 1935 a Lord Commissioner of the Admiralty as 4SL, Chief of Supplies and Transport. He was appointed to this position, 'in succession to Rear Admiral G. Blake'.

Vice Admiral: 9 May 1935.

Continued as a Lord Commissioner of the Admiralty.

KCB: 23 June 1936.

Appointed C. in C., China on 9 December 1937. In China Admiral Little had been ill with pleurisy consequently was to be invalided back home. On 27 December 1937, just before his departure from England, he wrote to a friend, Vice Admiral Sir Geoffrey Blake, who also was suffering from ill health. This letter of sympathy ends amusingly:-

> '... before I go however I would like to express to you the real regret I felt when Chatfield told me you were going to retire – I am so sad – both for you personally and for the service you loved so well. Why you should be visited with this bad luck I can't imagine. With all the care you took to keep fit and avoid girls – I feel that I am lucky to be alive at all (19).'

Assumed the command on 5 February 1938. First flew his Flag in the heavy cruiser *Cumberland*, 10,000 tons, 5CS, Flag Captain John C. Leach. His Flag Captain from 7 April 1938 in *Kent* was Leslie Haliburton Ashmore, (1893-1974), subsequently Vice Admiral, and father of the future First Sea Lord, Admiral of the Fleet Sir Edward Ashmore, (1919-2016).

In north China in January 1938 Japanese forces had occupied Tsingtao and vicinity.

Finally, after some fifteen years of vacillation, adequate funds had been made available and construction of the naval base up the Johore Strait at Singapore had progressed to the stage that on Monday, 14 February 1938 the new graving dock could be opened officially by HE The Governor, Sir Thomas Shenton Whitelegge Thomas (1879-1962). To reach this happy position, and in an effort to strengthen the resolve of successive governments in London, over the years considerable pressure had been applied by the governments of both Australia and New Zealand. These two Dominions long had perceived the future danger of Japanese aggression. As early as 22 February 1924, in a note on the subject of the base, Sir Maurice Hankey (1877-1963) recorded that New Zealand had voted GBP 100,000 towards the cost of the proposed facility (20). On 16 December 1924 the Governor of Hong Kong, Sir Reginald Stubbs (1876-1947), had offered that colony's contribution, the substantial sum of GBP 250,000 (21). Malaya itself had contributed an even greater sum, GBP 2,000,000. Even so, far from being an impregnable 'fortress', Singapore island was to remain open to assault by land down the Malay peninsula.

Although dating back to 24 February 1936 the following anecdote perhaps, in a rather sad way, sums up the torpid handling of the matter by successive British governments between the wars. The occasion was during a cocktail party held that evening in Hong Kong onboard *Tamar* in honour of General Sir William Edmund Ironside, from 1939 to 1940 to be CIGS, and a future Field Marshal:-

> 'He had been disgusted to find at Singapore that the 15" guns decided on ten years ago for its defence had not yet been placed, also that the 9.2" guns which are in position have no sights (22).'

Writing to the C. in C. from Hankow on 21 April 1938, RAY, who continued to be R.V. Holt, enclosed a copy of a report submitted on 7 February 1938 by the commanding officer of the gunboat *Aphis,* stationed at Wuhu. Two extracts follow from which examples of the behaviour of some of the Japanese military, as the occupying force, may be noted:-

> 'On arrival at Wuhu p.m. 28 January, a large fire was observed about eight miles N.N.E. of the city. I was informed ashore that the Japanese had set fire to a village in that direction having massacred many of the inhabitants in retaliation for the killing of two Japanese soldiers who had been molesting the women there two days previously. Some refugees from this village had made their way into the American Hospital and Mission compounds. Aware of this, the Japanese had notified the foreigners in charge of compounds that all refugees were to be cleared out of the compounds and that food supplies would be cut off from the compounds until they were clear of refugees. The foreigners concerned were anxious that all men and elderly women should be

discharged from their care but were reluctant to release the younger women in view of what was known to be happening to some twenty captured in the village mentioned above. The threat about food supplies did not materialise although much was commandeered on its way and several half grown bean crops were uprooted.'

'The situation is by no means normal. Only yesterday a Japanese soldier shot my fox-terrier on the bund abreast the ship because he barked at him (23).'

As a continuation of what might be described as a general softening up process, during mid 1938 the Japanese Army Air Force also commenced to bomb Canton. As an example of their success here follows an extract taken from a letter dated 3 June 1938. It was written to his London head office by Mr. W.H. Lock, Taipan of Messrs. Butterfield and Swire in Hong Kong:-

'Canton has been severely bombed during the past week. The principal objects of attack have been the Wongsha station, which is the terminus of the Hankow railway and which has been badly damaged, and government offices in the city.

The Saichuen cement works has only been damaged. There has been very great loss of life, particularly around Wongsha station, and a large exodus of population into the country and to Hong Kong (24).'

Outside Shanghai during the latter part of the previous year a number of Chinese army units had fought well against the Japanese invading military. Unfortunately the following example gives an account of the more usual form of leadership of the defending armies in the field.

By now Japan had advanced well up the Yangtse, taken Wuhu, and on 12 June 1938 had captured Anking, the capital of the Province of Anhwei. Continuing upstream, then a few miles below Kiukiang, which town is 493 sea miles from the open sea, at Matang the Chinese had constructed a massive boom across the River. The sorry tale continues:-

'The next obstacle (faced by the advancing Japanese) was the strongly fortified Matang boom. This position was considered impregnable. It was covered by fortified positions equipped with modern artillery and should have held up the Japanese advance indefinitely. Actually military units which left Anking on 22 June effected landings at two points on the right bank on 24 June, and by the evening of 26 June were concentrated five kilometres South of Matang. The Matang positions were occupied, allegedly without a shot being fired from the fortress guns, on 28 June. It was later reported that the Chinese general responsible for the defence, and many of his subordinates, had been executed (25).'

Once past Kiukiang then the Japanese were able to set their sights on another most important centre, Hankow in the tri-city of Wuhan. The Chinese however did have one useful ally, the climate. 'The campaign against Hankow took some time to gather force owing to the intense heat, and the prevalence of sickness – cholera, dysentery and malaria.'

Not surprisingly the fact that the atmosphere between Japan and Great Britain was strained could extend to the officers and men manning the warships of their respective Navies. A minute but revealing example took place late in July 1938 when the heavy cruiser *Dorsetshire*, Captain Francis R. Barry, was at Wei-Hai-Wei. The Japanese heavy cruiser *Ashigara*, 13,000 tons, also chanced to pay a short visit and, as was the usual custom, a small party of British officers went over to pay their respects to their opposite numbers. One of the British Lieutenants in the group subsequently was to record:-

'... in their Wardroom the Japanese were cold, aloof and unsmiling. It was a most difficult occasion and we were glad to return to *Dorsetshire* (26).'

Canton fell to Japan on 22 October 1938. To seize that important city the enemy forces first had landed in Bias Bay on 12 October. Foreigners resident in China had anticipated a wretched resistance and, sadly, this proved to be the case:-

'Sensational reports of counter-attacks upon, and the evacuation of, Canton were issued from Chungking and Canton but had no foundation in fact. Seeing that Canton had been preparing for resistance to a Japanese invasion for over a year, its capture with not more than a few score Japanese casualties, within nine days of landing, after an advance of about 175 kilometres over what was supposed to be a heavily fortified terrain, gave rise to rumours of treachery. These were denied by the Chinese authorities with the somewhat unconvincing explanation that resistance had been rendered impossible by the concentration of Cantonese units in the Wuhan sector (27).'

Writing to the Admiralty, Sir Percy summarised the above:-

'Japanese forces landed in Bias Bay on 12.10.38. Estimated that their forces landed from about sixty transports. The city was occupied without opposition on 22.10.38. However the retreating Chinese did destroy, or attempt to destroy, power plants, factories and so on (28).'

To look ahead just briefly it is relevant to note that on 4 October 1939 from Hong Kong, Messrs. Butterfield and Swire, writing to London, enclosed a copy of a report entitled, "A Letter from Canton". It was prepared by Mr. Ian Morrison, recently personal secretary to Sir Robert Craigie, British Ambassador to Tokyo. The contents reveal two aspects of the 'trade' which Japan was carrying on with their recently occupied territory in China:-

'Firstly large quantities of scrap iron are being shipped back to Japan. The wasted areas have been completely denuded of metal. Iron grids have been torn from the front of shops. Fire hydrants have been dug up from the streets. Coming up the river I saw the wheels and axles from coaches of the Canton-Hankow Railway being loaded onto a transport. Since the Japanese Railways have a different guage I presume that these wheels will be melted down.

Secondly, a certain amount of raw silk from the Delta, which again is paid for in military yen (they are printed in millions and have no exchange value), is being shipped direct to India by (I think) Mitsui (29).'

Meanwhile, the writing on the wall being perfectly clear, from Hankow on 20 October members of the British Diplomatic Mission to China embarked in the river gunboat *Tern*, 262 tons, to take passage at the start of their journey upriver which, in due course, was to end at Chungking.

Hankow, in the Wuhan sector, fell to Japanese forces on 26 October 1938. One Chinese source claims as follows. 'The campaign to defend Wuhan lasted over four months, including hundreds of big and small battles, inflicting 200,000 casualties on the Japanese.'

Comparing the forces utilised the same source mentions 350,000 men, 500 aircraft and 120 warships for Japan, being opposed by 1.1 million men, but only 40 warships and 'more than 100 aircraft' for the Nationalist government (30).

Just prior to the fall of Hankow/Wuhan, the new capital of China under Chiang Kai-shek was established at Chungking (31).

Well before Chiang's withdrawal up the River to Chungking a great exodus had commenced. Rather naturally at the foot of the Gorges, Ichang, a bottleneck situation rapidly developed. The Master of the China Navigation Company twin screw Upper River steamer *Wanliu*, 781 grt, has left a short description of his life during those several months from the late spring of 1938 on into 1939:-

'I arrived at Ichang to find it crowded with shipping which had reached the end of the line. They could go no further; the town was filled with refugees; all roads led to Ichang; and pressure on the Gorge shipping, steamers and junks, was building up. The Upper Yangtze was the slender thread that connected this human flood and its impedimenta with the promised land.

For the next fourteen months, that is until the summer of 1939 when the exodus was halted by the

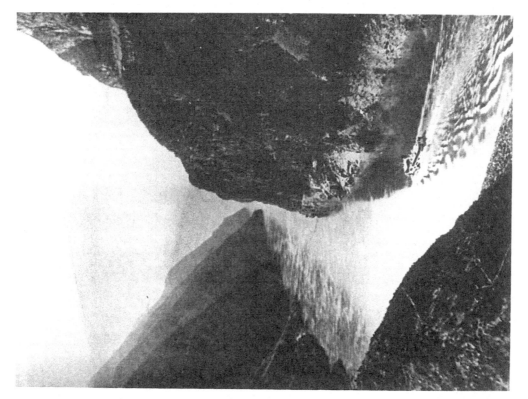

In the Yangtse Gorges below Chungking. Here is seen a ship streaming through the 24 mile long Wushan Gorge. In these waters no ship can come to anchor or turn therefore main propulsion systems must be reliable! Note that in these gorges between winter and summer the water level in those days might vary by as much as 180 to 190 feet. Today the gigantic dam structure accross the Rover at Sandouping has resulted in a great control of the river water level thus rate of flow upstream and through the gorges.

Admiral Thomas C. Hart, USN (1877-1971).
From 25 July 1939 he was appointed C. in C., Asiatic Fleet.
Necessarily the appointment expired following the Japanese assault in the East.

near approach of the Japanese, conditions on the Upper Yangtze were almost indescribable. Sleep became something from another age. One appeared at times to be almost too frightened to think. Ships ran non-stop, there were no facilities for repairs at Ichang or Chungking, the military seized the high quality coal at Chungking, leaving us to scratch for anything we could find along the way. Safety precautions like draught restrictions, watermark minimum and maximum regulations, delays to avoid freshets, all went by the board (32).'

In China by the end of 1938 the Japanese invasion forces had reached a position of stalemate which was to endure until the end of 1944. Neither side, Nationalist and Communist China in uneasy and loose association on the one hand, nor Japan on the other, was capable of overthrowing the other. As one authority has written:-

'In spite of the appearance of a victorious war, the Japanese army was able to control only major cities and railway lines, and its authority failed to penetrate the interior (33).'

By adopting these tactics of an army in being, and through guerrilla operations, the Chinese were to provide a most valuable service in keeping very appreciable Japanese forces on their guard and occupied until the eventual Allied victory. In part this explains the huge expenditure in lives, equipment and treasure by which the Allies, especially the U.S.A., were to do their best to ensure that China remained actively involved during WW2.

The Soviets too, fully appreciating the danger to their Siberian front from further Japanese assault, also sent military aid to China. This assistance commenced in 1938 and was increased in 1939. Pragmatically however, this aid was not sent to the Chinese communists, but was despatched overland to Chiang Kai-shek. Only later would the emphasis return in favour of their communist brethren.

In *Kent* in April 1939 the C. in C. visited Batavia. There he participated in talks with Dutch naval and military commanders from which it was made clear to him that in the event of Japanese aggression against those Dutch possessions then the Dutch immediately would declare war themselves. In addition the Dutch put informal proposals to him concerning possible spheres of co-operation with Britain in the event of any such aggression (34).

Admiral: 3 May 1939.

Back in north China late in August 1939 the C. in C., Asiatic Fleet, Admiral Thomas C. Hart, USN, arranged to visit Admiral Noble:-

'… Admiral Hart took the opportunity to go up to Weihaiwei (from Tsingtao) and return the call of Admiral Sir Percy Noble, the British naval commander in Chinese waters. He also intended to have a "very confidential" talk with Noble about possible actions "if this situation develops into actual hostilities with the Japs." When Hart arrived on 25 August he found that developments halfway around the globe had caused Noble to be more interested in the Germans than in the Japanese. Hitler was making menacing noises about Poland, and the Nazi-Soviet non aggression pact signed just two days earlier made it easier to convert those words into action. In response to these developments Sir Percy was going to concentrate his surface ships at Hong Kong. After coolly and matter-of-factly providing this disturbing news, Noble bid Hart goodbye and departed to lead the British ships, now battened down and in a state of war readiness, south towards Hong Kong (35).'

30 August 1939: Vice Admiral Yamamoto Isoroku was appointed C. in C., Combined Fleet, IJN.

In Wakanoura Bay, Kii Strait on 1 September 1939 his flag was hoisted in the Fleet Flagship, HIJMS *Nagato*, Captain Fukudome Shigeru (1891-1971), later Vice Admiral.

In Europe on 3 September 1939 that stage of WW2 commenced.

On receipt of the news in his flagship Admiral Yamamoto's own personal feelings may be gathered from the following quote taken from a letter he wrote to a friend on 4 September:-

'The great upheaval now occurring in Europe makes me feel terrified when I think of our relationship with Germany and Italy (36).'

Admiral Yamamoto Isoroku, (1884-1943)
On 30 August 1939 appointed C. in C., Combined Fleet, IJN.

From an Englishman, long resident in China and now living in the new, temporary capital of Nationalist China, Chungking, here follows two extracts taken from his memoirs:-

'On the 3ʳᵈ September we listened to Chamberlain's very moving speech, announcing a state of war between England and Germany. Later that night, after the First Alarm had sounded, we sat in our little drawing room with all lights out except for the glow from the indicator face of our radio set, hoping against hope that the Japanese would delay a little longer so as to enable us to listen to King George's speech. But at seven minutes to midnight, the hour set for it, the lights in the city were turned off at the main and we had to turn our attention to the war on our doorstep. That night in Chungking more than a thousand innocent people were killed, either being buried alive or trapped against the city wall in a raging inferno of flames. In the morning fallen masonry, plaster, shattered glass, broken telegraph wires and poles littered the streets, while flames and smoke rose high over Chungking's jagged ramparts. With hardly a breathing space the (air) raids followed each other.'

'Although the Chinese were terrified of the raids, they faced them, perhaps because they seemed to be inevitable, with that dogged endurance which is one of the most remarkable features of the race. Far from accomplishing their purpose of terrorizing the Chinese people into submission, the Japanese bombings heightened their determination to resist (37).'

24 September 1939. The seaplane tender *Langley* AV-3 arrived at the Cavite base in Manila Bay. She was the first such ship to serve with the U.S. Asiatic Fleet.

21 January 1940: the NYK passenger liner *Asama Maru*, Captain Y. Watanabe, on passage home from the west coast USA via Honolulu, was stopped at sea some thirty five miles off the Honshu coast at the entrance to Tokyo Bay. Twenty one German citizens, one time crew members from the scuttled Norddeutscher Lloyd liner *Columbus*, 32,581 grt, and who were endeavouring to return home to rejoin the German war effort, were removed from the ship by a boarding party from the British light cruiser *Liverpool*, 9,400 tons, Captain A.D. Read (38).

From 15 November 1939 to 10 April 1941 the chief of staff to Admiral Yamamoto Isoruku, Combined Fleet, was his old friend and now Rear Admiral Fukudome Shigeru. In the spring of 1940 it was to him that:-
> 'Yamamoto first mentioned the possibility of an attack on Hawaii: "Kokubokan ni yoru Hawai kogeki wa dekinai mono kanaa" – "Would an attack on Hawaii using aircraft carriers really be impossible" (39).'

From 21 March 1940 to 8 May 1945 Rear Admiral Paul Wenneker (1890-1979), later Admiral, was to serve as Naval Attache in the German Embassy, Tokyo, and as Admiral, East Asia. The genial and most competent Wenneker, as a younger officer previously had held that office between 28 December 1933 and 23 August 1937. Dating back to this earlier appointment to Tokyo he had been on excellent terms with the then assistant British Naval Attache, Commander (E) George Ross, subsequently to retire as a Rear Admiral. In his memoirs the late Admiral Ross left this rather charming vignette:-
> 'Paul Wenneker was a bachelor with a great sense of humour and never took life too seriously. We became good friends. After Hitler came to power I noticed that Wenneker had added a small swastika to the decorations on his uniform.
> "What on earth is that?" I asked him.
> "Affenteater (monkey business)", he replied with a smile and a wink (40).'

30 March 1940, at Nanking the installation of Wang Ching-wei (1883-1944), former associate of Dr. Sun Yat-sen and Chiang Kai-shek, by Japan as the nominal head of their regime in occupied China.

Following his admirable handling of the heavy cruiser *Exeter*, 8,300 tons, at the successful Battle of the River Plate on 13 December 1939, from 24 May 1940 Captain Frederick Secker Bell (1897-1973) was to be appointed Flag Captain in the base ship at Singapore, *Sultan*.

After an absence of barely a year, during the spring of 1940 that British diplomat of very many years experience in Japan, Sir George Bailey Sansom, returned to Tokyo on a special mission from the Foreign Office. He was dismayed by what he found. Relevant extracts taken from a series of letters to his wife follow:-
> 'Tokyo, June 8, 1940. The general atmosphere in Tokyo is not at all agreeable. The town looks drab, and the people look rather melancholy. (-) The internal political situation is rather tense.'
> 'Tokyo, June 1940. Japan is well advanced on the totalitarian road now. The change since last year is very marked; and recent German victories have given tremendous impetus to the movement. I doubt very much if Japan will keep quiet now. She is trying desperately to finish off the "China Incident" somehow or other, so as to be free for other adventures. I don't see how she can resist such a tempting morsel as the Dutch East Indies, to say nothing of Indo-China. (-) The atmosphere is not agreeable.

I catch myself being quite gratified when I get a glimpse of old fashioned politeness.'

'Tokyo, June 20, 1940. Things look rather bad here, as the Japanese military, who anticipate our defeat or at least a struggle which will leave us helpless, are increasing pressure on us. I think it *may* end in a state of war, though we hope this can be avoided. They want to stake a claim in French Indo-China, and have their eyes on Hong Kong and the Burma frontier. It is an uneasy situation, to say the least of it.'

'Tokyo, July 1, 1940. It is remarkable to see how Japan has changed in a year. Manners of course have sadly deteriorated, and they tell me that pilfering is on the increase. (-) It's sad to see virtue disappearing from the scene. Everyone talks of the New Order, which to me looks as if it would be a kind of chaos under regulations. Yoshida said to me that, if events in Europe show that Might is Right, then Japan will adopt the doctrine wholeheartedly he fears (41).'

'Nikko, July 27, 1940. It is infuriating to see the rude, tough kind of Japanese in the ascendant, and to know that all the time in this country there are immense reserves of decency and kindliness and the essential things of civilization (42).'

As can be imagined, up until the time that he left Japan a few weeks later, Sir George, sadly disillusioned, in his correspondence was to continue to include such comments as, 'there are no standards of behaviour left', 'the most innocent persons are being arrested', and, 'the authorities are making a drive against "economic sabotage"', in other words many of the ghastly signs of the imposition of a totalitarian regime.

In the interim on 10 June 1940 Italy entered the war as an ally of Germany.

Then on 22 June 1940 France signed an Armistice with Germany. Even before this armistice was signed, on 20 June France had submitted to Japanese pressure and agreed that Japan should control the nature of the rail freight being transported north from Hanoi in French Indo-China to Kunming in Nationalist controlled China. This left the Burma Road as the one overland supply route remaining for Britain and the USA to use into China to forces controlled by Chiang Kai-shek.

On Tuesday, 2 July 1940 in the British built Australian owned motorship *Kanimbla*, the C. in C. arrived at Singapore from Hong Kong via Saigon. At Saigon talks had taken place with the French authorities (43).

In mid July Britain too submitted to Japanese pressure and agreed that for three months, until 18 October 1940, the Burma Road between Lashio and Kunming would be closed. There was a degree of subtlety associated with this diplomatic gesture however, as that was the season of the South West monsoon so in practical terms little traffic in any case could or would have passed over the Road.

Meanwhile in their aerial campaign against the Nationalist Chinese in Chungking, gradually the IJN began to suffer greater casualties from the steadily improving capability of the Chinese Air Force. From Hankow the IJN 'Claude' fighter did not have an adequate range to escort the bombers for that long distance. The answer rested with the new IJN fighter, an aircraft which in due course was to astonish the Allies with its speed, manoeuvrability and range, the Mitsubishi Navy Type O 'Zero' or 'Zeke'. On 19 August 1940 twelve of these machines first escorted bombers in a raid against Chungking, a round trip of some one thousand nautical miles. On that occasion no Chinese aircraft were encountered. However within a month, on 13 September, success was to be achieved when thirteen Zero aircraft, model A6M2, led by Lieutenant Shindo Saburo, shot down twenty seven Russian built fighters of the Chinese Air Force. This date was the occasion of the thirty fifth raid made by aircraft of the Japanese 12th Air Corps operating from Hankow against Chungking. (44).

On 20 August 1940 Japan, having subjected the new French Vichy government to additional pressure, signed an agreement which was to give her two important and additional advantages in her war with Nationalist China. Both concerned North French Indo-China. Firstly Japan was granted the use of air bases from which to launch bombing attacks against targets in China. Such targets would include the Burma Road. Secondly she was granted the use of military bases from which her army would be better positioned to launch attacks against Chiang Kai-shek from the south.

However matters did not move entirely in Japan's favour. Initially the French colonial authorities resisted these terms and, largely as a face saving gesture, fought briefly until capitulation on 22 September. In addition, and of greater importance, the United States took two steps, firstly increasing financial aid to Chiang and, secondly, placing an embargo on the sale of scrap iron and steel to nations outside the British Empire and Western Hemisphere.

The new C. in C., Vice Admiral Sir Geoffrey Layton, arrived at Hong Kong on 29 August 1940 in the CPR steamer *Empress of Asia*, 16,909 grt. In turn on 5 September Sir Geoffrey continued to Singapore in the China Navigation (Butterfield and Swire) steamer *Anhui*, 3,494 grt. Finally at Singapore on 12 September he assumed command of the Station in succession to Sir Percy (45).

In Berlin Japan signed the Tripartite Pact on 27 September 1940, the three nations bound together being Germany, Italy and Japan. Although on behalf of Japan the necessary negotiations had been undertaken by Foreign Minister Matsuoka Yosuke, signing for Japan was their ambassador to Berlin, Kurusu Saburo (1886-1954).

As was reported from Hong Kong, '4 October 1940: Admiral Sir Percy Noble left Hong Kong in s.s. *Empress of Russia* on passage to U.K. (46).'

From 18 November 1940 he served in *President*, the Admiralty.

In succession to Admiral Sir Martin E. Dunbar-Nasmith, VC, between 17 February 1941 and 1 November 1942 he filled the important post of C. in C., Western Approaches, HMS *Eaglet* (47). There at Derby House in Liverpool his presence was felt quickly:-

> 'There was the impression of many and various threads in the battle (of the Atlantic) being drawn together into one firm controlling hand (48).'

It was during this period at Liverpool that his most valuable work, including the re-organization of escort groups and the establishment of training groups such as the school at Tobermory, served to lay the foundation which his successor, the ex-submariner Admiral Sir Max K. Horton, was to find invaluable. In addition:-

> 'He took particular care to liaise with RAF Coastal Command (49).'

In succession to Rear Admiral Wilfrid Rupert Patterson (1893-1954) next appointed as head of the British Admiralty Delegation, BAD, in Washington, DC, HMS *Saker*: 3 December 1942 – 20 November 1944. In due course there he was to be succeeded by Admiral Sir James Somerville who reached New York in RMS *Queen Mary* on 28 October 1944.

As may be imagined this position in Washington was most significant, both before and after the United States actively entered WW2, therefore a little elaboration follows. As a Captain, Wilfrid R. Patterson had commanded the battleship *King George V* at the time of the sinking of *Bismarck* in May 1941. Promoted Rear Admiral on 28 July 1942, then for just a few weeks, interregnum, he had been head of BAD in Washington in succession to Admiral Sir Andrew Browne Cunningham who from October 1942 had been appointed Naval C. in C. of the Allied Expeditionary Force, North Africa and Mediterranean. Sir Andrew, mentioned earlier, is the future First Sea Lord and Admiral of the Fleet Viscount Cunninghham of Hyndhope (1883-1963).

In Washington the Chief of Staff to President Roosevelt was Admiral William D. Leahy, later Fleet Admiral. At just about the time of the turning of the tide, so to speak, of the anti U-boat campaign, on 14 April 1943 Admiral Noble called on him, '.. to discuss the possibility of increasing the rate of production of escort vessels that were being used against German submarines in the Battle of the Atlantic'. The Americans themselves then were, '... much concerned with the slow delivery of both planes and escort vessels (50).'

During the Pacific War in WW2 the Chief of Operations and C. in C., U.S. Fleet was the straight speaking, fiery Admiral Ernest J. King, also later to be Fleet Admiral (51). On occasion Admiral Leahy was able to pour oil on stormy waters:-

Fleet Admiral Ernest J. King, USN (1878-1956)
Chief of Naval Operations from 26 March 1942 to 15
December 1945.
Also Commander in Chief, United States Fleet.
In this capacity most successfully he directed U.S.N.
operations worldwide during WW2.

'The plain-spoken Admiral (King) did not hide his irritation at some of the tactics of our British ally, and Admiral Sir Percy Noble (--) complained to me personally and confidentially that he was not getting "courteous cooperation" from the American Admiral. I got King in a corner soon after, passed on Sir Percy's complaint, and asked him to be more polite. King did quiet down, for a while at least (52).'

First and Principal ADC to H.M. King George VI: 21 October 1943-1945.
GBE: 1 January 1944.
From 27 December 1944 to April 1946 served in *President*, 'for miscellaneous services at the Admiralty'.
Having reached the age of sixty five years, on 16 January 1945 placed on the Retired List, but was re-appointed on retirement.

On 11 March 1946 he wrote to inform The Admiralty that he had, 'Received Hon. Degree of LL.D from the University of Liverpool.'
Eventually he reverted to the Retired List on 21 March 1947 (53).

Following his death on 25 July 1955 the usual obituary notices appeared in the national press.
Two days later *The Times* informed their readers:-
    'Funeral private and no memorial service, by his request. No flowers, but donations, if desired, to King George's Fund for Sailors (54).'

This was followed in London on 1 August 1955 by a fine tribute paid by one of his WW2 escort group commanders dating from his time in office as C. in C, Western Approaches in Liverpool in 1941. An extract follows:-

'Victory in the Atlantic was only made possible by the perfection of the base organisation instituted by Admiral Noble in 1941. Developments in this organisation in later years were comparatively simple since the whole edifice was solidly and soundly based. The secret lay in the fact that Sir Percy was one of the rare admirals who really understood how to use a staff. He had a gift for selecting the right man for the right job and having put him there he gave him his entire trust. He took a personal interest in his staff and made each one feel he was dependent on him. (-)

As commander of one of the first escort groups I used to visit the C. in C. on return from every convoy. We would talk for an hour and he gave the impression that every word you said was important and that he had unlimited time to spare for you. So it was with all. His life and his staff were so well organised that he gave a feeling of tranquillity. The effect of these interviews was to raise one's morale immediately... (55)'

At the request of the late Professor Arthur Marder, on 17 October 1979 Sir Percy's son, Commander the Rt. Hon. Sir Allan Noble, PC KCMG DSO DSC DL, prepared a few notes covering aspects of his father's life. Arthur Marder also asked for any papers or information concerning Sir Percy and the "redoubtable Ernie King". As the following extracts indicate, he commenced with comments on the Admiral's enthusiasm for sport and on his determination to keep fit, and then continued:-

'As a young man he played rugger for the Navy versus the Army at fly-half, and was a Scotland Reserve. He continued as a physical fitness enthusiast doing Sandow's exercises. During the first world war he always went for long walks when Executive Officer of a cruiser, be it Rosyth or Scapa Flow, which habit he continued as an Admiral. When C. in C., Western Approaches he had set walks in Sefton Park , his car taking him to the "start" and picking him up at the "finish", thus getting the maximum exercise in the shortest time. In Washington he used to play tennis in Henry Spenser's group. A naval officer has to be prepared to take part in what is offered by the "station", from polo to fishing, so he was good at tennis, golf, squash racquets and cricket (--).

He was fond of riding but could not really afford hunting, except the Dartmoor from Devonport and the Calpe at Gibraltar, both of which he enjoyed to the full. He won a naval officers' "scurry" at Gibraltar as a Captain. The same really applied to polo, except for Malta as a young man. This meant, of course, that he kept his good figure, and fitted in with his reputation of being the "best dressed officer in the Navy".

He went to a good tailor, and took great trouble over his clothes, while many naval officers did not care a hoot. When he died of a heart attack at 75, people said how good it was to remember him walking smartly down St. James's Street, and not as an invalid. He was a man of commanding presence and appearance, and was a fine seaman and administrator. He was a master of his profession at all stages, for he believed that a happy ship had to be an efficient ship. As regards discipline, he believed that not only should the individual sailor get a fair deal, but should feel and know that he had. He therefore took great trouble with "defaulters" and "requestmen". He believed that you must like your men, and know all about them, which would lead to them respecting and indeed liking you. All this lead to his great success as C. in C., Western Approaches, because it filtered down to the youngest sailor or Wren that the C. in C. was human and knew all about them and their difficulties. As in his ship commands earlier, his Headquarters in Liverpool was a happy family, and it was always fun and enjoyable to do anything with or for him. When his first wife died after they had been married for two years, he volunteered to go to the Antarctic with Captain Scott, but this was not to be. He went to the China Station, and on his return was appointed to the Royal Yacht for the second time. His second marriage took place a year before the first world war.

He had a great admiration and affection for the Royal Family from that time, and later became First and Principal Naval ADC, and on his retirement, Rear Admiral of the United Kingdom. With this background no better man could have been chosen to lead the British Admiralty Delegation in Washington, in 1942. His urbanity, dignity, and charm of manner, coupled with his wide knowledge and experience, made him popular with his American colleagues and in a position when the utmost tact and delicacy was often required.

Like others he, of course, had his difficulties with Admiral King, but at the Second Quebec Conference, did not the President accept Mr. Churchill's offer of the British Pacific Fleet, of which it was known that King did not approve? (56)'

Earlier, on 6 June 1979, Professor Marder had written to Sir Allan. On the reverse of this letter, in Sir Allan's own hand, is an amusing note in which is indicated the opinion held by Ernie King in respect of three of the heads of the British Admiralty Delegation in Washington during WW2. These had been Admirals Cunningham who is "ABC", Noble who is "Daddy", and Somerville who is "James S":-

"ABC as 'the old sea-dog'.

Daddy as the 'diplomat'.

James S called him 'an old b.......' and won the day."

NOTES

1. NA ADM 196/45. *Service Record.*
2. Archives Centre, Churchill College, Cambridge. Ref: *NBLE 1/2.* Journals kept by PLH Noble, Midshipman.
   Single screw steamer *Shanghai*, completed in Greenock in June 1889. One of a class of four. Thirty passengers. Early in January 1904 sold to the French owner, Messageries Maritimes, and re-named *Crimee*. Scrapped at Genoa in 1923.
3. NA ADM 53/14062. Log Book *Immortalite.*
4. Ibid.
5. Churchill College. Ref: *NBLE 1/2.* G.A.D. Hay and T.R. Fforde together with Lieut. C. Seymour.
   James Alexander **Swettenham**. Born: 1846. Died: 19 April 1933. Scholar of Clare College, Cambridge. Ceylon Service: 1868-1883. Receiver-General, Cyprus: 1884-1891. Auditor-General, Ceylon: 1891-1895. Colonial Secretary, Singapore: 1895. KCMG: 1898. Acting Governor, Straits Settlements in 1898 and 1900. Governor, British Guiana: 1901-1904. Governor, Jamaica: 1904-1907. *Colonial Office List. Who's Who.* His younger brother was Sir Frank Athelstane **Swettenham** (1850-1946).
6. Ibid.
7. *Service Record.* Single screw steamer *Victoria*, 6,522 grt, completed in 1887, and sold in 1909 for breaking up.
8. Lord Sysonby, *Recollections of Three Reigns,* (London, 1951), 90.
9. Percy Noble, *Funeral of Queen Victoria at Windsor, 2 February 1901,* (Mariner's Mirror, Vol. 37, 1951), 80/1.
10. *Service Record.*
11. David Lyon and Rif Winfield, *The Sail and Steam Navy List,* (London, 2004), 286.
12. Gordon Brook-Shepherd, *Uncle of Europe,* (New York and London, 1975), 325/7. *Recollections of Three Reigns,* 194/6. *Service Record.*
13. *Service Record.*
14. *The Daily Telegraph,* 12 November 1988.
15. *Dictionary of National Biography,* Vol. 40, (OUP, 2004), 958.
16. Captain Arthur L. Cay. At the Battle of Jutland, 31 May 1916, to lose his life when commanding the battlecruiser *Invincible*, sunk by gunfire received from SMS *Lutzow* and *Derfflinger*. Admiral of the Fleet Viscount Jellicoe of Scapa, *The Grand Fleet 1914-1916,* (London, 1919), 466 and 490.
17. After the Great War *Courageous* and her sister, *Glorious*, were to be converted to aircraft carriers. In this new role

Courageous was to commission on 5 May 1928. Under the command of Captain William T. Makeig-Jones, to be torpedoed and sunk in the Western Approaches on 17 September 1939 by *U-29*, Otto Schuhart.

18. *Service Record.*

19. National Maritime Museum, Greenwich. Caird Library. Ref: *BLE/7.*

20. NA CAB 27/236.

21. NA CO 129/485 f. 441.

22. NA ADM 1/9558. Ref. No. 67/194. As SNO, Wuhu, the commanding officer of *Aphis* was Lieut. Commander Robert Basil Stewart Tennant (1905-1969).

23. Diary entry, Monday, 24 February 1936. Captain Arthur John Layard Murray (1886-1959), a future Admiral but then commanding the heavy cruiser *Dorsetshire.* By kind permission of the late Dame Rosemary Murray.

24. B&S Records, SOAS, London: *Box 52.* By kind permission. Mr. Lock also was Deputy Chairman of the Hong Kong and Shanghai Banking Corporation.

25. China Year Book, 1939. 406. Matang is just a short distance downstream from that marvellous sight, the high conical rock feature, in the stream just off the left bank of the River known as 'Little Orphan'.

26. Letter dated 21 August 1997 received by the author from the late Lieut. Commander A.M. Nagle, RN.

27. China Year Book, 1939. 408.

28. NA ADM 116/3902.

29. B&S Records, SOAS, London: *Box 53.* By kind permission.

30. Ed. Bai Shouji, *An Outline History of China, 1919-1949*, (Beijing, 1993), 162/3. The same source suggests that by the end of 1938 Japanese casualties incurred during their invasion of China amounted to 447,000 in total. 172. On the other hand Max Hastings in *All Hell Let Loose*, (London, 2011), 191, gives a very different picture. Regarding the Japanese in China from 1937: '185,000 dead by the end of 1941'.

31. On 28 April 2008 the author and his wife visited the park, a short distance outside Chungking (Chongqing), in which is situated the WW2 Headquarters of General Chiang Kai-shek. It is beautifully maintained. The Chinese certainly have not forgotten the Japanese assault on their country as outside the entrance to the park a huge and colourful sign proclaims both in Chinese and English, "Chongqing Anti – Japanese War Site Museum".

32. Captain Graham Torrible, *Yangtze Reminiscences*, (Hong Kong, 1990), 74.

33. Tsuzuki Chushichi, *The Pursuit of Power in Modern Japan, 1825-1995*, (OUP, 2000), 288.

34. Herman Bussemaker, *Australian War Memorial Journal*, (Issue 29 – November 1996), para. 15.

35. James Leutze, *A Different Kind of Victory*, (Annapolis, 1981), 152/3.

36. Agawa Hiroyuki, *The Reluctant Admiral*, (Tokyo and New York, 1979), 13.

37. G.R.G. Worcester, *The Junkman Smiles*, (London, 1959), 156/8. George Raleigh Gray **Worcester**. Known to many as 'Paul'. Born: 9 August 1890. Died: 5 January 1969. Entered the RN with seniority as a Midshipman: 1 January 1909. Between August 1914 and March 1915, as an acting Sub Lieut., served in the AMC *Empress of Asia*, the CPR liner taken up in Hong Kong for war service. Sub Lieut.: 2 August 1915. Also spent some time in the AMC *Suva*. In 1916, 'Given Gunnery Cert. by Captain (G) Devonport'. Service in AMC *Orvieto*, in peacetime the Orient Line vessel. Lieutenant: 2 August 1917. AMC *Macedonia*, in peacetime the P. & O. liner: 14 January 1918. Submarine Depot Ship *Maidstone*: 15 August 1918 followed by service in submarine *H29* upon commissioning: 14 September 1918. Later service in submarine depot ships *Dolphin* and *Alecto.* Demobilised from date of arrival at Shanghai: 24 April 1919. Subsequently employed by the Chinese Maritime Customs. Assembled and created much of the Maze Collection of Chinese Junks, Kensington Science Museum. Editor, *The Mariner's Mirror*: 1954-1961. For many years resided at Windlesham, Surrey. Obituary, *The Mariner's Mirror*, Vol. 55, 1969, No. 2, 114. NA ADM 340/149: *Service Record.*

38. Arthur Duncan **Read**. Born: 1889. Died: 29 October 1976. Subsequently to command the battleship *Ramilles*: 27 November 1940. Rear Admiral: 6 February 1942. Flag Officer, Ceylon: 1 June 1942 and in this capacity served under Admiral Layton (see C. in C., July 1940). Rear Admiral, 4CS with his flag in *Newcastle*: 15 October 1943. Vice Admiral: 1 June 1945, and retired. *Who's Who. Navy List.*

39. Peter Wetzler, *Hirohito at War*, (Hawaii, 1998), 27/8. Professor Wetzler quotes from *Senshi sosho*, Vol. 10, 7. Gordon W. Prange, *At Dawn We Slept*, (New York, 1981), 14/15. Mr. Prange interviewed Admiral Fukudome on 27 April 1950, 'To the best of Fukudome's recollection, Yamamoto first spoke to him about his daring plan in either March or April 1940'.

40. Library, Imperial War Museum, London. Ref: *86/60/1*, page 254.

41. **Yoshida** Shigeru. Born: 22 September 1878. Died: 20 October 1967. In July 1906 graduated from Tokyo Imperial University and entered the diplomatic corps. Baron in 1921 and an ally of Saionji Kinmochi in his policy of endeavouring to protect the Emperor from direct involvement in political affairs. Served in various diplomatic posts in Europe and China. In the early 1930s Ambassador to Italy, and then, following the attempted coup d'etat by the Army in Tokyo in February 1936, to Great Britain, retiring from the latter position in 1938. In 1936, following the ultranationalist disgrace in Tokyo his name had been put forward for Foreign Minister but the Army had opposed the appointment. During WW2 to put forward various peace proposals. In January 1945 briefly arrested by the Tojo authorities. On 17 October 1945 succeeded Shigemitsu Mamoru as Minister for Foreign Affairs. Prime Minister: May 1946 to May 1947, and from October 1948 to December 1954. As is clear he and Sir George Sansom enjoyed most friendly relations. *Encyclopaedia Britannica*. Yuki Yoshida, *Whispering Leaves in Grosvenor Square: 1936- 1937*, (Folkestone, Kent, 1997), 33-49. Ed. Ian Nish, *Britain and Japan: Biographical Portraits*, II (Richmond, Surrey, 1997), 233/244.

42. Katharine Sansom, *Sir George Sansom and Japan*, (Tallahassee, FL., 1972), 109-115. Also see Sir Hugh Cortazzi and Gordon Daniels, *Britain and Japan: 1859-1991*, (London, 1991), Chapter 22, *Sir George Sansom*.

43. NA ADM 199/374. *Kanimbla*, 10,985 grt, twin screw motor passenger and cargo vessel, registered in Melbourne, taken up for war time service. *Lloyd's Register*.

44. Masatake Okumiya, Jiro Horikoshi and Martin Caidin, *Zero*, (London, 1957), 13/14.

45. NA ADM 199/374. Hong Kong letter dated 25 October 1940.

46. Ibid. Hong Kong letter dated 25 November 1940. *Empress of Russia*, 16,810 grt, quadruple screw steam turbine. Launched in Glasgow on 28 August 1912. Back at Hong Kong, on 28 November 1940 she was requisitioned for war time service as a troopship. Survived the war. At Barrow on 8 September 1945 to be destroyed by fire during a refit. W. Kaye Lamb, *Empress to the Orient*, (Vancouver, 1991), 123/130.

47. Martin Eric **Dunbar-Nasmith**. Born: 1 April 1883. Died: 29 June 1965. His Victoria Cross was awarded: 25 June 1915, following his patrol in the sea of Marmora between 20 May and 8 June 1915 in *E.11*. Captain 30 June 1916. Rear Admiral: 16 January 1928. RA Submarines: 1929-1931. C. in C., East Indies: 1932-1934. Vice Admiral: 12 October 1932. KCB: 4 June 1934. Admiral: 2 January 1936. C. in C., Plymouth and Western Approaches: 1938- 1941. KCMG: 1 January 1955. *Navy List*. Richard Compton-Hall, *Submarines and the War at Sea: 1914-1918*, (London, 1991), 175-181.

48. John Winton, *Convoy*, (London, 1983), 172.

49. Alastair Wilson and Joseph F. Callo, *Who's Who in Naval History*, (Abingdon, Oxon., 2004), 229.

50. Fleet Admiral William D. Leahy, *I Was There*, (New York, 1950), 150.

51. Ernest Joseph **King**. Born in Lorain, OH: 23 November 1878. Died at Portsmouth, NH: 25 June 1956. Annapolis: 1897. Ensign: 7 June 1903. Lieutenant: 7 June 1906. Commander: 1 July 1917. For much of the time that the U.S. was involved in WW1 served on the staff of Admiral H.T. Mayo, C. in C., Atlantic Fleet. A Captain at age forty, from 20 November 1922 commanded Submarine Division Eleven. Air experience followed in command of aircraft tender *Wright*: 28 July 1926. From January 1927 flight training at Pensacola: Naval Aviator #3368: 26 May 1927. In command *Lexington* CV-2: 2 June 1930. Rear Admiral at age fifty four and Chief of the Bureau of Aeronautics in April 1933 in succession to Admiral William A. Moffett. Commander Aircraft, Battle Force: 29 January 1938. As Admiral, from 1 February 1941 C. in C., Atlantic Fleet. C. in C., U.S. Fleet: 30 December 1941. CNO: 13 March 1942. Taking the first step back across the Pacific, US Marines assaulted Guadalcanal: 7 August 1942. Fleet Admiral: 17 December 1944. On 15 December 1945 succeeded as CNO by Fleet Admiral Chester W. Nimitz. Thomas B. Buell, *Master of Sea Power*, (Boston, 1980). Ernest J. King and Walter Muir Whitehill, *Fleet Admiral King*, (New York, 1976). Naval Historical Center, Washington, DC.

52. William D. Leahy, 224.

53. *Service Record*.

54. *The Times*, Wednesday, July 27, 1955.

55. *The Times*. The tribute was written by AJBC.

56. Archives Centre, Churchill College, Cambridge. Ref: *NBLE 1/6*.

The Antarctic expedition to which reference is made is that lead by Captain Robert Falcon Scott in *Terra Nova* who sailed from Cardiff on 15 June 1910. Admiral Sir Edward Evans, *South With Scott*, (London & Glasgow), 13. Scott and his party reached the South Pole on 18 January 1912 but they did not survive the return journey.

10 July 1940 to 8 December 1941
Vice Admiral Sir Geoffrey **Layton**

Geoffrey was born on 20 April 1884 at Glendale, Leyfield Road, West Derby, Liverpool by Sarah Greene, wife of George Layton, who practiced as a solicitor (1). He was one of nine children.

He died in the Royal Naval Hospital, Haslar, Gosport on 4 September 1964.

Eastman's, then entered *Britannia* as a **Cadet** on 15 May 1899 (2).

Midshipman: 30 September 1900. From 15 September 1900 he had been serving in cruiser *Niobe*, 11,000 tons, Channel Squadron, and remained in her. From 19 August 1901 to 1 October 1903 in cruiser *Cambrian*, 4,360 tons, 'Senior Officers' Ship, South East coast of America'. **Sub Lieutenant**: 30 November 1903. On 19 January 1904, 'Joined College', studying at RNC, Greenwich, then at Portsmouth. He achieved the fine total of four 'Firsts'. From 5 April 1905 in cruiser *Thames*, 4,050 tons, 'For course of instruction in Submarine Boats' (3). **Lieutenant**: 30 November 1905. From 1 November 1906 in *Forth*, 'For Command of Submarines'. Later in *Forth* in command submarine *B.7*. To remain based in depot ship *Forth* until 1 January 1909.

On 17 December 1908 he married Eleanor Gwladys Langley of Tettenhall, Wolverhampton, daughter of Frederick Theobald Langley, a solicitor. They were to have three daughters. The two elder were Winifred, later Lady Riches, wife of General Sir Ian Riches, one time Commandant General, Royal Marines, and Diana, later wife of a Bishop of Bermuda, the Rt. Rev. John Armstrong. The youngest, Suzanne, as her second husband, in 1947 was to marry Rear Admiral Michael Kyrle Pope (1916-2008) (4). From Suzanne's writings it is clear that her father ran their home, and the lives of his daughters, along very strict lines (5).

From 1 January 1909 in 'Sea Going Depot Ship for Submarines' *Vulcan*, 6,620 tons, Home Fleet, The Nore, in command submarine *C.21*. From 8 August 1910 to 30 October 1911 he served as Lieutenant in the battleship *Venerable*, 15,000 tons, Atlantic Fleet, then from 17 November 1911 to 5 March 1912 in the armoured cruiser *Shannon*, 14,600 tons. She was the flagship of RA 2CS, Home Fleet, Sir George J.S. Warrender. From 5 March 1912 Lieutenant in the battlecruiser *Indomitable*, 17,250 tons, Flagship, RA 2CS. From 15 August 1912 returned to *Vulcan*, now Depot Ship, Patrol Flotillas, Dundee.

As far as the submarine service was concerned then, slowly, 'the usefulness of submarines for scouting and reporting enemy movements by radio began to be apparent'. In addition:-

> 'In 1912 Lieutenant Geoffrey Layton, commanding *D.2*, made a stronger point by entering the Firth of Forth and making his way unobserved past the patrols. In spite of all the navigational difficulties in a narrow fairway beset by strong tides, he slipped submerged beneath the Forth Bridge and torpedoed his own Depot Ship anchored off Rosyth Dockyard (6).'

Subsequently appointed in command of submarine *C.23*. **Lieutenant Commander**: 30 November 1913.

Remained in command of *C.23*, Depot Ship *Vulcan* at Dundee. From 2 September 1914 in Submarine Depot Ship *Maidstone*, 3,600 tons, Captain Arthur K. Waistell (see C. in C., 1929), in command submarine *E.13*: Eighth S/M Flotilla, Harwich.

In August 1915 he was ordered to enter the Baltic in *E.13*. Unfortunately at night on Wednesday 18/Thursday 19 August, while passing through Ore Sund in the vicinity of the Danish island of Saltholm, speed about seven knots, a malfunctioning gyro compass resulted in her taking the ground badly. Although the boat was in neutral waters, and in spite of Danish protests, German naval forces destroyed her, in the process killing fifteen members of her company and wounding others. With local authorities appearing to turn a blind eye, and with assistance from Danish friends, Layton was able to escape, first to Sweden, then, as Mr. George Perkins, an American, across to Newcastle and the Admiralty via Bergen, Norway (7). He crossed the North Sea from Bergen, 'by s.s. *Venus* due 1 November (8).'

From 4 November 1915 in *Dolphin*, Gosport, 'For Command of Submarines'. At the time Commander Charles J.C. Little (see C. in C., 1936) was serving in the ship as Assistant to Commodore (S). From July 1916 in Depot Ship *Titania*, 'For Command of Submarines'. From 15 November 1916 in light cruiser *Fearless*, 3,440 tons, 'For Command of Submarines', Commander Charles J.C. Little being 'In Command of the Flotilla'.

Commander: 31 December 1916. Continued in *Fearless*.

During the evening of 31 January 1918, when in command of *K.6* in the Firth of Forth, unfortunately in collision with *K.4*, sinking her with much loss of life. Mayhem had arisen on the occasion of the Rosyth Squadron proceeding to sea to rendezvous for exercises with the Grand Fleet. The steam driven submarine boats of the 'K' class were a dangerous aberration. Fortunately their period of service in the Navy was to be short.

Immediately following that unfortunate incident he was borne in *Dolphin*, Gosport on the staff of Commodore (S), and later as Assistant to Rear Admiral (S), but actually served at the Admiralty. From September 1916 the Assistant to the Commodore had been another submariner of note, Commander Cecil Ponsonby Talbot, DSO.

DSO: London Gazette of 17 April 1918. Awarded in recognition of his service in submarines.

To summarise, during the Great War/WW1 he had commanded submarines *C.23*, *E.13*, *Swordfish*, *K.7* and *K.6* (9).

From July 1920 in command Submarine Depot Ship *Maidstone*, 3,600 tons, 'And for Command of Flotilla'.

From 14 July 1921 in command Submarine Depot Ship *Lucia*, 6,005 tons, 'and in Command of Eleventh Submarine Flotilla'.

Captain: 31 December 1922. Continued in *Lucia* as Captain (S).

From 15 April 1924 in command light cruiser *Conquest*, 3,750 tons, as Captain (S), First Submarine Flotilla.

From 31 December 1924 served as Chief of Staff to RA, Submarines in *Dolphin*. From 1 September 1925 RA (S) was Vernon H.S. Haggard.

From 2 August 1927 to 1 August 1929 in the Admiralty as Deputy Director, Operations Division. From 1 March 1928 the Director was Captain Percy L.H. Noble (see C. in C., 1938).

Between 12 August and 13 December 1929 attending Senior Officers' Technical Course at Portsmouth. Also attending the course was Vice Admiral F.C. Dreyer (see C. in C., 1933).

Between 14 January and 19 December 1930 he attended a course at the Imperial Defence College, 9 Buckingham Gate, London S.W. (10).

From 9 January 1931 Flag Captain in heavy cruiser *Suffolk*, 10,000 tons, Flagship, China Station: Vice Admiral Sir William A.H. Kelly.

On 16 November 1931 *Suffolk* was replaced as Flagship by *Kent* 10,000 tons. He continued as Flag Captain to the C. in C., newly promoted Admiral Sir W.A. Howard Kelly, as now he preferred to be known.

From 13 January 1932 to 11 March 1933 continued in *Kent* but as Chief of Staff, and now as **Commodore** second class.

From 18 August 1933 to 3 May 1934 in command battlecruiser *Renown*, 26,500 tons, Battlecruiser Squadron, Home Fleet.

From 4 May 1934, as Commodore second class in *Victory*, in command Royal Naval Barracks, Portsmouth. The C. in C. was Admiral Sir John D. Kelly, brother of his recent C. in C. in China.

Rear Admiral: 24 January 1935.
Continued in command RNB, Portsmouth to 17 February 1936.
From 18 February 1936 to 2 May 1938 at the Admiralty as Director of Personal Services.
CB: 1936.
From 9 May 1938 attending 'Tactical Course' at Portsmouth.
On 22 August 1938 at Malta succeeded Admiral Sir Andrew B. Cunningham in command Battle Cruiser Squadron with his flag in *Hood*, 42,200 tons. The C. in C., Mediterranean, was the future First Sea Lord, Admiral Sir A. Dudley P.R. Pound, flag in the battleship *Warspite*, 27,500 tons.

Vice Admiral: 22 October 1938.
From 1 June 1939 VA 1BS in the battleship *Barham*. From that date the C. in C., Mediterranean was Admiral Sir Andrew B. Cunningham, appointed in succession to Dudley Pound, and in due course also to be First Sea Lord.
From 20 November 1939 Flag in light cruiser *Manchester*, 9,400 tons, 18CS, and second in command, Home Fleet (11). As such he was much involved during the campaign in Norway.
KCB: 1940.
On 10 July 1940 appointed C. in C., China Station and on 12 September 1940 he assumed that command in succession to Sir Percy Noble.

In Berlin on 27 September 1940 Japan signed the Tripartite Pact, the three nations bound together being Germany, Italy and Japan. In Tokyo at the time the Foreign Minister was Matsuoka Yosuke (1880-1946).
During November 1940 Captain Matsunaga Sadaichi of the Imperial Japanese Navy was promoted Rear Admiral.
In November 1940 in Chungking, correctly anticipating that war between Japan and the U.S.A. was becoming inevitable, Chiang Kai-shek shrewdly declared the firm alignment of Nationalist China with Great Britain and the United States of America.

On 11 November 1940 the Royal Navy achieved a great success with their carrier launched torpedo attack against capital ships of the Italian Navy at their moorings at Taranto. Lieut. Commander Takeshi Naito, IJN especially flew from Berlin to Taranto to study the results of this operation. Nearly a year later, at Kagoshima in October 1941, he was to personally discuss the details of this successful British carrier operation with Commander Fuchida Mitsuo, shortly thereafter to be the leader of the IJN air strike over Hawaii.

Also on 11 November 1940 Japanese naval forces occupied Wei-Hai-Wei thus forcing the final British departure (12).
In the Indian Ocean, the southern waters of the Bay of Bengal, again on 11 November 1940, the German raider *Atlantis*, Captain Bernhard Rogge, captured then later sank the Blue Funnel cargo liner *Automedon*, 7,268 grt. In apprehending the ship Captain Rogge had been forced to open fire thereby killing the Master, Captain W.B. Ewan, and a number of other personnel. One result was that much of the most secret mail and documentation, intended for senior military and colonial officials in Singapore, was not destroyed. This material reached the German Naval Attache in Tokyo, Rear Admiral Paul Wenneker (1890-1979), on 5 December. In turn on 12 December he passed copies to a senior IJN General Staff Officer, Vice Admiral Kondo Nobutake (1886-1953). After initial doubts, feeling that such extraordinarily comprehensive data had been 'planted' by the British, the IJN were to make great use of the valuable material.
Naturally following the destruction of *Automedon* a great effort, by both sea and air, was made to ascertain

the whereabouts of the German raider. These included the provision, from RAF Seletar on Singapore Island, of two Short S. 19 'Singapore' III biplane flying boats. Unfortunately, with their limited range and patrol speed, with the best will in the world these two aircraft offered only a very limited search capability. The hunt was unsuccessful and Captain Rogge took his ship safely to Kerguelen, there to remain in Bassin de la Gazelle from 14 December 1940 to 11 January 1941.

15 November 1940: Vice Admiral Yamamoto Isoroku was promoted Admiral. With his flag in the battleship *Nagato*, 38,500 tons, he continued to command the Combined Fleet.

In London on 23 November 1940 the Chairman of Far Eastern Committee of the War Cabinet, Rt. Hon. R.A. Butler, MP, circulated a memorandum which had been prepared by the Far Eastern Department. This document was headed 'Far Eastern Situation'. Extracts follow:-

> 'In their appreciation of 31 July 1940 the Chiefs of Staff stated that the foundation of our strategy in the Far East must remain the basing of an adequate fleet on Singapore. They expressed the view however that "until we have defeated Germany and Italy, or drastically reduced their naval strength, we are faced with the problem of defending our interests in the Far East without an adequate fleet."
>
> There is reason to believe that discussions are in progress for the conclusion of an agreement of some kind – possibly a non-aggression pact – between Japan and the Soviet Union. Were such an agreement to be concluded, it is probable that Japan would feel encouraged to accelerate the pace of her southward advance (--). In these circumstances there is an urgent need to strengthen our defences in the Far East, not only with the object of offering successful resistance to any attack which may be made, but even more for the purpose of showing Japan by our preparedness that she would be unwise to make the attempt (--).
>
> Some progress is being made with the strengthening of our land and air defenses in Malaya, but our naval weakness in the Far East remains without remedy or visible sign of remedy, and now that the successful action by the Fleet Air Arm at Taranto has materially reduced the capital ship strength of the Italian Navy it is for consideration, in the light of the threatening situation in the Far East, whether the time has not come to augment our naval forces in that part of the world by the despatch of one or two capital ships (13).

Just one example of some of the very different experiences undergone by expatriate British civilians in north Europe during the early years of WW2 may be seen from the following extract of a report written in Hong Kong on 25 November 1940:-

> 'Evacuation of British refugees from Baltic States. s.s. *Haiten* was chartered from Douglas Shipping Company and sailed from Hong Kong for Vladivostok on 25 October to embark about 180 British subjects evacuated from Baltic States and brought by rail across Siberia (14).'

Meanwhile the Royal Navy finally completed arrangements to withdraw from Wei-Hai-Wei:-

> 'The evacuation of Wei-Hai-Wei was completed on 5 November (1940). s.s. *Chungking* and *Chengtu* arrived at Hong Kong from Wei-Hai-Wei on 12 November, loaded with stores and each towing one lighter (15).'

In January 1941 Rear Admiral Matsunaga Sadaichi of the IJN was appointed in command of the Twenty Second Air Flotilla. This was a shore based unit of the Navy.

On 27 January 1941 the U.S. Ambassador to Tokyo, Joseph Clark Grew (1880-1965) noted, 'There is a lot of talk around town to the effect that the Japanese, in case of a break with the United States, are planning to go all out in a surprise mass attack on Pearl Harbour. Of course I informed our Government (16).'

The U.S. authorities were well aware that such a possibility existed, and, furthermore, that a surprise attack by Japan could well be launched over a weekend or during a public holiday.

Nevertheless, as examples of the confused thinking emanating from Washington DC at the time, two conflicting letters were despatched to Admiral Husband Edward Kimmel, USN (1882-1968), C. in C., Pacific or CinCPAC. The first, dated 24 January 1941, was a copy of an internal note from Frank Knox (1874-1944), Secretary of the Navy, to the Secretary of War, Henry L. Stimson (1867-1950). The relevant sentence reads, 'If war eventuates with Japan, it is believed easily possible that hostilities would be initiated by a surprise attack upon the Fleet or the Naval Base at Pearl Harbor (17).'

In astonishing contrast from Admiral Stark:-

> 'Yet a strange ambivalence was at work. Stark's concern over the Fleet as a result of the Taranto raid had initiated a chain of awareness which on January 24 culminated in Knox's letter to Stimson. But eight days later the CNO dispatch went off to Kimmel quoting Grew's famous warning, placing "no credence in these rumours", and declaring that, "no move against Pearl Harbour appears imminent or planned for in the foreseeable future." (18)'

At Singapore on 23 March 1941 an important step was taken to modernise the aerial ocean reconnaissance capability of the RAF. On that date the first U.S. built Consolidated Catalina flying boat arrived at the 'fortress' via Australia. Thereafter the obsolete Short Singapore III machines gradually were to be replaced (19).

10 April 1941. Formation by the Imperial Japanese Navy of their First Air Fleet. With his flag in *Akagi* the C. in C. was Vice Admiral Nagumo Chuichi.

Vice Admiral Nagumo Chuichi, (1887-1944).

On 13 April 1941 the Soviet Union signed a five year neutrality pact with Japan. Chiang Kai-shek was astounded. On the one hand Soviet Russia was sending him military supplies to be used in his struggle against Japan and now, here on the other, the Soviets appeared to be supporting Japan.

From the point of view of the Soviets this new agreement could be regarded as strengthening their pact with Germany and at the same time, on the face of it, gave them some sort of guarantee against attack in the East.

In Japan clearly the 'Strike South' group received much benefit. As seen above, in London on 23 November 1940 the probability of such a new southern emphasis had been anticipated.

As the political atmosphere in the East gradually became more tense then at Singapore between 21 and 27 April 1941 'Most Secret: American-Dutch-British Conversations' – ADB – were held. Those involved were of senior status and included delegate representatives from Australia, New Zealand and India. Unfortunately few decisions of merit were to be reached, indeed subsequently it was to be written that:-

'It is enough here to say that no ADB naval operational plan was in effect when the Japanese struck (20).'

On 29 April 1941 the C. in C., Asiatic Fleet, Admiral Thomas C. Hart, USN, in a letter to Admiral Harold R. Stark in Washington, included this comment:-

'Vice Admiral Layton has my people's entire liking and respect – as a fine example of the blue water school of the Royal Navy. He is direct, frank and forceful (21).'

In London on 1 May 1941 the Joint Intelligence Sub Committee of the British War Cabinet prepared a study from which extracts follow. Apart from Japanese capability in the air, on which point in London they were sadly misled by inaccurate information received from British diplomatic and other representatives in the Far East, it was to prove to be a fine effort:-

'Future Strategy of Japan.

1) Japanese policy, which is strongly nationalistic and which aims at strategic self sufficiency, is influenced by two conflicting views: the one advocating a continental policy to watch Russia and to persevere in China, the other favouring a maritime policy of expansion Southwards meanwhile standing fast in China. Both schools of thought are represented in the present Government and the Prime Minister endeavours to preserve a balance between them. The recent pact with Russia, while making little practical difference, may be expected to have a psychological reaction in favour of those who advocate Southward expansion.

2) Japan is extremely susceptible to economic pressure and is therefore continually striving to gain control of the supply of essential raw materials.

4) Japan's greatest need is for oil. If outside sources of supply were cut off, her stocks are probably sufficient for nine months' active warfare.

7) Japan could make available some 450 shore based aircraft, and sufficient aerodromes exist for these in Indo-China, Thailand and the Kra peninsula. These aircraft could not be used from shore bases for operations against Borneo or Java, but another 340 could be carrier borne. The operational value of the Japanese Air Force is probably akin to that of the Italians. If the capture of Singapore were attempted the most probable method would be a landing near the frontier on the East coast of the Kra peninsula in conjunction with landings at suitable points on the East coast of Malaya, the whole developing into a Southward move on Singapore. It would not be an easy operation and would become virtually impossible in the face of strong British naval and air forces. An attempt by special service troops to seize control of oil facilities of Borneo is likely at the same time. Owing to the present British and U.S. economic pressure, which is likely to increase, Japan's economic capacity for waging war will progressively deteriorate, while our own position in Singapore should strengthen, particularly in aircraft. If Japan should decide to run the risk of war with the British Empire which may also bring in the U.S., she may well decide to take the risk sooner rather than later (22).'

At this point it should be recorded that at that time and in general neither the British nor the Dutch held the overall direction of U.S. Far Eastern naval operations in much regard. As examples two quotes follow. The first is taken from Sir Geoffrey Layton to the Admiralty on 20 January 1942. The second is earlier, Vice Admiral Conrad E.L. Helfrich, RNN to Geoffrey Layton on 23 December 1941:-

'Such difficulties as I have had in the way of co-operation have been almost exclusively with the United States representatives. This has certainly not extended to personal relations, which have

6 May 1940. Admiral Osami Nagano, IJN with foreign attaches at the Tokyo Naval Club. Vice Admiral Nobutake Kondo is seaset in the front row, third from the left.

been most cordial, nor to the loyalty of liaison staffs, which have been excellent. What I have found is that the American naval authorities have produced in practice policies and conceptions of co-operation which are very different from those fore-shadowed in pre-war conferences. As far as the officers in this area are concerned, this is due in greater part to interference from above (23).'
'I certainly dislike the orders from Washington and I cannot understand that they come from an 'Admiral'. I have the strong impression that the American flag-officers out here do not agree with these orders at all, but they have to obey. Still I have not yet the impression of an offensive mind as far as the Americans are concerned. The great tragedy in my opinion is that we thought too much of the value of the American Navy and spirit (24).'

1 July 1941. In Tokyo Foreign Minister Matsuoka lost the struggle as leader of the 'Strike North' faction. Thereafter within ruling government circles the 'Strike South' element was to direct proceedings. Matsuoka resigned on 15 July.

21 July 1941. Japan and the Vichy reached agreement permitting the establishment by Japan of certain air and naval bases in south French Indo-China. Ten days later President Roosevelt introduced further economic measures against Japan. With immediate effect he announced an embargo on the supply of all high octane gasoline (avgas) and crude oil to Japan.

Already on 28 July the Dutch government in Batavia had ordered the restriction of oil exports to Japan.

To illustrate the importance of this embargo decided upon by the USA, for the years from 1935 to 1937 Japan had obtained 67% of her petroleum and 74% of her crude oil from that country. For Japan a particular advantage to her on the occasion of the signing of the Tripartite Pact on 27 September the previous year had been that Japan then had access to the technology which Germany had developed for the synthetic production of oil (25).

In the Blue Funnel Line steamer *Ulysses*, 14,499 grt, Captain J.A. Russell, Rear Admiral Ernest John Spooner arrived at Singapore on 22 August 1941, his fifty fourth birthday, to take up his new post as Admiral Superintendent, Singapore Naval Dockyard, HMS *Sultan*, and Rear Admiral, Malaya (26). Accompanied by his wife they had embarked at Gourock on the evening of 11 June 1941. Their voyage to the East via Halifax, Capetown, Durban, Colombo and Penang had been lengthy. At Singapore he succeeded Rear Admiral Thomas B. Drew, he who from January 1932 had been Flag Captain to Admiral Sir Howard Kelly in *Kent* (see C. in C., 1931).

In her private diary the Admiral's wife, Mrs. Megan Spooner, has left her opinions of a number of the characters holding senior positions in Singapore at the time:-

'8 September 1941. Dined with Governor – Sir Shelton Thomas – a nice man but not a leader of men. I should say rather a rigid insensitive brain.'

29 November 1941. We want more brains in Singapore. B.P. (Brooke Popham, the C. in C.) is unusual but he has a first class mind – Percival (Army) may have brains but certainly is short of guts and decision. Layton has plenty of guts but no first class grey matter. Pulford (RAF) is good – brain keen and subtle, and character firm and steady. Keith Simmons (Army) – steady brain, great tact, considerable charm and judgement but lacking in drive and not a first class brain. Governor seems a poor reed. Col. Sec. (Colonial Secretary Stanley Wilson Jones) reputed to be a bottleneck and obstructor and also to be revengeful – certainly unbalanced – I think he has ophthalmic goitre.

30 November 1941. Acting Admiral Sir Tom S.V. Phillips and his Staff Officer (Plans), Commander M.G. Goodenough having arrived on 29 November, stayed at Navy House with the Spooners.

TSV (the Admiral) looks tired and worn but is as modest and gentle as ever.

Cdr. Goodenough is a nice young man.

TSV Ph. Is charming and so willing to talk to anyone (27).'

In September 1941 Vice Admiral Kondo Nobutake hoisted his flag in the heavy cruiser *Atago* as C. in C., Second Fleet (28). During the Japanese assault of the Malay peninsula in December he was to operate in the South China Sea in overall command of IJN support activity.

In Tokyo on 12 September 1941 the C. in C., Combined Fleet, Admiral Yamamoto Isoruku attended a meeting with Prime Minister Konoe Fumimaro. In reply to a question concerning the position of the Navy should hostilities be opened against the U.S.A. the Admiral replied:-

'If you insist on my going ahead I can promise to give them hell for a year or a year and a half, but can guarantee nothing as to what will happen after that (29).'

This is not the place to eleborate regarding opinions held amongst senior officers of the IJN over the question of any future conflict with the U.S.A., including Great Britain and the Netherlands for that matter. Nevertheless it is useful to record that in contrast to the aggressive notions held by a number of his peers Admiral Yamamoto Isoroku himself was not in favour of the idea but, if so ordered and as just seen above, naturally would do his very best to serve the Emperor. As just one example of the pragmatic attitude held by a number of officers here follows the opinion put forward by Rear Admiral Onishi Takijiro (1891-1945), Chief of Staff, 11th Air Fleet, IJN (30). The date and place was at the end of September 1941 at the IJN air base, Kanoya, southern Kyushu:-

'It would be impossible in any war with the U.S. for Japan to bring the other side to its knees. Going into a war with America without this ability means that we must consider ways to bring it to an early end, which means in turn that at some point we'll have to reach a compromise. For that reason, whether we land in the Philippines or anywhere else, we should avoid anything like the Hawaiian operation that would put America's back up too badly (31).'

In Japan on 25 September 1941 the large aircraft carrier *Zuikaku*, 25,675 tons and a sister to *Shokaku*, was commissioned. These two carriers, both of whom were to work up quickly, constituted the Fifth Carrier Division, IJN. Now the First Air Fleet consisted of six large Fleet carriers.

During September 1941 Alfred Duff-Cooper, newly despatched from London as the Resident Cabinet Minister in Singapore, arrived in the colony. Also appointed to Singapore, but who had arrived a little earlier, was Sir George Sansom, Civilian Representative on the Singapore War Council. In 1957 Sir George recounted a short conversation which then had taken place between the two of them:-

'Soon after his (Duff Cooper's) arrival he asked me, "Are the Japanese going to attack?"
I said, "Of course. There isn't any question about it. You had better make sure that the soldiers and sailors are fully aware."
He looked surprised, and said later that I'd spoken in a calm, sad voice. At all events he decided to believe me, and did everything he could to ginger up preparations for dealing with the – to me – inevitable attack.

Sir George continued with the following account of a similar conversation which had taken place shortly before that with Duff-Cooper:-

'The Admiral in charge of the Navy Base at Singapore was Jack Spooner, an old friend, who had only arrived from war duties elsewhere in August 1941. (--) Immediately on arrival he had asked me what the true position was: "George, here I am at Singapore, and the place seems to be in a state of frightful confusion. And nobody seems to know what should be done. How long have I got?"
I said, "Well, Jack, I think you've till about the end of November" (32).'

18 October 1941. The War Minister, General Tojo Hideki, was appointed Prime Minister of Japan (33). In addition now he became Home Minister.

Tojo replaced Prince Konoe Fumimaro (1891-1945) who, although desiring to control the army, was in the unfortunate position of knowing that, '... right now the civilian government is too weak to do anything.' The establishment of the supreme war council in November 1937 had greatly limited the authority of any government over the conduct of both the Army and Navy. Always in that immediate pre WW2 era it was the aggressive attitude of the Army that caused alarm in realistic, informed Japanese circles. In this connection as early as 21 July 1938, during Prince Konoe's first term in office as Prime Minister, the American Ambassador to Tokyo, had written:-

'Prince Konoye (Konoe) and other members of the Government realized that if progress were to be made in consolidating Japan's position in China and in avoiding serious friction with Great Britain and the United States the conduct of everything except purely military affairs must be taken out of the hands of the Army and lodged in the civil part of the Government (34).'

In London on 31 October 1941 the Far Eastern Committee of the War Cabinet discussed developments. Short extracts follow:-

'The Committee heard a statement regarding developments in Japan. The most notable event since the last meeting of the committee had been the change of government of that country. Statements by the spokesman of the new government had been imprecise but referred particularly:-

a) to the determination to go forward with the policy of establishing the "East Asia Co-Prosperity Sphere".

b) to the intention to liquidate the "China incident".

c) to the desireability of a complete adherence to the Tripartite Pact.

It seemed clear that the Army were in control of the new government, but it would be premature to assume that any decision had yet been reached to embark upon war (35).'

26 November 1941. Departure from Hitokappu Bay, Etorofu, Kurile Islands of the IJN, First Air Fleet and escorting warships. Vice Admiral Nagumo Chuichi flew his flag in *Akagi* as Commander, Carrier Strike Force, 'Kido Butai'. He steamed in an easterly direction out across the Pacific.

At 01:15 hours on Monday, 8 December 1941 at Singapore Sir Geoffrey recorded in a rough diary which he maintained:-

'Information received of an attempted Japanese landing at Kota Bharu (36).'

At sunset on 8 December 1941 hauled down his Flag and the appointment of C. in C., China Station lapsed.

NOTES

1. *Dictionary of National Biography*, Vol. 32, (OUP, 2004), 931.
2. NA ADM 196/49. *Service Record.*
3. Ibid. On 13 November 1920 HMS *Thames* was to be acquired privately by Mr. T.B.F. Davis of Durban and to be presented by him to South Africa as the training ship *General Botha*. As an exercise on 13 May 1947, some sixty seven years from the date her keel had been laid, to be sunk in Simon's Bay by coastal battery gunfire.
4. Rear Admiral Michael Kyrle Pope. Obituary, *The Times,* Wednesday, September 24, 2008.
5. Suzanne Kyrle-Pope, *The Same Wife in Every Port,* (Co. Durham, 2002).
6. Richard Compton-Hall, *Submarines and the War at Sea, 1914-18,* (London, 1991), 19.
7. Ibid. 147/9.
8. *Service Record.*
9. Obituary, *The Times,* September 7, 1964.
10. *Service Record.*
11. Ibid.
12. For an insight into the behaviour of Japanese forces at Wei-Hai-Wei in 1940 see the volume by Carlene Pomfret, *Cabin*

Trunks and Far Horizons, (Ware, Herts, 1991), 92/98. Her husband, latterly Surgeon Rear Admiral Arnold Ashworh Pomfret, then was SNO, Wei-Hai-Wei.

13. NA CAB 96/1. Notation No. 65. It is of interest to note that at the time a member of the committee, and representing the Ministry of Economic Warfare, was Mr. J. Keswick of Jardine Matheson.

14. NA ADM 199/374. *Haitan*, 3,554 grt, built in Danzig in 1909 for Russian owners. Following an interesting, even exciting life, in 1935 acquired by Douglas interests. To survive WW2. *Beancaker to Boxboat*, 142.

15. Ibid. Letter 173/HK.0345 dated at Hong Kong, 23 December 1940. *Chungking*, 2,141 grt, built in 1914. *Chengtu*, 2,219 grt, built 1914. Both owned by Butterfield and Swire's China Navigation. Only the former was to survive WW2. *Beancaker to Boxboat*, 89.

16. Joseph C. Grew, *Ten Years in Japan*, (London, 1944), 318.

17. Gordon W. Prange, *At Dawn We Slept*, (New York, 1983), 45.

Admiral Kimmel was C. in C., U.S. Fleet and Pacific Fleet from February to December 1941. His predecessor, Admiral James Otto Richardson (1878-1974), who had taken the Pacific Fleet from San Diego to Pearl Harbour, the 'forward deployment', subsequently had had a disagreement with President Franklin D. Roosevelt (1882-1945) hence Admiral Kimmel's appointment in February 1941. In turn as C. in C., U.S. Fleet Kimmel was succeeded on 30 December 1941 by Admiral Ernest Joseph King (1878-1956). As C. in C., Pacific Fleet on 31 December 1941 he was succeeded by Admiral Chester William Nimitz (1885-1966). Department of the Navy, Navy Historical Center, Washington DC.

18. Ibid. 47. Stark is the Chief of Naval Operations USN (equivalent then to the British First Sea Lord), Admiral Harold Rainsford **Stark** (1880-1972). CNO from 1 August 1939 to 26 March 1942 when succeeded by Admiral Ernest Joseph King. The reference to Taranto is in respect of the most successful carrier launched air attack carried out on 11 November 1940 by the RN against the Italian Fleet moored in Taranto harbour.

19. NA ADM 199/411.

20. Arthur J. Marder, *Old Friends, New Enemies: The Royal Navy and the Imperial Japanese Navy: Strategic Illusions 1936-1941*, (OUP, 1981), 211. Together with assistant staff members the delegates included:-

For the USA: Captain W.R. Purnell, USN, Chief of Staff, Asiatic Fleet.

For the Netherlands East Indies: Major General H. ter Poorten, Chief of General Staff.

For Great Britain: Air Chief Marshall Sir Robert Brooke-Popham, Commander in Chief, Far East.

Vice Admiral Sir Geoffrey Layton, Commander in Chief, China.

For Australia: Admiral Sir Ragnar M. Colvin, First Naval Member.

For New Zealand: Commodore W.E. Parry, Chief of Naval Staff.

For India: Major General G.N. Molesworth, Deputy Chief of General Staff.

21. James Leutze, *A Different Kind of Victory*, (Annapolis, 1981), 196.

22. NA CAB 79/11: J.I.C. (41) 175. The signatories were V. Cavendish Bentinck, Foreign Office. Rear Admiral J.H. Godfrey, D.N.I. (Director Naval Intelligence). Major General F.H.N. Davidson, War Office. Air Vice Marshall C.E.H. Medhurst, Air Ministry, and Col. C.G. Vickers, Ministry of Economic Warfare.

As one example, although Japan had been at war with China since July 1937, as late as in his message to the Foreign Office dated 26 November 1941 the British Ambassador to Tokyo, Sir Robert Craigie, continued to include remarks such as:-

'Air Force. Technical and flying efficiency of the Japanese Air Force is believed to be similar to that of the Italians, although Japanese held their own against U.S.S.R. at Nomomhan.'

NA FO 371/27971. In London this entire message was given War Cabinet distribution.

Unfortunately In London it appears clear that, with very considerable justification, on the whole minds were concentrated elsewhere than on the possibility of future Eastern conflict.

Paragraph 4, oil. Precise figures in respect of IJN oil reserves are not easy to obtain. One source indicates that by 1936 the Navy had brought its stockpile to some 3.5 million tons of oil. Thereafter with the outbreak of the 'China Incident' and the subsequent US embargoes on their supply, both of aviation fuel and of oil, the question of oil reserves became more serious. However by 1 December 1941, 'the Navy had on hand 6,500,000 tons of petroleum' products of all kinds including bunker oil and aviation fuel. At that time the IJN estimated that once hostilities commenced then average consumption would amount to some 2,800,000 tons p.a., a figure which in practice was to prove woefully incorrect as in just the first year of war consumption was to amount to 4,850,000 tons. David C. Evans and Mark R. Peattie, *Kaigun*, (Annapolis, MD, 1997), 407 – 410.

Another source confirms the figure available to the IJN at the outbreak of the Pacific War, 6.5 million tons of all oil products, but makes the additional point that, 'these domestic reserves included nothing for either the Imperial Japanese Army or for civilian use'. Arthur J. Marder asnd associates, *Old Friends New Enemies*, Vol. II, (OUP, 1990), 376.

23. NA ADM 199/1389. Letter 11/4682.

24. NA ADM 199/1472A. In due course on behalf of The Netherlands in Tokyo Bay onboard USS *Missouri* BB-63, Captain Stuart S. Murray, on 2 September 1945 Admiral Helfrich (1886-1962) was to have the pleasure of signing the Japanese surrender documentation.

25. Tsuzuki Chushichi, *The Pursuit of Power in Modern Japan, 1825-1995)*, (OUP, 2000), 294.

26. Ernest John **Spooner**. Born: 22 August 1887. Died: 15 April 1942. As a Captain from 19 December 1938 had commanded the battlecruiser *Repulse*, 26,500 tons. Succeeded in command of her on 18 June 1940 by Captain William George Tennant. Rear Admiral: 25 June 1940. From 16 July 1940 Flag Officer Commanding Northern Patrol in the stone frigate *Fortitude*, Adrossan. With the Japanese success in Malaya and Singapore, in *ML 310* he and his party were to attempt to escape to the Dutch East Indies but off Tjebia Island in the Tujoh Group north of Bangka during the afternoon of 15 February were intercepted by the enemy. Of fever and other illness there he died. Of the party of forty five who had embarked in *ML 310*, sadly eighteen were to join him by remaining in that isolated place. NA ADM 1/17363. Author's notes. Also see 'Appendix One'.

27. Diary: Mrs. Megan Spooner. King's College, London. Ref: *GB KCLMA Spooner*. She was the well known soprano, Megan Foster, who had married Jack Spooner in 1926.

28. Misao Toyama, *Rikukaigun Shokan Jinji Soran: Kaigun Hen*, (Japan, 1981). HIJMS *Atago*, 13,400 tons. Ten 8", ten 5" DP, and lighter guns. Sixteen 24" T.T. 34 knots. In the Palawan Passage on 23 October 1944 to be torpedoed and sunk by US S/M *Darter* SS-227, Commander D.H. McClintock. Theodore Roscoe, *United States Submarine Operations in WW2*, (Annapolis, 1988), 392/3.

29. Agawa Hiroyuki, *The Reluctant Admiral: Yamamoto and the Imperial Navy*, (Tokyo and New York, 1979), 232.

30. Onishi Takijiro. Born: 2 June 1891. Death by traditional seppuku: 16 August 1945. Graduated from Etajima in 1912. Early service included at sea in seaplane tender *Wakamiya*. Always a far sighted promoter of Naval 'air', to the extent of outspokenly criticizing the building of super battleships. Rear Admiral: November 1939. Vice Admiral: May 1943. As the newly appointed C. in C., Third Air Fleet, Philippine Islands, in October 1944 the first IJN senior officer to advocate the use of suicide air attacks, kamikaze. Vice Chief, IJN General Staff: May 1945. Mark R. Peattie, *Sunburst*, (Annapolis, MD., 2001), 81-83. Richard Fuller, *Shokan*, (London, 1992), 280. Masatake Okumiya, Jiro Horikoshi and Martin Caidin, *Zero*, (London, 1957), 271-273, 282. Tsuzuki, 313.

31. Agawa Hiroyuki, 229.

32. Katharine Sansom, *Sir George Sansom and Japan*, (Tallahassee, Fla., 1972), 123.
Sir George Sansom – see Moore, C. in C., 1905, reference (30).
Rear Admiral Ernest John Spooner: see Appendix One.

33. Prime Minister Konoe Fumimaro had resigned on 16 October 1941. This period of open military dictatorship in Japan was to endure until 19 July 1944. Then, with the resignation of General Tojo following the successful conquest of the Marianas by the U.S. Fifth Fleet, Admiral Raymond A. Spruance, that disastrous experiment was to end. Tojo was hanged for war crimes: 23 December 1948.

34. Joseph Clark Grew (1880-1965), Ambassador from February 1932 to December 1941. *Ten Years in Japan*, 218.

35. NA CAB 96/2. Notation No. 36.

36. NA ADM 199/1743.

3 to 10 December 1941
Acting Admiral Sir Tom Spencer Vaughan **Phillips**

As C. in C., Eastern Fleet

He was born on 19 February 1888 in Pendennis Castle, Budock Roads, Falmouth. His father was a gunner, Lt. Col. Thomas Vaughan Wynn Phillips, Royal Artillery (1). His mother was Louisa May Adeline, daughter of Admiral Sir Algernon F.R. de Horsey (2).

Died in the South China Sea in *Prince of Wales* on 10 December 1941.

With initial preparation for a Naval career at Stubbington House, Fareham then later he entered the Royal Navy in the training ship *Britannia* on 15 January 1903. **Midshipman**: 15 May 1904. From 15 May 1904 in cruiser *Drake*, 14,100 tons, Flagship 2CS, Atlantic Fleet, Rear Admiral HSH Prince Louis of Battenberg. **Sub Lieutenant**: 15 July 1907. Continued in *Drake* until 17 September 1907, then studied at Portsmouth, and subsequently at RNC, Greenwich. **Lieutenant**: 15 July 1908. In January 1909 awarded, 'GBP 10 prize for six First Class certificates', this being a most noteworthy academic achievement. From 6 February 1909 served in cruiser *Black Prince*, 13,550 tons, 5CS, Atlantic Fleet. From 2 August 1909 in *Dryad*, Navigational School Ship, Portsmouth, 'Lieutenant Qualifying as a Navigator'. He 'qualified for navigational duties' on 3 December 1909. From 1 January 1910 as Assistant to Navigation Officer in *Drake*, Flagship, RA 5CS, Atlantic Fleet. From 5 April 1910 Lieut. (N) in TBD *Halcyon*, 1,070 tons, Coast Guard and Reserves. Between 1 January and 1 August 1911 Lieut. (N) in cruiser *Thetis*, 3,400 tons, and then transferred to the small cruiser *Pyramus*, 2,135 tons, for passage out to Australia. There from 27 October 1911 served as Lieut. (N) in cruiser *Pegasus*, 2,135 tons, Australia but, 'Detailed temporarily for service China Station'. From 7 March 1913 Lieut. (N) at Glasgow standing by new building Depot Ship for TBDs *Woolwich*, 3,380 tons. She commissioned at Portsmouth: 12 December 1913. Remained in her until 15 January 1915. From that date Lieut. (N) in cruiser *Bacchante*, 12,000 tons at the Dardanelles. From 9 February 1916 in cruiser *Lancaster*, 9,800 tons, Captain John R. Segrave, Far East. **Lieutenant Commander**: 15 July 1916. Remained in *Lancaster* as Lieut. Commander (N). In the second quarter of 1917 off the Chilean coast actively involved in the hunt for the German raider *Seeadler*, 1,571 grt, herself the captured British square rigged ship, *Pass of Balmaha*. Under the German flag, and commanded by Felix Count von Luckner, she had a most successful raiding career in 1917 until wrecked on a reef at Mopelia (Maupihaa) in the Society Islands on 2 August 1917.

Also during that year, 1917, for local defense purposes *Lancaster* landed two of her fourteen six inch guns at the Falkland Islands. 'One of these had been positioned on Mount Low, just to the North of Sparrow Cove off Port William. Port William provides the northerly entrance through the Narrows into Stanley harbour itself (3).'

On returning to England as acting Captain of the cruiser *Euryalus*, from 17 April 1919 he was 'granted 90 days leave (4)'. However the furtherance of his career was to intervene as from 6 May 1919 he attended the RN Staff College, Greenwich.

Also in 1919 he married Gladys Metcalfe, daughter of the late Captain F.G. Griffith Griffin, DCLI, and the widow of J.H. Brownrigg. They were to have one son who was to follow his father into the Royal Navy.

From 15 June 1920 borne in *President*, the Admiralty, 'To assist Captain Segrave', who was 'Chief of Staff to British Naval Representative in League of Nations'. From 22 November 1920 rather similarly, 'For duty with League of Nations Committee'.

Commander: 30 June 1921. Continued with League of Nations Committee.

From 15 June 1923 with Plans Division at the Admiralty.

From 1 November 1924 in command sloop *Verbena*, 1,250 tons, Africa Station.

From 1 July 1925 Staff Officer (Operations) in battleship *Warspite*, 27,500 tons, staff of the C. in C., Mediterranean, Admiral Sir Roger J.B. Keyes. To take up this position he arrived at Malta on 27 July 1925.

Captain: 30 June 1927. From 1 February 1928 on the staff of Admiral Sir Roger J.B. Keyes, C. in C., Mediterranean, now in battleship *Queen Elizabeth*, 27,500 tons, a sister ship to *Warspite*.

From 4 September 1928 Captain (D), 6DF, Atlantic Fleet, in destroyer leader *Campbell*, 1,600 tons.

Admiralty as Assistant Director, Plans Division: 24 April 1930 – 21 September 1932.

From 21 September 1932 Flag Captain light cruiser *Hawkins*, 9,800 tons, Flagship, East Indies, Vice Admiral Martin Eric Dunbar-Nasmith, VC (1883-1965). The C. in C. joined her at Bombay on 25 November 1932, transferring his flag from *Enterprise*. From 26 October 1934 the new C. in C. was Vice Admiral Frank Forrester Rose (1878-1955) who arrived at Colombo in the P. & O. s.s. *Maloja*, 20,837 grt, on 9 December and assumed the command on 12 December 1934. Very shortly thereafter Admiral Dunbar-Nasmith sailed for home in the Orient Line s.s. *Orontes*, 20,097 grt. To assume her duties in the East Indies *Hawkins* had sailed from Portsmouth on 11 October 1932 and eventually was to return on 1 March 1935. During the commission she visited the China Station at Penang and Singapore very briefly between 11 and 29 January 1934, and the Africa Station at Durban, again very briefly between 2 and 14 July 1934 (5).

Admiralty as Director, Plans Division: 8 August 1935 – April 1938.

CB: 1937.

From 20 April 1938 as **Commodore** First Class in cruiser *Aurora*, 5,270 tons, 'Commanding Home Fleet Destroyer Flotillas.'

Rear Admiral: 10 January 1939.

Continued in *Aurora* commanding Home Fleet Destroyer Flotillas.

From 1 June 1939 a Lord Commissioner of the Admiralty and Deputy Chief of Naval Staff.

From 12 June 1939 the First Sea Lord was Admiral of the Fleet Sir Alfred Dudley Pickman Rogers Pound (1877-1943).

One historian of note has this to say on the subject of what might be described as the conservative attitude which prevailed on the occasion of the outbreak of the European aspect of WW2 on 3 September 1939:-

> '... nevertheless, I think it fair to say that many of the lessons of 1914-1918 were forgotten, neglected, not thoroughly absorbed, or were misread in the interwar years. Why was this the case? The simple explanation is that armies and navies rarely learn from success, and the Royal Navy had been successful in its main objective. Also, there was a school of thought that said: "We did it in the last war, therefore we must do it in the next war", irrespective of why they had done it, or what the results were.
> (Rear Admiral Tom Phillips, who was DCNS at the outbreak of the Second War, has been called "the High Priest" of this cult) (6).'

At the outbreak of WW2 the most senior officers of all Navies still were wedded to the historical view of battleships being the capital ships of all fleets. It is to the First Lord's credit, he then being Winston Churchill, that he proposed the suspension in construction of those new battleships of the proposed *Lion* class as other greater priorities existed. The First Lord also made known his awareness of developments in the air, '... must have all armour capacity which can be spared for strengthening H.M. Ships against air attack'. The writer, already just quoted above, continues:-

> 'The debate came to centre upon the *Conqueror* and *Thunderer* (two of the proposed *Lion* class), on which no work was yet being done. Churchill continued to argue the importance of concentrating personnel and materiel resources on the production of ships that could be used in this war: *Conqueror* and *Thunderer* could not qualify. (--)
>
> He was resisted on both issues by the Naval Staff, including the First Sea Lord, and by the Controller. The Staff repeated earlier arguments about the need for a strong battle fleet after the war, especially in view of Far Eastern contingencies and the necessity, as the DCNS, Phillips, declared, of achieving the prewar goal of maintaining "an adequate fleet to go to the Far East plus the necessary minimum to retain in Home Waters to balance any one European Power (7)'.

Acting Vice Admiral: 7 February 1940.

On 9 April 1940 Germany invaded Norway. The British were surprised by the degree of success enjoyed by German forces in the air:-

> 'As Admiral Forbes put it, "the scale of air attack that would be developed against our military forces on shore and our naval forces off the Norwegian coast was grievously underestimated when the operations were undertaken". This blind confidence in sea power was the responsibility of the Chiefs of Staff, specifically, of Ironside and Pound. The Navy itself, from Churchill, Pound, and Phillips down, had excessive faith in the effectiveness of a warship's A.A. defences. (--) Phillips was perhaps the most dedicated disbeliever in the air threat (8)'.

Next, in May 1940, followed the impressively coordinated German blitzkreig attack on the Low Countries and France. French resistance was inadequate and on 22 June 1940 they signed an armistice with Germany. In London it was perceived as being extremely important that the warships of the French fleet, under Admiral Darlan, did not fall into enemy hands. Darlan gave a guarantee that France would not permit such an occurance but, with good reason, his word was not trusted by the British. The affair at Oran took place on 3 July 1940. Rather neatly Admiral Phillips summed up the British need to have acted against France in that manner:-

> 'While having no reason to doubt Admiral Darlan's good faith, it was clear that events might put it beyond his power to control the future of the Fleet if it was not handed over to us. Further, when vital matters which might govern the whole future of the world were at stake, it could not be accepted that the British Government could place itself in a position of having to rely on the word of one man, however much they trusted him (9)'.

Up until around this period he had enjoyed a good relationship with Prime Minister Churchill but as is recorded in the Dictionary of National Biography:-

> 'Churchill records in his second volume (of *The Second World War*) that in September 1940 Phillips demurred to the suggestion of retaliatory bombing of German cities.
>
> Early in 1941 he expressed and maintained the view that to divert forces from Cyrenaica to Greece would be unsound and probably disastrous. That diversion took place in March, and from that time, according to his own statement to an intimate, Phillip's personal contact with the prime minister practically ceased (10)'.

KCB: gazetted on 1 July 1941.

Following the resignation of Prime Minister Konoe Fumimaro the previous day, on 17 October 1941 General Tojo Hideki became Prime Minister of Japan. Also he retained his previous appointment as Minister of War.

Up to 21 October 1941 he continued as a Lord Commissioner of the Admiralty latterly as Vice Chief of Naval Staff.

In London, following a Defence Committee meeting on 20 October 1941, he was ordered to his new position as C. in C., Eastern Fleet, and as an acting Admiral.

As indicated above earlier he and the Prime Minister had achieved an excellent rapport however subsequently he had fallen out with Mr. Churchill over the matter of the diversion of sparse military resources from North Africa to Greece. Attacking through Bulgaria, Germany had invaded Greece on 6 April 1941 and, for a number of reasons, Great Britain wished to be seen to be supporting that country. As briefly mentioned above, this was a strategic move which Sir Tom had felt unable to support (11). Also Sir Tom had felt unable to support the Prime Minister's enthusiasm for the carpet bombing of German cities. Possibly for these two reasons the First Sea Lord felt that he would prefer to promote Sir Tom away from the Naval Staff at the Admiralty.

To proceed East he joined *Prince of Wales* at Greenock on 24 October 1941 and, escorted by the destroyers *Express* and *Electra*, steamed to Colombo via Freetown, the Cape, Mauritius, and Addu Atoll. The latter otherwise was known as Port 'T' and was where the British authorities were constructing a secret Naval refuelling and watering facility.

While at Capetown between 16 and Tuesday, 18 Novemer 1941, he took the opportunity to fly to Pretoria to meet Field Marshal Jan Christiaan Smuts (1870-1950), the Prime Minister of the Union. After their meeting, during which Jan Smuts had been impressed by Sir Tom, the Field Marshal was to cable London. Concerning the naval reinforcements being sent East by Britain, which included the old battlecruiser *Repulse* but no aircraft carriers, taken together with the existing US Pacific Fleet at Honolulu, the IJN battlefleet being more formidable than both, Jan Smuts was to include the following prescient comment:-

'... there was an opening for a first class disaster if the Japanese were really nippy (12).'

After *Prince of Wales* had sailed, on 29 November 1941 the Japanese Consul General in Capetown sent a telegram, 'Secret to the Department', addressed to the Foreign Minister in Tokyo. In this message the battleship's camouflage paintwork details, and other information, were passed on. In turn British Intelligence, by 4 December 1941, had de-coded the Japanese message, translated the contents, and passed this information to the Admiralty and other interested parties (13).

On 29 November he arrived at Singapore by air from Koggala, Ceylon (14). This was a long non-stop flight of some thirteen hours. The navigator of his RAF Catalina aircraft later was to write:-

'... the Admiral was an outstanding passenger. He showed a most knowledgeable interest in navigation and, informally, checked each station of the crew. After landing he visited each crew station and bade farewell to each member. He was an outstanding gentleman whom I've not forgotten (15).'

Tuesday, 2 December 1941: H.M. Ships *Prince of Wales*, Captain John C. Leach, and *Repulse*, Captain W.G. Tennant, arrived at Singapore.

The following day he hoisted his flag in *Prince of Wales* as C. in C., Eastern Fleet.

Having decided to confer with the Americans he left Singapore on 4 December in RAF 205 Squadron Catalina *FV-V*, Flight Lieut. S.G. Stilling. After an overnight stop at Labuan, then at 1225 hours the following day, 5 December, he arrived at Manila to confer with Admiral Thomas C. Hart, C. in C., US Asiatic Fleet (16).

Admiral Hart was impressed favourably:-

'What he found he liked. Phillips was "good stuff", he wrote, "decidedly the intellectual type with a first rate brain." Moreover, Phillips agreed that Manila was a better base than Singapore for conducting offensive operations and said that he would plan on basing the British battle fleet there. He also agreed to form several "striking forces" whose primary role would be offensive and only secondarily the protection of convoys.

As Hart advised Stark, Phillip's ideas were similar "in general" to those "previously encountered out here but perhaps less extreme." The British were still of a mind to "disperse forces, guard everything and be so thin that nothing is really guarded." The most encouraging things from Hart's point of view were Phillips's offensive spirit and his candour. "We were quite frank," wrote Hart, "laid our cards down and wore no gloves." Hart found Phillips a man whom he liked, respected, and would be happy to serve under (17).'

Saturday, 6 December 1941. Japanese convoys steaming in a westerly direction across the southern waters of the Gulf of Siam were sighted, first at 12:12 hours then again at 12:46 hours local Malay time, by Flight Lieut. J.C. Ramshaw, in his Hudson aircraft, No. 1 RAAF Squadron then based at Kota Bharu, north east Malaya (18). The second sighting revealed the presence of twenty five merchantmen in addition to warships. In Singapore Admiral Layton kept a rough diary from which later he was able to prepare official reports. This diary has survived. An entry dated 6 December states:-

'14:40 (hours)   Report received of two large Japanese escorted convoys off the S. coast of Indo-China (19).'

In response, at 18:40 local time RAF 205 Squadron Catalina *FV-S* took off from Seletar with orders to search the waters towards the Gulf of Siam in the direction of the Ramshaw sightings. Unfortunately it was a particularly stormy night with poor visibility and nothing was sighted. After a patrol flight of thirteen hours and twenty minutes the aircraft returned safely to Seletar at 08:00 hours the following morning (20).

Sunday, 7 December 1941. Meanwhile, to replace aircraft *FV-S* out on patrol, at 00:50 hours local time on 7 December, another Catalina, *FV-W*, Flight Sergeant William Edward Webb, took off from Seletar. The last signal from her was received at Seletar later that morning, at 0720. At 09:50 Tokyo time, thus 08:20 local Malay time, *FV-W* was sighted by a 'Jake' reconnaissance floatplane from the seaplane tender *Kamikawa Maru* (21). The position was, 'Panjang Island twenty miles distant bearing 300 deg.', from which it will be seen that *FV-W* had penetrated rather far north into the Gulf of Siam. In his 'Jake' machine Reserve Ensign Eiichi Ogata fired just twenty rounds from one of his 7.7mm machine guns following which, at 10:15 Tokyo time, 08:45 local, *FV-W* was taken under fire by an Army fighter aircraft flown by First Lieut. Toshirou Kuboya. *FV-W* was shot down with there being no survivors (22). In this manner did Catalina *FV-W* and her crew become war casualties, possibly the first of the Pacific War about to commence at 01:15 Malay local time on Monday, 8 December (23).

Following the above mentioned Japanese shipping movements, information in respect of which had been received while he was in conference with Admiral Hart in Manila, overnight 6/7 December Admiral Phillips returned by Catalina aircraft direct from Manila to Seletar, Singapore.

Very early on Monday, 8 December 1941 Japanese forces, the 23rd Brigade of the 18th Division, Major General Takumi Hiroshi, commenced to come ashore through the surf onto the open beaches of Sabak and Badang at Kota Bharu. They lost some one third of their initial assault force to machine gun fire received from troops of the 3/17 Dogra Regiment of the 8th Indian Brigade. Nevertheless by midnight on 9 December the town, and especially the two all important air bases, were to be in Japanese hands (24).

Forty minutes later, also early on 8 December 1941 Malaya time but on Sunday, 7 December in Hawaii, Japanese Naval forces commenced their attack on Pearl Harbour. Over Oahu Commander Fuchida Mitsuo was in command of the air attack (25). The first attack wave of dive bombers was led by Lieut. Commander Takahashi Kakuichi and commenced at 03.25 hours Japan time on 8 December 1941. This was 07.55 hours on 7 December Hawaii time.

At Shanghai, after first being invited by a Japanese boarding party to surrender, at 07:45 on 8 December the river gunboat *Peterel*, 185 tons, Lieutenant Stephen Polkinghorn RNR, at her moorings in the river, was taken under fire by the cruiser *Idzumo* and sank rapidly thereafter.

With his Flag in *Prince of Wales*, and as Commander of Force 'Z', the C. in C. sailed from Singapore shortly after 17:00 hours on 8 December 1941 with the objective of bringing Japanese invasion forces to action.

Originally it had been intended that the carrier *Indomitable*, first commissioned on 10 October 1941, would have accompanied *Prince of Wales* and *Repulse* to the Far East. Unfortunately however, while working up in the West Indies, on Monday, 3 November 1941 she had run aground on Rackham Cay near Kingston, Jamaica. Subsequent repairs to the ship took place at Norfolk, VA. The time taken to carry out this work made it impossible for her to steam East until much later, in fact eventually it was only on 2 January 1942 that she was to leave Capetown bound for Aden (26).

Wednesday, 10 December 1941: lost at sea on the occasion of the sinking of his two heavy ships by IJN air attack, shore based forces of the Twenty Second Air Flotilla, Rear Admiral Matsunaga Sadaichi, the first such aerial success of this nature against capital ships. No divebombers were used in this attack. *Prince of Wales* and *Repulse* were sunk by bombs and torpedoes dropped by type 96 'Nell', and type 1 'Betty' Navy machines, both of Mitsubishi manufacture. Captain Tennant of *Repulse* was among the survivors (27).

On the subject of his belief in the A.A. fire protection afforded to men of war by their own such weapons, after the event another authority was to write:-

> 'Peter Kemp, who worked closely with Phillips and knew him well, thinks that he "was a bit contemptuous of air attacks on ships and reckoned that any ship worth her salt could shoot any aircraft out of the sky". Kemp continues: "I am forced to the conclusion that, when the Japanese aircraft were sighted, Phillips believed the ships could defend themselves adequately with their own A/A fire. A decision not to ask for air cover seems to me to be entirely in character with the man as I knew him (28).'

NOTES

1. NA ADM 196/51. *Service Record.* Colonel Phillips was born: 3 May 1855, first commissioned: 28 January 1875, promoted Lieut. Colonel: 17 July 1901, and retired from the Royal Artillery on 17 July 1906. *Army List,* July 1908.

2. *Dictionary of National Biography.*

3. Author's notes, *The Life and Times of His Majesty's Light Cruiser Durban: 1921-1944.* 122. In 1931 a party from *Durban* was to shift this aged weapon to a new position on Sapper's Hill to the south west of Stanley.

4. *Dictionary of National Biography.* Also S*ervice Record.*

5. Chaplain W.E. Rea, *Nil Desperandum, H.M.S. Hawkins, Flagship of the East Indies Station,* (Privately, 1935), 299, 300, 311, and 313. Copy kindly loaned to the author by Mr. Nigel Hughes.

6. Arthur J. Marder, *From the Dardanelles to Oran,* (OUP, 1974), 57.

7. Ibid. 117/118.

8. Ibid. 166/167. Later the then Major General Sir Hastings Ismay, who had worked closely with him in London, was to write as follows regarding the blind spot held by Tom Phillips concerning air power, 'In particular, he refused to admit that properly armed and well fought ships had anything to fear from air power.' Lord Ismay, *The Memoirs of General The Lord Hastings Lionel Ismay,* (London, 1960), 240.

9. Ibid. 216.

10. The author of the *Dictionary* entry is Rear Admiral Henry George Thursfield (1882-1963), naval historian and author, and Naval correspondent of *The Times* from 1936 to 1952.

11. Arthur J. Marder, *Old Friends New Enemies,* 1, (OUP, 1981), 367.
    The late Professor Marder, academically speaking, rated Sir Tom very highly. As regards his lack of sea going experience, and junior permanent rank, many brother officers were less than impressed by his selection for this new position in the East. Although he could be charming, professionally speaking all seem agreed that he was difficult to get on with, frequently curt, even rude, too opinionated, and, in his own view, almost always right.

12. Arthur Nicholson, *Hostages to Fortune,* (Stroud, 2005), 31.

13. NA HW 1/296.

14. In RAF 205 Squadron Catalina flying boat *FV-S*, Flight Lieut. R. Atkinson. Co-pilot: Pilot Officer S.E. Scales.

15. Kind communication of 14 December 1998 received by the author from Mr. David B. Babineau.

16. Details of this flight from a copy of the log book kindly made available to the writer by Mr. J.E. Cason, Flight Engineer in *FV-V* at the time.

17. James Leutze, *A Different Kind of Victory*, (Annapolis, 1981), 225/6.

18. Third Supplement, *The London Gazette*, Friday, 20 February 1948.

19. NA ADM 199/1473, with additional detail given in ADM 199/1185.

20. Copy of log book kindly made available to the writer in January 1999 by Mr. David B. Babineau, at the time Pilot Officer and Navigator in *FV-S*.

21. m.v. *Kamikawa Maru*, 6,853 grt, built in 1937 at Kawasaki Dockyard, Kobe, a freighter owned by 'K' Line, Kawasaki Kisen Kaisha Ltd. When new placed in service on their prestigious New York route. Taken up for war service. On 28 May 1943 to be sunk by USS *Scamp* SS-277, Commander W.G. Ebert, at position 1.36S 150.24E, just to the north of the Saint Matthias Group off Papua New Guinea. *Lloyd's Register*. Theodore Roscoe, *United States Submarine Operations in WW2*, (Annapolis, 1988), 551.

22. **Eiichi** Ogata. Born: 10 January 1916. Called up for IJN service: 12 April 1940. 'Jake' aircraft – Aichi E13A1 Navy Type reconnaissance seaplane. Two or three seat low wing monoplane, twin float, radial engine. Max. speed: 222 m.p.h. Range: 1,415 miles. Other details per *Kamikawa Maru*: Combat Report No. 1: 7 to 12 December 1941. Letter to the writer dated 29 March 1999, National Institute for Defense Studies, Tokyo.

23. In addition to Flight Sergeant Webb the other members of his crew were co-pilot Flying Officer Patrick Edwin Bedell, Sgt. Colin Burns Treloar, Sgt. Edwin Alexander Bailey, Sgt. Stanley Abram, Sgt. Peter Eaton, LAC Arthur Henry Chapman, and AC1 William Thomas David Burnett.

24. Henry Frei, *Guns of February*, (Singapore, 2004), 44.

25. **Fuchida** Mitsuo. Born in Nara Prefecture: 2 December 1902. Died at Kashiwara near Osaka: 30 May 1976. Entered the IJN, Etajima Naval College: 26 August 1921. At Kasumiga Ura assigned to the Naval Air Arm: December 1927. Joined Yokosuka Air Corps for training in horizontal bombing: 1 November 1933. Promoted Lieut. Commander and selected for Naval Staff College: 1 December 1936. Appointed Flight Commander in *Akagi*: 1939. Appointed in command Air Groups, Carrier Division 1: August 1941. In command of the air attack at Pearl Harbour, HI: 7 December 1941. Planned air attack against Rabaul: January 1942. Led the first air attack against Darwin: 19 February 1942. In command air attacks over Colombo: 5 April 1942. Suffering from appendicitis he took no operational role at Midway and, although wounded, survived the sinking of *Akagi*: 5 June 1942. For the remainder of WW2 served as a staff officer. Post war spent many years as a Christian missionary. In 1960 he became a US citizen. Gordon W. Prange, *At Dawn We Slept*, (New York, NY: 1983), 195-201, and elsewhere. It should be noted that USN air attack on 4 June so badly damaged *Akagi* (*Red Castle*) that early on 5 June the burning hulk was scuttled by the IJN.

26. NA ADM 199/426: *War Diary, East Indies, 1942*.
    With hindsight there is little doubt that it was just as well that *Indomitable* did not form the air arm of Force 'Z'. Firstly the ship would not have been adequately worked up so would not have been operating in a truly efficient manner, and most of her aircrew would have been inexperienced. Secondly, her aircraft mostly would have been antiques of out of date design with poor range and wretched performance capability. In the circumstances had she been with the two heavy ships there is a very great likelihood that she would have joined them both on the bottom of the China Sea.

27. There are a number of accounts of this disaster. For example, Martin Middlebrook and Patrick Mahoney, *Battleship*, (London, 1977), and Geoffrey Brooke, *Alarm to Starboard*, (Cambridge, 1982). A recent comprehensive and most useful volume is by Arthur Nicholson, *Hostages to Fortune*, (Stroud, 2005).

28. Richard Hough, *The Longest Battle*, (London, 1986), 141.

10 December 1941 to 16 January 1942

Vice Admiral Sir Geoffrey **Layton**,

for his second and short period in office

At Singapore Admiral and Lady Layton had embarked in the peacetime Shaw Savill Line m.v. *Dominion Monarch*, 27,155 grt. Early on 10 December, as soon as he received the news of the sinking of *Prince of Wales* and *Repulse*, Rear Admiral Ernest John Spooner, 'rushed off to stop Geoffrey Layton who had gone onboard *Dominion Monarch* which was taking him home (1).'

At 0833 on 11 December 1941 Vice Admiral Sir Geoffrey Layton made a broad policy signal on assuming command of the Eastern Fleet. He was under no illusions as to the abilities and likely characteristics of the new enemy, Japan:-

> 'He expected them to fight with fanatical determination, and to carefully laid plans. He thought their ships and aircraft would be good and likely to be formidable, and that their forces would be fully equipped and trained for any operations they had in mind.
>
> He only made the proviso that the Japanese would not be very good at retrieving a situation which went wrong, nor at exploiting a situation which opened unexpected opportunities. They were too concerned with pursuing fixed plans to the bitter end. (--)
>
> He did not think the Japanese would be very good at operating submarines and they weren't …
> (2).'

25 December 1941. The Governor of Hong Kong, His Excellency Sir Mark Young, surrendered the colony to Japanese forces under the command of Lieut. General T. Sakai of the Twenty Third Army.

On 27 December 1941 General Sir Henry Pownall succeeded Air Chief Marshall Sir Robert Brooke-Popham in Singapore as C. in C., Far East. That day he sent a telegram to the Chief of the Imperial General Staff in London. The first of the following extracts covers the Japanese landing on the beaches at Kota Bharu during the N.W. monsoon. The second is of interest considering the forthcoming generally wretched performance by British Imperial forces in the heavily forested jungle conditions prevalent over much of the peninsula, especially down the mountainous centre and on the east coast:-

> 'From para. 5: They can carry out combined operations in surf conditions we should consider impossible.'
> 'From para. 10: Hardly any part of country is impassable for lightly equipped infantry, except jungle covered hills only fit for small parties (3).'

Following the debacle at Pearl Harbour the week before, in Washington, DC on Monday, 15 December 1941 President Franklin Delano Roosevelt (1882-1945) and Secretary of the Navy Frank Knox (1874-1944) agreed to appoint Admiral Ernest Joseph King, USN as the new C. in C., US Fleet. Officially he was to assume this new position in Washington, DC on Tuesday, 30 December 1941.

On the following morning, 16 December, the President and Secretary decided that the new C. in C., Pacific Fleet would be Admiral Chester William Nimitz, USN. Onboard *Grayling* SS-209 at Pearl Harbour he was to assume command on 31 December 1941.

Admiral Raymond Ames Spruance, USN (1886-1969)
Victor of the Battle of Midway, 4-7 June 1942.
Regarded as 'one of the greatest Admirals in American naval history'

Admiral Marc Andrew Mitscher, USN (1887-1947)
During the latter half of WW2 to command the Fast Carrier Task Force in the Pacific.

On 7 December 1941, in addition to the above, the five other USN and Marine officers of whom reference was made in July 1937, were employed as follows. To these names is added that of the submariner and future Commander, Submarines, Pacific Fleet, Charles Andrews Lockwood (1890-1967). Also the vital matter of logistical support is mentioned:-

William F. Halsey	Vice Admiral commanding Aircraft, Battle Force in the Pacific Fleet with his flag in *Enterprise* CV-6.
Raymond A. Spruance	Rear Admiral commanding Cruiser Division Five, Pacific Fleet with his flag in *Northampton* CA-26.
John H. Towers	Rear Admiral, Chief of the Bureau of Aeronautics.
Marc A. Mitscher	Captain in command *Hornet* CV-8 then being completed at Newport News, VA.
Charles A. Lockwood	Captain, Naval Attache, U.S. Embassy, London.
Alexander A. Vandegrift	Brigadier General USMC, First Marine Division.

Especially in and across the Pacific, where distances are enormous, the fleet and military supply chain was of the very greatest importance. The Commander of this Service Force, USN, throughout the Pacific War was

Vice Admiral William L. Calhoun. At the time of the Pearl Harbour attack, as a Rear Admiral he had been commanding the Base Force (4).

By the end of December 1941 troops of the Japanese army had advanced far down the Malay peninsula. Roughly speaking the front line extended across from the mouth of the Perak River, well to the south of Penang on the West coast, to Kuantan on the East coast.

The outlook for the New Year was poor.

From Singapore on 1 January 1942 in the 'Nederland' Line passenger motor ship *Marnix van Sint Aldegonde,* 19,129 grt, Lady Layton, together with Sir Robert and Lady Brooke-Popham, sailed for Batavia (5). Many other service wives departed from Singapore in this sailing.

On 4 January 1942 in position 9.12S 111.10E, or 200 odd miles south of Java, the China Navigation steamer *Kwangtung*, 2,626 grt, was the first ship to be sunk in the Indian Ocean by Japanese submarine in WW2. The victor was *I-156* who achieved this success by gunfire (6).

The British and their Allies by now had agreed to certain changes in the Eastern command structure. Accordingly in the light cruiser *Dragon*, Captain R.J. Shaw, and with *Durban*, Captain P.G.L. Cazalet, in company he left Singapore at noon on Monday, 5 January 1942, arriving the following afternoon at Tangjong Priok, the port of Batavia, Java. At Singapore the SNO now was Rear Admiral E.J. Spooner – see Appendix One.

On his departure from Singapore for Batavia Sir Geoffrey made an unfortunate general signal to those he was leaving behind. A quote follows, together with the comment subsequently made by one authority:-

"With your heads held high and your hearts beating proudly, I leave the defence of Singapore in your strong and capable hands. I am off to Colombo to collect a new fleet".

Although it was an eminently sensible move, the signal was criticized as one of the worst examples of British wartime leadership, a grandiloquent "I'm all right, Jack" (7).

This critical comment is justified. To illustrate with just one example, on 20 January 1942 the Chaplain in *Sultan*, Rev. P.B. Clear, RNVR, was to write officially on the subject, his letter being addressed to the base ship commander. Extracts follow:-

'I have been gravely disquieted during the past few days by conversations and the tone of certain letters, which appear to reveal among the ship's company the seeds of possible disaffection:-

"… the loss of the two capital ships was due to recklessness."

"… the C. in C's staff have found it healthy to leave."

Further, numbers of ratings were questioning the need to keep the existing number of men in the Naval base since, " there are no defences to man", "there are not sufficient arms for the numbers here", and that, "ships have recently gone away empty". Other phrases heard were, "another Hong Kong", "rats in a trap", and "can't hit back" (8).'

On the other hand the same authority, quoted above at the time of the Admiral's departure for Batavia, also writes about him:-

'His powerful personality was reflected in his appearance. This short, thickset, well built man, with a jutting chin and a tight lipped mouth turned down noticeably at the corners, and with clear grey-blue eyes, gave an impression of rugged determination.'

Later, in Ceylon, "… did not hesitate to use the whiplash of his tongue when he felt people were not pulling their weight in the war effort."

'Mentally and physically alert, energetic and tough, on the whole a shrewd judge of men, he could be very firm, ruthless even, and a bully when dealing with subordinates.

But experienced and level headed officers who stood up to him never regretted it, and he gave subordinates he knew a free hand in carrying out work entrusted to them, together with his backing when required. He certainly possessed the two qualities that he believed were essential to a good leader: a determination to succeed, and not to let go, and the ability to make quick decisions and stick to them (9).'

Meanwhile on 5 January 1942 the Bibby Line motor ship *Devonshire*, 11,275 grt, who had arrived at Singapore in convoy on 3 January with 1,599 troop reinforcements, sailed for Colombo. Amongst the personnel taking passage in her were members of the F.E.C.B. or Far East Combined Bureau, the most secret British signals interception intelligence organisation (10). As the Japanese had begun to make their intentions clear, then first, at the end of August 1938, they had been moved from Hong Kong to Singapore. In due course, and as a further precaution, they were to be moved again, on from Colombo to East Africa. By 22 July 1942, with the arrival of H.M.S. *Ranchi* at Kilindini, this latter move was to be complete (11). During much of that period a senior officer within the FECB organisation was acting Captain Stephen Barry, RN (retired).

Also in the interim ABDA, American -British- Dutch- Australian command, had been formed on 10 January 1942. Based in Java, on 15 January 1942 the British General Wavell took overall command.

In overall command of the ABDA naval forces was Admiral Thomas C. Hart, USN.

However, from the outbreak of the Pacific War and during the first few weeks of that titanic struggle, it was the small number of submarines serving with the Royal Netherlands East Indies Navy who were to sink a useful tonnage of Japanese shipping. Energetically led by Vice Admiral Conrad E. L. Helfrich, RNN, and although as a Naval force greatly outnumbered, they performed most satisfactorily (12).

From 16 January 1942 the few remaining warships of the British China Squadron, now re-named Force, came under the authority of ABDA in Java, specifically Commodore J.A. Collins, RAN.

Also on 16 January 1942 Sir Geoffrey left Tanjong Priok in the cruiser *Emerald*, 7,550 tons, Captain F.C. Flynn, bound for Colombo where he arrived on 21 January.

In the Sunda Strait on 17 January 1942 the destroyer *Jupiter*, 1,690 tons, Lieut. Commander N.V.J.T. Thew, was the first British warship in WW2 to destroy a Japanese submarine. On that day she disposed of *I-60*, Lieut. Commander Hasegawa Shun, first by blowing her to the surface with depth charges, and then by engaging her with gunfire.

Sunday, 15 February 1942. Fall of Singapore, the victor being Lieut. General Yamashita Tomoyuki (1885-1946), Twenty Fifth Army.

Japan re-named the island city Syonan, 'Light of the South'.

C. in C., Ceylon: 5 March 1942 – 8 January 1945. Naturally this position as supremo had been authorised at a high level, the Chiefs of Staff Committee of the War Cabinet. Clause one of the relevant directive read as follows:-

'You are appointed Commander in Chief, Ceylon. All naval, military, air and civil authorities in the area including the Governor and civil administration will be subject to your direction (13).'

On Easter Sunday, 5 April 1942 aircraft flown off five Japanese carriers attacked Colombo. Vice Admiral Nagumo Chuichi continued to fly his Flag in HIJMS *Akagi*.

9 April 1942: Admiral Nagumo launched his attack against Trincomalee.

Fortunately at that stage of the war the IJN had not mastered the technicalities of radar so had not been able to equip their ships accordingly. Also they did not know of the existence of the secret RN refuelling base, Port "T" at Addu in the Maldives. By the most narrow of margins Admiral Nagumo did not come up with the

British Eastern Fleet under Admiral Sir James Somerville (1882-1949). So, 'it was Providence alone,' who saved the latter from a consequence which in all likelihood must have been close to annihilation.

The second in command of the Eastern Fleet at the time was acting Vice Admiral Algernon Willis (1889-1976). From the battleship *Resolution* on 10 April 1942 he drafted a letter to be sent to the C. in C., Mediterranean, Admiral Sir Andrew Cunningham (1883-1963). Extracts follow, the capital letters being in the original:-

'Out of it all emerges that the Jap. F.A.A. (Fleet Air Arm) is much superior to us
in numbers carrier for carrier, speed, range and performance and therefore we're
in a pretty fair mess. (--).
'So here we are, Naval Strategy dominated once AGAIN by the air or as usual the
lack of it (14).'

Admiral: 15 September 1942.

KCMG: 1 January 1945.

C. in C., Portsmouth: 29 September 1945 – 29 June 1947. At the Portsmouth command he succeeded Admiral Sir Charles Little (see C. in C., 1936), and in turn was to be succeeded by Admiral The Lord Fraser of North Cape.

GBE: 1 January 1947.

Retired in 1947. For thirteen years until his death lived in 'Tower Cottage', Rowlands Castle, Hampshire. He was a keen gardener.

Shortly after his death on 4 September 1964 it was reported in the local press that his funeral had taken place at Blendworth Parish Church on Tuesday, 8 September, and had been followed by a cremation. The next day, from the frigate *Tenby*, Captain N.E.F. Dalrymple-Hamilton, his ashes had been committed to the sea off Portsmouth, the ceremony being conducted by his son-in-law, the Bishop of Bermuda, Rt. Rev. John Armstrong. Subsequently, on Friday, 11 September 1964 at 2 p.m., a memorial service was held in St. Ann's Church, Portsmouth Dockyard. Among the mourners at St. Ann's were a great many naval officers, these including Admiral Sir John Eccles, GCB (1898-1966), one time C. in C., Home Fleet and a veteran of the Pacific War (15).

NOTES

1. Diary: Mrs. Megan Spooner. King's College, London. Ref: *GB KCLMA Spooner.*
   Dominion Monarch. When built she was the highest powered motor ship in the world. Shaw Savill & Albion. Maiden voyage to the Antipodes: 16 February 1939, her passenger accommodation being all first class. In August 1940 taken up for troop ship service, being returned to her owners in 1946. Refit. Post war commercial service commenced: 17 December 1948. Final sailing to Wellington: 30 December 1961. Floating hotel at Seattle, WA in 1962 then broken up. William H. Miller, *The Last Blue Water Liners*, (London, 1986), 160-162.

2. Arthur J. Marder and associates, *Old Friends New Enemies*, II, (OUP, 1990), 8. The authors are quoting from a paper prepared for Professor Marder in 1979 by Captain D.H. Doig, Secretary to Admiral Layton for nine years until the Admiral's retirement.

3. Archives Centre, Churchill College, Cambridge. Ref: *DUFC 3/8.* War Cabinet Documents, May 1942.

4. Rear Admiral Worrall Reed Carter, *Beans, Bullets, and Black Oil*, (Washington, DC, 1953), ix, 7.
   To give just one example of the huge supply needs of the Fleet at war, in the very short period September/October 1944, Philippines Campaign, Admiral Carter on page 251 relates that Supply Task Group 30.8, 'of 29 oilers with escorts fed the Fast Carrier Force alone 3,567,000 barrels of fuel and other petroleum products.' That figure equates to some 486,500 short tons. During the Pacific War their failure to attend to logistical matters correctly was to cost Japan dearly.

5. Twin screw *Marnix van Sint Aldegonde*, launched at Amsterdam on 21 December 1929 and completed on 10 Sept. 1930 for the regular service to the East Indies. Taken up for war service and on 6 November 1943, while transporting

2,924 troops from Liverpool into the Mediterranean, she was attacked by German aircraft and torpedoed, sinking the following day when rather over six miles off Cape Bougaroni in Algeria. Happily there was no loss of life. When built she and her sister ship, *Johan van Oldenbarneveldt,* were the largest Dutch liners. In 1602 Johan van Oldenbarneveldt (1547-1619) had been one of the founders of the VOC, Vereenidge Oost-Indische Compagnie or United East India Company. Thus was laid the foundation for the Dutch colonial empire in the East.

6. Hans-Joachim Krug, Yoichi Hirama, Berthold J. Sander-Nagashima and Axel Niestle, *Reluctant Allies,* (Annapolis, MD, 2001), 43. Other sources suggest that the sinking took place on 5 January 1942. Sadly also there exist allegations that the submarine commander may have committed atrocities against the survivors. At that stage of the war, correctly *I-56.*

7. Marder, II, 19/20.

8. NA ADM 199/1472A. Rev. Clear had been appointed to *Sultan* on 19 August 1940 so was well experienced in the position.

9. Marder, II, 7.

10. NA HW 4/24 and 25. *Devonshire,* launched on the Clyde on 20 December 1938 as a troopship. In 1942 converted into a Landing Ship Infantry. Refitted and modernised in 1953. In January 1962 sold to B.I. as their educational cruise ship *Devonia.* Arrived at La Spezia for breaking up: 14 December 1967.

11. NA HW 4/27. Steam ship *Ranchi,* 16,738 grt. In peacetime the P. & O. liner, built in 1925 for their Bombay service. In August 1939 requisitioned for service as an AMC, Armed Merchant Cruiser. In March 1943 converted to a troopship. In June 1948 completed her refit for return to commercial service, the emigrant traffic to Australia. In January 1953 to arrive at Newport, Wales for breaking up.

12. Conrad Emil Lambert **Helfrich**. Born in Semarang, Java: 11 October 1886. Died in The Hague: 20 September 1962. Between 1903 and 1907 studied at the Naval Institute, Den Helder. Commanded the Netherlands East Indies Squadron: 1935–1937, thereafter Director, Higher Naval Military School. As a Rear Admiral, in October 1939 appointed Commander of all forces in the Netherlands East Indies. Vice Admiral: 31 August 1940. On 12 February 1942 succeeded Admiral Thomas C. Hart, USN in command of ABDA naval forces. Just six days prior to the fall of the Dutch East Indies, on 2 March 1942 flew to Ceylon and for the remainder of WW2 commanded the remaining Dutch forces in the East. Admiral and commander of all Dutch Naval Forces: August 1945. In Tokyo Bay in U.S.S. *Missouri* BB-63, and on behalf of the Netherlands, on 2 September 1945 signed the Japanese Instrument of Surrender. Retired: 1 January 1949.

13. NA CAB 79/19. Signal from The Admiralty, No. 0159a dated 5 March 1942. The directive consisted of seven clauses in total.

14. Archives Centre, Churchill College. Ref: *WLLS 5/5 – part I of II.*

15. *The News*, Portsmouth, Saturday, 12 September 1964.

16 January to 1 March 1942
Commodore John Augustine **Collins**, RAN

(Commodore China Force, based in Batavia, Java)

He was born in Deloraine, Tasmania on 7 January 1899, the son of Dr. M.J. and Mrs Collins. Sir John died in Sydney on 3 September 1989.

Educated at Christian Brothers College, Melbourne.

Joined the first class of **Cadets**, Royal Australian Naval College, Geelong on 13 February 1913. **Midshipman**: 1 January 1917. From 4 April 1917 served in battleship *Canada*, 28,000 tons. The Captain of the ship from 13 February 1918 was Hugh D.R. Watson, he of the Yangtse Gorges pioneering voyage in 1900. **Sub Lieutenant**: 1 September 1918. From 19 November 1918 in destroyer leader *Spencer*, 1,740 tons. **Lieutenant**: 1 December 1919. From 1 January 1920 in *Cerberus II* 'Naval Depot, London', attending courses. From 23 April 1921 in light cruiser *Melbourne*, 5,400 tons. From 25 September 1924 attending RNC, Greenwich, 'Officer Qualifying for (G)'. From 27 March 1925 Lieut. (G) in Gunnery School Ship, *Excellent*, Portsmouth. Also he qualified as a deep sea diver. From 20 June 1925 Lieut. (G) in coal fired surveying sloop *Moresby*, 1,650 tons, the ex RN minesweeper *Silvio* who from that day had been commissioned into the RAN (1). She sailed from England on 28 June and arrived in Australian waters in September, there to be employed for several years in surveying the waters of the Great Barrier Reef. However surveying duties were not to come his way as from 8 October 1925 he was appointed Lieut. (G) in another coal fired man of war, light cruiser *Melbourne*, 5,400 tons. She recommissioned on that day for a voyage from Sydney, leaving on 23 November for England. En route briefly joined the 1CS, Mediterranean fleet, and then continued her voyage to arrive at Portsmouth on 30 March 1926. Subsequently she returned to Australia in August 1926. In her idle moments could be whiled away as related here:-

> 'Like many coal burning ships our cruiser became infested with rats and our solitary ship's cat could not compete with them. We had an air rifle in the Wardroom and used to take pot shots at them as they ran along the top of the ventilation shafts but we seldom did them much damage (2).'

1927: Naval Liaison Officer during the Royal Visit by T.R.H. The Duke and Duchess of York in battlecruiser *Renown*, 26,500 tons, Captain Norton A. Sulivan. The ship arrived at Sydney on 26 March 1927. Homeward bound and sailing without escort on passage from Fremantle to Mauritius, it was on 26 May that a serious fire broke out onboard. Although there followed some tense hours fortunately by 2200 hours that evening it had been brought under control (3). Back in the British Isles from 26 August 1927 Lieut. (G) standing by new building, the heavy cruiser *Australia* at John Brown & Co. Yard, Clydebank. **Lieutenant Commander**: 1 December 1927. Lieut. Commander (G) in the heavy cruiser *Australia*, 10,570 tons, who commissioned at Clydebank on 24 April 1928. Naturally she worked up in the waters of Great Britain and then, sailing on 2

August, steamed out to Australia via North America and the Pacific. From 24 July 1930 in command destroyer leader *Anzac*, 1,670 tons. From 3 January 1931 in *Cerberus*, Flinders Naval Depot, '... for charge of Gunnery School'. From 12 January 1932 attending the staff course for a year at Royal Naval Staff College, Greenwich.

Commander: 30 June 1932. Continued on Staff Course.

From 9 January 1933 at the Admiralty, Plans Division for two years.

From 9 January 1935 standing by new building, light cruiser *Sydney*, 6,830 tons, at Swan Hunter and Wigham Richardson Yard, Wallsend-on-Tyne. Commander of *Sydney* when she commissioned on 24 September 1935. Owing to the invasion of Abyssinia by Italy she remained in the Mediterranean for several months, finally departing for Australia on 14 July 1936.

Captain: 31 December 1937. Early in 1938 to Navy Office, Melbourne as Assistant Chief of Naval Staff and Director of Naval Intelligence.

From 16 November 1939 to 13 May 1941 in command *Sydney*. He joined her at Fremantle. Home waters and in the Indian Ocean. Subsequently arrived Alexandria: 26 May 1940.

11 June 1940: hostilities commenced against Italy.

West of Crete on 28 June 1940 he participated in the sinking of Italian destroyer *Espero*, 1,090 tons.

On 19 July 1940, northwest of Crete, he achieved another success which resulted in the sinking of light cruiser *Bartolomeo Colleoni*, 5,200 tons, and the damaging of sister ship *Giovanni Delle Bande Nere* (4).

CB: 26 July 1940

12 November 1940. Participated in a most successful action against an Italian convoy bound across the Strait of Otranto:-

> '.... to the Italian mainland from Valona Bay (5).'

Just before midnight on Sunday, 9 February 1941 *Sydney* returned to Sydney.

17 June 1941, '.... assumed duty at Singapore as Assistant Chief of staff to Admiral Layton for combined planning operations.'

On 15 January 1942 in Java Admiral Thomas C. Hart, USN assumed command as ABDAFLOAT, the Naval arm of the short lived ABDA concept (6). Under him:-

> 'Collins assumed his appointment on the 16th (of January 1942), and hoisted his broad pendant in
> the depot ship *Anking* at Tanjong Priok (7).'

With the collapse of ABDA on 25 February, he left Java from the south coast port of Tjilatjap in corvette minesweeper HMAS *Burnie*, 733 tons, at 20:15 hours, Monday, 2 March 1942 (8).

1942: Naval Officer in charge, Western Australia.

Subsequently actively involved in the Pacific War.

From 7 April 1943 – June 1944: in command heavy cruiser HMAS *Shropshire*, 9,830 tons, concerning which as early as 27 August 1942 in London Prime Minister Churchill had submitted to the War Cabinet a proposal:-

> 'If the shortage of cruisers in British areas is balanced against the apparent position in the American
> areas, there is good reason for retaining all British construction of cruisers under Admiralty
> control. On the other hand, the most serious consideration must be given to the maintenance of
> the Royal Australian Navy. The losses the Royal Australian Navy have sustained have been very
> heavy especially in cruisers which are the backbone of their Fleet.'

The very next day, in Cabinet, he continued:-

> 'My War Cabinet colleagues will be aware that the Royal Australian Navy has recently lost
> HMAS *Canberra*, one of her last two remaining 8-inch cruisers. Thus, in the past year the Royal

Australian Navy has lost three out of the six cruisers with which they began the war. I consider that it might have a lasting effect on Australian sentiment if His Majesty's government gave freely and outright to the Royal Australian Navy one of our similar ships. The Admiralty are willing to offer HMS *Shropshire* which will be available in six months' time after refit (9).'

So it was that the ship came under the command of Captain Collins. In turn on 10 April 1943 in a letter to the C. in C., the Nore, concerning the transfer of the ship to the RAN, Collins expressed himself as follows:-

'It is assumed that, in the circumstances, publicity is undesirable, particularly as the destination of the ship will be apparent.

It is suggested that any extensive ceremonial entailing travel for numerous participants, e.g. Representative of the Country of Shropshire, would be inappropriate at this time. Furthermore, in view of the necessity for preparing the ship for war at utmost speed, it would appear inappropriate to arrange any ceremonial that would require time spent in rehearsal (10).'

On 25 June 1943, and following this extensive refit at Chatham, the ship officially was transferred from the RN to RAN (11). On 1 July 1943 she proceeded to Scapa Flow to work up. There on 12 August she was inspected by HM King George VI and the C. in C., Home Fleet, Admiral Sir Bruce Fraser. On the following day she sailed for Fremantle where she arrived on 24 September. Finally at Brisbane at the end of October 1943 she joined TF (Task Force) 74.

13 June 1944 – 21 October 1944: Commodore R.A.N. squadron in the Pacific War. In *Australia* he relieved Rear Admiral Victor A.C. Crutchley, VC, RN on 13 June 1944, just in time to participate in the USN Seventh Fleet operation on 2 July to secure Noemfoor, west of Biak. The Seventh Fleet commander was Vice Admiral Thomas C. Kinkaid (12).

Between 22 July 1944 and 3 September 1944 *Australia* proceeded to Australia to refit whereupon he transferred his pendant to *Shropshire*. Subsequently, on re-hoisting his pendant in *Australia* at Seeadler Harbour, Manus, Admiralty Islands in September, the ship was assigned to TG (Task Group) 75.2.

15 September 1944 in *Australia* participated in the successful USN led assault on Morotai.

US landings on islands in Leyte Gulf commenced from 17 October 1944 when minesweepers first began operations to clear the waters. He was wounded in action at 0605 hours on Trafalgar Day, 21 October 1944 during a 'Val' Aichi divebomber suicide aircraft attack against *Australia*. Captain Emile F.V. Dechaineux, six other officers and twenty three ratings were killed, and sixty four officers and men wounded (13).

1945: Naval officer in charge, Western Australia.

Now recovered from his wounds, as **Commodore** commanding Australian Squadron, an appointment was which to endure to 6 November 1946, his pendant was hoisted in *Shropshire* at Manila on 22 July 1945. In her he entered Tokyo Bay on 31 August 1945 (14).

In the interim, flying from Tinian in the Mariana Islands, on 6 August the atomic bomb 'Little Boy' had been dropped over Hiroshima by USAAF B-29 bomber *Enola Gay* flown by Colonel Paul Tibbets (15). Similarly on 9 August atomic bomb 'Fat Man' had been dropped over Nagasaki by another B-29, *Bockscar* flown by Major Charles Sweeney.

2 September 1945: in *Shropshire* he was present in Tokyo Bay on the occasion of the surrender of Japan. During that memorable day he attended the ceremony onboard USS *Missouri* BB-63, 54,900 tons, Captain Stuart S. Murray (16).

Early on 20 September Admiral William F. Halsey left to return home to the U.S.A. As Commander, Fifth Fleet, USN, Admiral Raymond A. Spruance assumed Naval command in the theatre.

Subsequently he was much involved with organising the future presence of the British Commonwealth Occupational Forces, Japan. These troops, from Britain, Australia, New Zealand and India, took up their duties from January 1946 after which in February he returned to Australia. The Commodore already had sensed future problems however. An extract taken from his reminiscences follows:-

'This time we had no illusions about the war to end war and there were already signs of trouble brewing in Korea (17).'

4 July 1946: Represented Australia at the inauguration of the Philippines Republic.

Rear Admiral: 8 January 1947.
First Naval Member and Chief of Australian Naval Staff: 24 February 1948 – 23 February 1955. He was the first graduate from the RAN College to attain this, the highest post in the RAN.

Vice Admiral: 10 May 1950.
KBE: 1 January 1951.
Australian High Commissioner to New Zealand: 1956-1962
On the occasion of his funeral in September 1989 his countrymen showed their respect for and pride in their distinguished Admiral:-

'In the largest Naval funeral ever conducted in the city, Sir John was farewelled with a procession along George Street (Sydney) comprising a funeral firing party of 24 sailors, a Naval band of 40 musicians, 200 officers and sailors, and 150 personnel from HMAS *Nirimba* manning the gun carriage carrying his White Ensign draped casket (18).'

NOTES

1. HMAS *Moresby* named for Admiral John Moresby (1830-1922). See Kuper, C. in C., 1862, reference (20).
2. Vice Admiral Sir John Collins, *As Luck Would Have It,* (Sydney, 1965), 35/36.
3. Ibid, 41. Peter C. Smith, *Hit First, Hit Hard,* (London, 1979), 51/52.
4. G. Hermon Gill, *Royal Australian Navy, 1939-1942,* (Canberra, 1957), 190, 235, 432, 517/8.
5. Ibid. Valona today is Vlore, Albania.
6. Thomas Charles **Hart**. Born in Davison, MI: 12 June 1877. Died in Sharon, CT: 4 July 1971. Entered U.S. Naval Academy: May 1893. Spent much of WW1 involved with submarines. Assumed command *Mississippi* BB-41: 6 June 1925. Superintendent, U.S. Naval Academy, Annapolis: 1 May 1931 – 18 June 1934. Appointed C. in C., U.S. Asiatic Fleet: April 1939. With his flag in heavy cruiser *Augusta* CA-31, 9,050 tons, assumed command: 25 July 1939. Following the success of Japanese military operations in the Philippines arrived at Surabaja in USS *Shark* SS- 174, Lieut. Commander Lewis Shane Jr.: 2 January 1942. ABDA formally constituted on 10 January 1942 with Admiral Hart in command of Naval forces. Relinquished this position: 14 February 1942. Tanjong Priok to Colombo in HMS *Durban*: 16 – 22 February 1942. ABDA concept dissolved: 25 February 1942. Back home officially transferred to the Retired List in the rank of Admiral: 1 July 1942. Subsequently assisted with a Pearl Harbour inquiry, and served on the General Board. U.S. Senator for Connecticut: 1945-1947. James Leutze, *A Different Kind of Victory,* (Annapolis, 1981). Naval Historical Center, Washington, DC.
7. s.s. *Anking*, 3,472 grt. Built at Greenock in 1925 for The China Navigation Co., (Butterfield and Swire). In December 1941 at Singapore taken up for wartime service by the RN as a depot ship, Malta. In 1942 transferred back East as a communications ship, initially at Tanjong Priok, the port at Batavia, then at Tjilatjap, south coast of Java. Later, when bound for Fremantle, sunk by IJN gunfire when some 200 miles East of Christmas Island: 3 March 1942. Only three survivors. John Swire & Sons, *The China Navigation Company Limited,* (Hong Kong, 1992), 65.
8. Hugh Campbell and Ron Lovell, *So Long, Singapore,* (Hobart, 2000), 194. HMAS *Burnie*. 16 knots. One 3", one 20mm Oerlikon and machine guns.
9. NA ADM 116/4848.
10. Ibid.

11. G. Hermon Gill, *Royal Australian Navy, 1942-1945,* (Canberra, 1968), 292/3. At the time the C. in C., The Nore was Admiral Sir George d'Oyly Lyon.

12. Gerald E. Wheeler, *Kinkaid of the Seventh Fleet,* (Annapolis, 1996), 372. This operation took place to secure airfields prior to the advance on Morotai and, ultimately, the U.S. return to the Philippines.
Thomas Cassin **Kinkaid**. Born in Hanover, NH: 3 April 1888. Died in Bethesda, MD: 17 November 1972. Midshipman, USN: July 1904. Executive Officer *Colorado* BB-45: 3 February 1933. Commanding Officer heavy cruiser *Indianapolis,* 9,950 tons: 7 June 1937. Rear Admiral: 27 November 1941. As a Vice Admiral assumed command of the Seventh Fleet: 26 November 1943. Admiral: 6 April 1945. At Keijo (Seoul) on 9 September 1945 on behalf of the Allies accepted the Japanese surrender of their colony of Chosen (Korea). Retired as a full Admiral: 28 April 1950.

13. Gill, 512/3. Among the wounded in *Australia* was gunnery officer Richard Innes **Peek** (1914-2010) who was badly burned by the effect of this kamikaze attack. In due course he too was to reach the top of the tree in the RAN as First Naval Member and Chief of the Naval Staff between 1970 and 1973, then being Vice Admiral. KBE: 1 Jan. 1972.

14. Collins, 156.

15. Today (written in 2010) the B-29 *Enola Gay* may be seen in the Udvar-Hazy Center, a facility of the Smithsonian adjacent to Washington Dulles International Airport. Their collection is impressive.

16. Seapower Centre, Australia: email dated 14 April 2005 received from duncan.perryman@defence.gov.au.
On behalf of Australia the Japanese surrender document was signed by General Sir Thomas Blamey.

17. Collins, 162.

18. Obituary, *The Sydney Morning Herald,* Saturday, September 9, 1989. HMAS *Nirimba*: shore establishment – a 'stone frigate'.

Appendix One

Rear Admiral Ernest John **Spooner**:

R/A, *Sultan*, Naval Base, Singapore: August 1941

to February 1942

Born in Winchester: 22 August 1887, son of John Douglas Spooner and his wife, Mary E. Spooner of 'The Homestead', Winchester.

Died on Tjebia Island, Tujoh group to the north of Bangka: 15 April 1942.

Educated from 1898 at West Downs School, Winchester, and then between September 1901 and December 1902 in the Navy Class at Bradfield College, Berkshire (1).

Entered the Royal Navy, training ship *Britannia*, on 15 January 1903 (2).

Midshipman: 30 May 1904.

Already from 16 May 1904 appointed to the armoured cruiser *Leviathan*, 14,100 tons, China Station. From 27 December 1904 in armoured cruiser *Sutlej*, 12,000 tons, also on the China Station. Her Captain was William L. Grant who, between July 1915 and July 1917, was to serve in the East again, but then as C. in C., China Station. Her Commander was John D. Kelly, and a Lieutenant was James F. Somerville, both in due course to reach the highest rank.

In June 1905 joined *Ocean* to return home and pay off on 16 August 1905 (3).

From 1 September 1905 appointed to battleship *Goliath*, 12,950 tons, Captain Henry C. Kingsford, Channel Fleet. Present in the ship at Portsmouth on Saturday, 10 February 1906, the occasion when H.M. King Edward VII launched a warship of radical new design, the battleship *Dreadnought*, 17,900 tons (4). Her first commanding officer was Captain Reginald H.S. Bacon.

In *Goliath* the normal routine with the Fleet consisted of cruising in English, Irish and Portuguese waters with frequent gunnery target practice, the landing of guns ashore, running torpedoes, manoeuvres, and other war related exercises. Naturally coaling ship was a regular part of the routine, for example at Portland on Tuesday, 5 June 1906 when she took in 1,300 tons at an average of 101 tons per hour, 'the collier shoving off at 9 p.m.'. On the following morning, 'hands were employed cleaning ship after coaling.'

On Monday, 1 October 1906, at Portland, 'Captain Robert H.J. Stewart joined ship to relieve Captain Kingsford who left to the strains of "Auld Lang Syne" from the Band.'

The horrible task of coaling ship was a most regular and unpleasant feature of life. Here again, at Portland once more on 12 October 1906:-

'The collier *Greenhill* came alongside at 11.30. We commenced coaling at 1.0 p.m.

This proved a very slow and arduous task as we had to sweep the collier. The after holds having little left in them and what was there was quickly disposed of. But in No. 2 hold 100 tons was left after the rest had been cleared and it was 3 a.m. before this was inboard. It rained during the night which did not add pleasure (5).'

At Arosa Bay, Finisterre on Tuesday, 29 January 1907 *Goliath* was inspected by the Vice Admiral, Second in Command, Channel Fleet, The Hon. Sir Assheton G. Curzon Howe who flew his flag in the battleship *Caesar*, 14,900 tons, Captain Sydney Robert Fremantle (1867-1958). He was the eldest son of Admiral The Hon. Sir Edmund Robert Fremantle who had been C. in C., China Station from February 1892 to May 1895.

Just over a fortnight later the combined Channel and Atlantic Fleets, with a squadron from the Mediterranean Fleet also there present, a total of fifty seven warships, anchored in Lagos Bay, south Portugal. Then on Friday, 16 February 1907:-

'At 08.45 combined Battle Fleets proceeded to sea and carried out steam tactics under Admiral Sir Arthur K. Wilson, VC at 14 knots. Returning to harbour fleets anchored at 5.20 p.m. firing a Royal salute of 21 guns in honour of the King of Portugal who had arrived.'

It is difficult today to imagine such a magnificent occasion.

Admiral Sir Arthur Knyvet Wilson (1842-1921), was awarded his Victoria Cross following the Battle of El Teb in the Sudan, 29 February 1884. As C. in C., Home and Channel Fleets, in February 1907 he was flying his flag in the battleship *Exmouth*, 14,000 tons. To be promoted Admiral of the Fleet just a few days later, on 1 March 1907, and from 25 January 1910 to succeed Admiral of the Fleet Lord Fisher as First Sea Lord.

Also serving under his command at the time, with his flag in the cruiser *Sapphire*, 3,000 tons, was Rear Admiral Alfred L. Winsloe, in due course to be C. in C., China Station from January 1910 to January 1913.

The Vice Admiral, Atlantic Fleet, was Sir William H. May with his flag in the battleship *King Edward VII*, 16,350 tons. She was commanded by Arthur C. Leveson, from September 1922 to September 1924 yet another officer to be C. in C., China Station.

With his flag in the battleship *Venerable*, 15,000 tons, the Vice Admiral, Mediterranean Fleet, was Francis C.B. Bridgeman (1848-1929), in December 1911 in turn to succeed Arthur Wilson as First Sea Lord.

HRH The King of Portugal was Carlos I, born on 28 September 1863. Within the year he was to be assassinated in Lisbon, on 1 February 1908.

While in Lagos Bay numerous other exercises took place at various times, and involving various different squadrons of ships. In his Journal on 17 February 1907 Midshipman Spooner made the following entry:-

'In the afternoon the Private rig race was run for the King of Portugal's cup and was won by *Irresistible*'s gig. In the evening the King and Queen of Portugal and Crown Prince attended the 'At Home' of *Caesar* where he presented the cup to the winner of the race.'

Irresistible, a battleship of 15,000 tons, Captain Lionel G. Tufnell, a signals expert, then was serving with the Mediterranean Fleet.

From 5 March 1907 he was appointed to the new battleship *Hibernia*, 16,350 tons, and actually joined her at Portland on Saturday, 9 March 1907. She had commissioned at Devonport as recently as on 2 January 1907, flagship of Second in Command, Channel Fleet, Vice Admiral Sir Reginald N. Custance. A Lieutenant then serving in the ship was Charles J.C. Little, from January 1936 to February 1938 to be C. in C., China Station.

Midshipman Spooner's Journal closes on Sunday, 14 July 1907, at the time *Hibernia* being at anchor at Cromarty.

Sub Lieutenant: 30 July 1907.

He continued to serve in *Hibernia* until 17 September 1907.

Then studied at Portsmouth until, later in 1908, at the RNC, Greenwich.

From 7 January 1909 appointed to battleship *Prince of Wales*, 15,000 tons, Flagship, Atlantic Fleet. The C. in C. was Vice Admiral HSH Prince Louis of Battenberg.

Lieutenant: 30 January 1909.

Continued to serve in *Prince of Wales*.

From 29 January 1910 in *Dryad*, Navigation School Ship, Portsmouth, for 'Navigation Course'. On 10 June 1910 he passed the necessary examination.

From 4 August 1910 as Lieutenant (N), assistant to Navigation Officer in battleship *Agamemnon*, 16,500 tons, Home Fleet.

From 1 January 1911 Lieutenant (N) in Torpedo Gun Boat *Halcyon*, 1,070 tons, Coast Guard Service.

Between 15 February 1913 and 3 January 1914 Lieutenant (N) in the light cruiser *Sappho*, 3,400 tons, 'for service with First Fleet'. Then he returned to Navigation School, on this occasion to *Druid*, and on 13 February 1914, 'Passed for First Class Ships – 2nd Class (6)'.

From 31 March 1914 Lieutenant (N) in light cruiser *Bellona*, 3,350 tons.

For Great Britain and her Empire the Great War commenced on 4 August 1914.

The log book in the new light cruiser *Constance*, 3,750 tons, records that at Birkenhead on Wednesday, 26 January 1916, 'Ship commissioned by Captain C.S. Townsend'. She had been launched just a few months earlier, 12 September 1915. On 29 January she carried out her full power trials during which she achieved 29.2 knots, and at 4 p.m. that afternoon was handed over to the Royal Navy by her builders, Messrs. Cammell Laird & Co., together with 685 tons of oil fuel remaining in her tanks. The log book was signed by E.J. Spooner, Navigating Officer (7).

On Sunday morning, 30 January *Constance* sailed from Birkenhead for Scapa Flow where she arrived the following afternoon. For the entire month of February she worked up at Scapa Flow. Under the command of Captain Cyril Samuel Townsend *Constance* participated in the Battle of Jutland on 31 May 1916.

From 13 June 1916 he served as Lieutenant (N) in the light cruiser *Calliope*, 3,750 tons.

Lieutenant Commander: 30 January 1917.

Continued to serve in *Calliope*. From 15 October 1918 her Captain was Percy L.H. Noble who, between February 1938 and July 1940, was to be C. in C., China Station.

Armistice Day on 11 November 1918 signalled the end of the Great War, WW1.

From 22 January 1919 appointed Navigator in the battlecruiser *New Zealand*, 18,800 tons. This was the occasion of the Empire Tour undertaken by Admiral of the Fleet Lord Jellicoe who flew his flag in the ship. She sailed from Portsmouth on 21 February and with a call at Gibraltar, 24/25 February, made her transit of the Suez Canal, 3/5 March, and arrived at Bombay on 14 March. Thereafter, with a call at Colombo and another at the Cocos Islands, she reached Albany, West Australia on 15 May. From Sydney, NSW on 16 August the ship crossed the Tasman Sea and arrived at Wellington on 20 August 1919. From Auckland, North Island on 3 October, and following very short calls at various Pacific Islands, she arrived at Esquimalt, BC on 8 November. From Esquimalt on 25 November she made her transit of the Panama Canal between 13 and 18 December. Christmas 1919 was spent at Kingston, Jamaica. Finally, and via Port of Spain, Trinidad from 17 to 21 January 1920, *New Zealand* returned to Portsmouth on 3 February 1920.

Meanwhile, in the London Gazette of 21 June 1919, notification was given that his DSO had been awarded for distinguished service during the Great War as Navigator of two light cruisers, respectively *Constance* and *Calliope*.

From 6 August 1920 he served as Navigator in the 'large light cruiser' *Courageous*, Reserve Fleet, Portsmouth. Only in 1923 was work to commence on her conversion to become an aircraft carrier.

From 5 May 1921 borne in the Flotilla Leader *Shakespeare*, 1,750 tons, Port Edgar, the destroyer base on the south bank of the Firth of Forth a very short distance upstream from the modern road bridge, 'for duty with TBDs'.

Commander: 31 December 1922.

From 18 April 1923 as Commander (N) and Fleet Navigating Officer in the light cruiser *Lowestoft*, 5,440 tons, Flagship, Africa Station. The C. in C. was Rear Admiral Sir Rudolf Walter Bentinck (1869-1947), and his Flag Captain was Henry J.S. Brownrigg.

By the end of the year she was replaced by *Birmingham*, a sister ship also of four funnels and who re-commissioned at Chatham on 15 November 1923. From 12 December 1924 the new C. in C., Africa Station was Rear Admiral M.S. Fitzmaurice, with, from 23 December 1924, Flag Captain R.H.L. Bevan.

From 26 October 1925 he was appointed Commander of the Dockyard, and King's Harbour Master at Gibraltar.

On 20 April 1926 at the English Cathedral, Gibraltar he married the well known soprano, Megan Gwladys Foster (8). She was born on 16 July 1898 and was to die in August 1987.

From 10 April 1928 attending courses in *Victory*, Portsmouth.

Between 1 January and 9 April 1929 in *President*, Admiralty, for duty with the Department of Navigation.

From 9 April 1929 served as Commander (N) and Fleet Navigating Officer in the battleship *Nelson*, 33,500 tons, Flagship, Atlantic Fleet. The C. in C., was Admiral Sir A. Ernle M. Chatfield, subsequently to be promoted Admiral of the Fleet and, as Baron Chatfield, at the outbreak of WW2 to be Minister for Coordination of Defence in the Chamberlain government.

Captain: 30 June 1930.

From 2 October 1930 appointed in command of the light cruiser *Dragon*, 4,850 tons, America and West Indies Station. He joined her at Bermuda on 29 October 1930. Sadly his predecessor, Captain L.H.B. Bevan had died at Valparaiso on 5 September whereupon Commander P.W. Nelles, RCN had assumed command temporarily (9). Commander Nelles was to leave the ship at Bermuda on 4 January 1931 in order to return home in readiness to assume command of the new destroyer HMCS *Saguenay* when she was completed in May 1931 (10).

Christmas 1930 was spent at Bermuda then during the first three months of 1931 she cruised south to Grenada, Trinidad, the Virgin Islands, Puerto Rico, Jamaica, Haiti, Cuba and Key West in Florida. She returned to Bermuda on 24 March 1931. Her following cruise, from May to October 1931 took her through the Panama Canal and north towards the Pacific coast of Canada and the U.S.A. during which she steamed as far to the north as Ketchikan, Alaska.

Between 1930 and 1932 the C. in C. on the station was Vice Admiral Sir Vernon H.S. Haggard.

At the conclusion of this commission he brought *Dragon* home to reach Sheerness on 2 September 1932.

His and Mrs. Spooner's son, James Douglas Spooner, was born on 11 July 1932. Subsequently he was to attend Eton and Christ Church, Oxford.

From 5 December 1932 appointed Deputy Director, Operations Division, Admiralty, London.

From 27 July 1934 to August 1936 in command of *Dryad*, Navigation School, Portsmouth.

Then from 21 September 1936 he attended a Senior Officers' Tactical Course in *Victory*.

From 18 December 1936 he commanded the Cadet Training Cruiser *Frobisher*, 9,860 tons. This was followed, from 17 August 1937, by his command of the Cadet Training Cruiser *Vindictive*, 9,100 tons. The latter was an interesting hybrid in some respects in that originally it was intended that she should enter service as the cruiser *Cavendish*. Launched on 17 January 1918 she was commissioned in October that year as the seaplane tender cum aircraft carrier *Vindictive*. As such she had seen service in the Baltic after the Great War in the campaign against the Bolsheviks. Between 1923 and 1925 she had been re-converted as a cruiser once more, but retained a hangar forward of the bridge and the capability to handle three seaplanes. In this capacity, for two years from early in 1926, and under the command of Captain Ronald Howard, she had seen service for one commission on the China Station. There out East, for just a few months until October 1926 and even with her modest aerial capacity, she was called upon to replace the carrier *Hermes*. In her new role as a Cadet Training Cruiser, Captain Spooner was her first commanding officer.

From 19 December 1938, in succession to Captain John Henry Godfrey, appointed in command of the battlecruiser *Repulse*, 26,500 tons. Completed in August 1916 unfortunately owing to financial constraints she had been inadequately modernised during her long refit between 1934 and 1936. Between 1936 and 1938 she had served in the Mediterranean. She re-commissioned at Portsmouth on 3 January 1939. On 18 June 1940 he was to be succeeded in command of the ship by Captain William George Tennant.

In Europe WW2 commenced on 3 September 1939.

Rear Admiral: 25 June 1940.

From 16 July 1940, in succession to Vice Admiral Robert Henry Taunton Raikes (1885-1953), a submariner, flag in *Pyramus*, Kirkwall parent ship, as Flag Officer Commanding Northern Patrol. A short while later his headquarters were transferred to *Fortitude*, stone frigate, Ardrossan, Firth of Clyde. Appropriate accommodation was provided at the Hollywood Hotel in Largs, later to be used by the Commandant, Combined Training Centre.

In view of what was to come, here, writing on the eve of his departure to Singapore, Saturday, 26 October 1940, is the newly appointed C. in C., Far East, Air Chief Marshall Sir Robert Brooke-Popham. This and other comments are addressed to the Secretary, Chiefs of the Staff Sub-Committee, Committee of Imperial Defence, Whitehall. The Secretary, who in 1936 had been especially selected by Lord Hankey to succeed him in that position, was Major General Sir Hastings Ismay (11). From this extract it is clear that the new C. in C. held few illusions concerning the relative status of his new post:-

'2. I fully realise that at the present time the requirements of Singapore must come
a bad third to those of the British Isles and of the Middle East (12).'

Sir Robert arrived at Singapore on 14 November 1940. In due course, between December 1941 and February 1942, Imperial military performance when engaging Japanese forces in the thick jungles and elsewhere in the Malay peninsula was to be unimpressive. Therefore, as an airman, it is of interest to read that as early as 5 December 1940 he was to include the following comment in another report to General Ismay in London:-

'I have also realised that the word 'impenetrable' as applied to jungle has many
interpretations and that it is dangerous to rest one's flank on it thinking that nothing
will get through (13).'

From 10 June 1941 Ernest Spooner was appointed Admiral Superintendent, Singapore Naval Dock Yard (DY) and Rear Admiral, Malaya with his flag in the stone frigate (shore base) *Sultan*.

———

His wife was to join him for their voyage East. Extracts taken from her diary follow.
Wednesday, 11 June 1941 (14).

> In order to proceed East to take up his new position he and his wife ended their association with the Largs Naval offices and off Gourock that evening embarked in s.s. *Ulysses*, Captain James Appleton Russell, and were settled in by 8.30 p.m.
> Coal fired *Ulysses*, 14,499 grt, was completed on 22 October 1913 for the Australian service of the Blue Funnel Line. When homeward bound frrom Australia, on Saturday, 11 April 1942 to be torpedoed and sunk forty five miles south of Cape Hatteras by *U-160*, Lieut. Commander Georg Lassen. Happily there was to be no loss of life as Captain Russell, and the 189 crew members, five gunners and ninety five passengers were rescued by USS *Manley* APD 1 and the next day landed at Charleston, NC.

Thursday, 12 June 1941: by breakfast time steaming off the Mull of Kintyre.

26-27 June 1941: in Halifax, N. S. where the C. in C. was Rear Admiral Bonham-Carter (15). A fellow passenger in the ship was Lady Northcote, wife of the Governor of Hong Kong (16).

3 July 1941: steamed through Mona Passage with Puerto Rico to port and the Dominican Republic, Hispaniola to starboard.

Saturday, 5 July 1941: steamed between Trinidad and Tobago. *Ulysses* steamed at thirteen knots.

At sea: 'Jack' Spooner was musical. He played the piano and joined his wife in singing duets. Megan Spooner was forty three on 16 July 1941.

21 July 1941: Japan signed an agreement with the Vichy French government of Marshall Petain. One important consequence was the granting to Japan of considerable military concessions in south French Indo-China included the use of airfields, and of Saigon and Camranh Bay as Naval bases.

Wednesday, 23 July 1941: arrived Cape Town. Journeyed to Admiralty House, Simon's Town. "It is a charming house with a delightful garden. Admiral Budgeon is an experienced gardener (17). Spent the night in *Ulysses*."

The C. in C., South Atlantic only was to shift from Freetown to Simon's Town in 1942. By then he was to be Vice Admiral William E. C. Tait who was to hoist his flag at Simon's Town on Friday, 27 March 1942 (18).

Thursday, 24 July 1941: returned to Simon's Town and lunched in his old command, the light cruiser *Dragon*, Captain R.J. Shaw, MBE (19). Spent that night at the Mount Nelson Hotel, Cape Town.

Friday, 25 July 1941: at Mount Nelson Hotel.

Saturday, 26 July 1941: a.m. Off by train to Johannesburg.

Sunday, 27 July 1941: arrived at Johannesburg and stayed at the Carlton Hotel.

Monday, 28 July 1941: to Pretoria by train and returned to Johannesburg that evening to catch the overnight train to Durban.

Tuesday, 29 July 1941: arrived Durban and stayed at the Edward Hotel.
Socialised with various friends.

Thursday, 31 July 1941: embarked in *Ulysses* who had been at the Bluff for two days coaling. Sailed from Durban at 16.30 on 31 July.

Wednesday, 13 August 1941: arrived at Colombo and stayed at the Galle Face Hotel.
"Jack saw the C. in C. at the Navy offices. (Since 16 July 1941 the C. in C. was Vice Admiral G.S. Arbuthnot, CB, DSO)."
"Dined with C. in C. at 8.30. Awful dinner."

Thursday, 14 August 1941: sailed from Colombo at about 3.00 p.m.

Monday, 18 August 1941: arrived at Penang and spent two nights ashore at the Eastern and Oriental Hotel.

20 August 1941: sailed from Penang.

22 August 1941: arrived at Singapore, "Jack's 54th birthday".
   Admiral Spooner was to succeed Rear Admiral T.B. Drew (20).
   Megan Spooner wrote:-
   "Admiral Drew not very bright specimen – he has the breezy assured manner of many Naval Officers and gets away with it."

Thursday, 28 August 1941: dined at Layton's (the C. in C. which see above).

Tuesday: 2 September 1941: Drew's sailed.

Monday, 8 September 1941.
   "Dined with Governor – Sir Shenton Thomas – a nice man but not a leader of men.
   I should say rather a rigid insensitive brain (21)."
   "Lady Shenton T – small gentle charming. Easy atmosphere."

20 September 1941: in order to attend the Brooke family celebrations sailed from Singapore to Sarawak in s.s. *Marudu* (22).

22 September 1941: anchored at Pending at about 2 p.m. In Kuching stayed as a guest of the Chief Secretary, C.D. Les Gros Clark (23).

24 September 1941. Centenary of the rule of the White Rajahs in Sarawak (24).
   "We breakfasted just after 7.30 and in our best bibs and tuckers went down for the Celebration Ceremony. It was staged near the landing quay."
   "The Rajah and Ranee walked from their palace, the Astana, to the river and entered a long white boat manned by about a dozen Malays with paddles and crossed over to the landing opposite the Government buildings – Le Gros Clark accompanied them."
   "They walked from the quay between lines of Malay soldiers and British sailors to two chairs on the steps of the Gov. Bldgs. Gold curtains were hung on either side and a gold rug at their feet. (-) The ceremony went without a hitch (25)."

On the occasion of this Centenary Admiral Layton, the C. in C., was represented by Captain J.A.S. Eccles (26). H.M. Ships present were the merchantman *Kedah*, taken up for war service, and the destroyer *Tenedos* (27).

Saturday, 27 September 1941: departure from Kuching.
   "At just after 11 a.m. we pushed off from the bank, waved to our very kind host (Le Gros Clark) and moved downstream in the tender m.v. *Rejang* (28). We anchored at the mouth of the Sarawak River at about 12 noon and had to wait until 4 p.m. before s.s. *Tajang* appeared on the horizon."
   "By 4.30 we were aboard the *Tajang* and sailed immediately. The ship is small but clean (29)."

Monday, 29 September 1941: her visit to Sarawak ended with the ship's return to Singapore at about 2.30 p.m., and her return to Navy House by 3.30 p.m.

17 October 1941: in Japan General Tojo Hideki replaced Prince Konoe Fumimaro as Prime Minister. Already he held the position of War Minister. In addition now he became Home Minister. Finally and openly Japan was governed by the right wing military, the fulfillment of a trend which had commenced with the Manchurian 'affair' of September 1931. For Japan the experiment, which was to endure until 18 July 1944, was to prove disastrous.

Wednesday, 26 November 1941: unknown to Britain or the U.S.A. at 0600 hours Tokyo time, which was 1030 a.m. on 25 November in Hawaii, a Japanese fleet based around their six fleet carriers supported by two battleships, weighed at Hitokappu Bay, Etorofu Island and proceeded out to sea in an easterly direction (30).
Vice Admiral Nagumo Chuichi flew his flag in H.I.J.M.S. *Akagi*, 'Red Castle', 36,500 tons.

Saturday, 29 November 1941: war warning.
"Jack picked me up (from the city) at about 12.45. Arrived Navy house to find signals saying 'Awake': code word for 'be prepared', and another saying (Admiral) Tom Phillips (the new C. in C., Eastern Fleet) was flying from Colombo with two staff officers."
"We want more brains in Singapore. B.P. (Brooke-Popham, C. in C.) is unusual but he has a first class mind – Percival (Army) may have brains but certainly is short of guts and decision. Layton has plenty of guts but no first class grey matter.
Pulford (RAF) is good – brain keen and subtle, and character firm and steady.
Keith Simmons (Army) – steady brain, great tact, considerable charm and judgement but lacking in drive and not a first class brain. Governor seems a poor reed. Col. Sec. reputed to be a bottleneck and obstructor and also to be revengeful - certainly unbalanced – I think he has ophthalmic goiter (31)."

Meanwhile on 27 November the Chief of Naval Operations of the United States Navy (equivalent to the British First Sea Lord), Admiral Harold R. Stark, had sent his 'war warning' message from Washington. This was followed up by specific instructions addressed to Admiral Husband E. Kimmel, C. in C., Pacific Fleet in Honolulu, and to Admiral Thomas C. Hart, C. in C., Asiatic Fleet in Manila (32). As one result of his frequent visits to Washington, DC, the last as recently as on 26 November, Admiral Ernest J. King, C. in C., Atlantic Fleet, was well acquainted with the extremely tense atmosphere prevailing as regards Japanese intentions.

Sunday, 30 November 1941: acting Admiral Sir Tom S.V. Phillips and Commander M.G. Goodenough, his Staff Officer (Plans), having arrived at Seletar the night before by Catalina *FV-S* (Flight Lieut. R. Atkinson) of RAF 205 Squadron, were accommodated at Navy House. His Chief of Staff, Rear Admiral Arthur Palliser, flew with him in the same aircraft but stayed elsewhere.
"TSV (the Admiral) looks tired and worn but is as modest and gentle as ever.
Cdr. Goodenough is a nice young man."
"TSV Ph. is charming and so willing to talk to anyone."

Tuesday, 2 December 1941.
"The Eastern fleet ! arrived at Naval Base at about 5.30 p.m. i.e. *Prince of Wales* and *Repulse* arrived accompanied by 4 destroyers. They passed Singapore harbour early afternoon and all Singapore stopped work to watch. When they came to the Johore Straits the evening was still

and clear – the ships with their strange exotic camouflage looked very fine against the green hills of Johore."

"Never before surely can two ships of H.M. Navy have been more welcome nor given more confidence. Malaya is pleased."

After the war, in April 1947 so for what it is worth, and writing of this event, Lieut. General A.E. Percival was to comment:-

'... on 2 December the battleship *Prince of Wales* and battlecruiser *Repulse*, escorted by four destroyers, arrived at Singapore. This was an historic occasion. It was the first time that a battle fleet had been based on Singapore. I can remember now the thrill it gave us all as we watched those majestic ships steaming up the eastern channel of the Johore Straits and coming to anchor at the Naval Base. But yet one wondered. When I had been a student at the Royal Naval Staff College I had been told that the essence of naval warfare was a balanced fleet, i.e. a fleet consisting of all types of warships, each with their own part to play, and here we saw those two great ships arriving accompanied by only a few destroyers. We knew that there were only a few light cruisers and a few destroyers at Singapore and that none of them were modern ships. There were no aircraft carriers, without which a battle fleet loses most of its value in modern war, no heavy cruisers, and no submarines. Obviously this was not sound strategy and obviously a great risk was being taken. All the same we were glad to see the big ships and we assumed that they had been sent in an eleventh-hour effort to deter the Japanese from going to war. (--). I think it was the next evening that I was invited to dinner with Admiral Spooner and his charming wife to meet the new arrivals. It was a delightful evening as I already knew most of them intimately. Admiral Sir Tom Phillips I had met when I was at the War Office and he at the Admiralty. John Leach, the Captain of *Prince of Wales* and one of the finest of men, had been an instructor at the Royal Naval Staff College when I was a student there and was a great personal friend of mine. So also was Bill (now Sir William) Tennant, the Captain of *Repulse* (--). I felt that here at any rate was a group of men who could do the trick if anybody could do it (33).'

Wednesday, 3 December 1941: in Navy House, their last large formal dinner party.

"Dinner to the Duff Coopers (briefly, Resident Cabinet Minister in Singapore) and to new C. in C., Eastern Fleet. Other guests were the Brooke Pophams, the (Sir George and Lady Katharine) Sansoms, General Percival, Air Vice Marshall Pulford, General Keith Simmons, Rear Admiral Palliser, Captains Tennant (*Repulse*), Leach *Prince of Wales*), and Atkinson (Royal Navy Captain of the Port), Lt. Col. Cole and wife and the Flag Lieut. (34). Quite a gala evening. The men were in uniform as owing to the war scare soldiers and airmen had to wear uniform always. Everyone was very pleasant. The Duff Coopers were gracious. She is a completely self confident woman. Every whim is gratified. Her manners are not very polished. She looked remarkably lovely but her face is unattractive and after an hour or so and the enamel had worn off the face fell away. He is quiet, unmoved and rather unyielding but easy and willing to talk. I found Sir Robert B. Popham improve on acquaintance – I think he is a little shy. Now he feels comfortable with me. He is certainly an aloof bird by nature. She is always gracious. Altogether an evening to remember and a happy one. The house was full of flowers, the garden bright with lights and everyone was cheerful and seemed to enjoy themselves."

Earlier that day Admiral Phillips had hoisted his flag in *Prince of Wales* as C. in C., Eastern Fleet. Vice Admiral Layton continued to command the China Station.

Thursday, 4 December 1941.

"(Captain) Bill Tennant to dinner. He is a nice person. He told of how Dudley Pound (in 1941 the

First Sea Lord) had spitefully given him a poor flimsy (confidential report). One realises more and more how D.P. is a place seeker and time server and lasts by virtue of extreme patience and calmness and a determination always to 'serve' his superiors and never take responsibility."

At 0700, in Catalina *FV-V* (Flight Lieut. S.G. Stilling) of RAF 205 Squadron, Admiral Phillips flew from Seletar via Labuan to Manila, there to confer with his American counterpart, Admiral Thomas C. Hart, C. in C., Asiatic Fleet. He was accompanied by his secretary, Paymaster Captain S.T. Beardsworth, and Staff Officer (Plans), Commander M.G. Goodenough.

> Friday, 5 December 1941.
> "Dined with Captain (John Augustine) and Mrs. Collins (RAN. Since August 1941 the Assistant Chief of Staff to Admiral Layton as C. in C., China Station) at Rimau. Very delicious dinner beautifully cooked. Other guests Mr. and Mrs. Bowden (35). Rear Admiral Palliser. Had long pleasant chat with the latter. A charming man straight from Regency Times."

As an aside of relevance Vice Admiral Sir John Collins, as he became, subsequently was to write that Captain Leach, in command of *Prince of Wales* and an old friend, told him that upon the arrival of the ship at Singapore, '*Prince of Wales* wanted at least a month in which to work up (36).'

Also on 5 December *Repulse*, escortd by *Vampire* and *Tenedos*, sailed for Darwin in North Australia, a political gesture made with the intention of re-assuring labour Prime Minister John Curtin (1885-1945), his government and his countrymen.

> Saturday, 6 December 1941.
> "6 p.m. Admiral Sir Guy Royle arrived to stay (37). He looks worried but is as charming as ever."

First at 1212 and again at 1246 hours local, two convoys of Japanese ships were sighted by Flight Lieut. J.C. Ramshaw, RAAF from his Hudson aircraft, RAAF No. 1 Squadron flying out of Kota Bharu (38). Already these ships had rounded the southernmost point of French Indo-China and were steaming in a westerly direction. The ships sighted on the second occasion consisted of twenty five merchantmen in addition to warships.

In the rough diary which he maintained in Singapore, an entry made by Admiral Layton on 6 December reads:-

> '1440   Report received of two large Japanese escorted convoys off the S. coast of Indo-China (39).'

Sunday, 7 December 1941: Mrs. Spooner was present with her party at a fund raiser at the Naval Base. This was held in the evening when the, ".. band of *Prince of Wales* played from 8 – 9."

> The late Professor Arthur Marder gives the reason for the presence of Admiral Royle, and others, at Singapore. The whole business may well have been unavoidable in the circumstances, nevertheless it was to prove to be another case of too little, too late:-
> 'When Phillips returned to Singapore from Manila in the forenoon of Sunday, 7 December (*Repulse* returned at noon that day), he plunged into a series of conferences with British and other officers, including Vice Admiral Sir Guy Royle, the First Naval Member of the Australian Navy Board, and Commodore W.E. Parry, the First Naval Member of the New Zealand Navy Board (40). These officers had just arrived for an inter-Allied (anticipating the Americans and Dutch as Allies) conference of Naval commanders which was projected, but which circumstances were to prevent. In the same context Phillips conferred with the Dutch and American Naval Liaison Officers at Singapore, Captains L.G.L. van der Kun and J.M. Creighton.'

Meanwhile the Blue Funnel vessel *Ulysses* had been refiting at the Taikoo Dockyard in Hong Kong. Great efforts to get her ready for sea were made successfully and by 6 December she had been ready to sail:-

'However a good deal of very valuable cargo remained to be loaded and the naval authorities therefore ordered the ship to remain a further 24 hours. At 2 p.m. on Sunday, 7 December, the day of the Japanese attack, the *Ulysses* sailed. A number of fitters from the dockyard went with her, in order to complete her machinery repairs while on passage, as did some of the staff of Messrs. Butterfield and Swire (41).'

Monday, 8 December 1941.

"Approx. 1 a.m. Jack 'phoned by Duty Staff Officer to announce rumour that Japanese had landed at Kota Bharu on north coast of Malaya. Some time later, 4 a.m., another call with report that unidentified aircraft were off Mersing. Half an hour later the air raid siren went. Jack rushed down to the office and we were in the middle of an air raid and it was war with Japan. At 8 a.m. (?) Japan declared war against Britain and America. The air raid did damage in Singapore to the shops in Battery Road and in Raffles Place. Some people were killed and many hurt. Unexploded bombs are in many quarters."

The time of this landing in north east Malaya also was recorded in the rough diary maintained by Admiral Layton:-

'0115   Information received of an attempted Japanese landing at Kota Bharu (42).'

Concerning the air raid over Singapore made early that morning, the Japanese were well informed regarding at least some of the British signal systems. Serving in the light cruiser *Durban*, then at the Singapore Naval Base, *Sultan*, was Surgeon Commander D.R. Goodfellow, RNVR. Amongst other comments he recorded:-

'It was a perfectly glorious night with a brilliant moon and visibility of about twelve miles, when aircraft were reported approaching. The alarm rattlers were sounded as a routine procedure and, on my way to my action station, I came up onto the quarterdeck where there were several officers moving off to their various places of duty. We stopped for a few moments to look at the aircraft thinking they were British. They had already been picked up by the searchlights and our impression that they were friendly was further strengthened by the fact that there was no gunfire, and that the leading machine of the formation of about twenty dropped three red Very lights in succession, which was the British rercognition signal for that night (43).'

Sir Robert Brooke-Popham merely was to report the attack, making no mention of the apparent lapse in signals security:-

'At 0300 hours on 8 December Singapore was attacked by Japanese bombers, which, in all probability, came from Southern Indo-China (44).'

From the log book in *Durban* it may be noted that at 0300 hours on Monday, 8 December, 'Port Watch to A.A. defence stations'. Then at 0340 hours, 'Air Raid warning Red. Hands to Action Stations'. Only at 0515 hours was she to secure from this A.A. action station (45).

Shortly after 1700 that afternoon, with his flag in *Prince of Wales* and with *Repulse* and four escorting destroyers in company, Admiral Phillips sailed with his Force 'Z'. He proceeded in the direction of N.E. Malaya with the intention of bringing the Japanese invasion forces to action and of disrupting their landings.

At sunset Vice Admiral Sir Geoffrey Layton hauled down his flag and the appointment of C. in C., China Station lapsed.

Admiral Phillips, C. in C., Eastern Fleet, assumed overall command of Britain's naval affairs in the Far East.

Admiral Layton and his wife were to leave Singapore as soon as their ship, m.v. *Dominion Monarch*, 26,463 grt and the peacetime flagship of the Shaw Savill Line, was ready to sail.

In the meantime C. in C., Far East had cabled London with an urgent request for more aerial reinforcements. On Tuesday, 9 December the Chiefs of Staff Committee of the War Cabinet replied as follows:-

'Your 423/6 cipher 8.12.

We regret that it is impossible to provide two squadrons of night fighters in the immediate future.

We are doing everything possible to sustain your day fighter force and your short range bombers, and are also expediting A.A. reinforcements (46).'

Tuesday, 9 December 1941.

"4.30 p.m. Admiral Royle left (from the Navy Base) for Singapore to be on hand for 'plane at 7 a.m. Many air raid warnings but no attack. Jack very tired and worried – mentioned he hoped Tom Phillips would be all right. 6 p.m. called to say farewell to Laytons."

Wednesday, 10 December 1941.

"Jack 'phoned about 11.30 a.m. and I had a premonition of disaster. He returned to lunch at 1.30 and told me *Prince of Wales* and *Repulse* had been sunk by aerial attack. He swallowed some food and rushed off to stop Geoffrey Layton who had gone aboard *Dominion Monarch* which was taking him home."

Later in the day Mrs. Spooner took some papers to the Navy office:-

"Geoffrey L(ayton) there – sad but I think fundamentally a little glad. Lady L prostrate with shock and exhaustion. No news yet of Tom Phillips or Bill Tennant. 11 p.m. Jack 'phoned from office to say Bill T(ennant) was saved and would be coming in shortly. Before midnight Bill, Cdr. Goodenough and Captain Bell (Captain of the Fleet) came up. We fed them and put them to bed. They all were exhausted. We went to bed about 2 a.m."

Indeed the two British capital ships had been sunk at sea off the east coast of Malaya by high level and torpedo bombers of the IJN Twenty Second Air Flotilla, Rear Admiral Matsunaga Sadaichi. At the time this Air Flotilla consisted of three Air Corps, being Genzan, Bihoro and Kanoya, all of whom were based in south French Indo-China. Admiral Phillips and Captain John C. Leach went down with *Prince of Wales* (47). As mentioned, Captain Tennant of *Repulse* was among the survivors.

Thursday, 11 December 1941: at 0833 Vice Admiral Sir Geoffrey Layton made a broad policy signal on assuming command of the Eastern Fleet.

Sunday, 14 December 1941.

"Jack also worried: the Army and Air Force seem ill equipped to say nothing of the naval disaster. Army according to one staff officer never made a defensive line in the north as they had expected to move forwards into Thailand (48). Our Air Force here is puerile – inexperienced and insufficient (49). Many lads have been killed. Evacuations of mothers and children is afoot. Penang is the first – it has been very badly bombed and set on fire."

Monday, 15 December 1941.

"Jack never stops. He starts at 8 a.m. and goes on until about 11 p.m. to say nothing of calls in the night. But he keeps very cheerful though news from the north is bad. We started this war with 160 fighters here. Why oh why didn't Brooke-P resign when nothing was forthcoming?"

Thursday, 18 December 1941.

"Bill (Tennant) sad over his going and the general situation which seems Bloody.

He is flying home with a report from all concerned – Duff Cooper, General Percival, AVM Pulford, Layton and Jack, and possibly Brooke-Popham. He said Duff C. and Layton want martial law – the governor and Percival wouldn't have it. Duff C. very disillusioned about the civil authorities here. Pathetic to hear Jack say what he is needing here – he is short of everything."

Friday, 19 December 1941.

"Penang is evacuated. Chaos reigned there. Everyone failed – the initial air raids completely stunned everyone so that afterwards for two and a half days nothing was done. Then the evacuation was carried out too quickly and things were left undone. (--) At Penang the military asked to have soldiers evacuated and were told by C. in C. to put them on mainland to fight! This eventually happened. Aeroplanes and petrol were left on the quay on the mainland: no one remembered to destroy them."

Also on 19 December 1941 many survivors from *Prince of Wales* and *Repulse,* together with a number of other personnel, some 900 persons in total, were evacuated in the B.I. cargo passenger steamer *Erinpura,* 5,143 grt. She was escorted from Singapore by the light cruisers *Durban* and *Dragon* together with the destroyer *Vampire.* Owing to the rapid Japanese advance down the West coast of the peninsula no longer was it safe to proceed towards Ceylon through the Strait of Malacca. Instead the convoy proceeded south, made their transit of the Sunda Strait on 21 December, only then altering course in a westerly direction. At sea on 24 December the escort of *Erinpura* was transferred to the heavy cruiser *Exeter* and those two ships continued to Colombo to arrive safely on 27 December 1941 (50). While standing by for their next escort duty with further reinforcements for Singapore, *Durban, Dragon* and *Vampire* spent Christmas 1941 at Padang, west coast of Sumatra.

On 27 December 1941 General Sir Henry Pownall succeeded Air Chief Marshall Sir Robert Brooke-Popham in Singapore as C. in C., Far East. That day he sent a telegram to the Chief of the Imperial General Staff in London.

The first of the following extracts refers to the Japanese landings on the beaches at Kota Bharu during the North East monsoon season.

The second is of interest when taking into consideration the generally wretched performance by British Imperial forces in the heavily forested jungle conditions prevalent over much of the Malay peninsula, especially down the mountainous centre and on the East coast:-

'From para. 5:   they can carry out combined operations in surf conditions we should consider impossible.'

'From para. 10:   hardly any part of country is impassable for lightly equipped infantry, except jungle covered hills only fit for small parties (51).'

From various extracts and other sources mentioned above a clear picture emerges of the unpleasant situation, for the British that is, which prevailed in Singapore and Malaya following the Japanese assault.

The capital city of Malaya, Kuala Lumpur, fell on 11 January 1942 and the forces of the British Empire continued to withdraw towards Singapore Island. With a few relatively small exceptions units of the Imperial Japanese Army outfought their opponents on a steady basis and this in spite of the fact that the forces in defence considerably outnumbered the aggressors.

The whole question of morale, and what was in many circles regarded as a lack of 'spine', combined with a state of mental un-preparedness, was commented upon in a short letter addressed to the Secretary to the Admiralty by Admiral Spooner on 19 January 1942. Extracts follow, reference especially being made to the oft resulting desertions by Malay ratings:-

'There was a general absence of ability to take charge and much more strenuous action should have been taken by the officers to prevent desertions. This lack of leadership was also evident in Captain Fraser whom I had to relieve of his appointment as Naval Officer-in-Charge, Penang.

While not seeking to excuse the above, there is no doubt that the complete failure of the Civil Authorities to function on shore aggravated the desertions of the native ratings onboard the ships. There have since been several examples of devotion to duty on the part of Malay ratings, but I am not confident that they will as a whole remain at their posts even if well led, and further desertions from ships must be anticipated when they are put to the test.

I have taken such action as is possible with the European ratings at my disposal to stiffen the Malay ships' companies (52).'

With a month to go before the fall of Singapore extracts from Mrs. Spooner's diary resume.

Thursday, 15 January 1942: among their dinner guests that night was Captain Peter G.L. Cazalet, commanding the light cruiser *Durban*.

> 19 January 1942.
> "Jack feels that Percival has lost his grip – if he ever had it! He is charming and easy but has no drive."

In a diary maintained by H.E. The Governor, Sir Shenton Whitelegge Thomas (1879-1962), an extract taken from his entry of 21 January 1942 reads as follows:-

> 'After War Council today Spooner (Rear Admiral) blazed out and said, 'we had just walked out of Malaya'. And yet they have the nerve to criticize my officers. The behaviour 'of the military' ever since the retreat began has been disgraceful ... If Singapore falls it will be the army's fault; they have been incredibly inefficient (53).'

Again, on 4 and 5 February His Excellency made notes in his diary. Those which are relevant to the Navy follow:-

> 'February 4. Col. Bretherton rang to ask did we know that if you want anything out of the Naval Base you have only got to go and get it. Apparently since Navy evacuated it a few days ago it has been at the mercy of anyone in uniform.
> February 5. Brought up Naval Base evacuation at War Council with Percival and Spooner. Spooner said the military told him they wanted no navy personnel in operational area, so he took them all away. Percival said he had never been consulted in the matter at all. I said I could not understand how a great Base could be handed over by the Navy at the request of anyone but the GOC. Bretheron says the whole place looks as if the staff had left for lunch and never returned. Maps and plans left on office tables and so on. A dreadful thing (54).'

In the interim, on 30 January 1942 Sir Shenton had written to Sir Charles Parkinson, Colonial Office, London. The main purpose appears to have been to include in the package his diary, and some files covering the work of the War Council in Singapore. The following extracts are useful:-

> 'The rest of our troops cross over from the mainland tonight, so in just under 8 weeks the Japs have walked us out of Malaya. 50 miles a week. It has been a very inglorious show with bad and timid leadership. There are many who think that we ought still to have been in Kedah. Murray Lyon lost us that, and since then we seem all the time to have been looking over our shoulder for the next step back. Then we had the break through in Perak, which Wavell himself told me should never have happened if proper dispositions had been made. And so it has gone on. I fear the Army

has become a byword throughout Malaya for incompetence and muddle, and its indiscipline has scared the people out of their wits.

Here there is the same sort of defeatist talk, how that we must be sure to destroy this or that, and get this or that away, so that the Japs shan't get it. I refuse to accept that sort of thing. It ought to be the assumption that we shall hold Singapore, not lose it. What we want here are some first rate fighting commanders and we haven't got them. The only one with that spirit is Spooner. I had better stop or I shall be indiscreet (55).'

Tuesday, 10 February 1942: in the destroyer *Scout*, Lieut. Commander H. Lambton, from her berth at Godown 17, Mrs. Spooner embarked and left Singapore. She was accompanied by her husband's ADC, Lieut. Gordon Peters, RNVR, who was a *Repulse* survivor. He had served under Admiral Spooner previously when, prior to his promotion to flag rank, he had commanded that ship.

Gordon Peters relates that *Scout* was crowded with naval personnel including several other *Repulse* survivors (56).

In Singapore by 10 February it was clear to many that the defences were crumbling. On that day Admiral Spooner stated as much in a hand written note addressed to Captain Cazalet and which was to be given to him very shortly:-

'Singapore will probably be captured tonight or tomorrow (57).'

Wednesday, 11 February 1942: as *Scout* steamed south towards Batavia Mrs. Spooner noted:-

"Passed *Durban*, *Kedah* and two destroyers going north to the rescue."

At 1100 on 11 February the ships passed just to the north of the Bangka Strait.

Thursday, 12 February 1942. *Kedah* was commanded by Commander J.L. Sinclair, DSO, RD, RNR, in peacetime a Singapore harbour pilot. Consequently as she and *Durban* neared Singapore then at 0052 hours early that morning of 12 February Captain Cazalet ordered *Kedah* into the van so that, at a gentle twelve knots, Commander Sinclair could guide both ships on through waters which to him were very familiar. It was not easy. Captain Cazalet subsequently was to record:-

'The glare from burning oil tanks round Singapore and a huge pall of black smoke hanging over the city were sighted from fifty miles away, when still South of the Durian Strait, and as had been anticipated this smoke seriously reduced visibility as we approached (58).'

Accompanied by the two destroyers, *Jupiter*, Lieut. Commander N.V.J.T. Thew, and *Stronghold*, Lieut. Commander Pretor Pinney (ret'd), the four ships duly berthed in Keppel Harbour, Singapore opposite Godowns 53 and 54. Naval and military personnel embarked and the ships sailed, at 0405 hours *Durban* following the destroyers and *Kedah*. Captain Cazalet later noted:-

'When *Durban* left, Keppel Harbour area was utterly deserted and the town itself, lit up by the glare of many fires, appeared quiet. Gunfire on the outskirts of the town was, however, continuous.'

Also Captain Cazalet took with him trunks of personal effects, the property of Admiral Spooner.

One of the Army officers who had embarked in *Durban* was Captain David Wilson of the Second Argylls. He too made a note of the conditions prevailing as the ship sailed:-

'I went on deck again to catch a last sight of the island, which was blazing more and more furiously, with the flicker of gunfire as a sort of background to the whole scene. It was soon obscured by a dense pall of smoke (59).'

Owing to this smoke and murk neither Commandr Sinclair nor Captain Cazalet could find the buoy marking the entrance to the safe passage South through the Durian Strait minefields consequently the ships anchored until first light at 0635. In the vicinity were two merchantmen, also laden with refugees, *Gorgon*, Captain E. Marriott, and *Empire Star* (60). At daylight the four ships proceeded together.

By 12 February 1942 most of the land based bombers of the IJN Twenty Second Air Flotilla had moved to new advanced bases consequently now were available as follows:-
Genzan Air Corps: 17 machines at Kuching, Sarawak.
Bihoro Air Corps: 26 machines at Kuantan, Malaya.
Kanoya Air Corps: 27 machines still at their base near Saigon.
Such was the flexibility of IJN air operations that by now these bombers were supported by up to thirty six Yamada Air Corps Navy type 'O' Zeke fighters plus six reconnaissance machines. Their rapid advance had taken them to Kuantan on 6 February, Kahang by 10 February, and to Kuching by 12 February. Commencing at 0803 hours, just after the British ships cleared Durian Strait, aircraft of this Air Flotilla took these ships under attack, commencing with the largest, *Empire Star*. Subsequent attacks caused damage and casualties on some of the ships, including *Durban*, but their ability to steam was not affected. These attacks ceased at 1300 that afternoon and fortunately no further effort was attempted by the enemy that day. No dive nor torpedo bombers were used by the IJN (61).

Friday, 13 February 1942. Subsequently Mrs. Spooner recorded her safe arrival at Batavia where they, "… went alongside a dirty old ship called *City of Canterbury* (62)."

However here at Batavia Mrs. Spooner wisely accepted the advice given to her by Commodore Collins and embarked in the 'dirty old ship'. She sailed that afternoon at 4.30 p.m. bound for Colombo, a vessel in convoy 'SJ.1'.

That same night at 2300 hours Rear Admiral Spooner and his party left Singapore in the Fairmile launch *ML. 310* commanded by Lieut. H.J. Bull, RNZNVR. Included in his party was the one time Naval officer but now Air Vice Marshal C.W.H. Pulford, AOC, RAF Far East Command (63).

When writing of this occasion after the war, Lieut. General Percival was to state:-
'There were still a number of small ships and sea going craft lying in Singapore Harbour including some naval patrol vessels. On the morning of the thirteenth Rear Admiral Spooner decided that it was no longer safe to keep these at Singapore and that they would be of more use for the general prosecution of the war at Java. Accordingly he decided to sail them all for Java that night and to go with them himself. There were in all about fifty of these little ships with accommodation for about 3,000 persons in addition to the crews. It was the last opportunity that could be foreseen for any organized parties to leave Singapore and vacancies were allotted to the Services and to the civil government at a conference held by the Rear Admiral. The army was allotted 1,800 vacancies. This was no evacuation comparable to our evacuations from Dunkirk, Greece, Crete or elsewhere. It was an attept to get out from Singapore a number of highly trained men and women (staff officers now surplus to our requirements, technicians, business men etc.), whose knowledge would be of value to the Allies for the further prosecution of the war (64).'

As can only be expected in a time of defeat many persons involved held critical opinions. As will be seen now the Navy too was not without fault in at least one important aspect of defence preparation. Some of the following information was provided by Captain F.W. Chamberlin, after the war between the years 1951 to 1962 to be the Marine Superintendent of the Straits Steamship Company, therefore a Merchant Navy officer of considerable stature. Of the evacuation and general period of retreat down the Malay peninsula it was to be written that:-

> 'During the previous days and nights (prior to 15 February 1942), a stream of small craft had poured across the Straits. Some, under Naval orders, who handled their evacuation badly, headed for Java; the remainder to Sumatra.
>
> F.W. Chamberlin recalls that the Navy Base was constantly telephoning the Marine Department's office of Straits Steamships Company from December onwards for tide and other information on the harbours, rivers and beaches of the peninsula. They did not know and had collected no information on the waters and coastline of the country they were defending (65).'

On Saturday, 14 February 1942 Mrs. Spooner noted that, "*Dorsetshire* joined .... who has come to strengthen our escort."

> Indeed the heavy cruiser *Dorsetshire*, Captain A.W.S. Agar, VC, during the previous afternoon having handed over the escort of the Orient liner/troopship *Orcades*, 23,456 grt, to *Dragon*, at 0929 on the Saturday off the south west coast of Sumatra sighted the vessels of convoy 'SJ.1', all crowded with refugees and personnel being evacuated from the East Indies (66). So rapid had been the speed of the Japanese advance that two of H.M. Ships under refit had had to be taken in tow to escape. Thus it was that another Ellerman steamer, *City of Pretoria*, 8,049 grt, had the submarine *Rover* in tow, and the Brocklebank steamer *Malancha*, 8,124 grt, similarly was looking after the destroyer *Isis*. The convoy even included five small Dutch flag vessels of their Batavian based colonial steamship company, K.P.M., Koninklijke Paketvaart Maatschappij.

> Admiral Spooner and party in *ML.310*, having passed safely through the Durian Strait swept channel, then from 1000 to 1700 hours on the Saturday remained at anchor very close inshore off a suitable island. In addition, in case of enemy air patrols, the precaution was taken to camouflage their launch.

Sunday, 15 February 1942: Mrs. Spooner, "Sent a signal to Agar in *Dorsetshire*."

> Singapore fell this day. It was during the afternoon that Lieut. General Arthur E. Percival surrendered his forces to General Yamashita Tomoyuki of the Japanese Twenty Fifth Army. Onboard the IJN Combined Fleet, 'Rengo Kantai', battleship *Yamato*, 68,200 tons, Captain Takayanagi Gihachi, appointed to Admiral Yamamoto's flagship just three days earlier and still in Japanese waters, news of the surrender was received after dinner. The Chief of Staff, Rear Admiral Ugaki Matome, 'sent for *Yamato*'s skipper and a few other officers, and they celebrated until around midnight (67).'
>
> The victors new name for Singapore was Syonan or Shonan, 'Light of the South' or 'Bright South'.

> At 1515 that Sunday afternoon *ML. 310* was sighted by a group of enemy warships from which a destroyer was detached to close and investigate. In addition, now being about four miles from Tjebia Island in the Tujuh (Seven) Group north of Bangka, they were bombed by Japanese aircraft. Fortunately the bomb missed however shortly thereafter the destroyer took them under fire. In the circumstancs it was decided to beach *ML. 310* on Tjebia in order to land the Staff parties (68). Now the first Japanese destroyer was replaced by another. She

took the grounded launch under accurate fire causing Lieut. Bull to order his crew ashore. Shortly thereafter an enemy boarding party crossed from this second destroyer and to them Lieut. Bull, Sub Lieut. Pool and two other officers surrendered. However it appeared that the Japanese were unable to accommodate them in their ship and so, after rendering *ML. 310* immobile, they returned to their destroyer leaving Lieut. Bull and his party free to rejoin the remainder of his ship's company, and passengers, ashore.

Monday, 16 February 1942: at 1000 at Tjebia a Japanese seaplane bombed and strafed *ML. 310*. However a working party from the shore was able to salvage some stores and gear. Fortunately on the island some deserted native housing was found. These were cleaned out and used by the survivors as temporary quarters. Also an old native prau (boat) was found.

Tuesday, 17 February 1942: Mrs. Spooner recorded that, "The *Dorsetshire* sailed off on Tuesday 17th after sending me a kind message."

Indeed at noon Captain Agar parted company with convoy 'SJ.1; and at nineteen knots proceeded on to Colombo.

Thursday, 19 February 1942: *Dorsetshire* arrived safely and at 1322 hours that afternoon anchored and secured to her buoys in Colombo harbour (69).

Friday, 20 February 1942: having carried out repairs to the prau, at 1800 hours from Tjebia Lieut. Bull departed for Batavia to seek assistance. With him were two of his ratings, Leading Seaman Brough and AB Hill, together with two islanders.

Saturday, 21 February 1942: *City of Canterbury* and other vessels of convoy 'SJ.1' arrived safely at Colombo. Mrs. Spooner noted that:-
"During the morning Captain Agar came to see me and brought the only gleam of warmth I had received. He was sweet and said I was to stay with his wife in Winchester if I wanted to. He was so kind and sympathetic."

That afternoon at 1607 hours *Dorsetshire* returned to sea.

Sunday, 22 February 1942: *Durban* arrived from Batavia and at 1020 berthed at Colombo harbour alongside the cruiser *Enterprise*, Captain J.C. Annersley. With her came mail from Rear Admiral Spooner and the personal effects for Mrs. Spooner. Apart from several lines of correspondence of a personal nature, from Singapore Rear Admiral Spooner also had included phrases such as:-
    'The story is rapidly closing with the same ineptitude and lack of decision etc.'
    'The A.I.F. let us down again last night. Hence the debacle.'
    'I have never seen such hopeless ineptitude.'
    'This has been a hopeless muddlesome day. Chaos in all directions. A.I.F. rushing sampans.'

In Colombo Mrs. Spooner recorded that, "Actually everyone is kind only the Arbuthnots freeze me."

Friends were sailing on from Colombo in *City of Canterbury* for Bombay and South Africa.
Also the Captain of the ship, Percival, "... had 'phoned earlier to say he was due to sail at 4 p.m. but he wouldn't leave till he had heard if I wanted to go with him". Having friends onboard helped her to decide and so:-

"I will be in a good place to meet Jack in Durban and it is good to have people one knows to travel with today. Also I have faith in Captain Percival. So I announced my decision. Poor Gordon (Peters) got into very hot water from Arbuthnot who had been 'phoned by Layton who asked, '... what was this all about – Mrs. Spooner being flung out of the island.' A(rbuthnot) was foaming with rage and sent for Gordon (Peters) ….. Fortunately the business was resolved and, as Mrs. Spooner was to continue in her diary:-

"I'm sure A(rbuthnot) feels he has been wrong. He was very smarmy after lunch. But he's too old: he looks a real old man – his walk is dead and lifeless – and he can't be more than about 56 or 57 (70)."

Prior to her depature from Colombo Mrs. Spooner attended to a few matters:-

"We first called on *Durban* and I fetched the three tin trunks Jack had salvaged, also my shoe box. Captain Cazalet was very kind and pleasant. Then to *City of Canterbury* and goodbye to Colombo and to Gordon. (--) We sailed at 4.30 but spent two hours going over the degaussing range."

Monday, 23 February 1942: Mrs. Spooner noted that, "Ship much less full and consequently much more comfortable. Slept on deck and at least could breathe. But didn't sleep very soundly."

Tuesday and Wednesday, 24/25 February 1942: she diarised, "Weather cooler – life goes on." Mrs. Spooner read, played deck quoits and bridge as the ship steamed up the Malabar coast towards Bombay.

Thursday, 26 February 1942: Bombay, where she noted:-

"We arrived about 10 a.m. A misty morning so little view unfortunately. Ship anchored in the bay for about two hours. Some sailors corded the trunks securely for me. (--) I dreamt of Jack for the first time this morning early. He said they'd had difficulty in getting away but had managed it. Oh can it be true."

Later Mrs. Spooner moved ashore to stay in the Taj Mahal Hotel.

Friday, 27 February 1942.

Meanwhile in their prau Lieut. Bull and his party had sailed down the east coast of Bangka towards Batavia. For the final six hours of their journey they were forced to row in order to reach Merak, in the extreme north west of Java, at 1100 on 27 February, a voyage of just under a week. There Lieut. Bull reported to acting Commander Glen Loftus Cant, RAN of the Australian sloop *Maryborough* (71). Immediately appropriate signals were sent giving the whereabouts of Rear Admiral Spooner and his party on Tjebia.

Shortly thereafter the old submarine, U.S.S. *S-39*, Lieut. J.W. Coe, USN, was ordered to assist. One account has her arriving off Tjebia that same evening, 27 February (72). Lieut. Coe made a valiant effort:-

'Locating a fly-speck island in a zone teeming with enemy patrols demanded a high order of submarining. Locating a party of refugees in an island hideout demanded something more. Coe and company answered the demand by reaching the island on February 27 in plenty of time for the rendezvous. Periscope view showed a palm jungled shoreline, a strip of white beach, no sign of Japs. No sign of refugees either, but Coe assumed they were hiding in the bush. After nightfall he maneuvered the old S-boat close in and flashed a message through the tropic dark. No answer. He kept the signal going while all hands waited with crossed fingers, hoping the light would not be spotted by lurking enemies. The light remained unanswered. At daybreak Coe withdrew. The sun blazed up, and *S-39* waited offshore, submerged.

> At nightfall she moved in for a repeat performance – furtive signals – no answer – another flash of code – finally a radio call. Chebia (Tjebia) Island remained as silent as an oil painting. "Tomorrow night", Coe told he crew, "we go ashore." There was no lack of volunteers. Special missions had their drawbacks, but an opportunity to get out in the air and stretch one's legs on a tropic beach was not one of them. The men crowded forward. Automatics were buckled on. Coe briefed them on what might happen – Japs – anything. They launched a boat, Coe with them, and paddled in. Beginning at one end of the island, they started working through the bush to the other end. (--) Its nocturnal slumbers remained undisturbed. The submariners could find no human occupant. All they found was a trample of footprints on a sandy beach – footprints driven to the water's edge where undoubtedly a Japanese small boat had been grounded.'

After a very short while on the island not unexpectedly fever and other illnesses began to take their toll. It is sad to have to record that Admiral Spooner died in that isolated place on 15 April 1942, just over two months after his departure from Singapore.

Eventually from the group of forty four who had sailed in *ML. 310* from Singapore, eighteen were to die on that unhealthy island (73).

Before the fact of his death could be ascertained, from 'Jack' Spooner's Service Record it may be noted that:- 'Placed on Retired List and promoted to Vice Admiral on Retired List 22.10.43'.

NOTES

1. Information kindly provided by the College Archivist.
2. National Archives, Kew. NA ADM 196/51. *Service Record.*
3. Ibid.
4. RN Museum Library, Portsmouth. Ref: *181/91 (1).*
5. Ibid. Midshipman's Journals. A wretched task in October, but one can imagine undertaking the work in a very cold month such as February. s.s. *Greenhill*, 1,900 grt, built in 1901 and owned by W.J. Tillett & Co. Registered: Cardiff. *Lloyds Register.*
6. *Service Record.*
7. NA ADM 53/38433.
8. *Service Record.*
9. Privately printed. *With H.M.S. Dragon Around the New World: 1930-1932,* (Lowestoft, 1932), 45.
    Percy Walker **Nelles**. Born: Brantford, Ontario: 7 January 1892. Died: Victoria, B.C.: 13 June 1951. In 1908, there being no Canadian Naval Service, he joined the Fisheries Protection Service. In 1910 transferred to the newly founded Canadian Navy. Chief of the Canadian Naval Staff: 1934-1944 and responsible for the extraordinarily successful expansion of the RCN during WW2. Vice Admiral: 19 November 1941. As a full Admiral, retired: 7 January 1945. *Navy List. Who's Who.* Also see Michael Whitby, Richard H. Gimblett and Peter Haydon, *The Admirals,* (Toronto, 2006), Chapter Three by Roger Sarty.
10. *The Admirals*, 73.
11. Hastings Lionel 'Pug' **Ismay**. Born: 21 June 1887. Died: 17 December 1965. Charterhouse and R.M.A. Sandhurst. Indian Army. Assistant Secretary, CID: 1925. Subsequently Military Secretary, Viceroy of India before returning to the War Office, then CID. From May 1940 chief military assistant to Prime Minister Churchill. KCB: June 1940. Lieut. General: 16 August 1942. General: 20 May 1944. GCB: June 1946. Created Baron: 1 January 1947. Served under the last Viceroy, Lord Mountbatten, at the Partition of India in 1947. Secretary of State for Commonwealth Relations: 1951-1952. Secretary General of NATO: 1952-1957. *Who's Who.*

12. King's College, London. Ref: *6/2/1 Brooke-Popham Papers.*

13. Ibid. Ref: *6/2/3 Brooke-Popham Papers.*

14. Diary of Mrs. Megan Spooner. King's College, London. Ref: *GB KCLMA Spooner.*

15. Stuart Sumner **Bonham-Carter**. Born: 1889. Died: 5 September 1972. Rear Admiral: 10 January 1939. Vice Admiral, Malta: 1 December 1942 to 7 May 1943. KCB: 1943. Retired in 1944 but served for the remainder of WW2 as Commodore of Convoys. *Navy List. Who's Who.*

16. Geoffry Alexander Stafford **Northcote** (1881-1948). Blundell's. Balliol College, Oxford. His Excellency, of the Iddesleigh family, was Governor of the Colony from 28 October 1937 to 6 September 1941. On 27 October 1910 he had married Edith Juliet Mary Adams. As a young man served in Kenya, Northern Rhodesia and the Gold Coast. Governor of British Guiana: 1935-1937. KCMG: 1935. War service in East Africa. *Who's Who.*

17. Douglas Adams **Bugden** (not Budgeon). As Commodore First Class on 15 November 1939 appointed Captain in command, Simon's Town. From 15 March 1940, as a retired Rear Admiral, continued to serve as Flag Officer in command and SNO, Simon's Town. Died: 13 January 1947. *Navy List. Who's Who.*

18. Simon's Town Historical Society, *Bulletin*, Vol. XXI No. 2, July 2000. *Navy List.*
    William Eric Campbell **Tait**. Born: 12 August 1886. Died in Government House, Salisbury: 17 July 1946. Entered the RN in 1902. Captain: 1926. Consecutively commanded *Dragon*, *Capetown* and *Delhi*. Deputy Director of Naval Intelligence: 1932-1933. Staff of C. in C., China Station: 1933-1934. Commanded heavy cruiser *Shropshire*: 1934-1937. Rear Admiral: 1938. Vice Admiral: 1941. C. in C., South Atlantic: 1942-1944. KCB: 1943. Admiral: May 1945. Governor of Southern Rhodesia: 20 February 1945. In failing health he relinquished that post in February 1946. *Who's Who.*

19. Robert John **Shaw**. Born in High Wycombe: 10 February 1900. Died in Hindhead: 5 August 1995. Entered the RN: 1 January 1913. As a Midshipman served at the Battle of Jutland, 31 May 1916, in battleship *Hercules*, 20,000 tons, Captain Lewis Clinton-Baker. In the 30s he had been Navy squash champion, also Captain of the Navy Cricket XI. Promoted Captain: 30 June 1939, and to *Dragon*: 27 August 1940. By the end of WW2 in command *Osprey*, Anti Submarine Establishment, Portland. In command battleship *Howe*: 25 August 1947 to 6 July 1948. Retired: 20 September 1948. *Navy List.*

20. Thomas Bernard **Drew**, CB, CVO, OBE. Entered the RN: 1901. Captain: 30 June 1928. Flag Captain heavy cruiser *Kent*, China Station: 13 January 1932. During her period of modernization commanded battleship *Royal Oak*: June 1936. Commodore Malaya and in command of Naval Establishments at Singapore: 10 October 1938. Rear Admiral: 1 August 1939. Appointed to *President*, Admiralty, London: 22 December 1941. Vice Admiral: 1943. In retirement, from 1946 to 1956 private secretary to successive Lord Mayors of London. On 22 April 1960 died suddenly at his residence, Cedar Cottage, Bembridge, Isle of Wight, aged 73. *Navy List. Who's Who.* Obituary, *The Times*, Thursday, 28 April 1960. (*Who's Who* gives his date of death as 27 April 1960).

21. Thomas Shenton Whitelegge **Thomas**. Born: 10 October 1879. Died: 15 January 1962. St. John's, Leatherhead and Scholar of Queen's College, Cambridge. A school master for seven years prior to joining the Kenya Colonial Service in 1909. Subsequent service in Uganda, Nigeria and the Gold Coast. In 1929 appointed Governor of Nyasaland. KCMG: 1931. From 1932 Governor of the Gold Coast. Governor of the Straits Settlements: 9 November 1934 – 15 February 1942, then a prisoner of the Japanese occupying forces. Resumed gubernatorial duties: 12 September 1945 – 1 April 1946. GCMG: 1937. Sir Shenton was a useful cricketer. *Colonial Office List. Who's Who.*

22. m.v. *Marudu*, 1,926 grt. Built in Belfast: 1924. Owned by the Straits Steamship Co. Ltd. K.G. Tregonning, *Home Port Singapore*, (OUP, 1967), 109.

23. Cyril Drummond Le Gros **Clark**. Born: 1894. Interned by the Japanese occupying forces and in North Borneo executed by them: 6 July 1945. Amongst other accomplishments a Chinese scholar. Robert Reece, *The White Rajahs of Sarawak*, (Singapore, 2004), 109.

24. Sir James **Brooke** (1803-1868), Sir Charles Anthoni Johnson Brooke (1829-1917), and Sir Charles Vyner Brooke (1874-1963). The actual dynasty endured from 1841 to 1946. Vyner Brooke's Ranee was Sylvia, nee Brett. Steven Runciman, *The White Rajahs*, (Cambridge, 1960).
    The graves of the three Rajahs may be found together at Sheepstor, Devon, in the churchyard of the Church of St. Leonard. Also appropriate memorials may be seen within the church itself. Sir James died nearby, at his beloved

Burrator, on 11 June 1868. Sheepstor visited by the author, and respects paid, on 13 and 14 May 2011.

25. Extracts from the Megan Spooner diary, 50-62.

26. John Arthur Symons **Eccles** (1898-1966). At the time commanding the light cruiser *Durban* who was refitting at Singapore. Ended WW2 in command of the aircraft carrier *Indomitable*. KCVO: 1953. KCB: 1955. Admiral: 1 December 1955. From 5 January 1956 C. in C., Home Fleet and C. in C., Allied Forces, Eastern Atlantic. Retired in 1958. GCB: 1958. *Navy List. Who's Who.*

27. s.s. *Kedah,* 2,499 grt. In peacetime flagship of the Straits Steamship Company fleet serving on their prestigious express Singapore/Penang route. Capable of twenty knots. Tregonning, 141.

    Tenedos, 905 tons. Launched 21 October 1918. *Navy List.*

28. Passenger tender *Rejang,* 288 grt. Owned by Sarawak Steamship Co. Ltd., a subsidiary company of Straits Steamship. Built in 1934 by the Singapore Harbour Board. *Lloyds Register.*

29. Diary, 67-69. Actually s.s. *Kajang,* 2,082 grt. Straits Steamship Co. Ltd. Built in Hong Kong in 1916 by Taikoo Dockyard. *Lloyds Register.*

30. An island in the Kurile chain north of Hokkaido. After WW2 occupied by the Soviet Union and today known as Iturup Island.

31. Diary, 121-123.

    Air Chief Marshall Henry Robert Moore **Brooke-Popham**. Born: 18 September 1878. Died: 20 October 1953. Haileybury and Sandhurst. Entered Army: 1898. Royal Flying Corps: 1912. RAF: 1919. KCB: 1927. Finally A.O.C. in C., Middle East: 1935-1936. GCVO: 1935. Retired: 1937. Governor of Kenya: 1937-1939. C. in C., Far East: 1940- 1941. Reverted to Retired List: 1942. President NAAFI Council: 1944-1946. *Who's Who.*

    Early in 1941 Sir Robert had paid a visit to Australia and on 28 February 1941 wrote to 'Pug' Ismay in London to give him some opinions concerning his findings. The following entertaining extract is included as some might say that his comments continue to be valid today (written in the year 2009):-

    > 'Then I noticed the same difficulty in getting good men to become politicians as is evident in Canada. It is partly because the capable man wants to go in for business or industry and partly because many people are unwilling to become a target for the personal abuse that is so freely directed to everyone in public life in Australia. Consequently one finds that the majority of politicians have but little moral courage and are much influenced by any press campaign.'

    King's College, London. Ref: *Brooke-Popham Papers: 6/2/7.* Para. 7.

    Lieut. General Arthur Ernest **Percival**. Born: 26 December 1887. Died: 31 January 1966. Enlisted as a private on the first day of WW1 thus in this manner entered the Army from civilian life. By March 1936 a Colonel. In April 1941 promoted acting Lieut. General and appointed GOC, Malaya. *Who's Who.*

    Stanley Wilson **Jones**. Born: 1 July 1888. Died: 17 January 1962. Entered Malayan Civil Service: 1911. Colonial Secretary, Straits Settlements: 1940-1942. *Who's Who.*

32. B. Mitchell Simpson III, *Admiral Harold R. Stark,* (University of South Carolina, 1989), 110.

33. Lieut. General A.E. Percival, *The War in Malaya,* (London, 1949), 95 and 98.

34. Sir George Bailey **Sansom** and his wife Katharine, nee Slingsby. Sir George was born in London: 28 November 1883. Died in Tucson, AZ: 8 March 1965. Palmer's School, Grays. Lycee Malherbe, Caen. Giessen and Marburg, both in Hessen. Appointed Student Interpreter in Japan: 28 October 1903. Prior to the Great War served in Yokohama, Chemulpo, Tokyo and Hakodate. Employed at the Admiralty, London: 26 July 1915 to 30 June 1917. Then Intelligence Directorate at the War Office: 1 July 1917 to 30 October 1919. Returned to Japan: Shimonoseki, Yokohama, Osaka and Tokyo. Commercial Secretary at Tokyo: 2 September 1923. By 7 March 1925 Commercial Counsellor, Tokyo. KCMG: 3 June 1935. Retired: 8 September 1940. Visiting Professor at Columbia University, New York: 1935-1936 and 1940-1941. Adviser to Far Eastern Mission, Ministry of Economic Warfare, Singapore: 1941. Civilian Member of Far Eastern War Council, Singapore: 1941-1942, then at Java in 1942. Minister, British Embassy, Washington DC: 1942-1947. United Kingdom Member of Allied Far Eastern Commission: 1946-1947. GBE: 1947. Professor between 1947 and 1953, and Director, East Asian Institute, Columbia University: 1949-1953. Retired to Stanford, CA. Distinguished author of works on Japan such as *The Western World and Japan,* (London, 1950). *Foreign Office List,* 1941. *Who's Who.* Writing of his period in Singapore in 1941 one authority states:-

'Sansom was also appointed to be the civilian representative on the Singapore War Council and appears to have shocked his superiors by clearly stating that a Japanese attack was inevitable. Indeed Sansom's forecast, that the war would begin 'about the end of November' was extremely accurate, for the attack on Pearl Harbour came a mere week later. Sansom also transmitted a message to Washington warning that Japanese forces in Indo-China were preparing to advance into Thailand and Malaya.'

Ed. Hugh Cortazzi, *British Envoys in Japan: 1859-1972,* (Folkestone, Kent, 2004). Chapter 25, Dr. Gordon Daniels, 255.

Major General F. Keith **Simmons**. Commander of the Singapore Fortress.

Rear Admiral Arthur Francis Eric **Palliser**. Born in Richmond, Surrey: 20 July 1890. As Commodore Second Class, Chief of Staff to C. in C., China Station: 20 November 1936. Rear Admiral: 8 July 1941. Ordered to remain ashore in Singapore at the time of the Force 'Z' disaster. Following the collapse of ABDA , on 2 March 1942 escaped in a USN Catalina from Tjilatjap, south coast of Java, to Exmouth Bay, West Australia. Thence from Fremantle on 8 March 1942 in battleship *Warspite*, Captain Douglas Fisher, to Trincomalee where arrived 22 March. Fortress Commander, Trincomalee: 26 March 1942. Subsequently Naval Aide to the Viceroy of India, New Delhi. Vice Admiral, 1CS with flag in *Kent*: 29 August 1943. Confirmed as Vice Admiral: 7 February 1944. A Lord Commissioner of the Admiralty and Chief of Supplies and Transport: 1944-1946. KCB: 1945. C. in C., East Indies: 1946-1948. Admiral: 16 May 1947. Retired: 1948. Died in Kensington: 22 February 1956. *Navy List. Who's Who.*

35. Vivian Gordon **Bowden** (1884-1942), Official Representative at Singapore to Dr. E.V. Evatt, Australian Minister for External Affairs. In 1935 he had been appointed Australian Trade Commissioner in China. *Who's Who.*

36. Vice Admiral Sir John Collins, *As Luck Would Have It,* (Sydney, 1965), 101.

An easy remark to make but, at the same time, one can only wonder as to the nature of the wartime exercises carried out onboard during the long voyage from Britain. From a private source, for example, the author has been given to understand that during this passage to the East only minimal attention was paid to the exercising of her light A.A. weapon defences.

37. Admiral Sir Guy Charles Cecil **Royle**, RN (1886-1954). From 18 July 1941 to 28 June 1945 First Naval Member, Australian Commonwealth Naval Board, i.e. professional head of the R.A.N.

38. Third supplement, *The London Gazette*, Friday, 20 February 1948.

39. NA ADM 199/1473 with more detail in ADM 199/1185.

40. Arthur J. Marder, *Old Friends, New Enemies,* (OUP, 1981), 405/6.

In command of the light cruiser *Achilles*, Captain William Edward **Parry** had participated in the Battle of the River Plate, 13 December 1939, the successful engagement against *Admiral Graf Spee*. Born: 8 April 1893. Died: 21 August 1972. Joined RN: 1905. Captain: 1934. Commanded Anti Submarine Establishment *Osprey*: 1936-1937. First Naval Member of New Zealand Navy Board: 1940-1942. Commanded *Renown*: 1943. Rear Admiral: 1944. Control Commission for Germany, Berlin: 1945-1946. Director of Naval Intelligence: 1946-1948. Vice Admiral: 1948. C. in C., Indian Navy: 14 August 1948 – 13 October 1951. KCB: 1950. Admiral: 1951. Retired: 1952. *Who's Who. Navy List.*

41. Captain S.W. Roskill, RN, *A Merchant Fleet in War: Alfred Holt & Co., 1939-1945,* (London, 1962), 153.

Roskill errs since the attack on Hong Kong commenced shortly after 0800 on Monday, 8 December, local time.

42. NA ADM 199/1743.

43. Imperial War Museum. Goodfellow papers studied by the author: 19 April 1995.

44. King's College, London. Ref: *6/11/17 – Despatch on Far East: XI The Start of Hostilities.* Para. 101, page 38 dated 25 June 1942.

45. NA ADM 53/114185.

46. NA CAB 79/16: C.O.S. (41) 414th meeting.

47. At the time of the loss of *Prince of Wales* Captain Leach's third son, Henry Conyers Leach (1923-2011) was serving as a Midshipman in the light cruiser *Mauritius*, 8,000 tons, who then was undergoing a refit at Singapore. In due course to be First Sea Lord at the time of the Falklands War in 1982. After a most successful career Sir Henry was to retire as an Admiral of the Fleet. Obituary, *The Daily Telegraph,* 27 April 2011.

48. To take advantage of useful topographical features known as 'The Ledge', this military advance a short distance over the border into Thailand, Operation 'Matador', had been planned beforehand. During the night of 7 December 1941

Sir Robert Brooke-Popham declined to authorize the commencement of this essential defensive operation.

49. In a democracy the armed forces ultimately are controlled by elected civilians. As had the other Services in the Thirties, the Air Force too had been starved of adequate funding to prepare for the advent of hostilities. In addition both in Britain and in the U.S.A. there existed a completely unrealistic appreciation of the ability of Japan in the air, both men and machines, this in spite of the war which Japan had waged against China since July 1937.

50. NA ADM 199/408. Report 599/E.I. 03203 for December 1941 dated 14 May 1942.

51. Archives Centre, Churchill College, Cambridge. Ref: *DUFC 3/8*. War Cabinet Documents, May 1942.

52. NA ADM 199/357. Letter No. 17/351.

53. Brian Montgomery, *Shenton of Singapore,* (London, 1984), 124.

54. Ibid. 129/130.

55. Ibid. 134. Sir Charles Parkinson is Arthur Charles Cosmo **Parkinson**. Born: 18 November 1884. Died: 16 August 1967. Epsom and Magdalen College, Oxford. First Class Mods. and First Class Lit. Hum. Joined Admiralty: February 1908. Transferred to Colonial Office: 19 April 1909. Military service: 16 May 1915 to 26 May 1919. Major, K.A.R. Principal: 1 April 1920. Private Secretary to Lord Milner: 1 October 1920. Assistant Secretary: 1 October 1925. Assistant Under Secretary of State: 15 August 1931. KCMG: 1935. Permanent Under Secretary of State for the Colonies: 2 July 1937. KCB: 1938. Permanent Under Secretary of State for Dominion Affairs: 1 February 1940. GCMG: 1942. Retired: 31 December 1944. 'Re-employed 1 January to 30 December 1945 on special duty for the Secretary of State for the Colonies.' *Who's Who. Colonial Office List.*

56. Letter dated 12 August 1998 received by the author from Mr. Gordon Peters.

57. Cazalet Papers. Viewed at the Imperial War Museum: 19 April 1995.

58. Ibid. Also NA ADM 1/17359. Stocks of fuel at the Singapore Naval Base, *Sultan,* alone amounted to 816,000 tons of furnace oil and 40,000 tons of diesel. Such was the speed of the Japanese advance that by no means was all this huge stock denied to the enemy.

59. Wilson Papers, also interview kindly granted to the author by Brigadier Wilson: 29 April 1995.

60. s.s. *Gorgon,* 3,533 grt. Built in Dundee in 1933 for the Ocean S.S. Co. Ltd. (The Blue Funnel Line) service between Singapore and West Australia. In August 1964 to be sold in Hong Kong for breaking up. Duncan Haws, *Merchant Fleets: The Blue Funnel Line,* (Burwash, East Sussex, 1986), 104. Captain S.W. Roskill, RN, *A Merchant Fleet at War: 1939-1945,* (London, 1962), 155/6.

    m.v. *Empire Star,* 10,800 grt., Captain Selwyn N. Capon. Blue Star Line. North of the Azores on 23 October 1942 to be torpedoed and sunk by *U-615,* Rolf Kapitzky. Taffrail, *Blue Star Line at war: 1939-1945,* (Blue Star Line, 1973), 61-64 and 109-133.

61. The reasons for this lack of aggression follow. Firstly, dive bombers: at the outbreak of hostilities those machines that were available, relatively few in number, were all assigned to the fleet carriers. Secondly, torpedoes were scarce so their use was confined to really important targets. In addition frequently it was the case that the surfaces of recently occupied airfields were uneven. In those circumstances aircraft heavily laden with torpedoes were unable to take off safely.

62. *City of Canterbury,* 8,331 grt. A coal burning steamer built in 1922 for Ellerman Lines. At the time of the fall of Greece carried the Greek Royal Family safely to South Africa. Survived WW2 as a troopship, and sold for scrapping in 1953. David Hughes and Peter Humphries, *In South African Waters,* (OUP, Capetown, 1977), 39.

63. Conway Walter Heath **Pulford** (1892-1942). Joined the RN and by 15 January 1910 a Midshipman in the battleship *Russell,* 14,000 tons, Mediterranean. Sub Lieut.: 15 March 1913. Transferred to ther RNAS and by 15 December 1914 a Flight Lieut. attending the Central Flying School. Flight Commander: 30 June 1916. Squadron Commander: 31 December 1917. The RAF was formed on 1 April 1918 to which service subsequently he transferred. Group Captain: 1 July 1932. Air Commodore: 1 July 1936. Air Vice Marshal: 1 April 1939. AOC RAF Far East Command: 6 March 1941. *Navy List. Who's Who.*

64. Percival, 285.

65. Tregonning, 174.

66. *Orcades,* Captain C. Fox. On 10 October 1942, so just a few months later and while on passage from Egypt to England, and having left Capetown the previous afternoon, to be torpedoed and sunk by *U-172,* Carl Emmermann. Fortunately

from some 1,300 persons in the ship the loss of life was to amount to just forty five. L.C.F. Turner, H.R. Gordon-Cumming and J.E. Betzler, *War in the Southern Oceans: 1939-1945*, (OUP, 1961), 179/180.

67. Donald M. Goldstein, Katherine V. Dillon, Masataka Chihaya, *Fading Victory*, (Annapolis, MD, 2008), 90.

68. NA ADM 199/1473. Subsequent report prepared for Commodore John Collins, RAN by Lieut. H.J. Bull, Batavia, 28 February 1942.

69. NA ADM 53/114140. Log book, *Dorsetshire*.

70. Geoffrey Schomberg Arbuthnot. Born: 18 January 1885. Died: 4 October 1957. Therefore in February 1942 he was fifty seven years of age.

71. NA ADM 199/622A. report by Commander Cant: S.M. 7/42 dated 15 March 1942.

72. Theodore Roscoe, *United States Submarine Operations in WW2*, (Annapolis, MD, 1988), 81.
As a Lieut. Commander, and with a record of several successful sinkings behind him while in command of USS *Skipjack* SS-184, James Wiggins Coe and all hands were to be lost on 28 September 1943. On that date his new command, USS *Cisco* SS-290, was sunk in the Sulu Sea by Japanese aircraft and gunboat bomb and depth charge attack.

73. NA ADM 1/17363. Also a survivor, Lieut. Richard Pool, RN, subsequently was to write, *Course for Disaster*, (London, 1987). Pages 103 – 163 are especially relevant. The names of the members of the ship's company in *ML.310* and of the party taking passage in her from Singapore appear on pages 193/4.

Bibliography

Agawa Hiroyuki, *The Reluctant Admiral*, (Tokyo and New York, 1979)

Agar, Captain Augustus, VC, *Baltic Episode*, (London, 1963)

Akashi Yoji and Yoshimura Mako, Ed., *New Perspectives on the Japanese Occupation in Malaya and Singapore, 1941-1945*, (Singapore, 2008).

Albert Victor, Prince and Prince George of Wales, *The Cruise of HMS Bacchante: 1879-1882*, (London, 1886)

Andrews, Adolphus, Jnr., *Admiral with Wings*, (Princeton University, 1943)

Axelson, Eric, *Vasco da Gama: The Diary of His Travels through African Waters: 1497-1499*, (Somerset West, Cape, 1998)

Bacon, Admiral Sir R.H., *The Life of Lord Fisher of Kilverstone*, (London, 1929)
 The Life of John Rushworth, Earl Jellicoe, (London, 1936)
 From 1900 Onward, (London, 1940)

Bai Shouyi, Ed., *An Outline History of China 1919-1949*, (Beijing, 1993)

Beesly, Patrick, *Very Special Admiral*, (London, 1980)

Belcher, Captain Sir Edward, *Narrative of the Voyage of H.M.S. Samarang During the Years 1843-1846*, (London, 1848)

Beresford, Lord, *The Memoirs of Admiral Lord Beresford*, (London, 1916)

Black, John R., *Young Japan*, Vols. I and II, (London and Yokohama, 1880/1881)

Black, Nicholas, *The British Naval Staff in the First World War*, (Woodbridge, Suffolk, 2009)

Blake, Clagette, *Charles Elliot, RN: 1801-1875*, (London, 1960)

Blake, George, *B.I. Centenary*, (London, 1956)
 The Ben Line, (Edinburgh, 1956)

Blakiston, Captain Thomas Wright, *Five Months on the Yangtse*, (London, 1862)

Bodley, R.V.C., *Togo*, (London, 1935)

Bonner-Smith, D and Lumby, E.W.R., Eds., *The Second China War: 1856-1860*, (London, 1954)

Bowie, Christopher J., *Great Britain and the use of Force in China, 1919-1931*, (Ph.D thesis, Oxford, 1983)

Boxer, C.R., *The Portuguese Seaborne Empire: 1415-1825*, (London, 1991)

Boyce, Ed. D. George, *The Crisis of British Power, The Imperial and Naval Papers of the Second Earl of Selborne, 1895-1910*, (London, 1990)

Brackley, Frida, *Brackles: Memoirs of a Pioneer of Civil Aviation*, (London, 1952)

Bradford, Admiral Sir Edward E., *Life of Admiral of the Fleet Sir Arthur Knyvet Wilson*, (London, 1923)

Brassey, T.A., *The British Navy*, III, (London, 1883)
 The Naval Annual, (Portsmouth, 1905)

Brice, Martin H., *The Royal Navy and the Sino-Japanese Incident: 1937-1941*, (Shepperton, Surrey, 1973)

Bridge, Admiral Sir Cyprian, *Some Recollections*, (London, 1918)

Brook, Peter, *Warships for Export*, (Gravesend, 1999)

Brook-Shepherd, Gordon, *Uncle of Europe,* (New York and London, 1975)

Brooks, Barbara J., *Japan's Imperial Diplomacy,* (Hawaii, 2000)

Brown, David, *Warship Losses of World War Two,* (London, 1996)

Buell, Thomas B., *Master of Sea Power,* (Boston, 1980)

    The Quiet Warrior, (Annapolis, MD, 1988)

Burke-Gaffney, Brian, *Nagasaki, The British Experience, 1854-1945,* (Folkestone, Kent, 2009)

Bush, Lewis, *The Illustrious Captain Brown,* (Tokyo and Rutland, VT, 1969)

Butterworth, A.E., *The Commission of HMS Glory: 1900-1904,* (London, 1904)

Cable, Boyd, *A Hundred Year History of the P. & O.,* (London, 1937)

Campbell, Hugh and Ron Lovell, *So Long, Singapore,* (Hobart, 2000)

Candlin, Enid Saunders, *The Breach in the Wall – a Memoir of the Old China,* (London, 1974)

Carroll, John M., *Edge of Empires,* (Harvard, 2005)

Carter, Rear Admiral Worrall Reed, *Beans, Bullets, and Black Oil,* (Washington, DC, 1953)

Chalmers, Rear Admiral W.S., *Full Cycle,* (London, 1959)

    The Life and Letters of David Beatty, (London, 1951)

    Max Horton and the Western Approaches, (London, 1954)

Chamberlin, William Henry, *Japan Over Asia,* (London, 1938)

Chavasse, E.H., *Up and Down the Yangtse,* (Privately)

Clements, Jonathan, *Prince Saionji,* (London, 2008)

Clowes, William Laird, *The Royal Navy – a History,* Vol. VI, (London, 1901) and other volumes

Coates, P.D., *The China Consuls,* (OUP, 1988)

Coles, Alan, *Invergordon Scapegoat,* (Stroud, 1993)

Collins, Vice Admiral Sir John, *As Luck Would Have It,* (Sydney, 1965)

Collis, Maurice, *Wayfoong: The Hongkong and Shanghai Banking Corporation,* (London, 1965)

Compton-Hall, Richard, *Submarines and the War at Sea, 1914-1918,* (London, 1991)

Cook, Christopher, *The Lion and the Dragon,* (London, 1985)

Cork and Orrery, Admiral of the Fleet the Earl of, *My Naval Life,* (London)

Cortazzi, Hugh, *The Japanese Achievement,* (London, 1990)

    Ed., *British Envoys to Japan: 1859-1972,* (Folkestone, Kent, 2004)

    Ed., *Biographical Portraits, V,* (Folkestone, Kent, 2005)

Cortazzi, Sir Hugh and Gordon Daniels, *Britain and Japan: 1859-1991,* (London and New York, 1991)

Creagh, Sir O'Moore and E.M. Humphris, *The VC and DSO,* (London)

Crisswell, Colin, N., *The Taipans,* (OUP, 1981)

Crowe, George, *The Commission of HMS Terrible,* (London, 1903)

Cunningham, Admiral of the Fleet Viscount, of Hyndhope, *A Sailor's Odyssey,* (London, 1951)

Cunyngham-Brown, Sjovald, *The Traders,* (London, 1971)

Daniels, Gordon, *Sir Harry Parkes,* (Richmond, Surrey, 1996)

Davidson-Houston, J.V., *The Piracy of the Nanchang,* (London, 1961)

Davies, Richard Bell, *Sailor in the Air,* (Barnsley, England, 2008)

Dawson, L.S., *Memoirs of Hydrography,* (London, 1885)

Dawson, Lionel, *Sound of the Guns,* (Oxford, 1949)

de Chair, Admiral Sir Dudley, *The Sea is Strong,* (London, 1961)

Delgado, James P., *Across the Top of the World,* (New York, 1999)

Des Voeux, George William, *My Colonial Service,* (London, 1903)

Devereux, W. Cope, *A Cruise in the 'Gorgon',* (London, 1968)

Dick, H.W. and S.A. Kentwell, *Beancaker to Boxboat,* (Canberra, 1988)

Dilks, David, *Curzon in India,* two vols. (London, 1969 and 1970)

Dilks, Ed. David, *The Diaries of Sir Alexander Cadogan: 1938-1945,* (London, 1971)

Dodge, Ernest S., *Beyond the Capes,* (London, 1971)

Dreyer, Admiral Sir Frederic, *The Sea Heritage,* (London, 1955)

Duberly, Frances Isabella, *Journal kept during the Russian War,* (London, 1855)

Dundas of Dundas, Admiral Sir Charles, *An Admiral's Yarns,* (London, 1922)

Dunmore, John, *Who's Who in Pacific Navigation,* (Hawaii, 1991)

Eiichi Kiyooka as Translator, *The Autobiography of Yukichi Fukuzawa,* (New York and London, 1966)

Eitel, E.J., *Europe in China,* (London and Hong Kong, 1895)

Evans, David Chris, *The Satsuma Faction and Professionalism in the Japanese Naval Officer Corps of the Meiji Period, 1868-1912,* (Stanford, 1978)
>   Together with Mark R. Peattie, *Kaigun,* (Annapolis, MD, 1997)

Falkus, Malcolm, *The Blue Funnel Legend*, (Basingstoke and London, 1990)

Featherstone, Donald, *Victorian Colonial Warfare – Africa,* (London, 1992)

Field, Colonel C., *Britain's Sea Soldiers,* (Liverpool, 1924)

Finn, Dallas, *Meiji Revisited,* (New York, 1995)

Fisher, Admiral Sir Frederick William, *Naval Reminiscences,* (London, 1938)

Fisher, Admiral of the Fleet Lord, *Records,* (London, 1919)
>   *Memories,* (London, 1919)

Fitzgerald, Rear Admiral C.C. Penrose, *Sir George Tryon, KCB,* (Edinburgh and London, 1903)

Fleet, Vice Admiral H.L., *My Life, and a Few Yarns,* (London, 1922)

Fleming, Peter, *One's Company,* (London, 1934).

Forbes Munro, J., *Maritime Enterprise and Empire,* (Woodbridge, Suffolk, 2003)

Fortune, Robert, *A Journey to the Tea Countries,* (London, 1852)
>   *Yedo and Peking,* (London, 1863)

Fox, Grace, *Britain and Japan, 1858-1883,* (OUP, 1969)

Fraser, Edward and L.G. Carr-Laughton, *The Royal Marine Artillery, 1804-1923,* (RUSI London, 1930)

Frei, Henry, *Guns of February,* (Singapore, 2004)

Fremantle, Admiral The Hon. Sir Edmund R., *The Navy as I have Known it, 1849-1899,* (London, 1904)

Friendly, Alfred, *Beaufort of the Admiralty: The Life of Sir Francis Beaufort, 1774-1857,* (London, 1977)

Friends of English Harbour, *The Romance of English Harbour,* (Antigua, 1959)

Gandt, Robert L., *China Clipper,* (Annapolis, 1991)

Garrett, Valery M., *Heaven is High, the Emperor Far Away,* (OUP, 2002)

Gill, G. Hermon, *Royal Australian Navy, 1939-1942,* (Canberra, 1957)
>   *Royal Australian Navy, 1942-1945,* (Canberra, 1968)

Gill, William John, *The River of Golden Sand,* (London, 1883)

Goodenough, Admiral Sir William, *A Rough Record,* (London, 1946)

Goodman, Jordan, *The Rattlesnake,* (London, 2005)

Gorlitz, Walter, Ed., *The Kaiser and His Court,* (London, 1961)

Gough, Barry M., *The Royal Navy and the Northwest Coast of North America: 1810-1914,* (Vancouver, 1971)
>   *To the Pacific and Arctic with Beechey,* (Hakluyt Society, 1973)

Graham, Gerald S., *The China Station,* (OUP, 1978)

Green, Daniel, *A Plantation Family,* (Ipswich, 1979)

Grew, Joseph, C., *Ten Years in Japan,* (London, 1944)

Gwynn, Stephen, Ed., *The Letters and Friendships of Sir Cecil Spring Rice,* (London, 1929)

Hahn, Emily, *China Only Yesterday*, (London, 1963)

Haines, Gregory, *Gunboats on the Great River*, (London, 1976)

Harding, Richard, Adrian Jarvis and Alston Kennerley, Ed., *British Ships in China Seas*, (Liverpool, 2004)

Hastings, Max, *All Hell Let Loose*, (London, 2011)

Haviland, Edward Kenneth, *American Steam Navigation in China: 1845-1878*, (Salem, Mass., 1956-1958)

Hawes, Duncan, *Merchant Fleets: The Blue Funnel Line*, (Burwash, 1986)
    Merchant Fleets: Canadian Pacific, (Hereford, 1992)

Herwig, Holger H., *Luxury Fleet – The Imperial German Navy, 1888-1918*, (London, 1980)

Hewlett, Sir Meyrick, *Forty Years in China*, (London, 1943)

Hezel, Francis X., *Strangers in Their Own Land*, (Hawaii, 2003)
    The First Taint of Civilization, (Hawaii, 1994)

Hibbert, Christopher, *The Dragon Wakes, China and the West, 1793-1911*, (London, 1970)

Higham, Robin and Karen Cox Wing, *The Consolidated Author and Subject Index to The Journal of the Royal United Service Institution, 1857-1963*, (Ann Arbor, Michigan, 1964)

Hoare, J.E., Ed., *Biographical Portraits, III*, (Richmond, Surrey, 1999)
    Embassies in the East, (Richmond, Surrey, 1999)

Hough, Richard, *Dreadnought*, (London, 1965)
    First Sea Lord, (London, 1969)
    Louis and Victoria, (London, 1974)
    The Great War at Sea, 1914-1918, (OUP, 1983)
    Former Naval Person, (London, 1985)
    The Longest Battle, (London, 1986)

Howard, R.G., et al, *H.M.S. Suffolk, Third Commission*, (Hong Kong, 1935)

Howell, Glenn F., Ed. Dennis L. Noble, *Gunboat on the Yangtze*, (Jefferson, NC., 2002)

Hussin, Nordin, *Trade and Society in the Straits of Melaka*, (Singapore, 2007)

Hyde, Francis E., *Far Eastern Trade 1860-1914*, (London, 1973)
    Blue Funnel, (Liverpool, 1957)

Ingleton, Geoffrey C., *Charting a Continent*, (Sydney, 1944)

Inglis, Robin, *Historical Dictionary of the Discovery and Exploration of the Northwest Coast of America*, (Lanham, MD., 2008)

James, Admiral Sir William, *The Sky was Always Blue*, (London, 1951)
    A Great Seaman, the Life of Admiral of the Fleet Sir Henry Oliver, (London, 1956)

Jameson, Thomas Henry, *Expedition to Siberia – 1919*, (Royal Marines Historical Society, 1987)

Jameson, William, *The Fleet that Jack Built*, (London, 1962)

Jane, Fred T., *The Imperial Japanese Navy*, (London, 1904)

Jellicoe of Scapa, Admiral Viscount, *The Grand Fleet, 1914-1916*, (London, 1919)

Jennings, Eric, *Cargoes*, (Singapore, 1980)
    Mansfields, (Singapore, 1973)

Jentschura, Hansgeorg et al, *Warships of the Imperial Japanese Navy: 1869-1945*, (London, 1977)

Jones, Mary, *A Naval Life*, Dulverton, Somerset, 2007)

Keir, David, *The Bowring Story*, (London, 1962)

Kennedy, Greg, Ed., *British Naval Strategy East of Suez, 1900-2000*, (Abingdon, Oxon, 2005)

Kennedy, Vice Admiral Sir William R., *Hurrah For The Life of a Sailor*, (Edinburgh and London, 1900)

Keppel, Henry, *The Adventures to Borneo of HMS Dido*, (OUP, 1991)

Keswick, Maggie, Ed., *The Thistle and the Jade*, (London, 1982)

Keyes, Admiral of the Fleet Sir Roger, *Adventures Ashore and Afloat*, (London, 1939)

King, Ernest J., and Walter Muir Whitehill, *Fleet Admiral King,* (New York, 1976)

Kiyooka, Eiichi, translator, *The Autobiography of Yukichi Fukuzawa,* (Columbia University Press, 1966)

Kouwenhoven, Arlette and Matthi Forrer, *Siebold and Japan: His life and work,* (Leiden, 2000)

Krug, Hans-Joachim et al, *Reluctant Allies,* (Annapolis, MD, 2001)

Kyrle-Pope, Suzanne, *The Same Wife in Every Port,* (Co. Durham, 2002)

Lamb, W. Kaye, *Empress to the Orient,* (Vancouver, 1991)

Lambert, Andrew, *Admirals,* (London, 2008)

Lauridsen, Peter, *Vitus Bering,* (New York, 1969)

Layman, R.D., *Before the Aircraft Carrier,* (London, 1989)
    Naval Aviation in the First World War, (London, 2002)

Leahy, Fleet Admiral William D., *I Was There,* (New York, 1950)

LeFevour, Edward, *Western Enterprise in Late Ch'ing China,* (Harvard, 1968)

Le Hunte, J. Ruthven, *Six Letters from the Western Pacific,* (Colombo, 1883)

Leutze, James, *A Different Kind of Victory,* (Annapolis, MD, 1981)

Levien, Ed. Michael, *The Cree Journals,* (Exeter, Devon, 1881)

Little, Alicia Helen Neva, *Li Hung-chang: His Life and Times,* (London, 1903)

Liu, Kwang-ching, *Anglo-American Steamship Rivalry in China, 1862-1874,* (Harvard, 1962)

Livock, G.E., *To the Ends of the Air,* (London, 1973)

Lloyd, Christopher, *Mr. Barrow of the Admiralty,* (London, 1970)

Lo Hui-min, *The Correspondence of G.E. Morrison, Vols. I, 1895-1912, and II, 1912-1920,* (Cambridge University Press, 1976/1978)

Loadman, John, *Tears of the Tree,* (OUP, 2005)

Longhurst, Henry, *The Borneo Story,* (London, 1956)

Lowis, Commander Geoffrey L., *Fabulous Admirals,* (London, 1957)

Lum, Yansheng Ma and Raymond Mum Kong, *Sun Yat-sen in Hawaii,* (Hawaii, 1999)

Lumby, E.W.R., Ed., *Policy and Operations in the Mediterranean: 1912-1914,* (Naval Records Society, 1970)

Lundstrom, John B., *Black Shoe Carrier Admiral,* (Annapolis, 2006)

Lyon, David and Rif Winfield, *The Sail and Steam Navy List,* (London, 2004)

McCrae, Alister and Alan Prentice, *Irrawaddy Flotilla,* (Paisley, 1978)

McKay, Alexander, *Scottish Samurai, Thomas Blake Glover 1838-1911,* (Edinburgh, 1997)

Mackay, Ruddock F., *Fisher of Kilverstone,* (OUP, 1973)

Marder, Arthur, J., *Portrait of an Admiral,* (London, 1952)
    From the Dreadnought to Scapa Flow, (OUP, five volumes, 1961, 1965, 1966, 1969, 1970)
    From the Dardanelles to Oran, (OUP, 1974)
    With associates, *Old Friends New Enemies,* (OUP, Vol. I in 1981 and Vol. II in 1990)

Marriner, Sheila and Francis E. Hyde, *The Senior, John Samuel Swire 1825-1898,* (Liverpool, 1967)

Martin, W.E.R., *The Adventures of a Naval Paymaster,* (London, 1924)

Maugham, W. Somerset, *On a Chinese Screen,* (OUP, 1985)

May, W.A., *The Commission of HMS Talbot: 1901-1904,* (London, 1904)

Miller, Harry, *Pirates of the Far East,* (London, 1970)

Miller, William H., *The Last Blue Water Liners,* (London, 1986)

Mitsui OSK Lines Ltd., *The First Century of Mitsui OSK Lines Ltd.,* (Japan, 1985)

Moore, E. Marjorie, *Adventure in the Royal Navy,* (Liverpool, 1964)

Moore, Captain W.J., *Shanghai Century,* (Ilfracombe, 1966)

Moresby, John, *Two Admirals,* (London, 1913)

Neatby, L.H., *Arctic Profiles,* (University of Calgary, ASTIS 32861)

Nicholson, Arthur, *Hostages to Fortune*, (Stroud, 2005)

Nish, Ian, Ed., *Biographical Portraits, II*, (Richmond, Surrey, 1997)

Notehelfer, F.G., Ed., *Japan Through American Eyes: 1859-1866*, (Boulder, CO., 2001)

Nunn, Wilfred, *Tigris Gunboats*, (London, 2007)

O'Byrne, William R., *A Naval Biographical Dictionary*, (Reprint at Polstead, Suffolk, 1986)

O'Connor, V.C. Scott, *The Empire Cruise*, (London, 1925)

Okumiya, Masatake, et al, *Zero*, (London, 1957)

O'Regan, John, *From Empire to Commonwealth*, (London, 1994)

Pack, S.W.C., *Cunningham the Commander*, (London, 1974)

Paludan, Ann, *Chronicle of the Chinese Emperors*, (London, 2005)

Parkes, Oscar, *British Battleships*, (Annapolis, MD, 1990)

Parkinson, Jonathan, *The First Steam Powered Ascent Through the Yangtse Gorges*, (Journal of the Royal Asiatic Society Hong Kong Branch, Vol. 46, 2006)
    Early Steam Powered Navigation on the Lower Yangtse, (Journal of the Royal Asiatic Society Hong Kong Branch, Vol. 51, 2011)

Parry, Ann, *The Admirals Fremantle, 1788-1920*, (London, 1971)

Patience, Kevin, *Zanzibar: Slavery and the Royal Navy*, (Bahrain, 2000)

Paton, James R., *Wide Eyed in Old China*, (Edinburgh, 1974)

Patterson, A. Temple, *Tyrwhitt of the Harwich Force*, (London, 1973)

Peattie, Mark R., *Nanyo*, (Hawaii, 1988)
    Sunburst, the Rise of Japanese Naval Air Power, 1909-1941, (Annapolis, 2001)
    Together with David C. Evans, *Kaigun*, (Annapolis, 1997)

Percival, Lieut. General A.E., *The War in Malaya*, (London, 1949)

Perry, John Curtis, *Great Britain and the Imperial Japanese Navy: 1858-1905*, (Harvard, 1962)

Pierce, R.A. and J.H. Winslow, Eds., *H.M.S. Sulphur on the Northwest and Californian Coasts, 1837 and 1839*, (Kingston, Ontario, 1979)

Pochhammer, Captain Hans, *Before Jutland*, (London, 1931)

Pomfret, Carlene, *Cabin Trunks and Far Horizons*, (Ware, Herts., 1991)

Pool, Richard, *Course for Disaster*, (London, 1987)

Potter, E.B., *Nimitz*, (Annapolis, MD, 1987)

Pottinger, George, *Sir Henry Pottinger*, (Stroud, 1997)

Prange, Gordon W., *At Dawn We Slept*, (New York, 1983)

Rea, W.E. *Nil Desperandum*, (Privately, 1935)

Reece, Robert, *The White Rajahs of Sarawak*, (Singapore, 2004)

Reynolds, Clark G., *Admiral John H. Towers*, (Annapolis, MD, 1991)

Ridley, Jasper, *Lord Palmerston*, (London, 1970)

Ritchie, G.S., *The Admiralty Chart*, (Bishop Auckland, 1995)

Roberts, John G., *Mitsui*, (New York and Tokyo, 1989)

Roff, William R., Ed., *Stories and Sketches by Sir Frank Swettenham*, (OUP, 1967)

Roscoe, Theodore, *United States Submarine Operations in WW2*, (Annapolis, MD, 1988)

Roskill, Stephen, *Hankey, Man of Secrets*, (London, three volumes , 1970, 1972, 1974)
    A Merchant Fleet in War: Alfred Holt & Co., 1939-1945, (London, 1962)

Rotberg, Robert I., *The Founder*, (Johannesburg, 1988)

Runciman, Steven, *The White Rajahs*, (Cambridge, 1960)

Ruxton, Ian D., *The Diaries and Letters of Sir Ernest Mason Satow (1843-1929)*, (Lewiston, NY, 1998)

Sansom, G.B., *The Western World and Japan*, (London, 1950)

Sansom, Katharine, *Sir George Sansom and Japan*, (Tallahassee, Fla., 1972)

Satow, Sir Ernest, *A Diplomat in Japan*, (London, 1921)

Savours, Ann, *The Search for the North West Passage*, (London, 1999)

Sayer, Geoffrey Robley, *Hong Kong, 1841-1862*, (Hong Kong, 1980)

Hong Kong: 1862-1919, (Hong Kong, 1975)

Schencking, J. Charles, *Making Waves*, (Stanford, 2005)

Seymour, E.H., Admiral of the Fleet, *My Naval Career and Travels*, (London, 1911)

Shiba, Ryotaro, *The Last Shogun, The Life of Tokugawa Yoshinobu*, (New York and Tokyo, 2004)

Shore, Hon. Henry Noel, *The Flight of the Lapwing*, (London, 1881)

Simpson, B. Mitchell III, *Admiral Harold R. Stark*, (University of South Carolina, 1989)

Smith, George and successors, *Dictionary of National Biography*, (OUP, various)

Smith, Peter C., *Hit First, Hit Hard*, (London, 1979)

Spence, Jonathan D., *Emperor of China*, (London, 1974)

The China Helpers, ((London, 1969)

St. John, Henry Craven, *The Wild Coasts of Nipon*, (Edinburgh, 1880)

Statham-Drew, Pamela, *James Stirling*, (Crawley, West Australia, 2003)

Staunton, George, *An Historical Account of the Embassy to the Emperor of China*, (London, 1797)

Stephenson, Charles, *Germany's Asia-Pacific Empire*, (Woodbridge, Suffolk, 2009)

Stuart, Vivian, *The Beloved Little Admiral*, (London, 1967)

Swire, John and Sons, *The China Navigation Company Limited*, (Hong Kong, 1992)

Sysonby, Lord, *Recollections of Three Reigns*, (London, 1951)

Tate, E. Mowbray, *Transpacific Steam*, (Cranbury, NJ, 1986)

The Journal of Commerce and Shipping Telegraph, *Seventy Adventurous Years*, (Liverpool, 1956)

Tolley, Rear Admiral Kemp, USN, *Yangtze Patrol*, (Annapolis, 1987)

Torrible, Captain Graham, *Yangtze Reminiscences*, (Hong Kong, 1990)

Tracey, Nicholas, Ed., *The Collective Naval Defence of the Empire, 1900-1940*, (Naval Records Society, 1997)

Tregonning, K.G., *Home Port Singapore*, (OUP, 1967)

Tsuzuki, Chushichi, *The Pursuit of Power in Modern Japan*, (OUP, 2000)

Tweedie, Admiral Hugh, *The Story of a Naval Life*, (London, 1939)

Tyler, William Ferdinand, *Pulling Strings in China*, (London, 1929)

Urban, Frank, *Ned's Navy*, (Shrewsbury, 1998)

van Slyke, Lyman P., *Yangtze*, (Stamford, CA., 1988)

Walder, David, *The Short Victorious War*, (London, 1973)

Wall, Greg, *The Book of South Brent*, (Tiverton, Devon, 2005)

Welch, John C., *John Goodridge – Naval Surgeon*, (Mariner's Mirror, November 2004)

Wells, John, *The Royal Navy: An Illustrated Social History 1870-1982*, (London, 1999)

Wells Williams, Dr. S., *The Middle Kingdom*, (London, 1883)

Welsh, Frank, *A History of Hong Kong*, (London, 1997)

Wemyss, Lady Wester, *The Life and Letters of Lord Wester Wemyss*, (London, 1935)

West, Algernon, *Harry Keppel*, (London, 1905)

Wetzler, Peter, *Hirohito at War*, (Hawaii, 1998)

Wheeler, Gerald E., *Kinkaid of the Seventh Fleet*, (Annapolis, 1996)

Whitby, Michael, et al, Eds., *The Admirals, Canada's Senior Naval Leadership in the Twentieth Century*, (Toronto, 2006)

Wildenberg, Thomas, *All the Factors of Victory, Admiral Joseph Mason Reeves and the Origins of Carrier Airpower*, (Washington, DC, 2003)

Williams, Harold S., *Shades of the Past*, (Tokyo and Rutland, VT., 1959)

Williams, Stephanie, *Running the Show*, (London, 2011)

Williamson, Captain A.R., *Eastern Traders*, (Jardine, Matheson & Co., 1975)

Wilson, Alastair, and Joseph F. Callo, *Who's Who in Naval History*, (Abingdon, Oxford, 2004)

Wilson, Andrew, *The Ever Victorious Army*, (Edinburgh and London, 1868)

Wilson, H.W., *Battships in Action*, two volumes, (London)

Winton, John, *Jellicoe*, (London, 1981)

    Convoy, (London, 1983)

Wonham, Albert R., *Spun Yarns of a Naval Officer*, (Westminster, 1917)

Worcester, G.R.G., *The Junkman Smiles*, (London, 1959)

Wright, Richard N.J., *The Chinese Steam Navy, 1862-1945*, (London, 2000)

Yoshida, Takashi, *The Making of the "Rape of Nanking"*, (OUP, 2006)

Yoshida, Yuki, *Whispering Leaves in Grosvenor Square: 1936-37*, (Folkestone, Kent, 1997)

Zandvliet, Kees, *The Dutch Encounter with Asia: 1600-1950*, (Rijksmuseum, Amsterdam, 2002)

Publications

Australian Dictionary of Biography

Bideford Gazette

Blackwood's Edinburgh Magazine

Bristol Times and Mirror

British Army List

Camberley News

Chronicle (Bulletin) of the Simon's Town Historical Society

Colonial Office List

Darlington and Stockton Times

Dictionary of American Naval Fighting Ships

Dictionary of Canadian Biography Online

Dictionary of National Biography

Encyclopaedia Britannica

Foreign Office List

Hampshire Chronicle & General Advertiser for the South and West of England

Illustrated London News

International Journal of Maritime History, St. John's, Newfoundland

Japan Times

John O'Groat Journal

Journal of the Hong Kong Branch of the Royal Asiatic Society – RASHKB

Journal of the Royal Geographical Society

Journal of the Royal United Service Institution

Kent Messenger

Lloyds Register

Lynn News

Midhurst Times

Midland Tribune

Naval History, Annapolis

Naval and Military Record

Navy List

New York Times

North China Herald

North Devon Journal

Proceedings/Journal of the Royal Geographical Society, London

Ships Monthly

South China Morning Post, Hong Kong

South China and Yangtze Patroller

Standard Encyclopaedia of South Africa

Straits Settlements Government Gazette

The China Journal

The China Year Book

The Daily Telegraph, London

The Encyclopaedia of Plymouth History

The Evening News, Portsmouth and Southsea

The Hertfordshire Mercury

The Isle of Wight County Press

The London Gazette

The Maidenhead Advertiser

The Mariner's Mirror

The Naval Review, London

The News, Portsmouth

The Northern Mariner, Canadian Nautical Research Society

The Straits Calendar and Directory

The Straits Times, Singapore

The Surrey Comet

The Sydney Morning Herald

The Times, London

The World Book Encyclopaedia

Tipperary Free Press

Transactions of the Devonshire Association

Vancouver Daily Province

Warship International, Holden, MA

Western Morning News

Who's Who

Wiltshire Gazette

Sources

Aberdeen City Archives

Aberdeen Maritime Museum

Archives Centre, Churchill College, Cambridge

Australian Antarctic Data Centre

Bitterne Local History Society

Bracknell Heritage, Berkshire

British Horseracing Authority, London

Caird Library, National Maritime Museum, Greenwich

Cambridge University Library, especially for the Jardine Matheson records, with kind permission

Canadian Army Historical Section

Centre for Buckinghamshire Studies, Aylesbury

Chipping Sodbury Historical Society

City Library, Johannesburg

City Library, Victoria, Hong Kong

Cornwall Family History Society, Truro

Devon County Council Archives, Exeter

Devon Record Office

Hampshire County Council

Hong Kong Museum of History, Kowloon

Imperial War Museum, London

King's College, London

Local and Naval Studies, Central Library, Plymouth

Maritime Museum of British Columbia Society

Melksham and District Historical Association

National Institute for Defense Studies, Tokyo

National Library, Singapore

Naval Historical Center, Washington, DC

Nederlands Scheepvaartmuseum, Amsterdam

North Devon Record Office

Northallerton and District Local History Society

Plymouth and West Devon Record Office

Royal Astronomical Society, London

Royal Marines Museum, Southsea

Royal Society, London

Russo-Japanese War Research Society

Sandon Hall Archives, Staffordshire

Scott Polar Research Institute, Cambridge

Seapower Centre, Australia
Seeley G. Mudd Manuscript Library, Princeton, NJ
Simon's Town Historical Society
SOAS, London, especially for the Butterfield and Swire records, with kind permission.
Surrey Heath Museum, Camberley
Surrey History Centre, Woking
The Bodleian, Oxford
The British Library
The Churchill Archives, Cambridge
The Historical Association, Isle of Wight Branch
The Institution of Civil Engineers, London
The National Archives, Kew
The Royal Artillery Museum, Woolwich
The Royal Naval Museum Library, Portsmouth
Torpoint Archives, Cornwall
UMI Dissertation Services, Ann Arbor, Michigan
United Kingdom Hydrographic Office, Taunton
West Sussex Record Office
Whangpoo Conservancy Board
Wiltshire and Swindon History Centre
Wiltshire and Swindon Record Office

J.M. Parkinson
Email: jmpiafrica@gmail.com
Dunkeld
March 2012

Index

Please note: The ranks of naval and military officers are shown as the highest attained.

Here follows an explanation in respect of theMeiji, 'enlightened government', era which in Japan covered the years 1868-1912. This too is the era covered by the reign of H.I.M. Emperor Mutsuhito. Thus in the script both references can be applicable, generally in accordance with the context.

M